Student Teaching and Field Experiences Handbook

THIRD EDITION

Betty D. Roe
Tennessee Technological University

Elinor P. Ross
Tennessee Technological University

Merrill, an imprint of
Macmillan Publishing Company
New York

Maxwell Macmillan Canada
Toronto

Maxwell Macmillan International
New York   Oxford   Singapore   Sydney

Cover photo: Dennis MacDonald/Unicorn Stock Photos
Editor: Linda James Scharp
Production Editor: Stephen C. Robb
Art Coordinator: Ruth A. Kimpel
Photo Editor: Anne Vega
Text Designer: Jill E. Bonar
Cover Designer: Robert Vega
Production Buyer: Pamela D. Bennett
Artist: Steve Botts

Photo credits: Ben Chandler/Macmillan, pp. 11 and 226; Paul Conklin, pp. 103, 116, 128, 160, and 177; Vivienne Della Grotta, p. 2; Matthew Fearing, p. 185; Robert Finken, pp. 26, 83, 97, and 137; Larry Hamill/Macmillan, p. 45; Jean-Claude Lejeune, pp. 52, 62, and 75; Harvey Phillips/Macmillan, p. 266; Charles Quinlan, pp. 56, 180, 220, and 244; Michael H. Roe, p. 190; Barbara Stimpert, p. 72; David Strickler/Strix Pix, pp. 8 and 188; Tom Watson/Macmillan, p. 222.

This book was set in Century and Franklin Gothic by Carlisle Communications, Ltd. and was printed and bound by Semline, Inc., a Quebecor America Book Group Company. The cover was printed by Phoenix Color Corp.

Macmillan Publishing Company
866 Third Avenue
New York, New York 10022

Macmillan Publishing Company is part of the
Maxwell Communication Group of Companies.

Maxwell Macmillan Canada, Inc.
1200 Eglinton Avenue East, Suite 200
Don Mills, Ontario M3C 3N1

Library of Congress Cataloging-in-Publication Data
Roe, Betty D.
    Student teaching and field experiences handbook / Betty D. Roe,
    Elinor P. Ross.— 3rd ed.
        p.   cm.
    Includes bibliographical references and index.
    ISBN 0-02-402661-1
    1. Student teaching--Handbooks, manuals, etc.   I. Ross, Elinor P.
    II. Title
    LB2157.A3R59   1994
    370'.7'33—dc20   92-42859
                                                                          CIP

Printing: 1   2   3   4   5   6   7   8   9   Year: 4   5   6   7

Preface

Student Teaching and Field Experiences Handbook is designed for students who are teaching in schools during their teacher-preparation programs, either in pre-student teaching practicum courses or as actual student teachers. The text is a practical guide for college students who are directly involved with elementary and secondary students.

Each chapter opens with an introductory vignette to initiate discussion of the material in the chapter. Questions following each vignette and discussion questions at the ends of the chapters encourage reflection about all the material in the chapters as well as ways to apply the information. Selected references guide students to additional reading.

The first three chapters help the student get ready to teach. The first chapter addresses professional ethics and legal status, stress, teacher effectiveness, and extracurricular activities, all issues students need to know about as background for engaging in teaching activities. Chapter 2 focuses on the relationships a student teacher or practicum student will have with other people in the school. Chapter 3 gives practical suggestions about observation, planning, and use of instructional resources.

The next six chapters address specific teaching challenges. Chapter 4 offers practical suggestions about discipline—many student teachers' number one worry. Chapter 5 provides information on several important aspects of classroom management: grouping, scheduling, record keeping, student supervision, and classroom environment. Chapters 6 and 7 cover teaching strategies and other school activities—motivation, teaching techniques, activities for developing higher-order thinking skills, use

of study skills, and functional learning activities. The exceptional student receives attention in Chapter 8. Because of mainstreaming, all student teachers need information on this topic. Chapter 9 deals with methods of evaluation, and student teachers are asked to evaluate both their students and themselves. The final chapter provides information about entering the teaching profession, giving suggestions for locating and applying for positions and information about continuing one's professional growth after obtaining a position.

Five appendixes offer helpful information in the form of assessment instruments, code of ethics for educators, sample lesson plans, sample unit plans, and a sample learning center. The appendix on assessment instruments is new to this edition.

This third edition has many new or expanded sections that reflect current topics of interest in education. Some of the more prominent ones are the sections on cultural diversity, computer applications, student-centered learning, literature across the curriculum, cooperative learning, whole language theory and applications, portfolio assessment, and reflective teaching through journal writing. Activities related to topics in each chapter enable students to apply information from the text to actual teaching situations. A special listing of these application activities follows the table of contents.

Throughout the text, case studies focus on situations that student teachers may encounter. Analyzing these case studies and considering the other discussion questions in the chapter are good seminar activities for student teachers and practicum students.

This book is not meant to supply all the information students generally require in their methods courses. Rather, it will remind them of what they already know, fill in some gaps that are often not covered by methods courses, offer practical suggestions, and provide a setting for critical analysis of teaching activities. The orientation is toward practical suggestions rather than theory.

We hope that this handbook will give prospective teachers greater confidence as they prepare for their profession and that it will make the preparation more enjoyable.

Acknowledgments

The authors thank Maxine Harrow, University of Maine; Mark Freer, University of Idaho; and Toni M. Sills, Murray State University, for their helpful reviews of this manuscript. Their insightful comments were greatly appreciated.

We also express our gratitude to Alice Bedford and Kathy Dooley for permission to use excerpts from their student teaching journals.

Contents

Application Activities

1

General Background

Miss Cooper, the student teacher, notices that Debbie is dull and listless in class and sometimes has bruises on her body. Miss Cooper is concerned about Debbie and wants to help. Mr. Huang is the cooperating teacher.

Miss Cooper (trying to gain Debbie's confidence): Debbie, tell me what you like to do when school is out.

Debbie: Nothing.

Miss Cooper: Where do you live?

Debbie: Over by the cannery.

Miss Cooper: You must do some things for fun.

Debbie: Nope.

Miss Cooper (two weeks later, still patiently trying to bring Debbie out of her shell): Debbie, you really look nice today.

Debbie: Yeah. My cousin gave me this new shirt.

Miss Cooper: I think you could be a really good student in class, but sometimes you look so sleepy. What time do you go to bed?

Debbie: About midnight, sometimes later.

Miss Cooper: Couldn't you try to get to bed earlier than that? I'll bet you could really do well if you got enough sleep.

Debbie: I can't never get to sleep before then.

Miss Cooper: Why? Surely you can go to bed earlier than that?

Debbie: I don't want to talk about it.

Miss Cooper (after another two weeks): Debbie, have you tried to get to bed any earlier? You know, it would really help you. You fell asleep during English today.

Debbie: I know. I really want to, but I just can't.

Miss Cooper: Why don't you tell me about it?

Debbie (sighing and looking doubtful): Would you promise you wouldn't tell nobody? Nobody at all?

Miss Cooper: I promise. I won't ever tell anybody.

Debbie: Well, see, it's like this. My dad comes home; then he starts drinking. He's O.K. at first, but then he starts getting real loud and mean. Then he starts beating on me and my mom. We try to get away from him, but he's too strong. There ain't nothing we can do about it. Now don't tell nobody, or that'll only make it worse.

Miss Cooper (very concerned after this disclosure): Mr. Huang, do you know anything about Debbie and her family?

Mr. Huang: I know something about them.

Miss Cooper decides to tell Mr. Huang Debbie's story. He shares her concern and realizes that this is probably a case of wife and child abuse. Mr. Huang notifies people at the Department of Human Services at once, and they agree to investigate the matter. Miss Cooper is now worried that Debbie will think she told them and asks them to be discreet.

Debbie (one week later with dark bruises on her arms and a bruise under her left eye): I thought I could trust you not to tell. I should've knowed better. All you teachers are just alike. You sent the welfare person out, and she asked my dad a bunch of questions. He figured I'd been blabbing, so he really laid into me and my mom last night. Now it's worse than ever. I wish I'd never told you!

1. Do you think Miss Cooper did the right thing? Are there laws about reporting suspected child abuse? Check with your local agency, and find out how this situation should be handled.
2. Is there anything Miss Cooper can do to restore Debbie's trust? How might she try to do this?
3. Do you believe it is ever right to share a student's confidences with someone else after you promise not to tell? If so, under what circumstances?
4. What would you have done in a similar situation?

GETTING READY

You are about to enter the teaching profession. Before you become a fully qualified teacher, you will have many experiences working with students under the guidance of a cooperating teacher and a university supervisor. With their suggestions and your knowledge, you will discover many techniques for helping students learn. Your introduction to teaching will be gradual, so you will be prepared to assume additional responsibilities as you encounter them.

When you begin teaching, your point of view will change. As a student, you have worried about paying attention to dull teachers, spending long hours doing homework, and taking tests. As a teacher, you will have different concerns. How do you prepare informative lessons that will keep each student interested? How do you find the time to plan tomorrow's lessons after teaching all day? How do you make up tests that will truly evaluate what each student has learned?

Teaching is both a wonderful opportunity and a serious responsibility. Teachers never really know the extent of their influence. What you teach may affect students in such a way that they will, in turn, influence others. As you teach, be sensitive to the needs and feelings of your students, and let them know that you believe in their ability to succeed.

PROFESSIONAL ETHICS AND LEGAL STATUS

Am I allowed to express my own political opinions when I teach? Can I do anything I want to do in my free time? Should I talk about my students with other teachers? What should I do if I suspect a student in my class is using drugs? You may be wondering about the answers to questions such as these. A professional code of ethics (see Appendix B) and school law should serve as guides for your behavior.

Ethical Responsibilities to Students

Your primary concern as a student teacher should be for the students you teach. A good student teacher can enrich the students' education; a poor student teacher merely wastes valuable learning time. As a guest of the school, you owe the students your very best efforts in providing worthwhile learning experiences.

Each student is entitled to your courtesy and consideration, regardless of her or his physical appearance, socioeconomic status, race, creed, or ethnic origin. You will find that it is much easier to get along with some students than with others, and you will be tempted to have "teacher's pets." Students may compete for your attention with notes and little gifts, but you should be impartial in the way you treat your students. Never embarrass or humiliate students who do not measure up to your expectations.

Your classroom should have a democratic atmosphere. Students should be allowed to express their opinions and different points of view. Don't impose your own religious or political views on your students, and be careful to present both sides of controversial issues.

Students who confide in you expect you to keep their secrets. It would be unethical to take advantage of the information they share with you, or to embarrass them by revealing their information to other people. There may be times, however, when you feel the information they confide in you may bring harm to them or to others. They may be concealing information sought by the police or may need psychological help you cannot provide. In these cases, and in the case of Debbie and Miss Cooper, it is usually a good idea to discuss the information with someone in authority who will respect the student's confidence and know what to do.

You may overhear teachers talking, particularly in the faculty lounge, about some of the students. It is unethical for you to openly and informally discuss a student's character, personality, appearance, or behavior in a disparaging way. Such conversations violate students' rights to privacy, and you should avoid them.

Students also have the right to confidentiality in the grades they receive. You shouldn't post grades or read them aloud unless you use some identification other than the students' names. When you return papers, make sure that only the student receiving the paper can see the grade.

Ethical Responsibilities to the Profession

You should be proud to be entering the teaching profession, and you will want to act appropriately. Dress and behave in such a way that your students and colleagues will respect you. Try to get along with your coworkers. Show respect for people in authority, even if you don't always agree with them. Be sure to express appreciation to the school in which you do your student teaching for assisting you in your education. Remember also that you are a representative of your college or university, and your behavior is a reflection on that institution.

You should also observe certain ethical standards regarding tutoring. Don't tutor students assigned to your classes for pay unless no other qualified person is available.

When you look for a teaching job, be completely honest with school district personnel about your qualifications and professional preparation. Don't apply for any position already held by a qualified teacher.

You have a responsibility to support your profession and to stay up-to-date. One way to become professionally active is to join a professional organization. Many professional organizations offer student memberships at reduced rates. Your university supervisor can probably suggest one or two appropriate organizations for you to join and can help you find information about them. Chapter 10 gives information about professional associations for educators.

The Law and Student Teaching

You will need to know your legal rights, responsibilities, and liabilities as a student teacher. Since local and state laws differ and change frequently, be sure to find out what your legal status is in the school system where you are teaching. (See Activity 1.1.)

If a serious problem arises, document the evidence as soon as possible. Record the time, date, place, names of those involved, and a brief account of the event. Be objective and accurate in your report, and avoid personal opinions and judgments. Such evidence is useful for later reference and in some cases may be used as court evidence.

Child Abuse Laws in most states specifically direct school personnel to report suspected child abuse. Since many child abuse cases involve school-aged children, educators can play a key role in identifying and reporting individuals who have been abused. If school personnel neglect this responsibility, they may endanger a child's well-being and contribute to the recurrence of abuse.[1]

Learn to recognize these signs of possible child abuse:

1 *Physical abuse*—Lacerations, missing teeth, fractures, rope burns, cigarette burns, bruises
2 *Neglect*—Constant fatigue, excessive hunger, lack of cleanliness, body odor
3 *Sexual abuse*—Difficulty in walking or sitting, torn or stained underclothes
4 *Emotional maltreatment*—Low self-concept, behavioral extremes, frequent temper tantrums, demand for affection

[1]Samuel B. London and Stephen W. Stile. *The School's Role in the Prevention of Child Abuse.* Bloomington, Ind.: Phi Delta Kappa Educational Foundation, 1982.

Not every child who exhibits one of these characteristics has been abused, but a combination of these factors, frequent recurrence of injuries, or excessive behavioral maladjustment may justify your suspicion. If you have reason to suspect a student is being abused, first talk it over with your cooperating teacher. Perhaps he or she is already aware of the problem or has noticed the same symptoms. Then a school employee—perhaps a teacher, school nurse, or principal—should interview the student in a relaxed, nonthreatening manner. The interview should be conducted privately, and the school authority should assure the child that the conversation will be confidential unless it becomes necessary to contact an agency for help. If further action is necessary, school authorities will then follow appropriate procedures for reporting the situation.

If there are abused children in your classroom, you can offer support in a number of ways. Be understanding and patient with them. Be a model of behavior for them to follow so they realize there are better ways to deal with frustrations and disappointments than by using physical violence. Focus on their strengths, and find ways for them to experience success. Praise them whenever there is cause. Be sensitive to their problems and willing to listen if they need to talk about their feelings.

Negligence   School personnel are responsible for the protection of students while they are in school. When an accident or injury occurs to a student, you may be held liable if you are in charge and negligence, or extreme carelessness, can be proved. In determining negligence, a court of law considers whether or not the person in charge exercised reasonable care and acted sensibly. If, for example, on a day when you are responsible for the class, an accident occurs while you are out of the classroom, you could be found negligent if your presence most likely would have prevented the accident from happening.

Accidents are apt to occur when unusual events are taking place. When animals are brought to school, you are responsible for seeing that they are kept under control so that no students are injured. When the class goes on a field trip, each student should return a signed parental permission form that shows the date, place, and type of transportation. The note should include a statement that frees the teacher and school from liability in case of an accident, but, even so, you could be held liable if you were negligent. If there is no note, make arrangements for the student to stay at school instead. Do not accept a phone call instead of a signed note, because you will not have a written record of permission.

Discipline   Recent U.S. Supreme Court decisions held that corporal punishment does not violate the Eighth Amendment barring cruel and unusual punishment. The Court supported your right as a teacher to use corporal punishment even over parental objections. Although corporal punishment has been banned by some states and in some local districts, other school systems permit corporal punishment as a way of controlling student behavior.

The Supreme Court has established certain due process procedures for administering corporal punishment.

1 Corporal punishment should rarely be used in a first-offense situation.
2 Students should know what types of misconduct could lead to corporal punishment.
3 An adult witness should be present when someone administers corporal punishment.
4 The student should be informed in front of the adult witness of the reasons for the punishment.
5 The disciplinarian should inform the student's parents of the reason for administering corporal punishment, if requested to do so.[2]

[2]Eugene J. Connors. *Student Discipline and the Law.* Bloomington, Ind.: Phi Delta Kappa Educational Foundation, 1979, p. 10.

Activity 1.1   Legal Status of Teachers

Because states differ in their laws and new legal decisions are made from time to time, it is important for you to know your legal rights and responsibilities. Check the law on the following issues and write a brief statement about each.

Child abuse (responsibility for reporting and to whom to report):

Negligence (use of permission notes, extent of reponsibility):

Discipline (status on corporal punishment):

Individuals with Disabilities Education Act (IDEA) (involvement in preparing an IEP):

Liability insurance (availability, coverage, cost):

Self-defense (reporting procedures, what is considered "excessive force"):

First aid and medication (when to act, administering medication):

Copyright laws (photocopying rights, "fair use"):

Private lives of teachers (rights and responsibilities):

Academic freedom (censorship; prayer and other religious issues):

Many individuals with disabilities are "mainstreamed" into regular classrooms instead of being placed in special classes.

Corporal punishment may take forms other than spanking or striking a student. It is sometimes interpreted as any action that could cause physical or emotional damage to a student, such as having a student stand with arms outstretched while holding a book in either hand.

As a student teacher, you should avoid using corporal punishment. If a student doesn't seem to respond to any other form of discipline, you might consult with your cooperating teacher about how to handle the problem.

There are other forms of discipline that can also result in legal action. Courts generally oppose a decision to punish all of the students for the misbehavior of one when the culprit cannot be identified. Such mass discipline affects the innocent as well as the guilty. In some situations you may wish to keep a student after school, but if this detention causes the student to miss the school bus and an accident occurs later en route to home, you may be held liable.

Individuals with Disabilities Education Act (IDEA)   The federal law known as Public Law 94–142, the Education for All Handicapped Children Act, has significantly affected service delivery to all students with disabilities in public schools. In 1990 Congress reauthorized this act by passing the Individuals with Disabilities Education Act (IDEA) (Public Law 101–476). The new law incorporates changes in terminology and additional categories of disabilities. Both laws mandate that individuals with disabilities be "mainstreamed" into regular classrooms to the greatest extent possible instead of being placed in special classes. The rationale for this policy is that both disabled and "normal" individuals benefit from the increased academic and social interaction.

You will have an opportunity to observe and work with these students on a daily basis. Because the law requires each student with a disability to have an Individual Educational Program (IEP), you may participate in developing and implementing such a plan.

Search and Seizure   Courts have generally ruled in favor of allowing school officials to conduct searches and seizures. Searches consist of looking for illegal goods; seizures involve confiscating illegal goods. Some of the items usually prohibited in schools are drugs and drug paraphernalia, weapons such as knives and guns, and obscene materials.

The Fourth Amendment to the Constitution gives individuals freedom from unreasonable searches and seizures. Weighing this freedom against a safe and drug-free school environment, however, the courts usually rule in favor of the schools. Searches and seizures are increasing as drug use and violence in schools become greater problems.

If you suspect a student possesses something illegal, discuss the matter with your cooperating teacher. If evidence warrants an investigation, a school official can be asked to search the student's locker. Do not conduct the search yourself, and do not search a student's body or clothing for suspected harmful items.

You may find that your students are bringing things to school that distract their attention and interfere with their school work, such as comic books, toys, or water pistols. You have a right to remove these things from them, but you must return them to the students at the end of a period of time or to parents whom you ask to come to school for them. Otherwise, you are confiscating the students' personal property permanently.

Liability Insurance   You can purchase liability insurance to protect yourself from lawsuits. Liability insurance is available through professional societies at greatly reduced student rates, or you may include it as part of your homeowner's general policy. (See Chapter 10 for professional societies.)

Before you drive students anywhere in your own vehicle, make sure that you have adequate insurance coverage. If there is an accident and you are found negligent, you could be sued. Your school may provide coverage for you, but otherwise you should not transport students in your personal vehicle.

You should check the school's insurance policies regarding coverage of personal losses or damages. You may want to bring your own tape player or Uncle Jack's priceless African mask to enrich your lessons, but if these items are stolen or damaged, you may have no recourse.

Self-Defense   Self-defense generally takes one of three forms: protecting yourself against a student who threatens bodily harm, preventing one student from physically injuring another, and stopping a student from destroying school property. If a student is injured as a result of any of these actions, the courts will generally support you if you used "reasonable force." However, if you act out of anger and lose control of your temper, you may apply unreasonable force and eventually lose a court case. Whenever possible, avoid a physical confrontation, but if you must intervene, avoid excessive force when dealing with a physically aggressive student.

Consider any threats made against you for their potential danger. For example, a student to whom you have given a bad grade may say, "I'm gonna kill you!" This is very likely an exaggeration. On the other hand, you may need to consider some threats to you or your personal property seriously and report them to the proper authorities.

First Aid and Medication   The best guideline to follow in administering first aid is to act only in case of emergency, such as choking or profuse bleeding. Whenever there is an injury, inform your cooperating teacher immediately. If that is impossible, notify someone in the school, such as the school nurse (if there is one), another teacher, or the principal. Try to make the student as comfortable as possible, but avoid treating an injury unless absolutely necessary, since you could be sued for improper treatment.

Some students must take medication under certain conditions, but it is better for the school nurse or regular teacher to administer this medication than for you to do it. There are risks in administering medication, particularly if the directions are unclear or inaccurate. Don't give students aspirin or cough drops either, because they could be harmful for some students. If a student needs an insulin shot during the school day, the school nurse or parent should give the injection. It is generally inadvisable for teachers to give medication.

Copyright law does not permit duplication of consumable materials (worksheets, standardized tests, ditto sheets) without permission from the publisher.

Copyright Laws   The U.S. Copyright Act contains certain provisions for photocopying material. You need to know what you can copy and how many copies you can make without violating the copyright law. Some magazines and journals state their photocopying policies on the title page of each issue. When reproduction of certain material is clearly prohibited, you may still write to the publisher for permission to use the material.

There are several guidelines for determining if material can be photocopied under the "fair use" policy. Generally, "fair use" is observed when photocopying material has no effect on its demand. For instance, you can make a copy of an article or selection, but you can make multiple copies of only a very small portion of a work. You are not permitted to copy consumable materials, such as workbook pages, standardized tests, and ditto sheets, unless permission is granted by the publishers. You cannot reproduce substantial parts of materials for public performances, including sheet music and plays. If a work is out of print or unavailable, however, the policy of "fair use" generally allows you to photocopy it.

Private Lives of Teachers   Teachers have advanced considerably since the days when they were forbidden to drink or smoke, and married women were not permitted to teach. Today, teachers are granted a great many privileges, but their behavior is still sometimes challenged and brought before the courts.

Some general guidelines for behavior have been established as a result of case law. As you begin your student teaching, you should find out if there are any published or generally accepted rules regarding these matters. Dress, grooming, and sexual behavior usually come under the teacher's right to privacy, unless it can be proved that the teacher's appearance or lifestyle affects her or his teaching. Teachers, as well as students, have the right to refuse to participate in patriotic ceremonies. They are also free to oppose school policies by speaking out against them or writing letters that appear in local newspapers. As a student teacher, however, you would be wise to act with discretion and avoid antagonizing people.

Academic Freedom

Congress shall make no law respecting an establishment of religion, or prohibiting the free exercise thereof; or abridging the freedom of speech, or of the press; or the right of the people peaceably to assemble, and to petition the government for a re-dress of grievances.

—First Amendment, United States Constitution

A great deal of controversy has arisen over recent interpretations of the First Amendment. There have been many court cases dealing with censorship of mate-rials and subjects for instruction, as well as with school prayer and Bible reading. The issues of morality, politics, racism, and religion form the basis of most attacks by censors.

Teachers sometimes face the dilemma of using uncontroversial and generally acceptable materials, or materials relevant to living in contemporary society that may offend some citizens of the community. When you deal with controversial issues, you risk confrontations with parents and public criticism. Teachers who use books or teach subjects that have been specifically forbidden by the board of edu-cation may be dismissed. These are some points to consider in determining whether or not to use controversial materials in your classroom:

1 Is the material you plan to use appropriate for the maturity and age level of the students?
2 Is there a valid educational reason for using the material?
3 Is there any policy established by the board of education to prohibit use of the material?

In *Abington Township School District* v. *Schempp,* 1963, the U.S. Supreme Court ruled that school prayer and Bible reading violated the constitutional provi-sion for separation of church and state. Due to different interpretations of the law, however, schools in some states permit silent periods of meditation or voluntary school prayer.

STRESS

As a student teacher, you face many pressures: teaching lessons for the first time, preparing to enter the job market, and handling social, family, and monetary de-mands. These pressures can cause stress, and stress can affect your teaching per-formance. It can also affect your physical and emotional well-being. How you deal with stress will determine to a great extent how successful you will be in teaching.

Understanding Stress

Stress is an intense degree of nervous tension that results from anxiety. It occurs when people are unable to cope with the demands of a situation. The most stressful situations are those that people are least able to control. An increase in teacher stress and subsequent "burnout" has become a major concern in the teaching pro-fession. In a survey of 9,000 teachers, 75 percent indicated that their absences from school were often related to stress and tension.[3]

This high rate of stress is caused by many factors, including lack of respect from students, potential student violence, run-down school buildings, and unreasonable expectations from the public. Teachers are held accountable for helping students attain certain levels of achievement; yet, they find they must also act as counselors and stand-in parents. They are pressured to individualize, evaluate, motivate, and

[3]William C. Miller. *Dealing with Stress: A Challenge for Educators.* Bloomington, Ind.: Phi Delta Kappa Educational Foundation, 1979, p. 7.

maintain discipline. Good teachers combine all their knowledge, skill, and training in their daily encounters with students.

Although too much stress can cause physical and emotional problems, a certain amount of stress is desirable. Stress can give you a burst of energy and get your adrenalin flowing. In the right amount, stress will enable you to "rise to the occasion" and put forth the extra energy to get the job done. People react differently to potentially stressful situations. You may consider these situations challenging and stimulating, or you may become anxious and tense. How would you react if your cooperating teacher asked you to take over the class unexpectedly when a parent came for an unscheduled conference?

Sources of Stress

Any situation involving worry or tension may cause stress. You may encounter some of these sources of stress:

1 *Choice of career*—You may be wondering if you should be in the field of education after all. Perhaps you are finding it more difficult to work with students and to help them learn than you expected.

2 *Expectations of others*—Your parents, your former teachers, or family friends may have always expected you to grow up to be a teacher. You may be worried now that you are not able to live up to their expectations.

3 *Effectiveness of teaching*—The range of interests and abilities within any classroom is so wide that it is nearly impossible to fully meet the needs of every student. You may become frustrated because you cannot reach each student, regardless of how hard you try.

4 *Evaluation by supervisors*—Being evaluated is probably a stressful time for you. You worry about how your supervisors regard your efforts, especially if they observe one of your less successful lessons.

5 *Appreciation for your efforts*—Teaching requires a great deal of outside preparation: writing daily lesson plans, grading papers, making up tests and worksheets, setting up audiovisual equipment, developing materials, and planning units. It may seem that your efforts go unnoticed and unappreciated.

6 *Job market*—The job market may be tight when you graduate and seek employment. You may worry about how you will support yourself if you can't get a teaching job.

Some sources of stress originate in situations outside yourself. Clouds gather, and thunder booms. Jackhammers reverberate as construction begins on the new addition. Tony interrupts to tell you he's going to be sick. The first snowflake drifts down lazily. A parent enters with the cupcakes for this afternoon's Halloween party. The principal makes an announcement over the intercom. Any of these events can turn a well-ordered classroom into chaos, and chaos is a cause of stress.

Other external sources of stress generally center on circumstances such as these:

1 *Too much work for the time available*—You find you are staying up late at night and working weekends to get everything done. You have practically no free time and not enough social life. The day moves too quickly, and extra responsibilities—working on the school newspaper, bus duty, playground supervision—further intrude on your time.

2 *Unpleasant working environment*—Not everyone faces this problem, but those who do are disturbed by overcrowded classrooms; poorly maintained buildings; and/or old, drab schools with poor lighting in potentially dangerous inner-city neighborhoods.

3 *Lack of resources*—Some schools have old audiovisual equipment in need of repair. Books and materials you would like to use with your unit may be

Avoid worrying. Many things you worry about never happen. Other things work themselves out without the serious consequences you feared. Worrying doesn't solve problems; it only makes you less effective as a teacher. Don't worry about things you can't change; do something about things you *can* change. Feeling guilty or worrying about something you did earlier doesn't change what happened. Remembering unpleasant scenes only makes you uncomfortable. Things won't always go well, but it's important to keep the day's events in perspective. Perhaps only three things went wrong, but as many as twenty went well. Focus on the good things that happened.

Relationships   Find time to be with friends during student teaching. Some friends should be outside the field of education so that you can get your mind off school. You need to forget your students and teaching obligations for a while and laugh and talk about other things. You will also want some friends in whom you can confide about problems with your student teaching. By sharing your difficulties with each other, you may see things from a different point of view and be willing to try a new approach.

Your working relationships with supervisory personnel and other student teachers are also important. If you have a conflict with someone, it is usually best to discuss the problem with that person instead of worrying about it. Perhaps it is based on a misunderstanding and can be readily resolved. If there is simply a personality conflict or a basic difference in point of view, accept the situation, and get along the best you can. The relationship is only temporary.

Don't forget that your students may also be under stress. They don't know exactly what to expect from you. Let them know what your standards of behavior are and what will happen if they violate them. Give warnings only when you are prepared to act on them. Give assignments clearly so students will know what to do. Show them that you care and are willing to help. Be fair and consistent. If you can relieve your students' stress, they will perform better for you.

Dealing with Stress   One of the first steps in dealing with a problem that produces stress is to decide if the problem is really *yours*. If it isn't, turn it over to the person responsible for it. If it is your problem, brainstorm ways to solve it. If you don't know how to solve it, get help. Then proceed to solve the problem the best way you can.

When you feel stress because you have so many things to do, make a list of what must be done, in order of importance. Consider what must be done right away so that it will be completed when it is needed, such as starting a science experiment that takes two weeks to reach fruition. Set deadlines for getting these things done, and stick to your schedule. As you finish each task, check it off. This way you are aware of your accomplishments and aren't as likely to fall behind.

Don't worry about assignments because they seem too big. Break them into manageable chunks, and work on them a piece at a time. Do the hardest parts first, and save the most interesting tasks until the end. Each time you successfully complete one portion of the assignment, you will be motivated to try another until you are finished.

Keep your sense of humor. Be able to laugh with the children at your own mistakes. It is better to laugh with them when something goes wrong than to get angry. Even though it may not seem funny when it happens, you may see the humor later. Besides, laughter reduces stress, while anger increases it.

Feel free to say "no" to people when you feel you can't handle another responsibility. Do what is required of you and a little more, but don't accept unreasonable demands on your time. Someone may be taking advantage of your good nature. If you take on more responsibilities than you can manage, you will not do well in anything.

Taking Action   Some activities will keep stress from getting the better of you. Exercise—jogging, walking briskly, playing tennis or racquetball, working out in the gym—is good for you as a change of pace. Even though these forms of exercise can

Activity 1.2   One Day of Student Teaching

Time	Stressful Situation	Reactions	Rating	Avoidance/ Management Strategies

Typical extracurricular activities center around clubs (science, photography, mathematics, drama, foreign language, community action, future teachers, future homemakers, etc.); school publications (magazines, annuals, newspapers); athletic teams (football, basketball, baseball, track, golf, volleyball, wrestling); musical groups (marching band, jazz band, orchestra, chorus); and scholastic honor societies (Beta Club, Quill and Scroll, National Honor Society). School-sponsored dances, carnivals, and festivals also qualify as extracurricular activities. This variety gives you a wide range from which to choose if you are asked to participate. The list of possibilities for after-hours involvement seems endless. You may help with science fair projects or work at a book fair; you may judge a storytelling contest or a debate; you may coach intramural sports, accompany students on special trips, mend costumes for a play, paint sets, move band equipment, organize the safety patrol—the list goes on and on. Students involved in extracurricular activities are usually highly motivated in the chosen areas and therefore make the sessions enjoyable, so go ahead and give a chosen activity a try.

You may think of extracurricular activities as just another intrusion on your already vanishing free time, or you may remember that extracurricular activities were really important to you when you were your students' age. Contribute some time and effort to give your students some valuable experiences.

If your school has a handbook, read the section on extracurricular activities. Find out what roles faculty members play and the rules and restrictions for each activity. Then you will be able to choose activities or assist with assigned activities knowledgeably.

You should encourage students to participate in extracurricular activities because they gain experience that helps them succeed in college.[4] You might point out that these activities provide opportunities for gaining recognition, engaging in new experiences, developing talents, and extending textbook learning into meaningful experiences. You should also watch that some students don't become too involved, however, and thereby place their academic progress at risk.

When you apply for a job, be sure to mention any extracurricular activities that you supported during student teaching. Direct experience with such activities as editing the school paper or constructing sets for a play may make you a more viable candidate for a teaching position.

DISCUSSION QUESTIONS

These discussion questions and those near the end of each chapter in this text may be handled in different ways. Questions may be discussed by the entire class, shared with partners, considered in small groups, or adapted for role playing.

1 Role play what you should do if you join the teachers in the faculty lounge and hear them discussing one of your students in a way you feel is unfair to the student. Should you get up quietly and leave, sit there quietly and not enter into the discussion, speak out and defend the student, or mention that you think it is wrong to talk about students that way?

2 Do you believe the school is responsible for providing education in values, sex, systems of government (including communism), morality, and religion? If so, how should these matters be handled? What would your approach be? Discuss this issue in small groups.

3 What are some things that cause stress? What are some ways you can reduce these stressors? Can you think of a time when you handled a stressful situation especially well?

[4]William J. Bennett. *What Works: Research about Teaching and Learning.* Washington, D.C.: United States Department of Education, 1986.

Activity 1.3   Analyzing Stress

1. Identify a recent stressful situation. _____

_____

_____

2. Why did this particular situation cause you to feel stress? _____

_____

_____

3. How did you react? _____

_____

_____

4. Could the situation have been avoided? If so, how? What else could you have done? _____

_____

_____

5. Should you have reacted differently? What else could you have done? _____

_____

_____

6. What was most effective in helping you overcome your feelings of stress? _____

_____

_____

7. Could you have used this situation in a positive way? How? _____

_____

_____

8. How could you have reduced the intensity of the stress? _____

_____

_____

9. If the same thing happens again, how can you manage the stress better? _____

_____

_____

Activity 1.4   Practices for Good Teaching

Read the list of guidelines related to good teaching practices near the end of the chapter. Periodically, consider your quality of performance in each of these areas and rate yourself on a scale of 1 (lowest) to 5 (highest) for each guideline.

Guidelines	Rating Periods			
	1	2	3	4
1. Organize content around concepts.				
2. Support and respond to students.				
3. Encourage meaning making.				
4. Make authentic assignments.				
5. Integrate thinking skills.				
6. Create a learning community.				
7. Stress conceptual understanding.				
8. Use teachable moments.				
9. Relate material to prior knowledge.				
10. Actively engage students.				

For each rating period, identify your strengths and weaknesses according to the guidelines. Consider how you might develop your strengths and reduce your weaknesses.

First period:

   Strengths:

   Weaknesses:

Second period:

   Strengths:

   Weaknesses:

Third period:

  Strengths:

  Weaknesses:

Fourth period:

  Strengths:

  Weaknesses:

  Reflect on your overall teaching style and identify those guidelines that you follow most closely.

4 What are some common areas of stress that you can share with other student teachers? Can any changes be made in policies or assignments to reduce the stress?

5 Consider the guidelines for good teaching. What are your reactions to them? Which ones are in accord with your personal philosophy of teaching? Which ones might cause you difficulty?

6 Think of the teachers you have had. Which characteristics of good teaching did they possess? Which characteristics were often lacking? Do you think you would have learned more if your teachers had implemented the guidelines identified in this chapter?

7 What can you do to help with extracurricular activities? What have you done so far? Can you think of a way to help that no one else is doing? What is it?

8 What special talents or interests do you have that could help you become involved with extracurricular activities?

SELECTED REFERENCES

Bennett, William J. *What Works: Research about Teaching and Learning*. Washington, D.C.: United States Department of Education, 1986.

"Beyond 'Effective Teaching'." *Educational Leadership* 49 (April 1992) (series of articles).

Blair, Timothy R. "Teacher Effectiveness: The Know-How to Improve Student Learning." *The Reading Teacher* 38 (November 1984): 138–42.

Brophy, Jere. "Probing the Subtleties of Subject-Matter Teaching." *Educational Leadership* 49 (April 1992): 4–8.

Connors, Eugene T. *Student Discipline and the Law*. Bloomington, Ind.: Phi Delta Kappa Educational Foundation, 1979.

London, Samuel B., and Stephen W. Stile. *The School's Role in the Prevention of Child Abuse*. Bloomington, Ind.: Phi Delta Kappa Educational Foundation, 1982.

Miller, William C. *Dealing with Stress: A Challenge for Educators*. Bloomington, Ind.: Phi Delta Kappa Educational Foundation, 1979.

Monks, Robert L., and Ernest I. Proulx. *Legal Basics for Teachers*. Bloomington, Ind.: Phi Delta Kappa Educational Foundation, 1986.

Otto, Wayne, Anne Wolf, and Roger G. Eldridge. "Managing Instruction." In *Handbook of Reading Research*. P. David Pearson, Ed. New York: Longman, 1984, pp. 799–828.

Rosenshine, Barak, and Robert Stevens. "Classroom Instruction in Reading." In *Handbook of Reading Research*. P. David Pearson, Ed. New York: Longman, 1984, pp. 745–98.

Rossow, Lawrence, and Janice Hininger. *Students and the Law*. Bloomington, Ind.: Phi Delta Kappa Educational Foundation, 1991.

Rupley, William H., Beth S. Wise, and John W. Logan. "Research in Effective Teaching: An Overview of Its Development." In *Effective Teaching of Reading: Research and Practice*. James V. Hoffman, Ed. Newark, Del.: International Reading Association, 1986, pp. 3–36.

Selye, Hans. *Stress without Distress*. Philadelphia: J. B. Lippincott, 1974.

2

Human Relations

Mrs. Sanchez is a cooperating teacher. Miss Mosley is her student teacher.

Mrs. Sanchez: Miss Mosley, there is going to be a special in-service education program at the teacher center Thursday evening at 8:00. Would you like to attend the session with me?

Miss Mosley: What is the topic?

Mrs. Sanchez: Our reading program. I know you aren't required to attend, but this is an excellent opportunity for you to learn about the materials you will be using for the remainder of the semester. I thought you would want to take advantage of it. I'll be glad to drive you over there, if you need transportation.

Miss Mosley: Yes, I would like to go. Thank you for inviting me.

At the end of the semester, Miss Mosley is pleased to see that Mrs. Sanchez has made the comment: "Interested in self-improvement of teaching skills."

1. Did Mrs. Sanchez have a good basis for her evaluative comment? Why or why not?
2. Do you show interest in self-improvement of teaching skills when opportunities are presented?

FOCUS ON SPECIFIC RELATIONSHIPS

An important part of the student teaching experience is developing appropriate relationships with a variety of people—students, college supervisors, cooperating teachers, other school personnel, other student teachers, and parents. Your inter-action with these people can be a major factor in your overall success as a student teacher. Let us first look at each of these relationships separately.

STUDENTS

The most important and most demanding set of relationships you must handle as a student teacher is the one with your students. They are the ones to whom you hope to impart the knowledge you have gleaned from your program of preparation. It is important to develop a positive and cooperative relationship with each student in the class. Some student teachers misunderstand the nature of this relationship. They want to be "buddies" with the students because this seems the best way to be liked. Unfortunately, being liked is not sufficient for a student/teacher relationship; respect is also important, as is recognition of the student teacher as an authority figure. The students' respect must be earned, and it takes time to earn it. This respect is not automatically accorded. Development of a "buddy" relationship can undermine the students' respect for you as an authority figure, and thus adversely affect classroom control. We will consider the topic of classroom control more thoroughly at a later time.

What, then, should your relationship with your students be? An appropriate relationship will require a great deal of perceptiveness and understanding on your part.

General Guidelines

First, you must treat each student as a worthwhile individual. You must react pos-itively to all students and show them you care about their progress and well-being. Something so simple as learning the students' names quickly can have a positive effect on your relationships with them. Noticing that a student was absent the day before and inquiring about her health or indicating that she was missed shows the student that you care. When students perform well, your approving comments help establish a positive relationship.

It is important to let the students know you respect them as individuals. You can do this by listening to their opinions and expressions of feelings and responding to them in a way that shows you have given careful thought to their ideas. Dismissing students' ideas as trivial or worthless will indicate that you feel they are unable to contribute effectively to the class. Such actions can cause students to withdraw from the learning environment, rather than participate in classroom activities.

Nonverbal behavior can also promote good relationships with students. *Smile* at them often. Show them that you enjoy them. Let all the students know you are there to help them. *Listen* to them when they voice problems, and try to help each one. Let them know that you are on their side.

One important aspect of respecting students' individuality is to avoid labeling them according to racial, ethnic, socioeconomic, or sex stereotypes. Expectations should not be the same for all African-Americans, all whites, all Hispanics, all people of Polish extraction, all Jews, all poor people, all rich people, all boys, or all girls. Each of these groups has industrious individuals and others who are lazy; bright individuals and others who are dull; honest individuals and others who are dishon-est; clean individuals and others who are not; athletic individuals and some who are not; and so on. Each member of a group should be looked upon as an individual with a variety of traits acquired through interaction with the environment. As a student teacher, you are an important part of that environment, and, therefore, you help to shape some of the traits your students develop. Don't be so narrow-minded as to expect all members of a group to be alike.

Avoiding Sexism   The following case study shows a situation involving sex stereotypes.

Case Study: Sex Stereotypes

Miss Chambers was a student teacher in a fifth-grade class that was studying Mexico. She thought that staging a fiesta, which would give the children the opportunity to sample many Mexican foods, would be a good teaching device.

She told the boys to plan and construct a set to look like a festive Mexican home, while the girls located and prepared the foods to be tried. Darren, who was an excellent cook, wanted to prepare the tamales. Miss Chambers admonished him with the reply, "Cooking is women's work. You help the boys with the construction."

1. What is your analysis of Miss Chambers' reply to Darren?
2. What would you have said?
3. Do you suppose some of the girls might have enjoyed the construction project better than the cooking?
4. How would you have handled the entire project?

Sex stereotypes, such as the one Miss Chambers voiced, are unfortunately not uncommon. Certain activities, toys, and manners of speaking are arbitrarily attributed to boys and others to girls. A boy or girl who fails to fit the stereotype is treated as abnormal, instead of as an individual with a right to behave in a way that does not fit the stereotype. Teachers often discourage boys from crying, cooking, or sewing, saying that they are not appropriate activities for boys, just as other activities are considered inappropriate for girls.

Sexism is an issue you should be aware of when you choose materials and work with male and female students. It is a way of treating males and females differently solely on the basis of their sex. The practice of sexism can restrict what a person becomes by limiting choices of behavior and careers. Title IX of the Education Amendments Act of 1972 was enacted by Congress to prohibit discrimination against males or females in federally assisted education programs. Even though it is no longer legal to discriminate, many people continue to do so through their attitudes toward sex roles.

Consider your own feelings by answering the following questions: Are men or women more likely to cry? Should the wife or husband be the primary provider for a family? Are girls or boys likely to be better at each of the following: reading, math, science, cooking, industrial arts, or sewing? Who will cause the most discipline problems—boys or girls? If you have definite choices of one sex in each of your answers, you are probably reflecting the sex role stereotypes in our society.

According to research, there are very few innate differences between the sexes. Although biological factors are significant in shaping some masculine behavior, cultural factors can override biological impulses.[1] Some of the differences that appear to exist may be the result of different expectations for boys and girls as they grow

---

[1]D. Cooper Thompson. "A New View of Masculinity." *Educational Leadership*, (December 1985/January 1986): 55.

up. You may be helping to cause the differences. Instead, you should be helping both boys and girls recognize the breadth of their behavioral and career choices. Boys should be permitted to try cooking and sewing as well as carpentry, and they should be allowed to show emotions, ask for help, and be gentle and cooperative, without having their masculinity questioned. Girls should not just be allowed to engage in athletic activities, but should be encouraged to do so. They should also be encouraged in studies of math and science, for this is one way of acknowledging that girls may wish to enter technical fields that require knowledge of these subjects.

It may be desirable for you to talk about how men and women are beginning to explore nontraditional career choices, such as nursing for males and construction work for females. A girl who says she wants to be an airplane pilot should be given as much reinforcement as a boy who says the same thing.

In addition, you should try to give your attention to girls and boys equally. All students need to be given chances to respond and receive teacher feedback.

Your language may unintentionally support sexist stereotypes. When you speak of the builders of our nation as forefathers, for example, it may seem to young children that women had no part. Use of the generic *he* may also cause young, and even adolescent, students to assume that only males are the topic of conversation. Use of terms such as *mailman* and *policeman* to refer to letter carriers and police officers seems to close these careers to females. Much of this language has probably been ingrained since childhood and may be difficult to avoid. Considering the possible effects of such usage on your students, however, you should attempt to eliminate it from your speech patterns.

Dealing with Cultural Diversity   Some people have grown up hearing language that is derogatory toward certain racial, ethnic, or socioeconomic groups. This language must also be eliminated from your vocabulary, or you can do real damage to some of your students' self-concepts.

The classes you are asked to teach will be culturally diverse. It is part of your responsibility to help the students develop positive cultural identities and accept classmates with other cultural backgrounds. They need to have opportunities to read material by and about people from their own cultural backgrounds and from a variety of other backgrounds. They also need to be led to see that there are many ways that people from other cultures are like them: they often share similar dreams, emotions, and experiences. Students also need to be helped to understand why some differences exist and to learn to value those differences for the variety and interest that culturally diverse people add to our nation and the world.

Classrooms that have culturally diverse populations should direct attention to the contributions and values of all cultures represented, as well as some that are not, in order to allow the students involved to feel a part of the educational experience and to experience an increased sense of self-worth. In social studies classes, for example, inclusion of such material should be a natural occurrence. Contributions to our society, other societies, and the world at large made by people from different cultures, as well as difficulties faced by these people, can be emphasized as you teach history, geography, political science, and current events. In science, scientific contributions of people from varying cultures should be emphasized. You may need to point out the cultural background of the scientist in question, or else the students may simply assume that the person was from their own culture or the culture that they expect to produce scientists. In literature, selections by and about people from different cultures should be included. (Complete Activity 2.1 to see how your classroom rates in this area.)

On special occasions in school, students from different cultural backgrounds should sometimes be called upon to explain how celebrations of those occasions differ for them or how they celebrate similar things at different times of the year. Special attention to the effects that the settlement of the Pilgrims in America had on the Native American inhabitants, for example, or consideration of the points of

Activity 2.1   Checking for Cultural Bias and Stereotypes in Reading Materials

1. Are a variety of cultures represented in the illustrations in the materials? _____

2. Are a variety of cultures represented in the written texts of the materials? _____

3. In the illustrations, are the people from any particular cultures shown in stereotyped occupations or activities? _____ If so, which ones? _____

   _____

   _____

4. In the written texts, are the people from any particular cultures described or represented in stereotyped occupations or activities? _____ If so, which ones? _____

   _____

   _____

5. From what cultures do the main characters in stories or featured characters in expository text come?

   _____

   _____

6. Are any of the materials written by people from other cultures? _____ If so, which ones?

   _____

   _____

7. Are any of the materials illustrated by people from other cultures? _____ If so, which ones?

   _____

   _____

8. What do the results of your analysis of the reading materials in your classroom indicate that you need to do in order to provide your students with positive multicultural reading experiences? _____

   _____

   _____

view that groups such as the Tories, Native Americans, British, and French had toward the American Revolution may be appropriate in expanding multicultural awareness and understanding.

Instructional materials in the classroom should be free of cultural bias. Even math activities may show cultural bias by the situations described in statement problems. Teachers must be vigilant and de-emphasize material that could cause some children to feel as if they do not "fit in" with the class.

Cooperative learning groups (described in Chapter 5) should be formed in a way that results in multicultural groupings. In such situations, the students will learn from each other and come to respect the contributions made by the other group members.

In classrooms where there is little or no cultural diversity, an even more urgent need exists to make students aware of the ways in which people may be different from them, while sharing some characteristics with them. They need to realize that not all contributions to society have come from their own restricted group, but that all kinds of people have influenced their world. Not only printed materials, but also audiovisual resources, should be brought to class to help make the discussions of other cultures as vivid and complete as possible.

Understanding of the culture or cultures represented in your classroom is very important for you as a student teacher. For example, a child from one culture may look down and fail to meet your eye as a sign of respect, and you may use your cultural background to misinterpret this action negatively. One beginning teacher gave a test to a group of Navaho children and was aghast when she saw them helping each other. She interpreted their actions as cheating, but in their culture cooperation and helping each other are considered to be desirable. (Complete the Class Culture Survey in Activity 2.2 to help you plan ways to adjust for multicultural class membership.)

Some of your students may speak little or no English but speak another language, while you may not speak that other language. How can you relate positively to such a student? It takes persistence and effort, but you can have a positive impact. Include the student in classroom activities that require little language from the first moment he or she enters the classroom. At the elementary level, these activities may include playing action games at recess, drawing and painting, and viewing displays and demonstrations. At the secondary level, the activities may include almost all aspects of a physical education class or some vocational classes and viewing displays and demonstrations in other areas. You should attempt to communicate with the student through gestures, pictures, and any words you know from her or his language. Whatever you do, even though attempting to communicate with this student may be frustrating, always be positive. Encourage other students to include the new student in their activities, explaining that they are already at home in this school and can make the new student comfortable by helping him or her learn the standard procedures and popular activities. Students often take behavioral cues from their teachers.

Some of the students in your class are likely to speak nonstandard dialects of English. Part of your job as a teacher is to expose them to standard English so that they can become upwardly mobile in society. On the other hand, you must model standard English and reinforce its use in school settings without discrediting their home language. Home language should be treated as one communication system and standard English ("school language") as an alternate system that can be useful for them to know. Students should not be reprimanded for using their home language for communications with other students in informal settings, but should practice standard English in formal situations, such as giving oral reports and producing written reports. Elementary classroom teachers and secondary English teachers especially must approach this task with understanding and sensitivity.

It is the purpose of multicultural education to promote understanding among the varied people in our country. Teachers have to find ways to accomplish this in their own classrooms.

Showing Respect for and Fairness to All Students   You can show respect for your students by allowing them to take on responsibilities. Giving students tasks for which they are responsible, no matter how small the tasks may be, shows that you trust them to fulfill the duties and recognize their capabilities to do so. This attitude can have an enormous effect upon the way a student responds to you. Let us look at the case of Randy as an example.

Case Study: Showing Respect for Students

Randy was a sixth-grade student who had failed two previous grades. As a consequence, he was 14 years old in a classroom with many 11- and 12-year-olds. He was larger than any of the other students and had different interests. To make matters worse, he was poor, and most of his clothing was worn and faded. The heels of his boots were run over, and his sleeves were a little too short for his arms. His general style of dress was reminiscent of a stereotypical motorcycle gang member in late-night movies.

Randy was generally quiet and obedient in class, but rarely made any attempt to do his assignments. He displayed an extremely negative self-concept, informing the student teacher, Miss Davis, "I'm too dumb to do that," when she encouraged him to try some of the work.

Miss Davis tried very hard to treat Randy the same way she treated the other students. She called on him to respond in class and listened respectfully to his replies. She greeted him when he entered the classroom in the morning. She smiled and spoke when she passed him in the hall. She gave him much encouragement and assistance during directed study periods. Still, she felt she was making little headway. To be sure, he talked a *little* more in class than he had previously, and turned in a few more assignments, but

Miss Davis still did not feel she had reached Randy.

One day, as Randy was leaving the classroom to go home for lunch, Miss Davis realized she had a letter that needed to be mailed and remembered that Randy passed by a mailbox on his way home. She called to him and asked him if he would do her a favor and mail the letter. Randy looked at her in disbelief. *Nobody* at school had ever trusted him to take responsibility for *anything*. He hesitated and said, "You want *me* to mail it?"

Miss Davis replied, "I would appreciate your doing it, if you don't mind."

Randy walked over and picked up the letter, glancing around to see if others had heard this exchange. "I'll be sure it gets mailed," he told Miss Davis rather loudly, and walked out of the room proudly holding the letter.

Upon returning to the room after lunch, the first thing he told Miss Davis was, "I mailed your letter." He said it with a smile of satisfaction.

Thereafter, Randy began to respond more and more to Miss Davis' encouragement to do assignments. He seemed to try much harder to do what she thought he could do. He did not become an overnight scholar, but he improved in all his work and once even scored a "100" in mathematics. And he continued to carry Miss Davis' letters with pride.

1. What is your analysis of the way Miss Davis handled Randy?
2. Would you have treated the situation differently in any way?

It is important to give attention to all students. Do not favor a few with your attention and ignore or avoid others. This may be difficult, for some students are not as appealing as others. Some dress carelessly or shabbily, fail to wash, or have belligerent attitudes. It is your challenge to be as accepting of and positive about the appropriate behaviors these students exhibit as you are of the neat, clean, and cooperative students. This does not mean you should accept behavior that deviates from school rules, but it does mean you should show acceptance of the individual,

Activity 2.2   Class Culture Survey

1. What different cultural backgrounds are represented by the students in your classroom?

    Cultures   **Number of Students**

    a.

    b.

    c.

    d.

    e.

    f.

2. What are some important holidays or events for the various cultural groups in your class?

    a.

    b.

    c.

    d.

    e.

    f.

3. List any students in your class who speak a language other than English as their primary language.
    Make a checkmark by the language if you can speak it.

    Student's Name   **Other Language**   **Can You Speak It?**

    a.

    b.

    c.

    d.

    e.

    f.

even when you show disapproval of her or his behavior. It also means you should find traits in each person to which you can react positively. Try to develop a sense of community in your classroom—a feeling of togetherness in which all students can feel they are valued members of the class. Now complete Activity 2.3 to help you focus on this behavior.

After you have completed Activity 2.3, attempt to use as many of the comments from the activity as you can. Then do Activity 2.4 as a follow-up procedure to help you analyze your results.

To have a good relationship with your students, absolute fairness is important. If you have a rule, enforce it equally for all students. Any hint that you have "teacher's pets" will cause poor relationships between you and the majority of the class.

Honesty is also important in your relationship with your students. Students quickly recognize insincerity and resent it.

Therefore, to establish good relationships with students, you should do the following:

1 Treat each student as a worthwhile individual, worthy of respect.
2 Use appropriate nonverbal behavior in your interactions with students.
3 Avoid labels and stereotypes when working with students.
4 Offer students chances to take on responsibilities.
5 Give attention to all students.
6 Be positive toward all students.
7 Be fair to all students.
8 Be honest with all students.

COLLEGE SUPERVISORS

Your relationship with your college supervisor is also important. He or she has the responsibility for overseeing and critiquing your work in the classroom. The college supervisor is there to help you throughout the student teaching experience, as well as to determine your grade at the end. Therefore, the college supervisor will be offering, either orally or in writing, suggestions for improving your teaching. These suggestions are intended to help you analyze what you are doing and make the most of your field experience. They are not meant as personal attacks upon your competence. Try to consider the suggestions objectively and ask questions about points that may be unclear, rather than react defensively and produce excuses for mistakes you may have made. If you show your college supervisor that you are open to suggestions and will make an effort to benefit from constructive criticism, your relationship is likely to be a good one.

A way to show that you are eager to improve and that you welcome your college supervisor's help is to try to put his or her suggestions into practice as soon as possible. When your supervisor makes a suggestion and subsequently sees no attempt on your part to change, he or she is likely to become irritated with your behavior. On the other hand, if your supervisor sees you working to incorporate the suggestion into your teaching, he or she is likely to perceive you as a serious student with a desire to become a good teacher.

Asking pertinent questions of your college supervisor shows a desire to improve and an interest in seeking new knowledge. These attributes are desirable in a student teacher and are likely to be appreciated. After observing your teaching, your college supervisor will probably hold a conference with you or with both you and your cooperating teacher. It is a good idea to take the written comments your college supervisor has made about your performance to these scheduled conferences. If conferences are not automatic, don't hesitate to request them if you feel the need for more feedback.

Case Study: Fear of Exposure

Dale Martin was a secondary school teacher, assigned to two classes of algebra, a class of plane geometry, and a class of trigonometry. His college supervisor had visited him several times, but all visits had been during one of his algebra classes. Dale felt very confident and comfortable teaching the algebra classes, and his comments from his college supervisor had all been positive. He was really struggling with the trigonometry class, however, and could sense that his cooperating teacher was displeased with his efforts. Dale confessed his concern to Alvin James, a student teacher in physical education.

Alvin suggested that Dale ask Mr. Walsky, their college supervisor, to make a point of sitting in on the trigonometry class on his next visit to the school, so that he could give Dale some feedback. Dale told Alvin that he thought he had better leave well enough alone—Mr. Walsky had only seen him in successful experiences. Perhaps if he saw the trigonometry class, Mr. Walsky's overall evaluation at the end of the quarter would be lower. Acting on this reasoning, Dale said nothing to Mr. Walsky.

1. How do you feel about Dale's situation?
2. What is your opinion of Alvin's advice?
3. What would you have done?
4. What is likely to be the result of Dale's decision?

When speaking with your college supervisor, it is important to be straightforward about your problems. He or she is the person best equipped to act as liaison between you and your cooperating teacher or other school personnel, if the need arises. Your honesty will make the supervisor's job easier and will probably ultimately improve your situation. Your openness about problems will also improve the rapport between you and the college supervisor.

The college supervisor is there to help you. Your openness, honesty, and willingness to accept suggestions will create a good relationship that makes it easier for the supervisor to help.

COOPERATING TEACHERS

A good relationship with your cooperating teacher is vital for achieving maximum benefit from the student teaching experience. Whereas your college supervisor may be in contact with you once or twice a week for a period or two, your cooperating teacher is with you every day. You and your cooperating teacher will be working together for the best interest of the students.

It is important to remember that the cooperating teacher has ultimate responsibility for the classroom to which you are assigned. She or he is legally responsible, and because of the responsibility, some cooperating teachers are more hesitant than others to relinquish control. The way you conduct yourself initially will have a strong influence upon how the cooperating teacher feels about leaving you in control. Taking an interest in everything that is going on in the classroom, asking questions about appropriate procedures and classroom rules, and making notes of information the cooperating teacher offers may be helpful. Being responsive to requests for assistance (putting up bulletin boards, grading test papers, etc.) will show the cooperating teacher that you are a willing worker.

Your appearance and manner are also important. Your cooperating teacher will feel more comfortable entrusting you with her or his charges if you dress appropriately (look more like a teacher than a student), speak correctly (use standard English), and exhibit self-confidence.

Activity 2.3   Attending to Students*

List the students in your class (if you have a self-contained classroom) or one of your classes (if your students change classes throughout the day). After each student's name, note something that you could say to this student to make him or her feel accepted and appreciated. Consider positive comments about schoolwork, athletic exploits, personal appearance, behavior, or family.

	Student's Name	Comments
1.		
2.		
3.		
4.		
5.		
6.		
7.		
8.		
9.		
10.		
11.		
12.		
13.		
14.		
15.		
16.		
17.		
18.		
19.		
20.		
21.		
22.		

*If you have several classes with different students, you may want to duplicate these pages and carry out this activity for each class.

Student's Name	**Comments**
23.	
24.	
25.	
26.	
27.	
28.	
29.	
30.	
31.	
32.	
33.	
34.	
35.	
36.	

Activity 2.4   Analyzing Student Interactions*

Examine the list of students and possible comments that you made for Activity 2.3. Below, write down the name of each student for whom you tried the comments. After the student's name, indicate her or his reaction to the comment. Did she or he smile, frown, make a positive comment in response, make a negative comment in response, make a gesture of acceptance, or ignore the comment? Consider what the student's response indicates to you about future interactions with her or him. Did you strike a responsive chord, or do you need to think of another approach? Why did your comment elicit the reaction that it did?

	Student's Name	Result of Interaction
1.		
2.		
3.		
4.		
5.		
6.		
7.		
8.		
9.		
10.		
11.		
12.		
13.		
14.		
15.		
16.		
17.		
18.		
19.		
20.		
21.		

*If you have several classes with different students, you may want to duplicate these pages and carry out this activity for each class.

	Student's Name	**Result of Interaction**
22.	_____	_____
23.	_____	_____
24.	_____	_____
25.	_____	_____
26.	_____	_____
27.	_____	_____
28.	_____	_____
29.	_____	_____
30.	_____	_____
31.	_____	_____
32.	_____	_____
33.	_____	_____
34.	_____	_____
35.	_____	_____
36.	_____	_____

Notes for the future based on my results:

Case Study: Appropriate Dress

Susan Granger was a secondary English student teacher. Her cooperating teacher was Mrs. Barfield, a 50-year-old English teacher.

On the first day of student teaching, Susan reported to her assignment wearing a pair of jeans, a tee shirt, and a pair of tennis shoes. Mrs. Barfield made the mistake of asking Susan if she was a new student in the class before she had a chance to introduce herself. When she learned who Susan was, Mrs. Barfield said, "Ms. Granger, I believe you need to dress more appropriately for teaching in the future."

Susan, noticing that Mrs. Barfield was clad in casual slacks and shirt, was furious. Later that day she said to her roommate, "Who does she think she is, telling me what to wear? She had on pants herself."

1. What do you think about Mrs. Barfield's comment to Susan?
2. Was it justified?
3. Was there a difference in Mrs. Barfield's dressing as she did and Susan being dressed as she was? If so, what was the difference?
4. Might Susan's attire affect her relationship with Mrs. Barfield? Might it affect her relationship with her secondary students?

When you are given an actual teaching assignment, careful planning is likely to evoke a positive response from your cooperating teacher. Showing responsibility in small ways will encourage the cooperating teacher to give you larger responsibilities. (Chapter 3 has tips for good planning.)

Although you may be very eager to begin teaching, do not *demand* that your teacher let you start. Demonstrate your readiness; then *suggest* that you are ready. If this fails, you may wish to consult your college supervisor, who can act as a liaison.

You may find that your cooperating teacher does some things differently from the way you would do them and/or the way you have been taught. Do not criticize her or his methods; ask *why* she or he does things that way. Weigh the pros and cons of the teacher's method. If you feel it is not the best way, simply ask if you can try another way in which you have some background. Most cooperating teachers expect some experimentation and will allow this without your resorting to an attack on an existing procedure. This approach can certainly help your relationship with the teacher, and, upon examination, you may find things of value in the teacher's approach that you will wish to use also. Just because you have not been exposed to an idea or approach before does not mean it is not a good one.

Most programs have specified minimum requirements that student teachers are expected to meet. If you are willing to do only the *minimum* expected of you, your relationship with the cooperating teacher may be less than perfect. Dedicated educators do not settle for doing the least they can get by with doing.

Your cooperating teacher, like your college supervisor, will be giving you oral and/or written suggestions and constructive criticism. Accepting these comments as avenues to improvement will enhance the rapport between you and your cooperating teacher. If the teacher sees that you are attempting to put the suggestions to work, she or he will be more likely to have positive feelings toward you as a prospective member of the profession. Ignoring suggestions or indicating that you cannot or will not change will not promote a good relationship.

Case Study: No Desire to Change

In his first conference with his cooperating teacher, Leon Garritt was told, "Mr. Garritt, you must watch your English when you are speaking to the class. I noticed you saying 'he don't' and 'I seen' several times during this single lesson."

Leon responded, "That's the way everybody talks back home. I've talked that way all my life. It's too late to change now. Besides, I'm going back home to teach. I want to sound like everyone else."

1. How do you think Leon's teacher responded to Leon's explanation?
2. Do you think Leon's reaction affected his relationship with the teacher? In what way?
3. How would you have responded if you had been Leon?
4. How would you have responded if you had been Leon's teacher?
5. Does where Leon plans to teach have any relevance to the issue at hand?

Taking the initiative and offering assistance before it is requested shows the teacher that you are ready to be a part of classroom activities. Waiting to be told every move to make is a sign of lack of maturity and confidence.

You can see that showing the cooperative teacher your preparedness, willingness, and ability to perform in the classroom can do much to enhance your relationship. Appropriate reactions to suggestions and criticism and willingness to work cooperatively are also important.

OTHER SCHOOL PERSONNEL

In addition to building a good relationship with your cooperating teacher, you need to develop positive relationships with other school personnel, including other teachers, administrators, counselors, supervisors, secretaries, custodial staff members, and cafeteria workers. From time to time you will have occasion to interact with all of these people.

On your first day in the school, introduce yourself to the school personnel with whom you come in contact. Explain that, since you are a student teacher and may need their assistance in the future, you are pleased to meet them. They will appreciate your acknowledgment that you may need their help, and they may seek opportunities to help you. Even if you do not need their aid, just knowing them and realizing that they know who you are will make life in the school more comfortable.

Case Study: Pleasantness Pays Off

Miss Garcia, a student teacher in first grade, had gone out of her way to meet and be pleasant to the school custodian, Mr. Nabors, who had a reputation among some of the teachers of being uncooperative. She had cause to be glad she had done so on the first day her cooperating teacher left her in charge of the class.

The children were moving down the hall toward their classroom following a milk break, when Mario became sick at his stomach. The children squealed and scattered as Mario's snack gushed onto the floor. Mario burst into tears.

Mr. Nabors, hearing the commotion, hurried over to help Miss Garcia. He made certain that the remainder of the class lined up again and became quiet, while Miss Garcia calmed Mario. Then he assured Miss Garcia that he would take care of cleaning the hall immediately, while she continued with her normal procedures.

1. Do you think Miss Garcia's friendly approach to the custodian worked in her favor?
2. In your opinion, is it possible that the custodian's reputation is unjust?
3. How might the other teachers elicit more cooperation from him?

Sharing experiences with other student teachers can help you analyze and solve problems.

Other teachers may offer valuable suggestions about teaching or disciplinary actions and may provide you with support and counsel in the absence of your cooperating teacher. Administrators can help you become acclimated to the school and school policies and may also offer useful information about your responsibilities as a member of the profession. Supervisors may offer critiques of your teaching procedures, or they may provide materials that will be helpful to you in your lessons. Custodians may help with incidents such as the one cited in the previous case study, as well as with major and minor spills of food, paints, or other materials in the classroom. Cafeteria workers may alert you to problems developing in the cafeteria before they are beyond control.

In brief, you should be pleasant to all school personnel and cooperate with them as necessary. Your friendliness and cooperation will be returned in kind.

OTHER STUDENT TEACHERS

There are probably other student teachers assigned to your school; if not, you have probably been assigned to a seminar with student teachers from other schools. These peers are facing the same challenges that you are, even though the different situations make each assignment unique. If you are willing to share your experiences openly with these peers, you may find that they can help you analyze and solve the problems you face. At the same time, solutions you have discovered yourself may benefit others in the group. Openness and willingness to cooperate can make your relationships with the other student teachers very rewarding.

Just because another student teacher is teaching in an elementary school and you are teaching in a secondary school, or another teacher is a physical education teacher and you are a chemistry teacher, do not assume you cannot learn from each other. Regardless of level or subject area, many of the problems student teachers encounter, especially in the area of human relations, are similar.

Case Study: Learning from Others

Troy was assigned to a secondary geography class for his student teaching experience. He had planned for and taught several lessons, but had had trouble estimating the amount of time his plans were going to take. As a result, he had twice run out of instructional material before the period ended. He hadn't known what to do, so he had just let the students have a study period each time. He mentioned his problem in his student teaching seminar.

Carol was teaching in a sixth-grade self-contained classroom, but was expected to conduct certain classes during specified periods of the day. She had run into the same problem that Troy had. Her cooperating teacher had suggested planning several extra filler, or sponge, activities for each subject area in case her lessons did not take as much time as she expected. The practice had worked well for her. She mentioned several filler activities she had used for social studies, including blank outline maps to be filled in with data pertinent to the current topic, vocabulary card games, and construction of time lines. Troy adapted several of her ideas to meet the needs of his particular class and found that they worked well for him too. (See Chapter 5 for suggestions for filler activities.)

1. Do elementary and secondary student teachers have many common concerns such as the one Troy and Carol shared?
2. What are some of the common concerns?

Treat your fellow student teachers with the same respect you show the other teachers with whom you have contact. Listen to what they have to say in your seminars, and share your knowledge with them. The relationships can be mutually beneficial.

PARENTS

As a student teacher, you may or may not have a great deal of contact with parents. If such contact occurs, however, it is vitally important that you develop good relationships with them.

One factor in effective interaction with parents is knowing about the community in which you are student teaching. Awareness of the types of businesses, industries, and recreational facilities in the community will give you some insight into the background from which the parents come. Awareness of the general socioeconomic, racial, and ethnic balance of the community also will be helpful. Knowing that the people in the town are generally avid football fans and enthusiastically support the local high school team or realizing that they work in the coal mines and may have associated health problems can give you a basis for interacting with community members with greater understanding and empathy. For this reason, it is a good idea to spend some time familiarizing yourself with the community and its people. Walk around the downtown area and observe the businesses and the people. Attend recreational activities, such as ball games, concerts, dances, and festivals, and note community interests. Drive around the residential section, and observe the types of homes in which your students live. These experiences will help prepare you for encounters with parents.

Many parents are uncomfortable in the school environment, so when parents come to the school to discuss their child's progress, the teacher (or you as the student teacher) must make an effort to put them at ease. Open the conversation with a nonthreatening comment, perhaps about the weather or some recent local event. Then express your appreciation to the parent for taking the time to come to the school. It is difficult for many parents to schedule such visits, and your acknowledgment of this fact may put the parent more at ease. It is also best to begin the discussion of the student on a positive note. Almost all students have attributes that can be praised—a pleasant manner, creativity, talent in art or music, athletic ability, cooperativeness, or excellence in a particular academic area. Be honest with parents about problems, but do not be abrupt or unkind in your comments. Explain the procedures you plan to implement to correct the problem, and express anticipation of improvement. Try to end the interview with another positive note. Always stress your desire to help the child in any way you can, and urge the parents to consult you if they have any concerns. Throughout the conference, remain pleasant, calm, and objective.

It is important that the parents perceive you as a competent professional who is truly concerned about their child. If you put your best foot forward in any encounter with parents, they are more likely to be supportive of what you attempt to do with the students.

Listen to what parents have to tell you about their children. They can often give you information that will help you understand the students' strengths and weaknesses and thus help you plan instruction that will be most beneficial to the students. Parents will also be favorably impressed with your willingness to listen to what they have to say.

If you meet parents outside the school setting, smile and speak to them. Do not bring up problems at chance meetings. These should be covered in carefully planned conferences.

Case Study: Careless Comments Cause Problems

Mr. Meadows, a student teacher in the junior high school, saw the father of Joe Mills, one of his general science students, in the supermarket. Mr. Meadows walked over to Mr. Mills and said, "If Joe doesn't start coming to class more regularly, I will have to give him a failing grade. I think he cuts class to sneak off and smoke."

Mr. Mills was visibly upset. "Why haven't I been notified of this?" he demanded. "Why don't you keep parents adequately informed?" Then he turned and stalked away.

The next day, Mr. Meadows' cooperating teacher, Mrs. Daily, told him that Mr. Mills had called the principal and spoken angrily to him about the way the general science class was being handled. The principal demanded an explanation from Mrs. Daily. Now Mrs. Daily demanded an explanation from Mr. Meadows.

1. What mistakes did Mr. Meadows make in his contact with Mr. Mills?
2. What should he have done instead?
3. What would you have done?

Parents are potential allies. If you make an effort to communicate with them appropriately, they can help you better understand your students. Parents have their children's best interests at heart and will respond favorably to you if they believe you do too.

DISCUSSION QUESTIONS

1 What conditions could cause you to have problems in developing good relationships with your students? How might you work to overcome these difficulties?

2 Are there any special problems in developing good relationships with students of different racial or ethnic groups from yours? What are they? How can they be overcome?

3 How may the fact that the college supervisor is giving you a grade affect your relationship with him or her? Should this happen? Why or why not?

4 Why should you avoid criticism of your cooperating teacher's methods?

5 Why is it a good policy to develop positive relationships with many school personnel?

6 How can your relationships with other student teachers benefit your student teaching?

7 How could your poor relationships with parents inhibit a student's progress?

8 What will you do if:

    (a) You are student teaching in second grade, and an apparently bright and curious Vietnamese boy, who speaks no English, is in your class. Your cooperating teacher has ignored him, letting him entertain himself during lessons. The boy's father is an engineering student at the university who speaks broken English. The boy's mother is free during the day, but she speaks only a few words of English. No one in your school speaks any Vietnamese.

    (b) You are student teaching in sixth grade and have a girl in your class who comes from an impoverished home with no running water. The child's clothes are filthy. Her face and hands are encrusted with grime, and she smells bad. The other children make fun of her and refuse to sit next to her.

9 A student teacher in a secondary school located in an area with little racial diversity wrote the following entry in the journal she kept of her reactions to daily events at school:

"Students from other counties were visiting the school for some FFA event. One of my students walked out in the hallway (before class) and spoke to a visiting student, using a racial slur. I'm so tired of all these racial problems. They seem to get worse every year."

How should she have handled this situation?

10 The student teacher in Question 9 was told by her supervisor, "You could approach a situation like this by asking the student to put himself in the other person's place and think how the remarks would make him feel."

    (a) Do you think this advice would work? Why, or why not?

    (b) What other advice could have helped her to deal with such a situation?

SELECTED REFERENCES

Arthur, Beth M. "Working with New ESL Students in a Junior High School Reading Class." *Journal of Reading* 34 (May 1991): 628–31.

The ASCD Multicultural Education Commission. "Encouraging Multicultural Education." *Educational Leadership* 34 (January 1977): 288–91.

Au, Kathryn Heu-Pei, and Alice J. Kawakami. "Reviews and Reflections: Understanding and Celebrating Diversity in the Classroom." *Language Arts* 67 (October 1990): 607–10.

Banks, James A. "Integrating the Curriculum with Ethnic Content: Approaches and Guidelines." In *Multicultural Education: Issues and Perspectives.* J. A. Banks and C. A. McGee Banks, Eds. Boston: Allyn & Bacon, 1989, pp. 189–207.

Banks, James. *Multiethnic Education: Practices and Promises.* Bloomington, Ind.: Phi Delta Kappa Educational Foundation, 1977.

Barnes, Willie J. "How to Improve Teacher Behavior in Multiethnic Classrooms." *Educational Leadership* 34 (April 1977): 511–15.

Bennett, Christine. "A Case for Pluralism in the Schools," *Phi Delta Kappan* 62 (April 1981): 589–91.

Bowman, Barbara T. "Educating Language-Minority Children: Challenges and Opportunities." *Phi Delta Kappan* 71 (October 1989): 118–20.

Brophy, Jere, and Carolyn Evertson. *Student Characteristics and Teaching.* New York: Longman, 1981.

Campbell, Patricia B. "What's a Nice Girl Like You Doing in a Math Class?" *Phi Delta Kappan* 67 (March 1986): 516–20.

Carney, Janet. "The Language of Sexism: Sugar, Spice and Semantics." *Journal of Reading* 21 (October 1977): 51–56.

Computerworld staff writer. "Women Seen Suffering 'Subtle' Discrimination." *Computerworld* (June 1979): 16.

Early, Margaret. "Enabling First and Second Language Learners in the Classroom." *Language Arts* 67 (October 1990): 567–75.

Gilbert, Shirl E., II, and Geneva Gay. "Improving the Success in School of Poor Black Children." *Phi Delta Kappan* 67 (October 1985): 127–32.

Glenn, Charles L. "Just Schools for Minority Children." *Phi Delta Kappan* 70 (June 1989): 777–79.

Goldenberg, Claude. "Research Directions: Beginning Literacy Instruction for Spanish-Speaking Children." *Language Arts* 67 (October 1990): 590–98.

Gough, Pauline. *Sexism: New Issue in American Education.* Bloomington, Ind.: Phi Delta Kappa Educational Foundation, 1976.

Graening, Joyce. "Sexism: Does the American School Structure and Curriculum Promote It?" *Kappa Delta Pi Record* 17 (April 1981): 105–6.

Harvey, Glen. "Finding Reality among the Myths: Why What You Thought about Sex Equity in Education Isn't So." *Phi Delta Kappan* 67 (March 1986): 509–12.

Heathington, Betty S., Ed. *Breaking Barriers: Overcoming Career Stereotyping in Early Childhood.* College Park, Md.: University of Maryland, 1981.

Holliday, Bertha. "Towards a Model of Teacher-Child Transactional Processes Affecting Black Children's Academic Achievement." In *Beginnings: The Social and Affective Development of Black Children.* M. Spencer, G. Brookins, and W. Allen, Eds. Hillsdale, N.J.: Erlbaum, 1985, pp. 117–30.

Klein, S., Ed. *Handbook for Achieving Sex Equity through Education.* Baltimore, Md.: Johns Hopkins University Press, 1985.

Krupp, Judy-Arin. "No, You Can't Build Someone Else's Self-Esteem." *Teaching K–8* 21 (October 1991): 67–68.

Meek, Anne. "Supervision." *Educational Leadership* 43 (April 1986): 80–81.

Moore, Sharon Arthur, and David W. Moore. "Linguistic Diversity and Reading." *The Reading Teacher* 45 (December 1991): 326–27.

Morrison, James L., and Jerry M. Goldstein. "On Educational Inequality." *The Education Digest* 42 (September 1976): 31–33.

Nilsen, Alleen Pace, et al. *Sexism and Language.* Urbana, Ill.: NCTE, 1977.

Norton, Donna E. "Teaching Multicultural Literature in the Reading Curriculum." *The Reading Teacher* 44 (September 1990): 28–40.

Pine, Gerald J., and Asa G. Hilliard III. "Rx for Racism: Imperatives for America's Schools." *Phi Delta Kappan* 71 (April 1990): 593–600.

Pritchard, Robert. "The Effects of Cultural Schemata on Reading Processing Strategies." *Reading Research Quarterly* 25 (Fall 1990): 273–93.

Pugh, Sharon L., and Jesus Garcia. "Portraits in Black: Establishing African American Identity through Nonfiction Books." *Journal of Reading* 34 (September 1990): 20–25.

Ramsey, Patricia G. *Teaching and Learning in a Diverse World: Multicultural Education for Young Children.* New York: Teachers College Press, 1987.

Rasinski, Timothy V., and Nancy D. Padak. "Multicultural Learning through Children's Literature." *Language Arts* 67 (October 1990): 576–80.

Reimer, Kathryn Meyer. "Multiethnic Literature: Hold Fast to Dreams." *Language Arts* 69 (January 1992): 14–21.

Reyes, Maria de la Luz, and Linda A. Molner. "Instructional Strategies for Second-Language Learners in the Content Areas." *Journal of Reading* 35 (October 1991): 96–103.

Rigg, Pat, and Virginia G. Allen. *When They Don't All Speak English: Integrating the ESL Student into the Regular Classroom.* Urbana, Ill.: National Council of Teachers of English, 1989.

Sadker, Myra, and David Sadker. "Sexism in the Classroom: From Grade School to Graduate School." *Phi Delta Kappan* 67 (March 1986): 512–15.

Scott-Jones, Diane, and Maxine L. Clark. "The School Experiences of Black Girls: The Interaction of Gender, Race, and Socioeconomic Status." *Phi Delta Kappan* 67 (March 1986): 520–26.

Shakeshaft, Carol. "A Gender at Risk." *Phi Delta Kappan* 67 (March 1986): 499–503.

Sheridan, E. Marcia, Ed. *Sex Stereotypes and Reading: Research and Strategies.* Newark, Del.: International Reading Association, 1982.

Tarvin, William L., and Ali Yahya Al-Arishi. "Literature in EFL: Communicative Alternatives to Audiolingual Assumptions." *Journal of Reading* 34 (September 1990): 30–36.

Thomas, M. Donald. "The Limits of Pluralism," *Phi Delta Kappan* 62 (April 1981): 589–92.

Thompson, D. Cooper. "A New View of Masculinity." *Educational Leadership* 43 (December 1985/January 1986): 53–56.

"Toward a Nonsexist School." *American Education* 13 (April 1977): 7–9.

Trachtenberg, Stephen Joel. "Multiculturalism Can Be Taught Only by Multicultural People." *Phi Delta Kappan* 71 (April 1990): 610–11.

3

Introduction to the Classroom

Mr. Wiley is the cooperating teacher; Mr. Allen is his student teacher; and Mrs. Paris is the principal.

Mrs. Paris: Mr. Allen, I just received a call from Mr. Wiley. He is having car trouble and won't be able to get here on time. I realize you didn't expect to be in charge of the class this morning, but you have been observing for a week. You should be able to take care of the attendance and lunch records with no problem. He said the first two classes will be easy to handle, too. In one, you just have to give the test he left in his file cabinet, already duplicated. He should be here before the students finish the test. Good luck! Call on me if you have any problems.

Mr. Allen: Thank you, Mrs. Paris. I'll do my best. (Mrs. Paris exits. Mr. Allen goes to Mr. Wiley's desk and begins searching for his register. He finds it and looks at it in dismay. He can't remember how to fill it out. He *watched* Mr. Allen do it before, but he hadn't attended carefully enough. Embarrassed, he goes next door to ask another teacher, rather than sending a child to get the principal. In the meantime, the children, left alone in the classroom, go wild. They run around the room, throw things, and yell. When Mr. Allen returns to the room with information about how to fill out his records, chaos reigns. "How does Mr. Wiley quiet them down?" he thinks in panic. "I have to do something quick.")

Mr. Allen (in a loud voice): Class! Be quiet! Return to your seats! (Mr. Allen's voice is hardly heard above the racket and has little effect. He suddenly remembers what he has seen Mr. Wiley do before, in a less chaotic situation. Mr. Allen quickly walks over and flips the classroom lights off, waits a few seconds, and flips them on again. The noise and movement slowly begin to abate. He flips the switch off and on again, and it becomes quieter still. Now his voice can be heard.)

Mr. Allen: Go to your seats, and listen for your name as I call the roll. (To his surprise and relief, the students comply. The record keeping proceeds smoothly, and Mr. Allen feels more confident. Then he realizes he doesn't remember which class is first on Thursday mornings, since every day is not the same. Once again embarrassed, he turns to the students.)

Mr. Allen: What do we do first on Thursdays?

Chorus of answers: Spelling! Recess! (Mr. Allen knows recess isn't first, so he looks for the spelling book, wondering what activity to do on Thursday. Then he remembers the lesson planner Mr. Wiley keeps in his desk drawer. He finds the planner and verifies that the spelling lesson comes first. He also discovers that Mr. Wiley has planned a trial test for today. He saw Mr. Wiley give a trial test last week, but he doesn't remember the exact procedure. He leaps into the activity anyway, giving each word and a sentence with it as he vaguely remembers Mr. Wiley doing.)

Randy: You're supposed to say the word again after you give the sentence. That's the way Mr. Wiley does it.

Mr. Allen (frustrated and upset): Well, I'm doing it today, and I'll do it my way.

Rachel: What was the word again?

Mr. Allen: Clothes.

Randy: Mr. Wiley never repeats a word after we've passed it.

Rachel: Like you close a door?

Mr. Allen: Didn't you listen to my sentence, Rachel? Just do your best. (The test proceeds along these lines until it is finished.)

Mr. Allen: Pass your papers to the front.

Joe: But we grade our own trial tests so we'll learn the words better. (Suddenly remembering that this is so, Mr. Allen decides to do it the way Mr. Wiley would. Half the papers have already been passed to the front.)

Mr. Allen: Okay. I'll let you check your own papers. Pass them back to their owners. (Papers are passed back, amid much murmuring. Mr. Allen has to flip the lights off and on again. While this is happening, Mr. Wiley walks in.)

Mr. Wiley: I'm sorry I'm late. I had car trouble. How did things go?

Mr. Allen: Okay.

Mr. Wiley: If you've finished that English test, that's perfect. We can go right on to math.

Mr. Allen: We didn't get to the English test yet. These are the spelling papers.

Mr. Wiley: You took all this time on spelling? I'm going to have to help you budget your time better.

Mr. Allen (shamefacedly): Yes, sir.

1. Is there a difference between just watching and truly observing? What is it?
2. Had Mr. Allen been a good observer? Why do you say so?
3. Do you observe procedures carefully enough to be able to perform them alone, if necessary?

OBSERVING THE CLASSROOM TEACHER

When you first begin student teaching, you will probably not be placed immediately in a direct teaching situation. On the contrary, you will probably be given a period of time to observe your cooperating teacher and perhaps other teachers in the school, to orient you to the teaching situation before you are in charge of one. It is important to try to derive maximum benefit from this observation time.

To benefit fully from your observation period, you need to realize that "observing" and "looking at" are not the same. Observation involves close attention to detail, analysis of what is happening, evaluation of what is happening, and assimilation of new ideas into your existing store of information.

In the opening vignette of this chapter, Mr. Allen had spent a week *looking at* what was going on in the classroom, not carefully *observing* it. Therefore, he did not gain the maximum benefit from his observation time. If *you* are to use your observation time to best advantage, you need to know *what* to look for and *how* to look at what you are observing.

When you enter the classroom for your first day of student teaching, your cooperating teacher will probably introduce you to the class and suggest that you spend the next few days observing to get the "feel" of the classroom and learn the general procedures of a typical day. The cooperating teacher may mention that you should become aware of the teaching and disciplinary techniques in use, with a view toward developing your own teaching approach. Whether or not this is mentioned, you should indeed be alert for these techniques, examining them analytically and critically, as you consider them for possible use when *you* are teaching.

It is a good idea to ask your cooperating teacher if there is a seating chart to use as you observe. If such a chart exists, copy it, so that you can take it home and study it at night. If one is not available, construct one, with your teacher's help, before the next observation. Learning the students' names is extremely important for developing rapport with them and maintaining classroom control. At the secondary level, with several different sets of students' names to learn, it is extremely important to apply yourself immediately to the task. Learning names is usually easier at the elementary level, because you generally see fewer students each day, but it is no less important to your success.

Your cooperating teacher will probably first check attendance, and, at the elementary levels, collect lunch money. Don't just *look at* the process. Observe it. Notice how the teacher marks the register. Make notes, if necessary. If there is roll call, look at each student when his or her name is called. Try to fix the students in mind. Note features that will help you remember the students. You may miss a few students on the first round, but study as many as you can; fill in others later in the day or on subsequent days of observations, adding to your notes each day. Study these notes after school, and try to connect all of your students with their names as quickly as possible.

Get a daily schedule from the cooperating teacher so you will be aware of the order of classes, times for breaks and special activities, and beginning and dismissal times. Secondary student teachers may find that each day's schedule is essentially the same with the exception of variations for assembly schedules, test schedules, and other special events. Elementary student teachers may have a different schedule for each day of the week. Whichever is the case for you, familiarize yourself with the schedule as quickly as possible. Don't be left, as Mr. Allen was, wondering what comes next.

As your cooperating teacher begins to teach, once again, don't just be a *looker*, be an observer. To observe properly, you need to know *what* to look for. Activity 3.1 is a form that contains questions that can help you focus on important aspects of your observations. It covers 11 observation areas. Complete it for one of the observations that you do as your cooperating teacher presents a lesson. You may wish to photocopy the blank form to use with other observations for your own benefit or at the request of your college supervisor.

You can facilitate notetaking when you observe by making a separate page for each of these 11 observation areas. Merely recording carefully the details of the lessons you observe will be beneficial, but it is not enough. At this point, you must analyze what you have seen and evaluate it critically. Below the notes you make on each observation area, write a brief analysis and evaluation (or do this mentally). Once again, some structure may help. Here are some questions you can ask yourself about each of the 11 observation areas.

Area 1 Did the students seem to grasp how the lesson tied to previous learning? Did the motivational activities seem to arouse students' interest successfully? Why do you think they did or did not accomplish their goal?

Area 2 Were the purpose and relevance of the lesson made clear to the students? Why or why not? How might they have been better clarified?

Area 3 Were the teacher's procedures effective for presenting the content? Might some other procedures have been more effective? Why do you think so?

Area 4 Were the lesson materials appropriate and effective? Would other materials have been more effective? Why do you think so?

Area 5 Was the teaching style effective with this particular group and for this particular lesson? Why do you think so? If the style was ineffective, what might have worked better?

Area 6 Did the teacher seem to have adequate knowledge of the subject matter? Was enough outside knowledge brought into the lesson? If not, what else should have been included? Was content effectively related to the students' lives? If not, how might this aspect of the lesson have been improved?

Area 7 Were adequate provisions made for individual differences? If not, what steps might have been taken to improve the situation?

Area 8 Were disciplinary techniques appropriate and effective? Why do you think so? If they were inappropriate or ineffective, what techniques might have been better?

Area 9 Did the teacher's personal qualities advance the lesson effectively? Why do you think so? Might changes in this area be helpful to future lessons?

Area 10 Was the conclusion of the lesson effective? Why? If not, what might have been done to improve it?

Area 11 Were the teacher's evaluation techniques appropriate and effective? Why do you think so? If not, what techniques might have been better?

Even after this analysis and evaluation, you are not through with your observation. Now you must once again examine each observation area and ask yourself these questions: "How can I incorporate this into my teaching? Will I want to use this technique, or an alternative I think would be better? How does what I have seen fit into what I have learned in my methods courses? Are there areas in which I need clarification?" If you answer "yes" to the last question, you should seek clarification immediately from your cooperating teacher, college supervisor, college textbooks, or all of these sources.

You should be observing more than lesson presentations. We have already pointed out the need to observe record-keeping processes, but there are many other areas you need to observe carefully: procedures for carrying out bus, lunchroom, hall, or playground duty, or any of the other duties teachers are frequently called upon to perform. Watch for time factors, control methods, procedures for handling special cases, and so on. Inquire about schoolwide rules, if you have not been

Before actually beginning to teach, take advantage of opportunities to observe your cooperating teacher—observe, don't just look.

supplied with a handbook outlining them. Take notes on what you see and hear so that you can adhere strictly to school policy in the future.

Since teachers are also expected to attend faculty meetings, parent-teacher meetings, in-service sessions, and professional meetings, you would do well to attend these with your cooperating teacher for the purpose of observation. Your cooperating teacher may be asked to chaperone a school dance or take tickets for an extracurricular activity, such as a play, concert, dance, or athletic event. Observing these activities will help you better understand just what working as a teacher entails.

Such small details as the method of dismissal in the afternoon are worthy of note. In many schools, not all students leave the room at the same time. If this is true in your school, make it a point to know who leaves when and why. In many schools, you also need to find out how hall passes are handled. Observe your teacher, and ask questions about general procedures if they do not seem clear.

If you observe carefully, you won't end up like Mr. Allen, and you'll be more ready for teaching when your opportunity comes.

PLANNING FOR INSTRUCTION

Without planning for instruction, your teaching experiences are likely to turn into disasters. Planning offers organization and direction to your teaching efforts. It can help you make sure that you cover all important aspects of a lesson, while avoiding overemphasis on isolated points that interest you but do not merit extensive coverage. Planning can save you from not having enough to do in a lesson, especially if you practice "overplanning." (By overplanning, we mean planning extra related and purposeful activities that you don't expect to have time for, but have ready in case the rest of the lesson progresses rapidly and time is available. See Chapter 5 for some suggested filler, or sponge, activities. Planning can also help you avoid trying to cover too much material at one time. As you look at the complexity of the concepts you plan to present in a lesson format, you may find that you have selected more material than the students can readily absorb at once and that certain complex concepts need much elaboration, rather than a hasty mention.

Activity 3.1 Observation Form

Date: _____ Class observed: _____

Area 1   How did the teacher:

1. Start the lesson? _____

   _____

2. Tie it to previous learning? _____

   _____

3. Arouse students' interest? _____

   _____

Area 2   How did the teacher make the purpose and relevance of the lesson apparent?

1. Through direct teacher statements? _____

2. By eliciting reactions from students? _____

3. Other? (Specify.) _____

Area 3   What procedures were incorporated into the body of the lesson?

1. Lecture? _____

2. Discussion? _____

3. Audiovisual presentation? _____

4. Demonstration? _____

5. Student activities? _____

Area 4   What materials were used in the course of the lesson?

1. Textbooks? _____

2. Supplementary books? _____

3. Films? _____

4. Filmstrips? _____

5. Audiotapes? _____

6. Videotapes? _____

7. Television? _____

8. Records? _____

9. Concrete objects? _____

10. Illustrations? _____

11. Models? _____

12. Other? (Specify.) _____

Area 5   What was the teacher's style of teaching?

1. Direct? _____

2. Indirect? _____

Area 6   Did the teacher show a broad knowledge of the subject area? _____ Did she or he stick to the textbook or bring in information from other sources as well? _____

Did she or he relate the subject matter to other content the students had studied, to current events, or to students' personal needs? _____ If so, how was this accomplished? _____

_____

_____

Area 7   What provisions were made for individual differences?

1. Small group work? _____
2. Individualized assignments? _____
3. Differentiated reading materials? _____
4. Other? (Specify.) _____

Area 8   What disciplinary techniques did the teacher use?

1. Light flipping? _____
2. Penalty points? _____
3. Deprivation of privileges? _____
4. Other? (Specify.) _____

Area 9   How did the teacher's personal qualities help advance the lesson?

1. Dressed appropriately, so that apparel did not distract from subject matter? _____
2. Displayed no distracting mannerisms? _____
3. Used correct grammar? _____
4. Used appropriate voice volume and pitch? _____

Area 10 How did the teacher end the lesson?

1. Summarized the day's learning? _____
2. Assigned homework? _____ If so, specify the kind of assignment. _____
3. Other? (Specify.) _____

Area 11 What evaluation techniques did the teacher use in the course of the lesson?

1. Oral questions? _____
2. Written questions? _____
3. Observation of students' verbal responses? _____
4. Observation of students' application skills? _____
5. Other? (Specify.) _____

Good planning also enhances your poise and confidence, and, as a result, class control will tend to be positively affected. Since class control is a major problem for student teachers, this advantage alone should encourage planning.

Written plans allow you to consult your cooperating teacher and college supervisor about the likelihood of a successful teaching experience. They can give you valuable feedback which may avert a teaching disaster brought on by inexperience. Some cooperating teachers and college supervisors *require* written plans. If yours don't, we highly recommend that you do them anyway, for your personal benefit. It will pay off.

When you are actually assigned to teach, it is vitally important that you plan for instruction, whether or not you actually write down the plans. Your instructional plans should always relate directly to the course of study for your class and should always build upon previous learnings.

One good way to ease into your teaching experience is to work jointly with your cooperating teacher in planning a lesson, watch your cooperating teacher teach the lesson in an early class, and then try it yourself in a later class. This arrangement gives you the benefit of seeing an experienced teacher move from plan to execution. Obviously, this procedure will only work in departmentalized settings where a teacher has several sections of the same course.

At first you will probably be assigned responsibility for single, isolated lessons. Later, as you progress, you will probably be assigned to teach entire units of instruction. These two planning tasks will be considered separately, in the order in which you are likely to encounter them, even though, obviously, lesson planning is an integral part of unit planning.

Lesson Planning

Your lesson plans should be detailed enough that you or another person qualified to teach your grade or subject can teach from them with ease, yet brief enough that they do not become cumbersome. Usually, more detailed plans are needed at the beginning of your student teaching experience than at the end or after you become a regular classroom teacher. More detail gives an inexperienced person greater confidence and makes the inclusion of all important material more likely. Too much detail, however, can inhibit flexibility in a lesson. Do not, for example, plan to get one particular answer from students and build all your subsequent plans on this answer. That answer may not come. Plan to accommodate a variety of student responses.

What belongs in a good lesson plan? Opinions vary, and each teacher generally has to evolve a planning scheme that fits his or her personality. Certain ingredients appear almost universally, however, and you would do well to use these in initial planning activities. (See Figure 3–1.)

When you write objectives for a specific lesson you have been asked to teach, be sure to study the overall objectives of the unit of which the lesson is a part, and check on the instruction that has previously taken place in that unit. Your chosen objectives should build upon previously taught material and lay a groundwork for future instruction, either by you or your cooperating teacher. Be specific in your objectives. Don't use a vague objective, such as "To help them understand verbs better"; instead, say "To help the students understand and apply the concept of subject-verb agreement" or in more behavioral terms, "In 20 consecutive trials the student will demonstrate accurate use of subject-verb agreement."

In the content section of your plan, list the major concepts you plan to cover. Don't just write "Causes of the Civil War"; list specific causes. Consult resources other than the textbook when planning this part of the lesson.

Make your materials list include *everything* you will need. If you need a transparency marker and an acetate sheet for the overhead projector, list them. You can use this list to help you accumulate all necessary materials before the lesson begins,

FIGURE 3–1   Ingredients for a Lesson Plan*

 1. Subject
 2. Grade
 3. Date (not always essential)
 4. Time (useful for secondary teachers who teach more than one section of a subject and grade)
 5. Objectives (be specific)
 6. Content to be covered (be specific)
 7. Materials and equipment needed
 8. Activities and procedures with time allocations (keeps you from running out of time in the middle of something)
 9. Alternative activities (in case a piece of audiovisual equipment won't work, a film doesn't arrive on time, or you overestimated how long other activities would take)
10. Method of evaluation (to determine if the students really learned the material)
11. Assignments (to provide practice on a taught skill, to prepare for a future lesson, or to achieve some very specific purpose)
12. Self-evaluation (Put this section in your written lesson plan, to be filled out after you teach the lesson.)
13. Supervisory feedback (Put this section in your written lesson plan, to be filled out after you have been critiqued by your cooperating teacher, your college supervisor, or both.)

*See Appendix C for sample lesson plans.

so you won't have to disrupt your lesson while you search the room for an appropriate pen for writing on transparencies.

Under the activities and procedures section, you may wish to list questions you plan to raise, motivational techniques you plan to use, what you plan to do, and what you are going to ask the students to do. Consult your college methods textbooks when you plan this part of your lesson. Vary activities. Students become bored with lessons that require one type of response. Plan to have students do some combination of listening, watching, reading, speaking, and writing in each lesson. Don't forget to develop background for the lesson before you begin the new material, and model for the students the skill or strategy you want them to acquire.

By estimating how much time each activity should take, you minimize the risk of finishing an hour lesson in 20 minutes or of getting only halfway through a 30-minute lesson before the time has elapsed. At first, of course, your time estimates may not be extremely accurate, but the very act of keeping up with them in each lesson helps you learn how to judge time needs better. A common problem for student teachers is finishing all the planned material early and being forced to "wing it." This will not be a problem for you if you plan some good alternative activities to use in such an eventuality, or in case a projector bulb burns out and there is not another one in the school, or if some other unforeseen difficulty occurs.

You should always consider how to determine whether or not your pupils have learned the lesson material. You can evaluate through oral or written questions, observation of pupil performance, or some other means, but you *must* evaluate. Planning future lessons depends upon whether or not students learned the material in the current one.

The assignments you give students for independent work should be carefully planned to meet a specific purpose. An assignment might be designed to offer further practice in a skill just taught, to help fix it in the students' minds. Another assignment might be designed to prepare the students for a future lesson. Any materials that students are assigned to read independently must be chosen carefully. Students will be unable to complete independent assignments in materials that are too difficult for them to read, and, for this reason, differentiated reading assignments may be necessary.

After you have taught the lesson, you should evaluate your effectiveness much as you evaluated lessons you observed others teach. When you recognize weaknesses, consider how you would teach the lesson differently if you taught it a second time. Those of you in departmentalized settings who are assigned to two sections of the same class may even have a chance to try out your ideas for improvement later in the day. If you do, remember to evaluate the second presentation also. When you receive feedback from your cooperating teacher and your college supervisor about your lesson, compare their comments to your self-evaluation. If you noticed the same things they did, your evaluation skills are probably good. If they mention many things you missed, you may need to work at evaluating your performance more critically and objectively.

Complete the Lesson Plan Outline in Activity 3.2 for one lesson that you plan to teach this term. You may wish to photocopy the blank form to use with other observations for your own benefit or at the request of your cooperating teacher or college supervisor. Although this is only one possible lesson plan form, completing it can help you determine important components for your lesson that would need to be included on any form that you might use for future lessons.

Once you have presented the lesson specified in Activity 3.2, complete Activity 3.3 to help you analyze it.

Unit Planning

After you have achieved some success at planning individual lessons, your cooperating teacher will probably move you into unit planning. Unit plans are coordinated sets of lessons built around central themes. In the elementary school, a unit plan frequently cuts across disciplines and includes activities in language arts, mathematics, social studies, science, art, music, and other areas. An example of this type of unit might be one on the Westward Movement. Although this unit has basically a social studies theme, the teacher can incorporate language arts instruction through reference reading, oral and written reports, and class discussions; mathematics instruction in figuring distances and calculating amounts of needed supplies and prices of supplies in those days to discover the cost of a journey; science and health instruction through comparing disease remedies used then with those used today; art, in illustrating modes of transportation, clothing, or other features of the times, and in constructing dioramas and models; music instruction through singing and playing songs of the time; and even home economics instruction, by making recipes of that era (which also requires mathematics skills) and performing sewing tasks appropriate to the times, such as quilting and making samplers. Secondary level units, especially in social studies and literature classes, may cut across disciplines, but this is not as common as at the elementary level. Most units at the secondary level and many at the elementary level are based upon major topics within single disciplines. A mathematics class, for example, may have a unit on measurement, incorporating a multitude of mathematical concepts and skills. You should review your methods textbooks for types of units appropriate to your grade and/or discipline.

Different situations require different types of units; that is, there is no one form for all units. Different reference books promote different formats, some of which are harder and some easier to use in a particular situation. You should examine these options and pick the one that best fits *your* situation.

Despite the variations in form suggested for unit preparation, there are certain important considerations you should not overlook when preparing any unit.

Make your unit plan fit into the class's overall course of study. If you are allowed to pick your own unit topic, examine the course of study and pick a topic that fits into the long-term plans for the class. Whether you pick the topic or your cooperating teacher does, check to see how your unit fits into the overall instructional plan. Locate the prior learnings upon which your unit can build. Check on the relationships between your unit and the previous and succeeding units. Decide what things you must include to ensure students' success in succeeding units.

After you have learned how to plan individual lessons, you may be asked to plan a unit.

Find out from your cooperating teacher the time allotment for your unit, and make your plans conform to this allotment. You will probably not be able to include every aspect of your chosen topic within the given time frame. You must decide, either independently or in conjunction with the students, which aspects to include.

Consider carefully the students who will be studying the unit. Find out their backgrounds of experience in relation to the topic, their general levels of achievement in school and/or in your subject area, their levels of interest in the unit topic, their reading levels, their attitudes toward school and the subject area or areas involved, their study habits and ability to work independently or engage in group work, and their special talents. Plan all your activities with these characteristics in mind. It may be useful to actually write down a profile of your class, including all these characteristics, to refer to as you develop objectives, teaching methods, activities, and evaluation methods.

Collect ideas for the unit from a variety of sources: students' textbooks, your college textbooks, professional journals, local resources (businesses and individuals), resource units on file in your school or college media center, and, of course, your cooperating teacher. Make lists of helpful books, periodicals, audiovisual aids, and resource people for future reference. One caution is in order here: do not lecture straight from your old college notes. Remember that your students are not yet ready for material as advanced as the material in your college classes. Use the

Activity 3.2   Lesson Plan Form

Name: _____ Subject: _____

Grade level: _____ Date: _____ Time: _____

Objectives (Be specific.)

Content to be covered (Be specific.)

Materials and equipment needed (Indicate sources.)

Activities and procedures (Include time allocations.)

Introductory activities

Developmental activities

Concluding activities

Alternative activities—emergency fillers

Method of evaluation

Assignments—homework or in-class supervised study

Self-evaluation

Supervisory feedback

Activity 3.3   Personal Lesson Analysis Form

Name: _____ Date: _____

Class: _____

Area 1 Did the students seem to grasp how the lesson was tied to previous learning? _____ Did the motivational activities seem to arouse students' interest successfully? _____ Why do you think they did or did not accomplish their goal? _____

_____

_____

Area 2 Were the purpose and relevance of the lesson made clear to the students? _____ Why, or why not? _____

_____

_____

How might they have been better clarified? _____

_____

_____

Area 3 Were your procedures effective for presenting the content? _____ Might some other procedures have been more effective? _____ Why do you think so? _____

_____

_____

Area 4 Were the lesson materials appropriate and effective? _____ Would other materials have been more effective? _____ Why do you think so? _____

_____

_____

Area 5 Was your teaching style effective with this particular group and for this particular lesson? _____ Why do you think so? _____

_____

_____

Area 6 Did you have adequate knowledge of the subject matter? _____ Was enough outside knowledge brought into the lesson? _____ If not, what else might have been included? _____

_____

_____

Was content effectively related to the students' lives? _____ If not, how might this have been accomplished? _____

_____

_____

Area 7 Were adequate provisions made for individual differences? _____ If so, how? _____

_____

_____

If not, what steps might have been taken to improve the situation? _____

_____

_____

Area 8 Were disciplinary techniques appropriate and effective? _____ Why do you think so? ____

_____

_____

If they were inappropriate or ineffective, what techniques might have been better? _____

_____

_____

Area 9 Did your personal qualities advance the lesson effectively? _____ Why do you think so?

_____

_____

Might changes in this area be helpful to future lessons? _____ How? _____

_____

_____

Area 10 Was the conclusion of the lesson effective? _____ Why, or why not? _____

_____

_____

If not, what might have been done to improve it? _____

_____

_____

Area 11 Were your evaluation techniques appropriate and effective? _____ Why do you think so?

_____

_____

If not, what techniques might have been better? _____

_____

_____

college notes as background material, and work in information from them only as it is directly applicable and appropriate for your particular students.

Draft your objectives for the unit according to the content you want to cover and the students with whom you will be working. You may wish to refer to your methods textbooks to refresh your memory on writing clear objectives. Include both cognitive and affective objectives when appropriate.

Organize the procedures section of your unit plan to include the unit introduction, the body of the unit, and culminating activities: (a) The introductory part of the unit should connect this unit with prior learning or backgrounds of experience, diagnose the needs of the students and their strengths in this area of study (through pretests or informal discussions), and arouse interest in the topic and motivate students to study it. Methods and activities for this part of the unit should be of high interest; frequently, they should vary from usual classroom routine. (b) The body of the unit should address the teaching of each objective, matching teaching procedures and student activities, including assignments, to objectives. Include evaluative measures as needed. (c) Culminating activities for the unit should tie together all the previous learnings. Frequently, culminating activities include practical applications of the concepts acquired in the unit, interrelating the various concepts. Overall evaluative measures may be a part of the culminating activities.

Vary your planned activities. This will help keep the students' attention and can help your unit progress more smoothly, because certain activities suit certain types of learning better than others. Consider use of audiovisual aids, field trips, resource people, class discussions, library research activities, simulations and dramatizations, construction activities, oral and written reports, games, demonstrations, and creative applications. Be sure, however, that all activities relate directly to unit objectives.

Case Study: Failure to Follow Through

Jerry Clement was planning a unit on law enforcement. Jerry's cooperating teacher, Mrs. Granger, knew an excellent resource person, Mr. McDonald, whom Jerry might use in the course of his unit. She told Jerry about Mr. McDonald and, to her surprise, discovered that Jerry was a friend of Mr. McDonald. She strongly suggested that Jerry ask Mr. McDonald to come to the class and share his knowledge with the students. Jerry seemed to think this was a good idea, but he never actually contacted Mr. McDonald. At the end of the term, Jerry was surprised that his cooperating teacher rated him lower than he would have liked on use of community resources.

1. Do you believe the use of a resource person would have enhanced Jerry's unit? Why, or why not?
2. If you had been Jerry, what would you have done if you decided that having Mr. McDonald would not add substantially to your unit?

Decide on the different forms of evaluation you intend to use during the course of the unit, to be sure you haven't overrelied on a single type. Consider the use of formal and informal paper-and-pencil tests, oral or performance tests, observation of student performance in activities and discussions, evaluation of daily in-class and homework assignments, and individual pupil conferences, among other evaluation methods.

Estimate the time needed for the various instructional procedures and student activities, and make tentative decisions about daily coverage. Make adjustments if your plans do not fit the allotted time.

Consult your cooperating teacher about the plan you have constructed. If it meets with the teacher's approval, you are ready to make detailed daily lesson plans based on your unit plan.

Figure 3–2 shows a brief outline to use in unit planning.

**FIGURE 3–2 Unit
Plan Outline***

A. Topic and overall time allotment
B. Students' characteristics and backgrounds
C. Resources and materials
D. Unit objectives
E. Unit procedures
   1. Introduction
   2. Body
   3. Culminating activities
F. Evaluation

*See Appendix D for sample unit plans.

If you remember that a unit of work is a series of interrelated lessons clustered around a central theme, then you will probably plan a good unit. Poor units are characterized by lack of continuity and interrelatedness and by irrelevant activities.

Complete Activity 3.4 as you plan your first unit. You may wish to photocopy this activity form and use it on other units as well.

INSTRUCTIONAL RESOURCES

People learn best the things that they experience. Much learning takes place through the vicarious (indirect) experiences of listening, reading, and viewing pictures and films, but learning is likely to be more meaningful and lasting if it is supplemented with direct experiences.

You can find instructional resources in a wide variety of places. You can obtain audiovisual materials through the school, public library, college resource center, and local and state agencies. Industries, farms, and parks provide opportunities for field trips. People in various occupations can serve as resources.

You may wish to make games and activities for teaching specific skills. The community is rich in resources to use in constructing such materials. For example, many home decorating and home supply stores give away scraps of materials that can be used for various purposes in the classroom. Newspapers may be a source of newsprint for murals and posters, and restaurants may provide placemats that have educational themes. If you use your imagination, you will find ways to take advantage of the resources that abound in your school and community.

Audiovisual Media

A wide variety of audiovisual media is used in many ways in schools today. You should plan to use these media as alternatives to, or along with, other teaching approaches. If you are going to use audiovisual media effectively, you need to know *where* to obtain them, *when* to make use of them, *how* to use them, *why* they can enhance your lessons, and *which types* are most appropriate for your purposes.

Selecting Audiovisual Media When you meet with your cooperating teacher, discuss what units, skills, and activities you will be expected to teach. Decide what materials you might want to use in connection with these teaching areas; then check to see what materials are available. Some materials may have to be reserved or ordered well in advance of the time you actually plan to use them.

One of the first things you should do is to become acquainted with the school librarian or media specialist. Find out what resources are available in your school. Most school media centers have supplementary reading materials, newspapers and periodicals, reference books, maps and globes, files of photographs and slides, filmstrips,

Activity 3.4   Unit Planning Form

Unit topic:

Overall time allotment:

Student characteristics that need to be considered in teaching this unit:

List of resources and materials:

Unit objectives:

Unit procedures:

    Introduction:

    Body (list of lessons—*not* complete lesson plans, activities, and assignments)

    Culminating activities:

    Evaluation:

FIGURE 3–3 Teacher-Made Language Arts Game

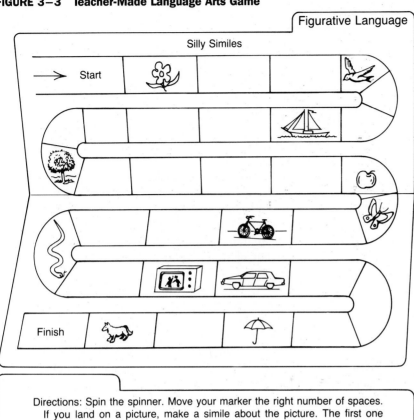

art prints, audiotapes, videotapes, transparencies, charts and posters, models and exhibits, and a limited supply of films.

After assessing the holdings of the school media center, you may wish to explore other possibilities. One place to look for additional materials is the school system's central office, which may have a systemwide file of resource materials. Another source is the public or regional library. You may be able to order films or obtain computer software from the state Department of Education. In addition, don't overlook your university's resources in your search for appropriate teaching materials.

Materials are also available from other places. The Public Documents Distribution Center (Pueblo, Colorado 81009), various state departments and agencies, and businesses and industries will send you free or inexpensive materials. Locally, you can get maps and other printed materials from the Chamber of Commerce, banks, local industries, and the Department of Health.

If you still can't find what you need, you may want to make simple materials yourself, such as transparencies, slides, mounted pictures, or teaching games. Some of these materials should be protected by laminating them or covering them with clear contact paper. A good way to begin a collection of teacher-made games and activities is to make some on the insides of file folders. Write the directions on the outside of each folder. You can then label and organize these activities according to skills. (See Figure 3–3 for an example of a teacher-made language arts game.)

There are a number of factors to consider in selecting audiovisual materials to use with a particular lesson. Be sure you do not decide to use them simply to impress your cooperating teacher, fill up instructional time, or entertain the students. Consider these criteria in choosing materials:

1 *Relevance to lesson*—Make sure the audiovisual material actually helps carry out the objectives of the lesson you are teaching. The material should be the most appropriate medium for your purpose, making the necessary points in the clearest possible manner. It should stimulate discussion and lead the way to further study.

2 *Appeal to students*—Be sure the material is suitable for the students' age level and that it will hold their attention. Students should have sufficient background information to appreciate the presentation.

3 *Quality of materials*—Check your materials to make sure they are well designed and of high technical quality. The material should be accurate, current, and in good taste.

4 *Objectivity*—Examine your material for bias, propaganda, and controversy. If there is bias, help your students to see the other point of view. Point out misconceptions that arise as a result of propaganda techniques. If the material is controversial, be sure that each side receives equal emphasis. Free materials are often available to classroom teachers for the purpose of advertising a product or advancing a particular point of view. Be cautious about using these materials.

5 *Practical considerations*—Be sure you know how to operate the equipment you need for presenting your material. Check in advance to see that both material and equipment will be available when you need them. Allow enough time to introduce the lesson, present the audiovisual material, and follow it up. Allow extra time in case something goes wrong. Prepare a suitable place for your presentation. Use the checklist in Activity 3.5 to help you use audiovisual materials efficiently.

Choosing computer software requires a few more decisions than are necessary in choosing most other audiovisual materials. For example, most people know to

Be sure to familiarize yourself with audiovisual equipment before you use it in class.

Activity 3.5   Checklist for Using Audiovisual Equipment

Preparation

_____ Reserve or check out necessary materials and equipment.

_____ Preview material to make sure it is appropriate and in good condition.

_____ Prepare related materials for introduction or follow-up activities.

_____ If each student is to receive a copy of related materials, count the copies to make sure you have enough. Plan for efficient distribution.

_____ Arrange audience seats so that everyone can see.

_____ Consider the location of handicapped students by placing those with visual or auditory difficulties near the front and providing places for students in wheelchairs.

_____ Check the room's temperature, ventilation, and lighting.

_____ Eliminate distractions as much as possible.

Equipment

_____ Practice operating equipment until you feel sure of yourself.

_____ Set equipment up in advance so that it is ready to use (check focus, position on screen, size of image, etc.).

_____ Have an extra bulb on hand, and know how to replace the old one.

_____ Get an extension cord or an adapter if you need one.

_____ Avoid having cords where the students will trip over them.

_____ Check the cleanliness of the lens and other vital parts of the equipment.

choose a cassette tape—rather than a reel-to-reel tape—to play on a cassette tape recorder. However, many people do not have the knowledge of computers necessary to choose the correct software. These additional considerations are necessary when choosing computer software for use in your classes:

1 *Make sure the format of the software is appropriate for the computer hardware.* In other words, if you have a computer with a cassette drive, make sure the software is on a cassette; if you have a computer with a floppy disk drive, make certain the software is on a diskette of the appropriate size; and if you have a computer that accepts cartridges, look for software on cartridges.

2 *Make sure the software was designed to be used on the type of computer you have in your class.* If you have an Apple IIe computer with a floppy disk drive, you will not be able to use a program on a diskette that was designed to be used on an IBM or IBM-compatible computer. The documentation accompanying the software will tell you with which computer or computers the program was designed to be used.

3 *Make sure the program is easy for your students to use.* Some programs have useful information on them, but they are not "user friendly"—they are hard to use due to missing or inadequate instructions about how to enter information, how to progress through the program by moving from screen to screen, how to exit the program, how to adjust the program's rate of presentation or difficulty level, or where to obtain assistance when problems arise. If the programs are hard for *you* to use, you can be sure they will be hard for some of your students. Therefore, you should try programs out before using them for a class, even though reviews have indicated that they are just what you need. The reviewers may never have had a class like yours.

Make sure that the computer software you choose for your students is easy for them to use.

4 *Make sure the time available for use of the program is sufficient for all of the students to complete the lesson.* Availability of a limited number of computers may make the use of some very good programs impractical on a whole-class or large-group scale.

5 *Check the program out for sound effects.* Decide if they are likely to be disturbing to the part of the class not working on the program at the moment. If you think that they may be distracting, check to see if the sound can be turned down or even off. If you plan to turn the sound off, make sure the program is still effective without it. Maybe you can use the program with earphones for the students involved. Try to take all possibilities into account.

Effective Use of Audiovisual Media   Audiovisual media can be used for many purposes: introduction and orientation to a new area of study, representation of events and processes, and individualized learning experiences. They can arouse students' interest and curiosity as you introduce a new topic. A display of brightly colored photographs of wild animals, a recording of medieval madrigal music, or a film of a slowly opening flower can be a stimulus for learning. Since students have become accustomed to acquiring ideas and information through television, an audiovisual presentation, such as a videotape, film, or television program, can often command their attention more effectively than a textbook or lecture. In addition, because students have become accustomed to playing video games in arcades and on home game machines and computers, computer programs may excite interest not generated by other classroom presentations.

You can use certain types of audiovisual media to individualize instruction according to the learner's style or special needs. If the same information is available in the classroom in different forms, learners can choose the forms that best suit their ways of learning. For instance, a student who has great difficulty with reading can listen to a tape about the African jungle. Another student who has trouble visualizing what is read might operate a filmstrip or film projector or videotape recorder and watch either still or motion pictures of the jungle. A third student who is an excellent reader might prefer to read about the jungles of Africa from several reference books. Visually handicapped students may need to use recordings or large-print materials. A student who learns best through active participation may best gain information about the African jungle or any other habitat through a computer simulation related to this area.

When you use audiovisual material, prepare carefully for your lesson by previewing the material and reading the accompanying study guide or lesson plan. Create a feeling of readiness and anticipation among the students by raising questions and telling them what they can expect to learn. Relate the audiovisual material to what they are studying; make it a part of your overall instructional plan. Explain any unfamiliar terms or concepts that will be used.

During the presentation, observe the students' reactions. There may be some points they do not seem to understand or some parts that do not hold their interest. You may be able to interrupt the presentation, but more likely you will need to address these matters during your follow-up discussion. You should take notes of your observations so that you can recall anything that needs to be mentioned later.

The follow-up activities are based on the audiovisual presentation, but are not limited to it. In fact, the presentation may serve primarily as a taking-off point. Follow-up activities may consist of lively discussions, the application of concepts to real situations, or experiments, projects, and reports. Students may be divided into groups to pursue special interests, and the projects may continue over an extended period of time. Pupil participation in follow-up activities is essential for learning to take place.

Case Study: Breakdown of a Lesson

Mr. Ray, the student teacher, is introducing a unit on Scandinavia in social studies by showing his students a film about the region. He has reserved the film and equipment, set it up, and is ready to begin. Mrs. Colby is the cooperating teacher.

Mr. Ray: Everybody sit down and be quiet. We're going to see a film.

Students (shuffling to their seats and mumbling): Wonder what it's about. Probably something dumb. Who wants to see a film anyway? They're always so dull and boring in school.

Mr. Ray: Okay. We're ready to start. Oh—just a minute. I forgot to pull down the shades. (Students wait restlessly while Mr. Ray pulls down the shades. One group starts giggling in the corner.)

Mr. Ray: Hey, you guys. Keep quiet. Okay. Ellen, turn out the lights please. Here we go. (Film starts, and students settle down. Suddenly the screen goes blank. Mr. Ray stares at the projector and wonders what happened.)

Mrs. Colby: I believe the bulb has burned out. Do you have another one?

Mr. Ray: I don't think so. Let me look. (Pause while students start whispering, poking each other, and laughing) I can't find one. Do you think they'd have one at the resource center?

Mrs. Colby: They probably do, but the librarian is out today, and I doubt if the substitute would know where to find one.

Mr. Ray: Peter, would you go to the resource center for me and ask the substitute librarian if she can find a projector bulb? (Peter starts off in search of a bulb. By now the class is throwing paper wads and paper airplanes. Some students are getting out of their seats. Carmelita trips over the projector cord and falls against the filing cabinet. She cuts her lip, and it starts bleeding.)

Mr. Ray (speaking in an excited, almost angry tone): All of you get back in your seats! Stop throwing things! Shut up! Peter should be back soon.

Students: Oh, look! Carmelita's lip is bleeding!

Carmelita (wailing slightly as she looks at the bloodstained hand she has just removed from her mouth): My mouth is bleeding!

Mr. Ray glances helplessly at Mrs. Colby, starts to say something and then stops.

Mrs. Colby (speaking calmly and turning the lights back on): All of you get back to your seats now. Get out your math books, and work on your assignment for tomorrow. (Students do as she says.)

Mrs. Colby: Let me see your lip, Carmelita. I believe it will be okay if you go to the girls' room and put a cold, wet paper towel over it until the bleeding stops. Kim, you go with her.

Peter (just returning to the room): She looked for a bulb but couldn't find one. She says we'd better wait and show the film tomorrow when the regular librarian will be back.

Mr. Ray: Thank you, Peter. Class, I guess you might as well keep working on your math, and we'll do social studies tomorrow when we can see the film.

1. Did Mr. Ray succeed in his objective of introducing his unit on Scandinavia? Could he have introduced the unit anyway, even if he couldn't show the film?
2. Did Mr. Ray ever make clear to the students his purpose in showing the film? If the film had been shown, do you think the students would have gained much from it? What could Mr. Ray have done to create interest in the film and make sure the students learned all they could from it?
3. What could Mr. Ray have done to prevent the class from becoming unruly?
4. How could Carmelita's accident have been prevented? How might Mr. Ray have handled the incident?
5. What would you do to avoid making the same kinds of mistakes Mr. Ray made?
6. Is there anything you think Mr. Ray did correctly? If so, what?

Case Study: Salvaging a Lesson

Mr. Carson, the student teacher, is introducing a unit on Africa in social studies by showing his students a film on the region. He has reserved the film and equipment, set it up, and is ready to begin. Miss Rios is the media specialist.

Mr. Carson: This afternoon we are going to see a film. The film is about Africa, the unit we are going to begin studying today. Africa is the second-largest continent and is made up of many different countries. As you watch the film, I want you to notice the different kinds of land regions you can find in Africa. Also, be sure to look for the natural resources that Africa has. Kim, will you please pull down the shades? I believe we're ready to start. (Film begins, but suddenly the screen goes blank.)

Students: Oh, no. What happened? Hey, it was just getting interesting.

Mr. Carson: I'm afraid the bulb has burned out. I tried to get a spare just in case, but there wasn't one. I'll try to get one by tomorrow.

Mike: Oh good. No film. Can we play a game?

Susan: Let's have free time.

Sally (jumping out of her seat): I think I know where there's an extra bulb. I'll go ask Miss Rios.

Mr. Carson: Never mind, Sally. I already checked with Miss Rios, and she doesn't have one. We'll have to do something else instead.

Anthony: I want to get my math homework done. Is it okay if I do that?

Chris: No, let's play 20 questions.

Mr. Carson: Wait a minute, everybody. We can still begin learning about Africa today even if we can't see the film. We'll begin by finding Africa on the globe. Who can come up and show us where it is?

Sonya (raising her hand): I can see it from here. Let me show them.

Mr. Carson (after discussing the features of Africa on the globe and on a pull-down map): Africa has been in the news quite a bit lately, and I've been clipping some items from the newspapers. I'm going to divide you into groups of four and let each group take one clipping. I want you to read your clipping and select someone from your group to report to the class about the article. Select another person to point to the country or region in Africa that is mentioned in your article. You may use either the map or the globe. I will give you a few minutes to do this work in your groups, and then I will call on you to make your reports. Do you have any questions?

Jimmy: Who's going to be in my group?

Mr. Carson: I'll put you into groups just as soon as I'm sure you understand what to do.

Jake: What if we can't find our country on the map?

Mr. Carson: I'll help you. You may come up ahead of time to try to find it. Any other questions? (pause) I think we're ready to start now.

1. Suppose that Mr. Carson had not thought to use the map and globe and that he had not brought the clippings. What would have happened to his lesson?
2. What are some other ways that Mr. Carson might have introduced his unit without the film?
3. At what point was Mr. Carson about to lose control of the class? How did he manage to retain control?
4. Compare and contrast the lessons of Mr. Ray and Mr. Carson according to the following criteria: preparation, class management, effectiveness of introducing a unit, and flexibility.

Types of Audiovisual Media   Since the days of the cave dwellers, humans have communicated through audiovisual means. The human race has progressed from grunting sounds and crude drawings on rock walls to sophisticated electronic media. Various kinds of print materials and audiovisual media you can use for communicating ideas to your students are discussed in this section.

Print materials—Basal readers (series of graded reading instructional books) and content area textbooks can provide structure and sequence in the school curriculum. They may be the framework for learning experiences, but they should never be considered as the total instructional program. You will want to use trade books, or library books, to supplement the material in textbooks, and reference books to provide factual material related to specific areas of study. You may want to use magazines that focus on single topics of current interest for both informational and recreational reading. You may also want to begin a collection of leaflets and pamphlets on various topics. Additionally, you can find some pictures and photographs to mount and cover with laminating film or clear contact paper to add to your collection of resource materials.

Chalkboards—The chalkboard is one of the most familiar visual devices in the classroom. Both students and teachers can use the chalkboard in a number of ways. As a change of pace, students enjoy going to the board individually or in groups to do their work. For teachers, the chalkboard is a readily available place to record information, write seatwork and homework assignments, and use in teaching lessons.

Although you are accustomed to seeing the chalkboard used in the classroom, you may not feel comfortable using it yourself. It is difficult to write a lot of material on the board while you are teaching, since you cannot watch the students when you are facing the board. If you have work to put on the board, you may want to do it the night before or early in the morning, when you are not rushed. It is important to form your letters correctly so that your writing will be a good model for the students to follow. You may need guidelines to keep your writing straight. You can soak chalk for 20 minutes in a mixture of three parts water and one part saturated sugar water to use for drawing lines along a straightedge as guides. These lines will not erase, but will wash off easily with water.

Models, globes, and maps—Models are three-dimensional replicas of actual objects that may be smaller (an airplane) or larger (the ear) than actual size. Globes are models of the earth, and maps are two-dimensional representations of the earth's geographic and/or political features. Both globes and maps can help students visualize geographic relationships and understand world affairs. Be sure that the globes and maps are current, because political boundaries change.

Audio media—You should use audio media when sound is of primary importance for learning or appreciation. You can use recordings of folk songs, important historical speeches, famous symphony concerts, or performances by military bands. You might want to play recordings of town meetings or forums to use as a basis for discussions of controversial issues. In many schools, students learn foreign languages in language labs that use audio media for instructional purposes. Dramatizations, documentaries, poetry readings, and great moments from history are also particularly well suited to audio presentations.

There are three major types of audio media: radios, phonographs, and audiotape recorders. Each has certain features that make it particularly appropriate for given situations. Radios are readily available and provide immediate communication on specific national or international affairs, such as a space launch. Many stations broadcast outstanding educational programs, but scheduling these programs into your instructional periods can be a problem. Phonographs have certain advantages over radios in that the same selection can be played more than once and whenever the time is right. Phonographs are not as versatile as audiotape recorders, however, for instructional purposes. Audiotape recorders have many features that make them desirable for classroom use. Students can record themselves when they read orally or make speeches, play back the tapes to listen for errors, and make efforts to improve. You can record classroom activities such as dramatizations, interviews, panel discussions, or musical programs, and play them back later. You can also record some stories or lessons for students to use individually or in groups at listening stations while you are working directly with other groups of students.

You may want to have your own audiotape recorder because there are so many good opportunities for using it during the school day. An audiotape recorder is fairly inexpensive, and tapes made in class can be erased and reused. Your school may have a tape library where you can find tapes for various purposes.

Projected still pictures—Four types of projected still pictures are generally available for classroom use: slides, filmstrips, overhead transparencies, and opaque projections. Slides can be selected and arranged to suit your purpose. After you assemble them, you can add a commentary tape with background sound effects, or instead of a prepared narrative, you may prefer to discuss the slides as you go, taking as much time with each slide as you wish. Remote control projectors allow you to stand at the front of the class and point to details you want the students to notice.

Filmstrips may be used by individual students or with the entire class. You can use them with synchronized records or tapes, or you may prefer to read from the accompanying guides. When you use the filmstrips without synchronized sound, you can hold them on each frame for any length of time. You can also roll them forward or backward while the students discuss the filmstrip with you. If there are captions on the bottoms of the frames, you may want to cover them and discuss the pictures before revealing the captions.

The overhead projector is simple to operate, and it can be used to project images on a screen in a normally lighted classroom. You can easily create your own transparencies by writing with a grease pencil or transparency marking pen on a clear sheet of acetate, or you can use commercially prepared transparencies designed for use with your textbook or units. If you have never used an overhead projector, become acquainted with it during your student teaching. Practice using it by yourself before using it with your class. Remember three important points: (1) check the placement and focus of the projector before the lesson starts, (2) know how to place the transparencies so the images are readable on the screen, and (3) identify items by pointing on the transparencies, not on the screen.

An opaque projector produces full-color images from materials that are not transparent, such as maps, mounted pictures, newspaper or magazine clippings, sheet music, or concrete materials. It can also be used to create enlargements. To accomplish this, you project an image onto a large surface (such as a sheet of newsprint or cardboard) and trace it. If you decide to use this projector, the classroom must be darkened in order to see the image clearly. Be sure to place the bulky machine so that it does not block anyone's view of the screen. You can move it forward to give a smaller image, or back to make a larger image. The bulb becomes very hot; it can easily overheat and actually destroy materials if you leave them in place too long. The fan may cause the paper to flutter, so you may need to hold it in place by mounting it on stiff cardboard.

Videotapes and films—You can use videotapes and films to create interest in a unit, review and reinforce a subject under study, provide a vicarious experience, or initiate discussion. Many useful lessons and other types of programs can be found on videotape or film, and these are often available through the school system from the central office. For example, there are videotapes and films of Shakespearean plays and other literature selections. Some videotapes and films are springboards for creative activities; others are straightforward presentations of subject matter through illustrated lectures. As processes are speeded up or slowed down on tape or film, students can watch changes occur that would otherwise be unobservable. Using videotape recorders, you can record television programs and play them back later, but you must be sure to observe the copyright laws concerning use of videotapes of commercial programs.

You can also record students' performances with portable videotape recorders and play those performances back for the students to see. The students can use these videotape recordings for self-analysis. They are particularly useful in speech, drama, dance, and physical education classes. The recordings may also be used as visible evidence of improvement in these and other areas. For example, creative dramatic performances can be recorded over a period of time, and all of the performances played back in a single viewing. The students can see how their actions and speech have changed over time.

Videotape recorders are relatively easy to operate, and they can be used to provide focused instruction for the whole class or targeted groups of students. Older students can learn to use the recorders and then assist in documenting class presentations or special programs.

Television—Two types of television programming are appropriate for instructional use: educational television programming, which is generally on the Public Broadcasting System, and commercial television programming that happens to cover areas of educational interest. Students may have access to either of these types of programming during the school day, depending upon scheduling consider-ations, or students may be assigned to watch programs at home, outside of school hours, with the understanding that these programs will be discussed in class later.

Whether or not you make use of instructional television will probably be deter-mined by your cooperating teacher and the availability of a television set in your classroom. Unlike filmstrips, films, and videotapes, television programs cannot be previewed if they are watched live. Therefore, you must study the manual to develop your lesson. When using a television program, turn on the set at least 15 minutes before the scheduled starting time to make sure it is operating correctly. Introduce vocabulary and concepts by writing them on the chalkboard and discussing them, and thoroughly prepare your students for what they will see. When the program starts, encourage students to respond to the television teacher by participating actively in the lesson yourself. During the lesson, take notes on points that you want to discuss later. Walk around among the students to make sure that they are actively involved in the lesson. After the program is over, don't reteach the lesson, but follow through with related activities.

If you assign the students to watch regular television programs (e.g., documen-taries, cultural programs, or series of educational significance) at home during the evenings or on weekends, you should provide the students with specific objectives. Television guides are often available for teachers to use for these types of programs. With the help of a guide, you can assign students to watch for certain points or ideas as they view the programs. The next class day, you should follow up with a discus-sion or other experiences related to the programs.

Computers—"Computer literacy" refers to knowledge of and experience with computers. It covers familiarity with computer hardware (equipment) and software (programs) and understanding of the functions of computers in carrying out various jobs, presenting school lessons, solving problems, and providing recreation. Some schools include some computer programming instruction in computer literacy classes. In recent years, computer literacy has become part of the curriculum of many schools at all grade levels.

Schools use microcomputers for a variety of purposes. Although computer literacy is the primary goal of computer use in many schools, computer-assisted instruction (CAI) and computer-managed instruction (CMI) are also frequently used.

Computer-assisted instructional applications include drill-and-practice pro-grams, tutorial programs, simulations, and game programs. Drill-and-practice pro-grams do not teach new material; they simply offer practice on skills that you or your cooperating teacher have previously taught. Tutorial programs do offer skill instruc-tion, and they also generally include a practice component. Simulations replicate on the computer the important aspects of real-life situations to which the students have an opportunity to respond. Games provide recreation, but, if they require content knowledge to be played, they may also reinforce classroom learning.

Microcomputers can be used outside of computer classes to provide enrich-ment in school subjects for all students, to offer challenges for bright students, and to give special assistance for remedial and compensatory purposes. Students are often provided with drill-and-practice programs on mathematics, language, reading and other skills in order to free the teacher from the repetitive drill and allow her or him to work at *instructing* students who need extra explanation and attention. Tutorial programs may be used for students who need extra instruction in an area that has been covered in class already, for students who were absent when initial instruction occurred, or for gifted students who are ready for more advanced materials than is the class as a whole. Simulations are available in fairly large numbers in the areas of science, health, and social studies, and they can offer students many experiences that the students could not have otherwise had. For example, simulations of chemistry experiments that use dangerous materials can provide learning experiences without the danger. Games are often used as rewards for successful completion of work, although they may offer skill practice as well as the game element.

In some schools, computers with word processing software may be available to students to use in preparing class assignments in creative writing, reports in content areas, or class or school newspapers or magazines. These computers may be located in individual classrooms or in a computer laboratory. Such availability is a plus for your students, because word-processing programs allow students to make corrections in their written assignments quickly and easily, thereby making it more likely that they will attempt to make such corrections. These programs make inserting or deleting material and moving chunks of text easy, and many programs have spelling checkers and/or grammar checkers that help students find problems with their papers.

Computers with word processing programs can be helpful to you, as a teacher, as well. You can use them to prepare study guides, review sheets, and tests and to write letters to parents. For the benefit of both you and your students, learn about the word processing software available to you, and make use of it.

Computer databases are also becoming an important part of instruction in schools where computers are available. A computer "database is an organized collection of information which can be electronically searched and sorted according to its various categories."[1] The information within a database is filed under categories for easy access. There are many preexisting databases that may be used in schools; as a matter of fact, some entire encyclopedias are available on computer. Some school libraries are putting their card catalogs on computer, resulting in very useful databases. Students can also create their own databases on topics of study with appropriate software. Doing so gives students experience in categorization of material. Students need to know how to search existing databases and how to create their own databases for class projects, if such software is available. If your school has database software, learn how to use it so that you can help your students to use it effectively. You might also use database software to record information about your students or units that you plan to teach, making the learning process pay off for you personally.

In some classes, students may be learning to use spreadsheet programs. A spreadsheet program is an electronic accounting pad that can automatically perform calculations such as addition and subtraction on rows and columns of numbers.

As a student teacher, you may find that computer-assisted instruction and other computer applications are a part of the classes you are assigned to teach. You should have your cooperating teacher or the media specialist orient you to the particular computer used in your school. You will need to know how to load a commercial courseware package (the program that tells the computer what to do) and what the special keys on the computer keyboard mean. You also need to know what to do if a student "crashes" a program (causes it to cease to operate).

You should also know the proper way to handle and care for the courseware. If your system has a disk drive, you may find this information on the protective sleeve of the diskette. If your system uses a cassette drive, you should care for the cassettes the same way you care for the audio cassettes you use for recorded speech or music. Diskettes, cassettes, and plug-in modules must all be kept as clean as possible—dust-free and uncontaminated by food substances or drinks.

Be sure to read the documentation for each program your students are using. This will enable you to help students load programs, enter answers properly, and understand error messages. Some programs can be adjusted to the particular student; for example, response time or number of items can be varied. Usually, the accompanying documentation tells the teacher how to make these adjustments.

---

[1]Kent Layton and Martha E. Irwin. "Enriching Your Reading Program with Databases." *The Reading Teacher* 42 (May 1989): 724.

Some CAI programs have a computer-managed instruction (CMI) component. These programs provide you with an analysis of student performances, may suggest further instructional needs, and may move the students through new instructional sequences without your direct intervention. Obviously, this component can be a valuable aid. If such a component is not included in the program, however, you may wish to check the results on the screen for each student before he or she ends the program.

Community Resources

The community in which your school is located offers many opportunities for purposeful learning experiences. Through resource people and field trips, it provides links between the basic skills taught in the classroom and the application of these skills in the outside world. As a student teacher, your community involvement will be limited, but you can still utilize many resources if you begin early to explore the possibilities.

Resource People   A resource person can often attract students' attention more than the classroom teacher can. Due to the resource person's direct experience with

A resource person can often attract students' attention more than the classroom teacher can, and he or she is more likely to make a lasting impression.

a topic, the presentation is usually more credible and more likely to make a lasting impression. Since you cannot be an expert in every field, other people can sometimes supplement your knowledge. A resource person can be especially effective at the beginning of a unit to create interest or near the end of a unit to reinforce and extend concepts.

The first step in using resource people is to consider who has expertise in the topics you plan to cover. Your personal friends may have hobbies or experiences that would make them valuable resource people. If you are student teaching in your hometown, you may already know people who could contribute to your unit. School personnel may discuss their work experiences or offer special knowledge. Your university employs specialists in many fields who may be willing to work with you. People from varied cultural, ethnic, and religious backgrounds may be available to share their heritage. Businesses and industries, banks, protective service agencies, public utilities, and government agencies at all levels often have representatives who go into the schools to provide information.

Resource people can be identified through various approaches. Your school may have a volunteer services program or a file with the names of resource people and their areas of expertise. Your cooperating teacher or other school personnel may be able to recommend a suitable resource person for your subject. Senior citizens can be recruited from retirement centers and church and community organizations. You may wish to survey your students to see if their parents or someone else they know can be helpful. A sample survey form is provided in Activity 3.6. Before you take a survey, be sure to get permission from school authorities.

After you select someone with the appropriate specialized knowledge, you will have to contact her or him concerning the proposed school visit. Tactfully discuss the type of presentation, the need to adjust to the students' level, and the amount of time available. Discuss the students' background knowledge, attention span, and probable questions. The visitor may prefer to lecture, show slides, demonstrate a process, or talk informally. Be sure she or he understands the purpose of the visit and how it relates to what you are teaching.

You must also prepare students for resource visitors. They should be involved in the planning and may want to make lists of questions prior to visits. Students can issue invitations, arrange for any special equipment, meet guests upon their arrival, introduce them, and assist them in their presentations. Students should be encouraged to show their appreciation at the time of the visit and later in the form of thank-you letters. As the teacher, you must relate the presentations of resource people to your unit by preparing the students for visits and following them up with reinforcing activities.

Some business and civic leaders may not be willing to come to the school but will grant interviews to students who come to see them. The experience of conducting an interview is worthwhile; however, careful and detailed arrangements need to be made prior to the interview. School personnel must approve the interview. Consent must also be given by the prospective interviewee and by the parents of the students participating in the interview. The students should draw up questions in advance, practice note-taking skills, and learn proper conduct in handling an interview. After the interview, students need to organize their notes and write summaries of the information to share with their classmates.

Students at the secondary level can become involved with resource people by taking surveys. The students can identify an issue in which they are interested and design a simple questionnaire to give to people they know. Topics might include whether or not to build a new gymnasium, establish a teen center, or extend the city limits. Students can get additional information about their topics by searching through records and interviewing city employees. The students can summarize their findings and draw conclusions that might have implications for community action. They can submit the results to the media for dissemination to the public.

Activity 3.6   Survey of Resource People

Date _____

Student's name _____ Grade _____ Phone _____

Teacher's name _____ School _____

Address of student _____

Parent's name _____

Address (if different) _____

Are you willing to volunteer your help in your son's or daughter's classroom?_____

If so, what days and hours are most convenient? _____

Do you have any special knowledge, talents, or skills that you can share with the class? _____ If so,

what are they? _____

_____

Perhaps you know someone who would be able to contribute something worthwhile to the school. If so, please fill in the information below. (Use other side for additional suggestions.)

Name _____ Phone _____

Address _____

Possible contribution _____

Thank you for your cooperation!

Field Trips A field trip is an organized class excursion for the purpose of obtaining information through direct observation. A child's experiences with field trips usually begin with visits to places like a fire station or dairy farm. Some classes take end-of-year trips to zoos or museums. Older students may "run" City Hall for one day of the year—each student is appointed to a position and assumes the responsibilities of the person who occupies the corresponding position in city government. Participation in field experiences during their school years gives students many opportunities to understand how their community operates and to broaden their knowledge of specific subjects. Acquaintance with different occupations can also give students direction in choosing careers.

Although a field trip can be a valuable learning experience, it requires a great deal of planning; otherwise, it can be a fiasco. Students may become disorderly and disruptive, get injured, destroy property, and generally damage school–community relations. Unless you make careful preparations, students may not see the reason for the trip, and its educational value is therefore lost. The checklist in Activity 3.7 can help you plan a successful field trip.

Other problems beset the field trip from a different point of view. With school budgets tightening, many school districts no longer provide free bus transportation for field trips. Increased concern about liability and lawsuits has made many teachers wary of the risk involved in taking students away from the school. In self-contained classrooms, scheduling a field trip is usually fairly simple because only one teacher is involved. It is far more difficult, however, to arrange trips in secondary schools, due to the short class periods. Sometimes teachers of other subjects will cooperate to permit the absence of your students, but it may be necessary to plan trips at this level for after school or Saturdays.

Students who know what to expect are likely to learn more from a field trip than students who have no background information. The class should be involved in planning each trip. Even though you may have the idea in the back of your mind, you may want to let the students think the idea is theirs. For young children, a discussion about the subject and the proposed field trip may result in a set of questions on a language experience chart. These questions can be used as objectives for the trip. Older students can research the subject and develop individual lists of questions which may ultimately result in written reports.

Field trips are valuable only when they are an integral part of a total learning situation. You need to make adequate preparation and reinforce the educational value of the field trip with a variety of follow-up activities. These activities often spill over into many areas of the curriculum—social studies, science, reading, language arts, art, and music.

One example of an integrated learning experience is the neighborhood field trip.[2] This trip can be taken within walking distance of the school and can provide students with experiences in observing, collecting data, and making inferences. Before setting out on the walking tour, students should be told what data to collect for later analysis. After returning to the classroom, they may work in teams of three to five students to share their data and draw conclusions from their observations. The students may want to record some of the data in the form of bar graphs or pictographs. These are some questions the students can consider:

1 Which houses do or do not have people inside them now? How do you know?
2 How many and what types of trees are growing in this block?
3 Which houses have pets and/or children? What makes you think so?
4 What kind of people live in each house? How do you know?
5 How many houses are constructed of brick, wood, stone, or something else?

[2]Kenneth W. Kelsey. "A Neighborhood Field Trip." *Science and Children* 16 (April 1979): 14–15.

Examples of School–Community Experiences

1 A visit from an Antarctic scientist became an annual tradition for children in an elementary school in Virginia. His presentation was part of a "Winter Holiday" theme and tied in with the Science Curriculum Improvement Study (SCIS) Science Material. Children examined a stuffed penguin and looked at pictures of the scientist's trips to Antarctica. In conjunction with his visit, they found Antarctica on maps and globes, read about Antarctica, and watched films of animals native to Antarctica.[3]

2 A retired bicycle mechanic in Tennessee worked with reluctant remedial students to create an interest in learning. All students in the school were encouraged to bring to school any bicycles that needed repair. Under the direction of the mechanic, the remedial students studied repair manuals, mulled over catalogs, placed orders, and followed directions for repairing bicycles. The students' interest in school and their achievement levels soared.

3 Photography was the key ingredient in a community studies program for a class of junior high school students. The teacher was especially interested in photography and encouraged her students to use their cameras to photograph community sites. At the same time, they collected historical photographs of the town. As they excitedly compared the old pictures with the new, they became aware of the many changes that had taken place in their community over the years.[4]

4 Second-year chemistry students in a Pennsylvania high school were released from class two or three times a week to work in a host industry or medical center. The class was scheduled for the last period of the day, and students left school at 1:30 to work until 5:00 in the community job. The students worked in laboratories, where they used the latest techniques and equipment available.[5]

You may find an opportunity to develop a plan for using resources creatively in your teaching situation. Talk it over with your cooperating teacher; then make it work!

SUGGESTIONS TO HELP YOU BE SUCCESSFUL

During your first days in the classroom, you may feel somewhat unsure of how to act or dress. Following these general tips will help alleviate some of your anxiety. Some have been mentioned earlier but bear repeating here because of their importance to your success.

- Be pleasant and polite toward everyone with whom you come in contact—students, parents, your cooperating teacher, other teachers, administrators, and support personnel. In your anxiety about the new situation, don't forget how to *smile*.
- Be enthusiastic about the prospect of teaching. Show your cooperating teacher that you are energetic and willing, rather than lethargic and reluctant. Volunteer to help with tasks such as grading papers, giving individual assistance, and making instructional aids, as the opportunity arises. The greater and earlier your involvement, the more comfortable you will be when you begin teaching.

[3]Helenmarie Hofman. "Resource People." *Science and Children* 15 (February 1978): 20–21.
[4]Casey Murrow. "The Classroom Goes to Town." *National Elementary Principal* 58 (June 1979): 21–24.
[5]Thomas W. Clapper. "A School–Community Science Experience." *Journal of Chemical Education* 57 (February 1980): 143–44.

Activity 3.7 Checklist for Field Trip

1. _____ Permission to take a field trip has been granted by the school.

2. _____ Personnel at the destination have been contacted, and a time has been set for the visit.

3. _____ Transportation arrangements have been made.

4. _____ If you are using private cars, insurance and liability regulations have been checked.

5. _____ An adequate number of adults have agreed to accompany the students.

6. _____ Proper arrangements have been made regarding the facilities at the destination: restrooms, cafeteria, picnic tables, parking areas, size of observation areas.

7. _____ Lunch money and other fees have been collected (if applicable).

8. _____ Parental permission notes have been sent home.

9. _____ Parental permission notes have been returned.

10. _____ Students have been told how to behave and what to wear.

11. _____ Students have been told what to expect and have adequate background knowledge to understand what they will see.

12. _____ A list of questions has been prepared to set purposes for the visit.

13. _____ Tape recorders and note pads are available for recording specific information.

14. _____ Safety hazards, if any, have been noted and appropriate precautions taken.

15. _____ A first aid kit is available for emergencies.

16. _____ A signal (such as a whistle or raised arm) has been agreed upon for getting students' attention.

17. _____ Students have been paired and assigned buddies (if appropriate).

18. _____ Policy manual regarding field trips has been read, and policies have been followed.

- Be punctual. Punctuality reflects a professional attitude.
- Dress like a teacher dresses. Don't wear faded jeans and sweatshirts. If you don't look like a teacher, the students won't treat you like one. This aspect becomes more and more important as the grade level increases. It is easy for a secondary student teacher to look like "just one of the gang," but classroom management suffers when this happens. In most cases, you can take your cue from your cooperating teacher or other teachers in the school. Remember, however, that they are probably older than you and have already established their authority, whereas you are in the process of trying to establish yours.
- Check with your cooperating teacher about school policies *before* a crisis occurs in which you need to know those policies.
- Learn the students' names quickly. This helps you build rapport and maintain class control.
- Always use good grammar. You are supposed to be a model for the students, so you must take care to meet this responsibility in speaking and writing.
- Write legibly. You may be asked to construct worksheets or study guides for the students or write assignments on the chalkboard. Use the form of writing appropriate for your students (manuscript or cursive), and make sure you form the letters properly, that spacing and size of letters is appropriate, and that the overall product is legible. Once again, you are a model for the students.
- Keep calm. Do not allow yourself angry outbursts in school, even if things are not going well.
- Observe all school policies related to teachers, especially those about smoking (which is a trouble area for some student teachers).
- Never criticize your cooperating teacher to another teacher or criticize other teachers in the school to each other. This is unprofessional behavior.
- Learn the school's resources well before you are expected to take charge, so that you will be able to locate the things you need when you need them.
- Learn the daily routine thoroughly, so that you can manage it smoothly when you take over responsibility.
- Speak with pride about becoming a teacher. In these days of criticism of education, you should stand up for your chosen profession.

Later, when you begin teaching, you will need to remember these tips, which apply to the entire student teaching setting, plus the following additional ones, which apply to your direct teaching activities. Learn them so that you can perform acceptably.

- Be aware of the students' comfort. Adjust the temperature if the room is too hot or too cold. Adjust the blinds if there is a glare from the sunlight. See that there is adequate ventilation. Before, your cooperating teacher saw to these details; now, they are your responsibility.
- Don't lecture about something you have written or drawn on the board while standing in such a way that you block the students' view of the material.
- Use your voice well when teaching. A droning monotone bores students. An overly loud voice may intimidate some students, especially younger ones. A too-quiet voice may not carry well enough to reach students at the back of the room.
- Use only disciplinary methods sanctioned by your cooperating teacher. Avoid inappropriate practices such as punishing everyone for the misbehavior of a few and making unrealistic threats.
- Don't call on the same students all the time. Distribute classroom participation as evenly as possible.
- Vary activities to keep students' interest. Avoid leaning exclusively upon one teaching approach, such as the lecture method.

- Plan each lesson thoroughly, no matter how well you think you know the material. Consider the level of the students, and adjust your explanations and procedures accordingly. For example, a one-hour lecture is completely inappropriate for use with a second-grade class.
- Make clear and unambiguous assignments, and allow students the opportunity to ask for clarification if they need it.
- Grade and return all assignments promptly. Students will learn more from assignments with immediate feedback.
- Don't assign busywork. Make sure that all assignments contribute to classroom goals.

If you take these suggestions seriously, you will greatly enhance your chances of success in student teaching.

DISCUSSION QUESTIONS

1 How can you make your observations of your cooperating teacher and/or other teachers most useful to you? Would keeping a log of "Ideas for Future Use" help?
2 Do all the teachers you have observed use the same teaching and disciplinary techniques? Why do you believe this might be so?
3 What are some different lesson plan forms you might use? What are advantages and disadvantages of each form?
4 Are units more effective in your teaching situation when they cut across disciplines or when they are chosen from content within a single discipline? Why do you think so? Is there a place for both types of units?
5 Should you use a free, current, and interesting film from a company that uses the film to advertise its product? If you decide to use the film, what are some ways to handle the advertising message?
6 How can you use the resources in your community? What people, places, or agencies are available that relate to your subjects? How can you find out?
7 What do you do if one student's parents offer to share information with your class that you feel is inappropriate? How can you avoid offending the parent and the student? Is there another way you could use the parent's services?
8 What is the policy regarding field trips in your school? Are they permitted? How is transportation arranged? What regulations are in effect? Would a field trip be a good learning experience for your students?
9 Choose one of the selected references below that is concerned with use of computers or videotechnology. Read it and answer this question: How can the ideas presented in this source help me in my teaching assignment?

SELECTED REFERENCES

Allen, Denise. "Byte Size: Blue Ribbon Software." *Teaching K–8* 22 (May 1992): 16–23.
Allen, Denise. "Byte Size: Three Math Games." *Teaching K–8* 21 (January 1992): 14–16.
Artesani, Mary Ann. "Teaching's Videoclub Exchange: Winter Taping." *Teaching K–8* 22 (February 1992): 7.
Baker, Justine. *Microcomputers in the Classroom.* Bloomington, Ind.: Phi Delta Kappa Educational Foundation, 1982.
Balajthy, Ernest. *Microcomputers in Reading & Language Arts.* Englewood Cliffs, N.J.: Prentice-Hall, 1986.
Balajthy, Ernest, and Gordon Link. "Desktop Publishing in the Classroom." *The Reading Teacher* 41 (February 1988): 586–87.
Blanchard, Jay S., and George E. Mason. "Using Computers in Content Area Reading Instruction." *Journal of Reading* 29 (November 1985): 112–17.
Borden, Christopher III. "Helping Print-Oriented Teachers to Use Other Media." *Educational Technology* 18 (December 1978): 41–42.

Busse, Norman L. "Revealed: How Classroom Teachers Use Media." *Audiovisual Instruction* 21 (October 1976): 44–45.

Clapper, Thomas W. "A School–Community Science Experience." *Journal of Chemical Education* 57 (February 1980): 143–44.

Collins, Allan. "The Role of Computer Technology in Restructuring Schools." *Phi Delta Kappan* 73 (September 1991): 28–36.

Cooter, Robert B., Jr., and Robert Griffith. "Thematic Units for Middle School: An Honorable Seduction." *Journal of Reading* 32 (May 1989): 676–81.

DeGroff, Linda. "Is There a Place for Computers in Whole Language Classrooms?" *The Reading Teacher* 43 (April 1990): 568–72.

Dowd, Cornelia A., and Richard Sinatra. "Computer Programs and the Learning of Text Structure." *Journal of Reading* 34 (October 1990): 104–12.

Doyle, Claire. "Creative Applications of Computer Assisted Reading and Writing Instruction." *Journal of Reading* 32 (December 1988): 239.

DuBey, Robert E., et al. *A Performance-Based Guide to Student Teaching.* Danville, Ill.: Interstate, 1975.

Evans, Christopher, et al. "Microcomputers in the Classroom." *Today's Education* 71 (April/May 1982): 11–28.

Hofman, Helenmarie, "Resource People." *Science and Children* 15 (February 1978): 20–21.

Hydrick, Janie. "DISKovery: Kids and Technology—Revelry or Rivalry?" *Language Arts* 67 (September 1990): 518–19.

Kelsey, Kenneth W. "A Neighborhood Field Trip." *Science and Children* 16 (April 1979): 14–15.

Kemp, Jerrold E. *Planning, Producing, and Using Instructional Media,* 6th ed. New York: Harper Collins, 1989.

Layton, Kent, and Martha E. Irwin. "Enriching Your Reading Program with Databases." *The Reading Teacher* 42 (May 1989): 724.

Lindroth, Linda. "Have Computer, Will Travel." *Teaching K–8* 21 (October 1990): 64–66.

Lowe, Janis Lindley. "Building Self-Esteem—Computer Style." *Teaching K–8* 21 (October 1990): 69–70.

"Macintosh Generates Excitement and Profits for Journalism Program." *Curriculum Product News* 25 (May 1991): 19, 38.

Mathison, Carla, and Linda Lungren. "Using Computers Effectively in Content Area Classes." In *Content Area Reading and Learning: Instructional Strategies.* Diane Lapp, James Flood, and Nancy Farnan, Eds. Englewood Cliffs, N.J.: Prentice-Hall, 1989, pp. 304–18.

Miklethun, Betsey A. "The Young Reach Out to the Old in Shaker Heights." *Today's Education* 70 (April/May 1981): 34E–35E.

Morgan, Mary. "Using Computers in the Language Arts." *Language Arts* 68 (January 1991): 74–77.

Murrow, Casey. "The Classroom Goes to Town." *National Elementary Principal* 58 (June 1979): 21–24.

Oley, Elizabeth. "Information Retrieval in the Classroom." *Journal of Reading* 32 (April 1989): 590–97.

Phenix, Katharine. "Software for Libraries." *Wilson Library Bulletin* 66 (April 1992): 83–84.

Ramondetta, June. "Using Computers: Learning from Lunchroom Trash." *Learning92* 20 (April/May 1992): 59.

Rude, Robert T. *Teaching Reading Using Microcomputers.* Englewood Cliffs, N.J.: Prentice-Hall, 1986.

Schmid, William T. "The Teacher and the Media Specialist." *Media and Methods* 13 (October 1976): 22–24.

Solomon, Gwen. "Interdisciplinary Writing—Down East Style." *Electronic Learning* 11 (May/June 1992): 8.

Solomon, Gwen. *Teaching Writing with Computers: The Power Process.* Englewood Cliffs, N.J.: Prentice-Hall, 1986.

"Turned on to Reading and Writing." *Electronic Learning* 11 (May/June 1992): 12–18.

Ventura, Fred. "Computers and Manipulatives: Making the Connection." *Teaching K–8* 21 (October 1990): 71–72.

Wegner, Hart. *Teaching with Film*. Bloomington, Ind.: Phi Delta Kappa Educational Foun-
    dation, 1977.
Wepner, Shelley B. "Holistic Computer Applications in Literature-Based Classrooms." *The
    Reading Teacher* 44 (September 1990): 12–19.
Wepner, Shelley B. "Technology between the Lines." *Teaching K–8* 21 (October 1990): 61–
    63.
Woodbury, Marda. *Selecting Instructional Materials*. Bloomington, Ind.: Phi Delta Kappa
    Educational Foundation, 1978.

4

Discipline

In science class, Mrs. Goldberg was doing a unit on reptiles, and Miss Yeatch, the student teacher, was helping her. For the culminating activity, the children were to bring some specimens to class. Maria had brought an unusual lizard, and Frank had brought a frog. Manuel had contributed a garter snake he had found near his house. These animals were placed in separate cages on a counter in the back of the room that the students called their "zoo." Most of the students were curious about the reptiles and liked watching them. A few boys and girls, however, seemed timid about approaching the cages and avoided looking in their direction. The day before the reptiles were to be taken home, Mrs. Goldberg was called to the office for an emergency meeting with a parent. Miss Yeatch was in charge.

Manuel (whispering to some friends in the back of the room): Hey, Mrs. Goldberg's gone. Have you noticed the way Benjy and Tony and Karen are scared to death of those animals? Let's give the three of them a real good scare. When Miss Yeatch isn't looking, let's sneak over and let the animals out of their cages.

Rachel (also in a whisper): Yeah, let's each get one of the cages on a signal and let them all out at once.

Jake: What a blast! Let's do it!

Miss Yeatch (trying to introduce a lesson on pronouns): Quiet down in the back of the room. There's no need for any talking. Do you have your English books out yet? Turn to page 79.

Manuel, Rachel, Jake (mumbling): Yeah, sure, we're with you. (The three send secret messages to one another with their eyes, waiting for the right opportunity.)

Miss Yeatch: All of you get on with your work. Try to have this finished before Mrs. Goldberg returns. (She bends down to help a student who is having trouble with a sentence.)

Manuel, Rachel, Jake (in a mutual, excited whisper): Now! (They sneak quickly and quietly to the cages, unfasten the hooks and open the doors, and return to their seats. A few children who notice begin to giggle.)

Dottie: Oh my goodness! The frog's loose. He's hopping over to the window.

Allen: Look out. Here comes the snake!

Benjy: Oh no! I'm getting out of here! (He runs for the door and makes a quick exit down the hall.)

Miss Yeatch: What's happening? Oh no! Who let those animals out? Put them back. Manuel, get your snake back in its cage. Somebody catch that frog. (The lizard is hiding under a leaf; the snake is crawling toward a dark spot in the corner.)

By now, several of the children are screaming and standing on their desks. Miss Yeatch, who is terrified of snakes, is now speechless and can only stand rooted to the spot. Some of the children are grinning slyly at each other as they stand around the snake, watching it glide across the room.

Mrs. Goldberg (just returning to the room): What's going on in here? I heard the racket all the way down at the principal's office.

Miss Yeatch (in a weak voice): Somebody let the animals out.

Mrs. Goldberg (in a firm voice): All right. All of you return to your seats. Manuel, put the snake back and fasten the cage. Cathy, you catch the frog, and Mark, close the lizard's cage before it gets out too. Now get on with your work. I believe you're supposed to be studying pronouns.

1. Could Miss Yeatch have anticipated the problem? If so, how? Were there any preventive measures she might have taken?
2. What are some ways Miss Yeatch might have handled the situation when she first noticed the reptiles were out of the cages?
3. Can you think of a way Miss Yeatch could have regained control of the class before Mrs. Goldberg returned?
4. Do you think Mrs. Goldberg got the class under control when she returned and spoke to the students? Why or why not?

DILEMMAS IN DISCIPLINE

Students occasionally misbehave in every classroom. How to deal with them can be a problem for you. Consider the following situations. None of the answers is necessarily the right one; in fact, you might be able to come up with a better solution. In some cases, you might choose more than one answer. Consider what the circumstances might be and the probable consequences of each alternative. After you read this chapter, reconsider your answers.

1 Billy sticks out his tongue at you and gives you a smart answer. What do you do?
   (a) Paddle him.
   (b) Tell him to shut up and sit down.
   (c) Ignore his behavior this time.
   (d) Speak to him calmly, explaining why you cannot tolerate this kind of behavior.
   (e) Punish him by making him stay in at recess.
   (f) Laugh at him. He really was sort of cute.

2 Chrissy throws an eraser at Tammy and hits her on the head. What do you do?
   (a) Check to see if Tammy is hurt. If not, ignore the situation.
   (b) Let Tammy throw an eraser at Chrissy and hit *her* on the head.
   (c) Warn Chrissy that, if she does it again, she'll have to miss lunch for one week.
   (d) Make an example of Chrissy. Scold her severely in front of the class, and make her stand in the corner for an hour.
   (e) Stop what you are doing. Quietly point out that throwing things can be dangerous and that this behavior is unacceptable.
   (f) Go on with your lesson as if nothing happened.

3 At the precise moment of 10:07 (according to the clock on the wall) all students bend down to tie their shoes, even those who don't have shoelaces. What do you do?
   (a) Ignore this event, and go on with your lesson.
   (b) Stop the lesson, and demand to know who is responsible for instigating this diversion.
   (c) Punish the entire class by making them write 100 times, "I will not tie my shoes during class."
   (d) Deny the students an anticipated privilege.
   (e) Pass the episode off with a humorous remark, such as "Next time you'd better wear self-tying shoelaces," and then go on with your lesson.
   (f) Lecture the class on the importance of paying attention and concentrating on the lesson.

4 Two students are talking and giggling in the back of the room while you are trying to conduct a discussion. What do you do?
   (a) Move closer to the students, pause, and look at them significantly.
   (b) Call on one of them to answer a question you have just asked.
   (c) Stop and wait as long as necessary until everyone is quiet.
   (d) Call them by name, and ask them to pay attention.
   (e) Say in a loud and angry voice, "Your talking is disturbing to the rest of the class. I want you to stop this minute. If I hear one more word out of either of you, I'll send you both to the office."
   (f) Wait until after class; then talk to the students, and explain that their talking was very disturbing.

5 Carol is eating potato chips during reading group. You ask her to stop, and she defiantly tells you "No." What do you do?
   (a) Try to take the bag away from her by force.
   (b) Tell her that if she is going to eat potato chips in front of the other students, she will have to bring enough for everyone.

    (c) Tell her that if she'll put the potato chips away now, she can eat them during recess.

    (d) Ask her to return to her seat until she is finished.

    (e) Insist that she stop eating. Warn her that she will be punished if she does not stop right now. Continue until you win your point.

    (f) Drop the request for the moment. Get the children interested in an exciting part of the story, and then quietly ask Carol to put the chips away for now.

6 Judy and Jerry are passing notes during math class. What do you do?

    (a) Pick up the notes from their desks, and read the notes aloud to the class.

    (b) Pick up the notes from their desks, tear them into shreds, and drop them into the wastebasket.

    (c) In front of the class, say sarcastically, "Judy and Jerry seem to know all there is to know about math since they aren't paying attention." Then send them to the board, and give them a difficult problem to work in front of the other students.

    (d) Assign Jerry and Judy ten extra problems for homework, and threaten to do the same to anyone else who doesn't pay attention.

    (e) Walk toward their desks; look at them intently until they understand they are not to write notes any more; then continue your lesson.

    (f) Have them stay after school and pick up all the scraps of paper in the room.

To deal with situations such as these, you should begin by understanding what discipline is and what it is not. Discipline is controlled behavior. It is the ability to get attention when you need it. It does not call for an absolutely quiet and rigidly controlled class, although some degree of order is implied. There is often quiet, purposeful talking in a well-disciplined classroom, with students moving freely about as they work on projects.

Teachers often consider discipline their number one problem. Why is it so difficult to establish and maintain classroom control? The answer probably lies partly in the complexity of the causes of discipline problems. You must consider the students' personalities and backgrounds, the type of learning situation in which they are involved, and the distractions that may interfere with their concentration. Discipline is also difficult because, in most cases, you must decide what to do on the spot, and you cannot be sure of the consequences of your actions.

Even though effective classroom discipline may be difficult to achieve, you must have it to accomplish any of your objectives. Without it, too much time is wasted, and too many students never get the message. Without it, students never learn to control their own behavior so as to become productive citizens later in life. Finally, without it, you will not survive. Teacher burnout is often the result of a breakdown in discipline.

CAUSES OF DISCIPLINE PROBLEMS

Who or what might cause discipline problems? Maybe society, maybe something in the classroom environment, maybe the students themselves—or maybe you! Let's look at some of the causes.

Society may need to shoulder part of the blame. At one time, teachers were highly respected, and their word was law, but this situation is no longer true. Parents today seem to be more permissive toward their children and do not train them to practice self-discipline at home. Law enforcement agencies do not always support the schools in dealing with juvenile offenders. There is little you can do about society's changing attitudes toward the teaching profession, except to show through your actions that you are worthy of respect.

You *can* do something about your classroom environment, however. When there are so many other things to think about, it's easy to forget such apparently obvious factors as lighting, temperature control, room arrangement, and distracting elements. Analyze your classroom. Is there something in the room you could change that might reduce the number of discipline problems?

The students bring with them such a bewildering array of emotional, physical, and social problems that it's no wonder they sometimes misbehave. Sometimes you may be able to help them solve problems or accept what's troubling them. Sometimes just knowing that you care makes a difference to them. Students whose personal problems no longer interfere with their concentration are less likely to cause problems for you.

Without realizing it, you may be responsible for some of the discipline problems that arise. Can you answer all of these questions affirmatively?

1 Is my lesson well planned and purposeful?
2 Am I meeting the interests and needs of the students? Are they motivated to learn?
3 Are the students actively involved in learning?
4 Is the material at an appropriate level of difficulty, and do I have reasonable expectations for each student?
5 Do the students understand exactly how I expect them to behave and know the consequences of misbehavior?
6 Am I fair and consistent with discipline, and do I carry out my promises?

"Yes" to each of these questions will go a long way toward preventing discipline problems from developing.

Your situation as a student teacher is slightly different from that of the classroom teacher. No matter who is doing the teaching, the standards of discipline set by the regular teacher usually prevail (see Activity 4.1). This condition can work to your advantage if your cooperating teacher is a good disciplinarian, or to your disadvantage if she or he is poor with discipline. The students realize that even if you're in charge of this lesson, they will ultimately have to answer to their regular teacher. You also have not had the experience of a regular teacher and must pay attention to many things that are routine for the experienced teacher. This predicament makes it difficult for you to notice all the small incidents that could lead to trouble in time to stop discipline problems from occurring. Finally, as a student teacher, you may overlook occasional infractions because you want the students to like you. When they find out they can get away with misbehaving, they will take advantage of you, and your control will disappear.

PREVENTION OF DISCIPLINE PROBLEMS

Learning how to prevent discipline problems is one secret of classroom control. Some problems may develop anyway, but if you know when to anticipate trouble, you can prevent minor skirmishes from erupting into full-fledged battles.

Student Relationships

Your relationship with the students is of primary importance. They are amazingly perceptive and can tell if you truly care about them and want to help. Try to learn something about their home environments, their special needs and problems, and what interests them. They will respect you if you patiently show them how to do something they want to learn. They will appreciate your recognition of their successes and achievements. You will win a loyal supporter if you find out that a student's mother is in the hospital and remember to ask about her progress. When you earn their support and respect, students are likely to cooperate with you in maintaining order in the classroom.

Activity 4.1   Observation Sheet for Classroom Management

Carefully observe your cooperating teacher for classroom management strategies. Note nonverbal behavior, preventive actions, and disciplinary techniques.

Classroom management strategies:

Most effective strategies:

Least effective strategies:

Conclusions about strategies I may want to use with this class:

Verbal and nonverbal reinforcers are good ways to establish a warm relationship with your students. These reinforcers are words and signals that influence students' behavior. Verbal reinforcers can be comments such as "good work" and "nice going, Timmy." Light, kidding conversations before or after class, offers of help, and friendly greetings are good social reinforcers. Examples of nonverbal reinforcers are approving facial expressions and gestures. Use these reinforcers frequently during the school day.

Student self-control, or self-discipline, is the center of good classroom control. As long as the students rely on you to control their behavior, they are apt to lapse into poor behavior if you do not constantly direct their actions. Instead, teach them to be responsible for their own behavior. Self-control develops gradually, and your students probably have it in varying degrees, ranging all the way from the well-controlled individual to one who frequently seems totally out of control. If you can get your students to develop self-discipline, both you and the students are the winners. You will have fewer discipline problems, and the students will acquire a skill they will need all their lives.

You can help students develop self-control in a variety of ways. Keep in mind that all students are not at the same level of self-discipline, and you will have to vary your strategies accordingly. Hold students responsible for performing classroom duties. Give them opportunities to be responsible for guiding someone else's progress by setting up a tutoring program. Encourage them to keep records of their own progress.

All students should be able to make some choices of their own—what books to read, interests to pursue, friends to be with, and behavior patterns to follow. The students should know and be prepared to live with the consequences of their choices. They should be granted privileges as long as they honor them; if they abuse a privilege, it should be taken away.

Remember to start with small tasks and work up to larger ones as students demonstrate readiness to assume more responsibility. You can experiment with making long-term assignments occasionally, without checking daily, to see if students can direct their own activities. If assignments aren't completed on time, you may need to revert to daily evaluation. Among your teaching strategies, include independent activities such as projects and lab work, where students must carry an

Students know when you truly care about them and want to help.

activity through to completion. If you show the students you believe they are capable of directing many of their own activities, they are likely to live up to your expectations.

Students feel responsible for their actions when they have a hand in planning activities and making their own rules for behavior. They realize that limits must be set for behavior, and they may understand what works better than you do. You will probably continue many of the policies already in effect in your classroom, but you might also work with the students to develop some rules of your own to take care of problems that seem to be arising. It is a good strategy for you and the students to agree on a signal to get instant attention, such as raising your hand, ringing a bell, or saying "Freeze!" After rules have been established, help your students evaluate their effectiveness. If a rule is frequently violated, perhaps the rule is unnecessary, or perhaps there is something else wrong with it. If a penalty seems unfair, perhaps there is a more appropriate consequence.

Your relationships with students are also important in other ways. Learn your students' names, and use them as soon as you can. Use a seating chart or name tags to help you. Calling students by name gets their attention quickly. Expect them to say Mr., Mrs., Ms., or Miss before addressing you by name, to maintain a respectful relationship.

Observe the seating arrangement in your room to see if you might eliminate some centers of disturbance by relocating some students. Learn which students are likely to instigate trouble, and watch them more closely. Even though you find yourself liking some students better than others, treat them all fairly and consistently. Don't let anyone accuse you of having "teacher's pets." Avoid confrontations with students in front of their peers. It's better to discuss problems rationally, later, during a one-to-one conference. Whenever you can, try to help students work out their problems without having to send them to an outside source.

It doesn't take students long to figure out what kind of disciplinarian you are. Some will deliberately test you to find out how far they can go. You need to be firm from the first day if you expect to have good classroom control.

Presentation of Lessons

If you use the following suggestions, your lessons should give little cause for misbehavior. Make sure the classroom is as comfortable and free from distractions as you can make it. Get everyone's attention before you begin, and be sure that desks or tables are cleared of everything except what the students will need during the lesson. Be well prepared. Know your lesson well enough that you don't have to read from the manual while you teach. It's important to have good eye contact with the students during a lesson. Be ready to switch to another method if one strategy isn't working. Watch for students who may have trouble understanding the work, and be ready to help them over their hurdles; otherwise, their frustration can erupt in behavior problems.

Start and end your lessons promptly, and make transitions from one lesson to another quickly and smoothly. In discussion lessons, let only one student answer at a time to prevent the confusion that results when students call out answers. Keep your lessons interesting and fast-paced. Be enthusiastic, and the students will catch your enthusiasm. Get the students actively involved in your lessons, and keep them motivated, because highly motivated students seldom cause discipline problems. Have more than enough material for the entire class period. In case you still run short, keep ideas in mind for filling in the remaining minutes productively.

Give directions clearly and precisely. Reinforce important directions by writing them on the chalkboard. Be sure the students know what choices they have when they finish their work. If they don't know what to do next, they may become disruptive. Be patient with slow learners. If necessary, explain things more than once, so that everyone understands. Put things in simple words for young children.

Your teaching style makes a difference in how students respond to you. Move around the room, and use nonverbal communication to interact with various students as you teach. Call on students who seem inattentive to get them to stay with you. If a crisis occurs, keep your composure. Remain in charge of the situation, and calmly decide what to do. Develop a sense of humor. Laugh with the students and occasionally at yourself. A good laugh reduces tension.

The volume of your voice can set the noise level of the class. If you raise your voice to be heard, the students will only get noisier. If you lower your voice, they will become quiet to hear what you have to say. Be sure, however, that you can be heard in the back of the room and that you speak distinctly. After a week of teaching classes, try Activity 4.2.

Reacting to Danger Signals

If you're alert to impending trouble, you can often stop problems just as they start. Boredom, daydreaming, restlessness, and long periods of inactivity breed discipline problems. Danger signals include a paper wad shot across the room, a half-smothered giggle, or a quick exchange of glances between students.

When you sense trouble brewing, nip it in the bud. Try these ideas:

1 Change your tactics fast. Switch to a different approach, read a story, play a rhythm game, or talk about an event in which students share an interest.

2 Use nonverbal communication to arrest the problem. Catch the instigator's eye and hold it. Pause in midsentence, and look intently at the potential troublemakers. Shake your head slowly to indicate disapproval.

3 Remind the students of a privilege or reward that will be the consequence of good behavior, while looking in the direction of the potential problem.

4 Move closer to the source of trouble. Indicate that you are aware of what's going on.

5 Speak softer and slower. You will get the students' attention for the moment, as they try to figure out why you shifted your speech.

6 Catch them off guard by saying something like, "I surely hope no one in here is thinking about throwing a pencil" or "Did I tell you what is going to happen this Friday?"

7 Use humor. Laugh off a minor incident instead of making a big deal of it. For example, to a student who has just thrown a paper airplane, say "Billy, I'll bet the Air Force could use you to help design airplanes. Now let's get back to work."

8 Call on students you believe are about to cause a problem to answer a question. Or simply insert a student's name in midsentence to bring attention back to the lesson; for example, "The next question, Johnny, is number seven."

9 In response to an irritating noise, say, "Distracting noises interfere with what we need to accomplish in here. I guess we won't have time to play '20 Questions.' "

10 Confiscate distracting materials, especially toys or food, that are diverting students' attention.

MODELS OF DISCIPLINE

In recent years, many writers have proposed models of discipline. You may be able to draw from these writers' ideas to solve discipline problems in your classroom. We will discuss five of these models briefly and illustrate their correct and incorrect use. Refer to these models as you do Activity 4.3.

Glasser

Let's look first at Glasser. He represents two views, one that he expressed prior to 1985 and the other after 1985. His earlier view is based on student responsibility for behavior. Students examine problems and seek solutions; they also participate in making reasonable rules for behavior that they are then expected to observe. If they choose inappropriate behavior, the teacher accepts no excuses and the student must accept the consequences.

Glasser's later view supports the teacher's need to make the classroom a desirable place to learn. He believes that students have four basic needs: the need to belong, the need for power, the need for freedom, and the need for fun. Therefore, school should be structured so that schoolwork helps satisfy these needs in order for students to make the effort to learn. How can teachers do this? This can be accomplished by having students work together in small learning teams of about four students, according to Glasser. When students' needs are met, they are likely to increase their work output and create fewer discipline problems.

Comparing Glasser's two views, we can see a shift of responsibility from student to teacher. Actually, both views are viable in that it is indeed a teacher's obligation to provide stimulating, student-oriented situations for learning. It is also, however, the student's responsibility to assume control over his or her behavior.

Case Study: A Joint Endeavor

Mrs. Burks likes an orderly, quiet classroom with each student in her or his seat. She constantly has to remind Yvonne, a gregarious student, to stay in her seat, stop talking, and finish her work.

Mrs. Burks: Yvonne, you're out of your seat again. I've told you not to leave it without permission. Why do you keep getting up?

Yvonne: I get so tired of sitting still—I just *need* to get up sometimes.

Mrs. Burks: Let me think. . . . Would it help if you could work with other students sometimes on group projects?

Yvonne: I think it would be a lot easier if I could talk sometimes about my work to my friends. Could we do that?

Mrs. Burks: I'll try to work something out, but you must agree to do your share of the work if we plan some group activities. You can't just talk and move around unless you are working on your project. Do you understand?

Yvonne: Yes. I'll really try.

Mrs. Burks: I'll give group work a try, but remember that I hold you responsible for working cooperatively with your group.

Although she was reluctant to do so, Mrs. Burks was willing to modify her class structure in order to make it more satisfying for Yvonne, as well as for other students with similar tendencies. At the same time, she will expect the students to do their part in working cooperatively to achieve learning goals.

Case Study: Teacher Authority

Dennis constantly shows off to the other students, rarely does his work, and is always jumping up to do or say something.

Mr. Olsen: Dennis, come up to my desk. I want to talk to you.

Dennis: What did I do now?

Mr. Olsen: You know perfectly well. You were about to throw that paper wad toward the trash can.

Dennis: Oh, that. Well, I had to get rid of it somehow—and I'm usually a pretty good shot.

Mr. Olsen: That's beside the point. I expect you to sit in your seat and do your work. Is that clear?

Dennis: Yes, Mr. Olsen.

Mr. Olsen: Go back to your seat and stay there until the end of class.

Activity 4.2   Self-Analysis of Classroom Management Techniques

After your first week of teaching classes, analyze the effectiveness of your classroom management techniques. Identify each technique and rate it on a scale of 1 (worst) to 5 (best). (You may want to repeat this activity periodically.)

Technique	Rating

Briefly summarize your most and least effective techniques.

What are some other techniques you might want to use?

Activity 4.3   Case Study of a Student with Behavior Problems

As you observe a class, identify one student who appears to have behavior problems. Notice how the teacher handles each situation with this student. Study the different models for discipline and decide which techniques might be useful for improving the student's behavior. With your cooperating teacher's approval, try some of the techniques when you begin teaching. Analyze the results.

Thumbnail sketch of case study:

Techniques the teacher uses:

Techniques I want to try (based on models of discipline):

Effectiveness of my techniques and future recommendations:

This encounter resolved nothing. Mr. Olsen was unwilling to consider any changes in structuring his class and did not help Dennis take responsibility for his actions. Dennis will probably continue his inappropriate behavior.

Kounin

One aspect of Kounin's discipline theory is the ripple effect—the effect of a disciplinary measure on the rest of the class. When a teacher corrects one pupil, other students are influenced by the example that is set. You can make good use of this ripple effect if you know how. When you correct a student, clearly identify the student, what she is doing, and what she should be doing instead. Vague generalizations have little effect. For instance, say "Cathy, stop playing with those cards, and finish your spelling paper." Simply saying "Class, get busy" makes little difference in students' behavior. Students learn how to behave by listening to your comments to other students. Correcting the behavior of classroom leaders instead of followers generally has a greater ripple effect. Rough physical treatment is generally ineffective since it usually makes the class uneasy and fearful.

Kounin also advocates smooth lesson transitions and effective teaching strategies as deterrents to behavior problems. Teachers must keep their lessons moving along without interrupting themselves with "dangles" (leaving a lesson hanging while tending to something else) and "flip flops" (changing back and forth from one subject to another). They must keep their students alert by calling on them randomly and occasionally calling for unison responses. They should become skilled at "overlapping," the ability to handle two or more students or groups at one time. Finally, they should be "withit" by using their sixth sense to react quickly and accurately to class disturbances.

Case Study: Withitness

Mr. Wiseman had taught algebra for 14 years and knew pretty well what to expect of his students. They rarely tried to take advantage of him because it was said that he had eyes in the back of his head. One day he was writing an equation on the board for the students to work during class. The class was quiet as he began writing, but as he continued, he heard some whispers and movement in one corner of the room where Karen was usually the instigator of any trouble. As he turned around, Edna jumped up from her seat and demanded angrily, "All right, whoever has my calculator had better give it back." Two or three students got out of their seats to help her look for her calculator. Mr. Wiseman looked directly at Karen, who was secretly passing the calculator to Paul. Mr. Wiseman said, "Karen, return the calculator to Edna. Class, get to work on these problems." The students settled down to work.

Mr. Wiseman handled the situation well. He anticipated trouble when he first heard the whispering and turned quickly to nip it in the bud. By knowing his students, he was able to locate the source of the trouble, correct the problem, and get the students back on task with only a small interruption. The students respected him for knowing who the culprit was and dispensing with the problem quickly.

Case Study: Un-Withitness

In the class next door, Mr. Dole was preoccupied with assembling a science experiment, while the students waited with nothing to do. He heard some commotion in the classroom, but hoped it would subside without his intervention. He continued connecting the hose to the pump, but eventually the hubbub became so loud that he looked up. Mike and Bonnie were throwing an eraser to each other, and Alex was running between them trying to intercept it. Students were shouting encouragement, and one or two others were moving into the game. Mr. Dole couldn't understand how things had gotten so out of hand in such a short time. He tried to yell over the noise, but only a few students heard his voice, and they ignored him. He frantically flipped the light switch, threatened the students with expulsion, and eventually got them back into their seats. He told Bonnie, Mike, and Alex to go to the principal's office, even though they protested that it wasn't their idea to play Catch the Eraser. He told the rest of the class that there would be no experiment and that they should read Chapter 4 for a test the next day.

Mr. Dole made a number of mistakes. He was unprepared when class started, and he left his students with nothing to do. He ignored the first signs of trouble when he could still have prevented a major disruption from occurring. He was unable to deal with more than one issue at a time. In his panic to restore order, he made a threat that he had no intention of carrying out. He wasn't sure how many students were really at fault, so he chose the three who were participating in the game and punished them by sending them to the office. In effect, he punished the rest of the class as well by assigning a test for the next day. The students were resentful and felt they had been unfairly treated.

Redl and Wattenburg

Redl and Wattenburg examine the effects of group dynamics on behavior. They believe the behavior of individuals affects the group, and that group expectations sway individual behavior. Understanding the psychological forces underlying group behavior helps the teacher maintain classroom control.

Teachers can influence group behavior in four ways. In *supporting self-control,* a low-keyed approach, teachers help students to help themselves. *Situational assistance* requires the teacher to help the student regain self-control; an example is "hurdle help," or helping the student overcome a specific problem that is preventing learning. Another example is restructuring the situation when the present approach is not working. In *reality appraisal,* students are made aware of what behavior is acceptable and the consequences of breaking rules. Finally, the *pain-pleasure principle* provides for rewards to be given for good behavior and threats for unacceptable behavior. Punishment is used only as a last resort for those occasions when a student completely loses self-control.

Case Study: Restructuring the Situation

Mrs. Keen was teaching an American history lesson to her general curriculum students. It was the last period of the day, and the students were tired and restless. Mrs. Keen tried to involve her students in a discussion about the landing of the Pilgrims at Plymouth Rock. When she called on Kirk, usually a good student, he told her he hadn't heard the question. Randy didn't know the answer either, but he whispered a few words to his neighbors that made them laugh. Mrs. Keen looked at Susan, who was watching Dennis try to balance his pencil on an eraser. Susan wouldn't know the answer either. As Mrs. Keen surveyed her class, she realized that no one seemed the least bit interested in what happened to the Pilgrims.

Mrs. Keen racked her brain for a way to get the students to respond. She suddenly thought of simulating this event, of having each person in the room become involved in the story by acting it out. She stopped her lesson, told the students that for the rest of the afternoon they were going to do something different, and began explaining the procedure. The class gradually got caught up in acting out the landing of the Pilgrims and their attempts to survive in a cold and primitive new world.

Mrs. Keen was perceptive enough to realize that if her students were to get anything out of the landing of the Pilgrims, she would have to change her tactics at once. Since her students appeared totally uninterested in the lesson, she tried to think of a way to get them all involved. Her change of pace worked, and she added simulation to her repertoire of teaching techniques.

Case Study: Maintaining the Status Quo

Mrs. Lee had planned her English lesson carefully. First she was going to tell her class about adjectives and how they are used. Then she planned to have the class complete a worksheet on the use of adjectives.

Outside, there was a terrible storm with thunder and lightning. Some of the students were frightened, especially when one blinding flash of lightning was followed instantly by a loud crash of thunder. Mrs. Lee continued discussing adjec- tives, although she noticed that nearly all the children were pointing out the window at a tree that had been knocked down by the heavy winds. When Mrs. Lee had concluded her lesson, she asked the students if they had any questions about adjectives. They looked at her blankly, but said nothing. Mrs. Lee was disappointed to find that the children did not do well on the worksheet that followed her well-presented lesson.

Mrs. Lee was totally inflexible. She was unable to deviate from her lesson plan even when circumstances clearly called for a change. Instead of ignoring the storm, she could have talked about what causes thunder and lightning and allowed the children to observe what was happening. Afterward, she could have asked them to think of all the adjectives they could use to describe the storm. The lesson would then have been meaningful to the class.

Canter and Canter

The Canters advocate assertive discipline as a means for establishing effective classroom control. Assertive discipline is based on the concept that teachers have the right to insist on appropriate behavior from students. From the beginning of the school year, teachers establish rules for behavior along with logical consequences for both proper and improper behavior. These expectations are communicated clearly to the students. Failure to behave well results in negative consequences, such as losing privileges or preferred activities, remaining after school, being sent to the principal's office, or time out (isolation). Good behavior brings positive consequences, such as material rewards, positive notes to parents, special privileges or awards, and personal attention from the teacher. Teachers can also elicit the support of parents and administrators.

Case Study: Playing It by the Rules

It was raining, and Mr. Arrow's students were staying inside for recess. They had requested free time and were well aware of the rules for behavior. Mr. Arrow had suggested that the students might like to go to the reading corner, play one of the games, or work on their mural. As Mr. Arrow was talking with a group of children, he noticed that Ken had snatched Dottie's lunch box and begun to run around the room with it. Dottie started to chase him, but soon realized she couldn't catch him. She whined, "Give me back my lunch box." Ken taunted, "You'll have to catch me first."

At that point, Mr. Arrow said firmly, "Ken, come here." When Ken reached him, Mr. Arrow continued, looking Ken directly in the eye. "Ken, I don't like what you have done. You know the rules in here. There is to be no running in the classroom. Also, you are not to take something that belongs to someone else. You have broken both of these rules. I want you to return Dottie's lunch box. Then I want you to sit in that chair by the counter until recess is over." Ken reluctantly did as Mr. Arrow told him.

Limits for behavior had been set early in the year in Mr. Arrow's class. The students were well aware of the limits and the consequences of going beyond those limits. Occasionally, a student slipped, and Mr. Arrow asserted himself, as in the case of Ken. He spoke to Ken firmly, maintained eye contact, explained the inappropriate behavior, and followed through with a reasonable consequence.

Case Study: Anything Goes

Mr. Wilson was a new teacher. He knew classroom control was important, but he felt it was even more important for the students to like him. In an effort to be a pal to his students, he overlooked many inconsequential incidents at the beginning of the year. One day, he realized that he had to enforce some rules of behavior or he would lose control of the class altogether. He told the students, "You'd better settle down now" and "Please get quiet." These requests didn't seem to make any difference.

The next time the noise level rose, Mr. Wilson threatened to send all the students to detention hall. They were confused by this unnatural behavior and responded with complaints of unfairness and pleas for another chance. Hating to lose the friendship of his students, Mr. Wilson gave in to their requests and withdrew his threat.

A similar situation occurred the next day, so Mr. Wilson told the students to put their heads down on their desks for 10 minutes. After a minute or two, some students began looking up. They said they thought they'd been punished long enough, so Mr. Wilson let them keep their heads up.

Mr. Wilson's students took advantage of his nonassertiveness by kidding around in class. His requests for good behavior were vague and unclear, so the students ignored him. They soon realized they could talk him out of any threats he made. They liked Mr. Wilson, but had little respect for him due to his inability to set and enforce limits for behavior.

Behavior Modification

All discipline deals with modifying behavior in some way, but behavior modification is a specific model of discipline based on B. F. Skinner's ideas. The basic premise is that all behavior is shaped by what happens to the students following an action. In this model, reinforcement is used systematically to change student behavior. Students who perform well are given reinforcers, or rewards. The rewards may be words of approval, awards, grades, or even such tangible items as raisins or candy. Students who perform badly receive no reinforcers; their behavior is ignored. Some systems of reinforcement are quite complex, but the concept of rewarding good behavior and ignoring bad behavior can be observed in any classroom.

Case Study: Catch More Flies with Honey

Mr. Sahai had studied about behavior modification in his psychology class and decided to put it into action. He realized that his classroom control wasn't as good as it could be and thought that a system of reinforcement might help. He introduced the plan to his class, announcing that points would be awarded to the class for good behavior. He pointed to a poster showing the maximum number of points that could be earned for each function. For instance, if everyone was seated and ready to work when the bell rang for class to start, the class would earn 10 points. If Mr. Sahai didn't have to correct anyone's behavior during an entire class period, the class would earn 15 points. He continued with other examples, then explained that the number of points would be totaled at the end of each week. Then Mr. Sahai showed the class another chart indicating the number of points required to earn certain privileges.

The students were very responsive to this plan. They cared more about behaving well when they were rewarded for doing so. The only problem was that Jon kept calling out during class, and Mr. Sahai sometimes had to correct him. No points were earned during these classes. The other students decided to take matters into their own hands and make Jon stop interrupting. This peer pressure changed Jon's behavior so that the class was soon earning the full number of points.

Mr. Sahai's experiment with behavior modification was successful. He had carefully thought out his plan and made the rules clear to the class. He kept careful records and never forgot to let the students choose their reward. The students soon began to enjoy working for points that earned them rewards. They responded more actively in class, liked the quieter, more businesslike atmosphere, and respected Mr. Sahai for thinking of this plan. By exerting peer pressure, the students helped their teacher control the misbehavior of individual students.

Case Study: Catch Fewer Flies with Vinegar

Mr. Wynne decided it was time to crack down on his class. He was tired of the myriad interruptions and the inattentiveness of his students. He believed in giving them fair warning, so he told them that beginning Monday morning, he was going to expect them to behave themselves, or else!

The students came to school Monday in their usual carefree way, entirely forgetting Mr. Wynne's threat. Mr. Wynne remembered, however, and wasted no time in carrying out his intentions.

"Bobby, stop talking and sit down," he snapped. Bobby looked bewildered. He was only talking to Terry while he put his jacket away. "Anyone who talks in here before the bell rings will have to come straight back to the room after lunch," Mr. Wynne said. The students looked at each other in confusion. Until now, they had always been permitted to talk before school started. Mr. Wynne continued, "We're going to run a tight ship from now on. I don't want to hear a sound in this room."

The students resented Mr. Wynne's treatment and thought he was being unfair. He had not even discussed with them the new rules of conduct he was imposing. Although they were afraid not to comply with his demands, the students no longer cared about the quality of the work they turned in to him. Mr. Wynne had tried to improve his classroom control through threats and punishments; in doing so, he had lost the willing cooperation and respect of his students.

APPROPRIATE DISCIPLINARY MEASURES

As a student, you may have wondered why some teachers seemed to be aware of everything that went on in the classroom, even when they didn't appear to be looking. This is a knack good teachers develop, a sort of sixth sense that enables them to pick up the vibrations from their classes so that they always know what's happening. You can acquire this ability if you develop a sensitivity to the sounds, movements, voices, and behavior patterns within your classroom.

Teachers "with eyes in the backs of their heads" are usually good disciplinarians. In fact, it is difficult to observe the techniques they use because their methods are subtle and unobtrusive. A quiet nod, the mention of a student's name, or a warning glance usually suffices. Don't worry if you haven't yet mastered this technique—it often takes years of practice.

Even these master disciplinarians occasionally have problems that require more attention, as you probably will also. When problems do develop, you must consider several factors before taking action. It is important to keep in mind the purpose of discipline: to restore order by helping the student regain control of his or her behavior, not to seek revenge for violation of the rules. You should also consider the reason for misbehavior and the personal circumstances of the misbehaving student. Appropriate disciplinary measures vary according to the student's grade level, degree of motivation for learning, ability level, and personality. As you can see, there is no single solution for any problem.

Before deciding what to do, you must also consider your school's policy regarding discipline. Check with your cooperating teacher to find out what types of disciplinary action are permitted if a student misbehaves. Can you keep students after school, or do bus schedules prohibit this? Can you deny a student recess, or is a certain amount of free time compulsory? Is there a detention hall, and do you have the option of sending a student there? Is paddling permitted? Are hall passes required, and what is the penalty for failing to have one?

Remember that the purpose of discipline is to restore order by helping the student regain control of his or her behavior.

Knowing Some Options

Tuck all of these considerations away somewhere in your mind so you can pull them out when a problem arises. You may sometimes reach the point that you must discipline a class or an individual student. You may want to ask the advice of your cooperating teacher first, but there are some appropriate consequences for specific types of misbehavior.

1 If a student tries to be the class clown . . .
  (a) Explain that there are times when that kind of behavior is appreciated, but it is not appropriate during class.
  (b) Give the clown special assignments to show your confidence in her or his ability to assume responsibility.
  (c) Praise the clown for completion of serious work while ignoring the clowning.
  (d) If the behavior persists, isolate the clown temporarily.
2 If students talk at inappropriate times . . .
  (a) Ignore the interruption, if possible.
  (b) Change the seating arrangement. Some students may encourage those who sit near them to talk during class.
  (c) Give students a few minutes of free time to get talking out of their systems.
  (d) Stop your lesson, and wait until everything quiets down.
  (e) Divide the class into groups. Reward the group that does the least amount of unnecessary talking.
3 If students litter or mess up things . . .
  (a) Provide time for them to clean up their desks and work areas.
  (b) Provide incentives for neat work.
  (c) Brainstorm all the ways to make the room neater, cleaner, and more attractive.
  (d) Let students be messy sometimes; then give them a chance to clean up.
  (e) Confiscate articles left carelessly around the room. Return them at the end of the week.
  (f) Use creative dramatics. Turn young children into robots, and see how quickly they can run around and put everything in its place.
4 If students push, shove, and make noise when forming lines . . .
  (a) Appoint a different leader each week.
  (b) Dismiss one row or group at a time. Choose the best-behaved group first.
  (c) Line up according to some plan, such as alphabetical order, height, or color of clothing.
  (d) Have young children pretend to be Native Americans gliding quietly through the halls in soft moccasins.
5 If a student tattles . . .
  (a) Explain that you don't want to hear personal information about another student (gossiping), but only news of rules that have been broken or of someone who has been hurt (reporting).
  (b) Ask the offender to write down the information for you to read at the end of the day, because you do not have time to listen. Writing should discourage the tattler.
  (c) If there are several tattlers in your class, ask them to save all their tales to tell on Friday afternoon. By then, they will probably consider the matters too trivial to share.
  (d) Role play a tattletale incident so students can understand why this behavior is undesirable.

6 If a student lies ...

    (a) Ignore this student if you know he or she is just fantasizing or exaggerating. To a young child, say "Oh, what a nice story."

    (b) Praise this student whenever he or she tells the truth. Point out on these occasions how important it is to be able to trust another person.

    (c) Have a one-to-one conference with a student who lies habitually to discuss the importance of being truthful.

    (d) For serious and persistent lying, impose a penalty (such as demerits) that has been agreed upon by the class.

7 If students cheat ...

    (a) Rearrange the seats to separate those who "help" each other.

    (b) Take the cheating students' tests away, and retest the students at another time.

    (c) Give open-book or essay tests.

    (d) Use alternate forms of a test so students seated beside each other will be taking different tests.

    (e) Move close to students who are cheating. Whisper comments such as, "I want to find out what *you* know. Please write your own answers."

8 If students fight ...

    (a) Stop the fight. It may be necessary to restrain the fighters physically.

    (b) Encourage the fighters to make up, shake hands, and be friends.

    (c) Have each student write or tape record her or his side of the story.

    (d) Give students who repeatedly get into fights opportunities to fight with supervision. Let them Indian wrestle or use physical education equipment.

    (e) Discuss or role play situations that make students angry. Find solutions.

9 If a student steals ...

    (This is a touchy problem with many circumstances to consider!)

    (a) If you see a student take something that belongs in the classroom, such as a pen or a pair of scissors, discuss the matter with him or her privately. Ask that the student return the item.

    (b) If you think you know who is guilty of taking something that belongs to someone else, speak to that student privately. If the student admits taking the item, ask him or her to please return it. You might suggest that the student apologize for his or her behavior. If the student doesn't admit taking anything, tactfully suggest that you look through his or her things together.

    (c) If you don't know who is guilty, you might hold a class meeting to discuss the problem.

    (d) Role playing may help students understand the problem and prevent future thefts.

    (e) If a student has admitted to taking something of value, the student should be asked to return it, replace it, pay for it, or work long enough to cover the expense of the stolen item.

    (f) If thievery persists, you will probably need to get outside help from the guidance counselor or parents (if you know the student's identity).

10 If a student is using drugs or alcohol ...

    Pass along this information to your cooperating teacher who, in turn, should notify school authorities and parents.

Testing the Technique

Some common disciplinary practices are considered generally effective; some are considered good or bad depending on the circumstances; others are thought to be inappropriate. Do Activity 4.4 to analyze the effectiveness of the strategies you use.

Activity 4.4 Self-Analysis of Classroom Management Techniques

Near the conclusion of your student teaching, assess your effectiveness as a classroom manager. What strategies did you find most or least useful in managing student behavior? On the basis of your analysis, make a list of strategies you plan to use in your own classroom.

Effective Techniques

Reinforcers—Both verbal and nonverbal reinforcers are effective for encouraging good behavior and discouraging improper conduct.

Restitution—A student who takes or destroys something should be expected to return or restore it. If this is impossible, the student should compensate for the loss in some other way.

Role playing—Students appreciate the feelings of other students and see incidents in a new light when they role play (see Chapter 7).

Contracts—The use of contracts works well for intermediate and secondary level students. Contracts are agreements that deal with specified behaviors, tasks, responsibilities, and rewards. They give the effect of a legal commitment and are signed by both the teacher and the student.

Group discussions—Guided, open discussions are good ways to handle disputes and discipline problems. Students feel involved and responsible for carrying out their own recommendations.

Gripe box—A suggestion box or gripe box allows students to express their dissatisfactions. After reading the students' notes, you might want to make some changes.

Nonverbal signals—Effective use of nonverbal signals and body language is one of the best forms of discipline. Examples are a frown, a smile, a nod, movement toward a student, an intent look, a raised hand, and a wink.

Time out—Time out can be used to remove a student who is highly distracting to the rest of the class or who is acting in such a way that she or he could harm others. The teacher isolates the student from the rest of the class for five to ten minutes until she or he can regain control of her or his behavior. The isolation area should be secluded, quiet, and dull.

Appeal to reason—Explaining why good behavior is necessary often convinces students to act well. You might say, "Be careful with the equipment so we don't break anything" or "Work quickly so we'll have time to plan our party."

Approval of behavior—This method generally works well in the elementary school. The teacher notices students who are "ready to begin," "sitting up nicely," or "have their books open to the right page." Other students follow suit because they also want recognition.

Grounding—This technique is effective for a student who can't work well or cooperate at an interest center. The student must return to his or her seat to work until ready to rejoin the group.

Matching the penalty to the offense—A penalty should relate to the offense so the student can see the seriousness of it.

Borderline Techniques

Planned ignoring—This technique may work for a while. Sometimes if you ignore the problem, it will go away; other times, it only becomes worse, until you are forced to deal with it.

Apologies—If apologies are genuine, they are effective. If you force students to say words they don't mean, you are only teaching them to lie. Their apologies mean nothing.

Removal of students from the classroom—Removal may seem the best procedure when a student is out of control; however, it is always better to try to settle the matter yourself. You and your cooperating teacher probably know the situation better than anyone else. If a student is sent from the room, someone should chaperone her or him to her or his destination. Arrangements should be made beforehand with the person to whom the student is being sent.

Merits and demerits—This system consists of awarding or taking away points for certain kinds of behavior. This technique generally works well if it is carefully structured, especially when it is used on a temporary basis. Students should eventually learn to control their own behavior, however, rather than rely on outside incentives.

Remaining after school—Keeping a student after school, either in your own room or in detention hall, may have some value as a penalty for misbehavior. Unless some educational experience is planned for this time, however, this method will waste time for both you and the student. Remaining after school can also interfere with bus schedules or a worthwhile extracurricular activity.

Denial of privileges—A denied privilege is usually an effective penalty. It can have a negative effect, however, if a student is being denied something important for him or her. For instance, a hyperactive child who is denied recess probably needs this outlet for his or her surplus energy.

Scoldings—An occasional reprimand is often necessary, but a bitter harangue has a negative effect on the whole class. Avoid nagging, constant faultfinding, and long discourses on behavior.

Personal conferences—A private, one-to-one conference often clears up problems. It helps the student and teacher understand each other. Privacy is necessary for a free exchange of views and for keeping a matter confidential. Conferences are ineffective when the teacher simply makes accusations and the student is unresponsive, and they can be destructive if they deteriorate into arguments.

Ineffective Techniques

Assignment of additional classwork or homework—This practice generally results in the student's disliking the subject.

Use of ridicule or sarcasm—Students who are embarrassed or humiliated by their teachers may suffer serious psychological damage.

Grade reduction—Grades for academic achievement should not be affected by behavior.

Punishments like wearing dunce caps, holding books at arm's length, standing with nose in a circle drawn on the board, writing sentences, and other such bugaboos—These techniques belong back in the Dark Ages. While they may deter students from certain kinds of behavior, they do nothing to rehabilitate the student or solve the problem.

Threats—It's usually better to act than to threaten. If you do make threats, be sure you are prepared to follow through. Generally, threats cause students to become upset and suspicious.

Corporal punishment—Corporal punishment rarely corrects a problem. Like threats, it usually has a negative effect on students and should be used only as a last resort, if ever. Improper use of corporal punishment can result in legal problems.

EVALUATING FIVE CASE STUDIES

The following case studies are based on actual situations. Read them, and evaluate the teacher's action in each case. Were other options available? How would you have handled these students?

Case Study: The Last Straw

Jeff, a twelfth-grade student, came from a low socioeconomic level home where he was taught the value of a good education. His parents were interested in his progress and encouraged him to do well.

In industrial arts class, Jeff was a reasonably good student, but he often caused minor disruptions. He would distract other students by sticking his foot out to trip them, making wisecracks, laughing raucously at nothing, and occasionally defying his teacher, Mr. Hamlin. Mr. Hamlin put up with his behavior for several weeks. He knew that Jeff was basically a good student and did not feel that Jeff's interruptions warranted a confrontation.

One morning, Jeff decided he would go to the cosmetology class to get a haircut during industrial arts. When he told Mr. Hamlin he was going, Mr. Hamlin refused to give him permission. Jeff told Mr. Hamlin to go to hell, and that he was going anyway. At this point, Mr. Hamlin realized he had been too lenient with Jeff. He knew something would have to be done, or there would be a total breakdown in discipline in his class. Mr. Hamlin took Jeff to the office, where the principal suspended him for his defiant and discourteous behavior.

Following his suspension, Jeff returned to school with his father. During a conference with the guidance counselor, Mr. Carlin, the entire situation was reviewed and correct standards of be-havior were discussed. A contract was drawn up which allowed Jeff to return to class as long as he acted like a gentleman. Mr. Carlin went over the contract with Jeff and his father in detail. If Jeff failed to live up to his commitment, he would be dropped from the class roll. Jeff seemed to hold no malice toward his teacher or the counselor and willingly agreed to sign the contract, along with his father and Mr. Carlin. The counselor also requested that Jeff apologize to Mr. Hamlin and the rest of the class, but only if he felt he owed them an apology.

Mr. Hamlin later reported that Jeff had been much less disruptive in class and that he was behaving more maturely.

Case Study: Reaching a Truce

Ann is a large, unattractive eighth grader. She is rarely a discipline problem for her teachers, but has a record of tardiness and unexcused absences. Her home background is extremely poor, and her father is unknown. Miss Horne is her guidance counselor.

Ann came to Miss Horne's attention because she smoked in areas where smoking was prohibited. She had a smoking permit that her mother had signed, but she failed to restrict her smoking to areas designated for that purpose. Miss Horne forbade Ann to visit a particular restroom and threatened to send her home if she smoked in there. When Miss Horne found Ann smoking there again, she sent her home.

After Ann returned to school, she continued to smoke in forbidden areas. Miss Horne observed her on three occasions in a single day smoking in the restroom that was off limits to her. Ann denied that she did it and then said she had permission to smoke there. Both of these statements were untrue. Miss Horne had written down the exact times she had seen Ann and the names of witnesses who were with her at the time. Ann was sent home again. She was warned that the next time she defied the rules, she would have to face the school board.

Ann has returned to school again on a probationary status. She realizes that Miss Horne means what she says and will follow through with her warnings. Ann has not been observed smoking again, but she still has a poor attitude toward school. She does speak to Miss Horne, however, and a temporary truce seems to have been established between them.

Case Study: Moving toward Acceptable Behavior

Jill is a fifth grader who lives with her mother and stepfather. She was abused by her father as a young child, and her stepfather has helped her make adjustments. Jill is much like her mother, and they do not get along well. Both parents are beginning to lose patience with her.

At the beginning of the year, Jill threw temper tantrums when things didn't go her way. She nearly went into convulsions sometimes and had to be taken from the room. At other times, she was told to stand in the corner as punishment for her fits of temper. She hated standing in the corner, so the number of tantrums gradually decreased.

Jill was hostile toward the teacher, Mrs. Lynch, and the other children. She was loud and aggressive when she came to school in the morning. She called people names and frequently told lies. She was easily distracted and rushed through her work, not caring if it was done correctly. On the playground, she tried to get control of the ball and take it away from the other children. She had no remorse about hurting people, even when she caused them to bleed.

During the year, three things seemed to help Jill. First, Jill enjoyed getting the attention of the other students. She was beginning to discover that when she was nice to them, they would be friendly toward her. To win friends, she began to change her attention-getting strategies to more acceptable behavior patterns.

Jill's relationship with Mrs. Lynch also helped her. Mrs. Lynch and Jill talked frequently in private about why Jill acted as she did and how she might get along better with the other children. Jill began to trust Mrs. Lynch and stopped feeling that Mrs. Lynch was picking on her.

Jill was also helped by the school psychologist with whom she met each week. The psychologist required her to earn points for satisfactory achievement. Jill's teachers had to sign a paper each time she earned a point. Jill then took the paper to the psychologist, who granted her a privilege if she had earned at least 16 points in a week.

Jill is still immature and demands attention in unacceptable ways, but her behavior is much better than it was at the beginning of the year.

Case Study: Parental Restitution

Troy is a rather homely and unpopular fourth grader whose parents have a lot of money. His mother places a great deal of importance on wealth and continually brags about recent trips and acquisitions. It seems to Troy that money can buy anything.

Troy wanted more than anything to be accepted by his friends. He decided to ask Sheila, the cutest girl in class, to "go with" him for $10 a week. This seemed like a lot of money to Sheila, but she was doubtful about the arrangement. She discussed Troy's proposition with her friends before deciding what to do. She really didn't want to be Troy's girl, even for the money. She finally agreed, however, and Troy brought $10 to school for her.

Until this time, Sheila had barely spoken to Troy, but now she occasionally sat with him during lunch and talked to him during the day. She allowed him to call her at night, but they never went anyplace together. This arrangement satisfied Troy. He boasted to his classmates about his new girl friend. They were properly impressed, and Troy gained status among his peers.

After two or three weeks, Troy's teacher, Mrs. Hobson, became suspicious. She had observed the new relationship between Troy and Sheila and thought it was unusual. One day she glimpsed Troy handing $10 to Sheila. She talked to the two quietly and found out about their arrangement.

Mrs. Hobson felt that the only thing to do was to bring both sets of parents to school and discuss the matter with them. During the conference, the parents agreed to talk to their children about ending the arrangement. Sheila's parents returned the money to Troy's parents, and the matter ended. Troy and Sheila resumed their original relationship. Troy did not seem depressed over losing Sheila's attention.

Case Study: Peer Pressure Does the Trick

Dan came from a high socioeconomic-level home and had the support of his family. He didn't believe in law enforcement, school regulations, or God. He was an excellent student academically, but had begun using drugs as a high school sophomore.

As a junior, Dan became even more strongly hooked on drugs. His guidance counselor, Mrs. Tilton, was aware of Dan's dependence on drugs and talked to him about this problem on several occasions. Dan insisted that it was his right to use drugs and that no one could tell him what to do. He claimed that all the students used drugs, but Mrs. Tilton denied this. Mrs. Tilton warned him that drugs could eventually ruin him, but nothing she said made any difference. Dan continued to be cooperative and do well in his classes, but was beginning to go downhill by the end of the year.

Despite his heavy use of drugs, Dan won the history prize in his junior year. As he walked across the stage to receive his award, the students booed him. They had no respect for him due to his involvement with drugs.

For some reason, this rejection by his peers turned Dan around. He cared about his fellow students and their feelings toward him. He stopped using drugs and was elected president of the student body in his senior year. According to some, he was the best student body president the school had had. He went on to the local university, where he carried a double major and made the Dean's List each semester.

DISCUSSION QUESTIONS

1 Which model of discipline do you think would have been effective in the vignette at the beginning of this chapter? Why?

2 Select one or two students who tend to be disruptive in class. Can you determine the reasons for their behavior? Is there anything you can do to change this disruptive behavior?

3 Analyze the five models of discipline. Which model, if any, does your cooperating teacher use? Which model do you prefer? Can you put together parts of the different models and come up with a plan you think would work for you? Can you identify some basic concepts that appear to be true of all five models?

4 Watch your cooperating teacher carefully. How does she or he control behavior? Do the teacher's signals, warnings, nonverbal messages, or other subtle measures prevent discipline problems from arising? Which techniques seem most successful? Do all students respond the same way?

5 Develop a plan for helping your students acquire self-discipline. What reasonable responsibilities can you give them? Can you vary the responsibilities to meet the capabilities of each student? How can you check students' progress toward developing self-discipline?

6 What kinds of verbal and nonverbal reinforcers do you use during the day? Do you reinforce each student's good behavior, or do you reserve reinforcers for just a few? How might you make better use of reinforcers to encourage good academic work and proper behavior?

SELECTED REFERENCES

Axelrod, S. *Behavior Modification for the Classroom Teacher.* New York: McGraw-Hill, 1977.

Canter, Lee, and Marlene Canter. *Assertive Discipline: A Take-Charge Approach for Today's Educator.* Seal Beach, Calif.: Canter and Associates, 1976.

Carter, Mildred. *A Model for Effective Discipline.* Bloomington, Ind.: Phi Delta Kappa Educational Foundation, 1987.

Charles, C. M. *Building Classroom Discipline,* 3rd ed. New York: Longman, 1989.

Collins, Myrtle T., and Dwane R. Collins. *Survival Kit for Teachers (And Parents).* Pacific Palisades, Calif.: Goodyear, 1975.

Duke, Daniel L., and Vernon F. Jones. "Two Decades of Discipline—Assessing the Development of an Educational Specialization." *Journal of Research and Development in Education* 17, no. 4 (1984): 25–35.

Faust, Naomi F. *Discipline and the Classroom Teacher.* Port Washington, N.Y.: Kennikat Press, 1977.

Glasser, William. *Control Theory in the Classroom.* New York: Perennial Library, 1985.

Glasser, William. *Schools without Failure.* New York: Harper and Row, 1969.

Gnagey, William J. *Maintaining Discipline in Classroom Instruction.* New York: Macmillan, 1975.

House, Ernest R., and Stephen D. Lapan. *Survival in the Classroom.* Boston: Allyn and Bacon, 1978.

Johnson, Simon O. *Better Discipline: A Practical Approach.* Springfield, Ill.: Charles C. Thomas, 1980.

Jones, Frederic. "The Gentle Art of Classroom Discipline." *National Elementary Principal* 58 (June 1979): 26–32.

Kounin, Jacob. *Discipline and Group Management in Classrooms.* New York: Holt, Rinehart and Winston, 1970.

Long, James D., and Virginia H. Frye. *Making It Till Friday: A Guide to Successful Classroom Management.* Princeton, N.J.: Princeton Book Company, 1977.

Martin, Reed, and David Lauridsen. *Developing Student Discipline and Motivation.* Champaign, Ill.: Research Press, 1975.

Pearson, Craig. *Resolving Classroom Conflict.* Palo Alto, Calif.: Learning Handbooks, 1974.

Redl, Fritz, and William W. Wattenberg. *Mental Hygiene in Teaching.* New York: Harcourt, Brace and World, 1959.

Steinback, Susan Bray, and William Clarence Steinback. *Classroom Discipline.* Springfield, Ill.: Charles C. Thomas, 1977.

Tanner, Laurel N. *Classroom Discipline for Effective Teaching and Learning.* New York: Holt, Rinehart and Winston, 1978.

Volkmann, Christina S. *The Last Straw.* San Francisco: R. & E. Research Associates, 1978.

5

Classroom Management

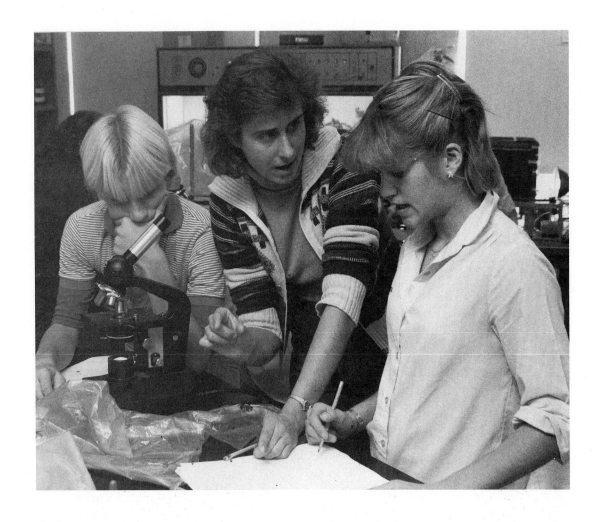

Miss Collins, a student teacher, has been successfully using the Newspaper in Education program with her ninth-grade students. As a culminating activity for the unit, she expects the students to publish a newspaper of their own. They have been divided into groups and are writing their paper.

Li-Jan: Miss Collins, what am I supposed to do?

Miss Collins: What is your job?

Li-Jan: I'm supposed to be the sports editor.

Tony: Miss Collins, where are we supposed to work?

Miss Collins: What is your group, Tony?

Tony: Feature stories.

Miss Collins: Well, try to find a place over by the bulletin board.

David: That's where you said we could work, Miss Collins.

Miss Collins: Well, find another place then, Tony. What is your group, David?

Li-Jan: Miss Collins—

Miss Collins: Just a minute, Li-Jan. What did you say, David?

David: We're writing the ads.

Miss Collins: Oh, that's right. Now, Li-Jan, what did you want?

Li-Jan: What is the sports editor supposed to do?

Miss Collins: Look at the sports section of the paper, and see if you can figure out what's supposed to be in there.

Li-Jan: Who's supposed to be in my group? I can't find anyone to work with me.

Miss Collins: Let's see. I know I have that list here somewhere. It must be under these papers.

Linda: Miss Collins, Joe says he's in charge of the news stories, but yesterday you said I could do that.

Miss Collins (to the whole class in a raised, agitated voice): Boys and girls. You must get quiet! We can't work in here with all that noise. Get busy now.

Li-Jan: Is it okay if I just write something about what our softball team did over the weekend?

Miss Collins: Yes, that'll be fine, Li-Jan. Just do that. I can't seem to find who the other members of your group are.

Phil and Steve: Miss Collins, you said we needed to go interview some other teachers. Is it okay if we do that now?

Miss Collins: I'm not sure.

Joe (approaching Miss Collins angrily): How come Linda says she's supposed to do news stories? I thought you told me to do that.

Linda (addressing Joe): She told me to do them!

Miss Collins: Why don't you two work together on them?

Joe (shuffling off and muttering under his breath): I can't stand that girl. She's a creep. She can do it by herself for all I care.

Phil and Steve: What about it? Can we go?

Miss Collins: Go where? Oh yes, I remember. Did you make appointments with anyone?

Phil and Steve: No, were we supposed to?

Miss Collins: Well, you really should.

Diane: It's almost time for my bus. Shall I get ready?

Miss Collins: I had no idea it was that late already. Yes, go get ready.

Miss Collins (addressing the class): Class! (no one hears) Class! (still no one hears amidst the laughter, talking, and running around the room) Boys and girls!!! (now shouting to be heard) Clean up your work, and get in your seats. The buses are coming.

The students finally hear her and begin to gather their things together. The buses arrive before they finish, and Miss Collins must straighten up the rest of the room herself. At this point, her cooperating teacher walks in and asks, "Well, how did everything go?"

Miss Collins (with a heavy sigh): I'll never try that again. These kids don't know how to work in groups.

1. Was Miss Collins's idea for a culminating activity a good one? How might it have been handled more successfully?

2. What mistakes did Miss Collins make in assigning group activities? How could she have prevented some of the problems from arising?

3. Why do you think Miss Collins ran out of time? What factors should be considered in scheduling activities such as this one to be sure there is enough time?

4. What could Miss Collins have done to get the children's attention instead of shouting at them? How could she have reduced the noise level while the boys and girls were working?
5. Do you agree with Miss Collins that these children can't work in groups? Do you think she was right to say she'll never try group work again?

SUPPORT SYSTEM FOR TEACHING

Knowing your subject and how to teach it is important, but students won't learn if your plans go awry because of poor classroom management. What can you do about providing a classroom environment conducive to learning, scheduling activities within limited time frames, grouping students for different purposes, and keeping records for future reference? Unfortunately, there are no easy answers to these questions. Each situation is unique. You *can*, however, observe your cooperating teacher and read this chapter for some useful ideas on classroom management.

STRUCTURED AND FLEXIBLE CLASSROOMS

Schools and individual teachers within the same school observe different degrees of formality in their approaches to learning. They may have anything from highly structured classrooms to extremely flexible ones. The degree of formality in your school can affect the way you teach. In many schools, however, individual classroom teachers set the level of flexibility. One may have assigned seats arranged in perfect rows, whereas another may have a room filled with clusters of chairs for small group work and areas designated for learning centers.

In some classrooms there is an emphasis on exploration, discovery, and spontaneity. Students may plan learning experiences with their teachers and take a more active part in classroom decision making. If students express interest in a particular aspect of a lesson, the teacher may allow them to pursue that special interest, rather than conforming rigidly to the lesson plan. Differences of opinion are permitted and even encouraged in such classrooms.

Regardless of the amount of structure or flexibility in your classroom, you must do a great deal of planning and classroom management. The rules are already established pretty clearly in the structured classroom, and it will be your responsibility to enforce them. You will need to prepare your lesson plans carefully and keep the students on the subject during discussions. You should try to meet each objective and cover the material adequately. In a less structured classroom, where the students move and speak more freely, you will have to know how to help students resolve disagreements and conflicts. You should also set up situations and make resources available to stimulate the desire to learn. You must be sufficiently knowledgeable in your subject to expand on your lesson in response to the interest your students show. You should develop an atmosphere of mutual trust and responsibility and guard against permissiveness and chaos.

ORGANIZATIONAL PLANS

Individualization

Each student is unique in terms of personality, experience, language facility, academic potential, attitude, and home environment. It would be ideal if teachers could work with each student as an individual, but such an idea is impractical, of course. Nevertheless, teachers should provide opportunities for students to work individually on some occasions in order to pursue special interests and work at their own paces. Some ideas for independent activities follow.

1 *Sustained silent reading (SSR)*—In this program, students, teachers, and the entire school staff read materials of their choice during an agreed-upon period each school day (generally between 15 and 30 minutes long).

2 *Journal writing*—Each student writes a daily entry in a notebook. Entries may consist of reactions to lessons, communications with the teacher, or special concerns. More information on journal writing is given in Chapters 7 and 9.

3 *Computer-assisted instruction*—Students work on computer programs to practice skills, play games, write compositions, or solve puzzles.

4 *Learning centers*—Students work independently on special projects at learning centers that teachers have designed. Learning centers are useful for giving students choices of activities that extend classroom learning.

5 *Research reports*—Students choose topics to investigate. They find reference materials in the library, organize the content, and prepare oral or written reports.

6 *Seatwork*—Students work independently at their seats, often while the teacher is engaged with other students. Seatwork activities include doing workbooks, practicing skills, reading library books, and completing assignments.

Grouping

Grouping is an attempt to compromise between totally individualizing instruction and treating the entire class as a single unit. Individual differences can be reduced to some extent by some types of grouping, but many differences remain.

Types of Grouping By this time, you are probably well acquainted with your school. You may already know whether students are grouped homogeneously (according to ability) or heterogeneously (without regard to ability). Secondary schools may offer a multiple-track curriculum that groups students into a college preparatory, business, or general curriculum. There may also be special programs for groups of students with different needs. For instance, your school may group students who are learning English as a second language, have been identified as potential dropouts, or are recognized as gifted. Grouping patterns that cut across classrooms and grade levels are known as *interclass* groupings.

You will be concerned primarily with *intraclass* groupings (grouping within the classroom), however. Your cooperating teacher may already use small groups. As you teach, you may want to try grouping as a way to meet your objectives.

You can set up groups for different purposes. Most groups are established in an attempt to place students of similar achievement levels together. Groups are sometimes arranged for other subject-related purposes as well. Students having difficulty with a particular math skill may meet together two or three times to relearn the concept and do practice exercises. In social studies, students may work together in research groups. Science classes may be broken into groups to perform an experiment that illustrates a certain concept. Physical education classes may be divided into homogeneous groups according to skill level, or into heterogeneous groups so that less able students can benefit from interaction with more proficient students. Groups may be short term or long term, depending on the length of time required to meet objectives.

You might want to try establishing friendship groups that allow friends to work together. Students in these groups are often highly motivated because they enjoy being with each other. You need to be careful of two things when allowing friendship groups. First, students may enjoy one another's company so much that they won't get any work done, so you will have to warn them that they can work with their friends only as long as they produce results. When they cease to work, the groups will be disbanded and other activities substituted. Second, there will probably be some students who do not seem to have any friends. You might tactfully approach one or two popular students about including these isolates in their groups.

Interest grouping is another kind of classroom organization you may wish to try. You might begin forming this type of group after you've gotten to know the students well enough to know their interests. You can also discover their interests by asking them to list three things they would like to know more about. After you have compiled the results of this informal survey, you can divide the class into several groups. If some students did not choose one of the topics selected for an interest group, allow them to join one of the other groups.

Since many groups are set up on the basis of achievement levels, low-achieving students often develop poor self-concepts. They think of themselves and others in their group as "dummies." Ethnic groups tend to stay together and not mingle with other students. By forming project and interest groups, you encourage students of differing achievement levels and ethnic origins to work together, and students contribute according to their particular knowledge, skills, or talents.

Implementation of Groups   In many classrooms, grouping is not used to best advantage. Consider a situation you may meet in an elementary classroom: As you observe the class, you notice that the teacher does group for reading instruction in the morning; however, no other groups are held during the day. You notice that the children in the low group tend to goof off during the day and stick together during lunch and free time. Students in the high group seem to be cliquish and ignore the other students.

Another situation may exist in a secondary classroom: As you observe the teacher leading the class discussion, you notice that the same six or eight students participate each day. The other students daydream, stare out the window, pass notes, and occasionally doze off.

Now let's see what might happen if you tried grouping the students in these two classes. In the elementary classroom, you set up interest groups that meet from 1:00 to 1:40 each day. It happens that three children from the low group, two from the middle group, and four from the high group have chosen dinosaurs as their topic. Their assignment is to create a room display and give a 20-minute presentation at the end of two weeks. Before they realize what's happening, the students are excitedly delving into books, working on drawings, sharing models from home, and planning their presentation. At least during this period, achievement levels are forgotten.

At the secondary level, you decide to abandon whole class discussion for the time being and break the class into four groups. You include in each group one or two leaders and five or six students who have not been participating actively in class. The assignment for each group is to decide which invention has had the greatest impact on the progress of the human race. Working secretly in their groups, the students investigate inventions, select the one they feel is most influential, and build a case to support their choice. Instead of only a small number of students participating, everyone is working creatively to prove to the rest of the class that their group's invention is most significant.

If you decide to create groups within your classroom, don't begin impulsively. Think your plan through carefully before you start. Try to make your groups a workable size, small enough that everyone must participate but large enough to develop a worthy project. Avoid putting in the same group students who cause trouble when they are together. Be sure resource materials—references and supplies—are available and that students know how to use them.

The following pointers can help you with group management. Set up guidelines so that students know their privileges and limitations. Make sure before starting that all the students understand exactly what they are to do. Allow them freedom to talk quietly and move around the room. If possible, let them go to the library for additional information. Suggest that each group appoint a leader who will be responsible for the group's activities. Experiment with the length of time; allow enough time to get something accomplished but not so much that students lose interest and stray off task. Give each group space to carry out its activity without interfering with the other students. Be available to offer ideas. (Miss Collins should have observed some of these pointers!)

Reading groups are probably the most common form of grouping, and they operate somewhat differently from interest or project groups. Reading groups are often composed of students who read at approximately the same level. The groups are teacher guided and generally follow an established procedure. There are usually two, three, or four groups in a class, depending on the range of levels within that class. If you are an elementary major, you may begin your field experiences by teaching a reading group. You will quickly become accustomed to the way the group operates by observing your cooperating teacher and studying the basal reader manual.

The procedure and the students who make up the group were probably already established when you arrived, but here are some techniques that will help the group operate smoothly. If you have any choice, sit in a corner of the room facing the group, with the rest of the class beyond the group. This forces the children in the group to watch you instead of their classmates, and you can see both your group and the rest of the class. Sit next to a chalkboard or an easel with a chart tablet so that you can write important words or examples as you say them. Unless it is a dire emergency, don't allow children from the rest of the class to interrupt you during a group lesson. Have all the materials you will need during the lesson ready before you start. Don't let children bring anything with them to the group except what they will need. Toys and food should be strictly forbidden.

Observe your students carefully during the reading groups to see if they are comfortable in their groups or if they might perform better with different groups. As a general rule, if pupils miss more than one word out of twenty, they should move to an easier level. If they always finish first and know all the answers, they might work better at a higher level. Grouping should always be flexible, to allow for variations in students' learning rates, so don't hesitate to suggest a move to your cooperating teacher if you think a change is warranted.

Complete Activity 5.1 on grouping patterns to help you analyze the uses of grouping in your classroom situation.

FIGURE 5–1 Methods of Student Team Learning (STL)

Student Teams-Achievement Divisions (STAD)—After the teacher has presented the lesson, four-member student teams of mixed ability help each other learn the material. Each member takes an individual test, and scores are computed to arrive at team scores. Teams that meet certain criteria earn rewards, which are usually certificates.

Teams-Games-Tournament (TGT)—This procedure is similar to that of STAD, but weekly tournaments replace quizzes. Groups of three students of similar achievement levels compete at tournament tables. The winner at each table gets points for his or her team, and winning teams earn rewards.

Team Assisted Individualization (TAI)—Combining cooperative learning with individualized instruction, TAI is used to teach math to students in grades three through six. Team members usually work on different units, but help each other with problems and check answers. Groups earn points as members complete units and do extra work.

Cooperative Integrated Reading and Composition (CIRC)—Teachers use CIRC to teach reading and writing from literature-based readers to students in grades three through five. Students work in pairs as they read to each other, make predictions, write responses to stories, and so on. They take quizzes and may also "publish" team books.

Cooperative Learning

Cooperative learning is a form of classroom organization in which students work in groups or as teams to help each other acquire academic information. Sometimes students discuss material or practice skills that the teacher has presented; at other times they use cooperative methods to discover information on their own. Two key elements for improving academic achievement are individual accountability and group goals. Benefits from cooperative learning include increased self-esteem, better intergroup relations, more positive attitudes toward school, and acceptance of academically mainstreamed students.

Because cooperative learning promises both academic and social benefits, you may want to try it with your classes. Workshops and courses can provide training, but some self-study and guidance from other teachers may be enough to help you get started. You need to become familiar with some of the most widely used models of cooperative learning so that you can choose one that is appropriate.

Figure 5–1 shows four methods of Student Team Learning (STL). Common to each of these models are individual accountability, team rewards, and equal opportunities for success.

If you decide to implement cooperative learning, here are some general guidelines to follow:

1 Make sure students have the necessary social skills to work cooperatively in group situations.
2 Arrange the classroom so that groups of students can sit facing each other during cooperative learning sessions.
3 Group students heterogeneously, with high, low, and average achievers in each group.
4 Encourage students to assume responsibility for individual and group learning by offering rewards for achievement.
5 Make sure each group understands goals, procedures, tasks, and methods of evaluation.
6 Decide how long groups will remain intact. (Four to six weeks works well.)

Cooperative learning has been used successfully at all grade levels and in every subject area. The following ideas are examples of purposeful cooperative learning:[1]

1 *Study guides*—Fourth graders write study guides by working either in pairs or individually, later sharing their work in groups of two to four. These guides are useful for reviewing before tests.
2 *Vocabulary study*—Junior high students look up word meanings independently and then review them in groups of three. The students first take a group test and then an individual test over the vocabulary. By studying together they can practice and reinforce word meanings, but individual testing holds each student accountable for learning the vocabulary.
3 *Television news*—Groups of three or four high school students put on simulated videotaped telecasts of news programs with news, weather, sports, commercials, and "happy talk." Group members must plan the order of events, time each segment according to predetermined schedules, include visual aids, and observe FCC regulations.
4 *Medieval newspaper*—Ninth graders, in groups of four, research aspects of medieval life for history class and write a newspaper. Each paper has a theme, and each student must contribute a major piece of writing. Students help other group members and receive one grade for their newspaper.

[1]Roy A. Smith. "A Teacher's Views on Cooperative Learning." *Phi Delta Kappan* 68 (May 1987): 663–66. (Based on the work of David Johnson and Roger Johnson, Cooperative Learning Center, University of Minnesota.); Marian Houseman and Frederick A. Duffelmeyer. "Textbook Related Methods in Social Studies." *The Reading Teacher* 40 (April 1987): 820–22; and Donna Niday. "Collaborative Writing." 10 pp. (mimeographed, n.d.).

Activity 5.1   Grouping Patterns

Place a check mark beside each type of grouping that is currently being used in your classroom. Place a plus sign (+) beside any type of grouping not currently being used that you intend to try. Note your reasons at the bottom of the page.

_____ Achievement or ability grouping (to put students of similar achievement or ability together)

_____ Needs (or skills) grouping (to correct problems)

_____ Research grouping (to investigate topics or themes)

_____ Project (or performance) grouping (to perform experiments or carry out construction activities)

_____ Friendship grouping (to increase motivation)

_____ Interest grouping (to increase motivation)

Watching a demonstration is usually a whole class activity.

5 *Writing support groups*—High school students collaborate on their writing projects both in and out of school. In-school activities include writing newspaper articles, research reports, short stories, one-act plays, and computer programs. Out-of-school writings include skits, special purpose letters, 4-H projects, anniversary poems, and posters for a family business.

Whole Class Instruction

On many occasions whole class instruction is most effective. Good activities for the entire class include listening to a resource visitor, being introduced to a unit, seeing a film, participating in a discussion, watching a demonstration, listening to an ongoing story, and taking a field trip. Whole class activities have the advantage of building an esprit de corps, so that all students are likely to feel a sense of belonging and share the concerns of their classmates. Whole class instruction is also efficient, because the teacher presents information to all students at the same time.

Integration of Organizational Plans

During the day, you will probably want to spend some time with whole class instruction, some time with small groups, and the remainder of the time individualizing instruction. A day in an elementary classroom might proceed this way: You make announcements and explain assignments to the whole class. Then groups of children come to you for reading instruction while others work independently at their seats. After reading groups, the whole class goes to the gym for physical education. When the students return to the classroom, you instruct the whole class in adding fractions. After lunch, some children work in project groups to compile booklets on the solar system, while others work individually at learning centers. During this time, you are holding individual conferences with children who need to do make-up work. At the end of the day, you meet with the whole class again to give a trial spelling test and, finally, to review what has happened during the day.

A secondary class might also involve whole class, group, and individual activities. Usually, you will want to meet with the entire class at the beginning of the period to review old material, introduce new information, and give directions. You should also pull the whole class together again near the end of the period to evaluate progress, make further assignments, and clear up any confusion. During the remainder of the class time, students might work together on group projects, such as making mock investments in the stock market, tracing the development of amphibians for a class presentation, or writing a play about good citizenship. The students could work in pairs as they review for a test or proofread each other's creative writing. They might also do assignments or research independently.

SCHEDULING

The use of time enters into nearly every phase of your teaching. It has a lot to do with how much you accomplish, how well you hold the interest of your students, and how you feel as you proceed through the day. Good time management will make teaching a lot easier, as well as more effective, than if you rush helter-skelter through the day.

Flexibility within a Routine

Routine and flexibility seem to be contradictory ideas, but you need some of each to build a balanced program. You will probably begin teaching by following the schedule already set by your cooperating teacher. A well-planned routine helps you cover everything you are supposed to accomplish, fosters good classroom control because students feel secure when they know what to expect next, and is comfortable because you don't have to wonder all day long what to do next.

Don't be a slave to your schedule, however. The schedule is for your convenience; don't let it become an obstruction to learning. Sometimes you will need more time than what is scheduled to develop a concept fully. You may want to use audiovisual media, invite a resource person, or take a short field trip. You may get into an activity and realize that some really creative experiences are taking place. Whenever possible, allow these learning experiences to continue, even if it means extending them beyond the scheduled time limit.

One way to have flexible scheduling within a fixed schedule at the elementary level is to plan on a weekly instead of a daily basis. Perhaps you will spend 20 minutes extra on math today because you are working with manipulative materials and cut 20 minutes out of language arts. You can pay back this time later in the week.

Some schools provide for flexibility through modular scheduling. Modules are uniform blocks of time arranged to meet instructional needs. For instance, a field trip would require several connected modules, whereas reviewing a test might require only one module. Check with your cooperating teacher to see if your school uses this plan or a similar one.

Some students report to supportive classes. A handful may go to remedial reading from 10:05 to 10:40 three times a week; another group may go to the gifted class from 1:15 to 2:15 every Friday. Don't plan an activity for the whole class when some students will be elsewhere.

Your school may support a Youth Participation program, through which young people engage in service or learning activities that are not a regular part of the school curriculum. Students involved in Youth Participation programs have served as teachers, medical assistants, mechanics, journalists, and tour guides. Although many of these programs are beneficial, finding flexible ways to schedule them is a problem. Some school systems have found solutions in these ways:

1 Enrichment and creative activity periods
2 Elective or noncredit courses

3 Scheduling of two classes with consecutive double periods once a week
4 Use of before- and after-school hours, weekends, and summer programs
5 Releasing of students for a certain amount of time one day a week on a temporary basis

Using Time Effectively

Your time, both in and out of the classroom, is precious. You'll get more done in the classroom if you use your time well, and you'll have more free time out of the classroom if you plan efficiently.

Evenings and weekends are not entirely your own during student teaching. You may be working with your cooperating teacher on the yearbook, sharing late afternoon bus duty, or coaching the football team well into the evening. Sometimes you will have a parent-teacher conference after school or a meeting in the evening. Planning and record keeping also take a great deal of time. For these and other reasons, many universities do not permit student teachers to take additional courses. If you have held a part-time job during your college years, you may have to quit or reduce your hours. Avoid committing too much time to extracurricular or social activities. Full-time student teaching is generally much more demanding on your time than 15 or 18 hours of coursework.

Planning will probably take more time than you expect. Many of the procedures that have become habit for experienced teachers will require detailed planning for you. Whenever possible, make use of planning time during school. Don't depend on this time, however, as unexpected interruptions frequently occur during any school day.

Good organization will enable you to plan thoroughly for your lessons and still have time for yourself. Plan well ahead. Order or reserve materials in advance. If you will need to make several games or posters, buy all the materials at once. A single trip to the library can serve many purposes if you get resource material you will need over a period of time. Instead of spending hours searching through curriculum guides for ideas, sit down and think hard for a few minutes. Your own idea is often as good as or better than one you find in another source. Combine social activities with school functions—take your date, a friend, or your family with you on a Sunday afternoon hike while you collect specimens for a terrarium.

You should use time efficiently in the classroom, also. The most effective teachers are those who spend most of their time giving direct instruction to students and waste little time with disruptions and periods of confusion. These teachers give presentations, explanations, and reinforcement to students to help them learn. They encourage students to spend time on assignments, because the more time students spend on academic tasks, the more likely they are to learn.

The following tips will help you keep things moving in the classroom:

1 Have learning centers ready for action, fully equipped and neatly arranged.
2 Put markers in your books so you can turn quickly to the right page.
3 Be sure all the resource materials you will need for the day are readily available, including supplies you will ask students to distribute.
4 Erase the chalkboards as soon as you finish one lesson so that you will be ready for the next.
5 Have everything ready for the next day's lessons before you go home in the afternoon. If you are an early riser, however, you may prefer to come early and get things ready in the morning.

Your expectations of your students have a lot to do with efficiency. Do the students take five minutes to change from one lesson to another as they yawn, stretch, sharpen pencils, drop books, and make remarks to each other, or do they quietly put away one book and get out another? Do you have to repeat instructions three or four times before everyone knows what to do, or do they listen the first time? When you ask them to line up or get into groups, do they make a mad dash, or sit and stare in confusion, or do they do what you expect of them? When it's time for class to start, are they still roaming around the room, or do they know to get into their seats?

Negative behaviors are big time wasters. You can avoid problems with them, however, by setting realistic expectations for your students and holding them responsible. If it takes too long for students to change from one book to another, practice doing this one day. Have a race against time to see if they can make the change in 45 seconds, 30 seconds, or less. They won't always work this quickly, but knowing what they *can* do should speed things up.

It's important to train students to listen well the first time you say something. Not only is repeating yourself a time waster, but it also teaches students that they don't really have to listen the first or second time; they know you'll keep repeating what you want them to hear. You can break this habit by warning them that from now on you will say something only once. Get their attention, speak clearly, and don't repeat yourself. Some students may do the wrong assignments or miss out altogether on an activity, but if you really mean it, most of them will eventually learn to hear you the first time.

If the students don't know what to do when you tell them to line up or get into groups, the fault is probably yours. This was undoubtedly the case with Miss Collins. Have you told the students what you expect? Are your directions clear? You may have to practice these activities one day so you won't waste time on other occasions. Students must also realize that, at a certain signal, they are expected to get into their seats and be ready to begin.

Establishing routine procedures saves time during the day. Assign responsibilities to different students, and be sure they can carry them out efficiently. Minimize interruptions by letting students know in advance what you expect. For example, students won't need to raise their hands and interrupt the lesson if they already know what they are permitted to do. With young children, establish regular times for using the restrooms. After that, if a child really has to go, allow her or him to go alone without asking permission. Encourage students to sharpen pencils before school starts, but if a point breaks, allow a student to sharpen the pencil again without first asking you. If a student interrupts discussion with an irrelevant story, ask him or her to tell you later. Responding this way allows you to continue the lesson and satisfies the student by letting him or her know you will listen later.

While it's true that some students need more individual attention than others, you must be careful to attend to all students' needs. Guard against spending so much time with an individual student that you neglect the rest of your class. Perhaps you can help a particularly needy student by arranging peer tutoring, working with the student before or after school, or conferring with a parent to get assistance at home.

If you are planning to introduce a new approach, do it gradually. It can be chaotic to plunge the entire class at once into something that has never been done before. For example, if you want to try individualized reading, begin with your top group. Explain exactly what they are to do, and work out the problems before introducing the program to the other groups. This procedure avoids wasting class time during an adjustment period.

No class must always operate on schedule, however. Sometimes something funny happens, and everyone needs to take time for a good laugh. You may lose some time from a scheduled activity by taking advantage of a "teachable moment," but this time is well spent. For instance, when the first snow falls, let the students go to the window and watch. Then share a poem or a song about snow, or talk about how snowflakes form, and note their delicate beauty. After a particularly tense test-taking session, students may need time to relax. Remember—schedules do keep things moving along, but they are not cast in concrete.

Filler, or Sponge, Activities

Even the most experienced teacher cannot predict exactly how long a lesson will take. As a relatively inexperienced teacher, you will often find yourself running out of time—or having time left over. When you realize your lesson will end five or ten minutes before the class is over, you should have some ideas in the back of your mind. The best filler (or sponge) activities are those that directly relate to your lesson or unit. For instance, if you are teaching a unit on energy, the students could brainstorm several ways to conserve or produce energy. Try to plan one or more filler activities for each lesson in case you have too much time. These are some general activities that could be adapted to specific subject matter areas or used for other occasions:

1 Read or tell a story—good at any age level.
2 Put a long word on the board, and see how many words students can make from it (e.g., Thanksgiving, revolutionary).
3 Play "20 Questions." Students try to guess what you're thinking by asking questions that can be answered only by yes or no.
4 Get a paperback book of brainteasers, riddles, and puzzles, and ask the class for answers.
5 Ask students to do mental addition or subtraction.
6 Let students play storybook charades by acting out favorite stories.
7 Introduce a new vocabulary word that has an interesting meaning or origin. This can be a "Word of the Week" activity.
8 Sing a folk song or round with the class.
9 Let students dictate headlines about current news stories for you to write on the board.
10 Write a cinquain, a simple five-line poem. First line is the title (topic), second line is two descriptive words, third line is three action words, fourth line is a descriptive phrase, and fifth line is a repeat of the title or a synonym for it.
11 Name a topic, and see how many facts the students can tell you about it.
12 Scramble the letters in a word, and see how many words the students can make from it (e.g., otps, mtae).
13 Let students pantomime their favorite sport or hobby, and have the class guess what they are doing.
14 Start a story with a one-line introduction, and have each student add a line to the story. (A good starter: "It was cold and dark and dreary, and suddenly I heard a noise.")
15 Have a question box, and let a student pick a question. It could be serious (What can we do for senior citizens?) or silly (Why would a grasshopper make a good pet?). Students answer the question.
16 Role play a recent classroom conflict.
17 Build word families from such phonograms as -it, -at, -ill (e.g., -an, can, fan, ran, pan, Stan, than, bran).
18 Play "Gossip." Whisper a sentence to one student, who whispers it to the next, and so on. Compare the original sentence with the final result.
19 Look for geometric shapes in the classroom (e.g., chalkboards as rectangles and pencils as cylinders).
20 Give students, one at a time, a series of directions to follow, and see if they can remember to do everything in the correct sequence.
21 Write the months of the year on the board. Poll the class to find out how many students' birthdays fall in each month.
22 Rearrange the seating in the classroom.
23 Divide the class in half to create two teams. Name a country, and let a student from each team try to locate it on a world map within 10 seconds.
24 Make a list of all the things to do on a rainy day.

25 Brainstorm solutions to a problem. (See Chapter 7 for suggested topics.)
26 Review assignments.
27 Discuss plans for an upcoming event.
28 Let students have free reading time, finish their class work, do their homework, or clean out their desks.

RECORD KEEPING

Every teacher has the responsibility of keeping records. The amount and type of record keeping varies from one school system to another, and your cooperating teacher will show you what records your school requires. When you are responsible for keeping records, record the information promptly so that you don't forget to do it later. Keeping accurate records is an important aspect of professionalism.

Personal Record Keeping

As part of your student teaching assignment, you may be asked to keep a diary or log of your daily experiences. If it is required, your university supervisor will give you directions for doing this. Even if it is not a requirement, you may want to keep track of the lessons you teach and your feelings about teaching. You can also write down some of the funny things the students say or insights about teaching you don't want to forget. Looking back at the end of your experience, you will probably notice how your attitudes changed and your confidence grew as the weeks passed.

School Records

The attendance register is one of the most important school records. Class roll must be taken daily or every period of the day, and all absences and cases of tardiness recorded. These records are used for various purposes, including computing average daily attendance for state funding. The state allocates a certain amount of money for each child counted in the average daily attendance record. Records are sometimes used in court cases to verify a student's presence in school on a particular day. This information is summarized at the end of every month. Even though these records may be handled by a computer or by office personnel, you should learn how to do them yourself.

You will have to keep other records when you are teaching. Many schools require each teacher to turn in a milk money or lunch money report every morning. Some schools have fund-raising activities that require a great deal of bookkeeping, and, if you are involved in these efforts, you will have to keep an accurate account of the money collected and each student's sales record. If you (through your cooperating teacher) sponsor an extracurricular activity, you may be responsible for keeping membership and financial records. You also need to keep records of students with special programs or problems, such as those who are excused from physical education or who go to special classes at specific times during the day. Additional records are required for students in federally funded programs.

As a student teacher, you may have very little responsibility for ordering books and supplies or keeping inventory. It would be a good idea to learn these procedures anyway, so that you will know what to do when you are in your own classroom. Supplies, such as paper and chalk, should be ordered well in advance of running out. You will probably be limited as to how many supplies you can order, so don't order unnecessary items. Become familiar with school supply catalogs so that you know what materials are available, their prices, and how to order them. Learn how to requisition new materials that can be ordered when funds are available. It is difficult for school systems to reimburse you for money you have already spent for school supplies.

You will also have to keep records related to your teaching. You will need a daily lesson plan book to record brief outlines of your lessons and page numbers of material you expect to cover in each class. You can never be sure exactly how far you will get in your lesson, so you will probably have to modify these plans slightly from day to day. You will also need to make up a broad course or unit outline as a framework for daily plans. If you schedule a field trip in connection with a lesson, you will be responsible for keeping records of parent permission notes and any money you collect. If you use audiovisual media, you may need to fill out request forms. You may want to give the school media specialist a list of topics you will be covering and request help in locating appropriate books and materials. At the conclusion of a unit, you may want to write about your culminating activity and invite the local newspapers to print the story.

Reporting Students' Progress

Keeping track of students' progress is one of the most important forms of record keeping. You should keep records of daily quizzes and completed daily assignments, as well as scores of major tests. Your cooperating teacher probably has a grade book with the scores of each student before you arrived. You may be expected to record your grades in this book, or you may have your own grade book.

Some teachers keep tests in folders at school in order to have a record of each pupil's progress throughout the year. Teachers who feel parents should be kept aware of their child's performance may send tests home. If you decide to send papers home but are not sure all the students are showing the papers to their parents, ask the students to have a parent sign each test paper and then return it to you.

Some computer-managed instructional systems in areas such as reading and mathematics generate reports on student progress. These reports may indicate the skill needs of each student, skills that have been mastered, and sometimes assignments that have been given. Some of these programs generate reports designed primarily for use by you as a teacher, but you can use them as a basis for producing reports to the parents. Other programs generate a report that is designed to go to the parents. These reports can be very helpful to you in communicating with parents.

Reporting to parents is usually done through report cards, although it is sometimes done with descriptive letters or orally at parent-teacher conferences. Your cooperating teacher may ask you to assist in assigning grades on report cards or to assume the full responsibility for grades during the period you do most of the teaching. In either case, be sure you thoroughly understand the school's grading system. Most schools give grades according to achievement, but some give marks for attitude and effort, and some grade on the basis of student ability. Most report cards have a place for comments, which you may or may not wish to use. Putting grades on report cards requires some hard decision making. If the responsibility is yours, be sure to have good records of student work on which to base decisions.

You may want to send notes to parents of students who have behaved or achieved unusually well. Notes of this type are always welcome and help build positive relationships among the student, parents, school, and you. These notes will be especially appreciated by students who rarely receive praise and are often in trouble. If you make a practice of sending favorable comments home, the students are likely to do better work for you.

Case Study: No Records for Support

Miss Patel is the student teacher. She has been concerned about Vinetta's behavior recently. Vinetta doesn't do her homework and doesn't seem to be doing good work in class. Miss Patel decides to ask Vinetta's mother, Mrs. Kolsky, to come for a conference. Mr. Kent is the cooperating teacher.

Miss Patel: Good afternoon, Mrs. Kolsky. I'm glad you were able to come talk with me about Vinetta. I'm Miss Patel, Vinetta's student teacher.

Mrs. Kolsky: Yes. Naturally I hope Vinetta is getting along all right.

Miss Patel: That's just it, Mrs. Kolsky. Vinetta doesn't seem to be doing as well as she could be.

Mrs. Kolsky: Why not? What's wrong? Is there a problem?

Miss Patel: She isn't doing her homework, and she isn't doing very well in her classwork, either.

Mrs. Kolsky: Well, this is the first I've known anything about homework. And what do you mean she isn't doing well in her classwork?

Miss Patel: I've been sending homework home each night, but Vinetta never has hers done. As far as classwork is concerned, she just doesn't seem to be doing her best work any more.

Mrs. Kolsky: May I see her grades on her classwork?

Miss Patel: I'm afraid I don't have any records of her grades. I've given some quizzes, but I've let the students take them home with them. I can remember, though, that she didn't do very well. Didn't she bring her tests home?

Mrs. Kolsky: No, she hasn't brought any of them home. It seems to me you don't really know what you're talking about. You say she isn't doing well, but you can't show me any grades. When I ask you what she isn't doing well in, you don't seem to have any definite answers. I don't think there's anything wrong with Vinetta at all. I think you just don't have your facts straight. I'd better talk to Mr. Kent.

1. Was it a good idea for Miss Patel to have a conference with Vinetta's mother if she felt Vinetta could be doing better work?
2. What went wrong with Miss Patel's conference?
3. What could she have done to back up her statements to Mrs. Kolsky?
4. Is there any way to make sure parents know their child has homework assignments? How can you be sure parents actually see the test papers you return?

You may want to record information about a student in an anecdotal report—an objective, detailed account of a pupil's behavior. During your period of observation, you have an excellent opportunity to study a student's behavior. Your reasons for selecting particular students may vary. You may choose a student who is different in some way, perhaps due to achievement level, relationships with other children, or ethnic origin. You may want to observe a student who is being recommended for an award or one who is being considered for disciplinary action. You may want to collect data on a student whose parents are concerned about her or his progress, or you may select any student simply to learn about typical behavior patterns.

Be accurate and objective in recording your observations. Don't let your feelings affect what you select to record or how you write your observations. Write the date and time of each observation, and try to include everything that happens, both good and bad. It is better if the student doesn't realize what you are doing, so that she or he will continue to act naturally. Choose a child to study and complete Activity 5.2, an anecdotal report.

Your classroom organization determines to some extent how you keep records. If you use an individualized or independent study plan, you will probably need a manila folder in which to record each student's program and progress. Your class may use a systems-management program that has a checklist of concepts or skills to be mastered. In this plan, quizzes are given frequently to make certain a student has reached an acceptable level of mastery on a particular skill before moving on to the next skill. If your class uses learning centers most of the day, your cooperating teacher has probably already set up a way to check each student's work at the different centers. In science classes, you may need to keep progress charts on lab projects. Portfolio assessment (see Chapter 9) is currently being used by many teachers.

Records of students' progress sometimes motivate the students to do better work. They may want to chart their spelling test scores and see if they can improve

Activity 5.2   Anecdotal Report

Name of child selected:

Reason(s) for selection:

Types of information you are seeking:

Begin your anecdotal records below with your first entry. Don't forget to date it and indicate the time when it occurred. If there is not enough room on the bottom of this page, use the back of the page to finish the first record. Continue with other entries on separate sheets of paper. Staple them, in order, to this cover sheet.

their records. You might want to average the scores from weekly math quizzes and make a class chart comparing the scores from different weeks. Students can also be motivated to do more recreational reading by using devices to record the number and sometimes the types of books they read.

All the records a school has concerning a student are generally kept in a cumulative record file in the school office. This file contains health and attendance records, comments by school personnel, and standardized intelligence and achievement test scores. As a student teacher, you will probably be allowed to see this information, but remember that it is confidential.

Case Study: To Look or Not to Look

Three student teachers, Miss Luke, Mr. Feinstein, and Mrs. Tsai, are talking while waiting for their student teaching seminar to begin. They have been student teaching for four weeks.

Miss Luke: Do you know what cumulative records are?

Mr. Feinstein: I think they are some records in the office files that nobody ever looks at.

Mrs. Tsai: They *are* files that are kept in the office, but I've looked at the ones on my students. My cooperating teacher took me right down on the first day I got my classes and told me where they were and that he expected me to read them all the first week. Some of them are really eye-openers, I'll tell you!

Miss Luke: What do you mean?

Mrs. Tsai: I really learned a lot about my students, and I knew just how to treat them right from the beginning. Linda's file said that one time they caught her stealing a transistor radio, so I don't trust her for a minute. Any time anything disappears, I feel sure Linda had something to do with it. And Tad. They said all through the grades that Tad has been a discipline problem, and they're surely right. He's always causing trouble.

Mr. Feinstein: I'm not sure it's right to read all that personal information about your students. Doesn't that influence how you feel about them?

Mrs. Tsai: Sure, it influences how I feel. But this way I know right away all I need to know about the students instead of waiting until the end of the semester to find out.

Miss Luke: I'm not going to look at my students' cumulative records. I want to make up my own mind about them and not go by what other teachers have said.

Mr. Feinstein: But suppose there's something really important in there? Something we *should* know about? Maybe one of the students had psychological testing or something and the psychologist made recommendations about how he or she learns best. Wouldn't that be helpful?

Mrs. Tsai: Definitely! It said in one of my records that Chad's parents had been divorced a couple of years ago and he had a real emotional problem with that. The teacher suggested that we all be patient with him and consider his feelings.

Miss Luke: I'm just not sure if it's a good idea to read all those records. It still might do more harm than good.

1. How do you feel about reading your students' cumulative records? If you feel you should read them, should you look at them as soon as you meet the students or at some later time?
2. How could the information in cumulative records be helpful? How could it be misused?
3. What is the purpose of keeping cumulative records?
4. Do you think Mrs. Tsai is able to treat Linda and Tad objectively? Would she have arrived at the same conclusions about these two students if she hadn't read their files? Do students tend to live up to our expectations of them?
5. Who is allowed to read cumulative records? Do you know what the law says about this?

In regard to examining students' cumulative records, it is a good policy to give yourself enough time to evaluate the students for yourself, then look at the records to learn more about them. When you read the files, keep in mind that test scores do not always accurately reflect a student's capability. Also, be sure to look for factual information and specific situations. Avoid being swayed by unsupported generalizations and statements of opinion previous teachers may have made. Using cumulative records wisely can help you understand your students better and help you plan appropriate learning activities for those with special needs.

Since passage of the Family Educational Rights and Privacy Act of 1974 (PL 93–380), control of student records has changed. Now, students over 18 years old or parents of students under 18 may examine these records—they have access to all teacher comments, test scores, and special reports in the file. On the other hand, the law forbids anyone except those directly involved in the students' education to see the records without written consent.

STUDENT SUPERVISION

You are likely to share your cooperating teacher's assigned supervisory responsibilities, such as performing cafeteria, hall, or bus duty, or keeping detention hall. Each school has its own policies regarding supervision of students waiting for buses, moving through hallways, eating in the cafeteria, and working in study or detention halls. Observe your cooperating teacher closely, and learn the ground rules for these situations so that you can handle them properly.

Supervision of students in the lunchroom is more likely to be a responsibility of an elementary or middle school teacher than of a secondary school teacher. If you are lucky, even at the lower levels, cafeteria supervision will be handled by staff members or volunteers so that you can enjoy a quiet, uninterrupted meal.

A nutritious and relaxing lunch is important for helping students make it through the afternoon. Routine procedures are usually followed, so students know where to sit and what rules are in effect. If you are helping to supervise students in the cafeteria, you need to know what to do if any one of these situations arises: the noise level gets too high, a student drops a tray, a child breaks a Thermos®, a slow eater doesn't finish in time, a student loses a lunch box or bag, a student forgets lunch money, students want to trade food, or someone offers you a sandwich. If there is no policy concerning such matters, keep in mind that students need to eat a nourishing lunch in an atmosphere that enables them to digest it!

Bus and hall duty may exist in your school. Hall duty simply means that teachers are stationed in school corridors when students change classes to keep an orderly flow of traffic, direct new students, and help with problems. In some schools, bus duty is handled by each student's homeroom teacher; in other schools, students assemble in a central location, where they are supervised by one or more teachers. If you must assist your cooperating teacher in supervising groups of students from different classes, you might suggest ideas for passing the time constructively. Students may be asked to bring library books to read, or you can read to them, show films, lead singing, or let them play guessing games.

Some secondary teachers may have responsibility for supervising a study hall during a period when they do not have a scheduled class. The study hall provides a place for students to study during free periods, and the study hall supervisor is generally expected to maintain a quiet, orderly study environment. Students will sometimes ask for help with assignments. If your school has formal study halls, find out what rules the students are expected to obey and the responsibilities of the supervisor. You may be called upon to supervise a study hall with your cooperating teacher or alone.

Some schools still use detention after school hours as punishment for minor infractions of school rules. Generally in the elementary grades, each teacher supervises the students she or he has detained. In secondary schools, there are often detention halls to which all misbehaving students are sent. Responsibility for supervising detention halls usually rotates among the teachers. If your cooperating teacher is assigned to supervise detention hall, you will probably be expected to help check the roll, hand out special assignments to be completed as a condition of the detention, take up any special detention assignments, and monitor the students' behavior. Many schools do not use detention as a means of punishment due to bus schedules and interference with extracurricular activities or after-school employment.

CLASSROOM ENVIRONMENT

As a student teacher, you will take some responsibility for the appearance and comfort of your classroom from the early days of your experience. By the time you take over full teaching responsibilities, the appearance and comfort of the classroom will, in most cases, be completely your responsibility. Naturally, in many matters you will follow the procedures established by your cooperating teacher. In some areas, however, you may want to try variations, with the teacher's approval.

Neatness and Cleanliness

Although in years past teachers were expected to sweep and mop their classrooms, chances are good that you will not be expected to perform these duties. Most schools hire maintenance personnel to care for such matters. These people generally work before or after school hours to clean classrooms, although some schools have maintenance personnel on duty during the school day. In some schools, you may be expected to handle emergency situations (e.g., paint, ink, or sand spills) yourself, so you should know where cleaning materials are located. In other schools, you may not be expected to do the cleaning; instead, you may simply need to know how to summon the custodian for assistance. Where custodians perform these duties during class hours, it is especially important to develop a good relationship with them. Let them know that you value their help and that their work contributes to your effectiveness. Even if the custodians work only after hours, showing appreciation for a well-cleaned room is likely to pay dividends in the care your room receives.

Cooperation with these support personnel is also important. You may be asked to have students put their chairs on their desks so that it will be easier to clean the floors. Be sure to comply with such a request.

A neat room requires floors free of paper and other trash and supplies put away instead of left out where they were last used. Make students responsible for keeping the floor clear of trash and putting away supplies, and make sure they fulfill these responsibilities. Be sure that there are designated places for storing all supplies and that these places are easily accessible. This kind of planning greatly enhances the functionality of a classroom. It is more pleasant for both teacher and students to work in a neat and clean classroom.

Control of Temperature, Ventilation, and Lighting

Proper temperature, ventilation, and lighting in a classroom promote comfort and the ability to concentrate. Students are easily distracted when a classroom is too hot, too cold, or too stuffy, or when the lighting is too dim or there is a glare on work surfaces. The students focus on their discomfort rather than on their assignments. They may become drowsy from excess heat or insufficient ventilation, or they may develop headaches and eyestrain from inappropriate lighting. It is your responsibility to adjust these factors or to see that they are adjusted by the proper person. If your room has an uncomfortable temperature or poor ventilation, you may need to adjust thermostats, windows, or vents, or you may need to summon the custodian to make appropriate changes. Be sure to follow the school's regulations. If you are not supposed to change the thermostat setting, don't do it, but, if it needs doing, see that the person designated to take care of such matters makes the adjustment before valuable class time is wasted. You can handle lighting problems yourself by turning on more lights, rearranging students' seats, and adjusting blinds or curtains to provide enough light without glare.

Case Study: Not Attuned to the Students

Ms. Jordan, a cold-natured student teacher, entered her empty classroom at 7:45 one morning, took off her coat, shivered, and turned up the room's thermostat. This was the first day she had full responsibility for the classroom, and she didn't want to be uncomfortable all day. At 8:00, the students poured into the room. The body heat of 30 extra people, plus the higher thermostat setting, resulted in a very warm room. Ms. Jordan, who enjoyed the warmth, at first failed to notice how lethargic the class seemed as she began her first complete day of teaching. As time passed, however, the signs were unmistakable. Students were inattentive, and many seemed to be drowsy.

"What is the matter with you?" Ms. Jordan snapped irritably. "Did you all stay up all night watching television?"

"No! No!" came a chorus of answers.

"Then what is wrong?" Ms. Jordan asked again.

A boy in the back of the room finally replied, "It's too hot in here to work."

"That's ridiculous!" Ms. Jordan responded. "I'm perfectly comfortable. Now pay attention."

It was Ms. Jordan who was not paying attention. She was seeing the signs of an overheated room but doing nothing about them. Furthermore, she failed to pay attention to the fact that, due to her tendency to feel cold, she could be comfortable when the students were not, despite a direct verbal cue. Don't be a teacher like Ms. Jordan.

1. Are you extremely hot- or cold-natured? How may this affect your ability to keep your classroom at a comfortable temperature for your students?
2. What clues in the students' behavior may help you determine if the classroom is comfortable for them?

Bulletin Boards/Displays

Bulletin boards and displays can add much to the attractiveness of a classroom; however, they should not be limited to this function. The best bulletin boards and displays are both attractive and informative. They add color and interest to the room while conveying useful information in a content area or while providing motivation to study a particular topic.

All bulletin boards and displays must be carefully constructed to maintain their effectiveness. Inaccurate data, material inappropriate for the age group, sloppy drawing and lettering, or faded or torn background material on bulletin boards and displays make them undesirable rather than helpful additions to the classroom. Even carefully executed displays lose their effectiveness if they are left up too long. Thanksgiving turkeys are out of place in January, even if the display has an excellent instructional focus.

You can make effective bulletin boards and displays for your classroom by following a few simple guidelines:

1 Choose material appropriate to your students' learning and maturity levels.
2 Make sure all the information is accurate.
3 Choose a central theme for a focus.
4 Organize the materials carefully to show their relationship to the central theme.
5 Choose a pleasing color scheme.
6 Do not use faded or torn background material.

7 Use a variety of materials, such as construction paper, crepe paper, yarn, cloth, and cardboard to give the displays texture. Consider use of three-dimensional effects.

8 Change your bulletin boards and displays regularly. They become faded as time passes and cease to generate interest. Never leave seasonal displays up past their time of relevance.

9 Make some bulletin boards manipulative. Students at lower grade levels particularly enjoy such boards. Examples are boards that require activities such as matching synonyms with yarn strips and opening cardboard doors for answers to riddles.

Bulletin boards and displays can be great learning experiences because they help make concepts more concrete. They can sometimes provide even more learning opportunities if you let the students construct the displays themselves or assist you in the construction. It is also easier to keep fresh displays in the classroom when you have student assistance.

Bulletin boards and displays should occasionally include examples of students' work. Don't succumb to the temptation of putting up only the best work. Put up any work of which an individual can be proud, even if it lacks the precision of more advanced students' offerings. On the other hand, do not display especially poor work in an effort to embarrass a student into doing better work. This practice is psychologically unsound. Do not display a student's work if the reason for the display is negative rather than positive.

Use bulletin boards and displays as teaching tools that enhance the attractiveness of your classroom. Keep a file of good ideas as you observe your cooperating teacher and other teachers and as you read professional materials. This file will prove valuable when you have your own classroom.

Learning Centers

Learning centers are areas of the classroom set aside for development and practice of specific skills. You can develop learning centers for any grade level or content area. They usually consist of a skill objective, materials that have been collected to help students meet that objective, task cards or assignment sheets explaining what students are supposed to do in the centers, and a means of evaluating the completed work. Students are frequently assigned to center work on the basis of tests the teacher has administered. Posttests may be provided at the center to determine if students have acquired the indicated skill.

Learning centers may be designed to introduce new skills, offer practice in skills already taught, or provide students with motivation for studying a particular topic. The particular objective of a specific center should be made clear to the students who are expected to use the center. If you help them see the importance of completing the center activities, the activities will have more value for them.

You must assemble the necessary materials for meeting the objective of a center and arrange them so that they are accessible. You may need to label some materials as to purpose, but not all of them will need to be labeled.

You must prepare the task cards or assignment sheets with directions for the center activities carefully. They may need accompanying cassette tapes for younger children or older students with reading disabilities. You can include tasks at different levels of difficulty and code them so that you can differentiate assignments. If you include more than one task in a center, each should be labeled clearly and located in a separate part of the center.

Whenever possible, center activities should be self-checking. In many cases, answer sheets will suffice. Some work may not lend itself to self-checking. In these cases, you should collect the work, evaluate it, and return it to the students as promptly as possible.

Some routines related to center use should be made clear from the outset. Students need to know when they can use the centers, the number of people allowed to use a center simultaneously, how to care for materials, when assignments from centers are due, what personal codes they must use to choose activities, and what they should do when center activities are completed.

You may have one or many centers set up in your room at any given time. They can be set up on tables, in large containers such as refrigerator boxes, on the floor or carpet, in corners, behind bookshelves, or behind folding screens. Your ingenuity is the only limiting factor.

An elementary-level learning center might be based on a skill objective like this one: The student will be able to answer multiplication problems containing the multiplier 9 and multiplicands from 1 through 12 with 100 percent accuracy. Materials for developing this skill might include multiplication study sheets containing the appropriate multiplication facts and multiplication skill tapes to which the child listens and responds, checking his or her answers with answers supplied on the tape later. Obviously, a tape recorder would have to be located at the center for playing the tapes, and it would be best to have headphones so that the center activity does not disturb the rest of the class. The task card for the center would direct students to study the facts, using the multiplication study sheet, then listen to the multiplication skill tapes, respond as directed on the tapes, and, finally, check their answers.

A secondary center might have this as an objective: The student will be able to complete analogies with one missing element with 90 percent accuracy. A microcomputer program to offer instruction on what analogies are and to provide practice in completing them might be the material chosen for this center. Naturally, a microcomputer compatible with the designated program would have to be provided. A duplicated test on analogies could be available as an evaluation technique. The task card would give directions for loading the program and interacting with it, as well as instructions to complete the test located in the center and turn it in to the teacher.

Setting up centers with microcomputers presents some special problems. The microcomputers need to be

1 convenient to electrical outlets.
2 located in a place that is relatively dust-free. (Chalk dust can be lethal to disk drives.)
3 positioned so that glare on the screens is minimized.
4 positioned so that the screens are not facing the part of the class that is not working on the microcomputers. (Students are easily distracted by graphics on the screens.)

Learning centers have been prevalent at the elementary level for a long time, but, in recent years, applications have been made with excellent results at the secondary level. Don't write off the idea without trying it. You may be amazed at the results. Now complete Activity 5.3 on creating a learning center.

Seating Arrangements

Few classrooms today have stationary furniture. The moveable furniture in your classroom represents another responsibility—proper arrangement of this furniture for instructional purposes. You may want one arrangement for whole class instruction, another for small group instruction, and still another when students are working on individual projects. Moveable furniture makes this flexibility possible. An instructional group that requires a chalkboard can cluster around the chalkboard for that lesson, then disperse when another learning activity begins. Chairs can be turned to face a film shown on a side wall, a follow-up discussion using a chalkboard on a different side wall, and a demonstration at the front of the room, all within the space of a single class.

Activity 5.3   Learning Center Idea

Decide upon an idea for a learning center in one of the subjects that you teach. Fill out the following form about this idea.

Subject area:

Objective(s) of the center:

Materials and/or equipment needed:

Sketch the center below, indicating the placement of the center (on a table, in a container, behind a shelf or screen, etc.), locations of the different materials to be used in the center (on a pegboard, in folders, in boxes, etc.), and any decorations that will be used to make the center attractive.

With all this mobility, there are other considerations about seating that you must not overlook. Students with certain handicaps must be seated in the most advantageous positions possible. For example, students who have hearing difficulties should usually be seated near you; those who are nearsighted may need to be seated close to boardwork, displays, and demonstrations; and so on. Potentially disruptive students should also be seated where they are less likely to cause trouble, which may mean seating them near you or making sure certain students do not sit beside each other. Activity 5.4 gives you a chance to work on seating arrangements in one of your classes.

Case Study: Arbitrary Seating Arrangements

When Miss Gomez first came into the seventh-grade business mathematics class in which she was assigned to student teach, the students seemed to be arranged in no logical order. One day, Susie Carter would sit in the front row; the next day, she might sit near the back bulletin board. Furthermore, Susie and several other students seemed to change seats frequently in the middle of class. Miss Gomez felt she would find that distracting when she was teaching.

When Miss Gomez took over the class, she announced that the seating would be alphabetical for the rest of the year. When Susie raised her hand to protest, Miss Gomez said, "There will be no discussion of this matter. Take your assigned seat as I indicate it."

Susie was seated near the back of the room. When Miss Gomez wrote the assignment for the next day on the board, Susie stood up to move to the front of the room as she had been accustomed to doing.

Miss Gomez said abruptly, "Susie, didn't I make it clear that you must stay in your assigned seat?"

Susie replied, "I can't see the board from this seat. Our regular teacher let me sit in the room wherever I needed to so I could see. Whoever was in a seat I needed was supposed to swap until I could get the information I needed. I didn't mean to cause problems."

Miss Gomez was embarrassed. She didn't know what to do. She seemed to have backed herself into an uncomfortable corner.

1. What would you have done at this point?
2. What should Miss Gomez have done to prevent this from happening?
3. Could anyone other than Miss Gomez have helped to avoid this problem? If so, who?

Another concern for teachers, particularly those of younger children, is making sure each child has a chair and desk of suitable size. Small children should not be allowed to choose large desks just because they are attracted to these desks. The children will be in a strained position most of the time if they do. For the same reason, larger children should not have desks too small for them. The children in a single grade will vary greatly in size, and one desk size will not be suitable for all of them. If necessary, swap with other teachers to get a desk appropriate for each student.

The days of nothing but straight lines, exclusively alphabetical seating, and desks bolted to the floor seem to be behind us. The future for teachers and students is much more flexible. Use this flexibility for your benefit and that of your students.

DISCUSSION QUESTIONS

1 Observe the groups that have been set up in your class. Can you see the reason for each type of grouping? Do you think it would be helpful to have additional groups? How might grouping be used to better advantage? If

there are no groups now, can you see any reasons for forming them? If so, how would you do this?

2 Do you see any indications of student discouragement due to their group placement? If so, how could you try to correct this situation?

3 Investigate your school's grouping patterns. Are classes homogeneously or heterogeneously grouped? Do some students move from one class to another for instruction? Do low achievers meet together? Is there a program for gifted students? Are there other ways interclass grouping takes place in your school?

4 Did you waste any time today during your classes? What did you spend time doing that wasn't really important to achieving your goals?

5 Can you think of a better way to organize your class periods or your day? What factors should you consider if you decide to use a different schedule?

6 Why is it extremely important for teachers to be accurate and objective in the material they include in a student's cumulative record? What might happen if a teacher makes careless, negative generalizations about a student?

7 What special reports and records does your school require? What is your responsibility for keeping these records?

8 What is the school's grading system? Is there any provision for giving information to a student's parents about effort, attitude, or interest? Is it important for parents to know this information?

9 How can a neat and clean classroom be an asset to your teaching?

10 Why is control of the classroom's temperature, ventilation, and lighting an important responsibility?

11 Could there be situations in which you might not have control of temperature and ventilation? Why might this happen?

12 Do all bulletin boards and displays serve the same purpose? What purposes do they serve?

13 How often should bulletin boards and displays be changed? Why do you think so?

14 What are some bulletin board or display ideas for your grade or content area?

15 How can learning centers enhance instruction in your classroom?

16 How can classroom seating arrangements be used to best advantage?

17 Is your classroom highly structured or very flexible? What aspects of your classroom reflect this structure or flexibility?

SELECTED REFERENCES

Beach, Don M. *Reaching Teenagers: Learning Centers for the Secondary Classroom.* Santa Monica, Calif.: Goodyear, 1977.

Bennie, Francis. *Learning Centers: Development and Operation.* Englewood Cliffs, N.J.: Educational Technology Publications, 1977.

Burns, Paul C., and Betty D. Roe. *Reading Activities for Today's Elementary Schools.* Lanham, Md.: University Press of America, 1991.

"Cooperative Learning." *Educational Leadership* 47 (December 1989/January 1990): entire issue.

Drayer, Adam M. *Problems in Middle and High School Teaching.* Boston: Allyn and Bacon, 1979.

Dubey, Robert E., et al. *A Performance-Based Guide to Student Teaching.* Danville, Ill.: Interstate, 1975.

Duke, Daniel L., ed. *Helping Teachers Manage Classrooms.* Alexandria, Va.: Association for Supervision and Curriculum Development, 1982.

Gere, Ann Ruggles, and Robert D. Abbott. "Talking about Writing: The Language of Writing Groups." *Research in the Teaching of English* 19 (December 1985): 362–81.

Activity 5.4   Seating Arrangements

Draw a seating chart for use with one of your classes during whole group instruction. Circle the names of students with special needs who should have special consideration in seating arrangements. Explain the reasons for the particular placements of these students in the space below your seating chart.

Houle, Georgia B. *Learning Centers for Young Children,* 3rd ed. West Greenwich, R.I.: Consortium Publishing, 1987.

Houseman, Marian, and Frederick A. Duffelmeyer. "Textbook Related Methods in Social Studies." *The Reading Teacher* 40 (April 1987): 820–22.

Johnson, Hiram, et al. *Learning Center Ideabook: Activities for the Elementary and Middle Grades.* Boston: Allyn and Bacon, 1977.

Kozoll, Charles E. *Time Management for Educators.* Bloomington, Ind.: Phi Delta Kappa Educational Foundation, 1982.

Learning Center Handbook. Temple City, Calif.: Pacific Shoreline Press, 1986.

Levin, Tamar, and Ruth Long. *Effective Instruction.* Alexandria, Va.: Association for Supervision and Curriculum Development, 1981.

Ptreshene, Susan S. *A Complete Guide to Learning Centers.* Palo Alto, Calif.: Pendrogen House, 1977.

Slavin, Robert E. "Cooperative Learning." *Review of Educational Research* 50 (Summer 1980): 315–42.

Slavin, Robert E. *Cooperative Learning: Theory, Research, and Practice.* Englewood Cliffs, N.J.: Prentice-Hall. 1990.

Slavin, Robert E. "Synthesis of Research on Cooperative Learning." *Educational Leadership* 48 (February 1991): 72–82.

Smith, Roy A. "A Teacher's Views on Cooperative Learning." *Phi Delta Kappan* 68 (May 1987): 663–66.

Zumwalt, Karen K., ed. *Improving Teaching.* Alexandria, Va.: Association for Supervision and Curriculum Development, 1986.

6

Teaching Strategies

Ralph is a ninth grader reading at a fourth-grade level in Mrs. Kelsey's remedial reading class. During the year, Mrs. Kelsey and Mr. Sunas, the intern, tried to encourage Ralph to read by finding him easy materials and offering rewards for progress. Ralph didn't respond and showed no interest in reading. Mr. Sunas was determined to find some way to reach Ralph before the end of the year. One morning Ralph came to school unusually tired.

Mr. Sunas: What's the matter, Ralph? You seem so tired today. Did you have a rough weekend?

Ralph: We was out planting soybeans all weekend, Mr. Sunas. I'm beat.

Mr. Sunas: I don't know much about growing soybeans, Ralph. Tell me about it.

Ralph: Gosh, there's so much to tell. I don't know where to begin. My folks've been raising soybeans for as far back as I can remember.

Mr. Sunas: Is that what you plan to do, too?

Ralph: You bet! I want to grow the very best soybeans in these here parts. That's why I'm just waiting to be 16 so I can drop out of school. I want to get out and work with the soybeans and not just sit here all day doing nothing.

Mr. Sunas: Ralph, if you really want to be the best producer of soybeans in the area, how are you going to go about it?

Ralph: I don't know—guess I'll just do what my dad and his folks have always done.

Mr. Sunas: But Ralph, the Agricultural Experiment Station is developing more efficient ways of raising soybeans all the time. There's a lot to know about disease control, fertilizers, soil con-

servation, and marketing. I'll bring you some information about it.

Ralph: Naw, don't bother. I don't want to read nothing about it.

Mr. Sunas (a few days later): I found some pamphlets on how to raise soybeans. I thought you might want to look at them.

Ralph: Maybe later. (Ralph yawns, leans back in his chair, and stares out the window.)

Mr. Sunas (20 minutes later): Ralph, have you looked at those pamphlets yet?

Ralph: No, not yet. (He picks up his pencil and starts doodling on a scrap of paper.)

Mr. Sunas (10 minutes later): Did you have any trouble with blister beetles last year? I hear they're supposed to be bad again this year.

Ralph: Yeah. They really gave us problems last year. (pause) Why? Does it say something about them in here?

Mr. Sunas: Yes. It tells you what to do to prevent having so many and how to control the ones you do have.

Ralph: No foolin'? I bet my dad would really like to know about this.

Mr. Sunas: Why don't you read about it for the rest of the period? I'll help you with the words you don't know.

Ralph: Hey, here's a picture of one of them beetles. This is really neat. What's this say here, Mr. Sunas? I really need to know this stuff.

Florinda was a bright, eager child who came to first grade already knowing how to read. At age three, she was reading signs on franchises along the highway, and at age four, she was picking words out of the storybooks her father read to her. By the time she was five, she could read simple books by herself. Mrs. Cho, Florinda's teacher, had 29 students in first grade that year and had her hands full working with a large number of immature children. She realized Florinda knew how to read, but Mrs. Cho certainly couldn't take the time to work with Florinda on a different level. Florinda was placed in a readiness group, then in a preprimer group.

Florinda (one morning before school starts): Look, Mrs. Cho, this is the book my daddy read me

last night—Where The Wild Things Are! It's so exciting, and I can read it all by myself.

Mrs. Cho: That's fine, Florinda. It is a good book. Now put it away. It will be time for reading group soon.

Florinda: But Mrs. Cho, those stories in reading group are too easy. I already know all the words. They're no fun to read.

Mrs. Cho: I'm sorry, Florinda, but you'll just have to read what the other boys and girls are reading. I don't have time to listen to you read your books.

Florinda: Well, okay.

Mrs. Cho (observing Florinda reading her book during class time later that morning): Florinda, I told you to put that book away. This isn't the time to read. You have four worksheets to do.

Florinda: But I don't want to do them. They're dumb.

Mrs. Cho: Give me your book, Florinda. Do your work like the other boys and girls. I don't want you causing any trouble.

1. What motivational techniques were mentioned in the vignette about Ralph? Which one seemed to be successful? Why do you think it worked?
2. Was Ralph internally motivated? If so, why didn't he respond positively to the school situation? How are both intrinsic and extrinsic motivation a part of the story about Ralph?
3. Does Ralph's interest in the blister beetle mean that he is now motivated to learn? Is there a danger that his interest in learning will pass? How could his interest be extended until it becomes a part of his internal motivation?
4. How could Ralph's interest in soybeans be used to increase his achievement in other areas, such as math and science?
5. What was Mrs. Cho doing to Florinda's internal motivation? What might happen to Florinda as a result of her teacher's attitude? What are some choices Mrs. Cho had for keeping alive Florinda's interest in reading?
6. How did these two teachers differ in dealing with their students' needs and interests? What long-term effects do you think their different strategies might have on their students?

HELPING THEM LEARN

Now the groundwork has been laid. You know about lesson plans and discipline, as well as your resources, coworkers, and students. It's time to start teaching. In this chapter, you'll find some traditional approaches to teaching along with some creative and student-centered activities. You'll also find some ways to motivate students and help them learn effectively. Student teaching is a good time to experiment with new ideas and find out what works for you.

Remember that you cannot teach your students all there is to know. Such a feat would be impossible in view of the current knowledge explosion. What is important is that, through your teaching, you help students discover how to learn. Provide them with skills for solving problems, and teach them to think for themselves.

STUDENT-CENTERED LEARNING

When students plan cooperatively and make decisions about their own learning experiences, they are assuming the kinds of responsibilities that will enable them to become productive citizens in a democratic society. Students at all levels have the capacity and right to make some decisions about their learning. If given such opportunities, they are likely to improve their problem-solving skills, critical thinking ability, and language fluency. In addition, they will be more motivated to learn because they are actively involved.

Student-centered learning does not mean that you should abandon all plans and preparations; after all, you have knowledge and experience that are useful for helping students learn. It does mean, however, that you should find opportunities to let students grow in their ability to direct their own learning. The term *negotiated learning* means that you, with your expertise, and the students, with their increasing ability to assume responsibility, work together to plan, direct, and assess learning experiences (see Activity 6.1).

An example of negotiated learning is the theme cycle, a way of integrating the curriculum. Together, students and teacher select a topic for study. The teacher offers choices based on the curriculum for that grade level, and the students select the topic of greatest interest to them. For example, if the curriculum mandates study

Activity 6.1   Student-Centered Learning Activity Sheet—Plan for Negotiated Learning

Date:

Type of activity:

Teacher involvement:

Student involvement:

Assessment of activity:

Recommendations for improving student responsibilities and decision making:

of states within the United States, the students might choose Hawaii. Instead of providing the plan for the unit and related resources, the teacher asks students such questions as:

What do we already know?

What do we want to find out?

Where can we find resources?

How can we organize the class to get the information we need?

What are some ways to present the findings of individuals or groups to the rest of the class?

What time frame should we establish?

At the end, how should we evaluate what we learned?

As a result of these problem-solving and decision-making activities, students not only learn content, but also discover ways to work independently and cooperatively.

It would be a mistake to assume that all students are ready for negotiated learning, because some may never have had opportunities to make choices and decisions at school. Cooperative teacher-student planning and decision making works best if the teacher makes careful preparations and follows guidelines, such as:

1 Create learning environments that enable students to make reasonable choices, take risks, assume responsibilities, and use their imaginations.
2 Act as a facilitator, not a director, of learning, and be ready to serve as a resource person as needed.
3 Begin with small tasks, building gradually to larger tasks as you observe that the students are ready.
4 Involve each student as much as possible, and encourage each one to hold a leadership role at some time.
5 Be sure that students perceive their activities as meaningful and important.
6 Before involving the students, be well prepared yourself by knowing the subject, available resources, and desirable outcomes.
7 Be accepting of students' attempts, providing guidance or intervention only when requested or necessary.
8 Participate with the students in evaluating the final product.

Beginning in kindergarten, children can make choices, lead "show-and-tell" activities, work with partners, and so forth. As children mature, they are able to assume more complex roles in classroom planning and decision making. Grade level alone, however, does not indicate students' preparation for directing their own learning; their prior experiences, personalities, and social interactions, as well as the teacher's attitude toward student-centered learning, are also important considerations. In the following list, you will find some types of negotiated activities. Remember, even when you turn a great deal of the responsibility over to the students, your guidance and support are essential components of successful student-centered learning.

Student-Centered Learning Activities

1 Determine what learning strategies to use (e.g., brainstorming, demonstrating, sharing, interviewing, using reference materials, etc.).
2 Identify reasonable time frames for projects, allowing for flexibility.
3 Decide what forms final products will take.
4 Lead activities, workshops, and games.
5 Direct own independent studies with student-teacher input.
6 Set daily schedules and rules for behavior.
7 Participate in projects, such as making videos, writing computer programs, and conducting science experiments.
8 Be responsible for establishing and managing learning centers.

9 Participate in record keeping and evaluation.
10 Provide peer assistance.
11 Create bulletin boards, displays, and visuals for the classroom.
12 Choose topics for investigation.

MOTIVATION

One of your greatest challenges as a teacher will be to motivate your students. All learning is motivated in one way or another. Highly motivated pupils almost teach themselves in their eagerness to learn. Poorly motivated students are unlikely to learn much of anything, no matter how well you teach.

Intrinsic versus Extrinsic Motivation

Motivation comes both from the student's inner self and from external forces. Internal or intrinsic motivation arises out of a student's needs, personality, attitudes, and values. Students who are internally motivated are driven by the need to be popular, the desire to excel, or the fear of failure. Intrinsic motivation is generally long lasting; it is a part of the individual that drives that person toward her or his goals. Successful experiences tend to increase a student's internal drives, but repeated failures may eventually destroy inner motivation.

Intrinsic motivation is part of a student's basic personality and changes very slowly, if at all. This means you will have little opportunity to change the underlying motivational patterns of students in the short time you will work with them. By stimulating their curiosity and building on their interests, however, you can lay the foundation for lasting internal changes.

External or extrinsic motivation originates in the learning environment and causes the student to want to do certain things. As the teacher, you may want to employ various types of external motivation to modify student behavior. Be aware, however, that this type of motivation is usually short term and may disappear when the student reaches the immediate goal.

You can use incentives as extrinsic motivators to make students want to work or behave better. Rewards are generally more effective incentives than punishments. Positive incentives that you may find useful are free time, extended recess periods, recognition on the classroom bulletin board, or prizes and awards. Students can also be motivated by earning good grades and seeing their names on the honor roll.

Keep in mind that external incentives are only artificial ways of getting students to try harder. They should never become the major reason for doing schoolwork, or students will value the reward more than the learning. Most learning tasks don't require incentives. Students should develop self-discipline to get their work done. If you decide to use incentives, learn which types work best for your students; then use them sparingly and for only short periods of time.

Be careful about giving awards or prizes as incentives for top achievers. These students are usually internally motivated anyway, and poor achievers become even more frustrated when competing against them. One way to overcome this problem is by having students compete against their own records instead of trying to be the best in the class. For instance, students can keep charts of their daily or weekly grades and try to show improvement. Another way to avoid the problem is to have one group or class compete against another group or class. Students work together to win a reward, and all students have a chance to win. Recognition can also be given for increased effort and for improvement in attitude.

Who Is Motivated?

You will be able to observe different levels of motivation among your students. Those who seem poorly motivated will need more patience and skill to get them interested.

If you aren't sure which students are well motivated and which are not, use the following lists of questions as you observe students. The more "yes" answers you get on the first list, the more positively motivated the student is. On the second list, a large number of "yes" answers indicates a poorly motivated student.

Highly Motivated Students   Does the student:

_____   **1** Appear to use good study skills?
_____   **2** Read or seek information during free time?
_____   **3** Ask questions in class?
_____   **4** Listen attentively?
_____   **5** Express curiosity and interest when given new ideas?
_____   **6** Take a lively part in class discussion?
_____   **7** Do extra work beyond regular class assignments?
_____   **8** Think independently instead of following the crowd?
_____   **9** Persist in solving problems until reaching a solution?
_____   **10** Send off for information?

Poorly Motivated Students   Does the student:

_____   **1** Seem inattentive and appear to daydream a lot?
_____   **2** Give up on a test or just guess at answers?
_____   **3** Try to avoid participating in class activities?
_____   **4** Cause disruptions by distracting other students?
_____   **5** Waste time?
_____   **6** Not do homework or other assignments?
_____   **7** Jump to conclusions instead of thinking something through?
_____   **8** Seem bored and uninterested most of the time?
_____   **9** Seem unable to work independently?
_____   **10** Read assigned pages without understanding what has been read?

Setting Goals

All your students need approval, acceptance, and achievement. Most of them also have special interests, such as taking care of a new puppy or rebuilding a car engine. These needs and interests become the basis for setting goals. If you can develop a relationship between their goals and your instructional program, the students will be motivated to learn. That is what Mr. Sunas tried to do with Ralph.

You can set goals for your pupils, but if you expect them to work toward those goals, your students must accept them as their own. The students should see that *your* instructional goals will help them achieve something *they* want; otherwise they will not be motivated to do their best work.

One eighth-grade teacher was frustrated because, even though her students could pass tests on the correct use of English, as soon as they were outside the classroom, they used poor grammar. She realized they didn't see any point in speaking Standard English. One day she asked them, "Can you think of any reasons for needing to speak correct English?" Finally, one student said, "Well, I guess so. I plan to earn money next summer by selling books. If I can't speak right, no one will buy books from me." Another student said, "When I go to church, sometimes they call on me to make a prayer. I get embarrassed in front of the preacher if I make a mistake in English."

Using their interests in establishing goals is a good way to motivate students. You can learn about students' interests by taking a simple written or oral survey. You may have a problem if the interests in your class vary widely, but students' interests usually tend to cluster around a few general topics. Once you identify these topics, you can begin to relate instructional objectives to them. If you find this procedure difficult, build on the students' interests until you make a connection with what you need to teach. For instance, if several students are interested in race cars, let them: (1) read books about race cars, (2) solve math problems that involve the speed of race cars, (3) do research reports on the history of race cars, and (4) investigate the construction of race car engines. Common interests, such as holidays or community and school events, also make good focal points for setting instructional goals.

Students must also view goals as reasonable and attainable. Unreasonably long assignments will only frustrate them and discourage most of them from trying. If you want to assign work that will take a period of time to complete, break the work down into small steps. For instance, research reports can be broken down like this: (1) select a topic, (2) read about it in different sources and take notes, (3) outline the report, (4) make a rough draft, and (5) write the final report. Goals do not seem so difficult to reach when they become a series of small, related tasks.

Motivational Strategies

You may want to use some of these specific suggestions for motivating students.

1 Keep records of progress made, books reviewed, or tasks completed, so students can see what they have accomplished.
2 Encourage students to identify their own problems; then help them solve the problems creatively.
3 Use variety and occasional surprise in your lessons. Vary teaching strategies so that students will be eager to see what you do next.
4 Work in some riddles and jokes. It takes intelligence to appreciate humor, and you will keep the students interested.
5 Arouse their curiosity. Bring a praying mantis to school, and don't say anything. Let them observe and ask questions.
6 Vary the activities. Follow a quiet study session with a song or physical activity.
7 Have plenty of scrap materials, games, audiovisual media, and manipulative devices. Use them in your lessons and let students use them for independent learning.
8 Be enthusiastic. Enthusiasm is contagious, and your students will catch it.
9 Create failure-proof situations for slow learners and poorly motivated students. Offer challenges to highly motivated students.
10 Use educational games, concrete objects, and audiovisual media to create interest.
11 Write brief messages to students when you return their papers instead of assigning only a letter grade.
12 Videotape a special presentation, debate, panel discussion, or activity.
13 Set up a mailbox or communications bulletin board for each class so that you and the students can exchange messages.
14 Use a popular song (choose carefully!) as a basis for a lesson in language arts. Look for new vocabulary words, synonyms, antonyms, rhyming words, alliteration, and special meanings.
15 Instead of the textbook, teach from a newspaper. It can be used for any content area.
16 In a foreign language class, translate the school menu each day from English to the foreign language, or play "Password" in the foreign language.
17 Encourage home economics students to prepare projects for competitions, such as county fairs.
18 Compute averages, figure percentages, and make graphs in math class from data the students collect. Sample topics include height of students, size of rooms, students on the honor roll, and male and female faculty members.

19 Let students set up and carry out experiments in science class. Be sure the students can explain what is happening and why.

20 In social studies class, assign different groups of students to present daily news broadcasts.

Now do Activity 6.2.

RELATING INSTRUCTION TO STUDENTS' BACKGROUNDS

Schema theory is a term in education that may sound technical and theoretical, but it actually is very simple in meaning and application. Essentially, your schema for a particular idea or thing is a combination of your knowledge, experiences, and impressions related to it. For instance, your schema for *teacher* includes memories of teachers you have had, information from your education classes about what teachers should do and be, and your own thoughts based on experiences in which you were the teacher. It may also include sensory impressions, such as the smell of chalk dust and the ache of hurting feet. Your schema for teacher should be rich and full due to your association with the teaching profession, but your schema may be limited or nonexistent for *paleontologist* or *philatelist*.

A student's schemata (plural of schema), or clusters of information about various topics, are important factors in determining how well that student learns the material you are presenting. Students with many well-developed schemata bring a great deal of knowledge and understanding to the learning situation and are likely to absorb related information readily. On the other hand, students who have poorly developed schemata will generally have difficulty understanding new concepts. In other words, they cannot relate new learning to old when they have little prior knowledge or understanding of a subject.

If students lack relevant schemata for a unit you are teaching, they will be seriously limited in their ability to understand your presentations, the textbook, or other instructional materials. Therefore, it is important to assess the knowledge the students already have of the topic and then, if necessary, provide additional experiences to fill in gaps in their knowledge before proceeding with the lesson or unit.

There are two simple ways to determine your students' prior knowledge of a subject.[1] One way is to list key vocabulary words on the chalkboard and ask the students what they know about each term. Another way, sometimes referred to as semantic mapping, is to put the main topic in the center of the chalkboard and have students provide information that can be clustered around the main topic. In Figure 6–1, the main topic is farms, and related clusters are farm buildings, farm animals, farm work, and crops. Students who contribute answers such as these evidently have some background knowledge of farms, and you will not need to provide much additional information. However, you will need to enrich the backgrounds of students who could tell you little or nothing about farms. A semantic map such as

FIGURE 6–1 Semantic Map for Farms

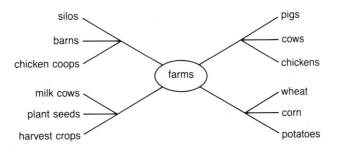

[1] P. David Pearson and Rand Spiro. "The New Buzz Word in Reading Is Schema." *Instructor* 91 (May 1982): 46–48.

Figure 6–1 not only checks prior knowledge, but it also serves as a good introduction or overview for a unit.

If you discover that your students have very little prior knowledge of a topic, you may wish to provide vicarious or direct experiences for them. In the example of farms, you might take a class to a dairy farm, have a farmer visit the class, view a film on farms, read stories and show pictures about farms, or do some other activity that would help students understand what a farm is.

In any situation, you should try to relate new knowledge to what students already understand by making meaningful connections. For instance, you might point out how one concept is similar to or different from another by comparing a familiar concept, such as democracy, with another form of government, such as communism. As students build bridges of meaning between new concepts and old, they are expanding their schemata and establishing a base of knowledge for acquiring new ideas.

ADJUSTING INSTRUCTION TO STUDENTS' LEARNING STYLES

Not all students learn in the same way. Just as you probably learn better in some situations than others, all students have preferred ways of learning. Each person has a unique learning style, a set of strategies for acquiring information, that remains fairly constant throughout life. You can improve the effectiveness of your teaching by understanding how each student learns best and using that knowledge to individualize instruction whenever possible.

There are three major areas in which learning styles may differ: cognitive, affective, and physiological. Cognitive factors relate to how a person acquires and uses information. Some students are analytical and learn best by examining details and studying each element of a situation; others are global or holistic learners who look at large chunks of information. Therefore, analytical students are likely to learn better with instruction in discrete basic skills, whereas global or holistic learners may learn better by first considering an entire problem or reading selection and then breaking it down into smaller elements.

Affective factors deal with a learner's personality and emotional characteristics, including such aspects as sociability, willingness to take risks, sense of responsibility, and motivation. Important instructional considerations related to the affective style are use of appropriate motivational strategies and provision of opportunities for group or individual work. You may need to experiment with various techniques before finding those that work best for each student.

The third area of learning style consists of physiological or environmental factors. Students vary widely in their preference for strong or dim lighting, time of day when they learn best, need to eat and move about while working, desire for a quiet or noisy classroom, and preference for cool or warm temperatures.[2] Although it is impossible to consider all of these variables for each student, you can provide a variety of learning situations and sometimes give choices for working conditions.

CLASSROOM TECHNIQUES

There are many techniques available for helping students learn. Some are more appropriate for slow learners than for bright students, for younger children than for older students, or for some subject areas than for others. As a student teacher, you

[2]Kenneth Dunn and Rita Dunn. "Dispelling Outmoded Beliefs about Student Learning." *Educational Leadership* 44 (March 1987): 55–62.

Activity 6.2   Motivational Strategies

Read the following list of motivational strategies, taken from the list in the text, and check those you have tried. Put a check (√) beside those that have worked well and the letter X beside those that have been ineffective.

1. _____ Keep progress records.

2. _____ Encourage student participation in solving their problems.

3. _____ Use variety and occasional surprises in your lessons.

4. _____ Add humor—jokes and riddles.

5. _____ Arouse curiosity.

6. _____ Alternate quiet and active periods.

7. _____ Let students use manipulatives and media for independent learning.

8. _____ Be enthusiastic.

9. _____ Challenge motivated students and guarantee success for slow learners.

10. _____ Create interest in a variety of ways.

11. _____ Write messages on papers you return to students.

12. _____ Videotape special events.

13. _____ Exchange messages with students.

14. _____ Teach with popular songs.

15. _____ Teach with a newspaper.

16. _____ Use foreign language lessons for authentic purposes.

17. _____ Let home economics students prepare special meals.

18. _____ Make math lessons meaningful by using real data.

19. _____ Let students conduct science experiments.

20. _____ Ask students to present daily newscasts.

should try a variety of techniques to find out which ones work best for you. Then complete Activity 6.3.

Lecture

"Good morning, class. Today I will be telling you about. . . ." And so the familiar lecture technique begins. The teacher does the telling, and the students listen.

Lectures can be divided into two types: formal and informal. You can probably recall some of your college professors who delivered highly structured, carefully worded, inflexible, and uninterrupted lectures. The formal lecture is generally inappropriate for public school teaching, except occasionally for classes of college-bound students who are good listeners. On the other hand, informal lectures are often effective for getting information across. An informal lecture is usually brief and often involves use of audiovisual materials along with minimal student participation.

You will probably want to do some lecturing in your teaching because it is often the most direct and efficient way to convey the message. Lecture is particularly appropriate for history and literature classes and can also be used to explain an experiment in science. Brief, informal lectures can provide background information when you introduce a new topic, or summarize what has happened during a learning experience.

When you prepare to lecture, keep certain points in mind. Remember that elementary children and slow learners have short attention spans and cannot listen very long. Even older, bright students probably won't want to listen for more than about 20 minutes without a change of pace. Get to know your students well enough so that you can adapt your lectures to their interests and needs and relate the lectures to their background experiences. Then prepare and organize your material carefully so you can make a concise, easy-to-understand presentation.

Delivery makes the difference between a boring and a stimulating lecture. Keep your voice pitched low, use expression, and make sure every student can hear you. Maintain eye contact, and occasionally interject a student's name to recapture the attention of a student who appears to be drifting away from you. Speak in Standard English, and use vocabulary words each student understands.

You can use several techniques to hold students' interest as you lecture. Begin by making sure that students remove all unnecessary items from their desks so that they will not be distracted. Introduce your topic in such a way that you arouse curiosity. Use audiovisual materials or demonstrations to supplement the lecture. Emphasize major points by writing them on the chalkboard, and encourage secondary students to take notes. Occasionally ask a question to get students involved and to check on how well they are listening to your presentation.

Although lecture is often a quick way to transmit information, it has many dangers. It does not allow for student creativity or problem solving, nor does it enable students to practice applying the knowledge that is being passed along to them. During this one-way communication process, many teachers get carried away with their own speech making while students sit passively and daydream.

Discussion

Guided discussion is also a teacher-centered technique, but it affords greater opportunities for students to participate than does lecture. Students can exchange ideas and consider the pros and cons of issues. Guided discussion is a natural and informal way for students to communicate their thoughts.

By engaging students in guided discussions, you can help them achieve many worthwhile goals. They learn to see different points of view and to keep their minds open. They begin to think critically about important issues and question whatever they are told or see in print. They develop speaking and listening skills by reacting to what their classmates say. They also develop tolerance for other people's ideas when they hear different opinions expressed.

If you want to conduct a guided discussion in your class, first decide whether you want a whole class discussion or several small group discussions. In the latter case, you will need to divide your class into three or four groups and appoint a leader for each group. You should move from one group to the next, checking to see that students are making relevant comments. Small groups should meet for 20 to 30 minutes, after which the leader can summarize the group's ideas for the rest of the class. Students who are afraid to speak out in front of the entire class are usually willing to participate in small group discussions.

In a discussion with the whole class, you have several responsibilities as the discussion leader. Choose a controversial topic familiar to your students so they can discuss it intelligently. Create a supportive atmosphere where students are not afraid to say what is on their minds, but control the discussion so that it doesn't deteriorate into pointless conversation. Encourage widespread participation by asking questions directed toward students of different ability levels. Conclude the discussion by summarizing the points that were made and suggesting a solution that seems acceptable to most of the class.

A good topic for discussion might be "What sources of energy should we pursue for future development?" Possible answers include solar, nuclear, geothermal, synthetic fuel, wind, and biological sources. You could consider these sources in terms of their cost to develop, the length of time before they would be available for independent use, their impact on the environment, and their safety. The whole class could consider these issues, or you could divide the class into groups with each group discussing one source and making recommendations as to its feasibility.

During a guided discussion or other type of lesson, students may raise questions you cannot answer. Rather than take a chance and give a wrong answer, admit that you don't know the answer. Then, depending on the situation, you can look it up in a reference source immediately, tell the students you will try to find the answer, or suggest that they find the answer and discuss it in class the next day. Of course you should know your lesson, but no one knows all of the answers all of the time.

Panel discussions and debates are variations of the discussion approach. In panel discussions, students prepare in advance to discuss issues related to a specific topic in front of the class. One student usually serves as chairperson and directs the discussion. Debates are similar to panel discussions, but call for two teams of students to present opposing sides of a topic. With both procedures, make sure the participants understand the ground rules and are well prepared. At the conclusion of the activity, ask the rest of the class to respond to the presentation.

Demonstration

Another teacher-centered instructional activity is demonstration. With this technique, students learn by watching as well as by listening. You can use demonstrations in every part of the curriculum and at any age level. In the elementary grades, you might need to show some children how to tie their shoes or demonstrate to a baseball player how to pitch a ball. At the secondary level, you can demonstrate how to make a soufflé in home economics or show the correct position for the fingers on the keys of a typewriter in typing class. If you teach science classes, you will have many opportunities to demonstrate scientific processes by performing experiments yourself or helping students set them up.

Demonstrations have a special attraction for students. They create a feeling of anticipation. Students welcome the change from routine lessons and give their full attention to what you are doing.

In preparing for a demonstration, make sure it relates clearly to your objectives. Try to keep it simple and to the point—it's a mistake to try to teach too many

Activity 6.3   Classroom Techniques

In order to meet the diverse needs and interests of the students in your class, you should use a variety of teaching strategies. Listed below are several classroom techniques that you might try. For each technique you attempt, write a statement about its effectiveness.

Lecture:

Discussion:

Demonstration:

Guided study activities—supervised study:

Guided study activities—drill:

Guided study activities—review:

Guided study activities—project:

Homework:

Questioning:

Programmed instruction:

Case method:

Can you think of other teaching strategies to use? If so, what are they?

Reflect on the methods that you have used and identify the most effective ones. Why do you think these methods work best? What methods will you want to learn to use better? Which ones might you want to discard?

concepts in a single demonstration. If your demonstration could cause injury, be sure to take safety precautions; then practice it several times until you are sure nothing can go wrong.

Now you are ready to present the demonstration to your class. Collect all the materials you need, and provide a good viewing area for the students. Prepare them for what you will be doing so that they will know what to expect. During the demonstration, you can ask questions or point out what is taking place. Afterward, review what happened and why it occurred as it did. If something went wrong, ask the students if they can tell you why.

Guided Study Activities

Give an assignment and then have students study the text, discuss the material, memorize the important facts, and take a test. You know the routine. It is not much fun, but it is sometimes useful for helping students acquire specific knowledge in a short time.

Supervised Study   As the teacher, you may want to supervise occasional study sessions in which students are responsible for mastering content you have assigned.

Constructing models is one type of guided study activity on which children can work individually or in groups.

Be sure to make reasonable assignments that all students can complete successfully if they apply themselves to the task. You may have to individualize some assignments according to students' different ability levels. You should walk around among the students while they study, stopping occasionally to answer questions, offer suggestions, and head them in the right direction. Your guidance during a supervised study session can help students learn to use study time efficiently when they are on their own.

Supervised study during class time is a useful teaching technique if you are introducing a new subject or type of assignment. You are there to offer encouragement and make sure students are getting off to a good start. It is also valuable if the assignment requires the use of resources in the classroom or the school library.

Because of its limitations, you should use this approach infrequently. It can easily become boring and routine, seldom involves the student in creative or critical thinking, and may seem unrelated to real-life situations. This procedure has little power to motivate the slow learner, and the bright student learns, not for the purpose of gaining information, but for the reward of a good grade.

Drill   Nine times two is eighteen, nine times three is twenty-seven, nine times four is thirty-six. On and on, over and over. This is known as *drill*, or organized practice. Is it really necessary? Why do we do it?

Drill can be a valuable instructional technique when it is based on solid understanding of a concept. It provides practice through repetition to the point of overlearning. In such areas as math, spelling, grammar, and motor development, repeated practice is helpful for mastering skills.

Although drill is often boring, it doesn't have to be. Here are some ways to keep drill from becoming tedious. Think up games for practicing skills. Keep drill periods short—don't go beyond the time when it ceases to hold the students' attention. Vary the amount and kind of drill according to students' needs. Give slow learners more repetition than fast learners—because they generally need it. Make sure students see the reason for complete mastery of the concept. Let students keep individual charts to record their progress. Intersperse drill with other types of instruction to avoid monotony.

Review   Review is similar to drill. It is based on previously learned concepts and makes use of recall. While drill simply provides practice in skills, however, review explores students' attitudes, understandings, and appreciations. Review is essentially a group process that extends initial learnings by bringing out relationships and applications of the topic. Use review before tests and whenever you want to pull together the major concepts you have been teaching.

Project   Another type of guided study activity is the project technique. In this approach, students have more freedom to direct their own activities and can become more actively involved in the learning process. Usually several groups work simultaneously on different but related projects. Groups may conduct research, construct models, or solve problems, and then prepare a report to present to the class. Your role as the teacher is to support, encourage, and assist as groups work toward completing their projects. Quite often, course content is not covered as thoroughly in this approach, so you will need to fill in the gaps with other techniques.

Homework

"Can't tonight. I've got tons of homework to do." Sound familiar? Educators dispute the value of homework; it may or may not do any good. Research reports indicate, however, that student achievement increases when students conscientiously do regularly assigned homework.[3] To be most effective, homework should relate to and go beyond what students are learning in the classroom. Also, teachers should care-

---

[3]William J. Bennett. *What Works.* Washington, D.C.: United States Department of Education, 1986, pp. 41–42.

fully prepare the assignments, thoroughly explain them, give reasons for doing them in terms of enhanced learning, and promptly return them with comments.

To keep your assignments from becoming boring and meaningless, vary the type of homework that you give. There are two major types of homework: (1) practice and preparation and (2) extension activities. Practice and preparation homework includes most reading and writing assignments, practice and drill exercises, and individual work. The individual work allows you to provide extra practice for students who need it and to give assignments that are compatible with the learning styles of different students. However, it is often difficult to manage individualized assignments. Extension activities often involve group work on such projects as making maps, conducting surveys, doing long-term science experiments, and working on community projects. Use a combination of these types of homework so that students don't always have to work math problems or answer questions from the text. Instead, allow the students sometimes to investigate, discover, interview, work on projects, do computer programs, and solve problems dealing with real-life situations.

Remember that some students have little time or opportunity to do homework. They may have jobs or chores to do after school. The home may be so crowded and have such poor study facilities that doing homework is impossible. There may be no one at home for some students to turn to for assistance or clarification. If you are uncertain about the homework you assign, ask some of the dependable students how much time they are spending on homework and if the assignments seem beneficial. Their answers may guide you in making realistic assignments.

Questioning

You can use questioning with almost any type of lesson, including informal lecture, discussion, demonstration, recitation, discovery, and inquiry. Sometimes questions are rapid-fire; one question comes quickly upon the heels of another, giving students little chance to think and reflect on meanings. On other occasions questioning sessions may proceed more slowly, with fewer questions and more time for thoughtful, reflective responses. Questioning is a useful instructional technique in almost any situation, but students benefit more from slower-paced recitations in which there is time to consider the implications of higher-order questions.

Suppose you want to try your skill at leading a question session. How would you start? First, choose an appropriate topic. It should be one your students already know something about, that is important and interesting to them, and that is within their level of understanding. Get their attention before you begin, and then ask your questions clearly. Ask each question only once, so that they will know they must listen carefully. Once the session begins, keep to the subject, and don't get too far off the track. Try to include all the students in the questioning, even those who don't volunteer.

One way of ensuring participation by all students is to use the every-pupil-response technique. In this approach, you ask questions that all pupils can answer at the same time by indicating one of two or more choices. You may read a list of statements and ask students to put their thumbs up if they agree, down if they disagree, and to the side if they aren't sure. Or you may make cardboard strips with "yes" or "true" on one end and "no" or "false" on the other end for each student to hold up in response to questions or statements. Other applications for cardboard strips include the following:

1 "Long" and "short" to indicate the vowel sound
2 Two strips with "add," "subtract," "multiply," or "divide" to show the appropriate mathematical process
3 "Fact" or "opinion" to indicate the truth of a statement
4 "Vertebrate" or "invertebrate" to indicate the type of animal

Divergent questions encourage reflection and discovery.

5 "Acid" or "base" for the appropriate chemical property
6 "Deciduous" or "evergreen" to indicate the type of tree
7 "Before" or "after" to show the place of an event in history

Although this technique affords full student participation and offers a fast-paced review, it does not allow for thoughtful responses.

It is not easy to ask good questions. Write down in advance some questions designed to achieve certain purposes. Phrase them simply and clearly so students will know exactly what you want. Don't be afraid to include a question for which you don't know the answer—you and the students can seek it together. As the session progresses, you may find yourself discarding your prepared list and asking spontaneous questions that arise from student responses.

The types of questions you ask determine the kind of thinking your students will learn to do. Include diverse types of questions, stressing critical-creative thinking and avoiding questions with "yes" or "no" answers in most cases. Table 6–1 lists purposes for various types of questions and words or phrases to use to begin appropriate questions that meet these purposes. Activity 6.4 helps you know the kinds of questions you ask.

Asking questions is only half the process; the other half is knowing how to respond. Give your students plenty of time to answer—at least three seconds or more. Wait-time encourages more students to consider the answer, to grope and ponder, and to think through the question. Don't rush on after an answer has been given, but leave the door open for other students to express their views. Extend a thought by asking "Are you sure?" and "How do you know?" Be willing to accept reasonable answers even if they don't agree with your interpretations.

One aim of a good questioning session is to let students ask questions of you and each other. Foster this purpose by setting an accepting, noncritical classroom atmosphere in which honest questions, no matter how silly they seem, are welcome. Students may ask you something you don't know. Don't be afraid to admit that you don't know the answer, but encourage them to join you in finding the answer. A really productive questioning session involves a lively exchange of ideas in an effort to reach a logical and satisfying conclusion.

You can use questions to promote convergent or divergent thinking. When things converge, they come to a point. When they diverge, they go off in many

TABLE 6–1 Questions and How to Begin Them

Purpose	Questions
If you want to:	Ask questions that begin with:
Assess knowledge	Define, Describe, Tell, List, Who, When, Where, Identify
Check understanding	Compare, Contrast, Explain the relationships, How do you know
Help analyze problems	How, Why, What procedures, What causes, What steps in the process
Lead students to explore values	Why do you feel, What is important, Why do you prefer
Promote creative thinking	How else, What if, Just suppose, Create a new, Design an original
Help evaluate situations	Judge the following, Select, Evaluate the result, Rate as to good or bad
Show how to apply knowledge	Demonstrate, Show how to solve, Construct, Use the information to

directions. A convergent question is narrowly focused and usually has a single correct answer. An example of a convergent question is "Who was the first president of the United States?" If you use many convergent questions, you will be checking knowledge of facts, but you will not be helping your students think creatively or critically.

Divergent questions, on the other hand, challenge students to think of many possible solutions. These questions are the type used in reflective thinking or discovery inquiry. A good divergent question is "How many ways can we think of to help make our community more attractive?" You may want to begin a questioning session with divergent questions, then move toward more convergent questions as students approach a decision or reach a conclusion.

Deductive and Inductive Teaching

You should also be familiar with deductive and inductive teaching. Both types are useful, but a great deal of teaching is deductive. You can probably remember that many of your teachers told you rules and even made you memorize them; then you applied them, probably by completing workbook pages and worksheets. Most of the time, you didn't have a chance to discover for yourself; therefore, you have probably forgotten much of what you were taught. Here is an example of a deductive lesson on syllabication.

Deductive Lesson: Syllabication Say: "Today we are going to learn a new rule for dividing words into syllables. The rule states that whenever a word has two consonants with a vowel on either side, you divide the word between the two consonants. Here is an example. In the word *comfort*, we divide the word between the *m* and the *f*. Now I want you to divide the words on this worksheet into syllables." (See Figure 6–2 for a sample worksheet.) Say: "When you finish your worksheet, be sure you can say the rule that tells you how to divide these words into syllables."

WORKSHEET
Divide the following words into syllables:

butter   after   problem   hammer   sermon

FIGURE 6–2 Sample Syllabication Worksheet

Inductive teaching calls for an inquiring mind and leads students to make their own discoveries. It is based on the use of examples. By asking students questions about the examples or helping students form their own questions, you can guide them toward a solution. The discovery inquiry approach challenges students to think for themselves and pull together clues for discovering the answer. Students internalize what they discover for themselves; it becomes a part of them, and they aren't likely to forget it. An example of an inductive lesson follows. By using your ingenuity, you will be able to come up with other examples of inductive lessons that are pertinent for your class.

Inductive Lesson: Syllabication   Say: "Sometimes we need to divide words into syllables. How do we know where to divide them? Look at these examples on the board."

but/ter   af/ter   prob/lem   ham/mer   ser/mon

"How many syllables are in each word?"
"What do you think the slash mark means?"
"What do you notice about the position of the slash mark in each word in relation to consonants and vowels?"
"Does it make any difference whether the two consonants in the middle of the word are alike or different?"
"Can you give me a rule that tells where to divide words into syllables? Using this rule, can you divide these words into syllables?"

suppose   sister   content   channel   blunder

Programmed Instruction

Programmed instruction is implemented through many types and combinations of media. It may be administered through workbooks, teaching machines, or computers. (See Chapter 3 for information on computer-assisted instruction.) Programs are either *linear* or *branching*. Linear programs consist of a series of small steps in the development of a skill or concept, with frequent provisions for student responses. These programs are easy to use and provide good practice in areas such as spelling and word recognition, math problems, and literal translations of foreign words. Linear programs allow for only one "right" answer, however, and do not provide for creative thinking.

Branching programs are much more complex. Students answer multiple-choice questions, and each answer determines what question they see next. If the student answers incorrectly, he or she leaves the main line of the program and is branched to a track where the concept is retaught. When the student is able to answer the questions on the branched track correctly, he or she returns to the main line to continue the work. With branching programs, a student selects answers and moves to the next step based upon his or her answer.

If you plan to use computer programs for skill practice, you will need to evaluate the software carefully in order to choose programs that give clear directions and are "user friendly." The software you select should offer practice on skills related to classwork at levels of difficulty appropriate for your students. Programs should be interesting enough to sustain attention, and they should provide immediate feedback.

The effectiveness of programmed instruction depends on how you use it. You should not grade programmed materials, but use them simply for providing practice in skills that will be tested later. Don't expect programmed instruction to be the total instructional program; it should be used along with other learning activities. While students are engaged in programmed learning, you need to check their progress and help them with any difficulties they may be having.

Activity 6.4   Types of Questions

Tape record one of your discussion or question-answer lessons. Play back the tape and write down the questions you asked. Listen for the opening words of each question, and identify the purpose for the type of question you asked (see Table 6–1). Count the number of questions for each category and fill in the second column for each of the purposes listed below.

Purpose	Number of Questions
1 Assess knowledge	
2 Check understanding	
3 Help analyze problems	
4 Lead students to explore values	
5 Promote creative thinking	
6 Help evaluate situations	
7 Show how to apply knowledge	

Look at the numbers of questions for each purpose and find out what purposes you are meeting with the questions you ask. Consider whether you are selecting your questions to meet just one or two purposes or covering a wide variety of purposes. Are there any types of questions you should add? Do your types of questions relate to your instructional goals? Write a statement about your use of questions and any changes you might make.

The Case Method

The case method is suitable for training young people to analyze real-life situations. Case study allows students to extend and apply information from their textbooks. To discuss the issues of each case, the students also must pull together knowledge from different subject areas. The case method encourages them to think critically and acquaints them with problem-solving techniques.

Cases are built around problem situations. They describe actual problems and supply facts related to the situations. Some cases may be open-ended, with no solution given; others may be closed, with one solution or several alternate solutions. The incident case, a short, three- to five-paragraph description of a situation, is more appropriate for young students than the more complex case studies used at the college level. Some of the vignettes and case studies in this book could be used as incident cases. The case method is appropriate for almost any subject area, but is particularly effective in history, economics, sociology, psychology, and business courses.

If you want to try the case method with your students, first select a fairly simple situation that will interest them, such as the development of a well-known fast-food franchise or the promotion of a famous rock star. Then learn all you can about the subject. Draw up a set of questions that will lead students to define the problem, analyze different aspects of it, reach one or more possible solutions, and evaluate the possible consequences of their conclusions. You can start with a simple case that can be completed in one class period, then work up to a more complicated case that could last for several days.

Programs for skill practice should be interesting and provide immediate feedback.

As the teacher, you must play an active role in presenting and developing an incident case. Lively discussion is the key to learning through this method. You must be knowledgeable about all aspects of the subject so you can supply additional information as the students begin asking questions about the case. After students have arrived at a tentative solution, you may need to offer alternate proposals to stimulate further critical analysis of the problem. You should guide the class in making a decision based on facts rather than personal prejudices or hunches. Finally, you will need to help the students evaluate their decision and look at its long-range implications.

DISCUSSION QUESTIONS

1 How can you involve your students more in your lessons? What kinds of responsibilities can they assume?
2 Are you motivated to be a good teacher? What motivates you to do your best? Is your motivation primarily intrinsic or extrinsic? Explain your answer.
3 Select a student in your class who appears to be unmotivated. What are some ways you might try to motivate her or him? Looking back through this chapter, can you find some strategies that might work with this student?
4 How would you assign homework so that it relates to what you are studying but doesn't involve the use of textbooks? Can you design it so that it requires problem-solving or creative-thinking skills?
5 Select a goal that you and your students would like to achieve. From Table 6–1, find the purpose that most closely relates to that goal. Can you compose a set of questions appropriate for reaching your goal?
6 Why are schemata important for understanding topics presented in school? What schemata are directly related to the next unit you plan to teach? How will you enrich the experiences of students who may be deficient in their knowledge of essential concepts?
7 What are some characteristics of your preferred learning style? What indications of differences in learning styles do you see among your students? What are some ways that you might accommodate these differences?
8 What are some lessons in which you could use the every-pupil-response technique for answering questions? How would you implement this technique?
9 What kinds of homework could you assign that would extend learning through group work on long-term projects? How would such assignments benefit the students?

SELECTED REFERENCES

Bennett, William J. *What Works*. Washington, D.C.: United States Department of Education, 1986.
Cornett, Claudia E. *What You Should Know about Teaching and Learning Styles*. Bloomington, Ind.: Phi Delta Kappa Educational Foundation, 1983.
Dillon, J. T. "Research on Questioning and Discussion." *Educational Leadership* 42 (November 1984): 50–56.
Dillon, J. T. *Teaching and the Art of Questioning*. Bloomington, Ind.: Phi Delta Kappa Educational Foundation, 1983.
Drayer, Adam M. *Problems in Middle and High School Teaching*. Boston: Allyn and Bacon, 1979.
Dunn, Kenneth, and Rita Dunn. "Dispelling Outmoded Beliefs about Student Learning." *Educational Leadership* 44 (March 1987): 55–62.
England, David A., and Joannis K. Flatley. *Homework—And Why*. Bloomington, Ind.: Phi Delta Kappa Educational Foundation, 1985.

Gall, Meredith. "Synthesis of Research on Teachers' Questioning." *Educational Leadership* 42 (November 1984): 40–47.

Harste, Jerome, Kathy Short, and Carolyn Burke. *Creating Classrooms for Authors: The Reading-Writing Connection.* Portsmouth, N.H.: Heinemann, 1988.

Kourilsky, Marilyn, and Lory Quaranta. *Effective Teaching.* Glenview, Ill.: Scott, Foresman, 1987.

Pearson, P. David, and Rand Spiro. "The New Buzz Word in Reading Is Schema." *Instructor* 91 (May 1982): 46–48.

Stewart, William, ed. *How to Involve the Student in Classroom Decision Making.* Saratoga, Calif.: R & E Publishers, 1985.

Strother, Deborah B. "Homework: Too Much, Just Right, or Not Enough?" *Phi Delta Kappan* 65 (February 1984): 423–25.

7

Language, Thinking, and Learning across the Curriculum

Ms. Jamison, the student teacher in a fifth-grade class, had assigned each class member to write a report on a famous historical figure. As a first step in collecting information, class members were to check encyclopedia accounts and seek additional information. Ricky had been asked to report on James Otis.

Ricky: Ms. Jamison, James Otis isn't in the encyclopedia. I checked all three sets.

Ms. Jamison (puzzled): I'm sure you just overlooked his name, Ricky. I know it is there.

Ricky: No, it's not. I'm sure.

Ms. Jamison (suddenly realizing what she should do): Let's go to the encyclopedia together, and you can show me how you looked for his name.

Ricky (walking toward the reference books): Okay. Oh! I can't show you now. All the *J* encyclopedias are being used.

Ms. Jamison: Why did you look under *J*?

Ricky: His name starts with a *J*.

Ms. Jamison: It's his first name that starts with a *J*. In the encyclopedia, people's names are alphabetized according to their last names. That's why you couldn't find James Otis in the *J* encyclopedia. You should have looked for Otis in the *O* encyclopedia. Nobody is using the *O* encyclopedia now. Why don't you try it while I watch?

Ricky (picking up the encyclopedia): Okay. Let's see. Here it is—Otis, James! Thank you, Ms. Jamison.

At this point Ms. Jamison notices that several students seem to be wandering around aimlessly. Several are scanning books in the biography section. The section near the card catalog is strangely empty.

Ms. Jamison: Bryan, what are you doing?

Bryan: Looking for a book on Thomas Jefferson. I've already used the encyclopedia.

Ms. Jamison: Did you try the card catalog?

Bryan: No. Where is it?

Ms. Jamison (pointing): Over by the wall.

Bryan: There aren't books in those drawers, are there?

Ms. Jamison (feeling frustrated): Jana, can you show Bryan how to use the card catalog?

Jana: What is it?

Ms. Jamison (raising her voice): How many of you have checked the card catalog? (three hands) How many of you know how to use the card catalog? (eight hands)

Ms. Jamison (walking toward the card catalog): Please come over here with me for a few minutes, class. . . .

1. What assumption had Ms. Jamison made about the students' research skills when she assigned the lesson? Was it valid? Why do you say so?
2. What might you do before making an assignment like this one to avoid a similar occurrence in your class?
3. Have students always mastered the study skills they have had presented in class?

LANGUAGE SKILLS

Language skills are vital to your students' success in all curricular areas. If you are an elementary grade teacher, you will have a special period devoted to language arts instruction, during which you will teach listening, speaking, reading, and writing skills. Secondary English teachers will also be expected to include these skill areas in their instruction. Simply focusing on these skills in a separate period is not sufficient for their complete assimilation, however. Language skills are used daily in all classes. Elementary teachers should help students apply language skills throughout the day as the students read to complete assignments, give and listen to oral reports, participate in discussions, and complete written assignments. Secondary teachers of content areas other than English should try to reinforce language skills as they are needed for assignments.

Reading Proficiency and School Assignments

Students are expected to learn much content from their textbooks and other supplementary printed materials. Often, however, the textbooks chosen for use in particular classes are too difficult for many of the students to handle with ease. It is important for you, as the instructional leader, to be aware of the difficulty of the materials the students are asked to read and to provide appropriate alternate materials for students who cannot handle the standard assignments. You may wish to check the difficulty levels of the textbooks and supplementary reading materials with a readability formula. The Fry Readability Graph (Figure 7–1) is a relatively quick and easy formula to use. Estimates of students' reading proficiency can be obtained from the results of informal or formal tests. With a knowledge of the approximate difficulty levels of the materials and the approximate reading levels of your students, you can attempt to match students to appropriate reading material more effectively.

Reading assignments may be adjusted for students who are unable to read the text or other assignments by providing those students with easier texts or materials that cover the same topics or by rewriting key passages at easier reading levels for their use. It is also possible for you to tape—or have a good reader from the class

Teachers should be prepared to help students apply their language skills as they read and complete written and oral assignments.

tape—the assignments and make the tapes available to poor readers to listen to as they "read" the assignments. By following along in their books as they listen, they should pick up some of the key terms and add them to their sight vocabularies, easing the reading of further assignments in this subject area.

If you want to promote comprehension of reading assignments that you make, give students purposes for the reading. Purpose questions help students focus on important information and promote comprehension and retention of the material, but remember that good purposes will be of no value if assignments are too difficult for the students to handle.

You can also enhance reading comprehension by building background for reading assignments that you are about to make. Class discussions, films or videotapes, filmstrips, pictures, computer simulations, and class demonstrations can all provide background concepts that will make understanding the reading assignment easier. Introduction of new vocabulary terms related to the concepts at this point can help students acquire the information in the assignment more readily. This approach

FIGURE 7–1   Graph of Estimating Readability—Extended*
Average number of syllables per 100 words

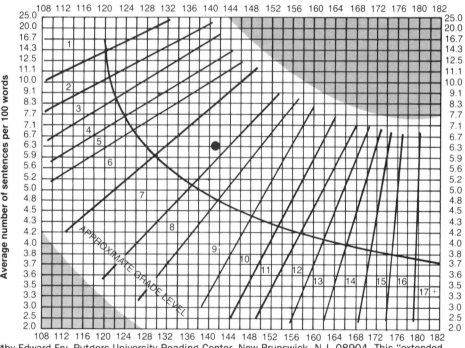

*by Edward Fry, Rutgers University Reading Center, New Brunswick, N.J. 08904. This "extended graph" does not outmode or render the earlier (1968) version inoperative or inaccurate; it is an extension. (Reproduction permitted, no copyright)

1. Randomly select 3 sample passages and count out exactly 100 words each, beginning with the beginning of a sentence. Do count proper nouns, initializations, and numerals.
2. Count the number of sentences in the 100 words, estimating length of the fraction of the last sentence to the nearest one-tenth.
3. Count the total number of syllables in the 100-word passage. If you don't have a hand counter available, an easy way is to simply put a mark above every syllable over one in each word; when you get to the end of the passage, count the number of marks and add 100.
4. Enter on graph the *average* sentence length and *average* number of syllables; plot dot where the two lines intersect. Area where dot is plotted will give you the approximate grade level.
5. If a great deal of variability is found in syllable count or sentence count, putting more samples into the average is desirable.
6. A word is defined as a group of symbols with a space on either side; thus, *Joe, IRA, 1945,* and & are each one word.
7. A syllable is defined as a phonetic syllable. Generally, there are as many syllables as vowel sounds. For example, *stopped* is one syllable and *wanted* is two syllables. When counting syllables for numerals and initializations, count one syllable for each symbol. For example, *1945* is four syllables, *IRA* is three syllables, and & is one syllable.

works because vocabulary terms are labels for the concepts that are presented, and knowing the proper labels makes discussion of the concepts easier.

Writing across the Curriculum

Writing is a skill that is also used in every curricular area. In English and language arts classes, students are taught how to write effectively, but in all classes writing provides an effective technique for learning. You should take advantage of this technique in your classes. Although you will focus upon composition skills and mechanics of writing if you are an English teacher, you should be willing to employ some writing assignments that are primarily designed to help students learn other things that you are teaching. If you teach another content area subject, you may not find it quite as difficult to ignore split infinitives and comma splices occasionally in favor of focusing exclusively upon the student's message. Of course, if the message is obscured by the poor mechanics, a teachable moment for this skill area exists. Students will not succeed in many future endeavors if their writing skills are not sufficient for clear communication.

Some of the ways to use writing as a tool for learning in different curricular areas include having students write summaries of class lectures, which can sometimes be shared with the class and revised as needed; explanations of new concepts presented in the textbook or in class; descriptions of processes being studied; reactions to curricular material; and applications for ideas presented in class. In a literature class the students might be asked to write imaginative newspaper accounts of happenings in a novel they are reading, character sketches of major characters, or diary entries that a character might have written. In a science course students might be asked to write up the results of an experiment, compose an essay about the impact of a scientific discovery on society, or trace the development of an area of technology over a specified period of time. In a social studies class students might be asked to produce imaginary letters from one historical character to another, written reactions to the actions of a historical character, or written explanations about the causes of certain historical events. In a physical education class students might be asked to write directions for a sports activity or an exercise or write about the benefits of an exercise program. In art and music classes students might be asked to write descriptions of techniques or reactions to paintings, sculptures, and compositions. In home economics classes students might be asked to write case studies related to child care techniques or nutritional practices, or write about advantages and disadvantages of certain home management practices.

There is no area in which writing opportunities are not abundant, and these activities can help students organize the knowledge they possess about topics, as well as clarify their feelings about these areas. Having students write about their studies gives you a chance to see each student's current level of understanding of the topics and allows you to plan instruction to overcome misconceptions. The writing activities also make students more aware of what they already know and what they need to find out. Personal journals, which may be read by others only at the invitation of the students who produced them, may allow students to explore their feelings and clarify their personal beliefs.

Consider possible writing activities as you plan each lesson. Think about possible benefits of each activity, and choose judiciously. These activities—if they are handled well—can offer dividends in initial learning and retention and may even improve attitudes toward the area of study. Complete Activity 7.1 to help you analyze your use of writing in your classes.

Literature across the Curriculum

Literature is often relegated to English class alone, especially in secondary schools. Many teachers have found, however, that literature can enrich other curricular areas

Activity 7.1   Writing across the Curriculum

Place a check mark (√) before the writing activities that you have used or intend to use in your class or classes. After you have tried each activity, place a plus (+) after the activity if it worked well or a minus (−) after the activity if it was not successful in meeting your goals.

_____ Summaries of class lectures _____

_____ Summaries of textbook readings _____

_____ Summaries of outside reading assignments _____

_____ Explanations of new concepts _____

_____ Descriptions of processes being studied _____

_____ Reactions to material in the textbook or presented in class _____

_____ Applications of ideas presented in class or in the textbook _____

_____ Newspaper accounts based on material read _____

_____ Character sketches of real or fictional characters _____

_____ Diary entries that real or fictional characters might have written _____

_____ Results of experiments _____

_____ Explanation of impact on society of a scientific discovery or political action _____

_____ Account of the development of an area of technology over a period of time _____

_____ Imaginary letters from one historical or fictional character to another _____

_____ Written reactions to the actions of one historical or fictional character _____

_____ Written explanations about the causes of historical events _____

_____ Written directions for a game or other activity _____

_____ Explanation of benefits of an exercise program or particular diet _____

_____ Written description of an artistic technique _____

_____ Written reactions to works of art _____

_____ Case studies _____

_____ Personal journals _____

_____ Other _____

Please describe:

_____ Other _____

Please describe:

_____ Other _____

Please describe:

as well. Integrating literature across the curriculum can be accomplished more easily in self-contained classroom situations, rather than departmentalized settings, but it can provide rewarding results for teachers in departmentalized settings who analyze its possibilities.

Social studies classes are a natural place to use literature to enrich the curriculum. Both fiction and nonfiction selections set in specific historical periods can make these times come alive for the readers. Many stories in books, for example, are set during wars, and they can help the students see how the wars affected the lives of the people in a way that history textbooks cannot. Similarly, stories in books that are set in a particular geographic region can add to the understanding of the material presented in a geography text. Books are also available that clarify lifestyles and occupations for readers. Biographies of important historical figures can make these people's contributions to civilization clearer, and books about people from diverse cultures can help students to understand themselves and others better.

Literature selections can also help students in science classes understand scientific concepts and obtain insight into the lives of inventors and innovators. Finding out the painstaking experimentation behind many scientific discoveries can put the textbook information in perspective. Reading books that focus upon a single aspect of science, such as the solar system, also can be helpful to students, since material in textbooks has often been condensed so much that its clarity has suffered. A book on a single topic has the space to elaborate and flesh out spare textbook discussions. Books that contain experiments for the students to perform allow hands-on experiences that promote motivation and understanding of concepts. Many books for young children highlight the cycles of the seasons and life cycles of plants and animals. Many newer books focus on conservation and the environment.

In physical education classes students may read books about the sports that they are playing or biographies of sports personalities. Both factual how-to-play books and fictional and factual stories about sports can add interest and motivation to these classes.

Even in mathematics classes, literature selections can be useful. Books are available for young children that emphasize counting, concepts of numbers, telling time, understanding calendars, learning about measurements, and comprehending size concepts. Older students may enjoy and learn from mathematical puzzle books.

Applications of literature selections in English classes are numerous. Literature selections can be used to study genres, characterization, plots, settings, themes, and writing styles. They can be used to promote literary appreciation, or they can serve as stimuli for writing. Comparisons and contrasts of literature selections can reveal information about genres, cultures, and points of view, among other things. An English class without literature would be unthinkable, but many uses of literature may not be included in English classes, if the teacher fails to examine the many possibilities that exist. Activity 7.2 gives you a chance to assess your use of literature in the class(es) that you teach.

Whole Language Theory and Applications

Following the lead of schools in other English-speaking countries around the world, many schools in the United States have begun to adopt a whole language, or holistic, philosophy. Depending on the area in which you live, classrooms you have observed, and lessons from your methods teachers, you may already be familiar with whole language theory. For some of you, however, a whole language philosophy may still be unclear.

It is important for you to know something about whole language so that you can choose the philosophy that supports your beliefs about teaching and learning. As long as you are student teaching, you may have to follow the procedures of your cooperating teacher, but knowing alternatives will enable you to implement the

FIGURE 7-2 Comparison of Whole Language Instruction and Skill-Based Instruction

Whole Language Instruction	Skill-Based Instruction
Learning from whole to part	Learning from part to whole
Student-centered	Teacher-directed
Natural learning (like home)	School learning (unlike home)
Discovery-based learning	Formal, systematic instruction
Flexible grouping for various purposes	More use of achievement or needs grouping
Student participation in planning	Teacher-planned lessons
Use of library books (without worksheets) for reading instruction	Primary reliance on basals and worksheets for reading instruction
Encouragement of risk taking	Insistence on correct work
Freedom to make choices	Teacher-selected activities
Some student self-evaluation	Teacher-only evaluation
Room filled with children's work	Teacher-designed environment (may be limited to perfect papers, commercial bulletin boards)

kinds of instruction that work best for you when you are in charge of your own classroom. Following is a list of basic concepts about whole language:

1 Writing and reading should be learned together in meaningful, purposeful, authentic situations.

2 Language is best learned with other children through cooperative learning and social interaction.

3 The curriculum is child-centered, focusing on students' interests and their active involvement.

4 The classroom environment includes walls covered with children's work, tables and shelves filled with books, and collections of reading and writing materials.

5 The curriculum is integrated, with reading, writing, and thinking skills being used in every subject.

6 Assessment includes teacher observation (kid-watching), portfolios, conferencing, and self-evaluation.

7 Whole language means learning from whole to part, not part to whole. (Example: Students learn reading skills by reading whole stories and discovering skills within the framework of a story instead of learning isolated skills and then applying the skills to story reading.)

8 Children learn to read and write naturally, as they learned to listen and speak. Reading and writing are a continuation of what they have already learned in the home instead of mastery of a series of skills.

9 Students spend a great deal of time each day in purposeful reading-writing activities.

10 Teachers hold high expectations for children and believe that they will succeed.

Whole language classrooms are more often found in elementary schools than in secondary schools. Whereas some schools may consistently follow a whole language view, in other schools some teachers have whole language classrooms and some are teaching traditionally. Many teachers consider themselves to be in the process of becoming whole language teachers and are implementing various whole language strategies while still adhering to some traditional methods. Figure 7-2 gives a comparison of some whole language instruction and some skill-based approaches.

Some teachers feel more comfortable in a skill-based, structured teaching situation, whereas other teachers prefer holistic classrooms. To find out which is likely to work best for you, complete Activity 7.3.

Activity 7.2   Literature across the Curriculum

List four literature selections related to a class or several classes that you are teaching. Note how the use of each of these selections could enrich the teaching of your class(es).

1. Class:

   Literature selection   **Usefulness**

2. Class:

   Literature selection   **Usefulness**

3. Class:

   Literature selection   **Usefulness**

4. Class:

   Literature selection   **Usefulness**

Activity 7.3 Aptitude for Whole Language versus Skill-Based Instruction

Respond to each of the following statements by writing *true* or *false*.

I believe . . .

1. _____ Students should help plan their curriculum.

2. _____ Teachers should place student work on bulletin boards even if it is not perfect.

3. _____ Students should participate in the evaluation of their own work.

4. _____ Reading and writing should be taught together.

5. _____ Students should be free to make some choices during the day.

6. _____ Students learn language best by experimenting with it, using it purposefully with others, and taking risks.

7. _____ Teachers should read aloud to children often.

8. _____ During most of the day, children should work together in flexible groups instead of working individually at their seats.

9. _____ When they read and write, children need real audiences to respond to them.

10. _____ Lots of good books are important for a reading program, as opposed to basal readers only.

11. _____ Language should be learned naturally in real situations instead of through the use of skill and drill.

12. _____ Most instruction should be informal.

13. _____ The emphasis in reading and writing should be on meaning.

14. _____ Reading instruction should begin with whole stories instead of isolated skills.

15. _____ Teachers should model the kind of behavior they expect from their students.

16. _____ Children can and should help each other learn.

17. _____ Children are capable of making reasonable decisions and taking responsibility for much of their own learning.

18. _____ The curriculum should be integrated around a topic or theme.

19. _____ Students should be involved in authentic reading-writing activities during much of the day.

20. _____ Teachers are facilitators of learning.

21. _____ Learning often occurs through discovery.

Each statement represents a whole language belief. In evaluating your aptitude for whole language teaching, count the number of *true* responses. If it exceeds the number of *false* responses, you are leaning toward the whole language philosophy.

HIGHER-ORDER THINKING SKILLS

The current interest in higher-order thinking skills in education is making many teachers aware of the need to help students learn how to think, not just recall information. Thought processes, including learning how to learn, are far more useful for dealing with life situations than knowledge of facts. In and of themselves, facts have little value, but a person trained in the use of thinking skills can act on knowledge of facts to solve problems, make decisions, and generate new ideas. Knowledge-level skills, such as recognition and recall, are not included in this discussion.

The rapid growth of interest in thinking skills recently has led to the development of several models for teaching thinking skills. Various educators have considered teaching thinking skills as (1) enrichment with thinking exercises added to the curriculum, (2) discrete skills to be taught directly as content (courses in logic or problem solving, for example), or (3) skills to be integrated with subjects across the curriculum. Most educators support the latter view because thinking skills then become a natural part of learning. Students not only learn information in each content area, but they also learn how to think about what they are learning.

A Framework

Higher-order thinking skills can be organized in many ways, but the framework for thinking skills in this handbook is relatively simple. It looks like this:

Higher-Order Thinking Skills

Inferential thinking
   Making inferences
   Generalizing and drawing conclusions
   Observing relationships

Creative thinking
   Synthesis
   Fluency and flexibility
   Imagination
   Originality

Critical thinking
   Analysis
   Evaluation

Combinations of thinking skills
   Problem solving
   Decision making

Before looking at ways to implement instruction in thinking skills, you need to understand the meanings of some of these terms. *Inferential thinking* means that the learner must put together clues in order to understand information that is not directly stated, but implied. *Generalizing* is the process of grasping an overall meaning or purpose from limited information, and *drawing conclusions* is making decisions based on evidence. *Observing relationships* is the mental ability to perceive similar or dissimilar features of ideas or objects. These relationships may be in the form of (1) *classifications* (ways of categorizing according to systems), (2) *comparisons and contrasts* (awareness of similarities and differences), or (3) *cause and effect* (observance of the relationships between actions and their consequences).

Critical thinking is the process of mentally acting on something that already exists by interpreting, analyzing, or evaluating it in some way. *Analysis* is the act of critically examining and/or reacting to something, and *evaluation* is the process of questioning and making judgments based on existing information.

Unlike inferential and critical thinking, which are reactions to existing ideas, *creative thinking* leads to the development of new and unusual ideas or products. *Synthesis*, like inventiveness, is the process of combining simple ideas or elements into larger concepts or products. In school, synthesis often occurs when students write stories or poems, collaborate on projects, find different solutions to problems, or express ideas or emotions in art. *Fluency* is the skill of generating many ideas, and *flexibility* is the creation of ideas that fit into many different systems or categories. *Imagination* enables the learner to create mental pictures or patterns of things that are not actually present, and *originality* is the ability to produce unique responses.

Some thinking processes, such as *problem solving* and *decision making,* are actually complex combinations of various types of thinking skills. Problem solving consists of several steps, including the following:

1 Identifying a problem
2 Obtaining information related to the problem
3 Forming hypotheses
4 Testing the hypotheses and forming a conclusion
5 Applying the solution and evaluating its effectiveness

Decision making is similar to problem solving, but it involves the following steps:

1 Identifying a goal
2 Collecting relevant data
3 Recognizing obstacles to reaching the goal
4 Identifying alternatives
5 Analyzing and ranking alternatives
6 Choosing the best alternative

You can integrate thinking skills with your teaching in every area of the curriculum from kindergarten through twelfth grade, but be aware that young children are limited in their ability to think abstractly. Not until the age of 10 or 11 are they able to deal successfully with abstract thought and concepts beyond their experiences. Therefore, in the lower grades you should teach the rudiments of various thinking skills by having youngsters manipulate concrete objects or apply these skills to what they already know and understand. In the middle grades students are better prepared for learning higher-order thinking skills because they are now capable of some degree of abstract reasoning and can think outside the realm of personal experiences. By the time they are in high school, students are capable of analyzing situations in greater depth, creating more complex thoughts and products, solving problems logically, making rational decisions, and evaluating concepts more critically.

If you consider thinking skills to be a high priority in your teaching, you may wish to establish the kind of classroom climate that is conducive to developing these skills. In order to do this, you need to show respect for your students by accepting their ideas and tolerating their mistakes. Listen to them, help them find alternatives, and show them that there may not be a single correct answer for every situation. Give them time to work through real problems, and provide opportunities to experiment with ideas and materials. Encourage your students by providing constructive feedback, and build their confidence by enabling them to succeed with simple tasks. Perhaps most important of all, learn to think and create along with them so that they can sometimes see you struggle and make mistakes, but then try again and eventually reach a conclusion.

Once you have decided to use thinking skills in your instruction, you will consciously need to structure activities and ask questions that cause students to think critically and creatively. On the next several pages you will find samples of activities for promoting thinking at different grade levels and in different content areas.

Inferential Thinking Activities

Two types of inferential thinking activities—classification and making inferences—are presented here with suggestions for using them at lower and upper grade levels. You should be able to think of other possibilities as you plan your lessons and units.

Classification   Classification is the process of organizing items or concepts with similar features into categories. In classifying, you first scan the material to get a general impression, then select a characteristic common to more than one item, and finally group together items that share this feature. (Some items may fit logically into more than one category.) You repeat this process until you categorize all of the items to be considered. Classifying is based on making comparisons and is one of several ways to see relationships and make meaningful connections.

Children who begin to classify at an early age might group objects with common characteristics together, while slightly older children might categorize pictures that have been cut from magazines or catalogs. Still older students might classify words, concepts, literary works, or artistic masterpieces according to common features. At whatever level students are working, it is important for them to give reasons for their classifications. In order to clarify their thinking and justify their choices of categories, students need to explain the relationships they perceive.

Suppose you give an envelope of pictures of the following items to a group of second graders and ask them to group the pictures that belong together. The children will probably consider many possibilities and find that some items could be placed in more than one category. Likely categories are given immediately following the items.

Items

set of drums	toy box
chalkboard	computer
television set	stove
box of cheese	doll carriage
chair	roller skates
tape player	lawn mower
recipe book	harmonica

Possible Classifications

Things with wheels—lawn mower, roller skates, doll carriage

Food-related items—box of cheese, stove, recipe book

Toys—doll carriage, set of drums, harmonica, toy box, roller skates, chalkboard

Household furnishings—stove, chair, television set, tape player, computer, toy box

Electronics—television set, computer, tape player, stove

Music—set of drums, tape player, harmonica

Things for reading and writing—computer, recipe book, chalkboard

Given the following words to classify for a social studies lesson, high school students might group them according to the classifications that follow the list of words.

Words

creativity	newspapers
corruption	propaganda
politics	starvation
freedom	honesty
leadership	books
crime	people

Possible Classifications

Sources of information—newspapers, books, people, propaganda

Personal attributes—honesty, leadership, creativity

Negative social issues—crime, starvation, corruption

Features of government—freedom, politics, propaganda, corruption, leadership, people

Education—people, leadership, freedom, creativity, newspapers, books

You can use classification skills as you teach subjects in any area of the curriculum. Some types of classification activities are:

Math—Group objects, pictures, or line drawings by classifications of geometric shapes.

Science—Classify animals according to various attributes.

Political science—Categorize types of governments by salient features.

Music—Classify musical recordings by such types as country, rock, classical, big band, and gospel.

Art—Classify works of art according to their historical periods.

Literature—Group literary works by genre, author's style, or some other characteristic.

Geography—Classify cities by the continents where they are located.

History—Make categories of great people through history (e.g., military leaders, philosophers, artists, heads of state, scientists, and religious leaders).

Making Inferences   Making inferences calls for the ability to observe clues and use them to get implied meanings. It involves thought processes that are similar to those used in drawing conclusions, making predictions, and making generalizations. When you read a murder mystery, you look for clues in order to determine who did it. If you want to know if someone likes you, you watch for behavioral clues, such as a wink or a shared smile. Frequently, the information you need is not clearly given, so you have to "read between the lines" and then make reasonable assumptions as to the full meaning. Making inferences is an important skill for critical reading and thinking, but students often have a great deal of difficulty learning to use it.

One technique you can use when teaching inferences is the "grab bag" approach in which you give a bag of objects to a group of students. The objects can be readily available materials that you may have around your home. Students read the directions on the bag and create a story from the objects by making inferences about the objects' relationships to each other. You can use sets of pictures or sets of words and phrases, as well as sets of objects, to teach students to infer. Examples follow.

Grab Bag #1

Contents—an old wallet with three pennies, a "help wanted" ad asking for someone to deliver papers, a handwritten note that says "Do you know anybody who wants firewood for this winter?" and an ad from a catalog with a stereo system circled

Directions—Someone has a problem. Can you figure out what the problem is from these clues?

Possible answer—A young person wants to earn money to buy a stereo system.

Grab Bag #2

Contents—family photograph, receipt from a store in Greeneville, a page ripped out of a telephone directory with a moving company circled, a real estate page from a Spring City newspaper with checks beside three house ads

Directions—Look at all of these items, and give as many details as you can about what you think is happening.

Possible answer—A family is moving from Greeneville to Spring City. (Many details can be added.)

Grab Bag #3

Contents—airline schedule with a flight circled from Los Angeles to Monterrey, Mexico; a Canadian nickel; a golf tee; a tube of skin ointment; a stick of name brand chewing gum; a pack of matches from a barber shop in Los Angeles

Directions—Pretend you are a detective. A crime has been committed, and you find these objects near the site of the crime. What clues can you use that might lead you to the criminal?

Possible answer—Check the golf courses near Monterrey, Mexico, for a Canadian male with a skin problem who chews gum.

It is important for students to understand *how* they made inferences from the clues in order to transfer this thinking skill to other learning tasks. Students need to use the same thought processes for making inferences with word clues in reading as they used for making inferences from objects. Having students underline word clues in reading selections is a good way to help them make inferences in their reading.

Critical Thinking Activities: Recognizing Propaganda

One way to develop critical thinking skills is by teaching students to recognize propaganda, a form of persuasion that is intended to influence the audience by the use of exaggerations and emotional appeals. Both you and the students can enjoy this activity as you look for examples of propaganda that are readily found in political promotions and product advertisements. If you are teaching during a political campaign, you can find brochures and newspaper articles to bring to class, or you may wish to videotape messages by the candidates and play them during class. In order to choose the best candidate, students should critically analyze material for evidence of misleading statements, biased or one-sided reports, false assumptions, avoidance of issues, exaggerated statements, and emotional appeals.

Advertising contains a great deal of propaganda, and you can obtain samples from newspapers, magazines, and television. Some types of propaganda are name calling (using negative words to produce an undesirable effect), transfer (associating a worthy concept with a product), testimonial (having a celebrity endorse a product), plain folks (identifying with ordinary people), and band wagon (accepting something because everyone else does).

Some suggested propaganda-detection activities that will help stimulate students to think critically include having the students:

1 Distinguish between advertisements that simply make emotional appeals and those that give information.
2 Find examples of propaganda techniques, and make displays of them.
3 Learn to recognize "emotional" words by circling them as they appear.
4 Look for examples of exaggerations, emotional appeals, and propaganda techniques for a type of product or service in which the students are particularly interested (e.g., films or videotapes).
5 Compare ads that are for the same products, such as cereals or motorcycles, but produced by different companies. Tell students to look for use of fact versus opinion, propaganda techniques, and emotional appeals.

Creative Thinking Activities

For the following activities, students will need to use creative thinking skills. Brainstorming requires students to think fluently as they generate many ideas and flexibly as they think of divergent ideas. Their responses to brainstorming situations are often original or unique. In simulation, role playing, and creative dramatics, students need to use their imaginations to project themselves into situations that differ in some respect from their own experiences. You can use these and other creative activities to encourage children to use higher-order thinking skills.

Brainstorming

Brainstorming can be used to develop creative thinking at any grade level. Students are given a real or imaginary problem and asked to think of as many ways as they can to solve it. You will probably have to direct the activity yourself the first time you try it, but later a student can lead it.

Here's how it works. First, identify a *specific* problem, one that is limited in scope. Then divide the class into groups of six to ten students. Appoint a recorder for each group to write down the ideas. Brainstorming sessions are brief and are usually most productive in the morning. You may want to ask students to meet again the following day for additional "afterthoughts" and to select those ideas that are worth following up.

Students must understand how the session will be conducted before they start brainstorming. Tell them to think of as many ideas as they can, the wilder the better. They should build on the ideas of others, combining and modifying what other students suggest. They can offer only one idea at a time, and only one person can speak at a time. Most important of all, there must be no criticism of any ideas during the session. You may ask anyone who criticizes or ridicules someone's idea to leave the group, because such criticism destroys creative thinking.

You may want to use brainstorming to solve real problems, or you may want to use fantasy situations simply to promote creative thinking. Here are suggested topics for both types of brainstorming sessions:

Realistic Situations

1 What are some things we can do to make our classroom more attractive?
2 How can we become more considerate of Jorge? (Conduct session on a day when Jorge, a student with a disability, is absent.)
3 How can we show our appreciation to the parents who have given us parties and helped in our classroom during the year?
4 How can we prevent a group of ninth-grade bullies from picking on the seventh graders?

Fantasy Situations

1 What would happen if we learned to create energy from sand?
2 In what ways are a steam engine and a chain saw alike?
3 How many ways are there to kill a mosquito?
4 How many ways could you change a bicycle to make it more fun to ride?
5 What would be different if you woke up one morning and discovered that it was a hundred years from now?

Simulation

An interesting way to involve your students in real-life situations is through simulation activities. In simulation, a realistic situation is created in which students play various roles or act out scientific processes. It is a "learning by doing" activity. By acting out a situation, students come to understand what processes are involved and how problems are solved.

Simulation offers many advantages over textbook learning, but it has disadvantages, too. You will find that most students are enthusiastic about participating in simulation and are highly motivated to learn all they can about the roles they are playing. They are using high-level communication skills and thinking creatively. They need freedom to move around and negotiate with each other, though, so your classroom may become noisy and disorderly at times. Some students may remain on the fringe of the activity and not get the full benefit of the experience. The entire simulation can be a waste of time unless the experience and the follow-up discussions are skillfully directed.

If you decide to try simulation, your first problem will be to locate an activity appropriate for the students' age level, the time available, and the lesson topic. You may want to use computer simulations or commercial games similar to Monopoly that require students to think about what they are learning. Many simulations involve students in realistic situations that cause them to make decisions and solve problems related to content area materials. They provide opportunities for students to learn by discovery and to apply their knowledge to actual situations. Some computer simulations deal with running a lemonade stand, investigating underwater ecology, and traveling the Oregon Trail during pioneer days.

You may wish instead to plan an activity yourself. In this case, you need to become thoroughly familiar with the activity, preferably by trying it out first with some of your friends. When you present it to the class, give the directions simply and clearly. At the close of the activity, be prepared to lead a discussion based on the students' experiences. During the discussion, encourage students to express different points of view and explain their reasoning. Simulation may be followed with related assignments to reinforce and extend the learning experience.

Controversial subjects are often the subject of simulation activities. Conducting a political campaign followed by a mock election is an excellent way for students to understand political maneuvering and strategic campaigning, especially during an election year. Other simulations can deal with zoning decisions, race relations, profits and losses, and ecology. Students discover why people hold certain values and attitudes as they play out the roles they have assumed.

These are possible simulation activities:

1 You are a tiny seed planted in the ground. The sun is shining and makes you feel warm. Now the rain comes and helps you to grow. You become a small plant and push through the earth. You grow taller and stronger. The wind blows gently, and you move. A small bud forms on your stem. Slowly the bud opens, and you are a beautiful flower.

2 Five of you are being sent to an uninhabited island for two years to pass a survival test. You are allowed to take 10 things (not to exceed $100 in value) with you, besides the clothes you are wearing. What will you take? Why?

3 A spaceship lands in your neighborhood. Three crimson creatures emerge and let you know they want to stay in your community. Some concerned citizens call a meeting. Those at the meeting are the PTA president, a television agent, an environmentalist, a medical doctor, a civil rights representative, and a journalist. You must decide if the creatures can stay. If the answer is no, how will you persuade them to leave?

4 The city council is meeting to decide whether or not to legalize gambling to bring in more revenue. Members of the council include a minister, a businessperson connected with organized crime, a motel developer, an unemployed construction worker, an independently wealthy playboy, a young mother, a school teacher, a banker, and a farmer. Discuss your feelings about the proposal, and reach a decision.

5 A site location simulation is described in Figure 7–3.

Role Playing

Role playing is closely related to simulation. During role playing, a student assumes the role of another person in order to understand the other's feelings and attitudes. Role playing that involves solving problems is sometimes called *sociodrama*. Role playing can develop communication skills, creative thinking processes, and clarification of values.

FIGURE 7–3   Site Location Simulation

The Speedwheel Bicycle Manufacturing Co. wants to build a new plant. Members of the Site Selection Committee are meeting to select a desirable location. They are considering four sites. As members of the committee, discuss the advantages and disadvantages of each location, and reach a decision.

Criteria	City A	City B	City C	City D
General information	Population 90,000 Industrial part of a megalopolis	Population 450,000 State capital	Population 2,800 Isolated rural town	Population 25,000 Center of a generally rural area
Transportation facilities	On major tidal river, on major rail lines, near large metropolitan airport, on N–S interstate	On major railroad and interstate routes River running through city	On old E–W highway and railroad spur line Limited air service 30 miles away	On major N–S interstate and railroad freight line Small local airport
Tax situation	Extremely high taxes on individuals and industry	No state income tax Low municipal rates Adequate for services	High, progressive state income tax Heavy industrial taxes	Low tax rates No state income tax Inadequate for services
Labor force	Heavily unionized Poor productivity Highly skilled Adequate supply	Unskilled or semiskilled Chiefly nonunion Short supply	Heavily unionized with coal mining background Unskilled to highly skilled Adequate supply	Large supply of unskilled and semiskilled Unions active
Utilities	Electricity, water adequate; low supply of gas; all expensive	Low rates Abundant supplies	Adequate supplies High rates	Low-priced electricity Adequate supplies of natural gas and water
Plant sites available	Existing old factory sites available No open land	Six well-developed industrial parks Land reasonably priced	Hilly forestland available No industrial park Expensive	Two industrial parks Reasonably priced
City management	Expects kickbacks from industry	Generally favorable to recruiting industry	Inactive in industrial recruiting	Selective recruiting of industry
School system	Meets state standards Old buildings and outdated facilities	Quality varies, but generally adequate	Good-quality education Limited facilities	Good quality but low funding
Cultural activities	None in city, but full range available in adjacent cities	New Arts Center Symphony Orchestra Several universities	Nothing local Concert series and extension courses 30 miles away	University town Small orchestra Well-developed arts programs
Parks and recreation	Organized sports No local parks Eighty miles from ocean	Several city parks Lakes nearby	Good hunting, fishing Ski resort nearby	Lakes, waterfalls, and parks within an hour's drive, but not much locally

In directing role playing situations, you should observe certain guidelines. Encourage the players to speak distinctly and make their actions clear to the audience. Remind students who are not participating to be good listeners and not interrupt or carry on side conversations. When you choose students to play certain parts, assign them to play roles that are unlike their own personalities; for instance, let the well-mannered student be the class bully.

Usually, in role playing situations, two or more characters become involved in a conflict. There should be plenty of action and dialogue. The characters are led to a point where they must choose from among several possible courses of action. After students play the situation, you should discuss what took place and whether or not the problem was solved.

Role playing helps students see emotional situations clearly and objectively. In playing out a situation, they experience the emotions connected with it. Good subjects for role playing include conflicts on the playground, family disagreements, misuse of drugs, disobedience to rules, and peer relationships.

You can develop role playing situations from real life or create imaginary circumstances. Here are some suggestions:

Nick doesn't do his share—Mrs. Miller's ninth-grade class has been studying different systems of government. As their final project, the students have been divided into groups to make presentations. All students in each group will receive the same grade. Janie, Roger, Mel, Sandy, and Nick are investigating socialism. They agree to research certain aspects of socialism and combine their information into a final report. The day before the presentation is due, all the students are ready except Nick. When they ask him to do his part, he says he has a job after school and doesn't have time. The other four students are concerned that their presentation will be incomplete because Nick hasn't done his assignment.

What courses of action are open to the four students? What is the best way to resolve this problem?

A lucky find—Freda and Elena were following Mrs. Gomez, a wealthy widow, out of the grocery store one day. As she put her change back in her purse, a $10 bill drifted down. Mrs. Gomez didn't notice she had lost the money, but Freda and Elena saw the bill fall to the sidewalk. They looked at each other; then Freda walked over and picked it up. They had never had so much money at one time before. Freda started to catch up to Mrs. Gomez to return the money to her, but Elena put her hand on Freda's arm and stopped her.

What do they say to each other? What do they finally decide to do?

Creative Dramatics

Creative dramatics is similar to simulation and role playing, and you can use it effectively in the classroom for interpreting literature and reenacting episodes from history. Students can become totally involved in creative dramatics through their thinking, speaking, listening, movement, and imaginations. Therefore, they are more likely to understand and remember what they portray than if they were merely to read from a textbook or listen to a lecture.

The procedure for creative dramatics is fairly simple. You do not need props, settings, or scripts, but you do need some space. The students should become totally familiar with a story or historical event, including its sequence of action and the feelings of the characters. Sometimes students do additional research to learn more about the story. Then you choose students to play the parts. If there are not enough parts to go around, some students can be extra villagers or even animals. The students improvise the dialogue as the story unfolds. After the play is over, help them evaluate the performance by asking them what was good about the presentation and what could be done to improve it. Usually, half the class participates while the other half is the audience, and then the play is performed again with students reversing roles.

Almost any historical event can be dramatized. Here are some good scenes to try:

1 The signing of the Magna Carta or the Declaration of Independence
2 Encounters between Native Americans and the white settlers, including the first Thanksgiving
3 The arrival of the missionaries in Hawaii
4 The Boston Tea Party
5 The assassination of Lincoln or Kennedy

Some stories are better suited to dramatization than others, and in some cases you will want to dramatize just one or two scenes from a story. Most folktales move quickly, show conflict, and have strong characterizations. Scenes from Shakespeare's plays are also good sources for classroom creative dramatics. These are some other good selections, ranging from primary to secondary levels:

Ask Mr. Bear by Marjorie Flack (New York: Macmillan, 1932)

The Three Billy Goats Gruff by Asbjornsen and Moe (New York: Harcourt Brace Jovanovich, 1957)

Peddler and His Caps by Esphyr Slobodkina (New York: William R. Scott, 1947)

The Pied Piper of Hamelin by Robert Browning (New York: Scroll, 1970)

Stone Soup by Marcia Brown (New York: Scribner, 1947)

Anne Frank: The Diary of a Young Girl by Anne Frank (New York: Doubleday, 1967)

To Kill a Mockingbird by Harper Lee (Philadelphia: Lippincott, 1960)

The Pearl by John Steinbeck (New York: Viking, 1953)

The Glass Menagerie by Tennessee Williams (New York: Random House, 1945)

The Count of Monte Cristo by Alexandre Dumas (St. Louis: Webster, 1949)

Combinations of Thinking Skills

Students solve problems and make decisions every day, but seldom do they approach problem solving and decision making in logical, systematic ways. Both processes require the use of many different thinking skills, and examples of procedures and topics for each appear below.

Problem Solving   When introducing problem solving to your class, start by having the students identify a real problem. The following example for a fifth-grade class will help you understand the procedure.

Step 1. Identifying a problem—The children brainstorm several problems to solve, including ways to improve the food in the cafeteria, get better playground equipment, and eliminate homework on weekends. After some discussion, the students agree to solve the problem of wanting to take an end-of-year field trip, even though no funds are available for transportation. They decide they want to go to the Space Center and figure the approximate cost for hiring the school bus. The problem is that they need to find a way to get the money.

Step 2. Obtaining information related to the problem—Once again, the students brainstorm. This time they generate many ideas for getting money, including various ways of asking for it and earning it.

Step 3. Forming hypotheses—The students consider advantages and disadvantages to each option and check with persons in authority about the merits of each alternative. They make a list of several possibilities, discuss the practicality of each one, and choose the three best ideas.

Step 4. Testing the hypotheses and forming a conclusion—The three best possibilities are (1) asking the principal to take the money from a special fund,

(2) earning the money individually by doing chores at home, and (3) earning the money through a class project of writing a school newspaper and selling it. The students make inquiries about the special fund and find that it is only to be used for schoolwide projects, and they find that the parents of several of the students will not pay them for doing chores. The students check about the newspaper and find that, although they will have to pay for the paper, the school office will reproduce copies of the newspaper. They decide that if they can sell 300 copies for 25 cents each, they can cover the cost of the paper and have enough money for the trip. Therefore, they decide that writing a school paper is their best option.

Step 5. Applying the solution and evaluating its effectiveness — The students begin writing the paper and advertising it. Due to their enthusiasm for the project, everyone in the school wants a copy of the paper. When the paper is ready, the students sell 429 copies and have more than enough money for the trip. The solution was therefore satisfactory.

A similar process can be followed at almost any level, and it can be integrated with content areas. You will want to use fairly simple problem situations with fewer options for primary grades, such as rearranging the classroom to improve traffic patterns or finding ways to thank parent volunteers, but you will be able to deal with more complex situations in the upper grades.

You can use the following ideas for involving students in problem solving by telling the students to

1 Design an attractive display to fill a large empty space at the school entrance. (math, art)
2 Discover why plants die in the school library and correct the situation. (biology)
3 Survey the community to find volunteers and tutors. (social studies)
4 Find ways that the school can save money to alleviate the budget deficit. (math, business)
5 Find a solution to uneven heat distribution in the school. (physics)
6 Plan a physical fitness program for your school to raise the fitness of students to an acceptable level. (physical education)
7 Identify a problem in your school and find a way to solve it. (many possibilities, depending on type of problem)

Hypothetical Problem-Solving Situations

1 As community leaders, develop a plan to reduce unemployment in the area. (social studies)
2 As engineers, find practical alternatives for energy sources. (science)
3 As food service managers, plan a month of school cafeteria menus with food that is nutritious, delicious, attractive, and affordable. (health, home economics, business, math)
4 As curriculum designers, develop an annotated list of recommended reading for specific grade levels. (English, reading)
5 As architects, design a functional and aesthetically pleasing mall for your community. (art, math, business)
6 As directors of a cultural center, plan a series of concerts with famous performers that will offer a wide variety of good music to the citizens. (music)

Decision Making   Imagine that you have decided to work through the process of decision making, according to the steps given earlier, by helping your tenth-grade students decide on suitable careers. You might begin by discussing various career options and inviting a guidance counselor to answer questions about career opportunities. Then you could let individual students find out about educational requirements, advancement opportunities, employment prospects, salaries, job satisfaction, and other information for their chosen fields. The students should realistically as-

FIGURE 7−4   Sample Decision Tree

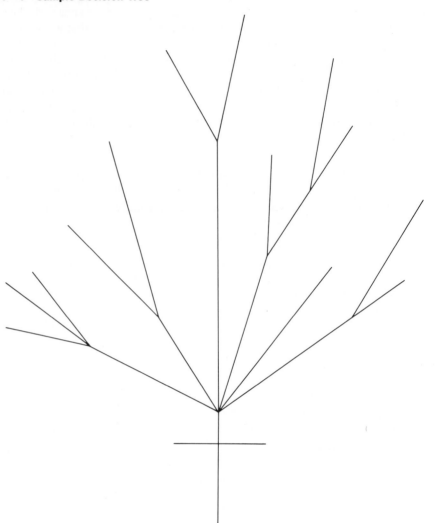

sess their likelihood of achieving success by examining such possible obstacles as financial resources, length of preparation time, access to specialized training, their current grade averages, geographical location, and parental support. For each potential obstacle they can find alternatives.

Now imagine that Bob, one of your students, has chosen a business career and has identified some obstacles to reaching it, including lack of education and lack of financial resources. As he identifies alternatives, he considers overcoming financial problems by getting a scholarship, working part-time, or getting a loan. He can overcome his lack of education by going to college full-time or part-time, or by going to night school. In ranking his alternatives, he finds that the most practical solution for him is to go to college part-time, work part-time, and take out a small loan.

You might help Bob and the other students analyze their options more carefully by teaching them to make decision trees, a way of graphically organizing their alternatives. The students might list their alternatives and then place them on blank "trees" that you have given them (see Figure 7−4), or they may wish to create their own trees. Bob's tree might look something like the one in Figure 7−5.

Some ideas to use with your students follow. You can simplify or expand these ideas to serve different ages, and you can integrate them with various content areas. Reading is necessary for nearly all of these ideas.

FIGURE 7–5   Decision Tree (Completed)

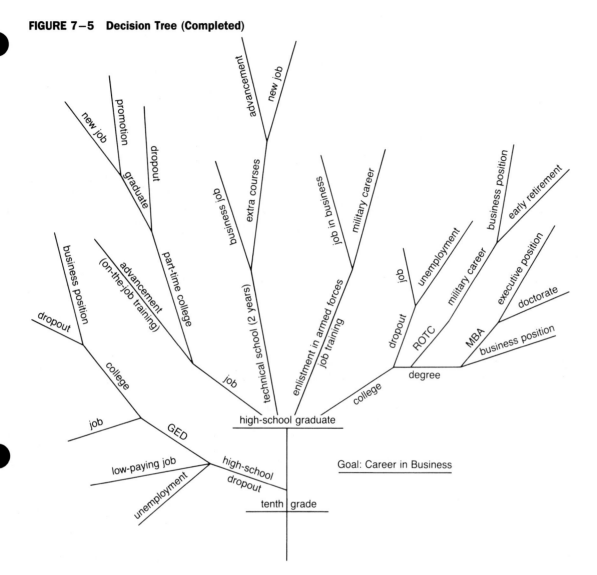

Decision-Making Goals

1 Identify the best political system in which to live. (social studies)

2 Decide which novelist (or scientist, philosopher, artist, musician, etc.) made the greatest contribution to literature (or the related field of study). (literature or any other subject)

3 Calculate the best form(s) of transportation (or the best routes) to take to reach various destinations. (math, geography)

4 Decide which car would be the best purchase for you or your parents. (math, social studies)

5 Decide which region of the world has the best climate in which to live. (geography, science)

6 Identify the best form of energy to use. (science)

7 Decide which animal has the best defense system. (biology)

8 Decide on the best way to catch a mouse. (science)

9 Decide on the best way to spend the $100 given to your class by the school. (math, social studies)

10 Identify the best language to use for worldwide communication. (language).

Complete Activity 7.4 to help you focus on your use of such activities.

STUDY SKILLS

In the vignette at the beginning of the chapter, Ms. Jamison faced difficulties in teaching a social studies class because the students had not mastered crucial study skills. Students at all levels and in all disciplines need to master a set of basic study skills that will enhance their abilities to learn from content area materials. It is, of course, beyond the scope of this book to teach you *how* to teach study skills; the purpose of this discussion is to make you aware of *what* the important study skills are, so that you will not fail to help your students acquire them. Don't assume that students have learned these skills simply because they have been previously exposed to them. Check to see—through pretests, oral questions, and observation of classroom performance—if the students have actually acquired them. Many students have been exposed to the skills, but the exposure has not "taken."

Location Skills

Starting with the problem posed by Ms. Jamison's class, you should first consider the study skill of locating information. To carry out many routine assignments in content classes, students need to be able to locate information in trade books (non-textbook reading materials), textbooks, and reference books, as well as to be able to locate the books in libraries.

If students are to use trade books and textbooks to best advantage, you must ensure that they understand how to use prefaces and/or introductions, tables of contents, indexes, appendixes, glossaries, footnotes, and bibliographies. Many students do not even know the functions of these book parts; therefore, their chances of using them effectively to locate information are poor. Before some students can use indexes and glossaries effectively, they may need instruction in the prerequisite skill of alphabetization. For use of the glossary, they may also need instruction in use of guide words and pronunciation keys and in choosing the meaning that fits the context. Some students also need instruction in identifying key words under which to look when using the index. You need to assess the students' knowledge of the skills they need for using trade books and textbooks, and offer information, instruction, and practice as necessary. Informal assessment measures will usually suffice. You can ask students to use each of the book parts and observe their performance, or you can ask them to explain the function of each part. Primary level students will be concerned only with tables of contents and, by second or third grade, glossaries. Intermediate level students should use all book parts, with the possible exception of the preface and/or introduction, and students in junior and senior high schools should use these parts as well.

Reference books call for a wide variety of skills. Knowledge of alphabetical order and the ability to use guide words are necessary for use of most reference books, especially encyclopedias and dictionaries. Most secondary level students have mastered the use of alphabetical order, which receives initial attention in first grade, but some will have difficulty with alphabetizing beyond the first letter. Many secondary students, however, still have trouble with use of guide words, although most have had repeated exposure to them since at least fourth grade. The ability to use cross references is particularly important for using an encyclopedia. Of course, for use of the dictionary, students need the same skills they need for use of a glossary, including ability to use pronunciation keys and to choose the meaning that fits the particular context. To use encyclopedias, students must be able to determine which volume of a set contains the information they seek, which was Ricky's problem at the beginning of this chapter. Encyclopedia users must also be able to determine key words under which they can find related information. To use atlases, students need to know how to interpret a map's legend and scale, and locate directions on a map.

Activity 7.4   Creative Thinking Activities

Examine the following list of creative thinking activities. Place a check mark (√) by the ones you have used in your class. Place a plus (+) by the ones you intend to use. Under each activity you have used or intend to use, briefly explain how you applied or plan to apply it in your class(es).

_____ Brainstorming

_____ Simulation

_____ Role playing

_____ Creative dramatics

_____ Problem solving

_____ Decision making

Reference books are often written on relatively high readability levels, considering the populations for which they are intended. Guard against assigning students to look up information in reference books with readability levels far above their reading abilities. Students will not learn from such assignments and are likely either to do nothing or merely copy from the reference book without understanding. These responses will not result in the learning outcomes you anticipated. Readability information on some reference books may already be available, but if it is not, you may wish to use a readability formula on selected portions of the books to estimate their levels of difficulty. The Fry Readability Graph (Figure 7–1) is a possible choice.

Even if students know how to use trade books, textbooks, and reference books effectively, they may not have an opportunity to do so because they do not know how to locate the books in the library. At the beginning of this chapter, Ms. Jamison gave a library assignment before assessing the students' ability to use the library facilities to best advantage. She at least recognized her error and began to try to rectify her mistake, but she had already essentially wasted a period of instruction that was irretrievable. A check-up on library knowledge *before* the class went to the library would have been in order. Areas in which students showed weaknesses — library arrangement (location of books and magazines, reference materials, and card catalog), Dewey Decimal System or Library of Congress System of shelving books, and use of the card catalog—could then have been given attention before the trip to the library or in the initial portion of the trip.

You could plan cooperatively with the librarian or media specialist to do initial teaching of library skills or to review them. He or she may have access to teaching aids of which you are not aware, such as special mini-card catalogs, posters on catalog cards and/or such topics as the Dewey Decimal System, films, or filmstrips. In addition, his or her high degree of familiarity with the library may have made the librarian or media specialist aware of potential uses you have overlooked. Consider this resource person, as all support personnel in the school, an ally in your teaching endeavor.

Organizational Skills

Organizational skills are highly important to students working on reports for content area classes. These skills include notetaking, outlining, and summarizing. They are most easily taught in conjunction with an assignment on report writing, since students can best see the need to learn them at such a time. These skills are usually not taught before the intermediate grade levels, but ordinarily receive attention then. Still, many secondary students have not mastered these skills, perhaps because they were never taught in a functional setting. If you are teaching above the primary level, you need to assess students' mastery of these skills and help them acquire the skills if they have not yet done so. Primary teachers lay the groundwork for these skills, especially outlining, when they help students determine main ideas and supporting details. They lay the groundwork for notetaking and summarizing especially, when they encourage students to paraphrase what they have just read.

Retention

A major goal of content area learning is retention of subject matter. Teaching students how to study so that they will retain what they read will be an important task for you. Here are some ways you can help students retain content, coded as to the appropriate levels: A = all levels, primary through secondary grades; I = intermediate grades; and S = secondary grades.

1 Have class discussions over all material you assign students to read. (A)
2 Encourage students to evaluate what they read. (A)
3 Give the students an opportunity to apply what they have read. (A)
4 Use audiovisual aids to illuminate concepts presented in the reading. (A)

5 Prepare students before they read by giving them background about the topic. (A)

6 Encourage students to picture in their minds what the author is trying to describe. (A)

7 Have students retell what they have read, in their own words, to you or a classmate soon after they finish reading. (A)

8 Always give students purposes for which to read. Never just say, "Read pages 2–9 for tomorrow." Tell them what to look for as they read. (A)

9 Teach your students a study method such as SQ3R[1], SQRQCQ[2], or EVOKER[3]. (I, S)

10 Encourage students to analyze the author's organization. (I, S)

11 Have students take notes on the main points in the material. (I, S)

12 Have students write summaries of the material after they finish reading. (I, S)

13 Hold periodic classroom review sessions on material that has been read. (A)

14 Prepare study guides for students to use as they read the material. (I, S)

15 Have students apply mnemonic devices to aid memory. (I, S)

16 Give students immediate feedback on correctness of oral or written responses to the reading material. (A)

17 Encourage students to classify the ideas in their reading material. (A)

These techniques will bolster the students' retention.

Reading Rate

Another useful study skill your students need to acquire is the ability to adjust reading rate to fit the purpose for reading and the material. Many students have never had help in developing flexibility in reading rates. As a result, they frequently read everything at the same rate. Some employ a painstakingly slow rate that is inappropriate for reading light fiction, for locating isolated facts, or for seeking only general themes. Others use a rapid rate that is inappropriate for reading mathematics story problems, science experiments they must perform, or any type of intensive study material.

Make the students aware that good readers use many different reading rates, matching the rate to the purpose for reading and the nature of the material. Offer them opportunities to practice varying reading rates in the classroom; for example, have them scan for isolated details, skim for main ideas, and read slowly and carefully to solve a mathematics problem.

Interpreting Graphic Aids

The ability to interpret graphic aids in content materials is another vital area. Students need to be able to interpret maps, graphs, tables, and illustrations in their textbooks, or they will not gain all they should from the content. Students tend to skip graphic aids when they encounter them in textbooks, perhaps because their teachers have never explained the informative nature of these aids, or because they have never been shown *how* to interpret these aids. We have already mentioned the skills necessary for reading maps. When reading graphs, students must be able to decide what is being compared, the units of measure involved, and how to extract specific information from the graph and make overall generalizations based on the graph. When reading tables, students must be able to decide what type of information is included, the meanings of the columns and rows, and how to extract specific facts. Illustrations such as diagrams present problems due to their abstract nature,

[1]Francis P. Robinson. *Effective Study.* New York: Harper & Row, 1961, Chapter 2.

[2]Leo Fay. "Reading Study Skills: Math and Science." In *Reading and Inquiry,* J. Allen Figurel, ed. Newark, Del. International Reading Association, 1965, pp. 93–94.

[3]Walter Pauk. "On Scholarship: Advice to High School Students." *The Reading Teacher* 17 (November 1963): 73–78.

distortion of reality, and oversimplification. Realistic illustrations may be looked upon as decorative features, when they really convey information.

You should assess the students' ability to deal with graphic aids and help them interpret those that present problems. Students at all levels need appropriate instruction in these important skills.

Metacognitive Skills

Metacognitive skills are ones that allow a person to monitor her or his intellectual functioning. They are important for comprehension and retention of content material. Metacognition includes awareness of what you already know, knowledge of when you have achieved understanding of new information, and realization of how you accomplished the understanding.

You can help your students learn to monitor their comprehension of material presented in your classes. You should be aware, however, that the ability to do this monitoring is a developmental skill only fully acquired during adolescence and that low-ability students do not always benefit from metacognitive strategies. Therefore, you should take your students' maturational levels into consideration when planning to work on the area of metacognition.

In order to exercise metacognitive skills, students must become active learners, setting goals for their learning tasks, planning ways to meet their goals, monitoring their success in meeting their goals, and remedying the situation when they fail to meet the goals. You can help them acquire techniques to do these things. Teaching them to relate new information to things that they already know, to preview material that they are about to read, to paraphrase ideas presented, to identify the organizational patterns in written materials, and to question themselves periodically will help them to monitor their comprehension effectively. You should teach them to expect their reading assignments to make sense and, if they cannot make sense out of the material, to attempt to find out why this situation has occurred. They may ask themselves whether the words in the material are unfamiliar, the sentence structure is confusing, or some other problem exists. After the specific problem area has been determined, they should decide what reading skills need to be applied (for example, use of context clues) and apply the skills. Some ways to remedy the situation when material has not been understood are to read on and try to use subsequent context to help make sense of the material, to reread the material, and to use the glossary or a dictionary to clarify word pronunciations or meanings.

You can help students learn to monitor their comprehension by modeling the monitoring skills for them. You can take a content passage and read it aloud to them, pausing to tell them how you are checking your own comprehension internally at frequent points in the reading. You should tell them the questions you are asking yourself about the material and how you can tell when you have found the answers. This technique is very powerful and effective, if used appropriately.

Study Habits

You may also find that your students have very poor study habits. They must learn that study should take place in an environment that is as distraction-free as possible (many may not have a distraction-free option), that they should gather their study tools (books, pens, pencils, paper) *before* they start to study, that they should budget their study time so that nothing is left out, and that they should set aside a time for study that they will not be constantly relinquishing to other activities. Those who just do not have a good place to study at home should be encouraged to use school study periods as effectively as possible. Students who change classes should learn to gather all necessary study materials before they go to the study hall period, to have all homework assignments written down to take with them, and to concentrate on homework tasks during the study period rather than visit with other students.

Students at all levels must learn to master basic study skills.

DISCUSSION QUESTIONS

1 Using the Fry Readability Graph, figure the readability of a 100-word sample from this text. Compare your results with those of your classmates for the same passage, and reconcile any differences that occur. How easy is this readability measure to apply?

2 What can you do when there are students in your content classes who cannot read the assigned textbook? Would different techniques be better in different situations? Why, or why not?

3 Choose a chapter from a textbook that you are using with students. What are some ways you could build the students' background for reading this material?

4 How can you incorporate writing instruction into your classroom instruction?

5 What opportunities do the students in your class have for developing higher-order thinking skills? How do you and your cooperating teacher react to students' efforts to think critically and creatively?

6 What can you do to provide a classroom environment that is more conducive to higher-order thinking skills? Would you need to make any changes in the room arrangement, scheduling of class work, types of activities, or assignments?

7 What critical or creative thinking activities are you willing to try in your classroom? What problems can you foresee in doing them?

8 What would happen to our society if there were no creativity? Which is more important, knowledge or creativity?

9 How can you help students develop metacognitive skills?

10 What is the most appropriate time to teach outlining, summarizing, and notetaking skills? Why do you think so?

11 How can you and the librarian or media specialist cooperate to ensure that students master important library skills?

12 How can inappropriate and inflexible reading rates inhibit students' learning? What can you do to change these habits?

13 What study methods might you use in your grade or discipline? Why would these methods be appropriate?

14 What kinds of graphic aids are most common in your content area or areas?

SELECTED REFERENCES

Balajthy, Ernest. *Microcomputers in Reading and Language Arts.* Englewood Cliffs, N.J.: Prentice-Hall, 1986.

Beyer, Barry K. "Improving Thinking Skills—Practical Approaches." *Phi Delta Kappan* 65 (April 1984): 556–60.

Brizendine, Nancy Hanks, and James L. Thomas, eds. *Learning Through Dramatics.* Phoenix, Ariz.: Oryx Press, 1982.

Burns, Paul C., Betty D. Roe, and Elinor P. Ross. *Teaching Reading in Today's Elementary Schools.* Boston: Houghton Mifflin, 1992.

Chuska, Kenneth R. *Teaching the Process of Thinking, K–12.* Bloomington, Ind.: Phi Delta Kappa Educational Foundation, 1986.

DuBey, Robert E., et al. *A Performance-Based Guide to Student Teaching.* Danville, Ill.: Interstate, 1975.

Fay, Leo. "Reading Study Skills: Math and Science." In *Reading and Inquiry,* J. Allen Figurel, ed. Newark, Del.: International Reading Association, 1965, pp. 93–94.

"Frameworks for Teaching Thinking." *Educational Leadership* 43 (May 1986): 3–59 (series of articles).

Frymier, Jack. *Motivation and Learning in School.* Bloomington, Ind.: Phi Delta Kappa Educational Foundation, 1974.

Galda, Lee, and Linda DeGroff. "Across Time and Place: Books for Social Studies." *The Reading Teacher* 44 (November 1990): 240–46.

Galda, Lee, Linda DeGroff, and Meg Walworth. "Exploration and Discovery: Books for a Science Curriculum." *The Reading Teacher* 44 (December 1990): 316–25.

Goodman, Ken. *What's Whole in Whole Language?* Portsmouth, N.H.: Heinemann, 1986.

Greenlaw, M. Jean, Grace M. Shepperson, and Robert J. Nistler. "A Literature Approach to Teaching about the Middle Ages." *Language Arts* 69 (March 1992): 200–04.

Heyman, Mark. *Simulation Games for the Classroom.* Bloomington, Ind.: Phi Delta Kappa Educational Foundation, 1975.

Kobrin, B. *Eyeopeners! How to Choose and Use Children's Books about Real People, Places, and Things.* New York: Penguin, 1988.

Lamme, Linda Leonard. "Exploring the World of Music Through Picture Books." *The Reading Teacher* 44 (December 1990): 294–300.

McCaslin, Nellie. *Creative Drama in the Classroom,* 5th ed. White Plains, N.Y.: Longman, 1990.

Moss, J. F. *Focus Units in Literature: A Handbook for Elementary School Teachers.* Katonah, New York: Richard Owen, 1990.

Pauk, Walter. "On Scholarship: Advice to High School Students." *The Reading Teacher* 17 (November 1963): 73–78.

Raths, Louis E., Selma Wassermann, Arthur Jonas, and Arnold Rothstein. *Teaching for Thinking,* 2nd ed. New York: Teachers College, 1986.

Reed, Arthea J. S. *Comics to Classics.* Newark, Del.: International Reading Association, 1988.

Robinson, Francis P. *Effective Study.* New York: Harper and Row, 1961.

Roe, Betty D., Barbara D. Stoodt, and Paul C. Burns. *Secondary School Reading Instruction: The Content Areas.* Boston: Houghton Mifflin, 1991.

Routman, Regie. *Invitations.* Portsmouth, N.H.: Heinemann, 1991.

Thompson, John F. *Using Role Playing in the Classroom.* Bloomington, Ind.: Phi Delta Kappa Educational Foundation, 1978.

Walker-Dalhouse, Doris. "Using African-American Literature to Increase Ethnic Understanding." *The Reading Teacher* 45 (February 1992): 416–22.

"When Teachers Tackle Thinking Skills." *Educational Leadership* 42 (November 1984): 3–72 (series of articles).

Worsham, Antoinette M., and Anita J. Stockton. *A Model for Teaching Thinking Skills: The Inclusion Process.* Bloomington, Ind.: Phi Delta Kappa Educational Foundation, 1986.

8

The Exceptional Student

In January, Carlos, an eight-year-old boy from Cuba, enters a mostly white, middle-class school in a suburb of a northern city. Carlos is a shy child who knows only a little English. Mrs. Hearn, the cooperating teacher, and Carol Vaughn, the student teacher, encourage the class to accept Carlos and try to make him feel part of the class. Sam Ray is a student teacher in the fourth grade.

Mrs. Hearn: Boys and girls, I'd like you to meet Carlos. He has just moved here from Cuba, and I want you to make him feel welcome. Carlos, we're glad to have you. Here is your seat, right between Nancy and John.

John (at recess): Come on, Carlos. We're going to play kickball. You can be on my team.

Carlos: No. I no play ball.

Terry: We'll show you how. It's easy.

Carlos: No. (He moves away from the boys and stands off by himself.)

John: Suit yourself. Let's get started.

Hank (at lunch): Did you bring your lunch, Carlos?

Carlos: Sí.

Hank: Here, you can eat at our table.

Carlos: No. I eat over here. Myself.

Hank: Okay. Whatever you say.

Miss Vaughn (one week later): Mrs. Hearn, I'm worried about Carlos. I think the class tried to make him feel welcome at first, but now the children ignore him. He just stays by himself and looks so sad and lonely. We should be able to do something.

Mrs. Hearn: I'm concerned about him too, but I don't know what to do. I've talked to some of the children about him, and they say he never wants to do anything with them, so they don't ask him any more.

Miss Vaughn: What's even worse is that some of them are beginning to laugh at him and make fun of him because he brings unusual food to lunch and acts strangely sometimes. I'll try talking to him about it and see how he feels.

Miss Vaughn: Carlos, how are you getting along?

Carlos: Not so good. Boys and girls, they no like me.

Miss Vaughn: Sure, they like you. They want you to be their friend.

Carlos: No. I no like them.

Miss Vaughn (to herself): I didn't get any place with him. I've just got to think of something.

Miss Vaughn (a few days later): Sam, aren't you teaching a unit on Mexico?

Mr. Ray: I'm right in the middle of it.

Miss Vaughn: How would you like your children to learn some Spanish words?

Mr. Ray: That'd be great. What do you have in mind?

Miss Vaughn: I've got this little guy from Cuba who is having a really hard time in our class. I thought maybe you could ask him to help you with some Spanish words.

Mr. Ray: Sure. Could he come over tomorrow about 10:30?

Miss Vaughn: That'll be fine.

Miss Vaughn (back in her own class): Carlos, the class down the hall is learning about Mexico. The teacher can't speak Spanish. Could you go there and tell them some Spanish words tomorrow?

Carlos: I don't know. They no like me either.

Miss Vaughn: They'll like you. Don't worry about that. Anyway, you know Spanish words, and they don't know any.

Carlos: Well, maybe.

Mr. Ray (next day at 10:30): Class, this is Carlos from Mrs. Hearn's room. He knows how to speak Spanish and is going to tell us some words we need to know.

Jean: Terrific! I'm working on a scrapbook. I can put in some Spanish words. Carlos, how do you say *family* in Spanish? How about *dinner*? And *school*?

Barry: Can you teach us how to count in Spanish?

Elaine: Say something to us in Spanish.

Mr. Ray: Whoa. Wait a minute. Give Carlos a chance to answer. Carlos, can you tell Jean the words she wants to know first?

Carlos (beginning very cautiously): Sí. Word for *family* is *familia*. What else you want to know? (Carlos answers more questions, gradually builds confidence, then seems eager to answer questions about Spanish.)

Mr. Ray: That's great, Carlos. You've helped us a lot. Maybe you can come back again.

Carlos (with a big grin): Sí. I come back.

Mr. Ray (that afternoon): Thanks, Carol. Having Carlos come was really good for my class.

Miss Vaughn: It seemed to help Carlos, too.

John (three days later): Hey, Carlos. I hear you've been teaching the kids down the hall to speak Spanish. How about teaching us?

Carlos: Sí. I teach you. What you want to know?

Terry: I know. You teach us some Spanish, and we'll teach you how to play kickball. Is it a deal?

Carlos: Okay. Now we go play ball. You show me. Okay? Then I teach you Spanish.

1. Why do you think Carlos had trouble getting along with the boys and girls?
2. What are some indications that he is beginning to feel more comfortable in his new school?
3. Why did Miss Vaughn's idea about having Carlos teach Spanish to a group of children seem to help him when other attempts to help had failed?
4. Can you think of other plans that might have helped Carlos adjust to his new class?

RECOGNIZING THE EXCEPTIONAL STUDENT

It probably comes as no surprise that you will find all types of students when you enter the classroom. Taking one characteristic as an example, students will range in ability from academically gifted to slow learning. There may also be learning disabled, culturally different, and physically disabled students. With mainstreaming, many kinds of students will need your consideration. It will take your best efforts to challenge, help, provide for, and understand these youngsters.

CHALLENGING THE GIFTED STUDENT

Gifted students often make much faster academic progress in a year than do average students. They may make one and a fourth (or more) years' progress within a single year, whereas the average students show one year of academic growth each year. As a student teacher, you should, however, be aware that there are both "normal" achievers and underachievers among the gifted. They do not always reach their academic potentials. Usually, gifted students possess some of these characteristics:

1 They are interested in books and reading.
2 They possess relatively large vocabularies and the ability to express themselves verbally in a mature manner.
3 They are curious to learn and have relatively long attention spans.
4 They have achieved a high level of abstract thinking.
5 They exhibit a wide range of interests.

Gifted students have the same needs as other students in terms of acceptance, achievement, and interaction with others. They need the same basic academic tools as others, but to a different degree and at different times. While gifted students are able to direct many of their own activities, some teacher direction is needed.

Within the school program, you will find many opportunities to attend to the special needs of gifted students. These are some suggested instructional procedures:

1 Make use of trade (library) books in the program.
2 Develop units of work that provide opportunities for in-depth and long-term activities, as well as library research.
3 Utilize special tables and bulletin boards for interesting and challenging problems, puzzles, worksheets, etc.

FIGURE 8—1   Math Wizard: A Course in Informal Geometry

During the summer, I taught a mini-course in informal geometry geared to gifted children in grades 4—6, as part of the Summer Enrichment Program. Since geometry is an indispensable tool of mankind, used constantly in many professions—by the builder, the engineer, the navigator, the astronomer, the artist, the musician, the inventor—gifted children should learn this material to have a solid foundation on which to build more complex geometric skills as their education progresses.

Some of the concepts taught and investigated in this mini-course were the three basic shapes; the ideas of proximity, separation, order, and enclosure; the relationship of sides and angles; the ideas of congruent, similar, and different; the Platonic Solids and Euler's Formula; and the visualization and creation of two- and three-dimensional objects.

Gifted children need to begin by working with concrete objects, even though these students are quick to perceive the abstract. From concrete objects they can move to semiconcrete or pictorial representations and then to abstract thinking.

Integration of mind and body is also essential for the gifted student, and with this in mind, I made it a point to involve the students physically with the concepts we studied. For example, they used their and/or other students' bodies to demonstrate the ideas of proximity, separation, order, and enclosure, and we had a relay race as a follow-up to the section on visualization and creation of two- and three-dimensional objects.

Every few days we had a "Tricky Puzzle"—a mathematical brain-teaser—to serve as a follow-up of the lesson. These puzzles also served as a lesson carry-over to get things rolling the next day by having the students present their solutions of the previous day's puzzle. "Tricky Puzzle" time was definitely the highlight of the day!

As the culminating experience for this mini-course, the students created box sculptures from "garbage" they had been collecting since the first day of class. The only criteria were that (1) the students have a "guiding idea" for their construction, and that (2) they be able to name the geometric shapes involved in their sculptures. This exercise served as a good way to wrap up the course and ended things on a pleasant note.

4 Use special enrichment materials appropriate to the content areas.
5 Encourage oral and written reports on topics under discussion and related subjects.
6 Provide opportunities for participation in special clubs or groups designed to challenge gifted students.
7 Place gifted students in cooperative learning groups and special project groups where they can work with less able students.

Marty Williams describes her experiences in teaching some gifted students in Figure 8—1.

As a student teacher, you should begin collecting a file of creative and unusual ideas for use with gifted students. Figure 8—2 shows one card with which you can start your file.

Although our discussion has centered on intellectually gifted students, do not

FIGURE 8—2   Sample Activity Card for Gifted Students

File Card for Able Students

BOX O' BALLADS

Have a copy available of Carl Sandburg's book, *The American Songbag*. Provide time and materials for students to do one of the following related projects after discussing and enjoying some of the ballads:

1. Draw a panorama representing one of the cowboy ballads.
2. Write some imaginative ballads of your own about the pioneers or the railroad workers.
3. Create a shoe-box diorama representing one of the lumberjack ballads.
4. Plan and present a short creative drama representing the ballad of your choice.

Even gifted children need to begin by working with concrete objects.

overlook other types of talented students. These other talented students may be:

Students who engage in divergent thinking, differing from the "normal," "expected," or "standard"

Students with leadership abilities

Students with visual and performing arts abilities

Students with a specific ability, such as psychomotor ability

Obviously, recognition of various types of talents cannot be made only on the basis of intelligence or achievement tests. No tests exist to measure all of these areas. Still, students in all of the categories just listed have special needs and can profit from specifically planned activities beyond those normally provided by the standard school program.

Options to regular classroom instruction for gifted students may be available in the school in which you are student teaching. These options may include special programs outside the classroom, use of resource teachers, mini-courses, summer programs, independent study, advanced placement, community programs, and study groups. In addition, your school system may have a special teacher for the gifted and talented, who can give you a great deal of help with materials and program planning. As the student teacher, you will need to enjoy learning from gifted students, to respect their ideas, and to encourage a wide range of classroom activities (from independent study to much group interaction) as a way of individualizing instruction. In working with these students you will certainly need a sense of humor. How helpful it is to admit mistakes and be able to laugh at yourself!

HELPING THE SLOW LEARNER

The main characteristic of slow learners is that they do not learn as quickly as do others of the same age. You will have to make some adjustments for instructing students of low-normal ability, such as:

1 Carefully developing readiness for each learning task
2 Moving through instructional material more slowly and gradually than with the normal learning student
3 Developing ideas with concrete, manipulative, and visually oriented materials
4 Using simplified materials that do not demand too much at one time from the student
5 Varying activities due to short attention spans
6 Relating learnings to familiar experiences (such as school, lunchroom, gymnasium, current events, community projects, and holiday celebrations)
7 Providing for large amounts of practice to master new learnings
8 Reviewing with closely spaced, cumulative exercises to encourage retention

Many slow learners, accustomed to years of placement in low groups, have negative self-concepts. It is important for them to experience success in some way—perhaps through athletics, art, or some other talent or skill. Consider those students in your class who have less academic ability than others, and then do Activity 8.1.

To develop and maintain positive attitudes toward school subjects, it is necessary to provide slow learners with situations that relate to their experiences and to the real world in which they live. For example, where students have had experience with money, many of the computational operations can be approached in terms of money:

$$
\begin{array}{ccccc}
42 & & 4 \text{ dimes} + 2 \text{ cents} & & 3 \text{ dimes} + 12 \text{ cents} \\
-18 & \rightarrow & -1 \text{ dime } + 8 \text{ cents} & \rightarrow & -1 \text{ dime } + 8 \text{ cents} \\
\hline
& & & & 2 \text{ dimes} + 4 \text{ cents}
\end{array}
$$

Similarly, many student teachers have found ways to present subject matter concepts through newspapers and magazines, "how to" books, telephone directories, mail order catalogues, TV guides, scouting manuals, menus, greeting cards, hobby materials, food and medicine containers, road signs, and nature guide materials. If a slow learner is having difficulty with a particular concept or idea, you may need to utilize corrective exercises and materials, such as the one shown in Figure 8–3.

PROVIDING FOR THE LEARNING DISABLED STUDENT

Students with a learning disability usually demonstrate a significant discrepancy between intellectual potential and actual level of performance. They exhibit behaviors that point to an impairment, usually involving perceptual difficulties. In other words, there is difficulty in processing auditory and visual sensations or stimuli, resulting in a faulty interpretive response. On the other hand, these students are not below average in intelligence, visually or hearing impaired, or "educationally deprived."

Students with learning disabilities usually profit most from concrete, manipulative materials and direct, hands-on experiences, depending upon the specific learning disability. These are areas in which learning disabilities can occur:

Memory—Failure to remember newly presented information

Visual or auditory discrimination—Failure to see or hear likenesses and differences

Visual-auditory association—Failure to associate visual and auditory stimuli

Perceptual-motor skills—Failure of visual, auditory, tactile, and kinesthetic channels to interact appropriately with motor activity

Spatial orientation—Failure to master temporal, spatial, and orientation factors

FIGURE 8–3   Sample Corrective Exercise for Slow Learners

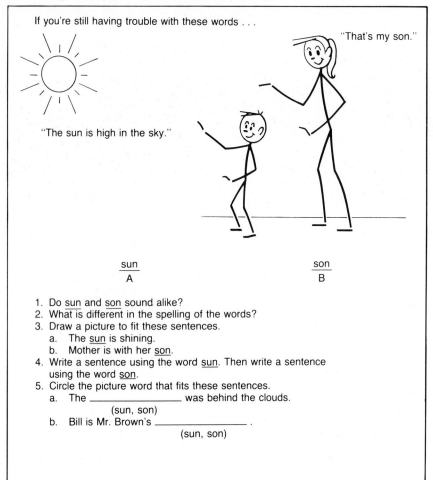

If you're still having trouble with these words . . .

"That's my son."

"The sun is high in the sky."

sun
A

son
B

1. Do sun and son sound alike?
2. What is different in the spelling of the words?
3. Draw a picture to fit these sentences.
   a. The sun is shining.
   b. Mother is with her son.
4. Write a sentence using the word sun. Then write a sentence using the word son.
5. Circle the picture word that fits these sentences.
   a. The _____ was behind the clouds.
      (sun, son)
   b. Bill is Mr. Brown's _____ .
      (sun, son)

Verbal expression—Failure to express ideas, communicate, or request information

Closure-generalization—Failure to extrapolate beyond an established set of data or information

Attending—Failure to attend selectively or focus upon tasks

General guidelines for working with learning disabled students usually involve ideas relating to attention span, hyperactivity, and related organizational patterns. These are useful ideas:

1 Increase attention span by removing distractions, including any materials other than those necessary for the assigned task.

2 Teach the student how to organize his or her desk, belongings, and materials.

3 Try to improve one behavior at a time, rewarding appropriate behavior and involving the student in recording behavioral progress. Discuss appropriate ways to expend extra energy.

4 Carefully structure the learning environment and tasks with specific standards, limits, and rules.

5 Be consistent. Consistency is an important ingredient—in rules, directions, and the like. Make consequences for rule infractions clear.

Activity 8.1   Building the Self-Esteem of Less Able Students

Some students may be less able than others in a class. List ways that you can help the less able students build their self-esteem and succeed, and try these techniques in the next two weeks.

Two weeks later: Identify the techniques that were most effective by putting an asterisk (*) in front of them. Put an x in front of the least effective techniques. Can you think of other strategies to use?

  6 Assign one task at a time, at first using a step-by-step procedure. In other
   words, use short, sequential assignments, with breaks between tasks.
  7 Use a variety of media to present content (such as films, tapes, and printed
   material).
  8 Utilize active methods (such as simulation games, experiments, and role
   playing) in the instructional strategies.
  9 Employ materials for differing learning styles (pictures, tapes, and concrete
   objects).
  10 Prepare peers or partners to serve as tutors in certain skills or content
   areas.

Practices frequently used with learning disabled students at the secondary level include teaching generalized learning strategies (such as notetaking, test taking, outlining, and study skills), putting greater emphasis on multimedia presentation of material (using items such as films, tapes, and transparencies) than upon lecture/ textbook, and making provision for alternatives (such as oral instead of written examinations).

Some secondary school programs focus instruction for the learning disabled on practical skill applications: for example, planning a budget; filling out job applications; learning social skills needed in family and job situations; and using independent living skills, such as food preparation, home management, attention to personal hygiene practices and safety practices. Other functional curriculum programs incorporate career education, prevocational study, specific vocational skills, and/or on-the-job training in certain areas.

Students with Attention Deficit Disorder (ADD)

You may have heard teachers discussing students with attention deficit disorder (ADD), a form of learning disability. Although ADD can occur without hyperactivity, these teachers are probably referring to hyperactive students who are difficult to manage in the classroom. ADD is most common among elementary-school-aged children and tends to slow down by adolescence. The ADD child is likely to:

  1 Be inattentive and unable to remain on task
  2 Become impatient while waiting for his or her turn during games
  3 Blurt out answers to questions
  4 Fidget with his or her hands or feet
  5 Be easily distracted
  6 Turn in careless or incomplete work
  7 Talk excessively and interrupt others
  8 Lose things necessary for school tasks (e.g., pencils, books, assignments)
  9 Engage in potentially dangerous acts without considering the consequences
   (e.g., darting into the street without looking)
  10 Shift from one activity to another without completing anything

Since this disorder occurs in about 3 percent of children, you are likely to have an ADD child in your class—one who constantly disrupts the class and has several of the characteristics listed above. A guidance counselor or your cooperating teacher may have some suggestions for dealing with such a student, and the following ideas can also be helpful:

  1 Reward the child for remaining on task and completing work.
  2 Set up study carrels or private areas where the child can work without
   distraction.
  3 Keep lessons short.
  4 Use progress charts and contracts.
  5 Ignore inappropriate behavior whenever possible.
  6 Stick to schedules and routines.

UNDERSTANDING THE NEEDS OF THE CULTURALLY AND LINGUISTICALLY DIFFERENT STUDENT

Many students may be different in terms of cultural background—students who are not native to the United States or students from the inner city or from rural areas, such as Southern Appalachia. Teachers should be aware of concerns related to culturally different students.

Ethnic groups—groups of people who are unique in ancestry, language, religion, physical characteristics, or customs—exist within a larger, dominant society. Among the ethnic groups with which you may deal are Hispanics, African-Americans, and Native Americans. Members of these and other groups may exhibit different language patterns, attitudes, and behaviors from those in the mainstream population. In dealing with students from these groups, your knowledge of their language and culture can be valuable. For example, some groups of Native American and African-American children function better in cooperative environments and do not perform well when placed in highly competitive instructional settings.

Each school setting will have a different cultural mixture. You should familiarize yourself with the cultural backgrounds of the specific students you are assigned to teach.

Students' backgrounds of experiences affect their ability to comprehend oral and written language in school. Culturally different students often do not have the same types of background experiences that students in the mainstream of our society have. Textbooks, however, are often written as if all students have certain background knowledge, and teachers' discussion sessions may reflect the same assumption. You must determine which students may be lacking particular background knowledge assumed by the textbook authors and take steps to develop such background if it does not exist.

Although some students from minority groups may come from low socioeconomic backgrounds, not all do. When the students are from low socioeconomic backgrounds, however, you should not use this fact to excuse poor achievement,[1] for the ability to learn is not decided by monetary circumstances.

In recent years, many people who do not speak English have entered the United States from a variety of nations. Students who only speak a language other than English need your help in learning English as quickly as possible in order to benefit from the educational experiences offered in an English-speaking school. You should purchase a foreign language dictionary to refer to when trying to communicate with these students. If a student reads her or his own language fluently, you should provide a dictionary with English equivalents of familiar words. In the lower grades, you can construct a picture dictionary of English words for such a student. You may make use of pictures and concrete objects to supply needed vocabulary words to a student. For example, you may show the student a picture of a dog or an actual dog and point to the picture or the animal while saying the word *dog*. Coloring books and picture books were successfully used with one eight-year-old child from Thailand: her vocabulary grew by leaps and bounds due to her desire to communicate. Classmates spent countless free hours identifying objects for her, listening to her repeat their names, and helping her correct her pronunciation. In return, she taught the names for the items in her own language to her highly receptive classmates. The result was mutual respect and enjoyment. Always remember that language-minority students have the right "not to have their culture denigrated by the school...."[2]

It is helpful to assign students who do not speak English, or who speak little English, buddies to guide them to the cafeteria, restrooms, and other classrooms. If

[1]Shirl E. Gilbert II and Geneva Gay. "Improving the Success in School of Poor Black Children." *Phi Delta Kappan* 67 (October 1985): 133–37.

[2]Charles L. Glenn. "New Challenges: A Civil Rights Agenda for the Public Schools." *Phi Delta Kappan* 67 (May 1986): 656.

other students speak the new students' languages at all, they would be good choices for guides. Including new students in many classroom activities in which they can listen to the language being used in conjunction with real situations can also be helpful. As the students learn English, they can help familiarize other students with a second language, as Carlos did in his school and as the eight-year-old girl did in her class.

In certain geographic areas, you will need to recognize the importance of the Bilingual Education Act. This act has been interpreted to require that a school district offer a bilingual program (education in two languages, one of which is English) where there are a number of limited English-speaking students. A well-known part of bilingual education is English as a Second Language (ESL). ESL focuses first upon helping students to understand and speak oral English, then to read and comprehend written English, and finally to write in English.

Multiethnic or multicultural education is a way of observing the rights of various cultural groups within the schools. It "is concerned with modifying the total educational environment, so that the environment is more reflective of the ethnic diversity of American Society."[3] Supporters of multicultural education believe that material related to ethnic groups should be an integral part of the curriculum, beginning in kindergarten and continuing throughout the grades. In social studies, you may want to have students study world events from different perspectives. Instead of having the students consider only the American point of view, you can lead them to consider also how Mexicans, Asians, or Arabs view international events. In literature, you can have them read stories with varied ethnic and racial content from the preprimer level onward. You can also incorporate multiethnic themes into the art, music, science, mathematics, and physical education portions of the curriculum.

A much less effective approach to multiethnic education that some teachers take is the "heroes and holidays" observance. Two or three times during the year, certain periods are set aside to celebrate a particular event related to an ethnic group. For example, at Thanksgiving children may dress as Native Americans and construct teepees, or in observance of Martin Luther King's death, students might prepare a "soul food" meal. Such observances do little to promote understanding of racial and ethnic groups, but rather reinforce misconceptions and stereotypes. As a student teacher, you should consider taking a more comprehensive approach to multiethnic education.

Multiethnic content in the curriculum can be more meaningful than material about Anglo-Saxons for students of particular ethnic groups. Your African-American students will be more interested in reading stories about Harriet Tubman's heroic efforts to free slaves or George Washington Carver's ingenuity in finding ways to use peanuts than about many situations involving no African-American characters. When students have greater interest in reading material, they are likely to develop more skill in reading. The same principle applies to other subject matter areas where students work with information pertaining to their own ethnic groups.

You also need to be conscious of ways to use multicultural content in your lessons. Keep in mind that multicultural education is not simply a matter of adding a bit of information about a minority group to your lessons now and then. It is a total commitment to presenting material from a global perspective that values the contributions and life styles of each ethnic group.

One aspect of multicultural education does not deal with the curriculum itself, but with attitudes toward ethnic groups. Research has shown that many preschool children are already aware of racial differences. These children have acquired negative impressions of various races from their parents, television, and movies. These negative attitudes become more widespread as students progress through school.

[3]James Banks. *Multiethnic Education: Practice and Promises.* Bloomington, Ind.: Phi Delta Kappa Educational Foundation, 1977, p. 21.

They are damaging to students of all groups, but they are particularly damaging to students who belong to those groups that are viewed negatively. These students often find the school environment hostile, unaccepting, and destructive to their self-concepts.

You need to be sensitive to the special needs of the minority students in your classroom. In your student teaching, you need to be aware of ways to work with these students that take into consideration their needs and feelings. You should respect their ethnic and racial backgrounds. While some students have no problems with their ethnicity, others feel insecure and ill at ease in a different culture. You should respond in helpful and constructive ways to students with ethnic identity problems.

Although you may not mean to offend minority students, you may unconsciously reveal negative feelings toward them. Here are behaviors to avoid in working with minority students:

1 Assigning them a large number of menial tasks
2 Using derogatory labels for different racial and ethnic groups
3 Referring to students according to negative stereotypes
4 Verbally or nonverbally expressing dislike or disapproval
5 Becoming impatient when they misinterpret your questions or fail to respond as quickly as other students
6 Ignoring them when they want your attention
7 Being condescending toward them (appearing to be nice while actually feeling superior)
8 Avoiding physical closeness or actual contact
9 Constantly criticizing their use of dialect
10 Failing to give them opportunities for leadership
11 Blaming the minority student when it is unclear who is at fault

In your daily work with these students, you should be able to find many ways to encourage and support them. Expressing interest in what they are doing or granting them a special privilege for work well done are examples of ways to show that you care.

Several strategies can be used to encourage students to accept their peers who come from different racial or ethnic origins. Role playing helps students understand how it feels to be a member of a different ethnic group. Assigning children of different ethnic heritages to work together on a committee helps them realize that each member of the group can make an important contribution. You can create other situations in which problems can be solved only through the cooperation of each member of an ethnically mixed group.

Culturally different students need to acquire the values and behaviors essential for success in the dominant society while retaining important aspects of their own subcultures. (See Activity 8.2 on valuing diversity.) Whereas you cannot do a great deal to further this ideal in a short period of time, your awareness of cultural differences, your attitudes toward your students, and the focus of your lessons can make a difference.

MAINSTREAMED STUDENTS

Because students who had previously been enrolled in special education classes are now being integrated into regular classes, you will probably be responsible for a number of exceptional students. This practice is referred to as "mainstreaming."

You should be familiar with Public Law 101–476, the Individuals with Disabilities Education Act (IDEA), which is the reauthorization of Public Law 94–142, the Education for All Handicapped Children Act. These laws affect services provided to

Activity 8.2   Valuing Student Diversity

Refer to the Class Culture Survey that you did in Activity 2.2 to focus on students who represent various ethnic backgrounds. Plan some experiences for valuing the diversity of these students. Briefly describe them here.
Experiences:

Reflection: How effective were the experiences? What else could you try?

individuals with disabilities in public schools and provided for mainstreaming students with disabilities into regular classrooms to the greatest extent possible.

On the basis of test materials and appropriate records, an evaluation is made by an "M-Team" (multidisciplinary team). The team is composed of the student's teacher, one or both of the parents, and a representative of the local education agency (other than the teacher). It may also include the student and additional professional personnel. The M-Team writes the Individual Education Program (IEP).

Due process must be observed in all evaluation and placement of the student. Parents (or guardians) must consent to formal evaluation, be informed of results, and be involved in developing the IEP. They have the right to examine records and to present complaints with respect to any matter related to evaluation or placement of the student. Additionally, the Buckley Amendment (Family Educational Rights and Privacy Act of 1974) prohibits the release of a student's records without parental consent and provides that all information be kept confidential.

One of the first steps you should take in working with a mainstreamed student is to become familiar with the IEP for the student. The IEP provides a synthesis of all assessment information, as well as classroom accommodations and instructional plans. The format will probably include items such as these:

1 A statement of the student's present levels of educational performance, including academic achievement, social adaptation, prevocational and vocational skills, psychomotor skills, and self-help skills
2 A specific statement describing the student's learning style
3 A statement of annual goals describing the educational performance to be achieved by the end of the school year
4 A statement of short-term instructional objectives, which must be measurable intermediate steps between present levels of educational performance and annual goals
5 A statement of specific educational services needed by the student (determined without regard to the availability of those services), with a description of all special education and related services necessary to meet the unique needs of the student, including the type of physical education program in which the student will participate and any special instructional media and materials needed to implement the individualized education program
6 The date when those services will begin and length of time the services will be given
7 A description of the extent to which the student will participate in regular education programs
8 A justification for the type of educational placement the student will have
9 A list of the individuals responsible for implementation of the individualized education program
10 Objective criteria, evaluation procedures, and schedules for determining, on at least an annual basis, if the short-term instructional objectives are being achieved. (Annual and short-term goals must be revised at least annually.)

The following ideas may be useful in teaching the mainstreamed student:

1 Build rapport with the student. Let the student know you are genuinely interested in seeing that he or she overcomes difficulties. A comfortable, relaxed atmosphere also enhances rapport.
2 Formulate a plan for alleviating the difficulty as much as possible. Instruction must be tailored to meet the needs of the individual student. Skills to be taught must relate to the student's learning characteristics and potential. Different approaches will succeed with different students, so you must be both flexible in your approaches and familiar with many different approaches.

3 Adjust the length of the instructional sessions to fit the student's attention span. In fairly long sessions, you will need frequent changes of activities. Repeated drill may be necessary due to poor retention.

4 Identify the basic life skills, and relate them to subject content. For example, in mathematics, note skills related to such everyday areas as reading price tags, calendars, road maps, recipes, timetables, thermometers, clocks, and sales slips; understanding money values and measurement units; making change; budgeting money; writing personal checks; and planning meals.

5 The mainstreamed student's interests need to be utilized. If a student is interested in a particular topic, she or he will tend to put forth much effort to master a particular concept or skill that relates to the interest.

Help is available for classroom teachers who work with mainstreamed students. These teachers should work closely with the special education teacher and other personnel to maximize the student's potential without duplication of effort (see Activity 8.3). A paraprofessional (such as a teacher's assistant) may be available. Peers may act as tutors—either student tutors from the same classroom or students from higher grade levels. Finally, a course in the education of exceptional children and courses dealing with diagnosis and correction of classroom problems in reading, mathematics, or language arts can be helpful.

Case Study: Planning for Differences

Mr. Hernandez, a student teacher, is planning a study of the Civil War for his American History class. He is aware of the need to adjust instruction for the students' varying achievement levels, as well as for some of their personal characteristics. For example, he plans to encourage several advanced students to read widely from a prepared bibliography and plan to present to the class some of the information they glean from their reading—through formal reports, panel discussions, dramatizations, and the like. Some students will be assigned chapters from the textbook in their search for answers to a list of questions prepared cooperatively by the students and teacher. The teacher will prepare reading aids, such as study guides, to help the students focus on particular information.

Several slower-learning students will use some easy-to-read books and other supplementary materials to prepare for a group discussion about the Civil War. They will also view several filmstrips as part of their study. A few of the slower learners will be assigned a student "tutor" to help when difficulties arise.

Students will also be assigned to cooperative learning groups with each group consisting of an advanced student, a slow learner, and two or three average students, so far as possible. Working as a team, these students will investigate different aspects of the Civil War.

An assignment for one set of students will include reading about Harriet Tubman's efforts in freeing the slaves and preparing a role-playing report. One student with a learning disability who has difficulty paying attention will be given an individual set of short, sequential assignments, with a specific "date due" schedule. A visually limited student will listen to several tape recordings prepared by the teacher. Also, Mr. Hernandez is planning to read key information aloud while the study is in progress. Through these and other ways, Mr. Hernandez hopes he has made appropriate adjustments for the needs of the students in the classroom.

1. What is your opinion of the way Mr. Hernandez adjusted assignments to meet differing needs?

2. What additional ideas can you suggest for adjusting to individual differences?

Activity 8.3   Support Personnel for Special Needs Students

Identify a special needs student in your class. Identify several people who might help you work with this student, such as your cooperating teacher, a resource teacher, or a guidance counselor. Interview them, and then write an informal plan for helping the student.

Comments from support personnel:

Informal plan:

Reflection: How effective is my plan? Who else might be able to help? What else could I try?

DISCUSSION QUESTIONS

1 How could you identify the following types of students: (a) gifted; (b) slow learner; (c) learning disabled; (d) culturally different?

2 Consider one content or subject area. How would you challenge the gifted student?

3 Again, consider one content area. How would you help the slow learner in this area?

4 How would you help the student with a learning disability? Relate your answer to a specific content area.

5 How can the needs of the culturally different be considered in the instructional program?

6 What are the teacher's responsibilities toward the mainstreamed student?

7 How can you and special resource personnel cooperate to ensure the best program for the exceptional student?

8 What would you do if in the ninth-grade history class where you are student teaching, there is a student named Pedro who speaks fluent Spanish, but refuses to try to learn more than the small amount of English he already knows? Many of the other students are Mexican-Americans like Pedro, but unlike him, they are learning English rapidly. When it is time to give a test over the unit you have been studying, Pedro is the only one who has difficulty reading the questions. Do you translate into Spanish for him (assuming you can), read the questions to him in English, or let him do the best he can with the test on his own? What is the reason for your answer?

SELECTED REFERENCES

Adelman, Howard S., and Linda Taylor. *An Introduction to Learning Disabilities.* Glenview, Ill.: Scott, Foresman, 1986.

Affleck, J. S., et al. *Teaching the Mildly Handicapped in the Regular Classroom,* 2nd ed. New York: Merrill/Macmillan, 1980.

Alexander, Clara Franklin. "Black English Dialect and the Classroom Teacher." *The Reading Teacher* 33 (February 1980): 571–77.

Bader, Lois A. "Instructional Adjustments to Vision Problems." *The Reading Teacher* 37 (March 1984): 566–69.

Banks, James. *Multiethnic Education: Practice and Promises.* Bloomington, Ind.: Phi Delta Kappa Educational Foundation, 1977.

Barbe, Walter B., and Joseph S. Renzulli, eds. *Psychology and Education of the Gifted,* 3rd ed. New York: Irvington, 1980.

Bloome, David, and Judith Green. "Directions in the Sociolinguistic Study of Reading." In *Handbook of Reading Research,* P. David Pearson, ed. New York: Longman, 1984, pp. 395–421.

Brophy, Jere. "Successful Teaching Strategies for the Inner-City Child." *Phi Delta Kappan* 63 (April 1982): 527–30.

Carlsen, Joanne M. "Between the Deaf Child and Reading: The Language Connection." *The Reading Teacher* 38 (January 1985): 424–26.

Carr, Kathryn S. "What Gifted Readers Need from Reading Instruction." *The Reading Teacher* 38 (November 1984): 144–46.

Fish, John. *Special Education: The Way Ahead.* Philadelphia: Open University Press, 1985.

Gilbert, Shirl E., II, and Geneva Gay. "Improving the Success in School of Poor Black Children." *Phi Delta Kappan* 67 (October 1985): 133–37.

Gillet, Jean Wallace, and J. Richard Gentry. "Bridges between Nonstandard and Standard English with Extensions of Dictated Stories." *The Reading Teacher* 36 (January 1983): 360–65.

Glenn, Charles L. "New Challenges: A Civil Rights Agenda for the Public Schools." *Phi Delta Kappan* 67 (May 1986): 653–56.

Hakuta, Kenji, and Laurie J. Gould. "Synthesis of Research on Bilingual Education." *Educational Leadership* 44 (March 1987): 38–45.

Hasazi, Susan E., et al. *Mainstreaming: Merging Regular and Special Education.* Bloomington, Ind.: Phi Delta Kappa Educational Foundation, 1979.

Henley, Martin. *Teaching Mildly Retarded Children in the Regular Classroom.* Bloomington, Ind.: Phi Delta Kappa Educational Foundation, 1985.

Herlihy, John G., and Myra T. Herlihy, eds. *Mainstreaming in the Social Studies.* Washington, D.C.: National Council for the Social Studies, 1980.

Herman, Barry E. *Winchester: A Community School for the Urbanvantaged.* Bloomington, Ind.: Phi Delta Kappa Educational Foundation, 1977.

Hewett, Frank M., with Steven R. Forness. *Education of Exceptional Learners,* 3rd ed. Boston: Allyn and Bacon, 1984.

Hough, Ruth A., Joanne R. Nurss, and D. Scott Enright. "Story Reading with Limited English Speaking Children in the Regular Classroom." *The Reading Teacher* 39 (February 1986): 510–14.

Johnson, Stanley. *Arithmetic and Learning Disabilities.* Boston: Allyn and Bacon, 1979.

Khatena, Joe. *The Creatively Gifted Child: Suggestions for Parents and Teachers.* New York: Vantage Press, 1978.

Kirk, Samuel A., and James J. Gallagher. *Educating Exceptional Children,* 6th ed. Boston: Houghton Mifflin, 1989.

Lerner, Janet W. *Learning Disabilities,* 5th ed. Boston: Houghton Mifflin, 1988.

Mallis, Jackie, ed. *Ideas for Teaching Gifted Students.* Blauvelt, N.Y.: Multimedia, 1979.

Maring, Gerald H., Gail Chase Furman, and Judy Blum-Anderson. "Five Cooperative Learning Strategies for Mainstreamed Youngsters in Content Area Classrooms." *The Reading Teacher* 39 (December 1985): 310–13.

Markoff, Annabelle M. *Teaching Low Achieving Children Reading, Spelling, and Handwriting.* Springfield, Ill.: Charles C. Thomas, 1976.

Ovando, Carlos J., and Virginia P. Collier. *Bilingual and ESL Classrooms.* New York: McGraw-Hill, 1985.

Ramirez, Arnulfo G. *Bilingualism through Schooling: Cross-Cultural Education for Minority and Majority Students.* Albany: State University of New York Press, 1985.

Reisman, Fredricka K., and Samuel H. Kauffman. *Teaching Mathematics to Children with Special Needs.* New York: Merrill/Macmillan, 1980.

Rhodes, Lynn, and Curt Dudley-Marling. *Readers and Writers with a Difference.* Portsmouth, N.H.: Heinemann, 1988.

Romney, David M. *Dealing with Abnormal Behavior in the Classroom.* Bloomington, Ind.: Phi Delta Kappa Educational Foundation, 1986.

Rouse, Michael W., and Julie B. Ryan. "Teacher's Guide to Vision Problems." *The Reading Teacher* 38 (December 1984): 306–07.

Schulz, Jane B., and Ann P. Turnbull. *Mainstreaming Handicapped Students,* 2nd ed. Boston: Allyn and Bacon, 1984.

Sedlak, Robert A., and Denise M. Sedlak. *Teaching the Educable Mentally Retarded.* Albany: State University of New York Press, 1985.

Smith, Deborah. *Teaching the Learning Disabled.* Englewood Cliffs, N.J.: Prentice-Hall, 1981.

Turnbull, A. P., Bonne Strickland, and John C. Brantley. *Developing and Implementing Individualized Education Programs.* New York: Merrill/Macmillan, 1978.

Warger, Cynthia L., et al. *Mainstreaming in the Secondary School: Role of the Regular Teacher.* Bloomington, Ind.: Phi Delta Kappa Educational Foundation, 1983.

Washburn, Winifred Y. *Vocational Mainstreaming.* Novato, Calif.: Academic Therapy Publications, 1979.

Wilkins, Gloria, and Suzanne Miller. *Strategies for Success: An Effective Guide for Teachers of Secondary-Level Slow Learners.* New York: Teachers College Press, 1983.

Woodward, Dolores M. *Mainstreaming the Learning Disabled Adolescent.* Rockville, Md.: Aspen Systems, 1980.

Ysseldyke, James, and Bob Algozzine. *Introduction to Special Education,* 2nd ed. Boston: Houghton Mifflin, 1990.

9

Evaluation

Mr. Todd has been student teaching in eighth grade for four weeks and has become aware that it is more difficult to evaluate student progress than he expected it to be. Instead of simply averaging test scores, Mr. Todd finds that he should probably consider a number of other factors as well. Five students in particular puzzle Mr. Todd.

Amy is alert, interested, outgoing, and talkative. She always has her hand up to answer questions, even though she sometimes can't answer correctly. Despite her eagerness and enthusiasm during class, however, Amy makes very low grades on tests. Her written work is below average for the class.

George appears bored during class, often gazes out the window, and seldom participates in class discussions. He makes average grades on tests. Mr. Todd notices, however, that George shows spurts of interest and creativity when the class works on special projects. He appears to be a natural leader during group work and can analyze and solve problems remarkably well.

Julie Beth is a straight-A student. She rarely participates in class discussions and seems very nervous when called on to respond in class. Her homework is meticulous, but she never shows any interest in class activities other than what is required for getting good grades.

Barry is a careful, thorough worker. He pays close attention to details and conscientiously and systematically completes all assignments. He is never able to finish a test within the time limits, however, so his test scores are low.

Carol races through her work so that she can read her library books. She catches on quickly to new material and readily grasps difficult concepts. Her work is sloppy and careless, however, and she seldom turns in her homework. Her test scores are average.

1. From the information given, what do you believe are the learning strengths and weaknesses of each student?
2. For which students, if any, do you think test scores accurately reflect ability?
3. What factors should a teacher consider when evaluating students?
4. How can evaluation help a teacher plan appropriate instruction to meet individual needs?

TWO TYPES OF EVALUATION

In terms of evaluation, as a student teacher you will wear two hats. You will wish to check student progress through various means—observation, informal techniques, and formal tests. At the same time, you will be monitoring your own performance through a variety of methods.

STUDENT PROGRESS

Teaching without evaluation is like taking a trip without checking the map to see that you are going in the right direction. Periodic assessment enables you to observe student progress and then make adjustments in your instruction that enable students to achieve instructional goals.

Evaluation is an important component of any instructional plan, but it is not an easy task. You may be asking yourself such questions as: How do I find out how well my students are learning? What kinds of tests should I give? How often should I give them? How difficult should the questions be? What happens if everyone fails? . . . or if everyone gets a perfect score? What can I learn from the test results that will help me plan instruction? How can I measure different types of learning, and how can I be sure that my assessment techniques are appropriate for measuring each student's ability in various situations? You already know some of the answers to these questions from courses in evaluation and measurement, from your own experiences as a student, and from observations of your cooperating teacher. In this chapter you should find the answers to other questions.

Informal Evaluation Techniques

As a student teacher, most of your evaluation of student progress will be informal, although you may occasionally give a major examination over a unit. The most useful information you are likely to get is from day-to-day observations, samples of students' work, and short quizzes for checking students' understanding of the material you are presenting.

Observation   You have many opportunities to observe students in different situations, both academic (during class) and social (before and after class or during extracurricular activities). If you observe purposefully, perhaps by using the Observation Guide in Activity 9.1, you can find out a lot about how students learn. You can determine which students are self-motivated, easily distracted, disinterested, quick to learn, or capable of better work. You'll find that some possess leadership qualities while others prefer to be part of a group, and that some are naturally attentive and eager to learn while others appear bored and disinterested. You can also observe their learning styles. As you systematically observe your students, you are acquiring information that will help you plan lessons and activities to meet the wide range of individual differences within any class.

Teacher-Made Quizzes   You need to consider certain factors when planning your testing program. After identifying the objectives and content to be covered in a test, make sure your test appropriately distributes the emphasis upon the objectives and content. For example, if most instructional time has been spent on identifying main ideas in novels, be sure the greater part of the test asks questions about main ideas in novels, not about interpreting the mood projected by the authors. After assigning relative importance to the objectives and topics to be tested, you must decide what type of test items to use—for example, completion, short answer, essay, true-false, matching, or multiple choice. Completion, true-false, multiple-choice, and short-answer items are often used for frequent and short assessments. Essay test items are best for major examinations that require students to organize and present careful discussion.

Activity 9.1   Observation Guide

This observation guide will help you make systematic observations of students, which will help you plan learning experiences. You may wish to make copies of this observation guide for all of your students, or you may prefer to make copies only for selected students.

Student's Name _____

_____ 1 Volunteers to answer questions posed to class	Key:
_____ 2 Listens carefully during class time; follows directions	A—Always occurs
_____ 3 Asks questions about what is not understood	B—Often occurs
_____ 4 Completes homework assignments	C—Occasionally occurs
_____ 5 Participates in voluntary projects	D—Seldom occurs
_____ 6 Likes to help others and share activities with them	E—Never occurs
_____ 7 Projects a good self-image	
_____ 8 Attends regularly	
_____ 9 Performs well on quizzes	
_____10 Uses resource materials well	

A review quiz can be part of a lesson plan. The quiz may be oral, or it may be a short paper-and-pencil one of usually three to five questions, limited to the material taught in the immediate lesson. The quiz should be varied, with true-false and short-answer items. The main purpose of such a quiz is to see what concepts each student has not grasped or perhaps has misunderstood. It may be marked by the students and then checked by you.

A longer test may be appropriate about once every 10 days. It may have 20 to 25 true-false, multiple-choice, and short-answer questions. Such a test should be duplicated, rather than written on the board or dictated.

A unit test covers a larger block of teaching and may require most of a class period to complete. You will want to have several parts, including short essay items. Prepare a standard answer sheet before marking the test.

Some teachers give midterms and final examinations to cover a half or whole semester of instruction. You may want to assign points to each part of the examination in terms of its percentage of the whole test.

Completion test items are often used to measure knowledge of names, dates, terms, and other simple associations. Choose only important concepts, and make sure only one response correctly completes the statement. Short-answer test items are similar in format to completion test items.

True-false test items should test only important objectives and content, not trivial items. Avoid use of words such as *all, never,* and others that may give clues to correct answers. Avoid use of negative statements, since students often miss the item through misreading it, rather than because they don't know the answer. To discourage guessing, a true-false test may call for inclusion of the correct answer to any item marked "false."

Matching test items are often used to test student knowledge of definitions or identification of objects presented graphically or pictorially. To help eliminate guessing, present more response items than are to be used.

Multiple-choice test items should be in the form of questions, involving complete ideas. The four or five possible responses should be grammatically and logically consistent and similar in length, and correct responses should appear in all positions in the course of the test.

Essay test items should be phrased carefully to limit the question, specifically defining the expectations for each answer. In other words, directions must be thorough and specific as to the relative time to be spent on each question, the relative score to be assigned to each question, and the like. The answer key should contain the essential components of the answer, and papers should be scored against these factors.

Traditional types of test questions are not always suitable for evaluating certain types of knowledge. For example, it is better to judge a student's writing competence by evaluating writing samples than by asking objective questions about placement of commas and spellings of words. Also, when evaluating higher-order thinking skills, teachers should design open-ended test questions that allow students to give various solutions or interpretations.

Some guidelines for administering informal tests are:

1 Make sure that your test is based on the material that you have taught.
2 Ask "fair" questions. Avoid using misleading, ambiguous questions or questions that relate to insignificant material.
3 Make sure that students have the materials they need for taking the test (i.e., sharpened pencils with erasers, enough paper, and so forth).
4 Give clear instructions, and make sure that students understand what they are to do. You may need to do an example with the students before they begin.
5 Be certain that students understand the purpose of the test.

6 Let students know your expectations regarding neatness and correct use of spelling and punctuation.

7 Space students so that they will not be tempted to cheat.

8 Walk quietly around the room while the students are taking the test, and make sure they are following directions.

9 Make sure that students understand your grading policy.

10 Make a scoring key on one copy of the test you are giving.

11 When grading papers, always give students the benefit of the doubt.

12 Return tests promptly, and go over them with the students so that they can learn from their mistakes.

13 Make sure that students understand the meanings of the scores they make in terms of letter grades and percentages of total grades.

14 Generally, do not change grades.

If all of your students made perfect or nearly perfect scores on the test, it means that either you taught very well, the students are very bright or studied very hard, the test was too easy, or some combination of these factors. If nearly all of the students did poorly on the test, it may mean they didn't understand the material, they didn't study, or the test was too difficult. If the problem seems to be that they didn't learn the material, you may need to reteach it. Your cooperating teacher may be able to advise you on these matters.

Computer Applications for Testing

Computers can be useful in assessing student progress, but school systems vary in the availability of computers and software designed for assessment and test analysis. If computers are available for your students to use, you may assess their knowledge of skills by letting them complete short practice activities. If a computer is available for your use, you may wish to use it for test construction and analysis of grades. Even if you are not a good typist, you can use a word processor for preparing your tests because you can readily make corrections. Word-processing programs allow you to edit test questions and move items from one section of the test to another easily and efficiently. Computer programs may also be available to help you average grades, analyze the difficulty of individual test items, and keep records of students' scores.

Formal Tests

Most school systems administer formal standardized tests only once or twice a year, so you may not have an opportunity to give one to your students. Nonetheless, you should be able to interpret the scores and understand the place of formal tests in measuring student progress.

Norms are averages of test scores based on the performance of students in the norming population. They are ordinarily applied to formal or standardized tests.

Group achievement tests serve the purpose of telling the teacher how the *class*, not individual class members, is performing in comparison with other groups of students. The most important score is the class average, which helps the teacher determine whether the class is average, below average, or above average.

Standardized tests report norms in several ways:

1 *Grade equivalents*—The grade level for which a given score is a real or estimated average. Scores are expressed in terms of grade and month of grade, such as 4.8 for fourth grade, eighth month.

2 *Percentile rank*—Expression of a test score in terms of its position within a group of 100 scores. The percentile rank of a score is the percentage of scores equal to or lower than the given score in its own or in some reference group.

3 *Stanine*—One of the steps in a nine-point scale of standard scores. The stanine scale has values from one to nine, with a mean (average) of five.

Table 9–1 summarizes the types of tests that are appropriate for different assessment purposes.

Portfolio Assessment

Many educators believe that test scores alone do not accurately reflect what students can do, so they are proposing an alternative—portfolio assessment. Portfolios are folders that contain varied, representative samples of students' work over a period of time. Although informal tests can be part of a portfolio, work samples—such as drafts of students' writing or audiotapes of oral reading—are more likely to be present. The following list provides some possible inclusions:

Writing samples

Project reports

List of books read

Tape recordings of oral reading

Student self-appraisals

Semantic maps

Checklists

Illustrations

Selected daily work

Informal quizzes

Teacher's observational notes

Literature logs (responses to reading)

Parents' comments

At the secondary level, portfolios can be designed specifically for a particular subject, as in the following examples:

Art—Collages, prints, portraits, still lifes, sketches from rough draft to finished form

Science—Reports on the progression of experiments, drawings (diagrams and charts), biographies of scientists, labeled earth samples, statistical data for projects

Composition—Initial and all other drafts through publication of articles, note cards, letters, poems, essays

TABLE 9–1   Guide for Selecting Tests

Purpose	Appropriate Types of Tests
To check short-term progress	Short, objective written quizzes; oral questioning sessions; computer drill and practice
To check depth of understanding of a subject	Thought-provoking essay questions
To evaluate writing ability	Writing samples, essay questions, journals
To assess problem-solving and thinking skills	Observation of performance, open-ended test questions
To evaluate learning over an extended time period	Typed or word-processed tests with a variety of questions (such as essay, true-false, multiple choice, and completion)
To assess skill mastery	Short answer or completion questions, computer practice
To get a quick estimate of reading ability or level	Observation of oral reading performance and answers to oral comprehension questions
To compare achievement with that of students across the nation	Standardized achievement tests

If you decide to use portfolios, you need to explain to the students what you are doing and why. Students need to understand that instead of simply averaging grades, you will be asking for their help in evaluating samples of their work. Together with the students, you should establish guidelines for the types of material to include. In most cases, selections should relate to instructional goals and represent the students' best work; otherwise, portfolios can become stuffed with all sorts of materials that may have little value for review purposes. Make sure that students date each piece of work so that you and they can see the progress they are making. You should plan to have a conference with each student about her or his portfolio every few weeks to discuss the items and assess progress.

Although you may require students to include certain samples of their work, they should be able to select most items for their portfolios. Making decisions about what to include and how to organize the contents causes them to use critical thinking skills and evaluate their progress. In fact, you may ask them to write on a card or large sticky-tab note why they selected a particular piece to include. When they do this, they must justify their selections, and you will see what they value about their work.

You may additionally want to place some of your observations in students' folders, such as anecdotal notes about their contributions during class discussions. You may also want to include checklists about their progress toward achieving literacy or their participation in a social studies unit. Some key ideas for using portfolios are given in Figure 9–1.

Portfolio assessment requires additional time and effort, but the results can be worthwhile, because you will learn more about how and what your students are learning. Portfolios are also useful for parent conferences because you can show examples of what students are actually doing in class. Additionally, portfolios provide you with supporting information when you fill out report cards. You may want to try portfolio assessment for just one six-week period to see how it goes. (See Activity 9.2 for using portfolio assessment.) If the system works well, you may want to continue using it. You and the students, along with your cooperating teacher, must decide what happens to the portfolios when you leave. Your cooperating teacher may wish to keep them, pass them along to next year's teacher, give them to the students to keep, or send them home to the parents.

SELF-ANALYSIS

As you move through your student teaching program, you should be constantly evaluating your own progress. Although the supervisory personnel with whom you work are providing feedback on your performance, you may be the best judge of your teaching. You can analyze the effectiveness of your lessons in a variety of ways.

FIGURE 9–1   Key Concepts for Using Portfolio Assessment

Portfolio inclusions relate to instructional goals.
Students engage in reflective and critical thinking as they select and review their work.
Both teacher and students select material for inclusion in portfolios.
Periodically, the teacher and student have a conference about the portfolio, noting changes and progress, discovering insights, and seeking new directions for growth and learning.
Portfolios combine instruction and assessment by looking at the learning process as well as the product.
Portfolios are accessible to students at any time; they are working folders.
Students and teachers become partners in learning as they cooperatively assess student work.

Activity 9.2   Summary Sheet for Portfolio Assessment

Complete this summary sheet for your conferences with your students. You will probably want to make enough photocopies of this page for all of your students.

Grade: Subject: Date:

List of items in portfolio:

Student assessment of portfolio items:

Teacher assessment of portfolio items:

Conclusions and recommendations:

Student's signature _____

Microteaching/Videotaping/Audiotaping

You may microteach prior to, or along with, your student teaching. The idea of microteaching is to teach a brief lesson (about five to fifteen minutes in length) to a small group of students. A microteaching lesson concentrates on only one or two specific skills, such as asking higher-order questions or incorporating planned repetition. After the teaching, a supervisor, teacher, or other student critiques the performance. Some evaluative summary may be provided by the students taught. If the lesson is videotaped, there will be opportunity for pre- and post-comments when the lesson is replanned for teaching to a new group of students. In brief, microteaching follows these steps:

1 The prospective teacher receives exposure to a specific teaching skill.
2 He or she practices the technique in a short lesson with four or five students.
3 The lesson is recorded or videotaped for review by the prospective teacher.
4 A supervisor critiques the lesson.
5 The prospective teacher has an opportunity to replan and reteach the lesson to another small group of students. This session may also be recorded and critiqued.

Instead of having only one person critique the lesson, you may wish to cooperate with other students in critiquing each others' lessons, or you may want to critique your lesson yourself. If videotaping equipment is not available, record your lesson on an audiotape, and listen to it later at home. By going over tapes of your lessons, you can become aware of your voice control (audibility, pitch, expression), speech patterns (overuse of certain terms, such as "okay?"), use of praise and positive reinforcement, and clarity of directions. You can determine the kinds of questions you ask and the proportion of "student talk" to "teacher talk" during your lessons. You can also become aware of your use of nonverbal communication, such as encouraging nods, nervous gestures, or facial expressions.

Critical Analysis of Lesson Success

You and your cooperating teacher may wish to collaborate on evaluating certain lessons by using a form such as that in Activity 9.3. You should agree on the components that are to be evaluated and then separately rate a lesson or series of lessons. Then you should get together to compare notes and reconcile any differences. Over a period of time, you should try to improve those components that are indicated as needing improvement.

Other components that you may wish to include for certain lessons are giving clear directions, considering individual differences, maintaining discipline, organizing activities well, modeling or demonstrating desired learning, using audiovisual aids and resources appropriately, maintaining positive classroom climate, asking higher-order questions, promoting positive self-concept in all students, encouraging wide student participation, using different teaching strategies, communicating effectively with students, and showing evidence of preparation.

Student Analysis

Your students observe your teaching on a daily basis, and you may be able to learn a great deal about your teaching effectiveness from them. They may volunteer remarks, such as "Can we do that again?" or "Tell us more about pirate ships," that can guide you in planning subsequent lessons. The students may also give you insights into your effectiveness by answering questions that you ask them, such as "What did you learn today?" and "Did you do better when you worked with a partner?"

FIGURE 9–2   Rating Instruction by Younger Students

A. Marking Responses:

1. My teacher usually looks like this:

2. When I ask the teacher for help, he or she looks like this:

3. After I finish the lesson, I feel like this:

B. Oral Interview:

1. If I were the teacher, I would:

2. When I go to the teacher for help, he or she. . .

3. I would understand my lessons better if:

To get a more formal type of evaluation from your students, administer a checklist to find out how they perceive you. For younger children, you may use a format similar to that in Figure 9–2. For older students, a format such as that in Figure 9–3 is appropriate.

Case Study: A Challenge to a Student Teacher's Evaluation

A student teacher, Ms. Downey, was teaching a chemistry class. She was trying to keep a close record of student performance in her class. Through observation and analysis of student responses, she quickly noted that three students appeared to have little interest in the subject. Also, their early work products were of rather poor quality. After checking the results of a couple of tests (each covering two weeks of instruction), it seemed clear that the students had not grasped the content presented during that period of time. Ms. Downey thought student-teacher conferences might be helpful. She brought the evidence of her concern to the conferences. During the three conferences, the students responded with comments such as these:

Activity 9.3   Rating Key Aspects of Instruction

Using the form below, rate yourself for each component of instruction according to the following symbols: plus ($+$) for good, zero (0) for no evidence, or minus ($-$) for needs improvement. You may want to make a copy for your cooperating teacher to complete so that you can compare ratings. You may also want to make extra copies so that you can rate yourself periodically as you grow in your ability to teach.

Component	Rating	Comments
1 Gaining and holding student attention		
2 Telling students what they are expected to learn		
3 Reminding students of related knowledge or skills		
4 Presenting new stimuli for learning		
5 Guiding student thinking and learning		
6 Providing feedback about correctness		
7 Judging or appraising the performance		
8 Helping to generalize what is learned		
9 Providing practice for retention		
10 Other		

1. "The tests were too hard, so I just guessed."
2. "Most of the students missed the same questions I missed."
3. "Chemistry is mostly for brainy students."
4. "You don't make it clear what I'm supposed to learn."
5. "You talk all the time."
6. "You don't show much interest in the students."

> What objective data could Ms. Downey present to respond to each of these comments? What could Ms. Downey learn from these responses?

Reflective Teaching

According to John Dewey, reflective teaching is "behavior which involves active, persistent, and careful consideration of any belief or practice in light of the grounds that support it and the further consequences to which it leads."[1] It is a thoughtful analysis of the teacher's actions, decisions, and results in the classroom. Although it requires time and effort, reflective teaching can provide insights for you about your effectiveness as a teacher. It also causes you to question your procedures and consider alternatives, change any nonproductive routines, and try new ideas. Activity 9.4 gives some questions to ask yourself as you reflect on a lesson that you have taught.

FIGURE 9–3   Rating Instruction by Older Students

Student Opinion Questionnaire

A.   Circle the best answer.

1. Are assignments and explanations clear? Are assignments reasonable?

   Rarely   Sometimes   Usually   Almost Always

2. Is treatment of all students fair? Are students' ideas treated with respect?

   Rarely   Sometimes   Usually   Almost Always

3. Do students behave well for the teacher?

   Rarely   Sometimes   Usually   Almost Always

4. Is the teaching interesting and challenging?

   Rarely   Sometimes   Usually   Almost Always

5. Do you feel free to raise questions?

   Rarely   Sometimes   Usually   Almost Always

B.   Write a short answer.

1. Mention one or two things you like about this teacher.

2. Mention one or two things this teacher might do to help you be a better student.

---

[1]Christine Canning. "What Teachers Say about Reflection." *Educational Leadership* 48 (March 1991): 18–21.

Reflection can occur through many types of educational experiences—microteaching with self-analysis, conferences with your cooperating teacher, feedback from students, observations of other teachers in which you compare their strategies with your own, and journal writing. Of these, journal writing may be the most helpful way to reflect on your teaching. When you first begin writing in your journal you may feel that you are just rambling, putting down random thoughts that occur to you. As you continue writing, however, you may find that you begin to question, explore, and, finally, focus.

To get the most from journal writing, write about incidents, problems, or issues that truly concern you—not your lesson plan or a list of the day's events. Express your feelings about your frustrations and your triumphs. Think deeply about causes for them and consider what you need to do now. Writing can help clarify your thinking and enable you to reach conclusions about your teaching. (See Figure 9–4 for an example of a practicum student's journal entry.)

Perhaps your cooperating teacher or university teacher may assign journal writing. In this case, writing would be not only for your personal benefit, but also so that someone with more experience could understand your needs and concerns in order to help you. Similarly, you may want to do journal writing with your students in order to get to know them better. To ensure that they won't simply recall the day's

FIGURE 9–4 Excerpts from a Reading Practicum Student's Journal

Oct. 19
I had to *re*teach what I taught yesterday. I really had to discipline a lot too. I feel that they understood the content of what we were doing better after we went over it again. We went over question by question to ensure that everyone was listening—learning? I really want to establish myself before I get off the strict basal lesson. When they deserve to do something fun, we will. I'm enjoying this. This is a real-life classroom. I am learning so much!

Oct. 20
They were so "bad" today, or was it me? It seemed those same three boys always cause so much trouble. I gave them something that really challenged them—it was obvious that they are not often challenged. They acted so completely confused. I took it up and they were doing, mostly, okay on it. The ones with the lower grades were obviously intentionally not trying. I will go over it tomorrow.

Nov. 4
I have to constantly tell them to be quiet!! Why won't they learn—they are going to get into trouble when they're loud. I gave them a skills test—they did great! No one has to retake it!! I felt so proud of my teaching!

Nov. 13
I almost lost it today. I had assigned them homework. Five of them had it and even remembered it. They never stopped talking! I didn't know what to do. It is so discouraging. Forget all the good stuff I've learned and heard to say and do. It makes me feel so bad.

Nov. 14
We started back on basal. Boy, did they hate it. This class is definitely "dynamic" and likes something besides plain old reading class. This will challenge me to add more creativity to these lessons.

Nov. 19
We had an interesting class today. First, Tommy was sent to alternative school . . . today. The teacher was out of the class at a meeting because of that. Another lady sat in while she was gone. Two girls from my class observed me. I got evaluated. The principal came in and out about Tommy. That makes five extra people in the classroom besides myself and the students. They managed to stay tuned in fairly well. And I think I had them challenged with interesting issues about the story.

Activity 9.4   Questions That Reflective Teachers Ask Themselves

Date:

Lesson:

Read and seriously consider the following questions. Choose several that pertain to your lesson and write answers for them.

1. Did the students learn anything? If so, why? If not, why not?

2. Did anything significant occur? If so, what and why?

3. Was the strategy I used the most effective one? What other strategies might have been effective?

4. How well did I relate the lesson to the students' knowledge, experiences, and interests? How might I have done this better?

5. How flexible was I in modifying the lesson according to the students' responses?

6. How well did I manage classroom behavior? What other behavioral techniques could I have used? What technique worked best and what didn't work? Why?

7. What connections were there between teaching strategies and learning effectiveness? What does this tell me about what I need to do in the future?

8. What are some alternatives for conducting today's lesson?

9. How did I motivate the students? What are some other ways I might have motivated them?

10. Did I consider learning theory in preparing and implementing the lesson? If so, what theories worked? If not, what theories should I have considered?

11. Did I give students opportunities to direct their own learning? If so, how? If not, how could I have done this?

12. As a result of this lesson, what have I learned about teaching? How might I change to become a better teacher?

Teacher's signature _____

events, you may need to model a šample journal entry based on your own reflections about the lesson. You may do this on the chalkboard, a chart tablet, or a transparency, and then discuss what you wrote and why. A practical procedure is to provide time for students to write in their journals each day and for you to write a response to them about once a week. Here are some guiding questions to help your students write in their journals:

1 What did I learn?
2 What do I want to know more about?
3 What don't I understand very well?

DISCUSSION QUESTIONS

1 How would you modify the observation guide (Activity 9.1) to fit your particular class(es)?
2 What types of tests would be appropriate for the following situations?
    a. To see if a group of third graders can divide words into syllables
    b. To discover the reasoning powers of high school students in relation to foreign policy
    c. To assess the knowledge gained during a six-week unit on plant life
    d. To find out how your class compares with the national average on mathematical computation
    e. To assess the creative writing abilities of students
    f. To check understanding of last night's homework assignment, which was to read part of a chapter from the textbook
3 Investigate the availability of computers in your school. If they are available, what capabilities do they have, and how might you use them?
4 How might test scores indicate which students are or are not working up to their ability levels?
5 How does evaluation enable a teacher to plan better instruction?
6 What are the most effective ways for student teachers to evaluate their own teaching performances?
7 How valid are students' evaluations of teacher performance?
8 In the grade or subject you teach, what items would be appropriate to include in an assessment portfolio? How would you guide students in selecting which items to include?
9 What can you learn from the journals your students write? How can your responses help them?

SELECTED REFERENCES

Anthony, Robert J., Terry D. Johnson, Norma I. Mickelson, and Alison Preece. *Evaluating Literacy.* Portsmouth, N.H.: Heinemann, 1991.

Balajthy, Ernest. *Microcomputers in Reading and Language Arts.* Englewood Cliffs, N.J.: Prentice-Hall, 1986.

Canning, Christine. "What Teachers Say about Reflection." *Educational Leadership* 48 (March 1991): 18–21.

Farr, Roger. "Portfolio Assessment." *The Reading Teacher* 43 (December 1989): 264–65.

Harp, Bill, ed. *Assessment and Evaluation in Whole Language Programs.* Norwood, Mass.: Christopher-Gordon, 1991.

Johnston, Peter H. *Constructive Evaluation of Literate Activity.* New York: Longman, 1992.

Kubiszyn, Tom, and Gary Borich. *Educational Testing and Measurement,* 2nd ed. Glenview, Ill.: Scott, Foresman, 1987.

"Progress in Evaluating Teaching." *Educational Leadership* 44 (April 1987): entire issue.

Raths, Louis E., Selma Wassermann, Arthur Jonas, and Arnold Rothstein. *Teaching for Thinking,* 2nd ed. New York: Teachers College, 1986.

"Redirecting Assessment." *Educational Leadership* 46 (April 1989): entire issue.

"The Reflective Educator." *Educational Leadership* 48 (March 1991): entire issue.

Routman, Regie. *Invitations.* Portsmouth, N.H.: Heinemann, 1991.

"The Search for Solutions to the Testing Problem." *Educational Leadership* 43 (October 1985): entire issue.

Valencia, Sheila. "A Portfolio Approach to Classroom Reading Assessment: The Whys, Whats, and Hows." *The Reading Teacher* 43 (January 1990): 338–40.

10

Employment and Continued Professional Growth

Mrs. Carruthers and Mr. Martinez are both student teachers. Miss Page and Mrs. Lansing are regular teachers in the school to which the student teachers are assigned.

Mr. Martinez: Have you done any observation in other classrooms yet?

Mrs. Carruthers: Yes, I have. I observed Miss Page and Mrs. Lansing. I guess I chose them because they were both my teachers when I attended Jefferson.

Mr. Martinez: I've observed both of them, too. Mrs. Lansing seems to be using all the latest ideas we studied at school, but Miss Page's class seemed to be strictly traditional. Mrs. Lansing's students were playing a simulation game when I was in there. Miss Page's students were looking up the definitions of five vocabulary words and copying them directly from the dictionary.

Mrs. Carruthers: I noticed the same thing. Miss Page taught her class exactly the way she did when she was my teacher years ago, but I hardly recognized Mrs. Lansing's class. Everything she did had been revised and updated. There was even a boy in the back working on a computer lesson. I mentioned to her something about how things had changed, and she said, "You never stop learning how to be a better teacher." She has gone back to the university and gotten a master's degree since I was her student, and she still takes occasional classes. She also showed me several professional journals she subscribes to. She said they have wonderful teaching ideas in them.

Mr. Martinez: Miss Page made a disparaging comment about college courses when I had my brief conference with her. I don't think she's done any advanced work at the university.

Mrs. Carruthers: I don't either. I also doubt that she gets many professional publications, because you have to join professional organizations to get many of them, and I heard her mention to another teacher that she wasn't going to waste her money on those useless organizations.

Mr. Martinez: My university supervisor said it's possible to get 20 years of experience in 20 years or to get one year of experience 20 times. It looks like he was right.

Mrs. Carruthers: It surely does. I want to make sure I get a new year's experience for every year I teach. I guess that will mean more school and participation in professional organizations.

1. Did Mr. Martinez and Mrs. Carruthers learn something from their observations besides teaching techniques? If so, what was it?
2. Do you agree with Mrs. Carruthers' summation of the situation? Why or why not?

BEYOND STUDENT TEACHING

After you complete your student teaching experience, you will need to search for employment and consider your continued professional growth. You would do well to consider both processes now, well ahead of time, so you will know how to proceed efficiently and effectively after you graduate.

EMPLOYMENT

In this section, we will talk about searching for employment—where to find a position, how to develop a resumé and inquiry letter, how to get letters of reference, and how to handle interviews. We will also mention some general tips for ensuring your best chances for employment.

Case Study: A Fruitless Interview

John has just graduated from college. He spent four hard years in the study of elementary education, and now he has a bachelor's degree in education. The next step for John is to find a teaching position. He wants to teach at an elementary school close to his home and work with fifth-grade students.

John was busy during his last quarter of school, so he did not get to visit any schools or superintendents. He looked in the newspapers' classified ads, but he didn't find a job opening in a fifth-grade classroom. He telephoned some teachers at the school where he wanted to teach and asked if they knew of any openings for the coming year. They indicated that an opening in a first-grade classroom might be available, but nobody was sure about it. John didn't follow up on the possibility.

One day at a party, John overhead someone discussing the possibility of a job opening in the fourth grade in a different elementary school in the school system. He wasn't really interested in that teaching position, but he decided to go to see the superintendent.

Before going for the interview, John decided he would compile some kind of resumé. He decided he did not need to make a detailed resumé, since he wasn't very interested in the job. He thought he would go to see the superintendent for an interview concerning the actual job opening but would then use the interview to try to get a job in the fifth grade in the school he preferred. "I've heard that they need male teachers in the elementary school," he thought. "There weren't many males in my major in my graduating class. They should be glad to get me. Maybe they will give me a fifth-grade job and move somebody else."

John took a few minutes to write his resumé. The resumé looked like this:

My name is John Johnson.
Age: 24   Sex: Male
College: City University
Degree: B.S. in Education
Experience: I student taught in the third grade at Cordell Elementary School. They were nice kids, but I like the higher grades, like the fifth, better.

After developing his resumé, John went to the superintendent's office. John walked into the office and asked to see the superintendent. The secretary told John he would need to make an appointment because the superintendent would be busy with meetings all day. John argued with the secretary in an attempt to see the superintendent immediately, but finally agreed to set an appointment for the next day.

John had all kinds of trouble on his way to the office the next day. His car stalled several times, causing him to be 15 minutes late. He had dressed in a suit, but it was rumpled and smudged with grease from working on his car.

When he arrived, John did not apologize for being late. The superintendent looked somewhat shocked at John's appearance, but proceeded to ask him questions about his school experience and his interest in the job.

While answering some routine questions, John admitted he was not really very interested in the open position, but that he would like to teach fifth grade in another school. The superintendent told John that he could not guarantee him a job teaching fifth grade in the school of his choice, although a first-grade position in that school might become available. John said he was not sure he wanted a job if he had to teach first graders or couldn't be assigned to a better school than the one with the fourth-grade opening. The superintendent said that he would do his best and would let John know if any openings became available.

Before John left, the superintendent asked him for references. John said he did not have a reference list, but would give the superintendent the names of teachers he had worked with in school who might give him a good recommendation.

As John left the office, he had the feeling that the superintendent did not expect to call him. He shrugged and thought, "I don't need either of those jobs. I can find a better one if I get in touch with the right people."

What suggestions would you make to John about the following?

1. How to go about finding a job
2. Developing a letter of inquiry and resumé
3. Procedures for applying to a school system
4. Getting letters of reference
5. Interviewing skills

Where to Find a Position

You need to be aware of employment opportunities for graduates. The data change over a period of time. Mobility and double certification make locating jobs easier. (You should check trends in your own area and in the latest issue of *ASCUS ANNUAL: A Job Search Handbook for Educators,* published by the Association for School, College and University Staffing, 301 South Swift Road, Addison, Illinois 60101.)

Some special job options that are frequently overlooked are the following:

State government—Educators are employed in state correctional institutions and the state department of education. (Visit the state employment office in your city, and discuss possibilities with your advisor or counselor.)

Federal government—Educators are employed in several federal agencies, such as the Bureau of Indian Affairs (teaching on reservations, etc.), the Bureau of Prisons, the Department of Education, and the National Institute of Education. (Consult directories of government agencies in a library, and discuss possibilities with your advisor or counselor.)

Overseas—Educators, usually with at least two years of full-time experience, are selected for overseas positions. (Consult your library, and discuss possibilities with your advisor or counselor.) Several sources of employment for overseas jobs are:

U.S. Department of Defense (DOD), Office of Overseas Dependent Schools, 2461 Eisenhower Ave., Alexandria, VA 22331

The Teacher Exchange Program (known as the Fullbright-Hays Act), Teacher Exchange Section, Division of International Education, U.S. Department of Education, Washington, DC 20202

Schools operated by American firms conducting business overseas. See: *Directory of American Firms Operating in Foreign Countries,* 11th ed., World Trade Academy Press, 1987

Textbook publishers—Educators are employed in several capacities. Specific opportunities include sales representative, demonstrator of materials, leader of in-service sessions when new textbooks are adopted, writer for manuals and workbooks, and the like.

Through your library, you will find a number of references dealing with employment for teachers, such as directories of public school systems, boarding schools, and private schools, and journals such as *Academic Journal: The Educators Em-*

ployment Magazine (published biweekly) and *Affirmative Action Register* (published monthly) .

Some private employment agencies specialize in teacher placement, but they vary widely in quality and types of services they provide. City newspapers also run classified ads for teaching positions in the employment section. The cooperating teacher or principal where you did student teaching may know of openings outside or within their school systems, and job vacancies are often advertised at professional meetings. One of the best sources of help is the college or university career planning and placement office; it should have a complete and current placement file. The placement office will probably offer services such as providing placement files to employers who request credentials, arranging on-campus interviews with school systems, providing current listings of job opportunities, and making available job-search resources.

If you are considering alternate and/or satellite careers for teachers, the career/placement office can probably give you a list of possibilities. Career counseling will be provided, and credentials (or placement papers) are filed in this office to support your applications to prospective employers. You will also find a career library in the placement office, with such materials as brochures and applications, directories of community service organizations, encyclopedias of associations, audiovisual tapes on interviewing, information on writing resumés, overseas teaching literature, and the *ASCUS ANNUAL*.

Developing a Resumé and Inquiry Letter

A resumé is a brief statement about your abilities and experiences to help a prospective employer assess your potential for future success in a school system. The resumé can serve as a general introduction to accompany your letter of inquiry or application.

Preparing a Letter of Inquiry   Here is a general outline for the cover letter:

Paragraph 1—Give reasons for writing, indicating the position for which you are applying.

Paragraph 2—State concrete reasons for wanting to work for the particular employer. Give evidence that you understand the requirements of the position and that you possess the necessary qualifications for success in the position.

Paragraph 3—Refer the reader to your enclosed resumé, and emphasize the relevant personal qualities not cited elsewhere.

Paragraph 4—Provide at least three references with complete addresses.

Paragraph 5—Request a response, and ask for an interview.

Figure 10–1 provides a sample letter of inquiry.

Resumé   The resumé should be confined to one page, if at all possible. A reference on details of resumé writing is Burdette Bostwick's *Resumé Writing: A Comprehensive How-To-Do-It-Guide* (New York: John Wiley, 1990). Figure 10–2 is a sample resumé showing an acceptable format and what data to provide; it can be modified according to your specific experiences and qualifications. Activity 10.1 will help you see what should be included in a good resumé.

Getting Letters of Reference

Letters of reference increase the employer's confidence in the applicant's ability. Avoid including references who might be considered biased, such as relatives. Letters from appropriate persons (your adviser, student teaching supervisor, cooperating teacher, professors of courses you have taken, and the like) should reflect the writer's knowledge of your academic preparation and career objectives and should

FIGURE 10—1 Sample Letter of Inquiry

Box 145
University of Parkersburg
Parkersburg, Tennessee 55519
May 2, 1993

Dr. John Doe
Superintendent of Schools
Cumberland County Schools
Hillside, Delaware 24970

Dear Dr. Doe:

It has come to my attention that a teaching position in mathematics will be open next year at the Parkview School. I plan to graduate in June from the University of Parkersburg with an M.S. Degree in Mathematics Education and would like to apply for this position.

Your school system is often cited as outstanding because of its strong instructional program. The extensive use of media in your school system and the availability of facilities and equipment are impressive. My program of study included media courses that provided practical information for using audiovisual aids and computers in the classroom. I am eager to put my educational experiences into practice in a full-time teaching position.

Enclosed is a copy of my resumé, which will give you some insight into my background, education, and experience. A videotape of my teaching performance is also available upon request, and a copy of my placement file can be obtained from our Career Planning and Placement Service.

Below you will find three references you may contact about my qualifications for the position. I have received permission from all three to use them as references.

Dr. Buford Jenkins   Mr. A. J. Metcalf
1245 Park City Hall   Jenkins Square
Park City, TN 55516   Barkley, TN 55542

Dr. Maria Fernandez
1111 Memphis Avenue
Jacksonville, TN 55503

I will be available at your convenience for an interview and will look forward to hearing from you. Thank you for your consideration.

Sincerely,

Bob Alfred

Bob Alfred

FIGURE 10-2 Sample Resumé

Bob Alfred
Johnson Avenue
Corbin, Maine 44407
(207) 123-4567

Professional Objective:
  To secure a mathematics teaching position in a secondary school that encourages innovation and creativity.

Education:
  1992-1993   Coursework toward M.S., Mathematics Education, University of Parkersburg, Parkersburg, Tennessee—anticipated completion date June 10, 1993
  1991   B.S., Mathematics Education—University of Highpoint, Greenville, North Dakota
              Certification: Grades 8-12
              Major: Mathematics Education
              Minor: Physical Science
              GPA: 3.8

Honors and Awards:
  Received Maxwell Student Teacher of the Year Award (1991)
  Was in top 10 percent of secondary education graduating seniors (1991)

Experience:
  Teaching Assistant (for tenth-grade class), Parkersburg Secondary School, Parkersburg, N.D., 1992
  Student Teacher, Marks Secondary School, Greenville, N.D., 1991
  Math tutor for gifted children during the summer, Greenville, N.D., 1991

Activities:
  Debate Captain
  Active member in Student Teacher Association
  Volunteer worker at Student Handicap Center

Interests:
  Sports
  Computers

Placement File:
  Available upon request from:
  Career Planning and Placement Service, University of Parkersburg, Parkersburg, Tennessee

be positive statements of support for the position you seek. With an "open file" (nonconfidential), you can read the letters; with a "closed file" (confidential), you are unable to read your letters of recommendation.

Interviewing Skills

The best advice for an interview is to *be prepared*. One way to prepare is to anticipate questions you may be asked.

Research the school system as much as possible. Find out about its reputation, school/community relationships, organizational structure, teacher-pupil ratio, benefits and services provided to teachers, and other considerations.

Activity 10.1   Resumé Writing

Study the sample resumé in Figure 10–2. Then note, for each heading below, the information that you would be able to include on a resumé if you had to write one now.

Professional objective:

Education:

Honors and awards:

Experience:

Activities:

Interests:

Placement file:

Think through some responses for the questions likely to be asked, such as: Why did you select teaching as a career? How would you handle certain problems—such as motivation, discipline, or parental concerns? Why do you want to teach in this particular system? How would you like to organize your class? How would you take care of individual differences? What instructional materials have you found helpful? How would you evaluate students? How would you diagnose difficulties of students? What magazines, periodicals, or books relative to your field do you subscribe to or read regularly? What are your long-range goals in the teaching field? What are your strengths and weaknesses in teaching? How are your human relations with principals, supervisors, and students in such extracurricular activities as athletics, dramatics, publications, etc.?

Think through some questions you may wish to ask an interviewer, such as: What are your homework and discipline policies? What incentive is there for advanced study? What kinds of in-service programs will be offered to help me during my first year? With what supervisory assistance will I be provided? What is the school's evaluation system for teachers? What types of schools/situations are new teachers placed in? What is the beginning salary, and what are other monetary benefits? May I read the system's contract?

For some school systems, memoranda of understanding between the board of education of the system and the local education association will be available for study. These memoranda contain information about agreements reached relative to association rights, management rights, work stoppage, dues deductions, student discipline procedures, personnel files, evaluation, right to representation, grievances, transfer policy, leaves of absence, sick leave, physical examinations, insurance, salary schedule, and other such matters. Study of the memoranda of understanding will provide further information about the particular school systems you are investigating.

You may wish to take several items with you for the interview session—resumé, transcript, student records, representative lesson/unit plans, audio/videotape of a teaching situation, and student evaluations. Consult with your placement office for videotapes or films on interviewing and books about interviewing skills. Use a mirror, or ask a friend to look for characteristics that could detract from an interview session. Completing Activity 10.2 will help you prepare for an interview.

General Tips for Employment Search

Letters should be:

1 Typewritten on good-quality bond paper
2 Immaculately clean (no smudges or fingerprints)
3 Attractively arranged
4 Grammatically perfect and properly punctuated, with spelling carefully checked

For interviews, you should:

1 Know the name and position of the interviewing official
2 Arrive promptly for your appointment
3 Know something about the school and the position for which you are applying
4 Write a letter of appreciation following the interview
5 Dress formally and moderately
6 Look the interviewer in the eye when answering questions, look alert and interested, and be a good listener
7 Use language well

Where interest is evident on the part of the student and the prospective employer, there will probably be follow-up telephone calls and letters, and specific materials may be called for, such as an application form and transcripts. If you observe the commonsense guidelines in this chapter, the chances are good that you will be successful in your search for a job.

CONTINUED PROFESSIONAL GROWTH

After you actually have a job as a teacher, you may be tempted to settle into a routine much like Miss Page at the beginning of this chapter. It is, after all, easier to use the same lesson plans year after year without bothering to revise and update them. If it worked the first time, it ought to be good enough now, right?

Wrong! Every year, you will have students with different abilities and needs, and you must adjust instruction if the students are to benefit maximally. There will always be changes going on within your discipline that could render your lessons inadequate and, in some cases, actually incorrect. A teacher like Miss Page will never know.

How, then, can you be sure to stay "on top" of your teaching assignment? Actually, there are many ways. Membership and participation in professional organizations is one excellent way. Reading the publications of professional organizations is another way. Attending workshops sponsored by your school and outside agencies (professional groups, industries, federal and state agencies) can add much to your professional growth, if you approach these workshops with a desire to learn and not a resentment at being asked or required to attend. Courses at a nearby college or university, if carefully chosen to meet your needs, can be extremely beneficial. In addition, there are growth opportunities within your own school. Serving on textbook selection and curriculum revision committees will expose you to new ideas and materials.

Professional Organizations and Publications

Professional organizations for teachers abound today—general organizations, encompassing all grade levels and disciplines, and specific organizations, focusing on particular grade or subject areas. These organizations frequently have local, state, regional, and national level activities, and your involvement can vary as you desire. Activities usually include regular meetings (discussions, speakers, panels), conferences and conventions, and service projects. Members often receive benefits such as reduced rates for conferences and conventions, journals and/or newsletters, and group study opportunities. Attending the regular meetings, conferences, and conventions and reading the journals and newsletters will keep you up to date. By helping with service projects, you can learn more about the discipline and the community. In addition, group study opportunities offer motivation to analyze content, methods, and materials.

Two large general professional organizations are the National Education Association (NEA) and the American Federation of Teachers (AFT). The NEA was formed to promote professional development of educators and improvement of educational practices. It has become politically active in recent years and has participated in teachers' collective bargaining efforts. The AFT was created as an affiliate of the American Federation of Labor, and it functions primarily as a teacher's union by promoting better working conditions and higher salaries. It participates in collective bargaining activities as a main function. You need to analyze the goals and functions of these organizations and decide which, if either, is more closely oriented toward your personal philosophy.

A list of some professional organizations available to educators follows. This list is far from comprehensive, but it gives you an idea of the diverse organizations from which you may choose.

Activity 10.2   Preparing for an Interview

Think about the following questions that you may be asked during an interview, and write some possible responses.

1. Why did you select teaching as a career?

2. How do you believe discipline should be maintained in a classroom?

3. What class organizational pattern do you prefer, and why?

4. How will you take individual differences into account in your classroom?

5. What are some instructional materials that you would like to use in your classroom? Why?

6. What types of student evaluation will you use? Why?

7. How do you plan to remain up to date in your field?

8. What is your philosophy of education?

American Association for the Advancement of Science (science teachers)

American Chemical Society (chemistry teachers)

American Home Economics Association

American Physical Society (physics teachers)

Association for Childhood Education International (early childhood education)

Association of Educational Communications and Technology

Council for Exceptional Children

International Reading Association

Modern Language Association (teachers of foreign languages)

National Association for the Education of Young Children (early childhood education)

National Association of Geology Teachers

National Association of Independent Schools (secondary teachers)

National Council for Social Studies

National Council of Teachers of English

National Council of Teachers of Mathematics

National Science Teachers Association

National Vocational Agriculture Teachers Association

Speech Association of America (speech teachers)

Many professional publications can benefit the individual teacher, and quite a few of them are connected with professional organizations. Although there is a limit to the number of professional organizations you can realistically join, there is no reason to limit the journals you consult to help improve your teaching. To round out your professional reading, you should obtain journals to which you do not subscribe from other sources. Other sources include fellow teachers, the school library's professional collection, the public library, the teacher center, and college or university libraries. Articles in journals cover a wide range of topics, including classroom management, methods, materials, teacher liability, accountability, curriculum revision, new developments in different disciplines, and many others. Search out articles related to your situations and needs, read them, and *grow.* Completing Activity 10.3 will help you to identify some organizations that would be most beneficial to you.

In-Service Opportunities and Graduate Work

To keep their teachers up to date, school systems budget a certain amount of money each year for in-service education. In-service programs can be as effective as you and your colleagues determine. Most systems allow teachers some voice in choosing in-service programs *if* the teachers express a desire to have such a voice. In many cases, programs are chosen without teacher input because teachers have said nothing and administrators assume that teachers don't want to be involved. This may be an inaccurate assumption that administrators should investigate, but often such an assumption *is made* and *no* attempt is made to test its accuracy. When teachers do not have input about in-service programs, the programs may not meet their needs, and some teachers will write off in-service education programs as irrelevant. Don't make this mistake. Tell your in-service planners what your needs are, and those needs are more likely to be met.

Some systems ask teachers to attend a variety of professional functions to earn in-service "points," of which a specific number must be earned during each school year. Such a plan can work to your benefit. You may be able to earn points by attending the meetings and conferences of the professional organizations of your choice, participating in specially planned activities at your school, or taking part in professional activities such as curriculum development workshops. You may also be able to earn points by taking related graduate courses at a nearby college or university.

Graduate courses can help you improve your teaching if you choose them wisely. Many states require a certain amount of graduate work for renewing teaching certificates. Some teachers take any convenient or reportedly easy course for this purpose. Don't fall into this trap. You are paying for this graduate work; make it pay you back with ideas for better instruction. Choose courses that will increase your skills in the areas in which you have felt some weakness, alert you to new methods and materials, or give you more insight into your students. If you actually enroll in a degree program and steadily take relevant courses, your activity will also lead, in time, to a salary increase on the basis of your new degree.

Personal Contributions

You can also grow while helping others. Speaking at professional meetings or writing for professional journals will help you clarify your thinking and stimulate your mental processes. Your help for others turns into helping yourself. Serving on curriculum revision or textbook selection committees adds extra hours to your workday, but you will find that you also gain new ideas and familiarity with new materials that can improve your teaching. Everybody gains.

DISCUSSION QUESTIONS

1 What options and resources should you consider when looking for a position?
2 What factors should you consider in developing a resumé and a letter of inquiry?
3 From whom and how should you secure letters of reference?
4 What are some necessary interviewing skills?
5 What opportunities for employment are available in your field? Do all of them involve teaching?
6 Where might you relocate to find the right position?
7 Do you have a responsibility to continue your education after you graduate from college and are certified as a teacher? Why or why not?
8 How can you keep up to date in your field after you leave the college classroom?
9 What contributions can professional organizations make to your growth as a teacher?
10 How can you obtain professional journals to read for new ideas? What journals are designed for your particular field?
11 Do in-service programs serve a useful function? Why or why not?
12 Are there any advantages to doing graduate study when you are employed as a teacher? If so, what are they?
13 Find a current directory of job opportunities, or check with your placement office about the availability of positions. What good prospects are available?
14 Role play an interview with a peer. How could you improve your performance?
15 Develop a sample resumé and letter you might use. Have you presented yourself effectively?

Activity 10.3   Professional Organizations and Publications

Research the professional organizations cited earlier in the chapter and others that you have heard about in class or from your cooperating teacher. Write down up to four organizations that you believe might be good for you to join. Indicate for each one the focus of the organization and its publication(s).

1. Name:

   Focus:

   Publication(s):

2. Name:

   Focus:

   Publication(s):

3. Name:

   Focus:

   Publication(s):

4. Name:

   Focus:

   Publication(s):

SELECTED REFERENCES

Bolles, Richard Nelson. *The Nineteen Ninety-Two What Color Is Your Parachute? A Practical Manual for Job-Hunters and Career Changers,* rev. ed. New York: Ten Speed Press, 1991.

Crystal, John C., and Richard N. Bolles. *Where Do I Go From Here With My Life?* New York: Ten Speed Press, 1980.

Dictionary of Occupational Titles, 3 vols. New York: Gordon Press, 1991.

Dubey, Robert E., et al. *A Performance-Based Guide to Student Teaching.* Danville, Ill.: Interstate, 1975.

Figler, Howard. *The Complete Job-Search Handbook.* New York: Henry Holt and Co., 1988.

Flygare, Thomas J. *Collective Bargaining in the Public Schools.* Bloomington, Ind.: Phi Delta Kappa Educational Foundation, 1977.

Itish, Richard K. *Go Hire Yourself an Employer,* 3rd ed. New York: Doubleday, 1987.

Lathrop, Richard. *Who's Hiring Who,* rev. ed. New York: Ten Speed Press, 1989.

Medley, Anthony. *Sweaty Palms Revised: The Neglected Art of Being Interviewed.* New York: Ten Speed Press, 1991.

Scheele, Adele M. *Skills for Success.* New York: Ballantine Books, 1987.

Schmidt, Peggy J. *Making It on Your First Job: When You're Young, Ambitious, and Inexperienced,* rev. ed. Princeton, N.J.: Peterson's Guides, 1991.

U.S. Government Printing Office. *The Occupational Outlook Handbook, 1990–91.* Washington, D.C.: U.S. Government Printing Office, 1990.

APPENDIX
A

Assessment Instruments

This appendix contains instruments for the cooperating teacher in the school and the university supervisor to use to aid in assessing the student teacher's or practicum student's performance.

Overall Assessment

Student's Name _____

Cooperating Teacher's Name _____

College Supervisor's Name _____

Grade Level and/or Subject Area _____

Date _____

Key to Abbreviations:

EE = Exceeds expectations

ME = Meets expectations

NI = Needs improvement

BE = Below expectations

	EE	ME	NI	BE
1. Conducts self in an ethical manner				
2. Handles the stress of teaching appropriately				
3. Has positive relationships with:				
a. Students				
b. Supervisors				
c. Peers				
d. Other school personnel				
e. Parents				
4. Learns from classroom observations				
5. Plans effectively for instruction				
6. Uses a wide range of instructional resources well				
7. Is effective in teaching content				
8. Handles discipline well				
9. Understands how to use various organizational plans				
10. Supervises study effectively				
11. Maintains a positive classroom environment				
12. Motivates students to learn				
13. Adjusts instruction to meet student needs				
14. Evaluates student progress well				
15. Assists with extracurricular activities as appropriate				
16. Has a good knowledge base				
17. Has good communication skills				

	EE	ME	NI	BE

18. Maintains a professional appearance (as signified by appropriate dress, neatness, and cleanliness)

19. Has a positive attitude toward teaching

20. Seeks continued professional growth through professional reading, attendance at meetings, and/or conferences with professionals

Early Progress Check

Student's Name _____

Cooperating Teacher's Name _____

College Supervisor's Name _____

Grade Level and/or Subject Area _____

Date _____

Key to Abbreviations:

EE = Exceeds expectations

ME = Meets expectations

NI = Needs improvement

BE = Below expectations

	EE	ME	NI	BE
1. Shows enthusiasm for student teaching				
2. Is punctual in arriving at school and for each class				
3. Is becoming familiar with the faculty of the school				
4. Has learned students' names				
5. Shows readiness to help in classroom in a variety of ways				
6. Asks questions designed to prepare him or her for teaching				
7. Investigates the instructional resources of the school				
8. Interacts positively with other student teachers				
9. Knows school rules, routines, and disciplinary procedures				
10. Is planning ahead for future participation				

Periodic Progress Check
(File sequentially for comparison purposes.)

Student's Name _____

Cooperating Teacher's Name _____

College Supervisor's Name _____

Grade Level and/or Subject Area _____

Date _____

Key to Abbreviations

EE = Exceeds expectations

ME = Meets expectations

NI = Needs improvement

BE = Below expectations

	EE	ME	NI	BE
1. Plans lessons thoroughly				
2. Has clear objectives for lessons				
3. Ties new material to previous learning				
4. Motivates students to study material				
5. Chooses content wisely				
6. Has good grasp of content				
7. Uses a variety of materials and resources				
8. Uses appropriate materials and resources				
9. Budgets time well				
10. Evaluates student learning appropriately and accurately				
11. Has enthusiasm for teaching				
12. Relates well to other school personnel				
13. Handles noninstructional activities willingly and effectively				
14. Accepts constructive criticism and learns from it				
15. Shows signs of effective self-evaluation				

DISCUSSION TOPICS FOR STUDENT TEACHER-COOPERATING TEACHER OR STUDENT TEACHER-COLLEGE SUPERVISOR CONFERENCES*

Questions for Cooperating Teachers or College Supervisors to Ask

Early in the Experience

1 Have you become familiar with the physical layout of the school? If not, how do you plan to accomplish this goal soon?
2 Have you met the other school personnel with whom you will be working? Do you have any questions or concerns about these working relationships?
3 Have you gotten to know the students whom you will be teaching? If not, how can you get to know them better in a short period of time? Do you have any concerns about dealing with any of the students to whom you have been assigned? If so, what are they?
4 Are you networking with the other student teachers or practicum students in your group to share concerns, problems, and solutions? If not, how could you begin to do this? Do you see the benefits of such networking?
5 Do you understand what is expected of you during your student teaching or practicum experience? If not, what things need to be clarified?

Later in the Experience

1 What have you learned from observing your cooperating teacher or other school personnel?
2 Have you been devoting enough time and effort to planning your lessons? What makes you think so?
3 Have problems surfaced during your teaching that you did not know how to handle? What were they? Where did you turn for help? What else might you have done?
4 Have you had any problems with class control? What kinds of problems? How might these problems be handled, considering both the structure of the class to which you have been assigned and your status as a student teacher or practicum student (rather than a regular classroom teacher)?
5 Have you been using a variety of instructional resources and teaching approaches in your lessons? What have you used? How could you make use of other strategies and resources to facilitate the learning of your content?
6 What have you learned about teachers' responsibilities that go beyond teaching?
7 Do your students have special needs that must be considered? What kinds? How have you tried to accommodate them?
8 Have you promoted a positive classroom atmosphere? How have you attempted to do this? How have the students responded?
9 Have you been able to evaluate your students' learning effectively? What problems have you had with evaluation? Are there appropriate forms of evaluation that you have not tried? What might you try next?

Near the End of the Experience

1 Do you feel comfortable performing the duties of a teacher? If not, with which ones are you uncomfortable? What can you do in the time remaining to correct this problem?

*Note: These are just some suggestions that can help to keep a conference focused on important concerns. No conference would be likely to use all of the questions in a category, but all of them might be addressed over time.

2 Have your students been learning from your lessons? If not, have you analyzed your lessons for possible flaws? Have you retaught lessons that were not effective?

3 Have you helped your students to enjoy learning? What are some ways in which you have accomplished this?

4 How have your career goals been affected by your experiences? Are you comfortable with the students and subject matter with which you have been working, or will you seek employment at another level or in another teaching area?

5 Has your philosophy of education been changed by this experience? If so, how? If not, how did the experience reinforce your original position?

Questions for Student Teachers or Practicum Students to Ask

Early in the Experience

1 Am I doing the types of things that will best prepare me for the responsibilities I will have?

2 Are there people who are using different strategies and materials in the school that I could observe?

3 Am I assuming the correct amount of responsibility for this point in the term? If not, what should I be doing?

4 How can I interact with students more effectively?

Later in the Experience

1 Do my plans look complete, coherent, and effective? If not, how do they need to be changed?

2 Am I overlooking resources that would enrich my lessons? If so, what are they?

3 Am I being responsive enough to my students? If not, what more should I be doing, or what should I be doing differently?

4 Do my evaluation procedures appear to be appropriate? If not, what should I try?

5 Is my classroom management plan appropriate and effective? If not, what do you suggest?

6 Am I carrying my share of the noninstructional responsibilities? If not, what should I be doing?

Near the End of the Experience

1 Have I met your expectations in my noninstructional activities? Please explain why or why not.

2 Have my lessons been well planned and delivered, so that you have felt that the students were learning? Please explain why or why not.

3 Have my evaluation procedures been good enough to provide you with the information about the students that you need for reporting purposes? Please explain why or why not.

4 Has my attitude promoted a positive feeling in the classroom? Please explain why you feel that way.

5 Do you believe that I have the qualities to be a successful teacher? Please explain why or why not.

DISCUSSION TOPICS FOR SEMINARS*

1 What different types of students does this school serve? What types of adjustments need to be made for this student body?

2 What things have happened in your classes that have caused stress? How have you handled them? In what other ways might they have been handled?

3 Should teachers be involved with extracurricular activities? Why or why not? What have you learned while working with extracurricular activities in your situation?

4 How have you seen teachers work together for common goals? Can you think of other ways that you could work with peers for common goals?

5 Why is it valuable to observe in the classrooms of a variety of teachers and at different grade levels? What have you learned from such observations?

6 What instructional resources have you used in your lessons besides textbooks? How effective were they? What other resources do you plan to use? Where will you obtain them?

7 What problems have you encountered with time management? How might you avoid these problems in the future?

8 What discipline problems have you encountered? How have you handled them? How effective were your techniques? What else could you have done?

9 In what ways have you organized your classes for instruction? Have you tried whole class, small group, and individual organizations? Have you tried cooperative learning? Were some patterns more effective for certain types of lessons than others?

10 What assessment procedures have you used? Did you encounter any problems in using any of them? Which ones were most effective?

11 What motivational techniques have you used in your classes? Which ones have been most effective? What else do you intend to try?

12 What teaching strategies have you used? Have you tried both teacher-centered and student-centered strategies? Do you see a difference in student involvement when different strategies are used? How will this affect your teaching?

13 What part does homework play in your teaching situation? What kinds of homework are most effective? Why?

14 How does your use of questions affect what students learn? Are you including enough higher-order questions in your lessons?

15 Do some of your students have trouble reading their textbooks with understanding? What can you do to improve their chances of learning the material?

16 Where can you obtain ideas for teaching strategies that will enhance your teaching skills?

---

*Note: One form of assessment is observation of the responses that students make during discussion of important topics. Here are some discussion topics that may be used in seminars, from which much assessment information can be gleaned. The discussion questions at the ends of each of the chapters in the book are also good for this purpose.

APPENDIX
B

Code of Ethics of the Education Profession, Adopted by 1975 Representative Assembly, National Education Association*

PREAMBLE

The educator, believing in the worth and dignity of each human being, recognizes the supreme importance of the pursuit of truth, devotion to excellence, and the nurture of democratic principles. Essential to these goals is the protection of freedom to learn and to teach and the guarantee of equal educational opportunity for all. The educator accepts the responsibility to adhere to the highest ethical standards.

The educator recognizes the magnitude of the responsibility inherent in the teaching process. The desire for the respect and confidence of one's colleagues, of students, of parents, and of the members of the community provides the incentive to attain and maintain the highest possible degree of ethical conduct. The *Code of Ethics of the Education Profession* indicates the aspiration of all educators and provides standards by which to judge conduct.

The remedies specified by the NEA and/or its affiliates for the violation of any provision of this *Code* shall be exclusive and no such provision shall be enforceable in any form other than one specifically designated by the NEA or its affiliates.

PRINCIPLE I

Commitment to the Student

The educator strives to help each student realize his or her potential as a worthy and effective member of society. The educator therefore works to stimulate the spirit of inquiry, the acquisition of knowledge and understanding, and the thoughtful formulation of worthy goals.

*Reprinted by permission of National Education Association, Washington, D.C.

In fulfillment of the obligation to the student, the educator—

1 Shall not unreasonably restrain the student from the independent action in the pursuit of learning.
2 Shall not unreasonably deny the student access to varying points of view.
3 Shall not deliberately suppress or distort subject matter relevant to the student's progress.
4 Shall make reasonable effort to protect the student from conditions harmful to learning or to health and safety.
5 Shall not intentionally expose the student to embarrassment or disparagement.
6 Shall not on the basis of race, color, creed, sex, national origin, marital status, political or religious beliefs, family, social or cultural background, or sexual orientation, unfairly—
   a Exclude any student from participation in any program
   b Deny benefits to any student
   c Grant any advantage to any student.
7 Shall not use professional relationships with students for private advantage.
8 Shall not disclose information about students obtained in the course of professional service, unless disclosure serves a compelling professional purpose or is required by law.

PRINCIPLE II

Commitment to the Profession

The education profession is vested by the public with a trust and responsibility requiring the highest ideals of professional service.

In the belief that the quality of the services of the education profession directly influences the nation and its citizens, the educator shall exert every effort to raise professional standards, to promote a climate that encourages the exercise of professional judgment, to achieve conditions which attract persons worthy of the trust to careers in education, and to assist in preventing the practice of the profession by unqualified persons.

In fulfillment of the obligation to the profession, the educator—

1 Shall not in any application for a professional position deliberately make a false statement or fail to disclose a material fact related to competency and qualifications.
2 Shall not misrepresent his/her professional qualifications.
3 Shall not assist any entry into the profession of a person known to be unqualified in respect to character, education, or other relevant attribute.
4 Shall not knowingly make a false statement concerning the qualifications of a candidate for a professional position.
5 Shall not assist a noneducator in the unauthorized practice of teaching.
6 Shall not disclose information about colleagues obtained in the course of professional service unless disclosure serves a compelling professional purpose or is required by law.
7 Shall not knowingly make false or malicious statements about a colleague.
8 Shall not accept any gratuity, gift, or favor that might impair or appear to influence professional decisions or action.

APPENDIX
C

Sample Lesson Plans

ELEMENTARY MATHEMATICS, GRADE 3

A. Performance (Behavioral) Objective
Given two numbers (two-digit numerals), the student will compute the sum when regrouping is required.

B. Major Concepts
Addition
Regrouping (renaming, "carrying")

C. Materials
Flannel board and felt cutouts
Counting men*
Place value chart
Instructional chart
(Beansticks*/abacus)

D. Activities and Procedures
1. Use the word problem: "I have 23 small red stars and 18 small blue stars. How many small stars do I have altogether?"
2. Represent the number sentence $23 + 18 = \square$ with felt cutouts on a flannel board.

---

*Counting men are sets of materials used for developing place value concepts and computational skills. Beansticks are sets of materials made of beans glued to sticks; they are also used for developing place value concepts and computational skills.

3. Ask the students to group the stars into sets of tens and ones. Ask the students to trade each group of ten small stars for one large star. (The sum will be represented by four large stars and one small star.)

4. Provide counting men as student aids, and verbally guide the students through the process of representing the problem on their counting men.

5. Use a place value chart to illustrate the solution:

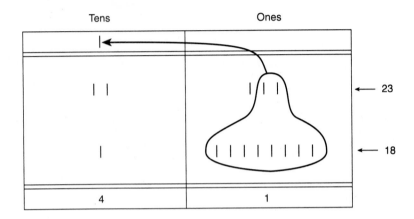

6. Use expanded notation, leading to the shortened form (on instructional charts)

			1
23	2 tens + 3 ones	23 = 20 + 3	23
+ 18	1 ten + 8 ones	+ 18 = 10 + 8	+ 18
	3 tens + 11 ones	30 + 11	41
	4 tens + 1 one	= 41	
	41		

7. *Alternative activity*—Use beansticks to represent the idea of regrouping of 26 + 19.

E. Evaluation

    1. Ask students to do the following with this word problem:

        Bill has 15 stamps, and Betty has 37 stamps. How many stamps do Bill and Betty have altogether?

        a. Write the number sentence.

        b. Use squares of paper to group into sets of tens and ones, trading each group of ten small squares for one large square of paper.

        c. Find sum, using counting men.

        d. Illustrate solution on a place value chart.

        e. Use expanded notation and shortened form.

F. Assignment

    Word problems and exercises on page 78 of textbook.

Plan Book Entry for Math Lesson

Objective—To add 2 two-digit numbers.

Materials—Flannel board, counting men, charts

Procedures—Give word problem for 23 + 18. Use flannel board to demonstrate problem. Use counting men and place value chart to solve problem.

Assignment—Do page 78 in text.

ELEMENTARY SCIENCE,* GRADES 4–6: ENERGY IN A NUTSHELL—USING A PEANUT TO ILLUSTRATE FORMS OF ENERGY

Scientific processes: Observing, describing, measuring (mass and temperature), questioning, collecting, recording and analyzing data, drawing conclusions, labeling diagrams

Rural issues and technology: Farm products are renewable resources that we are looking to now and in the future as fuel sources. Using a peanut as fuel demonstrates the science processes that can be used to discover new technologies.

Elementary science: Grades 4–6, Physical Science. Related Tennessee Science Curriculum Guide Objectives: 454N1, 551D4, 554N2, 651D1, 651C4, 654N3

Materials: Balance or scale for weighing equal amounts of peanut and peanut shell, empty soup can, metal coat hanger, paper clip, matches, thermometer, styrofoam cup, raw peanuts in the shell (roasted and salted in shell will work also)

Vocabulary: Temperature, thermometer, heat energy, light energy, potential energy

Instructional Procedures (Directions for Teachers)

Set   Show students a peanut in its shell, and ask them if it has energy stored in it. Tell students that today we will experiment to see if we can prove that a peanut has stored (potential) energy.

Lesson   If all students agree that the peanut has energy (they will usually say that it does because you can eat it and get energy), discuss the following questions before the experiment. If some questions cannot be answered by students, write the questions on the board, and say they will be answered by our experiment.

How could we measure the potential energy in a peanut? (Hint: How do we measure the potential energy in a stick of wood?)

When we burn a peanut, the potential energy is changed to what form(s) of energy? (heat energy and light energy)

When we eat a peanut, the potential energy is changed to what form of energy? (chemical energy)

Which do you think has more potential energy, a peanut or peanut shells? (Some students will say a peanut because it weighs more; some will say the shells because they burn faster.)

How can we make sure we are burning the same amount of peanut and peanut shells? (We can weigh them.)

What instrument do we use to measure heat energy?

How are we going to contain the heat energy given off by the burning peanut in order to measure it? (Listen to students' suggestions; then explain that we can use the burning peanut and shells to heat water and then measure the rise in temperature of the water.)

*"Energy in a Nutshell: Using a Peanut to Illustrate Forms of Energy," from *SPRITES*. Sponsored by TTU/TVA Environmental/Energy/Science Education Center, and TTU Rural Education Research and Service Consortium. Developed by Catherine Massengill, 1987.

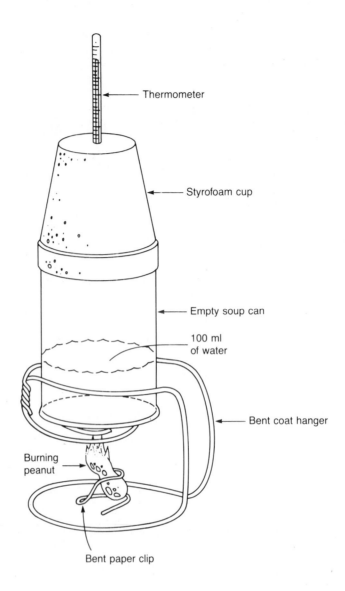

The Experiment   Show students the homemade apparatus that will be used, and have them draw and label it in their science notebooks.

Have students make a chart like the following to record the data.

Fuel	Temperature of Cold Water	Temperature After Burning	Difference in Temperature
Peanut			
Peanut shells			

Perform experiment

1 Weigh equal amounts of peanut and peanut shells, and attach paper clip stands to each.
2 Put 100 ml of cold water in can; record temperature in chart.
3 Burn peanut underneath. (You may also want to record time it takes to burn peanut.)
4 Take temperature of water, and record it.
5 Repeat with fresh water and peanut *shells*.

Closure:

Which had more potential energy, the peanut or the peanut shell?

Why?

Which burned the fastest?

What if we compared peanut oil and fuel oil? Could you design an experiment to do this?

Are peanuts a renewable or non-renewable resource?

Where did the peanut get its stored energy in the first place, and why is it there? (from the sun; stored for the young plant to get started)

What is gasohol? What agricultural products is this fuel made from?

Related Activities

Language arts: Who was George Washington Carver? Did he make a fuel from peanuts?

Math: Weigh your peanuts on a gram scale. Can you figure out how many peanuts are in a pound of peanut butter? (one pound = 454 grams)

Social studies/geography: Which state produces the most gasohol?

Plan Book Entry for Energy Lesson

Objective: To demonstrate forms of energy.

Materials: Balance scale, empty soup can, metal coat hanger, paper clip, matches, thermometer, styrofoam cup, peanuts

Procedures: Do experiment on energy with peanut (See Science Curriculum Guide, p. 97)

Assignment: Learn about George Washington Carver.

SECONDARY ENGLISH (WRITTEN COMPOSITION),* GRADE 11 OR 12

I. Objectives
General Aim: To make students aware of the fine distinctions in communication of language; to help them learn how to write more clearly and effectively.
Specific Aim: To teach students to recognize the ambiguous elements in our language and how to avoid using them in their writing.

II. Content
Old Knowledge: Students have already learned about stress, pitch, and juncture in their language study.
New Knowledge: Types of structurally ambiguous sentences, distinguishing between the two meanings that can be attributed to one ambiguous sentence, and how to avoid writing ambiguous sentences.

III. Materials: Mimeographed sheets, list of ambiguous sentences

IV. Activities and Procedures
When students come into class, this sentence will be written on the board:

Girl hunter says father sets example

*Reprinted with permission of Marsha Daugherty Grieve.

I will ask the class what this newspaper headline means to them. (I hope they will give me two different meanings; if they provide only one, I will tell them how it can have a completely different meaning from that one.)

To further introduce my subject for the lesson, I will tell them an amusing story about the misunderstanding by a coal deliveryman of the sentence "Empty sack in kitchen" and the funny consequences of this misunderstanding.

After I feel they sufficiently understand that sentences or even sequences of words they write may convey one meaning to themselves and quite another to someone else, I will enumerate and discuss with them six major sources of ambiguity and confusion in sentence structure.

I will ask students to add to the examples I give of each type of ambiguity. My examples will be on mimeographed sheets. The types of ambiguity are:

(1) One-stress pattern words—stress patterns of words are same, but certain words can function (grammatically) two ways in some sentences. Example:

Secondary stress-plus-primary
(gerund)

modifier → noun   verb → noun-object
She abhors scratching dógs.   She abhors scratching dógs.

(2) Overlap of stress patterns—some words have separate stress patterns for certain grammatical connotations. Examples:

Secondary-plus-primary	Primary-plus-third
↓	↓
modifier → noun	compound nouns
dârk róom	dárkroòm
bluê bóok	blúeboòk

(3) Form and position duality of certain words—same word can identify with two parts of speech and mean two entirely different things. Example:

The girl in the back seat looked *forward* (adverbial—ahead?)

or

(adjectival—brash and unladylike?)

(Verb *looked* also has two meanings in this connection.)
Example:
He likes to spear muskrats and fish.
(Fish—noun object or infinitive?)
(...to spear muskrats and fish?)

or

(...to spear muskrats and to fish?)

(4) Duality of sentence pattern
Example:
He found her an amateur. (indirect obj. plus direct obj.?)

or

(direct object plus obj. complement?)

(5) Absence of stress, pitch, and juncture signals carried by speaking voice to indicate which of two meanings implied.
Example:
Do you know how happy people ought to be?
Do you know how happy | → | people ought to be?
Wanted: Baby-sitting in my apartment
Wanted: Baby | → | sitting in my apartment
Did you ever stop to think how little men know about women?
Did you ever stop to think how little | → | men know about women?

(6) Modification by position—word order and position
(This is an easier one for students to correct in their writing.)
Example:
He washed the chair on the patio.
(On the patio he washed the chair?)
or

(The chair on the patio he washed?)
After this discussion, I will explain several ways by which errors in ambiguity of this type (6) can be corrected. They are:

gender	number	coordination
person—thing signals	position	punctuation
(pers—rel pronouns)		

To clarify this, I will give the students practice in trying to correct some ambiguous phrases. I will pass out sheets with these six phrases on them:

1. The man in the chair with the tattered look.
(the/its)—gender

2. The pet of the girl that was lying in the sand.
(who/which)—person—thing signals

3. The boats at the dock which seemed far from our house.
(was/were)—number

4. A discussion on gambling in the dormitory.
(in the dormitory on gambling)—position

5. The novel that stood beside his dictionary which he loved to pore over.
(and that he)—coordination

6. A small room heater
(small-room heater or small room-heater)—punctuation

V. Evaluation: I will give the students a list of sentences (much like the above-mentioned phrases) that are structurally ambiguous and ask them to improve them according to the six criteria above.

To make sure they understand this study of ambiguity thoroughly and completely, I will employ a reversal technique in which the students must deliberately think up about ten ambiguous sentences (including at least one to illustrate each of the six types of ambiguity I have introduced in class discussion) and be able to tell what is wrong with each of them.

VI. Assignments: The next day I will have the students read and discuss some of their made-up sentences in class. After that, we will discuss the best ways to correct the sentences on the sheet I gave them to work on the night before.

To make them more aware of structural ambiguity and its frequent occurrence in writing (magazines, books, their own themes), I will announce a standing assignment to be due every Friday throughout the term. For a few minutes on these days, students will tell the class about examples of ambiguity they have noticed in a book or magazine. Also, since themes are returned every Friday, I will bring to the students' attention the ambiguous statements I have discovered in their writing and have them tell me why the sentences are ambiguous and then correct them.

Plan Book Entry for Written Composition Lesson

Objective: To write clearly

Materials: Handout of ambiguous sentences

Procedures: Write sample ambiguous sentence on board. Discuss six sources of ambiguity (See text, pp. 27–29). Use handout to practice correcting ambiguities.

Assignment: Write ten ambiguous sentences.

APPENDIX
D
Sample Unit Plans

ENGLISH[*]

Title: Writing Paragraphs: Descriptive, Comparative, and Narrative

I. *Abstract*

    A. *Rationale*—A major focus of this writing unit is on the concept of revision of written material. Students learn that revision is a repetitive process and that original writings are rarely perfect. The emphasis on acceptability and desirability of revision is as important as the knowledge and understanding of the specific kinds of paragraphs which are presented in the unit.

        The writing practice done in this unit of study will help students in writing longer compositions in subsequent language lessons. Hopefully, students will transfer skills acquired in this unit to written assignments in other subjects.

    B. *Source*—County-adopted textbook for 5th grade language: Ragno, N. N., M. D. Toth, & B. G. Gray. *Silver Burdett English.* Morristown, N.J.: Silver Burdett Co., 1985.

    C. *Duration*—The unit will be taught in approximately 10 lessons of 45 minutes each.

[*]Adapted from Unit Outline on "Writing Paragraphs: Descriptive, Comparative, and Narrative," by Brenda Harrell, Capshaw Elementary School, Cookeville, Tennessee.

D. *Goals and related instructional objectives —*

1. The learner will understand the five steps of the writing process.

   a. Given a list of the five steps of the writing process, the learner will write at least one descriptive statement about each step.

   b. The learner will explain a rationale for each step in the writing process, including at least one reason for each step.

2. The learner will know how to write a descriptive paragraph.

   a. After a kite has been displayed, the learner will write a paragraph describing the kite, using at least four details.

   b. Having written a descriptive paragraph and having used a revision checklist, the learner will revise the paragraph for content, grammar, and form.

   c. After revising an original, descriptive paragraph, the learner will rewrite the paragraph to contain no more than two errors.

   d. After writing, revising, and rewriting a descriptive paragraph, the learner will read the paragraph aloud in a group of three to four students.

   e. Given two student-prepared descriptive paragraphs, the learner will orally critique the paragraphs based on content, grammar, and form.

3. The learner will know how to write a comparative paragraph.

   a. Given a kite and a balloon of identical colors, the learner will list at least four common qualities of the two objects.

   b. After listing qualities common to both a kite and a balloon, the learner will write a paragraph comparing the two objects in at least four ways.

   c. After writing a comparative paragraph, the learner will revise the paragraph for content, grammar, and form, using a revision checklist.

   d. After revising an original, comparative paragraph, the learner will rewrite the paragraph to contain no more than two errors in content, grammar, or spelling.

   e. After revising and rewriting an original, comparative paragraph, the learner will read the paragraph aloud in a group of three to four students.

   f. The learner will place his or her paragraph in a class notebook.

4. The learner will know how to write a narrative paragraph.

   a. The learner will tell how he or she thinks it would feel to be a kite or a balloon, stating at least one positive and one negative feeling.

   b. The learner will write a narrative paragraph from the point of view of either a kite or a balloon, following a logical sequence.

   c. After writing a narrative paragraph, the learner will revise the paragraph for errors in content, grammar, and form, using a revision checklist.

   d. After revising and rewriting an original, narrative paragraph, the learner will create an illustration of at least one event that happens in the paragraph to be displayed with the writing.

5. The learner will know the differences among descriptive, comparative, and narrative paragraphs and will be able to explain the characteristics of each.

   a. Given a worksheet with eight paragraphs, the student will correctly label at least seven of the paragraphs as descriptive, comparative, or narrative.

   b. The learner will write an explanation of the characteristics of descriptive, comparative, and narrative paragraphs, giving at least one characteristic of each.

E. *Procedures for introducing the unit*—

Show the class a kite and a helium-inflated balloon, both of which have strings attached (attention getter). Tell students to raise their hands if they have ever flown a kite. Then tell them to raise their hands if they have ever had a balloon similar to the one shown. Ask how many have ever lost such a balloon (student involvement). Tell the students that they will be using the kite and the balloon as subjects for some writing they are going to be doing in this unit. Tell the students they will be learning some steps in writing that they will find helpful in language class, as well as in other classes (relating to student's life). Remind students that they already have experience in writing paragraphs (relating to previous learning), and solicit examples of kinds of writing they have done. Inform the students that they will be writing paragraphs that describe; paragraphs that compare, or tell how things are alike; and paragraphs that narrate, or tell stories (stating objective).

II. *Instructional Considerations*

A. *Target group*—Fifth- through eighth-grade language classes

B. *Instructional environment*—Desk arrangement encourages small group sessions. Chalkboard and overhead projector are provided.

C. *Assessment of and provision for individual differences*—Some students will take much longer to complete writing assignments than others. These students will be allowed and encouraged to complete assignments between classes as homework, provided they have the skills necessary to do so.

When additional instruction is needed, individual tutoring by the teacher and/or peers will be provided.

Individual differences will be assessed by monitoring during formative evaluation.

III. *Materials and Media*

Display chart of steps in writing process

Worksheet with steps and descriptions

Kite, balloon

Student copies of revision checklist

Display chart of revision checklist

Art paper for illustrations

Extra crayons

Worksheet with eight paragraphs (colored paper)

Several examples of the three kinds of paragraphs in this unit

Picture of caterpillar

Dialogue for "Caterpillar Journey" from *Teaching Creativity Through Metaphor* by Donald and Judith Sanders

Overhead projector

Transparency of paragraph containing several errors

IV. *Assessment of Learner Understanding (Unit Evaluation)*

(F) Formative evaluation   (S) Summative evaluation

1.a. (F) Descriptions will be checked in class.
     (S) Unit test

  b. (F) Oral and written responses will be monitored.
     (S) Unit test

2.a. (F) Class observation (including teacher monitoring with individual students and small group self-checking followed by teacher monitoring of each group)
     (S) N/A

  b. (F) Class observation
     (S) N/A

  c. (F) Paragraphs will be checked by the teacher. Errors will be noted, and the paragraphs will be returned to the students.
     (S) N/A

  d. (F) Class observation
     (S) N/A

  e. (F) Class observation
     (S) N/A

3.a. (F) Class observation and monitoring through group signaling
     (S) N/A

  b. (F) Class observation (including teacher monitoring with individual students and small group self-checking followed by teacher monitoring of groups)
     (S) N/A

  c. (F) Class observation
     (S) N/A

  d. (F) Paragraphs will be checked by the teacher. Errors will be noted, and the paragraphs will be returned to the students.
     (S) N/A

  e. (F) Class observation
     (S) N/A

  f. (F) Class observation
     (S) N/A

4.a. (F) Class observation
     (S) N/A

  b. (F) Class observation (including teacher monitoring with individual students and small group self-checking followed by teacher monitoring of groups)
     (S) N/A

  c. (F) Class observation
     (S) N/A

    d. (F)   Class observation
       (S)   N/A

5.a. (F)   Monitoring throughout unit instruction
      (S)   Unit test

    b. (F)   Monitoring throughout unit instruction
      (S)   Unit test

Unit Test—Writing Paragraphs: Descriptive, Comparative, and Narrative

1.a. Write at least one statement to describe each of the steps of the writing process listed below:

    (1) prewriting:

    (2) writing:

    (3) revising:

    (4) rewriting:

    (5) publishing:

1.b. Why is it a good idea to do each of the steps listed below?

    (1) prewriting:

    (2) writing:

    (3) revising:

    (4) rewriting:

    (5) publishing:

2. Explain what content should be included in each of the following kinds of paragraphs:

   (1) narrative:

   (2) comparative:

   (3) descriptive:

Plan for Reporting Learner Progress

Students will be informed of their progress on a daily basis through verbal and/or written feedback.

   Learner progress will be reported on a weekly basis to parents by way of take-home folders containing graded/checked papers. Report cards will be sent home at the end of each six-week period. When individual parent-teacher conferences are desirable, they will be arranged through letters or phone calls.

SECONDARY SOCIAL STUDIES[*]

I. Topic
   The Spanish-American War is often glossed over or neglected entirely in surveys of American history, yet it is an excellent vehicle for examining American values at the turn of the century as well as America's perceived role in international affairs. The period itself (1898–1900) and its aftermath showcase a moral dilemma concerning American foreign policy, and eventually a resurgent "nationalism" that profoundly affects the events of ensuing decades. This is a five-day plan.

II. Students' background
   This unit is designed for a college-bound eleventh grade American history class with a small-town or suburban background.

III. Suggested resources for students
   A. Anti-Imperialism
   Twelve Against Empire, Robert Beisner ⎫   Copies in the library on
   U.S. Expansionism, David Healy   ⎬   reserve
   Textbook   ⎭
   Encyclopedia
   Photocopied material on resource table ⎫   May be used in class or
   Reader's Guide to Periodical Literature ⎬ checked out overnight

   B. Philippine Insurrection
   Little Brown Brother, Leon Wolff—Copies in library on reserve
   Textbook
   Encyclopedia
   Reader's Guide to Periodical Literature
   Photocopied material on resource table

---

*Reprinted with permission of Paul Aebischer, 122 Montana Ave., Oak Ridge, Tennessee 37830

C. 1900 Presidential Election
Encyclopedia
Various political histories in library
History of American Presidential Elections, ⎫   Library
  Arthur Schlesinger, editor   ⎬ reference area
Textbook   ⎭

D. Foreign Policy
U.S. Expansionism, David Healy—Copies in the library on reserve
Textbook
Encyclopedia
Reader's Guide to Periodical Literature

IV. Teacher's Bibliography
  A. Textbooks
  America! America!
  America: A Portrait in History

  B. Secondary Sources
  Richard Hofstedter, "Manifest Destiny..." in Daniel Aaron's *America in Crisis.*
  Robert Beisner, *Twelve Against Empire*
  Frank Friedel, *The Splendid Little War*
  David Healy, *U.S. Expansionism*
  Arthur Schlesinger, ed., *History of American Presidential Elections,* vol. III
  Joseph E. Wisah, *The Cuban Crisis as Reflected in the New York Press*
  Leon Wolff, *Little Brown Brother*

  C. Periodicals
  Robert Beisner, "30 Years After Manila: E. L. Godkin, Carl Schurz, and Anti-Imperialism in the Gilded Age," *The Historian,* vol. XXX, 1968, pp. 561–76. (Portion of this article will be photocopied for the resource table.)
  D. J. Tweton, "Imperialism vs. Prosperity," *North Dakota Quarterly,* vol. XXX, 1962, pp. 50–52.

  D. Primary sources: Published documents listed under W. J. Bryan, E. L. Godkin, Carl Schurz, and T. Roosevelt. Also copies of W. R. Hearst's *New York Journal* and J. Pulitzer's *World.*

  E. Audiovisual: Films dealing with destruction of battleship "Maine." Note: For further information on this topic, refer to "anti-imperialism" or "Spanish-American War" headings in *Harvard Guide to American History.*

V. Objectives
  A. To familiarize students with historical developments leading to the Spanish-American conflict.

  B. To trace the course of the Spanish-Cuban conflict prior to U.S. intervention.

  C. To recognize factors influencing the U.S. decision to enter the war.

D. To consider the role of the media and of public opinion as potent forces in politics.

E. To place the entire event in the context of the evolution of U.S. foreign policy.

F. To explore the consequences and implications of U.S. postwar policy, particularly in the Philippines.

G. To develop group discussion and problem-solving skills.

H. To develop research and writing skills.

VI. Procedures: Daily Activities
Introduction
A. Monday
   1. Introductory lecture. Topic is "Historical Background for the Spanish-American War." Lecture will cover the following:
   Spanish interests in the Caribbean—potential conflicts with the United States.
   Unrest in Cuba—the revolution in 1895 to throw off Spanish power.
   U.S. economic interests and humanitarian interests—developments in the Cuban-Spanish Conflict up to and including the explosion aboard *The Maine*. (twenty minutes)
   2. Show class the short film concerning activities surrounding the "Maine" incident. (twenty minutes)
   3. Introduce the class to the resource table where various documents, primary materials, and articles concerning the Spanish-American War can be found.
   Explain to class that unit grade will be determined by:
   Participation in discussions
   Quiz
   Unit exam
   Individual project
   Distribute ditto sheets explaining the project requirements (which follow).

PROJECTS FOR SPANISH-AMERICAN WAR UNIT (CULMINATING ACTIVITY)

Each student will complete one of the following:
A. After reading letters and articles concerning the anti-imperialists, summarize in a three–five page essay the sentiments of two of these people—Carl Schurz, E. L. Godkin, W. J. Bryan, Samuel Gompers.
B. Use outside resources to prepare a three–five page paper on the Philippine insurrection.
C. Use outside resources to prepare a three–five page paper on how the Spanish-American War affected the presidential campaign of 1900.
D. Write a three–five page essay explaining how the Spanish-American War might have been a turning point in American foreign policy. Use specific examples.
E. Prepare a bulletin board or other audiovisual presentation dealing with some aspect of the Spanish-American War.
F. Get teacher's approval to develop your own project.

Distribute ditto sheets of the student's bibliography and research guide. (ten minutes)

Assignment:
  Read Chapter 30 in textbook (*America! America!*) in preparation for a short cognitive quiz on Tuesday.

Body
B. Tuesday
  1. 20-point standardized cognitive quiz on Chapter 30 in textbook. (twenty minutes)
  2. Lecture. Topic is "U.S. Intervention: The Spanish-American War." Lecture will cover situations which convinced United States to enter the war, especially the "de Lome letter" and the "Maine" incident; President McKinley's role; suggestions that United States was eager to show off power, to seek "World Power" status; the course of the war before U.S. intervention; the course of the war after U.S. intervention; Admiral Dewey. (twenty minutes)
  3. Assignment/Activity. Distribute copies of an illustrative article from William Randolph Hearst's *New York Journal*. Allow remaining class time to read article. Distribute the following questions to be considered for discussion on Wednesday.
    a. Is the article biased? What does it intend its readers to believe? Isolate specific examples of "sensationalism."
    b. Do you think the media reflect public values or create them? Why?
    c. How important is public opinion in an event such as the Spanish-American War? Do you think President McKinley was pressured by public opinion?

C. Wednesday
  1. Class is broken into groups of eight for discussion of above questions. Teacher appoints discussion leader, discussion monitor (to record who participates and how often), secretary, and reporter (can be the same person). Groups will be allowed three minutes to report their conclusions to the entire group. (twenty minutes for discussion, ten minutes for reports)
  2. Lecture. Topic is "Public Opinion: Emerging Nationalism." Lecture will cover concept and philosophy of nativism, manifest destiny, and the "White Man's Burden"; review America's history as an isolationist nation (Declaration of Independence, Washington's Farewell Address, Monroe Doctrine); describe "yellow journalism," "jingoism," and the role of popular opinion; and introduce the anti-expansionist philosophy. (twenty minutes)

D. Thursday
  1. Lecture. Topic is "Moral Dilemma—The Question of Empire." Lecture will cover crux of the Philippine issue. McKinley wrestles with four alternatives; humanitarian or economic? The anti-imperialists—ideology, philosophy, distinguished members, methods used, results; William Jennings Bryan—election of 1900 as a last gasp for an anti-imperialistic administration, the "Bryan" dilemma for Democrats; the Philippine insurrection—why did it occur? Acquisition of Philippines as a crossroads in American foreign policy. Point to future events: Caribbean policy; World War I. (twenty minutes)

2. Explain nature of Friday's unit examination: Five out of eight identi-
   fications. (fifty points) and two out of three essays (fifty points). (five
   minutes)
3. Questioning techniques with entire group. Distribute handout on Philippine Islands.
   a. How does this account differ from what you've read? How would
      you account for differences?
   b. Main question: Should a nation be allowed the right of national
      self-determination? If they say "Yes," ask, "Do you suppose another
      powerful nation—such as Spain—would overrun the Philippines if
      the United States didn't acquire it?" If they say "No," ask "How
      would the United States have developed without this right? Could
      the Philippines develop similarly?" (twenty-five minutes)
      (If discussion stalls prematurely, time may be spent on projects.)

E. Friday—Unit Exam (Entire Period)
   (Remind students that projects are due Monday.)
   Part I. Identification
   Identify and briefly explain the significance of five (5) of the following:
      Isolationism
      de Lome letter
      William Jennings Bryan
      Manifest Destiny
      "jingoism"
      the anti-imperialists
      Admiral Dewey
   Part II. Essay
   Respond to two (2) of the following questions. Responses should be in
   the form of a concise (three–four paragraphs), well organized, and co-
   hesive essay.
   1. Support or attack the following statement:
      "The Spanish-American War was a blemish on the United States' dip-
      lomatic record. A misinformed nation acted on misperceived threats
      with territorial gains primarily in mind."
   2. "Theodore Roosevelt referred to the Spanish-American conflict as a
      'Splendid Little War.' In reality, this war—fought on Cuba's behalf,
      against Spain, in the Philippines—was a major turning point in Amer-
      ican foreign policy." Support or refute this statement.
   3. Trace the role of public opinion—both during the war itself and in
      ensuing events—in the Spanish-American War Period. What impor-
      tance would you ascribe to the power of public thinking? Be sure to
      consider political issues, economic aspirations, and "yellow journal-
      ism."
      Note: For those who finish before end of period—work on projects.

APPENDIX

E

Sample Learning Center:
Fabulous Fables*

OBJECTIVES

1 To acquaint students with fables
2 To encourage students to analyze and explore fables
3 To enable students to have fun with fables
4 To offer some creative challenges through fables
5 To relate fables to students' personal lives

MATERIALS AND RESOURCES

1 An area (counter or table) with activities and resources attractively displayed
2 Collections of fables
3 Tape recorder
4 Paper, pencil, scissors, glue
5 Activity packets, task cards, and/or assignment sheets
6 Resources for art project (such as cardboard cartons, old magazines, scraps of fabric and colored paper, and miniature animals)

DIRECTIONS

Work independently or with a partner on the activities that you find displayed here. Complete five of the seven activities. If an activity has * beside it, it is required. Take a file folder, write your name on it, and put your completed work in it (except for the

*Adapted from "Fabulous Fables," a Learning Center by Noralyn Parsons, Tennessee Technological University, Cookeville, Tennessee.

art project which you can leave on the table in the back of the room). You should finish your activities by _____ .

ACTIVITIES

*1 *Introduction*—Read "The Hare and the Tortoise," "The Town Mouse and the Country Mouse," and any other two fables. Then complete these statements about fables.
  a. A fable is usually a _____ (long, short) story.
  b. The main characters are usually _____ (people, animals, witches).
  c. A fable usually ends with a _____ (moral, joke, question).

  2 *Character traits*—Read "The Ant and the Grasshopper" and "The Fox and the Crow." Think about the main characters. When you finish reading these two fables, cut out the words at the bottom of the page. Then look at four of the characters from "The Ant and the Grasshopper," "The Fox and the Crow," and "The Hare and the Tortoise." Glue the words that you might use to describe each character in the appropriate column. (Some words might be used to describe more than one character.)

Ant	Grasshopper	Fox	Tortoise
Industrious	Slow	Lazy	Crafty	Frivolous
Hardworking	Sly	Steady	Foolish	Persistent

  3 *Find the moral*—Read "The Lion and the Mouse" and "The Fox and the Grapes." Consider the morals in the fables you have read. (A moral is a statement dealing with right and wrong behavior.) Then match the story to the appropriate moral.

_____ The Hare and the Tortoise

_____ The Ant and the Grasshopper

_____ The Town Mouse and the Country Mouse

_____ The Fox and the Crow

_____ The Fox and the Grapes

_____ The Lion and the Mouse

a. Better to eat plain food in safety than rich food in danger.

b. Slow and steady wins the race.

c. It is best to prepare for times of need.

d. Little friends may be great friends.

e. Do not trust flatterers.

f. It is easy to not want what you cannot get.

Read another fable, and write your own moral for it.

Name of fable: _____

Moral: _____

_____

4 *Art project*—Make a collage or diorama illustrating one of the fables. You may work with a partner. Use the materials at the center, or find other materials.

*5 *Think of it!* Choose one of the following ideas, and write a story.

    a. *Invent-a-fable.* Write an original fable to fit one of these morals:

        (1) It pays to be kind.

        (2) There is always a way.

        (3) Don't be greedy.

    b. *Add-a-character.* Pretend you are another hare in "The Hare and the Tortoise." What might you do or say? Would the race have a different winner? Rewrite the story with this character.

    c. *Change-an-ending.* Choose one of your favorite fables. Change the story so that it has a different ending.

6 *Characterize and vocalize*—Find a partner, and rehearse a scene from a fable. Say the parts the way you think the animals spoke them. When you think you know what to say and how to say it, tell your story into the tape recorder. Some sample scenes might be those that follow.

    a. The fox flattering the crow

    b. The hare challenging the tortoise

    c. The grasshopper persuading the ant to stop working so hard

    d. The town mouse persuading the country mouse to dine on fine food

*7 *It's a lesson for you*—Fables have been used for a long time to teach lessons to people. The morals from fables can help you make smarter decisions, be a better citizen, or be a better friend.

    Choose a moral from one of the fables you have read. Write the moral and the name of the fable it came from on your paper. How might you use this moral to help you make a decision in your life or solve a problem? Describe a situation (pretend or real) in which you might use this moral.

Moral: _____

_____

Fable: _____

Situation:

EVALUATION

The student should have completed five activities, and the activities should show the student's familiarity with several fables, knowledge of the characteristics of fables, appreciation of the worth of fables as a guide for living, and ability to relate morals to stories.

Index

Betty D. Roe is Professor of Curriculum and Instruction at Tennessee Technological University in Cookeville. She teaches reading and language arts methods courses and supervises reading practicum students and student teachers at all grade levels and in all subject areas. She received her Ed.D. in Curriculum and Instruction from the University of Tennessee, Knoxville. She is a former classroom teacher in the public schools and has worked with diagnosis and remediation of reading difficulties for students of all grade levels in clinical situations. She is the author or coauthor of twenty-seven books, most of which are college methods textbooks. She is also the author of numerous articles in professional journals. She makes professional presentations on reading and language arts instruction, as well as storytelling presentations for all age groups. She is active in several professional organizations at local, state, national, and international levels.

Elinor P. Ross is Professor of Curriculum and Instruction at Tennessee Technological University in Cookeville. She was a classroom teacher in Pennsylvania, Delaware, and Maryland before getting her Ed.D. at the University of Tennessee. She currently supervises practicum students and teaches methods courses in reading, children's literature, and whole language. She has supervised student teachers at various levels and in different subject areas. She works closely with the public schools by coordinating book fairs, providing in-service sessions, and organizing an annual literature conference. She is the coauthor of several textbooks and the author or coauthor of numerous articles that have appeared in professional journals. Her professional activities include making presentations at conferences; writing, editing, and reviewing for various publications; and serving on boards and committees of professional organizations.

ISBN 0-02-402661-1

Emergency
Care and Transportation of the Sick and Injured

Student Workbook

JONES & BARTLETT
LEARNING

World Headquarters
Jones & Bartlett Learning
5 Wall Street
Burlington, MA 01803
978-443-5000
info@jblearning.com
www.jblearning.com

Substantial discounts on bulk quantities of Jones & Bartlett Learning publications are available to corporations, professional associations, and other qualified organizations. For details and specific discount information, contact the special sales department at Jones & Bartlett Learning via the below contact information or send an email to specialsales@jblearning.com.

Jones & Bartlett Learning books and products are available through most bookstores and online booksellers. To contact Jones & Bartlett Learning directly, call 800-832-0034, fax 978-443-8000, or visit our website, www.jblearning.com.

Production Credits
General Manager, Executive Publisher: Kimberly Brophy
VP, Product Development and Executive Editor: Christine Emerton
Senior Development Editor: Alison Lozeau
Associate Director of Production: Jenny L. Corriveau
Production Editor: Kristen Rogers
VP, Sales, Public Safety Group: Matthew Maniscalco
Director of Sales, Public Safety Group: Patricia Einstein
Director of Marketing Operations: Brian Rooney
VP, Manufacturing and Inventory Control: Therese Connell

Composition: diacriTech
Cover Design: Kristin E. Parker
Rights & Media Specialist: Robert Boder
Media Development Editor: Shannon Sheehan
Cover Image: © Glen E. Ellman
Printing and Binding: Edwards Brothers Malloy
Cover Printing: Edwards Brothers Malloy

Editorial Credits
Authors: Alan Heckman, MSPAS, PA-C, NRP, NCEE
        Rhonda J. Hunt, NRP, BAS

ISBN: 978-1-284-13106-2

6048

Printed in the United States of America
22 21 20 19 18   10 9 8 7 6 5 4

Contents

EMS Systems

© Photos.com

General Knowledge

Matching

Match each of the items in the left column to the appropriate definition in the right column.

H	1. ALS	A. EMS professional with extensive training in ALS skills, such as intubation
N	2. BLS	B. A system of internal and external reviews and audits
M	3. EMT	C. A system that assists dispatchers with unit selection
G	4. AEMT	D. The physician who authorizes the EMT to provide care in the field
A	5. Paramedic	E. Responsibility of the medical director to ensure that appropriate care is delivered by an EMT
K	6. Medical control	F. Legislation that protects a patient's private health information
B	7. CQI	G. EMS professional trained in some ALS interventions
O	8. EMS	H. Advanced procedures, such as drug administration
L	9. MIH	I. Designated area in which the EMS agency is responsible for providing prehospital care
C	10. EMD	J. Protects disabled individuals from discrimination
I	11. Primary service area	K. Physician direction to an EMS team
D	12. Medical director	L. Providing health care within the community rather than in an office
J	13. Americans with Disabilities Act	M. EMS professional trained in BLS interventions
E	14. Quality control	N. Basic lifesaving interventions, such as CPR
F	15. HIPAA	O. A system to provide prehospital care to the sick and injured

Multiple Choice

Read each item carefully and then select the one best response.

____A____ 1. What year was the white paper, *Accidental Death and Disability: The Neglected Disease of Modern Society*, published?

    A. 1966

    B. 1970

    C. 1984

    D. 1992

____B____ 2. Which of the following is true of medical control?

    A. It is determined by the dispatcher.

    B. It may be written or "standing orders."

    C. It requires online radio or phone consultation.

    D. It only affects ALS providers.

____D____ 3. What is the purpose for providing Mobile Integrated Healthcare?

    A. To allow paramedics to function beyond the scope of practice

    B. To allow EMS agencies to respond to emergencies faster

    C. To educate the community on public health issues

    D. To facilitate improved access to health care at an affordable price

_C_   **4.** What is the major goal of continuous quality improvement?
   A. To perform quarterly audits of the EMS system
   B. To verify EMTs have received BLS/CPR training
   Ⓒ To ensure the public receives the highest standard of care
   D. To verify the proper information is received in the billing department

_A_   **5.** Which of the following involves federal legislation concerning patient confidentiality?
   Ⓐ HIPAA
   B. NAACS
   C. EMTALA
   D. FLCPC

Questions 6–10 are derived from the following scenario: After stocking the ambulance this morning, you and your partner go out for breakfast. While entering the restaurant, you see an older gentleman clutch his chest and collapse to the floor. When you get to him, he has no pulse and is not breathing.

_C_   **6.** Which of the following authorizes you, as an EMT, to provide emergency care to this patient?
   A. City council
   B. The EMS agency
   Ⓒ The medical director
   D. The fire chief

_C_   **7.** In order to treat this patient, what will you need to follow?
   A. Emergency Medical Dispatch
   B. Continuous Quality Improvement
   Ⓒ Protocols
   D. Quality Control

_D_   **8.** What level of training would allow you to perform cardiac monitoring and advanced life support on this patient?
   A. EMR
   B. EMT
   C. AEMT
   Ⓓ Paramedic

_A_   **9.** While you checked the patient's airway, breathing, and circulation, your partner considered the benefits of requesting a(n) _____ ambulance to assist with patient care.
   Ⓐ ALS
   B. CQI
   Ⓒ PSA
   D. EMD

_B_   **10.** While you performed CPR on this patient, your partner retrieved the _____, which will deliver an appropriate electrical shock.
   A. EMD
   Ⓑ AED
   C. PSA
   D. GPS

True/False

If you believe the statement to be more true than false, write the letter "T" in the space provided. If you believe the statement to be more false than true, write the letter "F."

_F_ 1. EMT personnel are the highest qualified members of the prehospital care team.

_T_ 2. The EMT scope of practice includes the use of an automated external defibrillator.

_T_ 3. Personnel trained as EMRs can include law enforcement officers, firefighters, and ski patrollers.

_T_ 4. A professional appearance and manner by the EMT will help build the patient's confidence and ease the patient's anxiety.

_T_ 5. Patient care should be focused on procedures that have proven useful in improving outcomes.

_F_ 6. As a health care professional and an extension of physician care, you are not bound by patient confidentiality.

_T_ 7. Most EMS training programs must adhere to national standards established by the accrediting organizations.

_F T_ 8. The medical director is responsible for authorizing and regulating all emergency medical services within the state.

_F_ 9. Advanced EMTs typically go through 1,000 to 1,300 hours of training.

_T_ 10. The development of the field medic and rapid helicopter evacuation took place during the Korean conflict.

Fill-in-the-Blank

Read each item carefully and then complete the statement by filling in the missing words.

1. _Continuous_ _quality_ _improvement_ is a circular system of continuous internal and external reviews and audits of all aspects of an EMS system.

2. Each EMS system has a physician _medical_ _director_ who authorizes the EMTs in the service to provide medical care in the field.

3. One of the most dramatic recent developments in prehospital emergency care is the use of a(n) _automated_ _electronic_ _external_ defibrillator.

4. The primary _service_ area is the main area in which an EMS agency operates.

5. A 9-1-1 dispatch center is called a public safety _access_ _point_, or PSAP.

Crossword Puzzle

The following crossword puzzle is an activity provided to reinforce correct spelling and understanding of medical terminology associated with emergency care and the EMT. Use the clues in the column to complete the puzzle.

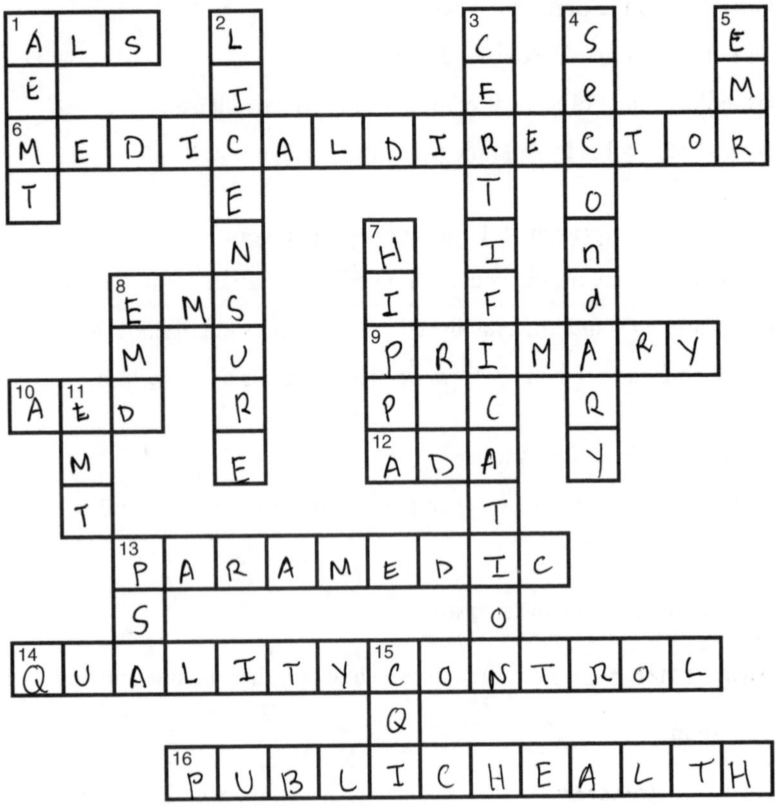
ALS
MEDICALDIRECTOR
EMS
PRIMARY
AED
ADA
PARAMEDIC
QUALITYCONTROL
PUBLICHEALTH
AEMT
LICENSURE
CERTIFICATION
SecondARY
EMR
HIPAA
EMD
EMT
PS
CQ

Across

1. Advanced lifesaving procedures.
6. The physician who authorizes or delegates to the EMT the authority to provide medical care in the field.
8. A multidisciplinary system that represents the combined efforts of several professionals and agencies to provide prehospital emergency care to the sick and the injured.
9. Efforts to prevent an injury or illness from ever occurring are known as ________________ prevention.
10. A device that detects treatable life-threatening cardiac arrhythmias (eg, ventricular fibrillation and ventricular tachycardia) and delivers the appropriate electrical shock to the patient.
12. Comprehensive legislation that is designed to protect individuals with disabilities against discrimination.
13. An individual who has extensive training in advanced life support, including endotracheal intubation, emergency pharmacology, cardiac monitoring, and other advanced assessment and treatment skills.
14. The responsibility of the medical director to ensure that the appropriate medical care standards are met by EMTs on each call.
16. Focused on examining the health needs of entire populations with the goal of preventing health problems.

Down

1. An individual who has training in specific aspects of advanced life support, such as intravenous therapy, and the administration of certain emergency medications.
2. The process whereby a state allows individuals to perform a regulated act.
3. A process in which a person, an institution, or a program is evaluated and recognized as meeting certain predetermined standards to provide safe and ethical care.
4. Efforts to limit the effects of an injury or illness that you cannot completely prevent are considered ________________ prevention.
5. The first trained individual, such as a police officer, firefighter, lifeguard, or other rescuer, to arrive at the scene of an emergency to provide initial medical assistance.
7. Federal legislation passed in 1996. Its main effect in EMS is in limiting availability of patients' health care information and penalizing violations of patient privacy.
8. A system that assists dispatchers in selecting appropriate units to respond to a particular call for assistance and in providing callers with vital instructions until the arrival of EMS crews.
11. An individual who has training in basic life support, including automated external defibrillation, use of a definitive airway adjunct, and assisting patients with certain medications.
13. The designated area in which the EMS agency is responsible for the provision of prehospital emergency care and transportation to the hospital.
15. A system of internal and external reviews and audits of all aspects of an EMS system.

Critical Thinking

Short Answer

Complete this section with short written answers using the space provided.

1. Describe the EMT's role in the EMS system.

_____

_____

_____

2. What role has the US Department of Transportation played in the development of EMS?

_____

_____

_____

3. List five roles and/or responsibilities of being an EMT.

_____

_____

_____

4. Describe the two basic types of medical direction that help the EMT provide care.

_____

_____

_____

Ambulance Calls

The following case scenarios provide an opportunity to explore the concerns associated with patient management and to enhance critical-thinking skills. Read each scenario and answer each question to the best of your ability.

1. You are dispatched to a two-car motor vehicle collision. On arrival, you see minimal damage to both vehicles because they were traveling less than 25 mph (40 kph) when the collision occurred. You and your partner interview and examine all of the patients and find no apparent injuries. Dispatch contacts you and asks if you need an ALS crew to respond to your location.

   Explain how you would respond and why.

   _____

   _____

   _____

2. You and your partner are both EMTs and are dispatched to a private residence for a hanging. You arrive to find a distraught man in the front yard who quickly explains that he found his teenaged daughter in the garage hanging by the neck from an extension cord. You enter the garage and find the patient unresponsive and not breathing but with a weak pulse. Using EMT airway skills, neither of you are able to successfully open the patient's airway enough to provide ventilations.

   What should you do?

   _____

   _____

   _____

Workforce Safety and Wellness

© Photos.com

General Knowledge

Matching

Match each of the items in the left column to the appropriate definition in the right column.

D	1. Communicable disease	A. Examples include gloves, gowns, and face shields
A	2. PPE	B. The process of alarm, reaction, and recovery
C	3. OSHA	C. Regulatory compliance agency
F	4. Posttraumatic stress disorder	D. Disease that can be spread from one person to another
B	5. General adaptation syndrome	E. Capable of causing disease in a susceptible host
KE	6. Pathogen	F. Delayed stress reaction
ØM	7. Transmission	G. Encompasses reporting, documentation, and treatment
G	8. Postexposure management	H. Unwelcome sexual advance
L	9. *Emergency Response Guidebook*	I. The use of objects to limit a person's visibility of you
JO	10. Indirect contact	J. Contact with blood, body fluids, tissues, or airborne particles
KJ	11. Exposure	K. The presence of infectious organisms in or on objects or a patient's body
N	12. Infection control	L. Resource detailing common hazards and proper responses
H	13. Sexual harassment	M. The way in which an infectious agent is spread
OK	14. Contamination	N. Procedures to reduce transmission of infection among patients and health care personnel
I	15. Concealment	O. Spread of infection through an inanimate object

Multiple Choice

Read each item carefully and then select the one best response.

C   **1.** If you are in the first unit to arrive at the scene of a motor vehicle collision, you should:

     A. immediately extricate patients from vehicles.

     B. disregard downed power lines.

     C. consider using the ambulance as a shield to protect the scene.

     D. park at least 10 feet away from the crash site.

C   **2.** The stage of the grieving process where an attempt is made to secure a prize for good behavior or promise to change one's lifestyle is known as:

     A. denial.

     B. acceptance.

     C. bargaining.

     D. depression.

A   **3.** The stage of the grieving process that involves refusal to accept diagnosis or care is known as:

     A. denial.

     B. acceptance.

     C. bargaining.

     D. depression.

D **4.** When tools are being used during extrication, you should:

  A. protect your eyes from ultraviolet light.

  B. wear eyeglasses with side shields.

  C. consider wearing body armor for added protection.

  D. wear a face shield or goggles.

B **5.** Which of the following is a sign that your sleep pattern is ineffective?

  A. You fall asleep within 5 to 10 minutes of lying down.

  B. You are unable to concentrate on repetitive tasks such as driving or completing paperwork.

  C. You are able to make it through the entire day without feeling severe fatigue.

  D. You find yourself still energized 1 to 2 hours after an EMS call.

A **6.** When providing support for a grieving person, it is okay to say:

  A. "I'm sorry."

  B. "Give it time."

  C. "I know how you feel."

  D. "You have to keep on going."

B **7.** What is the first thing you should do if exposed to a patient's blood or body fluids?

  A. Activate your department's infection control plan.

  B. Turn over patient care to another EMS provider.

  C. Wash the exposed area with soap and water.

  D. Seek immediate medical attention.

C **8.** _____ is a response to the anticipation of danger.

  A. Rage

  B. Anger

  C. Anxiety

  D. Despair

B **9.** Signs of anxiety include all of the following EXCEPT:

  A. diaphoresis.

  B. comfort.

  C. hyperventilation.

  D. tachycardia.

D **10.** What should you do if you suspect your patient has tuberculosis?

  A. Place a surgical mask on yourself and the patient.

  B. Place a particulate air respirator on the patient and a surgical mask on yourself.

  C. Place a particulate air respirator on the patient.

  D. Place a particulate air respirator on yourself and a surgical mask on the patient.

B **11.** Drug and alcohol use in the workplace causes:

  A. decreased stress for coworkers.

  B. increased accidents.

  C. increased decision-making ability.

  D. increased physical ability.

A **12.** Regardless of how stressful the situation, you must focus on several factors. Which of the following factors is your top priority?

  A. Personal safety

  B. Patient care

  C. Scene safety

  D. Safety of bystanders

_B_ **13.** When acknowledging the death of a child, reactions vary, but _____ is common.
- **A.** happiness
- **Ⓑ** disbelief
- **C.** apprehension
- **D.** psychosis

_C_ **14.** Which of the following is NOT a way an infectious disease is transmitted?
- **A.** Vector-borne
- **B.** Airborne
- **Ⓒ** Cyberborne
- **D.** Foodborne

_A_ **15.** What is the most common type of personal protective equipment?
- **Ⓐ** Gloves
- **B.** Masks
- **C.** Gowns
- **D.** Eye shields

_D_ **16.** Which of the following is NOT considered a common hazard in a fire?
- **A.** Smoke
- **B.** Building collapse
- **C.** Toxic gases
- **Ⓓ** Bystanders

_B_ **17.** _____ _____ occur(s) when insignificant stressors accumulate to a larger stress-related problem.
- **A.** Negative stress
- **Ⓑ** Cumulative stress
- **C.** Psychological stress
- **D.** Severe stressors

_A_ **18.** Events that can trigger critical incident stress include:
- **Ⓐ** mass-casualty incidents.
- **B.** serious damage to your ambulance at a scene.
- **C.** death or serious injury of a patient's friend.
- **D.** loss of equipment at the scene.

_A_ **19.** The quickest source of energy is _____; however, this supply will last less than a day.
- **Ⓐ** glucose
- **B.** carbohydrate
- **C.** protein
- **D.** fat

_B_ **20.** The safest, most reliable sources for long-term energy production are:
- **A.** sugars.
- **Ⓑ** carbohydrates.
- **C.** fats.
- **D.** proteins.

_A_ **21.** A CISD meeting is an opportunity to discuss:
- **Ⓐ** feelings about the incident.
- **B.** the operational critique.
- **C.** who to blame for the errors.
- **D.** opportunities for improvement.

B **22.** Sexual harassment is defined as:
  A. any welcomed sexual advance.
  B. unwelcome requests for sexual favors.
  C. welcomed verbal or physical conduct of a sexual nature.
  D. asking a coworker out for dinner.

A **23.** The CDC recommends immunizations for health care providers. Which of the following immunization is NOT recommended?
  A. Meningitis vaccine
  B. Hepatitis B vaccine
  C. Influenza vaccine
  D. Varicella vaccine

C **24.** Hazardous materials in vehicles and buildings should be clearly identified using:
  A. manifests.
  B. MSDS sheets.
  C. placards.
  D. beacons.

B **25.** Which of the following is a common characteristic found in patients with mental health problems?
  A. Contact with reality
  B. Regression
  C. Normal perception
  D. Lack of hallucinations

True/False

If you believe the statement to be more true than false, write the letter "T" in the space provided. If you believe the statement to be more false than true, write the letter "F."

F **1.** Recapping the needle from a syringe is the best way to dispose of it safely.

T F **2.** Gloves, eye protection, and handwashing are the main components of PPE.

T **3.** Denial is usually the first step in the grieving process.

F **4.** Body fluids are generally not considered infectious substances.

F **5.** Most EMTs never suffer from stress.

T **6.** Physical conditioning and nutrition are two factors the EMT can control in helping to reduce stress.

F **7.** The likelihood of you becoming infected during routine patient care is high.

T **8.** Construction-type helmets are not well suited for rescue situations.

T **9.** Religious customs or needs of the patient must be respected.

F **10.** Diversity is an ineffective way to strengthen a public safety workforce.

Fill-in-the-Blank

Read each item carefully and then complete the statement by filling in the missing words.

1. ___Stress___ is the impact of stressors on your physical and mental well-being.

2. ___Food born___ ___Transmission___ involves the contamination of food or water with an organism that can cause disease.

3. An ___infectious___ ___desies___ is a medical condition caused by the growth and spread of small, harmful organisms within the body.

4. Your safety is the most important consideration at a(n) ___hazardous___ materials incident.

5. Proper ___percautions___ (handwashing) is the simplest yet most effective way to control disease transmission.

6. ___Cover___ involves the tactical use of an impenetrable barrier for protection.

7. The ___death___ of a human being is one of the most ___traumatic___ (difficult) events for another human being to accept.

8. The term ___stress___ ___management___ refers to the tactics that have been shown to alleviate or eliminate stress reactions.

9. Good productive ___sleep___ is as important as eating well and exercise in the maintenance of good health.

10. ___eye___ ___protection___ is important in case blood splatters toward your eyes.

Crossword Puzzle

The following crossword puzzle is an activity provided to reinforce correct spelling and understanding of medical terminology associated with emergency care and the EMT. Use the clues in the column to complete the puzzle.

Across

1. _____ precautions are protective measures developed for use in dealing with objects, blood, body fluids, or other potential exposure risks of communicable disease.

5. The growth and spread of small, harmful organisms within the body is known as a(n) _____.

7. The body's ability to protect itself from acquiring a disease.

9. _____ stress reactions occur during a stressful situation.

10. _____ stress reactions occur after a stressful situation.

14. _____ pathogens are pathogenic microorganisms that are present in human blood and can cause disease in humans.

15. Transmission of a communicable disease from one person to another by physical contact.

18. Exposure or transmission of disease from one person to another by contact with a contaminated object is called _____ contact.

19. AIDS is caused by this virus, which damages the cells in the body's immune system.

Down

2. The individual in the department who is charged with managing exposures and infection control issues is known as the _____ officer.

3. A process that confronts the responses to critical incidents and defuses them.

4. The tactical use of an impenetrable barrier for protection is known as _____ and concealment.

6. Procedures to reduce transmission of infection among patients and health care personnel are known as infection _____.

8. Protective equipment that OSHA requires to be made available to the EMT.

11. The abnormal invasion of a host or host tissues by organisms such as bacteria, viruses, or parasites.

12. A delayed stress reaction to a prior incident.

13. The organism or individual that is attacked by the infecting agent.

16. The agency that conducts and supports public health activities and is part of the US Department of Health and Human Services.

17. The agency that develops, publishes, and enforces guidelines concerning safety in the workplace.

Critical Thinking

Multiple Choice
Read each critical-thinking item carefully and then select the one best response.

Questions 1–5 are derived from the following scenario: A 12-year-old boy told his grandmother he was going to collect the day's mail, located on the opposite side of the street, for her. As he was returning with the mail, he was struck by a vehicle and was found lying lifeless in the middle of the street.

_____ 1. Which of the following would be appropriate to say to the grandmother?
   A. "Don't worry. I'm sure he'll be fine."
   B. "What were you thinking? You will be reported!"
   C. "We're placing him on a backboard to protect his back, and we'll take him to the Columbus Community Hospital. Do you know who his doctor is?"
   D. It's best not to spend time talking to the grandmother.

_____ 2. As an EMT, you know these types of calls are coming. All of the following are ways to meet such stressful situations EXCEPT:
   A. eat a balanced diet.
   B. go for walks or other forms of exercise.
   C. cut down on caffeine and sugars.
   D. increase overtime hours.

_____ 3. You or your partner may develop _____ after experiencing this call.
   A. critical incident stress management
   B. posttraumatic stress disorder
   C. critical stress debriefing
   D. an acute stress reaction

_____ 4. What is NOT a sign of stress that you or your partner might exhibit?
   A. Irritability toward coworkers, family, and friends
   B. Loss of interest in work
   C. Guilt
   D. Feelings of relief.

_____ 5. When should you begin protecting yourself with standard precautions on this call?
   A. As soon as you are dispatched
   B. As soon as you arrive
   C. After you assess the victim and know what you need
   D. After speaking with the grandmother

Short Answer
Complete this section with short written answers using the space provided.

1. Describe the basic concept of standard precautions.

_____
_____
_____

2. List the five stages of the grieving process.

_____
_____
_____

3. List at least five warning signs of stress.

_____

_____

_____

4. List five strategies for managing stress.

_____

_____

_____

5. List the CDC-recommended immunizations for health care workers.

_____

_____

_____

6. List the three layers of clothing recommended for cold weather.

_____

_____

_____

7. List three signs/symptoms found in an anxious patient.

_____

_____

_____

8. What are some common hazards associated with a fire scene?

_____

_____

_____

Ambulance Calls

The following case scenarios provide an opportunity to explore the concerns associated with patient management and to enhance critical-thinking skills. Read each scenario and answer each question to the best of your ability.

1. In the process of working a motor vehicle collision, your arm is gashed open and you are exposed to the blood of a patient who tells you that he is HIV positive. You have no water supply in which to wash. Your patient is stable, and you are able to control his bleeding with direct pressure.

    How would you best manage this situation?

    _____

    _____

    _____

2. You are dispatched to a large apartment complex for a person in respiratory distress. You find the elderly patient living in a dark, messy apartment with many family members, both adults and children, and you know that there have been numerous cases of tuberculosis reported in this particular complex.

    With regard to infection control, how would you best manage this situation?

    _____

    _____

    _____

Fill-in-the-Patient Care Report

Read the incident scenario and then complete the following patient care report (PCR).

You and your partner are posted in the parking lot of a convenience store on McBride Avenue just west of Highway 9, cleaning and organizing the back of the ambulance, when emergency tones burst from the radio. "Truck three, emergency traffic," the dispatcher says.

"Go ahead to three," you respond.

"Truck three, priority one call to 7-9-7-9 Fisher Boulevard for a possible overdose. Show your time of dispatch at oh-nine-twelve."

You copy the assignment, activate the lights and siren, and roll off toward the address, about 14 minutes away.

As you pull up to the address, a towering grey concrete block, housing eight stories of single-room apartments, you are met by a police officer.

"So the mom calls us because she and her daughter were in the middle of a domestic issue," the officer says as he leads you through the lobby to the elevator. "By the time we got here, the 16-year-old girl had locked herself in the bathroom. I got in there and found her unconscious on the floor with a rig next to her."

"Rig?" your new partner whispers in your ear while you are waiting for the elevator to rumble to the sixth floor.

"Syringe," you say quietly as the officer steps off of the elevator and waves you to an open door.

The clock on the kitchenette microwave reads 9:29 as you enter the small, dimly lit apartment to the sounds of a woman wailing in the bathroom. Two police officers quickly move the distraught mother out of the tiny bathroom so you can get to the unresponsive girl.

"Let's get her out into the living room," you say, using the extremity lift to move the 48-kg (106-lb) patient into the wider floor of the living room. "And watch out for that needle next to her arm; there's no cap on it."

In the living room, you determine that the girl is breathing slowly but adequately and find that she has a slow pulse. You decide to get a full set of vital signs while your partner questions the mother about the girl's history and current drug use. At 0934, the patient's blood pressure is 116/76 mm Hg; her pulse is 46 beats/min; breathing is 8 breaths/min, but with good tidal volume; and she has a pulse oximetry reading of 96%. As you are placing a nonrebreathing mask on the unresponsive girl with 15 L/min of supplemental oxygen, your partner kneels next to you and looks at his notepad.

"She attempted suicide 2 years ago by taking an overdose of aspirin and has been struggling over the past year with a heroin addiction."

"Okay," you say. "Let's get her out to the stretcher and get going."

At 0947, your partner closes you into the back of the ambulance with the patient and climbs into the cab while you obtain a second set of vital signs: blood pressure 114/74 mm Hg, pulse 38 beats/min, respirations 8 breaths/min, and SpO_2 95%. Five minutes later, you arrive at the ambulance bay of the local hospital and quickly move the patient inside. You transfer her care to the emergency department staff after giving a full report to the receiving nurse. After cleaning and preparing the ambulance, you and your partner are clear at 1005.

Fill-in-the-Patient Care Report

EMS Patient Care Report (PCR)					
Date:	**Incident No.:**	**Nature of Call:**		**Location:**	
Dispatched:	**En Route:**	**At Scene:**	**Transport:**	**At Hospital:**	**In Service:**
Patient Information					
Age: **Sex:** **Weight (in kg [lb]):**			**Allergies:** **Medications:** **Past Medical History:** **Chief Complaint:**		
Vital Signs					
Time:	**BP:**	**Pulse:**	**Respirations:**	Spo_2:	
Time:	**BP:**	**Pulse:**	**Respirations:**	Spo_2:	
Time:	**BP:**	**Pulse:**	**Respirations:**	Spo_2:	
EMS Treatment **(circle all that apply)**					
Oxygen @ ____ L/min via (circle one): NC NRM BVM		**Assisted Ventilation**	**Airway Adjunct**		**CPR**
Defibrillation	**Bleeding Control**	**Bandaging**	**Splinting**		**Other:**
Narrative					

Skills

Skill Drills

Test your knowledge of this skill by filling in the correct words in the photo captions.

Skill Drill 2-1: Proper Glove Removal Technique

© Jones & Bartlett Learning.

© Jones & Bartlett Learning.

1. Partially remove the first glove by pinching at the _____. Be careful to touch only the _____ of the glove.

2. Remove the _____ glove by pinching the _____ with your partially gloved hand.

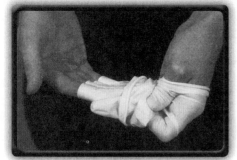

© Jones & Bartlett Learning.

© Jones & Bartlett Learning.

3. Pull the second glove inside out toward the _____.

4. Grasp both gloves with your _____ hand, touching only the clean, _____ surfaces.

PREPARATORY

Medical, Legal, and Ethical Issues

© Photos.com

General Knowledge

Matching

Match each of the items in the left column to the appropriate definition in the right column.

_____ **1.** Assault

_____ **2.** Abandonment

_____ **3.** Advance directive

_____ **4.** Battery

_____ **5.** Certification

_____ **6.** Competent

___O___ **7.** Consent

_____ **8.** Duty to act

_____ **9.** Ethics

_____ **10.** Expressed consent

_____ **11.** Forcible restraint

_____ **12.** Implied consent

_____ **13.** Medicolegal

_____ **14.** Negligence

_____ **15.** Standard of care

A. Able to make decisions

B. Specific authorization to provide care expressed by the patient

C. Confining a person from mental or physical action

D. Granted permission

E. Touching without consent

F. Legal responsibility to provide care

G. Written documentation that specifies treatment

H. Unlawfully placing a patient in fear of bodily harm

I. Unilateral termination of care

J. Failure to provide standard of care

K. Accepted level of care consistent with training

L. Process that recognizes that a person has met set standards

M. Legal assumption that treatment was desired

N. Relating to law or forensic medicine

Ø. Philosophy of right and wrong

Multiple Choice

Read each item carefully and then select the one best response.

_____ **1.** The care that an EMT is able to provide is most commonly defined as a:

　A. duty to act.

　B. competency.

　C. scope of practice.

　D. certification.

_____ **2.** How the EMT is required to act or behave is called:

　A. the standard of care.

　B. competency.

　C. the scope of practice.

　D. certification.

_____ **3.** The process by which an individual, an institution, or a program is evaluated and recognized as meeting certain standards is called:

　A. the standard of care.

　B. competency.

　C. the scope of practice.

　D. certification.

_____ **4.** Negligence is based on the EMT's duty to act, cause, breach of duty, and:

    A. expressed consent.

    B. termination of care.

    C. mode of transport.

    D. real or perceived damages.

_____ **5.** While treating a patient with a suspected head injury, he becomes verbally abusive and tells you to "leave me alone." If you stop treating him you may be guilty of:

    A. neglect.

    B. battery.

    C. abandonment.

    D. slander.

_____ **6.** Good Samaritan laws generally are designed to offer protection to people who render care in good faith. They do not offer protection from:

    A. properly performed CPR.

    B. acts of negligence.

    C. improvising splinting materials.

    D. providing supportive BLS to a DNR patient.

_____ **7.** Which of the following is generally NOT considered confidential?

    A. Assessment findings

    B. A patient's mental condition

    C. A patient's medical history

    D. The location of the emergency

_____ **8.** An important safeguard against legal implication is:

    A. responding to every call with lights and siren.

    B. checking ambulance equipment once a month.

    C. transporting every patient to an emergency department.

    D. writing a complete and accurate run report.

_____ **9.** Your responsibility to provide patient care is called:

    A. scope of practice.

    B. duty to act.

    C. DNR.

    D. standard of care.

_____ **10.** Which of the following is NOT considered a presumptive sign of death?

    A. Absence of pupil reactivity

    B. Profound cyanosis

    C. Dependent lividity

    D. Absence of chest rise

_____ **11.** Definitive or conclusive signs of death that are obvious and clear to even nonmedical people include all of the following EXCEPT:

    A. profound cyanosis.

    B. dependent lividity.

    C. rigor mortis.

    D. putrefaction.

_____ **12.** Medical examiners' cases include all of the following EXCEPT:

    A. violent death.

    B. suicide.

    C. suspicion of a criminal act.

    D. a physician's written orders for a DNR.

_____   **13.** HIPAA is the acronym for the Health Insurance Portability and Accountability Act of 1996. This act:

      A. makes ambulance services accountable for transporting patients in a safe manner.

      B. protects the privacy of health care information and safeguards patient confidentiality.

      C. allows health insurers to transfer an insurance policy to another carrier if a patient does not pay his or her premium.

      D. enables emergency personnel to transfer a patient to a lower level of care when resources are scarce.

True/False

If you believe the statement to be more true than false, write the letter "T" in the space provided. If you believe the statement to be more false than true, write the letter "F."

_____   **1.** Failure to provide care to a patient once you have been called to the scene is considered negligence.

_____   **2.** For expressed consent to be valid, the patient must be a minor.

_____   **3.** If a patient is unconscious and a true emergency exists, the doctrine of implied consent applies.

_____   **4.** EMTs can legally restrain patients against their will if they pose a threat to themselves or others.

_____   **5.** DNR orders give you permission not to attempt resuscitation at your discretion.

_____   **6.** A durable power of attorney for health care is a designated person who is authorized to make medical decisions on behalf of the patient.

_____   **7.** EMT textbooks are often used in court to establish standards of care.

_____   **8.** EMTs are not typically responsible for reporting suspected child abuse.

_____   **9.** When at a crime scene, you must be careful not to disturb the scene any more than absolutely necessary.

_____   **10.** Punitive damages are intended to compensate the plaintiff for the actual injuries sustained.

Fill-in-the-Blank

Read each item carefully and then complete the statement by filling in the missing words.

1. The _____ _____ _____ outlines the care you are able to provide.

2. The _____ _____ _____ is the manner in which the EMT must act when treating patients.

3. The legal responsibility to provide care is called the _____ _____ _____.

4. The determination of _____ is based on duty, breach of duty, damages, and cause.

5. Abandonment is _____ of care without transfer to someone of equal or higher training.

6. _____ consent is given directly by an informed patient, whereas _____ consent is assumed in the unconscious patient.

7. Unlawfully placing a person in fear of immediate harm is _____, whereas _____ is unlawfully touching a person without his or her consent.

8. A(n) _____ _____ is a written document that specifies authorized treatment in case a patient becomes unable to make decisions. A written document that authorizes the EMT not to attempt resuscitation efforts is a(n) _____ _____.

9. Mentally competent patients have the right to _____ _____.

10. Incidents involving child abuse, animal bites, childbirth, and assault have_____ _____

    requirements in many states.

Crossword Puzzle

The following crossword puzzle is an activity provided to reinforce correct spelling and understanding of medical terminology associated with emergency care and the EMT. Use the clues in the column to complete the puzzle.

Across

3. Basing current action on lessons, rules, or guidelines derived from previous similar experiences.
5. Unlawfully placing a patient in fear of bodily harm.
8. The philosophy of right and wrong, of moral duties, and of ideal professional behavior.
10. Any information about health status, provision of health care, or payment for health care that can be linked to an individual.
12. When a person who has a duty abuses it and causes harm to another individual, the EMT, the agency, and/or the medical director may be sued for negligence. This is called _____ causation.
13. A wrongful act that gives rise to a civil suit.
14. Oral questions asked of parties and witnesses under oath.
15. With _____ consent, a patient gives express authorization for provision of care or transport.

Down

1. A code of conduct that can be defined by society, religion, or a person, affecting character, conduct, and conscience.
2. Most commonly defined by state law; outlines the care you are able to provide for the patient.
4. Permission to render care.
6. False and damaging information about a person that is communicated by the spoken word.
7. False and damaging information about a person that is communicated in writing.
9. The study of ethics related to issues that arise in health care.
11. Written documentation by a physician giving permission to medical personnel not to attempt resuscitation in the event of cardiac arrest is called a(n) _____ order.

Critical Thinking

Multiple Choice

Read the scenarios carefully and select the best responses to the questions.

At 0200, a 17-year-old boy, accompanied by his 19-year-old girlfriend, had driven to the bar to give his father (who had been drinking large amounts of alcohol) a ride home. On the way back, they were involved in a motor vehicle collision. The boy has a large laceration with profuse bleeding on his forehead. His girlfriend is unconscious on the front passenger floor. The father is standing outside the vehicle, appearing heavily intoxicated, and is refusing care.

_____ **1.** Should the father be allowed to refuse care?

    A. Yes. Consent is required before care can be started.

    B. No. He is under the influence of drugs/alcohol and is therefore mentally incompetent.

    C. Yes. Consent is implied.

    D. No. You would be guilty of abandonment.

_____ **2.** Why is it permissible for you to begin treatment on the girlfriend?

    A. Consent is implied.

    B. Consent has been expressed.

    C. Consent was informed.

    D. Consent is not needed.

_____ **3.** As you progress in your care for the patients, the father becomes unconscious. Can you begin/continue care for him now?

    A. Yes. Consent is now implied.

    B. No. He made his wishes known before he fell unconscious.

    C. No. He just needs to sleep it off.

    D. Yes. Unconsciousness indicates informed consent.

_____ **4.** With the son being a minor, what is the best way to gain consent to begin care when his father has an altered mental status or is unconscious?

    A. Phone his mother for consent.

    B. Call his grandparents for consent.

    C. It is a true emergency, so consent is implied.

    D. You are covered under the Good Samaritan laws.

You respond to a single-vehicle crash on the highway west of town. On arrival, you find a 33-year-old man with an open forearm fracture who has self-extricated from his pickup truck, which is down the roadside embankment. He does not appear to have suffered any other injuries, is fully coherent, and refuses all medical care.

_____ **5.** You attempt to convince the patient to go to the hospital by explaining his injuries. In an effort to obtain consent to treat this patient, what else could you do to convince him?

    A. Summon law enforcement and threaten the patient that he'll be placed into protective custody.

    B. Clearly explain the consequences of not accepting medical treatment.

    C. Proceed with treatment; consent is not required because the patient is not being rational.

    D. Allow the patient to leave the scene without a signed refusal form.

_____ **6.** If you and your partner were out past the end of your scheduled shift and driving the ambulance back to base to go home when you came upon this accident, would you have a legal duty to act?

    A. No. If you were not specifically dispatched to the crash, you do not have an obligation to assist.

    B. Yes. As a trained and licensed EMT you must assist with every medical emergency that you encounter.

    C. No. Because it is past the end of your scheduled shift, you can decide whether you want to stop and help.

    D. Yes. As a trained EMT still on-duty for an EMS system, you would have a legal and ethical obligation to stop and assist.

Short Answer

Complete this section with short written answers using the space provided.

1. In many states, certain conditions allow an emancipated minor to be treated as an adult for the purpose of consenting to medical treatment. Give three examples of emancipated minors.

   _____

   _____

   _____

2. When does your responsibility as an EMT for patient care end?

   _____

   _____

3. There will be some instances when you will not be able to persuade the patient, guardian, or parent of a minor child or mentally incompetent patient to proceed with treatment. List the steps you should take to protect all parties involved.

   _____

   _____

   _____

4. List the two rules of thumb that courts consider regarding reports and records.

   _____

   _____

   _____

5. List the four elements that must be present for the legal doctrine of negligence to apply.

   _____

   _____

   _____

Ambulance Calls

The following case scenarios provide an opportunity to explore the concerns associated with patient management and to enhance critical-thinking skills. Read each scenario and answer each question to the best of your ability.

1. You are dispatched to a girl complaining of abdominal pain. You arrive to find the 17-year-old girl crying and holding her abdomen. She tells you that she fell down the stairs and that she is pregnant. She is not sure how long she's been pregnant, but she is experiencing cramping and spotting. She asks you not to tell anyone and says that if you tell her parents she will refuse transport to the hospital.

   What do you do?

   _____

   _____

   _____

2. You are off-duty when you see a child injured while riding his bike. You examine him and find abrasions on both knees but no other injuries. He needs help getting to his house up the street. He tells you that his mother is not home but his grandfather is (although he is bedridden). Looking through the window, you see the house is full of clothing, garbage, and papers.

What do you do?

_____

_____

_____

3. It is late at night when the police summon you to a motor vehicle collision. On arrival, the officer directs you to the back of his patrol car. Sitting on the seat is your patient, snoring loudly with blood covering his face. The officer states that the patient was involved in a drunk-driving accident in which he hit his head on the rearview mirror. The patient initially refused care at the scene. You were called because his wound continues to bleed. Assessment reveals a sleeping 56-year-old man with a deep, gaping wound over the right eye with moderate bleeding. During assessment, the patient wakes suddenly and pushes you away. He tells you to leave him alone.

What actions are necessary in the management of this situation?

_____

_____

_____

Fill-in-the-Patient Care Report

Read the incident scenario and then complete the following patient care report (PCR).

It is 2115 and you are just walking out of a grocery store with a small bag of apples when the dispatch tones blare from your portable radio.

"Truck Two," the dispatcher's voice blasts from the small speaker. "Emergency call."

You pick up the pace to the ambulance where your partner is fastening his seat belt, answering on the portable as you go. "Dispatch, go for Truck Two."

"Truck Two, I need you to head over to the intersection of Grand and Hopper for a motorcycle versus automobile." You repeat back the information, jump into the passenger seat, and pull your seat belt into position as your partner activates the lights and siren and pulls out onto the deserted street.

At 7 minutes after dispatch, you arrive at the intersection and see a small blue car with a shattered windshield sitting diagonally in the middle of the intersection. On the opposite side of the road there is a damaged and smoking motorcycle on its side; a person is lying motionless on the pavement nearby.

The driver of the car, who is standing on the side of the road and talking on his cell phone, shouts that he is not injured, so you proceed to the woman on the ground. She appears to be approximately 24 years old, is unresponsive to pain, has bleeding from a long forehead laceration, and has inadequate, snoring respirations.

At 9 minutes after dispatch, you have your partner manually immobilize the patient's head and neck while you insert an oropharyngeal airway and begin assisting her respirations with a bag-valve mask and 15 L/min of supplemental oxygen.

At 10 minutes after dispatch, a fire truck arrives on scene and one of the firefighters obtains the patient's vitals while the others prepare the cervical collar and long backboard.

Two minutes later, the firefighter reports the patient's vitals: blood pressure, systolic 90, diastolic 54; pulse of 100 beats/min, weak and irregular; respirations of 12 breaths/min with adequate assisted tidal volume; pale, cool, and diaphoretic skin; and a pulse oximetry reading of 94%.

About 5 minutes after obtaining vitals, the patient is appropriately secured to the long backboard and loaded into the ambulance for the short trip to the local university trauma center.

During the 6-minute transport to the trauma center ambulance entrance, you must continue assisting the patient's respirations and cannot repeat the vitals.

It takes a total of 14 minutes to move the patient from your gurney to the bed in the trauma bay, provide a verbal report to the nurse, and prepare the ambulance for your next call.

Fill-in-the-Patient Care Report

EMS Patient Care Report (PCR)			
Date:	Incident No.:	Nature of Call:	Location:

Dispatched:	En Route:	At Scene:	Transport:	At Hospital:	In Service:

Patient Information	
Age: Sex: Weight (in kg [lb]):	Allergies: Medications: Past Medical History: Chief Complaint:

Vital Signs				
Time:	BP:	Pulse: weak/irregular	Respirations:	SpO_2:
Time:	BP:	Pulse:	Respirations:	SpO_2:
Time:	BP:	Pulse:	Respirations:	SpO_2:

EMS Treatment (circle all that apply)				
Oxygen @ ___ L/min via (circle one): NC NRM BVM	Assisted Ventilation	Airway Adjunct	CPR
Defibrillation	Bleeding Control	Bandaging	Splinting	Other:

Narrative

Communications and Documentation

© Photos.com

General Knowledge

Matching

Match each of the items in the left column to the appropriate definition in the right column.

_____ **1.** Base station

_____ **2.** Mobile radio

_____ **3.** Portable radio

_____ **4.** Repeater

_____ **5.** Telemetry

_____ **6.** UHF

_____ **7.** VHF

_____ **8.** Cellular telephone

_____ **9.** Dedicated line

_____ **10.** MED channels

_____ **11.** Scanner

_____ **12.** Channel

_____ **13.** Rapport

A. "Hot line"

B. A trusting relationship built with your patient

C. Communication through an interconnected series of repeater stations

D. Assigned frequency used to carry voice and/or data communications

E. Radio receiver that searches across several frequencies until the message is completed

F. VHF and UHF channels designated exclusively for EMS use

G. Vehicle-mounted device that operates at a lower frequency than a base station

H. A process in which electronic signals are converted into coded, audible signals

I. Radio frequencies between 30 and 300 MHz

J. Hand-carried or handheld devices that operate at 1 to 5 watts

K. Special base station radio that receives messages and signals on one frequency and then automatically retransmits them on a second frequency

L. Radio frequencies between 300 and 3,000 MHz

M. Radio hardware containing a transmitter and receiver that is located in a fixed location

Multiple Choice

Read each item carefully and then select the one best response.

_____ **1.** Which of following is an example of a closed-ended question?

   A. What seems to be bothering you today?

   B. Has this ever happened before?

   C. What were you doing over the past few hours?

   D. Can you describe the pain for me?

_____ **2.** The transmission range of a(n) _____ _____ is more limited than that of mobile or base station radios.

   A. portable radio

   B. 800-MHz radio

   C. cellular phone

   D. UHF radio

_____ **3.** Which of the following is TRUE when communicating with a child?

   A. Children are easily fooled by lies and deception.

   B. Avoid eye contact when speaking to a child.

   C. Children are rarely frightened by EMS providers.

   D. Overly anxious parents can make the situation worse.

_____ **4.** What is your first step when initiating communication with a non–English-speaking patient?
- **A.** Find out how much English the patient can speak.
- **B.** Speak louder to see if the patient can understand you.
- **C.** Skip over obtaining a medical history and go to the secondary assessment.
- **D.** Wait on scene for a translator to arrive.

_____ **5.** Digital signals are also used in some kinds of paging and tone-alerting systems because they transmit _____ and allow for more choices and flexibility.
- **A.** numerically
- **B.** faster
- **C.** alphanumerically
- **D.** encoded messages

_____ **6.** The transfer of care officially occurs during:
- **A.** the documentation of the incident.
- **B.** the radio report to the hospital while en route.
- **C.** your oral report at the hospital.
- **D.** the restocking of the unit.

_____ **7.** Which of the following is FALSE with regard to simplex mode?
- **A.** When one party transmits, the other must wait to reply.
- **B.** You must push a button to talk.
- **C.** It is called a "pair of frequencies."
- **D.** Radio transmissions can occur in either direction but not simultaneously in both.

_____ **8.** Which of the following is NOT an FCC principal EMS-related responsibility?
- **A.** Monitoring radio operations
- **B.** Establishing limitations for transmitter power output
- **C.** Allocating specific radio frequencies for use by EMS providers
- **D.** Ensuring that all radios contain lithium batteries

_____ **9.** Information given to the responding unit(s) should include all of the following EXCEPT:
- **A.** the number of patients.
- **B.** a list of all patient medications.
- **C.** the exact location of the incident.
- **D.** responses by other public safety agencies.

_____ **10.** Which of the following is a reason to contact medical control?
- **A.** Notify the hospital of the patient's diet preference
- **B.** Direct orders needed to administer certain treatments
- **C.** Advise the hospital of the patient's primary care physician
- **D.** Discuss how to troubleshoot malfunctioning equipment

_____ **11.** The patient report commonly includes all of the following EXCEPT:
- **A.** a list of the patient's childhood illnesses.
- **B.** the patient's age and gender.
- **C.** a brief history of the patient's current problem.
- **D.** your estimated time of arrival.

_____ **12.** In most areas, medical control is provided by the _____ who work at the receiving hospital.
- **A.** nurses
- **B.** physicians
- **C.** interns
- **D.** staff

_____ **13.** Which of the following is NOT helpful when attempting to effectively communicate with a hearing impaired patient?

    A. Having paper and a pen available

    B. Learning some simple phrases in sign language

    C. Shouting

    D. Speaking slowly and distinctly

_____ **14.** In regard to therapeutic communication techniques, what does the term _reflection_ mean?

    A. Asking the patient to explain what he or she meant by an answer

    B. Being sensitive to the patient's feelings and thoughts

    C. Providing factual information to support a conversation

    D. Restating a patient's statement made to you to confirm your understanding

_____ **15.** When delivering a patient report, be sure that you report all patient information in a(n) _____ manner.

    A. objective

    B. accelerated

    C. sarcastic

    D. condescending

_____ **16.** Medical control guides the treatment of patients in the system through all of the following EXCEPT:

    A. hands-on care.

    B. protocols.

    C. direct orders.

    D. postcall review.

_____ **17.** When is using a closed-ended question appropriate?

    A. When patients are unable to provide long answers

    B. When you are trying to obtain the details of an event

    C. When asking about past medical history

    D. When patients are trying to explain their pain

_____ **18.** When you encounter a patient who is angry, you should:

    A. threaten the patient.

    B. assume an aggressive posture.

    C. stare down the patient.

    D. speak calmly and slowly.

_____ **19.** Which of the following is NOT included in the patient care report (PCR) narrative?

    A. Time of events

    B. Patient's address

    C. Assessment findings

    D. Care provided

_____ **20.** If you make an error when documenting in a patient's record, you should:

    A. erase the error, then correct it.

    B. cover it with correction fluid, then write over top.

    C. draw a single horizontal line through the error and initial it.

    D. highlight the error with a marker, then write the correction next to it.

_____ **21.** When caring for a visually impaired patient, you should:

    A. use sign language.

    B. touch the patient only when necessary to render care.

    C. try to avoid sudden movements.

    D. never walk him or her to the ambulance.

_____ **22.** Instances in which you may be required to file special reports with appropriate authorities include all of the following EXCEPT:
- **A.** gunshot wounds.
- **B.** dog bites.
- **C.** suspected physical, sexual, or substance abuse.
- **D.** diabetic emergencies.

True/False

If you believe the statement to be more true than false, write the letter "T" in the space provided. If you believe the statement to be more false than true, write the letter "F."

_____ **1.** The two-way radio is at least two units: a transmitter and a receiver.

_____ **2.** One of the most fundamental aspects of what EMTs do is to ask questions.

_____ **3.** Ethnocentrism occurs when you consider your own cultural values to be equal to those of others.

_____ **4.** Speaking louder to a non–English-speaking patient will increase his or her ability to understand you.

_____ **5.** If a patient refuses care and transport, you do not need to complete a PCR.

_____ **6.** Falsifying information on the PCR may result in suspension and/or revocation of your certification or license.

_____ **7.** EMS systems that use repeaters are unable to get good signals from portable radios.

_____ **8.** Children can easily see through lies or deception.

_____ **9.** When speaking on the radio, speak in plain English and avoid code words.

_____ **10.** Your PCR will reflect on you professionally and can be used as evidence in court.

Fill-in-the-Blank

Read each item carefully and then complete the statement by filling in the missing words.

1. The _____ section of the PCR is arguably the most important portion.

2. A two-way radio consists of two units: a(n) _____ and a(n) _____.

3. A(n) _____ _____, also known as a "hot line," is always open or under the control of the individuals at each end.

4. _____ is anything that dampens or obscures the true meaning of a message.

5. Refusal of care is a common source of _____ in EMS.

6. _____ are commonly used in EMS operations to alert on- and off-duty personnel.

7. When the first call to 9-1-1 comes in, the dispatcher must try to judge its relative _____ to begin the appropriate EMS response using emergency medical dispatch protocols.

8. The principal reason for radio communication is to facilitate communication between you and _____ _____.

9. A _____ is an assigned frequency or frequencies used to carry voice and/or data communications.

10. _____ _____ are important to use when patients are unable to provide long or complete answers to questions.

11. To ensure complete understanding, once you receive an order from medical control, you must _____ the order back, word for word, and then receive confirmation.

12. By their very nature, _____ _____ do not require direct communication with medical control.

13. The _____, pace, and _____ of the language will tell you about the mood of the person communicating.

14. Children can easily see through lies or deception, so you must always be _____ with them.

15. If the patient does not speak any English, in an emergency you can use a family member or friend to act as a(n) _____.

16. It is _____ _____ to use military time in EMS documentation.

17. _____ adult patients have the right to refuse treatment.

Crossword Puzzle

The following crossword puzzle is an activity provided to reinforce correct spelling and understanding of medical terminology associated with emergency care and the EMT. Use the clues in the column to complete the puzzle.

Across

2. A process in which electronic signals are converted into coded, audible signals.
7. Radio frequencies between 300 and 3,000 MHz.
9. _____ questions can be answered in short or single-word responses.
12. Anything that dampens or obscures the true meaning of a message.
13. An assigned frequency or frequencies that are used to carry voice and/or data communications.
14. Telecommunication systems that allow a computer to maximize utilization of a group of frequencies.
17. A special base station radio that receives messages and signals on one frequency and then automatically retransmits them on a second frequency.

Down

1. A low-power portable radio that communicates through an interconnected series of repeater stations called "cells" is known as a(n) _____ telephone.
3. A trusting relationship that you build with your patient.
4. The use of a radio signal and a voice or digital message that is transmitted to "beepers" or desktop monitor radios.
5. The ability to transmit and receive simultaneously.
6. Questions for which the patient must provide detail to give an answer are called _____ questions.
8. The federal agency that has jurisdiction over interstate and international telephone and telegraph services and satellite communications.
10. _____ imposition is when one person imposes his or her beliefs, values, and practices on another because he or she believes his or her ideals are superior.
11. A radio receiver that searches across several frequencies until the message is completed.
15. Small computer terminals inside ambulances that directly receive data from the dispatch center.
16. The legal document used to record all patient care activities.

Critical Thinking

Multiple Choice
Read each critical-thinking item carefully and then select the one best response.

Questions 1–5 are derived from the following scenario: You have just finished an ambulance run where a 45-year-old man had driven his SUV into a utility pole. The driver was found slumped over the steering wheel, unconscious. A large electrical wire was lying across the hood of the vehicle. After securing scene safety, you were able to approach the patient and complete a primary assessment, in which you found a 6-inch (15.4-cm) laceration across his forehead. The patient regained responsiveness, was alert and oriented, and refused care.

_____ 1. Should an EMT document this call, even though the patient refused care?
   A. No. You only need to document when you have actually provided care.
   B. No. This was not a billable run.
   C. Yes. Documentation is needed regardless.
   D. Both A and B.

_____ 2. Which of the following would NOT be important to document?
   A. That the scene needed to be made safe
   B. That ensuring scene safety delayed care
   C. That you completed a primary assessment
   D. What you and your partner were doing prior to receiving the call.

_____ 3. While writing the report, you made an error. How should this be corrected?
   A. Draw a single line through it.
   B. Erase the mistake.
   C. Cover up the mistake with correction fluid.
   D. Completely cross out the error by repeatedly drawing multiple lines through it.

_____ 4. What is NOT a consequence of falsifying a report?
   A. It may result in the suspension and/or revocation of your license.
   B. It gives other health care providers a false impression of assessment/findings.
   C. It results in poor patient care.
   D. It results in good patient care.

_____ 5. If the patient refuses to sign the refusal form:
   A. Sign it yourself and state: "Patient refused to sign."
   B. You cannot let the man leave the scene until he either goes with you or signs the form.
   C. Have a credible witness sign the form testifying that he or she witnessed the patient's refusal of care.
   D. If the patient refuses care, you don't have to document it.

Short Answer
Complete this section with short written answers using the space provided.

1. List the five principal FCC responsibilities related to EMS.

   _____

   _____

   _____

2. What are the 10 Golden Rules that will help calm a patient and establish a therapeutic rapport?

   _____

   _____

   _____

3. List the six functions of a patient care report.

_____

_____

_____

4. Describe the two types of written report forms generally in use in EMS systems.

_____

_____

_____

Ambulance Calls

The following case scenarios provide an opportunity to explore the concerns associated with patient management and to enhance critical-thinking skills. Read each scenario and answer each question to the best of your ability.

1. You are in the dispatch office filling in for the EMS dispatcher who needed to use the restroom. The phone rings and you answer it to hear a hysterical woman screaming about a child falling into an old well. The only information she is providing is that he is 5 years old and is not making any noise. The address is on the computer display.

How would you best manage this situation, and what additional help would you call for?

_____

_____

_____

2. You respond to an "unknown medical problem" in an area commonly populated by Hispanic Americans. You arrive to find several individuals speaking to a middle-aged man. They seem to be concerned about him and motion you toward the patient. You attempt to gain information about the situation, but your patient does not speak English and you do not speak Spanish. The patient has no outward appearance of any problems.

How would you best manage this situation?

_____

_____

_____

3. You are dispatched to the parking lot of a grocery store for a "confused child." You arrive to find a young boy who is developmentally disabled. He cannot communicate who he is or where he lives. He is frightened but appears otherwise unharmed.

How would you best manage this situation?

_____

_____

_____

Fill-in-the-Patient Care Report

Read the incident scenario and then complete the following patient care report (PCR).

You watch the digital clock on the dashboard change to 5:11 PM and flip through the stack of PCRs that you have accumulated during the past 10 hours of your busy shift, ensuring that they are all complete. Ten minutes later, the dispatcher contacts you on the radio and requests that you and your partner respond to 18553 Old Redwood Highway for a dirt bike accident.

Six minutes later, your partner pulls off the main road and into a sprawling green field dotted with motorcross riders in multicolored pads and helmets. One small group of riders off in the distance begins jumping up and down, waving their arms. The ambulance moves slowly across the smooth, solid ground, and a minute later you arrive at the group's location. You see a rider lying on the ground with blood covering his lower left leg.

"He ripped his foot off," a teenaged girl with long blonde hair shouts as you step out of the truck. "Please help him quick!"

You kneel next to the 19-year-old injured man as your partner gets the equipment from the back of the ambulance. The young man is pounding his fist on the ground and yelling in pain, holding his injured leg tightly with one gloved hand. The foot of his left leg is hanging limply, almost completely severed from the ankle and bleeding profusely.

You immediately apply pressure to the end of the patient's leg with a trauma dressing as three firefighters arrive. You direct two of the firefighters to remove the patient's helmet while you immobilize his spine. Your partner and the third firefighter prepare the cervical collar and long backboard.

Once the patient is completely immobilized on the backboard and your partner has initiated high-flow oxygen therapy with a nonrebreathing mask, you bandage the dressings in place (after noting that the bleeding has almost completely stopped) and direct the loading of the 73-kg (161-lb) patient into the ambulance. You make a mental note that you had been on scene for only 8 minutes.

You obtain a complete set of vital signs just as your partner is pulling away from the grass and back onto the road. You find the following: blood pressure is 104/66 mm Hg; heart rate is 102 beats/min; respirations are 18 breaths/min and unlabored; skin is pale, cool, and moist; and oxygen saturation is 97%. You immediately cover the patient with a blanket to preserve his body temperature.

After contacting the receiving trauma center with a verbal report and ETA, you repeat the vital signs about 5 minutes after the first set. You find his blood pressure is at 110/72 mm Hg, heart rate is 90 beats/min, respirations are 14 breaths/min and still unlabored, color is returning to his skin, and the pulse oximeter is showing 99%. Just as you finish obtaining the vitals, your partner opens the back doors and you deliver the patient to the waiting team in the trauma bay.

Twenty minutes later, after providing an appropriate report to the charge nurse, turning over care of the patient, and properly cleaning and disinfecting the ambulance, you call yourselves back in service and head back to the post.

Fill-in-the-Patient Care Report

EMS Patient Care Report (PCR)					
Date:	**Incident No.:**		**Nature of Call:**		**Location:**
Dispatched:	**En Route:**	**At Scene:**	**Transport:**	**At Hospital:**	**In Service:**
Patient Information					
Age: **Sex:** **Weight (in kg [lb]):**			**Allergies:** **Medications:** **Past Medical History:** **Chief Complaint:**		
Vital Signs					
Time:	**BP:**		**Pulse:**	**Respirations:**	**Spo$_2$:**
Time:	**BP:**		**Pulse:**	**Respirations:**	**Spo$_2$:**
Time:	**BP:**		**Pulse:**	**Respirations:**	**Spo$_2$:**
EMS Treatment **(circle all that apply)**					
Oxygen @ ____ L/min via (circle one): NC NRM BVM		**Assisted Ventilation**	**Airway Adjunct**		**CPR**
Defibrillation	**Bleeding Control**	**Bandaging**	**Splinting**		**Other:**
Narrative					

Medical Terminology

© Photos.com

General Knowledge

Matching

Match each of the items in the left column to the appropriate definition in the right column.

_D_	**1.** Prefix		**K.**	Bottom of the foot
_F_	**2.** Suffix		**B.**	Motion away from the midline
_J_	**3.** Superior		**C.**	Belly side of the body
_G_	**4.** Distal		**D.**	Occurs before the root word
_C_	**5.** Ventral		**E.**	Bending of a joint
_A_	**6.** Plantar		**F.**	Occurs after the root word
_B_	**7.** Abduction		**G.**	Farther from the trunk
_I_	**8.** Supine		**H.**	Back surface of the body
_E_	**9.** Flexion		**I.**	Lying face up
_H_	**10.** Posterior		**J.**	Nearer to the head

Match each of the prefixes in the left column to the appropriate definition in the right column.

_____	**11.** Tachy-	**A.**	Four
_____	**12.** Post-	**B.**	Over, excessive, high
_____	**13.** Quad-	**C.**	Rapid, fast
_E_	**14.** Bi-	**D.**	Before
_____	**15.** Brady-	**E.**	Two
_____	**16.** Pre-	**F.**	Slow
_____	**17.** Hyper-	**G.**	After, behind

Match each of the suffixes in the left column to the appropriate definition in the right column.

_____	**18.** –megaly	**A.**	Disease
_____	**19.** –oma	**B.**	Surgical removal of
_____	**20.** –ectomy	**C.**	Tumor
_____	**21.** –algia	**D.**	Inflammation
_____	**22.** –logist	**E.**	Pertaining to pain
_____	**23.** –pathy	**F.**	Enlargement
_____	**24.** –itis	**G.**	Specialist

Multiple Choice

Read each item carefully and then select the one best response.

_____   **1.** A patient was involved in a motor vehicle crash. He has abrasions to both arms. What word is used to describe this?

    A. Medial

    B. Bilateral

    C. Lateral

    D. Ventral

_____ 2. While assessing a patient, you note a slow pulse. How would you describe this?

A. Tachycardia

B. Brachiocardia

C. Retrocardia

D. Bradycardia

_____ 3. You are reviewing a patient care report and notice the abbreviation DOE. What does this mean?

A. Dead on extrication

B. Director of EMS

C. Dyspnea on exertion

D. Diabetes of elderly

_____ 4. You are transporting a 72-year-old female from a hospital to an extended care facility. When reviewing her chart, you note she underwent a pleurocentesis. What does this mean?

A. Removal of lung tissue

B. Draining fluid from the chest

C. Surgical opening of the chest

D. Examination of the lung with a scope

_____ 5. You arrive at the scene of a motorcycle crash. You find the patient lying prone on the ground. What does this mean?

A. The patient is lying face down.

B. The patient is lying face up.

C. The patient is sitting up at 45°.

D. The patient is sitting up at 90°.

_____ 6. While obtaining a history on a patient, she informs you that she has a carcinoma of the liver. What does this mean?

A. Enlargement of the liver

B. Inflammation of the liver

C. Cancerous tumor of the liver

D. Noncancerous tumor of the liver

_____ 7. You are preparing a patient for transport. A nurse informs you the patient has a history of AMI. What does this mean?

A. Acute marrow inflammation

B. Acute myocardial infarction

C. Acute musculoskeletal infection

D. Acute myocardial ischemia

_____ 8. Just prior to transporting a patient from a hospital to an extended care facility, the medical control physician informs you the patient is to remain NPO. What does this mean?

A. No pulmonary oxygen

B. Noting by parenteral route

C. No pulmonary obstructions

D. Nothing by mouth

_____ 9. You are examining a patient who experienced a TIA. What does this mean?

A. Transient ischemic attack

B. Total ischemic attack

C. Transient intestinal atrophy

D. Tissue inhibiting attack

_____ **10.** You are caring for a 6-year-old child with a recent diagnosis of pharyngitis. What does this mean?
    A. Pain in the throat
    B. Disease of the throat
    C. Inflammation of the throat
    D. Paralysis of the throat

True/False

If you believe the statement to be more true than false, write the letter "T" in the space provided. If you believe the statement to be more false than true, the letter "F."

_____ **1.** Not all medical terms will have a prefix.

_____ **2.** The ankle is proximal to the knee.

_____ **3.** The abbreviation CRNA means Certified Registered Nurse Anesthetist.

_____ **4.** The suffix "-megaly" means enlargement.

_____ **5.** The word root occurs before the prefix.

_____ **6.** When a term has more than one word root, a combining bowl must be placed between the two roots.

_____ **7.** Singular words that end in "a" change to "es" when plural.

_____ **8.** The wrist is proximal to the elbow.

_____ **9.** The abbreviation for deep vein thrombosis is DVT.

_____ **10.** The suffix "-plegia" refers to plastic surgery.

Fill-in-the-Blank

Read each item carefully and then complete the statement by filling in the missing words.

1. _____ means closer to or on the skin.

2. The _____ part of the body, or any body part, is the portion nearer to the head.

3. The bottom of the foot is referred to as the _____ surface.

4. The way to describe the sections of the abdominal cavity is by _____.

5. _____ is motion toward the midline.

6. The parts that lie closer to the midline are called _____ (inner) structures.

7. A patient who is sitting upright is said to be in the _____ _____.

8. When trying to define a term, begin with the _____ and work backward.

9. The body is in the _____ position when lying face down.

10. _____ take the place of words to shorten notes or documentation.

Labeling

Label the following diagrams with the correct terms.

1. Directional Terms

A. _____

B. _____

C. _____

D. _____

E. _____

F. _____

G. _____

H. _____

I. _____

J. _____

K. _____

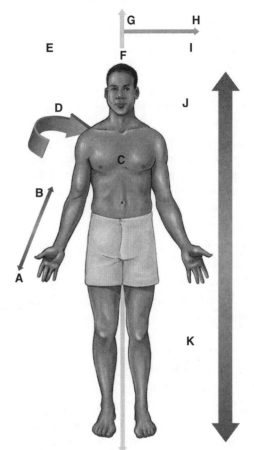

© Jones & Bartlett Learning.

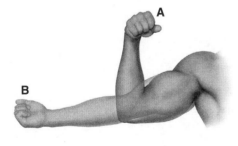

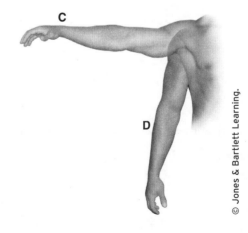

© Jones & Bartlett Learning.

2. Movement Terms

A. _____

B. _____

C. _____

D. _____

Critical Thinking

Multiple Choice

Read each critical-thinking item carefully and then select the one best response.

_____ 1. You respond to the home of a 38-year-old female who complains of nausea and vomiting. The patient informs you she has been ill for the past 3 days with nausea and vomiting, and states that she cannot "keep anything down." When questioned how many times she's vomited in the past 24 hours, she tells you at least 30 times. When giving a radio report to the receiving hospital, what term would you use to describe the patient's condition?

   A. Hypergastritis

   B. Hypernausea

   C. Hyperemesis

   D. Hypervomitus

_____ 2. You are examining a 28-year-old male who was stabbed following an altercation in a local bar. He has a stab wound to the right upper quadrant of the abdomen. You also notice a scar to the right lower quadrant. When you question the patient about the scar, he tells you his appendix was removed 3 years ago. What term can be used to describe the wound and the scar in reference to the abdomen?

   A. Contralateral

   B. Ipsilateral

   C. Bilateral

   D. Retrolateral

_____ 3. A 52-year-old male called for EMS because he is experiencing a headache. The patient tells you this is "the worse headache of my life." On examination, you note the patient has photophobia. What does this term mean?

   A. Fear of cameras

   B. Fear of photographs

   C. Fear of x-rays

   D. Fear of light

_____ 4. You are called to the home of a 60-year-old female with chest pain. The patient provides you with a paper listing her medical history. Most of the items on the list are abbreviated. The list includes: HTN, IDDM, GERD, CAD, MRSA, and PVD. Which abbreviation on that list describes a condition involving the gastrointestinal tract?

   A. IDDM

   B. MRSA

   C. GERD

   D. PVD

Short Answer

Complete this section with short written answers using the space provided.

1. List the four movement terms and their definitions.

_____

_____

_____

2. What are the five rules to use when converting terms from singular to plural?

_____

_____

_____

3. What are the four components that comprise a medical term?

_____

_____

_____

4. A combining vowel shown with the word root is called a combing form. List five of the most common combining forms found in EMS.

_____

_____

_____

Fill-in-the-Patient Care Report

Read the incident scenario and then complete the following patient care report (PCR) using medical terminology and abbreviations learned in this chapter.

You and your partner stop for something to eat at a local fast food restaurant. While eating your lunch, you look at your watch and notice it's exactly noon. You are amazed that you're actually eating lunch on time. In that instant, you are dispatched to 152 East Bramble Street for a male with chest pain. As you clean up from lunch, your partner acknowledges the call and marks your unit en route at 1202. The dispatcher tells you this is a 53-year-old male with a history of diabetes and hypertension who experienced chest pain while mowing his lawn.

You arrive on scene at 1210 and are greeting by the patient's wife. She tells you the patient was mowing the lawn and then experienced a sudden onset of central chest pain that radiated to his jaw. He informed his wife of his symptoms and she immediately called for EMS. You enter the patient's home and find him sitting on the couch. He appears short of breath and is holding his left hand to his chest. You introduce yourself to the patient and ask what's bothering him. He complains of chest pain and shortness of breath. As your partner places the patient on high-flow oxygen at 15 L/min via nonrebreathing mask, you request ALS and continue to get additional information from the patient and his wife. The patient tells you he has a history of hypertension, noninsulin-dependent diabetes, gastroesophageal reflux disease, and surgery to remove his appendix. His medications include Metformin, Lisinopril, and Omeprazole. He denies any allergies.

Your partner obtains vital signs at 1215 and tells you the following results: pulse 82/regular, respirations 16, blood pressure 148/92, SpO_2 98% on oxygen. You perform a secondary assessment and note the patient's lungs are clear in all fields and his abdomen is non-tender. In addition, he has equal pulses in all of his extremities.

Following your assessment, you package the patient in a semi-Fowler's position on the litter and transport him to the local hospital at 1220. You are only 2 minutes from the local hospital and cancel ALS due to your quick travel time. The unit arrives at the hospital at 1223. The patient reports that he is feeling better since he was placed on oxygen. You transfer care to the emergency department staff and provide the nurse with a verbal report as your partner restocks the unit for the next call. You call dispatch and mark your unit back in service at 1235.

Fill-in-the-Patient Care Report

EMS Patient Care Report (PCR)					
Date:	**Incident No.:**		**Nature of Call:**		**Location:**
Dispatched:	**En Route:**	**At Scene:**	**Transport:**	**At Hospital:**	**In Service:**

Patient Information	
Age:	**Allergies:**
Sex:	**Medications:**
Weight (in kg [lb]):	**Past Medical History:**
	Chief Complaint:

Vital Signs				
Time:	**BP:**	**Pulse:**	**Respirations:**	**Spo$_2$:**
Time:	**BP:**	**Pulse:**	**Respirations:**	**Spo$_2$:**
Time:	**BP:**	**Pulse:**	**Respirations:**	**Spo$_2$:**

EMS Treatment (circle all that apply)				
Oxygen @ ____ L/min via (circle one): NC NRM BVM	**Assisted Ventilation**	**Airway Adjunct**		**CPR**
Defibrillation	**Bleeding Control**	**Bandaging**	**Splinting**	**Other:**

Narrative

The Human Body

© Photos.com

General Knowledge

Matching

Match each of the items in the left column to the appropriate definition in the right column.

_____ **1.** Capillary

_____ **2.** Anatomic position

_____ **3.** Midline

_____ **4.** Flexion

_____ **5.** Tidal volume

_____ **6.** Hypoxic drive

_____ **7.** Epidermis

_____ **8.** Peristalsis

_____ **9.** Pathophysiology

_____ **10.** Ligament

_____ **11.** Symphysis

_____ **12.** Diffusion

_____ **13.** Residual volume

_____ **14.** Dead space

_____ **15.** Stoke volume

A. Outer layer of skin

B. Fibrous tissue that connects bones to bones

C. Amount of air moved in and out of the lungs in one relaxed breath

D. Study of how normal physiology is affected by disease

E. Standing, facing forward, palms facing forward

F. Wave-like contraction of smooth muscle

G. Connects arterioles to veins

H. Does not participate in gas exchange

I. Joint that has grown together to form a stable connection

J. Imaginary vertical line descending from the middle of the forehead to the floor

K. Air that remains in the lungs after maximum expiration

L. Volume of blood pumped with each contraction

M. Backup system to control respirations

N. Movement from higher concentration to lower concentration

O. Bending of a joint

For each of the bones listed in the left column, indicate whether it is an upper extremity bone (A) or a lower extremity bone (B).

_____ **16.** Talus

_____ **17.** Patella

_____ **18.** Clavicle

_____ **19.** Fibula

_____ **20.** Calcaneus

_____ **21.** Ulna

_____ **22.** Humerus

A. Upper extremity bone

B. Lower extremity bone

For each of the muscle characteristics described in the left column, select the type of muscle from the right column.

_____ **23.** Attaches to the bone

_____ **24.** Found in the walls of the gastrointestinal tract

_____ **25.** Forms the major muscle mass of the body

_____ **26.** Under the direct control of the brain

_____ **27.** Found only in the heart

_____ **28.** Can tolerate blood supply interruption for only a very short period

_____ **29.** Responsible for all bodily movement

_____ **30.** Has its own blood supply and electrical system

A. Skeletal

B. Smooth

C. Cardiac

For each of the parts of the nervous system in the left column, select the phrase in the right column with which it is associated.

_____ **31.** Spinal cord

_____ **32.** Central nervous system

_____ **33.** Sensory nerves

_____ **34.** Motor nerves

_____ **35.** Brain

_____ **36.** Peripheral nervous system

A. Exits the brain through an opening at the base of the skull

B. Transmit electrical impulses to the muscles, causing them to contract

C. Brain and spinal cord

D. Links the central nervous system to various organs in the body

E. Carry sensations of taste and touch to the brain

F. Controlling organ of the body

Multiple Choice

Read each item carefully and then select the one best response.

_____ **1.** Which of the following would be considered an underlying cause of shock?
- **A.** Increased blood volume
- **B.** Increased pumping ability of the heart
- **C.** Loss of blood vessel control
- **D.** Decrease in anaerobic metabolism

_____ **2.** In the female, what structure carries the ovum to the uterus?
- **A.** Ovary
- **B.** Fallopian tube
- **C.** Vas deferens
- **D.** Seminal vesicles

_____ **3.** The leaf-shaped flap of tissue that prevents food and liquid from entering the trachea is called the:
- **A.** uvula.
- **B.** epiglottis.
- **C.** laryngopharynx.
- **D.** cricothyroid membrane.

_____ **4.** Which of the following systems is responsible for releasing chemicals that regulate body activities?
- **A.** Nervous
- **B.** Endocrine
- **C.** Cardiovascular
- **D.** Skeletal

_____ **5.** Which of the following vessels does NOT carry blood to the heart?
- **A.** Inferior vena cava
- **B.** Superior vena cava
- **C.** Pulmonary vein
- **D.** Pulmonary artery

_____ **6.** The_____ is connected to the intestine by the bile ducts.
- **A.** Stomach
- **B.** Spleen
- **C.** Appendix
- **D.** Liver

_____ **7.** Which of the following is NOT a function of the urinary system?
- **A.** Fluid control
- **B.** Hormone regulation
- **C.** pH balancing
- **D.** Waste filtration

_____ **8.** What organ secretes enzymes that are used to digest fats, starches, and protein?
- **A.** Liver
- **B.** Gallbladder
- **C.** Pancreas
- **D.** Spleen

True/False

If you believe the statement to be more true than false, write the letter "T" in the space provided. If you believe the statement to be more false than true, write the letter "F."

_____   **1.** The aorta is the only artery that supplies the groin and lower extremities with blood.

_____   **2.** The knee is a ball-and-socket joint.

_____   **3.** The phalanges are the bones of the fingers and toes.

_____   **4.** The right atrium receives blood from the pulmonary veins.

_____   **5.** There are 10 ribs located in the thorax.

_____   **6.** Exhaled air contains 21% oxygen.

_____   **7.** The spleen is a muscle that is commonly injured in abdominal blunt-trauma injuries.

Fill-in-the-Blank

Read each item carefully and then complete the statement by filling in the missing words.

1. There is/are _____ cervical vertebrae.

2. The movable bone in the skull is the _____.

3. There is a total of _____ lobes in the right and left lungs.

4. There are _____ pairs of ribs in the thorax.

5. The spinal column has _____ vertebrae.

6. The ankle is formed by the _____,_____, and _____.

7. The cerebrum, which is the largest part of the brain, is composed of four lobes: _____,_____,_____,

and _____.

8. The _____ space is the space between the cells.

9. The movement of air between the lungs and the environment is called _____.

10. How much air is being effectively moved during ventilation and how much blood is gaining access to the alveoli is called

the _____ ratio.

Labeling

Label the following diagrams with the correct terms.

1. The Skull

A. _____

B. _____

C. _____

D. _____

E. _____

F. _____

G. _____

H. _____

I. _____

J. _____

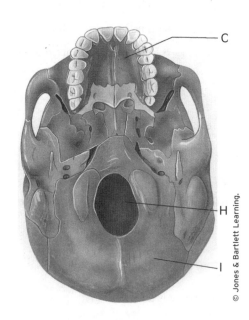

2. The Spinal Column

A. _____

B. _____

C. _____

D. _____

E. _____

F. _____

G. _____

H. _____

I. _____

J. _____

K. _____

L. _____

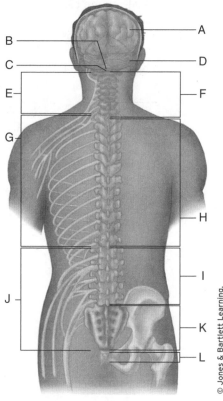

© Jones & Bartlett Learning.

3. The Thorax

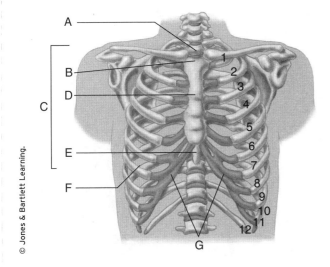

A. _____

B. _____

C. _____

D. _____

E. _____

F. _____

G. _____

4. The Shoulder Girdle

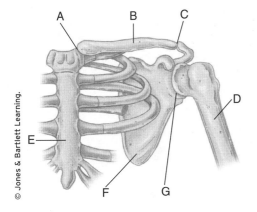

A. _____

B. _____

C. _____

D. _____

E. _____

F. _____

G. _____

5. The Wrist and Hand

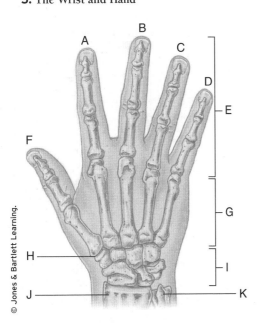

A. _____

B. _____

C. _____

D. _____

E. _____

F. _____

G. _____

H. _____

I. _____

J. _____

K. _____

6. The Pelvis

A. _____

B. _____

C. _____

D. _____

E. _____

F. _____

G. _____

H. _____

I. _____

J. _____

K. _____

L. _____

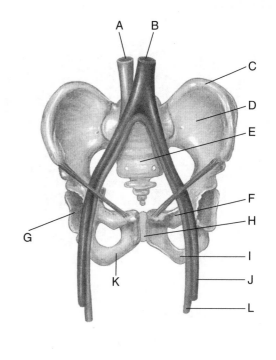

7. The Lower Extremity

A. _____

B. _____

C. _____

D. _____

E. _____

F. _____

G. _____

H. _____

I. _____

J. _____

K. _____

L. _____

M. _____

N. _____

O. _____

P. _____

Q. _____

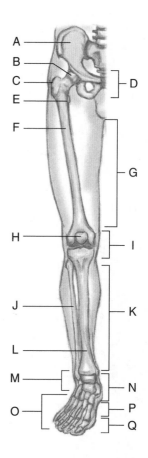

8. The Foot

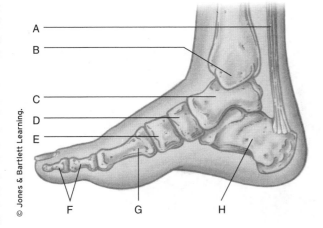

A. _____

B. _____

C. _____

D. _____

E. _____

F. _____

G. _____

H. _____

9. The Respiratory System

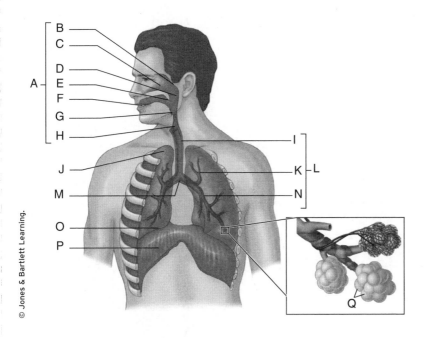

A. _____

B. _____

C. _____

D. _____

E. _____

F. _____

G. _____

H. _____

I. _____

J. _____

K. _____

L. _____

M. _____

N. _____

O. _____

P. _____

Q. _____

© Jones & Bartlett Learning.

10. The Circulatory System

A. _____

B. _____

C. _____

D. _____

E. _____

F. _____

G. _____

H. _____

I. _____

J. _____

K. _____

L. _____

M. _____

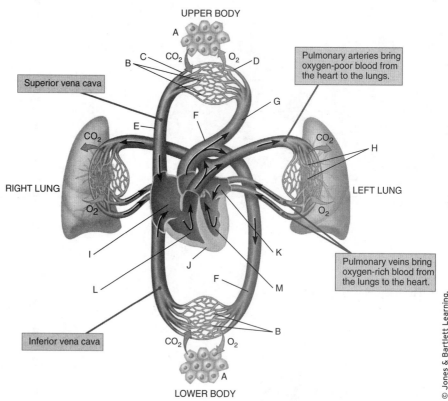

UPPER BODY

A

B C CO_2 O_2 D

Superior vena cava

G

E

F

CO₂

RIGHT LUNG

H

LEFT LUNG

O_2

O_2

Pulmonary arteries bring oxygen-poor blood from the heart to the lungs.

Pulmonary veins bring oxygen-rich blood from the lungs to the heart.

I

J

K

L

F

M

B

Inferior vena cava

CO_2 O_2

A

LOWER BODY

© Jones & Bartlett Learning.

11. Central and Peripheral Pulses

A. _____

B. _____

C. _____

D. _____

E. _____

F. _____

G. _____

H. _____

I. _____

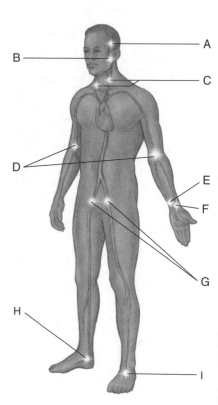

A

B

C

D

E

F

G

H

I

© Jones & Bartlett Learning.

12. The Brain

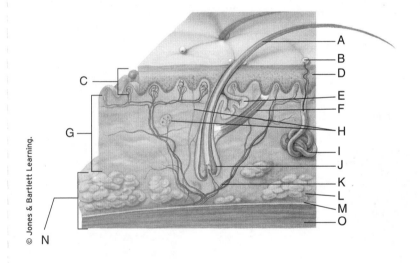

© Jones & Bartlett Learning.

A. _____

B. _____

C. _____

13. Anatomy of the Skin

© Jones & Bartlett Learning.

A. _____

B. _____

C. _____

D. _____

E. _____

F. _____

G. _____

H. _____

I. _____

J. _____

K. _____

L. _____

M. _____

N. _____

O. _____

14. The Male Reproductive System

A. _____

B. _____

C. _____

D. _____

E. _____

F. _____

G. _____

H. _____

I. _____

J. _____

K. _____

L. _____

M. _____

FRONT VIEW   SIDE VIEW

15. The Female Reproductive System

A. _____

B. _____

C. _____

D. _____

E. _____

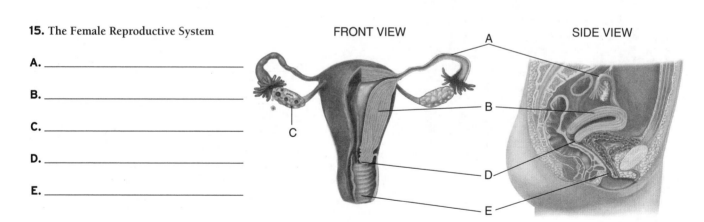

FRONT VIEW   SIDE VIEW

Crossword Puzzle

The following crossword puzzle is an activity provided to reinforce correct spelling and understanding of medical terminology associated with emergency care and the EMT. Use the clues in the column to complete the puzzle.

Across

1. The_____ artery leads from the right ventricle of the heart to the lungs; it carries oxygen-poor blood.
5. One of three bones that fuse to form the pelvic ring.
7. A portion of the medulla oblongata where the primary respiratory pacemaker is found.
9. To bend.
12. The breastbone.
13. The longest and one of the strongest bones in the body.
15. The part of the pharynx that lies above the level of the roof of the mouth.
17. Fluid produced in the ventricles of the brain that flows in the subarachnoid space and bathes the meninges.
18. An organ that lies below the midbrain and above the medulla and contains numerous important nerve fibers.

Down

1. One of three bones that fuse to form the pelvic ring.
2. The part of the skeleton comprising the skull, spinal column, and rib cage is known as the____ skeleton.
3. A portion of the medulla oblongata that is responsible for modulating breathing during speech.
4. The_____ position is the position of reference in which the patient stands facing you, arms at the side, with the palms of the hands forward.
6. One of three bones that fuse to form the pelvic ring.
7. Movement of a gas from an area of higher concentration to an area of lower concentration.
8. Seminal fluid ejaculated from the penis and containing sperm.
10. Any portion of the airway that contains air and cannot participate in gas exchange.
11. The_____ magnum is a large opening at the base of the skull through which the brain connects to the spinal cord.
13. The bending of a joint.
14. The brain and spinal cord.
16. The nucleotide involved in energy metabolism.

Critical Thinking

Multiple Choice

Read each critical-thinking item carefully and then select the one best response.

Questions 1–5 are derived from the following scenario: Kory, a 16-year-old boy, attempted to jump down a flight of stairs on his skateboard but landed face down on his chest and stomach, where he stayed until found. He was not wearing a helmet, and he hit the pavement with his head. Two bones were protruding from his right ankle.

_____ **1.** Which of the following bones are most likely fractured?

    A. Ulna/Radius

    B. Acromion/Humerus

    C. Tibia/Fibula

    D. Patella/Fibula

_____ **2.** What part of his spinal column do you want to keep immobilized so as not to move any of its seven vertebrae?

    A. Cervical

    B. Thoracic

    C. Sacrum

    D. Coccyx

_____ **3.** If Kory were to develop pain in his right upper quadrant, what organ may be causing the pain?

    A. Liver

    B. Stomach

    C. Spleen

    D. Appendix

_____ **4.** If Kory were to go into shock from his injuries, what type of shock will he most likely experience?

    A. Cardiogenic

    B. Obstructive

    C. Hypovolemic

    D. Septic

_____ **5.** Which of the following pulses is located near Kory's leg injury?

    A. Brachial

    B. Dorsalis pedis

    C. Ulnar

    D. Superficial temporal

Short Answer

Complete this section with short written answers using the space provided.

1. List the four components of blood and each of their functions.

   _____

   _____

   _____

2. List the five sections of the spinal column and indicate the number of vertebrae in each.

   _____

   _____

   _____

3. What organs are in each of the quadrants of the abdomen?

   RUQ: _____

   LUQ: _____

   RLQ: _____

   LLQ: _____

4. List in order the structures that blood flows through when circulating through the heart and lungs.

   1. _____

   2. _____

   3. _____

   4. _____

   5. _____

   6. _____

   7. _____

   8. _____

   9. _____

Ambulance Calls

The following case scenarios provide an opportunity to explore the concerns associated with patient management and to enhance critical-thinking skills. Read each scenario and answer each question to the best of your ability.

1. You are dispatched to the scene of a bar fight. A 34-year-old man has been stabbed in the right upper quadrant of the abdomen with a knife.

   What organs might be affected by this wound?

   _____

   _____

   _____

2. You are dispatched to a one-vehicle motor vehicle crash, car versus telephone pole. You arrive to find an unrestrained driver who is complaining of chest pain. You notice the steering wheel is deformed.

   Based on this information, what anatomic structures are potentially injured?

   _____

   _____

   _____

3. You are dispatched to a local BMX bike track just down the road from the fire station. You arrive to find a 14-year-old boy walking toward you, holding his left arm in place. He tells you that as he was turning a corner on the track, fell off his bike and landed on his shoulder.

   What anatomic structures are potentially injured?

   _____

   _____

   _____

Fill-in-the-Patient Care Report

Read the incident scenario and then complete the following patient care report (PCR).

You note that it has been far too quiet this evening as you and your partner sit overlooking the west end of the city. An approaching car's headlights briefly illuminate the cab of the ambulance before swinging around a curve, dropping you back into darkness again. The radio buzzes and you both snap to attention.

"Six-nineteen from central, I've got a priority-one call. Please proceed to the intersection of Alpha Street and 15th Avenue for an assault. Police reporting the scene as secure. I'm showing you assigned at 2312."

Your partner acknowledges the call as you pull out of the parking lot and begin the 17-minute cross-town trip to the scene location. On arrival, you are directed to a 38-year-old, 115-pound (52-kg) woman who is lying on the sidewalk, arms wrapped tightly around her torso.

"There was a fight over at Hank's bar," the police officer squatting next to the patient tells you. "Linda here was attacked by several other ladies and assaulted pretty severely in the street."

You kneel next to the moaning woman and explain that you are there to help her. After confirming a patent airway, you ask the police officer to hold the patient's head in a neutral, in-line position while you initiate high-flow oxygen therapy via a nonrebreathing mask set at 15 L/min. You and your partner then apply a cervical collar, secure the patient to a long backboard, and load her into the ambulance. You look at your watch and see that it has been 29 minutes since the initial dispatch.

Your partner jumps into the back of the ambulance with the patient while you slide into the cab, notify dispatch of your departure from the scene, and pull away, heading toward the university trauma center 13 minutes south on 15th Avenue. Your partner finds darkening bruises on the patient's upper arms, the left side of her chest, and down the front of both legs. Her stomach is distended and rigid, causing her to wince and cover her torso with her hands when touched.

By the time you pull to a stop in the hospital's ambulance bay, your partner has obtained two sets of vital signs—the first, 2 minutes following departure from the scene and the other 6 minutes later. The results were, in order: blood pressure, 108/56 mm Hg and 104/54 mm Hg; pulse, 96 beats/min and 104 beats/min; respirations, 16 breaths/min (good tidal volume but labored) and 18 breaths/min (adequate tidal volume and labored); and pulse oximetry 96% and 95%. The patient also seemed to be growing more anxious during the transport and was treated for shock with blankets and proper positioning.

You and your partner quickly transfer the patient to the open and waiting trauma room bed, provide the physician with a full report, and are back in service 15 minutes after initially arriving at the hospital.

Fill-in-the-Patient Care Report

EMS Patient Care Report (PCR)					
Date:	Incident No.:	Nature of Call:		Location:	
Dispatched:	En Route:	At Scene:	Transport:	At Hospital:	In Service:
Patient Information					
Age: Sex: Weight (in kg [lb]):		Allergies: Medications: Past Medical History: Chief Complaint:			
Vital Signs					
Time:	BP:	Pulse:	Respirations:		Spo_2:
Time:	BP:	Pulse:	Respirations:		Spo_2:
Time:	BP:	Pulse:	Respirations:		Spo_2:
EMS Treatment **(circle all that apply)**					
Oxygen @ ___ L/min via (circle one): NC NRM BVM		Assisted Ventilation	Airway Adjunct		CPR
Defibrillation	Bleeding Control	Bandaging	Splinting		Other:
Narrative					

PREPARATORY

Life Span Development

© Photos.com

General Knowledge

Matching

Match each of the items in the left column to the appropriate definition in the right column.

_____ 1. Preschoolers

_____ 2. Anxious-avoidant attachment

_____ 3. Nephrons

_____ 4. Toddlers

_____ 5. Atherosclerosis

_____ 6. School age

_____ 7. Conventional reasoning

_____ 8. Early adults

_____ 9. Moro reflex

_____ 10. Postconventional reasoning

_____ 11. Rooting reflex

_____ 12. Fontanelles

_____ 13. Secure attachment

_____ 14. Middle adults

A. The basic filtering units in the kidneys

B. Cholesterol and calcium buildup inside the walls of the blood vessels that forms plaque

C. Persons who are 19 to 40 years of age

D. Areas where the infant's skull has not fused together

E. Persons who are 1 to 3 years of age

F. A bond between an infant and his or her parents in which the infant understands that the parents will be responsive to his or her needs

G. Persons who are 41 to 60 years of age

H. An infant reflex in which the infant opens his or her arms wide, spreads the fingers, and seems to grab at things

I. A type of reasoning in which a child bases decisions on his or her conscience

J. A bond between an infant and his or her caregiver in which the infant is repeatedly rejected and develops an isolated lifestyle

K. A type of reasoning in which a child looks for approval from peers and society

L. Persons who are 3 to 6 years of age

M. An infant reflex that occurs when something touches an infant's cheek, and the infant instinctively turns his or her head toward the touch

N. Persons who are 6 to 12 years of age

Multiple Choice

Read each item carefully and then select the one best response.

_____ 1. What is the decline in kidney function between the ages of 20 and 90 years?

    A. 10%

    B. 50%

    C. 45%

    D. 20%

_____ 2. What is the typical age range for an adolescent?

    A. 6 to 12 years

    B. 3 to 6 years

    C. 12 to 18 years

    D. 10 to 19 years

_____ 3. Children who make decisions based on their conscience are using what type of reasoning?

    A. Postconventional

    B. Psychosocial

    C. Conventional

    D. Preconventional

_____ **4.** Which of the following is a nervous system change commonly found in older adults?
- **A.** Increase in brain weight
- **B.** Increase in peripheral nerve functioning
- **C.** Less space for cerebral spinal fluid
- **D.** Deterioration of nerve endings

_____ **5.** Maturation of the reproductive system usually takes place during:
- **A.** early adulthood.
- **B.** preschool.
- **C.** middle adulthood.
- **D.** adolescence.

_____ **6.** What term is used to identify a person who is from birth to 1 month old?
- **A.** Infant
- **B.** Toddler
- **C.** Neonate
- **D.** Newborn

_____ **7.** What is the estimated maximum life expectancy for humans?
- **A.** 120
- **B.** 78
- **C.** 67
- **D.** 56

_____ **8.** What do middle adults tend to focus their time and energy on?
- **A.** Raising a family
- **B.** Excelling in a career
- **C.** Achieving life goals
- **D.** Creating a self-image

_____ **9.** When encountering a patient with depressed fontanelles, you should suspect:
- **A.** respiratory distress.
- **B.** dehydration.
- **C.** atherosclerosis.
- **D.** nephrosis.

_____ **10.** What is "vital capacity"?
- **A.** The volume of blood moved by each contraction of the heart
- **B.** The maximum thickness of the meninges
- **C.** The volume of air moved during the deepest points of respiration
- **D.** The amount of air left in the lungs following exhalation

_____ **11.** Clingy behavior and the fear of unfamiliar people or places are normal among 10- to 18-month-old children and are commonly caused by _____ anxiety.
- **A.** bonding
- **B.** separation
- **C.** avoidant
- **D.** mistrust

_____ **12.** Diastolic blood pressure tends to _____ with age.
- **A.** decrease
- **B.** compensate
- **C.** increase
- **D.** decompensate

_____ 13. Into what age range do toddlers and preschoolers fit?

    A. 1 to 6 years

    B. 2 to 8 years

    C. 2 to 7 years

    D. 0 to 5 years

_____ 14. Work, family, and stress best describe the life stage known as:

    A. middle adulthood.

    B. adolescence.

    C. late adulthood.

    D. early adulthood.

_____ 15. At what age can an infant normally start tracking objects with his or her eyes and recognizing familiar faces?

    A. 7 months

    B. 2 months

    C. 4 months

    D. 10 months

True/False

If you believe the statement to be more true than false, write the letter "T" in the space provided. If you believe the statement to be more false than true, write the letter "F."

_____ 1. The majority of older adults live in assisted-living facilities.

_____ 2. The rooting reflex takes place when an infant's lips are stroked.

_____ 3. Toddlers should have pulse rates between 90 and 150 beats/min.

_____ 4. Men can produce sperm well into their 80s.

_____ 5. The older the patient is the larger his or her pupils will be.

_____ 6. Typically, antisocial behavior will peak around age 13.

_____ 7. Language is usually mastered by the 24th month.

_____ 8. Breastfeeding helps to boost an infant's immune system.

_____ 9. Teething in an infant typically begins around 6 months of age.

_____ 10. Adolescents are at less risk than other populations for suicide and depression.

Fill-in-the-Blank

Read each item carefully and then complete the statement by filling in the missing words.

1. _____ adults are those who are age 19 to _____ years.

2. In toddlers, the pulse rate is _____ to _____ beats/min and the respiratory rate is _____ to _____ breaths/min.

3. Middle adults tend to focus on achieving their _____ _____.

4. Most older adults can hear _____ and are able to see _____.

5. Rebellious behavior can be part of an adolescent trying to find his or her own _____.

6. A(n) _____ usually weighs 6 to _____ pounds at birth, and the head accounts for

_____% of its body weight.

7. An infant's lungs are _____, and providing bag-valve-mask ventilations that are too forceful can result in

trauma from pressure, or _____.

8. By _____ to 24 months, toddlers begin to understand cause and _____.

9. Changes in gastric and intestinal function may inhibit _____ intake and utilization in

_____ adults.

10. Among older adults, _____ function in the 5 years preceding death is presumed to decline.

Crossword Puzzle

The following crossword puzzle is an activity provided to reinforce correct spelling and understanding of medical terminology associated with emergency care and the EMT. Use the clues in the column to complete the puzzle.

Across

1. Persons who are from 1 month to 1 year of age.
5. _____ reflex is an infant reflex that occurs when something touches an infant's cheek, and the infant instinctively turns his or her head toward the touch.
6. Persons who are 1 to 3 years of age.
11. Persons who are 3 to 6 years of age.
12. In _____ reasoning, a child looks for approval from peers and society.
13. Areas where the infant's skull has not fused together.
14. Persons who are 12 to 18 years of age.

Down

2. The basic filtering units in the kidneys.
3. _____ grasp is an infant reflex that occurs when something is placed in the infant's palm.
4. Persons who are 41 to 60 years of age are known as _____ adults.
7. Persons who are 6 to 12 years of age.
8. Persons who are birth to 1 month of age.
9. The stage of development during which infants gain the trust of their parents or caregivers if their world is planned, organized, and routine is known as "trust and _____."
10. _____ attachment is a bond in which an infant understands that his or her parents or caregivers will be responsive to his or her needs.

Critical Thinking

Multiple Choice

Read each critical-thinking item carefully and then select the one best response.

You are dispatched to a public park in the middle of a sprawling subdivision for an arm injury. You arrive to find a crying 8-year-old boy cradling his swollen and deformed left forearm. His friends tell you that he was holding onto the bars of the play structure and that his arm "snapped" when he jumped into the sand below.

_____ 1. What would you expect this boy's normal pulse to be?
   A. Between 70 and 120 beats/min
   B. Higher than 150 beats/min
   C. Most likely below 70 beats/min
   D. Around 60 beats/min

_____ 2. An adult bystander tells you that the boy kept trying to impress his friends with more and more dangerous stunts on the play structure prior to the injury. This is an indication of _____ reasoning.
   A. conventional
   B. preconventional
   C. unconventional
   D. postconventional

_____ 3. You would expect to find a respiratory rate of between _____ and _____ breaths/min with this patient.
   A. 12, 20
   B. 15, 20
   C. 10, 15
   D. 20, 30

Short Answer

Complete this section with short written answers using the space provided.

1. Explain why breathing can become more labor intensive among older adults.

   _____

   _____

   _____

2. Describe conventional reasoning.

   _____

   _____

   _____

3. Explain the stage of development known as "trust and mistrust."

   _____

   _____

   _____

4. What is atherosclerosis and how does it affect older adults?

_____

_____

_____

5. List the nine basic stages of life.

_____

_____

_____

Ambulance Calls

The following case scenarios provide an opportunity to explore the concerns associated with patient management and to enhance critical-thinking skills. Read each scenario and answer each question to the best of your ability.

1. You are dispatched to a residential care facility for a "fall from bed" and arrive to find a 96-year-old man refusing assistance, even though he has a large, darkening hematoma above his left ear. He keeps telling the care facility staff and you that he doesn't want any of you "yahoos" touching him.

What would you be most concerned about with this patient?

_____

_____

_____

2. You respond to a local residence for a toddler who burned her arm by knocking a lit candle off a shelf. You have responded to numerous abuse situations as an EMT and now find yourself suspicious of any child's injury. You would like to speak to this 16-month-old patient alone, but both parents stay nearby and seem very concerned about the child's well-being.

Would you try to speak to the child alone? Explain your reason.

_____

_____

_____

3. You and your partner are requested to a high school for a teenaged boy who fell from the stage while rehearsing a play. You arrive to find him surrounded by concerned classmates. He is guarding the left side of his chest and breathing shallowly, but he refuses assistance and insists that he is doing fine.

How would you best manage this situation?

_____

_____

_____

Fill-in-the-Patient Care Report

Read the incident scenario and then complete the following patient care report (PCR).

The dispatch tones awaken you from a light sleep and you instinctively pull a notepad from your pocket and write down the key components of the following dispatch.

0345

Geary Residential Home

16654 Geary Street

Respiratory distress

Within 3 minutes you and your partner, Leticia, are pulling the ambulance from the fire station and moving off through the silent, early morning streets. At 0359 you arrive at the front entrance of the building and are escorted down several long, carpeted hallways to a small, dimly lit room.

"This is Mrs. Gershon," your escort tells you. "She started complaining about her breathing 20 minutes ago and it's just getting worse."

Mrs. Gershon is a 93-year-old woman who has been living at Geary for nearly 17 years. She used to share the room with her husband, Ronald, until his death 3 years ago. She has had three myocardial infarctions in the past and takes medication to regulate blood pressure. Based on her wristband, you see that she is allergic to penicillin. She is sitting on the edge of her bed in the tripod position, breathing through pursed lips, and you can clearly see accessory muscle use in her neck.

"Hello, Mrs. Gershon. We are from the fire department and we are here to help," you say to her. You speak loudly and clearly because her nurse told you that she has difficulty hearing. She looks up at you, inhales shallowly once, and then stops breathing.

"Mrs. Gershon, don't stop breathing now," you say, while Leticia quickly hands you the bag-valve mask, hissing with 15 L/min of oxygen. You begin ventilating the older woman, who is obviously exhausted after struggling to breathe for such a long period. You find no resistance to your assisted ventilations, and Mrs. Gershon just stares up at you as you continue squeezing the bag. Leticia and several nurses from the facility move the 44-kg (97-lb) patient onto the gurney and out to the ambulance as you continue ventilations. Before climbing into the driver's seat, Leticia places the pulse oximetry finger clip onto the patient. She then calls in your departure for the hospital at 0410 and provides a brief report to the receiving facility through dispatch. Within 7 minutes you hear the truck's backup alarm and the patient care compartment is flooded with the bright yellow light of the hospital's ambulance bay. The SpO$_2$ readout is showing 95%.

Several nurses and the emergency department physician come out to the ambulance and assist with getting Mrs. Gershon inside, where she is quickly sedated and intubated while you provide a verbal report to the charge nurse.

Eighteen minutes after arriving at the hospital, your ambulance is cleaned, stocked, and ready for the next call.

Fill-in-the-Patient Care Report

EMS Patient Care Report (PCR)			
Date:	**Incident No.:**	**Nature of Call:**	**Location:**

Dispatched:	**En Route:**	**At Scene:**	**Transport:**	**At Hospital:**	**In Service:**

Patient Information	
Age: **Sex:** **Weight (in kg [lb]):**	**Allergies:** **Medications:** **Past Medical History:** **Chief Complaint:**

Vital Signs				
Time:	**BP:**	**Pulse:**	**Respirations:**	**Spo$_2$:**
Time:	**BP:**	**Pulse:**	**Respirations:**	**Spo$_2$:**
Time:	**BP:**	**Pulse:**	**Respirations:**	**Spo$_2$:**

EMS Treatment (circle all that apply)				
Oxygen @ ____ L/min via (circle one): NC NRM BVM	**Assisted Ventilation**	**Airway Adjunct**		**CPR**
Defibrillation	**Bleeding Control**	**Bandaging**	**Splinting**	**Other:**

Narrative

PREPARATORY

Lifting and Moving Patients

© Photos.com

General Knowledge

Matching

Match each of the items in the left column to the appropriate definition in the right column.

_____ **1.** Extremity lift
_____ **2.** Flexible stretcher
_____ **3.** Stair chair
_____ **4.** Basket stretcher
_____ **5.** Scoop stretcher
_____ **6.** Backboard
_____ **7.** Direct ground lift
_____ **8.** Portable stretcher
_____ **9.** Wheeled ambulance stretcher
_____ **10.** Bariatrics

A. Separates into two or four pieces
B. Tubular framed stretcher with rigid fabric stretched across it
C. Used for patients who are supine or sitting without an extremity or spinal injury
D. Specifically designed stretcher that can be rolled along the ground
E. Commonly used in technical and water rescues; Stokes litter
F. Used for patients who are found lying supine with no suspected spinal injury
G. Concerned with management of obesity
H. Used to carry patients up and down stairs
I. Spine board or longboard
J. Can be folded or rolled up

Multiple Choice

Read each item carefully and then select the one best response.

_____ **1.** _____ safety depends on the use of proper lifting techniques and maintaining a proper hold when lifting or carrying a patient.

    A. Your
    B. Your team's
    C. The patient's
    D. Your, your team's, and your patient's

_____ **2.** You should perform an urgent move in all of the following situations EXCEPT:

    A. if a patient has an altered level of consciousness.
    B. if the patient is complaining of neck pain.
    C. in extreme weather conditions.
    D. if a patient has inadequate ventilation or shock.

_____ **3.** You may injure your back if you lift:

    A. with your back straight.
    B. using a power lift technique.
    C. with the shoulder girdle anterior to the pelvis.
    D. keeping the weight close to you.

_____ **4.** When lifting, you should:

    A. spread your legs past shoulder width.
    B. lift a patient while reaching far in front of your torso.
    C. keep the weight that you are lifting as close to your body as possible.
    D. use your back muscles by bending at the waist.

_____ 5. Which of the follow statements is FALSE regarding proper lifting?
   A. Avoid twisting.
   B. Bend at the waist.
   C. Keep the weight close to your body.
   D. Bend at the knees.

_____ 6. In lifting with the palm down, the weight is supported by the _____ rather than the palm.
   A. fingers
   B. forearm
   C. lower back
   D. wrist

_____ 7. When you must carry a patient up or down a flight of stairs or other significant incline, use a _____ if possible.
   A. backboard
   B. stair chair
   C. stretcher
   D. short backboard

_____ 8. Because of the weight distribution on backboards and stretchers, the stronger EMTs should be at the:
   A. head.
   B. foot.
   C. side.
   D. front corner.

_____ 9. A backboard is a device that provides support to patients who you suspect have all of the following EXCEPT:
   A. hip injuries.
   B. pelvic injuries.
   C. spinal injuries.
   D. symptoms of heart attack.

_____ 10. Before any lifting is initiated, the team leader should do all of the following EXCEPT:
   A. give a command of execution.
   B. indicate where each team member is to be located.
   C. rapidly describe the sequence of steps that will be performed.
   D. give a brief overview of the stages.

_____ 11. Special _____ are usually required to move any patient who weighs more than 350 pounds (159 kg) to an ambulance.
   A. techniques
   B. equipment
   C. resources
   D. techniques, equipment, and resources

_____ 12. Which of the following statements is FALSE regarding the use of a stair chair?
   A. Keep your back in a locked-in position.
   B. Lean back to help distribute the weight.
   C. Keep the patient's weight and your arms as close to your body as possible.
   D. Flex at the hips, not at the waist.

_____ 13. When you use a body drag to move a patient:
   A. your back should always be locked and straight.
   B. you should encourage twisting so that the vertebrae can flex during the move.
   C. consider hyperextending to gain more leverage.
   D. drag the patient by the ankles.

_____ **14.** When pulling a patient, you should do all of the following EXCEPT:

    A. extend your arms no more than about 15 inches to 20 inches (38 cm to 50 cm).

    B. reposition your feet so that the force of pull will be balanced equally.

    C. when you can pull no farther, lean forward another 15 inches to 20 inches (38 cm to 50 cm).

    D. pull the patient by slowly flexing your arms.

_____ **15.** When log rolling a patient, you should do all of the following EXCEPT:

    A. kneel as close to the patient's side as possible.

    B. lean solely from the hips.

    C. reach as far as possible to maintain stability.

    D. use your shoulder muscles to help with the roll.

_____ **16.** If the weight you are pushing is lower than your waist, you should push from:

    A. the waist.

    B. a kneeling position.

    C. the shoulder.

    D. a squatting position.

_____ **17.** If you are alone and must remove an unconscious patient from a car, you should first move the patient's:

    A. legs.

    B. head.

    C. torso.

    D. pelvis.

_____ **18.** Situations in which you should use an emergency move include all of the following EXCEPT:

    A. when fire, explosives, or hazardous materials are present.

    B. when the patient feels like he or she might pass out.

    C. when you are unable to gain access to others in a vehicle who need lifesaving care.

    D. when you are unable to protect the patient from other hazards.

_____ **19.** You can move a patient on his or her back along the floor or ground by using all of the following methods EXCEPT:

    A. pulling on the patient's clothing in the neck and shoulder area.

    B. placing the patient on a blanket, coat, or other item that can be pulled.

    C. pulling the patient by the legs if they are the most accessible part.

    D. placing your arms under the patient's shoulders and through the armpits, and while grasping the patient's arms, dragging the patient backward.

_____ **20.** The _____ is both the mechanical weight-bearing base of the spinal column and the fused central posterior section of the pelvic girdle.

    A. lumbar spine

    B. sacrum

    C. coccyx

    D. ileum

_____ **21.** Which of the following is NOT an indication for use of the rapid extrication technique?

    A. The patient is in severe pain.

    B. The patient's condition cannot be properly assessed before being removed from the vehicle.

    C. The patient blocks access to another seriously injured patient.

    D. The vehicle or the scene is unsafe.

_____ **22.** To avoid the strain of unnecessary lifting and carrying, you should use _____ or assist an able patient to the stretcher whenever possible.

    A. the direct ground lift

    B. the extremity lift

    C. the draw sheet method

    D. a scoop stretcher

_____ **23.** You should use a rigid _____, often called a Stokes litter, to carry a patient across uneven terrain from a remote location that is inaccessible by ambulance or other vehicle.

    A. basket stretcher

    B. scoop stretcher

    C. molded backboard

    D. flotation device

_____ **24.** You should not attempt to lift a patient who weighs more than _____ without at least four rescuers.

    A. 220 lbs (100 kg)

    B. 230 lbs (104 kg)

    C. 240 lbs (109 kg)

    D. 250 lbs (113 kg)

_____ **25.** Which of the following is FALSE regarding the lifting and moving of geriatric patients?

    A. Many geriatric patients have great fear when being transported.

    B. Most patients will be able to lie supine on a backboard without problems.

    C. Geriatric patients tend to have brittle bones.

    D. Some patients may require you to use towels and blankets to assist with immobilization.

_____ **26.** Bariatrics is:

    A. the branch of medicine concerned with the elderly.

    B. the branch of medicine concerned with the obese.

    C. the branch of medicine concerned with infants.

    D. the method used to assess blood pressure.

Questions 27-30 are derived from the following scenario: You have been called to the scene of a high-speed motor vehicle collision involving two compact cars. The first vehicle was a rollover, ejecting the driver. The second vehicle contained both a driver and a front-seat passenger who cannot be reached because the door is up against a building.

_____ **27.** What device will you use to put the rollover victim onto the wheeled ambulance stretcher?

    A. Extremity lift

    B. Scoop stretcher

    C. Short backboard

    D. Backboard

_____ **28.** For the passenger in the second vehicle, you may need to perform a(n) _____ on the driver in order to reach the patient.

    A. extremity lift

    B. emergency move

    C. short backboard

    D. You should do nothing different; treat each patient the same.

_____ **29.** Which of the following is an advantage of the diamond carry?

    A. It uses an even number of people (less likely to drop).

    B. It can be done with one person, freeing up others for patient care.

    C. The patient can be slid along the ground.

    D. It provides the best means of spinal immobilization.

_____ **30.** You'll likely use the _____ to transfer the patient from your stretcher to the hospital bed.

    A. diamond carry

    B. scoop stretcher

    C. portable stretcher

    D. draw sheet method

True/False

If you believe the statement to be more true than false, write the letter "T" in the space provided. If you believe the statement to be more false than true, write the letter "F."

_____ 1. A portable stretcher is typically a lightweight folding device that does not have the undercarriage and wheels of a true ambulance stretcher.

_____ 2. The term *power lift* refers to a posture that is safe and helpful for EMTs when they are lifting.

_____ 3. If you find that lifting a patient is a strain, try to move the patient to the ambulance as quickly as possible to minimize the possibility of back injury.

_____ 4. It is not important that you and your team use the correct lifting technique to lift a stretcher.

_____ 5. One-person techniques for moving patients should be used only when immediate patient movement is necessary due to a life-threatening hazard and only one EMT is available.

_____ 6. A scoop stretcher may be used alone for a standard immobilization of a patient with a spinal injury.

_____ 7. When carrying a patient down stairs or on an incline, make sure the stretcher is carried with the head end first.

_____ 8. The rapid extrication technique is the preferred technique to use on all sitting patients with possible spinal injuries.

_____ 9. It is unprofessional for you to discuss and plan a lift at the scene in front of the patient.

_____ 10. Bariatrics is a new field of medicine that deals with the care of the obese.

_____ 11. A minimum of five personnel should be present when restraining a combative patient.

_____ 12. An isolette is used to transport neonatal patients.

_____ 13. The flexible stretcher is the most comfortable of all of the various lifting devices.

_____ 14. Pneumatic stretchers were developed to increase patient comfort on the road.

_____ 15. The most important feature of the bariatric stretcher is the increased weight-lifting capacity.

Fill-in-the-Blank

Read each item carefully and then complete the statement by filling in the missing words.

1. To avoid injury to you, the patient, or your partners, you will have to learn how to lift and carry the patient properly,

   using proper _____ _____ and a power grip.

2. The key rule of lifting is to always keep the back in a straight, _____ position and to lift without twisting.

3. The safest and most powerful way to lift, lifting by extending the properly placed flexed legs, is called a(n)

   _____ _____.

4. The arm and hand have their greatest lifting strength when facing _____ up.

5. Be sure to pick up and carry the backboard with your back in the _____ position.

6. You should not attempt to lift a patient who weighs more than _____ pounds with fewer than four rescuers,

   regardless of individual strength.

7. During a body drag where you and your partner are on each side of the patient, you will have to alter the usual pulling

   technique to prevent pulling _____ and producing adverse lateral leverage against your lower back.

8. When you are rolling the wheeled ambulance stretcher, your back should be _____, straight, and untwisted.

9. A patient on a backboard or stretcher can be lifted and carried by four providers in a _____ carry.

10. Whenever a patient has been placed onto the stretcher, one EMT must hold the main frame to prevent

    _____.

11. The manual support and immobilization that you provide when using the rapid extrication technique produce a greater

    risk of _____ _____.

12. The _____ _____ _____ is used for patients with no suspected spinal injury who are found

    lying supine on the ground.

13. The _____ _____ may be especially helpful when the patient is in a very narrow space or when there is

    not enough room for the patient and a team of EMTs to stand side by side.

14. The mattress on a stretcher must be _____ _____ so that it does not absorb any type of potentially

    infectious material, including water, blood, or other body fluids.

15. It is essential that you _____ your equipment after use.

Crossword Puzzle

The following crossword puzzle is an activity provided to reinforce correct spelling and understanding of medical terminology associated with emergency care and the EMT. Use the clues in the column to complete the puzzle.

Across

2. A(n) _____ stretcher features a strong rectangular tubular metal frame with rigid fabric stretched across it.

6. A(n) _____ ambulance stretcher is a specially designed stretcher to be rolled along the ground.

7. A(n) _____ stretcher is designed to be split into two or four sections that can be fitted around a patient who is lying on the ground or other relatively flat surface.

9. A branch of medicine concerned with the management (prevention or control) of obesity and allied diseases.

11. A(n) _____ stretcher is a rigid carrying device when secured around a patient but can be folded or rolled when not in use.

12. The _____ ground lift is used for patients who are found lying supine on the ground with no suspected spinal injury.

Down

1. A device used to provide support to a patient who is suspected of having a hip, pelvic, spinal, or lower extremity injury.

3. A lifting technique in which the provider's back is held upright, with legs bent, and the patient is lifted when the provider straightens the legs to raise the upper body and arms.

4. A technique in which the litter or backboard is gripped by inserting each hand under the handle with the palm facing up and the thumb extended.

5. In a(n) _____ move, the patient is dragged or pulled from a dangerous scene before assessment and care are provided.

7. A lightweight folding device that is used to carry a conscious, seated patient up or down stairs.

8. The _____ carry technique involves one provider at the head end of the stretcher or backboard, one at the foot end, and one at each side of the patient; all are able to face forward as they walk.

9. A(n) _____ stretcher is commonly used in technical and water rescues.

10. A(n) _____ extrication technique is used to move a patient from a sitting position inside a vehicle to supine on a backboard in less than 1 minute.

Critical Thinking

Short Answer

Complete this section with short written answers using the space provided.

1. List the one-rescuer drags, carries, and lifts.

_____

_____

_____

2. List the situations where the rapid extrication technique is used.

_____

_____

_____

3. List three guidelines for loading the stretcher into the ambulance.

_____

_____

_____

4. List five guidelines for carrying a patient on a stretcher.

_____

_____

_____

5. Identify the key rule of lifting.

_____

_____

_____

Ambulance Calls

The following case scenarios provide an opportunity to explore the concerns associated with patient management and to enhance critical-thinking skills. Read each scenario and answer each question to the best of your ability.

1. You are dispatched to a construction site for a 26-year-old man who fell into a ravine. He is approximately 35 feet (11 m) down a rocky ledge. He is alert with an unstable pelvis and weak radial pulses. You have all the help you need from the construction crew and the volunteer fire department.

   How would you best manage this patient?

   _____

   _____

   _____

2. You are dispatched to an "unknown medical problem" at a local residence. You are met at the door by the wife of the patient who tells you that her husband is in the bathroom and is not acting right. You find the 350-pound (159-kg) patient lying in the bathroom, stuck between the toilet and the wall. He is not breathing and has no pulse.

   How would you best manage this patient?

   _____

   _____

   _____

3. You are dispatched to "difficulty breathing" at a nearby apartment complex. The patient's apartment is located on the top floor of a three-story building, is accessed through an exterior entryway, and no elevators are available. Your patient is morbidly obese and cannot walk.

   How would you best manage this patient?

   _____

   _____

   _____

Skills

Skill Drills

Skill Drill 8-1: Performing the Power Lift

Test your knowledge of this skill by filling in the correct words in the photo captions.

© Jones & Bartlett Learning.

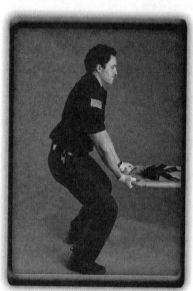

© Jones & Bartlett Learning.

1. Lock your back in a _____ curve. _____ and bend your legs. Grasp the backboard, palms up and just in front of you. _____ and _____ the weight between your arms.

2. Position your feet, _____ the object, and _____ your weight evenly. Lift by _____ your legs, keeping your back locked in.

Skill Drill 8-2: Performing the Diamond Carry

Test your knowledge of this skill by placing the following photos in the correct order. Number the first step with a "1," the second step with a "2," etc.

© Jones & Bartlett Learning.

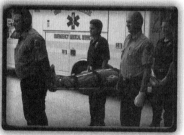

© Jones & Bartlett Learning.

© Jones & Bartlett Learning.

_____ The providers at each side turn the head-end hand palm down and release the other hand.

_____ The providers at each side turn toward the foot end. The provider at the foot end turns to face forward.

_____ Position yourselves facing the patient.

Skill Drill 8-3: Performing the One-Handed Carry

Test your knowledge of this skill by filling in the correct words in the photo captions.

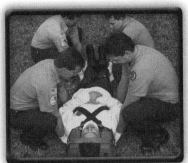

© Jones & Bartlett Learning.

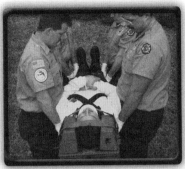

© Jones & Bartlett Learning.

© Jones & Bartlett Learning.

1. _____ each other and use both _____.

2. Lift the backboard to _____ _____.

3. _____ in the direction you will walk, and _____ to using one hand.

Skill Drill 8-7: Performing the Rapid Extrication Technique

Test your knowledge of this skill by placing the following photos in the correct order. Number the first step with a "1," the second step with a "2," etc.

© Jones & Bartlett Learning. Courtesy of MIEMSS.

_____ The second provider supports the torso. The third provider frees the patient's legs from the pedals and moves the legs together, without moving the pelvis or spine.

© Jones & Bartlett Learning. Courtesy of MIEMSS.

_____ The first provider provides in-line manual support of the head and cervical spine.

© Jones & Bartlett Learning. Courtesy of MIEMSS.

_____ The third provider exits the vehicle, moves to the backboard opposite the second provider, and they continue to slide the patient until the patient is fully on the board.

© Jones & Bartlett Learning. Courtesy of MIEMSS.

_____ The first (or fourth) provider places the backboard on the seat against the patient's buttocks. (Use of a backboard may depend on local protocols.)

© Jones & Bartlett Learning. Courtesy of MIEMSS.

_____ The third provider moves to an effective position for sliding the patient. The second and the third providers slide the patient along the backboard in coordinated, 8- to 12-inch (20 to 30-cm) moves until the patient's hips rest on the backboard.

© Jones & Bartlett Learning. Courtesy of MIEMSS.

_____ The first (or fourth) provider continues to stabilize the head and neck while the second provider and the third provider carry the patient away from the vehicle and onto the prepared stretcher.

© Jones & Bartlett Learning. Courtesy of MIEMSS.

_____ The second provider and the third provider rotate the patient as a unit in several short, coordinated moves. The first provider (relieved by the fourth provider as needed) supports the patient's head and neck during rotation (and later steps).

© Jones & Bartlett Learning. Courtesy of MIEMSS.

_____ The second provider gives commands, applies a cervical collar, and performs the primary assessment.

Skill Drill 8-9: Extremity Lift

Test your knowledge of this skill by filling in the correct words in the photo captions.

© Jones & Bartlett Learning. Courtesy of MIEMSS.

© Jones & Bartlett Learning. Courtesy of MIEMSS.

© Jones & Bartlett Learning. Courtesy of MIEMSS.

1. The patient's hands are _____ over the chest. Grasp the patient's wrists or _____ and pull the patient to a(n) _____ position.

2. Your partner moves to a position between the patient's_____, facing in the _____ direction as the patient, and places his or her hands under the _____.

3. Rise to a _____ position. On _____, lift and begin to move.

Skill Drill 8-10: Direct Carry

Test your knowledge of this skill by filling in the correct words in the photo captions.

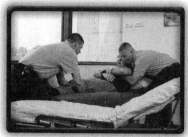

© Jones & Bartlett Learning.

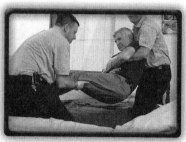

© Jones & Bartlett Learning.

1. Position the stretcher _____ to the bed. Secure the _____ to prevent movement. Face the patient while standing between the _____ and the _____. Position your arms under the patient's _____ and _____. Your partner should position his or her hands under the patient's _____.

2. Lift the patient from the bed in a smooth, _____ fashion.

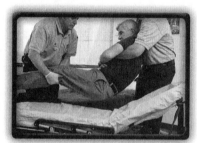

© Jones & Bartlett Learning.

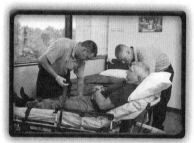

© Jones & Bartlett Learning.

3. Slowly carry the patient to the _____.

4. _____ lower the patient onto the stretcher and secure with _____.

General Knowledge

Matching

Match each of the items in the left column to the appropriate definition in the right column.

_____ 1. Triage

_____ 2. Cyanosis

_____ 3. Subcutaneous emphysema

_____ 4. Tachycardia

_____ 5. Conjunctiva

_____ 6. Symptom

_____ 7. Accessory muscles

_____ 8. Breath sounds

_____ 9. Chief complaint

_____ 10. Diaphoretic

_____ 11. Jaundice

_____ 12. Orientation

_____ 13. OPQRST

_____ 14. Palpate

_____ 15. Responsiveness

_____ 16. Retractions

_____ 17. Sclera

_____ 18. Frostbite

_____ 19. Crepitus

_____ 20. Paradoxical motion

A. Indication of air movement in the lungs

B. Lining of the eyelid

C. Indentation above the clavicles and in the spaces between the ribs during breathing

D. White of the eyes

E. The mental status of a patient

F. Mnemonic for gather information about a patient's symptoms

G. Yellow skin color due to liver disease or dysfunction

H. A crackling or grinding sound

I. Examine by touch

J. Damage to tissues as the result of exposure to cold

K. The way in which a patient responds to external stimuli

L. Secondary muscles of respiration

M. Air under the skin

N. Motion of a segment of chest wall that is opposite the normal movement during breathing

O. Most serious thing the patient is concerned about

P. The process of sorting patients based on severity of condition

Q. A blue-gray skin color associated with reduced oxygen levels

R. Profuse sweating

S. Subjective finding that the patient feels

T. A heart rate greater than 100 beats/min

Match the question with the corresponding assessment tool.

_____ 21. What does the pain feel like?

_____ 22. How long have you had the pain?

_____ 23. Are you taking any medications?

_____ 24. Did you eat this morning?

_____ 25. Does anything make the pain feel better or worse?

_____ 26. On a scale of 1 to 10, how do you rate your pain?

_____ 27. What were you doing before this happened?

_____ 28. What type of reaction do you have when you take medication?

_____ 29. Does the pain move anywhere?

_____ 30. When did the problem begin?

_____ 31. Does your chest hurt?

_____ 32. Have you been recently ill?

A. Signs and symptoms

B. Allergies

C. Medications

D. Past medical history

E. Last oral intake

F. Events leading up to illness

G. Onset

H. Provocation/palliation

I. Quality

J. Region/radiation

K. Severity

L. Timing

Multiple Choice

Read each item carefully and then select the one best response.

_____ **1.** Which of the following is NOT considered part of the scene size-up?
   A. Determining the mechanism of injury
   B. Requesting additional assistance
   C. Determining the level of responsiveness
   D. Determining the need for personal protective equipment (PPE)/standard precautions

_____ **2.** You should consider all women of childbearing years who are complaining of lower abdominal pain to be:
   A. pregnant until proven otherwise.
   B. experiencing cramps associated with menstruation.
   C. victims of sexual assault.
   D. suffering from a urinary tract infection.

_____ **3.** With _____, the force of the injury occurs over a broad area, and the skin is usually not broken.
   A. motor vehicle collisions
   B. blunt trauma
   C. penetrating trauma
   D. gunshot wounds

_____ **4.** Which of the following conditions is NOT known to cause a slow capillary refill?
   A. Local circulatory compromise
   B. Hypothermia
   C. Age
   D. Abdominal pain

_____ **5.** _____ is the measure of the amount of air that is moved into and out of the lungs in one breath.
   A. Residual volume
   B. Tidal volume
   C. Vital capacity
   D. Minute volume

_____ **6.** There are three elements to the physical exam. Which of the following is NOT one of those elements?
   A. Puncture
   B. Inspection
   C. Palpation
   D. Auscultation

_____ **7.** When determining the initial general impression, you should note all of the following EXCEPT:
   A. the patient's age.
   B. the level of distress.
   C. the events leading up to the incident.
   D. the patient's sex.

_____ **8.** When considering the need for additional resources, which of the following is NOT a question you should ask?
   A. How many patients are there?
   B. Is it raining?
   C. Who contacted EMS?
   D. Does the scene pose a threat to you or your patient's safety?

_____ **9.** Which of the following is included in the primary assessment?
   A. Blood pressure
   B. Pulse
   C. Breath sounds
   D. Pupils

_____ **10.** Which of the following conditions would be considered "high-priority" when determining the priority of transport?

    A. Uncomplicated childbirth

    B. Mild abdominal pain

    C. Difficulty breathing

    D. Pink skin color

_____ **11.** What does the "P" on the AVPU scale represent?

    A. Responsive to palpation

    B. Responsive to pain

    C. Responsive to provocation

    D. Responsive to palliation

_____ **12.** A normal respiratory rate for an adult is typically:

    A. 5 to 10 breaths per minute.

    B. 12 to 20 breaths per minute.

    C. 15 to 30 breaths per minute.

    D. 20 to 30 breaths per minute.

_____ **13.** For children younger than 1 year, you should palpate the _____ artery when assessing the pulse.

    A. carotid

    B. radial

    C. femoral

    D. brachial

_____ **14.** The automated external defibrillator (AED) with special pediatric pad and a dose attenuating system should be used on pediatric patients who are younger than _____ year(s) and who have been assessed to be unresponsive, apneic, and pulseless.

    A. 1

    B. 8

    C. 9

    D. 10

_____ **15.** When there are low levels of oxygen in the blood, the lips and mucous membranes appear blue or gray. What is the name of this condition?

    A. Cyanosis

    B. Pallor

    C. Jaundice

    D. Ashen

_____ **16.** Your first consideration when assessing a pulse is to determine:

    A. how fast the rate is.

    B. the quality.

    C. if one is present.

    D. if the rhythm is regular.

_____ **17.** To obtain the pulse rate in most patients, you should count the number of pulses felt in a _____ period and then multiply by two.

    A. 15-second

    B. 20-second

    C. 25-second

    D. 30-second

_____ **18.** In a patient with deeply pigmented skin, where should you look for changes in color?

    A. Ear canals

    B. External eyelids

    C. Groin

    D. Mucous membranes of the mouth

_____ **19.** With _____, the force of the injury occurs at a small point of contact between the skin and the object piercing the skin.
- **A.** motor vehicle collisions
- **B.** blunt trauma
- **C.** penetrating trauma
- **D.** falls

_____ **20.** Which of the following is NOT considered a method for controlling external bleeding?
- **A.** Direct pressure
- **B.** Tourniquet
- **C.** Cold water
- **D.** Elevation

_____ **21.** The _____ is/are the most serious thing that the patient is concerned about; the reason why they called 9-1-1.
- **A.** chief complaint
- **B.** pertinent negatives
- **C.** severity
- **D.** past medical history

_____ **22.** The four items used to assess the orientation of a patient's mental status include all of the following EXCEPT:
- **A.** person.
- **B.** place.
- **C.** history.
- **D.** events.

_____ **23.** An integral part of the rapid scan is evaluation using the mnemonic:
- **A.** AVPU.
- **B.** DCAP-BTLS.
- **C.** OPQRST.
- **D.** SAMPLE.

_____ **24.** In the absence of light, the pupils will:
- **A.** constrict.
- **B.** stay fixed.
- **C.** dilate.
- **D.** become unequal.

_____ **25.** _____ cause the pupils to constrict to a pinpoint.
- **A.** Opiates
- **B.** Antidepressants
- **C.** Antihypertensive medications
- **D.** Diabetic medications

_____ **26.** When assessing the respiratory system, which of the following is NOT considered essential to the assessment?
- **A.** Respiratory rate
- **B.** Depth of breathing
- **C.** Quality/character of breathing
- **D.** Breath odor

_____ **27.** Which of the following statements regarding assessment of the airway is true?
- **A.** The body will not be supplied the necessary oxygen if the airway is not managed.
- **B.** You should use the head tilt–chin lift maneuver to open the airway in trauma patients.
- **C.** The tongue is generally not a cause of airway obstruction.
- **D.** A conscious patient who cannot speak or cry is most likely hyperventilating.

_____ **28.** Which of the following is NOT considered a type of breath sound?
   A. Rhonchi
   B. Vibration
   C. Wheeze
   D. Stridor

_____ **29.** You are examining a 40-year-old female who you suspect might be a victim of abuse. Which of the following supports your suspicion?
   A. Mechanism of injury that matches the patient's history
   B. Unremarkable medical history with no previous injuries
   C. Multiple injuries in various stages of healing
   D. Consistent history reporting by the patient

_____ **30.** When using an interpreter to communicate with a patient, you should:
   A. maintain eye contact with the interpreter.
   B. maintain eye contact with the patient.
   C. feel free to make derogatory remarks.
   D. encourage the patient to learn English.

_____ **31.** _____ is an assessment tool used to evaluate the effectiveness of oxygenation.
   A. Capnography
   B. Capnometry
   C. Pulse oximetry
   D. Blood glucose

_____ **32.** The pressure felt along the wall of the artery when the ventricles of the heart contract is referred to as the:
   A. asystolic pressure.
   B. diastolic pressure.
   C. idiopathic pressure.
   D. systolic pressure.

_____ **33.** A blood pressure cuff that's too large for the patient:
   A. may result in a falsely low reading.
   B. may result in a falsely high reading.
   C. will not affect the reading.
   D. should be used in patients with arm pain.

_____ **34.** Which of the following is NOT typically found on an abdominal exam?
   A. Guarding
   B. Crepitation
   C. Tenderness
   D. Rigidity

_____ **35.** Crackling sounds produced by air bubbles under the skin are known as:
   A. subcutaneous ecchymosis.
   B. subcutaneous emphysema.
   C. subcutaneous erythema.
   D. subcutaneous emboli.

_____ **36.** Unstable patients should be reassessed every _____ minutes.
   A. 5
   B. 10
   C. 15
   D. 20

_____ **37.** In the _____ position, the patient sits leaning forward on outstretched arms with the head and chin thrust slightly forward.

    A. Fowler's

    B. tripod

    C. sniffing

    D. lithotomy

_____ **38.** In an unresponsive adult patient, the primary location to assess the pulse is the _____ artery.

    A. carotid

    B. femoral

    C. radial

    D. brachial

_____ **39.** Liver disease or dysfunction may cause _____, resulting in the patient's skin and sclera turning yellow.

    A. cyanosis

    B. jaundice

    C. diaphoresis

    D. lack of perfusion

_____ **40.** When obtaining a blood pressure by palpation in the arm, you should place your fingertips on the _____ artery.

    A. carotid

    B. brachial

    C. radial

    D. posterior tibial

_____ **41.** The _____ is performed at regular intervals during the assessment process, and its purpose is to identify and treat changes in a patient's condition.

    A. primary assessment

    B. reassessment

    C. secondary assessment

    D. scene size-up

_____ **42.** Which of the following is NOT considered a sign?

    A. Dizziness

    B. Marked deformities

    C. External bleeding

    D. Wounds

_____ **43.** When blood pressure drops, the body compensates to maintain perfusion to the vital organs by:

    A. decreasing the pulse rate.

    B. dilating the arteries.

    C. decreasing the respiratory rate.

    D. decreasing the blood flow to the skin and extremities.

_____ **44.** When assessing and treating a patient who is visually impaired, it is important that you do all of the following EXCEPT:

    A. speak loudly into the patient's ear because he or she can't see you.

    B. announce yourself when entering the residence.

    C. put items that were moved back into their previous position.

    D. explain to the patient what is happening.

_____ **45.** Which of the following statements is false regarding the assessment of patients with a language barrier?

    A. You should find an interpreter.

    B. You should determine whether the patient understands you.

    C. Your questioning should be lengthy and complex.

    D. You should be aware of the language diversity in your community.

True/False

If you believe the statement to be more true than false, write the letter "T" in the space provided. If you believe the statement to be more false than true, write the letter "F."

_____ 1. Responsiveness is evaluated with the mnemonic DCAP-BTLS.

_____ 2. Reassessment is not necessary for stable patients.

_____ 3. An assessment of the patient's musculoskeletal system typically is done because of a chief complaint associated with some type of trauma.

_____ 4. The apparent absence of a palpable pulse in an unresponsive patient is not a cause for concern.

_____ 5. A patient with a poor general impression is considered a priority patient.

_____ 6. When assessing the head, you should assess the patient's ears and nose for fluid.

_____ 7. Paradoxical motion of the chest wall is commonly associated with upper respiratory infections.

_____ 8. The abdomen is broken into six areas for assessment.

_____ 9. In the reassessment process, you should reevaluate everything that has been done to this point in the patient assessment process.

_____ 10. Law enforcement personnel may be needed at scenes to control traffic or intervene in domestic violence situations.

_____ 11. Determining the mental status and the level of consciousness of a patient take a great deal of time while on scene.

_____ 12. Depressed brain function can result from trauma or stroke.

_____ 13. PEARRL is used to describe skin color.

_____ 14. You should consider providing positive pressure ventilation in a conscious patient who has a respiratory rate of 14 breaths/min.

_____ 15. When documenting vital signs, you should note whether the patient's respirations are regular or irregular.

_____ 16. Patients with difficulty breathing, severe chest pain, and signs of poor perfusion should be transported immediately.

_____ 17. You should aim to assess, stabilize, and begin transport of trauma patients within 20 minutes.

_____ 18. Correct identification of high-priority patients is an essential aspect of the primary assessment and helps to improve patient outcome.

_____ 19. You should not interrupt patients when speaking, and you should be empathetic to their situations.

_____ 20. Being openly judgmental of patients who may have a chemical dependency is acceptable as long as you remain professional.

_____ 21. Scenes involving domestic violence can be extremely dangerous for EMS personnel.

_____ 22. You should consider all females of childbearing age who are reporting lower abdominal pain to be pregnant unless ruled out by history or other information.

_____ 23. Once you have allowed a talkative patient a chance to express himself or herself, you should allow the patient to continue talking about whatever he or she wants.

_____ 24. EMTs can expect anxious patients to exhibit signs of psychological shock.

_____ 25. It is unusual for a patient, family member, or friend to vent hostility toward EMS.

_____ 26. Information gathered from an intoxicated patient may be unreliable.

_____ 27. Your presence may make a crying patient feel more secure.

_____ 28. Depression is not a common reason for patients to call for EMS.

_____ **29.** When assessing a patient, you should inspect the pelvis for symmetry and any obvious signs of injury, bleeding, and deformity.

_____ **30.** Pulse and motor and sensory functions are typically assessed when examining a patient's extremities.

Fill-in-the-Blank

Read each item carefully and then complete the statement by filling in the missing words.

1. A(n) _____ is an objective condition that you can observe about the patient.

2. _____ _____ are protective measures for dealing with blood and bodily fluids.

3. When there are multiple patients, you should use the _____ _____ _____ to help organize the triage, logistics, and treatment of patients.

4. _____ _____ _____ should be requested for patients with severe injuries or complex medical problems.

5. Identifying and initiating treatment of immediate, potentially life-threatening conditions is the goal of the _____ _____.

6. You should think of the _____ _____ as a visual assessment, gathering information as you approach the patient.

7. _____ is the circulation of blood within an organ or tissue.

8. _____ tests the mental status of the patient by checking memory and thinking ability.

9. When light is shined into the eyes, the pupils should _____.

10. A brassy, crowing sound that is prominent on inspiration, suggesting a mildly occluded airway, is referred to as _____.

11. If there is a potential for trauma, use the modified _____ _____ to open the airway.

12. During _____ the chest muscles relax and air is released out of the lungs.

13. If a patient seems to develop difficulty breathing after your primary assessment, you should immediately reevaluate the _____.

14. If you hear fluid in the airway during your assessment, you should immediately _____ the airway to prevent aspiration.

15. A patient who coughs up thick yellow or green sputum most likely has a(n) _____ _____.

16. _____ _____ and see-saw breathing in a pediatric patient indicate inadequate breathing.

17. If you cannot palpate a pulse in an unresponsive patient, you should begin _____.

18. _____ is a heart rate greater than 100 beats/min.

19. The _____ is the delicate membrane lining the eyelids, and it covers the exposed surface of the eye.

20. Skin that is cool, clammy, and pale in your primary assessment typically indicates _____.

21. When the skin is bathed in sweat, it is described as _____.

22. A capillary refill time should be less than _____ second(s).

23. Direct pressure stops bleeding and helps the blood to _____, or clot, naturally.

24. A rapid scan to identify immediate threats should take _____ to _____ second(s).

25. The _____ _____ refers to the time from injury to definitive care.

26. The goal of the primary assessment is to identify and treat _____ _____.

27. _____ _____ provides details about the patient's chief complaint and an account of the patient's signs and symptoms.

28. You should use _____ questions when taking a history on a patient.

29. _____ is a mnemonic used to gather past medical or trauma history.

30. _____ _____ are negative findings used to help identify a patient's problem.

31. _____ _____ should be assessed in all known diabetic patients and all patients who are unresponsive for an unknown reason.

32. _____ describes the process of touching or feeling the patient for abnormalities.

33. _____ is a noninvasive method that can quickly and efficiently provide information on a patient's ventilatory status, circulation, and metabolism.

34. _____ _____ is the residual pressure that remains in the arteries during the relaxation phase of the heart.

35. A(n) _____ assessment should be performed any time you are confronted with a patient who has a change in mental status, a possible head injury, or syncope.

Crossword Puzzle

The following crossword puzzle is an activity provided to reinforce correct spelling and understanding of medical terminology associated with emergency care and the EMT. Use the clues in the column to complete the puzzle.

Across

1. Objective findings that can be seen, heard, felt, smelled, or measured.
3. The pressure wave that occurs as each heartbeat causes a surge in the blood circulating through the arteries.
7. A crackling, rattling breath sound that signals fluid in the air spaces of the lungs.
8. The way in which traumatic injuries occur.
9. The process of establishing treatment and transportation priorities according to severity of injury and medical need.
10. A step within the patient assessment process that provides details about the chief complaint is called _____ taking.
14. Flaring out of the nostrils, indicating that there is an airway obstruction.
16. _____ motion is the motion of the chest wall section that is detached in a flail chest.
17. Clothing or specialized equipment that provides protection to the wearer.
18. The general type of illness a patient is experiencing.

Down

2. Involuntary muscle contractions of the abdominal wall in an effort to protect an inflamed abdomen.
4. A harsh, high-pitched, crowing inspiratory sound.
5. Negative findings that warrant no care or intervention are known as _____ negatives.
6. A rapid heart rate, more than 100 beats/min.
11. A(n) _____ scan is performed during the secondary assessment.
12. To examine by touch.
13. Coarse, low-pitched breath sounds heard in patients with chronic mucus in the upper airway.
15. The _____ Period is the time from injury to definitive care.

Critical Thinking

Short Answer

Complete this section with short written answers using the space provided.

1. What is the single goal of primary assessment?

    _____

    _____

    _____

2. What is the general impression based on?

    _____

    _____

    _____

3. What do the letters ABC stand for in the assessment process?

    _____

    _____

    _____

4. What four kinds of questions are asked when assessing orientation, and what purpose do these questions serve?

    _____

    _____

    _____

5. What three questions should you ask yourself when assessing a patient's breathing?

    _____

    _____

    _____

6. List the elements of DCAP-BTLS.

    _____

    _____

    _____

7. What three questions should you ask yourself to determine if additional resources are needed at a scene?

_____

_____

_____

8. Define the acronym PEARRL.

_____

_____

_____

9. Explain the difference between a sign and a symptom.

_____

_____

_____

10. You are caring for a 24-year-old male with a pertinent sexual history. What questions should he be asked as part of your history taking?

_____

_____

_____

Ambulance Calls

The following case scenarios provide an opportunity to explore the concerns associated with patient management and to enhance critical-thinking skills. Read each scenario and answer each question to the best of your ability.

1. You are dispatched to a motor vehicle collision where you find a 32-year-old man with extensive trauma to the face and gurgling in his airway. He is responsive only to pain. You also note that the windshield is spider-webbed and that there is deformity to the steering wheel. He is not wearing a seat belt.

How would you best manage this patient? What clues tell you the transport status?

_____

_____

_____

2. You are dispatched to a local residence for "difficulty breathing." You find a man standing in his kitchen, leaning against a counter in a tripod position, and holding a metered-dose inhaler. As you question him, you see that he is working very hard to breathe, hear wheezing, and note that he can answer you with only one- or two-word responses.

What is the transport status of this patient?

_____

_____

_____

3. You are dispatched to "man fallen" at a private home. You arrive to find an older man who appears to have fallen down a flight of wooden stairs onto a cement basement floor. He is responsive to painful stimuli, has bruising, and has a small laceration above his left eye.

How would you best manage this patient?

_____

_____

_____

Skills

Skill Drills

Skill Drill 9-1: Rapid Scan

Test your knowledge of this skill by placing the following photos in the correct order. Number the first step with a "1," the second step with a "2," etc.

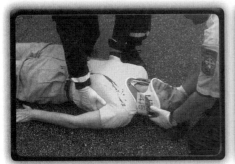

© Jones & Bartlett Learning. Courtesy of MIEMSS.

_____ Assess the chest. Listen to breath sounds on both sides of the chest.

© Jones & Bartlett Learning. Courtesy of MIEMSS.

_____ Assess the back. If spinal immobilization is indicated, do so with minimal movement to the patient's spine by log rolling the patient in one motion.

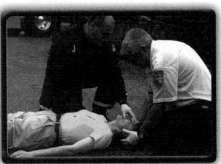

© Jones & Bartlett Learning. Courtesy of MIEMSS.

_____ Assess the head. Have your partner maintain in-line stabilization if indicated.

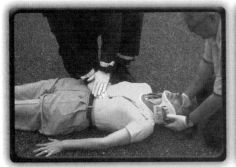

© Jones & Bartlett Learning. Courtesy of MIEMSS.

_____ Assess the abdomen.

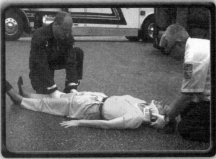

© Jones & Bartlett Learning. Courtesy of MIEMSS.

_____ Assess all four extremities. Assess pulse and motor and sensory function.

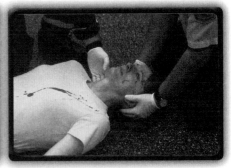

© Jones & Bartlett Learning. Courtesy of MIEMSS.

_____ Assess the neck.

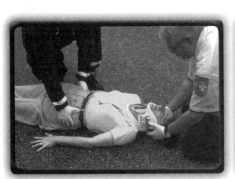

© Jones & Bartlett Learning. Courtesy of MIEMSS.

_____ Assess the pelvis. If there is no pain, gently compress the pelvis downward and inward to look for tenderness and instability.

© Jones & Bartlett Learning. Courtesy of MIEMSS.

_____ Apply a cervical collar if indicated.

Skill Drill 9-3: Obtaining Blood Pressure by Auscultation
Test your knowledge of this skill by placing the following photos in the correct order. Number the first step with a "1," the second step with a "2," etc.

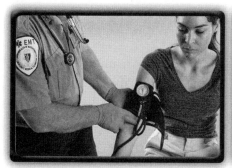
© Jones & Bartlett Learning.

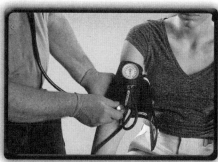
© Jones & Bartlett Learning.

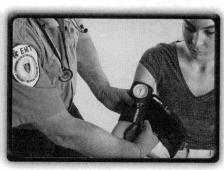
© Jones & Bartlett Learning.

_____ Support the exposed arm at the level of the heart. Palpate the brachial artery.

_____ Open the valve, and quickly release remaining air.

_____ Follow standard precautions. Check for a dialysis fistula, central line, previous mastectomy, and injury to the arm. If any are present, use the brachial artery on the other arm. Apply the cuff snugly. The lower border of the cuff should be about 1 inch (2.5 cm) above the antecubital space.

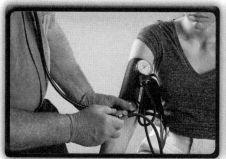
© Jones & Bartlett Learning.

_____ Close the valve, and pump to 30 mm Hg above the point at which you stop hearing pulse sounds. Note the systolic and diastolic pressures as you let air escape slowly.

_____ Place the stethoscope over the brachial artery, and grasp the ball-pump and turn-valve.

CHAPTER 10

Airway Management

General Knowledge

Matching

Match each of the items in the left column to the appropriate definition in the right column.

_____ 1. Inhalation
_____ 2. Exhalation

_____ 3. Alveoli
_____ 4. Mediastinum
_____ 5. Hypoxic drive
_____ 6. Tidal volume
_____ 7. Diaphragm
_____ 8. Intercostal muscle
_____ 9. Ventilation
_____ 10. Larynx
_____ 11. Hypoxia
_____ 12. Cheyne-Stokes

A. Moves down slightly when it contracts
B. Irregular breathing pattern with increased rate and depth followed by apnea
C. Active part of breathing
D. Where the upper airway ends and the lower airway begins
E. Amount of air moved during one breath
F. Raises ribs when it contracts
G. Space between the lungs
H. Functional site of oxygen and carbon dioxide exchange
I. Thorax size decreases
J. Insufficient oxygen for cells and tissues
K. Backup system to control respiration
L. Exchange of air between lungs and the environment

Multiple Choice

Read each item carefully and then select the one best response.

_____ 1. What percentage of the air we breathe is made up of oxygen?
A. 78%
B. 12%
C. 16%
D. 21%

_____ 2. What concentration of inspired oxygen is provided by a nasal cannula when the flowmeter is set at 1 to 6 L/min?
A. 10% to 18%
B. 24% to 44%
C. 52% to 84%
D. 89% to 98%

_____ 3. Which of the following statements regarding respiratory rate is true?
A. The respiratory rate is about equal to the person's heart rate.
B. The normal rate is 12 to 20 breaths/min.
C. The rate is faster when the person is sleeping.
D. The rate is the same as in infants and children.

_____ 4. Which of the following is a sign of inadequate breathing in an adult?
A. Respiratory rate of 18 breaths/min
B. Diminished breath sounds
C. Equal chest expansion
D. Warm, pink skin

_____   **5.** The brain stem normally triggers breathing by increasing respirations when:

   A. carbon dioxide levels increase.

   B. oxygen levels increase.

   C. carbon dioxide levels decrease.

   D. nitrogen levels decrease.

_____   **6.** Which of the following is a contraindication for placement of an oropharyngeal airway?

   A. Intact gag reflex

   B. Severe head injury

   C. Unconsciousness

   D. Fractured nasal bone

_____   **7.** The proper technique for sizing an oropharyngeal airway before insertion is to measure the device from:

   A. the tip of the nose to the earlobe.

   B. the bridge of the nose to the tip of the chin.

   C. the corner of the mouth to the earlobe.

   D. the center of the jaw to the earlobe.

_____   **8.** What is a common problem when a single EMT uses a bag-valve mask?

   A. Over-inflation of the lungs

   B. Delivering an inappropriate rate of ventilations

   C. Environmental conditions

   D. Maintaining an airtight mask seal

_____   **9.** When ventilating a patient with a bag-valve mask, you should:

   A. look for inflation of the cheeks.

   B. squeeze the bag hard and fast.

   C. look for rise and fall of the chest.

   D. only perform this with an advanced airway.

_____   **10.** Suctioning the oral cavity of an adult should be accomplished within:

   A. 5 seconds.

   B. 10 seconds.

   C. 15 seconds.

   D. 20 seconds.

_____   **11.** Which of the following is the most common method of assisting ventilations in the field?

   A. Mouth-to-mask with one-way valve

   B. Continuous positive airway pressure (CPAP)

   C. Flow-restricted, oxygen-powered ventilation device

   D. Bag-valve mask with oxygen reservoir and supplemental oxygen

_____   **12.** When a person goes _____ minutes without oxygen, brain damage is very likely.

   A. 0 to 4

   B. 4 to 6

   C. 6 to 10

   D. more than 10

_____   **13.** What is the most common airway obstruction in the unconscious patient?

   A. Food

   B. Tonsils

   C. Blood

   D. Tongue

_____ **14.** What are agonal gasps?

    A. Occasional gasping breaths but adequate to maintain life

    B. Occasional gasping breaths but unable to maintain life

    C. Painful respirations due to broken ribs

    D. Another name for ataxic respirations

_____ **15.** Which of the following could result in an inaccurate pulse oximetry reading?

    A. Warm extremities

    B. Carbon monoxide poisoning

    C. Vasodilation

    D. Hyperthermia

True/False

If you believe the statement to be more true than false, write the letter "T" in the space provided. If you believe the statement to be more false than true, write the letter "F."

_____ **1.** Nasal airways keep the tongue from blocking the upper airway and facilitate suctioning of the oropharynx.

_____ **2.** Nasal cannulas can deliver a maximum of 44% oxygen at 6 L/min.

_____ **3.** Oral airways should be measured from the tip of the nose to the earlobe.

_____ **4.** Compressed gas cylinders pose no unusual risk.

_____ **5.** The pin-indexing system is used to allow any gas regulator to be connected to an oxygen cylinder.

Fill-in-the-Blank

Read each item carefully and then complete the statement by filling in the missing words.

1. The upper airway consists of all anatomic airway structures above the level of the _____ _____.

2. In exhalation, air pressure in the lungs is _____ than the pressure outside.

3. The air we breathe contains _____ % oxygen and _____ % nitrogen.

4. The primary mechanism for triggering breathing is the level of _____ _____ in the blood.

5. During inhalation, the _____ and _____ _____ contract, causing the thorax to enlarge.

6. Continuous _____ airway _____ has proven to be immensely beneficial to patients experiencing respiratory

distress from acute pulmonary edema or obstructive pulmonary disease.

7. Insufficient oxygen in the cells and tissues is called _____.

8. _____ _____ is the act of air moving in and out the lungs during chest compressions.

Labeling

Label the following diagrams with the correct terms.

1. Upper and Lower Airways

A._____

B._____

C._____

D._____

E._____

F._____

G._____

H._____

I._____

J._____

K._____

L._____

M._____

N._____

O._____

P._____

Q._____

R._____

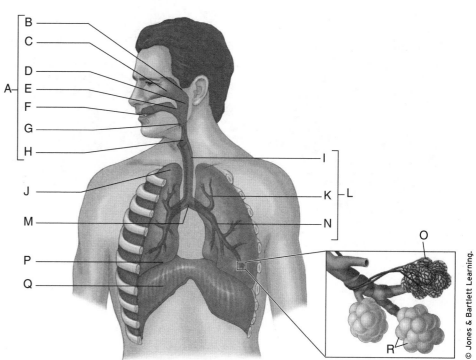

© Jones & Bartlett Learning.

2. Oral Cavity

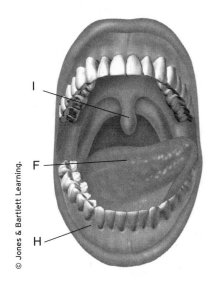

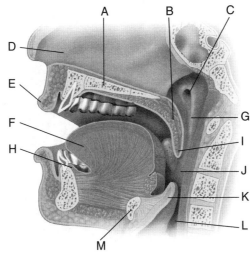

© Jones & Bartlett Learning.

A. _____

B. _____

C. _____

D. _____

E. _____

F. _____

G. _____

H. _____

I. _____

J. _____

K. _____

L. _____

M. _____

3. Thoracic Cavity

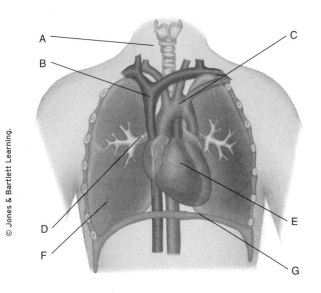

© Jones & Bartlett Learning.

A. _____

B. _____

C. _____

D. _____

E. _____

F. _____

G. _____

Crossword Puzzle

The following crossword puzzle is an activity provided to reinforce correct spelling and understanding of medical terminology associated with emergency care and the EMT. Use the clues in the column to complete the puzzle.

Across

4. Occasional, gasping breaths that occur after the heart has stopped are known as _____ respirations.

7. The space in between the vocal cords that is the narrowest portion of the adult's airway.

9. The amount of air that can be forcibly expelled from the lungs after breathing in as deeply as possible is known as the _____ capacity.

10. The metabolism that takes place in the absence of oxygen is called _____ metabolism; the principle product is lactic acid.

12. _____ respirations are irregular, ineffective respirations that may or may not have an identifiable pattern.

16. A safety system for large oxygen cylinders, designed to prevent the accidental attachment of a regulator to a cylinder containing the wrong type of gas, is known as the _____ Standard System.

17. _____ ventilation is the volume of air moved through the lungs in 1 minute, minus the dead space, and is calculated by multiplying tidal volume (minus dead space) and respiratory rate.

18. The point at which the trachea divides into the left and right mainstem bronchi.

Down

1. The process of delivering oxygen to the blood by diffusion from the alveoli following inhalation into the lungs.

2. The term used to describe the amount of gas in air or dissolved in fluid, such as blood, is _____ pressure.

3. _____ exchange is a term used to distinguish the degree of distress in a patient with a mild airway obstruction. The patient is still conscious and able to cough forcefully, although wheezing may be heard.

5. A ventilation device attached to a control box that allows the variables of ventilation to be set. It frees the EMT to perform other tasks while the patient is being ventilated.

6. A method of ventilation used primarily in the treatment of critically ill patients with respiratory distress; can prevent the need for endotracheal intubation.

8. A liquid protein substance that coats the alveoli in the lungs, decreases alveolar surface tension, and keeps the alveoli expanded; a low level in a premature infant contributes to respiratory distress syndrome.

11. _____ pressure can be applied to occlude the esophagus to inhibit gastric distention and regurgitation of vomitus in the unconscious patient.

13. The absence of spontaneous breathing.

14. A life-threatening collection of air within the pleural space is called a(n) _____ pneumothorax.

15. An opening through the skin and into an organ or other structure; one in the neck connects the trachea directly to the skin.

Critical Thinking

Multiple Choice

Read each critical-thinking item carefully and then select the one best response.

Questions 1-5 are derived from the following scenario: You respond to a construction site and find a worker lying supine in the dirt. He was struck by a heavy construction vehicle and flew more than 15 feet (4.6 m) before landing in his current position. There is discoloration and distention of his abdomen about the RUQ. He is unconscious and his respirations are 10 breaths/min and shallow, with noisy gurgling sounds.

_____ **1.** What airway technique will you use to open his airway?

  A. Head tilt–neck lift maneuver

  B. Jaw thrust

  C. Head tilt–chin lift maneuver

  D. Cross-finger technique

_____ **2.** After opening the airway, your next priority is to:

  A. provide oxygen at 6 L/min via nonrebreathing mask.

  B. provide oxygen at 15 L/min via nasal cannula.

  C. assist respirations.

  D. suction the airway.

_____ **3.** What method will you use to keep his airway open?

  A. Nasal cannula

  B. Jaw thrust

  C. Oropharyngeal airway

  D. Head tilt–chin lift maneuver

_____ **4.** While assisting with respirations, you note gastric distention. In order to prevent or alleviate the distention, you should do all of the following EXCEPT:

  A. ensure that the patient's airway is appropriately positioned.

  B. ventilate the patient at the appropriate rate.

  C. ventilate the patient at the appropriate volume.

  D. ventilate the patient at a faster rate.

_____ **5.** The patient is now apneic. What is the correct ventilation rate for assisting this adult patient?

  A. One breath every 5 to 6 seconds

  B. One breath every 3 to 5 seconds

  C. One breath every 10 to 12 seconds

  D. There is no need to assist with ventilations for this patient

Short Answer

Complete this section with short written answers using the space provided.

1. List the contraindications for continuous positive airway pressure (CPAP).

_____

_____

_____

2. What are the normal respiratory rates for adults, children, and infants?

_____

_____

_____

3. How can you avoid gastric distention while performing artificial ventilation?

_____

_____

_____

4. Identify the five ideal components of a manually triggered ventilation device.

_____

_____

_____

5. List six signs of inadequate breathing.

_____

_____

_____

6. What are accessory muscles? Name three.

_____

_____

_____

7. When should medical control be consulted before inserting a nasal airway?

_____

_____

_____

8. List the four steps in nasal airway insertion.

_____

_____

_____

9. What is the best suction tip for suctioning the oropharynx and why?

_____

_____

_____

10. What is the time limit for each episode of suctioning an adult?

_____

_____

_____

Ambulance Calls

The following case scenarios provide an opportunity to explore the concerns associated with patient management and to enhance critical-thinking skills. Read each scenario and answer each question to the best of your ability.

1. You are dispatched to a motor vehicle collision with multiple patients early one morning near the end of your shift. Your patient was the unrestrained driver of one of the vehicles. She is 38 years old and struck her face against the steering wheel and windshield. There is a large laceration on her nose and several teeth are missing. Although unconscious, she has vomited a large amount of food and blood, which is pooling in her mouth. You note gurgling noises as she attempts to breathe.

How would you best manage this patient?

_____

_____

_____

2. You are dispatched to a local restaurant for an unconscious woman. As you arrive, you are greeted by a frantic restaurant manager. She tells you that one of her staff members went into the restroom to complete the hourly cleaning routine and found a woman lying on the floor, motionless and apparently not breathing. You and your partner enter the cramped ladies' bathroom to find an older woman who is apneic and cyanotic but who has a carotid pulse. You attempt to ventilate the patient using a bag-valve mask but are unsuccessful.

How should you manage this patient?

_____

_____

_____

3. You are outside doing some yard work when you hear one of your neighbors call for help. As you cross the street, you see a husband standing over his wife, who is lying on the ground. He tells you that she complained of feeling lightheaded and then she suddenly passed out. He further tells you that he was able to help her to the ground without injury. When you assess her, you hear snoring sounds as she breathes.

How do you manage this patient?

_____

_____

_____

Fill-in-the-Patient Care Report

Read the incident scenario and en complete the following patient care report (PCR).

It is 1530, and you have just been dispatched to Market Street High School for a possible drug overdose. As your partner steers the ambulance into the nearly empty school parking lot at 1543, you see a woman waving her arms from near one of the low, gray buildings. You and your partner pull the equipment-laden gurney from the back of the truck and hurry across the grass.

"The janitor found her in the stall," the woman's voice trembles as you arrive at the restroom entrance where she is standing. "She's kind of breathing but I can't wake her up . . . she's had some troubles in the past with drugs."

You find the 14-year-old girl lying on her left side on the tile floor in the middle of three stalls, unresponsive to pain and with slow, snoring respirations.

"You see that?" your partner says, unzipping the airway bag and pointing toward the girl's bluish lips and fingernails.

"I'm going to drag her out here so we have room while you get the bag-valve mask set up," you say, carefully pulling the 110-pound (50-kg) girl from the stall and resting her on her back. You immediately open her airway with the head tilt–chin lift maneuver, which stops the snoring sound, but you still note that her breathing is very shallow. Just then your partner finishes assembling the oxygen tank and bag-mask device and inserts an oropharyngeal airway. Within 2 minutes of the time that you got out of the ambulance, your partner is assisting the patient's respirations, getting adequate chest rise, and you are getting a quick set of vitals signs.

You note that her blood pressure is 124/86 mm Hg, pulse is 112 beats/min and regular, respirations (with assistance) are 12 breaths/min, and her oxygen saturation is 93%.

Just as you are finishing vitals, the local fire crew arrives and helps place the patient onto the gurney and into the back of the ambulance. One of the firefighters even jumps into the back to continue assisting the girl's ventilations so that your partner can complete the assessment and obtain a second set of vitals en route to the receiving hospital.

You notify dispatch at 1556 that you are pulling away from the scene and headed to the hospital 12 minutes south of the school. The patient's second set of vitals, obtained 4 minutes after going en route, were as follows: blood pressure 122/86 mm Hg, pulse 110 beats/min, respirations 12 breaths/min (still being assisted), and a pulse oximetry reading of 96%.

On arrival at the hospital, you transfer the patient to the emergency department staff and clean and restock your equipment. Sixty-five minutes after receiving the initial dispatch, you go back in service.

Fill-in-the-Patient Care Report

EMS Patient Care Report (PCR)					
Date:	Incident No.:		Nature of Call:		Location:
Dispatched:	En Route:	At Scene:	Transport:	At Hospital:	In Service:
Patient Information					
Age: Sex: Weight (in kg [lb]):			Allergies: Medications: Past Medical History: Chief Complaint:		
Vital Signs					
Time:	BP:	Pulse:	Respirations:	Spo$_2$:	
Time:	BP:	Pulse:	Respirations:	Spo$_2$:	
Time:	BP:	Pulse:	Respirations:	Spo$_2$:	
EMS Treatment (circle all that apply)					
Oxygen @ ___ L/min via (circle one): NC NRM BVM		Assisted Ventilation	Airway Adjunct		CPR
Defibrillation	Bleeding Control	Bandaging	Splinting		Other:
Narrative					

Skills

Skill Drills

Test your knowledge of these skills by filling in the correct words in the photo captions.

Skill Drill 10-2: Positioning the Unconscious Patient

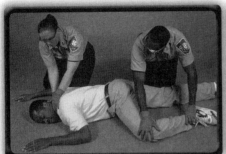

© Jones & Bartlett Learning. Courtesy of MIEMSS.

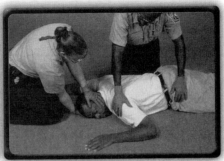

© Jones & Bartlett Learning. Courtesy of MIEMSS.

1. Support the _____ while your partner straightens the patient's legs.

2. Have your partner place his or her _____ on the patient's far _____ and hip.

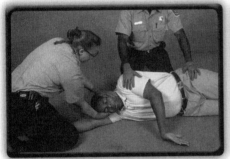

© Jones & Bartlett Learning. Courtesy of MIEMSS.

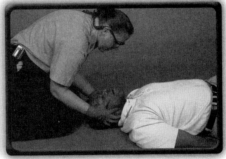

© Jones & Bartlett Learning. Courtesy of MIEMSS.

3. _____ the patient as a unit with the EMT at the patient's _____ calling the count to begin the move.

4. _____ and _____ the patient's airway and _____ status.

Skill Drill 10-4: Inserting an Oral Airway

© Jones & Bartlett Learning. Courtesy of MIEMSS.

© Jones & Bartlett Learning. Courtesy of MIEMSS.

© Jones & Bartlett Learning. Courtesy of MIEMSS.

1. Size the _____ by measuring from the patient's _____ to the corner of the _____.

2. Open the patient's _____ with the _____-finger technique. Hold the _____ upside down with your other hand. Insert the airway with the tip facing the _____ of the mouth.

3. _____ the airway _____. Insert the airway until the _____ rests on the patient's lips and teeth. In this position, the airway will hold the _____ forward.

Skill Drill 10-7: Placing an Oxygen Cylinder Into Service

© Jones & Bartlett Learning.

© Jones & Bartlett Learning.

1. Using an oxygen _____, turn the valve _____ to slowly "crack" the cylinder.

2. Attach the regulator/flowmeter to the _____ stem using the two pin-_____ holes and make sure that the _____ is in place over the larger hole.

© Jones & Bartlett Learning.

© Jones & Bartlett Learning.

3. Align the _____ so that the pins fit snugly into the correct holes on the _____ stem, and hand tighten the _____.

4. Attach the _____ connective tubing to the _____.

Skill Drill 10-8: Performing Mouth-to-Mask Ventilation

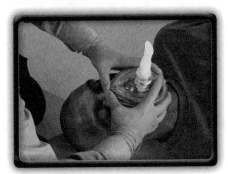

© Jones & Bartlett Learning.

© Jones & Bartlett Learning.

© Jones & Bartlett Learning.

1. Once the patient's head is properly _____ and an airway _____ is inserted, place the mask on the patient's face. _____ the mask to the face using both hands (EC_____).

2. _____ into the one-way valve until you note visible _____ rise.

3. Remove your _____ and watch the patient's chest fall during _____.

CHAPTER

11 Principles of Pharmacology

© Photos.com

General Knowledge

Matching

Match each of the items in the left column to the appropriate definition in the right column.

_____ 1. Absorption
_____ 2. Contraindication
_____ 3. Side effect
_____ 4. Adsorption
_____ 5. Dose
_____ 6. Indication
_____ 7. Action
_____ 8. Pharmacology
_____ 9. Capsules
_____ 10. Topical medications

A. Lotions, creams, ointments
B. Effect that a drug is expected to have
C. The science of drugs and their ingredients, uses, and actions
D. Amount of medication given
E. Gelatin shells filled with powdered or liquid medication
F. Any action of a drug other than the desired one
G. To bind or stick to a surface
H. Reason for which a medication is given
I. Process by which medications travel through body tissues
J. Situation in which a drug should not be given

Multiple Choice

Read each item carefully and then select the one best response.

_____ 1. Which of the following is taken into consideration when determining the dose of a medicine?
   A. Sex
   B. Occupation
   C. Ability to swallow
   D. Age

_____ 2. Nitroglycerin relieves the squeezing or crushing pain associated with angina by:
   A. dilating the arteries to increase the oxygen supply to the heart muscle.
   B. causing the heart to contract harder and increase cardiac output.
   C. causing the heart to beat faster to supply more oxygen to the heart.
   D. causing the heart to beat faster and more efficiently.

_____ 3. The brand name that a manufacturer gives to a medication is called the_____ name.
   A. trade
   B. generic
   C. chemical
   D. prescription

_____ 4. The fastest way to deliver a chemical substance is by the _____ route.
   A. intravenous
   B. oral
   C. sublingual
   D. intramuscular

_____ **5.** Which of the following is considered a relative contraindication to administration of aspirin?

    A. Hypersensitivity to aspirin

    B. History of asthma

    C. Preexisting liver damage

    D. History of nausea

_____ **6.** The most common technique for naloxone administration is via the:

    A. oral route.

    B. intramuscular route.

    C. intranasal route.

    D. intravenous route.

_____ **7.** Outside a hospital, a(n) _____ is the preferred method of giving oxygen to patients who are experiencing significant respiratory distress.

    A. nasal cannula

    B. nonrebreathing mask

    C. bag-valve mask

    D. endotracheal tube

_____ **8.** Which of the following is NOT a characteristic of epinephrine?

    A. Dilating passages in the lungs

    B. Secreted naturally by the pituitary gland

    C. Increasing the heart rate and blood pressure

    D. Dilating blood vessels

_____ **9.** What medication is commonly administered in a metered-dose inhaler (MDI)?

    A. Nitroglycerine

    B. Albuterol

    C. Activated charcoal

    D. Naloxone

_____ **10.** Nitroglycerin relieves pain because its purpose is to increase blood flow by relieving the spasms or causing the arteries to:

    A. dilate.

    B. constrict.

    C. thicken.

    D. contract.

_____ **11.** Which of the following routes of administration involves medication being absorbed in the fat tissue between the skin and muscle?

    A. Intravenous

    B. Intramuscular

    C. Subcutaneous

    D. Intranasal

Questions 12-16 are derived from the following scenario: You are called to a home of a 34-year-old male who is unresponsive. When you arrive, you find the patient supine and unconscious on the living room floor with snoring respirations.

_____ **12.** Which of the following medications might be useful in this situation?

    A. Nitroglycerin

    B. Activated charcoal

    C. Naloxone

    D. Aspirin

_____ **13.** Which medication commonly comes in gel form?

  A. Naloxone

  B. Epinephrine

  C. Glucose

  D. Activated charcoal

_____ **14.** The government publication listing all drugs in the United States is called the:

  A. *United States Pharmacopoeia.*

  B. *Department of Transportation Reference Guide.*

  C. *US Pharmacology.*

  D. *Nursing Drug Reference.*

_____ **15.** Oral glucose is _____ for this patient.

  A. indicated

  B. contraindicated

  C. not normally given

  D. prescribed

_____ **16.** Which of the following statements about oxygen is false?

  A. Most commonly administered medication in the prehospital setting

  B. Should be administered to all patients

  C. Is not flammable

  D. Is considered a suspension

True/False

If you believe the statement to be more true than false, write the letter "T" in the space provided. If you believe the statement to be more false than true, write the letter "F."

_____ **1.** Oxygen is a flammable substance.

_____ **2.** Glucose may be administered to an unconscious patient in order to save his or her life.

_____ **3.** Epinephrine is a hormone produced by the body to aid in digestion.

_____ **4.** Nitroglycerin decreases blood pressure.

_____ **5.** Sublingual medications are rapidly absorbed into the digestive tract.

_____ **6.** Adsorption means to bind to or stick to a surface.

_____ **7.** Enteral medications enter the body through the skin.

_____ **8.** Nitroglycerin should be administered only when the patient's systolic blood pressure is below 100 mm Hg.

Fill-in-the-Blank

Read each item carefully and then complete the statement by filling in the missing words.

1. _____ is a simple sugar that is readily absorbed by the bloodstream.

2. _____ is the main hormone that controls the body's fight-or-flight response.

3. Nitroglycerin is usually taken _____.

4. _____ _____ are the effects that are undesirable but pose little risk to the patient.

5. When given by mouth, _____ may be absorbed from the stomach fairly quickly because the medication is already dissolved.

6. A _____ is a chemical substance that is used to treat or prevent disease or relieve pain.

Crossword Puzzle

The following crossword puzzle is an activity provided to reinforce correct spelling and understanding of medical terminology associated with emergency care and the EMT. Use the clues in the column to complete the puzzle.

Across

1. A mixture of ground particles that are distributed evenly throughout a liquid but that do not dissolve.
5. The process by which medications travel through body tissues until they reach the bloodstream.
9. A delivery route in which a medication is pushed through a specialized atomizer device called a mucosal atomizer device (MAD) into the nare.
10. The amount of medication given on the basis of the patient's size and age.
12. A medication that causes stimulation of receptors.
13. Through the rectum.
15. By mouth.
16. A liquid mixture that cannot be separated by filtering or allowing the mixture to stand.

Down

2. Breathing into the lungs.
3. Activated _____ is an oral medication that binds and adsorbs ingested toxins in the gastrointestinal tract for treatment of some poisonings and medication overdoses.
4. A medication that binds to a receptor and blocks other medications.
6. Into the bone.
7. A semiliquid substance that is administered orally in capsule form or through plastic tubes.
8. A device that changes a liquid medication into a spray and pushes it into a nostril.
11. Medications that enter the body through the digestive system.
14. A miniature spray canister through which droplets or particles of medication may be inhaled.

Critical Thinking

Multiple Choice

Read each critical-thinking item carefully and then select the one best response.

_____ 1. You and your rookie partner are dispatched to a home on the east side of town for a possible poisoning. On arrival, you are met by a frantic mother who carries her crying 4-year-old boy up to your truck. "Please help him!" she pleads. "I was cleaning the garage and before I could stop him he drank a jar of gasoline that my husband uses to clean car parts." Your partner puts the truck in park and sets the parking brake. "I'll grab the activated charcoal," he says, climbing out of the cab. What should you do?

   A. Administer the activated charcoal and transport the child immediately.

   B. Ask to see the jar to determine how much gasoline was swallowed.

   C. Contact online medical direction while administering the activated charcoal.

   D. Do not administer activated charcoal.

_____ 2. Your patient is a 73-year-old man who complains of severe chest pressure with trouble breathing while having dinner at a local diner. He has a small vial of nitroglycerin in his pocket but says that he has not taken any in several days and needs you to help him to get the vial open. After administering oxygen, what is the first thing that you should do?

   A. Obtain the patient's blood pressure and ensure that his systolic pressure is not below 110 mm Hg.

   B. Begin assisting the patient's ventilations.

   C. Place him in the recovery position.

   D. Ask if he has taken any erectile dysfunction medications in the last 24 hours.

_____ 3. You are called to the beach for a 15-year-old boy who is having trouble breathing. He tells you between gasps that he was stung by something and that his body feels "swollen." Just then, his mother runs up to you and puts an EpiPen into your hand. "Here," she says breathlessly. "This is his EpiPen. He needs this!" Would you administer epinephrine to this patient?

   A. Yes. Push the EpiPen firmly against the patient's thigh for several seconds.

   B. No. The EpiPen will make his condition worse.

   C. Yes. Use the sublingual route.

   D. No. His signs and symptoms contraindicate an epinephrine injection.

_____ 4. "I think she's drunk!" a bystander yells, as you and your partner arrive on the scene of an unknown medical problem. You observe an approximately 45-year-old woman stumbling between several cars in the parking lot of a grocery store. As you catch up to the woman, you ask her if she is diabetic. She nods clumsily and leans against one of the cars. You test her blood glucose and obtain a reading of 49 mg/dL. What should you do?

   A. Administer glucose gel orally.

   B. Contact medical control for further instructions.

   C. Restrain her onto the gurney and insert a nasopharyngeal airway.

   D. Wait for an ALS response so that glucose can be administered intravenously.

_____ 5. You are dispatched to the county fair for a 54-year-old woman complaining of chest pain. You arrive to find her pressing on the center of her chest and note that she has pale, clammy skin. You ask if she has any cardiac history and she tells you, "No, I just have arthritis and my doctor says that I am prediabetic." Would you give this patient aspirin?

   A. No. Nitroglycerin would be more appropriate.

   B. Yes. Her signs and symptoms indicate a cardiac problem and aspirin could help.

   C. No. Aspirin is contraindicated for arthritis.

   D. Yes. Its analgesic properties may help with the discomfort.

Short Answer

Complete this section with short written answers using the space provided.

1. List seven routes of medication administration.

_____

_____

_____

2. What are the "six rights" of medication administration?

_____

_____

_____

3. Describe the action of activated charcoal and the steps of administration that are specific to this medication.

_____

_____

_____

4. List three characteristics of epinephrine.

_____

_____

_____

5. What are the steps for administering intranasal naloxone?

_____

_____

_____

6. List four effects of nitroglycerin.

_____

_____

_____

7. Explain why metered-dose inhalers are often used with a spacer.

_____

_____

_____

Ambulance Calls

The following case scenarios provide an opportunity to explore the concerns associated with patient management and to enhance critical-thinking skills. Read each scenario and answer each question to the best of your ability.

1. You are dispatched to "difficulty breathing" at one of your town's many parks. As you near the park entrance, you see a crowd of people who frantically wave for you. You arrive to find a city employee who was apparently mowing the park grounds when he accidentally mowed over a yellow jacket nest. He was wearing coveralls, but he was repeatedly stung around his neck and face. He appears to be somewhat confused; you can hear stridor with each inspiration and his blood pressure is 80/40 mm Hg. Your local protocols allow EMTs to carry EpiPens.

   How do you best manage this patient?

   _____

   _____

   _____

2. You are dispatched to an "unknown medical problem" at the Crosstown Mall. You were called after police were summoned to subdue a combative male shopper. Police officers were able to calm him down but felt that something was "not right" about him. You arrive to find a calm but confused man who is sweaty and pale. He has no complaints but keeps repeating, "I have to get home now." You notice a medical ID bracelet indicating that this patient is an insulin-dependent diabetic.

   How do you best manage this patient?

   _____

   _____

   _____

3. You are dispatched to the residence of a 68-year-old man who is complaining of "crushing" chest pain radiating down his left arm and trouble breathing for the past hour. He is pale, cool, diaphoretic, and is very nauseated. He tells you he had a heart attack several years ago and takes nitroglycerin as needed. He took two tablets prior to your arrival and reports no relief.

   How would you best manage this patient?

   _____

   _____

   _____

Fill-in-the-Patient Care Report

Read the incident scenario and then complete the following patient care report (PCR).

"Hey you! Medic!" It's 1300, and you are just finishing lunch at one of the picnic tables in Northern Park when you hear someone yelling from across the small duck pond. "This lady needs help!"

You whistle at your partner who is sitting in the ambulance reading a biology textbook and then begin the short walk to where a small crowd is gathering near an ivy-covered gazebo.

"I think she's having trouble breathing," a man says, moving aside so you can see a 38-year-old woman sitting in the tripod position on a wooden park bench. Her eyes are bulging, her lips and fingernails are beginning to turn blue, and you can immediately see accessory muscles moving in her neck as she struggles to breathe. You kneel in front of the bench, making eye contact with the panicked woman, and say, "I'm an EMT and I'm going to help you, okay?" She nods her head frantically.

"Does anyone know her?" you shout, looking at the confused faces around you. A teenaged girl appears and says, "I don't know her but she dropped this when she first started to freak out." The girl then hands you a blue plastic metered-dose inhaler labeled for asthma.

Approximately 4 minutes since first being alerted to the problem you quickly shake the metered-dose inhaler and hand it to the woman, who claws for it and pumps it once into her mouth and inhales weakly. Right then you partner arrives with the gurney and the equipment bags from the ambulance, and you instruct him to initiate oxygen therapy immediately with a nonrebreathing mask.

As you are helping the 45-kg (100-lb) woman onto the gurney, you notice that her lips and fingernails are returning to normal and that although she is still struggling to breath she is moving more air with each respiratory cycle. The high-concentration oxygen, set at 15 L/min, seems to be helping. Four minutes after the patient first used her inhaler, you and your partner load her into the ambulance for the 10-minute drive to the closest emergency department.

You obtain the patient's vital signs as soon as the ambulance rolls away from the scene, noting a blood pressure of 142/98 mm Hg, a heart rate of 110 beats/min, 28 labored respirations per minute, and a pulse oximetry reading of 88%. You are able to complete two more sets of vitals at 5-minute intervals prior to pulling into the hospital ambulance bay (138/90 mm Hg, 102 beats/min, 24 breaths/min labored, 92%; and 132/88 mm Hg, 96 beats/min, 20 breaths/min with good tidal volume, 96%) and between one more puff from the inhaler and the high-flow oxygen, the patient has improved tremendously.

You and your partner transfer the patient to an emergency department bed, provide the charge nurse with a full report, and are ready to go back into service 48 minutes from first being alerted to the emergency.

Fill-in-the-Patient Care Report

EMS Patient Care Report (PCR)					
Date:	Incident No.:	Nature of Call:		Location:	
Dispatched:	En Route:	At Scene:	Transport:	At Hospital:	In Service:
Patient Information					
Age: Sex: Weight (in kg [lb]):			Allergies: Medications: Past Medical History: Chief Complaint:		
Vital Signs					
Time:	BP:	Pulse:	Respirations:	Spo_2:	
Time:	BP:	Pulse:	Respirations:	Spo_2:	
Time:	BP:	Pulse:	Respirations:	Spo_2:	
EMS Treatment **(circle all that apply)**					
Oxygen @ ____ L/min via (circle one): NC NRM BVM		Assisted Ventilation	Airway Adjunct		CPR
Defibrillation	Bleeding Control	Bandaging	Splinting		Other:
Narrative					

Shock

© Photos.com

General Knowledge

Matching

Match each of the items in the left column to the appropriate definition in the right column.

_____ **1.** Shock

_____ **2.** Perfusion

_____ **3.** Sphincters

_____ **4.** Autonomic nervous system

_____ **5.** Blood pressure

_____ **6.** Anaphylaxis

_____ **7.** Septic shock

_____ **8.** Syncope

_____ **9.** Compensated shock

A. Severe allergic reaction

B. Hypoperfusion

C. Regulates involuntary body functions

D. Early stage of shock

E. Provides a rough measure of perfusion

F. Severe infection

G. Sufficient circulation to meet cell needs

H. Regulate blood flow in capillaries

I. Fainting

Multiple Choice

Read each item carefully and then select the one best response.

_____ **1.** What is the basic definition of shock?

  A. A state of collapse and failure of the cardiovascular system

  B. The loss of blood from the body

  C. An inadequate supply of oxygen in the lungs

  D. A state of low blood pressure

_____ **2.** Blood flow through the capillary beds is regulated by:

  A. systolic pressure.

  B. the capillary sphincters.

  C. perfusion.

  D. diastolic pressure.

_____ **3.** The autonomic nervous system regulates functions such as:

  A. running.

  B. digestion.

  C. eye movement.

  D. walking.

_____ **4.** Regulation of blood flow is determined by:

  A. oxygen intake.

  B. systolic pressure.

  C. cellular need.

  D. diastolic pressure.

_____ **5.** Patients in cardiogenic shock should not receive:

  A. oxygen.

  B. positive-pressure ventilation.

  C. ALS care.

  D. nitroglycerine.

_____   6. The action of hormones such as epinephrine and norepinephrine stimulates _____ to maintain pressure in the system and, as a result, perfusion of all vital organs.
    A. a decrease in heart rate
    B. an increase in the strength of cardiac contractions
    C. vasodilation in nonessential areas
    D. decrease in oxygen demand

_____   7. Which of the following is NOT a basic cause of shock?
    A. Poor pump function
    B. Blood or fluid loss
    C. Blood vessel dilation
    D. Release of norepinephrine

_____   8. Which of the following poisons affects the ability of cells to metabolize or carry oxygen?
    A. Bacterial toxins
    B. Insect stings
    C. Carbon monoxide
    D. Carbon dioxide

_____   9. _____ develops when the heart muscle can no longer generate enough pressure to circulate the blood to all organs.
    A. Pump failure
    B. Cardiogenic shock
    C. A myocardial infarction
    D. Congestive heart failure

_____   10. Neurogenic shock usually results from damage to the spinal cord at the:
    A. cervical level.
    B. thoracic level.
    C. lumbar level.
    D. sacral level.

_____   11. Which of the following statements about septic shock is false?
    A. There is an insufficient volume of fluid in the container.
    B. The fluid that has leaked out often collects in the respiratory system.
    C. There is a larger-than-normal vascular bed to contain the smaller-than-normal volume of intravascular fluid.
    D. There is damage to the spinal cord resulting in vasodilation.

_____   12. Neurogenic shock is caused by:
    A. a radical change in the size of the vascular system.
    B. massive vasoconstriction.
    C. low volume.
    D. fluid collecting around the spinal cord causing compression of the cord.

_____   13. Hypovolemic shock is a result of:
    A. widespread vasodilation.
    B. low volume.
    C. massive vasoconstriction.
    D. pump failure.

_____   14. An insufficient concentration of _____ in the blood can produce shock as rapidly as vascular causes.
    A. oxygen
    B. hormones
    C. epinephrine
    D. histamine

_____ **15.** Which of the following statements about anaphylactic shock is true?

    A. There is no blood loss in anaphylactic shock.

    B. It is caused by a lack of red blood cells.

    C. It is associated with bronchodilation.

    D. It can result from myocardia pump failure.

_____ **16.** You should suspect shock in all of the following EXCEPT:

    A. a mild allergic reaction.

    B. multiple severe fractures.

    C. a severe infection.

    D. abdominal or chest injury.

_____ **17.** When treating a suspected unstable shock patient, vital signs should be recorded approximately every _____ minutes.

    A. 2

    B. 5

    C. 10

    D. 15

_____ **18.** The Golden Period refers to the first 60 minutes after:

    A. medical help arrives on scene.

    B. transport begins.

    C. the injury occurs.

    D. 9-1-1 is called.

_____ **19.** Which of the following is NOT a sign of cardiogenic shock?

    A. Cyanosis

    B. Strong, bounding pulse

    C. Nausea

    D. Anxiety

_____ **20.** _____ is a sudden reaction of the nervous system that produces temporary vascular dilation and fainting.

    A. Neurogenic shock

    B. Psychogenic shock

    C. Vascular shock

    D. Cardiogenic shock

True/False

If you believe the statement to be more true than false, write the letter "T" in the space provided. If you believe the statement to be more false than true, write the letter "F."

_____ **1.** Life-threatening allergic reactions can occur in response to almost any substance that a patient may encounter.

_____ **2.** Bleeding is the most common cause of cardiogenic shock.

_____ **3.** Shock occurs when oxygen and nutrients cannot get to the body's cells.

_____ **4.** A person in shock, left untreated, will survive.

_____ **5.** Compensated shock is related to the last stages of shock.

_____ **6.** An injection of epinephrine is the only really effective treatment for anaphylactic shock.

_____ **7.** Septic shock occurs as a result of a severe infection.

_____ **8.** Metabolism is the cardiovascular system's circulation of blood and oxygen to all cells in different tissues and organs of the body.

_____ **9.** Shock occurs only with massive blood loss from the body.

_____ **10.** Decompensated shock occurs when the systolic blood pressure falls below 120 mm Hg.

Fill-in-the-Blank

Read each item carefully and then complete the statement by filling in the missing words.

1. _____ refers to the failure of the cardiovascular system.

2. Pressure in the arteries during cardiac _____ is known as systolic pressure.

3. The body responds to shock by directing blood flow away from organs that are more _____ of low flow.

4. Blood pressure is a rough measurement of _____.

5. Blood contains red blood cells, white blood cells, _____, and a liquid called _____.

6. Inadequate circulation that does not meet the body's needs is known as _____.

7. _____ are circular muscle walls in capillaries, causing the walls to _____

   and_____.

8. _____ pressure occurs during cardiac relaxation, while _____ pressure occurs during

   cardiac contractions.

9. As a result of the aging process, older patients generally have more serious _____ than younger patients.

10. The autonomic nervous system controls the _____ actions of the body.

Crossword Puzzle

The following crossword puzzle is an activity provided to reinforce correct spelling and understanding of medical terminology associated with emergency care and the EMT. Use the clues in the column to complete the puzzle.

Across

1. A condition in which the internal body temperature falls below 95°F (35°C).
6. Fainting.
7. Shock caused by inadequate function of the heart is called _____ shock.
8. Blue color of the skin resulting from poor oxygenation of the circulating blood.
10. The precontraction pressure in the heart as the volume of blood builds up.
12. Circular muscles that encircle and, by contracting, constrict a duct, tube, or opening.
13. Circulatory failure caused by paralysis of the nerves that control the size of the blood vessels is called _____ shock.
14. The presence of abnormally large amounts of fluid between cells in body tissues, causing swelling of the affected area.

Down

2. A balance of all systems of the body.
3. Hypoperfusion.
4. A swelling of a part of an artery, resulting from weakening of the arterial wall.
5. The final stage of shock, resulting in death, is called _____ shock.
7. The early stage of shock, in which the body can still compensate for blood loss, is called _____ shock.
9. The force or resistance against which the heart pumps.
11. Shock caused by severe infection is called _____ shock.

Critical Thinking

Multiple Choice

Read each critical-thinking item carefully and then select the one best response.

_____ 1. You are called to the residence of a 67-year-old man who is complaining of chest pain. He is alert and oriented. During your assessment, the patient tells you he has had two previous heart attacks. He is taking medication for fluid retention. As you listen to his lungs, you notice that he has fluid in his lungs. This is known as pulmonary:

   A. edema.

   B. overload.

   C. cessation.

   D. failure.

_____ 2. You are called to a construction site where a 27-year-old worker has fallen from the second floor. He landed on his back and is drifting in and out of consciousness. A quick assessment reveals no bleeding or blood loss. His blood pressure is 90/60 mm Hg with a pulse rate of 110 beats/min. His airway is open and breathing is within normal limits. You realize the patient is in shock. Based on this information, the patient's shock is most likely due to an injury to the:

   A. thoracic vertebrae.

   B. skull.

   C. spinal cord.

   D. peripheral nerves.

_____ 3. You respond to the local nursing home for an 85-year-old woman who has altered mental status. During your assessment, you notice that the patient has an elevated body temperature. She is hypotensive and her pulse is tachycardic. The nursing staff tells you that she has been sick for several days and that they called because her mental status continued to decline. You suspect the patient is in septic shock. This type of shock is due to:

   A. pump failure.

   B. massive vasoconstriction.

   C. widespread dilation.

   D. increased volume.

_____ 4. You are called to a motor vehicle collision. Your patient is a 19-year-old woman who was not wearing her seat belt. She is conscious but confused. Her airway is open and respirations are within normal limits. Her pulse is slightly tachycardic. Her blood pressure is within normal limits. She is complaining of being thirsty and appears very anxious. What is the last measurable factor to change that would indicate shock?

   A. Mental status

   B. Blood pressure

   C. Pulse rate

   D. Respirations

_____ 5. You respond to a 17-year-old football player who was hit by numerous opponents. While walking off the field, he became unconscious. You take cervical spine control and start your assessment. You know that in the treatment of shock you must do all of the following EXCEPT:

   A. secure and maintain an airway.

   B. provide respiratory support.

   C. assist ventilations.

   D. use hot water bottles or heating pads to keep the patient warm.

Short Answer

Complete this section with short written answers using the space provided.

1. List the causes, signs and symptoms, and treatment of anaphylactic shock.

_____

_____

_____

2. List the causes, signs and symptoms, and treatment of cardiogenic shock.

_____

_____

_____

3. List the causes, signs and symptoms, and treatment of hypovolemic shock.

_____

_____

_____

4. List the causes, signs and symptoms, and treatment of neurogenic shock.

_____

_____

_____

5. List the causes, signs and symptoms, and treatment of psychogenic shock.

_____

_____

_____

6. List the causes, signs and symptoms, and treatment of septic shock.

_____

_____

_____

7. List the three basic physiologic causes of shock.

_____

_____

_____

8. List the signs and symptoms of decompensated shock.

_____

_____

_____

Ambulance Calls

The following case scenarios provide an opportunity to explore the concerns associated with patient management and to enhance critical-thinking skills. Read each scenario and answer each question to the best of your ability.

1. You are dispatched to the victim of a fall at the local community college theater. One of the students involved in rigging the theater backgrounds fell from the platform above the stage. He landed directly on his back and is now complaining of numbness and tingling in his lower body.

How would you best manage this patient?

_____

_____

_____

2. You are dispatched to a local long-term care facility for an older man with a fever. You arrive to find an 80-year-old man who is responsive to painful stimuli and has the following vital signs: blood pressure of 80/40 mm Hg, weak radial pulse of 140 beats/min and irregular, respirations of 60 breaths/min and shallow, and pulse oximetry of 80% on 4 L/min nasal cannula. His temperature is 101.8°F (38.8°C).

How would you best manage this patient?

_____

_____

_____

3. You are dispatched to a residence where a 16-year-old girl was stung by a bee. Her mother tells you she is severely allergic to bees. She is voice responsive, covered in hives, and wheezing audibly. She has a very weak radial pulse and is blue around the lips.

How would you best manage this patient?

_____

_____

_____

Fill-in-the-Patient Care Report

Read the incident scenario and then complete the following patient care report (PCR).

You look at the glowing face of your watch in the darkness of the ambulance cab and realize that you have 4 hours until the end of your shift at 0200. At that moment, the dispatcher's voice bursts from the radio with a call for a motorcyclist down in the eastbound lanes of Highway 62 at exit 19, a 5-minute drive from your current location. Your partner copies the dispatch as you activate the lights and sirens and pull out of the parking lot, en route to the scene.

As you pull past the highway patrol's vehicle barricade, you see pieces of metal and plastic scattered down the freeway and a man lying motionless across both closed lanes. You and your partner approach to find the man responsive and coherent but complaining of "feeling odd" and not being able to move his legs. Along with the help of a responding fire crew, you and your partner are able to quickly remove the patient's helmet, apply a cervical collar, and immobilize the approximately 143-pound (65-kg) 18-year-old man to a long backboard after initiating oxygen therapy.

"Eight minute scene time!" your partner whistles, shutting you into the back of the ambulance with the immobilized patient. As your partner pulls away from the accident scene en route to the local trauma center minutes away, you obtain a set of vital signs (blood pressure 98/62 mm Hg; pulse 110 beats/min and weak; respirations 18 breaths/min, shallow but adequate; a pulse oximetry reading of 94% on high-flow oxygen via nonrebreathing mask; and pale, cool, moist skin). You cut away the patient's clothing to look for concealed injuries and find that both of his legs are pale, cooler than his torso, and not diaphoretic.

"I'm really feeling weird," the man says, panic evident in his eyes. "Am I dying?"

"We're doing everything we can to make sure that doesn't happen," you say, before asking your partner to upgrade to lights and sirens while you cover the patient with blankets. Exactly 5 minutes after leaving the scene you unload the patient and push him through the automatic doors of the university hospital where he is quickly enveloped by the trauma team.

Approximately 15 minutes later, you and your partner pull out of the ambulance bay and advise dispatch that you are back and available for another call.

Fill-in-the-Patient Care Report

EMS Patient Care Report (PCR)			
Date:	Incident No.:	Nature of Call:	Location:
Dispatched:	En Route:	At Scene:	Transport:	At Hospital:	In Service:

Patient Information	
Age: Sex: Weight (in kg [lb]):	Allergies: Medications: Past Medical History: Chief Complaint:

Vital Signs				
Time:	BP:	Pulse:	Respirations:	SpO_2:
Time:	BP:	Pulse:	Respirations:	SpO_2:
Time:	BP:	Pulse:	Respirations:	SpO_2:

EMS Treatment
(circle all that apply)

Oxygen @ ___ L/min via (circle one): NC NRM BVM	Assisted Ventilation	Airway Adjunct	CPR
Defibrillation	Bleeding Control	Bandaging	Splinting	Other:

Narrative

Assessment Review

Answer the following questions pertaining to the assessment of the types of emergencies discussed in this chapter.

_____ **1.** In the scene size-up for a patient(s) who you think may be susceptible to shock, you should:

  A. ensure scene safety.

  B. splint all potential fractures first.

  C. ask the patient if he or she has an EpiPen.

  D. immediately obtain a patient history.

_____ **2.** During the primary assessment of a patient in shock, you should:

  A. treat any immediate life threats.

  B. obtain a SAMPLE history.

  C. get a complete set of vital signs.

  D. inform medical control of the situation.

_____ **3.** You have completed your primary assessment of an embarrassed patient who fainted after seeing a coworker injure himself. Your next step should be:

  A. a rapid secondary assessment.

  B. to obtain a medical history.

  C. a detailed physical examination.

  D. a reassessment.

_____ **4.** Interventions for the treatment of shock should include:

  A. giving the patient something to drink.

  B. maintaining normal body temperature.

  C. withholding high-flow oxygen.

  D. delaying transport to splint fractures.

_____ **5.** You are transporting an unstable patient who you feel is going into shock. How often do you recheck his vital signs?

  A. Every 3 minutes

  B. Every 10 minutes

  C. Every 5 minutes

  D. Every 15 minutes

CHAPTER

13

BLS Resuscitation

© Photos.com

General Knowledge

Matching

Match each of the items in the left column to the appropriate definition in the right column.

_____ 1. Mechanical piston device

_____ 2. Abdominal-thrust maneuver

_____ 3. Basic life support (BLS)

_____ 4. Advanced life support (ALS)

_____ 5. Cardiopulmonary resuscitation (CPR)

_____ 6. Gastric distention

_____ 7. Impedance threshold device

_____ 8. Head tilt–chin lift maneuver

_____ 9. Jaw-thrust maneuver

_____ 10. Recovery position

A. Steps used to establish artificial ventilation and circulation in a patient who is not breathing and has no pulse

B. Opening the airway without causing manipulation to the cervical spine

C. Noninvasive emergency lifesaving care used to treat airway obstructions, respiratory arrest, and cardiac arrest

D. Procedures such as cardiac monitoring, intravenous medications, and advanced airway adjuncts

E. Method of dislodging food or other material from the throat of a conscious choking victim

F. Stomach becoming filled with air

G. Depresses the sternum via a plunger mounted on a backboard

H. Used to maintain an open airway in an adequately breathing patient with a decreased level of consciousness

I. Opening the airway in a patient who has not sustained trauma to the cervical spine

J. Valve device that helps to draw more blood back to the heart during chest compressions

Multiple Choice

Read each item carefully and then select the one best response.

_____ 1. Basic life support is noninvasive emergency lifesaving care that is used to treat:

    A. airway obstruction.

    B. chest pain.

    C. respiratory distress

    D. hypovolemia.

_____ 2. After _____ without oxygen, brain damage is very likely.

    A. 1 minute

    B. 3 minutes

    C. 4 minutes

    D. 6 minutes

_____ 3. All of the following are considered advanced lifesaving procedures EXCEPT:

    A. cardiac monitoring.

    B. mouth-to-mouth.

    C. administration of intravenous (IV) fluids and medications.

    D. use of advanced airway adjuncts.

_____ **4.** In a conscious infant who is choking, you would first give five back slaps, followed by:

    A. attempting to breathe.

    B. five chest thrusts.

    C. checking a pulse.

    D. five abdominal thrusts.

_____ **5.** In addition to checking level of consciousness, it is also important to protect the _____ from further injury while assessing the patient and performing CPR.

    A. spinal cord

    B. ribs

    C. internal organs

    D. facial structures

_____ **6.** In most cases, cardiac arrest in children younger than 9 years results from:

    A. choking.

    B. aspiration.

    C. congenital heart disease.

    D. respiratory arrest.

_____ **7.** Causes of respiratory arrest in infants and children include:

    A. aspiration of foreign bodies.

    B. vomiting.

    C. poor feeding.

    D. chronic obstructive pulmonary disease (COPD).

_____ **8.** Signs of irreversible or biologic death include clinical death along with:

    A. bleeding.

    B. dependent edema.

    C. decapitation.

    D. pale skin.

_____ **9.** Once you begin CPR in the field, you must continue until:

    A. the fire department arrives.

    B. the funeral home arrives.

    C. a person of equal or higher training relieves you.

    D. law enforcement arrives and assumes responsibility.

_____ **10.** If you encounter a pregnant patient in cardiac arrest, your priorities are to provide high-quality CPR and:

    A. relieve pressure off the aorta and vena cava.

    B. rapid transport for emergency caesarian section.

    C. intermittent abdominal thrusts.

    D. increase pressure on the aorta and vena cava.

_____ **11.** To perform a _____, place your fingers behind the angles of the patient's lower jaw and then move the jaw forward.

    A. head tilt–chin lift maneuver

    B. jaw-thrust maneuver

    C. tongue–jaw lift maneuver

    D. head–jaw tilt maneuver

_____ **12.** Providing fast, aggressive ventilations could result in:

    A. excessive bleeding.

    B. rupture of the bronchial tree.

    C. gastric distention.

    D. damage to the oral pharynx.

_____ **13.** A _____ is an opening that connects the trachea directly to the skin.

    A. tracheostomy

    B. stoma

    C. laryngectomy

    D. colostomy

_____ **14.** _____ position helps to maintain a clear airway in a patient with a decreased level of consciousness who has not had traumatic injuries and is breathing on his or her own.

    A. The recovery

    B. The lithotomy

    C. Trendelenburg's

    D. Fowler's

_____ **15.** In the adult, cardiac arrest is determined by the absence of the pulse at the _____ artery.

    A. femoral

    B. radial

    C. ulnar

    D. carotid

_____ **16.** In the adult, the proper hand placement for chest compressions is accomplished by placing the heel of one hand:

    A. on the lower half of the sternum.

    B. near the clavicles.

    C. over the xiphoid process.

    D. between the nipples.

_____ **17.** Which of the following is NOT a common complication from performing chest compressions?

    A. Fractured ribs

    B. Lacerated liver

    C. Fractured sternum

    D. Lacerated pancreas

_____ **18.** When checking for a pulse in an infant, you should palpate the _____ artery.

    A. radial

    B. brachial

    C. carotid

    D. femoral

_____ **19.** The rate of compressions for an infant is _____ compressions per minute.

    A. 70 to 80

    B. 80 to 100

    C. 100 to 120

    D. 120 to 150

_____ **20.** The ratio of compression to ventilation for infants and children is _____ when performing two-rescuer CPR.

    A. 1:5

    B. 5:1

    C. 15:2

    D. 2:15

_____ **21.** Sudden airway obstruction is usually easy to recognize in someone who is eating or has just finished eating because they suddenly:

    A. are able to speak clearly.

    B. turn pink.

    C. make exaggerated efforts to breathe.

    D. start screaming.

_____ **22.** You should suspect an airway obstruction in the unresponsive patient if:
  A. the patient is breathing.
  B. you feel resistance when blowing into the patient's lungs.
  C. there is no pulse.
  D. you have adequate chest rise with each ventilation.
_____ **23.** You should use _____ for women in advanced stages of pregnancy who are conscious and suffering from a foreign body airway obstruction.
  A. the blind finger sweep
  B. back slaps
  C. the abdominal-thrust maneuver
  D. chest thrusts
_____ **24.** For a patient with a mild airway obstruction, you should:
  A. begin chest compressions.
  B. attempt a finger sweep to remove the foreign body.
  C. not interfere with the patient's attempt to expel the foreign body.
  D. immediately perform abdominal thrusts.

True/False

If you believe the statement to be more true than false, write the letter "T" in the space provided. If you believe the statement to be more false than true, write the letter "F."

_____ **1.** During the primary assessment, you need to quickly evaluate the patient's airway, breathing, circulation, and level of consciousness.
_____ **2.** All unconscious patients need all elements of BLS.
_____ **3.** A person who is unresponsive may or may not need CPR.
_____ **4.** The recovery position should be used to maintain an open airway in a patient with a head or spinal injury.
_____ **5.** A barrier device should be used in performing ventilation because it will prevent aspiration of foreign objects.
_____ **6.** You should not start CPR if the patient has obvious signs of irreversible death.
_____ **7.** After you apply pressure to depress the sternum, you must follow with an equal period of relaxation so that the chest returns to normal position.
_____ **8.** The ratio of compressions to ventilations for one-person CPR on an adult is 2:1.
_____ **9.** Short, jabbing compressions are more effective than rhythmic compressions.
_____ **10.** For infants, the preferred technique of artificial ventilation without a BVM device is with a mask or other barrier device.
_____ **11.** Families typically expect EMS providers to stop resuscitation and leave their loved one on scene.
_____ **12.** While an AED can be used in an infant, the preferred method is manual defibrillation.
_____ **13.** In the adult, the sternum should be depressed 1 inch to 1.5 inches (2.5 cm to 3.8 cm) during chest compressions.
_____ **14.** In adults, the compression-to-breath ratio is always 30:2 in two-rescuer CPR.
_____ **15.** A Physician Orders for Life-Sustaining Treatment (POLST) must be signed by an authorized medical provider to be valid.

Fill-in-the-Blank

Read each item carefully and then complete the statement by filling in the missing words.

1. Permanent brain damage is possible if the brain is without oxygen for _____ to _____ minutes.

2. If the patient's chest is _____, then the electrical current may move across the _____ rather than between the pads to the patient's heart.

3. Because of the urgent need to start CPR in a pulseless, nonbreathing patient, you must complete a primary assessment as soon as possible and begin CPR with _____ _____.

4. If you encounter a patient who has a hard lump beneath the skin in the chest near the heart, you should assume the patient has a _____.

5. _____ _____, such as living wills, may express the patient's wishes, but these documents are not binding for all health care providers.

6. For CPR to be effective, the patient must be lying supine on a _____, _____ surface.

7. Without an open _____, rescue breathing will not be effective.

8. The _____ _____ _____ should be applied to an adult cardiac arrest patient as soon as it is available.

9. Assess for a pulse in an adult patient by palpating the _____ artery.

10. A(n) _____ _____ _____ is a device that depresses the sternum via a compressed gas-powered or electric-powered plunger mounted on a backboard.

Crossword Puzzle

The following crossword puzzle is an activity provided to reinforce correct spelling and understanding of medical terminology associated with emergency care and the EMT. Use the clues in the column to complete the puzzle.

Across

3. A load-distributing _____ is a circumferential chest compression device that puts inward pressure on the thorax.
7. The _____–chin lift maneuver is a combination of two movements to open the airway by tilting the forehead back and lifting the chin.
8. Cardiopulmonary _____ is the combination of rescue breathing and chest compressions to establish adequate ventilation and circulation in a patient.
10. _____ threshold device limits the amount of air entering the lungs during the recoil phase between chest compressions.
11. The _____ position is used to maintain a clear airway in unconscious patients without injuries who are breathing adequately.

Down

1. The _____-thrust maneuver is the preferred method to dislodge a severe airway obstruction in adults and children.
2. The _____ maneuver is a technique to open the airway by placing the fingers behind the angle of the jaw and bringing the jaw forward.
4. _____ distention is a condition in which air fills the stomach.
5. A(n) _____ piston device depresses the sternum via a compressed gas-powered plunger mounted on a backboard.
6. Advanced lifesaving procedures are known as advanced _____.
9. _____ life support is noninvasive emergency lifesaving care that is used to treat medical conditions.

Critical Thinking

Short Answer

Complete this section with short written answers using the space provided.

1. List the four obvious signs of death, in addition to absence of pulse and breathing, that are used as a general rule against starting CPR.

_____

_____

_____

2. List the five components of the American Heart Association's chain of survival.

_____

_____

_____

3. List five respiratory problems leading to cardiac arrest in children.

_____

_____

_____

4. Describe how to perform the head tilt–chin lift maneuver.

_____

_____

_____

5. Describe how to perform the jaw-thrust maneuver.

_____

_____

_____

6. Describe the process of chest compressions during one-rescuer adult CPR.

_____

_____

_____

7. List and describe the method for "switching positions" during two-rescuer adult CPR.

_____

_____

_____

8. Describe the process of abdominal thrusts for a standing patient with a foreign body airway obstruction.

_____

_____

_____

9. Describe the process for chest thrusts on a standing and a supine patient.

_____

_____

_____

10. Describe the process for removing a foreign body airway obstruction in a responsive infant.

_____

_____

_____

Ambulance Calls

The following case scenarios provide an opportunity to explore the concerns associated with patient management and to enhance critical-thinking skills. Read each scenario and answer each question to the best of your ability.

1. You are dispatched to a "person down." The dispatcher informs you that the caller said the patient is not breathing. On arrival, you find a 78-year-old woman in bed, apneic, and pulseless. In the process of moving the patient to place a CPR board underneath her, you note the discoloration of her back and hips known as dependent lividity.

   How would you best manage this patient?

   _____

   _____

   _____

2. You are off duty when you hear a dispatch for "chest pain" at a private residence near you. You arrive to find the patient's family members attempting to apply an AED they bought over the Internet. The patient currently has a pulse and is breathing.

   How would you best manage this situation?

   _____

   _____

   _____

3. You are dispatched to an "unconscious man" at a private residence. You arrive to find the man lying in the grass in the backyard. There is a ladder and equipment on the rooftop. It appears he was working on the roof of his two-story home. No one witnessed the event. The man is breathing and has a pulse.

   How would you best manage this patient?

   _____

   _____

   _____

Skills

Skill Drills

Skill Drill 13-1: Performing Chest Compressions
Test your knowledge of this skill by filling in the correct words in the photo captions.

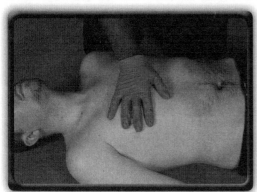

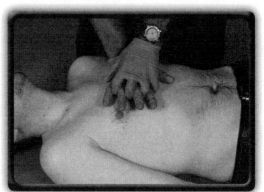

© Jones & Bartlett Learning. Courtesy of MIEMSS.

1. Take standard precautions. Place the
_____ of one hand on the
_____ of the chest.

2. Place the _____ of your other
_____ over the first hand.

© Jones & Bartlett Learning. Courtesy of MIEMSS.

3. With your arms straight, lock your
_____, and position your shoulders
directly over your _____. Depress
the sternum at a rate of _____
to _____ compressions per minute,
and to a depth of _____ to
_____ using a direct downward
movement. Allow the chest to return to its normal
position; do not lean on the chest between
compressions. _____ and relaxation
should be of equal duration.

Skill Drill 13-2: Performing One-Rescuer Adult CPR
Test your knowledge of this skill by placing the following photos in the correct order. Number the first step with a "1," the second step with a "2," etc.

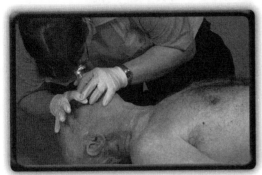

© Jones & Bartlett Learning. Courtesy of MIEMSS.

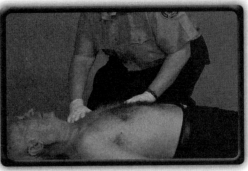

© Jones & Bartlett Learning. Courtesy of MIEMSS.

_____ Give two ventilations of 1 second each and observe for visible chest rise. Continue cycles of 30 chest compressions and two ventilations until additional personnel arrive or the patient starts to move.

_____ Take standard precautions. Establish unresponsiveness and call for help. Use your mobile phone if needed.

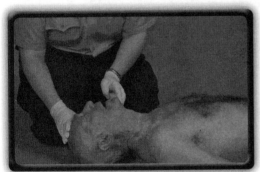

© Jones & Bartlett Learning. Courtesy of MIEMSS.

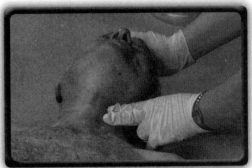

© Jones & Bartlett Learning. Courtesy of MIEMSS.

_____ Open the airway according to your suspicion of spinal injury.

_____ Check for breathing and a carotid pulse for no more than 10 seconds.

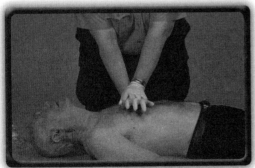

© Jones & Bartlett Learning. Courtesy of MIEMSS.

_____ If breathing and pulse are absent, begin CPR until an AED is available. Give 30 chest compressions at a rate of 100 to 120 per minute.

Skill Drill 13-3: Performing Two-Rescuer Adult CPR
Test your knowledge of this skill by filling in the correct words in the photo captions.

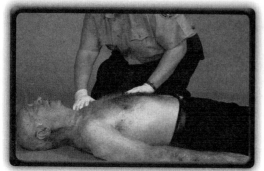

© Jones & Bartlett Learning. Courtesy of MIEMSS.

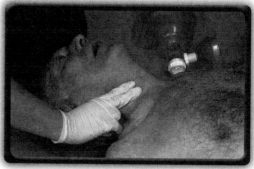

© Jones & Bartlett Learning. Courtesy of MIEMSS.

Take standard _____. Establish
_____ and take positions.

Check for breathing and a _____ pulse.

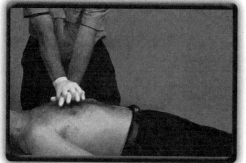

© Jones & Bartlett Learning. Courtesy of MIEMSS.

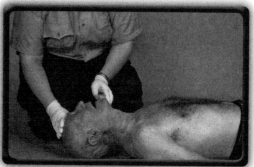

© Jones & Bartlett Learning. Courtesy of MIEMSS.

Begin CPR, starting with _____
_____. Give 30 chest compressions at a rate
of _____ to _____ per
minute. If the AED is available, then apply it and follow the
voice prompts.

_____ the airway according to your
suspicion of spinal injury.

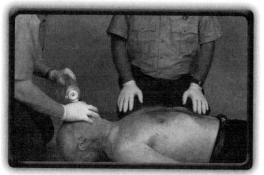

© Jones & Bartlett Learning. Courtesy of MIEMSS.

Give _____ _____ of 1 second each and
observe for _____ _____ _____.
Continue cycles of 30 chest compressions and two ventilations (switch
roles every five cycles [2 minutes]) until ALS providers take over or the
patient starts to move. Reanalyze the patient's cardiac rhythm with the
AED every 2 minutes and deliver a shock if indicated.

Medical Overview

© Photos.com

General Knowledge

Matching

Match each of the items in the left column to the related term in the right column.

_____ **1.** Asthma

_____ **2.** Hemophilia

_____ **3.** Congestive heart failure

_____ **4.** Substance abuse

_____ **5.** Chronic bronchitis

_____ **6.** Diabetes mellitus

_____ **7.** Pelvic inflammatory disease

_____ **8.** Syncope

_____ **9.** Depression

_____ **10.** Kidney stones

_____ **11.** Emphysema

_____ **12.** Appendicitis

_____ **13.** Anaphylactic reaction

_____ **14.** Heart attack

_____ **15.** Sickle cell disease

_____ **16.** Pancreatitis

_____ **17.** Vaginal bleeding

_____ **18.** Diverticulitis

_____ **19.** Plant poisoning

_____ **20.** Seizure

A. Respiratory

B. Cardiovascular

C. Neurologic

D. Gastrointestinal

E. Urologic

F. Endocrine

G. Hematologic

H. Immunologic

I. Toxicologic

J. Psychiatric

K. Gynecologic

Multiple Choice

Read each item carefully and then select the one best response.

_____ **1.** The most important aspect of the scene size-up is:

    A. determining the number of patients.

    B. calling for additional resources.

    C. ensuring scene safety.

    D. determining the nature of the illness.

_____ **2.** The _____ is your awareness of and concern for potentially serious underlying and unseen injuries or illnesses.

    A. nature of illness

    B. index of suspicion

    C. general impression

    D. clinical impression

_____ **3.** If your patient is alone and unresponsive, in order to obtain some form of medical history you should:

   A. ask people in the neighborhood.

   B. go through the patient's wallet.

   C. search the scene for medication containers or medical devices.

   D. search through the patient's bedroom drawers for hidden illegal drugs.

_____ **4.** "Has this ever happened before?" helps to determine the:

   A. chief complaint.

   B. history of present illness.

   C. medications.

   D. provocation of pain.

_____ **5.** You should assess pulse, motor, and sensation in all of the extremities and check for pupillary reactions if you suspect a(n) _____ problem.

   A. cardiovascular

   B. endocrine

   C. neurologic

   D. psychological

_____ **6.** When palpating the chest and abdomen, you are attempting to identify areas of:

   A. bruising.

   B. tenderness.

   C. crepitus.

   D. nausea.

_____ **7.** Patients with altered mental status should be considered _____ when determining transport options.

   A. nonemergency

   B. low priority

   C. moderate priority

   D. high priority

_____ **8.** A patient suffering from a heart attack should be transported to:

   A. a local clinic, 5 minutes away.

   B. a community hospital with no catheterization lab, 10 minutes away.

   C. a university hospital with a catheterization lab, 15 minutes away.

   D. a trauma center, 20 minutes away.

_____ **9.** Which statement regarding HIV is FALSE?

   A. It is not easily transmitted in your work environment.

   B. It is not considered a hazard when deposited on mucous membranes.

   C. You should always wear gloves when treating a patient with HIV.

   D. Many patients with HIV do not show symptoms.

_____ **10.** If you have been exposed to an HIV-positive patient's blood, you should:

   A. not worry about it because transmission rates are low.

   B. seek medical advice as soon as possible.

   C. wait until your next doctor visit to seek evaluation.

   D. wash the area thoroughly and get an updated tetanus shot.

_____ **11.** The incubation period for the Ebola virus is approximately:

   A. 1 to 3 days after exposure.

   B. 2 to 6 days after exposure.

   C. 6 to 12 days after exposure.

   D. 2 to 4 weeks after exposure.

_____ **12.** The incubation period for hepatitis B is typically:

    A. 1 to 2 weeks.

    B. 5 to 10 weeks.

    C. 4 to 12 weeks.

    D. 1 to 10 weeks.

_____ **13.** Vaccinations are NOT available for which form of hepatitis?

    A. Hepatitis A

    B. Hepatitis B

    C. Hepatitis C

    D. All forms of hepatitis.

_____ **14.** Which of the following statements about tuberculosis is FALSE?

    A. It is found in open, uncrowded living spaces.

    B. It can be found in crowded environments with poor ventilation.

    C. It is spread through the air via droplets.

    D. The primary infection is typically not serious.

_____ **15.** _____ is a bacterium that causes infections and is resistant to many antibiotics.

    A. Meningitis

    B. Tuberculosis

    C. Hepatitis C

    D. MRSA

_____ **16.** A(n) _____ is an outbreak that occurs on a global scale.

    A. epidemic

    B. pandemic

    C. endemic

    D. transdemic

True/False

If you believe the statement to be more true than false, write the letter "T" in the space provided. If you believe the statement to be more false than true, write the letter "F."

_____ **1.** You are obligated as a medical professional to refrain from labeling patients and displaying personal biases.

_____ **2.** In an unconscious adult patient, you should assess for a pulse in the carotid artery.

_____ **3.** An epidemic occurs when new cases of a disease in the human population exceeds the number of expected cases.

_____ **4.** History taking may be the only way to determine what the problem is or what may be causing the problem.

_____ **5.** Conscious medical patients will always need a full-body scan.

_____ **6.** A patient should be transported with lights and sirens activated when there is a life-threatening condition.

_____ **7.** Exposure to the virus that causes AIDS is a risk that EMTs face on a regular basis.

_____ **8.** EMTs can receive a vaccination against HIV to protect them from exposure.

_____ **9.** Middle East respiratory syndrome coronavirus (MERS-CoV) is a virus most commonly found in cats and birds living in the Middle East.

_____ **10.** Hepatitis A can only be transmitted from a patient who has an acute infection.

_____ **11.** HIV is far more contagious than hepatitis B.

_____ **12.** If you are exposed to a patient with pulmonary tuberculosis, you should be tested with a tuberculin skin test to see if you have been infected.

_____ **13.** MRSA is believed to be transmitted from patient to patient via the unwashed hands of health care providers.

_____ **14.** Whooping cough is an airborne disease caused by a virus.

_____ **15.** Meningococcal meningitis is highly contagious.

_____ **16.** All strains of influenza are transmitted through oral or fecal contamination.

_____ **17.** When examining the neck, you should assess for jugular vein distention and tracheal deviation.

_____ **18.** You should avoid asking family members for information regarding patient allergies and medication.

_____ **19.** Cardiac arrest patients should be transported to the closest appropriate facility.

_____ **20.** Differentiating a high-priority transport from a low-priority transport is often a skill developed with experience.

_____ **21.** Herpes simplex is primarily an animal respiratory disease that has mutated to infect humans.

Fill-in-the-Blank

Read each item carefully and then complete the statement by filling in the missing words.

1. _____ _____ may be the result of sickle cell disease or various blood clotting disorders, such as hemophilia.

2. _____ _____ occurs when you become focused on one aspect of the patient's condition and exclude all others.

3. As you approach a patient, you should determine the level of consciousness by using the _____ scale.

4. You should assess vital signs every _____ minutes in an unstable patient and every _____ minutes in a stable patient.

5. Permission to administer certain medication is usually obtained from _____ _____.

6. A(n) _____ should be used on a patient who is apneic and pulseless.

7. _____ patients include those with altered mental status, airway and breathing difficulties, or any sign of circulatory compromise.

8. Modes of transportation ultimately come in two categories: _____ or _____.

9. A(n) _____ _____ is a medical condition caused by the growth and spread of small harmful organisms within the body.

10. _____ refers to inflammation of the liver.

11. _____ _____ is transmitted orally through oral or fecal contamination.

12. You should note any _____ _____ along the veins that indicate potential IV drug use when examining the extremities.

13. _____ is the strength or ability of a pathogen to produce disease.

14. _____ is a chronic mycobacterial disease that usually strikes the lungs.

15. Patients with a fever, headache, stiff neck, and altered mental status may be suffering from _____.

Chapter 14

Fill-in-the-Table

Read each section of the chart and complete the missing areas.

Causes of Infectious Disease		
Type of Organism	**Description**	**Example**
Bacteria		*Salmonella*
	Smaller than bacteria; multiply only inside a host and die when exposed to the environment	
Fungi		
Protozoa (parasites)		Amoebas
	Invertebrates with long, flexible, rounded, or flattened bodies	

Crossword Puzzle

The following crossword puzzle is an activity provided to reinforce correct spelling and understanding of medical terminology associated with emergency care and the EMT. Use the clues in the column to complete the puzzle.

Across

2. Inflammation of the liver.
4. _____ emergencies are injuries that are the result of physical forces applied to the body.
6. A chronic bacterial disease that usually affects the lungs but can also affect other organs, such as the brain and kidneys.
7. An inflammation of the meningeal coverings of the brain and spinal cord.
8. Awareness that unseen life-threatening injuries or illness may exist is known as _____ of suspicion.
9. _____ simplex is a virus characterized by small blisters whose location depends on the type of virus.

Down

1. The general type of illness a patient is experiencing.
3. The strength or ability of a pathogen to produce disease.
5. _____ emergencies are life threats that require EMS attention because of illnesses or conditions not caused by an outside force.

Critical Thinking

Short Answer

Complete this section with short written answers using the space provided.

1. List four examples of how you can contract HIV while taking care of patients in EMS.

_____

_____

_____

2. What are the five major components of patient assessment for medical emergencies?

_____

_____

_____

3. Define each component of the acronym TACOS, which is used when determining factors that could complicate the chief complaint.

_____

_____

_____

4. List three conditions that are deemed serious and require rapid transport.

_____

_____

_____

5. List at least three important questions to ask a patient who potentially recently traveled.

_____

_____

_____

Ambulance Calls

The following case scenarios provide an opportunity to explore the concerns associated with patient management and to enhance critical-thinking skills. Read each scenario and answer each question to the best of your ability.

1. You respond to a local apartment building in the downtown area for a 42-year-old man with respiratory distress. On arrival, you notice the patient sitting in a chair with pale, diaphoretic skin. The patient tells you that he has been sick for several days and is too sick to drive himself to the hospital. When taking a history, the patient tells you that he has had night sweats and has been coughing up blood. His only complaint is fever and slight shortness of breath. He has no other significant history.

How would you best manage this patient?

_____

_____

_____

2. While driving back from a call, your unit is dispatched to a local recreation area for a 58-year-old woman with chest pain. On arrival, you notice a woman lying on the ground with several bystanders assisting her. The patient is alert and oriented and complains of chest pain.

What history-taking questions can you ask to help with your assessment of this patient?

_____

_____

_____

Respiratory Emergencies

© Photos.com

General Knowledge

Matching

Match each of the items in the left column to the appropriate definition in the right column.

_____ **1.** Respiration

_____ **2.** Pulmonary edema

_____ **3.** Epiglottitis

_____ **4.** Emphysema

_____ **5.** Pleural effusion

_____ **6.** Tuberculosis

_____ **7.** Dyspnea

_____ **8.** Pneumonia

_____ **9.** Hypoxia

_____ **10.** Chronic bronchitis

_____ **11.** Hyperventilation

_____ **12.** Allergen

_____ **13.** Embolus

_____ **14.** Asthma

_____ **15.** Pneumothorax

A. Ongoing irritation of the trachea and bronchi

B. Acute spasm of the bronchioles, associated with excessive mucus production and swelling of the mucous lining

C. Accumulation of air in the pleural space

D. Fluid buildup within the alveoli and lung tissue

E. An infection of the lung that damages lung tissue

F. A substance that leads to an allergic reaction

G. Difficulty breathing

H. Infection that can produce severe inflammation of the upper airway

I. A blood clot or other substance in the circulatory system that travels to a blood vessel where it causes blockage

J. Disease of the lungs in which the alveoli lose elasticity due to chronic stretching

K. Overbreathing to the point that the level of carbon dioxide in the blood falls below normal

L. Fluid outside the lung

M. Condition in which the body's cells and tissues do not have enough oxygen

N. The exchange of oxygen and carbon dioxide

O. A disease that can lay dormant in the lungs for decades, then reactivate

Multiple Choice

Read each item carefully and then select the one best response.

_____ **1.** A blood clot lodged in the pulmonary artery is referred to as a:
  A. myocardial infarction.
  B. stroke.
  C. pulmonary embolism.
  D. pulmonary effusion.

_____ **2.** The oxygen–carbon dioxide exchange takes place in the:
  A. trachea.
  B. bronchial tree.
  C. alveoli.
  D. blood.

_____ **3.** The letter "S" in the pneumonic PASTE refers to:
  A. symptoms.
  B. sputum.
  C. severity.
  D. sickness.

_____ **4.** If carbon dioxide levels drop too low, the person automatically breathes:
  A. normally.
  B. rapidly and deeply.
  C. slower and less deeply.
  D. fast and shallow.

_____ **5.** If the level of carbon dioxide in the arterial blood rises above normal, the patient breathes:
  A. normally.
  B. rapidly and deeply.
  C. slower and less deeply.
  D. fast and shallow.

_____ **6.** Inflammation and swelling of the pharynx, larynx, and trachea resulting in a "seal bark" is typically caused by:
  A. emphysema.
  B. chronic bronchitis.
  C. croup.
  D. epiglottitis.

_____ **7.** The rate of breathing is typically increased when:
  A. oxygen levels increase.
  B. oxygen levels decrease.
  C. carbon dioxide levels increase.
  D. carbon dioxide levels decrease.

_____ **8.** _____ is a sign of hypoxia to the brain.
  A. Altered mental status
  B. Decreased pulse rate
  C. Decreased respiratory rate
  D. Delayed capillary refill time

_____ **9.** An obstruction to the exchange of gases between the alveoli and the capillaries may result from:
  A. epiglottitis.
  B. pneumonia.
  C. a cold.
  D. croup.

_____ **10.** Pulmonary edema can develop quickly after a major:
  A. heart attack.
  B. episode of syncope.
  C. brain injury.
  D. trauma.

_____ **11.** Pulmonary edema may be produced by:
  A. cigarette smoking.
  B. seasonal allergies.
  C. inhaling toxic chemical fumes.
  D. carbon monoxide poisoning.

_____ **12.** _____ is a loss of the elastic material around the air spaces as a result of chronic stretching of the alveoli.
  A. Emphysema
  B. Bronchitis
  C. Pneumonia
  D. Diphtheria

_____ **13.** _____ is a genetic disorder that affects the lungs and digestive system.

    A. Chronic obstructive pulmonary disease

    B. Cystic fibrosis

    C. Pertussis

    D. Bronchiolitis

_____ **14.** Which of the following signs and symptoms will help distinguish COPD from congestive heart failure?

    A. Dyspnea

    B. Dependent edema

    C. Wheezing

    D. Skin color changes

_____ **15.** A pneumothorax is a partial or complete accumulation of air in the:

    A. pleural space.

    B. alveoli.

    C. abdomen.

    D. subcutaneous tissue.

_____ **16.** Asthma produces a characteristic _____ as patients attempt to exhale through partially obstructed air passages.

    A. rhonchi

    B. stridor

    C. wheezing

    D. rattle

_____ **17.** An allergic response to certain foods or some other allergen may produce an acute:

    A. bronchodilation.

    B. asthma attack.

    C. vasoconstriction.

    D. insulin release.

_____ **18.** In most cases, what is the treatment of choice for anaphylaxis?

    A. Epinephrine

    B. High-flow oxygen

    C. Antihistamines

    D. Albuterol

_____ **19.** A collection of fluid outside the lungs on one or both sides of the chest is called a:

    A. pulmonary edema.

    B. subcutaneous emphysema.

    C. pleural effusion.

    D. tension pneumothorax.

_____ **20.** Always consider _____ in patients who were eating just before becoming short of breath.

    A. upper airway obstruction

    B. anaphylaxis

    C. lower airway obstruction

    D. bronchoconstriction

_____ **21.** _____ is defined as overbreathing to the point that the level of arterial carbon dioxide falls below normal.

    A. Reactive airway syndrome

    B. Hyperventilation

    C. Tachypnea

    D. Pleural effusion

_____ **22.** Which of the following is NOT an indication of inadequate breathing?

    A. Accessory muscle use

    B. Cyanosis

    C. A regular pattern of inspiration and expiration

    D. Unequal chest expansion

Questions 23-27 are derived from the following scenario: You respond to the home of a 78-year-old man having difficulty breathing. He is sitting at the kitchen table in a classic tripod position, wearing a nasal cannula. He is cyanotic, smoking, and has his shirt unbuttoned. His respirations are 30 breaths/min and shallow, his pulse rate is 110 beats/min, and his blood pressure is 136/88 mm Hg.

_____ **23.** Your first thought as an EMT should be to:

    A. apply a nonrebreathing mask at 15 L/min.

    B. call for backup.

    C. assess the airway status.

    D. determine scene safety.

_____ **24.** His brain stem senses the level of _____ in the arterial blood, causing the rapid respirations.

    A. carbon dioxide

    B. oxygen

    C. insulin

    D. tobacco

_____ **25.** Proper management of this patient should include:

    A. supplemental oxygen.

    B. chest compressions.

    C. suctioning.

    D. epinephrine.

_____ **26.** Which of the following is NOT a sign or symptom of his inadequate breathing?

    A. He was cyanotic.

    B. His shirt was unbuttoned.

    C. He was in a tripod position.

    D. His pulse rate was over 100 beats/min (tachycardia).

_____ **27.** What should you do during the reassessment of this patient?

    A. Assess vital signs every 2 minutes.

    B. Repeat the initial and focused assessments.

    C. Reassess what time your shift ends.

    D. Repeat the initial history.

_____ **28.** Which of the following is a question you would NOT typically ask during the history taking of a patient with dyspnea?

    A. What has the patient already done for the breathing problem?

    B. Does the patient use a prescribed inhaler?

    C. Does the patient have any allergies?

    D. What time did the patient wake up this morning?

_____ **29.** Generic names for popular inhaled medications include:

    A. ventolin.

    B. flovent.

    C. albuterol.

    D. atrovent.

_____ **30.** Contraindications to helping a patient self-administer a metered-dose inhaler include all of the following EXCEPT:
   A. failure to obtain permission from medical control.
   B. noticing that the patient is in the tripod position.
   C. noticing that the patient has already taken the maximum dose of the medication.
   D. noticing that the medication has expired.

_____ **31.** Contraindications for continuous positive airway pressure (CPAP) include:
   A. being alert and able to follow commands.
   B. a pulse oximetry reading of less than 90%.
   C. a respiratory rate greater than 26 breaths/min.
   D. hypotension.

_____ **32.** A prolonged asthma attack that is unrelieved by epinephrine may progress into a condition known as:
   A. pleural effusion.
   B. status epilepticus.
   C. status asthmaticus.
   D. reactive airway disease.

_____ **33.** Which of following statements is FALSE regarding influenza?
   A. It may worsen chronic medical conditions.
   B. It is primarily a human respiratory disease that has mutated to infect animals.
   C. It is transmitted by direct contact with nasal secretions and aerosolized droplets.
   D. It has the potential to become a pandemic.

_____ **34.** Pulse oximeters measure the percentage of hemoglobin saturated with:
   A. carbon dioxide.
   B. carbon monoxide.
   C. oxygen.
   D. iron.

_____ **35.** An acute spasm of the smaller airways associated with excessive mucus production and swelling is characteristic of:
   A. asthma.
   B. chronic bronchitis.
   C. emphysema.
   D. severe acute respiratory syndrome (SARS).

True/False

If you believe the statement to be more true than false, write the letter "T" in the space provided. If you believe the statement to be more false than true, write the letter "F."

_____ **1.** Chronic bronchitis is characterized by spasm and narrowing of the bronchioles due to exposure to allergens.

_____ **2.** With pneumothorax, the lung collapses because the negative vacuum pressure in the pleural space is lost.

_____ **3.** Anaphylactic reactions occur only in patients with a previous history of asthma or allergies.

_____ **4.** Decreased breath sounds in asthma occur because fluid in the pleural space has moved the lung away from the chest wall.

_____ **5.** Patients with carbon monoxide poisoning initially complain of headache, fatigue, and nausea.

_____ **6.** Pulmonary edema is commonly associated with congestive heart failure.

_____ **7.** The distinction between hyperventilation and hyperventilation syndrome is straightforward and should guide the EMT's treatment choices.

_____ **8.** COPD most often results from cigarette smoking.

_____ **9.** COPD is characterized by long inspiratory times.

_____ **10.** In cystic fibrosis, mucus becomes thick, sticky, and hard to move.

_____ **11.** When assessing a patient, the general impression will help you decide whether the patient's condition is stable or unstable.

_____ **12.** The pulse oximeter can help you determine the severity of the respiratory component of a patient's problem.

_____ **13.** Oxygen is typically withheld from COPD patients regardless of their breathing status.

_____ **14.** Side effects of inhalers used for acute shortness of breath include increased pulse rate, nervousness, and muscle tremors.

_____ **15.** Patients who are hyperventilating should be treated by having them breathe into a paper bag.

_____ **16.** Epiglottitis is more predominant in the adult population.

_____ **17.** An RSV infection can cause respiratory illnesses such as bronchiolitis and pneumonia.

_____ **18.** When assisting a patient with a small-volume nebulizer, the oxygen flowmeter should be set to 10 L/min.

_____ **19.** Snoring sounds are indicative of a partial upper airway obstruction.

_____ **20.** Signs and symptoms of pulmonary emboli include dyspnea, hemoptysis, and tachycardia.

Fill-in-the-Blank

Read each item carefully and then complete the statement by filling in the missing words.

1. The level of _____ _____ sensed by the brain stem stimulates respiration.

2. The level of _____ in the blood is a secondary stimulus for respiration.

3. _____ passes from the blood through capillaries to tissue cells.

4. Carbon dioxide and oxygen are exchanged in the _____.

5. If you suspect a patient has tuberculosis, you should wear gloves, eye protection, and a(n) _____ _____.

6. Children with chronic pulmonary medical conditions may use a home ventilator that is connected by a _____ tube.

7. _____ _____ is an odorless, highly poisonous gas that results from incomplete oxidation of carbon in combustion.

8. High-pitched sounds heard on inspiration as air tries to pass through an obstruction in the upper airway is commonly referred to as _____.

9. _____ _____ are the sounds of air trying to pass through fluid in the alveoli.

10. When asking questions about the present illness during the history and secondary assessment, use the mnemonics _____ and _____ to guide you in your general questioning.

11. _____ _____, or allergic rhinitis, causes coldlike symptoms, including a runny nose, sneezing, congestion, and sinus pressure.

12. Medication from an _____ is delivered through the respiratory tract to the lung.

13. _____ is an airborne bacterial infection that is highly contagious and results in coughing attacks lasting longer than a minute.

14. _____ are lower pitched sounds caused by secretions or mucus in the larger airways.

15. A patient with a barrel chest and a "puffing" style of breathing most likely has _____.

Labeling

Label the following diagrams with the correct terms.

1. Obstruction, Scarring, and Dilation of the Alveolar Sac

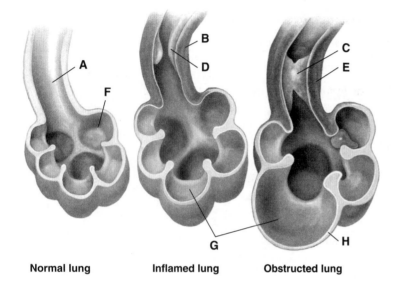

Normal lung   Inflamed lung   Obstructed lung

A. _____

B. _____

C. _____

D. _____

E. _____

F. _____

G. _____

H. _____

Crossword Puzzle

The following crossword puzzle is an activity provided to reinforce correct spelling and understanding of medical terminology associated with emergency care and the EMT. Use the clues in the column to complete the puzzle.

Across

1. Pulmonary _____ is a blood clot that breaks off from a large vein and travels to the blood vessels of the lung, causing obstruction of blood flow.
3. The exchange of oxygen and carbon dioxide.
6. A(n) _____ nebulizer is a respiratory device that holds liquid medicine that is turned into a fine mist.
8. Shortness of breath or difficulty breathing.
11. A virus that causes an infection of the lungs and breathing passages. This virus is highly contagious and spreads through droplets.
12. A disease of the lungs in which there is extreme dilation and eventual destruction of the pulmonary alveoli with poor exchange of oxygen and carbon dioxide; it is one form of chronic obstructive pulmonary disease.
13. A disease that can lay dormant in a person's lungs for decades, then reactivate; many strains are resistant to many antibiotics.
14. A slow process of dilation and disruption of the airways and alveoli caused by chronic bronchial obstruction.

Down

2. A miniature spray canister used to direct medications through the mouth and into the lungs.
4. Crackling, rattling breath sounds signaling fluid in the air spaces of the lungs.
5. A condition in which the body's cells and tissues do not have enough oxygen.
7. A high-pitched, whistling breath sound, characteristically heard on expiration in patients with asthma or chronic obstructive pulmonary disease.
9. _____ effusion is a collection of fluid between the lung and chest wall that may compress the lung.
10. A backup system to control respirations when oxygen levels fall is known as the _____ drive.
11. Coarse breath sounds heard in patients with chronic mucus in the airways.
13. Influenza _____ is a virus that has crossed the animal/human barrier and has infected humans, recently reaching a pandemic level with the H1N1 strain.

Critical Thinking

Short Answer

Complete this section with short written answers using the space provided.

1. List five characteristics of normal breathing.

_____

_____

_____

2. List six conditions where wheezing can be found.

_____

_____

_____

3. Under what conditions should you not assist a patient with a metered-dose inhaler?

_____

_____

_____

4. Describe chronic bronchitis.

_____

_____

_____

5. List complications associated with a tracheostomy tube.

_____

_____

_____

6. Explain carbon dioxide retention.

_____

_____

_____

7. When ventilating a patient, how would you determine whether your ventilations are adequate?

_____

_____

_____

Ambulance Calls

The following case scenarios provide an opportunity to explore the concerns associated with patient management and to enhance critical-thinking skills. Read each scenario and answer each question to the best of your ability.

1. You are called to the home of a young boy who is reportedly experiencing difficulty swallowing. You arrive to find concerned parents who tell you that their son seems to be "sick." He can't swallow, has a high fever, and refuses to lie down. As you enter the child's bedroom, you find him standing with arms outstretched onto the footboard of the bed, drooling and with a very frightened look on his face.

   How do you best manage this patient?

   _____

   _____

   _____

2. You are dispatched to a 36-year-old woman complaining of shortness of breath. You arrive to find a slightly overweight woman who tells you she "can't catch her breath." She is a smoker whose only medication is birth control pills.

   How would you best manage this patient?

   _____

   _____

   _____

3. You are called to the home of a 73-year-old man complaining of severe dyspnea. The patient has a history of COPD and is on home oxygen at 2 L/min via nasal cannula. His family tells you he has a long history of breathing problems and emphysema. He is cyanotic around his lips, and his respirations are 36 breaths/min and shallow.

   How would you best manage this patient?

   _____

   _____

   _____

4. You respond to a skilled nursing facility to find an 82-year-old man complaining of shortness of breath. The nursing staff tells you the patient has a cardiac history. The patient is using accessory muscles and can speak in two- to three-word sentences. You notice pink froth produced when the patient coughs and hear crackles when listening to the lungs.

   How would you best manage this patient?

   _____

   _____

   _____

Skills

Skill Drills

Test your knowledge of this skill by filling in the correct words in the photo captions.

Skill Drill 15-1: Assisting a Patient With a Metered-Dose Inhaler

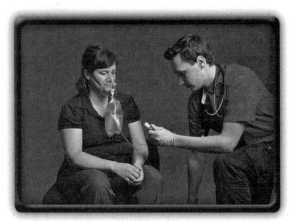

© Jones & Bartlett Learning.

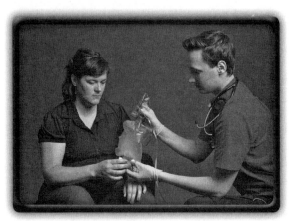

© Jones & Bartlett Learning.

1. Check to make sure you have the correct medication for the correct patient. Check the expiration date. Ensure inhaler is at room temperature or _____.

2. Remove oxygen mask. Hand inhaler to patient. Instruct about breathing and _____ _____.

© Jones & Bartlett Learning.

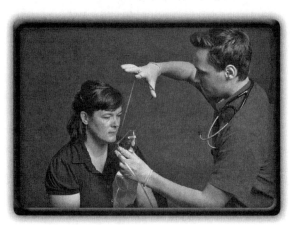

© Jones & Bartlett Learning.

3. Instruct patient to press inhaler and inhale one puff. Instruct about _____ _____.

4. Reapply _____. After a few _____, have patient repeat _____ if order or protocol allows.

Skill Drill 15-2: Assisting a Patient With a Small-Volume Nebulizer
Test your knowledge of this skill by placing the following photos in the correct order. Number the first step with a "1," the second step with a "2," etc.

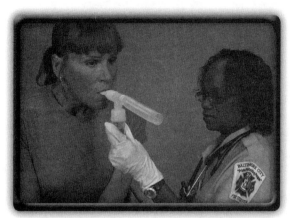

© Jones & Bartlett Learning. Courtesy of MIEMSS.

_____ Instruct the patient on how to breathe.

© Jones & Bartlett Learning. Courtesy of MIEMSS.

_____ Insert the medication into the container on the nebulizer. In some cases, sterile saline may be added (about 3 mL) to achieve the optimum volume of fluid for the nebulized application.

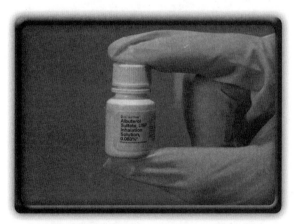

© Jones & Bartlett Learning. Courtesy of MIEMSS.

_____ Check to make sure you have the correct medication for the correct patient. Check the expiration date. Confirm you have the correct patient.

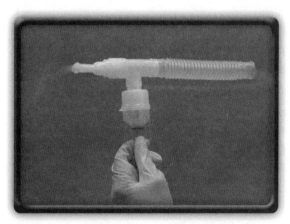

© Jones & Bartlett Learning. Courtesy of MIEMSS.

_____ Attach the medication container to the nebulizer, mouthpiece, and tubing. Attach oxygen tubing to the oxygen tank. Set the flowmeter at 6 L/min.

Assessment Review

Answer the following questions pertaining to the assessment of the types of emergencies discussed in this chapter.

_____ 1. You have been assessing a 17-year-old girl in respiratory distress and you have just completed the secondary assessment. Your next step is to:
   A. make a transport decision.
   B. consider a secondary assessment.
   C. contact medical control.
   D. make interventions.

_____ 2. You have determined that the patient in question 1 is hyperventilating. Your emergency care would include:
   A. having her breathe into a small paper sack.
   B. providing oxygen.
   C. having her run in place until the hyperventilation subsides.
   D. No interventions are necessary.

_____ 3. You have been called to a patient who resides in a long-term care facility and who is having difficulty breathing. After assessing and treating life threats to the patient's airway, breathing, and circulation, your next step in this case is to:
   A. make a transport decision.
   B. obtain a SAMPLE history.
   C. obtain an OPQRST history.
   D. obtain baseline vital signs.

_____ 4. During the reassessment, vital signs should be taken every _____ minutes for the unstable patient.
   A. 3
   B. 5
   C. 10
   D. 15

_____ 5. During the reassessment, vital signs should be taken every _____ minutes for the stable patient.
   A. 3
   B. 5
   C. 10
   D. 15

Emergency Care Summary

Complete the statements pertaining to emergency care for the types of emergencies discussed in this chapter by filling in the missing word(s).

NOTE: While the following steps are widely accepted, be sure to consult and follow your local protocol.

General Management of Respiratory Emergencies

Managing life threats to the patient's _____ and ensuring the delivery of high-flow oxygen are the primary concerns with any respiratory emergency. Patients breathing at a rate of less than _____ breaths/min or greater than _____ breaths/min should receive _____ _____. Continually assess the patient's mental status, and provide emotional support as needed. Transport in a position of comfort. For all respiratory emergencies, make sure you have taken the appropriate standard precautions, including the use of a(n) _____ _____ in a patient with suspected tuberculosis.

Upper or Lower Airway Infection

Dyspnea from an upper airway infection may be from _____ or _____. Patients should receive _____ oxygen if available. Patients who are sitting forward, seem lethargic, or are drooling may have _____. Do not force the patient to lie down or attempt to suction or insert a(n) _____ airway because this may cause a spasm and a complete airway obstruction. Transport should be rapid.
Lower airway infections may be from the common cold, bronchitis, or _____. Patients need supplemental oxygen, monitoring of vital signs, and transport to the hospital.

Asthma, Hay Fever, and Anaphylaxis

Not all wheezing is the result of asthma! Obtain a thorough _____ from the patient or family. If the patient is wheezing and has asthma, assist with the patient's prescribed _____ or administer a small-volume nebulizer containing _____. Provide supplemental oxygen and provide ventilatory support as needed. Patients whose asthma progresses to _____ _____ require immediate transportation. Be prepared to assist their ventilations because they may become too exhausted to breathe.
Hay fever usually requires only support and transport, but if the condition has worsened from generalized cold symptoms, the patient may require supplemental oxygen and _____ support.
Anaphylaxis is a true emergency that requires rapid intervention and _____. Airway, oxygen, and ventilatory support are paramount. Determine if the patient has a prescribed _____. Transport promptly. Reassess the patient's condition en route to the hospital.

Pneumothorax

A pneumothorax may occur spontaneously or may be the result of a(n) _____ _____. Place the patient in a position of comfort, and support the _____. Provide prompt transport, monitor the patient carefully, and be prepared to assist ventilations and provide _____ _____ if necessary.

Obstruction of the Airway

Managing an airway obstruction is a priority. Use age-appropriate _____ life support foreign body airway obstruction _____ to clear the airway. Administer supplemental oxygen, and transport the patient to the closest hospital. Some patients do not want to go to a hospital after the obstruction is cleared. Encourage them to be transported for evaluation of possible _____ to the airway.

Hyperventilation

Gather a thorough _____, and attempt to determine the _____ _____ because the hyperventilation may be the result of a serious problem. Do not have the patient breathe into a(n) _____ _____; this maneuver could make things worse. Instead, _____ the patient, administer supplemental oxygen, and provide prompt transport to the hospital.

CHAPTER 16

Cardiovascular Emergencies

© Photos.com

General Knowledge

Matching

Match each of the items in the left column to the appropriate definition in the right column.

_____ 1. Atria
_____ 2. Coronary arteries
_____ 3. Atrioventricular node
_____ 4. Myocardium
_____ 5. Sinus node
_____ 6. Venae cavae
_____ 7. Ventricles
_____ 8. Aorta
_____ 9. Atherosclerosis
_____ 10. Arrhythmia
_____ 11. Ischemia
_____ 12. Infarction
_____ 13. Tachycardia
_____ 14. Asystole
_____ 15. Bradycardia
_____ 16. Thromboembolism

A. Absence of heart electrical activity
B. Calcium and cholesterol buildup inside blood vessels
C. Blood vessels that supply blood to the myocardium
D. Abnormal heart rhythm
E. Unusually slow heart rhythm, less than 60 beats/min
F. Lack of oxygen
G. Heart muscle
H. Lower chambers of the heart
I. Tissue death
J. Rapid heart rhythm, greater than 100 beats/min
K. Carry oxygen-poor blood back to the heart
L. Upper chambers of the heart
M. Body's main artery
N. Electrical impulses begin here
O. Electrical impulses slow here to allow blood to move from the atria to the ventricles
P. Blood clot floating through blood vessels until it reaches a narrow area and blocks blood flow

Match each of the medical conditions in the left column to the appropriate description in the right column.

_____ 17. Acute myocardial infarction
_____ 18. Cardiac arrest
_____ 19. Angina pectoris
_____ 20. Cardiogenic shock
_____ 21. Congestive heart failure
_____ 22. Hypertensive emergency
_____ 23. Dissecting aneurysm

A. Swollen ankles, rales
B. Sudden tearing, separation of lining, potential for great blood loss
C. Heart lacks pumping power, low blood pressure
D. Severe headache, bounding pulses, ringing in ears
E. Pulseless, apneic
F. Exertional chest pain, relieved by nitroglycerin
G. Complete blockage of coronary artery

Multiple Choice

Read each item carefully and then select the one best response.

_____ 1. _____ allows a cardiac muscle cell to contract spontaneously without a stimulus from a nerve source.

   A. Repetition
   B. Reactivity
   C. Automaticity
   D. Autonomy

_____ 2. The aorta receives its blood supply from the:

   A. right atrium.
   B. left atrium.
   C. right ventricle.
   D. left ventricle.

_____ **3.** Blood enters the right atrium from the body through the:
- **A.** vena cava.
- **B.** aorta.
- **C.** pulmonary artery.
- **D.** pulmonary vein.

_____ **4.** The only vein(s) in the body that carry oxygenated blood is/are the:
- **A.** external jugular veins.
- **B.** pulmonary veins.
- **C.** subclavian veins.
- **D.** inferior vena cava.

_____ **5.** Normal electrical impulses originate in the sinus node, just above the:
- **A.** atria.
- **B.** ventricles.
- **C.** AV junction.
- **D.** bundle of His.

_____ **6.** Dilation of the coronary arteries _____ blood flow.
- **A.** shuts off
- **B.** increases
- **C.** decreases
- **D.** regulates

_____ **7.** The _____ are tiny blood vessels that are approximately one cell thick.
- **A.** arterioles
- **B.** venules
- **C.** capillaries
- **D.** ventricles

_____ **8.** _____ carry oxygen to the body's tissues and then remove carbon dioxide.
- **A.** Red blood cells
- **B.** White blood cells
- **C.** Platelets
- **D.** Veins

_____ **9.** _____ is the maximum pressure exerted by the left ventricle as it contracts.
- **A.** Cardiac output
- **B.** Diastolic blood pressure
- **C.** Systolic blood pressure
- **D.** Stroke volume

_____ **10.** Atherosclerosis can lead to a complete _____ of a coronary artery.
- **A.** occlusion
- **B.** disintegration
- **C.** dilation
- **D.** contraction

_____ **11.** The lumen of an artery may be partially or completely blocked by the blood-clotting system due to a _____ that exposes the inside of the atherosclerotic wall.
- **A.** tear
- **B.** crack
- **C.** clot
- **D.** rupture

_____ **12.** Tissues downstream from a blood clot will suffer from lack of oxygen. If blood flow is resumed in a short time, the _____ tissues will recover.

    A. dead

    B. ischemic

    C. necrosed

    D. dry

_____ **13.** Risk factors for myocardial infarction include all of the following EXCEPT:

    A. male gender.

    B. high blood pressure.

    C. stress.

    D. increased activity level.

_____ **14.** When, for a brief period of time, heart tissues do not get enough oxygen, the pain is called:

    A. AMI.

    B. angina.

    C. ischemia.

    D. CAD.

_____ **15.** Angina pain may be felt in the:

    A. epigastrium.

    B. legs.

    C. lower back.

    D. lower abdomen.

_____ **16.** The underlying cause of a dissecting aortic aneurysm is:

    A. controlled hypertension.

    B. uncontrolled hypertension.

    C. malignant hypertension.

    D. benign hypertension.

_____ **17.** Because the oxygen supply to the heart is diminished with angina, the _____ can become compromised, putting the person at risk for significant cardiac rhythm problems.

    A. circulation

    B. cardiac output

    C. electrical system

    D. vasculature

_____ **18.** About _____ minutes after blood flow is cut off, some heart muscle cells begin to die.

    A. 10

    B. 20

    C. 30

    D. 40

_____ **19.** An acute myocardial infarction is more likely to occur in the larger, thick-walled left ventricle, which needs more _____ than the right ventricle.

    A. oxygen and glucose

    B. force to pump

    C. blood and oxygen

    D. electrical activity

_____ **20.** Which of the following statements regarding congestive heart failure is FALSE?

    A. Stridor is a common lung sound heard on exam.

    B. It can be caused by diseased heart valves.

    C. It can be treated with nitroglycerin.

    D. Ankle edema is a common finding.

_____ **21.** Cardiogenic shock can occur within 24 hours of a(n):

    A. hypertensive emergency.

    B. acute myocardial infarction.

    C. aortic aneurysm.

    D. unstable angina attack.

_____ **22.** Sudden death is usually the result of _____, in which the heart fails to generate an effective blood flow.

    A. AMI

    B. atherosclerosis

    C. PVCs

    D. cardiac arrest

_____ **23.** Disorganized, ineffective quivering of the ventricles is known as:

    A. ventricular fibrillation.

    B. asystole.

    C. ventricular stand still.

    D. ventricular tachycardia.

_____ **24.** Which of the following is NOT a cause of congestive heart failure?

    A. Chronic hypotension

    B. Heart valve damage

    C. Myocardial infarction

    D. Long-standing high blood pressure

_____ **25.** Signs and symptoms of shock include all of the following EXCEPT:

    A. elevated heart rate.

    B. pale, clammy skin.

    C. air hunger.

    D. elevated blood pressure.

_____ **26.** Which of the following changes in heart function occur in patients with congestive heart failure?

    A. A decrease in heart rate

    B. Enlargement of the left ventricle

    C. Enlargement of the right ventricle

    D. A decrease in blood pressure

_____ **27.** Physical findings of AMI include skin that is _____ because of poor cardiac output and the loss of perfusion.

    A. pink

    B. white

    C. gray

    D. red

_____ **28.** All patient assessments begin by determining whether the patient:

    A. is breathing.

    B. can talk.

    C. is responsive.

    D. has a pulse.

_____ **29.** To assess chest pain, use the mnemonic:

    A. AVPU.

    B. OPQRST.

    C. SAMPLE.

    D. CHART.

_____ **30.** When using the mnemonic OPQRST, the "P" stands for:

    A. parasthesia.

    B. pain.

    C. provocation.

    D. predisposing factors.

_____ **31.** In addition to angina and myocardial infarction, nitroglycerin can be used to treat:
    A. congestive heart failure.
    B. cardiogenic shock.
    C. aortic aneurysm.
    D. hypertensive emergency.

_____ **32.** When administering nitroglycerin to a patient, you should make sure the patient has not taken any medications for _____ in the last 24 hours.
    A. angina
    B. erectile dysfunction
    C. migraine headaches
    D. gallbladder dysfunction

_____ **33.** In general, a maximum of _____ dose(s) of nitroglycerin is/are given for any one episode of chest pain.
    A. one
    B. two
    C. three
    D. four

_____ **34.** _____ are inserted when the electrical control system of the heart is so damaged that it cannot function properly.
    A. Stents
    B. Pacemakers
    C. Balloon angioplasties
    D. Defibrillations

_____ **35.** When the battery wears out in a pacemaker, the patient may experience:
    A. syncope.
    B. chest pain.
    C. nausea.
    D. tachycardia.

_____ **36.** The computer inside the AED is specifically programmed to recognize rhythms that require defibrillation to correct, most commonly:
    A. asystole.
    B. ventricular tachycardia.
    C. ventricular fibrillation.
    D. supraventricular tachycardia.

_____ **37.** The AED should be applied only to unresponsive patients with no:
    A. significant medical problems.
    B. cardiac history.
    C. pulse.
    D. brain activity.

_____ **38.** _____ usually refers to a state of cardiac arrest despite an organized electrical complex.
    A. Asystole
    B. Pulseless electrical activity
    C. Ventricular fibrillation
    D. Ventricular tachycardia

_____ **39.** The links in the chain of survival include all of the following EXCEPT:
    A. immediate high-quality CPR.
    B. ALS and postarrest care.
    C. administration of nitroglycerin.
    D. rapid defibrillation.

_____ **40.** Defibrillation works best if it takes place within _____ minutes of the onset of cardiac arrest.

    A. 2

    B. 4

    C. 6

    D. 10

Questions 41–45 are derived from the following scenario: At 0500, you respond to the home of a 76-year-old man complaining of chest pain. On arrival, the patient states that he had been sleeping in the recliner all night due to indigestion. He also tells you he has taken two nitroglycerin tablets. He continues to have pain and reports trouble breathing.

_____ **41.** Your first priority is to:

    A. apply an AED.

    B. provide high-flow oxygen.

    C. evaluate the need to administer a third nitroglycerin tablet.

    D. size up the scene.

_____ **42.** His vital signs are as follows: respirations, 16 breaths/min; pulse, 98 beats/min; blood pressure, 92/76 mm Hg. He is still complaining of chest pain. What actions should you take to intervene?

    A. Provide high-flow oxygen.

    B. Administer a third nitroglycerin tablet.

    C. Apply an AED.

    D. Begin chest compressions.

_____ **43.** Your patient suddenly becomes unresponsive. Assessment reveals no breathing and no pulse. Your partner begins chest compressions while you apply the AED. When operating an AED, what is the first step in the defibrillation sequence?

    A. Plug the pads connector to the AED.

    B. Apply the AED pads to the patient's chest.

    C. Remove clothing from the patient's chest.

    D. Turn on the AED.

_____ **44.** After applying an AED to this patient, the AED states, "No shock advised." What is your next step of action?

    A. Load and transport the patient.

    B. Push to reanalyze.

    C. Perform CPR for 2 minutes starting with chest compressions, then have the AED reanalyze.

    D. Consider termination.

_____ **45.** Your patient is now conscious, and you are en route to the hospital. You are six blocks away when the patient stops breathing again and no longer has a pulse. You should:

    A. continue to the hospital.

    B. continue to the hospital and analyze the rhythm.

    C. stop the vehicle and analyze the rhythm.

    D. only perform chest compressions.

True/False

If you believe the statement to be more true than false, write the letter "T" in the space provided. If you believe the statement to be more false than true, write the letter "F."

_____ **1.** The right side of the heart pumps oxygen-rich blood to the body.

_____ **2.** In the normal heart, the need for increased blood flow to the myocardium is easily met by an increase in heart rate.

_____ **3.** Atherosclerosis results in narrowing of the lumen of coronary arteries.

_____ **4.** Infarction is a temporary interruption of the blood supply to the tissues.

_____ **5.** Angina can result from a spasm of the artery.

_____ **6.** The pain of angina and the pain of AMI are easily distinguishable.

_____ **7.** Nitroglycerin works in most patients within 5 minutes to relieve the pain of AMI.

_____ **8.** If an AED malfunctions during use, you must report that problem to the manufacturer and to human resources.

_____ **9.** Angina occurs when the heart's need for oxygen exceeds its supply.

_____ **10.** White blood cells are the most numerous cells in the blood and help the blood to clot.

_____ **11.** Cardiac arrest in younger children is less common than in older children and is usually caused by a breathing problem.

_____ **12.** An AED with special pediatric pads may be used on pediatric medical patients between the ages of 1 month and 8 years who have been assessed to be unresponsive, not breathing, and pulseless.

_____ **13.** Dissecting aortic aneurysms are rarely considered life threatening.

_____ **14.** Heart disease is the number one killer of women in the United States.

_____ **15.** If a patient complaining of chest pain has a history of a previous AMI, you should ask if this pain feels similar to the previous AMI.

Fill-in-the-Blank

Read each item carefully and then complete the statement by filling in the missing words.

1. The heart is divided down the middle by a wall called the _____.

2. The _____ is the body's main artery.

3. The _____ ventricle pumps blood in through the pulmonary circulation.

4. Electrical impulses spread from the _____ node to the ventricles.

5. Blood supply to the heart is increased by _____ of the coronary arteries.

6. _____ _____ cells remove carbon dioxide from the body's tissues.

7. _____ blood pressure reflects the pressure on the walls of the arteries when the ventricle is at rest.

8. The heart has _____ chambers.

9. The _____ side of the heart is more muscular because it must pump blood into the aorta and all the other arteries of the body.

10. _____ is the most effective way to assist a person with CHF to breathe effectively and to prevent an invasive airway management technique.

11. The collection of fluid in the part of the body that is closest to the ground is called _____ _____.

12. A hypertensive emergency usually occurs only with a systolic pressure greater than _____.

13. In CHF, blood tends to back up in the _____ _____, increasing the pressure in the capillaries of the lungs.

14. A late finding in cardiogenic shock would be a systolic blood pressure of less than _____.

15. Damage to the _____ area of the heart often presents with bradycardia.

Labeling

Label the following diagrams with the correct terms.

1. **Right and Left Sides of the Heart**

Where arrows appear, also indicate the origin and destination of the blood.

A. _____

B. _____

C. _____

D. _____

E. _____

F. _____

G. _____

H. _____

I. _____

J. _____

K. _____

L. _____

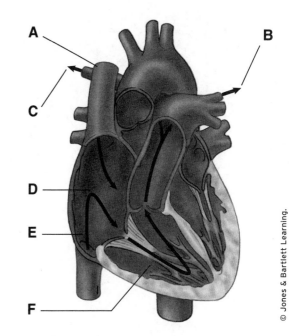

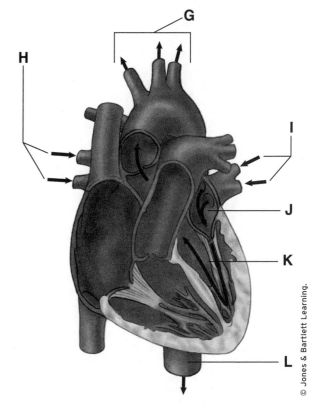

172

2. Electrical Conduction System

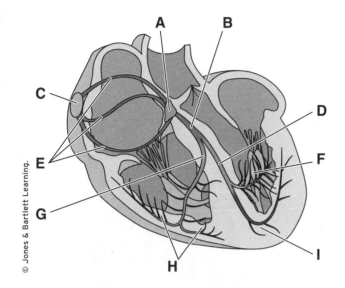

A. _____

B. _____

C. _____

D. _____

E. _____

F. _____

G. _____

H. _____

I. _____

3. Pulse Points

State the name of the artery that is being assessed at each of the following pulse points:

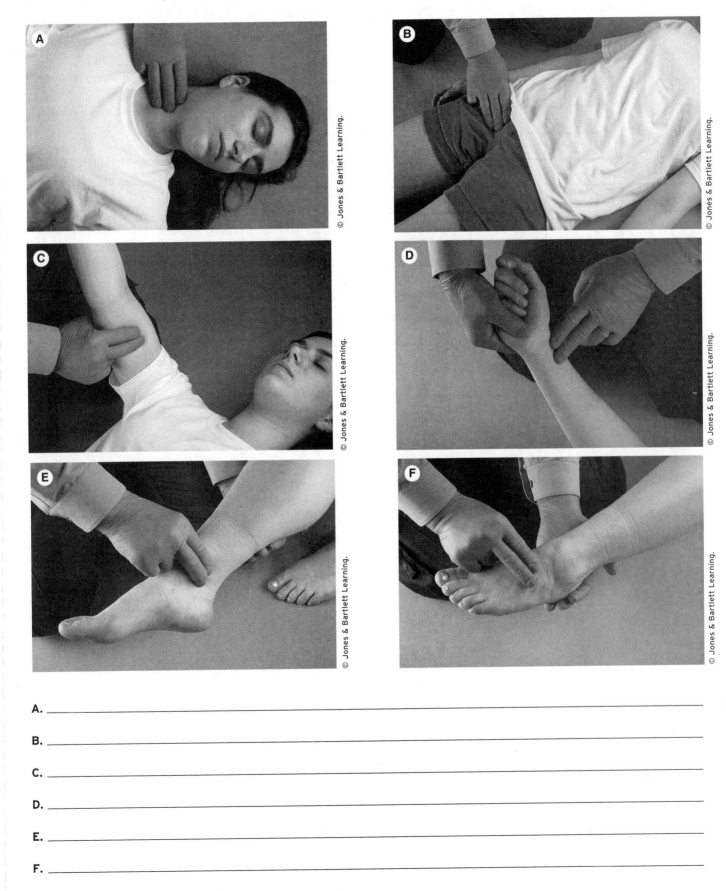

© Jones & Bartlett Learning.

A. _____

B. _____

C. _____

D. _____

E. _____

F. _____

Crossword Puzzle

The following crossword puzzle is an activity provided to reinforce correct spelling and understanding of medical terminology associated with emergency care and the EMT. Use the clues in the column to complete the puzzle.

Across

1. An irregular or abnormal heart rhythm.
4. A rapid heart rate, greater than 100 beats/min.
8. One of two (right and left) upper chambers of the heart.
9. A state in which the heart fails to generate effective and detectable blood flow.
12. The flow of blood through body tissues and vessels.
14. The _____ nervous system controls the involuntary activities of the body, such as heart rate, blood pressure, and digestion of food.
15. A fainting spell or transient loss of consciousness.

Down

2. Death of heart muscle following obstruction of blood flow to it.
3. Death of a body tissue, usually caused by interruption of its blood supply.
5. The main artery, which receives blood from the left ventricle and delivers it to all of the other arteries.
6. _____ syndrome is a term used to describe a group of symptoms caused by myocardial ischemia.
7. The complete absence of heart electrical activity.
10. _____ edema is swelling in the part of the body closest to the ground, caused by collection of fluid in the tissues.
11. A disorder in which the heart loses part of its ability to effectively pump blood.
13. The inside diameter of an artery or other hollow structure.

Critical Thinking

Short Answer

Complete this section with short written answers using the space provided.

1. Explain the differentiating features between an AMI and a dissecting aortic aneurysm.

_____

_____

_____

2. What are the three most common errors of AED use?

_____

_____

_____

3. If ALS is not responding to the scene, what are the three points at which transport should be initiated for a cardiac arrest patient?

_____

_____

_____

4. List four safety considerations for operating an AED.

_____

_____

_____

5. Explain the difference between stable angina and unstable angina.

_____

_____

_____

6. List three ways in which AMI pain differs from angina pain.

_____

_____

_____

7. List three serious consequences of AMI.

_____

_____

_____

8. Name at least five signs and symptoms associated with AMI.

_____

_____

_____

9. List six steps in the treatment of a patient with CHF.

_____

_____

_____

Ambulance Calls

The following case scenarios provide an opportunity to explore the concerns associated with patient management and to enhance critical-thinking skills. Read each scenario and answer each question to the best of your ability.

1. You are dispatched to the residence of a 58-year-old man complaining of chest pain. He states that it feels like "somebody is standing on my chest." He sat down when it started and took a nitroglycerin tablet. He is still a little nauseated and sweaty but feels better. He is very anxious.

How would you best manage this patient?

_____

_____

_____

2. You are dispatched to the home of a 45-year-old man experiencing chest pain. He told his wife that he was fine, but she decided to call 9-1-1. When you arrive, you find your patient sitting in the living room looking anxious. He is sweaty and pale and admits the pain is worse than just a few moments ago. He tells you that he is a very athletic person, so the pain must just be stress related and it will go away after he relaxes for a while. He tells you he does not want to be taken to the hospital.

How would you best manage this patient?

_____

_____

_____

3. You are dispatched to the home of a 60-year-old woman complaining of sudden weakness. She tells you that she usually has enough energy to perform daily tasks around the house, but today she's suddenly very tired, has some pain in her jaw, and has some nausea. She denies any history of recent illness, including cough, cold, or fever. She is otherwise healthy and does not take any medications.

How would you best manage this patient?

_____

_____

_____

Fill-in-the-Patient Care Report

Read the incident scenario and then complete the following patient care report (PCR).

Your shift ends at 1900 and you have 10 minutes to go. As you sit there daydreaming about your plans for the evening, the tones go off. "Unit 6291, respond to 1574 S. Main Street for a 58-year-old man with chest pain; time 1901."

You immediately acknowledge the call and note the incident number of 011543. You arrive on the scene 8 minutes later and notice a woman standing on the front porch. Your partner grabs the gear as you approach the woman. She tells you that her husband has had chest pain for about 30 minutes and has taken two nitroglycerin tablets but is not feeling any better.

As you enter the residence, you see a man sitting up on the living room couch. The man looks like he is having difficulty breathing. You introduce yourself to the patient and ask what is wrong. "I have horrible pressure in my chest," the patient replies. "Please help me." Because you are less than 5 minutes from the hospital, you elect not to request ALS.

"I was just sitting here on the couch when I began to feel incredible constant pressure in my chest. Then I began to get short of breath. I initially thought it was my angina, but this feels different and my nitro doesn't seem to be helping."

Your partner applies 15 L/min of oxygen via nonrebreathing mask, and you note that you have been on scene for 2 minutes. You note that the patient has an intact airway, and although he is a little short of breath, he seems to be breathing adequately.

As you continue with your assessment, you note clear lung sounds and good pulses in all of his extremities.

"Does your pressure go anywhere?" you ask.

"No," replies the patient.

"On a scale from 1 to 10, can you rate that pressure for me?" The patient responds with a 5 out of 10.

Your partner hands you a piece of paper indicating the vital signs: pulse, 88 beats/min; respirations, 22 breaths/min; blood pressure, 136/88 mm Hg; SpO_2, 99%; time, 1914.

The patient tells you he has a history of hypertension, angina, and diabetes. He takes Lisinopril, nitroglycerin, metformin, and metoprolol. When you ask him about allergies, he says, "I can't have aspirin—my throat closes up."

Your local protocol allows you to assist with administration of nitroglycerin. You check the patient's nitro and verify that it is indeed prescribed to him and that it is not expired. Because his systolic blood pressure is above 100 mm Hg, you elect to give the patient a nitro tablet. You explain to the patient that he is to place the tablet under his tongue and that he is not to chew or swallow it. You note the time as 1916.

You finish your secondary assessment and package the patient onto your litter.

The patient is loaded into your ambulance and transported to the local hospital. Just as you start en route to the hospital, you notice that it has been 5 minutes since you administered the nitro. You reassess his vital signs: pulse, 84 beats/min; respirations, 18 breaths/min; blood pressure, 122/74 mm Hg; SpO_2, 98%. The patient now rates his pain as a 4 out of 10.

In 5 minutes, you arrive at the local hospital with a stable patient and transfer care to the emergency department staff.

After giving your report to the ED staff and restocking/cleaning the unit, your partner looks at you and says, "Hey, you're only 35 minutes late." After his comment, you mark your unit available and return to the station.

Fill-in-the-Patient Care Report

EMS Patient Care Report (PCR)					
Date:	Incident No.:	Nature of Call:		Location:	
Dispatched:	En Route:	At Scene:	Transport:	At Hospital:	In Service:
Patient Information					
Age: Sex: Weight (in kg [lb]):			Allergies: Medications: Past Medical History: Chief Complaint:		
Vital Signs					
Time:	BP:	Pulse:	Respirations:		Spo$_2$:
Time:	BP:	Pulse:	Respirations:		Spo$_2$:
Time:	BP:	Pulse:	Respirations:		Spo$_2$:
EMS Treatment (circle all that apply)					
Oxygen @ ____ L/min via (circle one): NC NRM BVM		Assisted Ventilation	Airway Adjunct		CPR
Defibrillation	Bleeding Control	Bandaging	Splinting		Other:
Narrative					

Skills

Skill Drills

Skill Drill 16-1: Administration of Nitroglycerin
Test your knowledge of this skill by filling in the correct words in the photo captions.

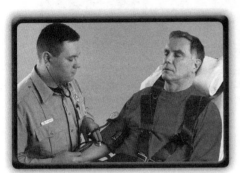

Jones & Bartlett Learning.

Jones & Bartlett Learning.

1. Obtain an order from _____
_____. Take the patient's
blood pressure. Administer
_____ only if the
_____ blood pressure is
greater than 100 mm Hg.

2. Check the medication and expiration date.
Ask the patient about the last dose he or
she took and its _____.
Make sure that the patient understands the
route of _____. Prepare
to have the patient lie down to prevent
_____.

Jones & Bartlett Learning.

Jones & Bartlett Learning.

3. Ask the patient to lift his or her
_____. Place the tablet or
spray the dose under the _____
(while wearing gloves), or have the patient do
so. Have the patient keep his or her mouth
_____ with the tablet or
spray under the tongue until it is dissolved
and absorbed. Caution the patient against
_____ or swallowing the
tablet.

4. Recheck the blood pressure within
_____ minutes.
Record each medication and the
time of administration. Reevaluate
the _____
_____ and blood
pressure, and repeat treatment, if necessary.

Skill Drill 16-3: AED and CPR
Test your knowledge of this skill by placing the following photos in the correct order. Number the first step with a "1," the second step with a "2," etc.

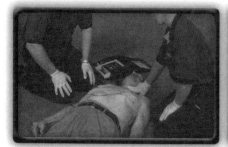

© Jones & Bartlett Learning. Courtesy of MIEMSS.

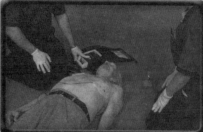

© Jones & Bartlett Learning. Courtesy of MIEMSS.

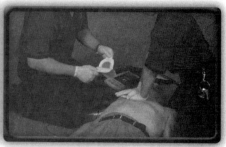

© Jones & Bartlett Learning. Courtesy of MIEMSS.

_____ If shock is advised, clear the patient, push the Shock button, and immediately resume CPR compressions. If no shock is advised, immediately resume CPR compressions and be sure to switch rescuers. After five cycles (2 minutes) of CPR, reanalyze the cardiac rhythm. Repeat the cycle of five cycles (2 minutes) of CPR, one shock (if indicated), and 2 minutes of CPR. Transport, and contact medical control as needed.

_____ Verbally and visually clear the patient. Push the Analyze button, if there is one. Wait for the AED to analyze the cardiac rhythm. If no shock is advised, perform five cycles (2 minutes) of CPR and then reanalyze the cardiac rhythm. If a shock is advised, recheck that all are clear, and push the Shock button. After the shock is delivered, immediately resume CPR beginning with chest compressions and remember to switch rescuers.

_____ Turn on the AED. Apply the AED pads to the chest and attach the pads to the AED. Stop CPR. If a shock is not advised, perform five cycles (about 2 minutes) of CPR, beginning with chest compressions, and then reanalyze the cardiac rhythm. If a shock is advised, reconfirm that no one is touching the patient and push the Shock button. If at any time the AED advises to check the patient, quickly assess for a carotid or femoral pulse. This should not take longer than 5 to 10 seconds. If you feel a pulse, the patient has experienced ROSC (return of spontaneous circulation). Continue to monitor the patient.

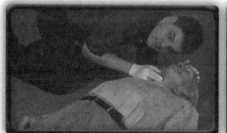

© Jones & Bartlett Learning. Courtesy of MIEMSS.

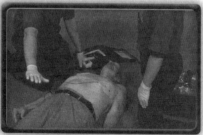

© Jones & Bartlett Learning. Courtesy of MIEMSS.

_____ Take standard precautions. Determine scene safety. Question bystanders. Determine responsiveness. Assess compression effectiveness if CPR is already in progress. If the patient is unresponsive and CPR has not been started yet, begin providing chest compressions and rescue breaths at a rate of 30 compressions to two breaths and a rate of 100 to 120 compressions per minute, continuing until an AED arrives and is ready for use.

_____ After five cycles (2 minutes) of CPR, reanalyze the cardiac rhythm. Do not interrupt chest compressions for more than 10 seconds.

Assessment Review

Answer the following questions pertaining to the assessment of the types of emergencies discussed in this chapter.

_____ 1. What type of additional resource is typically required for someone with chest pain?

   A. Lift assistance

   B. Advanced life support

   C. Police

   D. Rescue team

_____ 2. When taking a SAMPLE history of a conscious person with chest pain, what specific question should the EMT ask of the patient?

   A. Has he or she had a heart attack before?

   B. How long does he or she want to stay in the hospital?

   C. Did the patient's physician inform him or her of risk factors associated with heart disease?

   D. Does he or she exercise on a regular basis?

_____ 3. Which step should NOT be taken to complete a history and physical exam on an unconscious patient with a suspected cardiac problem?

   A. Perform a full-body scan.

   B. Obtain vital signs.

   C. Obtain history from family or bystanders.

   D. Look through the patient's wallet for medical information.

_____ 4. A patient taking medications such as Lasix or digoxin is likely to have which of the following underlying medical conditions?

   A. Hypertension

   B. Hyperglycemia

   C. Congestive heart failure

   D. Cerebral vascular accident

_____ 5. When assessing a cardiac arrest patient, you notice what appears to be a pacemaker implanted in the upper left chest. Care for this patient should include:

   A. attempting to deactivate the device by placing a magnet over it.

   B. making sure the AED patches are not directly over the pacemaker device.

   C. waiting for ALS to arrive before applying the AED.

   D. not using the AED in this situation.

CHAPTER 17

Neurologic Emergencies

© Photos.com

General Knowledge

Matching

Match each of the items in the left column to the appropriate definition in the right column.

_____ 1. Aneurysm

_____ 2. Aphasia

_____ 3. Aura

_____ 4. Brain stem

_____ 5. Cerebellum

_____ 6. Cerebrum

_____ 7. Hemiparesis

_____ 8. Hypoglycemia

_____ 9. Incontinence

_____ 10. Ischemia

_____ 11. Postictal state

_____ 12. Seizure

_____ 13. Status epilepticus

_____ 14. Stroke

_____ 15. Transient ischemic attack

A. A period following a seizure that typically includes labored respirations and altered mental status

B. Low blood glucose levels

C. A temporary alteration in consciousness, classified as generalized, partial, or status epilepticus

D. Experiencing a warning sense prior to an event

E. Part of the brain located above the cerebellum; divided into right and left hemispheres

F. Loss of bowel or bladder control

G. Stroke symptoms that go away in less than 24 hours

H. Weakness of one side of the body

 I. A seizure lasting longer than 30 minutes

J. An interruption of blood flow to the brain that results in a loss of brain function

K. Controls muscle and body coordination

L. A lack of oxygen that causes cells to not function properly

M. A swelling or enlargement of part of an artery resulting from weakness of the arterial wall

N. An inability to produce or understand speech

O. Controls basic functions of the body, such as breathing and blood pressure

Multiple Choice

Read each item carefully and then select the one best response.

_____ 1. A _____ is typically characterized by unconsciousness and a generalized severe twitching of all of the body's muscles that lasts several minutes or longer.

    A. stroke

    B. postictal state

    C. simple partial seizure

    D. generalized seizure

_____ 2. The _____ controls the most basic functions of the body, such as breathing, blood pressure, swallowing, and pupil constriction.

    A. brain stem

    B. cerebellum

    C. cerebrum

    D. spinal cord

_____ **3.** At each vertebra in the neck and back, _____ nerves, called spinal nerves, branch out from the spinal cord and carry signals to and from the body.

    A. two

    B. three

    C. four

    D. five

_____ **4.** All of the following are associated with altered mental status EXCEPT:

    A. coma.

    B. seizure.

    C. incontinence.

    D. intoxication.

_____ **5.** When blood flow to a particular part of the brain is cut off by a blockage inside a blood vessel, the result is:

    A. a hemorrhagic stroke.

    B. atherosclerosis.

    C. an ischemic stroke.

    D. a cerebral embolism.

_____ **6.** Patients who are at the highest risk of hemorrhagic stroke are those who have:

    A. untreated hypertension.

    B. hypotension.

    C. diabetes.

    D. atherosclerosis.

_____ **7.** Patients with a subarachnoid hemorrhage typically complain of a sudden severe:

    A. bout of dizziness.

    B. headache.

    C. altered mental status.

    D. thirst.

_____ **8.** The plaque that builds up in atherosclerosis obstructs blood flow and interferes with the vessel's ability to:

    A. constrict.

    B. dilate.

    C. diffuse.

    D. exchange gases.

_____ **9.** A TIA, or mini-stroke, is the name given to a stroke when symptoms go away on their own in less than:

    A. half an hour.

    B. 1 hour.

    C. 12 hours.

    D. 24 hours.

_____ **10.** Patients with a decreased level of consciousness:

    A. should not be given anything by mouth.

    B. should be given glucose regardless of the underlying condition.

    C. do not require medical care.

    D. require immediate assessment of their pupils.

_____ **11.** Hypoglycemia can mimic conditions such as:

    A. cystic fibrosis.

    B. myocardial infarction.

    C. high fevers.

    D. stroke.

_____ **12.** When assessing a patient with a history of seizure activity, it is important to:

    A. determine whether this episode differs from any previous ones.

    B. ask if the patient has had any recent surgeries.

    C. assess whether the patient has swallowed his or her tongue.

    D. ask whether anyone else in the household has had a seizure.

_____ **13.** Signs and symptoms of possible seizure activity include all the following EXCEPT:

    A. altered mental status.

    B. incontinence.

    C. muscle rigidity and twitching.

    D. petechiae.

_____ **14.** Common causes of altered mental status include all of the following EXCEPT:

    A. body temperature abnormalities.

    B. hypoxia.

    C. unequal pupils.

    D. hypoglycemia.

_____ **15.** The principal difference between a patient who has had a stroke and a patient with hypoglycemia almost always has to do with the:

    A. papillary response.

    B. mental status.

    C. blood pressure.

    D. capillary refill time.

_____ **16.** Consider the possibility of _____ in a patient who has had a seizure.

    A. hyperkalemia

    B. hyperglycemia

    C. hypoglycemia

    D. hypertension

_____ **17.** _____ are the second most common type of headache and are thought to be caused by changes in blood vessel size in the base of the brain.

    A. Sinus headaches

    B. Tension headaches

    C. Migraine headaches

    D. Compression headaches

_____ **18.** Headache, vomiting, altered mental status, and seizures are all considered early signs of:

    A. increased intracranial pressure.

    B. decreased intracranial pressure.

    C. increased extracranial pressure.

    D. decreased extracranial pressure.

_____ **19.** People with _____ have a higher risk of hemorrhagic stroke.

    A. uncontrolled hyperglycemia

    B. uncontrolled hypertension

    C. high fevers

    D. meningitis

_____ **20.** Headaches caused by muscle contractions in the head and neck are typically associated with:

    A. sinus headaches.

    B. migraine headaches.

    C. compression headaches.

    D. tension headaches.

_____ **21.** The following conditions may simulate a stroke EXCEPT:

    A. hyperglycemia.

    B. a postictal state.

    C. hypoglycemia.

    D. subdural bleeding.

_____ **22.** When assessing a patient with a possible CVA, you should check the _____ first.

    A. pulse

    B. airway

    C. pupils

    D. blood pressure

_____ **23.** A _____ is usually a warning sign that a larger, significant stroke may occur in the future.

    A. heart attack

    B. seizure

    C. transient ischemic attack

    D. migraine headache

_____ **24.** Which mnemonic is used to check a patient's mental status?

    A. OPQRST

    B. SAMPLE

    C. AVPU

    D. PEARRL

Questions 25-29 are derived from the following scenario: You are called to a home and find a 56-year-old woman supine in her bed. She appears alert but has slurred speech. Her family tells you she has a history of TIAs and hypertension.

_____ **25.** How would you best determine the probability of this patient having a stroke?

    A. By using AVPU

    B. By using the Cincinnati Prehospital Stroke Scale

    C. By using the Glasgow Coma Scale

    D. By assessing her blood glucose

_____ **26.** Which of the following would NOT be pertinent information regarding her condition?

    A. Knowing the time of onset of symptoms

    B. Gathering a list of patient medications

    C. Determining if the patient has a facial droop

    D. Asking the patient about childhood illnesses

_____ **27.** You ask the patient, "What day is it today?" Her reply is "butterfly." Which area of the brain is likely affected?

    A. Occipital lobe

    B. Left hemisphere

    C. Cerebellum

    D. Right hemisphere

_____ **28.** If the receiving facility told you the cause of her stroke was due to a buildup of calcium and cholesterol, forming a plaque inside the walls of her blood vessels, you would know that this patient has:

    A. atherosclerosis.

    B. multiple sclerosis.

    C. polyarteritis.

    D. liver dysfunction.

_____ **29.** Treatment for this patient should include all of the following EXCEPT:

    A. providing oxygen to maintain Sp_{O_2} of at least 94%.

    B. providing rapid transport.

    C. continuously talking to the patient.

    D. providing oral glucose.

True/False

If you believe the statement to be more true than false, write the letter "T" in the space provided. If you believe the statement to be more false than true, write the letter "F."

_____ **1.** The postictal state following a seizure commonly lasts only about 3 to 5 minutes.

_____ **2.** A low oxygen level can affect the entire brain, often causing anxiety, restlessness, and confusion.

_____ **3.** Febrile seizures result from sudden high fevers and are generally well tolerated by children.

_____ **4.** Hemiparesis is the inability to speak or understand speech.

_____ **5.** Patients with migraine headaches are sometimes sensitive to light and sound.

_____ **6.** Right-sided facial droop is most likely an indication of a problem in the right cerebral hemisphere.

_____ **7.** Serious conditions that include headache as a symptom are hemorrhagic stroke, brain tumors, and meningitis.

_____ **8.** A cerebral embolism is an obstruction of a cerebral artery caused by a clot that was formed somewhere else and traveled to the brain.

_____ **9.** Hemorrhagic stroke is the most common type of stroke.

_____ **10.** Patients with a stroke affecting the right hemisphere of the brain can usually understand language but their speech may be slurred.

_____ **11.** A patient who has bleeding in the brain may have very low blood pressure.

_____ **12.** All seizures involve muscle twitching and general convulsions.

_____ **13.** A patient having a seizure may become cyanotic from a lack of oxygen.

_____ **14.** Patients with a decreased level of consciousness should not be given anything by mouth.

_____ **15.** Hyperglycemia should be considered in a patient following an MVC with an altered mental status.

_____ **16.** Psychological problems and complications of medications can cause altered mental status.

_____ **17.** Patients who have had a stroke can lose their airway or stop breathing without warning.

_____ **18.** You should wait until you get an accurate pulse oximeter reading on a seizure patient before administering oxygen.

_____ **19.** Letting the hospital know the specifics regarding the patient's neurologic symptoms is generally not important.

_____ **20.** A key piece of information to document is the time of onset of the patient's signs and symptoms.

Fill-in-the-Blank

Read each item carefully and then complete the statement by filling in the missing words.

1. There are _____ cranial nerves.

2. Playing the piano is coordinated by the _____.

3. The two main types of strokes are _____ and _____.

4. The brain is most sensitive to _____, _____, and _____ levels.

5. An incident in which you have more than one patient complaining of a headache may indicate _____

   _____ _____.

6. A(n) _____ _____ seizure may cause twitching of the extremity muscles that may spread slowly to

   another body part.

7. Each hemisphere of the cerebrum controls activities on the _____ side of the body.

8. Complex partial seizures result from abnormal discharges from the _____ lobe of the brain.

9. _____ is a loss of bowel and bladder control and can be due to a generalized seizure.

10. Dilantin and Tegretol are medicines used to control _____ _____.

11. A period following a seizure in which the muscles relax and the breathing becomes labored is called a(n) _____

    _____.

12. Weakness on one side of the body is known as _____.

13. A person who was eating prior to having a seizure may have a(n) _____ _____ _____.

14. All patients with an altered mental status should have a(n) _____ _____ _____ score

    calculated.

15. _____ _____ may reverse stroke symptoms and even stop the stroke if given within 3 to 6 hours of the

    onset of symptoms.

Labeling

Label the following diagrams with the correct terms.

1. Brain

A. _____

B. _____

C. _____

D. _____

E. _____

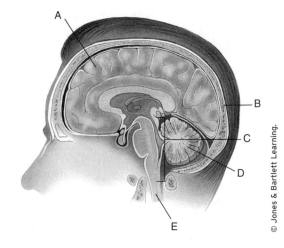

© Jones & Bartlett Learning.

2. Spinal Cord

A. _____

B. _____

C. _____

D. _____

E. _____

F. _____

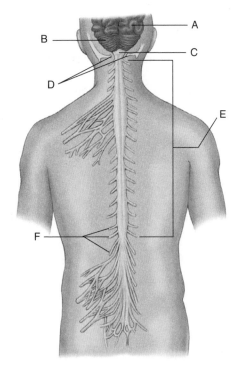

© Jones & Bartlett Learning.

Crossword Puzzle

The following crossword puzzle is an activity provided to reinforce correct spelling and understanding of medical terminology associated with emergency care and the EMT. Use the clues in the column to complete the puzzle.

Across

1. A(n) _____ seizure features rhythmic back-and-forth motion of an extremity and body stiffness.
3. Slurred speech.
6. _____ seizures result from sudden high fevers, particularly in children.
11. Clotting that forms in a remote area and travels to the site of blockage.
13. Weakness on one side of the body.
15. A disorder of the brain in which brain cells temporarily stop working because of insufficient oxygen, causing strokelike symptoms that resolve completely within 24 hours of onset.
16. A state of profound unconsciousness from which one cannot be roused.
17. A(n) _____ seizure is characterized by severe twitching of all of the body's muscles that may last several minutes or more.

Down

2. A stroke.
4. Clotting of the cerebral arteries that may result in the interruption of cerebral blood flow and subsequent stroke.
5. A sensation that serves as a warning sign that a seizure is about to occur.
7. A lack of oxygen in the cells of the brain that causes them not to function properly.
8. A swelling or enlargement of part of a blood vessel, resulting from weakening of the vessel wall.
9. A(n) _____ seizure affects a limited portion of the brain.
10. The inability to understand and/or produce speech.
12. Generalized, uncoordinated muscular activity associated with loss of consciousness.
14. An interruption of blood flow to the brain that results in the loss of brain function.

Critical Thinking

Short Answer

Complete this section with short written answers using the space provided.

1. Discuss the Cincinnati Prehospital Stroke Scale, including normal and abnormal findings.

   _____

   _____

   _____

2. Why is prompt transport of stroke patients critical?

   _____

   _____

   _____

3. Describe the characteristics of a postictal state.

   _____

   _____

   _____

4. What is the difference between a simple partial and a complex partial seizure?

   _____

   _____

   _____

5. List three conditions that may simulate stroke.

   _____

   _____

   _____

6. Determine the Glasgow Coma Scale score for the following patients.

_____ **A.** You respond to the scene of a 45-year-old woman with hypoglycemia. As you walk into the room, the patient looks at you and smiles. The patient is oriented to place but does not know the day of the week or the year. When you ask the patient to raise her arms, she smiles at you. When you pinch her hand, she pushes your hand away and says, "Ouch."

_____ **B.** You are at a nursing home where an 84-year-old man was found on the floor next to his bed having a seizure. The patient is now postictal and opens his eyes when you pinch his hand. When you ask the patient whether he remembers what happened, he responds with garbled speech. The patient is unable to follow your commands but pulls away when you pinch his hand.

        C. You respond to the scene of an MVC. On arrival, you find a 25-year-old man who was ejected from his vehicle as it rolled down an embankment. The patient fails to open his eyes to any external stimuli. The bystanders state that he has been unresponsive since the crash and has not moved. You place an oral airway into the patient and continue to manage his airway and provide cervical spine immobilization. You attempt multiple times to elicit a painful response; however, the patient does not move his extremities or open his eyes.

_____ **D.** You and your partner are eating at a local restaurant when your server tells you the manager is not feeling well. As you approach the manager, he apologizes to you for interrupting your meal. The patient tells you that he has not felt right since he opened the restaurant this morning. The manager is able to tell you the daily specials on the menu and is able to roll up his sleeves so you can take a blood pressure.

Ambulance Calls

The following case scenarios provide an opportunity to explore the concerns associated with patient management and to enhance critical-thinking skills. Read each scenario and answer each question to the best of your ability.

1. You are dispatched to a private residence for a "confused man." You arrive to find an older man sitting in a recliner. As you begin your assessment, you notice that he has right-sided weakness and does not seem to understand your questions. He is alone in the home, and it appears that no one lives with him in the residence.

   How would you best manage this patient?

   _____

   _____

   _____

2. You are dispatched to a 36-year-old man who had seizure activity at least an hour ago. The patient is incontinent, cold, clammy, and unresponsive. His friends tell you that the "shaking" stopped and he has not woken up. They thought he might just be tired until they discovered they could not wake him. He has no history of seizure activity. He has diabetes for which he takes medication.

   How would you best manage this patient?

   _____

   _____

   _____

3. You are dispatched to a local business for "woman with severe headache." The 55-year-old patient states that she has had headaches in the past, but this headache is the worst she has ever had in her life. She feels like the room is spinning around, she is seeing "double," and she feels sick to her stomach. She has a history of hypertension. She tells you that she stopped taking her blood pressure medicine about 6 to 8 months ago because she could no longer afford it.

   How would you best manage this patient?

   _____

   _____

   _____

4. You are dispatched to a local shopping center for a 42-year-old woman who is having a seizure. On arrival, you find your patient alert and sitting in a chair. The patient has a GCS score of 15 and states that it has been a few months since she has had a seizure. The patient states that she feels fine and does not want to go to the hospital.

   How would you manage this situation?

   _____

   _____

   _____

Skills

Assessment Review

Answer the following questions pertaining to the types of emergencies discussed in this chapter.

Questions 1–4 are derived from the following scenario: You are dispatched to a local residence for a change in mental status. On arrival, you find a 67-year-old man sitting at his kitchen table. The patient seems to be having trouble speaking and is leaning to his left. The patient's wife called 9-1-1 because she thought her husband was having a stroke.

_____   **1.** Which of the following is NOT part of the Cincinnati Prehospital Stroke Scale criteria?

    A. Facial droop

    B. Speech

    C. Gait

    D. Arm drift

_____   **2.** The patient's wife tells you the patient has a history of hypertension, myocardial infarction, renal failure, diabetes, and GERD. Based on the patient's history, what are possible conditions that could explain his symptoms?

    A. Heart attack

    B. Hypoglycemia

    C. Hyperglycemia

    D. Hyperkalemia

_____   **3.** As you are packaging the patient, the wife says she called 9-1-1 right away because she read about how time was an important factor with stroke patients. With regard to thrombolytic therapy at the hospital, what is the timeline that will allow this therapy to be most effective?

    A. Given within 3 hours of symptom onset

    B. Given within 12 hours of symptom onset

    C. Given within the first 24 hours of symptom onset

    D. There is no optimal time requirement for this treatment.

_____   **4.** While transporting the patient to the hospital, his left-sided weakness and speech improve. By the time you reach the hospital, the patient appears almost normal. Which of the following is most likely to be the underlying cause of the patient's condition?

    A. Hemorrhagic stroke

    B. Ischemic stroke

    C. Transient ischemic attack

    D. Partial simple seizure

CHAPTER

18

Gastrointestinal and Urologic Emergencies

© Photos.com

General Knowledge

Matching

Match each of the items in the left column to the appropriate definition in the right column.

_____ 1. Aneurysm

_____ 2. Cholecystitis

_____ 3. Retroperitoneal

_____ 4. Ulcer

_____ 5. Hernia

_____ 6. Ileus

_____ 7. Guarding

_____ 8. Uremia

_____ 9. Emesis

_____ 10. Referred pain

_____ 11. Acute abdomen

_____ 12. Cystitis

_____ 13. Strangulation

_____ 14. Peritonitis

_____ 15. Peritoneum

A. Paralysis of the bowel

B. Pain felt in an area of the body other than the actual source

C. Protective, involuntary abdominal muscle contractions

D. Inflammation of the gallbladder

E. Behind the peritoneum

F. Vomiting

G. A condition of sudden onset of pain within the abdomen

H. A membrane lining the abdomen

I. Swelling or enlargement of a weakened arterial wall

J. Buildup of waste products in the blood as a result of kidney failure

K. Protrusion of a loop of an organ or tissue through an abnormal body opening

L. Obstruction of blood circulation resulting from compression or entrapment of organ tissue

M. Erosion of the stomach or small intestinal lining

N. Inflammation of the bladder

O. Inflammation of the peritoneum

Match the condition in the left column with the appropriate localization of pain in the right column.

_____ 16. Appendicitis

_____ 17. Cholecystitis

_____ 18. Ulcer

_____ 19. Diverticulitis

_____ 20. Abdominal aortic aneurysm

_____ 21. Cystitis

_____ 22. Kidney infection

_____ 23. Kidney stone

_____ 24. Pancreatitis

_____ 25. Peritonitis

A. Lower midabdomen (retropubic)

B. Right upper quadrant (direct); right shoulder (referred)

C. Upper abdomen (both quadrants); back

D. Costovertebral angle

E. Low part of back and lower quadrants

F. Right lower quadrant (direct); around navel (referred); rebounding pain

G. Anywhere in the abdominal area

H. Right or left flank, radiating to genitalia

I. Left lower quadrant

J. Upper midabdomen or upper part of back

Multiple Choice

Read each item carefully and then select the one best response.

_____ 1. Peritonitis, with associated fluid loss, is the result of:

A. abnormal shift of fluid from body tissue into the bloodstream.

B. abnormal shift of fluid from the bloodstream into body tissue.

C. normal shift of fluid from body tissue into the bloodstream.

D. normal shift of fluid from the bloodstream into body tissue.

_____ 2. Distention of the abdomen is gauged by:
  A. visualization.
  B. auscultation.
  C. palpation.
  D. the patient's complaint of pain around the umbilicus.

_____ 3. A hernia that returns to its proper body cavity is said to be:
  A. reducible.
  B. extractable.
  C. incarcerated.
  D. replaceable.

_____ 4. A patient who presents with vomiting, signs of shock, and history of eating disorder and alcohol abuse is likely to be suffering from:
  A. diverticulitis.
  B. Mallory-Weiss Syndrome.
  C. appendicitis.
  D. cholecystitis.

_____ 5. When an organ of the abdomen is enlarged, rough palpation may cause _____ of the organ.
  A. distention
  B. nausea
  C. swelling
  D. rupture

_____ 6. Severe back pain may be associated with which of the following conditions?
  A. Abdominal aortic aneurysm
  B. PID
  C. Appendicitis
  D. Mittelschmerz

_____ 7. The _____ are found in the retroperitoneal space.
  A. stomach and gallbladder
  B. kidneys, ovaries, and pancreas
  C. liver and pancreas
  D. adrenal glands and uterus

_____ 8. _____ can be caused by an obstructing gallstone, alcohol abuse, and other diseases.
  A. Appendicitis
  B. A peptic ulcer
  C. Pancreatitis
  D. Diverticulitis

_____ 9. _____ commonly produces symptoms about 30 minutes after a particularly fatty meal and usually at night.
  A. A peptic ulcer
  B. Cholecystitis
  C. Appendicitis
  D. Pancreatitis

_____ 10. Which of the following is NOT a common disease that produces signs of an acute abdomen?
  A. Diverticulitis
  B. Cholecystitis
  C. Acute appendicitis
  D. Glomerulonephritis

_____ **11.** _____ occur(s) when there is excess pressure within the portal system and surrounding vessel; may lead to life-threatening bleeding.

    A. Esophageal rupture

    B. Esophageal varices

    C. Esophageal ulcers

    D. Esophageal reflux

Questions 12–16 are derived from the following scenario: You have been dispatched to the home of a 52-year-old woman with severe flank pain.

_____ **12.** Which of the following would be an appropriate question to ask regarding the pain?

    A. Have you experienced any belching?

    B. Do you feel nauseous?

    C. Is the pain constant or intermittent?

    D. Have you been urinating more or less?

_____ **13.** The patient tells you that she has right flank pain that radiates into her groin. What is the most likely cause of her condition?

    A. Cholecystitis

    B. Ileus

    C. Appendicitis

    D. Kidney stone

_____ **14.** In addition to the patient's presentation, which of the following would NOT be an additional expected sign or symptom?

    A. Diarrhea

    B. Hematuria

    C. Nausea

    D. Vomiting

_____ **15.** You should transport her:

    A. in a position of comfort.

    B. supine.

    C. left lateral recumbent.

    D. in the recovery position.

_____ **16.** Which of the following is NOT a function of the liver?

    A. It filters toxic substances.

    B. It creates glucose stores.

    C. It acts as a reservoir for bile.

    D. It produces substances for blood clotting.

_____ **17.** A patient presents with lower quadrant abdominal pain, tenderness above the pubic bone, and frequent urination with urgency. What is the most likely underlying condition?

    A. Cholecystitis

    B. Cystitis

    C. Gastroenteritis

    D. Diverticulitis

_____ **18.** Infected pouches in the lining of the colon are described as:

    A. cholecystitis.

    B. cystitis.

    C. gastroenteritis.

    D. diverticulitis.

_____   **19.** Pregnancy, straining at stool, and chronic constipation cause increased pressure that could result in:

    A. Mallory-Weiss Syndrome.

    B. diverticulitis.

    C. hemorrhoids.

    D. gallstones.

_____   **20.** Diarrhea is the principal symptom in:

    A. gastroenteritis.

    B. esophagitis.

    C. pancreatitis.

    D. peptic ulcers.

_____   **21.** Bowel inflammation, diverticulitis, and hemorrhoids are common causes of bleeding in the:

    A. upper GI tract.

    B. middle GI tract.

    C. lower GI tract.

    D. urinary tract.

_____   **22.** A patient complains of heartburn, pain with swallowing, and feeling like an object is stuck in the throat. Which of the following is the most likely cause?

    A. Esophageal varices

    B. Esophagitis

    C. Peptic ulcer

    D. Gastroenteritis

_____   **23.** Pain that initially starts in the umbilical area and then later moves to the lower right quadrant is typically associated with:

    A. gastroenteritis.

    B. pancreatitis.

    C. appendicitis.

    D. diverticulitis.

_____   **24.** When the abdominal muscles become rigid in an effort to protect the abdomen from further irritation, this is referred to as:

    A. guarding.

    B. tenderness.

    C. rebound tenderness.

    D. referred pain.

_____   **25.** If a patient misses a dialysis treatment, weakness and _____ can be the first in a series of conditions that can become progressively more serious.

    A. diarrhea

    B. chest pain

    C. vomiting

    D. pulmonary edema

_____   **26.** _____ regulates the amount of glucose in the bloodstream.

    A. Bicarbonate

    B. Amylase

    C. Insulin

    D. Bile

_____   **27.** Regulation of acidity and blood pressure is largely attributed to the:

    A. liver.

    B. kidneys.

    C. gallbladder.

    D. pancreas.

_____ **28.** Which of the following organs is part of the lymphatic system and plays a role in regulation of red blood cells and the immune system?
  A. Bladder
  B. Liver
  C. Spleen
  D. Pancreas

_____ **29.** Which of the following is NOT part of the male reproductive system?
  A. Epididymis
  B. Prostate gland
  C. Seminal vesicles
  D. Fallopian tubes

_____ **30.** _____ is responsible for the breakdown of starches into sugar.
  A. Insulin
  B. Bile
  C. Amylase
  D. Bicarbonate

True/False

If you believe the statement to be more true than false, write the letter "T" in the space provided. If you believe the statement to be more false than true, write the letter "F."

_____ **1.** Referred pain is a result of connection between ligaments in the abdominal and chest cavities.

_____ **2.** The adverse effects of dialysis include hypotension, muscle cramps, nausea and vomiting, and hemorrhage and infection at the access site.

_____ **3.** Questioning about bowel habits and flatulence is not necessary and considered unprofessional.

_____ **4.** If a female is of childbearing age, you should question her about her last menstrual period.

_____ **5.** The parietal peritoneum lines the walls of the abdominal cavity.

_____ **6.** Peritonitis is associated with a loss of blood from the abdominal cavity.

_____ **7.** When palpating the abdomen, always start with the quadrant where the patient complains of the most severe pain.

_____ **8.** Massive hemorrhaging is associated with rupture of an abdominal aortic aneurysm.

_____ **9.** Peptic ulcer disease affects both men and women equally.

_____ **10.** Patients with abdominal pain should be placed in a position of comfort but should not be given oxygen unless they show signs of shock.

Labeling

Label the following diagrams with the correct terms.

1. Solid Organs

A. _____

B. _____

C. _____

D. _____

E. _____

F. _____

2. Hollow Organs

A. _____

B. _____

C. _____

D. _____

E. _____

F. _____

G. _____

H. _____

© Jones & Bartlett Learning.

3. Urinary System

A. _____

B. _____

C. _____

D. _____

E. _____

F. _____

G. _____

H. _____

© Jones & Bartlett Learning.

Crossword Puzzle

The following crossword puzzle is an activity provided to reinforce correct spelling and understanding of medical terminology associated with emergency care and the EMT. Use the clues in the column to complete the puzzle.

Across

4. Vomiting.

6. Involuntary muscle contractions (spasm) of the abdominal wall.

9. Inflammation in small pockets at weak areas in the muscle walls.

10. _____ abdomen is a condition of sudden onset of pain within the abdomen, usually indicating peritonitis.

12. The protrusion of a loop of an organ or tissue through an abnormal body opening.

13. Inflammation of the peritoneum.

Down

1. Paralysis of the bowel; stops contractions that move material through the intestine.

2. Pain felt in an area of the body other than the area where the cause of pain is located.

3. Solid crystalline masses formed in the kidney, resulting from an excess of insoluble salts or uric acid crystallizing in the urine.

5. Complete obstruction of blood circulation in a given organ as a result of compression or entrapment.

7. Severe kidney failure resulting in the buildup of waste products within the blood.

8. Inflammation of the bladder.

11. An infection, usually of the lower urinary tract (urethra and bladder), that occurs when normal bacterial flora enter the urethra and grow.

Critical Thinking

Short Answer

Complete this section with short written answers using the space provided.

1. Explain the phenomenon of referred pain.

_____

_____

_____

2. List questions to ask yourself when reassessing a patient with abdominal pain.

_____

_____

_____

3. Why does abdominal distention accompany ileus?

_____

_____

_____

4. Explain the steps used to physically assess the abdomen.

_____

_____

_____

Ambulance Calls

The following case scenarios provide an opportunity to explore the concerns associated with patient management and to enhance critical-thinking skills. Read each scenario and answer each question to the best of your ability.

1. You are called to the local high school nurse's office for a 16-year-old girl complaining of fever and abdominal pain that started around the umbilicus but now is localized to the right lower quadrant. The patient also complains of nausea and vomiting.

How would you best manage this patient?

_____

_____

_____

2. You are dispatched to a long-term care facility for a geriatric man with abdominal pain. On arrival, a staff member tells you that this patient has been bedridden and taking pain medications for the last several weeks. Recently, he's had problems passing a normal bowel movement. He now has a distended, tender abdomen with nausea, vomiting, and tachycardia.

How would you best manage this patient?

_____

_____

_____

3. You are dispatched to the home of another responder for "severe back pain." You arrive to find your coworker writhing in pain on the floor. He tells you that when he tried to urinate (unsuccessfully), he immediately experienced a sharp, cramping sensation in his right side. As you are talking to him he vomits. After vomiting, he tells you the pain is worse and is now spreading to his groin.

How would you best manage this patient?

_____

_____

_____

Skills

Assessment Review

Answer the following questions pertaining to the assessment of the types of emergencies discussed in this chapter.

Questions 1-5 are derived from the following scenario: You respond to the home of a 46-year-old male complaining of severe back pain. You find the patient in the fetal position in obvious pain. He tells you that his pain is along his right flank and radiates to his groin.

_____ 1. What will you NOT be able to determine during the primary assessment?

    A. The priority of care

    B. The patient's level of consciousness

    C. Finding and treating any life threats

    D. Patient history

_____ 2. Your partner obtains a SAMPLE history. Which question(s) should she ask?

    A. "Do you know what medications you are currently taking?"

    B. "Where is your wife?"

    C. "Have you traveled out of the country recently?"

    D. "Rate your pain on a scale from 1 to 10."

_____ 3. Which of the following questions would be appropriate given the patient's presentation?

    A. "Do you have a headache?"

    B. "Do you have pain when you urinate?"

    C. "How long have you lived here?"

    D. "When was your last tetanus shot?"

_____ 4. On examination of the abdomen, you should:

    A. expose the abdomen and visually assess it.

    B. palpate the painful area first.

    C. place the patient in a semi-Fowler's position.

    D. palpate without watching the patient's face.

_____ 5. During your reassessment, you should do all of the following EXCEPT:

    A. repeat the primary assessment.

    B. repeat the secondary assessment.

    C. reassure the patient.

    D. make your initial transport decision.

Endocrine and Hematologic Emergencies

© Photos.com

General Knowledge

Matching

Match each of the items in the left column to the appropriate definition in the right column.

_____ 1. Hormone
_____ 2. Sickle cell disease
_____ 3. Type 1 diabetes
_____ 4. Acidosis
_____ 5. Insulin
_____ 6. Symptomatic hyperglycemia
_____ 7. Polyuria
_____ 8. Thrombophilia
_____ 9. Polyphagia
_____ 10. Hematology
_____ 11. Glucose
_____ 12. Kussmaul respirations
_____ 13. Hyperglycemia
_____ 14. Diabetes mellitus
_____ 15. Polydipsia
_____ 16. Hemophilia
_____ 17. Type 2 diabetes

A. Inherited disease that affects red blood cells
B. Study of blood-related diseases
C. Diabetes that usually starts in childhood; requires insulin
D. Excessive eating
E. Deep, rapid breathing
F. Excessive urination
G. A tendency to develop blood clots
H. Excessive thirst persisting for a long period of time
I. Diabetes with onset later in life; may be controlled by diet and oral medication
J. Chemical produced by a gland that regulates body organs
K. Metabolic disorder in which the ability to metabolize carbohydrates is impaired
L. Extremely high blood glucose level
M. Pathologic condition resulting from the accumulation of acids in the body
N. Disorder that causes an inability to develop blood clots
O. Hormone that enables glucose to enter the cells
P. Primary fuel, along with oxygen, for cellular metabolism
Q. State of unconsciousness resulting from several problems, including ketoacidosis, dehydration, and hyperglycemia

Multiple Choice

Read each item carefully and then select the one best response.

_____ 1. When the body's cells do not receive the glucose they require, the body resorts to burning _____ for energy.
A. fats
B. proteins
C. blood cells
D. ketones

_____ 2. Normal blood glucose levels range from _____ mg/dL.
A. 80 to 120
B. 90 to 140
C. 70 to 110
D. 60 to 100

_____ 3. A sickle cell-related issue that results in unintentional clot formation is know as a(n):
A. hemolytic crisis.
B. aplastic crisis.
C. splenic sequestration crisis.
D. vasoocclusive crisis.

_____ 4. Diabetes mellitus is a metabolic disorder in which the hormone _____ is missing or ineffective.
   A. estrogen
   B. adrenaline
   C. insulin
   D. epinephrine

_____ 5. Emergency care of a patient with hematologic disorder includes all of the following EXCEPT:
   A. rapid transport for patients with an altered mental status.
   B. providing supportive and symptomatic care.
   C. oxygen at 4 L/min for patients with inadequate breathing.
   D. placing patients in a position of comfort.

_____ 6. The accumulation of ketones and fatty acids in blood tissue can lead to a dangerous condition in diabetic patients known as:
   A. diabetic ketoacidosis.
   B. insulin shock.
   C. HHNC.
   D. hypoglycemia.

_____ 7. The term for excessive eating as a result of cellular "hunger" is:
   A. polyuria.
   B. polydipsia.
   C. polyphagia.
   D. polyphony.

_____ 8. Insulin is produced by the:
   A. adrenal glands.
   B. hypothalamus.
   C. spleen.
   D. pancreas.

_____ 9. The patient with diabetic ketoacidosis (DKA) will generally have a fingerstick glucose level higher than:
   A. 100 mg/dL.
   B. 200 mg/dL.
   C. 300 mg/dL.
   D. 400 mg/dL.

_____ 10. Where is glycogen stored in the body?
   A. Liver
   B. Brain
   C. Pancreas
   D. Heart

_____ 11. The sweet or fruity odor on the breath of a patient is commonly found in what condition?
   A. Hypoglycemia
   B. Hyperglycemia
   C. Hemophilia
   D. Thrombophilia

_____ 12. What condition increases a patient's risk for developing thrombophilia?
   A. Diabetes
   B. Sickle cell disease
   C. Cirrhosis of the liver
   D. Cancer

_____ **13.** Oral diabetic medications do NOT include:

    A. Micronase.

    B. Glucotrol.

    C. Januvia.

    D. insulin.

_____ **14.** Which of the following is a contraindication to the administration of oral glucose?

    A. Inability to swallow

    B. History of diabetic ketoacidosis

    C. Active infection

    D. Recent abdominal surgery

_____ **15.** _____ is the hormone that is normally produced by the pancreas that enables glucose to enter the cells.

    A. Insulin

    B. Adrenaline

    C. Estrogen

    D. Epinephrine

_____ **16.** The term for excessive urination is:

    A. polyuria.

    B. polydipsia.

    C. polyphagia.

    D. polyphony.

_____ **17.** When fat is used as an immediate energy source, _____ and fatty acids are formed as waste products.

    A. dextrose

    B. sucrose

    C. ketones

    D. bicarbonate

_____ **18.** An African American patient complaining of severe, generalized pain may have undiagnosed:

    A. sickle cell disease.

    B. type 1 diabetes.

    C. thrombopenia.

    D. hemophilia.

_____ **19.** The onset of hypoglycemia can occur within:

    A. seconds.

    B. minutes.

    C. hours.

    D. days.

_____ **20.** Without _____, or with very low levels, brain cells rapidly suffer permanent damage.

    A. epinephrine

    B. ketones

    C. bicarbonate

    D. glucose

_____ **21.** _____ is/are a potentially life-threatening complication of hypoglycemia.

    A. Kussmaul respirations

    B. Hypotension

    C. Seizures

    D. Polydipsia

_____ **22.** Blood glucose levels are measured in:
   A. micrograms per deciliter.
   B. milligrams per deciliter.
   C. milliliters per decigram.
   D. microliters per decigram.

_____ **23.** Diabetic ketoacidosis may develop as a result of:
   A. too little insulin.
   B. too much insulin.
   C. overhydration.
   D. metabolic alkalosis.

_____ **24.** Always suspect hypoglycemia in any patient with:
   A. Kussmaul respirations.
   B. an altered mental status.
   C. nausea and vomiting.
   D. stridor.

_____ **25.** The most important step in caring for the unresponsive diabetic patient is to:
   A. give oral glucose immediately.
   B. perform a focused assessment.
   C. open the airway.
   D. obtain a SAMPLE history.

_____ **26.** Determination of hyperglycemia or hypoglycemia should be:
   A. made before transport of the patient.
   B. made before administration of oral glucose.
   C. determined by a urine glucose test.
   D. based on your knowledge of the signs and symptoms of each condition.

_____ **27.** When obtaining the medical history of a patient experiencing a sickle cell crisis, you should:
   A. determine the patient's level of consciousness.
   B. ask the patient about recent illnesses or stress.
   C. take the patient's vital signs.
   D. avoid asking about previous sickle cell crises.

_____ **28.** A DVT is a worrisome risk for patients who have had:
   A. gallbladder surgery.
   B. alcoholism.
   C. pneumonia.
   D. joint replacement surgery.

_____ **29.** When reassessing the diabetic patient after administration of oral glucose, watch for all of the following EXCEPT:
   A. airway problems.
   B. seizures.
   C. sudden loss of consciousness.
   D. joint pain.

_____ **30.** Signs and symptoms associated with hypoglycemia include:
   A. warm, dry skin.
   B. slow pulse.
   C. Kussmaul respirations.
   D. anxious or combative behavior.

_____   **31.** Hospital interventions for hemophilia may include all of the following EXCEPT:

    A. blood transfusions.

    B. analgesics for pain.

    C. intraveneous (IV) therapy.

    D. decontamination.

_____   **32.** Because hyperglycemia is a complex metabolic condition that usually develops over time and involves all of the tissues of the body, correcting this condition may:

    A. be accomplished quickly through the use of oral glucose.

    B. require rapid infusion of IV fluid to prevent permanent brain damage.

    C. take many hours in a hospital setting.

    D. include a reduction in the amount of insulin normally taken by the patient.

_____   **33.** A patient with hypoglycemia or hyperglycemia may appear to be:

    A. having a heart attack.

    B. perfectly normal.

    C. intoxicated.

    D. having a stroke.

True/False

If you believe the statement to be more true than false, write the letter "T" in the space provided. If you believe the statement to be more false than true, write the letter "F."

_____   **1.** When patients use fat for energy, the fat waste products increase the amount of acid in the blood and tissue.

_____   **2.** The glucose of a neonate patient should be above 70 mg/dL.

_____   **3.** The life span of a normal red blood cell is approximately 50 to 75 days.

_____   **4.** If blood glucose levels remain low, a patient may lose consciousness or have permanent brain damage.

_____   **5.** Higher glucose levels in the blood cause the excretion of glucose in urine.

_____   **6.** People with hemophilia A have an increased ability to create a clot after an injury.

_____   **7.** Diabetic emergencies can occur when a patient's blood glucose level gets too high or drops too low.

_____   **8.** Diabetic patients may require insulin to control their blood glucose.

_____   **9.** Insulin is one of the basic sugars essential for cell metabolism in humans.

_____   **10.** A clot that forms deep in a vein is called an aplastic crisis.

_____   **11.** Diabetes can cause kidney failure, blindness, and damage to blood vessels.

_____   **12.** Most children with diabetes are insulin dependent.

_____   **13.** Within the red blood cells, leukocytes are responsible for carrying oxygen.

_____   **14.** Many adults with diabetes can control their blood glucose levels with diet alone.

Fill-in-the-Blank

Read each item carefully and then complete the statement by filling in the missing words.

1. The full name of diabetes is _____ _____.

2. _____ is a general term for many different conditions that result in the blood clotting more easily than normal.

3. Type 1 diabetes is considered to be a(n) _____ problem, in which the body becomes allergic to its own tissues and literally destroys them.

4. An African American patient or any patient of _____ descent who complains of severe pain may have undiagnosed _____ _____ disease.

5. Diabetes is defined as a lack of or _____ action of insulin.

6. In _____, the patient cannot drink enough fluid to keep up with the exceedingly high glucose levels in the blood.

7. _____ is the study and prevention of blood-_____ diseases.

8. A patient with hypoglycemia needs _____ immediately, and a patient with hyperglycemia needs _____ and IV fluid therapy.

Fill-in-the-Table

	Hyperglycemia	Hypoglycemia
History		
Onset		
Skin		
Infection		
Gastrointestinal Tract		
Thirst		
Hunger		
Vomiting/abdominal pain		
Respiratory System		
Breathing		
Odor of breath		
Cardiovascular System		
Blood pressure		
Pulse		
Nervous System		
Consciousness		
Treatment		
Response		

Crossword Puzzle

The following crossword puzzle is an activity provided to reinforce correct spelling and understanding of medical terminology associated with emergency care and the EMT. Use the clues in the column to complete the puzzle.

Across

2. A tendency to develop blood clots as a result of an abnormality of the coagulation system.

4. The passage of an unusually large volume of urine in a given period.

9. The study and prevention of blood-related disorders.

10. Glands that secrete or release chemicals that are used inside the body are known as _____ glands.

12. _____ mellitus is a metabolic disorder in which the ability to metabolize carbohydrates is impaired.

Down

1. Excessive thirst that persists for long periods, despite reasonable fluid intake.

2. _____ diabetes typically develops in later life and often can be controlled through diet and oral medications.

3. A hormone produced by the islets of Langerhans that enables glucose in the blood to enter cells.

5. A pathologic condition that results from the accumulation of acids in the body.

6. The primary fuel, in conjunction with oxygen, for cellular metabolism.

7. _____ diabetes typically develops in childhood and requires synthetic insulin for proper treatment and control.

8. A chemical substance produced by a gland that regulates the activity of organs and tissues.

11. A form of hyperglycemia in uncontrolled diabetes in which certain acids accumulate when insulin is not available.

Critical Thinking

Multiple Choice

Read each critical-thinking item carefully and then select the one best response.

Questions 1-4 are derived from the following scenario: A 54-year-old golfer collapsed on the 17th green at the golf course. His friend said he wasn't feeling well after the eighth hole but insisted on walking and finishing out the game. His skin is pale, cool, and diaphoretic, and he provides incoherent answers to your questions.

_____ 1. During your rapid full-body scan, you discover a medical alert necklace around his neck that reads "Type 1 Diabetic." This tells you that he most likely:

      A. developed diabetes later in life.

      B. produces inadequate amounts of insulin.

      C. takes noninsulin-type oral medications.

      D. will develop HHNS.

_____ 2. His blood glucose level is 65 mg/dL. You:

      A. do not suspect hypoglycemia and begin to think that his condition is cardiac in nature.

      B. suspect hyperglycemia and proceed to give oral glucose.

      C. suspect hypoglycemia and proceed to give oral glucose.

      D. suspect hypoglycemia but oral glucose is contraindicated for him.

_____ 3. The patient loses consciousness and a second blood glucose level reads 48 mg/dL. You should do all of the following EXCEPT:

      A. call for, or rendezvous with, an ALS unit.

      B. ensure a patent airway.

      C. provide high-flow oxygen.

      D. give oral glucose.

_____ 4. Because the patient is unconscious and his blood glucose level is 48 mg/dL, how should the glucose be delivered?

      A. Between the cheek and gum

      B. Placed on the back of the tongue

      C. Placed on the tip of the tongue

      D. You should not deliver oral glucose.

Short Answer

Complete this section with short written answers using the space provided.

1. What is insulin, and what is its role in metabolism?

_____

_____

_____

2. What are the preparations of commercially available oral glucose?

_____

_____

_____

3. What two basic complications are caused by the shape of the red blood cells in people with sickle cell disease?

_____

_____

_____

4. When should you not give oral glucose to a patient experiencing a suspected diabetic emergency?

_____

_____

_____

5. How can thrombophilia lead to a pulmonary embolism?

_____

_____

_____

6. List at least four key signs and symptoms of HHNS.

_____

_____

_____

7. When taking a history on a patient with known diabetes, what questions should be asked?

_____

_____

_____

8. If a diabetic patient was "fine" 2 hours ago and now is unconscious and unresponsive, which diabetes-related condition would you suspect and why?

_____

_____

_____

Ambulance Calls

The following case scenarios provide an opportunity to explore the concerns associated with patient management and to enhance critical-thinking skills. Read each scenario and answer each question to the best of your ability.

1. You are called to a local residence where you find a 22-year-old woman supine in bed, unresponsive to your attempts to rouse her. She is cold and clammy with gurgling respirations. Her mother tells you that her only history is diabetes, which she has had since she was a small child.

   How would you best manage this patient?

   _____

   _____

   _____

2. You are requested to respond to a local convenience store for an unknown medical problem. On arrival, you find a young African American man sitting on the curb, clutching his torso, and crying. He tells you that he is in severe pain and has a history of sickle cell disease.

   How would you best manage this patient?

   _____

   _____

   _____

3. You are dispatched to assist with a diabetic patient well known in your department for being noncompliant with his medications and diet. You have responded numerous times to his residence, all for instances of low blood sugar. Family members greet you at the door and say, "It's Jon again. Just give him some sugar like you usually do." You walk into the patient's bedroom to discover him unconscious with snoring respirations.

   How would you best manage this patient?

   _____

   _____

   _____

Fill-in-the-Patient Care Report

Read the incident scenario and then complete the following patient care report (PCR).

"Truck nine, trauma emergency," the dispatcher's voice bursts from the radio on your hip, drawing glances from several people around you in the grocery store.

"Go ahead to nine," your partner, Jerry, responds over the radio from somewhere else in the store.

"Truck nine, trauma emergency at 12556 Old Lake House Drive, for a laceration with uncontrolled bleeding. Showing you dispatched at 1752."

Within 3 minutes, both of you converge on the ambulance parked outside under a line of spruce trees and are en route through rush hour traffic to the subdivision on the east end of the town lake.

"Central, truck nine, we are on scene," you say quickly into the mic before opening your door and climbing from the truck.

"Showing you on scene at 1803," comes the muffled reply from the cab radio.

You are quickly ushered into the home and led by a frantic woman to an upstairs bedroom. As you pass through the door, you see a 14-year-old boy holding a blood-soaked T-shirt against his forearm. In front of him on a desk is a half-completed wooden model of an old pirate ship, now sprinkled with darkening blood.

"The blade slipped and he cut his arm," the boy's mother says rapidly. "Oh, please help him, he's got hemophilia!" You gently move the soaked T-shirt and see a 1-inch (3-cm) laceration that is bleeding profusely, running steadily down his arm and onto the carpet. You immediately apply pressure to the wound and direct Jerry to start high-flow oxygen therapy. You position the patient onto the stair chair and move him down to the wheeled stretcher in the living room, happy that he weighs only 132 pounds (60 kg).

Once on the gurney, you and Jerry cover the boy with a blanket and load him into the ambulance. You look at your watch (1813) and ask Jerry to get a quick blood pressure on the patient while you continue holding pressure on the wound.

"108 over 60," he says, before closing you in with the patient and climbing into the cab of the truck while you check his pulse and count 98 beats/min, get a respiratory rate of 16 breaths/min with good tidal volume, and a pulse oximetry reading of 96%. While en route to the hospital, you realize that the bleeding is just not going to stop with pressure, so you apply a tourniquet on the patient's arm and clearly document the time.

At 1819, Jerry backs into the trauma center's ambulance parking and you both roll the patient into the waiting trauma bay, where you turn him over to the waiting team and provide a verbal report.

Fill-in-the-Patient Care Report

EMS Patient Care Report (PCR)					
Date:	**Incident No.:**	**Nature of Call:**		**Location:**	
Dispatched:	**En Route:**	**At Scene:**	**Transport:**	**At Hospital:**	**In Service:**
Patient Information					
Age: **Sex:** **Weight (in kg [lb]):**			**Allergies:** **Medications:** **Past Medical History:** **Chief Complaint:**		
Vital Signs					
Time:	**BP:**	**Pulse:**	**Respirations:**	**Spo$_2$:**	
Time:	**BP:**	**Pulse:**	**Respirations:**	**Spo$_2$:**	
Time:	**BP:**	**Pulse:**	**Respirations:**	**Spo$_2$:**	
EMS Treatment **(circle all that apply)**					
Oxygen @ ___ L/min via (circle one): NC NRM BVM		**Assisted Ventilation**	**Airway Adjunct**	**CPR**	
Defibrillation	**Bleeding Control**	**Bandaging**	**Splinting**	**Other:**	
Narrative					

Skills

Skill Drills

Test your knowledge of this skill by filling in the correct words in the photo captions.

Skill Drill 19-1: Administering Glucose

© Jones & Bartlett Learning. Courtesy of MIEMSS.

© Jones & Bartlett Learning. Courtesy of MIEMSS.

© Jones & Bartlett Learning. Courtesy of MIEMSS.

1. Make sure that the tube of glucose is intact and has not _____.

2. Squeeze a generous amount of oral glucose onto the _____ _____ of a _____ _____ tongue depressor.

3. Open the patient's _____. Place the tongue depressor on the _____ _____ between the cheek and the gum with the _____ _____ next to the cheek. Repeat until the entire tube has been used.

Assessment Review

Answer the following questions pertaining to the assessment of the types of emergencies discussed in this chapter.

Questions 1–5 are derived from the following scenario: While driving back to the station, you and your partner find an unconscious person lying on the grass in front of a home.

_____ **1.** After completing a scene size-up, your first step is to:
   A. take appropriate BSI precautions.
   B. form a general impression of the patient.
   C. apply oxygen.
   D. None of the above.

_____ **2.** The patient appears to be a woman in her mid 30s, and she is unresponsive to verbal or painful stimulus. Because there is no one around, you are unable to complete a patient history. Which physical examination should you perform first?
   A. Focused physical examination
   B. Rapid full-body scan
   C. Detailed physical examination
   D. Blood glucose level

_____ **3.** Her respirations are 28 breaths/min, her pulse is 110 beats/min, and her blood pressure is 94/52 mm Hg. How should you intervene for her?
   A. Give her oral glucose.
   B. Give her insulin.
   C. Provide high-flow oxygen.
   D. All of the above.

_____ **4.** Your protocols do not allow you to measure blood glucose levels, and you are unsure as to the nature of her illness. You should:

    A. provide oral glucose anyway.

    B. provide insulin found in her purse.

    C. provide nitroglycerin found in her purse.

    D. None of the above.

_____ **5.** When relaying information to medical control, you should inform them of:

    A. the patient's condition.

    B. any changes of consciousness.

    C. any difficulty the patient may experience in breathing.

    D. All of the above.

Immunologic Emergencies

© Photos.com

General Knowledge

Matching

Match each of the items in the left column to the appropriate definition in the right column.

_____ **1.** Allergic reaction

_____ **2.** Leukotrienes

_____ **3.** Wheezing

_____ **4.** Urticaria

_____ **5.** Stridor

_____ **6.** Allergen

_____ **7.** Wheal

_____ **8.** Toxin

A. Substance made by the body; released in anaphylaxis

B. Harsh, high-pitched inspiratory sound, usually resulting from upper airway obstruction

C. Raised, swollen area on the skin resulting from an insect bite or allergic reaction

D. An exaggerated immune response to any substance

E. Multiple raised areas on the skin that itch or burn

F. A poison or harmful substance

G. Substance that causes an allergic reaction

H. High-pitched, whistling breath sound usually resulting from blockage of the airway and typically heard on expiration

Multiple Choice

Read each item carefully and then select the one best response.

_____ **1.** Steps for assisting a patient with administration of an EpiPen include:

  A. taking body substance isolation precautions.

  B. placing the tip of the auto-injector against the medial part of the patient's thigh.

  C. recapping the injector before placing it in the trash.

  D. holding the injector in place for 30 seconds.

_____ **2.** Which of the following is NOT one of the five common allergen categories?

  A. Food

  B. Insect bites

  C. Plants

  D. Environments

_____ **3.** Anaphylaxis is not always life threatening, but it typically involves:

  A. multiple organ systems.

  B. wheezing.

  C. urticaria.

  D. wheals.

_____ **4.** Signs and symptoms of insect stings or bites include all of the following, EXCEPT:

  A. swelling.

  B. ecchymosis.

  C. localized heat.

  D. wheals.

_____ **5.** Prolonged respiratory difficulty can cause _____, shock, and even death.
   A. tachypnea
   B. pulmonary edema
   C. tachycardia
   D. airway obstruction

_____ **6.** Speed is essential because in severe cases of anaphylaxis, _____ can occur rapidly.
   A. urticaria
   B. compensation
   C. death
   D. recovery

_____ **7.** Questions to ask when obtaining a history from a patient appearing to have an allergic reaction include:
   A. whether the patient has recently traveled.
   B. what the patient ate yesterday.
   C. asking bystanders if anyone else is ill.
   D. how the patient was exposed.

_____ **8.** The dosage of epinephrine in an adult EpiPen is:
   A. 0.10 mg.
   B. 0.15 mg.
   C. 0.30 mg.
   D. 0.50 mg.

_____ **9.** Epinephrine, whether made by the body or by a drug manufacturer, works rapidly to:
   A. decrease the pulse rate and blood pressure.
   B. increase an allergic reaction.
   C. increase wheezing.
   D. relieve bronchospasm.

_____ **10.** Because the stinger of the honeybee is barbed and remains in the wound, it can continue to inject venom for up to:
   A. 1 minute.
   B. 15 minutes.
   C. 20 minutes.
   D. several hours.

_____ **11.** You should not use tweezers or forceps to remove an embedded stinger because:
   A. squeezing may cause the stinger to inject more venom into the wound.
   B. the stinger may break off in the wound.
   C. the tweezers are not sterile and may cause infection.
   D. removing the stinger may cause bleeding.

_____ **12.** Your assessment of the patient experiencing an allergic reaction should include evaluations of all of the following EXCEPT the:
   A. respiratory system.
   B. circulatory system.
   C. skin.
   D. reproductive system.

_____ **13.** Eating certain foods, such as shellfish or nuts, may result in a relatively _____ reaction that still can be quite severe.
   A. mild
   B. fast
   C. slow
   D. rapid

_____ **14.** In dealing with allergy-related emergencies, you must be aware of the possibility of acute _____ and cardiovascular collapse.

    A. hypotension

    B. tachypnea

    C. airway obstruction

    D. shock

_____ **15.** Wheezing occurs because excessive _____ and mucus are secreted into the bronchial passages.

    A. fluid

    B. carbon dioxide

    C. blood

    D. oxygen.

True/False

If you believe the statement to be more true than false, write the letter "T" in the space provided. If you believe the statement to be more false than true, write the letter "F."

_____ **1.** Allergic reactions can occur in response to almost any substance.

_____ **2.** An allergic reaction occurs when the body has an immune response to a substance.

_____ **3.** Wheezing is a high-pitched breath sound, usually resulting from blockage of the airway, and is heard on expiration.

_____ **4.** For a patient appearing to have an allergic reaction, give 100% oxygen via nasal cannula.

Fill-in-the-Blank

Read each item carefully and then complete the statement by filling in the missing words.

1. Wheezing, a high-pitched, whistling breath sound that is typically heard on _____.

2. Small areas of generalized itching or burning that appear as multiple, small, raised areas on the skin are called _____.

3. The stinger of the honeybee is _____, so the bee cannot withdraw it.

4. A reaction involving the entire body is called _____.

5. The presence of _____ or respiratory distress indicates that the patient is having a severe enough allergic reaction to lead to death.

6. Epinephrine inhibits the allergic reaction by constricting the _____ _____.

7. Your ability to recognize and manage the many signs and symptoms of allergic reactions may be the only thing standing between a patient and _____ _____.

Crossword Puzzle

The following crossword puzzle is an activity provided to reinforce correct spelling and understanding of medical terminology associated with emergency care and the EMT. Use the clues in the column to complete the puzzle.

Across

1. Substances released by the immune system that are responsible for many of the symptoms of anaphylaxis, such as vasodilation.
6. Small spots of generalized itching and/or burning that appear as multiple raised areas on the skin.
8. The _____ system includes all of the structures and processes designed to mount a defense against foreign substances and disease-causing agents.
10. A poison or harmful substance.
11. A raised, swollen, well-defined area on the skin resulting from an insect bite or allergic reaction.
12. Chemical substances that contribute to anaphylaxis.

Down

2. A harsh, high-pitched respiratory sound, generally heard during inspiration, that is caused by partial blockage or narrowing of the upper airway.
3. A substance produced by the body (commonly called adrenaline) and a drug produced by pharmaceutical companies that increase pulse rate and blood pressure.
4. The study of the body's immune system.
5. The act of injecting venom.
7. An extreme, life-threatening systemic allergic reaction that may include shock and respiratory failure.
9. Substances that cause an allergic reaction.

Critical Thinking

Multiple Choice

Read each critical-thinking item carefully and then select the one best response.

You have been called to a park where a local church is holding a potluck dinner. As you exit your ambulance, a woman approaches you holding her 7-year-old son who is wheezing and having difficulty breathing. She informs you that he had inadvertently eaten a brownie with nuts, and he is allergic to nuts.

_____ 1. You lift the child's shirt and find small, raised areas that he is trying to scratch. They are likely to be:
   A. leukotrienes.
   B. histamines.
   C. urticaria.
   D. toxins.

_____ 2. Why is this patient wheezing?
   A. He has had an envenomation.
   B. His bronchioles are constricting.
   C. His bronchioles are dilating.
   D. His uvula has swollen.

_____ 3. The child's mother has an EpiPen that contains the appropriate dose of epinephrine for a child. What dose would that be?
   A. 0.8 mg
   B. 0.5 mg
   C. 0.4 mg
   D. 0.15 mg

_____ 4. When assisting with an auto-injector, how long should you hold the pen against the thigh?
   A. 3 seconds
   B. 5 seconds
   C. 10 seconds
   D. 30 seconds.

_____ 5. After removing the auto-injector from the child's thigh, you should do all of the following EXCEPT:
   A. record the time.
   B. record the dose.
   C. reassess his vital signs.
   D. place ice over the injection site.

Short Answer

Complete this section with short written answers using the space provided.

1. List the common side effects of epinephrine.

   _____

   _____

   _____

2. What are the five stimuli that most often cause allergic reactions?

   _____

   _____

   _____

3. What are the steps for administering or assisting with administration of an EpiPen?

_____

_____

_____

4. What are the common respiratory and circulatory signs and symptoms of an allergic reaction?

_____

_____

_____

Ambulance Calls

The following case scenarios provide an opportunity to explore the concerns associated with patient management and to enhance critical-thinking skills. Read each scenario and answer each question to the best of your ability.

1. You are dispatched to assist a 12-year-old child who was climbing a tree and apparently disturbed a wasp nest. When you arrive, the child is lying under the tree, and the nest is on the ground next to her.

How would you best manage this patient?

_____

_____

_____

2. You are dispatched to a local seafood restaurant for a person who is having difficulty breathing. On arrival, you find a 22-year-old woman with facial edema, cyanosis around the lips, audible wheezing, and urticaria on her face and upper body. Her boyfriend tells you she ate shrimp and she is allergic to them. He also tells you she has some medicine in her purse and hands you an EpiPen prescribed to her.

How would you best manage this patient?

_____

_____

_____

Fill-in-the-Patient Care Report

Read the incident scenario and then complete the following patient care report (PCR).

"Unit six-twelve, emergency assignment, you're headed to Crab Town Restaurant at 231 Seaside Parkway for an allergic reaction. Showing you dispatched at 1734."

Your partner, Ed, confirms the dispatch over the radio as you activate the lights and sirens and steer toward Seaside Parkway.

"Six-twelve is on scene," Ed says, snapping the microphone back into its holder as you shift the ambulance into park and pull on a pair of exam gloves.

"Unit six-twelve, copying you on scene at 1742."

As you roll the gurney into the restaurant, you are met by a frantic waitress who leads you to a small table at the rear of the bustling restaurant. A 37-year-old man is holding the edge of the table so tightly that his knuckles are white as he struggles to breathe. His face, neck, and hands are obviously swollen; bright hives are visible just above the collar of his shirt; and there is a bluish tinge to his lips and fingernails.

"Get some oxygen on him, Ed, and get the bag-valve mask ready," you say, pulling the portable radio from your belt. "I'm going to call for an ALS crew."

As Ed places a nonrebreathing mask onto the patient with 15 L/min of oxygen, you request an ALS rendezvous and then turn to the small group of terrified diners who were sitting with the patient. "Does he have an EpiPen or anything for this allergy?"

"No," a woman says, tears smearing the mascara down her cheeks. "He's my husband and I've never seen him react like this to anything."

"Let's load him, Ed!" You pull the gurney over, and the two of you help the 63-kg (138-lb) patient onto it as he sucks noisily on the oxygen. About 6 minutes after arriving, Ed is pulling the ambulance out of the parking lot while you get a baseline set of vitals on the patient.

His blood pressure is 100/64 mm Hg, pulse is 116 beats/min, and you note that it is strong and rapid. His respirations are 26 breaths/min and becoming more labored by the minute, coupled with an obvious anxiety; the patient is becoming very restless. The digital pulse oximeter screen shows 92%.

"Okay, sir, I'm going to help you to breathe." You grab the bag-valve mask and show it to him. "I'm going to help your breathing with this. Try and relax, although I know that's tough right now."

You remove the nonrebreathing mask and attach the bag-valve mask to the truck oxygen supply and begin gently forcing air into the patient with every inhalation. He is beginning to panic, so you have to reassure him loudly and constantly every time that you squeeze the bag.

The back door suddenly pops open and a paramedic that you know climbs aboard with his jump kit. You feel the ambulance start rolling again.

"Great job, my friend," he says to you. "Keep it up while I get my stuff together." The paramedic quickly assembles a syringe and jabs it into the patient's upper arm and then begins to monitor his pulse and breathing. Within a few minutes, you can see that the swelling is reversing and the patient starts to take deeper breaths, exhaling in relieved yells. You look at your watch (1755) and get another set of vitals while the paramedic talks calmly to the patient. His blood pressure is now 140/94 mm Hg, pulse rate is 128 beats/min, and breathing is 18 breaths/min and much less labored. The SpO_2 is showing 96%, and you reconnect the nonrebreathing mask and place it onto the patient.

You call in a quick but thorough verbal report to the receiving facility and provide the ETA given by Ed.

At 1801, you arrive at the hospital followed closely by the ALS ambulance that the paramedic had come from and wheel the deeply breathing patient through the emergency department doors. You and the paramedic provide verbal reports to the physician, and he assumes care of the quickly recovering patient.

At 1814, your unit goes back into service.

Fill-in-the-Patient Care Report

EMS Patient Care Report (PCR)			
Date:	**Incident No.:**	**Nature of Call:**	**Location:**
Dispatched:	**En Route:**	**At Scene:**	**Transport:**	**At Hospital:**	**In Service:**

Patient Information	
Age: **Sex:** **Weight (in kg [lb]):**	**Allergies:** **Medications:** **Past Medical History:** **Chief Complaint:**

Vital Signs				
Time:	**BP:**	**Pulse:**	**Respirations:**	**Spo$_2$:**
Time:	**BP:**	**Pulse:**	**Respirations:**	**Spo$_2$:**
Time:	**BP:**	**Pulse:**	**Respirations:**	**Spo$_2$:**

EMS Treatment (circle all that apply)				
Oxygen @ ____ L/min via (circle one): NC NRM BVM	**Assisted Ventilation**	**Airway Adjunct**	**CPR**
Defibrillation	**Bleeding Control**	**Bandaging**	**Splinting**	**Other:**

Narrative

Skills

Skill Drill

Test your knowledge of this skill by filling in the correct words in the photo captions.

Skill Drill 20-1: Using an EpiPen Auto-injector

© Jones & Bartlett Learning.

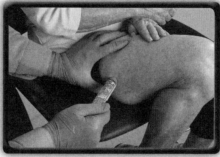

© Jones & Bartlett Learning.

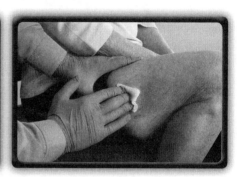

© Jones & Bartlett Learning.

1. Remove the _____ safety cap, and quickly wipe the thigh with _____, if possible.

2. Place the _____ of the auto-injector against the _____ part of the thigh. Push the auto-injector _____ against the thigh until a _____ is heard. Hold it in place until all the _____ has been injected (10 seconds).

3. Rub the area for _____ seconds.

Assessment Review

Answer the following questions pertaining to the assessment of the types of emergencies discussed in this chapter.

_____ **1.** As you begin to assess a patient suspected of anaphylactic shock, which of these steps would be done first?
   A. Assess and treat for life threats
   B. Assess lung sounds
   C. Provide high-flow oxygen
   D. Obtain a pulse oximetry reading

_____ **2.** After assisting with an EpiPen, what is the first thing that should be done?
   A. Make sure the medication is not expired.
   B. Take a set of vital signs.
   C. Place the used EpiPen in a biohazard container.
   D. Rub the area for 10 seconds.

_____ **3.** When using the EpiPen auto-injector, do all of the following EXCEPT:
   A. remove the safety cap.
   B. wipe the thigh with antiseptic.
   C. push the auto-injector firmly against the thigh for about 10 seconds.
   D. place ice over the injection site.

_____   **4.** What does the "M" stand for in SAMPLE?

    A. Mechanism—what substance caused the reaction?

    B. Maintenance—has the patient been compliant with his or her medications?

    C. Medications—what medications is the patient currently taking?

    D. Method—what method of medication administration is the patient using?

_____   **5.** What does the "P" stand for in SAMPLE?

    A. Pain—rate your pain from 1 to 10.

    B. Probable cause—what caused this to happen?

    C. Priority—is this a high- or low-priority patient?

    D. Past pertinent history.

Toxicology

21

General Knowledge

Matching

Match each of the items in the left column to the appropriate definition in the right column.

_____ **1.** Poison

_____ **2.** Substance abuse

_____ **3.** Antidote

_____ **4.** Tolerance

_____ **5.** Cholinergic

_____ **6.** Ingestion

_____ **7.** Hematemesis

_____ **8.** Stimulant

_____ **9.** Opioid

_____ **10.** Sedative

_____ **11.** Anticholinergic

A. Substance that decreases activity and excitement

B. Drug or agent with actions similar to morphine

C. Atropine, Benadryl, some cyclic antidepressants

D. Need for increasing amounts of a drug to obtain the same effect

E. Agent that produces an excited state

F. Substance whose chemical action can damage body structures or impair body functions

G. Substance that will counteract the effects of a particular poison

H. Misuse of any substance to produce a desired effect

I. Taking a substance by mouth

J. Overstimulates body functions controlled by parasympathetic nerves

K. Vomiting blood

Multiple Choice

Read each item carefully and then select the one best response.

_____ **1.** Activated charcoal is in the form of a(n):

    A. elixir.

    B. suspension.

    C. syrup.

    D. emulsion.

_____ **2.** The presence of burning of the mucous membranes around the mouth suggests:

    A. ingestion of depressants.

    B. ingestion of poison.

    C. overdose of heroin.

    D. that the patient may be a heavy smoker.

_____ **3.** Treatment for ingestion of poisonous plants includes all of the following EXCEPT:

    A. assessing the patient's airway and vital signs.

    B. taking the plant to the emergency department.

    C. administering activated charcoal.

    D. prompt transport.

_____ **4.** The most important consideration in caring for a patient who has been exposed to an organophosphate insecticide or some other cholinergic agent is to:

    A. maintain the airway.

    B. apply high-flow oxygen.

    C. avoid exposure yourself.

    D. initiate CPR.

_____ **5.** Which of the following would NOT provide clues to the nature of the poison?

    A. Open windows

    B. Scattered pills

    C. Chemicals

    D. A needle or syringe

_____ **6.** Which of the following is TRUE regarding injected poisons?

    A. Injected poisons cannot be diluted.

    B. Injected poisons can be easily removed from the body.

    C. Injected poisons are absorbed over time.

    D. Injected poisons only include intravenous drugs.

_____ **7.** The major side effect of ingesting activated charcoal is:

    A. depressed respirations.

    B. overproduction of stomach acid.

    C. black stools.

    D. increased blood pressure.

_____ **8.** Alcohol is a powerful central nervous system depressant. It:

    A. sharpens the sense of awareness.

    B. slows reflexes.

    C. increases reaction time.

    D. increases reflexes.

_____ **9.** Which of the following is NOT a narcotic?

    A. Heroin

    B. Morphine

    C. Ativan

    D. Codeine

_____ **10.** Which of the following is NOT part of treatment of patients who have overdosed with sedative-hypnotics and have respiratory depression?

    A. Provide airway clearance.

    B. Provide ventilatory assistance.

    C. Provide prompt transport.

    D. Administer syrup of ipecac.

_____ **11.** Anticholinergic medications have properties that block the _____ nerves.

    A. parasympathetic

    B. sympathetic

    C. adrenergic

    D. parasympatholytic

_____ **12.** _____ crack produces the most rapid means of absorption and therefore the most potent effect.

    A. Injected

    B. Absorbed

    C. Smoked

    D. Ingested

_____ **13.** Cholinergic agents overstimulate normal body functions that are controlled by parasympathetic nerves, causing:

    A. increased salivation.

    B. pupil dilation.

    C. decreased urination.

    D. decreased lacrimation.

_____ **14.** Signs and symptoms of staphylococcal food poisoning include:

      A. difficulty speaking.

      B. nausea, vomiting, and diarrhea.

      C. blurred vision.

      D. respiratory distress.

_____ **15.** Inhalant effects range from mild drowsiness to coma, but unlike most other sedative-hypnotics these agents may often cause:

      A. seizures.

      B. vomiting.

      C. swelling of the tongue.

      D. rashes.

_____ **16.** Cocaine is called all of the following EXCEPT:

      A. lady

      B. snow

      C. blow

      D. weed

_____ **17.** The effects of bath salts can last as long as:

      A. 12 hours.

      B. 24 hours.

      C. 48 hours.

      D. 72 hours.

_____ **18.** The ingestion of marijuana can lead to cannabinoid hyperemesis syndrome, resulting in extreme nausea and vomiting. How are these symptoms typically relieved?

      A. Hot showers

      B. Oxygen therapy

      C. Activated charcoal

      D. Massaging the feet

_____ **19.** Sympathomimetics are central nervous system stimulants that frequently cause:

      A. hypotension.

      B. tachycardia.

      C. pinpoint pupils.

      D. muscle weakness.

_____ **20.** Characteristics of carbon monoxide include all of the following EXCEPT:

      A. is odorless.

      B. produces severe hypoxia.

      C. does not damage or irritate the lungs.

      D. smells like rotten eggs.

_____ **21.** Chlorine:

      A. is odorless.

      B. does not damage or irritate the lungs.

      C. causes pulmonary edema.

      D. does not cause sore throat or hoarseness.

_____ **22.** Localized signs and symptoms of absorbed poisoning include:

      A. a history of exposure.

      B. burns, irritation of the skin.

      C. dyspnea.

      D. muscle weakness.

23. Which of the following statements regarding injected poisons is FALSE?

    A. They may result in dizziness, fever, and chills.

    B. They are frequently caused by a drug overdose.

    C. They are easily diluted once in the bloodstream.

    D. You should remove rings, watches, and bracelets in areas of swelling.

24. _____ is a highly toxic, colorless, and flammable gas with a distinctive rotten-egg odor.

    A. Carbon monoxide

    B. Hexane

    C. Chlorine

    D. Hydrogen sulfide

25. Injected poisons are impossible to dilute or remove because they are usually _____ or cause intense local tissue destruction.

    A. absorbed quickly into the body

    B. bound to hemoglobin

    C. large compounds

    D. combined with the cerebrospinal fluid

26. Medical problems that may cause the patient to present as intoxicated include all of the following EXCEPT:

    A. head trauma.

    B. diarrhea.

    C. uncontrolled diabetes.

    D. toxic reactions.

27. Which of the following is NOT considered a sign or symptom of alcohol withdrawal?

    A. Agitation and restlessness

    B. Fever and sweating

    C. Seizures

    D. Chest pain

28. Treatments for inhaled poisons include:

    A. removing the patient from the exposure.

    B. applying an SCBA to the patient.

    C. covering the patient to prevent spread of the poison.

    D. considering CPAP application.

29. Signs and symptoms of chlorine exposure include all of the following EXCEPT:

    A. cough.

    B. chest pain.

    C. rales.

    D. wheezing.

30. Which of the following is NOT a typical ingested poison?

    A. Aerosol propellants

    B. Household cleaners

    C. Plants

    D. Contaminated food

31. Naloxone (Narcan) should only be used in a patient with a suspected opiate or opioid overdose who has:

    A. an altered mental status.

    B. dilation of the pupils.

    C. carpopedal spasms.

    D. agonal respirations or apnea.

_____ **32.** Inhaled poisons include:
  A. chlorine.
  B. venom.
  C. *Dieffenbachia.*
  D. *Salmonella.*

_____ **33.** Which of the following is NOT considered a typical route of administration for naloxone?
  A. Intravenous
  B. Intranasal
  C. Intramuscular
  D. Intradermal

Questions 34–38 are derived from the following scenario: You have responded to the home of a 26-year-old woman who has reportedly taken a large number of pills in an attempt to commit suicide. As you enter the living room, you see her unresponsive in a chair, with several empty alcohol containers. She is breathing heavily.

_____ **34.** You are able to arouse her consciousness for a short period of time. Which course of action takes priority?
  A. Administer syrup of ipecac.
  B. Cover her with a blanket to maintain body temperature.
  C. Ensure scene safety.
  D. Attempt to administer naloxone.

_____ **35.** You have decided to give her activated charcoal. How much should you give her?
  A. Half a glass
  B. 12.5 to 25 g
  C. 30 to 100 g
  D. 30 to 100 mL

_____ **36.** What would be the desired goal of giving her activated charcoal?
  A. To vomit the drugs and alcohol
  B. To bind the toxin and prevent absorption
  C. To teach her a lesson
  D. To prevent excretion

_____ **37.** If she does not want to take the activated charcoal, you should:
  A. restrain her, pinch her nose, and make her drink it.
  B. have her sign a patient refusal form.
  C. attempt to persuade her.
  D. leave the scene.

_____ **38.** Side effects of ingesting activated charcoal include all of the following EXCEPT:
  A. vomiting.
  B. hematemesis.
  C. nausea.
  D. black stools.

_____ **39.** Which of the following is NOT commonly associated with an overdose from a cardiac medication?
  A. Cardiac arrhythmia
  B. Bleeding
  C. Unconsciousness
  D. Urinary incontinence

_____ **40.** Ringing in the ears is associated with an overdose of:
  A. acetaminophen.
  B. aspirin.
  C. ethylene alcohol.
  D. methyl alcohol.

True/False

If you believe the statement to be more true than false, write the letter "T" in the space provided. If you believe the statement to be more false than true, write the letter "F."

_____   **1.** The usual adult dose of activated charcoal is 30 to 100 g.

_____   **2.** The general treatment of a poisoned patient is to induce vomiting.

_____   **3.** Activated charcoal is a standard of care in all ingestions.

_____   **4.** Inhaled chlorine produces profound hypoxia without lung irritation.

_____   **5.** Shaking activated charcoal decreases its effectiveness.

_____   **6.** Opioid overdose typically presents with pinpoint pupils.

_____   **7.** Cholinergics include nerve gases used in chemical warfare and organophosphate insecticides.

_____   **8.** Alcohol is a stimulant.

_____   **9.** Dilaudid and Vicodin are examples of opioids.

_____   **10.** Cocaine is classically inhaled through the nose and absorbed in the nasal mucosa.

_____   **11.** Alcohol can result in significant respiratory depression.

_____   **12.** Ingestion of the plant dieffenbachia can cause irritation of the lower airway.

Fill-in-the-Blank

Read each item carefully and then complete the statement by filling in the missing words.

1. The most severe form of toxin ingestion is _____.

2. _____ _____ produce euphoria, increased mental clarity, and sexual arousal.

3. _____ _____ is the misuse of any substance to produce a desired effect.

4. If the patient has a liquid chemical agent on the skin, you should flood the affected part for _____

_____ _____ minutes.

5. Opioid analgesics are central nervous system depressants and can cause severe _____ _____.

6. Severe acute alcohol ingestion may cause _____.

7. Your primary responsibility to the patient who has been poisoned is to _____ that a poisoning occurred.

8. The usual dosage for activated charcoal for an adult or child is _____ _____ of activated charcoal per

_____ of body weight.

9. As you irrigate the eyes, make sure that the fluid runs from the bridge of the nose _____.

10. Approximately 80% of all poisoning is by _____, including plants, contaminated food, and most drugs.

11. Patients experiencing alcohol withdrawal may develop _____ _____ if they no longer have their daily

source of alcohol.

12. The _____ _____ is a single auto-injector containing 2 mg of atropine and 600 mg of

pralidoxime.

13. A person with an _____ has an overwhelming desire or need to continue using the substance, at whatever cost, with a tendency to increase the dose.

14. _____ may develop from sweating, fluid loss, insufficient fluid intake, or vomiting associated with delirium tremens.

Fill-in-the-Table

Fill in the missing parts of the table.

Toxidromes: Typical Signs and Symptoms of Specific Overdoses	
Agent	**Signs and Symptoms**
Opioid (Examples: heroin, oxycodone)	• Hypoventilation or respiratory arrest • _____ • Sedation or coma • _____
_____ (Examples: epinephrine, albuterol, cocaine, methamphetamine)	• Hypertension • _____ • Dilated pupils • Agitation or seizures • _____
Sedative-hypnotics (Examples: diazepam, secobarbital, flunitrazepam, midazolam)	• _____ • Sedation or coma • Hypoventilation • _____
_____ (Examples: atropine, diphenhydramine, chlorpheniramine, doxylamine, Datura stramonium [jimson weed])	• _____ • _____ • Hypertension • Dilated pupils • _____ • Sedation, agitation, seizures, coma, or delirium • _____
_____ (Examples: organophosphates, pilocarpine, nerve gas)	• _____ • _____ • Pinpoint pupils • Excess lacrimation (tearing) or salivation • _____ • _____

Crossword Puzzle

The following crossword puzzle is an activity provided to reinforce correct spelling and understanding of medical terminology associated with emergency care and the EMT. Use the clues in the column to complete the puzzle.

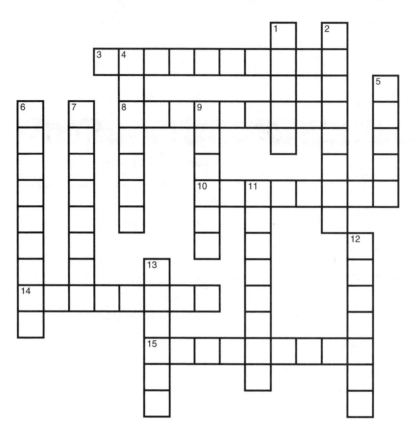

Across

3. The study of toxic or poisonous substances.

8. Swallowing; taking a substance by mouth.

10. A substance that decreases activity and excitement.

14. An excessive quantity of a drug that can have toxic or lethal consequences.

15. An agent that produces an excited state.

Down

1. A poison or harmful substance produced by bacteria, animals, or plants.

2. A sleep-inducing effect or agent.

4. Any drug or agent with actions similar to morphine.

5. Substance _____ is the misuse of any substance to produce some desired effect.

6. A state of overwhelming obsession or physical need to continue the use of a drug or agent.

7. A substance that is used to neutralize or counteract a poison.

9. Vomiting.

11. _____ tremens is a severe withdrawal syndrome seen in alcoholics who are deprived of ethyl alcohol.

12. Vomited material.

13. A substance whose chemical action could damage structures or impair function when introduced into the body.

Critical Thinking

Short Answer

Complete this section with short written answers using the space provided.

1. How does activated charcoal work to counteract ingested poison?

_____

_____

_____

2. What are four routes of contact for poisoning?

_____

_____

_____

3. List the typical signs and symptoms of an overdose of sympathomimetics.

_____

_____

_____

4. What are the two main types of food poisoning?

_____

_____

_____

5. What differentiates the presentation of acetaminophen poisoning from that of other substances? What does this mean to the prehospital caregiver?

_____

_____

_____

6. What condition do the mnemonics DUMBELS and SLUDGEM pertain to, and what do they mean?

_____

_____

_____

7. List at least five questions should you ask a possible poisoning victim.

_____

_____

_____

Ambulance Calls

The following case scenarios provide an opportunity to explore the concerns associated with patient management and to enhance critical-thinking skills. Read each scenario and answer each question to the best of your ability.

1. You are dispatched to a private residence for "accidental ingestion." You arrive to find a 3-year-old whose parents tell you "got into some rat poison." The child is alert, crying, and responding appropriately to parents and environmental stimuli.

   How would you best manage this patient?

   _____

   _____

   _____

2. You are dispatched to the sidewalk in front of a small business for "an intoxicated man." You arrive to find a 60-year-old man sitting on the curb, holding a bottle inside a paper bag. He is not fully alert and can only tell you that his name is Andy. He allows you to take his blood pressure, and as you roll up his sleeve you notice needle marks along his veins.

   How would you best manage this patient?

   _____

   _____

   _____

3. You are called to a possible suicide attempt. You arrive on the scene to find police and a neighbor in the home of a 25-year-old woman who is unresponsive, supine on her bed. The neighbor tells you that the patient recently broke up with her boyfriend and has been very distraught. There is an empty pill bottle on the nightstand. When you look at the label, you see that the prescription was filled yesterday and that 30 tablets were dispensed. An empty liquor bottle is on the floor.

   How would you best manage this patient?

   _____

   _____

   _____

Skills

Assessment Review

Answer the following questions pertaining to the assessment of the types of emergencies discussed in this chapter.

_____ 1. Which of the following would NOT be an appropriate question to ask regarding an ingested poison?
   A. What is the substance?
   B. How much did the patient ingest?
   C. What color was the substance?
   D. Have any interventions been performed?

_____ 2. "Hot as a hare, blind as a bat, dry as a bone, red as a beet, and mad as a hatter" describes which of the following conditions?
   A. Cholinergic poisoning
   B. Anticholinergic poisoning
   C. Delirium tremens
   D. Sympathomimetic poisoning

_____   **3.** *Shigella*, *Campylobacter*, and *Enterococcus* are associated with what type of poisoning?

    A. Plant

    B. Food

    C. Hallucinogen

    D. Sympathomimetic

_____   **4.** Ice, crank, speed, uppers, and meth are all street names for which type of poison?

    A. Hallucinogens

    B. Sympathomimetics

    C. Sedative-hypnotics

    D. Anticholinergics

_____   **5.** When would you NOT give activated charcoal?

    A. If the patient drank gasoline

    B. If the patient overdosed on aspirin

    C. If the patient overdosed on antidepressants

    D. If the patient overdosed on opiates

Psychiatric Emergencies

© Photos.com

General Knowledge

Matching

Match each of the items in the left column to the appropriate definition in the right column.

_____ **1.** Psychosis

_____ **2.** Schizophrenia

_____ **3.** Delirium

_____ **4.** Depression

_____ **5.** Psychiatric disorder

_____ **6.** Behavior

_____ **7.** Functional disorder

_____ **8.** Psychiatric emergency

_____ **9.** Behavioral crisis

_____ **10.** Organic brain syndrome

A. What you can see of a person's response to the environment; his or her actions

B. Temporary or permanent dysfunction of the brain caused by a disturbance in brain tissue function

C. Any reaction to events that interferes with activities of daily living or is unacceptable to the patient or others

D. A persistent feeling of sadness or despair

E. Abnormal operation of an organ that cannot be traced to an obvious change in structure or physiology of the organ

F. A complex disorder that involves delusions, hallucinations, a lack of interest in pleasure, and erratic speech

G. An illness with psychological or behavioral symptoms that may result in impaired functioning

H. The patient may show agitation or violence or become a threat to self or others

I. A state of delusion in which the person is out of touch with reality

J. Condition of impairment in cognitive function that can present with disorientation, hallucinations, or delusions

Multiple Choice

Read each item carefully and then select the one best response.

_____ **1.** Which of the following is NOT typically linked to a psychological or behavioral crisis?

    A. Mind-altering substances

    B. An underlying medical problem

    C. History of smoking

    D. Stress

_____ **2.** Which of the following is a normal reaction to a crisis situation?

    A. Monday morning blues that last until Friday

    B. Feeling blue after the break up of a long-term relationship

    C. Feeling depressed week after week with no discernible cause

    D. Thoughts of suicide

_____ **3.** Which of the following statements is FALSE?

    A. You may be able to predict whether a person will become violent.

    B. Scene safety is always your primary concern.

    C. Behavior problems may be the result of drug or alcohol abuse.

    D. Most people with a mental illness are dangerous.

_____ **4.** Learning to adapt to a variety of situations in daily life, including stresses and strains, is called:

   A. disruption.

   B. adjustment.

   C. behavior.

   D. functional.

_____ **5.** If the interruption of daily routine tends to recur on a regular basis, the behavior is also considered a _____ crisis.

   A. mental health

   B. functional

   C. behavioral

   D. psychogenic

_____ **6.** If an abnormal or disturbing pattern of behavior lasts for at least _____, it is regarded as a matter of concern from a mental health standpoint.

   A. 6 weeks

   B. 1 month

   C. 6 months

   D. 1 year

_____ **7.** Patients may show agitation, violence, or become a threat to themselves or others when they experience a(n) _____ emergency.

   A. psychiatric

   B. behavioral

   C. functional

   D. adjustment

_____ **8.** Which of the following is NOT considered a possible cause of a psychiatric disorder?

   A. Social disturbance

   B. Chemical disturbance

   C. Biologic disturbance

   D. Emotional disturbance

_____ **9.** An altered mental status may arise from:

   A. an oxygen saturation of 98%.

   B. moderate temperatures.

   C. inadequate blood flow to the brain.

   D. adequate glucose levels in the blood.

_____ **10.** Organic brain syndrome may be caused by:

   A. daily stress.

   B. seizure disorders.

   C. myocardial infarction.

   D. thoracic spinal cord injury.

_____ **11.** All of the following are examples of a functional disorder EXCEPT:

   A. anxiety.

   B. depression.

   C. organic brain syndrome.

   D. schizophrenia.

_____ **12.** When documenting abnormal behavior, it is important to:

   A. document restraints only when leather restraints are used.

   B. document everything that happened on the call.

   C. avoid quoting the patient's own words.

   D. interject your interpretations of the patient's thoughts.

_____ **13.** Safety guidelines for behavioral emergencies include all of the following EXCEPT:
   A. assessing the scene.
   B. being prepared to spend extra time.
   C. encouraging purposeful movement.
   D. determining the underlying psychiatric disorder.

_____ **14.** In evaluating a situation that is considered a behavioral emergency, the first things to consider are:
   A. airway and breathing.
   B. scene safety and patient response.
   C. history of medications.
   D. respiratory and circulatory status.

_____ **15.** _____ is a behavior that is characterized by restlessness and irregular physical activity.
   A. Agitation
   B. Aggression
   C. Anxiety
   D. Apathy

_____ **16.** Which of the following is NOT considered a risk factor for suicide?
   A. Alcohol abuse
   B. Recent marriage
   C. Family history of suicide
   D. Depression

_____ **17.** Which of the following is NOT a risk factor to consider when assessing a suicidal patient?
   A. Does the patient appear to be well groomed?
   B. Is the environment unsafe?
   C. Is there an imminent threat to the patient or others?
   D. Is there evidence of self-destructive behavior?

_____ **18.** Signs and symptoms of agitated delirium include all of the following EXCEPT:
   A. hyperventilation.
   B. tachycardia.
   C. vivid hallucinations.
   D. dilated pupils.

_____ **19.** You should request the assistance of a _____ when a mentally impaired patient refuses to go to the hospital.
   A. physician
   B. court order
   C. law enforcement officer
   D. psychologist

_____ **20.** When restraining a patient without an appropriate order, legal actions may involve charges of:
   A. abandonment.
   B. negligence.
   C. battery.
   D. breach of duty.

_____ **21.** When restraining a patient on a stretcher, it is necessary to constantly reassess the patient's:
   A. level of consciousness.
   B. respiration and circulation status.
   C. emotional status.
   D. pain status.

Questions 22–25 are derived from the following scenario: Dean, a man in his 50s, is acting irrationally. His wife states that he thinks he is the dictator of a small country, and he is wearing nothing but a baseball cap and a belt with a small handgun attached to it.

_____ **22.** What is your best course of action?
  A. Call ALS.
  B. Assess Dean from a distance.
  C. Have his wife take the gun from him.
  D. Call for police backup.

_____ **23.** The scene is safe. Dean now tells you he is "God" and can do anything he wants to. Which of the following should you NOT consider?
  A. He is probably not a threat to you.
  B. He may have a history of psychiatric problems.
  C. He could be suffering from an underlying medical problem.
  D. Alcohol or drugs could be a factor in his behavior.

_____ **24.** What are some tactics you can use to have Dean cooperate with your assessment?
  A. Reflective listening
  B. Threatening him with restraints
  C. Aggressive communication
  D. Passive listening

_____ **25.** Dean becomes agitated and states, "You'll never take me alive." A decision is made to restrain Dean. How many people should ideally be present to restrain Dean?
  A. Two
  B. Five
  C. Six
  D. Eight

True/False

If you believe the statement to be more true than false, write the letter "T" in the space provided. If you believe the statement to be more false than true, write the letter "F."

_____ **1.** Depression lasting 8 months after being fired from a job is a normal mental health response.

_____ **2.** Low blood glucose or lack of oxygen to the brain may cause behavioral changes to the degree that a psychiatric emergency could exist.

_____ **3.** From a mental health standpoint, a pattern of abnormal behavior must last at least 3 months to be a matter of concern.

_____ **4.** A disturbed patient should always be transported with restraints.

_____ **5.** It is sometimes helpful to allow a patient with a behavioral emergency some time alone to calm down and collect his or her thoughts.

_____ **6.** It is important to maintain eye contact with the patient when dealing with a behavioral crisis.

_____ **7.** A patient should never be asked if he or she is considering suicide.

_____ **8.** Urinary tract infections can cause behavioral changes in elderly patients.

_____ **9.** All individuals with mental health disorders are dangerous, violent, or otherwise unmanageable.

_____ **10.** When completing the documentation, it is important to record the reasons why you restrained a patient.

_____ **11.** When restraining a patient, at least three people should ideally be present to carry out the restraint.

_____ **12.** A patient should be placed face down when being restrained to a litter.

_____ **13.** Reassessment of restrained patients should take place every 5 minutes.

_____ **14.** Tears, sweating, and blushing may be significant indicators of state of mind, such as sadness, nervousness, or embarrassment.

_____ **15.** Almost every situation, medical or trauma, will have some behavioral component.

_____ **16.** Military personnel who experienced combat have a low incidence of PTSD.

_____ **17.** Flashbacks are uncontrolled events triggered by sound, sight, or smell.

_____ **18.** A competent adult may not refuse treatment when life-saving treatment is needed.

Fill-in-the-Blank

Read each item carefully and then complete the statement by filling in the missing words.

1. _____ is what you can see of a person's response to the environment; his or her actions.

2. A(n) _____ _____ or emergency is any reaction to events that interferes with the activities of daily living or has become unacceptable to the patient, family, or community.

3. Chronic _____, or a persistent feeling of sadness or despair, may be a symptom of a mental or physical disorder.

4. _____ _____ _____ is a temporary or permanent dysfunction of the brain caused by a disturbance in the physical or physiologic functioning of the brain.

5. Any time you encounter an emotionally depressed patient, you must consider the possibility of _____.

6. People with _____ may experience symptoms including delusions, hallucinations, a lack of interest in pleasure, and erratic speech.

7. Violent or dangerous people should be managed by _____ _____ before emergency care is rendered.

8. When a patient is not mentally competent to grant consent, the law assumes that there is _____ _____.

9. _____ _____ occurs when the person attempts to find an escape from constant internal distress or a particularly disturbing event.

10. In subduing a disturbed patient, use the _____ force necessary.

Crossword Puzzle

The following crossword puzzle is an activity provided to reinforce correct spelling and understanding of medical terminology associated with emergency care and the EMT. Use the clues in the column to complete the puzzle.

Across

2. How a person functions or acts in response to his or her environment.

3. A(n) _____ disorder has no known physiologic reason for the abnormal functioning of an organ or organ system.

8. A change in the way a person thinks and behaves that may signal disease in the central nervous system or elsewhere in the body is known as _____ mental status.

9. An emergency in which abnormal behavior threatens a person's own health and safety or the health and safety of another person is known as a(n) _____ emergency.

10. A persistent mood of sadness, despair, and discouragement.

Down

1. Activities of daily _____ are the basic activities a person usually accomplishes during a day.

2. _____ crisis is the point at which a person's reactions to events interfere with activities of daily living.

4. _____ brain syndrome is temporary or permanent dysfunction of the brain, caused by a disturbance in the physical or physiologic functioning of brain tissue.

5. _____ delirium is a condition of disorientation, confusion, and possible hallucinations coupled with purposeless, restless physical activity.

6. A mental disorder characterized by the loss of contact with reality.

7. A psychiatric _____ is an illness with psychological or behavioral symptoms and/or impairment in functioning.

Critical Thinking

Short Answer

Complete this section with short written answers using the space provided.

1. What is the distinction between a behavioral crisis and a psychiatric emergency?

   _____

   _____

   _____

2. What three major areas should be considered in evaluating the possible source of a behavioral crisis?

   _____

   _____

   _____

3. What are three factors to consider in determining the level of force required to restrain a patient?

   _____

   _____

   _____

4. List at least 10 safety guidelines for dealing with behavioral emergencies.

   _____

   _____

   _____

5. List at least 10 risk factors for suicide.

   _____

   _____

   _____

6. Explain the process for reflective listening.

   _____

   _____

   _____

7. List five risk factors to consider when dealing with a potentially violent patient.

   _____

   _____

   _____

Ambulance Calls

The following case scenarios provide an opportunity to explore the concerns associated with patient management and to enhance critical-thinking skills. Read each scenario and answer each question to the best of your ability.

1. You are dispatched to a nonemergency transport of a girl from a local hospital emergency department to a care facility that provides treatment for emotionally disturbed teenagers. She became violent in the emergency department and was placed in four-point restraints. As you begin transporting the patient, she begins to cry and asks you to remove the restraints.

   How would you best manage this patient?

   _____

   _____

   _____

2. You are dispatched to a "suicide attempt" at a private residence. When you arrive on scene, you are greeted by a calm, middle-aged man who appears to have been crying. He tells you that he was on the phone with his sister who lives out of state and that she must have called for the ambulance. The patient tells you that he was just upset, but he's fine now. Dispatch informed you via cell phone that this man recently lost his wife of 15 years to breast cancer.

   How would you best manage this patient?

   _____

   _____

   _____

3. You are dispatched to the residence of a 40-year-old woman who is upset over the loss of her mother 5 weeks ago. She tells you that she has no family and has cared for her elderly mother for the past 7 years. She has not eaten for several days and is severely depressed.

   How would you best manage this patient?

   _____

   _____

   _____

Skills

Assessment Review

Answer the following questions pertaining to the assessment of the types of emergencies discussed in this chapter. These questions are based on risk factors in assessing the level of danger in a behavior call.

_____ 1. When assessing the history, all of the following are past behaviors you want to know the patient has exhibited EXCEPT:

    A. hostile behavior

    B. overly aggressive behavior

    C. violent behavior

    D. cooperative behavior.

_____ 2. Physical tension is often a warning signal of impending hostility. What sign might warn you of physical tension?

    A. Posture

    B. Eye movement

    C. Facial expression

    D. Laughter

_____ 3. What warning signs can be detected from the scene?

    A. Hunting magazines on the table

    B. Known weapons in the outside shed

    C. Guns or knives near the patient

    D. Photos of hunting trips on the wall

_____ 4. What kind of speech may be an indicator of emotional distress?

    A. Quiet speech

    B. Obscene speech

    C. Rational speech

    D. Organized speech

_____ 5. What type of physical activity may be an indicator of risk to the EMT?

    A. Tense muscles

    B. Continuous stretching

    C. Lying down

    D. Vigorous exercise

Gynecologic Emergencies

© Photos.com

General Knowledge

Matching

Match each of the items in the left column to the appropriate definition in the right column.

_____ 1. Ovaries

_____ 2. Fallopian tubes

_____ 3. Uterus

_____ 4. Cervix

_____ 5. Vagina

_____ 6. Labia

_____ 7. Perineum

_____ 8. Chlamydia

_____ 9. Pelvic inflammatory disease (PID)

_____ 10. Bacterial vaginosis

_____ 11. Gonorrhea

A. Folds of tissue that surround the urethral and vaginal openings

B. Narrowest portion of the uterus; opens to the vagina

C. Disease causing lower abdominal and back pain, nausea, fever, pain during intercourse, and/or bleeding between menstrual cycles

D. Area of skin between the vagina and the anus

E. Connect(s) each ovary with the uterus

F. Infection of the uterus, ovaries, and fallopian tubes

G. Produce(s) an ovum, or an egg

H. Outermost cavity of a woman's reproductive system; forms the lower part of the birth canal

I. Condition in which bacteria can grow and multiply rapidly in the reproductive tract, mouth, throat, eyes, and anus

J. Condition in which normal bacteria is replaced by an overgrowth of other bacterial forms

K. Muscular organ where the fetus grows

Multiple Choice

Read each item carefully and then select the one best response.

_____ 1. Possible causes of vaginal bleeding include all of the following EXCEPT:

    A. ectopic pregnancy.

    B. cervical polyps.

    C. vaginal trauma.

    D. peptic ulcer.

_____ 2. Painful urination associated with burning and a yellowish discharge is associated with:

    A. chlamydia.

    B. gonorrhea.

    C. endometriosis.

    D. syphilis.

_____ 3. Which of the following statements is FALSE regarding assessment and treatment of a woman who was the victim of sexual assault?

    A. You may be called to testify in court regarding the incident.

    B. You should question the victim thoroughly about the assaulter in case the police missed any details.

    C. The patient should be given the option of being treated by a female responder.

    D. The patient should be discouraged from urinating or changing her clothes prior to examination at the hospital.

_____ **4.** The onset of menstruation usually occurs between the ages of:
   A. 8 and 10 years.
   B. 11 and 16 years.
   C. 16 and 18 years.
   D. 17 and 20 years.

_____ **5.** What is the most common presenting sign or symptom of PID?
   A. Vaginal discharge
   B. Fever
   C. Nausea and vomiting
   D. Lower abdominal pain

_____ **6.** In rare cases, _____ causes arthritis that may be accompanied with skin lesions and inflammation of the eyes and urethra.
   A. chlamydia
   B. gonorrhea
   C. PID
   D. vaginal bleeding

_____ **7.** Left untreated, _____ can lead to premature birth or low birth weight in pregnant women.
   A. chlamydia
   B. gonorrhea
   C. bacterial vaginosis
   D. vaginal bleeding

_____ **8.** If a patient with vaginal bleeding presents with a rapid pulse and pale or cool skin, you should:
   A. attempt to locate the source of bleeding and correct it.
   B. place the patient in a supine position.
   C. consider this to be a normal sign in a menstruating woman.
   D. inquire about recent problems with urination.

_____ **9.** When taking a history on a patient experiencing a gynecologic emergency, you should consider asking all of the following EXCEPT:
   A. Are you taking birth control?
   B. When was your last menstrual period?
   C. How many sexual partners have you had in the past?
   D. Do you have any history of sexually transmitted diseases?

_____ **10.** What does the "PID shuffle" refer to?
   A. A distinctive gait when the patient walks.
   B. Rotation of the microorganisms that cause PID.
   C. Symptoms that come and go.
   D. A structural abnormality in a patient's cervix.

_____ **11.** EMTs treating a patient of a sexual assault may not only be dealing with medical issues but with _____ issues as well.
   A. psychological
   B. physiological
   C. educational
   D. sociological

_____ **12.** When performing a physical exam on a victim of sexual assault, you should:
   A. expose and evaluate the patient's vaginal area regardless of whether there is bleeding.
   B. allow multiple people to observe the examination in case you have to testify.
   C. limit your examination to a brief survey for life-threatening injuries.
   D. place the patient's clothes into a paper bag.

_____ **13.** Rape is considered to be a _____ diagnosis, not a medical diagnosis.
   A. psychological
   B. surgical
   C. sociological
   D. legal

_____ **14.** Often the most important intervention for a sexual assault patient is _____ and transport to a facility with a staff specially trained to deal with this scenario.
   A. comforting reassurance
   B. excellent assessment skills
   C. bandaging skills
   D. emotional sympathy

_____ **15.** Your _____ is the best tool to gain the patient's confidence to seek medical help.
   A. professionalism
   B. content knowledge
   C. compassion
   D. empathy

Questions 16–18 are derived from the following scenario: You are called to the scene of a possible assault. On arrival, you are directed by police to a dark room where you find a 22-year-old woman who says she was sexually assaulted by a coworker this afternoon.

_____ **16.** Your first course of action should be to:
   A. determine whether the patient is physically injured.
   B. establish the exact events of what took place.
   C. allow the patient to use the restroom.
   D. let the police question the patient before conducting a primary assessment.

_____ **17.** The second course of action involves the psychological care of the patient. You should avoid:
   A. making attempts to get a female EMT to examine the patient.
   B. examination of the vaginal canal, even if active bleeding is taking place.
   C. attempting to gather information to assist the police.
   D. granting the patient's wishes for refusing care and transport.

_____ **18.** The patient tells you that she would really like to be transported to the hospital but refuses a physical examination. You should:
   A. explain to her that she cannot be transported without a physical exam.
   B. have the police take the patient into custody in order to legally force a physical exam.
   C. explain to her that this is a criminal case and that she must be examined.
   D. follow your system's refusal of treatment policy and respect the patient's wishes without judgment.

True/False

If you believe the statement to be more true than false, write the letter "T" in the space provided. If you believe the statement to be more false than true, write the letter "F."

_____ **1.** Chlamydial infection of the cervix can spread to the rectum, leading to rectal pain, discharge, or bleeding.

_____ **2.** If gonorrhea is not treated, the bacteria may enter the bloodstream and spread to other parts of the body, including the brain.

_____ **3.** Because menstrual bleeding is a monthly occurrence, it is not necessary to assess for other causes of vaginal bleeding.

_____ **4.** Obtaining an accurate and detailed patient assessment is critical when dealing with gynecologic issues.

_____ **5.** Most cases of gynecologic emergencies are not life threatening.

_____ **6.** Gynecologic emergencies are typically not embarrassing for women.

_____ 7. When taking a history of a woman with a gynecologic complaint, you should inquire about the possibility of pregnancy and exposure to sexually transmitted diseases.

_____ 8. Most presentations of tachycardia and hypotension are related to anxiety.

_____ 9. Any report of syncope in a woman complaining of vaginal bleeding is considered significant.

_____ 10. It is acceptable to place dressings into the vaginal canal to stop significant bleeding.

_____ 11. When examining a female, you should limit the number of people involved.

_____ 12. Gynecologic emergencies can occur at any age during a woman's lifetime.

_____ 13. Injuries to the external genitals are typically not painful due to the very sparse nerve supply.

_____ 14. When completing documentation of a sexual assault incident, adding your personal thoughts can help with the investigation.

_____ 15. Determining the cause of vaginal bleeding should be of less importance than treating for shock and transporting the patient to an appropriate facility.

Fill-in-the-Blank

Read each item carefully and then complete the statement by filling in the missing words.

1. The _____ are located on each side of the lower abdomen and produce the ovum, or egg.

2. When a female reaches _____, she begins to ovulate and experience menstruation.

3. _____ _____ _____ is an infection of the upper female reproductive organs.

4. _____ _____ can be very messy, sometimes involving large amounts of blood and bodily fluids.

5. _____ _____ and _____ _____ are two conditions that can cause vaginal bleeding in women who do not appear to be pregnant and who may not realize they are pregnant.

6. Make sure to use _____ _____ when attempting to control vaginal bleeding.

7. _____ _____ can cause significant blood loss and lead to hypovolemia.

8. You will need to work together with _____ _____ when dealing with a victim of sexual assault.

9. Symptoms of _____ appear approximately 2 to 10 days after exposure.

10. Women will continue to experience menstruation until they reach _____.

Labeling

Label the following diagrams with the correct terms.

1. Female Reproductive System

A. _____

B. _____

C. _____

D. _____

E. _____

FRONT VIEW

SIDE VIEW

© Jones & Bartlett Learning.

2. External Genitalia

A. _____

B. _____

C. _____

D. _____

E. _____

F. _____

© Jones & Bartlett Learning.

Crossword Puzzle

The following crossword puzzle is an activity provided to reinforce correct spelling and understanding of medical terminology associated with emergency care and the EMT. Use the clues in the column to complete the puzzle.

Across

5. The primary female reproductive organs that produce an ovum, or egg.

6. The lower third, or neck, of the uterus.

7. The muscular organ where the fetus grows.

9. Sexual intercourse inflicted forcibly on another person, against that person's will.

11. Outer fleshy "lips" covered with pubic hair that protect the vagina.

12. The outermost cavity of a woman's reproductive system; the lower part of the birth canal.

13. _____ tubes connect each ovary with the uterus and are the primary location for fertilization of the ovum.

Down

1. A sexually transmitted disease caused by *Neisseria gonorrhoeae*.

2. Inner fleshy "lips" devoid of pubic hair that protect the vagina.

3. _____ vaginosis is an overgrowth of bacteria in the vagina.

4. An attack against a person that is sexual in nature, the most common of which is rape.

8. A sexually transmitted disease caused by the bacterium *Chlamydia trachomatis*.

10. An infection of the fallopian tubes and the surrounding tissues of the pelvis.

Critical Thinking

Short Answer

Complete this section with short written answers using the space provided.

1. When performing your scene size-up, what questions should you ask yourself when dealing with a gynecologic emergency?

_____

_____

_____

2. List at least five signs and symptoms commonly found with a gonorrhea infection.

_____

_____

_____

3. Explain the general treatment strategies for vaginal bleeding.

_____

_____

_____

Ambulance Calls

The following case scenarios provide an opportunity to explore the concerns associated with patient management and to enhance critical-thinking skills. Read each scenario and answer each question to the best of your ability.

1. You are dispatched to a local college campus for a 21-year-old woman with abdominal pain. The dispatcher tells you the patient has lower abdominal pain, fever, nausea, and vomiting. When you arrive on the campus, you are directed by campus police to the health center. There you find your patient lying supine on a bed. The patient tells you she has had lower abdominal pain and a fever for the past 24 hours. She describes the pain as "achy" and says it gets worse with walking. She believes she has a "stomach virus" due to the fever and vomiting. Your partner obtains vital signs as you continue with your assessment. After finishing your SAMPLE history, you casually ask if she has had any other recent illnesses or if she has any other complaints. The patient says, "Well, since you mentioned it, I've been having some rather foul vaginal discharge lately. But I just thought it would go away." The patient denies pregnancy because she just finished her menstrual period last week.

What is the likely cause of this patient's condition and how is it treated?

_____

_____

_____

2. You are dispatched to an apartment complex at 538 N. 10th Street, Apartment 4-C, for an assault. You look at your watch and note the time as 2101. On the way to the unit your partner remarks, "689th call for the year so far. No doubt we'll hit 700 before the end of the night." You make note of the incident number at 011689, and mark responding 2 minutes after dispatch. The additional information states this is for a 32-year-old woman who was sexually assaulted.

You arrive on scene 8 minutes after the initial dispatch and notice the apartment is very well kept and is not cluttered. The police lead you to the back bedroom where you find your patient sitting up on the side of the bed speaking to the investigator. The patient appears alert, and you notice bleeding from the nose along with bruises to the patient's face. The patient tells you that she was raped by a maintenance worker at the apartment complex. She complains of pain to the nose, face, and groin. The patient says she is not sure whether she wants to go to the hospital, but she definitely wants to take a shower and change her clothes.

Explain the key issues to consider when treating a victim of sexual assault.

_____

_____

_____

Fill-in-the-Patient Care Report

Using the previous case (Ambulance Call 2) and the additional information provided, complete the patient care report (PCR) for this incident.

You explain to the patient that she should refrain from changing her clothes or washing because she could disrupt any potential evidence. The police agree with your statement.

As the police continue with some questions, you complete an initial assessment while your partner obtains the following vital signs at 2114: pulse, 102 beats/min; respirations, 22 breaths/min; blood pressure, 144/98 mm Hg; pulse oximetry, 98%.

You ask the patient if she would be more comfortable with a female EMT. Her response is a simple "No." The patient appears withdrawn and emotionally traumatized. You notice no obvious life-threatening injuries and ask the patient if she has bleeding anywhere. Her response, "No." The only visible external injuries you can find are multiple contusions to the face.

The patient does not make eye contact with you while questioning her medical history (diabetes), medications (lispro, Lantus, lisinopril), and allergies (none). When you ask her if she would like to tell you "what happened," she responds by saying, "Can't we just get going to the hospital? I would rather speak to the doctor."

You smile and say, "Absolutely."

Your partner applies oxygen at 2 L/min via nasal cannula. The patient is packaged on the litter and is loaded into the unit. Your partner verifies the hospital destination with the police so that they can continue with their investigation. You note that you were on scene a total of 11 minutes.

During transport, you notice that it has been 11 minutes since the vitals were assessed and ask the patient if she is having any pain. Her response, "No." You reassess the patient's vital signs: pulse, 108 beats/min; respirations, 20 breaths/min; blood pressure, 148/92 mm Hg; pulse oximetry, 97%.

Instead of calling in a report to the hospital, your partner calls in a basic update from the front of the cab so that the patient does not relive the experience.

You arrive at the hospital about 6 minutes after you reassessed the vitals. Care is transferred to the hospital staff, with no change in the patient's status. The nurse asks for a report, and you motion for her to leave the room with you. You give the report to the nurse away from the patient and any potential unnecessary personnel.

You and your partner don't have much to say to one another. The unit is cleaned and restocked, and you put yourself back in service at 2147.

Fill-in-the-Patient Care Report

EMS Patient Care Report (PCR)					
Date:	Incident No.:	Nature of Call:		Location:	
Dispatched:	En Route:	At Scene:	Transport:	At Hospital:	In Service:
Patient Information					
Age: Sex: Weight (in kg [lb]):			Allergies: Medications: Past Medical History: Chief Complaint:		
Vital Signs					
Time:	BP:	Pulse:	Respirations:	Spo_2:	
Time:	BP:	Pulse:	Respirations:	Spo_2:	
Time:	BP:	Pulse:	Respirations:	Spo_2:	
EMS Treatment (circle all that apply)					
Oxygen @ ____ L/min via (circle one): NC NRM BVM		Assisted Ventilation	Airway Adjunct		CPR
Defibrillation	Bleeding Control	Bandaging	Splinting		Other:
Narrative					

CHAPTER

Trauma Overview

24

© Photos.com

General Knowledge

Matching

Match each of the items in the left column to the appropriate definition in the right column.

_____ 1. Cavitation

_____ 2. Multisystem trauma

_____ 3. Kinetic energy

_____ 4. Mechanism of injury (MOI)

_____ 5. Potential energy

_____ 6. Blunt trauma

_____ 7. Penetrating trauma

_____ 8. Work

A. Result of force to the body that causes injury but does not penetrate soft tissue or internal organs and cavities

B. Force acting over a distance

C. Product of mass, gravity, and height

D. Injury caused by objects that pierce the surface of the body

E. How trauma occurs

F. Energy of a moving object

G. Significant MOI that causes injuries to more than one body system

H. Pressure waves that can damage nearby structures

Multiple Choice

Read each item carefully and then select the one best response.

_____ 1. Your awareness of and concern for potentially serious obvious and underlying injuries is referred to as the:
   A. mechanism of injury.
   B. index of suspicion.
   C. scene size-up.
   D. general impression.

_____ 2. The energy of a moving object is called:
   A. potential energy.
   B. thermal energy.
   C. kinetic energy.
   D. work.

_____ 3. Energy can be:
   A. created.
   B. destroyed.
   C. converted.
   D. lost.

_____ 4. The amount of kinetic energy that is converted to do work on the body dictates the _____ of the injury.
   A. location
   B. severity
   C. cause
   D. speed

_____ **5.** All of the following are considered types of motorcycle impacts EXCEPT:

    A. head-on collision.

    B. angular collision.

    C. controlled collision.

    D. rear collision.

_____ **6.** Which of the following is considered a type of impact from a motor vehicle collision?

    A. Ejection

    B. Rollover

    C. Crush

    D. Penetration

_____ **7.** The three collisions in a frontal impact include all of the following EXCEPT:

    A. car striking object.

    B. passenger striking vehicle.

    C. airbag striking passenger.

    D. internal organs striking solid structures of the body.

_____ **8.** Which of the following is NOT considered appropriate use of air medical services?

    A. The distance to a trauma center is greater than 25 miles.

    B. Traffic/road conditions make it unlikely to get the patient to the hospital in a timely manner.

    C. There is a mass-casualty incident.

    D. The closest trauma center is 10 minutes away by ground transport.

_____ **9.** Medium-velocity penetrating injuries may be caused by a:

    A. knife.

    B. military assault rifle.

    C. handgun.

    D. slingshot.

_____ **10.** In a motor vehicle collision, as the passenger's head hits the windshield, the brain continues to move forward until it strikes the inside of the skull, resulting in a _____ injury.

    A. compression

    B. laceration

    C. lateral

    D. motion

_____ **11.** Your quick primary assessment of the patient and evaluation of the _____ can help to direct lifesaving care and provide critical information to the hospital staff.

    A. environment

    B. index of suspicion

    C. mechanism of injury

    D. abdominal area

_____ **12.** A contusion to a patient's forehead along with a spider-webbed windshield suggests possible injury to the:

    A. nose.

    B. brain.

    C. face.

    D. heart.

_____ **13.** Which of the following is the most common cause of death from a blast injury?

    A. Amputation

    B. Burns

    C. Chest trauma

    D. Head trauma

_____ **14.** Significant clues to the possibility of severe injuries in motor vehicle collisions include:

    A. death of a passenger.

    B. a blown out tire.

    C. broken glass.

    D. a deployed airbag.

_____ **15.** Damage to the body that resulted from a pressure wave generated by an explosion is found in what type of blast injury?

    A. Primary

    B. Secondary

    C. Tertiary

    D. Miscellaneous

_____ **16.** Airbags decrease injury to all of the following EXCEPT:

    A. chest.

    B. heart.

    C. face.

    D. head.

_____ **17.** Optimally, on-scene time for critically injured patients should be less than _____ minutes.

    A. 5

    B. 10

    C. 15

    D. 20

_____ **18.** _____ impacts are commonly referred to as T-bone crashes.

    A. Frontal

    B. Lateral

    C. Rear-end

    D. Rollover

_____ **19.** The most common life-threatening event in a rollover is _____ or partial ejection of the passenger from the vehicle.

    A. vehicle intrusion

    B. centrifugal force

    C. ejection

    D. spinal cord injury

_____ **20.** A fall from more than _____ times the patient's height is considered to be significant.

    A. 1 to 2

    B. 2 to 3

    C. 3 to 4

    D. 4 to 5

Questions 21-24 are derived from the following scenario: A young boy was riding his bicycle down the street when he hit a parked car.

_____ **21.** How many collisions took place?

    A. One

    B. Two

    C. Three

    D. Four

_____ **22.** What was the first collision?

    A. The bike hitting the car

    B. The bike rider hitting his bike or the car

    C. The bike rider's internal organs against the solid structures of the body

    D. The bike rider striking the pavement

_____ **23.** What was the second collision?
  A. The bike hitting the car
  B. The bike rider hitting his bike or the car
  C. The bike rider's internal organs against the solid structures of the body
  D. The bike rider striking the pavement

_____ **24.** What will raise your index of suspicion for this collision?
  A. The mechanism of injury
  B. The type of bike
  C. How loudly he's crying
  D. A quick visual assessment

_____ **25.** "For every action, there is an equal and opposite reaction" is:
  A. Newton's first law.
  B. Newton's second law.
  C. Newton's third law.
  D. a false statement.

_____ **26.** "A comprehensive regional resource capable of providing every aspect of trauma care from prevention through rehabilitation" is the definition of a _____ trauma center.
  A. Level I
  B. Level II
  C. Level III
  D. Level IV

_____ **27.** Which of the following is NOT considered a type of impact associated with a motorcycle crash?
  A. Head-on
  B. Rotational
  C. Controlled
  D. Ejection

_____ **28.** Burns from hot gases and respiratory injuries from inhaling toxic gas are associated with which type of blast injury?
  A. Primary
  B. Secondary
  C. Tertiary
  D. Miscellaneous

_____ **29.** A patient complaining of chest tightness, coughing up blood, and subcutaneous emphysema following an explosion may be suffering from a:
  A. myocardial blast injury.
  B. ruptured tympanic membrane.
  C. ruptured peritoneal cavity.
  D. pulmonary blast injury.

_____ **30.** Patients suffering from an open wound to the neck may experience all of the following EXCEPT:
  A. significant bleeding.
  B. air embolism.
  C. tension pneumothorax.
  D. subcutaneous crepitation.

True/False

If you believe the statement to be more true than false, write the letter "T" in the space provided. If you believe the statement to be more false than true, write the letter "F."

_____ **1.** *Work* is defined as force acting over distance.

_____ **2.** Energy can be both created and destroyed.

_____ **3.** The energy of a moving object is called potential energy.

_____ **4.** Rear-end collisions often cause whiplash injuries.

_____ **5.** Penetration or perforation to the chest wall is called an open chest wound.

_____ **6.** The injury potential of a fall is related to the height from which the patient fell.

_____ **7.** In the United States, traumatic injuries are the leading cause of death for people younger than 44 years.

_____ **8.** Rapid transport of an unstable trauma patient takes priority over assessing and managing the ABCs.

_____ **9.** Injuries to the aorta are relatively common in lateral impacts from a motor vehicle collision.

_____ **10.** Headrests are the major cause of whiplash-type injuries in rear-impact collisions.

_____ **11.** In car-versus-pedestrian collisions, the speed of the vehicle should be the first step in determining the mechanism of injury.

_____ **12.** Helmets are reliable at protecting against cervical spine injuries.

_____ **13.** Tertiary blast injuries result from flying debris, such as glass or shrapnel, striking the patient.

_____ **14.** You should perform frequent neurologic assessments in patients with a presumed head injury.

_____ **15.** All patients with chest trauma, regardless of the injury, should be reassessed every 5 minutes.

Fill-in-the-Blank

Read each item carefully and then complete the statement by filling in the missing words.

1. Energy that is available to cause injury _____ when an object's weight doubles, but _____ when its speed doubles.

2. _____ _____ causes injury by objects that pierce the surface of the body and cause damage to soft tissues, internal organs, and body cavities.

3. A compression injury to the anterior portion of the brain and stretching of the posterior portion is called a(n) _____ brain injury.

4. The formula for calculating kinetic energy is _____.

5. Whiplash-type injuries are typically caused by _____ impacts.

6. Airbags provide the final capture point of the passengers and decrease the severity of _____ injuries.

7. _____ trauma is a term that describes a person who has been subjected to multiple traumatic injuries involving more than one body system.

8. A T-bone collision typically refers to a(n) _____ impact.

9. The most common life-threatening event in a rollover collision is _____.

10. The liver, spleen, pancreas, and kidneys are all considered _____ organs in the abdomen.

11. The _____ _____ Scale uses eye opening, verbal response, and motor response to rate a patient's level of consciousness.

12. Air collecting between the lung tissue and the chest wall is commonly referred to as a(n) _____.

13. _____ _____ describes the limited on-scene time for patients with multisystem trauma.

14. _____ _____ _____ states that an object at rest tends to stay at rest, and an object in motion

tends to stay in motion, unless acted on by some force.

15. A(n) _____ emergency occurs when the patient has an illness or condition that is not caused by an

outside force.

Fill-in-the-Table

Fill in the missing parts of the table.

Recognizing Developing Problems in Trauma Patients		
Mechanism of Injury	**Signs and Symptoms**	**Index of Suspicion**
Blunt or penetrating trauma to the neck	• • • • • • • •	• Significant bleeding or foreign bodies in the upper or lower airway, causing obstruction • Be alert for airway compromise.
Significant chest wall trauma from motor vehicle, car-versus-pedestrian, and other crashes; penetrating trauma to the chest wall	• • • • • • • • • • • •	• Cardiac or pulmonary contusion • Pneumothorax or hemothorax • Broken ribs, causing breathing compromise
Any significant blunt force trauma from motor vehicle crashes or penetrating injury	• • • • • •	• Injuries in these regions may tear and cause damage to the large blood vessels located in these body areas, resulting in significant internal and external bleeding. • Be alert to the possibility of bruising to the brain and bleeding in and around the brain tissue, which may cause the development of excess pressure inside the skull around the brain.
Any significant blunt force trauma, falls from a significant height, or penetrating trauma	• • •	• Injuries to the bones of the spinal column or to the spinal cord

Crossword Puzzle

The following crossword puzzle is an activity provided to reinforce correct spelling and understanding of medical terminology associated with emergency care and the EMT. Use the clues in the column to complete the puzzle.

Across

1. The path a projectile takes once it is propelled.
3. An impact on the body without penetrating soft tissues or internal organs and cavities.
5. Resistance that slows a projectile, such as air.
7. Pulmonary trauma resulting from short-range exposure to the detonation of explosives is known as pulmonary _____ injury.
9. The _____ membrane is the eardrum.
11. A scoring system used for patients with head trauma.
12. Emergencies that are the result of physical forces applied to a patient's body are known as _____ emergencies.
13. _____ energy is the energy of a moving object.
14. The forces or energy transmission that cause injury.
15. A phenomenon in which speed causes a bullet to generate pressure waves.

Down

2. A score that takes into account the GCS score, respiratory rate, respiratory expansion, systolic blood pressure, and capillary refill.
4. _____ trauma affects more than one body system.
5. The slowing of an object.
6. Index of _____ is an awareness that unseen life-threatening injuries may exist.
8. _____ emergencies are illnesses or conditions not caused by an outside force.
10. The product of force times distance.

Critical Thinking

Short Answer
Complete this section with short written answers using the space provided.

1. Describe potential energy.

_____

_____

_____

2. List the series of collisions typical with motor vehicles.

_____

_____

_____

3. List the three factors to consider when evaluating a fall.

_____

_____

_____

4. Describe the phenomenon of cavitation as it relates to an injury from a bullet.

_____

_____

_____

5. Why is it important to try to determine the type of gun and ammunition used when you are caring for a gunshot victim?

_____

_____

_____

6. What type of injuries can you expect from a motor vehicle collision with a lateral impact and substantial intrusion?

_____

_____

_____

7. List the information you should gather when determining the MOI of a motorcycle crash.

_____

_____

_____

8. What is the definition of a Level I trauma center?

_____

_____

_____

Ambulance Calls

The following case scenarios provide an opportunity to explore the concerns associated with patient management and to enhance critical-thinking skills. Read each scenario and answer each question to the best of your ability.

1. You are dispatched to a one-car crash As you arrive, you notice that the car hit a large deer, which is lying in the road, dead. Highway speed limits on this road are 65 mph (105 kph). The driver was restrained with a lap belt only, and his vehicle was not equipped with airbags. He is complaining of head and neck pain and tells you that he doesn't remember what happened.

How would you best manage this patient?

_____

_____

_____

2. You are dispatched to assist a man who fell from a ladder as he was repairing shingles on the roof of his two-story home. You arrive to find an unconscious middle-aged man lying on the ground. He is breathing and has a pulse. The call to 9-1-1 was placed after the man was found by a neighbor.

How would you best manage this patient?

_____

_____

_____

3. You are called to the residence of a 19-year-old man who was stabbed in the abdomen with an ice pick. The scene is safe, and the patient is lying on the floor with the ice pick impaled in his left lower quadrant. Bystanders tell you he did not fall. He is alert and complaining of severe pain.

How would you best manage this patient?

_____

_____

_____

4. You are called to the scene of a pedestrian struck by a motor vehicle in a residential neighborhood. As you approach the scene, you notice a vehicle pulled off to the side with damage to its bumper and hood and what appears to be a person lying unresponsive in the roadway.

What factors do you need to consider when determining the mechanism of injury?

_____

_____

_____

General Knowledge

Matching

Match each of the items in the left column to the appropriate definition in the right column.

_____ 1. Pulmonary artery

_____ 2. Heart

_____ 3. Ventricle

_____ 4. Aorta

_____ 5. Atrium

_____ 6. Pulmonary vein

_____ 7. Coagulation

_____ 8. Ecchymosis

_____ 9. Epistaxis

_____ 10. Hematoma

_____ 11. Hemophilia

_____ 12. Hemorrhage

_____ 13. Hypovolemic shock

A. Mass of blood in the soft tissues beneath the skin

B. Formation of a clot to plug an opening in an injured blood vessel, stopping blood flow

C. Upper chamber

D. A congenital condition in which a patient lacks one or more of the blood's normal clotting factors

E. Works as two paired pumps

F. Largest artery in the body

G. A condition in which low blood volume results in inadequate perfusion

H. Oxygenated blood travels through this back to the heart

I. Bruising

J. Blood flow to the lungs

K. Lower chamber

L. Bleeding

M. Nosebleed

Multiple Choice

Read each item carefully and then select the one best response.

_____ 1. The function of the blood is to _____ all of the body's cells and tissues.

    A. remove oxygen from

    B. deliver nutrients to

    C. carry waste products to

    D. hydrate

_____ 2. The cardiovascular system consists of all of the following EXCEPT:

    A. a pump.

    B. a container.

    C. fluid.

    D. a battery.

_____ 3. Blood leaves each chamber of a normal heart through a(n):

    A. vein.

    B. artery.

    C. one-way valve.

    D. capillary.

_____ 4. Blood enters the right atrium from the:

    A. coronary arteries.

    B. lungs.

    C. vena cava.

    D. coronary veins.

_____ **5.** Blood enters the left atrium from the:
  A. coronary arteries.
  B. lungs.
  C. vena cava.
  D. coronary veins.

_____ **6.** Which of the following is NOT a factor in the formation of blood clots?
  A. Pumping function of the heart
  B. Blood stasis
  C. Ability of blood to clot
  D. Changes to the walls of blood vessels

_____ **7.** The _____ is the thickest chamber of the heart.
  A. right atrium
  B. right ventricle
  C. left atrium
  D. left ventricle

_____ **8.** The _____ link(s) the arterioles and the venules.
  A. aorta
  B. capillaries
  C. vena cava
  D. valves

_____ **9.** _____ are the key to formation of blood clots.
  A. Capillaries
  B. White blood cells
  C. Red blood cells
  D. Platelets

_____ **10.** Blood contains all of the following EXCEPT:
  A. white blood cells.
  B. plasma.
  C. cerebrospinal fluid.
  D. platelets.

_____ **11.** _____ is the circulation of blood within an organ or tissue in adequate amounts to meet the cells' current needs for oxygen, nutrients, and waste removal.
  A. Anatomy
  B. Perfusion
  C. Physiology
  D. Conduction

_____ **12.** The _____ only require(s) a minimal blood supply when at rest.
  A. lungs
  B. kidneys
  C. muscles
  D. heart

_____ **13.** What part of the human body helps the cardiovascular system adapt to changes in order to maintain homeostasis?
  A. Respiratory system
  B. Central nervous system
  C. Autonomic nervous system
  D. Musculoskeletal system

_____ **14.** _____ is inadequate tissue perfusion.
   A. Shock
   B. Hyperperfusion
   C. Hypertension
   D. Contraction

_____ **15.** The brain and spinal cord usually cannot go for more than _____ minutes without perfusion, or the nerve cells will be permanently damaged.
   A. 30 to 45
   B. 12 to 20
   C. 8 to 10
   D. 4 to 6

_____ **16.** An organ or tissue that is considerably _____ is much better able to resist damage from hypoperfusion.
   A. warmer
   B. colder
   C. younger
   D. older

_____ **17.** The body will not tolerate an acute blood loss of greater than _____ of blood volume.
   A. 10%
   B. 20%
   C. 30%
   D. 40%

_____ **18.** If the typical adult loses more than 1 L of blood, significant changes in vital signs, such as _____, will occur.
   A. decreased heart rate
   B. increased respiratory rate
   C. increased blood pressure
   D. improved capillary refill time

_____ **19.** _____ shock is a condition in which low blood volume results in inadequate perfusion or even death.
   A. Hypovolemic
   B. Metabolic
   C. Septic
   D. Psychogenic

_____ **20.** You should consider bleeding to be serious if all of the following conditions are present EXCEPT:
   A. blood loss is rapid.
   B. there is no mechanism of injury.
   C. the patient has a poor general appearance.
   D. assessment reveals signs and symptoms of shock.

_____ **21.** Life-threatening external bleeding demands your immediate attention, even before the _____ has been managed.
   A. fracture
   B. extrication
   C. airway
   D. scene

_____ **22.** The process of blood clotting and plugging the hole is called:
   A. conglomeration.
   B. configuration.
   C. coagulation.
   D. coalition.

_____ **23.** Which of the following inhibits the body's ability to control bleeding?

    A. Medications that interfere with normal clotting

    B. Wounds that are extremely small in size

    C. Increased constriction of the blood vessels

    D. Shifting blood to protect organs

_____ **24.** A lack of one or more of the blood's clotting factors is called:

    A. a deficiency.

    B. hemophilia.

    C. platelet anomaly.

    D. anemia.

_____ **25.** You respond to a 25-year-old man who has cut his arm with a circular saw. The bleeding appears to be bright red and spurting. The patient is alert and oriented and converses with you freely. He appears to be stable at this point. What is your first step in controlling his bleeding?

    A. Direct pressure

    B. Maintain the airway

    C. Standard precautions

    D. Elevation

_____ **26.** When applying a bandage to hold a dressing in place, stretch the bandage tight enough to control the bleeding. You should still be able to _____ after the bandage is secure.

    A. palpate a distal pulse

    B. see bleeding through the dressing

    C. examine the wound

    D. remove the dressing

_____ **27.** If bleeding continues after applying a pressure dressing, you should do all of the following EXCEPT:

    A. remove the dressing and apply another sterile dressing.

    B. apply manual pressure through the dressing.

    C. add more gauze pads over the first dressing.

    D. secure both dressings tighter with a roller bandage.

_____ **28.** When using an air splint to control bleeding in a fractured extremity, you should reassess the _____ frequently.

    A. airway

    B. breathing

    C. circulation in the injured extremity

    D. fracture site

_____ **29.** When treating a patient with signs and symptoms of hypovolemic shock and no outward signs of bleeding, always consider the possibility of bleeding into the:

    A. thoracic cavity.

    B. abdomen.

    C. skull.

    D. chest.

_____ **30.** Which of the following is NOT a cause of nontraumatic internal bleeding?

    A. Ulcer

    B. Ruptured ectopic pregnancy

    C. Aneurysm

    D. Laceration

_____ **31.** The most common symptom of internal abdominal bleeding is:

    A. bruising around the abdomen.

    B. distention of the abdomen.

    C. rigidity of the abdomen.

    D. acute abdominal pain.

_____ **32.** Signs and symptoms of internal bleeding in both trauma and medical patients include:

    A. hematemesis.

    B. abrasions.

    C. lacerations.

    D. avulsions.

_____ **33.** The first sign of hypovolemic shock is a change in:

    A. respirations.

    B. heart rate.

    C. mental status.

    D. blood pressure.

True/False

If you believe the statement to be more true than false, write the letter "T" in the space provided. If you believe the statement to be more false than true, write the letter "F."

_____ **1.** Venous blood tends to spurt and is difficult to control.

_____ **2.** The human body is tolerant of blood losses greater than 20% of blood volume.

_____ **3.** The first step in controlling external bleeding is applying pressure to the proximal artery.

_____ **4.** The first step in preparing to treat a bleeding patient is standard precautions.

_____ **5.** A properly applied tourniquet should be loosened by the EMT every 10 minutes.

_____ **6.** A patient who has swallowed a lot of blood may become nauseated and vomit.

_____ **7.** You should contact medical control before applying a tourniquet.

_____ **8.** If a wound continues to bleed after it is bandaged, you should remove the bandage and start over again.

_____ **9.** A tourniquet is always required for massive spurting blood loss.

_____ **10.** You should provide high-flow oxygen whenever you suspect internal bleeding.

Fill-in-the-Blank

Read each item carefully and then complete the statement by filling in the missing words.

1. The _____ side of the heart receives oxygen-poor blood from the veins.

2. _____ is the circulation of blood within an organ or tissue in adequate amounts to meet the cells' current needs for oxygen, nutrients, and waste removal.

3. A(n) _____ is also called a contusion.

4. _____ bleeding is any bleeding in a cavity or space inside the body.

5. A systolic blood pressure of less than _____ mm Hg with a weak, rapid pulse suggests the presence of hypoperfusion in a patient who may have significant bleeding.

6. _____ is vomited blood.

7. _____ blood is dark red and oozes from a wound steadily but slowly.

8. The _____ _____ system monitors the body's needs from moment to moment and adjusts blood flow by changing the vascular tone, as needed.

9. _____ are small tubes that are about the same diameter as a single red blood cell.

10. All organs depend on the _____ to provide a rich blood supply.

Labeling

Label the following diagrams with the correct terms.

1. The Left and Right Sides of the Heart

A. _____

B. _____

C. _____

D. _____

E. _____

F. _____

G. _____

H. _____

I. _____

J. _____

K. _____

L. _____

M. _____

N. _____

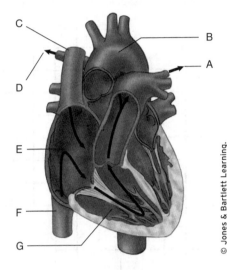

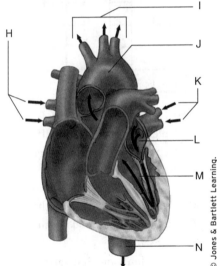

2. Perfusion

A. _____

B. _____

C. _____

D. _____

E. _____

F. _____

G. _____

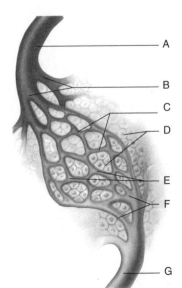

© Jones & Bartlett Learning.

Crossword Puzzle

The following crossword puzzle is an activity provided to reinforce correct spelling and understanding of medical terminology associated with emergency care and the EMT. Use the clues in the column to complete the puzzle.

Across

1. Discoloration of the skin associated with a closed wound.
4. Vomited blood.
5. A bruise, or ecchymosis.
9. A blood vessel that carries blood away from the heart.
11. The blood vessels that carry blood from the tissues to the heart.
12. A congenital condition in which the patient lacks one or more of the blood's normal clotting factors.
13. The main artery that receives blood from the left ventricle and delivers it to all of the other arteries that carry blood to the tissues of the body.

Down

2. A mass of blood in the soft tissues beneath the skin.
3. A condition in which the circulatory system fails to provide sufficient circulation so that every body part can perform its function.
4. _____ shock is a condition in which low blood volume results in inadequate perfusion.
6. The bleeding control method used when a wound continues to bleed despite the use of direct pressure and elevation.
7. Circulation of blood within an organ or tissue in adequate amounts to meet the current needs of the cells.
8. A nosebleed.
10. Black, foul-smelling, tarry stool containing digested blood.

Critical Thinking

Multiple Choice

Read each critical-thinking item carefully and then select the one best response.

_____ 1. You and your partner respond to a patient who has had his hand nearly severed by a drill press. As you approach, you note that the patient is pale and there appears to be a lot of blood on the floor. The wound continues to bleed copiously. After applying a tourniquet, you write _____ and _____ on a piece of adhesive tape and apply it to the patient's forehead.

    A. the patient's name; tourniquet location

    B. your last name; unit number

    C. the letters "TK"; the exact time applied

    D. the date and time; estimated amount of blood loss

_____ 2. In question 1, when applying the tourniquet you must be sure to:

    A. use the narrowest bandage possible to minimize the area restricted.

    B. cover the tourniquet with a bandage.

    C. never pad underneath the tourniquet.

    D. not loosen the tourniquet after you have applied it.

_____ 3. You are called to a playground for an 8-year-old girl who has an uncontrolled nosebleed. The child is crying and will not talk to you. The babysitter and other children present did not witness any trauma, but there is a bump on the temporal portion of the girl's head. The babysitter does state that the girl has had a cold for several days but can give you no further information on her medical history. What could NOT be the possible cause of the bleeding?

    A. A skull fracture

    B. Sinusitis

    C. Coagulation disorder

    D. A temper tantrum

_____ 4. You respond to a 33-year-old man who was hit in the ear by a line drive during a softball game. He is complaining of a severe headache, ringing in his ears, and dizziness. He has blood draining from his ear. Why would you not apply pressure to control bleeding?

    A. It should be collected to be reinfused at the hospital.

    B. It could collect within the head and increase the pressure on the brain.

    C. It is contaminated.

    D. You could fracture the skull with the pressure needed to staunch the flow of blood.

_____ 5. You are dispatched to a store in the downtown mall for an arm injury. When you arrive, you are directed to a small stock room where you find a teenaged girl holding a blood-soaked cloth tightly onto her left forearm. You notice blood droplets high up the wall and on the floor several feet from where she is sitting. "I was opening a shipment with a box cutter," she says, her skin noticeably pale. "And it slipped and cut my arm. The blood spurted everywhere." What type of bleeding should you anticipate?

    A. You should suspect heavy venous bleeding.

    B. She most likely has arterial bleeding.

    C. Internal bleeding is probably causing her skin to appear pale.

    D. Very sharp blades usually only cause capillary bleeding.

Short Answer

Complete this section with short written answers using the space provided.

1. Describe how the autonomic nervous system responds to severe bleeding.

_____

_____

_____

2. Describe the characteristics of bleeding from each type of vessel (artery, vein, capillary).

_____

_____

_____

3. List, in the proper sequence, the methods by which an EMT should attempt to control external bleeding of an extremity.

_____

_____

_____

4. List at least 10 signs and symptoms of hypovolemic shock.

_____

_____

_____

5. List, in the proper sequence, the general EMT emergency care for patients with internal bleeding.

_____

_____

_____

Ambulance Calls

The following case scenarios provide an opportunity to explore the concerns associated with patient management and to enhance critical-thinking skills. Read each scenario and answer each question to the best of your ability.

1. You arrive at a local school playground for a 9-year-old boy with a minor laceration on his left wrist. The teacher, who is holding a blood-soaked dressing on the boy's wound, tells you that she cannot stop the bleeding and that the boy has a history of hemophilia. The blood is steady, but not spurting, and dark in color.

    How would you best manage this patient?

    _____

    _____

    _____

2. You are dispatched to a local lumberyard for a machinery accident. When you arrive, you observe a man sitting on the ground, surrounded by coworkers. The very pale foreman runs up to you as you get out of the truck and says, "His shirt got caught in a chop saw. His arm got cut off just below the elbow." As you approach, you see that the man is holding a blood-soaked towel to the shortened end of his right arm.

    How would you best manage this patient?

    _____

    _____

    _____

3. Your team is called to the local jail for an inmate who has injured his arm with a ballpoint pen. You find that he is bleeding continuously from a wound that is in the area of the antecubital vein of his left arm.

    How would you best manage this patient?

    _____

    _____

    _____

Fill-in-the-Patient Care Report

Read the incident scenario and then complete the following patient care report (PCR).

You and your partner are posted at the corner of Seventh Street and Brogan Avenue, completing the paperwork for a recent respiratory distress call, when emergency tones burst from the radio:

"Two-fifty-three, priority traffic," the dispatcher says immediately. "Go ahead two-fifty-three," you respond.

"Two-fifty-three, code-three call to 1467 Abner Lane for a leg laceration. Show your time of dispatch at 1653."

You copy the assignment and slowly roll out into traffic after activating the lights and siren, proceeding to the address about six blocks away.

Five minutes later, you pull up outside of a well-kept home in a newly completed subdivision and are met by woman frantically waving her arms.

"Please hurry!" she shouts as you open your door. "My husband was chopping wood in the backyard and hit himself with the axe. He's bleeding badly!"

You and your partner grab your bags and walk quickly to the home's backyard. The man, whom you estimate to be about 170 pounds (77 kg), is sitting on the redwood deck, pale and shaking, holding a bloody T-shirt against his lower left leg; a huge circle of blood is soaking into the wood deck under him.

"Sir, we're from the city ambulance service and we're here to help you," you say, kneeling next to the man. "Can you tell me what happened?"

As the 42-year-old man describes how the axe glanced off a knot in the log that he was chopping, sending it deep into the flesh of his leg, you remove the T-shirt from the wound, observing a jagged laceration approximately 3.5 inches (9 cm) long, and replace it with a wide trauma dressing. Your partner begins assessing vitals.

At 1704, your partner reports the patient's vitals: blood pressure is 136/86 mm Hg; pulse is 88 beats/min, strong and regular; respirations are 16 breaths/min with good tidal volume; pale, cool, and diaphoretic skin; and pulse oximetry is 97%.

About 5 minutes after obtaining vitals, you have stopped the bleeding using a pressure bandage and are loading the patient into the ambulance, keeping him covered with a blanket and placing him in a position of comfort.

His wife tells you that he is allergic to amoxicillin and that he has been taking a cholesterol medication called Crestor ever since he suffered a transient ischemic attack in the spring of last year. You thank her for the information and climb into the patient compartment while your partner jumps into the driver's seat. Within a minute, you are en route to the Southside Medical Center emergency department and taking the patient's vitals again. This time they read: blood pressure is 122/76 mm Hg; pulse is 102 beats/min, weak and regular; respirations are 20 breaths/min and shallow but with adequate tidal volume; skin is still pale, cool, and diaphoretic; and pulse oximetry is 94%.

At 1715, you arrive at the ambulance bay of the Southside Medical Center, quickly move the patient inside, and transfer his care to the emergency department staff. After giving a full report to the receiving nurse and properly cleaning and preparing the ambulance, you and your partner go back available at 1735.

Fill-in-the-Patient Care Report

EMS Patient Care Report (PCR)				
Date:	Incident No.:	Nature of Call:		Location:
Dispatched:	En Route:	At Scene:	Transport:	At Hospital:	In Service:

Patient Information		
Age: Sex: Weight (in kg [lb]):		Allergies: Medications: Past Medical History: Chief Complaint:

Vital Signs				
Time:	BP:	Pulse:	Respirations:	SpO_2:
Time:	BP:	Pulse:	Respirations:	SpO_2:
Time:	BP:	Pulse:	Respirations:	SpO_2:

EMS Treatment (circle all that apply)				
Oxygen @ ____ L/min via (circle one): NC NRM BVM	Assisted Ventilation	Airway Adjunct	CPR
Defibrillation	Bleeding Control	Bandaging	Splinting	Other:

Narrative

Skills

Skill Drills

Test your knowledge of these skills by filling in the correct words in the photo captions.

Skill Drill 25-1: Controlling External Bleeding

© Jones & Bartlett Learning.

© Jones & Bartlett Learning.

1. Take standard _____.
Apply _____ _____
over the wound with a dry, sterile
dressing.

2. Apply a _____ _____.

© Jones & Bartlett Learning.

© Jones & Bartlett Learning.

3. If direct pressure with a
_____ _____ does
not control the bleeding, apply a
_____ above the level of the
_____.

4. Tighten the _____ until distal
_____ are no longer palpable.
Properly position the _____.
Apply _____ _____ as
necessary. Keep the patient _____.
Transport promptly.

Skill Drill 25-2: Applying a MAT Commercial Tourniquet

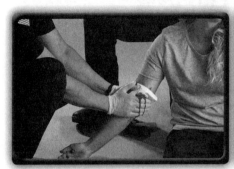

© Jones & Bartlett Learning.

© Jones & Bartlett Learning.

1. Apply _____ over the bleeding site and place the tourniquet _____ to the injury (in the axillary region for upper extremity injuries and at the groin for lower extremity injuries).

2. Click the buckle into place, pull the strap tight, and turn the tightening dial _____ until pulses are no longer palpable _____ to the tourniquet or until bleeding has been _____.

Assessment Review

Answer the following questions pertaining to the assessment of the types of emergencies discussed in this chapter.

_____ 1. When you are performing a scene size-up on a patient with external bleeding, the minimum standard precautions that should be taken are:
   A. gloves and gown.
   B. gown and eye protection.
   C. gloves and eye protection.
   D. gown and face mask.

_____ 2. For a patient with suspected internal bleeding, you should assess circulation by checking the pulse for:
   A. rate and quality.
   B. rate and rhythm.
   C. quality and rhythm.
   D. presence.

_____ 3. If you have completed your primary assessment and transport decision on an unresponsive patient with a significant mechanism of injury, what components should be included in the secondary assessment?
   A. Quick check for life-threatening injuries
   B. Detailed, comprehensive exam
   C. Determination of scene safety
   D. A comprehensive reassessment

_____ 4. Your severe external bleeding patient needs a detailed physical exam. When should it be performed?
   A. Immediately after the primary assessment
   B. During the reassessment
   C. When you arrive at the patient's side
   D. En route to the hospital

_____ 5. Why are proper communications to the hospital when dealing with a patient with significant bleeding needed?
   A. Prompts the staff when to schedule breaks
   B. Allows the hospital time to contact the patient's family
   C. Allows the hospital to prepare resources
   D. Encourages good rapport with the staff

CHAPTER
26

Soft-Tissue Injuries

© Photos.com

General Knowledge

Matching

Match each of the items in the left column to the appropriate definition in the right column.

_____ 1. Dermis

_____ 2. Sweat glands

_____ 3. Epidermis

_____ 4. Mucous membranes

_____ 5. Sebaceous glands

_____ 6. Abrasion

_____ 7. Laceration

_____ 8. Penetrating wound

_____ 9. Avulsion

_____ 10. Evisceration

A. Gunshot wound

B. Cool the body by discharging a substance through the pores

C. Tissue hanging as a flap from a wound

D. Tough external layer forming a watertight covering for the body

E. Razor cut

F. Secrete a watery substance that lubricates the openings of the mouth and nose

G. Inner layer of skin that contains the structures that give skin its characteristic appearance

H. Produce oil, which waterproofs the skin and keeps it supple

I. Exposed intestines

J. Skinned knee

Multiple Choice

Read each item carefully and then select the one best response.

_____ 1. The _____ is/are our first line of defense against external forces.

    A. extremities

    B. hair

    C. skin

    D. lips

_____ 2. The skin covering the _____ is quite thick.

    A. lips

    B. scalp

    C. ears

    D. eyelids

_____ 3. As the cells on the surface of the skin are worn away, new cells form in the _____ layer.

    A. dermal

    B. germinal

    C. epidermal

    D. subcutaneous

_____ 4. The hair follicles, sweat glands, and sebaceous glands are found in the:

    A. dermis.

    B. germinal layer.

    C. epidermis.

    D. subcutaneous layer.

_____ **5.** The skin regulates temperature in a cold environment by:

    A. secreting sweat through sweat glands.

    B. constricting the blood vessels.

    C. dilating the blood vessels.

    D. increasing the amount of heat that is radiated from the body's surface.

_____ **6.** Closed soft-tissue injuries are characterized by all of the following EXCEPT:

    A. pain at the site of injury.

    B. swelling beneath the skin.

    C. damage of the protective layer of skin.

    D. a history of blunt trauma.

_____ **7.** A(n) _____ occurs whenever a large blood vessel is damaged and bleeds.

    A. contusion

    B. hematoma

    C. crushing injury

    D. avulsion

_____ **8.** A(n) _____ is usually associated with extensive tissue damage.

    A. contusion

    B. hematoma

    C. crushing injury

    D. avulsion

_____ **9.** _____ develops when edema and swelling result in increased pressure within a closed soft-tissue space.

    A. A hematoma

    B. An avulsion

    C. Compartment syndrome

    D. Ecchymosis

_____ **10.** A(n) _____ occurs when a great amount of force is applied to the body for a long period of time.

    A. contusion

    B. hematoma

    C. crushing injury

    D. avulsion

_____ **11.** More extensive closed injuries may involve significant swelling and bleeding beneath the skin, which could lead to:

    A. compartment syndrome.

    B. contamination.

    C. hypovolemic shock.

    D. hemothorax.

_____ **12.** Open soft-tissue wounds include all of the following EXCEPT:

    A. abrasions.

    B. contusions.

    C. lacerations.

    D. avulsions.

_____ **13.** A laceration may be all of the following EXCEPT:

    A. linear.

    B. deep.

    C. jagged.

    D. a scrape.

_____ **14.** Because shootings usually end up in court, it is important to factually and completely document:
  A. the statements from witnesses.
  B. the suspect's description.
  C. the treatment given.
  D. the number of shots bystanders say were fired.

_____ **15.** All open wounds are assumed to be _____ and present a risk of infection.
  A. contaminated
  B. life threatening
  C. minimal
  D. extensive

_____ **16.** Before you begin caring for a patient with an open wound, you should:
  A. ensure standard precautions.
  B. splint potential fractures.
  C. notify the hospital.
  D. ask about patient medications.

_____ **17.** Splinting an extremity, even when there is no fracture, may:
  A. increase pain.
  B. increase damage to an already-injured extremity.
  C. make it easier to move the patient.
  D. cause any dressings to move.

_____ **18.** Treatment for an abdominal evisceration includes:
  A. pushing the exposed organs back into the abdominal cavity.
  B. covering the organs with dry dressings.
  C. flexing the knees and legs to relieve pressure on the abdomen.
  D. applying moist, adherent dressings.

_____ **19.** An open neck injury may result in _____ if enough air is sucked into a blood vessel.
  A. hypovolemic shock
  B. tracheal deviation
  C. air embolism
  D. subcutaneous emphysema

_____ **20.** Burns may result from all of the following EXCEPT:
  A. heat.
  B. toxic chemicals.
  C. electricity.
  D. choking.

_____ **21.** Which of the following is NOT a factor that can aid in determining the severity of a burn?
  A. The depth of the burn
  B. If the patient is between 20 and 30 years old
  C. The extent of the burn
  D. Whether critical areas are involved

_____ **22.** _____ burns involve only the epidermis.
  A. Full-thickness
  B. Second-degree
  C. Superficial
  D. Third-degree

_____ **23.** _____ burns cause intense pain.

    A. First-degree

    B. Second-degree

    C. Superficial

    D. Third-degree

_____ **24.** _____ burns may involve the subcutaneous layers, muscle, bone, or internal organs.

    A. Superficial

    B. Partial-thickness

    C. Full-thickness

    D. Second-degree

_____ **25.** Significant airway burns may be associated with all of the following EXCEPT:

    A. singeing of the hair within the nostrils.

    B. hoarseness.

    C. hypoxia.

    D. vomiting.

_____ **26.** The most important consideration when dealing with electrical burns is:

    A. standard precautions.

    B. scene safety.

    C. level of responsiveness.

    D. airway.

_____ **27.** Treatment of electrical burns includes all of the following EXCEPT:

    A. maintaining the airway.

    B. monitoring the patient closely for respiratory or cardiac arrest.

    C. splinting any suspected injuries.

    D. immersion in water.

_____ **28.** Which of the following should NOT be used as an occlusive dressing?

    A. Gauze pads

    B. Vaseline gauze

    C. Aluminum foil

    D. Plastic

_____ **29.** Using elastic bandages to secure dressings may result in _____ if the injury swells or if the bandages are applied improperly.

    A. additional tissue damage

    B. increased edema

    C. increased circulation

    D. further blood loss

_____ **30.** Burns are diffuse soft-tissue injuries created by destructive energy transfers from all of the following sources EXCEPT:

    A. thermal sources.

    B. kinetic sources.

    C. radiation sources.

    D. electrical sources.

_____ **31.** _____ is an acute, potentially fatal viral infection of the central nervous system that affects all warm-blooded animals.

    A. Streptococcus

    B. Rabies

    C. Tuberculosis

    D. Emboli

True/False

If you believe the statement to be more true than false, write the letter "T" in the space provided. If you believe the statement to be more false than true, write the letter "F."

_____ 1. Partial-thickness burns involve the epidermis and some portion of the dermis.

_____ 2. Blisters are commonly seen with superficial burns.

_____ 3. Severe burns are usually a combination of superficial, partial-thickness, and full-thickness burns.

_____ 4. The rule of nines allows you to estimate the percentage of body surface area that has been burned.

_____ 5. Two factors, depth and extent, are critical in assessing the severity of a burn.

_____ 6. Your first responsibility with a burn patient is to stop the burning process.

_____ 7. Burned areas should be immersed in cool water for up to 30 minutes.

_____ 8. Electrical burns are always more severe than the external signs indicate.

_____ 9. The hallmark sign of compartment syndrome is severe but painless swelling.

_____ 10. Occlusive dressings are usually made of Vaseline gauze, aluminum foil, or plastic.

_____ 11. Gauze pads prevent air and liquids from entering or exiting the wound.

_____ 12. Elastic bandages can be used to secure dressings.

_____ 13. Soft roller bandages are slightly elastic and the layers adhere somewhat to one another.

_____ 14. Ecchymosis is associated with open wounds.

_____ 15. A laceration is considered a closed wound.

Fill-in-the-Blank

Read each item carefully and then complete the statement by filling in the missing words.

1. There are three types of ionizing radiation: _____, _____, and _____.

2. A person will sweat in an effort to _____ the body.

3. Nerve endings are located in the _____.

4. When an area of the body is trapped for longer than 4 hours and arterial blood flow is compromised, _____ _____ can develop.

5. In cold weather, blood vessels in the skin will _____.

6. The only exceptions to the rule of not removing an impaled object are an object in the _____ that obstructs breathing and an object in the _____ that interferes with CPR.

7. _____ burns can occur when skin is exposed to temperatures higher than _____°F.

8. A(n) _____ is an injury in which part of the body is completely severed.

9. The external layer of skin is the _____ and the inner layer is the _____.

10. When the vessels of the skin dilate, heat is _____ from the body.

Labeling

Label the following diagram with the correct terms.

1. Skin

A. _____

B. _____

C. _____

D. _____

E. _____

F. _____

G. _____

H. _____

I. _____

J. _____

K. _____

L. _____

M. _____

N. _____

O. _____

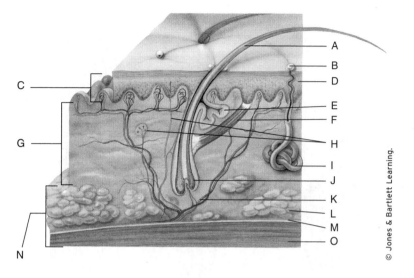

© Jones & Bartlett Learning.

2. Rule of Nines

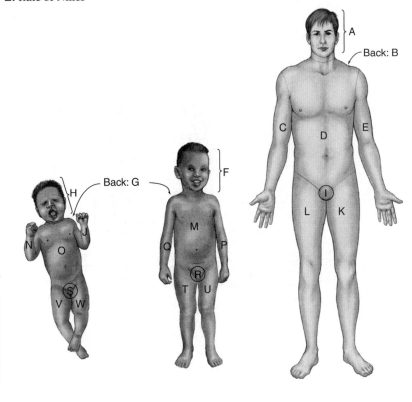

Label the following diagram with the correct percentage numbers.

A. _____

B. _____

C. _____

D. _____

E. _____

F. _____

G. _____

H. _____

I. _____

J. _____

K. _____

L. _____

M. _____

N. _____

O. _____

P. _____

Q. _____

R. _____

S. _____

T. _____

U. _____

V. _____

W. _____

Crossword Puzzle

The following crossword puzzle is an activity provided to reinforce correct spelling and understanding of medical terminology associated with emergency care and the EMT. Use the clues in the column to complete the puzzle.

Across

4. The inner layer of the skin; contains hair follicles, sweat glands, nerve endings, and blood vessels.
6. _____ burns affect only the epidermis.
9. Describes an animal that is infected with rabies.
11. The displacement of organs outside the body.
12. The linings of body cavities and passages that are in direct contact with the outside environment are known as _____ membranes.
14. A system that assigns percentages to sections of the body for calculating the burn area.

Down

1. The fiberlike connective tissue that covers arteries, veins, tendons, and ligaments.
2. An injury in which part of the body is completely severed.
3. An injury in which soft tissue is torn completely loose or is hanging as a flap.
5. The presence of infective organisms or foreign bodies, such as dirt, gravel, or metal.
7. The outer layer of skin that acts as a watertight protective covering.
8. A sharp, smooth cut.
10. A burn caused by an open flame.
13. Injuries in which damage occurs as a result from thermal heat, frictional heat, toxic chemicals, electricity, or nuclear radiation.

Critical Thinking

Multiple Choice

Read each critical-thinking item carefully and then select the one best response.

_____   1. You respond to a house fire with the local fire department. They bring a 48-year-old woman out of the house. She is unconscious but her airway is open. Her breathing is shallow at 30 breaths/min. Her pulse is 110 beats/min, strong and regular. Her blood pressure is 108/72 mm Hg. She has been burned over 40% of her body. The burned area appears to be dry and leathery. It looks charred and has pieces of fabric embedded in the flesh. You know that this type of burn is considered a:

   A. first-degree burn.

   B. second-degree burn.

   C. partial-thickness burn.

   D. third-degree burn.

_____   2. You respond to a scene where a 24-year-old man has been shot. Law enforcement is on scene, and the scene is safe. As you approach the patient, you notice that he is bleeding from the lower-right abdominal area. He is alert and oriented but seems confused. His airway is open, and he is breathing at a normal rate. His pulse is 120 beats/min, weak and regular. His blood pressure is 98/60 mm Hg. You ask the police officer about the weapon. You need this information because the amount of damage is related to the:

   A. size of the entrance wound.

   B. size of the bullet.

   C. size of the exit wound.

   D. speed of the bullet.

_____   3. You respond to a scene where a 14-year-old girl was playing softball and slid into second base. She states she felt and heard a loud pop. There is no obvious bleeding, but swelling is present. Her pulse is 86 beats/min, and her blood pressure is 114/74 mm Hg. In managing this situation you decide to use the RICES method of treatment. The "S" stands for:

   A. swelling.

   B. soft tissue.

   C. splinting.

   D. shock.

_____   4. In conducting a more detailed exam on the patient in question 3, you notice that she has an abrasion on her left knee that she sustained when she slid. The abrasion is covered with dirt and is oozing blood. You know that this injury is classified as:

   A. superficial.

   B. deep.

   C. full thickness.

   D. life-threatening.

_____   5. You decide to manage the injury found in question 4. You flush the site with sterile water, and it continues to bleed. What would be the best initial way to control the bleeding from this injury?

   A. Elevation

   B. Direct pressure

   C. Tourniquet

   D. Pressure points

Short Answer

Complete this section with short written answers using the space provided.

1. List the three major classifications of depth of burns.

_____

_____

_____

2. List the three general classifications of soft-tissue injuries.

_____

_____

_____

3. Define the acronym RICES.

R: _____

I: _____

C: _____

E: _____

S: _____

4. Describe the classification of a severe burn in infants and children.

_____

_____

_____

5. What treatment should be used with a patient who has been burned by a dry chemical?

_____

_____

_____

6. Why are electrical burns particularly dangerous to a patient?

_____

_____

_____

7. Identify the three general types of blast injuries.

_____

_____

_____

8. List the three primary functions of dressings and bandages.

_____

_____

_____

9. List the four types of open soft-tissue injuries.

_____

_____

_____

10. List the five factors used to determine the severity of a burn.

_____

_____

_____

Ambulance Calls

The following case scenarios provide an opportunity to explore the concerns associated with patient management and to enhance critical-thinking skills. Read each scenario and answer each question to the best of your ability.

1. You are dispatched to a residence where a 10-year-old girl fell onto a jagged piece of metal. She has a gaping laceration to the right upper arm that is spurting bright red blood. The mother tried to control the bleeding with a towel, but it kept soaking through.

How would you best manage this patient?

_____

_____

_____

2. You are dispatched to the home of a 3-year-old boy for an unknown problem. You arrive to find a young mother screaming for your help. She was cooking a meal for her other children when the phone rang. While she was talking, the 3-year-old child grabbed the pot handle, pulling boiling hot water onto his body.

How would you best manage this patient?

_____

_____

_____

3. You are watching television at the station when a firefighter comes into the room holding his left hand. His wedding ring got caught in a piece of small machinery at the stationhouse, resulting in an avulsion of his ring finger.

How would you best manage this patient?

_____

_____

_____

Fill-in-the-Patient Care Report

Read the incident scenario and then complete the following patient care report (PCR).

You are just getting back into the ambulance after throwing your lunch bag away when the dispatcher's voice comes across the radio. "Medic nineteen, priority call, police officer shot at 14th and Berry. Showing you dispatched and responding at 1321."

Your partner, Alicia, fastens her seat belt as you start the truck, and 8 minutes later you arrive at the scene of a traffic stop gone wrong. The intersection is in chaos, police cars block every lane, and you see an obviously dead man hanging from the driver's-side door of an old, rusted sedan on the opposite side of the street. You are met by a shaken sergeant who leads you over to a 24-year-old officer who is on the pavement, leaning against the flattened tire of a bullet-riddled patrol car. A motorcycle officer in tall, shining boots is kneeling next to him, holding his hand to the side of the other man's neck; his normally light blue uniform shirt now looks dark purple due to the blood saturation.

"Hang in there, officer," Alicia says, pulling a nonrebreathing mask from the airway bag and assembling the oxygen cylinder.

You place your gloved hand over the neck wound, and the sergeant has to make the motorcycle officer move away. You use your free hand to fish an occlusive dressing from the jump kit and apply it to the large hole in the officer's neck.

"Am I dying?" the officer asks quietly. His eyes are nearly closed and his face is pale and sweaty.

"I don't think so," you say, as you place a pressure dressing over the occlusive pad while Alicia places the nonrebreathing mask over the man's mouth and nose after setting the flow to 15 L/min. "We're going to do everything that we can for you, though."

Several firefighters on scene help you secure the injured 73-kg (161-lb) officer to a long backboard and load him into the ambulance. You climb into the back, and Alicia slides behind the steering wheel, preparing to drive behind a string of police cars that will be blocking intersections for the entire 9-minute drive to the trauma center.

A quick assessment of the patient shows that he has no injuries other than the apparent gunshot wound to the neck, so you take a baseline set of vital signs as the ambulance begins rolling, a mere 5 minutes after arriving on scene. His blood pressure is 92/60 mm Hg, pulse is 120 beats/min, respirations are 20 breaths/min and shallow, and pulse oximetry is 92%.

"We need to move it, Al," you say to your partner, and you hear the engine grow louder as you cover the officer with blankets and check to make sure that no blood is seeping through the dressing. You then make contact with the trauma center and provide a verbal report and ETA. Four minutes before arriving, you obtain a second set of vital signs and find his blood pressure is 92/58 mm Hg, pulse is 124 beats/min, respirations are still 20 breaths/min and shallow, and pulse oximetry is 94%.

Alicia pulls into the hospital ambulance zone 2 minutes sooner than normal for this transport and unloads the patient. You wheel him into the facility, flanked by grim-faced officers, and pass him to the capable trauma team, providing a brief verbal report to the trauma physician and the charge nurse.

Thirty minutes later, after cleaning and disinfecting the ambulance, you call yourselves available and pull back into the traffic around the downtown medical center.

Fill-in-the-Patient Care Report

EMS Patient Care Report (PCR)					
Date:	Incident No.:		Nature of Call:		Location:
Dispatched:	En Route:	At Scene:	Transport:	At Hospital:	In Service:
Patient Information					
Age: Sex: Weight (in kg [lb]):			Allergies: Medications: Past Medical History: Chief Complaint:		
Vital Signs					
Time:	BP:	Pulse:		Respirations:	Spo₂:
Time:	BP:	Pulse:		Respirations:	Spo₂:
Time:	BP:	Pulse:		Respirations:	Spo₂:
EMS Treatment **(circle all that apply)**					
Oxygen @ ___ L/min via (circle one): NC NRM BVM		Assisted Ventilation	Airway Adjunct		CPR
Defibrillation	Bleeding Control	Bandaging	Splinting		Other:
Narrative					

Skills

Skill Drills

Test your knowledge of these skills by filling in the correct words in the photo captions.

Skill Drill 26-1: Stabilizing an Impaled Object

© Jones & Bartlett Learning. Courtesy of MIEMSS.

© Jones & Bartlett Learning. Courtesy of MIEMSS.

© Jones & Bartlett Learning. Courtesy of MIEMSS.

1. Do not attempt to _____ or remove the object. _____ the impaled body part.

2. Control _____, and stabilize the object in place using _____ _____, gauze, and/or tape.

3. Tape a _____ item over the stabilized object to prevent it from _____ during transport.

Skill Drill 26-2: Caring for Burns

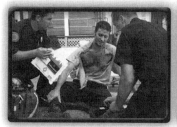
© Jones & Bartlett Learning.

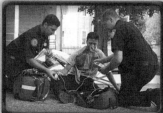
© Jones & Bartlett Learning.

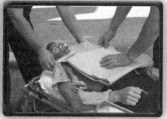
© Jones & Bartlett Learning.

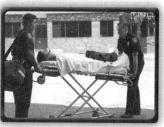
© Jones & Bartlett Learning.

1. Follow _____ precautions to help prevent _____. If safe to do so, remove the _____ from the burning area; extinguish or _____ hot clothing and jewelry as necessary. If the wound is still burning or hot, _____ the hot area in _____, sterile _____, or cover with a wet, cool _____.

2. Provide high-flow _____, and continue to assess the _____.

3. Estimate the _____ of the burn, and then cover the area with a(n) _____, sterile dressing or clean _____. Assess and treat the patient for any other _____.

4. Prepare for transport. Treat for _____. Cover the patient with _____ to prevent loss of _____ _____. Transport promptly.

Assessment Review

Answer the following questions pertaining to the assessment of the types of emergencies discussed in this chapter.

_____ **1.** During the primary assessment of burns, it is important to remember to:

  A. determine scene safety.

  B. obtain vital signs.

  C. prevent heat loss.

  D. estimate the amount of body surface injuries.

_____ **2.** You have been dispatched to a residence for a 24-year-old woman who splashed grease on her arm while cooking. As you approach her, she is crying and yelling that it hurts. Her pulse is 130 beats/min and regular. Her blood pressure is 126/86 mm Hg. You decide that she does not require immediate transport. The secondary assessment would include:

  A. proper interventions.

  B. an examination of the burned arm.

  C. deciding on the patient's priority for transport.

  D. an investigation of the chief complaint.

_____ **3.** During the reassessment of a burn patient with a significant MOI you should:

  A. splint all fractures.

  B. determine the transport decision.

  C. open all blisters.

  D. treat the patient for shock.

_____ **4.** During the intervention step of patient assessment for a burn patient, the first intervention should be to:

  A. stop the burning process.

  B. provide complete spinal stabilization.

  C. treat for shock.

  D. cover burns with moist sterile dressings.

_____ **5.** You respond to a patient who has been stabbed in the neck. You arrive to find the patient in police custody and bleeding moderately from the neck wound. The patient is alert, oriented, and swearing loudly. His pulse is 120 beats/min. His blood pressure is 124/76 mm Hg. You start to bandage the wound. What type of bandage should you use?

  A. Triangular bandage

  B. Adhesive bandage

  C. Roller bandage

  D. Occlusive bandage

Face and Neck Injuries

General Knowledge

Matching

Match each of the items in the left column to the appropriate definition in the right column.

_____ 1. Anisocoria

_____ 2. Cornea

_____ 3. Eustachian tube

_____ 4. Globe

_____ 5. Iris

_____ 6. Lens

_____ 7. Mastoid process

_____ 8. Pinna

_____ 9. Pupil

_____ 10. Retina

_____ 11. Sclera

_____ 12. Tragus

_____ 13. Turbinates

_____ 14. Tympanic membrane

_____ 15. Optic nerve

A. Layers of bone within the nasal cavity

B. Light-sensitive area of the eye where images are projected

C. Eyeball

D. Eardrum

E. External visible part of the ear

F. Tough, fibrous, white portion of the eye

G. Naturally occurring unequal pupils

H. Transparent tissue layer in front of the pupil and iris

I. Bony mass at the base of the skull about 1 inch (2.54 cm) behind the opening to the ear

J. Muscle and surrounding tissue behind the cornea that dilate and constrict the pupil

K. Transparent part of the eye through which images are focused on the retina

L. Connects the middle ear to the oropharynx

M. Small, rounded, fleshy bulge that lies immediately anterior to the ear canal

N. Cranial nerve that transmits visual information to the brain

O. Circular opening in the middle of the iris that admits light to the back of the eye

Multiple Choice

Read each item carefully and then select the one best response.

_____ 1. As an EMT, your objective when treating patients with face and neck injuries is to do all of the following EXCEPT:

    A. prevent further injury.

    B. manage any acute airway problems.

    C. control bleeding.

    D. disregard the cervical spine.

_____ 2. The head is divided into two parts: the cranium and the:

    A. brain.

    B. face.

    C. skull.

    D. medulla oblongata.

_____ 3. The brain connects to the spinal cord through a large opening at the base of the skull known as the:

    A. eustachian tube.

    B. spinous process.

    C. foramen magnum.

    D. vertebral foramina.

_____ **4.** Approximately _____ of the nose is composed of bone. The remainder is composed of cartilage.

    A. nine-tenths

    B. two-thirds

    C. three-quarters

    D. one-third

_____ **5.** Motion of the mandible occurs at the:

    A. temporomandibular joint.

    B. mastoid process.

    C. chin.

    D. mandibular angle.

_____ **6.** You respond to a 71-year-old woman who is unresponsive. You try to get her to respond but have no success. Her airway is open, and she is breathing at a rate of 14 breaths/min. You know you can check a pulse on either side of the neck. You know that the jugular veins and several nerves run through the neck next to the trachea. What structure are you trying to locate to take a pulse?

    A. Hypothalamus

    B. Subclavian arteries

    C. Cricoid cartilage

    D. Carotid arteries

_____ **7.** The _____ connects the cricoid cartilage and thyroid cartilage.

    A. larynx

    B. cricoid membrane

    C. cricothyroid membrane

    D. thyroid membrane

_____ **8.** You respond to a 68-year-old man who was involved in a motor vehicle collision. He is unresponsive, and as you approach you notice he is not breathing. He was unrestrained and has massive facial injuries. When you check his airway, it is obstructed. Which of the following is NOT likely to cause an upper airway obstruction in a patient with facial trauma?

    A. Heavy bleeding

    B. Loosened teeth or dentures

    C. Soft-tissue swelling

    D. Inflamed tonsils

_____ **9.** You are dispatched to a residential neighborhood for a 6-year-old girl who was bitten by the family pet. The mother meets you at the door with the girl, who is crying uncontrollably and has blood covering the right side of her head. You look at the child and notice that her lower right ear has been completely avulsed. You control the bleeding with direct pressure and bandage the injury. You follow the blood trail back to where the incident occurred and find the avulsed part. How do you manage the avulsed tissue?

    A. Wrap the skin in a moist, sterile dressing; place it in a plastic bag; and keep it cool.

    B. Place the skin in a plastic "biohazard" bag and dispose of it properly.

    C. Place the skin in a plastic bag filled with ice and transport it to the emergency department.

    D. Leave it at the scene to be disposed of later.

_____ **10.** The nasal cavity is divided into two chambers by the:

    A. frontal sinus.

    B. middle turbinate.

    C. zygoma.

    D. nasal septum.

_____ **11.** You are called to the home of a 48-year-old woman who has a history of high blood pressure and now has a major nose bleed. She is alert and oriented and converses freely with you. Her respirations and pulse are within normal limits. Her blood pressure is 194/108 mm Hg. You have been able to rule out trauma. How would you manage the nose bleed?

    A. Apply a sterile dressing.

    B. Pinch the nostrils together.

    C. Place the patient in a supine position.

    D. Have the patient hold ice in her mouth.

_____ **12.** The middle ear is connected to the nasal cavity by the:

    A. frontal sinus.

    B. zygomatic process.

    C. eustachian tube.

    D. superior trachea.

_____ **13.** Which of the following is NOT a sign or symptom of a laryngeal injury?

    A. Hoarseness

    B. Difficulty breathing

    C. Subcutaneous emphysema

    D. Wheezing

_____ **14.** Which of the following is NOT a sign of a possible facial fracture?

    A. Bleeding in the mouth

    B. Absent or loose teeth

    C. Bleeding from the forehead

    D. Loose and/or moveable bone fragments

_____ **15.** The presence of air in the soft tissues of the neck that produces a crackling sensation is called:

    A. the "Rice Krispy" effect.

    B. a pneumothorax.

    C. rales.

    D. subcutaneous emphysema.

_____ **16.** Which of the following statements is NOT true regarding the treatment of bleeding from a neck injury?

    A. Apply firm pressure to the carotid artery to reduce the amount of bleeding.

    B. Apply pressure to the bleeding site using a gloved fingertip.

    C. Apply a sterile occlusive dressing.

    D. Use gauze to secure the dressing in place.

_____ **17.** What is the main purpose of eye blinking?

    A. Clean the eye

    B. Prevent eye muscle atrophy

    C. Natural reflex to bright light

    D. Refocus the eye

_____ **18.** When flushing an eye with saline to remove a foreign object, it is important to remember to:

    A. flush from the outside of the eye in toward the nose.

    B. flush from the top of the eye toward the bottom.

    C. flush from the nose side of the eye toward the outside.

    D. flush only along the bottom of the eye.

_____ **19.** When stabilizing a large foreign object in the eye, you should first cover the eye with a moist dressing, then:

    A. irrigate the eye with saline.

    B. surround the object with a doughnut-shaped collar made from gauze.

    C. apply tape around the object and then secure the tape to the forehead.

    D. place an ice pack over the eye to reduce swelling.

_____ **20.** When a patient has a chemical burn to the eye, you should irrigate the eye for at least 5 minutes; however, if the burn was caused by an alkali or strong acid, you should irrigate for:

    A. 10 minutes.

    B. 15 minutes.

    C. 20 minutes.

    D. 25 minutes.

True/False

If you believe the statement to be more true than false, write the letter "T" in the space provided. If you believe the statement to be more false than true, write the letter "F."

_____ **1.** Injuries to the face often lead to airway problems.

_____ **2.** Care for facial injuries begins with standard precautions and the ABCs.

_____ **3.** Exposed eye or brain injuries are covered with a dry dressing.

_____ **4.** Clear fluid in the outer ear is normal.

_____ **5.** Any crushing injury of the upper part of the neck likely involves the larynx or the trachea.

_____ **6.** Soft-tissue injuries to the face are common.

_____ **7.** The opening through which the spinal cord leaves the head is called the occiput.

_____ **8.** The muscle that allows movement of the head is the temporomandibular.

_____ **9.** Standard precautions for assessing face and throat injuries should include eye and oral protection.

_____ **10.** The airway of choice with facial injuries is the nasopharyngeal.

_____ **11.** Stabilization and maintenance of an airway can be difficult in patients with facial injuries.

_____ **12.** Asymmetrical eyes could possibly indicate a brain injury.

_____ **13.** Gentle irrigation will usually wash out foreign material stuck in the cornea.

_____ **14.** Retinal injuries caused by exposure to extreme bright light are generally painful and result in permanent damage.

_____ **15.** You should never exert pressure on or manipulate an injured eye in any way.

_____ **16.** Bleeding into the anterior chamber of the eye is commonly called conjunctivitis.

_____ **17.** When dealing with an injured eye, you should always remove contact lenses before treatment.

_____ **18.** Open injuries to the larynx can occur as the result of a stabbing.

_____ **19.** Broken teeth and lacerations to the tongue cause minimal bleeding and are not concerning.

_____ **20.** Oxygen and airway management are important for all patients with face and neck injuries.

Fill-in-the-Blank

Read each item carefully and then complete the statement by filling in the missing words.

1. Pulsations in the neck are felt in the _____ vessels.

2. The _____ vertebrae are in the neck.

3. The _____ regions of the cranium are located on the lateral portion of the head.

4. The _____ connects the oropharynx and the larynx with the main air passages of the lungs.

5. The rings of the trachea are made of _____.

6. The Adam's apple is more prominent in _____ than in _____.

7. The _____ _____ is a large opening at the base of the skull.

8. Blunt trauma that causes fractures to the orbit are commonly called a(n) _____ _____.

9. Trauma to the face and skull that results in the posterior wall of the nasal cavity becoming unstable is caused by

_____ _____ _____.

10. When dealing with an avulsed tooth, handle it by its _____ and not by the _____.

11. A(n) _____ _____ results when an open vein sucks air into it and travels to the heart.

Labeling

Label the following diagrams with the correct terms.

1. The Face

A. _____

B. _____

C. _____

D. _____

© Jones & Bartlett Learning.

2. The Larynx

A. _____

B. _____

C. _____

D. _____

E. _____

© Jones & Bartlett Learning.

3. The Eye

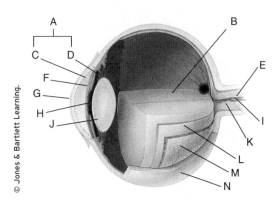

© Jones & Bartlett Learning.

A. _____

B. _____

C. _____

D. _____

E. _____

F. _____

G. _____

H. _____

I. _____

J. _____

K. _____

L. _____

M. _____

N. _____

4. The Ear

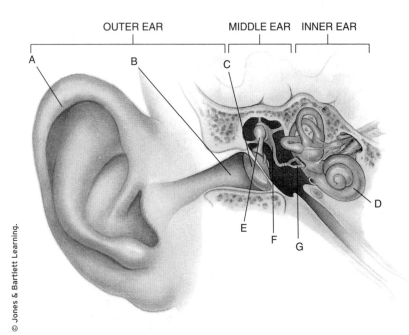

© Jones & Bartlett Learning.

A. _____

B. _____

C. _____

D. _____

E. _____

F. _____

G. _____

Crossword Puzzle

The following crossword puzzle is an activity provided to reinforce correct spelling and understanding of medical terminology associated with emergency care and the EMT. Use the clues in the column to complete the puzzle.

Across

2. A characteristic crackling sensation felt on palpation of the skin is known as _____ emphysema.
5. The light-sensitive area of the eye where images are projected.
7. The _____ glands produce fluids to keep the eye moist.
8. The transparent tissue layer in front of the pupil and iris of the eye.
13. The _____ process is the prominent bony mass at the base of the skull about 1 inch (2.5 cm) posterior to the external opening of the ear.
16. The delicate membrane that lines the eyelids and covers the exposed surface of the eye.
17. The transparent part of the eye through which images are focused on the retina.

Down

1. The circular opening in the middle of the iris that admits light to the back of the eye.
3. Naturally occurring uneven pupil size.
4. The tough, fibrous, white portion of the eye that protects the more delicate inner structures.
6. The small, rounded, fleshy bulge that lies immediately anterior to the ear canal.
9. The _____ tube is a branch of the internal auditory canal that connects the middle ear to the oropharynx.
10. The _____ membrane is the eardrum, which lies between the external and middle ear.
11. The eyeball.
12. The ear canal is known as the _____ auditory canal.
14. The external visible part of the ear.
15. The muscle and surrounding tissue behind the cornea that dilates and constricts the pupil, regulating the amount of light that enters the eye.

Critical Thinking

Short Answer

Complete this section with short written answers using the space provided.

1. Describe bleeding-control methods for facial injuries.

_____

_____

_____

2. Describe bleeding-control methods for lacerations to veins or arteries in the neck.

_____

_____

_____

3. Explain the physical exam process for evaluation of the eye.

_____

_____

_____

4. List three important guidelines to use when treating an eye laceration.

_____

_____

_____

5. List five eye indications that suggest a closed head injury.

_____

_____

_____

Ambulance Calls

The following case scenarios provide an opportunity to explore the concerns associated with patient management and to enhance critical-thinking skills. Read each scenario and answer each question to the best of your ability.

1. You are dispatched to assist a small child who was attacked by his family's dog. The dog bit the child's face and neck repeatedly, then grabbed him by the neck and shook him violently. The mother found the boy "making funny breathing sounds" and called for help. She has removed the dog from the area.

   How would you best manage this patient?

   _____

   _____

   _____

2. You are dispatched to a 37-year-old man with a large laceration to the right side of his neck. Bleeding is dark and heavy. He is alert but weak.

   How would you best manage this patient?

   _____

   _____

   _____

3. You are dispatched to a Little League baseball game to assist an assault victim. Apparently, emotions were running high when two parents began to argue. You arrive to find a 40-year-old man with a bloody nose.

   How would you best manage this patient?

   _____

   _____

   _____

Skills

Skill Drills

Skill Drill 27-1: Removing a Foreign Object From Under the Upper Eyelid
Test your knowledge of this skill by filling in the correct words in the photo captions.

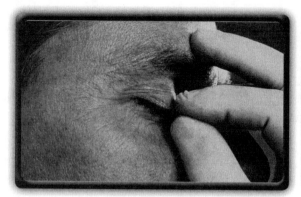

© Jones & Bartlett Learning. Courtesy of MIEMSS.

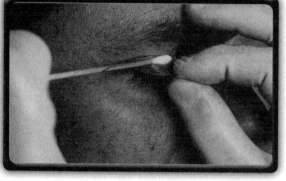

© Jones & Bartlett Learning. Courtesy of MIEMSS.

1. Have the patient look _____, grasp the upper _____, and gently pull the _____ away from the eye.

2. Place a cotton-tipped applicator on the _____ surface of the _____ lid.

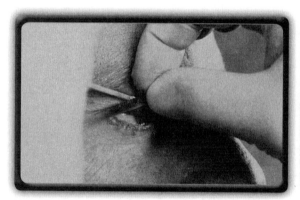

© Jones & Bartlett Learning. Courtesy of MIEMSS.

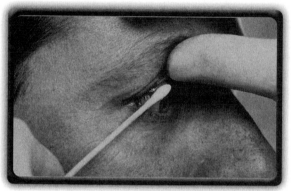

© Jones & Bartlett Learning. Courtesy of MIEMSS.

3. Pull the lid _____ and _____, folding it back over the applicator.

4. Gently remove the foreign object from the eyelid with a moistened, _____, cotton-tipped applicator.

Skill Drill 27-2: Stabilizing a Foreign Object Impaled in the Eye
Test your knowledge of this skill by placing the following photos in the correct order. Number the first step with a "1," the second step with a "2," etc.

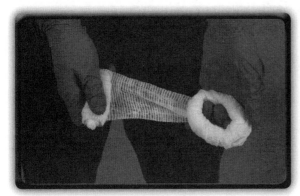

© Jones & Bartlett Learning. Courtesy of MIEMSS.

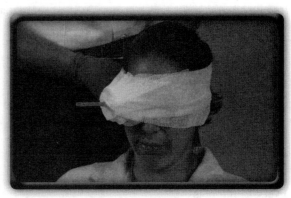

© Jones & Bartlett Learning. Courtesy of MIEMSS.

_____ Remove the gauze from your hand and wrap the remainder of the gauze roll radially around the ring that you have created.

_____ Place the dressing over the eye and impaled object to hold the impaled object in place, and then secure it with a roller bandage.

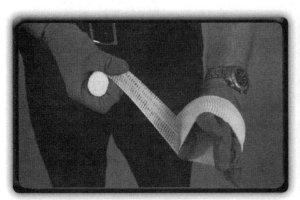

© Jones & Bartlett Learning. Courtesy of MIEMSS.

© Jones & Bartlett Learning. Courtesy of MIEMSS.

_____ To prepare a doughnut ring, wrap a 2-inch roll around your fingers and thumb seven or eight times. Adjust the diameter by spreading your fingers or squeezing them together.

_____ Work around the entire ring to form a doughnut.

Assessment Review

Answer the following questions pertaining to the assessment of the types of emergencies discussed in this chapter.

_____ 1. You have responded to a motor vehicle collision and find a 21-year-old man who has massive facial trauma. He is bleeding heavily and is unconscious. The first thing that you do in your treatment of this patient is to:

    A. take cervical spine precautions.

    B. open the airway.

    C. assess his breathing.

    D. take standard precautions.

_____ 2. For the patient described in question 1, how often would you reassess his vitals during your ongoing assessment?

    A. Every 3 minutes

    B. Every 5 minutes

    C. Every 10 minutes

    D. Every 15 minutes

_____ 3. You have a patient who has severe epistaxis. You have been able to rule out trauma. How would you position this patient to help control the bleeding?

    A. Supine

    B. Prone

    C. Sitting leaning back

    D. Sitting leaning forward

_____ 4. You have a patient who has had a tooth knocked out. You find the tooth. How would you transport it to the hospital?

    A. In saline

    B. In dextrose

    C. In ice

    D. In a dry sterile dressing

_____ 5. You respond to a child who has placed a pebble in his ear. He is complaining that his ear hurts. You should:

    A. remove the pebble with a cotton-tipped applicator.

    B. have the child try and shake the pebble out.

    C. leave the pebble in the ear and transport.

    D. not load the patient because this is not an emergency.

TRAUMA

Head and Spine Injuries

© Photos.com

General Knowledge

Matching

Match each of the items in the left column to the appropriate definition in the right column.

_____ 1. Epidural hematoma

_____ 2. Cushing reflex

_____ 3. Subdural hematoma

_____ 4. Retrograde amnesia

_____ 5. Concussion

_____ 6. Anterograde amnesia

_____ 7. Cerebral edema

_____ 8. Connecting nerves

_____ 9. Intervertebral disk

_____ 10. Meninges

A. Temporary loss of the brain's ability to function without actual physical damage

B. Swelling of the brain

C. Inability to remember events after an injury

D. Accumulation of blood between the skull and dura mater

E. Increased blood pressure, decreased pulse, irregular respirations

F. Three distinct layers of tissue that surround and protect the brain and spinal cord

G. Inability to remember events leading up to a head injury

H. Accumulation of blood beneath the dura mater but outside the brain

I. Located in the brain and spinal cord, these connect the motor and sensory nerves within the skull and spinal canal

J. Cushion that lies between the vertebrae

Multiple Choice

Read each item carefully and then select the one best response.

_____ 1. Which of the following is NOT part of the central nervous system?

    A. The brain

    B. The spinal cord

    C. Cerebrospinal fluid

    D. Cranial nerves

_____ 2. The nervous system is divided into the central nervous system and the:

    A. autonomic nervous system.

    B. peripheral nervous system.

    C. sympathetic nervous system.

    D. somatic nervous system.

_____ 3. The brain is divided into the cerebrum, the cerebellum, and the:

    A. foramen magnum.

    B. meninges.

    C. brain stem.

    D. spinal column.

_____ 4. Injury to the head and neck may indicate injury to the:

    A. thoracic spine.

    B. lumbar spine.

    C. cervical spine.

    D. sacral spine.

_____   **5.** The _____ is composed of three layers of tissue that suspend the brain and spinal cord within the skull and spinal canal.

    A. meninges

    B. dura mater

    C. pia mater

    D. arachnoid space

_____   **6.** The skull is divided into the cranium and the:

    A. occipital.

    B. face.

    C. parietal.

    D. foramen magnum.

_____   **7.** Peripheral nerves include all of the following EXCEPT:

    A. connecting nerves.

    B. sensory nerves.

    C. motor nerves.

    D. the spinal cord.

_____   **8.** Which of the following is NOT a function of cerebrospinal fluid?

    A. Acts as a shock absorber

    B. Bathes the brain and spinal cord

    C. Buffers the brain and spinal cord from injury

    D. Provides continuous oxygen to the brain

_____   **9.** The autonomic nervous system is composed of the sympathetic nervous system and the:

    A. peripheral nervous system.

    B. central nervous system.

    C. parasympathetic nervous system.

    D. somatic nervous system.

_____   **10.** The most prominent and the most easily palpable spinous process is at the _____ cervical vertebra at the base of the neck.

    A. 7th

    B. 6th

    C. 5th

    D. 4th

_____   **11.** You respond to a 14-year-old boy who fell out of a tree at a local park. He is unresponsive. His airway is open and respirations are 16 breaths/min and regular. His pulse is strong and regular. Distal pulses are present. You manage the cervical spine. Who should you NOT ask for help in determining how the injury happened?

    A. First responders

    B. Family members

    C. Bystanders

    D. Curious passersby that did not witness the accident.

_____   **12.** Emergency medical care of a patient with a possible spinal injury begins with:

    A. opening the airway.

    B. assessing level of consciousness.

    C. summoning law enforcement.

    D. standard precautions.

_____   **13.** The _____ is a tunnel running the length of the spine, which encloses and protects the spinal cord.

    A. foramen magnum

    B. spinal canal

    C. foramen foramina

    D. meninges

_____ 14. Once the head and neck are manually stabilized, you should assess for:

    A. pulse.

    B. motor function.

    C. sensation.

    D. All of the above.

_____ 15. You are called to a motor vehicle collision where a 27-year-old woman has a bump on her head. You immediately begin manual stabilization of the head. Her airway is open and respirations are within normal limits. Her pulse is a little fast but strong and regular. Distal pulses are present. You can release manual stabilization when:

    A. the patient's head and torso are in line.

    B. the patient is secured to a backboard with the head immobilized.

    C. the rigid cervical collar is in place.

    D. the patient arrives at the hospital.

_____ 16. The ideal procedure for moving a patient from the ground to the backboard is the:

    A. four-person log roll.

    B. lateral slide.

    C. four-person lift.

    D. push-and-pull maneuver.

_____ 17. You respond to a motor vehicle collision with a 29-year-old woman who struck the rearview mirror and has serious bleeding from the scalp. Her airway is open and respirations are normal. The pulse is a little rapid but strong and regular. Distal pulses are present, and there is no deformity to the skull. Most bleeding from the scalp can be controlled by:

    A. direct pressure.

    B. elevation.

    C. pressure point.

    D. tourniquet.

_____ 18. Exceptions to using a short spinal extrication device include all of the following EXCEPT:

    A. you or the patient is in danger.

    B. the patient is conscious and complaining of lumbar pain.

    C. you need to gain immediate access to other patients.

    D. the patient's injuries justify immediate removal.

_____ 19. Neck rigidity, bloody cerebrospinal fluid, and headache are associated with what kind of bleeding in the brain?

    A. Epidural hematoma

    B. Subdural hematoma

    C. Intracerebral hematoma

    D. Subarachnoid hemorrhage

_____ 20. A _____ is a temporary loss or alteration of a part or all of the brain's ability to function without actual physical damage to the brain.

    A. contusion

    B. concussion

    C. hematoma

    D. subdural hematoma

_____ 21. Which of the following is NOT a symptom of a concussion?

    A. Dizziness

    B. Weakness

    C. Muscle tremors

    D. Visual changes

_____ **22.** Intracranial bleeding outside of the dura mater and under the skull is known as a(n):

   A. concussion.

   B. intracerebral hemorrhage.

   C. subdural hematoma.

   D. epidural hematoma.

_____ **23.** The first step in securing a patient to a short backboard is to:

   A. assess pulse, motor function, and sensation.

   B. assess the cervical area.

   C. provide manual stabilization of the cervical spine.

   D. apply an appropriately sized cervical collar.

_____ **24.** _____ is the most reliable sign of a head injury.

   A. Vomiting

   B. Decreased level of consciousness

   C. Seizures

   D. Numbness and tingling in extremities

_____ **25.** Hyperventilation should be used with caution in head injury patients and only be attempted when _____ is/are available.

   A. pulse oximetry

   B. capnography

   C. air medical services

   D. noninvasive blood pressure monitoring

_____ **26.** Common causes of head injuries include all of the following EXCEPT:

   A. falls.

   B. motor vehicle collisions.

   C. seizure activity.

   D. sports injuries.

_____ **27.** Assessment of mental status is accomplished through the use of the mnemonic:

   A. SAMPLE.

   B. OPQRST.

   C. AVPU.

   D. AEIOU-TIPS.

_____ **28.** You respond to a 38-year-old man who fell while rock climbing. He is unconscious with an open airway. The respiration and pulse rates are within normal limits. His distal pulses are intact. You check his pupils and find that they are unequal. You know this could be a sign of:

   A. brain injury.

   B. hypoxia.

   C. seizure activity.

   D. chronic hypertension.

_____ **29.** Which of the following is NOT part of Cushing's triad?

   A. Increased blood pressure

   B. Decreased pulse rate

   C. Decreased pulse oximetry

   D. Irregular respirations

_____ **30.** How many EMTs are required to immobilize a standing patient?

   A. Two

   B. Three

   C. Four

   D. Five

_____ **31.** A cervical collar should be applied to a patient with a possible spinal injury based on:

    A. the mechanism of injury.

    B. the history.

    C. signs and symptoms.

    D. All of the above.

_____ **32.** Helmets must be removed in all of the following cases EXCEPT:

    A. cardiac arrest.

    B. when the helmet allows for excessive movement.

    C. when there are no impending airway or breathing problems.

    D. when a shield cannot be removed for access to the airway.

_____ **33.** A vacuum mattress molds to the specific contours of the patient's body and:

    A. reduces pressure point tenderness.

    B. provides better comfort.

    C. provides thermal insulation.

    D. All of the above.

True/False

If you believe the statement to be more true than false, write the letter "T" in the space provided. If you believe the statement to be more false than true, write the letter "F."

_____ **1.** An intracerebral hematoma involves bleeding outside the brain tissue.

_____ **2.** If a sensory nerve in the reflex arc detects an irritating stimulus, it will bypass the motor nerve and send a message directly to the brain.

_____ **3.** Voluntary activities are those actions we perform unconsciously.

_____ **4.** The autonomic nervous system is composed of the sympathetic nervous system and the parasympathetic nervous system.

_____ **5.** The parasympathetic nervous system reacts to stress with the fight-or-flight response whenever it is confronted with a threatening situation.

_____ **6.** All patients with suspected head and/or spine injuries should have their head realigned to an in-line, neutral position.

_____ **7.** When assessing a patient for possible spinal injury, you should begin with a full-body scan.

_____ **8.** One procedure for moving a patient from the ground to a backboard is the four-person log roll.

_____ **9.** You should not try to put a patient on a short backboard if the patient is in danger.

_____ **10.** To properly measure a cervical collar, use the manufacturer's specifications.

Fill-in-the-Blank

Read each item carefully and then complete the statement by filling in the missing words.

1. The _____ nerves carry information to the muscles.

2. The dura mater, arachnoid, and pia mater are layers of _____ within the skull and spinal canal.

3. The brain and spinal cord are part of the _____ nervous system.

4. The peripheral nervous system has _____ pairs of spinal nerves.

5. The _____ nerves are the 12 pairs of nerves that emerge from the brainstem and transmit information directly to or from the brain.

6. Vertebrae are separated by cushions called _____ _____.

7. The skull has two large structures of bone, the _____ and the _____.

8. The _____ and _____ _____ are the inner two layers of the meninges and are much thinner than the dura mater.

9. The _____ nervous system reacts to stress.

10. The _____ nervous system causes the body to relax.

11. A(n) _____ _____ involves bleeding within the brain tissue itself.

12. A(n) _____ is far more serious than a concussion because it involves physical injury to the brain tissue.

13. When immobilizing a small child, _____ may need to be added to maintain an in-line, neutral position.

14. On completion of spinal immobilization, reassessment of _____, _____, and _____ function in each extremity is necessary.

15. In a patient with a suspected head injury, you should use the _____ method for opening the airway.

Labeling

Label the following diagrams with the correct terms.

1. Brain

A. _____

B. _____

C. _____

D. _____

E. _____

F. _____

G. _____

H. _____

I. _____

© Jones & Bartlett Learning.

2. Connecting Nerves in the Spinal Cord

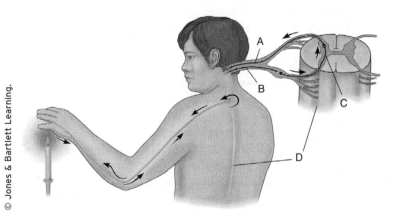

A. _____

B. _____

C. _____

D. _____

3. Spinal Column

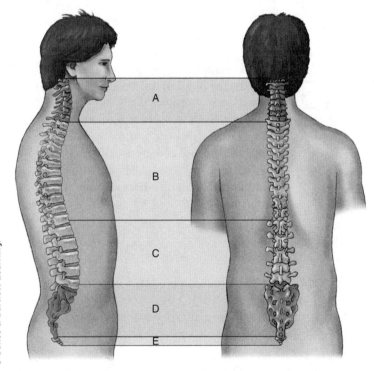

A. _____

B. _____

C. _____

D. _____

E. _____

© Jones & Bartlett Learning.

Crossword Puzzle

The following crossword puzzle is an activity provided to reinforce correct spelling and understanding of medical terminology associated with emergency care and the EMT. Use the clues in the column to complete the puzzle.

Across

1. Bruising under the eyes that may indicate a skull fracture.
3. The _____ log roll is the recommended procedure for moving a patient with a suspected spinal injury from the ground to a long backboard.
7. Bruising behind an ear over the mastoid process that may indicate a skull fracture.
10. Injury in which the brain has been injured but the skin has not been broken and there is no obvious bleeding is known as a(n) _____ head injury.
11. An accumulation of blood beneath the dura mater but outside the brain is known as a(n) _____ hematoma.
13. A traumatic insult to the brain capable of producing physical, intellectual, emotional, social, and vocational changes.
14. Three distinct layers of tissue that surround and protect the brain and the spinal cord within the skull and the spinal canal.
15. A(n) _____ hematoma is an accumulation of blood between the skull and the dura mater.

Down

2. Swelling of the brain.
4. Injury to the head often caused by a penetrating object in which there may be bleeding and exposed brain tissue is known as a(n) _____ head injury.
5. A temporary loss or alteration of part or all of the brain's ability to function without actual physical damage to the brain.
6. Actions of the body that are not under a person's conscious control are known as _____ activities.
8. The pressure within the cranial vault.
9. _____ skull fractures usually occur following diffuse impact to the head (such as falls and motor vehicle collisions).
12. _____ skull fractures are also referred to as nondisplaced skull fractures.

Critical Thinking

Short Answer
Complete this section with short written answers using the space provided.

1. List the 10 mechanisms of injury where you are likely to encounter a head injury.

_____

_____

_____

2. List the reasons for not placing the head and/or spine injury patient's head into a neutral in-line position.

_____

_____

_____

3. What is the difference between a primary brain injury and a secondary brain injury?

_____

_____

_____

4. List at least 10 signs and symptoms of a head injury.

_____

_____

_____

5. List the three general principles for treating a head injury.

_____

_____

_____

6. List the seven questions to ask yourself when deciding whether to remove a helmet.

_____

_____

_____

Ambulance Calls

The following case scenarios provide an opportunity to explore the concerns associated with patient management and to enhance critical-thinking skills. Read each scenario and answer each question to the best of your ability.

1. You are dispatched to a bicycle-versus-car collision. The driver of the car is uninjured, but the bicyclist is reported as "severely injured." You arrive to find the patient lying unconscious in the street and with an apparent head injury. The patient was not wearing a helmet when she was struck by the car. Witnesses say she was launched into the windshield and then landed in the road.

   How would you best manage this patient?

   _____

   _____

   _____

2. You are dispatched to assist a "young child fallen." You arrive to find a frantic parent who tells you her daughter was playing on the family's trampoline in the backyard. She was bouncing very high and accidentally launched herself off the trampoline, landing face down onto a concrete pad in the neighbor's yard. She responds to painful stimuli and has snoring respirations.

   How would you best manage this patient?

   _____

   _____

   _____

3. You are dispatched to a motor vehicle collision with major damage to the patient compartment. Your patient, an 18-month-old boy, is still in his car seat in the center of the back seat. He responds appropriately, and there is no damage to his seat. He has no visible injuries, but a front seat passenger was killed.

   How would you best manage this patient?

   _____

   _____

   _____

Skills

Skill Drills

Skill Drill 28-1: Performing Manual In-Line Stabilization

Test your knowledge of this skill by filling in the correct words in the photo captions.

  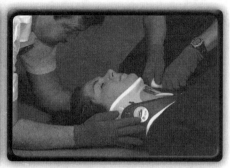

© Jones & Bartlett Learning. Courtesy of MIEMSS.   © Jones & Bartlett Learning. Courtesy of MIEMSS.   © Jones & Bartlett Learning. Courtesy of MIEMSS.

1. Take standard precautions. Kneel behind the patient and firmly place your hands around the _____ of the _____ on either _____.

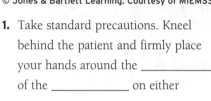

2. Support the lower jaw with your _____ and _____ fingers, and the head with your _____. Gently lift the head into a(n) _____, _____ position, aligned with the torso. Do not _____ the head or neck excessively, forcefully, or rapidly.

3. Continue to manually _____ the head while your partner places a rigid _____ _____ around the neck. Maintain _____ _____ until you have completely secured the patient to a backboard.

Skill Drill 28-3: Securing a Patient to a Long Backboard

Test your knowledge of this skill by placing the following photos in the correct order. Number the first step with a "1," the second step with a "2," etc.

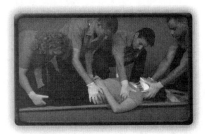

© Jones & Bartlett Learning. Courtesy of MIEMSS.

_____ Center the patient on the backboard.

© Jones & Bartlett Learning. Courtesy of MIEMSS.

_____ Secure the upper torso first.

© Jones & Bartlett Learning. Courtesy of MIEMSS.

_____ Begin to secure the patient's head using a commercial immobilization device or rolled towels.

© Jones & Bartlett Learning. Courtesy of MIEMSS.

_____ Apply and maintain cervical stabilization. Assess distal functions in all extremities.

© Jones & Bartlett Learning. Courtesy of MIEMSS.

_____ Apply a cervical collar.

© Jones & Bartlett Learning. Courtesy of MIEMSS.

_____ Secure the pelvis and upper legs.

© Jones & Bartlett Learning. Courtesy of MIEMSS.

_____ Rescuers kneel on one side of the patient and place hands on the far side of the patient.

© Jones & Bartlett Learning. Courtesy of MIEMSS.

_____ Place tape across the patient's forehead to secure the immobilization device.

© Jones & Bartlett Learning. Courtesy of MIEMSS.

_____ On command, rescuers roll the patient toward themselves, quickly examine the back, slide the backboard under the patient, and roll the patient onto the backboard.

© Jones & Bartlett Learning. Courtesy of MIEMSS.

_____ Check all straps and readjust as needed. Reassess distal functions in all extremities.

Skill Drill 28-5: Securing a Patient Found in a Sitting Position
Test your knowledge of this skill by filling in the correct words in the photo captions.

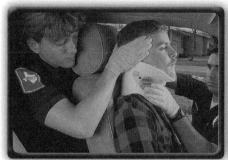

© Jones & Bartlett Learning. Courtesy of MIEMSS.

1. Take standard precautions. Stabilize the head and neck in a _____, _____ position. Assess pulse, motor, and sensory function in each extremity. Apply a _____ _____.

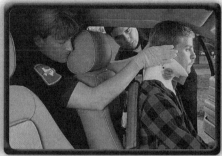

© Jones & Bartlett Learning. Courtesy of MIEMSS.

2. Insert an immobilization device between the patient's _____ _____ and the seat.

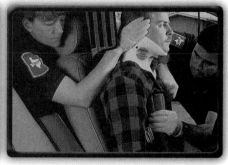

© Jones & Bartlett Learning. Courtesy of MIEMSS.

3. Open the side flaps, and position them around the patient's _____, snug around the armpits.

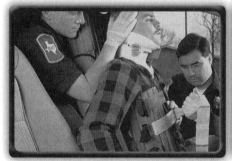

© Jones & Bartlett Learning. Courtesy of MIEMSS.

4. Secure the upper torso flaps, then the mid-torso flaps.

© Jones & Bartlett Learning. Courtesy of MIEMSS.

5. Secure the _____ (leg) straps. Check and adjust the _____ straps.

© Jones & Bartlett Learning. Courtesy of MIEMSS.

6. _____ between the head and the device as needed. Secure the forehead strap and fasten the _____ head strap around the cervical collar.

© Jones & Bartlett Learning. Courtesy of MIEMSS.

7. Place a long backboard next to the patient's buttocks, _____to the trunk.

© Jones & Bartlett Learning. Courtesy of MIEMSS.

8. Turn and lower the patient onto the long backboard. Lift the _____and slip the long backboard under the immobilization device.

© Jones & Bartlett Learning. Courtesy of MIEMSS.

9. Secure the immobilization device and long backboard to each other. _____ or _____ the groin straps. Reassess pulse, motor, and sensory function in each extremity.

Skill Drill 28-2: Application of a Cervical Collar

Test your knowledge of this skill by filling in the correct words in the photo captions.

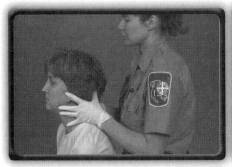

© Jones & Bartlett Learning. Courtesy of MIEMSS.

1. Apply in-line _____ .

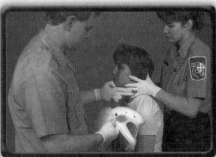

© Jones & Bartlett Learning. Courtesy of MIEMSS.

2. Measure the proper _____ _____ .

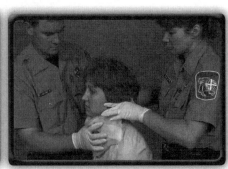

© Jones & Bartlett Learning. Courtesy of MIEMSS.

3. Place the _____ _____ first.

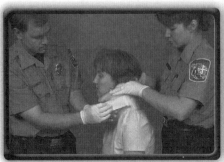

© Jones & Bartlett Learning. Courtesy of MIEMSS.

4. _____ the collar around the neck and _____ the collar.

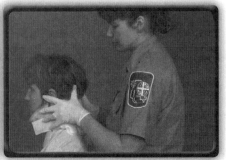

© Jones & Bartlett Learning. Courtesy of MIEMSS.

5. Ensure proper _____ and maintain _____, _____ stabilization until the patient is secured to a(n) _____.

Assessment Review

Answer the following questions pertaining to the assessment of the types of emergencies discussed in this chapter.

_____ **1.** You respond to a patient who was assaulted and is unconscious. On reaching his side, you check his airway and it is open. Breathing is at 18 breaths/min and regular. Pulse is strong and regular with distal pulses present. You want to administer oxygen. At what rate would you give it?

    A. 2 L/min

    B. 6 L/min

    C. 10 L/min

    D. 15 L/min

_____ **2.** You and your partner have determined that you need to put the patient from question 1 in full immobilization. When can your partner release manual stabilization of the head?

    A. When the cervical collar is applied

    B. When the torso is secured to the board

    C. When the patient is completely secured to the board

    D. When you arrive at the hospital

_____ **3.** You decide to put the patient on a long backboard and use the log-roll technique to accomplish the task. When do you check the patient's back?

    A. After securing the patient to the board

    B. As the patient is rolled onto his side

    C. Before any movement is attempted

    D. When you move the patient to the hospital bed

_____ **4.** If you respond to a patient who is in a sitting position and stable, how would you immobilize him or her?

    A. Lay the patient down and perform the log-roll technique.

    B. Use a scoop stretcher.

    C. Use a short backboard.

    D. Have the patient lie down on your backboard.

_____ **5.** You respond to a motorcycle accident. You decide that you need to remove the rider's helmet. What is the minimum number of people required to remove the helmet?

    A. Two

    B. Three

    C. Four

    D. Five

Emergency Care Summary

Fill in the following chart pertaining to the management of the types of emergencies discussed in this chapter.

NOTE: While the following steps are widely accepted, be sure to consult and follow your local protocol.

General Management of Head Injuries

1. Establish a(n) _____ airway. If necessary, begin and maintain _____ and provide _____ _____.
2. Control _____, and provide adequate _____ to maintain _____ perfusion. Begin _____ resuscitation, if necessary.
3. Assess the patient's baseline level of _____, and continuously monitor it.
4. Do not apply pressure to an open or _____ skull injury.
5. Assess and treat other injuries.
6. Anticipate and manage _____ to prevent aspiration.
7. Be prepared for _____ and changes in the patient's condition.
8. Transport the patient promptly and with extreme care.

General Management of Spine Injuries

1. Open and maintain a patent airway with the _____ maneuver.
2. Hold the head still in a(n) _____, in-line position until it can be fully immobilized.
3. Consider inserting a(n) _____ airway.
4. Have a(n) _____ unit available.
5. Provide supplemental oxygen.
6. Continuously monitor the patient's airway and be prepared for any changes in the patient's condition based on your treatment.

CHAPTER

29

Chest Injuries

© Photos.com

General Knowledge

Matching

Match each of the items in the left column to the appropriate definition in the right column.

_____ **1.** Thoracic cage   **A.** Delivering oxygen to the blood by diffusion

_____ **2.** Diaphragm   **B.** Chest

_____ **3.** Ventilation   **C.** Center cavity of the thorax

_____ **4.** Oxygenation   **D.** Separates the chest from the abdomen

_____ **5.** Aorta   **E.** Major artery in the chest

_____ **6.** Closed chest injury   **F.** Penetrating wound

_____ **7.** Hemoptysis   **G.** Rapid respirations

_____ **8.** Pericardium   **H.** Usually blunt trauma

_____ **9.** Open chest injury   **I.** Coughing up blood

_____ **10.** Tachypnea   **J.** Sac around the heart

_____ **11.** Mediastinum   **K.** Moving air in and out of the lungs

Multiple Choice

Read each item carefully and then select the one best response.

_____ **1.** Air is supplied to the lungs via the:

    A. esophagus.

    B. trachea.

    C. nares.

    D. oropharynx.

_____ **2.** The _____ separates the thoracic cavity from the abdominal cavity.

    A. diaphragm

    B. mediastinum

    C. xyphoid process

    D. inferior border of the ribs

_____ **3.** On inhalation, which of the following does NOT occur?

    A. The intercostal muscles contract, elevating the rib cage.

    B. The diaphragm contracts.

    C. The pressure inside the chest increases.

    D. Air enters through the nose and mouth.

_____ **4.** You respond to the local rodeo arena for a bull rider. The scene is safe, and the patient is lying unconscious in the middle of the arena. His airway is open, and he is breathing at 20 breaths/min. His pulse is 128 beats/min and blood pressure is 110/64 mm Hg. There is no obvious bleeding. Bystanders tell you he was thrown into the air and landed on the bull's head. He was not wearing a vest. Which of the following is NOT indicated in blunt trauma to the chest?

    A. Bruising of the lungs and heart

    B. Fracture of whole areas of the chest wall

    C. Damage to the aorta

    D. Dissection of the carotid arteries

_____ 5. You respond to a motor vehicle collision and find a 29-year-old woman who is complaining of chest pain. Her chest struck the steering wheel. Her airway is open, she is breathing at 24 breaths/min, and she is coughing up blood. Her pulse is 130 beats/min, rapid and weak, and her blood pressure is 90/58 mm Hg. You notice cyanosis around the lips and note that her fingers are also blue. When you expose the chest, she tells you it hurts and points to a bruised spot. Which of the following is a symptom?

   A. Cyanosis around the lips or fingertips

   B. Rapid, weak pulse

   C. Hemoptysis

   D. Pain at the site of injury

_____ 6. Which of the following is NOT a sign or symptom of a chest injury?

   A. Bruising of the chest wall

   B. Crepitus with palpation of the chest

   C. Clear and equal breath sounds

   D. Unequal expansion of the chest wall

_____ 7. You respond to an 18-year-old man who has been assaulted with a baseball bat. He was hit in the chest. He is unresponsive, apneic, and pulseless. This condition is most likely related to:

   A. commotio cordis.

   B. cardiac tamponade.

   C. pneumothorax.

   D. traumatic asphyxia.

_____ 8. Paradoxical motion of the chest refers to:

   A. rib fractures that move with the chest wall during breathing.

   B. one segment of the chest wall moving opposite the remainder of the chest.

   C. unequal expansion of the chest wall.

   D. one segment of the chest wall moving out on inspiration and in on exhalation.

_____ 9. A _____ results when an injury allows air to enter through a hole in the chest wall or the surface of the lung as the patient attempts to breathe, causing the lung on that side to collapse.

   A. tension pneumothorax

   B. hemothorax

   C. hemopneumothorax

   D. pneumothorax

_____ 10. A sucking chest wound should be treated with:

   A. a standard dressing.

   B. taping down the chest.

   C. an occlusive dressing.

   D. a sandbag over the wound.

_____ 11. You respond to a 20-year-old man who was playing basketball and suddenly developed chest pain and respiratory difficulty. He is alert and oriented and complaining of chest pain. He is breathing at 24 breaths/min. His pulse is 140 beats/min and blood pressure is 160/90 mm Hg. When listening to the chest, you notice diminished breath sounds on the left side. This patient is most likely suffering from a(n):

   A. simple pneumothorax.

   B. hemothorax.

   C. tension pneumothorax.

   D. open pneuomothorax.

_____ 12. Distended jugular veins, a narrowing pulse pressure, and muffled heart sounds are seen in which of the following conditions?

   A. Tension pneumothorax

   B. Cardiac tamponade

   C. Traumatic asphyxia

   D. Commotio cordis

_____ **13.** Common signs and symptoms of tension pneumothorax include all of the following EXCEPT:

    A. increasing respiratory distress.

    B. distended neck veins.

    C. high blood pressure.

    D. tracheal deviation away from the injured site.

_____ **14.** Which of the following statements regarding hemothorax is correct?

    A. It can only be treated by a surgeon.

    B. It results from a collection of air in the pleural space.

    C. Breath sounds tend to be equal.

    D. It is not typically associated with shock.

_____ **15.** A _____ is the result of blunt chest trauma and is associated with an irregular pulse and sometimes dangerous cardiac rhythms.

    A. cardiac tamponade

    B. pulmonary contusion

    C. myocardial contusion

    D. traumatic asphyxia

_____ **16.** A patient with blunt trauma who is holding the lateral side of his chest and has rapid and shallow respirations is most likely suffering from:

    A. rib fractures.

    B. a sternal fracture.

    C. a pneumothorax.

    D. a pulmonary contusion.

_____ **17.** Traumatic asphyxia:

    A. is bruising of the lung.

    B. occurs when three or more adjacent ribs are fractured in two or more places.

    C. is a sudden, severe compression of the chest.

    D. results from the pericardial sac filling with blood.

_____ **18.** _____ can increase intrathoracic pressure reducing cardiac output and potentially worsening chest injuries such as pneumothorax.

    A. Hypoventilation

    B. Positive pressure ventilation

    C. Hyperventilation

    D. Overventilation

_____ **19.** Which of the following is NOT a pertinent negative to note during your assessment of a patient with chest trauma?

    A. No heart murmurs

    B. No associated shortness of breath

    C. No rapid breathing

    D. No areas of deformity

_____ **20.** Large blood vessels in the chest that can result in massive hemorrhaging include all of the following EXCEPT:

    A. the pulmonary arteries.

    B. the femoral arteries.

    C. the aorta.

    D. the four main pulmonary veins.

True/False

If you believe the statement to be more true than false, write the letter "T" in the space provided. If you believe the statement to be more false than true, write the letter "F."

_____   **1.** Dyspnea is difficulty breathing.

_____   **2.** Tachypnea is slow respirations.

_____   **3.** Distended neck veins may be a sign of a tension pneumothorax.

_____   **4.** Rib fractures are especially common in children.

_____   **5.** Narrowing pulse pressure is related to spontaneous pneumothorax.

_____   **6.** Laceration of the large blood vessels in the chest can cause minimal hemorrhage.

_____   **7.** The thoracic cage extends from the lower end of the neck to the umbilicus.

_____   **8.** Patients with spinal cord injuries at C3 or above can lose their ability to breathe.

_____   **9.** A flutter valve is a three-way valve that allows air to leave the chest cavity.

_____   **10.** Open chest injury is caused by penetrating trauma.

_____   **11.** Paradoxical motion is an early sign of a flail segment.

_____   **12.** Because patients with chest injury have so many risks of mortality, they should be reassessed every 10 minutes.

_____   **13.** You should control external bleeding with direct pressure and a bulky dressing.

_____   **14.** Almost one-third of people who are killed immediately in car crashes die as a result of traumatic rupture of the aorta.

_____   **15.** The right lung contains two lobes, and the left lung contains three lobes.

Fill-in-the-Blank

Read each item carefully and then complete the statement by filling in the missing words.

1. The esophagus is located in the _____ of the chest.

2. During inhalation, the pressure in the chest _____.

3. In the anterior chest, ribs connect to the _____.

4. The trachea divides into the right and left main stem _____.

5. The _____ nerves supply the diaphragm.

6. Contents of the chest are protected by the _____.

7. The chest extends from the lower end of the neck to the _____.

8. _____ line the area between the lungs and chest wall.

9. An increase in CO_2 in the blood is known as _____.

10. During inhalation, the diaphragm _____.

11. _____ is the body's ability to move air in and out of the chest and lung tissue.

12. The intercostal muscles are innervated from spinal nerves originating in the cervical regions of _____ and

_____.

13. _____ _____ is the amount of air in mL that is moved into or out of the lungs during a single breath.

14. The _____ _____ may drop as the brain becomes starved for oxygen and overloaded with carbon dioxide and other waste products.

15. A severing of the aorta that can occur when the body is exposed to _____ _____.

Labeling

Label the following diagrams with the correct terms.

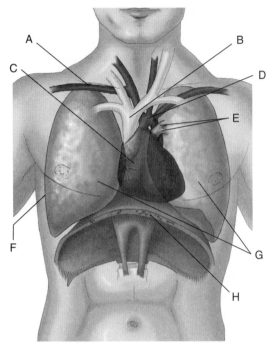

© Jones & Bartlett Learning.

1. Anterior Aspect of the Chest

A. _____

B. _____

C. _____

D. _____

E. _____

F. _____

G. _____

H. _____

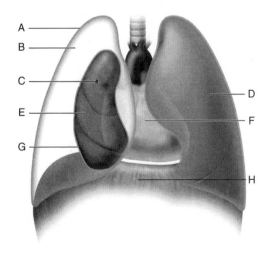

© Jones & Bartlett Learning.

2. Pneumothorax

A. _____

B. _____

C. _____

D. _____

E. _____

F. _____

G. _____

H. _____

Crossword Puzzle

The following crossword puzzle is an activity provided to reinforce correct spelling and understanding of medical terminology associated with emergency care and the EMT. Use the clues in the column to complete the puzzle.

Across

1. A collection of blood in the pleural cavity.
4. A(n) _____ chest injury is an injury in which the chest wall is penetrated by a fractured rib or by an external object.
5. Traumatic _____ is a pattern of injuries seen after a severe force is applied to the chest, forcing blood from the great vessels back into the head and neck.
8. A(n) _____ pneumothorax occurs when a weak area on the lung ruptures in the absence of major injury, allowing air to leak into the pleural space.
9. The fibrous sac that surrounds the heart.
11. A(n) _____ chest wound is a chest wall wound through which air passes during inspiration and expiration, creating a sucking sound.
12. A(n) _____ pneumothorax is an accumulation of air or gas in the pleural cavity that progressively increases pressure in the chest that interferes with cardiac function with potentially fatal results.
13. An accumulation of air or gas in the pleural cavity.

Down

2. Rapid respirations.
3. A(n) _____ dressing is made of Vaseline-impregnated gauze, aluminum foil, or plastic that protects a wound from air and bacteria.
6. A(n) _____ pneumothorax is any pneumothorax that is free from significant physiologic changes and does not cause drastic changes in the vital signs of the patient.
7. _____ cordis is a blunt chest injury caused by a sudden, direct blow to the chest that occurs only during the critical portion of a person's heartbeat.
10. A(n) _____ chest injury is usually caused by blunt trauma.

Critical Thinking

Short Answer

Complete this section with short written answers using the space provided.

1. List the signs and symptoms associated with a chest injury.

_____

_____

_____

2. Describe the two methods for sealing a sucking chest wound.

_____

_____

_____

3. Describe the method(s) for treating a flail chest segment.

_____

_____

_____

4. Define traumatic asphyxia and describe its signs.

_____

_____

_____

5. List the "deadly dozen" chest injuries.

_____

_____

_____

Ambulance Calls

The following case scenarios provide an opportunity to explore the concerns associated with patient management and to enhance critical-thinking skills. Read each scenario and answer each question to the best of your ability.

1. You are dispatched to an area horse ranch for an injury to a rider. You arrive to find that a horse has kicked one of the riders in the chest. The patient is having significant difficulty breathing and appears to be in extreme pain.

   How would you best manage this patient?

   _____

   _____

   _____

2. You are dispatched for a man trapped under a car. As you travel to the location, the dispatcher informs you that your patient is now free but is experiencing significant chest and midback pain.

   How would you best manage this patient?

   _____

   _____

   _____

3. You are dispatched to a lumberyard where a 27-year-old man was crushed by a piece of heavy equipment. Coworkers pulled the equipment off the patient. He presents with distended neck veins, cyanosis, and bloodshot eyes.

   How would you best manage this patient?

   _____

   _____

   _____

   _____

Skills

Assessment Review

Answer the following questions pertaining to the assessment of the types of emergencies discussed in this chapter.

_____ 1. You respond to an accidental shooting of a 37-year-old man. During the primary assessment, you find his airway to be open. His breathing is labored at 24 breaths/min. His pulse is rapid and weak. When exposing the chest you find a sucking chest wound. You should:

   A. take a blood pressure reading.

   B. cover the wound.

   C. continue your assessment.

   D. transport the patient immediately.

_____ 2. You respond to a 17-year-old girl who was hit in the chest with a lawn dart. On arrival, she is conscious and able to converse with you. Her airway is open, but her breathing is becoming progressively more difficult. Her pulse is rapid and weak. You can palpate a radial pulse. On examining the chest, you find that she has a penetrating injury to the chest and that there is a sucking sound as she breathes. How do you manage this wound?

   A. Apply oxygen by nasal cannula.

   B. Stabilize the cervical spine.

   C. Use a 4-inch by 4-inch gauze pad.

   D. Use an occlusive dressing.

_____ **3.** When bandaging an open chest wound, what is the minimum number of sides that have to be taped down?

    A. One

    B. Two

    C. Three

    D. Four

_____ **4.** Dispatch sends you to a farm on the edge of town. A 57-year-old man was kicked in the chest by a horse. He walked into his house and collapsed. He is confused and lethargic. His breathing is labored at 28 breaths/min, pulse is rapid and regular, and you are able to palpate a radial pulse. On examining his chest, you notice paradoxical movement on the right chest wall. You should:

    A. provide spinal immobilization.

    B. put the patient in a position of comfort.

    C. provide oxygen by nasal cannula.

    D. provide positive pressure ventilations.

_____ **5.** A 16-year-old boy walks into a pipe gate that hits him in the ribs on the left side. On arrival, he is alert and oriented. His breathing is shallow at 22 breaths/min. His pulse is regular and strong. You palpate a radial pulse. You are able to rule out spinal trauma. In which position do you transport him?

    A. Position of comfort

    B. Supine

    C. Prone

    D. Recovery

Abdominal and Genitourinary Injuries

© Photos.com

General Knowledge

Matching

Match each of the items in the left column to the appropriate definition in the right column.

_____ 1. Closed abdominal injury

_____ 2. Evisceration

_____ 3. Flank

_____ 4. Guarding

_____ 5. Hollow organs

_____ 6. Hematuria

_____ 7. Open abdominal injury

_____ 8. Peritoneal cavity

_____ 9. Solid organs

A. Contracting stomach muscles to minimize pain

B. Liver, pancreas, spleen

C. Blood in the urine

D. Injury in which a foreign object enters the abdomen and opens the peritoneal cavity to the outside

E. Soft-tissue damage inside the body, but the skin remains intact

F. Posterior region below the margin of the lower rib cage

G. Abdominal cavity

H. Stomach, small intestine, ureters

I. Displacement of organs outside the body

Multiple Choice

Read each item carefully and then select the one best response.

_____ 1. All of the following systems contain organs that make up the contents of the abdominal cavity EXCEPT:

   A. the digestive system.

   B. the urinary system.

   C. the genitourinary system.

   D. the limbic system.

_____ 2. Which of the following is NOT a hollow organ of the abdomen?

   A. Stomach

   B. Liver

   C. Bladder

   D. Ureters

_____ 3. Which of the following is NOT a solid organ of the abdomen?

   A. Liver

   B. Spleen

   C. Gallbladder

   D. Pancreas

_____ 4. The first signs of peritonitis include all of the following EXCEPT:

   A. severe abdominal pain.

   B. tenderness.

   C. muscular spasm.

   D. nausea.

_____ **5.** Late signs of peritonitis may include:

   A. a soft abdomen.

   B. nausea.

   C. normal bowel sounds.

   D. diarrhea.

_____ **6.** _____ takes place in the solid organs.

   A. Digestion

   B. Excretion

   C. Energy production

   D. Absorption

_____ **7.** Because solid organs have a rich supply of blood, any injury can result in major:

   A. hemorrhaging.

   B. damage.

   C. pain.

   D. guarding.

_____ **8.** The _____ is often injured during motor vehicle collisions, especially in the cases of improperly placed seat belts or impact from the steering wheel, falls from heights or onto sharp objects, and bicycle and motorcycle crashes where the patient hits the handlebars on impact.

   A. pancreas

   B. heart

   C. spleen

   D. liver

_____ **9.** Any air in the peritoneal cavity seeks the most _____ space or void; thus, the location of the air can change with positioning of the patient.

   A. inferior

   B. superior

   C. distal

   D. proximal

_____ **10.** The abdomen is divided into four:

   A. quadrants.

   B. planes.

   C. sections.

   D. angles.

_____ **11.** The largest organ in the abdomen is the:

   A. liver.

   B. spleen.

   C. pancreas.

   D. kidneys.

_____ **12.** Open abdominal injuries are also known as:

   A. blunt injuries.

   B. eviscerations.

   C. penetrating injuries.

   D. peritoneal injuries.

_____ **13.** Blunt abdominal injuries may result from:

   A. a stab wound.

   B. seat belts.

   C. a gunshot wound.

   D. an impaled object.

_____ 14. The major complaint of patients with abdominal injury is:
  A. pain.
  B. tachycardia.
  C. rigidity.
  D. swelling.

_____ 15. A very common early sign of a significant abdominal injury is:
  A. pain.
  B. tachycardia.
  C. rigidity.
  D. distention.

_____ 16. Late signs of abdominal injury include all of the following EXCEPT:
  A. distention.
  B. increased blood pressure.
  C. change in mental status.
  D. pale, cool, moist skin.

_____ 17. Your primary concern when dealing with an unresponsive patient with an open abdominal injury is:
  A. covering the wound with a moist dressing.
  B. maintaining the airway.
  C. controlling the bleeding.
  D. monitoring vital signs.

_____ 18. You respond to an 18-year-old high school football player who was hit in the right flank with a helmet several hours ago. He is complaining of pain in the area. He is alert and oriented. His airway is open, and his respirations are within normal limits. His pulse is rapid and regular. He has a radial pulse. He tells you that he is noticing blood in his urine. Based on this information, the patient is likely to have an injury to the:
  A. liver.
  B. kidney.
  C. gallbladder.
  D. appendix.

_____ 19. When performing a history on a patient with abdominal trauma, all of the following questions would be appropriate regarding trauma EXCEPT:
  A. Is there any blood in your stool?
  B. Does your pain go anywhere?
  C. Do you have any nausea, vomiting, or diarrhea?
  D. Are you having trouble with your hearing?

_____ 20. If the seat belt lies too high it can do all of the following EXCEPT:
  A. squeeze abdominal organs.
  B. compress the great vessels.
  C. fracture the lumbar spine.
  D. rupture the appendix.

_____ 21. You are dispatched to a motor vehicle collision. Your patient is a 42-year-old restrained woman. The air bag deployed, and the woman has abrasions on her face. She is complaining of pain to both her chest and abdomen. Her airway is open and respirations are within normal limits. Her pulse is a little rapid but strong and regular. She has distal pulses. In assessing this patient, which of the following statements is NOT true?
  A. Bowel sounds may help confirm findings.
  B. Palpation is typically performed first with light touch.
  C. If light touch elicits pain, perform deep palpation to assess further injury.
  D. If you find an entry wound, you should always assess for an exit wound.

_____ **22.** Patients with open abdominal injuries often complain of:
   A. pain.
   B. nausea.
   C. vomiting.
   D. dyspnea.

_____ **23.** You are called to the local bar where a fight has taken place. The police department tells you that you have a 36-year-old man who has been stabbed twice in the abdomen. On arrival, the patient is alert and oriented. His airway is open. His respirations are at 24 breaths/min; pulse is rapid, regular, and weak. He has distal pulses. With the penetrating trauma, you should assume that the object has done all of the following EXCEPT:
   A. has penetrated the peritoneum.
   B. has entered the abdominal cavity.
   C. has possibly injured one or more organs.
   D. has damaged only the skin.

_____ **24.** When treating a patient with an evisceration, you should:
   A. attempt to replace the abdominal contents.
   B. cover the protruding organs with a dry, sterile dressing.
   C. cover the protruding organs with moist, adherent dressings.
   D. cover the protruding contents with moist, sterile gauze compresses.

_____ **25.** The solid organs of the urinary system include the:
   A. kidneys.
   B. ureters.
   C. bladder.
   D. urethra.

_____ **26.** All of the following male genitalia lie outside the pelvic cavity EXCEPT:
   A. the urethra.
   B. the penis.
   C. the seminal vesicles.
   D. the testes.

_____ **27.** Suspect kidney damage if the patient has a history or physical evidence of all of the following EXCEPT:
   A. an abrasion, laceration, or contusion in the flank.
   B. a penetrating wound in the region of the lower rib cage or the upper abdomen.
   C. fractures on either side of the lower rib cage.
   D. a hematoma in the umbilical region.

_____ **28.** Signs of injury to the kidney may include any of the following EXCEPT:
   A. bruises or lacerations on the overlying skin.
   B. shock.
   C. increased urgency of urination.
   D. hematuria.

_____ **29.** Suspect a possible injury of the urinary bladder in all of the following findings EXCEPT:
   A. bruising to the left upper quadrant.
   B. blood at the urethral opening.
   C. blood at the tip of the penis or a stain on the patient's underwear.
   D. physical signs of trauma on the lower abdomen, pelvis, or perineum.

_____ **30.** When treating a patient with an amputation of the penile shaft, your top priority is:
   A. locating the amputated part.
   B. controlling bleeding.
   C. keeping the remaining tissue dry.
   D. delaying transport until bleeding is controlled.

_____ **31.** In any case of trauma to a female patient, you should always determine if the patient:

    A. is on birth control.

    B. is pregnant.

    C. is currently menstruating.

    D. has a history of ovarian cysts.

_____ **32.** In cases of sexual assault, which of the following is TRUE?

    A. You should always examine the genitalia for any sign of injury.

    B. Advise the patient not to wash, urinate, or defecate.

    C. In addition to recording the facts, it is important to include your personal thoughts.

    D. You should use plastic bags when collecting items such as clothes.

True/False

If you believe the statement to be more true than false, write the letter "T" in the space provided. If you believe the statement to be more false than true, write the letter "F."

_____ **1.** Hollow organs will bleed profusely if injured.

_____ **2.** One of the most common signs of a significant abdominal injury is an elevated pulse rate.

_____ **3.** Patients with abdominal injuries should be kept supine with the head elevated.

_____ **4.** Peritoneal irritation is in response to hollow organ injury.

_____ **5.** Eviscerated organs should be covered with a dry dressing.

_____ **6.** Injuries to the kidneys usually occur in isolation.

_____ **7.** Peritonitis is an inflammation of the peritoneum.

_____ **8.** The abdomen is divided into two quadrants.

_____ **9.** Swelling may involve the entire abdomen and indicates significant intra-abdominal injury.

_____ **10.** Patients with peritonitis will want to lie still with their legs drawn up.

Fill-in-the-Blank

Read each item carefully and then complete the statement by filling in the missing words.

1. Severe bleeding may occur with injury to _____ organs.

2. The _____ system is responsible for filtering waste.

3. Kidneys are located in the _____ space.

4. A penetrating wound that reaches the kidneys almost always involves _____ _____.

5. When ruptured, the organs of the abdominal cavity can spill their contents into the peritoneal cavity, causing an intense inflammatory reaction called _____.

6. Blood may irritate the _____ _____ and cause the patient to report abdominal pain.

7. Closed abdominal injuries are also known as _____ _____.

8. Open abdominal injuries are also known as _____ _____.

9. The region below the rib cage and above the hip is called the _____.

10. An open wound that allows internal organs or fat to protrude through the wound is called _____.

Labeling
Label the following diagrams with the correct terms.

1. Hollow Organs

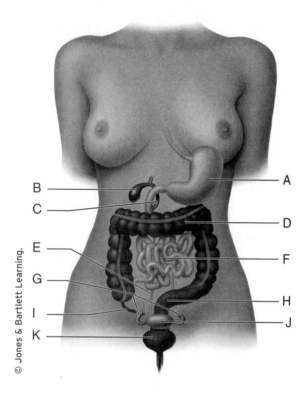

A. _____

B. _____

C. _____

D. _____

E. _____

F. _____

G. _____

H. _____

I. _____

J. _____

K. _____

2. Solid Organs

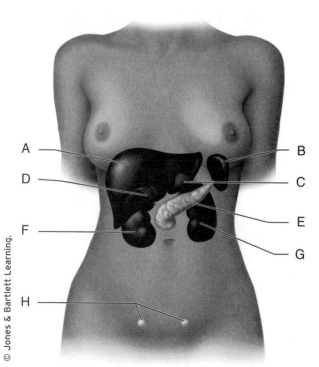

A. _____

B. _____

C. _____

D. _____

E. _____

F. _____

G. _____

H. _____

Crossword Puzzle

The following crossword puzzle is an activity provided to reinforce correct spelling and understanding of medical terminology associated with emergency care and the EMT. Use the clues in the column to complete the puzzle.

Across

3. Solid masses of tissue where much of the chemical work of the body takes place.
4. The abdominal cavity is known as the _____ cavity.
5. The posterior region below the margin of the lower rib cage.
7. Structures through which materials pass, such as the stomach, small intestines, large intestines, ureters, and bladder.
9. Black, tarry stools.

Down

1. Contracting the stomach muscles to minimize the pain of abdominal movement.
2. The displacement of organs outside the body.
6. In a(n) _____ abdominal injury, there is soft-tissue damage inside the body, but the skin remains intact.
8. In a(n) _____ abdominal injury, there is a break in the surface of the skin or mucous membrane, exposing deeper tissue to potential contamination.

Critical Thinking

Short Answer

Complete this section with short written answers using the space provided.

1. List the hollow organs of the abdomen and urinary system.

_____

_____

_____

2. List the solid organs of the abdomen and urinary system.

_____

_____

_____

3. List the signs and symptoms of an abdominal injury.

_____

_____

_____

4. List the steps to care for an open abdominal injury.

_____

_____

_____

5. List the steps to care for an open abdominal wound with exposed organs.

_____

_____

_____

6. List the major history or physical findings associated with possible kidney damage.

_____

_____

_____

Ambulance Calls

The following case scenarios provide an opportunity to explore the concerns associated with patient management and to enhance critical-thinking skills. Read each scenario and answer each question to the best of your ability.

1. You are dispatched to a local bar where your patient, a 26-year-old man, was involved in an altercation. He has several superficial lacerations to his arms, and a knife is impaled in his right upper quadrant. He is lying supine on the floor. He is alert. The bar patrons tell you that he did not fall, but that they helped him to the floor.

   How would you best manage this patient?

   _____

   _____

   _____

2. You are dispatched to assist police with a mentally ill patient who has threatened harm to himself and others. Police officers found the man running around his home with a knife and blood all over his lower body. The man tells you "the voices" told him to cut off his penis.

   How would you best manage this patient?

   _____

   _____

   _____

3. You are dispatched to a construction site, where a man has fallen onto a piece of rebar. You arrive to find a man sitting on the ground with his legs drawn toward his chest. He tells you that he fell from a ladder onto a piece of rebar. He says, "Something's sticking out of me." As you visualize his abdomen, you can clearly see a portion of his bowel on the outside of his body.

   How would you best manage this patient?

   _____

   _____

   _____

Skills

Assessment Review

Answer the following questions pertaining to the assessment of the types of emergencies discussed in this chapter.

_____ **1.** If you are treating a patient with an abdominal evisceration, you should use a(n):

A. moist, sterile dressing.

B. dry, sterile dressing.

C. adhesive dressing.

D. triangular bandage.

_____ **2.** You have a male patient who has no immediate life threat but does have bleeding genitalia. You should bandage with a(n):

A. dry dressing.

B. moist dressing.

C. occlusive dressing.

D. adhesive dressing.

_____ **3.** You have a patient with suspected kidney injury but no spinal injury. How should he be positioned?

A. Supine

B. Prone

C. Lateral recumbent

D. Position of comfort

_____ **4.** Your patient has his penis caught in his zipper. What do you need to do to relieve pressure?

A. Pull the pants off the patient.

B. Force the zipper open.

C. Remove the foreskin.

D. Cut the zipper out of the pants.

_____ **5.** Whenever possible, you should always provide the sexual assault patient with:

A. a police escort.

B. rape crisis intervention.

C. an attendant of the same gender.

D. the name of the assailant.

Emergency Care Summary

Fill in the following chart pertaining to the management of the types of emergencies discussed in this chapter.

NOTE: While the following steps are widely accepted, be sure to consult and follow your local protocol.

Abdominal Trauma

Blunt Abdominal Injuries

Log roll the patient to a _____ position on a backboard. If the patient vomits, turn him or her to one side and clear the mouth and throat of vomitus. Monitor the patient's vital signs for any indication of _____. If signs of shock are present, administer high-flow supplemental oxygen via a nonrebreathing mask, or a bag-valve mask if needed, and treat for shock. Keep the patient _____. Provide rapid transport to the emergency department.

Penetrating Abdominal Injuries

Patients with penetrating injuries generally have obvious wounds and _____ _____; however, significant external bleeding is not always present. As an EMT, you should have a high _____ _____ _____ that the patient has serious unseen blood loss occurring inside the body. Inspect the patient's back and sides for exit wounds, and apply a _____, sterile dressing to all open wounds. If the penetrating object is still in place, apply a _____ _____ around it to control external bleeding and to minimize movement of the object.

Abdominal Evisceration

Never attempt to replace protruding organs. Cover the exposed organs with a _____, sterile dressing. If local protocol allows, cover the sterile dressing with an _____ dressing. Maintain body temperature, treat for shock, and transport to the highest level trauma center available.

Genitourinary Trauma

Kidney Injuries

Damage to the kidneys may not be obvious on inspection of the patient. You may or may not see bruises or lacerations on the overlying skin. You will see signs of shock if the injury is associated with significant blood loss. Another sign of kidney damage is _____ in the urine (hematuria). Treat shock and associated injuries in the appropriate manner. Provide prompt transport to the hospital, monitoring the patient's vital signs carefully en route.

Urinary Bladder Injuries

Suspect a possible injury of the urinary bladder if you see blood at the _____ opening or physical signs of trauma on the lower abdomen, pelvis, or _____. There may be blood at the tip of the penis or a stain on the patient's underwear. The presence of associated injuries or of shock will dictate the urgency of transport. In most instances, provide prompt transport, and monitor the patient's vital signs en route.

Genitalia Injuries

_____ _____ with a dry, sterile dressing usually controls any external hemorrhage. Lacerations, abrasions, and avulsions should be treated with _____, sterile compresses. Contusions and other blunt injuries all require careful in-hospital evaluation. However, the urgency for transport will be determined by associated injuries, the amount of hemorrhage, and the presence of _____.

Rectal Bleeding

Bleeding from the rectum may present as blood stains or blood soaking through underwear or patients may report blood in the _____ after a bowel movement. Significant rectal bleeding can occur after hemorrhoid surgery and can lead to significant _____ _____ and _____.

Sexual Assault

Follow local protocol for crime scene management and _____ preservation. If available, an EMT of the same gender as the patient should perform the assessment and treatment. Advise the patient not to change clothes, _____, drink, or eat. Maintain patient privacy at all times. On some occasions, patients will have sustained multiple-system trauma and will also need treatment for shock. Do not examine the genitalia unless obvious bleeding must be managed.

General Knowledge

Matching

Match each of the items in the left column to the appropriate definition in the right column.

_____ **1.** Striated
_____ **2.** Fascia
_____ **3.** Smooth

_____ **4.** Joint
_____ **5.** Ligaments

_____ **6.** Closed fracture
_____ **7.** Point tenderness
_____ **8.** Displaced fracture
_____ **9.** Articular cartilage
_____ **10.** Open fracture
_____ **11.** Traction

A. Any injury that makes the limb appear in an unnatural position
B. Any fracture in which the skin has not been broken
C. A thin layer of cartilage, covering the articular surface of bones in synovial joints
D. Involuntary muscle
E. Any break in the bone in which the overlying skin has been damaged as well
F. Hold joints together
G. Skeletal muscle
H. The act of exerting a pulling force on a structure
I. Where two bones contact
J. Fibrous tissue that covers all skeletal muscle
K. Tenderness sharply located at the site of an injury

Multiple Choice

Read each item carefully and then select the one best response.

_____ **1.** Blood in the urine is known as:
   A. hematuria.
   B. hemotysis.
   C. hematocrit.
   D. hemoglobin.

_____ **2.** Smooth muscle is found in the:
   A. back.
   B. blood vessels.
   C. heart.
   D. leg.

_____ **3.** The bones in the skeleton produce _____ in the bone marrow.
   A. blood cells
   B. minerals
   C. electrolytes
   D. hormones

_____ **4.** _____ are held together in a tough fibrous structure known as a capsule.
   A. Tendons
   B. Joints
   C. Ligaments
   D. Bones

_____ **5.** Joints are bathed and lubricated by _____ fluid.
- **A.** cartilaginous
- **B.** articular
- **C.** synovial
- **D.** cerebrospinal

_____ **6.** A _____ is a disruption of a joint in which the bone ends are no longer in contact.
- **A.** torn ligament
- **B.** dislocation
- **C.** fracture dislocation
- **D.** sprain

_____ **7.** A _____ is an injury to the ligaments, the articular capsule, the synovial membrane, and the tendons crossing the joint.
- **A.** dislocation
- **B.** strain
- **C.** sprain
- **D.** torn ligament

_____ **8.** A _____ is a stretching or tearing of the muscle.
- **A.** strain
- **B.** sprain
- **C.** torn ligament
- **D.** split

_____ **9.** The zone of injury includes all of the following EXCEPT:
- **A.** adjacent nerves.
- **B.** adjacent blood vessels.
- **C.** surrounding soft tissue.
- **D.** the incident scene.

_____ **10.** A(n) _____ fractures the bone at the point of impact.
- **A.** direct blow
- **B.** indirect force
- **C.** twisting force
- **D.** high-energy injury

_____ **11.** A(n) _____ may cause a fracture or dislocation at a distant point.
- **A.** direct blow
- **B.** indirect force
- **C.** twisting force
- **D.** high-energy injury

_____ **12.** When caring for patients who have fallen, you must identify the _____ and the mechanism of injury so that you will not overlook associated injuries.
- **A.** site of injury
- **B.** height of fall
- **C.** point of contact
- **D.** twisting forces

_____ **13.** _____ produce severe damage to the skeleton, surrounding soft tissues, and vital internal organs.
- **A.** Direct blows
- **B.** Indirect forces
- **C.** Twisting forces
- **D.** High-energy injuries

_____ **14.** Regardless of the extent and severity of the damage to the skin, you should treat any injury that breaks the skin as a possible:

    A. closed fracture.

    B. open fracture.

    C. nondisplaced fracture.

    D. displaced fracture.

_____ **15.** A(n) _____ is also known as a hairline fracture.

    A. closed fracture

    B. open fracture

    C. nondisplaced fracture

    D. displaced fracture

_____ **16.** A(n) _____ produces actual deformity, or distortion, of the limb by shortening, rotating, or angulating it.

    A. closed fracture

    B. open fracture

    C. nondisplaced fracture

    D. displaced fracture

_____ **17.** You respond to a 19-year-old woman who was kicked in the leg by a horse. She is alert and oriented. Respirations are 20 breaths/min, regular and unlabored. Pulse is 110 beats/min and regular. Distal pulses are present. She has point tenderness at the site of the injury. You should compare the limb to:

    A. the opposite uninjured limb.

    B. one of your limbs or one of your partner's limbs.

    C. an injury chart.

    D. other limb injuries you have seen.

_____ **18.** _____ is the most reliable indicator of an underlying fracture.

    A. Crepitus

    B. Deformity

    C. Point tenderness

    D. Absence of distal pulse

_____ **19.** A(n) _____ fracture occurs in a growth section of a child's bone, which may prematurely stop growth if not properly treated.

    A. greenstick

    B. comminuted

    C. pathologic

    D. epiphyseal

_____ **20.** A(n) _____ fracture is an incomplete fracture that passes only partway through the shaft of a bone but may still cause severe angulation.

    A. greenstick

    B. comminuted

    C. pathologic

    D. epiphyseal

_____ **21.** You are called to the local assisted living facility where a 94-year-old man has fallen. He is alert and oriented and denies passing out. His respirations are 18 breaths/min and regular. Pulse is 106 beats/min, regular and strong. Distal pulses are present. He states that he was walking, heard a pop, and fell to the floor. You suspect a(n) _____ fracture.

    A. greenstick

    B. comminuted

    C. pathologic

    D. epiphyseal

_____ **22.** A(n) _____ fracture is a fracture in which the bone is broken into more than two fragments.

    A. greenstick

    B. comminuted

    C. pathologic

    D. epiphyseal

_____ **23.** Your 24-year-old patient fell off a balance beam and landed on his arm. He is complaining of pain in the upper arm, and there is obvious swelling. You know that swelling is a sign of:

    A. bleeding.

    B. laceration.

    C. a locked joint.

    D. compartment syndrome.

_____ **24.** Fractures are almost always associated with _____ of the surrounding soft tissue.

    A. laceration

    B. crepitus

    C. ecchymosis

    D. swelling

_____ **25.** Signs and symptoms of a dislocated joint include all of the following EXCEPT:

    A. marked deformity.

    B. tenderness or palpation.

    C. locked joint.

    D. ecchymosis.

_____ **26.** Signs and symptoms of sprains include all of the following EXCEPT:

    A. point tenderness.

    B. pain preventing the patient from moving or using the limb normally.

    C. marked deformity.

    D. instability of the joint indicated by increased motion.

_____ **27.** Which of the following is NOT considered one of the 6 Ps of the musculoskeletal assessment?

    A. Pain

    B. Pulselessness

    C. Pressure

    D. Peristalsis

_____ **28.** Which of the following statements about compartment syndrome is FALSE?

    A. It occurs 6 to 12 hours after an injury.

    B. It most commonly occurs with a fractured femur.

    C. It is usually a result of excessive bleeding, a severely crushed extremity, or the rapid return of blood to an ischemic limb.

    D. It is characterized by pain that is out of proportion to the injury.

_____ **29.** Always check neurovascular function at the following times EXCEPT:

    A. after any manipulation of the limb.

    B. before applying a splint.

    C. after applying a splint.

    D. during history taking.

_____ **30.** You respond to a 19-year-old woman who was involved in a motor vehicle collision. She is alert and oriented. Her airway is open, and respirations are 18 breaths/min and unlabored. Pulse is 94 beats/min and is strong and regular. Distal pulses are present. Her upper arm has obvious deformity. You splint the upper arm. You know that splinting will do all of the following EXCEPT:

    A. prevent the need for surgery.

    B. make it easier to transfer the patient.

    C. help prevent restriction of distal blood flow.

    D. reduce pain.

_____ **31.** In-line _____ is the act of exerting a pulling force on a body structure in the direction of its normal alignment.
   A. stabilization
   B. immobilization
   C. traction
   D. direction

_____ **32.** Which of the following is NOT a basic type of splint?
   A. Rigid
   B. Formable
   C. Traction
   D. Sling

_____ **33.** For which of the following should you use a traction splint?
   A. Injuries of the pelvis
   B. An isolated femur fracture
   C. Partial amputation or avulsions with bone separation
   D. Lower leg or ankle injury

_____ **34.** While transporting a patient, you continue to recheck the splint you applied. You know that improperly applying a splint can cause all of the following EXCEPT:
   A. an increase of distal circulation if the splint is too tight.
   B. a delay in transport of a patient with a life-threatening injury.
   C. a reduction of distal circulation.
   D. a compression of nerves, tissues, and blood vessels.

_____ **35.** The _____ is one of the most commonly fractured bones in the body.
   A. scapula
   B. clavicle
   C. humerus
   D. radius

_____ **36.** What joint is frequently separated during football and hockey when a player falls and lands on the point of the shoulder?
   A. Glenohumeral joint
   B. Acromioclavicular joint
   C. Sternoclavicular joint
   D. Sacroiliac joint

_____ **37.** Signs and symptoms associated with hip dislocation include all of the following EXCEPT:
   A. severe pain in the hip.
   B. lateral and posterior aspects of the hip region are tender on palpation.
   C. being able to palpate the femoral head deep within the muscles of the buttock.
   D. decreased resistance to any movement of the joint.

_____ **38.** There is often a significant amount of blood loss, as much as _____ mL, after a fracture of the shaft of the femur.
   A. 100 to 250
   B. 250 to 500
   C. 500 to 1,000
   D. 1,000 to 1,500

_____ **39.** The knee is especially susceptible to _____ injuries, which occur when abnormal bending or twisting forces are applied to the joint.
   A. tendon
   B. ligament
   C. dislocation
   D. fracture-dislocation

_____ **40.** Signs and symptoms of knee ligament injury include all of the following EXCEPT:

    A. swelling.

    B. point tenderness.

    C. joint effusion.

    D. the affected leg externally rotated.

_____ **41.** Although substantial ligament damage always occurs with a knee dislocation, the more urgent injury is to the _____ artery, which is often lacerated or compressed by the displaced tibia.

    A. tibial

    B. femoral

    C. popliteal

    D. dorsalis pedis

_____ **42.** Because of local tenderness and swelling, it is easy to confuse a nondisplaced or minimally displaced fracture at the knee with a:

    A. tendon injury.

    B. ligament injury.

    C. dislocation.

    D. fracture-dislocation.

_____ **43.** Fracture of the tibia and fibula are sometimes associated with _____ as a result of the distorted positions of the limb following injury.

    A. vascular injury

    B. muscular injury

    C. tendon injury

    D. ligament injury

_____ **44.** Dislocation of the _____ is usually associated with fractures of one or both malleoli.

    A. knee

    B. elbow

    C. ankle

    D. hip

_____ **45.** Which of the following statements regarding the treatment of an amputation is FALSE?

    A. You should sever any partial amputation because this will aid in the reattachment process.

    B. In some areas, wrapping the amputated part in a dry, sterile dressing is appropriate.

    C. In some areas, wrapping the amputated part in dressings moistened with sterile saline is appropriate.

    D. After wrapping the amputated part, place it in a plastic bag.

True/False

If you believe the statement to be more true than false, write the letter "T" in the space provided. If you believe the statement to be more false than true, write the letter "F."

_____ **1.** All extremity injuries should be splinted before moving a patient unless the patient's life is in immediate danger.

_____ **2.** Splinting reduces pain and prevents the motion of bone fragments.

_____ **3.** You should use traction to reduce a fracture and force all bone fragments back into alignment.

_____ **4.** When applying traction, the direction of pull is always along the axis of the limb.

_____ **5.** Cover wounds with a dry, sterile dressing before applying a splint.

_____ **6.** When splinting a fracture, you should be careful to immobilize only the joint above the injury site.

_____ **7.** One of the steps of the neurologic examination is to palpate the pulse distal to the site of injury.

_____ **8.** White blood cells and platelets are produced in the marrow cavity.

_____ **9.** Compartment syndrome can develop in the forearm in children with a fracture of the humerus.

_____ **10.** Fractures of the distal radius are known as Colles fractures.

Fill-in-the-Blank

Read each item carefully and then complete the statement by filling in the missing words.

1. The _____ is the largest of the tarsal bones.

2. Bone marrow produces _____ _____.

3. The humerus connects with the radius and ulna to form the _____ elbow joint.

4. The _____ is a slender, s-shaped bone attached by ligaments to the sternum on one end and to the acromion process on the other.

5. A patient who has a significant _____ _____ _____ but whose condition appears otherwise stable should also be transported promptly to the closest appropriate hospital.

6. Penetrating injury should alert you to the possibility of a(n) _____ _____.

7. The _____ _____ is the most important nerve in the lower extremity; it controls the activity of muscles in the thigh and below the knee.

8. _____ _____ are used to splint the bony pelvis to reduce hemorrhage from bone ends, venous disruption, and pain.

9. A grating or grinding sensation known as _____ can be felt and sometimes even heard when fractured bone ends rub together.

10. A dislocated joint sometimes will spontaneously _____, or return to its normal position.

11. If you suspect that a patient has compartment syndrome, splint the affected limb, keeping it at the level of the heart, and provide immediate transport, reassessing _____ _____ frequently during transport.

Labeling

Label the following diagrams with the correct terms.

1. Pectoral Girdle

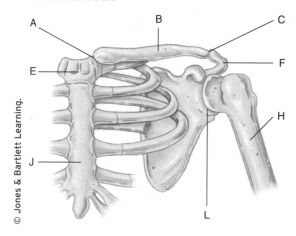

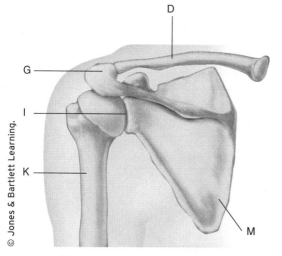

A. _____

B. _____

C. _____

D. _____

E. _____

F. _____

G. _____

H. _____

I. _____

J. _____

K. _____

L. _____

M. _____

2. Anatomy of the Wrist and Hand

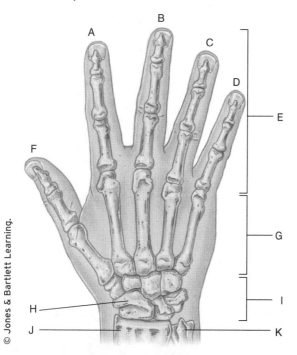

A. _____

B. _____

C. _____

D. _____

E. _____

F. _____

G. _____

H. _____

I. _____

J. _____

K. _____

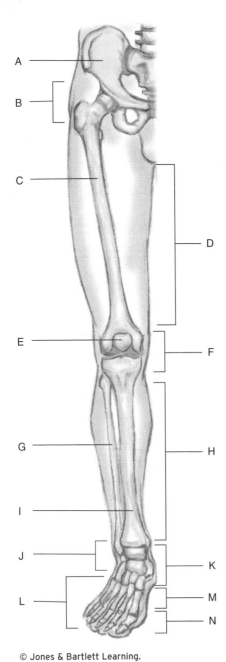

3. Bones of the Thigh, Leg, and Foot

A. _____

B. _____

C. _____

D. _____

E. _____

F. _____

G. _____

H. _____

I. _____

J. _____

K. _____

L. _____

M. _____

N. _____

Crossword Puzzle

The following crossword puzzle is an activity provided to reinforce correct spelling and understanding of medical terminology associated with emergency care and the EMT. Use the clues in the column to complete the puzzle.

Across

3. _____ cartilage is a pearly layer of specialized cartilage covering the articular surfaces of bones in synovial joints.

6. The zone of _____ is the area of potentially damaged soft tissue, adjacent nerves, and blood vessels surrounding an injury to a bone or a joint.

8. Blood in the urine.

10. Any break in a bone in which the overlying skin has been damaged.

13. A flexible or rigid appliance used to protect and maintain the position of an injured extremity.

14. The major nerve to the lower extremities.

15. _____ tenderness is sharply localized at the site of the injury, found by gently palpating along the bone.

Down

1. A bandage that passes around the chest to secure an injured arm to the chest.

2. The larger of the two lower leg bones responsible for supporting the major weight-bearing surface of the knee and the ankle.

4. The _____ space is between the abdominal cavity and the posterior abdominal wall.

5. A joint injury involving damage to supporting ligaments and sometimes partial or temporary dislocation of bone ends.

7. The place where two bones come into contact.

9. Longitudinal force applied to a structure.

11. The position of _____ is a hand position in which the wrist is slightly dorsiflexed and all finger joints are moderately flexed.

12. In a(n) _____ fracture, the skin is not broken.

13. A bandage or material that helps to support the weight of an injured upper extremity.

Critical Thinking

Short Answer

Complete this section with short written answers using the space provided.

1. List the four types of forces that may cause injury to a limb.

_____

_____

_____

2. List at least five of the signs associated with a possible fracture.

_____

_____

_____

3. List the 6 Ps of musculoskeletal assessment.

_____

_____

_____

4. List the general principles of splinting.

_____

_____

_____

5. What are the three goals of in-line traction?

_____

_____

_____

Ambulance Calls

The following case scenarios provide an opportunity to explore the concerns associated with patient management and to enhance critical-thinking skills. Read each scenario and answer each question to the best of your ability.

1. You are dispatched to care for a 17-year-old boy who jumped from the top of a three-story home into a pool. He landed directly on his feet just short of the pool. He is now complaining of low back pain and numbness and tingling of his legs.

How would you best manage this patient?

_____

_____

_____

2. You are called to a local park where an 11-year-old girl fell off the parallel bars onto her right elbow. She is cradling the arm to her chest. She has obvious swelling and deformity in the area. She has good pulse, motor, and sensation at the wrist. ABCs are normal.

How would you best manage this patient?

_____

_____

_____

3. You are dispatched to a fall at a local personal care home. You arrive to find an 82-year-old female complaining of severe pain to her right hip and the right leg is extended straight out and externally rotated.

How would you best manage this patient?

_____

_____

_____

Skills

Skill Drills

Skill Drill 31-1: Caring for Musculoskeletal Injuries
Test your knowledge of this skill by filling in the correct words in the photo captions.

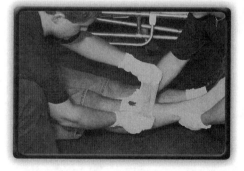

© Jones & Bartlett Learning. Courtesy of MIEMSS.

1. Cover open wounds with a _____, _____ dressing and apply pressure to control _____. Assess distal pulse and motor and sensory function. If bleeding cannot be controlled, quickly apply a tourniquet.

© Jones & Bartlett Learning. Courtesy of MIEMSS.

2. Apply a _____, and elevate the extremity about 6 inches (15 cm) (slightly above the level of the heart). Assess distal pulse and motor and sensory function.

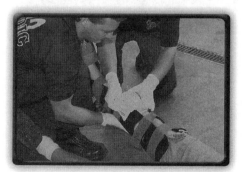

© Jones & Bartlett Learning. Courtesy of MIEMSS.

3. Apply cold packs if there is _____, but do not place them directly on the skin.

© Jones & Bartlett Learning. Courtesy of MIEMSS.

4. Position the patient for transport, and secure the _____ _____.

Skill Drill 31-2: Applying a Rigid Splint
Test your knowledge of this skill by filling in the correct words in the photo captions.

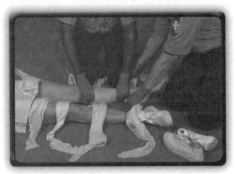

© Jones & Bartlett Learning. Courtesy of MIEMSS.

1. Provide gentle _____ and _____ _____ for the limb. Assess distal pulse and motor and sensory function.

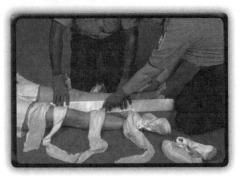

© Jones & Bartlett Learning. Courtesy of MIEMSS.

2. Place the splint _____ or _____ the limb. _____ between the limb and the splint as needed to ensure even pressure and contact.

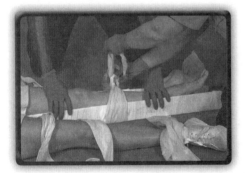

© Jones & Bartlett Learning. Courtesy of MIEMSS.

3. Secure the splint to the limb with _____.

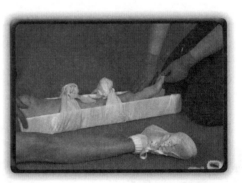

© Jones & Bartlett Learning. Courtesy of MIEMSS.

4. Assess and record _____ _____ function.

Skill Drill 31-5: Applying a Vacuum Splint
Test your knowledge of this skill by filling in the correct words in the photo captions.

© Jones & Bartlett Learning. Courtesy of MIEMSS.

1. Assess distal pulse and motor and sensory function. Your partner _____ and _____ the injury.

© Jones & Bartlett Learning. Courtesy of MIEMSS.

2. Place the splint, and _____ it around the limb.

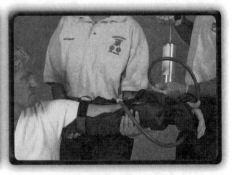

© Jones & Bartlett Learning. Courtesy of MIEMSS.

3. _____ the air out of the splint through the _____ _____, and then _____ the valve. Assess distal pulse and motor and sensory function.

Skill Drill 31-6: Applying a Hare Traction Splint
Test your knowledge of this skill by placing the following photos in the correct order. Number the first step with a "1," the second step with a "2," etc.

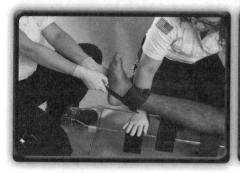

© Jones & Bartlett Learning.

_____ Slide the splint into position under the injured limb.

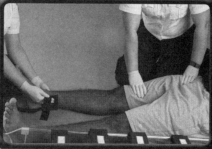

© Jones & Bartlett Learning.

_____ Support the injured limb as your partner fastens the ankle hitch about the foot and ankle.

© Jones & Bartlett Learning.

_____ Expose the injured limb and check pulse, motor, and sensory function. Place the splint beside the uninjured limb, adjust the splint to proper length, and prepare the straps.

© Jones & Bartlett Learning.

_____ Secure and check support straps. Assess pulse and motor and sensory functions.

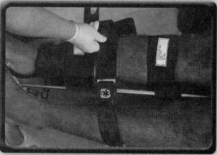

© Jones & Bartlett Learning.

_____ Secure the patient and splint to the backboard in a way that will prevent movement of the splint during patient movement and transport.

© Jones & Bartlett Learning.

_____ Connect the loops of the ankle hitch to the end of the splint as your partner continues to maintain traction. Carefully tighten the ratchet to the point that the splint holds adequate traction.

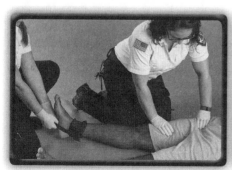

© Jones & Bartlett Learning.

_____ Continue to support the limb as your partner applies gentle in-line traction to the ankle hitch and foot.

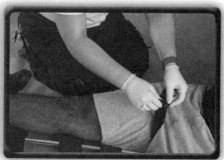

© Jones & Bartlett Learning.

_____ Pad the groin and fasten the ischial strap.

Skill Drill 31-8: Splinting the Hand and Wrist
Test your knowledge of this skill by filling in the correct words in the photo captions.

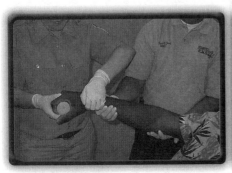

© Jones & Bartlett Learning. Courtesy of MIEMSS.

© Jones & Bartlett Learning. Courtesy of MIEMSS.

© Jones & Bartlett Learning. Courtesy of MIEMSS.

1. Support the injured limb and move the hand into the _____ of _____. Place a soft _____ _____ in the palm.

2. Apply a(n) _____ _____ splint on the _____ side with fingers _____.

3. Secure the splint with a(n) _____ _____.

Skills

Assessment Review

Answer the following questions pertaining to the assessment of the types of emergencies discussed in this chapter.

_____ 1. You respond to a motorcycle accident for a 41-year-old man who is unconscious. He has obvious deformity to both lower legs and is bleeding moderately from an open fracture. His airway is open, and he is making gurgling noises. Pulse is rapid and weak. Distal pulses are very weak. Your first priority with this patient is to:

    A. control bleeding.

    B. apply splints.

    C. maintain an airway.

    D. apply a pneumatic antishock garment.

_____ 2. You have loaded the patient in the question above and are en route to the hospital. You have secured the airway and immobilized the fractures. How often should you reassess his vital signs?

    A. Every 3 minutes

    B. Every 5 minutes

    C. Every 10 minutes

    D. Every 15 minutes

_____ 3. You are called to a 16-year-old girl who was injured in a basketball game. She is alert and oriented. Her airway is open, and respirations are within normal limits. Her pulse is strong and regular. Distal pulses are present. She states that she felt her ankle pop and immediately became nauseated. You decide to assess neurovascular status. When would you NOT perform the motor test?

    A. When you get a pain response

    B. When the patient walks away

    C. When you feel a distal pulse

    D. When the patient feels your touch

_____ **4.** You are called to the local junior high school where a 12-year-old boy fell and hurt his wrist. There is obvious deformity. He is alert and oriented. Respirations and pulse are within normal limits. Distal pulse is present. It is important to remember to:

    A. use a zippered air splint.

    B. splint in a position of function.

    C. splint the wrist only.

    D. completely cover the wrist and hand.

_____ **5.** When you have applied a traction splint, the last thing that you do is:

    A. check pulse, motor, and sensation.

    B. release traction if the pulse disappears.

    C. apply elasticized straps.

    D. secure the patient to a backboard.

CHAPTER 32

Environmental Emergencies

© Photos.com

General Knowledge

Matching

Match each of the items in the left column to the appropriate definition in the right column.

_____ 1. Conduction
_____ 2. Air embolism
_____ 3. Evaporation
_____ 4. Hyperthermia
_____ 5. Diving reflex
_____ 6. Core temperature
_____ 7. Convection
_____ 8. Laryngospasm
_____ 9. Turgor
_____ 10. Radiation
_____ 11. Hypothermia
_____ 12. Ambient temperature
_____ 13. Heat cramps
_____ 14. Drowning
_____ 15. Hymenoptera

A. Slowing of heart rate caused by submersion in cold water
B. Ability of the skin to resist deformation
C. Spasm of the larynx and vocal cords
D. Respiratory impairment from submersion in liquid
E. Heat loss resulting from standing in a cold room
F. Bees, wasps, ants, and yellow jackets
G. Condition when body temperature decreases
H. Condition caused by air bubbles in the blood vessels
I. Heat loss that occurs from helicopter rotor blade downwash
J. Heat loss resulting from sitting on snow
K. Heat loss resulting from sweating
L. Painful muscle spasms that occur after vigorous exercise
M. Temperature of the surrounding environment
N. Temperature of the heart, lungs, and vital organs
O. Core temperature greater than 101°F (38.3°C)

Multiple Choice

Read each item carefully and then select the one best response.

_____ 1. _____ causes body heat to be lost as warm air in the lungs is exhaled into the atmosphere and cooler air is inhaled.
   A. Convection
   B. Conduction
   C. Radiation
   D. Respiration

_____ 2. Evaporation, the conversion of a liquid to a gas, is a process that requires:
   A. energy.
   B. circulating air.
   C. a warmer ambient temperature.
   D. high humidity.

_____ 3. The rate and amount of heat loss by the body can be modified by all of the following EXCEPT:
   A. increasing heat production.
   B. moving to an area where heat loss is decreased.
   C. wearing insulated clothing.
   D. increasing fluid intake.

_____ **4.** The characteristic appearance of blue lips and/or fingertips seen in hypothermia is the result of:
  A. lack of oxygen in venous blood.
  B. frostbite.
  C. blood vessels constricting.
  D. bruising.

_____ **5.** Signs and symptoms of severe systemic hypothermia include all of the following EXCEPT:
  A. weak pulse.
  B. coma.
  C. shivering.
  D. very slow respirations.

_____ **6.** Hypothermia is more common among all of the following EXCEPT:
  A. older individuals.
  B. long-distance athletes.
  C. infants and children.
  D. those who are already ill.

_____ **7.** To assess a patient's core body temperature, pull back your glove and place the back of your hand on the patient's:
  A. abdomen, underneath the clothing.
  B. forehead.
  C. forearm, on the inside of the wrist.
  D. neck, at the area where you check the carotid pulse.

_____ **8.** Never assume that a(n) _____, pulseless patient is dead.
  A. apneic
  B. cyanotic
  C. cold
  D. hyperthermic

_____ **9.** Management of hypothermia in the field consists of all of the following EXCEPT:
  A. applying heat packs to the groin, axillary, and cervical regions.
  B. removing wet clothing.
  C. preventing further heat loss.
  D. massaging the cold extremities.

_____ **10.** All of the following conditions refer to when exposed parts of the body become very cold, but not frozen, EXCEPT:
  A. frostnip.
  B. trench foot.
  C. immersion foot.
  D. frostbite.

_____ **11.** When heat gain exceeds heat loss, _____ result(s).
  A. hyperthermia
  B. heat cramps
  C. heat exhaustion
  D. heatstroke

_____ **12.** Contributing factors to the development of heat illnesses include all of the following EXCEPT:
  A. high air temperature.
  B. vigorous exercise.
  C. high humidity.
  D. increased fluid intake.

_____ 13. When obtaining a SAMPLE history for a patient with a diving emergency, pay special attention to all of the following dive parameters EXCEPT:

    A. depth.

    B. length of time the patient was underwater.

    C. the time of onset of symptoms.

    D. time of day.

_____ 14. Which of the following statements about heat cramps is FALSE?

    A. They only occur when it is hot outdoors.

    B. They may be seen in well-conditioned athletes.

    C. The exact cause of heat cramps is not well understood.

    D. Dehydration may play a role in the development of heat cramps.

_____ 15. Signs and symptoms of heat exhaustion and associated hypovolemia include all of the following EXCEPT:

    A. cold, clammy skin with ashen pallor.

    B. dizziness, weakness, or faintness.

    C. normal vital signs.

    D. normal thirst.

_____ 16. Most spinal injuries in diving incidents affect the:

    A. cervical spine.

    B. thoracic spine.

    C. lumbar spine.

    D. sacrum/coccyx.

_____ 17. Often, the first sign of heatstroke is:

    A. a change in behavior.

    B. an increase in pulse rate.

    C. an increase in respirations.

    D. hot, dry, flushed skin.

_____ 18. The least common but most serious illness caused by heat exposure, occurring when the body is subjected to more heat than it can handle and normal mechanisms for getting rid of the excess heat are overwhelmed, is:

    A. hyperthermia.

    B. heat cramps.

    C. heat exhaustion.

    D. heatstroke.

_____ 19. _____ is the body's reaction to inhaling very small amounts of water.

    A. Bronchoconstriction

    B. Laryngospasm

    C. Esophageal spasms

    D. Swelling in the oropharynx

_____ 20. Treatment of drowning and/or near drowning begins with:

    A. opening the airway.

    B. ventilation with 100% oxygen via bag-valve mask.

    C. suctioning the lungs to remove the water.

    D. rescue and removal from the water.

_____ 21. In a diving emergency, _____ occurs when bubbles of gas, especially nitrogen, obstruct the blood vessels.

    A. compression sickness

    B. decompression sickness

    C. pulmonary sickness

    D. nitrogen toxicity

_____ **22.** Young children can drown in as little as _____ of water if left unattended.
   A. 1 inch
   B. 2 inches
   C. 3 inches
   D. 4 inches

_____ **23.** You should never give up on resuscitating a cold-water drowning victim because:
   A. when the patient is submerged in water colder than body temperature, heat is maintained in the body.
   B. the resulting hypothermia can protect vital organs from the lack of oxygen.
   C. the resulting hypothermia raises the metabolic rate.
   D. heat is conducted from the water to the body.

_____ **24.** The three phases of a dive, in the order they occur, are:
   A. ascent, descent, and bottom.
   B. descent, bottom, and ascent.
   C. orientation, bottom, and ascent.
   D. descent, orientation, and ascent.

_____ **25.** Areas usually affected by descent problems include:
   A. the lungs.
   B. the skin.
   C. the joints.
   D. vision.

_____ **26.** Potential problems associated with rupture of the lungs include all of the following EXCEPT:
   A. air emboli.
   B. pneumomediastinum.
   C. pneumothorax.
   D. hemopneumothorax.

_____ **27.** The organs most severely affected by air embolism are the:
   A. brain and spinal cord.
   B. brain and heart.
   C. heart and lungs.
   D. brain and lungs.

_____ **28.** Black widow spiders may be found in all of the following EXCEPT:
   A. New Hampshire.
   B. woodpiles.
   C. Georgia.
   D. Alaska.

_____ **29.** Coral snake venom is a powerful toxin that causes _____ of the nervous system.
   A. paralysis
   B. hyperactivity
   C. hypoactivity
   D. hemiparesis

_____ **30.** Rocky Mountain spotted fever and Lyme disease are both spread through the tick's:
   A. saliva.
   B. blood.
   C. hormones.
   D. excrement.

_____ **31.** Signs of envenomation by a pit viper include all of the following EXCEPT:

    A. swelling.

    B. chest pain.

    C. ecchymosis.

    D. severe burning pain at the site of the injury.

_____ **32.** Removal of a tick should be accomplished by:

    A. suffocating it with gasoline.

    B. burning it with a lighted match to cause it to release its grip.

    C. using fine tweezers to pull it straight out of the skin.

    D. suffocating it with Vaseline.

_____ **33.** Which of the following statements regarding the brown recluse spider is FALSE?

    A. It is larger than the black widow spider.

    B. It lives mostly in the southern and central parts of the country.

    C. Venom is not neurotoxic.

    D. Bites rarely cause systemic signs and symptoms.

_____ **34.** Treatment of a snake bite from a pit viper includes all of the following EXCEPT:

    A. calming the patient.

    B. not giving anything by mouth.

    C. marking the skin with a pen over the swollen area to note whether swelling is spreading.

    D. providing water to drink.

Questions 35-39 are derived from the following scenario: At 1400 in July, the weather is 105°F (41°C) and very humid. You have been called for a "man down" at the park. As you arrive, you recognize him as an alcoholic who has been a "frequent flyer" with your service. It looks like he had been sitting under a tree when he fell over, unconscious.

_____ **35.** As you assess the patient, he has cold, clammy skin and a dry tongue. You suspect that:

    A. he is well hydrated.

    B. he has suffered heat exhaustion.

    C. he is hypothermic.

    D. he has heatstroke.

_____ **36.** As you look closer, you note that he is shivering and his respirations are 20 breaths/min. You begin to have a stronger suspicion that he is now getting:

    A. hyperthermic.

    B. hypothermic.

    C. drunk.

    D. heatstroke.

_____ **37.** The direct transfer of heat from his body to the cold ground is called:

    A. conduction.

    B. convection.

    C. radiation.

    D. evaporation.

_____ **38.** You pull back on your glove and place the back of your hand on his skin at the abdomen, and the skin feels cool. Again, you suspect:

    A. hyperthermia.

    B. hypothermia.

    C. that he is drunk.

    D. heatstroke.

_____ **39.** Treat this patient by doing all of the following EXCEPT:

    A. Prevent conduction heat loss.

    B. Prevent convection heat loss.

    C. Remove the patient from the environment.

    D. Handle him roughly.

_____ **40.** Small infants have a poor ability to thermoregulate and are unable to shiver to control heat loss until about the age of:

    A. 4 to 6 months.

    B. 6 to 12 months.

    C. 12 to 18 months.

    D. 18 to 24 months.

_____ **41.** Most heat stroke cases occur when the temperature is around _____ and the humidity is 80%.

    A. 80°F (27°C)

    B. 90°F (32°C)

    C. 100°F (38°C)

    D. 110°F (43°C)

_____ **42.** Often, the first sign of heat stroke is a change in _____.

    A. behavior.

    B. skin turgor.

    C. blood pressure.

    D. perspiration.

True/False

If you believe the statement to be more true than false, write the letter "T" in the space provided. If you believe the statement to be more false than true, write the letter "F."

_____ **1.** Normal body temperature is 98.6°F (37.0°C).

_____ **2.** To assess the skin temperature in a patient experiencing a generalized cold emergency, you should feel the patient's skin.

_____ **3.** Mild hypothermia occurs when the core temperature drops to 85°F (29°C).

_____ **4.** The body's most efficient heat-regulating mechanisms are sweating and dilation of skin blood vessels.

_____ **5.** People who are at greatest risk for heat illnesses are the elderly and children.

_____ **6.** The strongest stimulus for breathing is an elevation of oxygen in the blood.

_____ **7.** Immediate bradycardia after jumping in cold water is called the diving reflex.

_____ **8.** Ice should be promptly applied to any insect sting or snake bite with swelling.

_____ **9.** The most common type of pit viper is the copperhead.

_____ **10.** Cottonmouths are known for aggressive behavior.

_____ **11.** Ticks should be removed by firmly grasping them with tweezers while rotating them counterclockwise.

_____ **12.** The pain of coelenterate stings may respond to flushing with cold water.

_____ **13.** If you are unsure as to whether a hypothermic patient has a pulse present, palpate the carotid artery for 15 to 20 seconds.

_____ **14.** The goal with the patient with moderate to severe hypothermia is to prevent further heat loss.

_____ **15.** After a lightning strike, you should practice reverse triage.

_____ **16.** Extremes in temperature and humidity are needed to produce hot or cold injuries.

_____ **17.** When approaching a water rescue scene, it is better to drive through moving water than through stagnant water.

_____ **18.** Potential safety hazards in the environment can include wet grass, mud, or icy streets.

_____ **19.** Long-sleeved shirts and long pants are considered dangerous for EMS responders in extreme heat and are not necessary because they provide only minimal protection from exposure.

Fill-in-the-Blank

Read each item carefully and then complete the statement by filling in the missing words.

1. Do not attempt to actively rewarm patients who have _____ to _____ hypothermia because they are prone to developing cardiac dysrhythmias unless handled very carefully.

2. Most serious diving injuries occur during _____.

3. When treating a patient with frostbite, never attempt _____ if there is any chance that the part may freeze again before the patient reaches the hospital.

4. A patient at an altitude above 8,000 feet (3,048 m) with shortness of breath and cough with pink sputum is likely to be suffering from _____ _____ _____.

5. _____, a common effect of hypothermia, is the body's attempt to increase its heat production.

6. Whenever a person dives or jumps into very cold water, the _____ _____ may cause immediate bradycardia.

7. _____ is the transfer of heat by radiant energy.

8. Mild hypothermia occurs when the core temperature is between _____ and _____.

9. The _____ and _____ systems are the most commonly injured during a lightning strike.

10. _____ is the third most common cause of death from isolated environmental phenomena.

11. _____ is a serum containing antibodies that counteracts venom.

12. _____ (bees, wasps, ants, and yellow jackets) stings are painful but are not medical emergencies unless the patient is allergic to the venom.

13. Most snake bites occur between _____ and _____, when the animals are active.

14. In the United States, the most common form of pit viper is the _____.

15. _____ are eight-legged arachnids with a venom gland and stinger at the end of their tails.

16. Tick bites occur most commonly during the _____ months.

17. The first symptoms of Lyme disease are generally fever and flulike symptoms, sometimes associated with a _____ rash.

18. To treat a sting from a jellyfish, pour _____ on the affected area.

19. Coelenterates are responsible for more _____ than any other marine animals.

20. Toxins from the spines of urchins and stingrays are _____ _____.

Crossword Puzzle

The following crossword puzzle is an activity provided to reinforce correct spelling and understanding of medical terminology associated with emergency care and the EMT. Use the clues in the column to complete the puzzle.

Across

1. The transfer of heat to colder objects in the environment by radiant energy.
7. The _____ temperature is the temperature of the central part of the body.
10. _____ injuries are caused by the difference between the surrounding atmospheric pressure and the total gas pressure in various tissues, fluids, and cavities of the body.
11. Conversion of water or another fluid from a liquid to a gas.
12. A serum that counteracts the effect of venom from an animal or insect.
13. The loss of heat by direct contact.

Down

2. The ability of the skin to resist deformation.
3. With heat _____, the body loses significant amounts of fluid and electrolytes because of heavy sweating.
4. Painful muscle spasms usually associated with vigorous activity in a hot environment.
5. The loss of body heat as warm air in the lungs is exhaled into the atmosphere and cooler air is inhaled.
6. Common name for decompression sickness.
8. The temperature of the surrounding environment is known as the _____ temperature.
9. A system that delivers air to the mouth and lungs at various atmospheric pressures, increasing with the depth of the dive.
10. The process of experiencing respiratory impairment from submersion or immersion in liquid.

Critical Thinking

Short Answer

Complete this section with short written answers using the space provided.

1. What are three ways to modify heat loss? Give an example of each.

   _____

   _____

   _____

2. What are the steps in treating heatstroke?

   _____

   _____

   _____

3. What is an air embolism and how does it occur?

   _____

   _____

   _____

4. For what diving emergencies are hyperbaric chambers used?

   _____

   _____

   _____

5. How should a frostbitten foot be treated?

   _____

   _____

   _____

6. What are four "Do Nots" in relation to local cold injuries?

   _____

   _____

   _____

7. What treatments for a snake bite assist with slowing and monitoring the spread of venom?

   _____

   _____

   _____

8. What are the two most common poisonous spiders in the United States and how do their bites differ?

_____

_____

_____

Ambulance Calls

The following case scenarios provide an opportunity to explore the concerns associated with patient management and to enhance critical-thinking skills. Read each scenario and answer each question to the best of your ability.

1. You are called to the local airport for a 52-year-old man who is the pilot of his own aircraft. He tells you he is having severe abdominal pain and joint pain. History reveals that the patient is returning from a dive trip off the coast. He says he has had "the bends" before and this feels similar.

How would you best manage this patient?

_____

_____

_____

2. You are dispatched to a long-term care facility for an Alzheimer's patient with an "unknown problem." You arrive to find a staff member who greets you at the front door and escorts you to a resident's room. He explains that the patient wandered out the back exit door of the Alzheimer's unit when the nurse was on her other rounds. They aren't sure how this happened because each patient wears a necklace that triggers an alarm if the patient leaves this specialized wing of the facility. They found the man outside in the snow, and he was possibly outdoors for 45 minutes.

How would you best manage this patient?

_____

_____

_____

3. You are dispatched to the local high school for a "person down." On arrival you are directed to the football field where the team is practicing for an upcoming game. You find a 16-year-old boy sitting on the bench, confused and lethargic. The coach tells you that they have been practicing for a couple of hours and the temperature is 97°F (36°C). He says he has encouraged the guys to drink continuously and he thought they were all well hydrated. During your assessment of the patient you notice that his skin is cool and clammy with a rapid, weak pulse. His temperature is 102.9°F (39.4°C) orally. He says he is thirsty but also feels nauseated so he stopped drinking a while ago.

How would you best manage this patient?

_____

_____

_____

Skills

Skill Drills

Skill Drill 32-1: Treating for Heat Exhaustion
Test your knowledge of this skill by filling in the correct words in the photo captions.

© Jones & Bartlett Learning. Courtesy of MIEMSS.

1. Move the patient to a(n) _____
   _____. Remove extra
   _____.

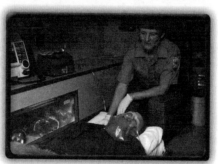

© Jones & Bartlett Learning. Courtesy of MIEMSS.

2. Give _____ if indicated. Check the patient's blood glucose level if indicated. Perform cold-water immersion or other cooling measures as available. Place the patient in a(n) _____ position and fan the patient.

© Jones & Bartlett Learning. Courtesy of MIEMSS.

3. If the patient is fully alert, give _____ by mouth.

© Jones & Bartlett Learning. Courtesy of MIEMSS.

4. If _____ develops, secure and transport the patient on his or her left side.

Skill Drill 32-2: Stabilizing a Suspected Spinal Injury in the Water
Test your knowledge of this skill by placing the following photos in the correct order. Number the first step with a "1," the second step with a "2," etc.

© Jones & Bartlett Learning. Courtesy of MIEMSS.

_____ Secure the patient to the backboard.

© Jones & Bartlett Learning. Courtesy of MIEMSS.

_____ Turn the patient to a supine position by rotating the entire upper half of the body as a single unit.

© Jones & Bartlett Learning. Courtesy of MIEMSS.

_____ Maintain the body's normal temperature and apply oxygen if the patient is breathing. Begin CPR if breathing and pulse are absent.

© Jones & Bartlett Learning. Courtesy of MIEMSS.

_____ Float a buoyant backboard under the patient.

© Jones & Bartlett Learning. Courtesy of MIEMSS.

_____ As soon as the patient is turned, begin artificial ventilation using the mouth-to-mouth method or a pocket mask.

© Jones & Bartlett Learning. Courtesy of MIEMSS.

_____ Remove the patient from the water.

Assessment Review

Answer the following questions pertaining to the assessment of the types of emergencies discussed in this chapter.

1. Most frostbitten parts are:
   A. soft and moist.
   B. hard and waxy.
   C. soft and waxy.
   D. hard and moist.

2. If a patient has a cold skin temperature, he or she likely is:
   A. hypothermic.
   B. hyperthermic.
   C. hypovolemic.
   D. hypoglycemic.

3. If a patient has a hot skin temperature, he or she likely is:
   A. hypothermic.
   B. hyperthermic.
   C. hypoglycemic.
   D. hypervolemic

4. When treating multiple victims of lightning strikes, who should you concentrate your efforts on first?
   A. Conscious patients
   B. Unconscious patients in respiratory or cardiac arrest
   C. All unconscious patients
   D. Conscious patients with burn wounds.

5. What is the best method of inactivating a jellyfish sting?
   A. Urinating on it
   B. Flushing the site with cold water
   C. Applying vinegar
   D. Applying an ice pack

Emergency Care Summary

Fill in the following chart pertaining to the management of the types of emergencies discussed in this chapter.

NOTE: While the following steps are widely accepted, be sure to consult and follow your local protocol.

Cold Exposure Emergency

1. Move the patient from the cold environment to prevent further _____ loss.
2. Remove any wet clothing, and place dry blankets over and under the patient.
3. If available, give the patient warm, _____ _____.
4. _____ _____ of a patient with moderate to severe hypothermia may cause the heart to go into ventricular fibrillation.
5. If the hypothermia is mild, begin _____ _____ slowly.

Diving Injuries

1. Remove the patient from the water.
2. Begin CPR if pulse and breathing are absent.
3. If pulse and breathing are present, administer _____.
4. Treat all drowning patients for _____ by removing wet clothing and wrapping them in warm blankets.
5. Provide prompt transport to the nearest _____ facility for treatment.

Spider Bites

1. Provide basic life support for respiratory distress.
2. Transport the patient and, if possible, the spider to the hospital.
3. If necessary, a physician can administer a specific _____, a serum containing antibodies that counteract the venom.

Snake Bites

1. Calm the patient and minimize movement.
2. Clean the bite area gently with soap and water or a mild _____. Do not apply _____.
3. Transport the patient and, if possible, the snake to the emergency department.
4. Notify the emergency department that you are bringing in a snake bite victim.

SPECIAL PATIENT POPULATIONS

Obstetrics and Neonatal Care

© Photos.com

General Knowledge

Matching

Match each of the items in the left column to the appropriate definition in the right column.

_____ **1.** Cervix

_____ **2.** Crowning

_____ **3.** Placenta

_____ **4.** Amniotic sac

_____ **5.** Fetus

_____ **6.** Embryo

_____ **7.** Primigravida

_____ **8.** Umbilical cord

_____ **9.** Lightening

_____ **10.** Breech presentation

_____ **11.** Limb presentation

_____ **12.** Multigravida

_____ **13.** Nuchal cord

_____ **14.** Presentation

_____ **15.** Miscarriage

A. An umbilical cord that is wrapped around the infant's neck

B. A fluid-filled, baglike membrane inside the uterus in which the fetus develops

C. Appearance of the infant's head at the vaginal opening during labor

D. The neck of the uterus

E. Connects mother and infant through the placenta

F. Sensation felt by a pregnant patient when the fetus positions itself for delivery

G. The body part of the infant that is delivered first

H. The stage from 0 to 10 weeks after fertilization

I. A woman who has had previous pregnancies

J. Spontaneous abortion

K. Delivery in which the presenting part is a single arm, leg, or foot

L. Provides nourishment to the fetus

M. First pregnancy

N. The stage from 10 weeks until delivery

O. Delivery in which the buttocks are delivered first

Multiple Choice

Read each item carefully and then select the one best response.

_____ **1.** Which of the following is NOT true regarding delivery with a nuchal cord?

 A. Gently slip the cord over the infant's head or shoulder.

 B. Encourage the woman to push harder and faster after cutting the cord.

 C. Clamp the cord, then suction the airway before cutting the cord.

 D. Clamp the cord and cut it, then gently unwind it from around the neck if wrapped around more than once.

_____ **2.** Which of the following refers to green or foul-smelling amniotic fluid?

 A. Nuchal rigidity

 B. Meconium staining

 C. Placenta previa

 D. Bloody show

_____ **3.** Approximately _____ of deliveries are complicated by the presence of meconium in the amniotic fluid.

 A. 8% to 12%

 B. 12% to 16%

 C. 16% to 20%

 D. 20% to 24%

_____ 4. You may help control bleeding by massaging the _____ after delivery of the placenta.
   A. perineum
   B. fundus
   C. lower back
   D. inner thighs

_____ 5. The Apgar score should be calculated at _____ minutes after birth.
   A. 1 and 5
   B. 3 and 7
   C. 2 and 10
   D. 4 and 8

_____ 6. Once the infant is delivered, feel for a brachial pulse or the pulsations in the umbilical cord. If the pulse rate is below _____ beats/min, begin assisted ventilations.
   A. 60
   B. 80
   C. 100
   D. 120

_____ 7. In situations where assisted ventilation is required, you should use a newborn BVM and ventilate with high-flow oxygen at a rate of _____ breaths/min.
   A. 20 to 30
   B. 30 to 50
   C. 35 to 45
   D. 40 to 60

_____ 8. When performing CPR on a newborn, a compression to ventilation ratio of 3:1 should be used; this will yield a total of _____ "actions" per minute.
   A. 90
   B. 100
   C. 110
   D. 120

_____ 9. You cannot successfully deliver a _____ presentation in the field.
   A. limb
   B. breech
   C. vertex
   D. cephalic

_____ 10. Which of the following is NOT performed when caring for a mother with a prolapsed cord?
   A. Clamp and cut the cord.
   B. Provide high-flow oxygen and rapid transport.
   C. Use your fingers to physically hold the infant's head off the cord.
   D. Position the mother to keep the weight of the infant off the cord.

_____ 11. When handling a delivery involving a drug- or alcohol-addicted mother, your first concern should be for:
   A. the mother's airway.
   B. your personal safety.
   C. the infant's airway.
   D. the need for CPR for the infant.

_____ 12. Which of the following is NOT a stage of labor?
   A. Rupture of amniotic fluid
   B. Expulsion of the baby
   C. Delivery of the placenta
   D. Dilation of the cervix

_____ **13.** The first stage of labor begins with the onset of contractions and ends when:

   A. the infant is born.

   B. the cervix is fully dilated.

   C. the water breaks.

   D. the placenta is delivered.

_____ **14.** Which of the following is NOT a sign of the beginning of labor?

   A. Bloody show

   B. Contractions of the uterus

   C. Crowning

   D. Rupture of the amniotic sac

_____ **15.** The second stage of labor begins when the cervix is fully dilated and ends when:

   A. the infant is born.

   B. the water breaks.

   C. the placenta delivers.

   D. the uterus stops contracting.

_____ **16.** The third stage of labor begins with the birth of the newborn and ends with the:

   A. release of milk from the breasts.

   B. cessation of uterine contractions.

   C. delivery of the placenta.

   D. cutting of the umbilical cord.

_____ **17.** The difference between preeclampsia and eclampsia is the onset of:

   A. seeing spots.

   B. seizures.

   C. swelling in the hands and feet.

   D. headaches.

_____ **18.** You should consider the possibility of a(n) _____ in women who have missed a menstrual cycle and complain of a sudden stabbing and usually unilateral pain in the lower abdomen.

   A. PID

   B. ectopic pregnancy

   C. miscarriage

   D. placenta abruptio

_____ **19.** Which of the following is NOT a reason for delivery of the fetus at the scene?

   A. Delivery can be expected within a few minutes.

   B. There is a natural disaster.

   C. There is severe inclement weather.

   D. The amniotic sac has ruptured.

_____ **20.** Which of the following statements regarding pregnancy is TRUE?

   A. A patient in the third trimester is at a decreased risk for aspiration.

   B. As the pregnancy continues, the patient will experience slower and deeper breathing.

   C. By the 20th week of pregnancy, the uterus is at or above the belly button.

   D. Maternal blood volume increases up to 10% by the end of pregnancy.

_____ **21.** Low blood pressure resulting from compression of the inferior vena cava by the weight of the fetus when the mother is supine is called:

   A. pregnancy-induced hypertension.

   B. placenta previa.

   C. placenta abruptio.

   D. supine hypotensive syndrome.

_____ 22. _____ is a situation in which the umbilical cord comes out of the vagina before the infant.
   A. Eclampsia
   B. Placenta previa
   C. Abruptio placenta
   D. Prolapsed cord

_____ 23. Premature separation of the placenta from the wall of the uterus is known as:
   A. eclampsia.
   B. placenta previa.
   C. placenta abruptio.
   D. prolapsed cord.

_____ 24. _____ is a condition in which the placenta develops over and covers the cervix.
   A. Eclampsia
   B. Placenta previa
   C. Placenta abruptio
   D. Prolapsed cord

_____ 25. _____ is heralded by the onset of convulsions, or seizures, resulting from severe hypertension in the pregnant woman.
   A. Eclampsia
   B. Placenta previa
   C. Placenta abruptio
   D. Supine hypotensive syndrome

_____ 26. Which of the following is NOT considered a possible effect to the fetus when the mother is a known substance abuser?
   A. Low birth weight
   B. Spina bifida
   C. Prematurity
   D. Severe respiratory depression

Questions 27-31 are derived from the following scenario: You have been dispatched to the side of a highway where a woman is reported to be delivering a baby. As you approach the vehicle, you see her lying down in the back seat.

_____ 27. Which of the following signs tells you that the birth is imminent?
   A. Her water has not broken.
   B. Her contractions are 3 to 6 minutes apart.
   C. She is a primigravida.
   D. The infant is crowning.

_____ 28. If the baby is crowning and the amniotic sac has not yet ruptured, you should:
   A. leave it in place and wait for ALS.
   B. puncture the sac only after ordered to do so by medical control.
   C. puncture the sac, allow the fluid to drain, and leave the sac in place.
   D. puncture the sac away from the head and then push the sac away from the infant's face.

_____ 29. As you perform a visual exam, you note crowning. This means that:
   A. the baby is making a crowing-type of sound.
   B. the baby cannot be visualized.
   C. the top of the head is visible.
   D. the father is excited and needs care.

_____ 30. Bleeding that exceeds approximately _____ mL is considered excessive.
   A. 100
   B. 250
   C. 500
   D. 1,000

_____ **31.** Concerning the delivery of the placenta, which of the following is NOT an emergency situation?

    A. More than 30 minutes have elapsed and the placenta has not delivered.

    B. There is more than 500 mL of bleeding before delivery of the placenta.

    C. There is significant bleeding after delivery of the placenta.

    D. Delivery of the placenta occurs 10 minutes after the birth.

_____ **32.** Ovulation occurs approximately _____ before menstruation.

    A. 1 week

    B. 2 weeks

    C. 3 weeks

    D. 4 weeks

_____ **33.** Fertilization usually occurs when the egg is inside the:

    A. ovary.

    B. uterus.

    C. fallopian tube.

    D. endometrium.

_____ **34.** Which of the following statements is FALSE?

    A. Gestational diabetes will clear up in most women after delivery.

    B. The leading cause of abruptio placenta is an ectopic pregnancy.

    C. As pregnancy progresses, the uterus enlarges and rises out of the pelvis.

    D. Some cultures may not permit male EMTs to examine a female patient.

_____ **35.** The "P" in Apgar stands for:

    A. perfusion

    B. pulse

    C. pupils

    D. position

_____ **36.** Which of the following statements regarding multiple gestations is FALSE?

    A. You should consider the possibility of twins when the first infant is small and the mother's abdomen remains fairly large after the birth.

    B. You should record the time of birth on each twin separately.

    C. There is only one placenta with the birth of twins.

    D. The second baby will usually be born within 45 minutes of the first.

_____ **37.** An infant delivered before _____ weeks is considered premature.

    A. 36

    B. 37

    C. 38

    D. 39

_____ **38.** All of the following are correct regarding postterm pregnancy EXCEPT:

    A. infants can be larger, sometimes weighing 10 pounds (4.5 kg) or more.

    B. there is an increased risk of meconium aspiration.

    C. postterm is considered past 2 weeks gestation.

    D. ultrasounds are not accurate at determining due dates.

_____ **39.** A patient presents with a sudden onset of shortness of breath 3 days following a delivery. What is the likely underlying cause of this condition?

    A. Pulmonary hypertension

    B. Pulmonary inflammation

    C. Pulmonary embolism

    D. Pulmonary fibrosis

_____ **40.** After delivery, if the infant does not begin breathing after _____ seconds, you should begin resuscitation efforts.

    A. 5 to 10

    B. 10 to 15

    C. 15 to 20

    D. 20 to 25

True/False

If you believe the statement to be more true than false, write the letter "T" in the space provided. If you believe the statement to be more false than true, write the letter "F."

_____ **1.** The small mucous plug from the cervix that is discharged from the vagina, often at the beginning of labor, is called a bloody show.

_____ **2.** Crowning occurs when the baby's head obstructs the birth canal, preventing normal delivery.

_____ **3.** Labor begins with the rupture of the amniotic sac and ends with the delivery of the baby's head.

_____ **4.** A woman who is having her first baby is called a multigravida.

_____ **5.** Once labor has begun, it can be slowed by holding the patient's legs together.

_____ **6.** Delivery of the buttocks before the baby's head is called a breech delivery.

_____ **7.** Massaging the abdomen after delivery helps to control bleeding.

_____ **8.** The placenta and cord should be properly disposed of in a biohazard container after delivery.

_____ **9.** The umbilical cord may be gently pulled to aid in delivery of the placenta.

_____ **10.** A limb presentation occurs when the baby's arm, leg, or foot is emerging from the vagina first.

_____ **11.** Multiple births may have more than one placenta.

_____ **12.** Pregnant teenagers may not know that they are pregnant.

_____ **13.** The secondary assessment of a pregnant patient should include a complete set of vital signs and pulse oximetry.

_____ **14.** Abuse during pregnancy increases the chance of miscarriage, premature delivery, and low birth weight.

_____ **15.** If called to deliver an infant who may have died in the uterus, you could notice skin blisters and dark discoloration to the infant.

_____ **16.** Most premature infants have vernix on their skin when delivered.

_____ **17.** Excessive bleeding after birth is usually caused by the muscles of the uterus not fully contracting.

Fill-in-the-Blank

Read each item carefully and then complete the statement by filling in the missing words.

1. After delivery, the _____, or afterbirth, separates from the uterus and is delivered.

2. The umbilical cord contains two _____ and one _____.

3. The amniotic sac contains about _____ to _____ mL of amniotic fluid, which helps to insulate and protect the floating fetus as it develops.

4. A pregnancy is considered full term once it reaches _____ weeks but has not gone beyond _____ weeks, _____ days.

5. By the end of pregnancy, the pregnant patient's heart rate increases up to 20%, or about _____ beats more per minute.

6. Blood volume may increase by as much as _____ by the end of the pregnancy.

7. The leading cause of maternal death in the first trimester is internal hemorrhage into the abdomen following rupture of a(n) _____ _____.

8. With a breech presentation, if the woman does not deliver within _____ minutes of the buttocks presentation, provide prompt transport.

9. During the delivery, be careful that you do not poke your fingers into the infant's eyes or into the two soft spots, called _____ on the head.

10. _____ _____ is a developmental defect in which a portion of the spinal cord protrudes outside the vertebrae.

11. Passage of the fetus and placenta before 20 weeks is called _____.

12. Preterm or false labor is commonly referred to as _____ contractions.

13. The _____ _____ carries oxygenated blood from the woman to the heart of the fetus.

14. The _____ is the area of skin between the vagina and the anus.

15. Due to hormonal changes that cause joints in the musculoskeletal system to "loosen," a pregnant patient has a greater risk of _____.

Fill-in-the-Table

Fill in the missing parts of the table.

Apgar Scoring System			
Area of Activity	**Score**		
	2	1	0
Appearance			
Pulse			
Grimace or irritability			
Activity or muscle tone			
Respiration			

Labeling

Label the following diagram with the correct terms.

1. Anatomic Structures of the Pregnant Woman

A. _____

B. _____

C. _____

D. _____

E. _____

F. _____

G. _____

H. _____

I. _____

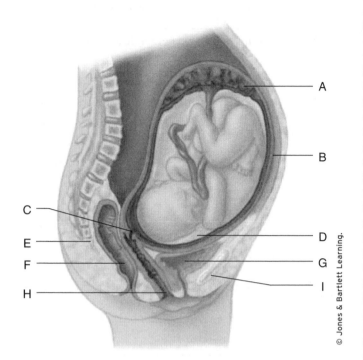

Crossword Puzzle

The following crossword puzzle is an activity provided to reinforce correct spelling and understanding of medical terminology associated with emergency care and the EMT. Use the clues in the column to complete the puzzle.

Across

1. The dome-shaped top of the uterus.
5. A dark green material in the amniotic fluid that can indicate distress or disease in the newborn.
6. _____ of the umbilical cord is a situation in which the umbilical cord comes out of the vagina before the infant.
8. Spontaneous passage of the fetus and placenta before 20 weeks.
10. _____ presentation is a delivery in which the buttocks come out first.
13. _____ pregnancy develops outside the uterus, typically in a fallopian tube.
14. The appearance of the infant's head at the vaginal opening during labor.
15. _____ show is a small amount of blood at the vagina that appears at the beginning of labor.

Down

2. The conduit connecting mother to infant via the placenta.
3. The fluid-filled, baglike membrane in which the fetus develops.
4. Narrowest portion of the uterus that opens into the vagina.
7. The developing, unborn infant inside the uterus.
9. _____ placenta is a premature separation of the placenta from the wall of the uterus.
11. The fertilized egg that is the early stages of a fetus.
12. _____ presentation is a delivery in which the presenting part is a single arm, leg, or foot.

Critical Thinking

Multiple Choice

Read each item carefully and then select the one best response. Determine the Apgar score for each of the following scenarios.

_____   1. You assess an infant newborn after delivery and note that the child has a loud cry and withdraws to pain. The heart rate is 94 beats/min, the extremities are cyanotic, respirations are rapid, and the newborn strongly resists your attempts to straighten the knees.

A. 2
B. 10
C. 8
D. 4

_____   2. You arrive at the scene of a home delivery. On entering the scene, the father appears upset and hands you a limp baby. The child has a weak cry, is completely cyanotic, and has a pulse of 70 beats/min. Respirations are slow.

A. 3
B. 9
C. 2
D. 7

_____   3. You arrive on scene to assist another crew with a delivery. On arrival, the crew on scene informs you that the delivery has already taken place and that you are going to be responsible for care of the newborn. As you approach, you hear a very loud cry. The newborn appears completely pink and moves his foot away when you flick the sole of his foot. The pulse is 120 beats/min and respirations are rapid. The newborn has excellent muscle tone and resists your attempt to straighten the hips.

A. 6
B. 10
C. 1
D. 8

Short Answer

Complete this section with short written answers using the space provided.

1. What are some possible causes of vaginal hemorrhage in early and late pregnancy?

_____

_____

_____

2. In what position should pregnant patients who are not delivering be transported and why?

_____

_____

_____

3. List three signs that indicate the beginning of labor.

_____

_____

_____

4. When determining whether delivery is imminent and whether there are complications, what questions should you ask the patient?

_____

_____

_____

5. Once the baby's head emerges, what actions should be taken to prevent too rapid a delivery?

_____

_____

_____

6. Why is it important to avoid pushing on the fontanelles?

_____

_____

_____

7. How can you help decrease perineal tearing?

_____

_____

_____

8. What are the two situations in which an EMT may insert his or her fingers into a patient's vagina?

_____

_____

_____

9. What are three fetal effects of maternal drug or alcohol addiction?

_____

_____

_____

10. List five signs/symptoms associated with preeclampsia.

_____

_____

_____

Ambulance Calls

The following case scenarios provide an opportunity to explore the concerns associated with patient management and to enhance critical-thinking skills. Read each scenario and answer each question to the best of your ability.

1. You are dispatched to a grocery store for an "unknown medical problem." You arrive to find a 20-year-old woman who is in her 32nd week of pregnancy. She tells you that this is her first pregnancy and she had made an appointment to see her obstetrician later that day because she was not feeling well. She's been experiencing a headache, swelling in her hands and feet, and transient problems with her vision. She states that she suddenly felt lightheaded and had to sit down. She appears unhurt.

   How would you best manage this patient?

   _____

   _____

   _____

2. You are enjoying a quiet lunch at the fire station when you hear the back doorbell ring. As you look out the window, you see a young woman running away from the building. You open the door to call to her and when you look down you see something bundled in a wet sheet. It's a newborn; she's wet with amniotic fluid, and she's not breathing very well.

   How would you best manage this patient?

   _____

   _____

   _____

3. You are on the scene with a 32-year-old woman who is 38 weeks pregnant. Delivery is imminent. As the infant starts to crown, you notice that the amniotic sac is still intact.

   How would you best manage this patient?

   _____

   _____

   _____

Skills

Skill Drills

Test your knowledge of this skill by placing the following photos in the correct order. Number the first step with a "1," the second step with a "2," etc.

Skill Drill 33-1: Delivering the Newborn

© University of Maryland Shock Trauma Center/MIEMSS.

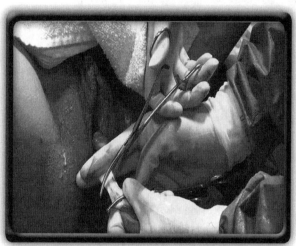

© University of Maryland Shock Trauma Center/MIEMSS.

_____ Support the head and upper body as the lower shoulder delivers, guide the head up if needed.

_____ Wait for the umbilical cord to stop pulsing. Place a clamp on the cord. Milk the blood from a small section of the cord on the placental side of the clamp. Place a second clamp 2 inches to 3 inches away from the first.

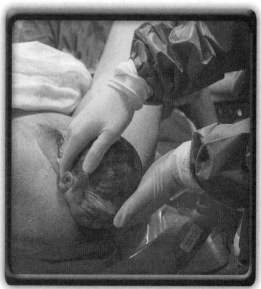

© University of Maryland Shock Trauma Center/MIEMSS.

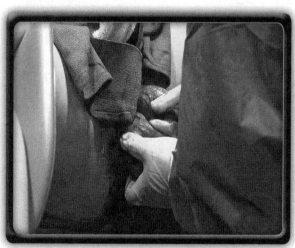

© University of Maryland Shock Trauma Center/MIEMSS.

_____ Use your hands to support the bony parts of the head as it emerges. The child's body will naturally rotate to the right or left at this point in the delivery. Continue to support the head to allow it to turn in the same direction.

_____ Allow the placenta to deliver itself. Do not pull on the cord to speed delivery.

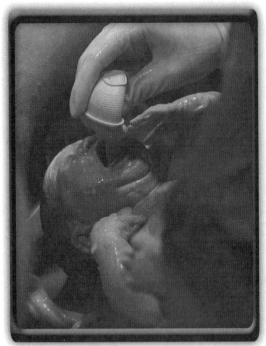

© University of Maryland Shock Trauma Center/MIEMSS.

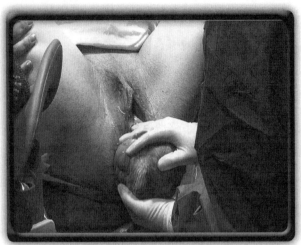

© University of Maryland Shock Trauma Center/MIEMSS.

_____ After delivery and prior to cutting the cord, if the child is gurgling or shows other signs of respiratory distress, suction the mouth and oropharynx to clear any amniotic fluid and ease the infant's initiation of air exchange.

_____ As the upper shoulder appears, guide the head down slightly by applying gentle downward traction to deliver the shoulder.

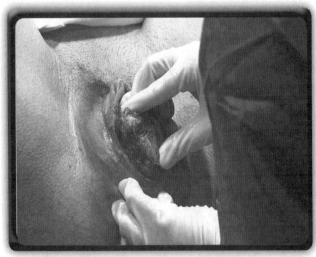

© University of Maryland Shock Trauma Center/MIEMSS.

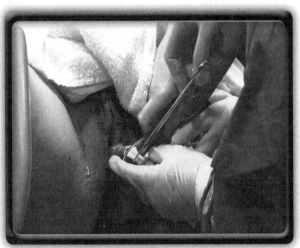

© University of Maryland Shock Trauma Center/MIEMSS.

_____ Crowning is the definitive sign that delivery is imminent and transport should be delayed until after the child has been born.

_____ Cut between the clamps.

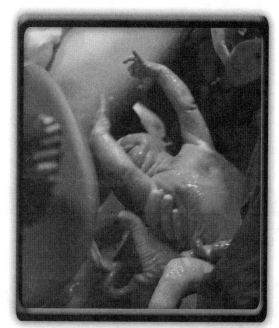

© University of Maryland Shock Trauma Center/MIEMSS.

_____ Handle the newborn firmly but gently, support the head, and keep the neck in a neutral position to maintain the airway. Consider placing the newborn on the mother's abdomen with the umbilical cord still intact, allow skin-to-skin contact to warm the newborn. Otherwise, keep the newborn approximately at the level of the vagina until the cord has been cut.

Assessment Review

Answer the following questions pertaining to the assessment of the types of emergencies discussed in this chapter.

_____ **1.** During delivery, after the head has been delivered and the shoulder appears:
   A. lower the head a little to deliver the upper shoulder.
   B. apply a nasal cannula to the infant.
   C. guide the head up slightly to deliver the shoulder.
   D. pull gently.

_____ **2.** If chest compressions are required for a newborn:
   A. use the hands-encircling technique for two-person resuscitation.
   B. press the palm of your hand over the sternum, compressing 1 inch to 1.5 inches (2.5 cm to 3 cm) deep.
   C. compress at a rate of 60 to 80 times a minute.
   D. compress the sternum one quarter the depth of the chest.

_____ **3.** Which of the following would NOT be a typical question to ask when taking a history on a woman in labor?
   A. Are you having a boy or a girl?
   B. When is your due date?
   C. Did your physician mention the possibility of any complications?
   D. Is there a possibility of multiples?

_____ **4.** Once the infant is completely delivered, you should do all of the following EXCEPT:
   A. dry and wrap the infant in a blanket.
   B. keep the infant at the level of the vagina until the umbilical cord is cut.
   C. use sterile gauze and wipe out the infant's mouth.
   D. Gently pull on the umbilical cord to speed up delivery of the placenta.

_____   **5.** When cutting the umbilical cord:

    A. place the clamps 7 inches to 10 inches (18 cm to 25 cm) apart.

    B. place the clamps 2 inches to 4 inches (5 cm to 10 cm) apart.

    C. tie the cord with shoelaces if you don't have any clamps.

    D. tie the cord with string if you don't have any clamps.

Emergency Care Summary

Fill in the following chart pertaining to the management of the types of emergencies discussed in this chapter.

NOTE: While the following steps are widely accepted, be sure to consult and follow your local protocol.

Special Considerations for Trauma and Pregnancy

Pregnant women have an increased overall total blood volume and an approximate _____ increase in their heart rate by the third trimester. A pregnant trauma patient may experience a significant amount of blood loss before you detect signs of _____. A traumatic injury to the abdomen can be life threatening to the woman and fetus because the pregnant uterus has a rich blood supply. If the woman is hypoxic, is in shock, or has _____, the fetus will be in distress. In most cases, the only chance to save the fetus is to adequately resuscitate the woman.

Delivery Complications

Nuchal Cord

When the _____ _____ is wrapped around the infant's neck, it is called a nuchal cord. If it is wound tightly it will strangle the infant, so it must be removed. Attempt to slip the cord over the infant's head or shoulder. If you are unable to slip the cord over the head or shoulder, you must clamp the cord in _____ places about 2 inches (5 cm) apart, if possible, and cut the cord between the clamps. After cutting the cord, you can unwrap it and continue with the delivery as usual.

Spontaneous Abortion (Miscarriage)

If the delivery is occurring before the _____ week of gestation, be prepared to treat the patient for bleeding and infection. Place a sterile pad/dressing on the _____. Collect any expelled tissue to take to the hospital, but never pull tissue out of the vagina. Transport immediately, continually monitoring the patient's ABCs while assessing for signs of shock.

Multiple Gestation

The procedure for delivering multiple infants is the same as that for a single fetus. Clamp and cut the cord for the first newborn as soon as it has been delivered and before the second newborn is delivered. There may be only one _____, or one for each fetus. Record the _____ _____ _____ for each infant separately, making sure to label them for identification after the delivery process is over. You can indicate the order of delivery by writing on a piece of tape and placing it on the blanket or towel that is wrapped around each newborn.

Postterm Pregnancy

Pregnancies lasting more than 42 weeks can lead to problems with the mother and the newborn. Newborns can be larger, leading to a more difficult delivery and injury to the newborn. _____ aspiration risk increases, as does infection and _____ birth. Respiratory and _____ functions may be affected, so be prepared to resuscitate the newborn.

SPECIAL PATIENT POPULATIONS
Pediatric Emergencies

© Photos.com

General Knowledge

Matching

Match each of the items in the left column to the appropriate definition in the right column.

_____ 1. Adolescents

_____ 2. Blanching

_____ 3. Infancy

_____ 4. Grunting

_____ 5. Neglect

_____ 6. Pediatrics

_____ 7. Pertussis

_____ 8. Preschool age

_____ 9. Sniffing position

_____ 10. Toddler

A. Sign of increased work of breathing

B. Optimal neutral head position for uninjured airway management

C. 12 to 18 years of age

D. Failure to provide life necessities

E. Infant to 3 years of age

F. First year of life

G. Medical practice devoted to care of the young

H. 3 to 6 years of age

I. Turning white

J. Caused by a bacterium that is spread through respiratory droplets

Multiple Choice

Read each item carefully and then select the one best response.

_____ 1. Making eye contact, recognizing caregivers, and following a bright light with their eyes are initially noticed in what age group?

   A. 0 to 2 months

   B. 2 to 6 months

   C. 6 to 12 months

   D. 12 to 18 months

_____ 2. Saying their first word, sitting without support, and teething are initially noticed in what age group?

   A. 0 to 2 months

   B. 2 to 6 months

   C. 6 to 12 months

   D. 12 to 18 months

_____ 3. Which of the following is NOT initially seen in children 12 to 18 months old?

   A. Speak four to six words

   B. Know the major body parts

   C. Can open doors

   D. Understand cause and effect

_____ 4. Toilet training is typically mastered at what age level?

   A. 6 to 12 months

   B. 12 to 18 months

   C. Preschool age

   D. School age

_____ 5. Which of the following is FALSE regarding the pediatric airway?
   A. The trachea is larger in diameter and shorter in length.
   B. The glottis opening is higher and positioned more anterior.
   C. The neck appears to be nonexistent.
   D. The lungs are smaller.

_____ 6. Breath sounds in the pediatric population are more easily heard because:
   A. their chest walls are thinner.
   B. the size of their lungs amplifies the sounds.
   C. the chest cavity is small in proportion to the rest of the body.
   D. children typically have upper airway problems.

_____ 7. An infant's heart can beat as many as _____ times or more per minute if the body needs to compensate for injury or illness.
   A. 110
   B. 120
   C. 140
   D. 160

_____ 8. Which of the following is NOT a common cause of altered mental status in pediatric patients?
   A. Drug and alcohol ingestion
   B. Hypertension
   C. Seizure
   D. Hypoglycemia

_____ 9. A fracture of the femur is rare and is a major source of _____ in the pediatric population.
   A. infection
   B. growth abnormalities
   C. blood loss
   D. nerve damage

_____ 10. When you assess a pediatric patient, it is best to place _____ on the patient's chest to feel the rise and fall of the chest wall.
   A. the left hand
   B. the right hand
   C. both hands
   D. the stethoscope

_____ 11. Tachycardia in pediatric patients may be an indication of all of the following EXCEPT:
   A. hypothermia.
   B. hypoxia.
   C. fever.
   D. pain.

_____ 12. When assessing capillary refill in pediatric patients, the color should return after:
   A. 1 second.
   B. 2 seconds.
   C. 3 seconds.
   D. 4 seconds.

_____ 13. Pupillary response in pediatric patients may be abnormal in the presence of all of the following EXCEPT:
   A. anxiety.
   B. hypoxia.
   C. brain injury.
   D. drugs.

_____ **14.** When obtaining information from the family regarding the pediatric patient's history, which of the following is NOT an appropriate inquiry?

    A. Does the child have any rashes?

    B. What has been the child's recent activity level?

    C. Has there been any vomiting or diarrhea?

    D. What types of toys does the child play with?

_____ **15.** When examining the head of a pediatric patient, which of the following statements is FALSE?

    A. You should look for bruising, swelling, and hematomas.

    B. Significant blood loss can come from the scalp.

    C. A bulging fontanelle suggests dehydration.

    D. The head is larger in proportion to the rest of the body.

_____ **16.** _____ may increase the effort or work of breathing.

    A. Anxiety

    B. Agitation

    C. Crying

    D. Anxiety, agitation, and crying

_____ **17.** Which of the following is NOT a sign of increased work of breathing in pediatric patients?

    A. Nasal flaring

    B. Grunting

    C. Equal chest expansion

    D. Retractions

_____ **18.** Which of the following is NOT an infection that can cause an airway obstruction in pediatric patients?

    A. Pneumonia

    B. Asthma

    C. Croup

    D. Epiglottitis

_____ **19.** Signs and symptoms of a lower airway obstruction in pediatric patients include:

    A. stridor.

    B. friction rub.

    C. drooling.

    D. wheezing.

_____ **20.** Exposure to cold air, infection, and emotional stress are all triggers of:

    A. pneumonia.

    B. asthma.

    C. bronchiolitis.

    D. epiglottitis.

_____ **21.** Which of the following statements regarding pediatric asthma is FALSE?

    A. Use strong, forceful breaths when ventilating to get air past the obstruction.

    B. The wheezing may be so loud that you can hear it without a stethoscope.

    C. The patient may be in the tripod position.

    D. A bronchodilator via a metered-dose inhaler may be helpful.

_____ **22.** All of the following are signs associated with pneumonia in pediatric patients EXCEPT:

    A. bradycardia.

    B. grunting.

    C. nasal flaring.

    D. hypothermia.

_____ **23.** Bronchiolitis usually occurs during the first _____ of life.

    A. 2 years

    B. 3 years

    C. 4 years

    D. 6 years

_____ **24.** Which of the following is NOT a common cause of shock in pediatric patients?

    A. Diseases of the heart

    B. Severe infection

    C. Dehydration

    D. Renal failure

_____ **25.** Signs of shock in children include all of the following EXCEPT:

    A. altered mental status.

    B. poor capillary refill.

    C. hypertension.

    D. tachycardia.

_____ **26.** A pediatric patient with hives, wheezing, increased work of breathing, and hypoperfusion is likely suffering from:

    A. pneumonia.

    B. bronchiolitis.

    C. asthma.

    D. anaphylaxis.

_____ **27.** Which of the following is NOT appropriate when treating pediatric patients with seizures?

    A. Clear the mouth with suction.

    B. Provide 100% oxygen.

    C. Consider placing the patient in the recovery position.

    D. Restrain the patient.

_____ **28.** Which of the following populations is at the greatest risk for contracting meningitis?

    A. Females

    B. Children who have had head trauma

    C. Children with preexisting heart conditions

    D. Children of parents with a history of meningitis

_____ **29.** A pediatric patient with a fever, pain on palpation of the right lower quadrant, and rebound tenderness is likely to be suffering from:

    A. cholecystitis.

    B. gastroenteritis.

    C. appendicitis.

    D. constipation.

_____ **30.** Which of the following is NOT a question you would ask if you suspected a poisoning emergency?

    A. Did the substance have an odor?

    B. Are there any changes in behavior or level of consciousness?

    C. What is the substance involved?

    D. Was there any choking or coughing after the exposure?

_____ **31.** Activated charcoal is indicated for pediatric patients who have ingested a(n):

    A. acid.

    B. alkali.

    C. petroleum product.

    D. poison.

_____ **32.** Which of the following is NOT a sign of severe dehydration in pediatric patients?

    A. Bulging fontanelles

    B. Very dry lips and gums

    C. Sunken eyes

    D. Sleepiness

_____ **33.** Young children can compensate for fluid losses by:

    A. decreasing blood flow to the brain and heart.

    B. decreasing blood flow to the extremities.

    C. increasing blood flow to the extremities.

    D. increasing blood flow to the gastrointestinal tract.

_____ **34.** All of the following are common causes of a fever in pediatric patients EXCEPT:

    A. infection.

    B. status epilepticus.

    C. drug ingestion.

    D. cholecystitis.

_____ **35.** A pediatric patient involved in a drowning emergency may present with:

    A. cerebral edema.

    B. hypoglycemia.

    C. abdominal distention.

    D. chest pain.

_____ **36.** Head and neck injuries are common after high-speed collisions in all of the following contact sports EXCEPT:

    A. wrestling.

    B. football.

    C. lacrosse.

    D. basketball.

_____ **37.** All children with abdominal injuries should be monitored for signs and symptoms of:

    A. pain.

    B. shock.

    C. hypothermia.

    D. nausea.

_____ **38.** Which of the following is NOT a common exposure when dealing with pediatric burns?

    A. Scalding water in a bathtub

    B. Electrocution from poor wiring

    C. Hot items on a stove

    D. Cleaning solvents

_____ **39.** How many triage categories are there in the JumpSTART system?

    A. Three

    B. Four

    C. Five

    D. Six

_____ **40.** Which of the following is NOT a known risk factor for SIDS?

    A. Mother younger than 20 years old

    B. Mother smoked during pregnancy

    C. Gestational diabetes

    D. Low birth weight

_____ 41. When you are performing a scene assessment at an incident involving SIDS, you should focus your attention on all of the following EXCEPT:

   A. signs of illness, including medication, humidifiers, and thermometers.

   B. the general condition of the house.

   C. the site where the infant was discovered.

   D. the temperature of the room.

_____ 42. Incidents involving the death of a child pose extra stress on EMS workers. Which of the following is NOT a sign of posttraumatic stress?

   A. Cold intolerance

   B. Nightmares

   C. Difficulty sleeping

   D. Loss of appetite

True/False

If you believe the statement to be more true than false, write the letter "T" in the space provided. If you believe the statement to be more false than true, write the letter "F."

_____ 1. You should avoid letting the parent or caregiver hold an infant during your assessment.

_____ 2. Toddlers have a hard time describing or localizing pain because they do not have the verbal ability to be precise.

_____ 3. It is considered acceptable to lie to a preschool-age child because he or she will not be able to understand their true medical condition.

_____ 4. Adolescence is a time for experimentation and risk-taking behaviors.

_____ 5. Some of the risks that adolescents take can ultimately facilitate development and judgment.

_____ 6. Congenital cardiovascular problems are the leading cause of cardiopulmonary arrest in the pediatric population.

_____ 7. Sprains are uncommon in the pediatric population.

_____ 8. Infants and young children should be kept warm during a transport or when the patient is exposed to assess or reassess an injury.

_____ 9. Bradypnea usually indicates that the pediatric patient's condition is improving.

_____ 10. Pediatric patients weighing less than 27 kg (60 lb) should be transported by car seat.

_____ 11. Blood pressure is usually not assessed in pediatric patients younger than 4 years.

_____ 12. A prolonged asthma attack that is unrelieved may progress to a condition known as status asthmaticus.

_____ 13. An oropharyngeal airway should be used for pediatric patients who are unconscious and in possible respiratory failure.

_____ 14. Blow-by oxygen is as effective as a face mask or nasal cannula for delivering oxygen to a pediatric patient.

_____ 15. A rectal temperature is the most accurate for infants to toddlers.

_____ 16. At around 8 to 10 years of age, children no longer require padding underneath the torso to create a neutral position.

_____ 17. Extremity injuries in the pediatric population are managed much differently than extremity injuries in adults.

_____ 18. EMTs in all states must report all cases of suspected abuse, even if the emergency department fails to do so.

_____ 19. Do not examine the genitalia of a young child unless there is evidence of bleeding or there is an injury that must be treated.

_____ 20. You should use a euphemism such as "passed away" when informing the family of a pediatric death to lessen their emotional pain.

Fill-in-the-Blank

Read each item carefully and then complete the statement by filling in the missing words.

1. Children not only have a higher metabolic rate but also a higher _____ _____, which is twice that of an adult.

2. Breathing requires the use of the _____ muscles and diaphragm.

3. Young children experience muscle fatigue much more quickly than older children, which can lead to _____ _____.

4. Located on the front (anterior) and back (posterior) portions of the head are soft spots, the _____.

5. The _____ _____ _____ is a structured assessment tool that allows you to rapidly form a general impression of the pediatric patient's condition without touching him or her.

6. Always position the airway in a neutral _____ _____.

7. Car seats are designed to be either _____ or _____; they cannot be mounted sideways on a bench seat.

8. A child in respiratory distress or possible respiratory failure needs supplemental _____.

9. _____ is an infection of the soft tissue in the area above the vocal cords.

10. _____ _____ are recommended to relieve a severe airway obstruction in an unconscious pediatric patient.

11. A prolonged asthma attack that is unrelieved may progress into _____ _____.

12. Inserting a(n) _____ _____ in a responsive patient may cause a spasm of the larynx and result in vomiting.

13. _____ is a congenital condition in which the patient lacks one or more of the normal clotting factors of blood.

14. _____ is common in pediatric patients and if left untreated can lead to peritonitis or shock.

15. _____ is the second most common cause of unintentional death among children in the United States.

16. In pediatric patients, chest injuries are usually the result of _____ _____, rather than penetrating trauma.

17. One common problem following burn injuries in children is _____.

18. _____ is refusal or failure on the part of the caregiver to provide life necessities.

Crossword Puzzle

The following crossword puzzle is an activity provided to reinforce correct spelling and understanding of medical terminology associated with emergency care and the EMT. Use the clues in the column to complete the puzzle.

Across

2. Increased respiratory rate.

5. Slow respiratory rate; ominous sign in a child that indicates impending respiratory arrest.

8. An acute infectious disease characterized by a catarrhal stage, followed by a paroxysmal cough that ends in a whooping inspiration. Also called whooping cough.

10. Refusal or failure on the part of the caregiver to provide life necessities.

11. Children between 12 to 18 years of age.

12. An event that causes unresponsiveness, cyanosis, and apnea in an infant, who then resumes breathing with stimulation.

13. The period following infancy until 3 years of age.

Down

1. Children between 6 to 12 years of age.

3. A specialized medical practice devoted to the care of the young.

4. The external openings of the nostrils.

6. An "uh" sound heard during exhalation, reflecting the child's attempt to keep the alveoli open.

7. A(n) _____ tonic-clonic seizure features rhythmic back-and-forth motion of an extremity and body stiffness.

8. A structured assessment tool that allows you to rapidly form a general impression of the infant or child without touching him or her; consists of assessing appearance, work of breathing, and circulation to the skin.

9. _____ syndrome is seen in abused infants and children.

Critical Thinking

Short Answer

Complete this section with short written answers using the space provided.

1. What does each letter in the mnemonic TICLS mean?

_____

_____

_____

2. What are the signs of increased work of breathing in a pediatric patient, and what do they mean?

_____

_____

_____

3. List the indications for immediate transport of a pediatric patient.

_____

_____

_____

4. What tool is used to determine the appropriate blood pressure for a pediatric patient between 1 and 10 years of age?

_____

_____

_____

5. When assessing for circulation, what are the specific areas to focus on, and what questions should you ask yourself?

_____

_____

_____

Ambulance Calls

The following case scenarios provide an opportunity to explore the concerns associated with patient management and to enhance critical-thinking skills. Read each scenario and answer each question to the best of your ability.

1. You are dispatched to the residence of a toddler who has a history of fever and who is now unresponsive. You arrive to find a 13-year-old babysitter who tells you that she is not sure what is wrong with the 2-year-old boy. She tells you that he started "shaking all over" and she didn't know what to do. He is currently responsive to painful stimuli and warm to the touch.

How would you best manage this patient?

_____

_____

_____

2. You are dispatched to the residence of a 3-year-old child with a history of lung problems. The child, a very small boy, is cyanotic and lethargic. He is pain responsive. He has copious mucous secretions in his airway. The grandmother, who was sitting with the child, is hysterical.

How would you best manage this patient?

_____

_____

_____

3. You are called to a residence for a 2-year-old child with difficulty breathing. The little girl has stridor and expiratory wheezes, as well as intercostal retractions. She is very upset by your arrival and clings to her mother. Her breathing worsens with agitation. Her mother tells you that she is currently taking medication for an upper respiratory infection and has spent much of her life in and out of hospitals with respiratory problems.

How would you best manage this patient?

_____

_____

_____

4. It's 0530, and you are dispatched to the home of a 6-month-old girl who is not breathing. You arrive to find a crying, young mother holding a lifeless baby. The infant is not breathing, is cold to the touch, and appears to have dependent lividity.

How would you best manage this patient?

_____

_____

_____

Skills

Skill Drills

Test your knowledge of this skill by filling in the correct words in the photo captions.

Skill Drill 34-1: Positioning the Airway in a Pediatric Patient

  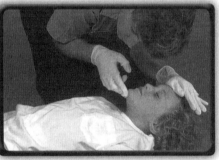

© Jones & Bartlett Learning. Courtesy of MIEMSS.   © Jones & Bartlett Learning. Courtesy of MIEMSS.   © Jones & Bartlett Learning. Courtesy of MIEMSS.

1. Position the pediatric patient on a(n) _____ surface.

2. Place a(n) _____ towel about 1-inch (2.5-cm) thick under the _____ and _____.

3. _____ the forehead to limit _____ and use the head tilt–chin lift maneuver to open the airway.

Test your knowledge of this skill by filling in the correct words in the photo captions.

Skill Drill 34-2: Inserting an Oropharyngeal Airway in a Pediatric Patient

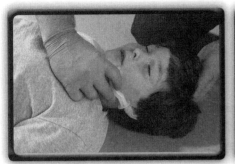
© Jones & Bartlett Learning.

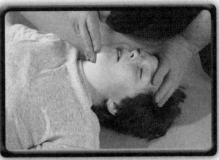
© Jones & Bartlett Learning.

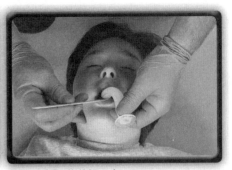
© Jones & Bartlett Learning.

1. Determine the appropriately _____ airway. Confirm the correct size _____, by placing it next to the pediatric patient's _____.

2. Position the pediatric patient's _____ with the appropriate method.

3. Open the mouth. Insert the airway until the _____ rests against the _____. _____ the airway.

Test your knowledge of this skill by filling in the correct words in the photo captions.

Skill Drill 34-3: Inserting a Nasopharyngeal Airway in a Pediatric Patient

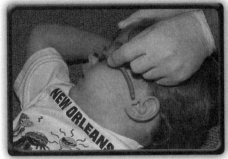
© Jones & Bartlett Learning. Courtesy of MIEMSS.

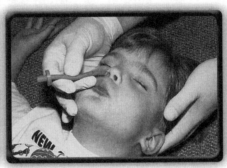
© Jones & Bartlett Learning. Courtesy of MIEMSS.

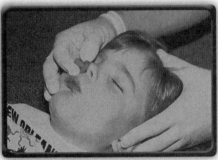
© Jones & Bartlett Learning. Courtesy of MIEMSS.

1. Determine the correct airway size by comparing its _____ to the opening of the _____ (nare). Place the airway next to the pediatric patient's _____ to confirm correct _____. _____ the airway.

2. _____ the airway. Insert the _____ into the right naris with the bevel pointing toward the _____.

3. Carefully move the tip forward until the _____ rests against the_____ of the nostril. Reassess the _____.

Skill Drill 34-4: One-Person Bag-Valve-Mask Ventilation on a Pediatric Patient
Test your knowledge of this skill by placing the following photos in the correct order. Number the first step with a "1," the second step with a "2," etc.

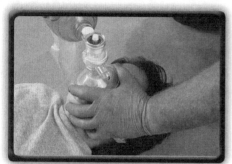

© Jones & Bartlett Learning.

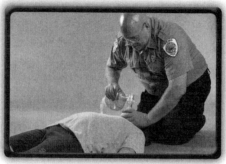

© Jones & Bartlett Learning.

_____ Hold the mask on the patient's face with a one-handed head tilt–chin lift technique (EC clamp method). Ensure a good mask–face seal while maintaining the airway.

_____ Assess effectiveness of ventilation by watching bilateral rise and fall of the chest.

© Jones & Bartlett Learning.

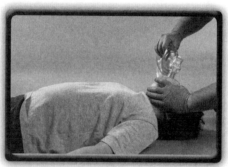

© Jones & Bartlett Learning.

_____ Open the airway and insert the appropriate airway adjunct.

_____ Squeeze the bag using the correct ventilation rate of 1 breath every 3 to 5 seconds, or 12 to 20 breaths/min. Allow adequate time for exhalation.

Test your knowledge of this skill by filling in the correct words in the photo captions.

Skill Drill 34-6: Immobilizing a Patient in a Car Seat

© Jones & Bartlett Learning. Courtesy of MIEMSS.

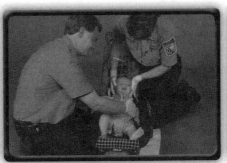

© Jones & Bartlett Learning. Courtesy of MIEMSS.

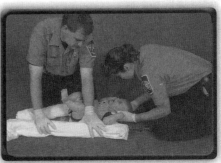

© Jones & Bartlett Learning. Courtesy of MIEMSS.

1. _____ the head in a(n) _____ position.

2. Place a(n) _____ _____ or pediatric _____ _____ between the patient and the surface he or she is resting on.

3. Slide the patient onto the _____ _____ or pediatric immobilization device.

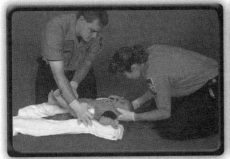

© Jones & Bartlett Learning. Courtesy of MIEMSS.

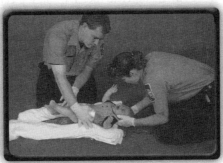

© Jones & Bartlett Learning. Courtesy of MIEMSS.

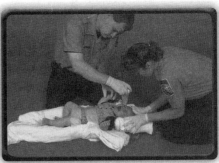

© Jones & Bartlett Learning. Courtesy of MIEMSS.

4. Place a _____ under the back, from the _____ to the _____, to ensure _____ head position.

5. Secure the _____ first; pad any_____.

6. Secure the head to the short backboard or pediatric _____ _____.

CHAPTER 35
Geriatric Emergencies

© Photos.com

General Knowledge

Matching

Match each of the items in the left column to the appropriate definition in the right column.

_____ 1. Aneurysm
_____ 2. Cataract
_____ 3. Delirium
_____ 4. Dementia
_____ 5. Syncopea
_____ 6. Dyspnea
_____ 7. Osteoporosis
_____ 8. Polypharmacy
_____ 9. Kyphosis
_____ 10. Ascites

A. Forward curling of the back
B. Fluid in the abdomen
C. Clouding of the lens of the eye
D. Reduced bone mass leading to fractures after minimal trauma
E. Abnormal blood-filled dilation of a blood vessel
F. Difficulty breathing
G. Inability to focus, think logically, or maintain attention
H. Use of multiple medications
I. Slow onset of progressive disorientation
J. Fainting

Multiple Choice

Read each item carefully and then select the one best response.

_____ 1. Which of the following is NOT one of the leading causes of death in the older population?
   A. Heart disease
   B. Diabetes
   C. AIDS
   D. Cancer

_____ 2. Geriatric patients present as a special problem for caregivers because:
   A. the classic presentation of disease is often altered.
   B. geriatric patients tend not to understand their underlying conditions.
   C. their medications are rather difficult to learn.
   D. the typical diseases of the geriatric population are uncommon.

_____ 3. Stereotyping of older adults that often leads to discrimination is called:
   A. geritism.
   B. geriographics.
   C. oldism.
   D. ageism.

_____ 4. Which of the following is NOT a common stereotype regarding geriatrics?
   A. Most older adults have dementia.
   B. Older adults are hard of hearing.
   C. Geriatric patients are likely to die on an EMS call.
   D. Older adults are immobile.

_____ 5. Which of the following is generally NOT acceptable when interviewing an older patient?
   A. Do not initiate eye contact because many geriatric patients might find this disrespectful.
   B. Speak slowly and distinctly.
   C. Give the patient time to respond unless the condition appears urgent.
   D. Explain what you are doing before you do it.

_____   6. Which of the following is NOT considered a common condition of older adults?

   A. Hypertension

   B. Asthma

   C. Gastroenteritis

   D. Arthritis

_____   7. Geriatric patients are commonly found living in all of the following locations EXCEPT:

   A. their homes.

   B. nursing homes.

   C. skilled nursing facilities.

   D. churches.

_____   8. You are responding to the dementia unit at a nursing home for respiratory distress. When you arrive, you notice that the patient is experiencing mild dyspnea and has an altered mental status. What can you do to help determine if the patient's altered mental status is appropriate for her underlying dementia?

   A. As long as the patient is alert and able to answer most questions there is no need to determine if this is normal behavior.

   B. Ask the patient's roommate if this is normal behavior for the patient.

   C. Find a staff member who can explain the patient's underlying mental status to you.

   D. Because the patient already has dementia, there is no need to investigate this further.

_____   9. Anatomic changes that occur as a person ages predisposes geriatric patients to:

   A. airway problems.

   B. fungal infections.

   C. communicable diseases.

   D. mental status changes.

_____   10. Which of the following statements regarding geriatrics is FALSE?

   A. Chronic mental status impairment is a normal process of aging.

   B. Multiple disease processes and complaints can make assessment complicated.

   C. Communication may be more complicated with an older adult.

   D. You should find and account for all patient medications.

_____   11. The last meal is particularly important in a patient with:

   A. hypertension.

   B. myocardial infarction.

   C. COPD.

   D. diabetes.

_____   12. The heart rate should be in the normal adult rage for a geriatric patient but can be altered by medications such as:

   A. insulin.

   B. beta-blockers.

   C. alpha-blockers.

   D. aspirin.

_____   13. Which of the following is NOT a factor that predisposes an older patient to a serious head injury?

   A. Long-term abuse of alcohol

   B. Recurrent falls

   C. Family history

   D. Anticoagulant medication

_____   14. The "E" of the GEMS diamond stands for:

   A. environmental assessment.

   B. events leading to the incident.

   C. extrication of the patient.

   D. emergency assessment.

_____ **15.** The alveoli in an older patient's lung tissue can become enlarged and less elastic, making it:

  A. easier to inhale air.

  B. harder to inhale air.

  C. easier to exhale air.

  D. harder to exhale air.

_____ **16.** _____ is the leading cause of death from infection in Americans older than 65 years.

  A. Chronic bronchitis

  B. Pneumonia

  C. Endocarditis

  D. Influenza

_____ **17.** A patient with leg pain who complains of sudden shortness of breath, tachycardia, fever, chest pain, and a feeling of impending doom is likely experiencing a(n):

  A. pulmonary embolism.

  B. pneumonia.

  C. myocardial infarction.

  D. aortic aneurysm.

_____ **18.** Geriatric patients are at risk for _____, an accumulation of fatty material in the arteries.

  A. vasculitis

  B. arteriosclerosis

  C. atherosclerosis

  D. varicose veins

_____ **19.** A drop in blood pressure with a change in position is referred to as:

  A. orthostatic hypotension.

  B. metastatic hypotension.

  C. malignant hypotension.

  D. psychogenic hypotension.

_____ **20.** Which of the following is NOT considered a risk factor for geriatric patients to develop a pulmonary embolism?

  A. Paralyzed extremities

  B. Sedentary behavior

  C. History of heart failure

  D. Exercise.

_____ **21.** All of the following are true of delirium EXCEPT:

  A. it may have metabolic causes.

  B. the patient may be hypoglycemic.

  C. it develops slowly over a period of years.

  D. the memory remains mostly intact.

_____ **22.** An 82-year-old woman has slurred speech, weakness on the left side of her body, visual disturbances, and a headache. This patient is likely to be suffering from a:

  A. myocardial infarction.

  B. stroke.

  C. diabetic emergency.

  D. spinal cord injury.

_____ **23.** The brain decreases in terms of _____ and volume as a person ages.

  A. length

  B. width

  C. size

  D. weight

_____ **24.** Older adults develop an inability to differentiate colors and have:

  A. increased sensitivity to light.

  B. decreased eye movement.

  C. decreased daytime vision.

  D. decreased night vision.

_____ **25.** _____ and long-term exposure to loud noises are the main factors that contribute to hearing loss.

  A. Heredity

  B. Injury

  C. Infection

  D. Medications

_____ **26.** Which of the following statements regarding dementia is FALSE?

  A. Patients may have anxiety about going to the hospital.

  B. Some patients are confused and angry.

  C. There may be a decreased ability to communicate.

  D. Due to memory loss, they are able to adapt easily to changes in their daily routine.

_____ **27.** Which of the following statements about changes to the gastrointestinal system is correct?

  A. Gastric secretions are reduced as a person ages.

  B. Dental loss is not a normal result of the aging process.

  C. Blood flow to the liver is increased as a person ages.

  D. Gastric motility increases and results in an increase in gastric emptying.

_____ **28.** All of the following are common specific gastrointestinal problems in older adults EXCEPT:

  A. ulcerative colitis.

  B. diverticulitis.

  C. peptic ulcer disease.

  D. gallbladder disease.

_____ **29.** A patient with an abdominal aortic aneurysm most commonly complains of abdominal pain that radiates to the:

  A. chest.

  B. lower legs.

  C. back.

  D. shoulders.

_____ **30.** Changes to the kidney and genitourinary tract in older patients can cause all of the following EXCEPT:

  A. urinary incontinence.

  B. urinary retention.

  C. an increased response to sodium deficiency.

  D. enlargement of the prostate.

_____ **31.** A patient experiencing weight gain, fatigue, cold intolerance, drier skin and hair, and a slower heart rate could be suffering from:

  A. hyperglycemia.

  B. ketosis.

  C. hyperthyroidism.

  D. hypothyroidism.

_____ **32.** Which of the following is NOT a factor that affects the development of osteoporosis?

  A. Hypertension

  B. Smoking

  C. Level of activity

  D. Alcohol consumption

_____ **33.** _____ is a progressive disease of the joints that destroys cartilage and leads to joint spurs and stiffness.

   A. Osteoporosis

   B. Osteosarcoma

   C. Osteoarthritis

   D. Osteoplegia

_____ **34.** All of the following are considered to be reasons for medication noncompliance EXCEPT:

   A. financial challenges.

   B. patient disagrees with the diagnosis.

   C. impaired cognitive ability.

   D. inability to open pill bottles.

_____ **35.** Which of the following statements regarding depression is TRUE?

   A. Treatment typically involves medication because counseling usually does not work.

   B. Older adults in skilled nursing facilities are less likely to develop depression.

   C. It generally does not interfere with ability to function in older adults.

   D. It is diagnosed three times more commonly in women than in men.

_____ **36.** Older pedestrians struck by a vehicle commonly sustain injuries to the:

   A. chest.

   B. abdomen.

   C. extremities.

   D. back.

_____ **37.** All of the following are common predisposing events that can lead to suicide in older adults EXCEPT:

   A. death of a loved one.

   B. hallucinations.

   C. alcohol abuse.

   D. physical illness.

_____ **38.** Older adults are more likely to experience burns because of all of the following EXCEPT:

   A. altered mental status.

   B. inattention.

   C. compromised neurologic status.

   D. osteoporosis.

_____ **39.** Signs and symptoms of possible abuse include all of the following EXCEPT:

   A. chronic pain with no medical explanation.

   B. no history of repeated visits to the emergency department or clinic.

   C. depression or lack of energy.

   D. self-destructive behavior.

_____ **40.** Because the brain tissue shrinks with age, older patients are more likely to sustain:

   A. basilar skull fractures.

   B. depressed skull fractures.

   C. open head injuries.

   D. closed head injuries.

_____ **41.** The most important piece of information to establish immediately when responding to a skilled nursing facility is determining:

   A. when someone last saw the patient.

   B. which nurse is overseeing patient care.

   C. what is wrong with the patient.

   D. how often this patient is transported to the hospital.

_____ **42.** MRSA is NOT commonly found on which of the following?
   A. Decubitus ulcers
   B. Feeding tubes
   C. Indwelling catheters
   D. Patient's charts.

_____ **43.** In the presence of a DNR order, if the patient is still alive, you are obligated to provide all of the following supportive measures EXCEPT:
   A. oxygen delivery.
   B. pain relief.
   C. comfort.
   D. resuscitation.

_____ **44.** Burns in elder abuse typically do NOT result from which of the following?
   A. Cigarettes
   B. Matches
   C. Hot liquids
   D. Fireplaces.

_____ **45.** Clues that might indicate elder abuse would include all of the following EXCEPT:
   A. bruises on the buttocks and lower back.
   B. weight gain.
   C. wounds in various stages of healing.
   D. lack of hygiene.

True/False

If you believe the statement to be more true than false, write the letter "T" in the space provided. If you believe the statement to be more false than true, write the letter "F."

_____ **1.** Some older adults may not take all of their medications to save money.

_____ **2.** Your first words to the patient and the attitude behind them can gain or lose a patient's trust.

_____ **3.** Hip fractures are less likely to occur when the patient has osteoporosis.

_____ **4.** The heart hypertrophies with age, likely in response to the chronically increased afterload imposed by stiffened blood vessels.

_____ **5.** A general complaint of weakness and dizziness can be an indication of something more serious, such as a heart problem or pneumonia.

_____ **6.** Multiple disease processes and multiple and/or vague complaints can make assessment complicated.

_____ **7.** The "S" in the GEMS diamond stands for social assessment.

_____ **8.** Loss of mechanisms to protect the upper airway include increased cough and gag reflexes.

_____ **9.** Changes in the cardiovascular performance of a geriatric patient are the direct consequence of aging.

_____ **10.** Respiratory rates in a geriatric patient with chest pain tend to be lower.

_____ **11.** The treatment goal of a stroke is to salvage as much brain tissue as possible.

_____ **12.** Glaucoma, macular degeneration, and retinal detachment can all cause vision problems in the geriatric patient.

_____ **13.** Taste can be diminished in an older patient due to a decrease in the number of taste buds.

_____ **14.** Neuropathy is a dysfunction of the central nervous system.

_____ **15.** Irritation of the lining of the stomach or ulcers can cause forceful vomiting that tears the esophagus.

_____ **16.** Inflammation of the gallbladder will present with left upper quadrant pain and fever.

_____ **17.** The blood glucose level will be greater than 600 mg/dL in DKA.

_____ **18.** Pneumonia and urinary tract infections are common in patients who are bedridden.

_____ **19.** Decreased liver function makes it easier for the liver to detoxify the blood.

_____ **20.** Most geriatric suicides occur in people who have recently been diagnosed with depression.

_____ **21.** There is a lower mortality from penetrating trauma in older adults.

_____ **22.** Trauma is always isolated to a single issue when you are assessing and caring for a geriatric patient.

_____ **23.** Broken bones are common in the geriatric population and should be splinted in a manner appropriate to the injury.

_____ **24.** Most indoor hypothermia deaths involve geriatric patients.

_____ **25.** A health care power of attorney is an advance directive that is exercised by a person who has been authorized by the patient to make medical decisions for the patient.

Fill-in-the-Blank

Read each item carefully and then complete the statement by filling in the missing words.

1. Using the patient's _____ shows respect and helps the patient to focus on your questions.

2. Hip fractures are more likely to occur when bones are weakened by _____ or infection.

3. _____ is a useful therapy for many geriatric problems, including vague complaints of weakness or dizziness.

4. _____ is an inflammation/infection of the lung from bacterial, viral, or fungal causes.

5. Increased _____ _____, pulmonary secretions, and the inflammatory effects of infection all interfere with the ability of the alveoli to oxygenate the blood.

6. _____ refers to stiffening of the blood vessel wall.

7. Severe blood loss can occur when a(n) _____ bursts.

8. With _____ heart failure, fluid backs up into the lungs.

9. _____ is the gradual hearing loss that occurs as we age.

10. An older person may have a decreased sense of _____ and _____ perception from the loss of end nerve fibers.

11. _____ is a condition in which small pouches protrude from the colon.

12. _____ _____ form when a patient is lying or sitting in the same position for a long time.

13. As you get older, the brain shrinks, leading to higher risk of _____ _____ following a minimal mechanism of injury.

14. _____ _____ may help determine if a loss of consciousness occurred before an accident.

15. Dentures may cause a(n) _____ _____ in a patient with an altered level of consciousness.

16. When assessing the abdomen, remember that geriatric patients have a _____ _____ _____ and may not show signs of rigidity in abdominal trauma.

17. Patients with _____ will require padding in order to keep the patient supine.

18. In addition to hip fractures, older adults with osteoporosis are at risk for _____ fractures.

19. _____ _____ are facilities that serve patients who need 24-hour care; they are sometimes a step down from a hospital.

20. _____ _____ are specific legal papers that direct relatives and caregivers about what kinds of medical treatment may by given to patients who cannot speak for themselves.

Fill-in-the-Table

Fill in the missing parts of the table.

Categories of Elder Abuse	
Physical	• _____ • _____ • _____ • _____ • _____ • _____
Psychological	• _____ • _____ • _____ • _____
Financial	• _____ • _____

Crossword Puzzle

The following crossword puzzle is an activity provided to reinforce correct spelling and understanding of medical terminology associated with emergency care and the EMT. Use the clues in the column to complete the puzzle.

Across

2. A disorder of the nerves of the peripheral nervous system in which function and structure of the peripheral motor, sensory, or autonomic neurons are impaired.

5. The assessment and treatment of disease in someone who is 65 years or older.

7. _____ ulcer disease is more common in older adults, especially people who use NSAIDS.

8. Any action on the part of an older person's family member, caregiver, or other associated person who takes advantage of the older person.

10. _____ infections are common among people who live in close quarters, such as nursing homes.

12. An inflammation/infection of the lung from a bacterial, viral, or fungal cause.

14. Respiratory _____ virus is highly contagious and causes an infection of the upper and lower respiratory system.

15. An abnormal blood-filled dilation of the wall of a blood vessel.

16. Shortness of breath or difficulty breathing.

Down

1. A sudden change in mental status marked by the inability to focus, think logically, and maintain attention.

3. A condition in which the walls of the aorta in the abdomen weaken and blood leaks into the layers of the vessel, causing it to bulge.

4. Fluid in the abdomen.

6. A pulmonary _____ is a condition that causes a sudden blockage of the pulmonary artery by a venous clot.

9. _____ directives are written documentation that specify medical treatment for a competent patient should the patient become unable to make decisions.

11. A fainting spell or transient loss of consciousness, often caused by an interruption of blood flow to the brain.

13. Black, tarry stools.

Critical Thinking

Short Answer

Complete this section with short written answers using the space provided.

1. List the eight most common conditions found in the geriatric patient.

   _____

   _____

   _____

2. What are the types of nerves affected in neuropathy, and what are the associated symptoms?

   _____

   _____

   _____

3. What are the differences between hyperosmolar hyperglycemic nonketotic syndrome (HHNS) and diabetic ketoacidosis (DKA)?

   _____

   _____

   _____

4. List at least five informational items that may be important in assessing possible elder abuse.

   _____

   _____

   _____

5. Briefly describe the three possible causes of syncope in the geriatric patient.

   _____

   _____

   _____

Ambulance Calls

The following case scenarios provide an opportunity to explore the concerns associated with patient management and to enhance critical-thinking skills. Read each scenario and answer each question to the best of your ability.

1. It is 0300, and you are dispatched to a long-term care facility for a geriatric woman with an "unknown emergency." You arrive to find no staff around, but you hear someone crying for help. You follow the voice and find an older woman lying on the floor holding her right hip. Her bed is made and the side rails are up. When a staff member finally appears, you ask how long she's been lying there. The staff member responds, "We don't know. How are we supposed to know that? We don't have enough help around here."

   How would you best manage this patient?

   _____

   _____

   _____

2. You are dispatched to the home of a 65-year-old woman who is complaining of severe back pain. She tells you that she tried to pick up the lawnmower when she "heard a pop and felt a crack in her back." She is experiencing intense pain in her lower back and feels some numbness in her legs.

   How would you best manage this patient?

   _____

   _____

   _____

3. You are dispatched to a private residence for a woman who has fallen. She tells you that she tripped over her granddaughter's toys and fell onto the hardwood floor. She tried to get up several times but couldn't. She denies any head, neck, or back pain or loss of consciousness. Her only complaint is pain in her right hip.

   How would you best manage this patient?

   _____

   _____

   _____

4. It is early evening, and you are dispatched to the parking lot of a popular shopping mall. Over the past several hours, local weather conditions have consisted of a combination of freezing rain and snow, making for very icy road conditions. Your patient is an older woman who has fallen and now complains of back pain and shortness of breath. She has severe kyphosis and will not tolerate traditional methods of spinal immobilization.

   How would you best manage this patient?

   _____

   _____

   _____

Fill-in-the-Patient Care Report

Read the incident scenario and then complete the following patient care report (PCR).

You are dispatched at 0843 to an unknown medical emergency at 222 Orchard Lane. You note the incident number as 011727 and immediately mark your unit as responding with the dispatcher. The dispatcher informs you that the fire department was also dispatched to assist you.

You arrive 6 minutes later to find an older woman who greets you at the front door. She tells you her 78-year-old husband is lying on the bathroom floor, and he's too heavy for her to lift. As you enter the small bathroom, you notice a large man on the floor with a laceration and hematoma on his forehead.

"I was on the toilet and must have fallen, but I don't remember exactly what happened," the patient tells you.

You immediately maintain cervical spine stabilization as the fire department personnel arrive on scene. Your partner grabs the necessary immobilization equipment as you interview the patient.

The patient continues to tell you that he does not remember what happened, but he states that his head hurts.

"I heard a loud 'thud' in the bathroom and came in to find him on the floor," the wife states. "He was awake when I came in, but I saw the blood and called 9-1-1."

You ask, "Are you having any other pain?"

"No, I feel OK other than my head," says the patient. The patient rates his pain as a 4 out of 10 and denies radiation. The patient also denies neck pain.

You inquire about dizziness, sweating, chest pain, shortness of breath, nausea, or vomiting, all of which the patient denies.

Your partner arrives, along with the fire personnel, with the immobilization equipment. While they immobilize the patient, you apply 15 L/min of oxygen via nonrebreathing mask at 0851 and place a bandage on the patient's forehead to control the bleeding.

After the patient is immobilized, you complete a rapid full-body scan of the patient and find no other deformities/abnormalities other than a hematoma and a 3-cm (1.2-inch) laceration noted to the patient's right forehead with minor bleeding, now controlled.

Your partner obtains vital signs 2 minutes after the patient is immobilized and finds the following: pulse, 86 beats/min; respirations, 20 breaths/min; blood pressure, 110/68 mm Hg; pulse oximetry, 98%.

The patient tells you that he is allergic to aspirin and that he takes metoprolol, Lisinopril, Actos, metformin, Zocor, Celebrex, allopurinol, Lasix, K-dur, Plavix, and a multivitamin. You're able to decipher much of the history from the medications, but you ask the patient to confirm. The patient tells you that he had a heart attack several years ago in which a stent was placed; he has congestive heart failure, hypertension, diabetes, arthritis, gout, and high cholesterol.

The fire personnel package the patient onto the litter and take the patient to the unit with your partner. The patient tells you that he wants to go to Mercy Hospital down the road. Because this is the closest trauma facility, you are happy to accommodate the patient's wishes.

You depart the scene at 0902 and reassess vital signs and physical exam. The vital signs are as follows: pulse, 84 beats/min; respirations, 18 breaths/min; blood pressure, 116/76 mm Hg; pulse oximetry, 100%. The patient's status remains stable through the transport, although he continues to complain about his head pain.

You arrive at Mercy Hospital 6 minutes later. The patient states that his head still hurts, but that he otherwise feels fine. He states that his pain is still 4/10.

You bring the patient to room 4 and give your report to the nurse. You state that it appears the patient had a syncopal episode and bumped his head; however, he's been stable throughout your care.

You replace the supplies while your partner cleans the unit. The unit is back in service at 0915.

Fill-in-the-Patient Care Report

EMS Patient Care Report (PCR)					
Date:	**Incident No.:**		**Nature of Call:**		**Location:**
Dispatched:	**En Route:**	**At Scene:**	**Transport:**	**At Hospital:**	**In Service:**
Patient Information					
Age: **Sex:** **Weight (in kg [lb]):**			**Allergies:** **Medications:** **Past Medical History:** **Chief Complaint:**		
Vital Signs					
Time:	**BP:**	**Pulse:**	**Respirations:**	**Spo$_2$:**	
Time:	**BP:**	**Pulse:**	**Respirations:**	**Spo$_2$:**	
Time:	**BP:**	**Pulse:**	**Respirations:**	**Spo$_2$:**	
EMS Treatment **(circle all that apply)**					
Oxygen @ ___ L/min via (circle one): NC NRM BVM		**Assisted Ventilation**	**Airway Adjunct**		**CPR**
Defibrillation	**Bleeding Control**	**Bandaging**	**Splinting:**		**Other:**
Narrative					

SPECIAL PATIENT POPULATIONS

Patients With Special Challenges

CHAPTER

36

© Photos.com

General Knowledge

Matching

Match each of the items in the left column to the appropriate definition in the right column.

_____ 1. Cerebral palsy	**A.** A surgical opening between the small intestine and the outside of the body
_____ 2. Colostomy	**B.** A portion of the spinal cord that protrudes outside of the vertebrae
_____ 3. Developmental disability	**C.** A group of disorders characterized by poorly controlled body movement
_____ 4. Down syndrome	**D.** An excessive amount of body fat
_____ 5. Ileostomy	**E.** A plastic tube placed in a stoma
_____ 6. Obesity	**F.** Insufficient development of the brain
_____ 7. Sensorineural deafness	**G.** Damage to the inner ear resulting in a permanent lack of hearing
_____ 8. Shunts	**H.** A surgical opening between the colon and the outside of the body
_____ 9. Spina bifida	**I.** Tubes that drain fluid from the ventricles of the brain
_____ 10. Tracheostomy tube	**J.** Round head with a flat occiput and slanted, wide-set eyes

Multiple Choice

Read each item carefully and then select the one best response.

_____ 1. Which of the following is NOT considered a potential cause of a developmental disability?

    A. Genetic factors

    B. Complications at birth

    C. Folic acid deficiency

    D. Malnutrition

_____ 2. Which of the following statements is FALSE regarding patients with autism?

    A. They fail to use or understand nonverbal communication.

    B. They will talk with normal tone and speech patterns.

    C. They may have extreme difficulty with complex tasks that require many steps.

    D. They have difficulty making eye-to-eye contact.

_____ 3. All of the following are associated with Down syndrome EXCEPT:

    A. a small face.

    B. short, wide hands.

    C. a protruding tongue.

    D. narrow-set eyes.

_____ 4. Down syndrome patients are at an increased risk for medical complications. Which of the following is NOT one of those potential complications?

    A. Respiratory complications

    B. Cardiovascular complications

    C. Gastrointestinal complications

    D. Endocrine complications

5. Which of the following is TRUE regarding airway management of patients with Down syndrome?
   A. Patients often have large tongues.
   B. Patients have large oral and nasal cavities.
   C. Mask ventilation is relatively easy to achieve.
   D. Use the head tilt–chin lift maneuver to open the airway.

6. When caring for a patient with a previous head injury, you should:
   A. speak in a loud, commanding tone.
   B. expect the patient to be able to walk.
   C. watch the patient for signs of anxiety.
   D. never consider restraining the patient.

7. Which of the following is NOT a possible cause of visual impairment?
   A. Disease
   B. Injury
   C. Congenital defect
   D. Regeneration of the eyeball, optic nerve, or nerve pathway

8. When caring for a patient with a visual impairment, which of the following is NOT appropriate?
   A. Identifying noises
   B. Always transporting the patient's service dog
   C. Describing the situation and surroundings
   D. Telling the patient what is happening

9. Conductive hearing loss can be caused by:
   A. advanced age.
   B. damage to the inner ear.
   C. nerve damage.
   D. a perforated eardrum.

10. Which of the following is NOT considered a clue that your patient might be hearing impaired?
    A. Slurred speech
    B. Presence of hearing aids
    C. Poor pronunciation of words
    D. Failure to respond to your questions

11. All of the following are possible causes of cerebral palsy EXCEPT:
    A. maternal preeclampsia.
    B. damage to the developing fetal brain in utero.
    C. traumatic brain injury at birth.
    D. postpartum infection.

12. Cerebral palsy is associated with all of the following conditions EXCEPT:
    A. epilepsy.
    B. cardiovascular complications.
    C. difficulty communicating.
    D. intellectual disabilities.

13. Which of the following statements is FALSE regarding the care of a patient with cerebral palsy?
    A. Do not assume these patients are mentally disabled.
    B. Limbs are often underdeveloped and are prone to injury.
    C. Walkers or wheelchairs should not be taken in the ambulance.
    D. Be prepared to care for a seizure if one occurs.

_____ **14.** Some patients with spina bifida have:

    A. partial or full paralysis of the lower extremities.

    B. multiple cardiovascular problems.

    C. daily episodes of neck pain.

    D. a tendency to resist sitting.

_____ **15.** When suctioning a tracheostomy tube, be sure not to suction for longer than:

    A. 5 seconds.

    B. 10 seconds.

    C. 15 seconds.

    D. 20 seconds.

_____ **16.** If a patient's home mechanical ventilator malfunctions, you should remove the patient from the ventilator and:

    A. place the patient on a nasal cannula.

    B. place the patient on a nonrebreathing mask.

    C. begin ventilations with a bag-valve mask.

    D. contact medical control.

_____ **17.** An apnea monitor is indicated in all of the following situations EXCEPT:

    A. premature birth.

    B. severe gastroesophageal reflux.

    C. family history of SIDS.

    D. asthma.

_____ **18.** Which of the following is NOT a risk factor associated with the implantation of a left ventricular assist device?

    A. Excessive bleeding

    B. Acute heart failure

    C. Renal failure

    D. Stroke

_____ **19.** Central venous catheters are located in all of the following areas EXCEPT:

    A. the upper arm.

    B. the lower leg.

    C. the chest.

    D. under the clavicle.

_____ **20.** Patients with gastric tubes who have difficulty breathing should be transported sitting or lying on the:

    A. left side, with the head elevated 30°.

    B. right side, with the head elevated 30°.

    C. right side, with the head elevated 45°.

    D. left side, with the head elevated 45°.

_____ **21.** A ventricular atrium shunt drains excess fluid from the ventricles of the brain into the:

    A. right atrium of the heart.

    B. left atrium of the heart.

    C. right ventricle of the heart.

    D. left ventricle of the heart.

_____ **22.** Services offered by home care agencies include all of the following EXCEPT:

    A. providing personal hygiene.

    B. wound care.

    C. taking the patient to restaurants.

    D. yard maintenance.

_____ **23.** All of the following are diseases or conditions that are associated with patients receiving hospice EXCEPT:

   A. AIDS.

   B. end-stage Alzheimer disease.

   C. cancer.

   D. pneumonia.

_____ **24.** Which of the following is NOT a disease prevention strategy that people living in poverty are lacking?

   A. Vaccinations

   B. Nutrition

   C. Exercise

   D. Dental care

_____ **25.** The term *obese* is used when someone is _____ or more over his or her ideal body weight.

   A. 20%

   B. 30%

   C. 40%

   D. 50%

True/False

If you believe the statement to be more true than false, write the letter "T" in the space provided. If you believe the statement to be more false than true, write the letter "F."

_____ **1.** It is important to make sure you are at eye level when communicating with patients.

_____ **2.** Visually impaired patients can be guided, pulled, or pushed to help them move.

_____ **3.** Some patients with paralysis will have normal sensation.

_____ **4.** In severe or morbid obesity, the person is 11 kg to 34 kg (25 lb to 75 lb) over his or her ideal weight.

_____ **5.** Tracheostomy tubes are prone to obstruction from mucus plugs or foreign bodies.

_____ **6.** You can estimate the size of a suction catheter for a tracheostomy tube by doubling the inner diameter of the tracheostomy tube.

_____ **7.** Patients with tracheostomies breathe through their mouths and noses.

_____ **8.** You should never place defibrillator paddles or pacing patches directly over an implanted defibrillation device.

_____ **9.** Patients who have a gastric tube in place may still be at increased risk of aspiration.

_____ **10.** Interaction with the caregiver of a child or adult with special needs will be an important part of the patient assessment process.

Fill-in-the-Blank

Read each item carefully and then complete the statement by filling in the missing word.

1. _____ is a pervasive developmental disorder characterized by impairment of social interaction.

2. You may allow a patient with a visual impairment to rest his or her hand on your _____ because this may help with balance and security while moving.

3. _____ _____ can be either external or internal, depending on the type of hearing damage.

4. The two most common forms of hearing loss are _____ deafness and _____ hearing loss.

5. _____ _____ is a term for a group of disorders characterized by poorly controlled body movement.

6. To reduce the occurrence of spina bifida, pregnant women are advised to take _____ _____.

7. A(n) _____ _____ _____ _____ is a special piece of medical equipment that takes over the function of either one or both heart ventricles.

8. _____ are tubes that drain excess cerebrospinal fluid from the ventricles of the brain to keep pressure from building up in the brain.

9. If you encounter a patient with a colostomy or ileostomy bag, assess for signs of _____ if the patient has been complaining of diarrhea or vomiting.

10. Comfort care, or _____ _____, improves the patient's quality of life before the patient dies.

Fill-in-the-Table
Complete the missing information to the right of the mnemonic.

DOPE Mnemonic	
D	
O	
P	
E	

Crossword Puzzle

The following crossword puzzle is an activity provided to reinforce correct spelling and understanding of medical terminology associated with emergency care and the EMT. Use the clues in the column to complete the puzzle.

Across

3. A(n) _____ tube is a plastic tube placed within the tracheostomy site.

5. A surgical procedure to establish an opening between the colon and the surface of the body.

7. A surgical procedure to create an opening between the small intestine and the surface of the body.

8. _____ syndrome is a genetic chromosomal defect that can occur during fetal development and that results in mental retardation.

9. Tubes that drain fluid from the brain to another part of the body outside of the brain.

10. Insufficient development of the brain, resulting in some level of dysfunction or impairment, is known as developmental _____.

Down

1. _____ palsy is a term for a group of disorders characterized by poorly controlled body movement.

2. _____ deafness is a permanent lack of hearing caused by a lesion or damage to the inner ear.

4. A developmental defect in which a portion of the spinal cord or meninges may protrude outside of the vertebrae.

6. A condition in which a person has an excessive amount of body fat.

Critical Thinking

Short Answer

Complete this section with short written answers using the space provided.

1. List at least four helpful hints for working with patients with hearing impairments.

_____

_____

_____

2. Describe the various troubleshooting methods for a hearing aid malfunction.

_____

_____

_____

3. List the four types of hearing aids.

_____

_____

_____

4. List at least eight helpful tips to use when moving a morbidly obese patient.

_____

_____

_____

5. List six questions you should ask when caring for a patient with an implanted pacemaker.

_____

_____

_____

Ambulance Calls

The following case scenarios provide an opportunity to explore the concerns associated with patient management and to enhance critical-thinking skills. Read each scenario and answer each question to the best of your ability.

1. You respond to a nursing home for a 75-year-old man whose internal defibrillator continues to fire. When you arrive on scene, you find the patient being assisted by the nursing staff. The patient is pale with an altered mental status. You notice he "jumps" every few minutes.

How would you best manage this patient?

_____

_____

_____

2. You are dispatched to a residence for a 12-year-old girl having a seizure. When you arrive on scene you are met at the door by the patient's mother. The mother tells you her daughter has Down syndrome and is prone to seizures. She states that her daughter has had two "tonic-clonic seizures" today. When you walk into the room, you see the patient lying on the floor in what appears to be a postictal state. The patient is being attended by other family members.

How would you best manage this patient?

_____

_____

_____

Skills

Assessment Review

Answer the following questions pertaining to the assessment of the types of emergencies discussed in this chapter.

_____ 1. When treating a patient with autism, remember that the patient:

    A. will be able to describe his or her underlying condition to you.

    B. will speak in a clear, inflected voice.

    C. is not likely to maintain eye contact with you.

    D. will be able to follow most of your commands without difficulty.

_____ 2. What sign found at a scene might indicate that your patient is visually impaired?

    A. No carpet

    B. Animals

    C. No stairs

    D. A cane

_____ 3. What can be done for a patient with a tracheostomy who needs oxygen when you do not have a proper tracheostomy collar?

    A. Immediately assist ventilations with a bag-valve mask.

    B. Place a nasal cannula on the patient.

    C. Place a face mask over the patient's mouth.

    D. Place a face mask over the stoma.

_____ 4. Which of the following is NOT a sign of infection at a colostomy site?

    A. Tenderness

    B. Bleeding

    C. Warm skin

    D. Redness

Transport Operations

© Photos.com

General Knowledge

Matching

Match each of the items in the left column to the appropriate definition in the right column.

_____ **1.** Medivac

_____ **2.** Type II Design

_____ **3.** Spotter

_____ **4.** Sterilization

_____ **5.** Ambulance

_____ **6.** Cleaning

_____ **7.** Disinfection

A. Standard van; forward-control integral cab-body ambulance

B. The killing of pathogenic agents by direct application of chemicals

C. The process of removing dirt, dust, blood, or other visible contaminants

D. Medical evacuation of a patient by helicopter

E. A person who assists a driver in backing up an ambulance

F. Specialized vehicle for treating and transporting sick and injured patients

G. Removes microbial contamination

Multiple Choice

Read each item carefully and then select the one best response.

_____ **1.** Ambulances today are designed according to strict government regulations based on _____ standards.

    A. local

    B. state

    C. national

    D. individual

_____ **2.** Features of the modern ambulance include all of the following EXCEPT:

    A. a self-contained breathing apparatus.

    B. a patient compartment.

    C. two-way radio communication.

    D. a driver's compartment.

_____ **3.** The first thing you do each day when you arrive at work is to make sure all equipment and supplies are functioning and in their assigned places. This is the _____ phase of transport operations.

    A. preparation

    B. dispatch

    C. arrival at scene

    D. transport

_____ **4.** The type _____ ambulance is a standard van with a forward-control integral cab body.

    A. I

    B. II

    C. III

    D. IV

_____ **5.** Suction units carried on ambulances must be powerful enough to generate a vacuum of _____ when the tube is clamped.

    A. 100 mm Hg

    B. 200 mm Hg

    C. 300 mm Hg

    D. 400 mm Hg

6. The following are all true regarding the use of oropharyngeal airways EXCEPT:

    A. Oropharyngeal airways can be used on adults.

    B. Oropharyngeal airways can be used on children.

    C. Oropharyngeal airways can be used on infants.

    D. Oropharyngeal airways cannot be used by EMTs.

7. When attached to oxygen supply with the oxygen reservoir in place, a bag-valve mask is able to supply almost _____ oxygen.

    A. 100%

    B. 95%

    C. 90%

    D. 85%

8. Extrication equipment carried on an ambulance may include all of the following EXCEPT:

    A. a rescue blanket.

    B. an adjustable wrench.

    C. duct tape.

    D. the jaws of life.

9. Basic wound care supplies include all of the following EXCEPT:

    A. sterile sheets.

    B. an OB kit.

    C. an assortment of adhesive bandages.

    D. aluminum foil.

10. Your supervisor asks you to make up jump kits for each ambulance. He has told you that he will leave it up to you as to what goes into the kit. You would want to include everything that you might need within the first _____ minutes of arrival at the patient's side.

    A. 2

    B. 3

    C. 4

    D. 5

11. Deceleration straps over the shoulders prevent the patient from continuing to move _____ in case the ambulance suddenly slows or stops.

    A. forward

    B. backward

    C. laterally

    D. down

12. The ambulance inspection should include checks of all of the following EXCEPT:

    A. fuel level.

    B. brake fluid.

    C. wheels and tires.

    D. spark plugs.

13. You are hired at the local EMS agency. During your orientation, you are given a tour of the station and the ambulances you will be riding on. Your duties include station cleanup and checking the unit for mechanical problems. You should also check all medical equipment and supplies:

    A. after every call.

    B. after every emergency transport.

    C. every 12 hours.

    D. every day.

_____ **14.** For every emergency request, the dispatcher should gather and record all of the following EXCEPT:

    A. the nature of the call.

    B. the patient's location.

    C. medications that the patient is currently taking.

    D. the number of patients and possible severity of their condition.

_____ **15.** During the _____ phase, the team should review dispatch information and assign specific initial duties and scene management tasks to each team member.

    A. preparation

    B. dispatch

    C. en route

    D. transport

_____ **16.** Basic requirements for the driver to operate an ambulance safely does NOT include:

    A. physical fitness.

    B. emotional fitness.

    C. proper attitude.

    D. the driver taking cold medication.

_____ **17.** The _____ phase may be the most dangerous part of the call.

    A. preparation

    B. en route

    C. transport

    D. on scene

_____ **18.** To operate an emergency vehicle safely, you must know how it responds to _____ under various conditions.

    A. steering

    B. braking

    C. acceleration

    D. steering, braking, and acceleration

_____ **19.** You must always drive:

    A. offensively.

    B. defensively.

    C. under the speed limit.

    D. recklessly.

_____ **20.** When driving with lights and siren, you are _____ drivers to yield the right-of-way.

    A. requesting

    B. demanding

    C. offering

    D. insisting

_____ **21.** Vehicle size and _____ will greatly influence braking and stopping distances.

    A. length

    B. height

    C. weight

    D. width

_____ **22.** When on an emergency call, before proceeding past a stopped school bus with its lights flashing, you should stop before reaching the bus and wait for the driver to do all of the following EXCEPT:

    A. make sure the children are safe.

    B. close the bus door.

    C. turn off the warning lights.

    D. An emergency vehicle does not need to stop for a school bus displaying its flashing lights.

_____ 23. _____ must be secured when the vehicle is in motion.

    A. All equipment and cabinets

    B. The patient

    C. Any passengers accompanying the patient

    D. All equipment, cabinets, the patient, and any passengers

_____ 24. The _____ is the most visible, effective warning device for clearing traffic in front of the vehicle.

    A. front light bar

    B. rear light bar

    C. high-beam flasher unit

    D. standard headlight

_____ 25. If you are involved in a motor vehicle collision while operating an emergency vehicle and are found to be at fault, you may be charged:

    A. civilly.

    B. criminally.

    C. both civilly and criminally.

    D. neither civilly nor criminally.

_____ 26. _____ crashes are the most common and usually the most serious type of collision in which ambulances are involved.

    A. T-bone

    B. Intersection

    C. Lateral

    D. Rollover

_____ 27. You respond to a multiple vehicle collision. You and your partner are reviewing dispatch information en route to the scene. You will be at a major intersection of two state highways. As you approach the scene, you review the guidelines for sizing up the scene. The guidelines include all of the following EXCEPT:

    A. looking for safety hazards.

    B. evaluating the need for additional units or other assistance.

    C. evaluating the need to stabilize the spine.

    D. entering the scene even if there are hazards.

_____ 28. The main objectives in directing traffic include all of the following EXCEPT:

    A. warning other drivers.

    B. preventing additional crashes.

    C. keeping vehicles moving in an orderly fashion.

    D. answering curious motorists' questions.

_____ 29. Transferring the patient to a receiving staff member occurs during the _____ phase.

    A. arrival

    B. transport

    C. delivery

    D. postrun

_____ 30. The decision to activate the emergency lights and siren depends on all of the following factors EXCEPT:

    A. local protocols

    B. patient condition

    C. the anticipated clinical outcome of the patient

    D. wanting to go faster.

_____ 31. You have called for an air ambulance. While your partner is monitoring the patient, he tells you to go set up a landing zone for the helicopter. When establishing a landing site for an approaching helicopter, ensure all of the following EXCEPT:

    A. that loose debris is cleared away.

    B. that the area is free of electric or telephone wires.

    C. that the area is free of telephone poles.

    D. that the area is on a hill.

True/False

If you believe the statement to be more true than false, write the letter "T" in the space provided. If you believe the statement to be more false than true, write the letter "F."

_____   **1.** Equipment and supplies should be placed in the unit according to their relative importance and frequency of use.

_____   **2.** A CPR board is a pocket-sized reminder that the EMT carries to help recall CPR procedures.

_____   **3.** Specially trained medical flight crews accompany all air ambulance flights.

_____   **4.** The en route or response phase of the emergency call is the least dangerous for the EMT.

_____   **5.** Using a police escort is a standard practice.

_____   **6.** Use the "4-second rule" to help you maintain a safe following distance.

_____   **7.** Always approach a helicopter from the front.

_____   **8.** Fixed-wing air ambulances are generally used for short-haul patient transfers.

_____   **9.** A clear landing zone of 50 feet by 50 feet (15 m by 15 m) is recommended for EMS helicopters.

Fill-in-the-Blank

Read each item carefully and then complete the statement by filling in the missing words.

1. A(n) _____ _____ is a portable kit containing items that are used in the initial care of the patient.

2. The six-pointed star that identifies vehicles that meet federal specifications as licensed or certified ambulances is known as the _____ _____ _____.

3. For many decades after 1906, a(n) _____ was the vehicle that was most often used as an ambulance.

4. _____ _____ respond initially to the scene with personnel and equipment to treat the sick and injured until an ambulance can arrive.

5. An ambulance call has _____ phases.

6. Some states allow you to proceed through a controlled intersection "_____ _____ _____," using flashing lights and siren.

7. Suction tubing must reach the patient's _____, regardless of the patient's position.

8. A(n) _____ _____ provides a firm surface under the patient's torso so that you can give effective chest compressions.

Labeling

Label the following diagrams with the correct terms.

1. Helicopter Hand Signals

A. _____

B. _____

C. _____

D. _____

E. _____

F. _____

Crossword Puzzle

The following crossword puzzle is an activity provided to reinforce correct spelling and understanding of medical terminology associated with emergency care and the EMT. Use the clues in the column to complete the puzzle.

Across

1. A specialized vehicle for treating and transporting sick and injured patients.
3. A(n) _____ board provides a firm surface under the patient's torso.
4. If you are the first EMT at the scene of a mass-casualty incident, quickly estimate the number of _____.
7. A person who assists a driver in backing up an ambulance to compensate for blind spots at the back of the vehicle.
9. A condition in which the tires of a vehicle may be lifted off the road surface as water "piles up" under them, making the vehicle feel as though it is floating.
10. A portable kit containing items that are used in the initial care of the patient.
12. The process of removing dirt, dust, blood, or other visible contaminants from a surface.
13. The killing of pathogenic agents by direct application of chemicals.

Down

2. Areas of the road that are blocked from your sight by your own vehicle or mirrors.
3. Keeping a safe distance between your vehicle and other vehicles on any side of you is known as a(n) _____ of safety.
5. _____ ambulances are fixed-wing aircraft and helicopters that have been modified for medical care.
6. A process, such as heating, that removes microbial contamination.
8. _____ disinfection is the killing of pathogenic agents by using potent means of disinfection.
11. The Star of _____ identifies vehicles that meet federal specifications as licensed or certified ambulances.

Critical Thinking

Multiple Choice

Read each critical-thinking item carefully and then select the one best response.

Questions 1–5 are derived from the following scenario: You are requested out to County Road 93 for a motor vehicle collision at a rural area known for serious crashes. After driving with lights and sirens for nearly 20 minutes to reach the scene, you arrive at the intersection at the east end of the county. As you pull up, you see two pickup trucks crushed into a mass of twisted, smoking metal. A sheriff's deputy is shouting and waving you over to the passenger side door of one of the demolished trucks. You quickly look down all four roads leading to the scene and note that they are deserted as far as you can see.

_____ 1. Specifically regarding the transport of patients from this scene, you should immediately consider _____ before stepping out of the ambulance.
    A. scene safety
    B. parking 100 feet (30 m) past the scene
    C. requesting a medical helicopter
    D. the risks versus benefits of using the siren

_____ **2.** Which phase of an ambulance call does this scenario demonstrate?
  A. Fifth
  B. Fourth
  C. Third
  D. Second
_____ **3.** Which of the following would you most likely NOT need for this incident?
  A. Jump kit
  B. Airway kit
  C. Extrication kit
  D. Obstetrics kit
_____ **4.** How would you ensure the proper control of traffic around this scene?
  A. Put out flares in a pattern that leads other vehicles safely around the involved vehicles.
  B. Because the roads were deserted when you arrived, it is not a priority.
  C. Ask the law enforcement officer to control any traffic.
  D. Pull completely off the roadway and leave your red emergency lights flashing.
_____ **5.** You end up transporting an unstable trauma patient from this scene. Assuming that the patient is breathing adequately, what should you be doing about every 5 minutes during the transport phase?
  A. Reassessing vital signs
  B. Providing an update to the receiving facility
  C. Checking your ETA with the navigational equipment
  D. Attempting to rendezvous with an ALS crew

Short Answer

Complete this section with short written answers using the space provided.

1. Describe the three basic ambulance designs.

_____

_____

_____

2. List the phases of an ambulance call.

_____

_____

_____

3. Define the term *siren syndrome*.

_____

_____

_____

4. Describe the three basic principles that govern the use of warning lights and siren.

_____

_____

_____

5. List four guidelines for safe ambulance driving.

_____

_____

_____

6. List the general considerations used for selecting a helicopter landing site.

_____

_____

_____

Ambulance Calls

The following case scenarios provide an opportunity to explore the concerns associated with patient management and to enhance critical-thinking skills. Read each scenario and answer each question to the best of your ability.

1. You are cross-trained as a firefighter, and your station has been dispatched to a working structure fire. As you near the scene, another call is dispatched for "an unknown medical emergency." You are the closest unit to the medical emergency.

How would you best manage this situation?

_____

_____

_____

2. Your department's coverage area is quite large, including ALS coverage for the entire county, as well as surrounding areas out of state. You are dispatched to an unfamiliar address for "CPR in progress" and are working with a newly hired partner who is not familiar with your coverage area.

How would you best manage this situation?

_____

_____

_____

3. You are called to the scene of a motor vehicle collision. The car is situated in a curve and traffic is heavy. Police are not on the scene. Your patient is alert and looking around but is stuck in the vehicle due to traffic. You see blood smeared across her face, but it appears to be minimal.

How would you best manage this situation?

_____

_____

_____

Fill-in-the-Patient Care Report

Read the incident scenario and then complete the following patient care report (PCR).

It is just before dawn (0512 by the clock on the dashboard), and the darkness is broken only by the occasional burst of lightning in the clouds above, which briefly illuminates the heavy rainfall that has been coming down all night long. You are just about to tell your partner, Alejandro, that you are surprised by the absence of vehicle collisions tonight with the weather the way it is when the dispatch tones burst from the speakers.

"4-0-9, Central Dispatch, emergency call to Highway 12 and Nest Creek Road for a motor vehicle collision."

"4-0-9 copies," Alejandro responds as you start the truck. "En route to Highway 12 and Nest Creek."

"Station time, 0513."

You drive carefully through the torrential rain, the flashing strobes mounted above the cab reflecting off the raindrops and reducing your visibility, turning what would normally be a 6-minute drive into 10. Thankfully, the heavy rain eases as you arrive on the scene, dissipating to a gentle shower. You park safely off the roadway, which has been shut down by highway patrol, and approach the scene while Alejandro pulls the equipment from the back.

"We've got two drivers and two cars involved," a highway patrol officer wearing a plastic-covered, wide-brimmed hat says as you approach. "One's not injured but the other is bleeding pretty good from her nose. I think she hit the steering wheel."

You walk over to the small white car where the injured woman is still in the driver's seat and see that the highway patrol has chocked the wheels and disconnected the battery. You approach from the front, so the 41-year-old woman can see you directly out of the windshield, and Alejandro moves to the rear door.

"Ma'am," you say loudly through the windshield. "Keep looking straight ahead at me and do not move your head. My partner is going to get in the back of your car right now and hold your head steady."

As soon as Alejandro is holding the woman's head in a neutral, in-line position, you set about applying a cervical collar and, finding no injuries other than a swollen (no longer bleeding) nose, you apply the vest-type extrication device and initiate high-flow oxygen therapy. Eight minutes after arriving on scene, and with the rain starting to fall harder again, you have the 90-kg (198-lb) patient secured to a long backboard and loaded into the back of the ambulance.

One minute after closing the back doors you have obtained a baseline set of vital signs, and Alejandro has pulled out onto the roadway and has started driving to the nearest emergency department, 14 minutes south. The patient's vital signs are: blood pressure, 142/100 mm Hg; pulse, 100 beats/min; respirations, 16 breaths/min and unlabored (but she cannot breathe through her nose); and SpO_2 of 98%.

"What is your blood pressure normally?" you ask while filling out the PCR.

"It's high," she says. "I'm supposed to take Lisinopril, but I always forget. I had something like a stroke when I was 36. They called it a TIA or something."

"Do you have any other medical issues or allergies?"

"No. But my nose and cheeks are killing me."

"Okay," you say, patting her arm. "I'm sorry about that. We'll be at the hospital in a few minutes, and they will be able to help with that."

You then pick up the radio and contact the hospital to provide a patient report and your ETA.

Three minutes before arriving at the emergency department, you get a second set of vital signs and find that they are the same as the first, except that the patient's breathing has slowed by two breaths per minute as she relaxed. You and Alejandro unload the gurney from the ambulance and deliver the patient to the waiting staff of County Medical Center, where you provide a verbal report to the accepting nurse and properly turn over care.

A total of 45 minutes after the initial dispatch, you notify the dispatch center that you are available and ready for more calls.

Fill-in-the-Patient Care Report

EMS Patient Care Report (PCR)					
Date:	Incident No.:	Nature of Call:		Location:	
Dispatched:	En Route:	At Scene:	Transport:	At Hospital:	In Service:

Patient Information	
Age: Sex: Weight (in kg [lb]):	Allergies: Medications: Past Medical History: Chief Complaint:

Vital Signs				
Time:	BP:	Pulse:	Respirations:	Spo$_2$:
Time:	BP:	Pulse:	Respirations:	Spo$_2$:
Time:	BP:	Pulse:	Respirations:	Spo$_2$:

EMS Treatment (circle all that apply)				
Oxygen @ ___ L/min via (circle one): NC NRM BVM	Assisted Ventilation	Airway Adjunct		CPR
Defibrillation	Bleeding Control	Bandaging	Splinting	Other:

Narrative

Vehicle Extrication and Special Rescue

© Photos.com

General Knowledge

Matching

Match each of the items in the left column to the appropriate definition in the right column.

_____ 1. Extrication
_____ 2. Simple access
_____ 3. Hazardous material

_____ 4. Access
_____ 5. Incident commander
_____ 6. SWAT
_____ 7. Complex access
_____ 8. Command post
_____ 9. Technical rescue group
_____ 10. Structure fire
_____ 11. SCBA
_____ 12. Danger zone

A. Access requiring no special tools or force
B. Individual who has overall command of the scene in the field
C. Area where individuals can be exposed to sharp objects and hazardous materials
D. Access requiring special tools and training
E. Removal from entrapment or a dangerous situation or position
F. The ability to reach patients
G. Fire in a house, apartment building, or other building
H. Location of the incident commander
I. Individuals trained to respond to special rescue situations
J. Special weapons and tactics team
K. Self-contained breathing apparatus
L. Toxic, poisonous, radioactive, flammable, or explosive

Multiple Choice

Read each item carefully and then select the one best response.

_____ 1. During all phases of rescue, your primary concern is:
- **A.** extrication.
- **B.** safety.
- **C.** patient care.
- **D.** rapid transport.

_____ 2. When you arrive at the scene where there is a potential for hazardous materials exposure:
- **A.** turn off your warning light.
- **B.** do not waste time waiting for the scene to be marked and protected.
- **C.** park your unit downhill of the scene.
- **D.** park your unit uphill of the scene.

_____ 3. _____ is the ability to recognize any possible issues once you arrive on the scene and to act proactively to avoid a negative impact.
- **A.** Situational awareness
- **B.** Situational consciousness
- **C.** Situational alertness
- **D.** Situational disregard

_____ 4. Controlling traffic at a scene is typically the responsibility of:
- **A.** a firefighter.
- **B.** law enforcement.
- **C.** the rescue group.
- **D.** EMS personnel.

_____ 5. During a 360° walk around at an accident scene, you should look for all of the following EXCEPT:

    A. the mechanism of injury.

    B. leaking fuels or fluids.

    C. trapped or ejected patients.

    D. the amount of air left in the tires.

_____ 6. You should communicate with members of _____ throughout the extrication process.

    A. law enforcement

    B. the media

    C. the rescue team

    D. the insurance company

_____ 7. If there are downed power lines near a vehicle involved in a crash, you should:

    A. attempt to move the power lines yourself.

    B. touch the power lines with an object to see if there is active electricity.

    C. have the patient slowly exit the vehicle.

    D. have the patient remain in the vehicle.

_____ 8. _____ is responsible for properly securing and stabilizing the vehicle and providing a safe entrance and access to the patient.

    A. Law enforcement

    B. The rescue team

    C. The EMS agency

    D. The HazMat unit

_____ 9. Prior to attempting to gain access into a vehicle, the parking brake should be on and the _____ should be disconnected.

    A. radio

    B. battery

    C. hydraulics

    D. brake lines

_____ 10. Lighting at a scene, establishing a tool and equipment area, and marking for a helicopter landing all fall under:

    A. logistic operations.

    B. EMS operations.

    C. support operations.

    D. law enforcement.

_____ 11. When removing an injured patient from a vehicle due to an environmental threat or the need to perform CPR, it is best to use the _____ technique.

    A. rapid extrication

    B. KED board

    C. upright chest compression

    D. intermediate extrication

_____ 12. When attempting simple access into a vehicle, you should:

    A. use complex tools.

    B. try opening the doors using the door handles first.

    C. break the windows initially.

    D. make sure that all the windows are rolled up.

_____ 13. Which of the following is NOT considered a specialized rescue situation?

    A. Cave rescue

    B. Dive rescue

    C. Truck rescue

    D. Mine rescue

_____ 14. When arriving at the scene of a cave-in or trench collapse, response vehicles should be parked at least _____ away from the scene.

A. 50 feet (15 m)

B. 150 feet (46 m)

C. 250 feet (76 m)

D. 500 feet (152 m)

_____ 15. Which of the following statements regarding tactical emergency medical support is FALSE?

A. Some incidents pose an increased risk to EMS.

B. Once you have checked in at the command post, you are free to roam the area looking for ways to help.

C. Lights and sirens should be turned off when nearing the scene.

D. Planning measures and working with the incident commander will reduce the potential for chaos.

True/False

If you believe the statement to be more true than false, write the letter "T" in the space provided. If you believe the statement to be more false than true, write the letter "F."

_____ 1. At a fire scene, you must ensure that your ambulance will not block or hinder other arriving equipment.

_____ 2. Ambulances are not typically summoned to search and rescue scenes.

_____ 3. When you arrive at the site of a technical rescue, you should identify the staging area where the technical rescue team will bring the patient.

_____ 4. Following the termination of a rescue incident, all equipment used at the scene must be checked before being reloaded onto the apparatus.

_____ 5. White-water rescue, structural collapse, and mountain-climbing rescue require specialized rescue teams.

_____ 6. You should put on proper protective gear before exiting your vehicle at an emergency scene.

_____ 7. Securing an injured arm to the body is generally considered to be acceptable until the patient is fully extricated.

_____ 8. When determining a rescue plan, your input will be essential so that the patient's injuries will be considered during the rescue process.

_____ 9. A short in a vehicle's electric system or a damaged battery may also cause a postcrash fire.

_____ 10. Hybrid batteries have a higher voltage than traditional automotive batteries, and it may take up to 10 minutes for a high-voltage system to de-energize after the main battery is turned off.

_____ 11. It is generally uncommon for EMTs to be in the vehicle with a patient during the disentanglement process.

_____ 12. Providing medical care to a patient who is trapped in a vehicle is principally the same as for any other patient.

_____ 13. Simple access typically involves breaking glass.

_____ 14. When there are multiple patients, you should locate and rapidly triage each patient to determine who needs urgent care.

_____ 15. A vehicle on its side is typically not a danger to you as long as the vehicle is not swaying.

_____ 16. Airbags can be located in the steering wheel, doors, or seats.

_____ 17. There are five phases to the extrication process.

Fill-in-the-Blank

Read each item carefully and then complete the statement by filling in the missing words.

1. In addition to posing a threat to you and others at the scene, _____ _____ may pose a threat to a much larger area and population.

2. A team of experienced EMTs should be able to perform _____ _____ in 1 minute or less.

3. _____ is the term used when a person is caught within a closed area with no way out or who has a limb or other body part trapped.

4. Once entrance and access to the patient have been provided and the scene is safe, you should perform a _____ _____ and provide care before further extrication begins.

5. _____ is the ongoing process of information gathering and scene evaluation to determine measures for managing an emergency.

6. Extrication is often extremely noisy, and appropriate _____ _____ should be worn by you and the patient.

7. _____ _____ are responsible for providing immediate assessment and treatment of injured people at rescue scenes.

8. Extinguishing fires, preventing additional ignition, and removing any spilled fuel is primarily the responsibility of _____.

9. The rescue team will set up a(n) _____ _____ that is off-limits to bystanders to protect their safety.

10. No matter what the fuel source of a crashed vehicle is, one common practice remains the same—the need to disconnect the _____.

11. You should not attempt to gain access into a vehicle until you are sure that it has been _____.

12. All EMS personnel should wear proper _____ _____ while in the working area.

13. The _____ _____ should provide you with the entrance you need to gain access to the patient.

14. _____ among team members and clear leadership are essential to safe, efficient provision of proper emergency care.

15. A lack of identifiable _____ at the scene hinders the rescue effort and patient care.

16. During disentanglement, cover the patient with a heavy, _____ _____ or place a _____ between the windshield and the patient to protect him or her from breaking glass or other hazards.

17. Cave rescue, confined space rescue, and search and rescue are all considered to be _____ _____ situations.

18. You should consider using _____ _____ if the patient will need to be transported an extensive distance.

19. Unless otherwise instructed, only the _____ _____ should communicate any news or progress of a search and rescue to a victim's family.

20. _____ is a primary cause of secondary collapse in a trench collapse.

21. At no time should medical personnel enter a trench deeper than _____ _____ without proper shoring in place.

22. In most areas, an ambulance is dispatched with the fire department to any _____ _____.

Crossword Puzzle

The following crossword puzzle is an activity provided to reinforce correct spelling and understanding of medical terminology associated with emergency care and the EMT. Use the clues in the column to complete the puzzle.

Across

1. Gaining entry to an enclosed area and reaching a patient.
5. A technical rescue _____ requires special technical skills and equipment in one of many specialized rescue areas.
10. Respirator with independent air supply used by firefighters to enter toxic and otherwise dangerous atmospheres.
12. To be caught (trapped) within a vehicle, room, or container with no way out or to have a limb or other body part trapped.
13. An area of protection providing safety from the danger zone (hot zone).
14. Complicated entry that requires special tools and training and includes breaking windows or using other force.

Down

2. A specialized law enforcement tactical unit.
3. Access that is easily achieved without the use of tools or force.
4. The incident _____ has overall command of the incident in the field.
6. Removal of a patient from entrapment or a dangerous situation or position.
7. Any substances that are toxic, poisonous, radioactive, flammable, or explosive and cause injury or death with exposure are _____ materials.
8. An area where individuals can be exposed to hazards, such as sharp metal edges, broken glass, toxic substances, lethal rays, or ignition or explosion of hazardous materials.
9. A team of individuals from one or more departments in a region who are trained and on call for certain types of technical rescue is known as a technical rescue _____.
11. The ongoing process of information gathering and scene evaluation to determine appropriate strategies and tactics to manage an emergency.

Critical Thinking

Short Answer

Complete this section with short written answers using the space provided.

1. Explain the individual responsibilities of EMS, firefighters, law enforcement, and rescue teams at a rescue scene.

_____

_____

_____

2. List the questions you and your team should consider whenever you need to determine the exact location and position of a patient.

_____

_____

_____

3. List the steps for assessing and caring for a patient who is entrapped once access has been gained.

_____

_____

_____

4. List the 10 phases of extrication.

_____

_____

_____

5. The reasons for rescue failure can be summarized by the mnemonic FAILURE. What does FAILURE stand for?

_____

_____

_____

Ambulance Calls

The following case scenarios provide an opportunity to explore the concerns associated with patient management and to enhance critical-thinking skills. Read each scenario and answer each question to the best of your ability.

1. You and your partner arrive on scene to find an extrication in progress. Your patient is a middle-aged female driver entrapped in a vehicle. One of the rescue team is yelling something about "bleeding" and waving you forward. The driver's side window is down and the woman is screaming in pain. You note bright red blood spurting from her left upper arm. There are no immediate scene hazards to prevent you from approaching.

   How would you best manage this situation?

   _____

   _____

   _____

2. It is spring, and the water runoff from melting snow has caused the local viaduct to swell with cold, fast-moving waters. You are off duty when you hear a tone out for "small boy swept away by flood waters." You arrive on the scene before your department's on-duty responders. You see a boy of approximately 13 years who is clinging to life in the middle of the channel, holding onto a trapped log. His mother is hysterical and screaming for you to "jump in and get him." You have no safety equipment available.

   How would you best manage this patient?

   _____

   _____

   _____

3. You are dispatched to a chemical spill where a train car derailed. The patient is the engineer; he was injured when he went to the back of the train to survey the damage. He is lying beside the tracks. From your vantage point at the staging area, he appears to be breathing. HazMat team members are suiting up to go in and retrieve the patient. They will decontaminate him before bringing him to the staging area.

   How would you best manage this patient?

   _____

   _____

   _____

CHAPTER

39

Incident Management

© Photos.com

General Knowledge

Matching

Match each of the items in the left column to the appropriate definition in the right column.

_____ 1. Carboys
_____ 2. Cold zone
_____ 3. Control zone
_____ 4. Freelancing
_____ 5. Decontamination

_____ 6. Demobilization
_____ 7. Disaster
_____ 8. Hot zone
_____ 9. Intermodal tanks

_____ 10. Placards

_____ 11. Primary triage
_____ 12. Secondary containment
_____ 13. Secondary triage
_____ 14. Span of control
_____ 15. Warm zone

A. Shipping and storage vessels that may or may not be pressurized
B. Areas designated as hot, warm, and cold
C. Initial triage done in the field
D. Patient sorting used in the treatment sector; involves retriage of patients
E. Removing or neutralizing hazardous materials from patients and equipment
F. Controlling spills when main containment vessel fails
G. Required on all four sides of vehicles transporting hazardous materials
H. Glass, plastic, or steel containers ranging in volume from 5 to 15 gallons
I. Area surrounding hazardous materials spill/incident that is the most contaminated area
J. Individual units or different organizations make independent and often inefficient decisions about the next appropriate action
K. Area located between hot zone and cold zone
L. Widespread event that disrupts community resources and function
M. The supervisor-to-worker ratio
N. Safe area at a hazardous materials incident
O. Responders return to their facilities when work at a disaster is completed.

Multiple Choice

Read each item carefully and then select the one best response.

_____ 1. Major incidents require the involvement and coordination of all of the following EXCEPT:
   A. multiple jurisdictions.
   B. local and national media.
   C. multiple agencies.
   D. emergency response disciplines.

_____ 2. Which of the following is NOT part of NIMS standardization?
   A. Personnel training
   B. Resource classification
   C. Terminology
   D. Funding

_____ 3. In the incident command system (ICS), organizational divisions may include sections, branches, divisions, and:
   A. groups.
   B. teams.
   C. platoons.
   D. squads.

_____ **4.** Which of the following is NOT considered a function of the finance section in the ICS?

    A. Time unit

    B. Procurement unit

    C. Cost unit

    D. Logistics unit

_____ **5.** Which of the following statements regarding the function of the public information officer is TRUE?

    A. Positions headquarters away from the incident

    B. Is not responsible for the safety of the media

    C. Monitors the scene for conditions that may be unsafe

    D. Relays information and concerns among the command and general staff

_____ **6.** What is one of the three main questions used during the scene size-up at a potential MCI?

    A. Is my ambulance stocked for an MCI?

    B. Where am I?

    C. What resources do I need?

    D. How long will it take to get help here?

_____ **7.** Which of the following is considered a priority when determining "what needs to be done" during the scene size-up?

    A. Rescue operations

    B. Incident stabilization

    C. Notifying hospitals

    D. Establishing operations

_____ **8.** Once you have performed a good scene size-up, _____ should be established by the most senior official.

    A. operations

    B. communications

    C. command

    D. rescue

_____ **9.** The primary duty of the triage division is to:

    A. begin basic treatment.

    B. establish zones for categorized patients.

    C. communicate with the treatment division.

    D. ensure that every patient receives an initial assessment.

_____ **10.** Documenting and tracking of transporting vehicles, transported patients, and facility destinations is the responsibility of the:

    A. operations supervisor.

    B. transportation supervisor.

    C. logistics supervisor.

    D. triage supervisor.

_____ **11.** Which of the following is NOT a sign of stress a rehabilitation supervisor is responsible for recognizing?

    A. Fatigue

    B. Headache

    C. Complete collapse

    D. Altered thinking patterns

_____ **12.** Which of the following definitions of MCI is correct?

    A. Any call that involves three or more patients

    B. Any situation that meets the demand of equipment or personnel

    C. Any incident that does not require mutual aid response

    D. Any call that has at least one motor vehicle involved

_____ 13. Triaged patients are primarily divided into how many categories?
   A. Two
   B. Four
   C. Six
   D. Eight

_____ 14. Delayed patients would be identified by using the color:
   A. black.
   B. red.
   C. yellow.
   D. green.

_____ 15. Immediate patients would be identified by using the color:
   A. black.
   B. red.
   C. yellow.
   D. green.

_____ 16. Minimal patients are the third priority and are identified using the color:
   A. black.
   B. red.
   C. yellow.
   D. green.

_____ 17. Patients who are dead or whose injuries are so severe that they have, at best, a minimal chance of survival, are categorized using what color?
   A. Black
   B. Grey
   C. White
   D. Brown

_____ 18. Facilities, food, lighting, and medical equipment are the responsibility of the:
   A. operations section.
   B. planning section.
   C. logistics section.
   D. finance section.

_____ 19. When using the START triage system, a patient who is breathing faster than 30 breaths/min is triaged as:
   A. immediate.
   B. delayed.
   C. minimal.
   D. expectant.

_____ 20. "If you can hear my voice and are able to walk . . ." is said to immediately identify patients categorized as:
   A. immediate.
   B. delayed.
   C. minimal.
   D. expectant.

_____ 21. A pediatric patient who is breathing 12 breaths/min would be categorized as:
   A. immediate.
   B. delayed.
   C. minimal.
   D. expectant.

_____ **22.** You are at the scene on a hazardous materials incident when your partner slips and falls, injuring his leg. He is alert and responds appropriately to your questions. His respirations are 20 breaths/min, and he has a radial pulse. What triage category does your partner fall into?
   A. Immediate
   B. Delayed
   C. Minimal
   D. Expectant

_____ **23.** Clues that you may be dealing with a hazardous material include all of the following EXCEPT:
   A. dead grass.
   B. animals near the scene.
   C. discolored pavement.
   D. visible vapors or puddles.

_____ **24.** Rail tank cars, intermodal tanks, and highway cargo tanks are all considered:
   A. oversize storage containers.
   B. gross storage containers.
   C. mass storage containers.
   D. bulk storage containers.

_____ **25.** Soap flakes, sodium hydroxide pellets, and food-grade materials are sometimes found in:
   A. bags.
   B. carboys.
   C. drums.
   D. cylinders.

_____ **26.** The US Department of Transportation (DOT) uses all of the following for hazardous identification EXCEPT:
   A. placards.
   B. labels.
   C. signals.
   D. markings.

_____ **27.** Some materials are so hazardous that shipping any amount of them requires a placard. Which of the following is NOT considered to be one of those hazards?
   A. Poison gases
   B. Low-level radioactive substances
   C. Water-reactive solids
   D. Explosives

_____ **28.** Which of the following statements regarding MSDS is FALSE?
   A. Facilities are no longer required by law to have an MSDS on file for each chemical used.
   B. They provide basic information about the chemical makeup of a substance.
   C. They list the potential hazards associated with a substance.
   D. They list appropriate first aid in the event of an exposure.

_____ **29.** Control zones at HazMat incidents are labeled as all of the following EXCEPT:
   A. hot.
   B. warm.
   C. cold.
   D. lukewarm.

_____ **30.** Nonencapsulated protective clothing, eye protection, and a breathing device that contains an air supply fall into what level of personal protective equipment?
   A. Level A
   B. Level B
   C. Level C
   D. Level D

True/False

If you believe the statement to be more true than false, write the letter "T" in the space provided. If you believe the statement to be more false than true, write the letter "F."

_____ **1.** Some of the most challenging situations you can be called to are disasters and mass-casualty incidents.

_____ **2.** The individuals who will participate in the many tasks in an MCI or a disaster should use the ICS.

_____ **3.** The purpose of the ICS is to designate the support agencies in several kinds of MCI.

_____ **4.** Safety priorities include your life, then your patient's, and then your partner's.

_____ **5.** A key role of the transportation supervisor is to communicate with the area hospitals to determine where to transport patients.

_____ **6.** The staging supervisor should be established near the scene.

_____ **7.** The morgue should be out of view of the living patients and other responders.

_____ **8.** A way of tracking and accounting for patients is to issue only 20 to 25 triage tags at a time with a scorecard.

_____ **9.** Infants and children not developed enough to walk or follow commands should be taken as soon as possible to the triage sector for immediate secondary triage.

_____ **10.** When you approach a hazardous scene, you should stay downhill and upwind.

_____ **11.** The farther you are from the incident when you notice a problem, the safer you will be.

_____ **12.** The nature of the chemical dictates the construction of the storage drum.

_____ **13.** The DOT system requires that all chemical shipments be marked with placards and labels.

_____ **14.** Some substances are not hazardous but can become highly toxic when mixed with another substance.

_____ **15.** If you are treating a patient who was partially decontaminated, you will not need to wear additional protective clothing.

Fill-in-the-Blank

Read each item carefully and then complete the statement by filling in the missing words.

1. Two important underlying principles of the NIMS are _____ and _____.

2. One of the organizing principles of the ICS is limiting the _____ _____ _____ of any one individual.

3. A(n) _____ command system is one in which one person is in charge, even if multiple agencies respond.

4. The _____ section solves problems as they arise during the MCI.

5. _____ involves the decisions made and basic planning done before an incident occurs.

6. The _____ _____ is ultimately in charge of counting and prioritizing patients.

7. _____ _____ ensure that secondary triage of patients is performed.

8. The main information needed on a triage tag is a unique _____ and a triage _____.

9. The _____ and type of _____ are two good indicators of the possible presence of a hazardous material.

10. Containers of material are divided into two categories: _____ and _____ storage containers.

11. _____ _____ may be constructed of plastic, paper, or plastic-lined paper.

12. _____ _____ are established at a HazMat incident based on the chemical and physical properties of the released material and the environmental factors.

13. The _____ _____ is where personnel and equipment transition into and out of the hot zone.

14. Anyone who leaves a hot zone must pass through the _____ area.

15. A(n) _____ _____ is shipped to a facility, where it is stored and used, and then returned to the shipper for refilling.

Fill-in-the-Table

Fill in the missing parts of the table.

Triage Priorities	
Triage Category	**Typical Injuries**
Red tag: first priority (immediate) Patients who need immediate care and transport Treat these patients first and transport as soon as possible	• _____ • _____ • _____ • _____ • _____ • _____
Yellow tag: second priority (delayed) Patients whose treatment and transport can be temporarily delayed	• _____ • _____ • _____
Green tag: third priority, minimal (walking wounded) Patients who require minimal or no treatment and whose transport can be delayed until last	• _____ • _____
Black tag: fourth priority (expectant) Patients who are already dead or have little chance for survival; treat salvageable patients before treating these patients	• _____ • _____ • _____ • _____

Crossword Puzzle

The following crossword puzzle is an activity provided to reinforce correct spelling and understanding of medical terminology associated with emergency care and the EMT. Use the clues in the column to complete the puzzle.

Across

1. A widespread event that disrupts community resources and functions, in turn threatening public safety, citizens' lives, and property.

3. A system designed to enable governments and private sector and nongovernmental organizations to effectively and efficiently prepare for, prevent, respond to, and recover from domestic incidents.

5. The _____ information center is an area designated by the incident commander, or a designee, in which public information officers disseminate information about the incident.

8. A system implemented to manage disasters and mass-casualty incidents in which section chiefs report to the incident commander.

10. In incident command, the _____ supervisor works with area medical examiners, coroners, and law enforcement agencies to coordinate the disposition of dead victims.

13. In incident command, the _____ officer gives the "go ahead" to a plan or may stop an operation when rescuer safety is an issue.

14. The process of removing or neutralizing and properly disposing of hazardous materials from equipment, patients, and rescue personnel.

15. _____ containment is an engineered method to control spilled or released product if the main containment vessel fails.

17. A safe area at a hazardous materials incident for the agencies involved in the operations.

18. An emergency situation involving three or more patients.

19. Glass, plastic, or steel containers ranging in volume from 5 to 15 gallons.

Down

2. The process of sorting patients based on the severity of injury and medical need to establish treatment and transportation priorities.

4. A form containing information about chemical composition, physical and chemical properties, health and safety hazards, emergency response, and waste disposal of a specific material.

6. In incident command, the _____ officer relays information, concerns, and requests among responding agencies.

7. In incident command, the person who keeps the public informed and relates any information to the press.

9. An incident _____ plan states general objectives reflecting the overall strategy for managing an incident.

11. In incident command, the _____ supervisor determines the type of equipment and resources needed for a situation involving extrication or special rescue.

12. The area located between the hot zone and the cold zone at a hazardous materials incident.

16. Barrel-like containers used to store a wide variety of substances, including food-grade materials, corrosives, flammable liquids, and grease.

Critical Thinking

Short Answer

Complete this section with short written answers using the space provided.

1. List the major components of the NIMS.

   _____

   _____

   _____

2. List the five factors included in mobilization and deployment.

   _____

   _____

   _____

3. What information should be communicated from the triage supervisor to the branch medical director?

   _____

   _____

   _____

4. Based on the HAZWOPER regulation, what are the competencies a first responder should be able to demonstrate at the awareness level?

   _____

   _____

   _____

5. What information is typically included on an MSDS?

   _____

   _____

   _____

Ambulance Calls

The following case scenarios provide an opportunity to explore the concerns associated with patient management and to enhance critical-thinking skills. Read each scenario and answer each question to the best of your ability.

1. You are dispatched to a multiple vehicle collision where you encounter three patients: a 4-year-old boy with bilateral femur fractures and absent radial pulse, a 27-year-old woman with a laceration to the head and a humerus fracture, and a 42-year-old man who is apneic and pulseless with an open skull fracture.

   How should you triage these patients?

   _____

   _____

   _____

2. Your response area contains a large portion of farming and other agricultural lands, including many orchards and vineyards. Right at shift change, there is a tone out for a "crop-duster accident" in a remote area of your jurisdiction. It appears that 15 to 30 agricultural workers were accidentally sprayed with pesticides and other chemicals from a crop-dusting plane. They are now experiencing a variety of signs and symptoms, including nausea, vomiting, and eye and upper airway irritation.

   How would you best manage this situation?

   _____

   _____

   _____

3. You and your partner are enjoying an unusually uneventful evening at work when you receive a dispatch for "overturned semitruck." As you approach the scene, you see a semitractor trailer that has left the roadway and rolled down a steep embankment. You see the driver attempting to climb up to the roadway, where many passersby have stopped to see what has happened. He is vigorously coughing, and you can see a liquid dripping from the truck's tank.

   How would you best manage this situation?

   _____

   _____

   _____

   _____

Skills

Assessment Review

Answer the following questions pertaining to the assessment of the types of emergencies discussed in this chapter.

_____ 1. You are at the scene of a multiple vehicle collision involving eight people. Your partner has established command and is requesting additional resources as you begin to triage patients. You see patients in various areas as you visually inspect the scene. "If any of you are able to walk to me, please do so," you state to the patients. Three of the eight people are able to walk to you. What category of triage do these patients initially fall into?

   A. Immediate

   B. Delayed

   C. Minimal

   D. Expectant

_____ **2.** As you continue moving through the scene, you come across two people in a vehicle. The first person has obvious bleeding from her forehead and is emotionally upset. She is slow to respond to your questions and cannot tell you what today's date is. When you ask her to show you "two fingers" she is able to but with some delay. Her radial pulse is 106 beats/min, and her respirations are 22 breaths/min and nonlabored. What category of triage does this patient initially fall into?

    A. Immediate

    B. Delayed

    C. Minimal

    D. Expectant

_____ **3.** The next patient in the vehicle has an obvious open femur fracture. The patient is breathing at a rate of 32 breaths/min but is completely alert, oriented, and able to follow commands without hesitation. The patient's radial pulse is 102 beats/min and weak. What category of triage does this patient initially fall into?

    A. Immediate

    B. Delayed

    C. Minimal

    D. Expectant

_____ **4.** Additional EMS have arrived on the scene, and you are being assisted by two other EMTs in the triage process. The last patient you encounter is a 7-year-old boy with neck and back pain. He is quite upset and keeps asking for his parents. His respirations are 38 breaths/min, and his radial pulse is 110 beats/min. What category of triage does this patient initially fall into?

    A. Immediate

    B. Delayed

    C. Minimal

    D. Expectant

CHAPTER

40

Terrorism Response and Disaster Management

© Photos.com

General Knowledge

Matching

Match each of the items in the left column to the appropriate definition in the right column.

_____ 1. Mutagen

_____ 2. Vesicants

_____ 3. Disease vector

_____ 4. Phosgene

_____ 5. Neurotoxins

_____ 6. Bacteria

_____ 7. Volatility

_____ 8. Cyanide

_____ 9. Vapor hazard

_____ 10. Lymph nodes

_____ 11. Incubation

_____ 12. Ricin

_____ 13. Dissemination

_____ 14. Radioactive material

_____ 15. Viruses

A. Substance that emits radiation

B. Describes how long a chemical agent will stay on a surface before it evaporates

C. Period of time from exposure to onset of symptoms

D. Agent that enters the body through the respiratory tract

E. Animal that, once infected, spreads the disease to another animal

F. Agent that affects the body's ability to use oxygen

G. Germs that require a living host to multiply and survive

H. Means by which a terrorist will spread a disease

I. Neurotoxin derived from mash that is left from the castor bean

J. Biologic agents that are the most deadly substances known to humans

K. Microorganisms that reproduce by binary fission

L. Substance that mutates and damages the structures of DNA in the body's cells

M. Area of the lymphatic system where infection-fighting cells are housed

N. Pulmonary agent that is a product of combustion

O. Blister agents

Multiple Choice

Read each item carefully and then select the one best response.

_____ 1. All of the following are examples of terrorist groups EXCEPT:

    A. doomsday cults.

    B. extremist political groups.

    C. single-issue groups.

    D. most organized religions.

_____ 2. An example of a single-issue group is:

    A. antiabortion groups.

    B. separatist groups.

    C. Aum Shinrikyo.

    D. the KKK.

_____ 3. When were chemical agents first introduced?

    A. Spanish-American War

    B. World War I

    C. World War II

    D. Korean War

_____ 4. During _____, Hiroshima and Nagasaki were devastated when they were targeted with nuclear bombs.
   A. World War I
   B. World War II
   C. Vietnam War
   D. Korean War

_____ 5. You are called to the scene of an unexplained explosion at the local shopping mall. The reports are that there are multiple injuries. You are the first unit to arrive on the scene. Your first responsibility is to:
   A. ensure scene safety.
   B. set up the incident command system.
   C. start triage.
   D. request additional resources.

_____ 6. In the previous scenario, you have been informed that there are numerous agencies responding with many different types of apparatus. They are approaching the scene from all directions and will be arriving shortly. You need to:
   A. set up a staging area.
   B. separate the different types of apparatus.
   C. let them continue as they are.
   D. have them come in from downwind.

_____ 7. _____ agents can remain on a surface for long periods, usually longer than 24 hours.
   A. Volatile
   B. Persistent
   C. Secondary
   D. Vapor

_____ 8. _____ is a brownish/yellowish oily substance that is generally considered very persistent.
   A. Lewisite
   B. Phosgene oxime
   C. Sulfur mustard
   D. Vesicant

_____ 9. An example of a pulmonary agent is:
   A. chlorine.
   B. phosgene oxime.
   C. G agents.
   D. lewisite.

_____ 10. The most lethal of all the nerve agents is:
   A. V agent.
   B. sarin.
   C. soman.
   D. tabun.

_____ 11. What two medications do DuoDote Auto-Injector antidote kits contain?
   A. Atropine and 2-PAM chloride
   B. Atropine and epinephrine
   C. Epinephrine and 2-PAM chloride
   D. Lidocaine and atropine

_____ 12. You are dispatched to a local farm where an unconscious 41-year-old man has been discovered. The patient's airway is open, but he has been vomiting. Respirations are within normal limits, and distal pulses are present. The patient has muscle twitches and has urinated on himself. There is a funny odor that seems to be coming from the patient's clothing. You would suspect:
   A. alcohol poisoning.
   B. organophosphate poisoning.
   C. drug overdose.
   D. respiratory agent.

_____ **13.** You are dispatched to a patient who is having respiratory problems. He is awake but is working so hard to breathe that he can't answer questions. His distal pulses are present and strong. There is an odor of almonds in the air. You would suspect:

    A. cyanide.

    B. sarin.

    C. soman.

    D. tabun.

_____ **14.** The period of time between the person becoming exposed to an agent and when symptoms begin is called:

    A. contagious.

    B. incubation.

    C. communicability.

    D. remission.

_____ **15.** Which of the following is NOT an example of a viral hemorrhagic fever?

    A. Ebola

    B. Rift Valley

    C. Yellow fever

    D. Smallpox

_____ **16.** Which of the following statements regarding anthrax is FALSE?

    A. It enters the body through inhalation, cutaneous, and gastrointestinal routes.

    B. It is caused by a deadly bacterium that lies dormant in a spore.

    C. A vaccine is available to prevent anthrax infections.

    D. Pulmonary anthrax is associated with the lowest risk of death if left untreated.

_____ **17.** Bubonic plague infects the:

    A. respiratory system.

    B. circulatory system.

    C. lymphatic system.

    D. digestive system.

_____ **18.** The deadliest substances know to humans are:

    A. neurotoxins.

    B. hemotoxins.

    C. plagues.

    D. bacteria.

_____ **19.** The least toxic route for ricin is:

    A. oral.

    B. inhalation.

    C. injection.

    D. absorption.

_____ **20.** The EMS role in helping to determine a biologic event is to:

    A. administer medications.

    B. be aware of an unusual number of calls for unexplainable symptom clusters.

    C. quarantine infected individuals.

    D. set up field hospitals.

_____ **21.** The most powerful of all radiation is:

    A. alpha.

    B. neutron.

    C. beta.

    D. gamma.

_____ **22.** To protect yourself from radiation exposure, you should do all of the following EXCEPT:
    A. limit the time of exposure.
    B. increase distance between yourself and the source.
    C. use shielding.
    D. wear a mask to prevent respiratory exposure.

_____ **23.** Which organ is most susceptible to pressure changes during an explosion?
    A. Liver
    B. Lung
    C. Heart
    D. Kidney

True/False

If you believe the statement to be more true than false, write the letter "T" in the space provided. If you believe the statement to be more false than true, write the letter "F."

_____ **1.** Atlanta's Centennial Park bombing during the 1996 Summer Olympics is an example of international terrorism.

_____ **2.** WMDs are easy to obtain or create.

_____ **3.** Most acts of terrorism occur after a warning is given to the general public.

_____ **4.** Understanding and being aware of the current threat is only the beginning of responding safely.

_____ **5.** Failure to park your ambulance in a safe location can place you and your partner in danger.

_____ **6.** You should have all units responding to an explosion converge on the main entrance to the building.

_____ **7.** Vapor hazards enter the body through the pores in the skin.

_____ **8.** The primary route of exposure of vesicants is through inhalation.

_____ **9.** Phosgene and phosgene oxime are two different classes of agents.

_____ **10.** Tabun looks like baby oil.

_____ **11.** Seizures are the most common symptom of nerve agent exposure.

_____ **12.** Organophosphate is the basic ingredient in nerve agents.

_____ **13.** Cyanide binds with the body's cells, preventing oxygen from being used.

_____ **14.** When dealing with smallpox, gloves are all the standard precautions you need.

_____ **15.** Outbreaks of the viral hemorrhagic fevers are extremely rare worldwide.

_____ **16.** Pulmonary anthrax infections are associated with a 90% death rate if untreated.

_____ **17.** Pneumonic plague is deadlier than bubonic plague.

_____ **18.** Ricin is deadlier than botulinum.

_____ **19.** Ingestion of ricin causes necrosis of the lungs.

_____ **20.** Large containers called life packs are delivered during a biologic event.

_____ **21.** The dirty bomb is an ineffective WMD.

_____ **22.** Being exposed to a radiation source does not make a patient contaminated or radioactive.

_____ **23.** Neurologic injuries and head trauma are common causes of death from blast injuries.

Fill-in-the Blank

Read each item carefully and then complete the statement by filling in the missing words.

1. The bombing of the Alfred P. Murrah Federal Building in Oklahoma City is an example of _____ _____.

2. Any agent designed to bring about mass death, casualties, and/or massive damage to property and infrastructure is a(n) _____ _____ _____ _____.

3. _____ _____ is when a nation has close ties with terrorist groups.

4. Like other burns, the primary complication associated with vesicant blisters is _____ _____.

5. _____ occurs when you come into contact with a contaminated person who has not been decontaminated.

6. _____ _____ _____ is a term used to describe how the agent most effectively enters the body.

7. An agent that gives off very little or no vapor and enters the body through the skin is called a(n) _____ _____.

8. _____ _____ are among the most deadly chemicals developed.

9. _____ means that vapors are continuously released over a period of time.

10. _____ is the means by which a terrorist will spread the agent.

11. _____ is a germ that requires a living host to multiply and survive.

12. The group of viruses that cause the blood in the body to seep out from the tissues and blood vessels is called _____ _____ _____.

13. _____ is a deadly bacterium that lies dormant in a spore.

14. Buboes are formed when the _____ _____ become infected and grow.

15. The most potent neurotoxin is _____.

16. _____ _____ _____ are existing facilities that are established in a time of need for the mass distribution of antibiotics, antidotes, vaccinations, and other medical supplies.

17. Any device that is designed to disperse a radioactive device is called a(n) _____ _____ _____.

18. A(n) _____ _____ _____ results from being struck by flying debris, such as projectiles or secondary missiles, that have been set in motion by the explosion.

Crossword Puzzle

The following crossword puzzle is an activity provided to reinforce correct spelling and understanding of medical terminology associated with emergency care and the EMT. Use the clues in the column to complete the puzzle.

Across

1. An animal that spreads a disease, once infected, to another animal is known as a disease _____.

3. A highly volatile, colorless, and odorless nerve agent that turns from liquid to gas within seconds to minutes at room temperature.

5. A type of energy that is emitted from a strong radiologic source and requires lead or several inches of concrete to prevent penetration.

7. A unique additive in GD causes it to bind to the cells that it attacks faster than any other agent. This irreversible binding is called _____.

9. A substance that mutates, damages, and changes the DNA in the body's cells.

10. A clear, oily agent that has no odor and looks like baby oil.

12. A neurotoxin derived from mash that is left from the castor bean.

14. Microorganisms that reproduce by binary fission.

15. Small suitcase-sized nuclear weapons that were designed to destroy individual targets, such as important buildings, bridges, tunnels, and large ships.

16. An agent that enters the body through the respiratory tract.

17. _____ terrorism is carried out by people in a country other than their own.

Down

2. An act in which the public safety community generally has no prior knowledge of the time, location, or nature of the attack.

3. A nerve agent that has a fruity odor, as a result of the type of alcohol used in the agent.

4. Phosgene _____ is a blistering agent that has a rapid onset of symptoms and produces immediate, intense pain and discomfort on contact.

6. Name given to a bomb that is used as a radiologic dispersal device.

7. A disease caused by deadly bacteria that lies dormant in a spore.

8. Early nerve agents that were developed by German scientists in the period after World War I and into World War II.

11. A natural process in which a material that is unstable attempts to stabilize itself by changing its structure.

13. A(n) _____ hazard gives off very little or no vapors; the skin is the primary route for this type of chemical to enter the body.

14. A type of energy that is emitted from a strong radiologic source and requires a layer of clothing to stop it.

Critical Thinking

Short Answer

Complete this section with short written answers using the space provided.

1. What are the key questions you should ask yourself when dealing with WMDs?

_____

_____

_____

2. List the four classes of chemical agents.

_____

_____

_____

3. What things should you observe on every call to determine the potential for a terrorist attack?

_____

_____

_____

4. List the signs of vesicant exposure to the skin.

_____

_____

_____

5. What are some of the later signs and symptoms of chlorine inhalation?

_____

_____

_____

6. What does the mnemonic SLUDGEM stand for?

_____

_____

_____

7. What are the signs and symptoms of high doses of cyanide?

_____

_____

_____

8. List the signs and symptoms of ricin ingestion.

_____

_____

_____

9. List three places that radioactive waste may be found.

_____

_____

_____

10. What should you use to best protect yourself from the effects of radiation?

_____

_____

_____

Ambulance Calls

The following case scenarios provide an opportunity to explore the concerns associated with patient management and to enhance critical-thinking skills. Read each scenario and answer each question to the best of your ability.

1. You are dispatched to an explosion at a nearby shopping mall. No other information is available regarding the nature of the explosion, only that there are possibly upwards of five fatally wounded and 50 severely injured.

How would you best manage this situation?

_____

_____

_____

2. Your emergency system is suddenly inundated with numerous calls for people experiencing fever, chills, headache, muscle aches, nausea/vomiting, diarrhea, severe abdominal cramping, and GI bleeding. All of the patients attended a local indoor sporting event 6 hours earlier.

How would you best manage this situation?

_____

_____

_____

3. You are dispatched to treat numerous patients with known exposure to cyanide. This occurred in a neighboring jurisdiction, and they have requested your assistance. The local fire department has set up a decontamination area, and you are asked to transport patients to the nearest appropriate medical facility.

What are important considerations to note about cyanide exposure?

_____

_____

_____

Skills

Assessment Review

Answer the following questions pertaining to the assessment of the types of emergencies discussed in this chapter.

_____ 1. A patient complains of a high fever for the past few days and now has blisters on the face and extremities. This is most consistent with:

   A. viral hemorrhagic fever.

   B. bubonic plague.

   C. smallpox.

   D. anthrax.

_____ 2. A patient complains of a fever, headache, muscle pain, shortness of breath, and extreme lymph node pain and enlargement. This is most consistent with:

   A. viral hemorrhagic fever.

   B. bubonic plague.

   C. smallpox.

   D. anthrax.

_____ 3. A patient was exposed to a package containing an unknown powder. The patient now complains of 3 to 5 days of flulike symptoms, difficulty breathing, and fever. The patient is also showing signs of shock, pulmonary edema, and respiratory failure. This is most consistent with:

   A. viral hemorrhagic fever.

   B. bubonic plague.

   C. smallpox.

   D. anthrax.

_____ 4. A patient complains of a sudden onset of fever, weakness, muscle pain, headache, and sore throat. Signs of external and internal hemorrhaging are noted, along with vomiting. This is most consistent with:

   A. viral hemorrhagic fever.

   B. bubonic plague.

   C. smallpox.

   D. anthrax.

THE TEAM APPROACH TO HEALTH CARE

A Team Approach to Health Care

© Photos.com

General Knowledge

Matching

Match each of the items in the left column to the appropriate definition in the right column.

_____ 1. Dependent groups

_____ 2. Gum elastic bougie

_____ 3. Oxygenation

_____ 4. Esophageal intubation

_____ 5. Vascular access

_____ 6. Independent groups

_____ 7. Laryngoscope

_____ 8. Macrodrip set

_____ 9. Saline lock

_____ 10. Situational awareness

_____ 11. Team leader

_____ 12. King LT

_____ 13. MIH technicians

_____ 14. Endotracheal intubation

_____ 15. Group

A. Each individual is responsible for his or her own area

B. Procedure that gains access to a patient's circulatory system

C. The knowledge and understanding of one's surroundings

D. Access device used to maintain an active IV site without running fluids

E. Team member who provides role assignments, coordination, oversight, etc.

F. Tube introducer

G. Mistakenly placing the advanced airway device into the esophagus instead of the trachea

H. Each individual is told what to do

I. Instrument used to view vocal cords

J. Insertion of a tube into the trachea

K. Loading oxygen molecules onto hemoglobin molecules

L. Consists of individual health care providers working independently to help the patient

M. Delivers 10 to 15 gtt/mL

N. Supraglottic airway

O. Special team whose members have particular knowledge and skills

Multiple Choice

Read each item carefully and then select the one best response.

_____ 1. A(n) _____ consists of a group of health care providers who are assigned specific roles and are working interdependently in a coordinated manner under a designated leader.

    A. group

    B. team

    C. dependent group

    D. independent group

_____ 2. The "C" in the PACE mnemonic stands for:

    A. choose.

    B. communication.

    C. challenge.

    D. clear.

_____ 3. Hyperventilating the patient may cause gastric distention and increase the risk of _____.

    A. barotrauma.

    B. pneumothorax.

    C. aspiration.

    D. hypertension.

_____   4. The appropriate ventilation rate for an infant or child is one breath every _____ seconds.
   A. 2 to 3
   B. 3 to 5
   C. 4 to 6
   D. 5 to 8

_____   5. Good oxygenation often includes BVM ventilation and ensuring a proper seal and all of the following EXCEPT:
   A. ventilation rate.
   B. volume of ventilation.
   C. time for patient exhalation.
   D. gastric distension.

_____   6. Physical signs of poor ventilation and perfusion include pale skin and:
   A. hypertension.
   B. cyanosis.
   C. moist mucus membranes.
   D. bulging fontanelles in infants.

_____   7. The "M" in the BE MAGIC mnemonic stands for:
   A. manipulate
   B. manage
   C. member
   D. minimal

_____   8. A(n) _____ consists of individual health care providers working independently to help the patient.
   A. group
   B. team
   C. dependent group
   D. independent group

_____   9. The appropriate ventilation rate for an adult is one breath every:
   A. 4 seconds.
   B. 6 seconds.
   C. 8 seconds.
   D. 10 seconds.

_____   10. The "C" in the BE MAGIC mnemonic stands for:
   A. confirm.
   B. challenge.
   C. commercial.
   D. colorimetric.

_____   11. _____ technique refers to minimizing the amount of pathogens or "unclean" materials that you pick up or transfer through the use of routine handwashing, nonsterile protective gloves, etc.
   A. Aseptic
   B. Hygienic
   C. Clean
   D. Sterile

_____   12. When conflicts arise among health care teams you should remember all of the following EXCEPT:
   A. that the patient comes first.
   B. to separate the person from the issue.
   C. to choose your battles.
   D. it is acceptable to shout at other providers.

_____ **13.** _____ entails emergency health care providers recognizing that by working together as a unified team from first patient contact to patient discharge, it is possible to improve individual and team performance, patient and provider safety, and ultimately, patient outcome.

    A. Mobile integrated health care

    B. Standard of care

    C. Continuum of care

    D. Community paramedicine

_____ **14.** In the _____ model, health care is provided within the community rather than at a physician's office or hospital.

    A. community paramedicine

    B. continuum of care

    C. mobile integrated health care

    D. team health care

_____ **15.** Pit crew CPR consists of defining each intervention that needs to be addressed during cardiac arrest and training providers before the call to _____ any areas that are not being addressed as soon as they arrive on scene.

    A. rapidly identify

    B. prioritize

    C. take over

    D. rapidly identify, prioritize, and take over

_____ **16.** The best way for a team to be effective during an emergency call is to practice with one another and become familiar with each other's _____ and preferences.

    A. tools

    B. techniques

    C. capabilities

    D. tools, techniques, capabilities,

_____ **17.** _____ technique refers to techniques and procedures that help ensure that pathogens are not introduced anywhere in the procedure.

    A. Clean

    B. Aseptic

    C. Sterile

    D. Hygienic

_____ **18.** It is your responsibility to understand what is allowed by the _____ where you work.

    A. scope of practice

    B. standard of care

    C. local protocols

    D. scope of practice, standard of care, and local protocols

_____ **19.** All of the following verify proper ET tube placement EXCEPT:

    A. breath sounds are present.

    B. gastric sounds are present.

    C. an end-tidal CO_2 waveform is visible during ventilation.

    D. Sp_{O_2} values are stable or rising.

_____ **20.** A microdrip administration set requires _____ drops to flow 1 mL.

    A. 15

    B. 30

    C. 45

    D. 60

_____ **21.** Use _____ to ramp, position, and otherwise manipulate the patient so that the first attempted intubation will be successful.

    A. towels

    B. blankets

    C. pillows

    D. towels, blankets, or pillows

_____ **22.** In _____, each individual is told what to do, and how often to do it, by his or her supervisor or group leader.

    A. groups

    B. teams

    C. dependent groups

    D. independent groups

_____ **23.** The team is NOT forced to move backward, resulting in a loss of valuable time and effort if:

    A. incorrect information is handed off.

    B. information is miscommunicated.

    C. care is interrupted.

    D. a proper transfer of patient care occurs.

_____ **24.** The "P" in the PACE mnemonic stands for:

    A. practice.

    B. probe.

    C. prepare.

    D. provide.

_____ **25.** The best administration set to use for general use and trauma is the:

    A. macrodrip.

    B. microdrip.

    C. Volutrol.

    D. minidrip.

_____ **26.** All of the following are supraglottic airway devices EXCEPT:

    A. the King LT.

    B. the laryngeal mask airway.

    C. the i-gel airway.

    D. the endotracheal tube.

_____ **27.** The ideal position for endotracheal intubation is achieved when the patient's _____ is on the same horizontal plane as his or her sternal notch.

    A. nose

    B. ear canal

    C. chin

    D. brow line

_____ **28.** The mnemonic used to remember the typical steps of endotracheal intubation is:

    A. BE MAGIC.

    B. SAVE ME.

    C. ENDO-T.

    D. TYPICAL.

_____ **29.** Assisting with an ALS skill does NOT include:

    A. patient preparation.

    B. equipment set up.

    C. continuing care.

    D. performing skills for which you are not authorized.

_____ **30.** All of the following are special teams EXCEPT:

    A. HazMat team

    B. MIH technicians

    C. Extracurricular EMS team

    D. EMS bike team

True/False

If you believe the statement to be more true than false, write the letter "T" in the space provided. If you believe the statement to be more false than true, write the letter "F."

_____ **1.** The cuff of the ET tube must pass through the vocal cords.

_____ **2.** Team members who train and work together infrequently rarely need more explicit verbal direction to accomplish their tasks.

_____ **3.** Temporary teams are unusual in volunteer EMS systems.

_____ **4.** The ET tube can be inserted through the mouth or through the nose.

_____ **5.** EMS providers often have varying levels of certification or licensure.

_____ **6.** When using any advanced tool or technique, the focus is always on achieving a goal rather than on simply completing a procedure.

_____ **7.** If a conflict arises from the behavior of another team member and the conflict cannot be delayed or avoided, then focus on the individual rather than on the behavior itself.

_____ **8.** Presence of breath sounds or absence of gastric sounds suggests the ET tube was improperly inserted into the esophagus.

_____ **9.** When the ET tube is placed in the esophagus, ventilation results in air being pumped into the lungs.

_____ **10.** The drip chamber should be filled to the piercing spike.

_____ **11.** The first step in preparing a patient for a vascular access procedure may involve positioning the patient and other EMS equipment so that the ALS provider has enough room to make the attempt.

_____ **12.** The procedure and equipment lists are completely different for IV and IO access.

_____ **13.** To successfully stabilize and treat the patient's condition, you must carefully coordinate your efforts with the advanced tools and techniques used by ALS providers.

_____ **14.** Excellent communication skills and teamwork are essential elements of emergency medicine.

_____ **15.** Carbon dioxide leaves the alveoli and enters the blood.

Fill-in-the-Blank

Read each item carefully and then complete the statement by filling in the missing words.

1. The National Incident Management System defines a _____ as "The organizational level that divides the incident according to functional levels of operation."

2. Team members who frequently _____ and _____ together are more likely to move smoothly from one step in the procedure to the next, performing as one seamless unit.

3. The _____ _____ is achieved when the patient's ear canal is on the same horizontal plane as his or her sternal notch.

4. Do not hyperventilate the patient during the preoxygenation phase because this may cause _____ _____.

5. _____ _____ _____ is a way for team members to work together with the team leader to develop and maintain a shared understanding of the emergency situation.

6. _____ _____ is visualization of the vocal cords with a laryngoscope.

7. While each provider may still be assigned to a particular area or task, everyone in a(n) _____ _____ works together with shared responsibilities, accountability, and a common goal, as opposed to focusing on the goals of their own individual areas.

8. _____ _____ allows for continuous oxygen delivery down the airways during all phases of the intubation procedure.

9. The _____ _____ is the team member who provides role assignments, coordination, oversight, centralized decision making, and support for the team to accomplish its goals and achieve desired results.

10. _____ _____ and mobile integrated health care teams may be the best example of the team concept of continuum of care.

11. _____ _____ are a way to maintain an active IV site without having to run fluids through the vein.

12. _____ _____ is a procedure that gains access to a patient's circulatory system in order to inject or remove fluids, medicines, or blood products.

13. _____ _____ are best used for rapid fluid replacement.

14. The position of the ET tube is _____ before the tube is secured with tape or a mechanical device.

15. _____ _____ is the insertion of a tube into the trachea to maintain and protect the airway.

Crossword Puzzle

The following crossword puzzle is an activity provided to reinforce correct spelling and understanding of medical terminology associated with emergency care and the EMT. Use the clues in the column to complete the puzzle.

Across

5. National Incident Management System.
8. The hard, sharpened plastic spike on the end of the administration set designed to pierce the sterile membrane of the intravenous bag is known as a(n) _____ spike.
10. Delivers 10 to 15 gtt/mL.
12. Loading oxygen molecules onto hemoglobin molecules in the bloodstream.
13. Each individual is told what to do in _____ groups.
14. Instrument used to view vocal cords.

Down

1. Special types of intravenous apparatus, also called heparin caps and heparin locks.
2. Supraglottic airway devices include the King LT and the _____ mask airway.
3. Procedure that gains access to a patient's circulatory system is _____ access.
4. Each individual is responsible for his or her own area in _____ groups.
6. _____ technicians are a special team whose members have particular knowledge and skills.
7. _____ intubation is mistakenly placing the advanced airway device into the esophagus instead of the trachea.
9. Delivers 60 gtt/mL.
11. A collection of individual health care providers working independently to help the patient.

Critical Thinking

Short Answer

Complete this section with short written answers using the space provided.

1. List five potential complications when monitoring a patient who has been successfully intubated.

_____

_____

_____

2. List the five techniques for handling team conflicts.

_____

_____

_____

3. What are the six typical steps of endotracheal intubation that can be remembered using the **BE MAGIC** mnemonic?

_____

_____

_____

4. What possible complications should you monitor the access site and IV tubing for once vascular access is established?

_____

_____

_____

5. List the five essential elements of a group that people must share as defined by the Research Center for Group Dynamics.

_____

_____

_____

Ambulance Calls

The following case scenarios provide an opportunity to explore the concerns associated with patient management and to enhance critical-thinking skills. Read each scenario and answer each question to the best of your ability.

1. You are dispatched to assist with a patient who is experiencing chest pain and dizziness. You notice another EMT on the scene assisting with the application of the ECG. As the paramedic's attention is focused on starting an IV, you see that the EMT has forgotten to attach one of the leads. The paramedic now begins assessing the patient's cardiac rhythm, but he appears confused by what he sees.

How would you best manage this situation?

_____

_____

_____

2. You are dispatched to a pulseless, apneic 45-year-old man. After assessing the patient, your paramedic partner decides to perform endotracheal intubation. This is the first field intubation your partner has attempted. Your partner tells you that he "thinks" he passed through the cords. As you auscultate the chest, you do not hear breath sounds, but you do hear gurgling over the epigastrium.

How would you best manage this situation?

_____

_____

_____

3. You are in the patient compartment with your AEMT partner who is caring for a patient with congestive heart failure. Your partner has initiated IV therapy and is now giving a radio report to the receiving hospital. You notice the IV tubing is still running wide open and that nearly the entire liter of fluid has been administered over a few minutes. The patient states his shortness of breath is worsening.

How would you best manage this situation?

_____

_____

_____

PREPARATORY
Chapter 1: EMS Systems

General Knowledge

Matching

1. H (page 6; Course Description)
2. N (page 6; Course Description)
3. M (page 6; Course Description)
4. G (page 6; Course Description)
5. A (page 6; Course Description)
6. K (page 18; Components of the EMS System)
7. B (page 20; Components of the EMS System)
8. O (page 5; Course Description)
9. L (page 19; Components of the EMS System)
10. C (page 17; Components of the EMS System)
11. I (page 17; Components of the EMS System)
12. D (page 18; Components of the EMS System)
13. J (page 8; Licensure Requirements)
14. E (page 20; Components of the EMS System)
15. F (page 27; Roles and Responsibilities of the EMT)

Multiple Choice

1. A (page 9; Overview of the EMS System)
2. B (page 18; Components of the EMS System)
3. D (page 19; Components of the EMS System)
4. C (page 20; Components of the EMS System)
5. A (page 27; Roles and Responsibilities of the EMT)
6. C (page 18; Components of the EMS System)
7. C (page 18; Components of the EMS System)
8. D (page 6; Course Description)
9. A (page 6; Course Description)
10. B (page 13; Levels of Training)

True/False

1. F (page 6; Course Description)
2. T (page 13; Levels of Training)
3. T (page 13; Levels of Training)
4. T (page 27; Roles and Responsibilities of the EMT)
5. T (page 24; Components of the EMS System)
6. F (page 27; Roles and Responsibilities of the EMT)
7. T (page 22; Components of the EMS System)
8. F (page 19; Components of the EMS System)
9. F (page 14; Levels of Training)
10. T (page 9; Overview of the EMS System)

Fill-in-the-Blank

1. Continuous quality improvement (page 20; Components of the EMS System)
2. medical director (page 18; Components of the EMS System)
3. automated external (page 13; Levels of Training)
4. service (page 17; Components of the EMS System)
5. access point (page 16; Components of the EMS System)

Crossword Puzzle

```
¹A  L  S      ²L         ³C   ⁴S         ⁵E
E            I         E    E          M
⁶M  E  D  I  C  A  L  D  I  R  E  C  T  O  R
T            E         T    O
             N   ⁷H    I    N
      ⁸E  M  S   I     F    D
      M      U   ⁹P  R  I  M  A  R  Y
¹⁰A ¹¹E  D   R   P         C    R
      M      E  ¹²A  D  A       Y
      T          T
      ¹³P  A  R  A  M  E  D  I  C
       S          O
¹⁴Q  U  A  L  I  T  Y ¹⁵C  O  N  T  R  O  L
                  Q
      ¹⁶P  U  B  L  I  C  H  E  A  L  T  H
```

Critical Thinking

Short Answer

1. The EMT is one of the four levels of prehospital care. The EMT provides basic life support, including automated external defibrillation, use of airway adjuncts, and assisting patients with certain medications. (page 6; Course Description)

2. The Department of Transportation has developed a series of guidelines, curricula, funding sources, and assessment tools designed to develop and improve EMS in the United States. (pages 9–10; Overview of the EMS System)

3. Keep vehicles and equipment ready for an emergency.

   Ensure the safety of yourself, your partner, the patient, and bystanders.

   Emergency vehicle operation.

   Be an on-scene leader.

   Perform an evaluation of the scene.

   Call for additional resources as needed.

   Gain patient access.

   Perform a patient assessment.

   Give emergency medical care to the patient while awaiting the arrival of additional medical resources.

   Only move patients when absolutely necessary to preserve life.

   Give emotional support to the patient, the patient's family, and other responders.

   Maintain continuity of care by working with other medical professionals.

   Resolve emergency incidents.

   Uphold medical and legal standards.

   Ensure and protect patient privacy.

   Provide administrative support.

   Constantly continue your professional development.

   Cultivate and sustain community relations.

   Give back to the profession.

   (page 26; Roles and Responsibilities of the EMT)

4. Online medical direction is provided through radio or telephone connections between the EMT and the medical control facility. Off-line medical direction is provided through written protocols, training, and standing orders. (page 18; Components of the EMS System)

Ambulance Calls

1. You would decline the assistance of an ALS ambulance crew. ALS, or advanced life support, means that the crew would have a higher level of training and could perform more advanced patient care procedures than you or your partner. Because there were no injuries resulting from this motor vehicle collision, there would be no reason to summon advanced care.

2. Because none of the EMT-level airway skills were successful, it is critical to request or rendezvous with a provider capable of using advanced airway techniques. You would contact dispatch and arrange to have an ALS crew either meet you at the patient's location or load the patient and meet up with an ALS crew while en route to the hospital.

Chapter 2: Workforce Safety and Wellness

General Knowledge

Matching

1. D (page 40; Infectious and Communicable Diseases)
2. A (page 43; Risk Reduction and Prevention for Infectious and Communicable Diseases)
3. C (page 42; Risk Reduction and Prevention for Infectious and Communicable Diseases)
4. F (page 69; Stress Management on the Job)
5. B (page 68; Stress Management on the Job)
6. E (page 40; Infectious and Communicable Diseases)
7. M (page 41; Infectious and Communicable Diseases)
8. G (page 52; Risk Reduction and Prevention for Infectious and Communicable Diseases)
9. L (page 54; Scene Safety)
10. O (page 73; Stress Management on the Job)
11. J (page 40; Infectious and Communicable Diseases)
12. N (page 42; Risk Reduction and Prevention for Infectious and Communicable Diseases)
13. H (page 75; Workplace Issues)
14. K (page 40; Infectious and Communicable Diseases)
15. I (page 41; Infectious and Communicable Diseases)

Multiple Choice

1. C (page 57; Scene Safety)
2. C (page 66; Death and Dying)
3. A (page 66; Death and Dying)
4. D (page 61; Protective Clothing: Preventing Injury)
5. B (page 38; General Health and Wellness)
6. A (page 67; Death and Dying)
7. B (page 52; Infectious and Communicable Diseases)
8. C (page 62; Caring for Critically Ill and Injured Patients)
9. B (page 62; Caring for Critically Ill and Injured Patients)
10. D (page 46; Infectious and Communicable Diseases)
11. B (page 76; Workplace Issues)
12. A (page 35; General Health and Wellness)
13. B (page 65; Caring for Critically Ill and Injured Patients)
14. C (page 41; Infectious and Communicable Diseases)
15. A (page 45; Infectious and Communicable Diseases)
16. D (page 56; Scene Safety)
17. B (page 68; Stress Management on the Job)
18. A (page 69; Stress Management on the Job)
19. A (page 36; General Health and Wellness)
20. B (page 37; General Health and Wellness)
21. A (page 70; Stress Management on the Job)
22. B (page 75; Workplace Issues)
23. A (page 52; Infectious and Communicable Diseases)
24. C (page 54; Scene Safety)
25. B (page 63; Caring for Critically Ill and Injured Patients)

True/False

1. F (page 47; Infectious and Communicable Diseases)
2. F (page 43; Infectious and Communicable Diseases)
3. T (page 66; Death and Dying)
4. F (page 41; Infectious and Communicable Diseases)
5. F (page 67; Stress Management on the Job)
6. T (pages 36–38; General Health and Wellness)
7. F (page 52; Infectious and Communicable Diseases)
8. T (page 60; Protective Clothing: Preventing Injury)
9. T (page 72; Stress Management on the Job)
10. F (page 74; Workplace Issues)

Fill-in-the-Blank

1. Stress (page 68; Stress Management on the Job)
2. Foodborne transmission (page 42; Infectious and Communicable Diseases)
3. infectious disease (page 40; Infectious and Communicable Diseases)

4. hazardous (page 54; Scene Safety)

5. handwashing (page 43; Infectious and Communicable Diseases)

6. Cover (page 73; Stress Management on the Job)

7. death, difficult (page 66; Death and Dying)

8. stress management (page 36; General Health and Wellness)

9. sleep (page 38; General Health and Wellness)

10. Eye protection (page 45; Infectious and Communicable Diseases)

Crossword Puzzle

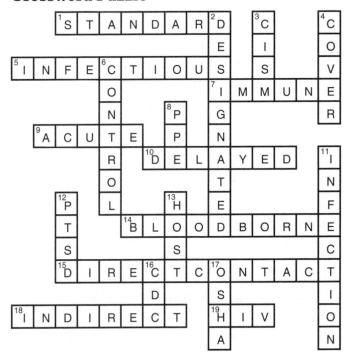

Critical Thinking

Multiple Choice

1. C (pages 63–64; Caring for Critically Ill and Injured Patients)

2. D (pages 35–40; General Health and Wellness)

3. B (page 69; Stress Management on the Job)

4. D (page 70; Stress Management on the Job)

5. A (page 48; Infectious and Communicable Diseases)

Short Answer

1. Standard precautions are protective measures based on the assumption that every person is potentially infected or can spread an organism that could be transmitted in the health care setting. Therefore, you must apply infection-control procedures to reduce infection in patients and health care personnel. (page 42; Infectious and Communicable Diseases)

2. 1. Denial

    2. Anger/hostility

    3. Bargaining

    4. Depression

    5. Acceptance (page 66; Death and Dying)

3. Irritability toward coworkers, family, and friends

Inability to concentrate

Difficulty sleeping, increased sleeping, or nightmares

Feelings of sadness, anxiety, or guilt

Loss of appetite (gastrointestinal disturbances)

Loss of interest in sexual activities

Isolation

Loss of interest in work

Increased use of alcohol

Recreational drug use

Physical symptoms such as chronic pain (headache, backache)

Feelings of hopelessness (page 70; Stress Management on the Job)

4. Minimize or eliminate stressors.

Change partners to avoid a negative or hostile personality.

Change work hours.

Change the work environment.

Cut back on overtime.

Change your attitude about the stressor.

Talk about your feelings with people you trust.

Seek professional counseling if needed.

Do not obsess over frustrating situations; focus on delivering high-quality care.

Try to adopt a more relaxed, philosophical outlook.

Expand your social support system apart from your coworkers.

Sustain friends and interests outside emergency services.

Minimize the physical response to stress by employing various techniques. (page 36; General Health and Wellness)

5. **1.** Hepatitis B

  2. Influenza (yearly)

  3. Measles, mumps, and rubella (MMR)

  4. Varicella (chickenpox) vaccine or having had chickenpox

  5. Tetanus, diphtheria, pertussis (Tdap) (every 10 years) (page 52; Infectious and Communicable Diseases)

6. **1.** Thin inner layer

  2. Thermal middle layer

  3. Outer layer (page 59; Protective Clothing: Preventing Injury)

7. **1.** Emotional upset

  2. Sweaty and cool skin (diaphoretic)

  3. Rapid breathing (hyperventilating)

  4. Fast pulse (tachycardia)

  5. Restlessness

  6. Tension

  7. Fear

  8. Shakiness (tremulous) (page 62; Caring for Critically Ill and Injured Patients)

8. Smoke

Oxygen deficiency

High ambient temperatures

Toxic gases

Building collapse

Equipment

Explosions (page 56; Scene Safety)

Ambulance Calls

1. Continue to treat the patient appropriately and transport. Allow the cut to bleed, as long as the bleeding is minimal. This will help to wash/clean it out. Clean the wound with an alcohol gel, if available. Once patient care has been transferred at the receiving facility, immediately wash thoroughly with soap and water and report to your supervisor. Follow up with prompt medical attention.

2. As always, you should wear exam gloves and consider eye protection. Because this call is for a respiratory issue and the possibility of tuberculosis is high, you should also don a HEPA respirator and place a surgical mask on the patient. Because the patient is complaining of respiratory distress, a nonrebreathing mask attached to oxygen will suffice as well. It is also very important that you pass the information about potential infection to the receiving facility staff in both your patient report while en route and again when you hand off care in the emergency department.

Fill-in-the-Patient Care Report

EMS Patient Care Report (PCR)				
Date: Today's date	**Incident No.:** 2011–1234	**Nature of Call:** Overdose		**Location:** 7979 Fisher Blvd.
Dispatched: 0912	**En Route:** 0912	**At Scene:** 0926	**Transport:** 0947	**At Hospital:** 0952	**In Service:** 1005

Patient Information	
Age: 16 years	**Allergies:** None
Sex: Female	**Medications:** None
Weight (in kg [lb]): 48 kg (106 lb)	**Past Medical History:** Attempted suicide 2 years ago—aspirin overdose
	Chief Complaint: Unresponsive/overdose

Vital Signs				
Time: 0934	**BP:** 116/76	**Pulse:** 46	**Respirations:** 8 GTV	**Spo$_2$:** 96%
Time: 0947	**BP:** 114/74	**Pulse:** 38	**Respirations:** 8 GTV	**Spo$_2$:** 95%

EMS Treatment

(circle all that apply)				
Oxygen @ _15_ L/min via (circle one): NC (NRM) BVM	**Assisted Ventilation**	**Airway Adjunct**		**CPR**
Defibrillation	**Bleeding Control**	**Bandaging**	**Splinting**	**Other:**

Narrative

Dispatched for an overdose. Arrived on scene to find the patient, a 16-year-old girl, unresponsive on the bathroom floor with a hypodermic needle next to her. Although unresponsive, she had a patent airway and was breathing adequately. She was moved out to the living room to allow better access. The patient's mother advised that the patient had attempted suicide 2 years ago with an aspirin overdose and had recently been struggling with heroin use. According to law enforcement on scene, the patient had apparently been arguing with her mother prior to today's events. Vital signs indicated that she was initially stable, but I chose to start her on high-flow oxygen therapy due to the potential for respiratory compromise. The patient was moved to the gurney and placed in the ambulance. I immediately obtained a second set of vitals, which showed a slight decrease in cardiac activity and oxygen saturation, and I continued to monitor her while en route to the receiving hospital without incident. While en route, I called the report in to the hospital and upon turning care of the patient over to the emergency department, I gave a verbal report to the charge nurse.**End of Report**

Skills

Skill Drills

Skill Drill 2-1: Proper Glove Removal Technique

1. Partially remove the first glove by pinching at the **wrist**. Be careful to touch only the **outside** of the glove.

2. Remove the **second** glove by pinching the **exterior** with your partially gloved hand.

3. Pull the second glove inside out toward the **fingertips**.

4. Grasp both gloves with your **free** hand, touching only the clean, **interior** surfaces. (page 45; Infectious and Communicable Diseases)

PREPARATORY

Chapter 3: Medical, Legal, and Ethical Issues

General Knowledge

Matching

1. H (page 99; Assault and Battery and Kidnapping)
2. I (page 98; Abandonment)
3. G (page 90; Advance Directives)
4. E (page 99; Assault and Battery and Kidnapping)
5. L (page 97; Standards of Care)
6. A (page 90; Advance Directives)
7. D (page 85; Consent)
8. F (page 97; Duty to Act)
9. O (page 102; Ethical Responsibilities)
10. B (page 86; Consent)
11. C (page 88; Consent)
12. M (page 86; Consent)
13. N (page 86; Consent)
14. J (page 98; Negligence)
15. K (page 95; Standards of Care)

Multiple Choice

1. C (page 94; Scope of Practice)
2. A (page 95; Standards of Care)
3. D (page 97; Standards of Care)
4. D (page 98; Negligence)
5. C (pages 98–99; Abandonment)
6. B (page 100; Good Samaritan Laws and Immunity)
7. D (page 90; Confidentiality)
8. D (page 101; Records and Reports)
9. B (page 97; Duty to Act)
10. C (pages 92–93; Physical Signs of Death)
11. A (page 93; Physical Signs of Death)
12. D (pages 93–94; Physical Signs of Death)
13. B (page 90; Confidentiality)

True/False

1. T (page 98; Negligence)
2. F (page 86; Consent)
3. T (page 86; Consent)
4. T (page 88; Consent)
5. F (page 90; Advance Directives)
6. T (page 91; Advance Directives)
7. T (page 97; Standards of Care)
8. F (page 101; Special Mandatory Reporting Requirements)
9. T (page 102; Special Mandatory Reporting Requirements)
10. F (page 105; The EMT in Court)

Fill-in-the-Blank

1. scope of practice (page 94; Scope of Practice)
2. standard of care (page 95; Standards of Care)
3. duty to act (page 97; Duty to Act)
4. negligence (page 98; Negligence)
5. termination (page 98; Negligence)
6. Expressed, implied (page 86; Consent)
7. assault, battery (page 99; Assault and Battery and Kidnapping)
8. advance directive, DNR order (page 90; Advance Directives)
9. refuse treatment (page 88; The Right to Refuse Treatment)
10. special reporting (page 101; Special Mandatory Reporting Requirements)

Crossword Puzzle

```
¹M              ²S
O          ³P R E C E D E N ⁴C E
R              C              O
⁵A S ⁶S A U ⁷L T   O          N
L   L     I   ⁸E T H I C S    S
I   A     B   O              E
T   N     E   F   ⁹B          N
Y   D     L   ¹⁰P H I          T
    E         R   O   ¹¹D
  ¹²P R O X I M I A T E   N
              C   ¹³T O R T
              T   H
          ¹⁴D E P O S I T I O N S
              C   C
          ¹⁵E X P R E S S E D
```

Critical Thinking

Multiple Choice

1. B (page 86; Consent)
2. A (page 86; Consent)
3. A (page 86; Consent)
4. C (page 87; Consent)
5. B (pages 88–89; The Right to Refuse Treatment)
6. D (page 98; Negligence)

Short Answer

1. Member of the armed services, married, a parent, or pregnant (page 87; Consent)
2. You must continue to care for the patient until the patient is transferred to another medical professional of equal or higher skill level or another medical facility. (page 98; Abandonment)
3.
   1. Obtain the refusing party's signature on an official medical release form that acknowledges refusal.
   2. Obtain a signature from a witness of the refusal.
   3. Keep the refusal form with the incident report.
   4. Note the refusal on the incident report.
   5. Keep a department copy of the records for future reference. (page 89; The Right to Refuse Treatment)
4.
   1. If it wasn't documented, it did not happen.
   2. Incomplete or disorderly records equate to incomplete or inexpert medical care. (page 101; Records and Reports)
5.
   1. Duty
   2. Breach of duty
   3. Damages
   4. Causation (page 98; Negligence)

Ambulance Calls

1. This patient needs to be evaluated at the hospital. Her parents will likely feel a right to be informed of their child's medical conditions and medical care. Laws regarding reproductive rights of minors vary from state to state. Some states allow minors to make decisions regarding birth control, prenatal care, or pregnancy termination without consenting parents, whereas others do not. You must know your local laws. You will have to provide information regarding the pregnancy to other health care providers directly involved in her care, and you should explain that fact and the necessity of such to the patient. Be tactful. Don't unnecessarily break your patient's trust by immediately sharing this knowledge with her parents. Document carefully and consult medical control.

2. The duty to act in this situation may vary from state to state; however, you did the right thing by stopping to help the child from an ethical perspective. Once you have initiated care, you must ensure that the child's parent(s) or legal guardian is notified. Although the grandfather is home, you now have another dilemma. The condition of the house/ capability of the grandfather to care for the child while the mother is away is such that the question of neglect arises. You should speak with the grandfather and attempt to contact the mother of the child. If you believe that neglect or abuse of a child is occurring, you are most likely legally required to intervene (most states require this by law). You should notify law enforcement and/or child protective serves in accordance with your local statues.

3. Assess the patient's mental status. If he is intoxicated or has an altered mental status, he is treated under implied consent. If he is alert and oriented, you may attempt to talk him into being treated by explaining what you feel is necessary and what may happen if he does not receive care. If he has an altered mental status, orders from medical control may be obtained to restrain the patient with the help of law enforcement and to transport him to the hospital.

Fill-in-the-Patient Care Report

EMS Patient Care Report (PCR)			
Date: Today's date	**Incident No.:** 2010-555	**Nature of Call:** MCA	**Location:** Grand and Hopper

Dispatched: 2115	**En Route:** 2116	**At Scene:** 2122	**Transport:** 2132	**At Hospital:** 2138	**In Service:** 2152

Patient Information	
Age: 24 years	**Allergies:** N/A
Sex: Female	**Medications:** N/A
Weight (in kg [lb]): 52 kg (114 lb)	**Past Medical History:** N/A
	Chief Complaint: N/A

Vital Signs				
Time: 2127	**BP:** 90/54	**Pulse:** 100 weak/irregular	**Respirations:** 12	**Spo₂:** 94%
Time: N/A	**BP:** N/A	**Pulse:** N/A	**Respirations:** N/A	**Spo₂:** N/A
Time: N/A	**BP:** N/A	**Pulse:** N/A	**Respirations:** N/A	**Spo₂:** N/A

EMS Treatment
(circle all that apply)

Oxygen @ _15_ L/min via (circle one): NC NRM (BVM)	(Assisted Ventilation)	(Airway Adjunct)	CPR
Defibrillation	(Bleeding Control) (Bandaging)	(Splinting)	Other:

Narrative

9-1-1 dispatch for a motorcycle versus automobile. On arrival, found the driver of the automobile unhurt and the motorcycle operator unresponsive in the street. She was bleeding heavily from a forehead laceration and did not have a patent airway—snoring respirations observed. Appropriate c-spine precautions taken, OPA inserted, and provided assisted ventilations using BVM with 15 L/min oxygen. Fire crew arrived on scene and assisted in bleeding control, obtaining vitals, and immobilizing patient to long backboard. Once adequately immobilized, patient was moved to the stretcher and loaded into the ambulance for transport to the University Trauma Center. Reassessment not completed while en route because of continuation of assisted ventilations. Delivered patient to trauma center and provided verbal report and copy of this written report to the charge nurse.
End of Report

PREPARATORY

Chapter 4: Communications and Documentation

General Knowledge

Matching

1. M (page 127; Written Communications and Documentation)
2. G (page 127; Written Communications and Documentation)
3. J (page 127; Written Communications and Documentation)
4. K (page 128; Written Communications and Documentation)
5. H (page 128; Written Communications and Documentation)
6. L (page 127; Written Communications and Documentation)
7. I (page 127; Written Communications and Documentation)
8. C (page 128; Written Communications and Documentation)
9. A (page 127; Written Communications and Documentation)
10. F (page 129; Written Communications and Documentation)
11. E (page 129; Written Communications and Documentation)
12. D (page 127; Written Communications and Documentation)
13. B (page 119; Therapeutic Communication)

Multiple Choice

1. B (pages 116–117; Therapeutic Communication)
2. A (page 136; Communications Systems and Equipment)
3. D (page 122; Therapeutic Communication)
4. A (page 124; Therapeutic Communication)
5. B (page 137; Communications Systems and Equipment)
6. C (page 124; Therapeutic Communication)
7. C (page 138; Communications Systems and Equipment)
8. D (pages 139–140; Radio Communications)
9. B (page 141; Radio Communications)
10. B (page 144; Radio Communications)
11. A (pages 142–143; Radio Communications)
12. B (page 144; Radio Communications)
13. C (page 123; Therapeutic Communication)
14. D (page 117; Therapeutic Communication)
15. A (page 143; Radio Communications)
16. A (page 144; Radio Communications)
17. A (page 116; Therapeutic Communication)
18. D (page 115; Therapeutic Communication)
19. B (page 128; Written Communications and Documentation)
20. C (page 131; Written Communications and Documentation)
21. C (page 123; Therapeutic Communication)
22. D (page 135; Written Communications and Documentation)

True/False

1. T (page 136; Communications Systems and Equipment)
2. T (page 116; Therapeutic Communication)
3. F (page 114; Therapeutic Communication)
4. F (page 124; Therapeutic Communication)
5. F (page 132; Written Communications and Documentation)
6. T (page 131; Written Communications and Documentation)
7. F (page 136; Communications Systems and Equipment)
8. T (page 122; Therapeutic Communication)
9. T (page 141; Radio Communications)
10. T (page 127; Written Communications and Documentation)

Fill-in-the-Blank

1. narrative (page 128; Written Communications and Documentation)
2. transmitter, receiver (page 136; Communications Systems and Equipment)
3. dedicated line (page 136; Communications Systems and Equipment)
4. Noise (page 116; Therapeutic Communication)
5. litigation (page 132; Written Communications and Documentation)
6. Pagers (page 140; Radio Communications)
7. importance (page 140; Radio Communications)
8. medical control (page 142; Radio Communications)
9. channel (page 136; Communications Systems and Equipment)
10. Closed-ended questions (page 116; Therapeutic Communication)
11. repeat (page 145; Radio Communications)
12. standing orders (page 145; Radio Communications)
13. tone, volume (page 114; Therapeutic Communication)
14. honest (page 122; Therapeutic Communication)
15. interpreter (page 124; Therapeutic Communication)
16. standard procedure (page 127; Written Communications and Documentation)
17. Competent (page 132; Written Communications and Documentation)

Crossword Puzzle

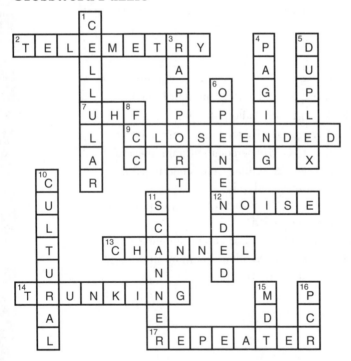

Critical Thinking

Multiple Choice

1. C (page 132; Written Communications and Documentation)
2. D (page 128; Written Communications and Documentation)
3. A (page 131; Written Communications and Documentation)
4. D (page 131; Written Communications and Documentation)
5. C (page 135; Written Communications and Documentation)

Short Answer

1.
   1. Allocating specific radio frequencies for use by EMS providers
   2. Licensing base stations and assigning appropriate radio call signs for those stations
   3. Establishing licensing standards and operating specifications for radio equipment used by EMS providers
   4. Establishing limitations for transmitter power output
   5. Monitoring radio operations (pages 139–140; Radio Communications)
2.
   1. Make and keep eye contact with your patient at all times.
   2. Provide your name and use the patient's proper name.
   3. Tell the patient the truth.
   4. Use language that the patient can understand.
   5. Be careful what you say about the patient to others.
   6. Be aware of your body language.
   7. Always speak slowly, clearly, and distinctly.
   8. If the patient is hard of hearing, face the person so that he or she can read your lips.
   9. Allow time for the patient to answer or respond to your questions.
   10. Act and speak in a calm, confident manner while caring for the patient. (pages 119–120; Therapeutic Communication)
3.
   1. Continuity of care
   2. Legal documentation
   3. Education
   4. Administrative information
   5. Essential research record
   6. Evaluation and continuous quality improvement (pages 126–127; Written Communications and Documentation)
4.
   1. Traditional, written form with check boxes and a narrative section
   2. Computerized, using electronic clipboard or similar device (pages 127–128; Written Communications and Documentation)

Ambulance Calls

1. Dispatch the closest ambulance for an emergency response. Call for assistance from the fire department and local law enforcement. Try to calm down the caller to obtain additional information. If the caller is still of no help, ask her to get someone else to the phone. Relay any additional information to the responding units.

2. You should determine whether anyone on scene can translate for you. (Children will often speak both English and Spanish.) If no one on scene can translate, you should contact a department translator. Every department should have a group of translators for different languages common to your community or an electronic translation device. (Ideally, you should speak languages commonly heard in your area.) If neither of these options are available, you should attempt as much nonverbal communication as possible, obtain baseline vital signs, and perform a primary assessment to determine the nature of the problem. If the patient appears to refuse your help, you are in a tough situation. You cannot leave without knowing what the medical emergency is (if any), and you cannot obtain an informed refusal if clear communication does not occur. Consider asking for law enforcement assistance as they have access to translation services as well.

3. Attempt to locate any identification that he may have on his person. If this is not possible or you cannot locate any forms of identification, you should notify law enforcement officers. The child should undergo a medical examination to ensure that no injuries or other medical emergencies are present. Take care to communicate in a nonintimidating manner (taking care in level/tone of voice and posture) and attempt to establish trust with the patient.

Fill-in-the-Patient Care Report

EMS Patient Care Report (PCR)			
Date: Today's date	**Incident No.:** 2011–8898	**Nature of Call:** Dirt bike crash/trauma	**Location:** 18553 Old Redwood Highway
Dispatched: 1721	**En Route:** 1721	**At Scene:** 1728	**Transport:** 1735	**At Hospital:** 1741	**In Service:** 1800

Patient Information	
Age: 19 years	**Allergies:** Unknown
Sex: Male	**Medications:** Unknown
Weight (in kg [lb]): 73 kg (161 lb)	**Past Medical History:** Unknown
	Chief Complaint: Partial amputation of left foot

Vital Signs				
Time: 1736	**BP:** 104/66	**Pulse:** 102	**Respirations:** 18 Unlabored	**Spo$_2$:** 97%
Time: 1741	**BP:** 110/72	**Pulse:** 90	**Respirations:** 14 Unlabored	**Spo$_2$:** 99%

EMS Treatment
(circle all that apply)

Oxygen @ _15_ L/min via (circle one): NC (NRM) BVM	Assisted Ventilation	Airway Adjunct	CPR
Defibrillation	(Bleeding Control)	(Bandaging)	(Splinting)	(Other: Shock Treatment)

Narrative

Responded to 9-1-1 dispatch to a motorcross park for a dirt bike crash. Arrived to find the patient, a 19-year-old man, lying supine on the ground and in obvious pain from near amputation of his left foot below the ankle. Patient had patent airway and adequate breathing, and I controlled the bleeding at the injury site with direct pressure. Patient was placed on high-flow oxygen therapy, secured to the backboard utilizing all appropriate spinal precautions, and loaded into ambulance. First set of vitals indicated possible onset of hypoperfusion, so I covered the patient with a blanket. Called report to the receiving facility and obtained a second set of vitals, which showed improvement when compared to the first. Patient was transported without incident and appropriately turned over to the trauma center staff after I provided a complete verbal report.**End of Report**

PREPARATORY

Chapter 5: Medical Terminology

General Knowledge

Matching

1. D (page 153; Anatomy of a Medical Term)
2. F (page 153; Anatomy of a Medical Term)
3. J (page 158; Common Direction, Movement, and Position Terms)
4. G (page 159; Common Direction, Movement, and Position Terms)
5. C (page 159; Common Direction, Movement, and Position Terms)
6. A (page 160; Common Direction, Movement, and Position Terms)
7. B (page 160; Common Direction, Movement, and Position Terms)
8. I (page 161; Common Direction, Movement, and Position Terms)
9. E (page 160; Common Direction, Movement, and Position Terms)
10. H (pages 159–160; Common Direction, Movement, and Position Terms)

11. C (page 154; Anatomy of a Medical Term)
12. G (page 154; Anatomy of a Medical Term)
13. A (page 156; Special Word Parts)
14. E (page 156; Special Word Parts)
15. F (page 154; Anatomy of a Medical Term)
16. D (page 154; Anatomy of a Medical Term)
17. B (page 154; Anatomy of a Medical Term)
18. F (page 155; Anatomy of a Medical Term)
19. C (page 155; Anatomy of a Medical Term)
20. B (page 155; Anatomy of a Medical Term)
21. E (page 155; Anatomy of a Medical Term)
22. G (page 155; Anatomy of a Medical Term)
23. A (page 155; Anatomy of a Medical Term)
24. D (page 155; Anatomy of a Medical Term)

Multiple Choice

1. B (page 160; Common Direction, Movement, and Position Terms)
2. D (pages 154, 164, 167; Master Tables)
3. C (page 168; Master Tables)
4. B (pages 165, 167; Master Tables)
5. A (page 161; Common Direction, Movement, and Position Terms)

6. C (pages 164, 167; Master Tables)
7. B (page 168; Master Tables)
8. D (page 170; Master Tables)
9. A (page 171; Master Tables)
10. C (pages 165, 167; Master Tables)

True/False

1. T (page 156; Word Building Rules)
2. F (page 159; Common Direction, Movement, and Position Terms)
3. T (page 168; Master Tables)
4. T (page 155; Anatomy of a Medical Term)
5. F (page 153; Anatomy of a Medical Term)

6. T (page 156; Word Building Rules)
7. F (page 156; Plural Endings)
8. F (page 159; Common Direction, Movement, and Position Terms)
9. T (page 169; Master Tables)
10. F (page 167; Master Tables)

Fill-in-the-Blank

1. Superficial (page 159; Common Direction, Movement, and Position Terms)
2. superior (page 158; Common Direction, Movement, and Position Terms)
3. plantar (page 160; Common Direction, Movement, and Position Terms)
4. quadrants (page 160; Common Direction, Movement, and Position Terms)
5. Adduction (page 160; Common Direction, Movement, and Position Terms)
6. medial (page 159; Common Direction, Movement, and Position Terms)
7. Fowler position (page 161; Common Direction, Movement, and Position Terms)
8. suffix (page 162; Breaking Terms Apart)
9. prone (page 161; Common Direction, Movement, and Position Terms)
10. Abbreviations (page 163; Abbreviations, Acronyms, and Symbols)

Labeling

1. Directional Terms (page 159; Common Direction, Movement, and Position Terms)

   A. Distal
   B. Proximal
   C. Anterior (front)
   D. Posterior (rear)
   E. Patient's right
   F. Midline
   G. Medial
   H. Lateral
   I. Patient's left
   J. Superior (nearer the head)
   K. Inferior (away from the head)

2. Movement Terms (page 160; Common Direction, Movement, and Position Terms)

   A. Flexion
   B. Extension
   C. Abduction
   D. Adduction

Critical Thinking

Multiple Choice

1. C (page 162; Breaking Terms Apart)
2. B (page 158; Special Word Parts)
3. D (pages 165, 167; Master Tables)
4. C (page 169; Master Tables)

Short Answer

1. Flexion: bending of a joint
   Extension: straightening of a joint
   Adduction: motion toward the midline
   Abduction: motion away from the midline (page 160; Common Direction, Movement, and Position Terms)

2. 1. Singular words that end in "a" change to "ae" when plural.
   2. Singular words that end in "is" change to "es" when plural.
   3. Singular words that end in "ex" or "ix" change to "ices."
   4. Singular words that end in "on" or "um" change to "a."
   5. Singular words that end in "us" change to "i." (page 156; Plural Endings)

3. 1. Word root
   2. Prefix
   3. Suffix
   4. Combining vowels (page 153; Anatomy of a Medical Term)

4. Cardi/o

   Gastr/o

   Hepat/o

   Arthr/o

   Oste/o

   Pulmon/o (page 155; Anatomy of a Medical Term)

Fill-in-the-Patient Care Report

EMS Patient Care Report (PCR)				
Date: Today's date	**Incident No.:** 2016-153	**Nature of Call:** MCA		**Location:** 152 East Bramble St.

Dispatched: 1200	**En Route:** 1202	**At Scene:** 1210	**Transport:** 1220	**At Hospital:** 1223	**In Service:** 1235

Patient Information		
Age: 53 years		**Allergies:** None known
Sex: Male		**Medications:** Metformin, Lisinopril, Omeprazole
Weight (in kg [lb]):		**Past Medical History:** HTN, NIDDM, GERD, appendectomy
		Chief Complaint: Chest pain

Vital Signs				
Time: 1215	**BP:** 148/92	**Pulse:** 82/regular	**Respirations:** 16	**Spo$_2$:** 98% on O$_2$

EMS Treatment (circle all that apply)				
Oxygen @ _15_ L/min via (circle one): NC (NRM) BVM		Assisted Ventilation	Airway Adjunct	CPR
Defibrillation	Bleeding Control	Bandaging	Splinting	Other:

Narrative

Dispatched to a residential home for a 53-year-old male with chest pain. Arrived on scene and was greeted by wife who informed the crew the patient experienced chest pain while mowing the lawn. On entering the residence, the patient was located in the living room, sitting on the couch. He appeared in respiratory distress. He complained of chest pain and shortness of breath. Patient was awake and able to communicate with crew. He was placed on high-flow oxygen via nonrebreathing mask while the initial assessment was performed. ALS was summoned due to patient experiencing chest pain. Vital signs were obtained and a secondary focused exam was performed. Lungs were clear and equal bilaterally. Abdomen was non-tender in all four quadrants. Pulses were equal bilaterally in all extremities. The patient was secured to the litter in a semi-Fowler's position. He was transported to the unit and secured. The patient was transported to the hospital located 2 minutes from his home. ALS was canceled due to the short ETA to the hospital. On arrival at the hospital, the patient stated he was beginning to feel better. Care was transferred to the ED staff. Verbal report was given to the nursing staff. Unit restocked and back in service without incident.**End of Report**

Chapter 6: The Human Body

General Knowledge

Matching

1. G (page 201; The Circulatory System: Anatomy)
2. E (page 179; Topographic Anatomy)
3. J (page 180; Topographic Anatomy)
4. O (page 183; The Skeletal System: Anatomy)
5. C (page 195; The Respiratory System: Physiology)
6. M (page 193; The Respiratory System: Physiology)
7. A (page 212; The Integumentary System (Skin): Anatomy)
8. F (page 220; The Urinary System: Anatomy and Physiology)
9. D (page 224; Pathophysiology)
10. B (page 180; The Skeletal System: Anatomy)
11. I (page 182; The Skeletal System: Anatomy)
12. N (page 192; The Respiratory System: Physiology)
13. K (page 195; The Respiratory System: Physiology)
14. H (page 195; The Respiratory System: Physiology)
15. L (page 198; The Circulatory System: Anatomy)
16. B (page 186; The Skeletal System: Anatomy)
17. B (page 186; The Skeletal System: Anatomy)
18. A (page 184; The Skeletal System: Anatomy)
19. B (page 185; The Skeletal System: Anatomy)
20. B (page 186; The Skeletal System: Anatomy)

21. A (page 184; The Skeletal System: Anatomy)
22. A (page 184; The Skeletal System: Anatomy)
23. A (page 186; The Musculoskeletal System: Anatomy)
24. B (page 186; The Musculoskeletal System: Anatomy)
25. A (page 186; The Musculoskeletal System: Anatomy)
26. A (page 186; The Musculoskeletal System: Anatomy)
27. C (page 186; The Musculoskeletal System: Anatomy)
28. C (page 197; The Circulatory System: Anatomy)
29. A (page 186; The Musculoskeletal System: Anatomy)
30. C (page 186; The Musculoskeletal System: Anatomy)
31. A (page 210; The Nervous System: Anatomy and Physiology)
32. C (page 208; The Nervous System: Anatomy and Physiology)
33. E (page 212; The Nervous System: Anatomy and Physiology)
34. B (page 212; The Nervous System: Anatomy and Physiology)
35. F (page 208; The Nervous System: Anatomy and Physiology)
36. D (page 208; The Nervous System: Anatomy and Physiology)

Multiple Choice

1. C (page 225; Pathophysiology)
2. B (page 221; The Genital System: Anatomy and Physiology)
3. B (page 189; The Respiratory System: Anatomy)
4. B (page 218; The Endocrine System: Anatomy and Physiology)

5. D (page 197; The Circulatory System: Anatomy)
6. D (page 217; The Digestive System: Anatomy)
7. B (page 220; The Urinary System: Anatomy and Physiology)
8. C (page 216; The Digestive System: Anatomy)

True/False

1. F (page 199; The Circulatory System: Anatomy)
2. F (page 183; The Skeletal System: Anatomy)
3. T (pages 184, 186; The Skeletal System: Anatomy)
4. F (page 193; The Circulatory System: Anatomy)

5. F (page 182; The Skeletal System: Anatomy)
6. F (page 192; The Respiratory System: Physiology)
7. F (page 215; The Digestive System: Anatomy)

Fill-in-the-Blank

1. seven (page 181; The Skeletal System: Anatomy)
2. mandible (page 181; The Skeletal System: Anatomy)
3. five (page 190; The Respiratory System: Anatomy)
4. twelve (page 182; The Skeletal System: Anatomy)
5. 33 (page 181; The Skeletal System: Anatomy)
6. talus, fibula, tibia (page 186; The Skeletal System: Anatomy)
7. frontal, parietal, temporal, occipital (page 208; The Nervous System: Anatomy and Physiology)
8. interstitial (page 205; The Circulatory System: Physiology)
9. ventilation (page 192; The Respiratory System: Physiology)
10. V/Q (page 225; Pathophysiology)

Labeling

1. The Skull (page 181; The Skeletal System: Anatomy)
   A. Parietal bone
   B. Frontal bone
   C. Maxilla
   D. Temporal bone
   E. Nasal bones
   F. Zygomatic bone
   G. Maxillae
   H. Foramen magnum
   I. Occipital bone
   J. Mandible

2. The Spinal Column (page 182; The Skeletal System: Anatomy)
   A. Cerebrum
   B. Foramen magnum
   C. Brain stem
   D. Cerebellum
   E. Cervical nerves
   F. Cervical vertebrae
   G. Thoracic nerves
   H. Thoracic vertebrae
   I. Lumbar vertebrae
   J. Lumbosacral nerves
   K. Sacral vertebrae
   L. Coccygeal vertebrae

3. The Thorax (page 182; The Skeletal System: Anatomy)
   A. Sternal notch
   B. Manubrium
   C. Sternum
   D. Body
   E. Xiphoid process
   F. Anterior ribs
   G. Costal arch

4. The Shoulder Girdle (page 184; The Skeletal System: Anatomy)
   A. Sternoclavicular joint
   B. Clavicle
   C. Acromioclavicular (A/C) joint
   D. Humerus
   E. Sternum
   F. Scapula
   G. Glenohumeral (shoulder) joint

5. The Wrist and Hand (page 185; The Skeletal System: Anatomy)
   A. Index
   B. Long
   C. Ring
   D. Small
   E. Phalanges
   F. Thumb
   G. Metacarpals
   H. Carpometacarpal joint
   I. Carpals
   J. Radius
   K. Ulna

6. The Pelvis (page 185; The Skeletal System: Anatomy)
   A. Inferior vena cava
   B. Descending aorta
   C. Iliac crest
   D. Ilium
   E. Sacrum
   F. Pubis
   G. Acetabulum
   H. Pubic symphysis
   I. Ischial tuberosity
   J. Femoral artery
   K. Ischium
   L. Femoral vein

7. The Lower Extremity (page 185; The Skeletal System: Anatomy)
   A. Pelvis
   B. Femoral head
   C. Greater trochanter
   D. Hip
   E. Lesser trochanter
   F. Femur
   G. Thigh
   H. Patella (knee cap)
   I. Knee
   J. Fibula
   K. Leg
   L. Tibia (shin bone)
   M. Ankle
   N. Tarsals
   O. Foot
   P. Metatarsals
   Q. Phalanges

8. The Foot (page 186; The Skeletal System: Anatomy)
   A. Achilles tendon
   B. Medial malleolus
   C. Talus
   D. Navicular
   E. Medial cuneiform
   F. Phalanges
   G. Metatarsal
   H. Calcaneus

9. The Respiratory System (page 189; The Respiratory System: Anatomy)
   A. Upper airway
   B. Nasopharynx
   C. Nasal air passage
   D. Pharynx
   E. Oropharynx
   F. Mouth
   G. Epiglottis
   H. Larynx
   I. Trachea
   J. Apex of the lung
   K. Bronchioles
   L. Lower airway
   M. Carina
   N. Main bronchi
   O. Base of the lung
   P. Diaphragm
   Q. Alveoli

10. The Circulatory System (page 197; The Circulatory System: Anatomy)
   A. Tissue cells
   B. Systemic (body) capillaries
   C. Venule
   D. Arteriole
   E. Vein
   F. Aorta
   G. Artery
   H. Pulmonary (lung) capillaries
   I. Right atrium
   J. Heart
   K. Left atrium
   L. Right ventricle
   M. Left ventricle

11. Central and Peripheral Pulses (page 201; The Circulatory System: Anatomy)
   A. Superficial temporal
   B. External maxillary
   C. Carotid
   D. Brachial
   E. Ulnar;
   F. Radial
   G. Femoral
   H. Posterior tibial
   I. Dorsalis pedis

12. The Brain (page 209; The Nervous System: Anatomy and Physiology)
   A. Cerebrum
   B. Brain stem
   C. Cerebellum

13. Anatomy of the Skin (page 213; The Integumentary System (Skin): Anatomy)
   A. Hair
   B. Pore
   C. Epidermis
   D. Germinal layer of epidermis
   E. Sebaceous gland
   F. Erector pillae muscle
   G. Dermis
   H. Nerve (sensory)
   I. Sweat gland
   J. Hair follicle
   K. Blood vessel
   L. Subcutaneous fat
   M. Fascia
   N. Subcutaneous tissue
   O. Muscle

14. The Male Reproductive System (page 222; The Genital System: Anatomy and Physiology)
   A. Ureter
   B. Urinary bladder
   C. Vasa deferentia
   D. Prostate gland
   E. Pubic bone
   F. Prostate gland
   G. Urethra
   H. Urethra
   I. Epididymis
   J. Testis
   K. Penis
   L. Glans penis
   M. Scrotum

15. The Female Reproductive System (page 222; The Genital System: Anatomy and Physiology)
   A. Uterine (fallopian) tube
   B. Uterus
   C. Ovary
   D. Cervix
   E. Vagina

Crossword Puzzle

```
              P  U  L  M  O  N  A² R  Y
        V³          U                 X
        R           B        A⁴    I⁵ L  I⁶ U  M
  D⁷ R  G           I     S⁸    N        A        S
  D                 S     E     A        L        C
  F⁹ L  E  X              M     T        O        H
  F                 D¹⁰   E     O        I        F¹¹
  U        S¹²  T  E  R  N  U  M         U        O
  S                 A     I        F¹³ E  M  U  R  R
  I        C¹⁴      D     C        L              A
  O        N        S              E              M
  N¹⁵ A¹⁶ S  O  P  H  A  R  Y  N  X               E
     T              A                 I           N
     P              C¹⁷ S  F           O
     E                    P¹⁸ O  N  S
```

Critical Thinking

Multiple Choice

1. C (page 186; The Skeletal System: Anatomy)
2. A (page 181; The Skeletal System: Anatomy)
3. A (page 215; The Digestive System: Anatomy)
4. C (page 227; Pathophysiology)
5. B (page 201; The Circulatory System: Anatomy)

Short Answer

1. 1. Plasma: A sticky, yellow fluid that carries the blood cells and nutrients.
   2. Red blood cells: Give blood its red color and carry oxygen
   3. White blood cells: Play a role in the body's immune defense mechanism against infection
   4. Platelets: Essential in the formation of blood clots. (page 203; The Circulatory System: Anatomy)

2. 1. Cervical spine: 7 vertebrae
   2. Thoracic spine: 12 vertebrae
   3. Lumbar spine: 5 vertebrae
   4. Sacrum: 5 vertebrae
   5. Coccyx: 4 vertebrae (pages 181–182; The Skeletal System: Anatomy)

3. **RUQ:** liver, gallbladder, large intestine, small intestine

   LUQ: stomach, spleen, large intestine, small intestine

   RLQ: large intestine, small intestine, appendix, ascending colon

   LLQ: large intestine, small intestine (page 215; The Digestive System: Anatomy)

4. 1. Superior and inferior vena cava
   2. Right atrium
   3. Right ventricle
   4. Pulmonary artery

5. Lungs

6. Pulmonary vein

7. Left atrium

8. Left ventricle

9. Aorta (pages 197–198; The Circulatory System: Anatomy)

Ambulance Calls

1. Liver, gallbladder, small intestine, large intestine, pancreas, diaphragm, right lung if the pathway is up, right kidney depending on length of knife. You could also have involvement of the other four quadrants based on the direction of travel of the blade.

2. Sternum, ribs, heart, aorta, pulmonary arteries, superior vena cava, inferior vena cava, lungs, pleura, esophagus, diaphragm

3. Humerus, ribs, scapula, clavicle, acromioclavicular joint, glenohumeral joint, sternoclavicular joint

Fill-in-the-Patient Care Report

EMS Patient Care Report (PCR)			
Date: Today's date	**Incident No.:** 2011-0000	**Nature of Call:** Assault	**Location:** Alpha St. and 15th Ave.
Dispatched: 2312	**En Route:** 2312	**At Scene:** 2329	**Transport:** 2341	**At Hospital:** 2354	**In Service:** 0009

Patient Information	
Age: 38 years	**Allergies:** Unknown
Sex: Female	**Medications:** Unknown
Weight (in kg [lb]): 52 kg (115 lb)	**Past Medical History:** Unknown
	Chief Complaint: Generalized pain

Vital Signs				
Time: 2343	**BP:** 108/56	**Pulse:** 96	**Respirations:** 16 GTV/labored	**Spo₂:** 96%
Time: 2349	**BP:** 104/54	**Pulse:** 104	**Respirations:** 18 adequate tidal volume/labored	**Spo₂:** 95%

EMS Treatment (circle all that apply)			
Oxygen @ _15_ L/min via (circle one): NC **(NRM)** BVM	**Assisted Ventilation**	**Airway Adjunct**	**CPR**
Defibrillation	**Bleeding Control**	**Bandaging**	**(Splinting)**	**(Other:** Shock Treatment**)**

Narrative

Dispatched to 9-1-1 scene for assault victim. Arrived to find 38-year-old woman lying on the sidewalk guarding her torso and moaning. Police officer on scene advised that the patient was assaulted by several people. Confirmed airway, breathing, and adequate circulation. Properly secured patient to long backboard after initiating oxygen therapy via nonrebreathing mask. Once en route to the trauma center, baseline vitals were obtained, indicating possible onset of hypoperfusion. Patient found to have contusions to both upper extremities, left lateral chest, anterior of both lower extremities, as well as abdominal rigidity and guarding. Subsequent vitals indicated continuing trend of possible hypoperfusion. Treated patient for shock and contacted receiving facility to give verbal report. Arrived at the trauma center and properly transferred patient to their care, providing a full verbal report to attending physician.**End of Report****

PREPARATORY

Chapter 7: Life Span Development

General Knowledge

Matching

1. L (page 245; Toddlers (1 to 3 Years) and Preschoolers (3 to 6 Years))
2. J (page 244; Neonates (Birth to 1 Month) and Infants (1 Month to 1 Year))
3. A (page 253; Older Adults (61 Years and Older))
4. E (page 245; Toddlers (1 to 3 Years) and Preschoolers (3 to 6 Years))
5. B (page 252; Older Adults (61 Years and Older))
6. N (page 247; School-Age Children (6 to 12 Years))
7. K (page 247; School-Age Children (6 to 12 Years))
8. C (page 249; Early Adults (19 to 40 Years))
9. H (page 243; Neonates (Birth to 1 Month) and Infants (1 Month to 1 Year))
10. I (page 247; School-Age Children (6 to 12 Years))
11. M (page 243; Neonates (Birth to 1 Month) and Infants (1 Month to 1 Year))
12. D (page 243; Neonates (Birth to 1 Month) and Infants (1 Month to 1 Year))
13. F (page 244; Neonates (Birth to 1 Month) and Infants (1 Month to 1 Year))
14. G (page 250; Middle Adults (41 to 60 Years))

Multiple Choice

1. B (page 253; Older Adults (61 Years and Older))
2. C (page 247; Adolescents (12 to 18 Years))
3. A (page 247; School-Age Children (6 to 12 Years))
4. D (pages 253–254; Older Adults (61 Years and Older))
5. D (page 248; Adolescents (12 to 18 Years))
6. C (page 241; Neonates (Birth to 1 Month) and Infants (1 Month to 1 Year))
7. A (page 251; Older Adults (61 Years and Older))
8. C (page 250; Middle Adults (41 to 60 Years))
9. B (page 243; Neonates (Birth to 1 Month) and Infants (1 Month to 1 Year))
10. C (page 253; Older Adults (61 Years and Older))
11. B (page 244; Neonates (Birth to 1 Month) and Infants (1 Month to 1 Year))
12. C (page 252; Older Adults (61 Years and Older))
13. A (page 245; Toddlers (1 to 3 Years) and Preschoolers (3 to 6 Years))
14. D (page 249; Middle Adults (41 to 60 Years))
15. B (page 244; Neonates (Birth to 1 Month) and Infants (1 Month to 1 Year))

True/False

1. F (page 255; Older Adults (61 Years and Older))
2. F (page 243; Neonates (Birth to 1 Month) and Infants (1 Month to 1 Year))
3. T (page 245; Toddlers (1 to 3 Years) and Preschoolers (3 to 6 Years))
4. T (page 253; Older Adults (61 Years and Older))
5. F (page 254; Older Adults (61 Years and Older))
6. F (page 249; Adolescents (12 to 18 Years))
7. F (page 246; Toddlers (1 to 3 Years) and Preschoolers (3 to 6 Years))
8. T (page 244; Neonates (Birth to 1 Month) and Infants (1 Month to 1 Year))
9. T (page 244; Neonates (Birth to 1 Month) and Infants (1 Month to 1 Year))
10. F (page 249; Adolescents (12 to 18 Years))

Fill-in-the-Blank

1. Early, 40 (page 249; Early Adults (19 to 40 Years))
2. 90, 150; 20, 30 (page 245; Toddlers (1 to 3 Years) and Preschoolers (3 to 6 Years))
3. life's goals (page 250; Middle Adults (41 to 60 Years))

4. well, clearly (page 254; Older Adults (61 Years and Older))

5. identity (page 249; Adolescents (12 to 18 Years))

6. neonate, 8, 25 (page 241; Neonates (Birth to 1 Month) and Infants (1 Month to 1 Year))

7. fragile, barotrauma (page 243; Neonates (Birth to 1 Month) and Infants (1 Month to 1 Year))

8. 18, effect (page 247; Toddlers (1 to 3 Years) and Preschoolers (3 to 6 Years))

9. nutritional, older (page 253; Older Adults (61 Years and Older))

10. mental (page 254; Older Adults (61 Years and Older))

Crossword Puzzle

Critical Thinking

Multiple Choice

1. A (page 247; School-Age Children (6 to 12 Years))

2. A (page 247; School-Age Children (6 to 12 Years))

3. B (page 247; School-Age Children (6 to 12 Years))

Short Answer

1. As people age, the size of the airway increases and the surface area of the alveoli decreases. The natural elasticity of the lungs also decreases, forcing individuals to increasingly use the muscles between their ribs, called intercostal muscles, to breathe. As the elasticity of the lungs decreases, the overall strength of the intercostal muscles and diaphragm also decreases. (page 252; Older Adults (61 Years and Older))

2. Conventional reasoning means that children are looking for approval from their peers and society. (page 247; School-Age Children (6 to 12 Years))

3. "Trust and mistrust" refers to a stage of development from birth to about 18 months of age that involves an infant's needs being met by his or her parents or caregivers. When caregivers and parents provide an organized, routine environment, the infant gains trust in those individuals. If the environment is not perceived as secure by the infant, a sense of mistrust will develop. (pages 244–245; Neonates (Birth to 1 Month) and Infants (1 Month to 1 Year))

4. Atherosclerosis most commonly affects coronary vessels. Cholesterol and calcium build up inside the walls of blood vessels, forming plaque. The accumulation of plaque eventually leads to a partial or complete blockage of blood flow. More than 60% of people older than 65 years have atherosclerotic disease. This can lead to decreased blood supply to the organs of the body. (page 252; Older Adults (61 Years and Older))

5. Neonate (0 to 1 month)
   Infant (1 month to 1 year)
   Toddler (1 to 3 years)
   Preschool age (3 to 6 years)
   School age (6 to 12 years)
   Adolescent (12 to 18 years)
   Early adult (19 to 40 years)
   Middle adult (41 to 60 years)
   Late adult (61 and older) (page 241; Introduction)

Ambulance Calls

1. You should be concerned about intracranial bleeding with this patient because he is at an age where brain shrinkage has likely occurred and the hematoma suggests that he hit his head after falling, which could have ruptured some of the bridging blood vessels.

2. The first thing that must be remembered is that our daily experiences as EMTs can "color" our responses. This means that you can begin to see similarities between calls where none actually exist. It is very important to treat each call as a new and different situation and not to make assumptions without very clear reasons. In this particular situation, you should not try to speak to the child alone. Children between the ages of 10 and 18 months are at the pinnacle of the separation anxiety stage, and removing the child from the parents will likely cause her to become noncommunicative and very upset. In this situation, you should keep the child with her parents, and if you truly suspect some type of abuse, you should report it afterward based on your local guidelines.

3. The best way to help this patient is to separate him from the other students before asking him about his injuries. Adolescents are very focused on their public image and are easily embarrassed. Falling off the stage in front of his peers would have embarrassed this teen enough, and publicly admitting to a subsequent injury would make it even worse for him.

Fill-in-the-Patient Care Report

EMS Patient Care Report (PCR)					
Date: Today's date	**Incident No.:** 2011-9999	**Nature of Call:** Respiratory distress		**Location:** 16654 Geary St.	
Dispatched: 0345	**En Route:** 0348	**At Scene:** 0359	**Transport:** 0410	**At Hospital:** 0417	**In Service:** 0435

Patient Information	
Age: 93 years **Sex:** Female **Weight (in kg [lb]):** 44 kg (97 lb)	**Allergies:** Penicillin **Medications:** Blood pressure **Past Medical History:** Three MIs **Chief Complaint:** Respiratory distress

Vital Signs				
Time: N/A	**BP:** N/A	**Pulse:** N/A	**Respirations:** N/A	**Spo₂:** 95%

EMS Treatment
(circle all that apply)

Oxygen @ _15_ L/min via (circle one):

NC NRM (BVM)	(Assisted Ventilation)	Airway Adjunct	CPR
Defibrillation	Bleeding Control	Bandaging	Splinting	Other:

Narrative

Dispatched on a 9-1-1 call for a respiratory distress patient. Arrived to find the patient, a 93-year-old woman, in the tripod position and clearly struggling to breathe. Just as patient contact was made, patient went into respiratory arrest and bag-valve-mask ventilations were immediately initiated. Patient was moved to the gurney and loaded into the ambulance for transport. Because of ongoing interventions, no vital signs were obtained except for a consistent Spo₂ reading of 95% while en route to the receiving facility. Patient report to the receiving facility was relayed through the dispatch center, and ventilations were continued during entire transport. At the receiving facility, patient care was properly transferred to the facility staff and a full verbal report was provided.**End of Report**

PREPARATORY
Chapter 8: Lifting and Moving Patients

General Knowledge

Matching

1. C (page 290; Nonurgent Moves)
2. J (page 298; Additional Patient-Moving Equipment)
3. H (page 274; Principles of Safe Lifting and Carrying)
4. E (page 299; Additional Patient-Moving Equipment)
5. A (page 300; Additional Patient-Moving Equipment)

6. I (page 262; Backboards)
7. F (page 288; Nonurgent Moves)
8. B (page 298; Additional Patient-Moving Equipment)
9. D (page 261; The Wheeled Ambulance Stretcher)
10. G (page 296; Bariatrics)

Multiple Choice

1. D (page 267; Principles of Safe Reaching and Pulling)
2. B (page 283; Urgent Moves)
3. C (page 264; Body Mechanics)
4. C (page 265; Body Mechanics)
5. B (pages 264–265; Body Mechanics)
6. A (page 267; Body Mechanics)
7. B (page 274; Principles of Safe Lifting and Carrying)
8. A (page 271; Principles of Safe Lifting and Carrying)
9. D (page 262; Backboards)
10. A (page 279; Directions and Commands)
11. D (page 271; Principles of Safe Lifting and Carrying)
12. B (page 276; Principles of Safe Lifting and Carrying)
13. A (page 267; Principles of Safe Reaching and Pulling)
14. C (page 268; Principles of Safe Reaching and Pulling)
15. C (page 269; Principles of Safe Reaching and Pulling)

16. B (page 274; Principles of Safe Lifting and Carrying)
17. A (page 281; Emergency Moves)
18. B (page 281; Emergency Moves)
19. C (page 281; Emergency Moves)
20. B (page 264; Body Mechanics)
21. A (pages 283–284; Urgent Moves)
22. C (page 292; Nonurgent Moves)
23. A (page 299; Additional Patient–Moving Equipment)
24. D (page 271; Principles of Safe Lifting and Carrying)
25. B (pages 293–294; Geriatrics)
26. B (page 296; Bariatrics)
27. D (page 262; Backboards)
28. B (page 281; Emergency Moves)
29. A (page 271; Principles of Safe Lifting and Carrying)
30. D (page 291; Nonurgent Moves)

True/False

1. T (page 298; Additional Patient-Moving Equipment)
2. T (page 265; Body Mechanics)
3. F (page 271; Principles of Safe Lifting and Carrying)
4. F (page 272; Principles of Safe Lifting and Carrying)
5. T (page 281; Emergency Moves)
6. F (page 292; Nonurgent Moves)
7. F (page 276; Principles of Safe Lifting and Carrying)
8. F (pages 283–284; Urgent Moves)

9. F (page 279; Directions and Commands)
10. T (page 296; Bariatrics)
11. T (page 301; Medical Restraints)
12. T (page 300; Additional Patient-Moving Equipment)
13. F (page 299; Additional Patient-Moving Equipment)
14. F (page 297; Additional Patient-Moving Equipment)
15. T (page 297; Additional Patient-Moving Equipment)

Fill-in-the-Blank

1. body mechanics (page 264; Body Mechanics)
2. upright (page 264; Body Mechanics)
3. power lift (page 265; Body Mechanics)
4. palm (page 267; Body Mechanics)
5. locked-in (page 273; Principles of Safe Lifting and Carrying)

6. 250 (page 271; Principles of Safe Lifting and Carrying)
7. sideways (page 268; Principles of Safe Reaching and Pulling)
8. locked (page 274; Principles of Safe Lifting and Carrying)
9. diamond (page 271; Principles of Safe Lifting and Carrying)
10. movement (page 276; Principles of Safe Lifting and Carrying)
11. spine movement (page 284; Urgent Moves)
12. direct ground lift (page 288; Nonurgent Moves)
13. extremity lift (page 290; Nonurgent Moves)
14. fluid resistant (page 262; The Wheeled Ambulance Stretcher)
15. decontaminate (page 300; Additional Patient-Moving Equipment)

Crossword Puzzle

Critical Thinking

Short Answer

1. 1. Emergency clothes drag
   2. Blanket drag
   3. Arm drag
   4. Arm-to-arm drag
   5. Firefighter's drag
   6. Front cradle
   7. One-person walking assist
   8. Firefighter's carry
   9. Pack strap (pages 282–283; Emergency Moves)

2. 1. The vehicle or scene is unsafe.
   2. Explosives or other hazardous materials are on the scene.
   3. There is a fire or a danger of fire.

4. The patient cannot be properly assessed before being removed from the vehicle.

5. The patient needs immediate intervention that requires a supine position.

6. The patient has a life-threatening condition that requires immediate transport to the hospital.

7. The patient blocks the EMT's access to another seriously injured patient. (page 284; Urgent Moves)

3. 1. Make sure there are enough providers for sufficient lifting power.

   2. Follow the manufacturer's directions for safe and proper use of the stretcher.

   3. Make sure that all stretchers and patients are fully secured before you move the ambulance. (page 278; Principles of Safe Lifting and Carrying)

4. 1. Estimate the weight of both the patient and the associated equipment to be lifted and gauge the limitations of the team's abilities.

   2. Coordinate your movements with those of the other team members while constantly communicating with them.

   3. Do not twist your body as you are carrying the patient.

   4. Keep the weight that you are carrying as close to your body as possible while keeping your back in a locked-in position.

   5. Do not bend at the waist; this could hyperextend your back. Instead, flex at the hips and bend at the knees. (page 271; Principles of Safe Lifting and Carrying)

5. Always keep your back in a straight, upright position and lift without twisting. (page 264; Body Mechanics)

Ambulance Calls

1. Immobilize the patient on a long backboard, apply high-flow oxygen, and consider the use of a basket stretcher. Use four people to carry the patient back up the ledge. Plan the route, and brief your helpers before moving the patient. Clarify whether you will move on "three" or count to three, then move. Coordinate the move until the patient is loaded into the ambulance.

2. It is highly unlikely that you will be able to move this patient, especially without significantly hurting yourself or your partner. You should immediately request additional personnel. You can attempt to move the patient, but if you cannot successfully do so, you will have to open his airway, in his current position. Do the best you can until the patient can be moved.

3. Patients whose conditions will be exacerbated by physical activity should not walk to the stretcher or ambulance. If a patient's condition is such that it is not medically necessary that you carry him or her, it is safer for the patient to walk on his or her own power to the ambulance. However, this patient should not/cannot walk. This produces a safety issue for you and your partner, especially given the fact that there is no elevator. Fortunately, this patient can sit upright; thus, the use of a stair chair would be appropriate in this situation. Regardless, you should ask for more personnel given the patient's large size. Back injuries are very common in EMS. For providers to avoid these injuries, correct lifting techniques should be used and assistance should be requested whenever the patient is large or in a position not conducive to correct lifting procedures.

Skills

Skill Drills

Skill Drill 8-1: Performing the Power Lift

1. Lock your back in a **slight** curve. **Spread** and bend your legs. Grasp the backboard, palms up and just in front of you. **Balance** and **center** the weight between your arms.

2. Position your feet, **straddle** the object, and **distribute** your weight evenly. Lift by **straightening** your legs, keeping your back locked in. (page 266; Body Mechanics)

Skill Drill 8-2: Performing the Diamond Carry

1. Position yourselves facing the patient.

2. The providers at each side turn the head-end hand palm down and release the other hand.

3. The providers at each side turn toward the foot end. The provider at the foot end turns to face forward. (page 272; Principles of Safe Lifting and Carrying)

Skill Drill 8-3: Performing the One-Handed Carry
1. **Face** each other and use both **hands**.
2. Lift the backboard to **carrying height**.
3. **Turn** in the direction you will walk, and **switch** to using one hand. (page 273; Principles of Safe Lifting and Carrying)

Skill Drill 8-7: Performing the Rapid Extrication Technique
1. The first provider provides in-line manual support of the head and cervical spine.
2. The second provider gives commands, applies a cervical collar, and performs the primary assessment.
3. The second provider supports the torso. The third provider frees the patient's legs from the pedals and moves the legs together, without moving the pelvis or spine.
4. The second provider and the third provider rotate the patient as a unit in several short, coordinated moves. The first provider (relieved by the fourth provider as needed) supports the patient's head and neck during rotation (and later steps).
5. The first (or fourth) provider places the backboard on the seat against the patient's buttocks. (Use of a backboard may depend on local protocols.)
6. The third provider moves to an effective position for sliding the patient. The second and third providers slide the patient along the backboard in coordinated, 8- to 12-inch (20- to 30-cm) moves until the patient's hips rest on the backboard.
7. The third provider exits the vehicle, moves to the backboard opposite the second provider, and they continue to slide the patient until the patient is fully on the board.
8. The first (or fourth) provider continues to stabilize the head and neck while the second provider and the third provider carry the patient away from the vehicle and onto the prepared stretcher. (pages 286–287; Urgent Moves)

Skill Drill 8-9: Extremity Lift
1. The patient's hands are **crossed** over the chest. Grasp the patient's wrists or **forearms** and pull the patient to a(n) **sitting** position.
2. Your partner moves to a position between the patient's **legs**, facing in the **same** direction as the patient, and places his or her hands under the **knees**.
3. Rise to a **crouching** position. On **command**, lift and begin to move. (page 290; Nonurgent Moves)

Skill Drill 8-10: Direct Carry
1. Position the stretcher **parallel** to the bed. Secure the **stretcher** to prevent movement. Face the patient while standing between the **bed** and the **stretcher**. Position your arms under the patient's **neck** and **shoulders**. Your partner should position his or her hands under the patient's **knees**.
2. Lift the patient from the bed in a smooth, **coordinated** fashion.
3. Slowly carry the patient to the **stretcher**.
4. **Gently** lower the patient onto the stretcher and secure with **straps**. (pages 291–292; Nonurgent Moves)

PATIENT ASSESSMENT
Chapter 9: Patient Assessment

General Knowledge

Matching

1. P (page 321; Scene Size-up)
2. Q (page 331; Primary Assessment)
3. M (page 368; Secondary Assessment)
4. T (page 357; Secondary Assessment)
5. B (page 331; Primary Assessment)
6. S (page 315; Introduction)
7. L (page 328; Primary Assessment)
8. A (pages 355–356; Secondary Assessment)
9. O (page 319; Scene Size-up)
10. R (page 331; Primary Assessment)
11. G (page 331; Primary Assessment)
12. E (page 325; Primary Assessment)
13. F (page 339; History Taking)
14. I (page 329; Primary Assessment)
15. K (page 324; Primary Assessment)
16. C (page 328; Primary Assessment)

17. D (page 331; Primary Assessment)
18. J (page 332; Primary Assessment)
19. H (page 333; Primary Assessment)
20. N (page 369; Secondary Assessment)
21. I (page 340; History Taking)
22. L (page 340; History Taking)
23. C (page 340; History Taking)
24. E (page 340; History Taking)
25. H (page 340; History Taking)
26. K (page 340; History Taking)
27. F (page 340; History Taking)
28. B (page 340; History Taking)
29. J (page 340; History Taking)
30. G (page 340; History Taking)
31. A (page 340; History Taking)
32. D (page 340; History Taking)

Multiple Choice

1. C (pages 317–321; Scene Size-up)
2. A (page 342; History Taking)
3. B (page 319; Scene Size-up)
4. D (page 332; Primary Assessment)
5. B (page 355; Secondary Assessment)
6. A (page 348; Secondary Assessment)
7. C (page 323; Primary Assessment)
8. B (page 321; Scene Size-up)
9. B (page 329; Primary Assessment)
10. C (page 335; Primary Assessment)
11. B (page 324; Primary Assessment)
12. B (page 354; Secondary Assessment)
13. D (page 330; Primary Assessment)
14. B (page 330; Primary Assessment)
15. A (page 331; Primary Assessment)
16. C (page 329; Primary Assessment)
17. D (page 357; Secondary Assessment)
18. D (page 331; Primary Assessment)
19. C (page 320; Scene Size-up)

20. C (page 332; Primary Assessment)
21. A (page 338; History Taking)
22. C (page 325; Primary Assessment)
23. B (page 333; Primary Assessment)
24. C (page 364; Secondary Assessment)
25. A (page 364; Secondary Assessment)
26. D (pages 354–356; Secondary Assessment)
27. A (page 327; Primary Assessment)
28. B (pages 355–356; Secondary Assessment)
29. C (page 342; History Taking)
30. B (page 346; History Taking)
31. C (page 371; Secondary Assessment)
32. D (page 358; Secondary Assessment)
33. A (pages 358–359; Secondary Assessment)
34. B (page 369; Secondary Assessment)
35. B (page 368; Secondary Assessment)
36. A (page 375; Reassessment)
37. B (page 328; Primary Assessment)
38. A (page 329; Primary Assessment)

39. B (page 331; Primary Assessment)

40. C (page 361; Secondary Assessment)

41. B (page 375; Reassessment)

42. A (page 315; Scene Size-up)

43. D (page 357; Secondary Assessment)

44. A (page 346; History Taking)

45. C (page 346; History Taking)

True/False

1. F (page 324; Primary Assessment)

2. F (page 375; Reassessment)

3. T (page 369; Secondary Assessment)

4. F (page 330; Primary Assessment)

5. T (page 335; Primary Assessment)

6. T (page 368; Secondary Assessment)

7. F (page 369; Secondary Assessment)

8. F (page 369; Secondary Assessment)

9. T (page 375; Reassessment)

10. T (page 321; Scene Size-up)

11. F (pages 324–325; Primary Assessment)

12. T (page 324; Primary Assessment)

13. F (page 365; Secondary Assessment)

14. F (page 328; Primary Assessment)

15. T (page 354; Secondary Assessment)

16. T (page 335; Primary Assessment)

17. F (page 336; Primary Assessment)

18. T (page 335; Primary Assessment)

19. T (page 338; History Taking)

20. F (page 341; History Taking)

21. T (page 342; History Taking)

22. T (page 342; History Taking)

23. F (page 344; History Taking)

24. T (page 344; History Taking)

25. F (page 344; History Taking)

26. T (page 344; History Taking)

27. T (page 345; History Taking)

28. F (page 345; History Taking)

29. T (page 369; Secondary Assessment)

30. T (page 370; Secondary Assessment)

Fill-in-the-Blank

1. sign (page 315; Introduction)

2. Standard precautions (page 320; Scene Size-up)

3. incident command system (page 320; Scene Size-up)

4. Advanced life support (page 321; Scene Size-up)

5. primary assessment (page 323; Primary Assessment)

6. general impression (page 323; Primary Assessment)

7. Perfusion (page 324; Primary Assessment)

8. Orientation (page 325; Primary Assessment)

9. constrict (page 364; Secondary Assessment)

10. stridor (page 354; Secondary Assessment)

11. jaw-thrust maneuver (page 327; Primary Assessment)

12. exhalation (page 354; Secondary Assessment)

13. airway (page 328; Primary Assessment)

14. suction (page 355; Secondary Assessment)

15. respiratory infection (page 355; Secondary Assessment)

16. Nasal flaring (page 328; Primary Assessment)

17. CPR (page 330; Primary Assessment)

18. Tachycardia (page 357; Secondary Assessment)

19. conjunctiva (page 331; Primary Assessment)

20. hypoperfusion (page 331; Primary Assessment)

21. diaphoretic (page 331; Primary Assessment)

22. 2 (page 332; Primary Assessment)

23. coagulate (page 332; Primary Assessment)

24. 60, 90 (page 332; Primary Assessment)

25. Golden Hour (pages 335–336; Primary Assessment)

26. life threats (page 323; Primary Assessment)
27. History taking (page 338; History Taking)
28. open-ended (page 338; History Taking)
29. SAMPLE (page 340; History Taking)
30. Pertinent negatives (page 340; History Taking)
31. Blood glucose (page 372; Secondary Assessment)
32. Palpation (page 348; Secondary Assessment)
33. Capnography (page 372; Secondary Assessment)
34. Diastolic pressure (page 358; Secondary Assessment)
35. neurologic (page 363; Secondary Assessment)

Crossword Puzzle

Critical Thinking

Short Answer

1. To identify and initiate treatment of immediate or potential life threats (page 323; Primary Assessment)
2. Age, sex, race, level of distress, and overall appearance (page 323; Primary Assessment)
3. A—Airway; B—Breathing; C—Circulation (page 323; Primary Assessment)
4. Orientation to person, place, time, and event. Person (name) evaluates long-term memory. Place and time evaluate intermediate-term memory. Event evaluates short-term memory. (page 325; Primary Assessment)
5. 1. Is the patient breathing?
   2. Is the patient breathing adequately?
   3. Is the patient hypoxic? (page 327; Primary Assessment)

6. D—Deformities
   C—Contusions
   A—Abrasions
   P—Punctures/penetrations
   B—Burns
   T—Tenderness
   L—Lacerations
   S—Swelling (page 333; Primary Assessment)
7. 1. Does the scene pose a threat to you, your patient, or others?
   2. How many patients are there?
   3. Do we have the resources to respond to their conditions? (page 321; Scene Size-up)

8. Pupils equal and round, regular in size, react to light (page 365; Secondary Assessment)

9. A sign is a condition that can be seen, heard, felt, smelled, or measured (objective). A symptom is something that the patient reports to you as a problem or feeling (subjective). (page 315; Introduction)

10. 1. Is there pain associated with urination?

    2. Do you have any discharge, sores, or an increase in urination?

    3. Do you have burning or difficulty voiding?

    4. Has there been any trauma?

    5. Have you had recent sexual encounters? (page 342; History Taking)

Ambulance Calls

1. Maintain cervical spine control and immediately manage the airway by suction and oxygen. Conduct a rapid survey and transport the patient to the nearest appropriate facility. This patient is a priority transport based on his mechanism of injury, level of consciousness, and airway compromise. Damage to the vehicle indicates possible occult injuries.

2. This patient is having a very serious asthma attack. Accessory muscle use (nasal flaring, tracheal tugging, suprasternal and intercostal muscle retractions), work of breathing, wheezing, and one- to two-word responses all point to the seriousness of his attack. You should transport immediately.

3. Mechanism of injury is significant for this patient. Not only did he fall down a flight of wooden stairs, but he landed on a cement floor. His head injury is likely more significant than the bruising and laceration you can see. He could also have skull fractures, contusions, or intracranial bleeding. With any significant trauma to the head comes the likelihood for cervical spine fractures. You should also question the mechanism of his fall because medical conditions can sometimes precipitate injuries. Full cervical spine precautions must be taken, along with application of high-flow oxygen and prompt transport.

Skills

Skill Drills

Skill Drill 9-1: Rapid Scan

1. Assess the head. Have your partner maintain in-line stabilization if indicated.

2. Assess the neck.

3. Apply a cervical collar if indicated.

4. Assess the chest. Listen to breath sounds on both sides of the chest.

5. Assess the abdomen.

6. Assess the pelvis. If there is no pain, gently compress the pelvis downward and inward to look for tenderness and instability.

7. Assess all four extremities. Assess pulse and motor and sensory function.

8. Assess the back. If spinal immobilization is indicated, do so with minimal movement to the patient's spine by log rolling the patient in one motion. (pages 334–335; Primary Assessment)

Skill Drill 9-3: Obtaining Blood Pressure by Auscultation

1. Follow standard precautions. Check for a dialysis fistula, central line, previous mastectomy, and injury to the arm. If any are present, use the brachial artery on the other arm. Apply the cuff snugly. The lower border of the cuff should be about 1 inch (2.5 cm) above the antecubital space.

2. Support the exposed arm at the level of the heart. Palpate the brachial artery.

3. Place the stethoscope over the brachial artery, and grasp the ball-pump and turn-valve.

4. Close the valve, and pump to 30 mm Hg above the point at which you stop hearing pulse sounds. Note the systolic and diastolic pressures as you let air escape slowly.

5. Open the valve, and quickly release remaining air. (pages 360–361; Secondary Assessment)

AIRWAY
Chapter 10: Airway Management

General Knowledge

Matching

1. C (page 393; Physiology of Breathing)
2. I (page 394; Physiology of Breathing)
3. H (page 392; Anatomy of the Respiratory System)
4. G (page 392; Anatomy of the Respiratory System)
5. K (page 395; Physiology of Breathing)
6. E (page 394; Physiology of Breathing)
7. A (page 393; Physiology of Breathing)
8. F (page 393; Physiology of Breathing)
9. L (page 393; Physiology of Breathing)
10. D (pages 389–390; Anatomy of the Respiratory System)
11. J (page 395; Physiology of Breathing)
12. B (page 402; Patient Assessment)

Multiple Choice

1. D (page 396; Physiology of Breathing)
2. B (page 423; Oxygen-Delivery Equipment)
3. B (page 400; Patient Assessment)
4. B (page 401; Patient Assessment)
5. A (page 395; Physiology of Breathing)
6. A (page 412; Basic Airway Adjuncts)
7. C (page 412; Basic Airway Adjuncts)
8. D (pages 430–431; Assisted and Artificial Ventilation)
9. C (page 431; Assisted and Artificial Ventilation)
10. C (page 410; Suctioning)
11. D (page 428; Assisted and Artificial Ventilation)
12. C (page 397; Physiology of Breathing)
13. D (page 398; Pathophysiology of Respiration)
14. B (page 401; Patient Assessment)
15. B (page 403; Patient Assessment)

True/False

1. F (page 411; Basic Airway Adjuncts)
2. T (page 423; Oxygen-Delivery Equipment)
3. F (page 412; Basic Airway Adjuncts)
4. F (page 418; Supplemental Oxygen)
5. F (page 418; Supplemental Oxygen)

Fill-in-the-Blank

1. vocal cords (page 388; Anatomy of the Respiratory System)
2. higher (page 394; Physiology of Breathing)
3. 21, 78 (page 396; Physiology of Breathing)
4. carbon dioxide (page 395; Physiology of Breathing)
5. diaphragm, intercostal muscles (page 393; Physiology of Breathing)
6. positive, pressure (page 436; Continuous Positive Airway Pressure)
7. hypoxia (page 395; Physiology of Breathing)
8. Passive ventilation (pages 433–434; Assisted and Artificial Ventilation)

Labeling

1. Upper and Lower Airways (page 388, Anatomy of the Respiratory System)

   A. Upper airway
   B. Nasopharynx
   C. Nasal air passage
   D. Pharynx
   E. Oropharynx
   F. Mouth
   G. Epiglottis
   H. Larynx
   I. Trachea
   J. Apex of the lung
   K. Bronchioles
   L. Lower airway
   M. Carina
   N. Main bronchus
   O. Pulmonary capillaries
   P. Base of the lung
   Q. Diaphragm
   R. Alveoli

2. Oral Cavity (page 389, Anatomy of the Respiratory System)

   A. Hard palate
   B. Soft palate
   C. Entrance to auditory tube
   D. Nasal cavity
   E. Upper lip
   F. Tongue
   G. Nasopharynx
   H. Gingiva
   I. Uvula
   J. Oropharynx
   K. Epiglottis
   L. Laryngopharynx
   M. Hyoid bone

3. Thoracic Cavity (page 392, Anatomy of the Respiratory System)

   A. Trachea
   B. Vena cava
   C. Aorta
   D. Bronchus
   E. Heart
   F. Lung
   G. Diaphragm

Crossword Puzzle

Critical Thinking

Multiple Choice

1. B (page 406; Opening the Airway)
2. D (page 408; Suctioning)
3. C (page 411; Basic Airway Adjuncts)
4. D (page 433; Assisted and Artificial Ventilation)
5. A (page 427; Assisted and Artificial Ventilation)

Short Answer

1. 1. A patient who is in respiratory arrest.
   2. Signs and symptoms of a pneumothorax or chest trauma.
   3. A patient who has a tracheostomy.
   4. Active gastrointestinal bleeding or vomiting.
   5. The patient is unable to follow verbal commands. (page 436; Continuous Positive Airway Pressure)
2. Adults: 12 to 20 breaths/min

   Children: 15 to 30 breaths/min

   Infants: 25 to 50 breaths/min (page 401; Patient Assessment)
3. Give slow, gentle breaths over 1 second (enough to see the chest rise). (page 433; Assisted and Artificial Ventilation)
4. 1. A peak flow rate of 100% oxygen at up to 40 L/min.
   2. An inspiratory pressure safety release valve that opens at approximately 60 cm of water and vents any remaining volume to the atmosphere or stops the flow of oxygen.
   3. An audible alarm that sounds whenever you exceed the relief valve pressure.
   4. The ability to operate satisfactorily under normal and varying environmental conditions.
   5. A trigger positioned so that both your hands can remain on the mask to provide an airtight seal while supporting and tilting the patient's head and keeping the jaw elevated. (pages 434–435; Assisted and Artificial Ventilation)
5. 1. Respiratory rate of less than 12 breaths/min or greater than 20 breaths/min in the presence of shortness of breath
   2. Irregular rhythm
   3. Diminished, absent, or noisy breath sounds
   4. Reduced flow of expired air at the nose and mouth
   5. Unequal or inadequate chest expansion
   6. Increased effort of breathing
   7. Shallow depth
   8. Pale, cyanotic, or cool (clammy) skin
   9. Skin pulling in around the ribs during inspiration (page 401; Patient Assessment)
6. They are the secondary muscles of respiration. They are not used in normal breathing. They include the sternocleidomastoid (neck) muscles, chest pectoralis major muscles, and abdominal muscles. (page 401; Patient Assessment)
7. When the patient has experienced severe trauma to the head or face (page 413; Basic Airway Adjuncts)
8. 1. Select the proper-size airway and apply a water-soluble lubricant.
   2. Place the airway in the larger nostril with the curvature following the curve of the floor of the nose.
   3. Advance the airway gently.
   4. Continue until the flange rests against the skin. (page 415; Basic Airway Adjuncts)
9. Tonsil tips are best because they have a large diameter and do not collapse. In addition, they are curved, which allows easy, rapid placement. (page 409; Suctioning)
10. 15 seconds (page 410; Suctioning)

Ambulance Calls

1. Maintain cervical spine stabilization. Immediately open the airway with the jaw-thrust maneuver. Suction to remove the obstruction. Assess the airway for breathing (rate, rhythm, quality) and provide oxygen via nonrebreathing mask or bag-valve mask. Continue initial assessment, rapid extrication, and rapid transport.

2. You should reposition the head and attempt to reventilate the patient. If you are unsuccessful in your second attempt, you must take action to clear her airway. If you fail to clear her airway, she will likely go into cardiac arrest as well. Choking victims have been known to walk away from others without indicating that they are choking, and when this occurs in a restaurant setting, many of these people will go into a bathroom. If you find a patient in a restroom who cannot be ventilated, they likely have a foreign body airway obstruction (FBAO), most often as a result of ingested food.

3. The most common cause of airway obstruction in an unconscious patient is the tongue. The patient's husband told you that he helped her to the ground without injury, so it is safe to open her airway using a head tilt–chin lift maneuver. If you were unsure of the presence of trauma, this position would not be used. Instead, you would use the jaw-thrust maneuver to manage her airway. In either case, you must continually monitor her condition and be prepared for vomitus.

Fill-in-the-Patient Care Report

EMS Patient Care Report (PCR)					
Date: Today's date	**Incident No.:** 2011-0000		**Nature of Call:** Possible overdose		**Location:** Market Street High School
Dispatched: 1530	**En Route:** 1530	**At Scene:** 1543	**Transport:** 1556	**At Hospital:** 1608	**In Service:** 1635
Patient Information					
Age: 14 years **Sex:** Female **Weight (in kg [lb]):** 50 kg (110 lb)			**Allergies:** Unknown **Medications:** Unknown **Past Medical History:** Unknown **Chief Complaint:** Unresponsive		
Vital Signs					
Time: 1545	**BP:** 124/86		**Pulse:** 112/regular	**Respirations:** : 12 shallow/inadequate tidal volume	**Spo₂:** 93%
EMS Treatment					
(circle all that apply)					
Oxygen @ _15_ **L/min via (circle one):** NC NRM (BVM)			(Assisted Ventilation)	(Airway Adjunct: OPA)	CPR
Defibrillation	Bleeding Control		Bandaging	Splinting	Other:
Narrative					
Responded to 9-1-1 call for possible drug overdose at Market Street High School. Arrived and was directed to an unresponsive 14-year-old girl on the floor of a restroom and was advised that patient had previous "troubles" with drugs, although no physical evidence was observed in the patient's immediate surroundings. Patient presented with no response to painful stimulus; cyanosis around lips and fingernails; and shallow, snoring respirations. Patient's respirations were immediately assisted with a BVM and 100% oxygen, and she was loaded into the ambulance where a firefighter rode along to assist. Vital signs, when compared to the baseline set, indicated that assisted ventilations and oxygen therapy were improving patient's Spo₂ levels. While en route, the receiving facility was updated with patient condition. On arrival she was transferred appropriately to the care of the ED staff, and a full verbal report was provided to the charge RN.**End of Report**					

Skills

Skill Drills

Skill Drill 10-2: Positioning the Unconscious Patient

1. Support the **head** while your partner straightens the patient's legs.

2. Have your partner place his or her **hand** on the patient's far **shoulder** and hip.

3. **Roll** the patient as a unit with the EMT at the patient's **head** calling the count to begin the move.

4. **Open** and **assess** the patient's airway and **breathing** status. (page 406; Opening the Airway)

Skill Drill 10-4: Inserting an Oral Airway

1. Size the **airway** by measuring from the patient's **earlobe** to the corner of the **mouth**.

2. Open the patient's **mouth** with the **cross**-finger technique. Hold the **airway** upside down with your other hand. Insert the airway with the tip facing the **roof** of the mouth.

3. **Rotate** the airway **180°**. Insert the airway until the **flange** rests on the patient's lips and teeth. In this position, the airway will hold the **tongue** forward. (page 413; Basic Airway Adjuncts)

Skill Drill 10-7: Placing an Oxygen Cylinder Into Service

1. Using an oxygen **wrench**, turn the valve **counterclockwise** to slowly "crack" the cylinder.

2. Attach the regulator/flowmeter to the **valve** stem using the two pin-**indexing** holes and make sure that the **washer** is in place over the larger hole.

3. Align the **regulator** so that the pins fit snugly into the correct holes on the **valve** stem, and hand tighten the **regulator**.

4. Attach the **oxygen** connective tubing to the **flowmeter**. (page 421; Supplemental Oxygen)

Skill Drill 10-8: Performing Mouth-to-Mask Ventilation

1. Once the patient's head is properly **positioned** and an airway **adjunct** is inserted, place the mask on the patient's face. **Seal** the mask to the face using both hands (EC **clamp**).

2. **Breathe** into the one-way valve until you note visible **chest** rise.

3. Remove your **mouth** and watch the patient's chest fall during **exhalation**. (page 429; Assisted and Artificial Ventilation)

Chapter 11: Principles of Pharmacology

General Knowledge

Matching

1. I (page 457; How Medications Work)
2. J (page 456; How Medications Work)
3. F (page 456; How Medications Work)
4. G (page 464; Medications Used by EMTs)
5. D (page 455; How Medications Work)

6. H (page 456; How Medications Work)
7. B (page 455; How Medications Work)
8. C (page 455; How Medications Work)
9. E (page 459; Medication Forms)
10. A (page 460; Medication Forms)

Multiple Choice

1. D (page 455; How Medications Work)
2. A (page 468; Medications Used by EMTs)
3. A (page 456; How Medications Work)
4. A (page 457; How Medications Work)
5. B (page 468; Medications Used by EMTs)
6. C (page 471; Medications Used by EMTs)
7. B (page 473; Medications Used by EMTs)
8. B (page 470; Medications Used by EMTs)

9. B (page 475; Medications Used by EMTs)
10. A (page 468; Medications Used by EMTs)
11. C (page 457; How Medications Work)
12. C (page 471; Medications Used by EMTs)
13. C (page 460; Medication Forms)
14. A (page 456; How Medications Work)
15. B (page 468; Medications Used by EMTs)
16. B (page 472; Medications Used by EMTs)

True/False

1. F (page 473; Medications Used by EMTs)
2. F (page 468; Medications Used by EMTs)
3. F (page 470; Medications Used by EMTs)
4. T (page 469; Medications Used by EMTs)

5. F (page 468; Medications Used by EMTs)
6. T (page 464; Medications Used by EMTs)
7. F (page 456; How Medications Work)
8. F (page 469; Medications Used by EMTs)

Fill-in-the-Blank

1. Glucose (page 468; Medications Used by EMTs)
2. Epinephrine (page 470; Medications Used by EMTs)
3. sublingually (page 469; Medications Used by EMTs)
4. Unintended effects (page 456; How Medications Work)
5. solutions (page 459; Medication Forms)
6. medication (page 455; How Medications Work)

Crossword Puzzle

Critical Thinking

Multiple Choice

1. D (page 467; Medications Used by EMTs)
2. D (page 469; Medications Used by EMTs)
3. A (page 471; Medications Used by EMTs)

4. A (page 468; Medications Used by EMTs)
5. B (page 468; Medications Used by EMTs)

Short Answer

1. 1. Intravenous
    2. Intramuscular
    3. Transcutaneous
    4. Oral
    5. Intraosseous
    6. Inhalation
    7. Sublingual
    8. Subcutaneous
    9. Per rectum
    10. Intranasal (pages 457–458; How Medications Work)

2. 1. Right patient
    2. Right medication
    3. Right dose
    4. Right route
    5. Right time
    6. Right documentation (pages 462–463; General Steps in Administering Medication)

3. Many drugs adsorb (stick to) activated charcoal, preventing the drugs from being absorbed by the body. It needs to be shaken because it is a suspension and should be given in a covered container with a straw. (pages 464, 467; Medications Used by EMTs)

4. 1. Secreted naturally by the adrenal glands

    2. Dilates lung passages

    3. Constricts blood vessels

    4. Increases heart rate and blood pressure (page 470; Medications Used by EMTs)

5. 1. Obtain medical direction per local protocol.

    2. Confirm correct medication and expiration date.

    3. Attempt to determine if the patient is allergic to any medications.

    4. Prepare the medication and attach the atomizer.

    5. Place the atomizer in one nostril, pointing up and slightly outward.

    6. Administer a half dose (1 mL maximum) into each nostril.

    7. Reassess the patient and document appropriately. (page 472; Medications Used by EMTs)

6. 1. Relaxes the muscular walls of the coronary arteries and veins

    2. Results in less blood returning to the heart

    3. Decreases blood pressure

    4. Relaxes arteries throughout the body

    5. Often causes a mild headache and/or burning under the tongue after administration (page 469; Medications Used by EMTs)

7. To avoid misdirecting the spay of the MDI and ensure inhalation of all medication (page 474; Medications Used by EMTs)

Ambulance Calls

1. This patient is in serious trouble. The history of the events combined with his level of consciousness, stridor, and hypotension are obvious signs of an anaphylactic reaction. You must immediately administer epinephrine in order to counteract the effects of the insect stings (ie, histamine release). If available, ALS providers should be requested. If not available, transport to the nearest appropriate facility should occur without delay. With the presence of multiple stings, this patient will likely need repeat doses of epinephrine as well as the administration of antihistamines, breathing treatments, and possibly advanced airway maneuvers. Your partner should apply high-flow oxygen and remove any remaining stingers in the neck or face by scraping them from the skin. Your prompt action is essential to patient survival.

2. This patient is most likely suffering from hypoglycemia. Although this patient is confused, he is able to talk and swallow. Some states allow EMTs to perform blood glucose tests, and this would provide information regarding this patient's blood glucose level. If your local protocols do not allow for this skill, you can gather much information about this patient through his physical signs and medical history (all indicative of low blood sugar). You should administer (at least) one tube of oral glucose and reassess his mentation and vital signs. Provide treatment and transport according to local protocols.

3. Place the patient in a position of comfort. Give 100% oxygen via nonrebreathing mask. Check blood pressure! Check the expiration date on the nitroglycerin. Contact medical control for permission to assist patient with one nitroglycerin tablet, SL. Monitor vital signs. Provide rapid transport.

Fill-in-the-Patient Care Report

EMS Patient Care Report (PCR)				
Date: Today's date	**Incident No.:** 2010-345	**Nature of Call:** Respiratory distress		**Location:** Northern Park
Dispatched: N/A	**En Route:** N/A	**At Scene:** 1300	**Transport:** 1308	**At Hospital:** 1318	**In Service:** 1348

Patient Information				
Age: 38 years **Sex:** Female **Weight (in kg [lb]):** 45 kg (100 lb)		**Allergies:** Unknown **Medications:** Metered-dose inhaler for asthma **Past Medical History:** Asthma **Chief Complaint:** Respiratory distress		

Vital Signs				
Time: 1308	**BP:** 142/98	**Pulse:** 110 regular	**Respirations:** 28 labored	**Spo$_2$:** 88%
Time: 1313	**BP:** 138/90	**Pulse:** 102 regular	**Respirations:** 24 labored	**Spo$_2$:** 92%
Time: 1318	**BP:** 132/88	**Pulse:** 96 regular	**Respirations:** 20 GTV	**Spo$_2$:** 96%

EMS Treatment (circle all that apply)				
Oxygen @ _15_ **L/min via (circle one):** NC (NRM) BVM		**Assisted Ventilation**	**Airway Adjunct**	**CPR**
Defibrillation	**Bleeding Control**	**Bandaging**	**Splinting**	**Other:**

Narrative
Summoned by civilian on scene for a respiratory distress. Arrived at patient's location to find a 38-year-old female on a park bench in the tripod position and struggling to breathe. Additionally, I observed a bluish hue around the patient's mouth and fingernails and accessory muscle use in her neck. A bystander handed me a metered-dose inhaler prescribed for asthma and told me that the patient had dropped it. The patient took the inhaler and inhaled one full puff of the device. The patient was then placed on high-concentration oxygen via nonrebreathing mask and prepared for transport. The patient was already beginning to show signs of improvement (bluish color fading, better tidal volume) as I obtained the first set of vitals and began transport to the emergency department. During transport, I was able to initiate reassessments, obtaining two more full sets of vital signs, which tended to show that the patient was improving as a result of the inhaler use and the oxygen therapy. While en route, I provided the receiving facility with a patient report, and the transport was uneventful. Once at the emergency department, the patient was properly transferred to their care and a full verbal report was provided.**End of Report**

SHOCK AND RESUSCITATION
Chapter 12: Shock

General Knowledge

Matching

1. B (page 487; Introduction)
2. G (page 487; Pathophysiology)
3. H (page 489; Pathophysiology)
4. C (page 489; Pathophysiology)
5. E (page 489; Pathophysiology)

6. A (page 494; Types of Shock)
7. F (page 493; Types of Shock)
8. I (page 494; Types of Shock)
9. D (page 496; The Progression of Shock)

Multiple Choice

1. A (page 487; Pathophysiology)
2. B (page 489; Pathophysiology)
3. B (page 489; Pathophysiology)
4. C (page 489; Pathophysiology)
5. D (page 500; Emergency Medical Care for Shock)
6. B (page 490; Pathophysiology)
7. D (page 490; Causes of Shock)
8. C (page 496; Types of Shock)
9. B (page 491; Types of Shock)
10. A (page 493; Types of Shock)

11. D (page 493; Types of Shock)
12. A (page 493; Types of Shock)
13. B (page 495; Types of Shock)
14. A (page 495; Types of Shock)
15. A (page 494; Types of Shock)
16. A (page 497; The Progression of Shock)
17. B (page 499; Patient Assessment for Shock)
18. C (page 500; Emergency Medical Care for Shock)
19. B (page 501; Emergency Medical Care for Shock)
20. B (page 494; Types of Shock)

True/False

1. T (page 494; Types of Shock)
2. F (page 491; Types of Shock)
3. T (page 487; Introduction)
4. F (page 487; Introduction)
5. F (page 496; The Progression of Shock)

6. T (page 503; Emergency Medical Care for Shock)
7. T (page 493; Types of Shock)
8. F (page 487; Pathophysiology)
9. F (page 490; Causes of Shock)
10. F (pages 496–497; The Progression of Shock)

Fill-in-the-Blank

1. Hypoperfusion (page 487; Introduction)
2. contraction (page 489; Pathophysiology)
3. tolerant (page 488; Pathophysiology)
4. perfusion (page 489; Pathophysiology)
5. platelets, plasma (page 489; Pathophysiology)
6. shock (hypoperfusion) (page 487; Introduction)
7. Sphincters, contract, dilate (page 489; Pathophysiology)
8. Diastolic, systolic (page 489; Pathophysiology)
9. complications (page 504; Emergency Medical Care for Shock)
10. involuntary (page 489; Pathophysiology)

Crossword Puzzle

The crossword grid contains the following answers:

Across:
1. HYPOTHERMIA
6. SYNCOPE
7. CARDIOGENIC
8. CYANOSIS
10. PRELOAD
12. SPHINCTERS
13. NEUROGENIC
14. EDEMA

Down:
1. HOMEOSTATIC
2. IRREVERSIBLE
3. SHOCK
4. ANEURYSM
5. COMPENSATED
9. AFTERLOAD
11. SEPTIC

Critical Thinking

Multiple Choice

1. A (page 491; Types of Shock)

2. C (page 493; Types of Shock)

3. C (page 493; Types of Shock)

4. B (page 496; The Progression of Shock)

5. D (page 499; Emergency Medical Care for Shock)

Short Answer

1. Causes: Extreme lift-threatening allergic reaction

Signs/Symptoms: Can develop within seconds, mild itching/rash, burning skin, vascular dilation, generalized edema, profound coma, rapid death

Treatment: Manage airway, assist ventilations, administer high-flow oxygen, determine cause, assist with administration of epinephrine, transport promptly, consider ALS (page 501; Emergency Medical Care for Shock)

2. Causes: Inadequate heart function, disease of muscle tissue, impaired electrical system, disease or injury

Signs/Symptoms: Chest pain; irregular pulse; weak pulse; low blood pressure; cyanosis (lips, under nails); cool, clammy skin; anxiety; rales; pulmonary edema

Treatment: Position comfortably, administer high-flow oxygen, assist ventilations, transport promptly, consider ALS (page 501; Emergency Medical Care for Shock)

3. Causes: Loss of blood or fluid

Signs/Symptoms: Rapid, weak pulse; low blood pressure; change in mental status; cyanosis (lips, under nails); cool, clammy skin; increased respiratory rate

Treatment: Secure airway, assist ventilations, administer high-flow oxygen, control external bleeding, keep warm, transport promptly, consider ALS (page 502; Emergency Medical Care for Shock)

4. Causes: Damaged cervical spine, which causes widespread blood vessel dilation

Signs/Symptoms: Bradycardia (slow pulse), low blood pressure, signs of neck injury

Treatment: Secure airway, spinal stabilization, assist ventilations, administer high-flow oxygen, preserve body heat, transport promptly, consider ALS (page 501; Emergency Medical Care for Shock)

5. **Causes:** Temporary, generalized vascular dilation; anxiety; bad news; sight of injury/blood; prospect of medical treatment; severe pain; illness; tiredness

   Signs/Symptoms: Rapid pulse, normal or low blood pressure

   Treatment: Determine duration of unconsciousness, position the patient supine, record initial vital signs and mental status, suspect head injury if patient is confused or slow to regain consciousness, transport promptly (page 502; Emergency Medical Care for Shock)

6. **Causes:** Severe bacterial infection

   Signs/Symptoms: Warm skin or fever, tachycardia, low blood pressure

   Treatment: Transport promptly, administer oxygen, assist ventilation, keep warm, consider ALS (page 501; Emergency Medical Care for Shock)

7. 1. Pump failure
   2. Blood or fluid loss from blood vessels
   3. Poor vessel function (blood vessels dilate) (page 490; Causes of Shock)

8. Falling blood pressure; labored or irregular breathing; ashen, mottled, or cyanotic skin; thready or absent peripheral pulses; dull eyes or dilated pupils; poor urinary output (page 496; The Progression of Shock)

Ambulance Calls

1. When assessing the victim of a fall, you must take into consideration not only the patient's complaints and obvious injuries but also the mechanism of injury, including the height of the fall, the surface on which he or she landed, the position in which he or she landed, and any medical and/or previous traumatic injuries that could exacerbate the injuries. This patient landed on a hard surface, most likely a wooden floor, and now presents with numbness and tingling of his lower body. These are all indicators of spinal cord injury. Assume spinal fractures are present; ensure that you assess pulse, motor, and sensation of all extremities prior to placing him in full spinal precautions; and reassess again after he is stabilized. Be alert for signs of neurogenic shock. Document your findings and continue this assessment en route to the hospital.

2. This patient is in shock and it seems to be related to an infectious organism (septic shock). In this case, although he has not lost blood volume through hemorrhage, his vessels, or "container," have become too large, making his available blood volume inadequate. Immediate transport is required. The patient should be given high-flow oxygen. Consider ALS.

3. Treat this patient for anaphylactic shock. Apply high-flow oxygen while inquiring if the patient has an EpiPen. Based on local protocols, obtain orders and administer the EpiPen, if available. Monitor the patient's vital signs. Rapid transport is required. Consider ALS.

Fill-in-the-Patient Care Report

EMS Patient Care Report (PCR)			
Date: Today's date	**Incident No.:** 2010-123	**Nature of Call:** MCA	**Location:** Highway 62 at Exit 19

Dispatched: 0200	**En Route:** 0200	**At Scene:** 0205	**Transport:** 0213	**At Hospital:** 0218	**In Service:** 0233

Patient Information	
Age: 18 years **Sex:** Male **Weight (in kg [lb]):** 65 kg (143 lb)	**Allergies:** Unknown **Medications:** Unknown **Past Medical History:** Unknown **Chief Complaint:** Unable to move legs

Vital Signs				
Time: 0213	**BP:** 98/62	**Pulse:** 110/weak	**Respirations:** 18/ shallow – adequate tidal volume	**Spo$_2$:** 94% on O$_2$

EMS Treatment (circle all that apply)			
Oxygen @ _15_ **L/min via (circle one):** NC (NRM) BVM	**Assisted Ventilation**	**Airway Adjunct**	**CPR**
Defibrillation	**Bleeding Control**	**Bandaging**	(Splinting)	(**Other:** Shock Treatment)

Narrative
Summoned by highway patrol for a motorcyclist down on Highway 62 at exit 19. Arrived to find an 18-year-old man supine on the highway, complaining of inability to move his legs and feeling "odd." Patient was alert, had a patent airway, and although his breathing was rapid and shallow it seemed to be producing adequate oxygenation. Initiated spinal stabilization and high-flow oxygen therapy via nonrebreathing mask prior to applying cervical collar and immobilizing patient to a long backboard. Once en route to the trauma center, I obtained vitals showing hypotension; increased heart rate; rapid breathing; decreased O$_2$ sat with high-flow oxygen; and pale, cool, moist skin. Removed patient's clothing to check for injuries and found that his lower extremities were cooler than his torso and that the skin on his legs was dry. Immediately upgraded transport to lights and sirens, treated patient for shock, and called verbal report to the receiving facility. Arrived at the trauma center prior to obtaining second set of vitals, and the patient was properly transferred to their care. A full verbal report was provided.**End of Report**

Assessment Review

1. A (page 497; Patient Assessment for Shock)
2. A (pages 497–498; Patient Assessment for Shock)
3. B (page 498; Patient Assessment for Shock)
4. B (page 499; Emergency Medical Care for Shock)
5. C (page 499; Patient Assessment for Shock)

SHOCK AND RESUSCITATION
Chapter 13: BLS Resuscitation

General Knowledge

Matching

1. G (page 532; Devices and Techniques to Assist Circulation)
2. E (page 542; Foreign Body Airway Obstruction in Adults)
3. C (page 514; Elements of BLS)
4. D (page 515; Elements of BLS)
5. A (page 514; Elements of BLS)
6. F (page 525; Opening the Airway and Providing Artificial Ventilation)
7. J (page 531; Devices and Techniques to Assist Circulation)
8. I (page 522; Opening the Airway and Providing Artificial Ventilation)
9. B (page 522; Opening the Airway and Providing Artificial Ventilation)
10. H (page 523; Opening the Airway and Providing Artificial Ventilation)

Multiple Choice

1. D (page 514; Elements of BLS)
2. D (page 514; Elements of BLS)
3. B (page 515; Elements of BLS)
4. B (page 548; Foreign Body Airway Obstruction in Infants and Children)
5. A (page 519; Positioning the Patient)
6. D (page 533; Infant and Child CPR)
7. D (page 534; Infant and Child CPR)
8. D (page 539; When Not to Start CPR)
9. C (page 540; When to Stop CPR)
10. D (page 548; Special Resuscitation Circumstances)
11. B (page 523; Opening the Airway and Providing Artificial Ventilation)
12. C (page 525; Opening the Airway and Providing Artificial Ventilation)
13. B (page 525; Opening the Airway and Providing Artificial Ventilation)
14. A (page 523; Opening the Airway and Providing Artificial Ventilation)
15. D (page 519; Check for Breathing and a Pulse)
16. A (page 520; Check for Breathing and a Pulse)
17. D (page 520; Check for Breathing and a Pulse)
18. B (page 534; Infant and Child CPR)
19. D (page 535; Infant and Child CPR)
20. C (page 535; Infant and Child CPR)
21. D (page 542; Foreign Body Airway Obstruction in Adults)
22. B (page 542; Foreign Body Airway Obstruction in Adults)
23. D (page 543; Foreign Body Airway Obstruction in Adults)
24. C (page 542; Foreign Body Airway Obstruction in Adults)

True/False

1. T (page 516; Assessing the Need for BLS)
2. F (pages 516–517; Assessing the Need for BLS)
3. T (pages 516–517; Assessing the Need for BLS)
4. F (pages 523–524; Opening the Airway and Providing Artificial Ventilation)
5. F (page 524; Opening the Airway and Providing Artificial Ventilation)
6. T (page 539; When Not to Start CPR)
7. T (page 520; Check for Breathing and a Pulse)
8. F (page 526; One-Rescuer Adult CPR)
9. F (page 520; Check for Breathing and a Pulse)
10. T (page 538; Infant and Child CPR)
11. F (page 549; Grief Support for Family Members and Loved Ones)
12. T (page 518; Automated External Defibrillation)
13. F (page 520; Check for Breathing and a Pulse)
14. T (page 526; Two-Rescuer Adult CPR)
15. T (page 540; When Not to Start CPR)

Fill-in-the-Blank

1. 4, 6 (page 514; Elements of BLS)
2. wet, skin (page 518; Automated External Defibrillation)
3. chest compressions (page 516; Assessing the Need for BLS)
4. pacemaker (page 518; Automated External Defibrillation)
5. Advance directives (page 540; When Not to Start CPR)
6. firm, flat (page 519; Positioning the Patient)
7. airway (page 522; Opening the Airway and Providing Artificial Ventilation)
8. automated external defibrillator (page 517; Automated External Defibrillation)
9. carotid (page 519; Check for Breathing and a Pulse)
10. mechanical piston device (page 532; Devices and Techniques to Assist Circulation)

Crossword Puzzle

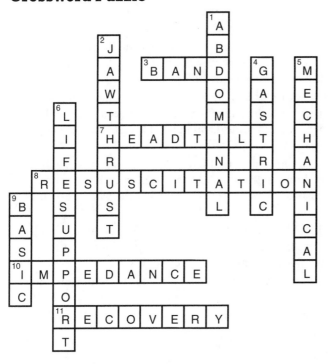

Critical Thinking

Short Answer

Complete this section with short written answers using the space provided.

1.
   1. Rigor mortis, or stiffening of the body after death
   2. Dependent lividity (livor mortis), a discoloration of the skin due to pooling of blood
   3. Putrefaction or decomposition of the body
   4. Evidence of nonsurvivable injury, such as decapitation (page 539; When Not to Start CPR)
2.
   1. Recognition and activation of the emergency response system
   2. Immediate, high-quality CPR
   3. Rapid defibrillation
   4. Basic and advanced emergency medical services
   5. Advanced life support and postarrest care (pages 515–516; The Components of CPR)
3.
   1. Injury, both blunt and penetrating
   2. Infections of the respiratory tract or another organ system
   3. A foreign body airway obstruction

   4. Submersion (drowning)

   5. Electrocution

   6. Poisoning or drug overdose

   7. Sudden infant death syndrome (SIDS) (page 534; Infant and Child CPR)

4. To perform the head tilt–chin lift maneuver, make sure the patient is supine. Place one hand on the patient's forehead and apply firm backward pressure with your palm to tilt the head back. Next, place the tips of your fingers of your other hand under the lower jaw near the bony part of the chin. Lift the chin upward, bringing the entire lower jaw with it, helping to tilt the head back. (page 523; Opening the Airway and Providing Artificial Ventilation)

5. To perform the jaw-thrust maneuver, place your fingers behind the angle of the lower jaw on both sides and move the jaw upward. Keep the head in a neutral position. If the mouth remains closed, use your thumbs to pull the patient's lower jaw down to allow breathing. (page 522; Opening the Airway and Providing Artificial Ventilation)

6. Take standard precautions. Once you have determined that the patient is unresponsive, call for additional help. Ensure that the patient is on a firm, flat surface in a supine position. Place your hands in the proper position. Give 30 compressions at a rate of 100 to 120 per minute for an adult. Using a rhythmic motion, apply pressure vertically from your shoulders down through both arms to depress the sternum 2 inches to 2.4 inches (5 cm to 6 cm) in an adult, then rise up gently and fully. Count the compressions aloud. (page 520; Check for Breathing and a Pulse)

7. Rescuer one should finish the cycle of 30 compressions while a second rescuer moves to the opposite side of the chest and moves into position to begin compressions. Rescuer one delivers two ventilations and then rescuer two should take over compressing by administering 30 compressions. (page 529; Two-Rescuer Adult CPR)

8. Standing: Stand behind the patient and wrap your arms around his or her abdomen. Make a fist with one hand, then grasp the fist with the other hand. Place the thumb side of the fist against the patient's abdomen between the umbilicus and the xiphoid process. Press your fist into the patient's abdomen in quick inward and upward thrusts until the object is expelled or the patient becomes unconscious. (page 543; Foreign Body Airway Obstruction in Adults)

9. Standing: Stand behind the patient and wrap your arms under the armpits and around the patient's chest. Make a fist with one hand, then grasp the fist with the other hand. Place the thumb side of the fist against the patient's sternum. Press your fist into the patient's chest and perform backward thrusts until the object is expelled or the patient becomes unconscious.

Supine: Kneel next to the patient. Place your hands as you would to deliver chest compressions. Deliver 30 chest compressions, open the airway, and look in the mouth. If the object is visible, remove it. If not, continue the cycle of chest compressions and opening the airway. (page 544; Foreign Body Airway Obstruction in Adults)

10.   **1.** Hold the infant face down, with the body resting on your forearm. Support the infant's jaw and face with your hand and keep the head lower than the body.

   2. Deliver five back slaps between the shoulder blades, using the heel of your hand.

   3. Place your free hand behind the infant's head/back and turn the infant face up.

   4. Give five quick chest thrusts on the sternum using two fingers.

   5. Check the airway. If the object is visible, then remove it. (pages 546, 548; Foreign Body Airway Obstruction in Infants and Children)

Ambulance Calls

1. Question the family about the last time they spoke with her. Explain that she has been down too long for CPR to be effective. Comfort family members. Notify your dispatcher to alert the supervisor and either law enforcement, the coroner, or a funeral home according to local protocols.

2. With the FDA's approval of AEDs for home use, it will become more common to see them being used by the lay provider. Simply purchasing an AED does not ensure appropriate usage during real-life events. Training by knowledgeable, skilled instructors is needed to minimize confusion and inappropriate AED use. Remove the AED and explain to them that AEDs are meant to be used only when a person is not breathing and has no pulse. Emphasize that it is appropriate to have the AED nearby in the event that a person goes into cardiorespiratory arrest, but that it is not to be applied until then. After the patient has been transported to the hospital, tell the friends and family that you appreciate their willingness to be prepared for emergencies, and that you would like to see them be successful in their usage of their AED. If you or your department offers CPR/AED courses, offer to train them and/or point them in the right direction to receive the appropriate training.

3. Given the scene, you must assume that there is the likelihood for trauma. This means that you must assess and maintain his airway without manipulating his spine. Use the jaw-thrust maneuver and apply full cervical spine precautions. Also, consider possible causes of his unconscious state, including any scene hazards and potential medical conditions.

Skills

Skill Drills

Skill Drill 13-1: Performing Chest Compressions

1. Take standard precautions. Place the **heel** of one hand on the **center** of the chest.
2. Place the **heel** of your other **hand** over the first hand.
3. With your arms straight, lock your **elbows**, and position your shoulders directly over your **hands**. Depress the sternum at a rate of **100** to **120** compressions per minute, and to a depth of **2 inches** to **2.4 inches (5 cm to 6 cm)** using a direct downward movement. Allow the chest to return to its normal position; do not lean on the chest between compressions. **Compression** and relaxation should be of equal duration. (page 521; Check for Breathing and a Pulse)

Skill Drill 13-2: Performing One-Rescuer Adult CPR

1. Take standard precautions. Establish unresponsiveness and call for help. Use your mobile phone if needed.
2. Check for breathing and a carotid pulse for no more than 10 seconds.
3. If breathing and pulse are absent, begin CPR until an AED is available. Give 30 chest compressions at a rate of 100 to 120 per minute.
4. Open the airway according to your suspicion of spinal injury.
5. Give two ventilations of 1 second each and observe for visible chest rise. Continue cycles of 30 chest compressions and two ventilations until additional personnel arrive or the patient starts to move. (page 527; One-Rescuer Adult CPR)

Skill Drill 13-3: Performing Two-Rescuer Adult CPR

1. Take standard **precautions**. Establish **unresponsiveness** and take positions.
2. Check for breathing and a **carotid** pulse.
3. Begin CPR, starting with **chest compressions**. Give 30 chest compressions at a rate of **100** to **120** per minute. If the AED is available, then apply it and follow the voice prompts.
4. **Open** the airway according to your suspicion of spinal injury.
5. Give **two ventilations** of 1 second each and observe **visible chest rise**. Continue cycles of 30 chest compressions and two ventilations (switch roles every five cycles [2 minutes]) until ALS providers take over or the patient starts to move. Reanalyze the patient's cardiac rhythm with the AED every 2 minutes and deliver a shock if indicated. (page 528; Two-Rescuer Adult CPR)

Chapter 14: Medical Overview

General Knowledge

Matching

1. A (page 561; Types of Medical Emergencies)
2. G (page 561; Types of Medical Emergencies)
3. B (page 561; Types of Medical Emergencies)
4. I (page 561; Types of Medical Emergencies)
5. A (page 561; Types of Medical Emergencies)
6. F (page 561; Types of Medical Emergencies)
7. K (page 561; Types of Medical Emergencies)
8. C (page 561; Types of Medical Emergencies)
9. J (page 561; Types of Medical Emergencies)
10. E (page 561; Types of Medical Emergencies)
11. A (page 561; Types of Medical Emergencies)
12. D (page 561; Types of Medical Emergencies)
13. H (page 561; Types of Medical Emergencies)
14. B (page 561; Types of Medical Emergencies)
15. G (page 561; Types of Medical Emergencies)
16. D (page 561; Types of Medical Emergencies)
17. K (page 561; Types of Medical Emergencies)
18. D (page 561; Types of Medical Emergencies)
19. I (page 561; Types of Medical Emergencies)
20. C (page 561; Types of Medical Emergencies)

Multiple Choice

1. C (page 562; Patient Assessment)
2. B (page 563; Patient Assessment)
3. C (page 564; Patient Assessment)
4. B (page 564; Patient Assessment)
5. C (page 565; Patient Assessment)
6. B (page 566; Patient Assessment)
7. D (page 568; Management, Transport, and Destination)
8. C (page 568; Management, Transport, and Destination)
9. B (page 570; Common or Serious Communicable Diseases)
10. B (page 571; Common or Serious Communicable Diseases)
11. C (page 575; Common or Serious Communicable Diseases)
12. C (page 572; Common or Serious Communicable Diseases)
13. C (page 572; Common or Serious Communicable Diseases)
14. A (pages 573–574; Common or Serious Communicable Diseases)
15. D (page 575; Common or Serious Communicable Diseases)
16. B (page 569; Infectious Diseases)

True/False

1. T (page 562; Patient Assessment)
2. T (page 564; Patient Assessment)
3. T (page 569; Infectious Diseases)
4. T (page 564; Patient Assessment)
5. F (page 565; Patient Assessment)
6. T (page 567; Management, Transport, and Destination)
7. T (page 570; Common or Serious Communicable Diseases)
8. F (page 570; Common or Serious Communicable Diseases)
9. F (page 575; Common or Serious Communicable Diseases)
10. T (page 573; Common or Serious Communicable Diseases)
11. F (page 573; Common or Serious Communicable Diseases)
12. T (page 574; Common or Serious Communicable Diseases)
13. T (page 575; Common or Serious Communicable Diseases)
14. F (page 575; Common or Serious Communicable Diseases)
15. T (page 573; Common or Serious Communicable Diseases)
16. F (page 569; Common or Serious Communicable Diseases)
17. T (page 565; Patient Assessment)
18. F (page 564; Patient Assessment)
19. T (page 568; Management, Transport, and Destination)
20. T (page 568; Management, Transport, and Destination)
21. F (page 569; Common or Serious Communicable Diseases)

Fill-in-the-Blank

1. Hematologic emergencies (page 561; Types of Medical Emergencies)
2. Tunnel vision (page 562; Patient Assessment)
3. AVPU (page 563; Patient Assessment)

4. 5, 15 (page 567; Patient Assessment)

5. medical control (page 567; Management, Transport, and Destination)

6. AED (page 567; Management, Transport, and Destination)

7. High-priority (page 568; Management, Transport, and Destination)

8. ground, air (page 568; Management, Transport, and Destination)

9. infectious disease (page 569; Infectious Diseases)

10. Hepatitis (page 571; Common or Serious Communicable Diseases)

11. Hepatitis A (page 573; Common or Serious Communicable Diseases)

12. track marks (page 566; Patient Assessment)

13. Virulence (page 573; Common or Serious Communicable Diseases)

14. Tuberculosis (page 573; Common or Serious Communicable Diseases)

15. meningitis (page 573; Common or Serious Communicable Diseases)

Fill-in-the-Table (page 570; Common or Serious Communicable Diseases)

Causes of Infectious Disease

Type of Organism	Description	Example
Bacteria	**Grow and reproduce outside the human cell in the appropriate temperature and with the appropriate nutrients**	*Salmonella*
Viruses	Smaller than bacteria; multiply only inside a host and die when exposed to the environment	**Human immunodeficiency virus**
Fungi	**Similar to bacteria in that they require the appropriate nutrients and organic material to grow**	**Mold**
Protozoa (parasites)	**One-celled microscopic organisms, some of which cause disease**	Amoebas
Helminths (parasites)	Invertebrates with long, flexible, rounded, or flattened bodies	**Worms**

Crossword Puzzle

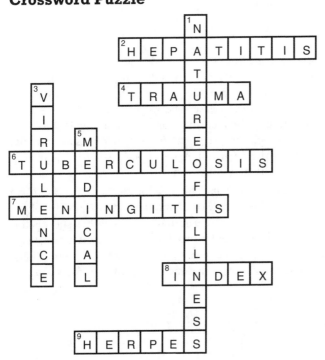

Critical Thinking

Short Answer

Complete this section with short written answers using the space provided.

1. 1. The patient's blood is splashed or sprayed into your eyes, nose, or mouth or into an open sore or cut; even microscopic openings in the skin are a possible source.

   2. You have blood from an infected patient on your hands and then touch your own eyes, nose, mouth, or an open sore or cut.

   3. A needle used to inject the patient breaks your skin.

   4. Broken glass at a motor vehicle collision or other incident may penetrate your glove (and skin), which may have already been covered with blood from an infected patient. (page 570; Common or Serious Communicable Diseases)

2. 1. Scene size-up

   2. Primary assessment

   3. History taking

   4. Secondary assessment

   5. Reassessment (page 562; Patient Assessment)

3. **T**–Tobacco

   A–Alcohol

   C–Caffeine

   O–Over-the-counter medications/herbal supplements

   S–Sexual and street drugs (page 565; Patient Assessment)

4. 1. Unresponsive/altered mental status

   2. Airway/breathing problems

   3. Circulatory problems, such as severe bleeding or signs of shock (page 568; Management, Transport, and Destination)

5. 1. Where did you recently travel?

   2. Did you receive any vaccinations before your trip?

   3. Were you exposed to any infectious diseases?

   4. Is there anyone else in your travel party who is sick?

   5. What types of food did you eat?

   6. What was your source of drinking water? (page 576; Common or Serious Communicable Diseases)

Ambulance Calls

1. It seems likely that this patient could be suffering from tuberculosis. You and your crew should apply protection immediately. You should place an N95 or HEPA mask on yourself and other crew members and a surgical mask on the patient. Although a surgical mask on the patient provides minimal protection, it provides a visual reminder to all who are involved in the patient's care of the possibility of an airborne communicable disease. The surgical mask should still allow for the placement of a nasal cannula for oxygen. Proper notification to the receiving hospital should be made so that isolation precautions can be in place when the patient arrives. Although the risk of contracting the illness is minimal to you and the crew, everyone should alert their management and follow their exposure-control plan. All crew members potentially exposed should receive a tuberculin skin test and follow up with a designated health care facility.

2. You should begin by verifying the chief complaint of chest pain. Ask the patient what she was doing when the pain began and whether anything potentially caused it. Does anything make the pain better or worse? Inquire as to the quality of the pain. Ask the patient to describe the pain, and determine if the pain is constant or intermittent. Where in her chest is the pain? Have the patient point to the painful area and determine whether the pain is localized to that area or if it radiates to other areas. Ask the patient to rate her pain on a scale from 1 to 10. Explain to her that 0 means no pain and that 10 means the worst pain. This will give you a baseline for reassessment after you begin treatment. Inquire as to how long she's had the pain. Is it just this incident or has she had previous episodes?

Critical Thinking

Short Answer

1. 1. Normal rate
    2. Regular pattern of inhalation and exhalation
    3. Clear and equal lung sounds on both sides of the chest
    4. Regular and equal chest rise and fall
    5. Adequate depth
    6. Unlabored; without adventitious breath sounds (page 587; Pathophysiology)

2. 1. Asthma
    2. Chronic obstructive pulmonary disease
    3. Congestive heart failure/pulmonary edema
    4. Pneumonia
    5. Bronchitis
    6. Anaphylaxis (page 605; Patient Assessment)

3. 1. Patient is unable to coordinate administration and inhalation.
    2. Inhaler is not prescribed for patient.
    3. You did not obtain permission from medical control or local protocol.
    4. Patient has already met maximum prescribed dose before your arrival.
    5. Medication is expired.
    6. There are other contraindications specific to the medication. (page 610; Emergency Medical Care)

4. An ongoing irritation of the respiratory tract; excess mucus production obstructs small airways and alveoli. Protective mechanisms are impaired. Repeated episodes of irritation and pneumonia can cause scarring and alveolar damage, leading to COPD. (page 594; Causes of Dyspnea)

5. Obstruction with secretions, mucus, foreign bodies, and/or airway swelling; Bleeding; Leaking; Dislodgement; Infection (page 618; Treatment of Specific Conditions)

6. A condition characterized by a chronically high blood level of carbon dioxide in which the respiratory center no longer responds to high blood levels of carbon dioxide. In these patients, low blood oxygen causes the respiratory center to respond and stimulate respiration. If the arterial level of oxygen is then raised, as happens when the patient is given additional oxygen, there is no longer any stimulus to breathe; both the high carbon dioxide and low oxygen drives are lost. (pages 587–589; Pathophysiology)

7. 1. Is the air going in?
    2. Does the chest rise and fall with each breath?
    3. Is the rate adequate for the age of your patient? (page 603; Patient Assessment)

Ambulance Calls

1. This child has all the classics signs of epiglottitis. You should do nothing to excite or frighten the child because doing so will likely cause his airway to spasm and close. Remember to use nonthreatening body language (place yourself below his eye level), give the child distance (until you establish trust), and perform any exam using a full-body scan. This is a true emergency that requires immediate transport to the hospital, but you must do so tactfully. Use parents to assist with patient care efforts, such as applying humidified oxygen (blow-by or mask).

2. This patient's chief complaint, age, weight, smoking, and birth control use all place her at risk of pulmonary embolism (PE). PE patients most often experience a sudden onset of shortness of breath that they describe as sharp and worsening with inspiration. You should provide high-flow oxygen, obtain vital signs, and perform a secondary assessment en route to the hospital (including auscultation of lung sounds). Provide prompt transport to the nearest appropriate facility.

3. Place the patient in a position of comfort. Provide high-flow oxygen via nonrebreathing mask and monitor his vital signs. This patient requires rapid transport to the nearest appropriate facility.

4. This patient is likely experiencing pulmonary edema associated with his cardiac history. Place the patient in a sitting-up position and administer 100% oxygen through a nonrebreathing mask. Suction the frothy secretions from the patient's airway, as necessary. Consider CPAP for this patient and be prepared to provide full ventilatory support for this patient should he deteriorate. This patient requires prompt transport to the nearest appropriate facility.

Skills

Skill Drills

Skill Drill 15-1: Assisting a Patient With a Metered-Dose Inhaler

1. Check to make sure you have the correct medication for the correct patient. Check the expiration date. Ensure inhaler is at room temperature or **warmer**.
2. Remove oxygen mask. Hand inhaler to patient. Instruct about breathing and **lip seal**.
3. Instruct patient to press inhaler and inhale one puff. Instruct about **breath holding**.
4. Reapply **oxygen**. After a few **breaths**, have patient repeat **dose** if order or protocol allows. (page 613; Emergency Medical Care)

Skill Drill 15-2: Assisting a Patient With a Small-Volume Nebulizer

1. Check to make sure you have the correct medication for the correct patient. Check the expiration date. Confirm you have the correct patient.
2. Insert the medication into the container on the nebulizer. In some cases, sterile saline may be added (about 3 mL) to achieve the optimum volume of fluid for the nebulized application.
3. Attach the medication container to the nebulizer, mouthpiece, and tubing. Attach oxygen tubing to the oxygen tank. Set the flowmeter at 6 L/min.
4. Instruct the patient on how to breathe. (page 614; Emergency Medical Care)

Assessment Review

1. D (page 609; Patient Assessment)
2. B (page 617; Treatment of Specific Conditions)
3. A (page 604; Patient Assessment)
4. B (page 608; Patient Assessment)
5. D (page 608; Patient Assessment)

Emergency Care Summary (pages 609-617; Emergency Medical Care, Treatment of Specific Conditions)

General Management of Respiratory Emergencies

Managing life threats to the patient's **ABCs** and ensuring the delivery of high-flow oxygen are the primary concerns with any respiratory emergency. Patients breathing at a rate of less than **12** breaths/min or greater than **20** breaths/min should receive **high-flow oxygen**. Continually assess the patient's mental status, and provide emotional support as needed. Transport in a position of comfort. For all respiratory emergencies, make sure you have taken the appropriate standard precautions, including the use of a(n) **N95 respirator** in a patient with suspected tuberculosis.

Upper or Lower Airway Infection

Dyspnea from an upper airway infection may be from **croup** or **epiglottitis**. Patients should receive **humified** oxygen if available. Patients who are sitting forward, seem lethargic, or are drooling may have **epiglottitis**. Do not force the patient to lie down or attempt to suction or insert a(n) **oropharyngeal** airway because this may cause a spasm and a complete airway obstruction. Transport should be rapid.

Lower airway infections may be from the common cold, bronchitis, or **pneumonia**. Patients need supplemental oxygen, monitoring of vital signs, and transport to the hospital.

Asthma, Hay Fever, and Anaphylaxis

Not all wheezing is the result of asthma! Obtain a thorough **history** from the patient or family. If the patient is wheezing and has asthma, assist with the patient's prescribed **inhaler** or administer a small-volume nebulizer containing **albuterol**. Provide supplemental oxygen and provide ventilatory support as needed. Patients whose asthma progresses to **status asthmaticus** require immediate transportation. Be prepared to assist their ventilations because they may become too exhausted to breathe. Hay fever usually requires only support and transport, but if the condition has worsened from generalized cold symptoms, the patient may require supplemental oxygen and **airway** support.

Anaphylaxis is a true emergency that requires rapid intervention and **transport**. Airway, oxygen, and ventilatory support are paramount. Determine if the patient has a prescribed **epinephrine.** Transport promptly. Reassess the patient's condition en route to the hospital.

Pneumothorax

A pneumothorax may occur spontaneously or may be the result of a(n) **traumatic event**. Place the patient in a position of comfort, and support the **ABCs**. Provide prompt transport, monitor the patient carefully, and be prepared to assist ventilations and provide **cardiopulmonary resuscitation** if necessary.

Obstruction of the Airway

Managing an airway obstruction is a priority. Use age-appropriate **basic** life support foreign body airway obstruction **maneuvers** to clear the airway. Administer supplemental oxygen, and transport the patient to the closest hospital. Some patients do not want to go to a hospital after the obstruction is cleared. Encourage them to be transported for evaluation of possible **injury** to the airway.

Hyperventilation

Gather a thorough **history**, and attempt to determine the **underlying cause** because the hyperventilation may be the result of a serious problem. Do not have the patient breathe into a(n) **paper bag**; this maneuver could make things worse. Instead, **reassure** the patient, administer supplemental oxygen, and provide prompt transport to the hospital.

Chapter 16: Cardiovascular Emergencies

General Knowledge

Matching

1. L (page 629; Anatomy and Physiology)
2. C (page 631; Anatomy and Physiology)
3. O (page 631; Anatomy and Physiology)
4. G (page 631; Anatomy and Physiology)
5. N (page 631; Anatomy and Physiology)
6. K (page 632; Anatomy and Physiology)
7. H (page 629; Anatomy and Physiology)
8. M (page 629; Anatomy and Physiology)
9. B (page 636; Pathophysiology)
10. D (page 639; Pathophysiology)
11. F (page 636; Pathophysiology)
12. I (page 637; Pathophysiology)
13. J (page 639; Pathophysiology)
14. A (page 639; Pathophysiology)
15. E (page 639; Pathophysiology)
16. P (page 636; Pathophysiology)
17. G (page 636; Pathophysiology)
18. E (page 637; Pathophysiology)
19. F (page 637; Pathophysiology)
20. C (page 640; Pathophysiology)
21. A (page 642; Pathophysiology)
22. D (page 642; Pathophysiology)
23. B (page 642; Pathophysiology)

Multiple Choice

1. C (page 631; Anatomy and Physiology)
2. D (page 629; Anatomy and Physiology)
3. A (page 632; Anatomy and Physiology)
4. B (page 630; Anatomy and Physiology)
5. A (page 631; Anatomy and Physiology)
6. B (page 631; Anatomy and Physiology)
7. C (page 632; Anatomy and Physiology)
8. A (page 632; Anatomy and Physiology)
9. C (page 632; Anatomy and Physiology)
10. A (page 636; Pathophysiology)
11. B (page 636; Pathophysiology)
12. B (page 636; Pathophysiology)
13. D (page 637; Pathophysiology)
14. B (page 637; Pathophysiology)
15. A (page 637; Pathophysiology)
16. B (page 642; Pathophysiology)
17. C (page 637; Pathophysiology)
18. C (page 638; Pathophysiology)
19. C (page 638; Pathophysiology)
20. A (page 641; Pathophysiology)
21. B (page 640; Pathophysiology)
22. D (page 639; Pathophysiology)
23. A (page 639; Pathophysiology)
24. A (page 640; Pathophysiology)
25. D (page 641; Pathophysiology)
26. B (page 640; Pathophysiology)
27. C (page 638; Pathophysiology)
28. C (page 643; Patient Assessment)
29. B (page 646; Patient Assessment)
30. C (page 646; Patient Assessment)
31. A (page 641; Pathophysiology)
32. B (page 648; Emergency Medical Care for Chest Pain or Discomfort)
33. C (page 648; Emergency Medical Care for Chest Pain or Discomfort)
34. B (page 653; Heart Surgeries and Cardiac Assistive Devices)
35. A (page 653; Heart Surgeries and Cardiac Assistive Devices)
36. C (page 655; Cardiac Arrest)
37. C (page 657; Cardiac Arrest)
38. B (page 656; Cardiac Arrest)
39. C (page 656; Cardiac Arrest)
40. A (page 657; Cardiac Arrest)
41. D (page 643; Patient Assessment)
42. A (page 643; Patient Assessment)
43. D (page 660; Emergency Medical Care for Cardiac Arrest)
44. C (page 660; Emergency Medical Care for Cardiac Arrest)
45. C (page 664; Emergency Medical Care for Cardiac Arrest)

True/False

1. F (page 630; Anatomy and Physiology)
2. F (page 631; Anatomy and Physiology)
3. T (page 636; Pathophysiology)
4. F (page 637; Pathophysiology)
5. T (page 637; Pathophysiology)
6. F (page 637; Pathophysiology)
7. F (page 648; Emergency Medical Care for Chest Pain or Discomfort)
8. F (page 659; Cardiac Arrest)
9. T (page 637; Pathophysiology)
10. F (page 632; Anatomy and Physiology)
11. T (page 655; Cardiac Arrest)
12. T (page 655; Cardiac Arrest)
13. F (page 642; Pathophysiology)
14. T (page 638; Pathophysiology)
15. T (page 645; Patient Assessment)

Fill-in-the-Blank

1. septum (page 629; Anatomy and Physiology)
2. aorta (page 629; Anatomy and Physiology)
3. right (page 630; Anatomy and Physiology)
4. atrioventricular (page 631; Anatomy and Physiology)
5. dilation (page 631; Anatomy and Physiology)
6. Red blood (page 632; Anatomy and Physiology)
7. Diastolic (page 634; Anatomy and Physiology)
8. four (page 630; Anatomy and Physiology)
9. left (page 630; Anatomy and Physiology)
10. CPAP (page 644; Patient Assessment)
11. dependent edema (page 642; Pathophysiology)
12. 180 mm Hg (page 642; Pathophysiology)
13. pulmonary veins (page 640; Pathophysiology)
14. 90 mm Hg (page 641; Pathophysiology)
15. inferior (page 638; Pathophysiology)

Labeling

1. Right and Left Sides of the Heart (page 630; Anatomy and Physiology)
   A. Superior vena cava (oxygen-poor blood from head and upper body)
   B. Left pulmonary artery (blood to left lung)
   C. Right pulmonary artery (blood to right lung)
   D. Right atrium
   E. Inferior vena cava (oxygen-poor blood from lower body)
   F. Right ventricle
   G. Oxygen-rich blood to head and upper body
   H. Right pulmonary veins (oxygen-rich blood from right lung)
   I. Left pulmonary veins (oxygen-rich blood from left lung)
   J. Left atrium
   K. Left ventricle
   L. Oxygen-rich blood to lower body

2. Electrical Conduction System (page 631; Anatomy and Physiology)
   A. Atrioventricular (AV) node
   B. Bundle of His
   C. SA node
   D. Left bundle branch
   E. Internodal pathways
   F. Left posterior fascicle
   G. Right bundle branch
   H. Purkinje fibers
   I. Left anterior fascicle

3. Pulse Points (page 635; Anatomy and Physiology)
   A. Carotid
   B. Femoral
   C. Brachial
   D. Radial
   E. Posterior tibial
   F. Dorsalis pedis

Crossword Puzzle

```
    ¹D Y S R H Y T H M I ²A
³I                        M
N       ⁴T ⁵A C H Y C ⁶A R D I ⁷A
F           O           C       S
A       ⁸A T R I U M    U       Y
R           T           T       S
⁹C A R ¹⁰D I ¹¹C A R R E S T    T
T       E       H       C       O
I      ¹²P E R F U S I O N       L
O       E           R   ¹³L     E
N       N           O   U
        D      ¹⁴A U T O N O M I C
        E           A   E
¹⁵S Y N C O P E     R   N
        T           Y
```

Critical Thinking

Short Answer

1. In an AMI, the onset of pain is gradual, with additional symptoms. The pain is typically described as a tightness or pressure. The severity of pain increases with time and may wax and wane. The pain is usually substernal and very rarely radiates to the back. Peripheral pulses are equal.

   With a dissecting aneurysm, the onset of pain is abrupt, without additional symptoms. The pain is typically described as sharp or tearing. The severity of pain is at its maximum from the onset and does not abate once started. The pain can be located in the chest with radiation to the back, between the shoulder blades. There can be a blood pressure discrepancy between the arms or a decrease in a femoral or carotid pulse. (page 642; Pathophysiology)

2. 1. Failure of the machine to not shock fine ventricular fibrillation
    2. Applying the AED to a patient who is moving, squirming, or being transported
    3. Turning off the AED before analysis or shock is complete (page 657; Cardiac Arrest)

3. 1. If the patient regains a pulse
    2. After six to nine shocks have been delivered
    3. If the machine gives three consecutive "no shock" messages (page 663; Emergency Medical Care for Cardiac Arrest)

4. 1. Be aware of the surface the patient is lying on. Wet and metal surfaces may conduct electricity, making defibrillation of the patient dangerous to EMTs.
    2. What is the age of the patient? Use pediatric AED pads when appropriate.
    3. Does the patient have a medication patch in the area where the AED pads will be placed? If so, remove the medication patch, wipe the area clean, and then attach the AED pad.
    4. Does the patient have an implantable pacemaker or internal defibrillator in the same area where the AED pads will be located? If so, place the AED pad below the pacemaker or defibrillator, or place the pads in anterior and posterior positions. (page 665; Emergency Medical Care for Cardiac Arrest)

5. Stable angina is characterized by pain in the chest of coronary origin that is relieved by rest or nitroglycerin. Unstable angina is characterized by pain in the chest of coronary origin that occurs in response to progressively less exercise or fewer stimuli than ordinarily required to produce angina. If untreated, it can lead to AMI. (page 637; Pathophysiology)

6. **1.** It may or may not be caused by exertion, but it can occur at any time.

   2. It does not resolve in a few minutes.

   3. It may or may not be relieved by rest or nitroglycerin. (page 638; Pathophysiology)

7. **1.** Sudden death

   2. Cardiogenic shock

   3. Congestive heart failure (CHF) (page 639; Pathophysiology)

8. **1.** Sudden onset of weakness, nausea, or sweating without an obvious cause

   2. Chest pain, discomfort, or pressure that is often crushing or squeezing and that does not change with each breath

   3. Pain, discomfort, or pressure in the lower jaw, arms, back, abdomen, or neck

   4. Irregular heartbeat with syncope

   5. Shortness of breath, or dyspnea

   6. Nausea/vomiting

   7. Pink, frothy sputum

   8. Sudden death (page 638; Pathophysiology)

9. **1.** Take vital signs, and give oxygen by nonrebreathing mask with an oxygen flow of 10 to 15 L/min. Medical control may order the use of CPAP.

   2. Allow the patient to remain sitting in an upright position with the legs down.

   3. Be reassuring; many patients with CHF are quite anxious because they cannot breathe.

   4. Patients who have had problems with CHF before will usually have specific medications for its treatment. Gather these medications and take them to the hospital.

   5. Nitroglycerin may be of value if the patient's systolic blood pressure is greater than 100 mm Hg. If the patient has been prescribed nitroglycerin, and medical control or standing orders advise you to do so, you can administer it sublingually.

   6. Prompt transport to the emergency department is essential. (page 641; Pathophysiology)

Ambulance Calls

1. The patient is feeling better, so it is likely that he was experiencing an episode of angina; however, because you cannot rule out an AMI, this patient should be strongly encouraged to go to the hospital for evaluation. Place the patient in a position of comfort. Provide oxygen therapy, if appropriate. Monitor his vital signs and provide normal transport. If the patient continues to have chest pain, reassess and consider administering an additional nitroglycerin tablet, if local protocol permits. In addition to BLS care, this patient will also benefit from ALS care; therefore, an attempt to rendezvous with an ALS unit should be made.

2. Denial is one of the biggest indicators of heart attack. Although this patient is considered "younger" and otherwise healthy, he is having signs and symptoms of a myocardial infarction. It may take some convincing of the need for treatment and transport, but you must be clear on the potential consequences of his refusal of care (informed refusal). If he initially refuses, explain what physical signs you see that lead you to believe he is likely having a heart attack, express genuine concern for his well-being, and allow him to speak directly with medical control. More often than not, when patients hear the same or similar information from a physician, it has a different effect. If he allows you to examine, treat, and transport him, apply oxygen (if appropriate), transport promptly, and follow local protocols.

3. This patient could be having a heart attack. A common symptom that women (especially postmenopausal women) experience when having a heart attack is the sudden onset of generalized weakness. Although chest pain is a common indicator of heart attack, if a patient is not experiencing pain or pressure it does not necessarily mean that he or she is not experiencing a cardiac event. It is important to note that heart disease is the number one killer of women in the United States, taking more lives than cancer and killing more women than men every year. If your patient exhibits any combination of the "associated symptoms" of heart attack, such as nausea, vomiting, shortness of breath, pain or numbness in the neck, jaw, back, or arm(s), or cool, pale, sweaty skin, you should suspect the possibility of a heart attack. You should apply oxygen (if appropriate), obtain vital signs, allow the patient to maintain a position of comfort, and provide immediate transport to the nearest appropriate facility.

Fill-in-the-Patient Care Report

EMS Patient Care Report (PCR)			
Date: Today's date	**Incident No.:** 011543	**Nature of Call:** Chest pain	**Location:** 1574 S. Main St.

Dispatched: 1901	**En Route:** 1901	**At Scene:** 1909	**Transport:** 1921	**At Hospital:** 1926	**In Service:** 1935

Patient Information	
Age: 58 years	**Allergies:** Aspirin
Sex: Male	**Medications:** Lisinopril, nitroglycerin, metformin, and metoprolol
Weight (in kg [lb]): Unknown	**Past Medical History:** Hypertension, angina, and diabetes
	Chief Complaint: Chest tightness

Vital Signs				
Time: 1914	**BP:** 136/88	**Pulse:** 88	**Respirations:** 22	**Spo₂:** 99%
Time: 1921	**BP:** 122/74	**Pulse:** 84	**Respirations:** 18	**Spo₂:** 98%

EMS Treatment
(circle all that apply)

Oxygen @ _15_ L/min via (circle one): NC **(NRM)** BVM	**Assisted Ventilation**	**Airway Adjunct**	**CPR**
Defibrillation	**Bleeding Control**	**Bandaging**	**Splinting**	**Other:**

Narrative

9-1-1 dispatch for 58-year-old man complaining of chest pain. Arrived on scene and was met by patient's wife at the front door who stated that patient has been experiencing chest pain for approximately 30 minutes with no relief from two nitroglycerin tablets. We were directed to the living room, where we found our patient sitting up on the couch with some obvious shortness of breath. Patient stated that he was sitting on the couch when he began to feel "incredible constant pressure" in his chest. Stated that he initially thought it was his angina but reported that "this feels different." Patient currently rates pain as a 5/10. Oxygen was applied at 15 L/min via nonrebreathing mask. Primary and secondary assessment performed, along with vital signs. Per local protocol, because the patient's systolic blood pressure was above 100 mm Hg, one tablet of nitroglycerin was administered sublingually to the patient. The patient was secured to stretcher and taken to unit. Patient was transported to local facility. Reassessment of patient indicated his pain was now a 4/10. On arrival at facility, patient was stable. Care was transferred to ED staff. Verbal report was given to staff. No further incidents. Unit cleaned and restocked. Crew went available and returned to station.**End of Report**

Skills

Skill Drills

Skill Drill 16-1: Administration of Nitroglycerin

1. Obtain an order from **medical control**. Take the patient's blood pressure. Administer **nitroglycerin** only if the **systolic** blood pressure is greater than 100 mm Hg.

2. Check the medication and expiration date. Ask the patient about the last dose he or she took and its **effects**. Make sure that the patient understands the route of **administration**. Prepare to have the patient lie down to prevent **fainting**.

3. Ask the patient to lift his or her **tongue**. Place the tablet or spray the dose under the **tongue** (while wearing gloves), or have the patient do so. Have the patient keep his or her mouth **closed** with the tablet or spray under the tongue until it is dissolved and absorbed. Caution the patient against **chewing** or swallowing the tablet.

4. Recheck the blood pressure within **5** minutes. Record each medication and the time of administration. Reevaluate the **chest pain** and blood pressure, and repeat treatment, if necessary. (page 649; Emergency Medical Care for Chest Pain or Discomfort)

Skill Drill 16-3: AED and CPR

1. Take standard precautions. Determine scene safety. Question bystanders. Determine responsiveness. Assess compression effectiveness if CPR is already in progress. If the patient is unresponsive and CPR has not been started yet, begin providing chest compressions and rescue breaths at a rate of 30 compressions to two breaths and a rate of 100 to 120 compressions per minute, continuing until an AED arrives and is ready for use.

2. Turn on the AED. Apply the AED pads to the chest and attach the pads to the AED. Stop CPR. If a shock is not advised, perform five cycles (about 2 minutes) of CPR, beginning with chest compressions, and then reanalyze the cardiac rhythm. If a shock is advised, reconfirm that no one is touching the patient and push the Shock button. If at any time the AED advises to check the patient, quickly assess for a carotid or femoral pulse. This should not take longer than 5 to 10 seconds. If you feel a pulse, the patient has experienced ROSC (return of spontaneous circulation). Continue to monitor the patient.

3. Verbally and visually clear the patient. Push the Analyze button, if there is one. Wait for the AED to analyze the cardiac rhythm. If no shock is advised, perform five cycles (2 minutes) of CPR and then reanalyze the cardiac rhythm. If a shock is advised, recheck that all are clear, and push the Shock button. After the shock is delivered, immediately resume CPR beginning with chest compressions and remember to switch rescuers.

4. After five cycles (2 minutes) of CPR, reanalyze the cardiac rhythm. Do not interrupt chest compressions for more than 10 seconds.

5. If shock is advised, clear the patient, push the Shock button, and immediately resume CPR compressions. If no shock is advised, immediately resume CPR compressions and be sure to switch rescuers. After five cycles (2 minutes) of CPR, reanalyze the cardiac rhythm. Repeat the cycle of five cycles (2 minutes) of CPR, one shock (if indicated), and 2 minutes of CPR. Transport, and contact medical control as needed. (pages 662–663; Emergency Medical Care for Cardiac Arrest)

Assessment Review

1. B (page 629; Introduction)
2. A (page 645; Patient Assessment)
3. D (page 643; Patient Assessment)
4. C (page 645; Patient Assessment)
5. B (page 653; Heart Surgeries and Cardiac Assistive Devices)

MEDICAL

Chapter 17: Neurologic Emergencies

General Knowledge

Matching

1. M (page 679; Stroke)
2. N (page 680; Stroke)
3. D (page 682; Seizures)
4. O (pages 675–676; Anatomy and Physiology)
5. K (page 676; Anatomy and Physiology)
6. E (page 676; Anatomy and Physiology)
7. H (page 685; Seizures)
8. B (page 683; Seizures)
9. F (page 684; Seizures)
10. L (page 678; Stroke)
11. A (page 681; Seizures)
12. C (pages 681–682; Seizures)
13. I (page 682; Seizures)
14. J (page 678; Stroke)
15. G (page 680; Stroke)

Multiple Choice

1. D (page 682; Seizures)
2. A (pages 675–676; Anatomy and Physiology)
3. A (page 676; Anatomy and Physiology)
4. C (page 685; Altered Mental Status)
5. C (page 678; Stroke)
6. A (page 679; Stroke)
7. B (pages 677–678; Headache)
8. B (page 678; Stroke)
9. D (page 680; Stroke)
10. A (page 685; Altered Mental Status)
11. D (page 685; Altered Mental Status)
12. A (page 684; Seizures)
13. D (page 684; Seizures)
14. C (page 685; Altered Mental Status)
15. B (page 685; Altered Mental Status)
16. C (page 683; Seizures)
17. C (page 677; Headache)
18. A (page 678; Headache)
19. B (page 679; Stroke)
20. D (page 676; Headache)
21. A (page 681; Stroke)
22. B (page 687; Patient Assessment)
23. C (page 680; Stroke)
24. C (page 687; Patient Assessment)
25. B (page 691; Patient Assessment)
26. D (page 689; Patient Assessment)
27. B (page 680; Stroke)
28. A (page 678; Stroke)
29. D (pages 695–696; Emergency Medical Care)

True/False

1. F (page 682; Seizures)
2. T (page 676; Pathophysiology)
3. T (page 684; Seizures)
4. F (page 680; Stroke)
5. T (page 695; Emergency Medical Care)
6. F (page 680; Stroke)
7. T (page 677; Headache)
8. T (pages 678–679; Stroke)
9. F (page 678; Stroke)
10. T (page 680; Stroke)
11. F (page 679; Stroke)
12. F (pages 681–682; Seizures)
13. T (page 684; Seizures)
14. T (page 685; Altered Mental Status)
15. F (page 686; Altered Mental Status)
16. T (page 686; Altered Mental Status)
17. T (page 687; Patient Assessment)
18. F (page 688; Patient Assessment)
19. F (page 694; Emergency Medical Care)
20. T (page 695; Emergency Medical Care)

Fill-in-the-Blank

1. 12 (page 676; Anatomy and Physiology)
2. cerebellum (page 676; Anatomy and Physiology)
3. ischemic, hemorrhagic (page 678; Stroke)
4. oxygen, glucose, temperature (page 676; Pathophysiology)
5. carbon monoxide poisoning (page 677; Headache)
6. simple partial (page 682; Seizures)
7. opposite (page 676; Anatomy and Physiology)
8. temporal (page 682; Seizures)
9. Incontinence (page 684; Seizures)
10. epileptic seizures (page 683; Seizures)
11. postictal state (page 684; Seizures)
12. hemiparesis (page 685; Seizures)
13. foreign body obstruction (pages 687–688; Patient Assessment)
14. Glasgow Coma Scale (page 692; Patient Assessment)
15. Thrombolytic therapy (page 696; Emergency Medical Care)

Labeling

1. Brain (page 675; Anatomy and Physiology)
   A. Cerebrum
   B. Skull
   C. Brain stem
   D. Cerebellum
   E. Spinal cord

2. Spinal Cord (page 676; Anatomy and Physiology)
   A. Cerebrum
   B. Cerebellum
   C. Brain stem
   D. Foramen magnum
   E. Spinal cord
   F. Spinal nerves

Crossword Puzzle

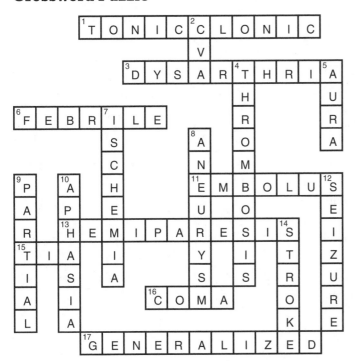

Critical Thinking

Short Answer

1. 1. Facial droop—Ask patient to show teeth or smile.

   Normal: Both sides of the face move equally well.

   Abnormal: One side of the face does not move as well as the other.

   2. Arm drift—Ask patient to close eyes and hold arms out with palms up.

   Normal: Both arms move the same, or both arms do not move.

   Abnormal: One arm does not move, or one arm drifts down compared to the other side.

   3. Speech—Ask patient to say, "The sky is blue in Cincinnati."

   Normal: Patient uses correct words with no slurring.

   Abnormal: Patient slurs words, uses inappropriate words, or is unable to speak. (page 691; Patient Assessment)

2. New therapies for stroke are available but must be used as soon as possible after the start of symptoms. You should minimize time on the scene, and notify the receiving hospital as soon as possible. (pages 694–695; Emergency Medical Care)

3. A period of time after a seizure, generally lasting from 5 to 30 minutes, in which a patient is unresponsive at first and gradually regains consciousness. The postictal state is over when the patient regains a complete return of his or her normal level of consciousness. The patient will likely appear dazed, confused, and fatigued. (page 682; Seizures)

4. A partial seizure begins in one part of the brain and is classified as simple or complex. In a simple partial seizure, there is no change in mental status. Patients may complain of numbness, weakness, or dizziness. The patient may report sensory disturbances. A simple partial seizure may also cause twitching of the muscles and extremities that may spread slowly from one part of the body to another, but it is not characterized by the dramatic severe twitching and muscle movements seen in a generalized seizure. In a complex partial seizure, the patient has an altered mental status and does not interact normally with his or her environment. This type of seizure results from abnormal discharges from the temporal lobe of the brain. Other characteristics may be lip smacking, eye blinking, and isolated convulsions or jerking of the body or one part of the body, such as an arm. (page 682; Seizures)

5. 1. Hypoglycemia

   2. Postictal state

   3. Subdural or epidural bleeding (page 681; Stroke)

6. **A.** Eye Opening—4—Patient is looking at you.

   Verbal—4—Patient is confused about the date/year.

   Motor—5—Patient does not respond to commands, localized to pain.

   Total: 13

   B. Eye Opening—2—Patient opens eyes to painful stimulus.

   Verbal—2—Patient uses incomprehensible sounds.

   Motor—4—Patient withdraws to pain.

   Total: 8

   C. Eye Opening—1—Patient does not open eyes to any stimuli.

   Verbal—1—Patient has no verbal response.

   Motor—1—Patient does not move extremities to any stimuli.

   Total: 3

   D. Eye Opening—4—Patient is looking at you.

   Verbal—5—Patient is able to have an oriented conversation.

   Motor—6—Patient is able to follow commands.

   Total: 15 (page 693; Patient Assessment)

Ambulance Calls

1. Given these signs, your patient is likely experiencing a left hemispheric stroke. Any problems related to his ability to understand or use language will be frustrating for both you and the patient. After performing your primary assessment, the Cincinnati Prehospital Stroke Scale can provide valuable information regarding the presence of a stroke. This assessment measures abnormalities in speech and the presence of facial droop and arm drift. Stroke is a true emergency that requires prompt transport. You should apply oxygen to maintain an SpO_2 of at least 94% and take care during transport to prevent injury of affected body parts because the patient will not be able to protect them on his own. It is helpful to place the patient on the affected side and elevate his head approximately 6 inches (15 cm) to facilitate swallowing. Be sure to relate your positive findings of stroke to the hospital to avoid any unnecessary delays in patient care on arrival to the emergency department.

2. Maintain the airway—assist ventilations with high-flow oxygen, if needed. Consider placement of an oral or nasal airway. Suction, if necessary, or position lateral recumbent to clear secretions.

   Check glucose level.

   Provide rapid transport.

3. This patient's signs and symptoms cause you to suspect the presence of a hemorrhagic stroke. You should consider applying oxygen (if appropriate) and provide immediate transport. This patient will be more likely to experience seizure activity than patients suffering from ischemic stroke. There is no way for you to determine the type or extent of her stroke because this can be accomplished only in the hospital. Your job is to recognize the seriousness of the situation, provide supportive measures within your scope of practice, provide prompt transport, and notify the receiving facility.

4. When a patient who experienced a seizure wants to refuse EMS care, the following questions need to be discussed and/or considered:

   1. Is the patient awake and completely oriented after the seizure (GCS score of 15)?
   2. Does your assessment show no evidence of trauma or complications from the seizure?
   3. Has the patient ever had a seizure before?
   4. Was this seizure the "usual" seizure in every way (length, activity, recovery)?
   5. Is the patient currently being treated with medications and receiving regular evaluations by a physician?

   If the answer to all of these questions is yes, you may consider agreeing to the patient's refusal for transport if the patient can be released to a responsible person and monitored. However, if the answer is no to any of these questions, you should strongly encourage the patient to be transported and evaluated.

Skills

Assessment Review

1. C (page 691; Patient Assessment)
2. B (page 685; Altered Mental Status)
3. A (pages 694–695; Emergency Medical Care)
4. C (page 680; Stroke)

MEDICAL

Chapter 18: Gastrointestinal and Urologic Emergencies

General Knowledge

Matching

1. I (page 713; Pathophysiology)
2. D (page 709; Pathophysiology)
3. E (page 705; Anatomy and Physiology)
4. M (pages 708–709; Pathophysiology)
5. K (page 713; Pathophysiology)
6. A (page 707; Pathophysiology)
7. C (page 716; Patient Assessment)
8. J (page 708; Pathophysiology)
9. F (page 708; Pathophysiology)
10. B (page 708; Pathophysiology)
11. G (page 707; Pathophysiology)
12. N (page 712; Pathophysiology)
13. L (page 714; Pathophysiology)

14. O (page 707; Pathophysiology)
15. H (page 707; Pathophysiology)
16. F (page 709; Pathophysiology)
17. B (page 709; Pathophysiology)
18. J (page 709; Pathophysiology)
19. I (page 709; Pathophysiology)
20. E (page 709; Pathophysiology)
21. A (page 709; Pathophysiology)
22. D (page 709; Pathophysiology)
23. H (page 709; Pathophysiology)
24. C (page 709; Pathophysiology)
25. G (page 709; Pathophysiology)

Multiple Choice

1. B (page 708; Pathophysiology)
2. A (page 717; Patient Assessment)
3. A (pages 713–714; Pathophysiology)
4. B (page 711; Pathophysiology)
5. D (page 717; Patient Assessment)
6. A (page 713; Pathophysiology)
7. B (page 705; Anatomy and Physiology)
8. C (page 710; Pathophysiology)
9. B (page 710; Pathophysiology)
10. D (page 709; Pathophysiology)
11. B (page 710; Pathophysiology)
12. C (page 716; Patient Assessment)
13. D (page 709; Pathophysiology)
14. A (page 713; Pathophysiology)
15. A (page 719; Emergency Medical Care)

16. C (page 706; Anatomy and Physiology)
17. B (page 712; Pathophysiology)
18. D (page 712; Pathophysiology)
19. C (page 712; Pathophysiology)
20. A (page 712; Pathophysiology)
21. C (page 712; Pathophysiology)
22. B (page 710; Pathophysiology)
23. C (page 710; Pathophysiology)
24. A (page 716; Patient Assessment)
25. D (page 719; Dialysis Emergencies)
26. C (page 706; Anatomy and Physiology)
27. B (page 706; Anatomy and Physiology)
28. C (page 706; Anatomy and Physiology)
29. D (page 706; Anatomy and Physiology)
30. C (page 706; Anatomy and Physiology)

True/False

1. F (page 708; Pathophysiology)
2. T (page 719; Dialysis Emergencies)
3. F (page 716; Patient Assessment)
4. T (page 716; Patient Assessment)
5. T (page 707; Pathophysiology)

6. F (page 707; Pathophysiology)
7. F (page 717; Patient Assessment)
8. T (page 713; Pathophysiology)
9. T (page 709; Pathophysiology)
10. F (page 719; Emergency Medical Care)

Labeling

1. Solid Organs (page 705; Anatomy and Physiology)
   A. Liver
   B. Spleen
   C. Pancreas
   D. Kidney
   E. Kidney
   F. Ovaries

2. Hollow Organs (page 705; Anatomy and Physiology)
   A. Gallbladder
   B. Stomach
   C. Ureter
   D. Small intestine
   E. Large intestine
   F. Fallopian tubes
   G. Urinary bladder
   H. Uterus

3. Urinary System (page 706; Anatomy and Physiology)
   A. Kidney
   B. Ureter
   C. Bladder
   D. Prostate gland
   E. Ureter opening
   F. Urethra
   G. Penis
   H. External urethral opening

Crossword Puzzle

Critical Thinking

Short Answer

1. Occurs because of connections between the body's two nervous systems. The abdominal organs are supplied by autonomic nerves that, when irritated, stimulate close-lying sensory (somatic) nerves. (page 708; Pathophysiology)

2. 1. Has the patient's level of consciousness changed?
   2. Has the patient become more anxious?
   3. Have the skin signs started to change?
   4. Has the pain gotten better or worse?
   5. Has the bleeding become worse or better?
   6. Is current treatment improving the patient's condition?
   7. Has an already identified problem gotten better or worse?
   8. What is the nature of any newly identified problems? (page 718; Patient Assessment)

3. Paralysis of muscular contractions in the bowel results in retained gas and feces. Nothing can pass through. (pages 707–708; Pathophysiology)

4. **1.** Explain to the patient what you are going to do in terms of assessing the abdomen.

    2. Place the patient in a supine position with the legs drawn up and flexed at the knees to relax the abdominal muscles, unless there is any trauma, in which case the patient will remain supine and stabilized. Determine whether the patient is restless or quiet and whether motion causes pain.

    3. Expose the abdomen and visually assess it. Does the abdomen appear distended (enlarged)? Do you see any pulsating masses? Is there bruising to the abdominal wall? Are there any surgical scars?

    4. Ask the patient where the pain is most intense. Palpate in a clockwise direction beginning with the quadrant after the one the patient indicates is tender or painful; end with the quadrant that the patient indicates is tender and painful. If the most painful area is palpated first, the patient may guard against further examination, making your assessment more difficult and less reliable.

    5. Remember to be very gentle when palpating the abdomen.

    6. Palpate the four quadrants of the abdomen gently to determine whether each quadrant is tense (guarded) or soft when palpated.

    7. Note whether the pain is localized to a particular quadrant or diffuse (widespread).

    8. Palpate and wait for the patient to respond, looking for a facial grimace or a verbal "ouch." Do not ask the patient "Does it hurt here?" as you palpate.

    9. Determine whether the patient exhibits rebound tenderness.

    10. Determine whether the patient can relax the abdominal wall on command. Guarding and rigidity may be detected. (pages 717–718; Patient Assessment)

Ambulance Calls

1. Appendicitis is a possibility. Place the patient in a position of comfort. Consider applying oxygen, if appropriate. Keep the patient warm and be prepared to manage shock. Provide rapid transport. Obtain a SAMPLE history. Document OPQRST. Monitor patient closely.

2. This patient is likely experiencing a bowel obstruction, secondary to an ileus, that is causing his pain and tenderness. If left untreated, his condition will deteriorate. When assessing his abdomen, explain what you will do, place him with knees slightly toward his abdomen, and gently palpate all four quadrants to determine the presence of rigidity or masses. If a patient points to a specific location of pain, palpate that area last. You must take great care in moving and transporting the patient because it will be particularly painful if he is bumped or jostled. Apply oxygen (if necessary), allow him to find a position of comfort, and move him gently. Do not delay transport to attempt to determine the cause of abdominal pain.

3. Individuals who have experienced a kidney stone(s) will tell you that it is an extremely painful experience. Provide prompt, gentle transport. Monitor his airway, breathing, and circulation. Be prepared for continued vomiting. Apply low-flow oxygen (which can ease nausea), obtain vital signs, do not give anything by mouth, and keep the patient as comfortable as possible. Be sure to thoroughly document all information regarding the patient's signs and symptoms, as well as any treatment you provide. Always follow local protocols.

Skills

Assessment Review

1. D (page 715; Patient Assessment)

2. A (page 716; Patient Assessment)

3. B (page 716; Patient Assessment)

4. A (page 717; Patient Assessment)

5. D (page 718; Patient Assessment)

MEDICAL
Chapter 19: Endocrine and Hematologic Emergencies

General Knowledge

Matching

1. J (page 727; Endocrine Emergencies)
2. A (page 742; Hematologic Emergencies)
3. C (page 730; Endocrine Emergencies)
4. M (page 737; Patient Assessment of Diabetes)
5. O (page 727; Endocrine Emergencies)
6. Q (page 733; Endocrine Emergencies)
7. F (page 731; Endocrine Emergencies)
8. G (page 743; Hematologic Emergencies)
9. D (page 731; Endocrine Emergencies)
10. B (page 741; Hematologic Emergencies)
11. P (page 727; Endocrine Emergencies)
12. E (page 731; Endocrine Emergencies)
13. L (page 729; Endocrine Emergencies)
14. K (page 728; Endocrine Emergencies)
15. H (page 731; Endocrine Emergencies)
16. N (pages 742–743; Hematologic Emergencies)
17. I (page 732; Endocrine Emergencies)

Multiple Choice

1. A (page 731; Endocrine Emergencies)
2. A (page 729; Endocrine Emergencies)
3. D (page 742; Hematologic Emergencies)
4. C (page 728; Endocrine Emergencies)
5. C (page 745; Emergency Medical Care for Hematologic Disorders)
6. A (page 732; Endocrine Emergencies)
7. C (page 731; Endocrine Emergencies)
8. D (page 727; Endocrine Emergencies)
9. D (page 732; Endocrine Emergencies)
10. A (page 727; Endocrine Emergencies)
11. B (page 730; Endocrine Emergencies)
12. D (page 743; Hematologic Emergencies)
13. D (page 732; Endocrine Emergencies)
14. A (page 738; Emergency Medical Care for Diabetic Emergencies)
15. A (page 727; Endocrine Emergencies)
16. A (page 731; Endocrine Emergencies)
17. C (page 731; Endocrine Emergencies)
18. A (page 744; Patient Assessment of Hematologic Disorders)
19. B (page 734; Endocrine Emergencies)
20. D (page 734; Endocrine Emergencies)
21. C (page 740; The Presentation of Hypoglycemia)
22. B (page 730; Endocrine Emergencies)
23. A (page 732; Endocrine Emergencies)
24. B (page 741; The Presentation of Hypoglycemia)
25. C (page 735; Patient Assessment of Diabetes)
26. D (pages 729–730; Endocrine Emergencies)
27. B (page 745; Patient Assessment of Hematologic Disorders)
28. D (page 744; Hematologic Emergencies)
29. D (page 740; Emergency Medical Care for Diabetic Emergencies)
30. D (page 734; Endocrine Emergencies)
31. D (page 745; Patient Assessment of Hematologic Disorders)
32. C (page 734; Endocrine Emergencies)
33. C (pages 729, 741; Endocrine Emergencies, The Presentation of Hypoglycemia)

True/False

1. T (page 731; Endocrine Emergencies)
2. F (page 736; Patient Assessment of Diabetes)
3. F (page 742; Hematologic Emergencies)
4. T (page 734; Endocrine Emergencies)
5. T (page 733; Endocrine Emergencies)
6. F (page 743; Hematologic Emergencies)
7. T (page 729; Endocrine Emergencies)
8. T (pages 730, 732; Endocrine Emergencies)

9. F (page 727; Endocrine Emergencies)

10. F (page 743; Hematologic Emergencies)

11. T (page 728; Endocrine Emergencies)

12. T (page 730; Endocrine Emergencies)

13. F (page 741; Hematologic Emergencies)

14. T (page 732; Endocrine Emergencies)

Fill-in-the-Blank

1. diabetes mellitus (page 728; Endocrine Emergencies)

2. Thrombophilia (page 743; Hematologic Emergencies)

3. autoimmune (page 730; Endocrine Emergencies)

4. Mediterranean, sickle cell (page 744; Patient Assessment of Hematologic Disorders)

5. impaired (page 728; Endocrine Emergencies)

6. HHNS (page 733; Endocrine Emergencies)

7. Hematology, related (page 741; Hematologic Emergencies)

8. sugar, insulin (page 737; Patient Assessment of Diabetes)

Fill-in-the-Table (page 730; Endocrine Emergencies)

	Hyperglycemia	Hypoglycemia
History		
Onset	Gradual (hours to days)	Rapid, within minutes
Skin	Warm and dry	Pale, cool, and moist
Infection	Common	Uncommon
Gastrointestinal Tract		
Thirst	Intense	Absent
Hunger	Present and increasing	Absent
Vomiting/abdominal pain	Common	Uncommon
Respiratory System		
Breathing	With DKA there are rapid, deep (Kussmaul) respirations	Normal; may become shallow or ineffective if hypoglycemia is severe and mental status is depressed
Odor of breath	With DKA there may be a sweet, fruity odor	Normal
Cardiovascular System		
Blood pressure	Normal to low	Normal to low
Pulse	Rapid, weak, and thready	Rapid and weak
Nervous System		
Consciousness	Restlessness, possibly progressing to coma; abnormal or slurred speech; unsteady gait	Irritability, confusion, seizure, or coma; unsteady gait
Treatment		
Response	Gradual, within 6 to 12 hours following medical treatment	Immediate improvement after administration of glucose

Crossword Puzzle

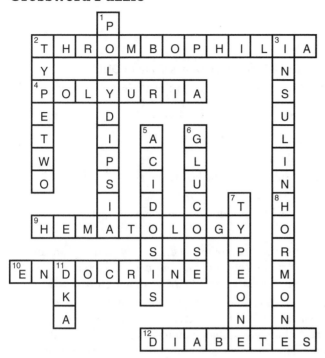

Critical Thinking

Multiple Choice

1. B (page 730; Endocrine Emergencies)
2. C (page 730; Endocrine Emergencies)
3. D (pages 736–737; Patient Assessment of Diabetes)
4. D (page 737; Patient Assessment of Diabetes)

Short Answer

1. Insulin is a hormone that enables glucose to enter the cells, which is essential for cellular metabolism. (page 727; Endocrine Emergencies)
2. 1. Dissolving gel
   2. Chewable tablet
   3. Liquid (page 738; Emergency Medical Care for Diabetic Emergencies)
3. Due to the oblong shape of the red blood cells, they are poor oxygen carriers and can become lodged in blood vessels and organs. (page 742; Hematologic Emergencies)
4. A patient who is unconscious or unable to swallow should not be given oral glucose. (page 738; Emergency Medical Care for Diabetic Emergencies)
5. A patient with thrombophilia has a tendency to develop clots in the blood vessels. These clots can travel through the circulatory system and become lodged in the lungs, obstructing blood flow and oxygen exchange. (page 744; Hematologic Emergencies)
6. 1. Hyperglycemia
   2. Altered mental status, drowsiness, lethargy
   3. Severe dehydration, thirst, dark urine
   4. Visual or sensory deficits
   5. Partial paralysis or muscle weakness
   6. Seizures (page 733; Endocrine Emergencies)

7. 1. Do you take insulin or any pills that lower your blood sugar?
   2. Do you wear an insulin pump? Is it working properly?
   3. Have you taken your usual dose of insulin (or pills) today?
   4. Have you eaten normally today?
   5. Have you had any illness, unusual amount of activity, or stress? (page 735; Patient Assessment of Diabetes)
8. Hypoglycemia; it develops rapidly as opposed to hyperglycemia, which takes longer to develop. (pages 733–734; Endocrine Emergencies)

Ambulance Calls

1. 1. Turn the patient on her side immediately or use suction to clear the airway.
   2. Insert an oral or nasal airway and support ventilations with a bag-valve mask attached to oxygen.
   3. Attempt to obtain a blood glucose level.
   4. Transport the patient rapidly because you should never give anything by mouth to an unresponsive patient.
   5. Monitor the patient closely.
2. The prehospital management of patients suffering from sickle cell crises will commonly include only comfort care and rapid transportation. You may also treat individual symptoms as they arise as per standard protocol. For example, a sickle cell patient presenting with difficulty breathing should receive oxygen therapy or ventilatory assistance if required.
3. You cannot give this patient anything by mouth because he is unconscious and therefore unable to protect his own airway. If available, you should request ALS providers because they can administer intravenous dextrose (glucose). If you have no emergency providers available with this scope of practice within your system, you must transport this patient immediately. You may encounter family members who do not understand why you cannot "just give him some sugar." Hopefully, there will be no delays in explaining his need for transport or the seriousness of his condition. Perform a thorough assessment (including blood glucose testing, if permitted), provide oxygen, monitor his ABCs (using airway adjuncts, positive pressure ventilations, and suctioning, as needed), and provide prompt transport.

Fill-in-the-Patient Care Report

EMS Patient Care Report (PCR)					
Date: Today's date	**Incident No.:** 2011-1234	**Nature of Call:** Laceration		**Location:** 12556 Old Lake House Drive	
Dispatched: 1752	**En Route:** 1755	**At Scene:** 1803	**Transport:** 1813	**At Hospital:** 1819	**In Service:** 1839

Patient Information	
Age: 14 years	**Allergies:** Unknown
Sex: Male	**Medications:** Unknown
Weight (in kg [lb]): 60 kg (132 lb)	**Past Medical History:** Hemophilia
	Chief Complaint: Bleeding laceration

Vital Signs				
Time: 1813	**BP:** 108/60	**Pulse:** 98	**Respirations:** 16/GTV	**Spo₂:** 96%

EMS Treatment
(circle all that apply)

Oxygen @ _15_ L/min via (circle one): NC (NRM) BVM	**Assisted Ventilation**	**Airway Adjunct**	**CPR**
Defibrillation / (**Bleeding Control**)	(**Bandaging:** Tourniquet)	**Splinting**	(**Other:** Shock Treatment)

Narrative

9-1-1 dispatch for an arm laceration with uncontrolled bleeding. Arrived on scene and was directed to a second-floor bedroom where the patient, a 14-year-old boy, was holding pressure on a left forearm laceration. Patient's mother advised that he had hemophilia. Observed steady bleeding and attempted to control with pressure. Initiated oxygen therapy at 15 L/min via nonrebreathing mask and used the stair chair to move the patient down to the gurney where he was covered with blankets to conserve body temperature and loaded into the ambulance. Obtained vitals, which indicated that the patient might be hypoperfusing. Because steady pressure didn't stop the bleeding, applied a tourniquet proximal to the laceration, which did stop the bleeding. Monitored the patient while en route to the hospital, continued oxygen therapy, and notified the facility of our impending arrival. Delivered the patient to the trauma department, gave a full report to the charge nurse, transferred patient care, and returned to service after cleaning/decontaminating the ambulance.**End of Report**

Skills

Skill Drills

1. Make sure that the tube of glucose is intact and has not **expired**.
2. Squeeze a generous amount of oral glucose onto the **bottom third** of a **bite stick** or tongue depressor.
3. Open the patient's **mouth**. Place the tongue depressor on the **mucous membranes** between the cheek and the gum with the **gel side** next to the cheek. Repeat until the entire tube has been used. (page 739; Emergency Medical Care for Diabetic Emergencies)

Assessment Review

1. B (page 734; Patient Assessment of Diabetes)
2. B (pages 735–736; Patient Assessment of Diabetes)
3. C (page 735; Patient Assessment of Diabetes)
4. D (page 738; Emergency Medical Care for Diabetic Emergencies)
5. D (page 738; Patient Assessment of Diabetes)

Chapter 20: Immunologic Emergencies

General Knowledge

Matching

1. D (page 753; Pathophysiology)
2. A (page 753; Pathophysiology)
3. H (page 755; Pathophysiology)
4. E (page 753; Pathophysiology)
5. B (page 757; Patient Assessment of an Immunologic Emergency)
6. G (page 753; Pathophysiology)
7. C (page 756; Common Allergens)
8. F (page 756; Common Allergens)

Multiple Choice

1. A (pages 761–762; Emergency Medical Care of Immunologic Emergencies)
2. D (page 755; Common Allergens)
3. A (page 757; Patient Assessment of an Immunologic Emergency)
4. B (page 756; Common Allergens)
5. C (page 758; Patient Assessment of an Immunologic Emergency)
6. C (page 753; Pathophysiology)
7. D (pages 758–759; Patient Assessment of an Immunologic Emergency)
8. C (page 761; Emergency Medical Care of Immunologic Emergencies)
9. D (page 761; Emergency Medical Care of Immunologic Emergencies)
10. C (page 755; Common Allergens)
11. A (page 761; Emergency Medical Care of Immunologic Emergencies)
12. D (page 758; Patient Assessment of an Immunologic Emergency)
13. C (page 755; Common Allergens)
14. C (page 753; Introduction)
15. A (page 757; Patient Assessment of an Immunologic Emergency)

True/False

1. T (page 753; Pathophysiology)
2. T (page 753; Pathophysiology)
3. F (page 755; Pathophysiology)
4. F (page 758; Patient Assessment of an Immunologic Emergency)

Fill-in-the-Blank

1. expiration (page 755; Pathophysiology)
2. urticaria (page 753; Pathophysiology)
3. barbed (page 755; Common Allergens)
4. anaphylaxis (page 753; Pathophysiology)
5. hypoperfusion (page 758; Patient Assessment of an Immunologic Emergency)
6. blood vessels (page 761; Emergency Medical Care of Immunologic Emergencies)
7. imminent death (page 753; Introduction)

Crossword Puzzle

```
            ¹H  I ²S  T  A  M  I  N ³E  S
      ⁴I           T                 P
      M       ⁵E ⁶U  R  T  I  C ⁷A  R  I  A
   ⁸I  M  M  U  N  E     I        N     N
      U        V        D        A     E
      N        E        O  ⁹A    P     P
   ¹⁰T  O  X  I  N        R  L    H     H
      L        O           L    Y     R
      O        M        ¹¹W  H  E  A  L  I
      G        A           R     A     N
      Y        T           G     X     E
               I           E     I
   ¹²L  E  U  K  O  T  R  I  E  N  E  S
               N           S
```

Critical Thinking

Multiple Choice

1. C (page 753; Pathophysiology)
2. B (page 755; Pathophysiology)
3. D (page 761; Emergency Medical Care of Immunologic Emergencies)
4. C (page 762; Emergency Medical Care of Immunologic Emergencies)
5. D (page 763; Emergency Medical Care of Immunologic Emergencies)

Short Answer

1. Increased blood pressure, tachycardia, pallor, dizziness, chest pain, headache, nausea, vomiting, anxiety, sweating, and palpitations (pages 761, 763; Emergency Medical Care of Immunologic Emergencies)
2. 1. Insect bites and stings
    2. Medications
    3. Plants
    4. Food
    5. Chemicals (page 755; Common Allergens)
3. 1. Obtain an order from medical control (or follow protocol or standing orders).
    2. Follow standard precautions.
    3. Make sure the medication was prescribed for that patient.
    4. Check for discoloration or expiration of medication.
    5. Remove the cap and wipe the thigh with alcohol, if possible.
    6. Place the tip of the auto-injector against the lateral part of the thigh.
    7. Push firmly until activation.
    8. Hold the auto-injector in place until the medication is injected (10 seconds).
    9. Remove and dispose.
    10. Rub the area for 10 seconds.

11. Record the time and dose.

12. Reassess and record the patient's vital signs.

13. Consider an additional administration (if possible) in 5 minutes if symptoms do not improve (pages 761–763; Emergency Medical Care of Immunologic Emergencies)

4. Respiratory: Shortness of breath (dyspnea); sneezing or itchy, runny nose; chest or throat tightness; dry cough; hoarseness; rapid, noisy, or labored respirations; wheezing and/or stridor

Circulatory: Decreased blood pressure (hypotension), increased pulse (tachycardia), pale skin, loss of consciousness and coma (page 758; Patient Assessment of an Immunologic Emergency)

Ambulance Calls

1. Based on the information you have, there is no way to determine if the child fell out of the tree or climbed down. You should assume that the child fell, which will require you to consider full spinal precautions. You also have the issue of scene safety because the damaged hive is now lying on the ground next to the patient. You must take care not to receive multiple stings yourself, so proceed with caution. If the child is having a severe allergic reaction, hopefully you will have access to an EpiPen Junior. Provide oxygen (if appropriate) and prompt transport according to local protocols.

2. Obtain a physician's order to administer the EpiPen to the patient (if required by local protocol). Check the EpiPen for clarity, expiration date, etc. Administer the EpiPen and promptly dispose of the auto-injector. Apply high-flow oxygen and provide rapid transport. Monitor the patient and assess vital signs frequently.

Fill-in-the-Patient Care Report

EMS Patient Care Report (PCR)			
Date: Today's date	**Incident No.:** 2011-0101	**Nature of Call:** Allergic reaction	**Location:** 231 Seaside Parkway
Dispatched: 1734	**En Route:** 1734 **At Scene:** 1742	**Transport:** 1748	**At Hospital:** 1801 **In Service:** 1814

Patient Information	
Age: 37 years	**Allergies:** Possible seafood
Sex: Male	**Medications:** N/A
Weight (in kg [lb]): 63 kg (138 lb)	**Past Medical History:** N/A
	Chief Complaint: Allergic reaction

Vital Signs				
Time: 1748	**BP:** 110/64	**Pulse:** 116	**Respirations:** 26 Labored	**Spo₂:** 92%
Time: 1755	**BP:** 140/94	**Pulse:** 128	**Respirations:** 18 Adequate Tidal Volume	**Spo₂:** 96%

EMS Treatment (circle all that apply)

Oxygen @ _15_ L/min via (circle one): NC (NRM) (BVM)   (Assisted Ventilation)   Airway Adjunct   CPR

Defibrillation   Bleeding Control   Bandaging   Splinting   (Other: Shock Treatment)

Narrative

Requested for an emergency response to a seafood restaurant for anaphylactic reaction. Arrived and led to patient—37-year-old man—who presented with generalized swelling of the face, neck, and hands; hives; and difficulty breathing. It was immediately apparent that the patient was becoming hypoxic, so we initiated oxygen therapy and requested an ALS rendezvous. We then began transport of the patient, and initial vitals indicated that the patient was anaphylactic. Began to assist ventilations with bag-valve mask until rendezvous with ALS crew. Paramedic Johnson boarded ambulance and administered epinephrine and patient responded to treatment quickly. Second set of vitals confirmed reversal of anaphylaxis. Provided verbal report and ETA to the receiving facility, and the rest of the transport was without incident. On arrival at the facility, patient was appropriately turned over to the receiving staff after we provided a complete verbal report to the charge nurse.**End of Report**

Skills

Skill Drill

Skill Drill 20-1: Using an EpiPen Auto-injector
1. Remove the **auto-injector's** safety cap, and quickly wipe the thigh with **antiseptic**, if possible.
2. Place the **tip** of the auto-injector against the **lateral** part of the thigh. Push the auto-injector **firmly** against the thigh until a **click** is heard. Hold it in place until all of the **medication** has been injected (10 seconds).
3. Rub the area for **10** seconds. (page 763; Emergency Medical Care of Immunologic Emergencies)

Assessment Review

1. A (page 757; Patient Assessment of an Immunologic Emergency)
2. C (page 762; Emergency Medical Care of Immunologic Emergencies)
3. D (page 762; Emergency Medical Care of Immunologic Emergencies)
4. C (page 758; Patient Assessment of an Immunologic Emergency)
5. D (page 758; Patient Assessment of an Immunologic Emergency)

Chapter 21: Toxicology

General Knowledge

Matching

1. F (page 771; Identifying the Patient and the Poison)
2. H (page 771; Identifying the Patient and the Poison)
3. G (page 773; How Poisons Enter the Body)
4. D (page 782; Specific Poisons)
5. J (page 789; Specific Poisons)
6. I (page 772; How Poisons Enter the Body)
7. K (page 783; Specific Poisons)
8. E (page 787; Specific Poisons)
9. B (page 784; Specific Poisons)
10. A (page 783; Specific Poisons)
11. C (page 789; Specific Poisons)

Multiple Choice

1. B (page 781; Emergency Medical Care)
2. B (page 772; Identifying the Patient and the Poison)
3. C (page 793; Plant Poisoning)
4. C (page 790; Specific Poisons)
5. A (page 779; Patient Assessment)
6. A (page 777; How Poisons Enter the Body)
7. C (page 782; Emergency Medical Care)
8. B (page 783; Specific Poisons)
9. C (page 784; Specific Poisons)
10. D (page 786; Specific Poisons)
11. A (page 789; Specific Poisons)
12. C (page 788; Specific Poisons)
13. A (page 789; Specific Poisons)
14. B (page 792; Food Poisoning)
15. A (page 786; Specific Poisons)
16. D (pages 787–788; Specific Poisons)
17. C (page 788; Specific Poisons)
18. A (page 788; Specific Poisons)
19. B (page 787; Specific Poisons)
20. D (page 775; How Poisons Enter the Body)
21. C (page 775; How Poisons Enter the Body)
22. B (page 776; How Poisons Enter the Body)
23. C (pages 777–778; How Poisons Enter the Body)
24. D (page 786; Specific Poisons)
25. A (page 777; How Poisons Enter the Body)
26. B (page 783; Specific Poisons)
27. D (page 784; Specific Poisons)
28. A (pages 774–775; How Poisons Enter the Body)
29. C (page 775; How Poisons Enter the Body)
30. A (page 777; How Poisons Enter the Body)
31. D (page 785; Specific Poisons)
32. A (page 774; How Poisons Enter the Body)
33. D (page 785; Specific Poisons)
34. C (page 781; Emergency Medical Care)
35. C (page 782; Emergency Medical Care)
36. B (page 781; Emergency Medical Care)
37. C (page 782; Emergency Medical Care)
38. B (page 782; Emergency Medical Care)
39. D (page 790; Specific Poisons)
40. B (page 790; Specific Poisons)

True/False

1. T (page 782; Emergency Medical Care)
2. F (page 781; Emergency Medical Care)
3. F (page 781; Emergency Medical Care)
4. F (page 775; How Poisons Enter the Body)
5. F (page 782; Emergency Medical Care)
6. T (page 784; Specific Poisons)
7. T (page 789; Specific Poisons)
8. F (page 783; Specific Poisons)
9. T (page 784; Specific Poisons)
10. T (page 787; Specific Poisons)
11. T (page 783; Specific Poisons)
12. F (page 793; Plant Poisoning)

Fill-in-the-Blank

1. botulism (page 792; Food Poisoning)
2. Bath salts (page 788; Specific Poisons)
3. Substance abuse (page 771; Identifying the Patient and the Poison)
4. 15 to 20 (page 776; How Poisons Enter the Body)
5. respiratory depression (page 784; Specific Poisons)
6. hypoglycemia (page 783; Specific Poisons)
7. recognize (page 771; Identifying the Patient and the Poison)
8. 1 gram, kilogram (pages 781–782; Emergency Medical Care)
9. outward (page 776; How Poisons Enter the Body)
10. ingestion (page 777; How Poisons Enter the Body)
11. delirium tremens (page 784; Specific Poisons)
12. DuoDote Auto-Injector (page 790; Specific Poisons)
13. addiction (page 782; Specific Poisons)
14. Hypovolemia (page 784; Specific Poisons)

Fill-in-the-Table (page 772; Identifying the Patient and the Poison)

Toxidromes: Typical Signs and Symptoms of Specific Overdoses	
Agent	**Signs and Symptoms**
Opioid (Examples: heroin, oxycodone)	• Hypoventilation or respiratory arrest • **Pinpoint pupils** • Sedation or coma • **Hypotension**
Sympathomimetics (Examples: epinephrine, albuterol, cocaine, methamphetamine)	• Hypertension • **Tachycardia** • Dilated pupils • Agitation or seizures • **Hyperthermia**
Sedative-hypnotics (Examples: diazepam, secobarbital, flunitrazepam, midazolam)	• **Slurred speech** • Sedation or coma • Hypoventilation • **Hypotension**
Anticholinergics (Examples: atropine, diphenhydramine, chlorpheniramine, doxylamine, Datura stramonium [jimson weed])	• **Tachycardia** • **Hyperthermia** • Hypertension • Dilated pupils • **Dry skin and mucous membranes** • Sedation, agitation, seizures, coma, or delirium • **Decreased bowel sounds**
Cholinergics (Examples: organophosphates, pilocarpine, nerve gas)	• **Excess defecation or urination** • **Muscle fasciculations** • Pinpoint pupils • Excess lacrimation (tearing) or salivation • **Airway compromise** • **Nausea or vomiting**

Crossword Puzzle

Critical Thinking

Short Answer

1. Activated charcoal adsorbs (binds to) the toxin and keeps it from being absorbed in the gastrointestinal tract. (page 781; Emergency Medical Care)

2. 1. Ingestion
   2. Inhalation
   3. Injection
   4. Absorption (surface contact) (page 773; How Poisons Enter the Body)

3. Hypertension, tachycardia, paranoia, and dilated pupils, along with irritability, agitation, anxiety, restlessness, or seizures (page 772; Identifying the Patient and the Poison)

4. 1. The organism itself causes the disease.
   2. The organism produces toxins that cause disease. (page 791; Food Poisoning)

5. Symptoms of acetaminophen overdose do not appear until the damage is irreversible, up to a week later. Finding evidence at the scene can save a patient's life. (page 790; Specific Poisons)

6. They describe patient presentation in cholinergic poisoning (ie, organophosphate insecticides, wild mushrooms).
   DUMBELS: Diarrhea, urination, miosis/muscle weakness, bradycardia/bronchospasm/bronchorrhea, emesis, lacrimation, salivation/seizures/sweating
   SLUDGEM: Salivation/sweating, lacrimation, urination, defecation/drooling/diarrhea, gastric upset/cramps, emesis, muscle twitching/miosis (page 790; Specific Poisons)

7. 1. What substance did you take?
   2. When did you take it or become exposed to it?
   3. How much did you ingest or were exposed to?
   4. How long ago did you take it or were exposed?
   5. What actions have been taken? Did it help?
   6. How much do you weigh? (page 780; Patient Assessment)

Ambulance Calls

1. You should attempt to identify the substance. Some rat poisons are actually blood-thinning agents or anticoagulants, such as warfarin. You should collect the substance and call the poison control center and/or the hospital emergency department for patient care instructions. Some substances require the administration of activated charcoal, whereas others do not. Perform your initial assessment, start oxygen (if appropriate), and provide prompt transport. Know your local protocols.

2. This patient potentially abuses alcohol and illegal substances. However, you cannot automatically assume that his decrease in mentation is directly related to alcohol intoxication or influence of other substances. He may have other medical conditions, which may mimic intoxication or even be obscured by it. You should perform a thorough assessment, take his vital signs, monitor his ABCs (because these could change at any time), and transport him to the nearest appropriate medical facility for evaluation. It is also important to be aware of the possibility of used needles when performing assessments and/or removing clothing when visualizing any potential injuries. Protect yourself.

3. Maintain the airway with an adjunct and high-flow oxygen via bag-valve mask or nonrebreathing mask with 100% oxygen. Monitor vital signs and provide supportive measures and rapid transport. Take the pill bottle along to the emergency department. Be alert for possible vomiting, monitor the patient closely, and be prepared for the possible need for CPR.

Skills

Assessment Review

1. C (page 780; Patient Assessment)
2. B (page 789; Specific Poisons)
3. B (pages 791–792; Food Poisoning)
4. B (page 787; Specific Poisons)
5. A (page 781; Emergency Medical Care)

MEDICAL

Chapter 22: Psychiatric Emergencies

General Knowledge

Matching

1. I (page 810; Acute Psychosis)
2. F (page 810; Acute Psychosis)
3. J (page 811; Excited Delirium)
4. D (page 804; Defining a Behavioral Crisis)
5. G (page 804; The Magnitude of Mental Health Disorders)
6. A (page 804; Defining a Behavioral Crisis)
7. E (page 805; Pathophysiology)
8. H (page 804; Defining a Behavioral Crisis)
9. C (page 804; Defining a Behavioral Crisis)
10. B (page 805; Pathophysiology)

Multiple Choice

1. C (page 803; Introduction)
2. B (page 803; Myth and Reality)
3. D (page 803; Myth and Reality)
4. B (page 804; Defining a Behavioral Crisis)
5. C (page 804; Defining a Behavioral Crisis)
6. B (page 804; Defining a Behavioral Crisis)
7. A (page 804; Defining a Behavioral Crisis)
8. D (pages 804–805; The Magnitude of Mental Health Disorders)
9. C (page 805; Pathophysiology)
10. B (page 805; Pathophysiology)
11. C (page 805; Pathophysiology)
12. B (page 810; Patient Assessment)
13. D (page 806; Safe Approach to a Behavioral Crisis)
14. B (page 807; Patient Assessment)
15. A (page 811; Excited Delirium)
16. B (page 817; Suicide)
17. A (page 817; Suicide)
18. A (page 811; Excited Delirium)
19. C (page 820; Medicolegal Considerations)
20. C (page 812; Restraint)
21. B (page 813; Restraint)
22. D (page 807; Patient Assessment)
23. A (pages 804–805; The Magnitude of Mental Health Disorders)
24. A (page 808; Patient Assessment)
25. B (page 812; Restraint)

True/False

1. F (page 804; Defining a Behavioral Crisis)
2. T (pages 804–805; The Magnitude of Mental Heath Disorders)
3. F (page 804; Defining a Behavioral Crisis)
4. F (page 812; Restraint)
5. F (page 807; Patient Assessment)
6. T (pages 808–809; Patient Assessment)
7. F (page 817; Suicide)
8. T (page 805; Pathophysiology)
9. F (page 803; Myth and Reality)
10. T (page 813; Restraint)
11. F (page 812; Restraint)
12. F (page 813; Restraint)
13. T (page 809; Patient Assessment)
14. T (page 808; Patient Assessment)
15. T (page 807; Patient Assessment)
16. F (page 818; Posttraumatic Stress Disorder and Returning Combat Veterans)
17. T (page 818; Posttraumatic Stress Disorder and Returning Combat Veterans)
18. F (page 820; Medicolegal Considerations)

Fill-in-the-Blank

1. Behavior (page 804; Defining a Behavioral Crisis)
2. behavioral crisis (page 804; Defining a Behavioral Crisis)
3. depression (page 804; Defining a Behavioral Crisis)
4. Organic brain syndrome (page 805; Pathophysiology)
5. suicide (page 817; Suicide)
6. schizophrenia (page 810; Acute Psychosis)
7. law enforcement (page 820; Medicolegal Considerations)
8. implied consent (page 820; Medicolegal Considerations)
9. Dissociative PTSD (page 818; Posttraumatic Stress Disorder and Returning Combat Veterans)
10. minimum (page 812; Restraint)

Crossword Puzzle

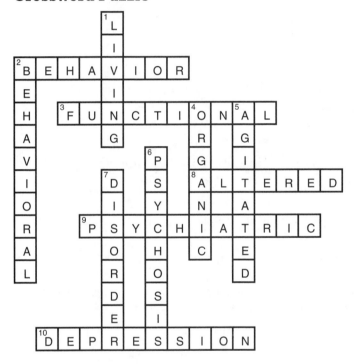

Critical Thinking

Short Answer

1. A behavioral crisis is a change in behavior that interferes with activities of daily living or that is unacceptable to the patient or others. A psychiatric emergency involves a patient showing violence, agitation, or a threat to self or others. (page 804; Defining a Behavioral Crisis)

2. 1. Improper functioning of the central nervous system
   2. Hallucinogens/drugs or alcohol
   3. Significant life changes, symptoms, or illness caused by a mental disorder (pages 807–808; Patient Assessment)

3. 1. The degree of force necessary to keep the patient from injuring self or others
   2. The patient's gender, size, strength, and mental status (including drug-induced states)
   3. The type of abnormal behavior the patient is exhibiting (page 812; Restraint)

4. 1. Assess the scene.
   2. Ensure that you have a means of communication.
   3. Know where the exits are.

    4. Don personal protective equipment.

    5. Have a definite plan of action.

    6. Urgently deescalate the patient's level of agitation.

    7. Calmly identify yourself.

    8. Be direct.

    9. Be prepared to spend extra time.

    10. Stay with the patient.

    11. Do not get too close to a potentially volatile patient.

    12. Express interest in the patient's story.

    13. Avoid fighting with the patient.

    14. Be honest and reassuring.

    15. Do not judge. (page 806; Safe Approach to a Behavioral Crisis)

5. **1.** Depression at any age

    2. Previous suicide attempt

    3. Current expression of wanting to commit suicide or sense of hopelessness

    4. Specific plan for suicide

    5. Family history of suicide

    6. Age older than 40 years, particularly for single, widowed, divorced, alcoholic, or depressed individuals

    7. Recent loss of spouse, significant other, family member, or support system

    8. Chronic debilitating illness or recent diagnosis of serious illness

    9. Feeling anxious, agitated, angry, reckless, or aggressive

    10. Financial setback, loss of job, police arrest, imprisonment, or some sort of social embarrassment

    11. Alcohol or substance abuse, particularly with increasing usage

    12. Children of an alcoholic or abusive parent

    13. Withdrawal from family and friends or a lack of social support, resulting in isolation

    14. Significant anniversaries of sentinel events

    15. Unusual gathering or new acquisition of things that can cause death, such as purchase of a gun, a large volume of pills (page 817; Suicide)

6. A technique used by mental health professionals to gain insight into a patient's thinking. It involves repeating, in question form, what the patient has said, encouraging the patient to expand on the thoughts. (page 808; Patient Assessment)

7. **1.** History

    2. Posture

    3. The scene

    4. Vocal activity

    5. Physical activity (pages 815–816; The Potentially Violent Patient)

Ambulance Calls

  1. Removing restraints (especially when the patient has a known history of recent violence) is ill-advised and potentially against local protocols. Restraints, although uncomfortable, afford you and your patient a safe environment. You should continually monitor the restraints to ensure that they are not too tight and that no manner of restraints (whether applied initially by you in the field or by hospital personnel for an interfacility transport) affects the patient's ability to breathe. Know your local laws regarding the use of restraints and your local protocols for appropriate use and discontinuation.

  2. Although he tells you that he is fine, you cannot simply walk away. Those individuals who contemplate suicide often tell people they are "fine." With information passed along by his sister, you must take action. Because there is no evidence that the patient has tried to harm himself and he did not express directly to you that he intends to, you must use persuasive techniques to gain consent to treatment and transport. If the patient refuses, consider contacting law enforcement for assistance.

  3. Be understanding and listen. Explain to the patient that she needs medical care. Monitor vital signs and reassure the patient en route.

Skills

Assessment Review

1. D (page 815; The Potentially Violent Patient)
2. A (page 815; The Potentially Violent Patient)
3. C (page 815; The Potentially Violent Patient)
4. B (page 815; The Potentially Violent Patient)
5. A (page 816; The Potentially Violent Patient)

Chapter 23: Gynecologic Emergencies

General Knowledge

Matching

1. G (page 829; Anatomy and Physiology)
2. E (page 829; Anatomy and Physiology)
3. K (page 829; Anatomy and Physiology)
4. B (page 829; Anatomy and Physiology)
5. H (page 829; Anatomy and Physiology)
6. A (page 829; Anatomy and Physiology)
7. D (page 829; Anatomy and Physiology)
8. C (page 832; Pathophysiology)
9. F (page 831; Pathophysiology)
10. J (page 832; Pathophysiology)
11. I (page 832; Pathophysiology)

Multiple Choice

1. D (page 832; Pathophysiology)
2. B (page 832; Pathophysiology)
3. B (page 837; Assessment and Management of Specific Conditions)
4. B (page 829; Anatomy and Physiology)
5. D (page 831; Pathophysiology)
6. A (page 832; Pathophysiology)
7. C (page 832; Pathophysiology)
8. B (page 833; Patient Assessment)
9. C (page 834; Patient Assessment)
10. A (page 836; Assessment and Management of Specific Conditions)
11. A (page 837; Assessment and Management of Specific Conditions)
12. D (page 837; Assessment and Management of Specific Conditions)
13. D (page 838; Assessment and Management of Specific Conditions)
14. A (page 838; Assessment and Management of Specific Conditions)
15. C (page 837; Assessment and Management of Specific Conditions)
16. A (page 837; Assessment and Management of Specific Conditions)
17. C (page 837; Assessment and Management of Specific Conditions)
18. D (page 838; Assessment and Management of Specific Conditions)

True/False

1. T (page 832; Pathophysiology)
2. T (page 832; Pathophysiology)
3. F (page 832; Pathophysiology)
4. T (page 832; Patient Assessment)
5. T (page 833; Patient Assessment)
6. F (page 833; Patient Assessment)
7. T (page 834; Patient Assessment)
8. F (page 835; Patient Assessment)
9. T (page 835; Patient Assessment)
10. F (page 836; Emergency Medical Care)
11. T (page 834; Patient Assessment)
12. T (page 835; Patient Assessment)
13. F (page 836; Emergency Medical Care)
14. F (page 838; Assessment and Management of Specific Conditions)
15. T (page 836; Emergency Medical Care)

Fill-in-the-Blank

1. ovaries (page 829; Anatomy and Physiology)
2. puberty (page 829; Anatomy and Physiology)
3. Pelvic inflammatory disease (page 831; Pathophysiology)

4. Gynecologic emergencies (page 833; Patient Assessment)
5. Ectopic pregnancy, spontaneous abortion (page 832; Pathophysiology)
6. external pads (page 835; Patient Assessment)
7. Vaginal bleeding (page 833; Patient Assessment)
8. law enforcement (page 837; Assessment and Management of Specific Conditions)
9. gonorrhea (page 832; Pathophysiology)
10. menopause (pages 829–830; Anatomy and Physiology)

Labeling

1. Female Reproductive System (page 830; Anatomy and Physiology)
   A. Uterine (fallopian) tube
   B. Uterus
   C. Ovary
   D. Cervix
   E. Vagina

2. External Genitalia (page 829; Anatomy and Physiology)
   A. Labia minora
   B. Labia majora
   C. Urethra
   D. Vaginal orifice
   E. Perineum
   F. Anus

Crossword Puzzle

Critical Thinking

Short Answer

1. Where or in what position is the patient found?
   What is the condition of the residence? Clean, filthy, or wrecked? Is there evidence of a fight?
   Are alcohol, tobacco products, or drug paraphernalia present?
   Are there pictures of loved ones? Is there a noticeable absence of pictures? Does the patient live alone or with other people? (page 833; Patient Assessment)

2. **1.** Painful urination

    2. Burning or itching

    3. Yellowish or bloody discharge associated with a foul odor

    4. Blood associated with vaginal intercourse

    5. Cramping and abdominal pain

    6. Nausea and vomiting

    7. Bleeding between menstrual periods (page 832; Pathophysiology)

3. Use external pads to control bleeding. Keep the patient warm, place her in a supine position, and provide her with supplemental oxygen, even if she is not experiencing any difficulty breathing. Provide prompt transport to the hospital and reassess her vital signs every 5 minutes. (pages 833, 835; Patient Assessment)

Ambulance Calls

1. The patient is most likely suffering from pelvic inflammatory disease (PID). A patient with PID will complain of abdominal pain. The pain is typically described as "achy" and can be worse with walking. Other symptoms include vaginal discharge, fever and chills, and pain or burning on urination.

    Prehospital treatment is limited to supportive care, and nonemergency transport is usually recommended. Place the patient in a position of comfort and monitor vital signs. Consider oxygen (if appropriate). Keep in mind that although this condition is typically not an emergency, these patients require monitoring for any signs of deterioration.

2. The first issue is the medical treatment of the patient. You should assess and treat life threats and inquire about pain. The second issue focuses on the psychological care of the patient. Many women report feeling violated when subjected to interrogation, so do not cross-examine the patient or pass judgment on her during the assessment. Take the patient's history, and limit any physical examination to a brief survey for life-threatening injuries. Keep in mind that this patient has been through a traumatic experience, and your compassion for her will help to gain the patient's confidence. Limit the number of people involved in the assessment/examination process to protect the patient's privacy and dignity. Remember that you are at a crime scene. Do not cut through any clothing or throw away anything from the scene. Place bloodstained articles in a separate paper bag. You should gently persuade the patient to refrain from cleaning herself, urinating, changing clothes, moving her bowels, or rinsing her mouth because this could potentially destroy evidence.

    When documenting this incident, keep the report concise and record only what the patient stated in her own words. Use quotations marks to indicate that you are reporting the patient's version of the events. Refrain from inserting your own opinion into the documentation. Record all of your observations during the physical exam, including the patient's emotional state, the condition of her clothing, obvious injuries, and so forth.

Fill-in-the-Patient Care Report

EMS Patient Care Report (PCR)

Date: Today's date	Incident No.: 011689	Nature of Call: Assault		Location: 538 N. 10th Street, Apartment 4-C	
Dispatched: 2101	En Route: 2103	At Scene: 2109	Transport: 2120	At Hospital: 2131	In Service: 2147

Patient Information

Age: 32 years	Allergies: None known
Sex: Female	Medications: lispro, Lantus, lisinopril
Weight (in kg [lb]): Unknown	Past Medical History: Diabetes
	Chief Complaint: Pain to the nose, face, and groin

Vital Signs

Time: 2114	BP: 144/98	Pulse: 102	Respirations: 22	Spo$_2$: 98%
Time: 2125	BP: 148/92	Pulse: 108	Respirations: 20	Spo$_2$: 97%

EMS Treatment
(circle all that apply)

Oxygen @ _2_ L/min via (circle one): (NC) NRM BVM	Assisted Ventilation	Airway Adjunct	CPR
Defibrillation	Bleeding Control	Bandaging	Splinting	Other:

Narrative

9-1-1 dispatch for 32-year-old assault victim. Dispatcher advised that police were already on scene. No other information was provided. On arrival, crew was directed by PD through a well-kept apartment into a dark room where we found our patient. The patient had obvious multiple contusions to her face and appeared to be emotionally upset. When inquired about the incident, the patient blurted out that she was "raped by a maintenance worker here at the apartment complex." The patient initially stated that she was unsure if she wanted to go to the hospital. She stated that she did want to "change her clothes" and "take a shower." Both EMS and PD stated to patient that she could potentially disrupt any evidence and that changing her clothes and showering were not advised. The patient complained of pain to the nose, face, and groin. She denied any bleeding. The patient appeared withdrawn and reluctant to speak with EMS. A female EMT was offered to the patient; however, the patient stated "No." No obvious life threats were noted on minimal exam. The patient was asked about the incident; however, she declined to comment. Due to the patient's status and limited injuries, no further examination was performed at this time. Patient was continuously monitored for any signs of hemorrhaging or deterioration. The patient was loaded into the unit and transported to the local facility. Radio report was carried out by partner/driver. On arrival at facility, the patient was stable with no change in status noted. Care was transferred to the ED staff. A verbal report was given to the nurse with patient privacy precautions taken. No further incidents. Unit cleaned and restocked. Crew available.**End of Report**

Chapter 24: Trauma Overview

General Knowledge

Matching

1. H (page 860; Penetrating Trauma)
2. G (page 850; Mechanism of Injury Profiles)
3. F (page 848; Energy and Trauma)
4. E (page 847; Energy and Trauma)
5. C (page 849; Energy and Trauma)
6. A (page 850; Blunt and Penetrating Trauma)
7. D (page 850; Blunt and Penetrating Trauma)
8. B (page 848; Energy and Trauma)

Multiple Choice

1. B (page 847; Introduction)
2. C (page 848; Energy and Trauma)
3. C (page 848; Energy and Trauma)
4. B (page 849; Energy and Trauma)
5. D (pages 857–858; Blunt Trauma)
6. B (page 850; Blunt Trauma)
7. C (pages 850–851; Blunt Trauma)
8. D (page 867; Management: Transport and Destination)
9. C (page 861; Penetrating Trauma)
10. A (page 851; Blunt Trauma)
11. C (page 851; Blunt Trauma)
12. B (pages 851–852; Blunt Trauma)
13. D (page 863; Blast Injuries)
14. A (page 852; Blunt Trauma)
15. A (page 862; Blast Injuries)
16. B (page 853; Blunt Trauma)
17. B (page 867; Management: Transport and Destination)
18. B (page 855; Blunt Trauma)
19. C (page 856; Blunt Trauma)
20. B (page 858; Blunt Trauma)
21. C (page 850; Blunt Trauma)
22. A (page 850; Blunt Trauma)
23. B (page 851; Blunt Trauma)
24. A (page 857; Blunt Trauma)
25. C (page 849; Energy and Trauma)
26. A (page 867; Management: Transport and Destination)
27. B (pages 857–858; Blunt Trauma)
28. D (page 862; Blast Injuries)
29. D (page 863; Blast Injuries)
30. C (page 865; Patient Assessment)

True/False

1. T (page 848; Energy and Trauma)
2. F (page 848; Energy and Trauma)
3. F (page 848; Energy and Trauma)
4. T (page 855; Blunt Trauma)
5. T (page 866; Patient Assessment)
6. T (page 858; Blunt Trauma)
7. T (page 847; Introduction)
8. F (page 867; Management: Transport and Destination)
9. T (page 856; Blunt Trauma)
10. F (page 855; Blunt Trauma)
11. T (page 857; Blunt Trauma)
12. F (page 857; Blunt Trauma)
13. F (page 862; Blast Injuries)
14. T (page 865; Patient Assessment)
15. T (page 866; Patient Assessment)

Fill-in-the-Blank

1. doubles, quadruples (pages 848–849; Energy and Trauma)
2. Penetrating trauma (page 850; Blunt and Penetrating Trauma)
3. coup-contrecoup (page 851; Blunt Trauma)
4. $KE = \frac{1}{2}\, m \times v^2$ (page 848; Energy and Trauma)

5. rear-end (page 855; Blunt Trauma)
6. deceleration (page 853; Blunt Trauma)
7. Multisystem (page 864; Multisystem Trauma)
8. lateral (page 855; Blunt Trauma)
9. ejection (page 856; Blunt Trauma)
10. solid (page 866; Patient Assessment)
11. Glasgow Coma (page 869; Management: Transport and Destination)
12. pneumothorax (pages 865–866; Patient Assessment)
13. Platinum 10 (page 864; Multisystem Trauma)
14. Newton's first law (page 848; Energy and Trauma)
15. medical (page 847; Introduction)

Fill-in-the-Table (page 861; Penetrating Trauma)

Recognizing Developing Problems in Trauma Patients		
Mechanism of Injury	**Signs and Symptoms**	**Index of Suspicion**
Blunt or penetrating trauma to the neck	• **Noisy or labored breathing** • **Increased respiratory rate** • **Swelling of the face or neck** • **Altered gag reflex** • **Decreasing/low Glasgow Coma Scale (GCS); <9 in severe** • **Decreasing/low Spo_2** • **Rapid, weak pulse** • **Decreasing/low blood pressure**	• Significant bleeding or foreign bodies in the upper or lower airway, causing obstruction • Be alert for airway compromise.
Significant chest wall trauma from motor vehicle, car-versus-pedestrian, and other crashes; penetrating trauma to the chest wall	• **Significant chest pain** • **Shortness of breath** • **Increased respiratory rate** • **Asymmetrical chest wall movement** • **Subcutaneous emphysema** • **Decreasing GCS (<9 is severe)** • **Decreasing/low Spo_2** • **Presence of jugular venous distention** • **Rapid, weak pulse** • **Decreasing/low blood pressure** • **Loss of peripheral pulses during respiration** • **Narrowing pulse pressures**	• Cardiac or pulmonary contusion • Pneumothorax or hemothorax • Broken ribs, causing breathing compromise
Any significant blunt force trauma from motor vehicle crashes or penetrating injury	• **Blunt or penetrating trauma to the neck, chest, abdomen, or groin** • **Blows to the head sustained during motor vehicle crashes, falls, or other incidents, producing loss of consciousness, altered mental status, inability to recall events, combativeness, or changes in speech patterns** • **Difficulty moving extremities; headache, especially with nausea and vomiting** • **Decreasing GCS (<9 is severe)** • **Decreasing/low Spo_2** • **Rapid, weak pulse** • **Decreasing/low blood pressure or increasing blood pressure with slow pulse**	• Injuries in these regions may tear and cause damage to the large blood vessels located in these body areas, resulting in significant internal and external bleeding. • Be alert to the possibility of bruising to the brain and bleeding in and around the brain tissue, which may cause the development of excess pressure inside the skull around the brain.
Any significant blunt force trauma, falls from a significant height, or penetrating trauma	• **Severe back and/or neck pain, history of difficulty moving extremities, loss of sensation or tingling in the extremities** • **Decreasing GCS (<9 is severe)** • **Rapid, weak pulse or slow pulse**	• Injuries to the bones of the spinal column or to the spinal cord

Crossword Puzzle

```
¹T R A J E C ²T O R Y
            R
³B L U N T T R A U ⁴M A
            U       U   ⁵D R A G
      ⁶S     M       L   E
      U   ⁷B L A S T  C       ⁸M
      S     S       I   E       E
⁹T Y M P A N I C     S   L       D
      I     O       Y   E       I
   ¹⁰W   C   ¹¹R T S     R       C
   O   I   E   ¹²T R A U M A
   R   O     E     T           L
   ¹³K I N E T I C ¹⁴M O I
                  O
      ¹⁵C A V I T A T I O N
```

Critical Thinking

Short Answer

1. Potential energy is the product of mass (weight), force of gravity, and height and is mostly associated with the energy of falling objects. (page 849; Energy and Trauma)

2. **1.** Collision of the car against another car or other object

   2. Collision of the passenger against the interior of the car

   3. Collision of the passenger's internal organs against the solid structures of the body (pages 850–851; Blunt Trauma)

3. **1.** The height of the fall

   2. The surface struck

   3. The part of the body that hit first, followed by the path of energy displacement (page 859; Blunt Trauma)

4. A bullet, because of its speed, creates pressure waves that emanate from its path, causing distant damage. (page 860; Penetrating Trauma)

5. The size (mass) and speed (velocity) of the projectile affect the potential damage. If the mass is doubled, the potential energy is doubled. If the velocity is doubled, the potential energy is quadrupled. (pages 848–849; Energy and Trauma)

6. Lateral chest and abdominal/internal organ injuries on the side of impact; fractures of the lower extremities, pelvis, and ribs; and injuries to the aorta (page 856; Blunt Trauma)

7. The deformity of the motorcycle, the side of most damage, the distance of skid in the road, the deformity of stationary objects or other vehicles, and the extent and location of deformity in the helmet (page 857; Blunt Trauma)

8. A comprehensive regional resource that is a tertiary care facility; capable of providing total care for every aspect of injury, from prevention through rehabilitation (page 868; Management: Transport and Destination)

Ambulance Calls

1. Given the highway speeds and lack of a shoulder belt and airbag, along with his complaints of head and neck pain, your index of suspicion for head and spinal injuries is very high. It is a positive sign that he is awake and able to communicate; however, this should not encourage you to spend any more time on scene than is necessary to extricate this patient and place him in full spinal precautions. His condition could change at any time, and his inability to remember the details of the event likely indicate the presence of a closed head injury. Provide high-flow oxygen (if appropriate) and prompt transport.

2. Each story is 10 feet (3 m), so this patient fell approximately 20 feet (6 m) from the ladder to the hard ground. He is now unconscious. Assume he has significant head and spinal injuries; determine if he is responsive and manage his airway because he will be unable to protect it. Provide high-flow oxygen and prompt transport to the nearest appropriate facility, taking care not to waste time in determining other injuries.

3. 1. Apply high-flow oxygen.

    2. Stabilize the object in place with bulky dressings.

    3. Monitor his vital signs.

    4. Transport the patient in a supine position. Provide rapid transport due to abdominal penetration.

4. 1. Estimate the speed of the vehicle that struck the patient.

    2. Determine whether the patient was thrown through the air and at what distance.

    3. Determine if the patient was struck and pulled under the vehicle.

    4. Evaluate the vehicle for structural damage that might indicate contact points with the patient and alert you to potential injuries.

Chapter 25: Bleeding

General Knowledge

Matching

1. J (page 880; Anatomy and Physiology of the Cardiovascular System)
2. E (page 880; Anatomy and Physiology of the Cardiovascular System)
3. K (page 880; Anatomy and Physiology of the Cardiovascular System)
4. F (page 880; Anatomy and Physiology of the Cardiovascular System)
5. C (page 880; Anatomy and Physiology of the Cardiovascular System)
6. H (page 880; Anatomy and Physiology of the Cardiovascular System)

7. B (page 883; External Bleeding)
8. I (page 885; Internal Bleeding)
9. M (page 895; Emergency Medical Care for External Bleeding)
10. A (page 885; Internal Bleeding)
11. D (page 884; External Bleeding)
12. L (page 882; External Bleeding)
13. G (page 883; External Bleeding)

Multiple Choice

1. B (page 881; Pathophysiology and Perfusion)
2. D (page 879; Anatomy and Physiology of the Cardiovascular System)
3. C (page 880; Anatomy and Physiology of the Cardiovascular System)
4. C (page 880; Anatomy and Physiology of the Cardiovascular System)
5. B (page 880; Anatomy and Physiology of the Cardiovascular System)
6. A (page 880; Anatomy and Physiology of the Cardiovascular System)
7. D (page 880; Anatomy and Physiology of the Cardiovascular System)
8. B (page 880; Anatomy and Physiology of the Cardiovascular System)
9. D (page 880; Anatomy and Physiology of the Cardiovascular System)
10. C (page 880; Anatomy and Physiology of the Cardiovascular System)
11. B (page 881; Pathophysiology and Perfusion)
12. C (page 881; Pathophysiology and Perfusion)
13. C (pages 880–881; Anatomy and Physiology of the Cardiovascular System)
14. A (page 881; Anatomy and Physiology of the Cardiovascular System)

15. D (page 882; Pathophysiology and Perfusion)
16. B (page 882; Pathophysiology and Perfusion)
17. B (page 882; External Bleeding)
18. B (pages 882–883; External Bleeding)
19. A (page 883; External Bleeding)
20. B (page 883; External Bleeding)
21. C (page 886; Patient Assessment for External and Internal Bleeding)
22. C (page 883; External Bleeding)
23. A (page 884; External Bleeding)
24. B (page 884; External Bleeding)
25. C (page 888; Emergency Medical Care for External Bleeding)
26. A (page 889; Emergency Medical Care for External Bleeding)
27. A (pages 889–890; Emergency Medical Care for External Bleeding)
28. C (page 894; Emergency Medical Care for External Bleeding)
29. B (page 884; Internal Bleeding)
30. D (page 885; Internal Bleeding)
31. D (page 885; Internal Bleeding)
32. A (page 885; Internal Bleeding)
33. C (page 885; Internal Bleeding)

True/False

1. F (page 883; External Bleeding)
2. F (page 882; External Bleeding)
3. F (page 888; Emergency Medical Care for External Bleeding)
4. T (page 888; Emergency Medical Care for External Bleeding)
5. F (page 893; Emergency Medical Care for External Bleeding)
6. T (page 895; Emergency Medical Care for External Bleeding)
7. F (page 891; Emergency Medical Care for External Bleeding)
8. F (page 890; Emergency Medical Care for External Bleeding)
9. F (page 890; Emergency Medical Care for External Bleeding)
10. T (page 888; Patient Assessment for External and Internal Bleeding)

Fill-in-the-Blank

1. right (page 880; Anatomy and Physiology of the Cardiovascular System)
2. Perfusion (page 881; Pathophysiology and Perfusion)
3. bruise (page 885; Internal Bleeding)
4. Internal (page 884; Internal Bleeding)
5. 100 (page 888; Patient Assessment for External and Internal Bleeding)
6. Hematemesis (page 885; Internal Bleeding)
7. Capillary (page 883; External Bleeding)
8. autonomic nervous (page 880; Anatomy and Physiology of the Cardiovascular System)
9. Capillaries (page 880; Anatomy and Physiology of the Cardiovascular System)
10. heart (page 880; Anatomy and Physiology of the Cardiovascular System)

Labeling

1. The Left and Right Sides of the Heart (page 880; Anatomy and Physiology of the Cardiovascular System)
   A. Left pulmonary artery
   B. Aorta
   C. Superior vena cava
   D. Right pulmonary artery
   E. Right atrium
   F. Inferior vena cava
   G. Right ventricle
   H. Right pulmonary veins
   I. Oxygen-rich blood to head and upper body
   J. Aorta
   K. Left pulmonary veins
   L. Left atrium
   M. Left ventricle
   N. Oxygen-rich blood to lower body
2. Perfusion (page 882; Pathophysiology and Perfusion)
   A. Artery
   B. Arterioles
   C. Capillaries
   D. Organ or tissue
   E. Capillaries
   F. Venules
   G. Vein

Crossword Puzzle

1. ECCHYMOSIS
2. HEMATOMA
3. SHOCK
4. HEMATEMESIS / HYP
5. CONTUSION
6. TOURNIQUE
7. PERFUSION
8. EPISTAXIS
9. ARTERY
10. MELENA
11. VEINS
12. HEMOPHILIA
13. AORTA

Critical Thinking

Multiple Choice

1. C (page 893; Emergency Medical Care for External Bleeding)
2. D (page 893; Emergency Medical Care for External Bleeding)
3. D (page 895; Emergency Medical Care for External Bleeding)
4. B (page 896; Emergency Medical Care for External Bleeding)
5. B (page 883; External Bleeding)

Short Answer

1. It redirects blood away from nonessential organs to the heart, brain, lungs, and kidneys. (page 880; Anatomy and Physiology of the Cardiovascular System)

2. **Artery:** Bright red, spurting
   Vein: Dark color with steady flow
   Capillary: Darker color, oozes (page 883; External Bleeding)

3. 1. Direct pressure and elevation
   2. Pressure dressings
   3. Tourniquets
   4. Hemostatic agent/splints (page 889; Emergency Medical Care for External Bleeding)

4. 1. Tachycardia
   2. Weakness, fainting, or dizziness on standing or at rest
   3. Thirst
   4. Nausea and vomiting
   5. Cold, moist (clammy) skin
   6. Shallow, rapid breathing
   7. Dull eyes
   8. Slightly dilated pupils, slow to respond to light

9. Capillary refill in infants and children of more than 2 seconds

10. Weak, rapid (thready) pulse

11. Decreasing blood pressure

12. Altered level of consciousness (pages 886; Internal Bleeding)

5. 1. Follow standard precautions.

2. Maintain the airway with cervical spine immobilization (if needed).

3. Administer high-flow oxygen and provide artificial ventilation as necessary.

4. Control all obvious external bleeding.

5. Treat suspected internal bleeding in an extremity by applying a splint.

6. Consider a pelvic compression device or splint for suspected internal bleeding from the pelvic area.

7. Monitor and record the patient's vital signs at least every 5 minutes.

8. Keep the patient warm.

9. Give nothing by mouth, not even small sips of water.

10. Provide prompt transport for all patients with sign and symptoms of hypoperfusion. Report changes in condition to the emergency department. (page 897; Emergency Medical Care for Internal Bleeding)

Ambulance Calls

1. Control bleeding with direct pressure, a pressure dressing, and a tourniquet as a last resort. Consider applying oxygen (if needed) and place the patient in a position of comfort. Monitor the patient's vital signs and provide rapid transport.

2. You must control bleeding through direct pressure, pressure dressings, and a tourniquet, as needed. You must also transport the amputated portion of the limb with the patient to the hospital. Quickly attempt to determine how much blood has been lost and assess his skin and vital signs because these will provide accurate indicators of the significance of blood loss. Place the patient in a position of comfort, consider applying oxygen as necessary, and provide prompt transport.

3. This is an isolated injury that, depending on the severity of the injury to the antecubital vein, can result in significant blood loss. Attempt to control bleeding through direct pressure, pressure dressings, and a tourniquet, as needed. Something as benign as a pen can cause significant damage in the hands of a determined person.

Fill-in-the-Patient Care Report

EMS Patient Care Report (PCR)			
Date: Today's date	**Incident No.:** 2010-123	**Nature of Call:** Laceration	**Location:** 1467 Abner Lane

Dispatched: 1653	**En Route:** 1653	**At Scene:** 1658	**Transport:** 1710	**At Hospital:** 1715	**In Service:** 1735

Patient Information	
Age: 42 years **Sex:** Male **Weight (in kg [lb]):** 77 kg (170 lb)	**Allergies:** Amoxicillin **Medications:** Crestor **Past Medical History:** TIA—1 year ago **Chief Complaint:** Laceration to lower left leg

Vital Signs				
Time: 1704	**BP:** 136/86	**Pulse:** 88 strong/regular	**Respirations:** 16 GTV	**Spo_2:** 97%
Time: 1710	**BP:** 122/76	**Pulse:** 102 weak/regular	**Respirations:** 20 shallow	**Spo_2:** 94%

EMS Treatment (circle all that apply)				
Oxygen @ ____ L/min via (circle one): NC NRM BVM		**Assisted Ventilation**	**Airway Adjunct**	**CPR**
Defibrillation	**Bleeding Control** (circled)	**Bandaging** (circled)	**Splinting**	**Other:** Shock treatment (circled)

Narrative
Dispatched for a leg laceration. Arrived on scene to find the patient, a 42-year-old man, on the back deck of his home. He was conscious and alert, had a patent airway, and was breathing with good tidal volume. The patient was holding a blood-soaked shirt on his lower leg and was sitting in a large pool of blood. Patient stated that he had been chopping wood when the axe blade bounced off the wood and struck his leg. I immediately applied direct pressure using a large sterile dressing and manually elevated the patient's leg. I then applied a pressure dressing to maintain bleeding control. We obtained the patient's vitals. The patient's skin was found to be pale, cool, and diaphoretic. Patient's wife disclosed patient history of TIA (1 year ago), amoxicillin allergy, and current Crestor use. Placed patient onto gurney, covered with a blanket, placed in a position of comfort, and moved him into the ambulance. I continued to monitor the patient's condition while en route. He remained conscious and alert but vital sign trending indicated possible hypoperfusion. Checked pressure dressing and found that bleeding was still controlled. Called in report to receiving facility and subsequently delivered patient without incident. Gave verbal report to the ED charge nurse.**End of Report**

Skills

Skill Drills

Skill Drill 25-1: Controlling External Bleeding

1. Take standard **precautions**. Apply **direct pressure** over the wound with a dry, sterile dressing.
2. Apply a **pressure dressing**.
3. If direct pressure with a **pressure dressing** does not control the bleeding, apply a **tourniquet** above the level of the **bleeding**.
4. Tighten the **tourniquet** until distal **pulses** are no longer palpable. Properly position the **patient**. Apply **high-flow oxygen** as necessary. Keep the patient **warm**. Transport promptly. (page 890; Emergency Medical Care for External Bleeding)

Skill Drill 25-2: Applying a MAT Commercial Tourniquet

1. Apply **pressure** over the bleeding site and place the tourniquet **proximal** to the injury (in the axillary region for upper extremity injuries and at the groin for lower extremity injuries).
2. Click the buckle into place, pull the strap tight, and turn the tightening dial **clockwise** until pulses are no longer palpable **distal** to the tourniquet or until bleeding has been **controlled**. (page 892; Emergency Medical Care for External Bleeding)

Assessment Review

1. C (page 888; Emergency Medical Care for External Bleeding)
2. A (page 887; Patient Assessment for External and Internal Bleeding)
3. B (page 888; Patient Assessment for External and Internal Bleeding)
4. D (page 888; Patient Assessment for External and Internal Bleeding)
5. C (page 888; Patient Assessment for External and Internal Bleeding)

Chapter 26: Soft-Tissue Injuries

General Knowledge

Matching

1. G (page 906; Anatomy and Physiology of the Skin)
2. B (page 906; Anatomy and Physiology of the Skin)
3. D (page 906; Anatomy and Physiology of the Skin)
4. F (page 906; Anatomy and Physiology of the Skin)
5. H (page 906; Anatomy and Physiology of the Skin)
6. J (page 909; Pathophysiology of Closed and Open Injuries)
7. E (page 909; Pathophysiology of Closed and Open Injuries)
8. A (page 910; Pathophysiology of Closed and Open Injuries)
9. C (page 909; Pathophysiology of Closed and Open Injuries)
10. I (page 919; Emergency Medical Care for Open Injuries)

Multiple Choice

1. C (page 905; Anatomy and Physiology of the Skin)
2. B (page 906; Anatomy and Physiology of the Skin)
3. B (page 906; Anatomy and Physiology of the Skin)
4. A (page 906; Anatomy and Physiology of the Skin)
5. B (page 906; Anatomy and Physiology of the Skin)
6. C (page 907; Pathophysiology of Closed and Open Injuries)
7. B (page 908; Pathophysiology of Closed and Open Injuries)
8. B (page 908; Pathophysiology of Closed and Open Injuries)
9. C (page 908; Pathophysiology of Closed and Open Injuries)
10. C (page 908; Pathophysiology of Closed and Open Injuries)
11. C (page 909; Pathophysiology of Closed and Open Injuries)
12. B (page 909; Pathophysiology of Closed and Open Injuries)
13. D (page 909; Pathophysiology of Closed and Open Injuries)
14. C (pages 911–912; Pathophysiology of Closed and Open Injuries)
15. A (page 909; Pathophysiology of Closed and Open Injuries)
16. A (page 912; Patient Assessment of Closed and Open Injuries)
17. C (page 919; Emergency Medical Care for Open Injuries)
18. C (pages 919–920; Emergency Medical Care for Open Injuries)
19. C (page 921; Emergency Medical Care for Open Injuries)
20. D (page 923; Burns)
21. B (page 924; Burns)
22. C (page 925; Burns)
23. B (page 925; Burns)
24. C (page 925; Burns)
25. D (page 925; Burns)
26. B (page 936; Emergency Medical Care for Burns)
27. D (page 937; Emergency Medical Care for Burns)
28. A (page 938; Dressing and Bandaging)
29. A (page 939; Dressing and Bandaging)
30. B (page 923; Burns)
31. B (page 922; Emergency Medical Care for Open Injuries)

True/False

1. T (page 925; Burns)
2. F (page 925; Burns)
3. T (page 925; Burns)
4. T (page 926; Burns)
5. T (page 924; Burns)
6. T (page 931; Emergency Medical Care for Burns)
7. F (page 931; Emergency Medical Care for Burns)
8. T (page 936; Emergency Medical Care for Burns)
9. F (pages 908–909; Pathophysiology of Closed and Open Injuries)

10. T (page 938; Dressing and Bandaging)

11. F (page 938; Dressing and Bandaging)

12. F (page 939; Dressing and Bandaging)

13. T (page 939; Dressing and Bandaging)

14. F (pages 907–908; Pathophysiology of Closed and Open Injuries)

15. F (page 909; Pathophysiology of Closed and Open Injuries)

Fill-in-the-Blank

1. alpha, beta, gamma (page 937; Emergency Medical Care for Burns)

2. cool (page 906; Anatomy and Physiology of the Skin)

3. dermis (page 906; Anatomy and Physiology of the Skin)

4. crush syndrome (page 908; Pathophysiology of Closed and Open Injuries)

5. constrict (page 906; Anatomy and Physiology of the Skin)

6. cheek, chest (page 920; Emergency Medical Care for Open Injuries)

7. Thermal, 111 (page 923; Burns)

8. amputation (page 910; Pathophysiology of Closed and Open Injuries)

9. epidermis, dermis (page 906; Anatomy and Physiology of the Skin)

10. radiated (page 906; Anatomy and Physiology of the Skin)

Labeling

1. Skin (page 906; Anatomy and Physiology of the Skin)

   A. Hair

   B. Pore

   C. Epidermis

   D. Germinal layer of epidermis

   E. Sebaceous gland

   F. Erector pillae muscle

   G. Dermis

   H. Nerve (sensory)

   I. Sweat gland

   J. Hair follicle

   K. Blood vessel

   L. Subcutaneous fat

   M. Fascia

   N. Subcutaneous tissue

   O. Muscle

2. Rule of Nines (page 927; Burns)

   A. 9

   B. 18

   C. 9

   D. 18

   E. 9

   F. 12

   G. 18

   H. 18

   I. 1

   J. 9

   K. 18

   L. 18

   M. 18

   N. 9

   O. 18

   P. 9

   Q. 9

   R. 1

   S. 1

   T. 16.5

   U. 16.5

   V. 13.5

   W. 13.5

Crossword Puzzle

Critical Thinking

Multiple Choice

1. D (page 925; Burns)
2. D (page 911; Pathophysiology of Closed and Open Injuries)
3. C (page 918; Emergency Medical Care for Closed Injuries)
4. A (page 909; Pathophysiology of Closed and Open Injuries)
5. B (page 919; Emergency Medical Care for Open Injuries)

Short Answer

1. 1. Superficial (first degree)
   2. Partial thickness (second degree)
   3. Full thickness (third degree) (page 925; Burns)
2. 1. Closed injuries
   2. Open injuries
   3. Burns (page 907; Anatomy and Physiology of the Skin)
3. **R:** rest

   I: ice

   C: compression

   E: elevation

   S: splinting (page 918; Emergency Medical Care for Closed Injuries)
4. Any full-thickness burn

   Partial-thickness burns covering more than 20% of the body's total surface area (page 927; Burns)
5. Brush off dry chemicals, and then remove the patient's clothing (including shoes, stockings, gloves, jewelry, and eyeglasses) because there may be small amounts of chemicals in the creases. (page 934; Emergency Medical Care for Burns)

6. First, there may be a deep tissue injury not visible on the outside. Second, there is a danger of cardiac arrest from the electrical shock. (page 936; Emergency Medical Care for Burns)

7. **1.** Primary
   2. Secondary
   3. Tertiary (page 912; Pathophysiology of Closed and Open Injuries)

8. **1.** To control bleeding
   2. To protect the wound from further damage
   3. To prevent further contamination and infection (page 938; Dressing and Bandaging)

9. **1.** Abrasions
   2. Lacerations
   3. Avulsions
   4. Penetrating wounds (page 909; Pathophysiology of Closed and Open Injuries)

10. **1.** Depth of the burn
    2. Extent of the burn
    3. Involvement of critical areas (face, upper airway, hands, feet, genitalia)
    4. Preexisting medical conditions or other injuries
    5. Age younger than 5 years or older than 55 years (page 924; Burns)

Ambulance Calls

1. Take standard precautions and apply direct pressure. Elevate the extremity and apply a pressure dressing. If the bleeding is not controlled, move to the use of a tourniquet. Once the bleeding is controlled, splint the arm to decrease movement. Apply high-flow oxygen (if appropriate) and transport the patient in a position of comfort. Monitor her vital signs en route to the hospital.

2. Unfortunately, this scenario has occurred in households throughout the country. This is why it is so important to "turn pot handles in" when cooking in the home of a small, inquisitive child. You must evaluate the child quickly to determine the extent and severity of the burns. Assess airway, breathing, and circulation, and quickly apply sterile dressings and high-flow oxygen. Promptly transport the patient according to local protocols.

3. Apply direct pressure to control any bleeding using sterile dressings. Have the patient lie down because this injury will be quite painful. Even the toughest person can suddenly feel faint, especially if he or she looks at the injury. Find the piece of avulsed tissue, wrap it in sterile dressings, and transport it with you to the hospital. Oxygen via nasal cannula can assist with any nausea that the patient may experience.

Fill-in-the-Patient Care Report

EMS Patient Care Report (PCR)					
Date: Today's date	**Incident No.:** 2011-2222		**Nature of Call:** Gunshot wound		**Location:** 14th and Berry
Dispatched: 1321	**En Route:** 1321	**At Scene:** 1329	**Transport:** 1334	**At Hospital:** 1341	**In Service:** 1411

Patient Information	
Age: 24 years **Sex:** Male **Weight (in kg [lb]):** 73 kg (161 lb)	**Allergies:** Unknown **Medications:** Unknown **Past Medical History:** Unknown **Chief Complaint:** Gunshot wound to neck

Vital Signs				
Time: 1334	**BP:** 92/60	**Pulse:** 120	**Respirations:** 20 Shallow	**Spo$_2$:** 92%
Time: 1337	**BP:** 92/58	**Pulse:** 124	**Respirations:** 20 Shallow	**Spo$_2$:** 94%

EMS Treatment (circle all that apply)				
Oxygen @ _15_ **L/min via (circle one):** NC (NRM) BVM		**Assisted Ventilation**	**Airway Adjunct**	**CPR**
Defibrillation	(Bleeding Control)	(Bandaging)	(Splinting)	(Other: Shock treatment)

Narrative
Medic 19 dispatched on emergency call for a police officer with a gunshot wound. Arrived on scene and was led to 24-year-old patient with a gunshot wound on left lateral neck. Bleeding was manually controlled, but evidence of severe blood loss was present. Patient was conscious and alert but subdued. Placed occlusive dressing and pressure dressing over wound and initiated high-flow oxygen therapy. Patient was secured to a long backboard due to MOI and immediate transport was initiated; no other wounds present. Baseline vital signs indicated that patient was hypoperfusing so we transported rapidly and covered the patient with blankets to retain body heat. Called report to the receiving trauma center and provided ETA. Subsequent vital signs showed no improvement of the shock condition but also no further deterioration. Remainder of transport was without incident, and we then delivered the patient to the emergency department and gave a verbal report to the attending physician and charge nurse. Medic 19 returned to service at 1411.**End of Report**

Skills

Skill Drills

Skill Drill 26-1: Stabilizing an Impaled Object

1. Do not attempted to **move** or remove the object. **Stabilize** the impaled body part.
2. Control **bleeding**, and stabilize the object in place using **soft dressings**, gauze, and/or tape.
3. Tape a **rigid** item over the stabilized object to prevent it from **moving** during transport. (page 921; Emergency Medical Care for Open Injuries)

Skill Drill 26-2: Caring for Burns

1. Follow **standard** precautions to help prevent **infection**. If safe to do so, remove the **patient** from the burning area; extinguish or **remove** hot clothing and jewelry as necessary. If the wound is still burning or hot, **immerse** the hot area in **cool**, sterile **water**, or cover with a wet, cool **dressing**.
2. Provide high-flow **oxygen**, and continue to assess the **airway**.
3. Estimate the **severity** of the burn, and then cover the area with a(n) **dry**, sterile dressing or clean **sheet**. Assess and treat the patient for any other **injuries**.
4. Prepare for transport. Treat for **shock**. Cover the patient with **blankets** to prevent loss of **body heat**. Transport promptly. (page 932; Emergency Medical Care for Burns)

Assessment Review

1. C (page 929; Patient Assessment of Burns)
2. B (page 929; Patient Assessment of Burns)
3. D (page 930; Patient Assessment of Burns)
4. A (page 930; Patient Assessment of Burns)
5. D (page 921; Emergency Medical Care for Open Injuries)

Chapter 27: Face and Neck Injuries

General Knowledge

Matching

1. G (page 950; Anatomy and Physiology)
2. H (page 950; Anatomy and Physiology)
3. L (pages 967–968; Emergency Medical Care for Specific Injuries)
4. C (page 949; Anatomy and Physiology)
5. J (page 950; Anatomy and Physiology)
6. K (page 950; Anatomy and Physiology)
7. I (page 947; Anatomy and Physiology)
8. E (page 947; Anatomy and Physiology)
9. O (page 950; Anatomy and Physiology)
10. B (page 950; Anatomy and Physiology)
11. F (page 949; Anatomy and Physiology)
12. M (page 947; Anatomy and Physiology)
13. A (page 966; Emergency Medical Care for Specific Injuries)
14. D (page 967; Emergency Medical Care for Specific Injuries)
15. N (page 950; Anatomy and Physiology)

Multiple Choice

1. D (page 947; Introduction)
2. B (page 947; Anatomy and Physiology)
3. C (page 947; Anatomy and Physiology)
4. D (page 947; Anatomy and Physiology)
5. A (page 947; Anatomy and Physiology)
6. D (page 948; Anatomy and Physiology)
7. C (page 948; Anatomy and Physiology)
8. D (page 950; Anatomy and Physiology)
9. A (page 956; Emergency Medical Care)
10. D (page 966; Emergency Medical Care for Specific Injuries)
11. B (pages 966–967; Emergency Medical Care for Specific Injuries)
12. C (pages 967–968; Emergency Medical Care for Specific Injuries)
13. D (page 972; Emergency Medical Care for Specific Injuries)
14. C (page 969; Emergency Medical Care for Specific Injuries)
15. D (page 970; Emergency Medical Care for Specific Injuries)
16. A (page 971; Emergency Medical Care for Specific Injuries)
17. A (page 949; Anatomy and Physiology)
18. C (pages 957–958; Emergency Medical Care for Specific Injuries)
19. B (page 959; Emergency Medical Care for Specific Injuries)
20. C (page 961; Emergency Medical Care for Specific Injuries)

True/False

1. T (page 950; Injuries of the Face and Neck)
2. T (page 955; Emergency Medical Care)
3. F (page 962; Emergency Medical Care for Specific Injuries)
4. F (page 969; Emergency Medical Care for Specific Injuries)
5. T (page 970; Emergency Medical Care for Specific Injuries)
6. T (page 951; Injuries of the Face and Neck)
7. F (page 947; Anatomy and Physiology)
8. F (page 948; Anatomy and Physiology)
9. T (pages 951–952; Patient Assessment)
10. F (page 952; Patient Assessment)
11. T (page 952; Patient Assessment)
12. T (page 950; Anatomy and Physiology)
13. F (page 958; Emergency Medical Care for Specific Injuries)
14. F (page 961; Emergency Medical Care for Specific Injuries)

15. T (page 962; Emergency Medical Care for Specific Injuries)

16. F (page 957; Emergency Medical Care for Specific Injuries)

17. F (page 964; Emergency Medical Care for Specific Injuries)

18. T (page 971; Emergency Medical Care for Specific Injuries)

19. F (pages 955–956; Emergency Medical Care)

20. T (page 955; Emergency Medical Care)

Fill-in-the-Blank

1. carotid (page 948; Anatomy and Physiology)
2. cervical (page 949; Anatomy and Physiology)
3. temporal (page 947; Anatomy and Physiology)
4. trachea (page 948; Anatomy and Physiology)
5. cartilage (page 948; Anatomy and Physiology)
6. men, women (page 948; Anatomy and Physiology)
7. foramen magnum (page 947; Anatomy and Physiology)
8. blowout fracture (page 963; Emergency Medical Care for Specific Injuries)
9. basilar skull fracture (page 965; Emergency Medical Care for Specific Injuries)
10. crown, root (page 970; Emergency Medical Care for Specific Injuries)
11. air embolism (page 971; Emergency Medical Care for Specific Injuries)

Labeling

1. The Face (page 948; Anatomy and Physiology)
   A. Nasal bone
   B. Zygoma
   C. Maxilla
   D. Mandible

2. The Larynx (page 949; Anatomy and Physiology)
   A. Laryngeal prominence (Adam's apple)
   B. Thyroid cartilage
   C. Cricothyroid membrane
   D. Cricoid cartilage
   E. Trachea

3. The Eye (page 949; Anatomy and Physiology)
   A. Anterior compartment filled with aqueous humor
   B. Posterior compartment filled with vitreous humor
   C. Anterior chamber
   D. Posterior chamber
   E. Vein
   F. Iris
   G. Cornea
   H. Pupil
   I. Artery
   J. Lens
   K. Optic nerve
   L. Retina
   M. Choroid
   N. Sclera

4. The Ear (page 968; Emergency Medical Care for Specific Injuries)
   A. Pinna
   B. External auditory canal
   C. Tympanic membrane
   D. Cochlea
   E. Hammer
   F. Anvil
   G. Stirrup

Crossword Puzzle

```
¹P        ²S  U  B  C  U  T  ³A  N  E  O  U  ⁴S
 U                             N              C
 P              ⁵R  E  T  I  N  A              L
 I        ⁶T                   S              E
⁷L  A  C  R  I  M  A  L         O              R
          A              ⁸C  O  R  N  ⁹E  A
¹⁰T       G     ¹¹G       O           U
 Y        U     L        R     ¹²E    S
¹³M  A  S  T  O  I  D     I     X     T
 P        B              A     T     A
 A     ¹⁴P  E            ¹⁵     E     C
 N     I                 I     R     H
 I     N                 R     N     I
¹⁶C  O  N  J  U  N  C  T  I  V  A     A
 A                       S     ¹⁷L  E  N  S
```

Critical Thinking

Short Answer

1. Apply direct manual pressure with a dry dressing. Use roller gauze around the circumference of the head to hold the pressure dressing in place. Make sure you do not apply excessive pressure if there is a possibility of an underlying skull fracture. (page 955; Emergency Medical Care)

2. 1. Apply direct pressure to the bleeding site using a gloved fingertip if necessary to control bleeding.
   2. Apply a sterile occlusive dressing to ensure that air does not enter a vein or artery.
   3. Secure the dressing in place with roller gauze, adding more dressings if needed.
   4. Wrap the gauze around and under the patient's shoulder. To avoid possible airway and circulation problems, do not wrap the gauze around the neck. (page 971; Emergency Medical Care for Specific Injuries)

3. Start on the outer aspect of the eye and work your way in toward the pupil. Examine the eye for any obvious foreign matter. Observe for discoloration of the eye. Evaluate the clarity of the patient's vision. Assess for redness of or bleeding into the iris. Look for symmetry between the two eyes. Assess the pupils for equal size and reaction to light. Determine if unequal pupils are caused by physiologic or pathologic issues. Determine if the patient is able to follow your finger with his or her eyes. Assess visual acuity by having the patient read normal print. Question about blurry vision or sensitivity to light. (page 954; Patient Assessment)

4. 1. Never exert pressure on or manipulate the injured eye (globe) in any way.
   2. If part of the eyeball is exposed, gently apply a moist, sterile dressing to prevent drying.
   3. Cover the injured eye with a protective metal eye shield, cup, or sterile dressing. Apply soft dressings to both eyes, and provide prompt transport to the hospital. (page 962; Emergency Medical Care for Specific Injuries)

5. 1. One pupil larger than the other
   2. The eyes not moving together or pointing in different directions
   3. Failure of the eyes to follow the movement of your finger as instructed
   4. Bleeding under the conjunctiva, which obscures the sclera of the eye
   5. Protrusion or bulging of one eye (page 964; Emergency Medical Care for Specific Injuries)

Ambulance Calls

1. Depending on where the dog's teeth have punctured the skin, you may have a variety of soft-tissue injuries and swelling. If you notice the presence of subcutaneous emphysema, the dog punctured or perforated the child's trachea. You must also assume the presence of cervical spine injuries and take appropriate precautions. Assess his level of consciousness, airway, breathing, and circulation. Control any bleeding and apply other dressings, as needed, after airway management is accomplished and while en route to the hospital. Always follow local protocols.

2. Apply direct pressure to the bleeding site using gloved fingertips and a sterile occlusive dressing. Secure the dressing in place and apply pressure, if necessary. You may need to treat for shock. Provide prompt transport with the patient immobilized to a long backboard and apply high-flow oxygen en route.

3. You should determine what objects were used to cause injury to this man's face. Baseball bats would be readily available and would increase your index of suspicion. You should determine the presence of head and neck pain. If the area of injury is limited to his nose, and the need for spinal precautions is not indicated, you can instruct the patient in controlling his bleeding by ensuring that he pushes on the cartilage of his nose and does not lean his head backward. Swallowing blood will cause nausea. Do not allow the patient to blow his nose, and consider using ice, as needed, to reduce swelling and pain. Transport according to local protocols.

Skills

Skill Drills

Skill Drill 27-1: Removing a Foreign Object From Under the Upper Eyelid

1. Have the patient look **down**, grasp the upper **lashes**, and gently pull the **lid** away from the eye.
2. Place a cotton-tipped applicator on the **outer** surface of the **upper** lid.
3. Pull the lid **forward** and **up**, folding it back over the applicator.
4. Gently remove the foreign object from the eyelid with a moistened, **sterile**, cotton-tipped applicator. (page 958; Emergency Medical Care for Specific Injuries)

Skill Drill 27-2: Stabilizing a Foreign Object Impaled in the Eye

1. To prepare a doughnut ring, wrap a 2-inch roll around your fingers and thumb seven or eight times. Adjust the diameter by spreading your fingers or squeezing them together.
2. Remove the gauze from your hand and wrap the remainder of the gauze roll radially around the ring that you have created.
3. Work around the entire ring to form a doughnut.
4. Place the dressing over the eye and impaled object to hold the impaled object in place, and then secure it with a roller bandage. (page 960; Emergency Medical Care for Specific Injuries)

Assessment Review

1. D (pages 951–952; Patient Assessment)
2. B (page 955; Patient Assessment)
3. D (pages 966–967; Emergency Medical Care for Specific Injuries)
4. A (page 970; Emergency Medical Care for Specific Injuries)
5. C (page 969; Emergency Medical Care for Specific Injuries)

Chapter 28: Head and Spine Injuries

General Knowledge

Matching

1. D (page 989; Head Injuries)
2. E (page 989; Head Injuries)
3. H (page 989; Head Injuries)
4. G (page 991; Head Injuries)
5. A (page 990; Head Injuries)
6. C (page 991; Head Injuries)
7. B (page 989; Head Injuries)
8. I (page 983; Anatomy and Physiology)
9. J (page 985; Anatomy and Physiology)
10. F (page 982; Anatomy and Physiology)

Multiple Choice

1. D (pages 981–983; Anatomy and Physiology)
2. B (page 981; Anatomy and Physiology)
3. C (page 981; Anatomy and Physiology)
4. C (page 986; Head Injuries)
5. A (page 982; Anatomy and Physiology)
6. B (page 984; Anatomy and Physiology)
7. D (page 983; Anatomy and Physiology)
8. D (page 983; Anatomy and Physiology)
9. C (page 984; Anatomy and Physiology)
10. A (page 986; Anatomy and Physiology)
11. D (page 996; Patient Assessment)
12. D (page 993; Patient Assessment)
13. B (page 985; Anatomy and Physiology)
14. D (page 1007; Preparation for Transport)
15. B (page 1004; Emergency Medical Care of Spinal Injuries)
16. A (page 1007; Preparation for Transport)
17. A (page 1002; Emergency Medical Care of Head Injuries)
18. B (page 1013; Preparation for Transport)
19. D (page 990; Head Injuries)
20. B (page 990; Head Injuries)
21. C (page 991; Head Injuries)
22. D (page 989; Head Injuries)
23. C (page 1016; Preparation for Transport)
24. B (page 996; Patient Assessment)
25. B (page 995; Patient Assessment)
26. C (page 986; Head Injuries)
27. C (page 994; Patient Assessment)
28. A (page 997; Patient Assessment)
29. C (page 1002; Emergency Medical Care of Head Injuries)
30. B (page 1014; Preparation for Transport)
31. D (page 1005; Emergency Medical Care of Spinal Injuries)
32. C (page 1018; Helmet Removal)
33. D (page 1007; Preparation for Transport)

True/False

1. F (page 990; Head Injuries)
2. F (page 984; Anatomy and Physiology)
3. F (page 983; Anatomy and Physiology)
4. T (page 984; Anatomy and Physiology)
5. F (page 984; Anatomy and Physiology)
6. F (pages 993–994; Patient Assessment)
7. F (page 994; Patient Assessment)
8. T (page 1007; Preparation for Transport)
9. T (page 1013; Preparation for Transport)
10. T (page 1005; Emergency Medical Care of Spinal Injuries)

Fill-in-the-Blank

1. motor (page 983; Anatomy and Physiology)
2. meninges (page 982; Anatomy and Physiology)
3. central (page 981; Anatomy and Physiology)
4. 31 (page 983; Anatomy and Physiology)
5. cranial (page 983; Anatomy and Physiology)
6. intervertebral disks (page 985; Anatomy and Physiology)
7. cranium, face (page 984; Anatomy and Physiology)
8. arachnoid, pia mater (page 983; Anatomy and Physiology)
9. sympathetic (page 984; Anatomy and Physiology)
10. parasympathetic (page 984; Anatomy and Physiology)
11. intracerebral hematoma (page 990; Head Injuries)
12. contusion (page 991; Head Injuries)
13. padding (page 1021; Helmet Removal)
14. pulse, motor, sensory (page 1007; Preparation for Transport)
15. jaw-thrust (page 1001; Emergency Medical Care of Head Injuries)

Labeling

1. Brain (page 982; Anatomy and Physiology)
   A. Cerebrum
   B. Parietal lobe
   C. Frontal lobe
   D. Occipital lobe
   E. Temporal lobe
   F. Brain stem
   G. Cerebellum
   H. Spinal cord
   I. Foramen magnum

2. Connecting Nerves in the Spinal Cord (page 984; Anatomy and Physiology)
   A. Motor nerve
   B. Sensory nerve
   C. Connecting nerve cell
   D. Spinal cord

3. Spinal Column (page 985; Anatomy and Physiology)
   A. Cervical (7)
   B. Thoracic (12)
   C. Lumbar (5)
   D. Sacrum (5)
   E. Coccyx (4)

Crossword Puzzle

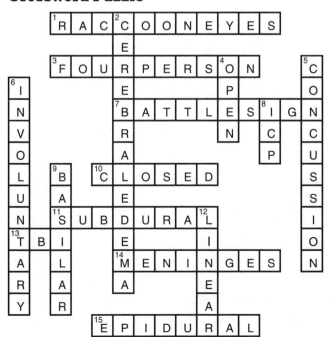

Critical Thinking

Short Answer

1. 1. Motor vehicle collision (including motorcycles, snowmobiles, and all-terrain vehicles)
   2. Pedestrian–motor vehicle collision
   3. Falls >20 feet (adult)
   4. Falls >10 feet (pediatric)
   5. Blunt trauma
   6. Penetrating trauma to the head, neck, back, or torso
   7. Rapid deceleration injuries
   8. Hangings
   9. Axial loading injuries
   10. Diving accidents (page 992; Patient Assessment)

2. Muscle spasms in the neck

   Substantial increased pain

   Numbness, tingling, or weakness in the arms or legs

   Compromised airway or ventilations (pages 1004–1005; Emergency Medical Care of Spinal Injuries)

3. Primary brain injury is injury to the brain and its associated structures that results instantaneously from impact to the head. Secondary brain injury refers to a multitude of processes that increase the severity of a primary brain injury and therefore negatively affect the outcome. Secondary brain injuries result from cerebral edema, intracranial hemorrhage, increased intracranial pressure, cerebral ischemia, and infection. Hypoxia and hypotension are the two most common causes of secondary brain injuries. (page 988; Head Injuries)

4. Lacerations, contusions, or hematomas to the scalp

   Soft area or depression on palpation

   Visible fractures or deformities of the skull

   Decreased mentation, irregular breathing pattern, widening pulse pressure, slow pulse rate

   Ecchymosis about the eyes or behind the ear over the mastoid process

   Clear or pink cerebrospinal fluid leakage from a scalp wound, the nose, or the ear

   Failure of the pupils to respond to light

   Unequal pupil size

   Loss of sensation and/or motor function

   A period of unconsciousness

   Amnesia

   Seizures

   Numbness or tingling in the extremities

   Irregular respirations

   Dizziness

   Visual complaints

   Combative or other abnormal behavior

   Nausea or vomiting

   Posturing (decorticate or decerebrate) (page 986; Head Injuries)

5. 1. Establish an adequate airway.
   2. Control bleeding.
   3. Assess the patient's baseline level of consciousness. (page 1001; Emergency Medical Care of Head Injuries)

6. 1. Is the patient's airway clear?
   2. Is the patient breathing adequately?
   3. Can you maintain the airway and assist ventilations if the helmet remains in place?
   4. Can the face guard be easily removed to allow access to the airway without removing the helmet?

5. How well does the helmet fit?

6. Can the patient move within the helmet?

7. Can the spine be immobilized in a neutral position with the helmet on? (page 1018; Helmet Removal)

Ambulance Calls

1. This incident involves a significant mechanism of injury. The impact with the car, the lack of a helmet, the obvious head trauma, and the patient's decreased level of consciousness all indicate significant life-threatening injuries. You must quickly apply full spinal precautions and manage her airway. Provide prompt transport and high-flow oxygen, and perform ongoing assessments while en route to the nearest appropriate medical facility.

2. This child landed face down on a concrete surface with significant force. She is now unconscious with a partially obstructed airway. You must move her to a supine position to manage her airway. Take note of any apparent injuries to her back as you reposition her. Ideally, you will have the appropriate equipment and adequate staffing to quickly and safely move her to a long backboard immediately. However, do not delay appropriately moving her to a supine position because you must do this to assess and manage her airway. This may be difficult because she likely has facial fractures and possibly broken teeth, blood, and secretions in her airway. Be prepared to suction her airway and apply positive-pressure ventilations (this may be especially challenging in the presence of significant facial fractures). Use high-flow oxygen and promptly transport her to the nearest appropriate facility according to your local protocols.

3. Leave the patient in his car seat. Pad appropriately to immobilize the patient. Use blow-by oxygen if the patient will tolerate it. Monitor vital signs. Continue assessment. Provide rapid transport due to mechanism of injury and death in vehicle.

Skills

Skill Drills

Skill Drill 28-1: Performing Manual In-Line Stabilization

1. Take standard precautions. Kneel behind the patient and firmly place your hands around the **base** of the **skull** on either **side**.

2. Support the lower jaw with your **index** and **long** fingers, and the head with your **palms**. Gently lift the head into a(n) **neutral**, **eyes-forward** position, aligned with the torso. Do not **move** the head or neck excessively, forcefully, or rapidly.

3. Continue to manually **support** the head while your partner places a rigid **cervical collar** around the neck. Maintain **manual support** until you have completely secured the patient to a backboard. (page 1004; Emergency Medical Care of Spinal Injuries)

Skill Drill 28-3: Securing a Patient to a Long Backboard

1. Apply and maintain cervical stabilization. Assess distal functions in all extremities.

2. Apply a cervical collar.

3. Rescuers kneel on one side of the patient and place hands on the far side of the patient.

4. On command, rescuers roll the patient toward themselves, quickly examine the back, slide the backboard under the patient, and roll the patient onto the backboard.

5. Center the patient on the backboard.

6. Secure the upper torso first.

7. Secure the pelvis and upper legs.

8. Begin to secure the patient's head using a commercial immobilization device or rolled towels.

9. Place tape across the patient's forehead to secure the immobilization device.

10. Check all straps and readjust as needed. Reassess distal functions in all extremities. (pages 1008–1009; Preparation for Transport)

Skill Drill 28-5: Securing a Patient Found in a Sitting Position

1. Take standard precautions. Stabilize the head and neck in a **neutral**, **in-line** position. Assess pulse, motor, and sensory function in each extremity. Apply a **cervical collar**.

2. Insert an immobilization device between the patient's **upper back** and the seat.

3. Open the side flaps, and position them around the patient's **torso**, snug around the armpits.

4. Secure the upper torso flaps, then the mid-torso flaps.

5. Secure the **groin** (leg) straps. Check and adjust the **torso** straps.

6. **Pad** between the head and the device as needed. Secure the forehead strap and fasten the **lower** head strap around the cervical collar.

7. Place a long backboard next to the patient's buttocks, **perpendicular** to the trunk.

8. Turn and lower the patient onto the long backboard. Lift the **patient**, and slip the long backboard under the immobilization device.

9. Secure the immobilization device and long backboard to each other. **Loosen** or **release** the groin straps. Reassess pulse, motor, and sensory function in each extremity. (pages 1014–1016; Preparation for Transport)

Assessment Review

1. D (page 995; Patient Assessment)
2. C (page 1004; Emergency Medical Care of Spinal Injuries)
3. B (page 1018; Preparation for Transport)
4. C (page 1013; Preparation for Transport)
5. A (page 1018; Helmet Removal)

Skill Drill 28-2: Application of a Cervical Collar

1. Apply in-line **stabilization**.
2. Measure the proper **collar size**.
3. Place the **chin support** first.
4. **Wrap** the collar around the neck and **secure** the collar.
5. Ensure proper **fit** and maintain **neutral**, **in-line** stabilization until the patient is secured to a(n) **backboard**. (page 1006; Emergency Medical Care of Spinal Injuries)

Emergency Care Summary

General Management of Head Injuries (page 1001; Emergency Medical Care of Head Injuries)

1. Establish an **adequate** airway. If necessary, begin and maintain **ventilation** and provide **supplemental oxygen**.
2. Control **bleeding**, and provide adequate **circulation** to maintain **cerebral** perfusion. Begin **cardiopulmonary** resuscitation, if necessary.
3. Assess the patient's baseline level of **consciousness**, and continuously monitor it.
4. Do not apply pressure to an open or **compressed** skull injury.
5. Assess and treat other injuries.
6. Anticipate and manage **vomiting** to prevent aspiration.
7. Be prepared for **convulsions** and changes in the patient's condition.
8. Transport the patient promptly and with extreme care.

General Management of Spine Injuries (page 1003; Emergency Medical Care of Spinal Injuries)

1. Open and maintain a patent airway with the **jaw-thrust** maneuver.
2. Hold the head still in a **neutral**, in-line position until it can be fully immobilized.
3. Consider inserting an **oropharyngeal** airway.
4. Have a **suctioning** unit available.
5. Provide supplemental oxygen.
6. Continuously monitor the patient's airway and be prepared for any changes in the patient's condition based on your treatment.

TRAUMA
Chapter 29: Chest Injuries

General Knowledge

Matching

1. B (page 1031; Anatomy and Physiology)
2. D (page 1033; Anatomy and Physiology)
3. K (page 1031; Anatomy and Physiology)
4. A (page 1031; Anatomy and Physiology)
5. E (page 1033; Anatomy and Physiology)
6. H (page 1034; Injuries of the Chest)
7. I (page 1036; Injuries of the Chest)
8. J (page 1045; Complications and Management of Chest Injuries)
9. F (page 1036; Injuries of the Chest)
10. G (page 1036; Injuries of the Chest)
11. C (page 1033; Anatomy and Physiology)

Multiple Choice

1. B (page 1032; Anatomy and Physiology)
2. A (page 1033; Anatomy and Physiology)
3. C (page 1033; Anatomy and Physiology)
4. D (page 1035; Injuries of the Chest)
5. D (page 1035; Injuries of the Chest)
6. C (pages 1035–1036; Injuries of the Chest)
7. A (page 1047; Other Chest Injuries)
8. C (page 1037; Patient Assessment)
9. D (page 1041; Complications and Management of Chest Injuries)
10. C (page 1041; Complications and Management of Chest Injuries)
11. A (page 1042; Complications and Management of Chest Injuries)
12. B (page 1045; Complications and Management of Chest Injuries)
13. C (page 1043; Complications and Management of Chest Injuries)
14. A (page 1044; Complications and Management of Chest Injuries)
15. C (page 1047; Other Chest Injuries)
16. A (page 1045; Complications and Management of Chest Injuries)
17. C (page 1047; Other Chest Injuries)
18. D (page 1034; Mechanics of Ventilation)
19. A (page 1039; Patient Assessment)
20. B (page 1048; Other Chest Injuries)

True/False

1. T (page 1036; Injuries of the Chest)
2. F (page 1036; Injuries of the Chest)
3. T (page 1043; Complications and Management of Chest Injuries)
4. F (page 1045; Complications and Management of Chest Injuries)
5. F (page 1045; Complications and Management of Chest Injuries)
6. F (page 1048; Other Chest Injuries)
7. F (page 1031; Anatomy and Physiology)
8. T (page 1033; Mechanics of Ventilation)
9. F (page 1041; Complications and Management of Chest Injuries)
10. T (page 1034; Injuries of the Chest)
11. F (page 1046; Complications and Management of Chest Injuries)
12. F (page 1039; Patient Assessment)
13. T (page 1038; Patient Assessment)
14. T (page 1035; Injuries of the Chest)
15. F (page 1032; Anatomy and Physiology)

Fill-in-the-Blank

1. back (page 1033; Anatomy and Physiology)
2. decreases (page 1033; Mechanics of Ventilation)
3. sternum (page 1032; Anatomy and Physiology)
4. bronchi (page 1032; Anatomy and Physiology)
5. phrenic (page 1033; Mechanics of Ventilation)
6. ribs (page 1032; Anatomy and Physiology)
7. diaphragm (page 1031; Anatomy and Physiology)
8. Pleura (page 1032; Anatomy and Physiology)
9. hypercarbia (page 1034; Injuries of the Chest)
10. contracts (page 1033; Mechanics of Ventilation)
11. Ventilation (page 1031; Anatomy and Physiology)
12. C6, C7 (page 1031; Anatomy and Physiology)
13. Tidal volume (page 1034; Mechanics of Ventilation)
14. respiratory rate (page 1040; Patient Assessment)
15. traumatic forces (page 1033; Anatomy and Physiology)

Labeling

1. Anterior Aspect of the Chest (page 1032; Anatomy and Physiology)
   A. Subclavian artery
   B. Superior vena cava
   C. Heart
   D. Aorta
   E. Pulmonary arteries
   F. Pleural lining
   G. Lungs
   H. Diaphragm

2. Pneumothorax (page 1041; Complications and Management of Chest Injuries)
   A. Parietal pleura
   B. Air in the pleural space
   C. Wound site
   D. Lung
   E. Collapsed lung
   F. Heart
   G. Visceral pleura
   H. Diaphragm

Crossword Puzzle

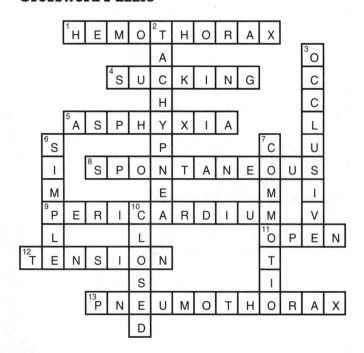

Critical Thinking

Short Answer

1. Pain at the site of injury

   Pain localized at the site of injury that is aggravated by or increased with breathing

   Bruising to the chest wall

   Crepitus with palpation of the chest

   Any penetrating injury to the chest

   Dyspnea (difficulty breathing, shortness of breath)

   Hemoptysis (coughing up blood)

   Failure of one or both sides of the chest to expand normally with inspiration

   Rapid, weak pulse and low blood pressure

   Cyanosis around the lips or fingernails (pages 1035–1036; Injuries of the Chest)

2.   1. Seal the wound with a large airtight dressing that seals all four sides.

     2. Seal the wound with a dressing that seals three sides, with the fourth side as a flutter valve. Your local protocol will dictate the way you are to care for this injury. (page 1041; Complications and Management of Chest Injuries)

3. Maintain the airway, provide respiratory support if necessary, and give supplemental oxygen. Perform an ongoing assessment for possible pneumothorax or other respiratory complications. Provide positive pressure ventilation with a bag-valve mask as needed. Use PPV in place of splinting with a bulky dressing. (page 1046; Complications and Management of Chest Injuries)

4. Sudden severe compression of the chest, causing a rapid increase of pressure within the chest. Characteristic signs include distended neck veins, facial and neck cyanosis, and hemorrhage in the sclera of the eye. (page 1047; Other Chest Injuries)

5.   1. Airway obstruction
     2. Bronchial disruption
     3. Diaphragmatic tear
     4. Esophageal injury
     5. Open pneumothorax
     6. Tension pneumothorax
     7. Massive hemothorax
     8. Flail chest
     9. Cardiac tamponade
     10. Thoracic aortic dissection
     11. Myocardial contusion
     12. Pulmonary contusion (page 1038; Patient Assessment)

Ambulance Calls

1. You should be concerned with the presence of rib and sternal fractures as well as pulmonary contusions and pneumothoraces. This patient may require assistance in breathing because it will be extremely painful for him to breathe in. If he requires assistance with a bag-valve mask, you must be careful not to become too aggressive in your ventilations. Time your ventilations with the patient's respirations and be gentle. Provide high-flow oxygen and take spinal precautions according to your local protocols.

2. This patient's chest has been crushed with a significant amount of weight. This mechanism of injury indicates the high potential for rib, sternal, and thoracic fractures as well as other soft-tissue injuries. Patients who experience sternal fractures will find it difficult to be placed supine because this will likely increase their pain. There will be little you can do to ease this pain because the patient should be immobilized on a long backboard. Provide prompt transport, high-flow oxygen, and monitor the pulse, motor, and sensations particularly distal to the suspected spinal injury.

3. Apply high-flow oxygen via nonrebreathing mask or bag-valve mask. Provide full cervical spine immobilization. Provide rapid transport and monitor vital signs en route.

Skills

Assessment Review

1. B (page 1037; Patient Assessment)
2. D (page 1041; Complications and Management of Chest Injuries)
3. C (page 1041; Complications and Management of Chest Injuries)
4. D (page 1046; Complications and Management of Chest Injuries)
5. A (pages 1045–1046; Complications and Management of Chest Injuries)

TRAUMA

Chapter 30: Abdominal and Genitourinary Injuries

General Knowledge

Matching

1. E (page 1059; Injuries to the abdomen)
2. I (page 1062; Injuries to the Abdomen)
3. F (page 1062; Injuries to the Abdomen)
4. A (page 1060; Injuries to the Abdomen)
5. H (page 1058; Anatomy and Physiology of the Abdomen)

6. C (page 1064; Injuries to the Abdomen)
7. D (page 1061; Injuries to the Abdomen)
8. G (page 1058; Anatomy and Physiology of the Abdomen)
9. B (page 1058; Anatomy and Physiology of the Abdomen)

Multiple Choice

1. D (page 1057; Introduction)
2. B (page 1058; Anatomy and Physiology of the Abdomen)
3. C (page 1058; Anatomy and Physiology of the Abdomen)
4. D (page 1058; Anatomy and Physiology of the Abdomen)
5. B (page 1058; Anatomy and Physiology of the Abdomen)
6. C (page 1059; Anatomy and Physiology of the Abdomen)
7. A (page 1059; Anatomy and Physiology of the Abdomen)
8. C (page 1064; Injuries to the Abdomen)
9. B (page 1063; Injuries to the Abdomen)
10. A (page 1057; Anatomy and Physiology of the Abdomen)
11. A (page 1064; Injuries to the Abdomen)
12. C (page 1061; Injuries to the Abdomen)
13. B (page 1059; Injuries to the Abdomen)
14. A (page 1062; Injuries to the Abdomen)
15. B (page 1062; Injuries to the Abdomen)

16. B (page 1062; Injuries to the Abdomen)
17. B (page 1065; Patient Assessment of Abdominal Injuries)
18. B (page 1073; Injuries of the Genitourinary System)
19. D (page 1066; Patient Assessment of Abdominal Injuries)
20. D (page 1060; Injuries to the Abdomen)
21. C (pages 1067–1068; Patient Assessment of Abdominal Injuries)
22. A (page 1062; Injuries to the Abdomen)
23. D (page 1061; Injuries to the Abdomen)
24. D (page 1071; Emergency Medical Care of Abdominal Injuries)
25. A (page 1072; Anatomy of the Genitourinary System)
26. C (page 1072; Anatomy of the Genitourinary System)
27. D (page 1073; Injuries of the Genitourinary System)
28. C (pages 1077–1078; Emergency Medical Care of Genitourinary Injuries)
29. A (page 1078; Emergency Medical Care of Genitourinary Injuries)
30. B (page 1078; Emergency Medical Care of Genitourinary Injuries)
31. B (page 1074; Injuries of the Genitourinary System)
32. B (page 1079; Sexual Assault and Rape)

True/False

1. F (page 1058; Anatomy and Physiology of the Abdomen)
2. T (page 1062; Injuries to the Abdomen)
3. F (page 1067; Patient Assessment of Abdominal Injuries)
4. T (page 1058; Anatomy and Physiology of the Abdomen)
5. F (page 1071; Emergency Medical Care of Abdominal Injuries)

6. F (page 1073; Injuries of the Genitourinary System)
7. T (page 1058; Anatomy and Physiology of the Abdomen)
8. F (page 1057; Anatomy and Physiology of the Abdomen)
9. T (page 1067; Patient Assessment of Abdominal Injuries)
10. T (page 1066; Patient Assessment of Abdominal Injuries)

Fill-in-the-Blank

1. solid (page 1059; Anatomy and Physiology of the Abdomen)
2. urinary (page 1072; Anatomy of the Genitourinary System)
3. retroperitoneal (page 1059; Anatomy and Physiology of the Abdomen)
4. other organs (page 1073; Injuries of the Genitourinary System)
5. peritonitis (page 1058; Anatomy and Physiology of the Abdomen)
6. peritoneal cavity (page 1059; Anatomy and Physiology of the Abdomen)
7. blunt injuries (page 1059; Injuries to the Abdomen)
8. penetrating injuries (page 1061; Injuries to the Abdomen)
9. flank (page 1062; Injuries to the Abdomen)
10. evisceration (page 1062; Injuries to the Abdomen)

Labeling

1. Hollow Organs (page 1058; Anatomy and Physiology of the Abdomen)
   A. Stomach
   B. Gallbladder
   C. Bile duct
   D. Large intestine
   E. Ureter
   F. Small intestine
   G. Fallopian tubes
   H. Rectum
   I. Appendix
   J. Uterus
   K. Urinary bladder

2. Solid Organs (page 1059; Anatomy and Physiology of the Abdomen)
   A. Liver
   B. Spleen
   C. Adrenal gland
   D. Adrenal gland
   E. Pancreas
   F. Kidney
   G. Kidney
   H. Ovaries

Crossword Puzzle

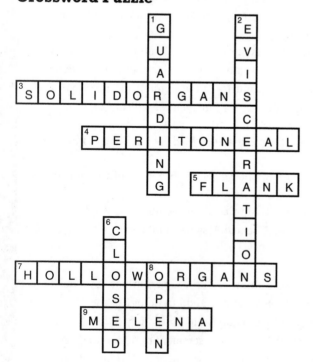

Critical Thinking

Short Answer

1. Stomach, intestines, ureters, bladder, gallbladder, bile duct, appendix, uterus, fallopian tubes, and rectum (page 1058; Anatomy and Physiology of the Abdomen)

2. Liver, spleen, pancreas, adrenal glands, ovaries, and kidneys (page 1058; Anatomy and Physiology of the Abdomen)

3. Pain

   Guarding

   Distention

   Tenderness

   Bruising and discoloration

   Abrasions

   Tachycardia

   Shock signs

   Lacerations

   Bleeding

   Difficulty with movement because of pain (pages 1059–1060, 1062; Injuries to the Abdomen)

4.   1. Log roll the patient to a supine position on a backboard.

   2. Inspect the patient's back and sides for exit wounds.

   3. Apply a dry, sterile dressing to all open wounds.

   4. If the penetrating object is still in place, apply a stabilizing bandage around it to control external bleeding and to minimize movement of the object.

   5. Monitor the patient's vital signs for indications of shock.

   6. Administer oxygen, if needed.

   7. Keep the patient warm with blankets.

   8. Provide prompt transport to the emergency department. (pages 1069–1071; Emergency Medical Care of Abdominal Injuries)

5.   1. Cover the wound with sterile dressings moistened with sterile saline solution.

   2. Secure the dressing with a dressing bandage and tape.

   3. Keep the organs moist and warm.

   4. Treat the patient for shock.

   5. Place the patient in a supine position.

   6. Provide high-flow oxygen.

   7. Transport the patient to the highest level trauma center available. (pages 1071–1072; Emergency Medical Care of Abdominal Injuries)

6. An abrasion, laceration, or contusion in the flank

   A penetrating wound in the flank (the region below the rib cage and above the hip) or the upper abdomen

   Fractures on either side of the lower rib cage or of the lower thoracic or upper lumbar vertebrae

   A hematoma in the flank region (page 1073; Injuries of the Genitourinary System)

Ambulance Calls

1. Assess the patient's ABCs and apply high-flow oxygen or a bag-valve mask if needed. Control any bleeding. Stabilize the knife in place with bulky dressings—do not remove it. Keep movement of the patient to the bare minimum so as not to create further injury. (Sliding the patient very carefully onto a backboard may help to minimize movement.) Monitor vital signs, and provide rapid transport. Keep warm and treat for shock if signs and symptoms present. Bandage minor lacerations en route.

2. Ensure that the scene is safe. Quickly visualize the area to determine how badly he has cut himself and whether he has in fact amputated any portion of his penis. You will need to control bleeding because blood loss in this area can be significant. Use direct pressure and/or pressure dressings to control bleeding. If a portion of the penis is amputated, wrap it in a moist, sterile dressing, place it in a plastic bag, and transport it in a cooled container. Do not allow it to come in direct contact with ice. Provide high-flow oxygen and prompt transport. Also, request the presence of a police officer during transport because this patient will likely need to be restrained and could be unpredictable during transport.

3. Cover the abdomen and the portion of the protruding bowel with a moistened, sterile dressing and/or an occlusive dressing. Secure these dressings with tape. Allow the patient to draw up his knees as needed for comfort. Apply high-flow oxygen, cover the patient to preserve warmth, treat for shock as needed, and promptly transport to the hospital.

Skills

Assessment Review

1. A (page 1071; Emergency Medical Care of Abdominal Injuries)
2. A (page 1078; Emergency Medical Care of Genitourinary Injuries)
3. D (page 1077; Patient Assessment of the Genitourinary System)
4. D (page 1078; Emergency Medical Care of Genitourinary Injuries)
5. C (page 1079; Sexual Assault and Rape)

Emergency Care Summary

Abdominal Trauma

Blunt Abdominal Injuries (pages 1069-1070; Emergency Medical Care of Abdominal Injuries)

Log roll the patient to a **supine** position on a backboard. If the patient vomits, turn him or her to one side and clear the mouth and throat of vomitus. Monitor the patient's vital signs for any indication of **shock**. If signs of shock are present, administer high-flow supplemental oxygen via a nonrebreathing mask, or a bag-valve mask if needed, and treat for shock. Keep the patient **warm**. Provide rapid transport to the emergency department.

Penetrating Abdominal Injuries (pages 1070-1071; Emergency Medical Care of Abdominal Injuries)

Patients with penetrating injuries generally have obvious wounds and **external bleeding**; however, significant external bleeding is not always present. As an EMT, you should have a high **index of suspicion** that the patient has serious unseen blood loss occurring inside the body. Inspect the patient's back and sides for exit wounds, and apply a **dry**, sterile dressing to all open wounds. If the penetrating object is still in place, apply a **stabilizing bandage** around it to control external bleeding and to minimize movement of the object.

Abdominal Evisceration (page 1071; Emergency Medical Care of Abdominal Injuries)

Never attempt to replace protruding organs. Cover the exposed organs with a **moist**, sterile dressing. If local protocol allows, cover the sterile dressing with an **occlusive** dressing. Maintain body temperature, treat for shock, and transport to the highest level trauma center available.

Genitourinary Trauma

Kidney Injuries (pages 1077-1078; Emergency Medical Care of Genitourinary Injuries)

Damage to the kidneys may not be obvious on inspection of the patient. You may or may not see bruises or lacerations on the overlying skin. You will see signs of shock if the injury is associated with significant blood loss. Another sign of kidney damage is **blood** in the urine (hematuria). Treat shock and associated injuries in the appropriate manner. Provide prompt transport to the hospital, monitoring the patient's vital signs carefully en route.

Urinary Bladder Injuries (page 1078; Emergency Medical Care of Genitourinary Injuries)

Suspect a possible injury of the urinary bladder if you see blood at the **urethral** opening or physical signs of trauma on the lower abdomen, pelvis, or **perineum**. There may be blood at the tip of the penis or a stain on the patient's underwear. The presence of associated injuries or of shock will dictate the urgency of transport. In most instances, provide prompt transport, and monitor the patient's vital signs en route.

Genitalia Injuries (pages 1078-1079; Emergency Medical Care of Genitourinary Injuries)

Direct pressure with a dry, sterile dressing usually controls any external hemorrhage. Lacerations, abrasions, and avulsions should be treated with **moist**, sterile compresses. Contusions and other blunt injuries all require careful in-hospital evaluation. However, the urgency for transport will be determined by associated injuries, the amount of hemorrhage, and the presence of **shock**.

Rectal Bleeding (page 1079; Emergency Medical Care of Genitourinary Injuries)

Bleeding from the rectum may present as blood stains or blood soaking through underwear or patients may report blood in the **toilet** after a bowel movement. Significant rectal bleeding can occur after hemorrhoid surgery and can lead to significant **blood loss** and **shock**.

Sexual Assault (page 1079; Sexual Assault and Rape)

Follow local protocol for crime scene management and **evidence** preservation. If available, an EMT of the same gender as the patient should perform the assessment and treatment. Advise the patient not to change clothes, **shower**, drink, or eat. Maintain patient privacy at all times. On some occasions, patients will have sustained multiple-system trauma and will also need treatment for shock. Do not examine the genitalia unless obvious bleeding must be managed.

Chapter 31: Orthopaedic Injuries

General Knowledge

Matching

1. G (page 1087; Anatomy and Physiology of the Musculoskeletal System)
2. J (page 1088; Anatomy and Physiology of the Musculoskeletal System)
3. D (page 1088; Anatomy and Physiology of the Musculoskeletal System)
4. I (page 1091; Anatomy and Physiology of the Musculoskeletal System)
5. F (page 1091; Anatomy and Physiology of the Musculoskeletal System)
6. B (page 1093; Musculoskeletal Injuries)
7. K (page 1094; Musculoskeletal Injuries)
8. A (page 1093; Musculoskeletal Injuries)
9. C (page 1091; Anatomy and Physiology of the Musculoskeletal System)
10. E (page 1093; Musculoskeletal Injuries)
11. H (page 1110; Emergency Medical Care)

Multiple Choice

1. A (page 1125; Specific Musculoskeletal Injuries)
2. B (page 1088; Anatomy and Physiology of the Musculoskeletal System)
3. A (pages 1088–1089; Anatomy and Physiology of the Musculoskeletal System)
4. B (page 1091; Anatomy and Physiology of the Musculoskeletal System)
5. C (page 1091; Anatomy and Physiology of the Musculoskeletal System)
6. B (page 1096; Musculoskeletal Injuries)
7. C (pages 1096–1097; Musculoskeletal Injuries)
8. A (page 1097; Musculoskeletal Injuries)
9. D (page 1092; Musculoskeletal Injuries)
10. A (page 1093; Musculoskeletal Injuries)
11. B (page 1093; Musculoskeletal Injuries)
12. C (page 1093; Musculoskeletal Injuries)
13. D (page 1093; Musculoskeletal Injuries)
14. B (page 1093; Musculoskeletal Injuries)
15. C (page 1093; Musculoskeletal Injuries)
16. D (page 1093; Musculoskeletal Injuries)
17. A (page 1093; Musculoskeletal Injuries)
18. C (page 1094; Musculoskeletal Injuries)
19. D (page 1093; Musculoskeletal Injuries)
20. A (page 1094; Musculoskeletal Injuries)
21. C (page 1094; Musculoskeletal Injuries)
22. B (page 1093; Musculoskeletal Injuries)
23. A (page 1095; Musculoskeletal Injuries)
24. C (page 1095; Musculoskeletal Injuries)
25. D (page 1096; Musculoskeletal Injuries)
26. C (page 1097; Musculoskeletal Injuries)
27. D (page 1102; Patient Assessment)
28. B (page 1132; Compartment Syndrome)
29. D (page 1104; Emergency Medical Care)
30. A (page 1104; Emergency Medical Care)
31. C (page 1110; Emergency Medical Care)
32. D (page 1104; Emergency Medical Care)
33. B (page 1110; Emergency Medical Care)
34. A (page 1115; Emergency Medical Care)
35. B (page 1115; Specific Musculoskeletal Injuries)
36. B (page 1116; Specific Musculoskeletal Injuries)
37. D (page 1126; Specific Musculoskeletal Injuries)
38. C (page 1127; Specific Musculoskeletal Injuries)
39. B (page 1127; Specific Musculoskeletal Injuries)
40. D (page 1127; Specific Musculoskeletal Injuries)
41. C (page 1128; Specific Musculoskeletal Injuries)
42. B (page 1128; Specific Musculoskeletal Injuries)
43. A (page 1130; Specific Musculoskeletal Injuries)
44. C (page 1130; Specific Musculoskeletal Injuries)
45. A (page 1132; Specific Musculoskeletal Injuries)

True/False

1. T (page 1104; Emergency Medical Care)
2. T (page 1104; Emergency Medical Care)
3. F (page 1110; Emergency Medical Care)
4. T (page 1110; Emergency Medical Care)
5. T (page 1105; Emergency Medical Care)
6. F (page 1105; Emergency Medical Care)
7. T (page 1105; Emergency Medical Care)
8. T (page 1091; Anatomy and Physiology of the Musculoskeletal System)
9. T (page 1118; Specific Musculoskeletal Injuries)
10. T (page 1121; Specific Musculoskeletal Injuries)

Fill-in-the-Blank

1. calcaneus (page 1091; Anatomy and Physiology of the Musculoskeletal System)
2. blood cells (pages 1088–1089; Anatomy and Physiology of the Musculoskeletal System)
3. hinged (page 1091; Anatomy and Physiology of the Musculoskeletal System)
4. clavicle (page 1089; Anatomy and Physiology of the Musculoskeletal System)
5. mechanism of injury (page 1100; Patient Assessment)
6. open fracture (page 1101; Patient Assessment)
7. sciatic nerve (page 1125; Specific Musculoskeletal Injuries)
8. Pelvic binders (pages 1114–1115; Emergency Medical Care)
9. crepitus (page 1095; Musculoskeletal Injuries)
10. reduce (page 1096; Musculoskeletal Injuries)
11. neurovascular status (page 1132; Compartment Syndrome)

Labeling

1. Pectoral Girdle (page 1089; Anatomy and Physiology of the Musculoskeletal System)

   A. Sternoclavicular joint
   B. Clavicle
   C. Acromioclavicular joint
   D. Clavicle
   E. Manubrium
   F. Acromion process
   G. Acromion process
   H. Humerus
   I. Glenoid fossa
   J. Sternum
   K. Humerus
   L. Glenohumeral (shoulder) joint
   M. Scapula

2. Anatomy of the Wrist and Hand (page 1090; Anatomy and Physiology of the Musculoskeletal System)

   A. Index
   B. Long
   C. Ring
   D. Little
   E. Phalanges
   F. Thumb
   G. Metacarpals
   H. Scaphoid
   I. Carpals
   J. Radius
   K. Ulna

3. Bones of the Thigh, Leg, and Foot (page 1090; Anatomy and Physiology of the Musculoskeletal System)

   A. Pelvis (hip bone)
   B. Hip
   C. Femur
   D. Thigh
   E. Patella (knee cap)
   F. Knee
   G. Fibula
   H. Leg
   I. Tibia (shin bone)
   J. Ankle
   K. Tarsals (ankle)
   L. Foot
   M. Metatarsals
   N. Phalanges

Crossword Puzzle

ARTICULAR · INJURY · HEMATURIA · OPEN FRACTURE · SPLINT · SCIATIC NERVE · POINT

(Down answers include: SWATHE, TIBIA, RETROPERITONEAL, SPRAIN, JOINT, PUNCTURE, CT, SLING, SED, COT)

Critical Thinking

Short Answer

1. 1. Direct blows
    2. Indirect forces
    3. Twisting forces
    4. High-energy injuries (pages 1092–1093; Musculoskeletal Injuries)

2. Deformity
    Tenderness (point)
    Guarding
    Swelling
    Bruising
    Crepitus
    False motion
    Exposed fragments
    Pain
    Locked joint (pages 1094–1096; Musculoskeletal Injuries)

3. 1. Pain
    2. Paralysis
    3. Paresthesia (numbness or tingling)
    4. Pulselessness
    5. Pallor
    6. Pressure (page 1102; Patient Assessment)

4. 1. Remove clothing from the area.
    2. Note and record the patient's neurovascular status distal to the site of the injury.
    3. Cover all wounds with a dry, sterile dressing before splinting.
    4. Do not move the patient before splinting.

5. For a suspected fracture of the shaft of any bone, immobilize the joints above and below the fracture.

6. For a joint injury, immobilize the bones above and below the injured joint.

7. Pad all rigid splints.

8. Maintain manual immobilization to minimize movement of the limb and to support the injury site.

9. If a fracture of a long-bone shaft has resulted in severe deformity, use a constant, gentle manual traction to align the limb.

10. If you encounter resistance to limb alignment, splint the limb in its deformed position.

11. Stabilize all suspected spinal injuries in a neutral in-line position on a backboard.

12. If the patient has signs of shock, align the limb in the normal anatomic position, and provide transport.

13. When in doubt, splint. (pages 1104–1105; Emergency Medical Care)

5. 1. Stabilize the fracture fragments to prevent excessive movement.

2. Align the limb sufficiently to allow it to be placed in a splint.

3. Avoid potential neurovascular compromise. (page 1110; Emergency Medical Care)

Ambulance Calls

1. This patient likely has a compression injury to his lumbar spine. The force exerted on his body from the landing will be transferred up from his feet through his legs to his pelvis and spine. You must take all spinal precautions, apply high-flow oxygen, and provide prompt transport to the nearest appropriate facility. Continue to monitor any changes in the pulse, motor, and sensation, specifically in his lower body.

2. Because circulation is intact, splint the arm in the position found. Use a board splint for support with a sling and swathe. Immobilize the hand in the position of function. Apply oxygen as needed and transport the patient in a position of comfort. Provide normal transport and monitor vital signs and neurovascular function.

3. This patient presents with signs of an anterior hip dislocation. Do not attempt to reduce the dislocation. It is preferable to use a scoop stretcher to move the patient to avoid any further injury. Manage her ABCs and give oxygen as needed. Assess for a pulse in the right foot before and after moving. Splint the dislocation in the position found and place the patient supine on the backboard using a scoop stretcher to lift her. Support her right leg with pillows and rolled blankets, then secure the entire limb to the backboard with long straps so that the hip region will not move. Provide prompt transport and reassess frequently.

Skills

Skill Drills

Skill Drill 31-1: Caring for Musculoskeletal Injuries

1. Cover open wounds with a **dry**, **sterile** dressing and apply pressure to control **bleeding**. Assess distal pulse and motor and sensory function. If bleeding cannot be controlled, quickly apply a tourniquet.

2. Apply a **splint**, and elevate the extremity about 6 inches (15 cm) (slightly above the level of the heart). Assess distal pulse and motor and sensory function.

3. Apply cold packs if there is **swelling**, but do not place them directly on the skin.

4. Position the patient for transport, and secure the **injured area**. (page 1103; Emergency Medical Care)

Skill Drill 31-2: Applying a Rigid Splint

1. Provide gentle **support** and **in-line traction** for the limb. Assess distal pulse and motor and sensory function.

2. Place the splint **alongside** or **under** the limb. **Pad** between the limb and the splint as needed to ensure even pressure and contact.

3. Secure the splint to the limb with **bindings**.

4. Assess and record **distal neurovascular** function. (page 1106; Emergency Medical Care)

Skill Drill 31-5: Applying a Vacuum Splint

1. Assess distal pulse and motor and sensory function. Your partner **stabilizes** and **supports** the injury.
2. Place the splint, and **wrap** it around the limb.
3. **Draw** the air out of the splint through the **suction valve**, and then **seal** the valve. Assess distal pulse and motor and sensory function. (page 1109; Emergency Medical Care)

Skill Drill 31-6: Applying a Hare Traction Splint

1. Expose the injured limb and check pulse and motor and sensory function. Place the splint beside the uninjured limb, adjust the splint to proper length, and prepare the straps.
2. Support the injured limb as your partner fastens the ankle hitch about the foot and ankle.
3. Continue to support the limb as your partner applies gentle in-line traction to the ankle hitch and foot.
4. Slide the splint into position under the injured limb.
5. Pad the groin and fasten the ischial strap.
6. Connect the loops of the ankle hitch to the end of the splint as your partner continues to maintain traction. Carefully tighten the ratchet to the point that the splint holds adequate traction.
7. Secure and check support straps. Assess pulse and motor and sensory functions.
8. Secure the patient and splint to the backboard in a way that will prevent movement of the splint during patient movement and transport. (pages 1111–1112; Emergency Medical Care)

Assessment Review

1. C (page 1099; Patient Assessment)
2. B (page 1102; Patient Assessment)
3. A (page 1101; Patient Assessment)
4. B (page 1123; Specific Musculoskeletal Injuries)
5. D (pages 1112–1113; Emergency Medical Care)

Skill Drill 31-8: Splinting the Hand and Wrist

1. Support the injured limb and move the hand into the **position** of **function**. Place a soft **roller bandage** in the palm.
2. Apply a(n) **padded board** splint on the **palmar** side with fingers **exposed**.
3. Secure the splint with a(n) **roller bandage**. (page 1123; Specific Musculoskeletal Injuries)

TRAUMA
Chapter 32: Environmental Emergencies

General Knowledge

Matching

1. J (page 1142; Cold Exposure)
2. H (page 1161; Diving Emergencies)
3. K (page 1143; Cold Exposure)
4. O (page 1151; Heat Exposure)
5. A (page 1160; Drowning)
6. N (page 1143; Cold Exposure)
7. I (page 1142; Cold Exposure)
8. C (page 1157; Drowning)

9. B (page 1153; Assessment of Heat Emergencies)
10. E (page 1143; Cold Exposure)
11. G (page 1143; Cold Exposure)
12. M (page 1142; Cold Exposure)
13. L (page 1151; Heat Exposure)
14. D (page 1157; Drowning)
15. F (page 1167; Bites and Envenomations)

Multiple Choice

1. D (page 1143; Cold Exposure)
2. A (page 1142; Cold Exposure)
3. D (page 1143; Cold Exposure)
4. C (page 1143; Cold Exposure)
5. C (page 1144; Cold Exposure)
6. B (page 1143; Cold Exposure)
7. A (page 1144; Cold Exposure)
8. C (page 1145; Cold Exposure)
9. D (page 1149; General Management of Cold Emergencies)
10. D (page 1145; Cold Exposure)
11. A (page 1150; Heat Exposure)
12. D (page 1151; Heat Exposure)
13. D (page 1163; Assessment of Drowning and Diving Emergencies)
14. A (page 1151; Heat Exposure)
15. D (pages 1151-1152; Heat Exposure)
16. A (page 1157; Drowning)
17. A (page 1152; Heat Exposure)
18. D (page 1152; Heat Exposure)
19. B (page 1157; Drowning)
20. D (page 1164; Emergency Care for Drowning or Diving Emergencies)

21. B (page 1161; Diving Emergencies)
22. A (page 1157; Drowning)
23. B (page 1160; Drowning)
24. B (pages 1160–1161; Diving Emergencies)
25. A (page 1160; Diving Emergencies)
26. D (page 1161; Diving Emergencies)
27. A (page 1161; Diving Emergencies)
28. D (page 1166; Bites and Envenomations)
29. A (page 1171; Bites and Envenomations)
30. A (page 1172; Bites and Envenomations)
31. B (page 1170; Bites and Envenomations)
32. C (page 1172; Bites and Envenomations)
33. A (page 1167; Bites and Envenomations)
34. D (page 1170; Bites and Envenomations)
35. B (pages 1151–1152; Heat Exposure)
36. B (page 1144; Cold Exposure)
37. A (page 1142; Cold Exposure)
38. B (page 1144; Cold Exposure)
39. D (page 1149; General Management of Cold Emergencies)
40. C (page 1142; Factors Affecting Exposure)
41. A (page 1142; Factors Affecting Exposure)
42. A (page 1152; Heat Exposure)

True/False

1. T (page 1150; Heat Exposure)
2. T (page 1144; Cold Exposure)
3. F (page 1144; Cold Exposure)
4. T (page 1150; Heat Exposure)
5. T (page 1151; Heat Exposure)
6. F (page 1165; Emergency Care for Drowning or Diving Emergencies)
7. T (page 1160; Drowning)
8. F (page 1170; Bites and Envenomations)
9. F (page 1169; Bites and Envenomations)
10. T (page 1170; Bites and Envenomations)
11. F (page 1172; Bites and Envenomations)
12. F (page 1173; Injuries From Marine Animals)
13. F (page 1147; Assessment of Cold Injuries)
14. T (page 1149; General Management of Cold Emergencies)
15. T (page 1166; Lightning)
16. F (page 1142; Factors Affecting Exposure)
17. F (page 1162; Assessment of Drowning and Diving Emergencies)
18. T (page 1146; Assessment of Cold Injuries)
19. F (page 1152; Assessment of Heat Emergencies)

Fill-in-the-Blank

1. moderate, severe (page 1149; General Management of Cold Emergencies)
2. ascent (page 1161; Diving Emergencies)
3. rewarming (page 1150; General Management of Cold Emergencies)
4. high-altitude pulmonary edema (page 1165; High Altitude)
5. Shivering (page 1143; Cold Exposure)
6. diving reflex (page 1160; Drowning)
7. Radiation (page 1143; Cold Exposure)
8. 90°F (32°C), 95°F (35°C) (page 1144; Cold Exposure)
9. cardiovascular, nervous (page 1165; Lightning)
10. Lightning (page 1165; Lightning)
11. Antivenin (page 1167; Bites and Envenomations)
12. Hymenoptera (page 1167; Bites and Envenomations)
13. April, October (page 1168; Bites and Envenomations)
14. rattlesnake (page 1169; Bites and Envenomations)
15. Scorpions (page 1171; Bites and Envenomations)
16. summer (page 1172; Bites and Envenomations)
17. bull's-eye (page 1172; Bites and Envenomations)
18. vinegar (page 1173; Injuries From Marine Animals)
19. envenomations (page 1173; Injuries From Marine Animals)
20. heat sensitive (page 1173; Injuries From Marine Animals)

Crossword Puzzle

Across: RADIATION, CORE, DYSBARISM, EVAPORATION, ANTIVENIN, CONDUCTION

Down: TURGOR, TRESPIRD, EXHAUST, HEATCRAMPS, AMBIENT, SCUBA, ENV, DROWNING

Critical Thinking

Short Answer

1. 1. Increase or decrease heat production: shiver, jump, walk around, etc.
   2. Move to an area where heat loss is decreased or increased: out of wind, into sun, etc.
   3. Wear insulated clothing, which helps decrease heat loss in several ways: layer with wool, down, synthetics, etc. (page 1143; Cold Exposure)

2. 1. Move the patient out of the hot environment and into the ambulance.
   2. Set the air conditioning to maximum cooling.
   3. Remove the patient's clothing.
   4. Administer high-flow oxygen if indicated. If needed, assist the patient's ventilations with a BVM and appropriate airway adjuncts as per your protocol.
   5. Provide cold-water immersion in an ice bath, if possible.
   6. Cover the patient with wet towels or sheets, or spray the patient with cool water and fan him or her to quickly evaporate the moisture on the skin.
   7. Aggressively and repeatedly fan the patient with or without dampening the skin.
   8. Exclude other causes of altered mental status and check blood glucose level, if possible.
   9. Provide rapid transport to the hospital.
   10. Notify the hospital as soon as possible so that the staff can prepare to treat the patient immediately on arrival.
   11. Do not overcool the patient. Call for ALS assistance if the patient begins to shiver. (pages 1156–1157; Management of Heat Emergencies)

3. An air embolism is a bubble of air in the blood vessels caused by breath-holding during rapid ascent. The air pressure in the lungs remains at a high level while the external pressure on the chest decreases. As a result, the air inside the lungs expands rapidly, causing the alveoli in the lungs to rupture. (page 1161; Diving Emergencies)

4. Treatment of air embolism and decompression sickness. The recompression treatment allows the bubbles of the gas to dissolve into the blood and equalize the pressures inside and outside the lungs. (page 1161; Diving Emergencies)

5. 1. Remove the patient from further exposure to the cold.
   2. Handle the injured part gently, and protect it from further injury.
   3. Remove any wet or restricting clothing from the patient, especially over the injured part.
   4. Remove any jewelry from the injured part and cover the injury loosely with a dry, sterile dressing.
   5. Splinting a frostbitten extremity may also help prevent secondary injury by limiting use.
   6. Evaluate the patient's general condition for the signs or symptoms of systemic hypothermia.
   7. Support the vital functions as necessary, and provide rapid transport to the hospital. (page 1150; General Management of Cold Emergencies)

6. 1. Do not break blisters.
   2. Do not rub or massage area.
   3. Do not apply heat or rewarm unless instructed by medical control.
   4. Do not allow patient to stand or walk on a frostbitten foot.
   5. Do not reexpose the injury to cold. (page 1150; General Management of Cold Emergencies)

7. 1. Have the patient lie flat and stay quiet.
   2. Wash the bite area with soapy water; consider a constricting band for hypotensive patients.
   3. Splint the extremity.
   4. Mark the skin with a pen to monitor advancing swelling. (page 1170; Bites and Envenomations)

8. 1. Black widow: Bite has a systemic effect (venom is neurotoxic).
   2. Brown recluse: Bite destroys tissue locally (venom is cytotoxic). (pages 1166–1167; Bites and Envenomations)

Ambulance Calls

1. Provide BLS. Administer oxygen. Transport the patient in the left lateral recumbent position with the head down. Transport to a facility with hyperbaric chamber access.

2. Your main concern for this patient is hypothermia. Although this patient could also likely have localized cold injuries such as frostbite or frostnip, hypothermia can be fatal. You must handle this patient carefully, remove any wet clothing, and prevent further heat loss. Assessing the extent of the hypothermia through mentation will be difficult in this case because your patient is likely confused. Take note of the presence of shivering (this protective mechanism stops at core temperatures > 90°F or 32°C), and, if possible, take his temperature (rectally). Assess airway, breathing, and circulation. Provide warm, humidified oxygen (if possible) and passive rewarming measures, such as increasing the heat in the patient compartment. Promptly transport.

3. This patient is suffering from heat exhaustion. The hot environment coupled with the strenuous activity and poor hydration has overwhelmed his ability to thermoregulate. Promptly move him to the back of the ambulance with the air conditioner on high. Remove any excessive clothing. Administer high-flow oxygen and assess his glucose level as his mental status is altered. Cover the patient with cool, wet towels and place ice packs on the trunk of the body—groin, axillae, neck. Because he is already nauseated, transport left lateral recumbent. Assess his skin turgor and call for ALS rendezvous for more aggressive treatment if his symptoms do not clear up promptly.

Skills

Skill Drills

Skill Drill 32-1: Treating for Heat Exhaustion

1. Move the patient to a(n) **cooler environment**. Remove extra **clothing**.

2. Give **oxygen** if indicated. Check the patient's blood glucose level if indicated. Perform cold-water immersion or other cooling measures as available. Place the patient in a(n) **supine** position and fan the patient.

3. If the patient is fully alert, give **water** by mouth.

4. If **nausea** develops, secure and transport the patient on his or her left side. (page 1155; Management of Heat Emergencies)

Skill Drill 32-2: Stabilizing a Suspected Spinal Injury in the Water

1. Turn the patient to a supine position by rotating the entire upper half of the body as a single unit.

2. As soon as the patient is turned, begin artificial ventilation using the mouth-to-mouth method or a pocket mask.

3. Float a buoyant backboard under the patient.

4. Secure the patient to the backboard.

5. Remove the patient from the water.

6. Maintain the body's normal temperature and apply oxygen if the patient is breathing. Begin CPR if breathing and pulse are absent. (page 1159; Drowning)

Assessment Review

1. B (page 1146; Cold Exposure)
2. A (page 1143; Cold Exposure)
3. B (pages 1150–1151; Heat Exposure)
4. B (page 1166; Lightning)
5. C (page 1173; Injuries From Marine Animals)

Emergency Care Summary

Cold Exposure Emergency (page 1149; General Management of Cold Emergencies)

1. Move the patient from the cold environment to prevent further **heat** loss.
2. Remove any wet clothing, and place dry blankets over and under the patient.
3. If available, give the patient warm, **humidified oxygen**.
4. **Rough handling** of a patient with moderate to severe hypothermia may cause the heart to go into ventricular fibrillation.
5. If the hypothermia is mild, begin **passive rewarming** slowly.

Diving Injuries (page 1164; Emergency Care for Drowning or Diving Emergencies)

1. Remove the patient from the water.
2. Begin CPR if pulse and breathing are absent.
3. If pulse and breathing are present, administer **oxygen**.
4. Treat all drowning patients for **hypothermia** by removing wet clothing and wrapping them in warm blankets.
5. Provide prompt transport to the nearest **recompression** facility for treatment.

Spider Bites (page 1167; Bites and Envenomations)

1. Provide basic life support for respiratory distress.
2. Transport the patient and, if possible, the spider to the hospital.
3. If necessary, a physician can administer a specific **antivenin**, a serum containing antibodies that counteract the venom.

Snake Bites (page 1170; Bites and Envenomations)

1. Calm the patient and minimize movement.
2. Clean the bite area gently with soap and water or a mild **antiseptic**. Do not apply **ice**.
3. Transport the patient and, if possible, the snake to the emergency department.
4. Notify the emergency department that you are bringing in a snake bite victim.

Chapter 33: Obstetrics and Neonatal Care

General Knowledge

Matching

1. D (page 1183; Anatomy and Physiology of the Female Reproductive System)
2. C (page 1194; Stages of Labor)
3. L (page 1184; Anatomy and Physiology of the Female Reproductive System)
4. B (page 1185; Anatomy and Physiology of the Female Reproductive System)
5. N (page 1183; Anatomy and Physiology of the Female Reproductive System)
6. H (page 1183; Anatomy and Physiology of the Female Reproductive System)
7. M (page 1194; Stages of Labor)
8. E (page 1185; Anatomy and Physiology of the Female Reproductive System)
9. F (page 1194; Stages of Labor)
10. O (page 1206; Complicated Delivery Emergencies)
11. K (page 1207; Complicated Delivery Emergencies)
12. I (page 1194; Stages of Labor)
13. A (page 1200; Normal Delivery Management)
14. G (page 1206; Complicated Delivery Emergencies)
15. J (page 1187; Complications of Pregnancy)

Multiple Choice

1. C (page 1200; Normal Delivery Management)
2. B (page 1192; Patient Assessment)
3. B (page 1204; Neonatal Assessment and Resuscitation)
4. B (page 1202; Normal Delivery Management)
5. A (page 1205; Neonatal Assessment and Resuscitation)
6. C (page 1204; Neonatal Assessment and Resuscitation)
7. D (page 1206; Neonatal Assessment and Resuscitation)
8. D (page 1204; Neonatal Assessment and Resuscitation)
9. A (page 1207; Complicated Delivery Emergencies)
10. A (pages 1207–1208; Complicated Delivery Emergencies)
11. B (page 1189; Complications of Pregnancy)
12. A (page 1193; Stages of Labor)
13. B (page 1193; Stages of Labor)
14. C (page 1193; Stages of Labor)
15. A (page 1194; Stages of Labor)
16. C (page 1194; Stages of Labor)
17. B (page 1187; Complications of Pregnancy)
18. B (page 1187; Complications of Pregnancy)
19. D (page 1194; Normal Delivery Management)
20. C (page 1185; Normal Changes in Pregnancy)
21. D (page 1187; Complications of Pregnancy)
22. D (page 1207; Complicated Delivery Emergencies)
23. C (page 1187; Complications of Pregnancy)
24. B (page 1188; Complications of Pregnancy)
25. A (page 1187; Complications of Pregnancy)
26. B (page 1189; Complications of Pregnancy)
27. D (page 1197; Normal Delivery Management)
28. D (page 1200; Normal Delivery Management)
29. C (page 1194; Stages of Labor)
30. C (page 1209; Postpartum Complications)
31. D (page 1202; Normal Delivery Management)
32. B (page 1183; Anatomy and Physiology of the Female Reproductive System)
33. C (page 1183; Anatomy and Physiology of the Female Reproductive System)
34. B (page 1187; Complications of Pregnancy)
35. B (page 1205; Neonatal Assessment and Resuscitation)
36. C (page 1208; Complicated Delivery Emergencies)
37. A (page 1208; Complicated Delivery Emergencies)
38. D (page 1209; Complicated Delivery Emergencies)
39. C (page 1210; Postpartum Complications)
40. B (page 1203; Neonatal Assessment and Resuscitation)

True/False

1. T (page 1183; Anatomy and Physiology of the Female Reproductive System)
2. F (page 1194; Stages of Labor)
3. F (page 1193; Stages of Labor)
4. F (page 1194; Stages of Labor)
5. F (page 1195; Normal Delivery Management)

6. T (page 1206; Complicated Delivery Emergencies)

7. T (page 1202; Normal Delivery Management)

8. F (page 1202; Normal Delivery Management)

9. F (page 1202; Normal Delivery Management)

10. T (page 1207; Complicated Delivery Emergencies)

11. T (page 1208; Complicated Delivery Emergencies)

12. T (page 1191; Teenage Pregnancy)

13. T (page 1193; Patient Assessment)

14. T (page 1188; Complications of Pregnancy)

15. T (page 1209; Complicated Delivery Emergencies)

16. F (page 1208; Complicated Delivery Emergencies)

17. T (page 1209; Postpartum Complications)

Fill-in-the-Blank

1. placenta (page 1201; Normal Delivery Management)

2. arteries, vein (page 1185; Anatomy and Physiology of the Female Reproductive System)

3. 500, 1,000 (page 1185; Anatomy and Physiology of the Female Reproductive System)

4. 39, 40, 6 (page 1185; Anatomy and Physiology of the Female Reproductive System)

5. 20 (page 1185; Normal Changes in Pregnancy)

6. 50% (page 1185; Normal Changes in Pregnancy)

7. ectopic pregnancy (page 1187; Complications of Pregnancy)

8. 10 (page 1206; Complicated Delivery Emergencies)

9. fontanelles (page 1200; Normal Delivery Management)

10. Spina bifida (page 1208; Complicated Delivery Emergencies)

11. abortion (page 1188; Complications of Pregnancy)

12. Braxton-Hicks (page 1194; Stages of Labor)

13. umbilical vein (page 1185; Anatomy and Physiology of the Female Reproductive System)

14. perineum (page 1184; Anatomy and Physiology of the Female Reproductive System)

15. falls (page 1189; Special Considerations for Trauma and Pregnancy)

Fill-in-the-Table (page 1205; Neonatal Assessment and Resuscitation)

Apgar Scoring System			
Area of Activity	**Score**		
	2	**1**	**0**
Appearance	**Entire newborn is pink.**	**Body is pink, but hands and feet remain blue.**	**Entire newborn is blue or pale.**
Pulse	**More than 100 beats/min.**	**Fewer than 100 beats/min.**	**Absent pulse.**
Grimace or irritability	**Newborn cries and tries to move foot away from finger snapped against sole of foot.**	**Newborn gives a weak cry in response to stimulus.**	**Newborn does not cry or react to stimulus.**
Activity or muscle tone	**Newborn resists attempts to straighten hips and knees.**	**Newborn makes weak attempts to resist straightening.**	**Newborn is completely limp, with no muscle tone.**
Respiration	**Rapid respirations.**	**Slow respirations.**	**Absent respirations.**

Labeling

1. Anatomic Structures of the Pregnant Woman (page 1184; Anatomy and Physiology of the Female Reproductive System)

A. Placenta

B. Uterus

C. Cervix

D. Amniotic fluid

E. Sacrum

F. Rectum

G. Bladder

H. Vagina

I. Pubic symphysis

Crossword Puzzle

1. FUNDUS
2. (down) M B I L I A L (AMBILICAL...)
3. (down) AMNIOTICSA (AMNIOTIC SAC)
4. (down) CERVIX
5. MECONIUM
6. PROLAPSE
7. (down) FETUS
8. MISCARRIAGE
9. (down) ABRUPTI...
10. BREECH
11. (down) EMBRYO
12. LIMB
13. ECTOPIC
14. CROWNING
15. BLOODY

Critical Thinking

Multiple Choice

1. C (page 1205; Neonatal Assessment and Resuscitation)
2. A (page 1205; Neonatal Assessment and Resuscitation)
3. B (page 1205; Neonatal Assessment and Resuscitation)

Short Answer

1. Early: spontaneous abortion (miscarriage) or ectopic pregnancy
   Late: Placenta previa or abruptio placenta (pages 1187–1188; Complications of Pregnancy)
2. On the left side, to prevent supine hypotensive syndrome (low blood pressure occurring from the weight of the fetus compressing the inferior vena cava) (page 1187; Complications of Pregnancy)
3. 1. Uterine contractions
   2. Bloody show
   3. Rupture of amniotic sac (pages 1183, 1185; Anatomy and Physiology of the Female Reproductive System)
4. 1. How long have you been pregnant?
   2. When are you due?
   3. Is this your first baby?
   4. Are you having contractions? If so, how far apart are the contractions? How long do the contractions last?
   5. Do you feel as though you will have a bowel movement?
   6. Have you had any spotting or bleeding?
   7. Has your water broken?
   8. Do you feel the need to push?
   9. Were any of your previous children delivered by cesarean section?
   10. Did you have any problems in this or any previous pregnancy?
   11. Do you use drugs, drink alcohol, or take any medications?
   12. Is there a chance you will have multiple deliveries (having more than one baby)?
   13. Does your physician expect any other complications? (page 1195; Normal Delivery Management)

5. Place your sterile gloved hand over the emerging bony parts of the head, avoid the eyes and fontanelles, and, by exerting minimal pressure, control the delivery of the head. (page 1200; Normal Delivery Management)

6. The brain is covered by only skin and membrane at the fontanelles. (page 1200; Normal Delivery Management)

7. Apply gentle pressure across the perineum with a sterile gauze pad. (page 1200; Normal Delivery Management)

8. 1. During a breech delivery to protect the infant's airway
   2. When the umbilical cord is prolapsed (pages 1207; Complicated Delivery Emergencies)

9. 1. Prematurity
   2. Low birth weight
   3. Severe respiratory depression (page 1189; Complications of Pregnancy)

10. 1. Severe or persistent headache
    2. Visual abnormalities such as seeing spots, blurred vision, or sensitivity to light
    3. Swelling in the hands and feet (edema)
    4. Anxiety
    5. Severe hypertension (page 1187; Complications of Pregnancy)

Ambulance Calls

1. This patient has classic signs of preeclampsia. If she does not receive medical care soon to control her hypertension, she will likely experience a seizure. Provide high-flow oxygen, obtain a set of vital signs (especially blood pressure), and provide prompt transport with the patient on her left side. Consider ALS intercept, if available.

2. Recent laws have been enacted to provide protection for new mothers who do not wish to keep their babies. They can release their newborns and infants to fire stations and hospitals without fear of criminal charges (as the young woman in this scenario chose to do). You should notify other providers in your station as you begin measures to dry, warm, stimulate, and suction the baby's airway if needed. These measures are very effective in improving a newborn's oxygenation and perfusion status. Blow-by oxygen will help immensely, but if those measures fail to quickly improve the newborn's status, bag-valve mask ventilations should be initiated. Provide chest compressions if the newborn's heart rate is less than 60 beats/min, and take note of the condition of the umbilical cord to ensure no blood loss occurs. Provide prompt transport and notify the hospital of the incoming patient.

3. Position the mother for delivery and apply high-flow oxygen. As crowning occurs, use a clamp to puncture the sac or tear it by twisting it between your fingers, away from the baby's face. Push the ruptured sac away from the infant's face as the head is delivered. Clear the newborn's mouth and nose, using the bulb syringe if required by your protocols, and wipe the mouth and nose with gauze. Continue with the delivery as normal.

Skills

Skill Drill

Skill Drill 33-1: Delivering the Newborn

1. Crowning is the definitive sign that delivery is imminent and transport should be delayed until after the child has been born.

2. Use your hands to support the bony parts of the head as it emerges. The child's body will naturally rotate to the right or left at this point in the delivery. Continue to support the head to allow it to turn in the same direction.

3. As the upper shoulder appears, guide the head down slightly by applying gentle downward traction to deliver the shoulder.

4. Support the head and upper body as the lower shoulder delivers, guide the head up if needed.

5. Handle the newborn firmly but gently, support the head, and keep the neck in a neutral position to maintain the airway. Consider placing the newborn on the mother's abdomen with the umbilical cord still intact, allow skin-to-skin contact to warm the newborn. Otherwise, keep the newborn approximately at the level of the vagina until the cord has been cut.

6. After delivery and prior to cutting the cord, if the child is gurgling or shows other signs of respiratory distress, suction the mouth and oropharynx to clear any amniotic fluid and ease the infant's initiation of air exchange.

7. Wait for the umbilical cord to stop pulsing. Place a clamp on the cord. Milk the blood from a small section of the cord on the placental side of the clamp. Place a second clamp 2 inches to 3 inches away from the first.

8. Cut between the clamps.

9. Allow the placenta to deliver itself. Do not pull on the cord to speed delivery. (pages 1198–1199; Normal Delivery Management)

Assessment Review

1. A (page 1200; Normal Delivery Management)
2. A (page 1203; Neonatal Assessment and Resuscitation)
3. A (page 1192; Patient Assessment)
4. D (page 1201; Normal Delivery Management)
5. B (page 1201; Normal Delivery management)

Emergency Care Summary (pages 1188–1209)

Special Considerations for Trauma and Pregnancy

Pregnant women have an increased overall total blood volume and an approximate **20%** increase in their heart rate by the third trimester. A pregnant trauma patient may experience a significant amount of blood loss before you detect signs of **shock**. A traumatic injury to the abdomen can be life threatening to the woman and fetus because the pregnant uterus has a rich blood supply. If the woman is hypoxic, is in shock, or has **hypovolemia**, the fetus will be in distress. In most cases, the only chance to save the fetus is to adequately resuscitate the woman.

Delivery Complications

Nuchal Cord (page 1200; Normal Delivery Management)
When the **umbilical cord** is wrapped around the infant's neck, it is called a nuchal cord. If it is wound tightly it will strangle the infant, so it must be removed. Attempt to slip the cord over the infant's head or shoulder. If you are unable to slip the cord over the head or shoulder, you must clamp the cord in **two** places about 2 inches (5 cm) apart, if possible, and cut the cord between the clamps. After cutting the cord, you can unwrap it and continue with the delivery as usual.

Spontaneous Abortion (Miscarriage) (page 1188; Complications of Pregnancy)
If the delivery is occurring before the **20th** week of gestation, be prepared to treat the patient for bleeding and infection. Place a sterile pad/dressing on the **vagina.** Collect any expelled tissue to take to the hospital, but never pull tissue out of the vagina. Transport immediately, continually monitoring the patient's ABCs while assessing for signs of shock.

Multiple Gestation (page 1208; Complicated Delivery Emergencies)
The procedure for delivering multiple infants is the same as that for a single fetus. Clamp and cut the cord for the first newborn as soon as it has been delivered and before the second newborn is delivered. There may be only one **placenta**, or one for each fetus. Record the **time of birth** for each infant separately, making sure to label them for identification after the delivery process is over. You can indicate the order of delivery by writing on a piece of tape and placing it on the blanket or towel that is wrapped around each newborn.

Postterm Pregnancy (page 1209; Complicated Delivery Emergencies)
Pregnancies lasting more than 42 weeks can lead to problems with the mother and the newborn. Newborns can be larger, leading to a more difficult delivery and injury to the newborn. **Meconium** aspiration risk increases, as does infection and **stillborn** birth. Respiratory and **neurologic** functions may be affected, so be prepared to resuscitate the newborn.

SPECIAL PATIENT POPULATIONS
Chapter 34: Pediatric Emergencies

General Knowledge

Matching

1. C (page 1222; Growth and Development)
2. I (page 1233; Patient Assessment)
3. F (page 1219; Growth and Development)
4. A (page 1228; Patient Assessment)
5. D (page 1270; Child Abuse and Neglect)
6. G (page 1218; Introduction)
7. J (page 1245; Respiratory Emergencies and Management)
8. H (page 1221; Growth and Development)
9. B (page 1230; Patient Assessment)
10. E (page 1220; Growth and Development)

Multiple Choice

1. B (page 1219; Growth and Development)
2. C (page 1219; Growth and Development)
3. D (page 1220; Growth and Development)
4. C (page 1221; Growth and Development)
5. A (page 1224; Anatomy and Physiology)
6. A (page 1225; Anatomy and Physiology)
7. D (page 1225; Anatomy and Physiology)
8. B (page 1255; Neurologic Emergencies and Management)
9. C (page 1262; Pediatric Trauma Emergencies and Management)
10. C (page 1232; Patient Assessment)
11. A (page 1232; Patient Assessment)
12. B (page 1233; Patient Assessment)
13. A (page 1233; Patient Assessment)
14. D (page 1236; Patient Assessment)
15. C (page 1226; Anatomy and Physiology)
16. D (page 1241; Respiratory Emergencies and Management)
17. C (page 1228; Patient Assessment)
18. B (page 1241; Respiratory Emergencies and Management)
19. D (page 1242; Respiratory Emergencies and Management)
20. B (page 1243; Respiratory Emergencies and Management)
21. A (page 1243; Respiratory Emergencies and Management)
22. A (page 1244; Respiratory Emergencies and Management)
23. A (page 1244; Respiratory Emergencies and Management)
24. D (page 1254; Circulation Emergencies and Management)
25. C (page 1254; Circulation Emergencies and Management)
26. D (page 1255; Circulation Emergencies and Management)
27. D (page 1256; Neurologic Emergencies and Management)
28. B (page 1256; Neurologic Emergencies and Management)
29. C (page 1257; Gastrointestinal Emergencies and Management)
30. A (page 1258; Poisoning Emergencies and Management)
31. D (page 1259; Poisoning Emergencies and Management)
32. A (page 1260; Poisoning Emergencies and Management)
33. B (page 1260; Poisoning Emergencies and Management)
34. D (page 1260; Fever Emergencies and Management)
35. C (page 1261; Drowning Emergencies and Management)
36. D (page 1262; Pediatric Trauma Emergencies and Management)
37. B (page 1264; Pediatric Trauma Emergencies and Management)
38. B (page 1266; Pediatric Trauma Emergencies and Management)
39. B (page 1268; Disaster Management)
40. C (page 1271; Sudden Infant Death Syndrome)
41. D (page 1272; Sudden Infant Death Syndrome)
42. A (page 1273; Sudden Infant Death Syndrome)

True/False

1. F (page 1219; Growth and Development)
2. T (page 1220; Growth and Development)
3. F (page 1221; Growth and Development)
4. T (page 1223; Growth and Development)

5. T (page 1223; Growth and Development)
6. F (page 1253; Respiratory Emergencies and Management)
7. T (page 1262; Pediatric Trauma Emergencies and Management)
8. T (page 1235; Patient Assessment)
9. F (page 1232; Patient Assessment)
10. F (page 1235; Patient Assessment)
11. F (page 1238; Patient Assessment)
12. T (page 1244; Respiratory Emergencies and Management)

13. T (page 1245; Respiratory Emergencies and Management)
14. F (page 1249; Respiratory Emergencies and Management)
15. T (page 1260; Fever Emergencies and Management)
16. T (page 1264; Pediatric Trauma Emergencies and Management)
17. F (page 1267; Pediatric Trauma Emergencies and Management)
18. T (page 1271; Child Abuse and Neglect)
19. T (page 1271; Child Abuse and Neglect)
20. F (page 1272; Sudden Infant Death Syndrome)

Fill-in-the-Blank

1. oxygen demand (page 1224; Anatomy and Physiology)
2. chest (page 1225; Anatomy and Physiology)
3. respiratory failure (page 1225; Anatomy and Physiology)
4. fontanelles (page 1226; Anatomy and Physiology)
5. pediatric assessment triangle (page 1227; Patient Assessment)
6. sniffing position (page 1230; Patient Assessment)
7. forward-facing, rear-facing (page 1235; Patient Assessment)
8. oxygen (page 1241; Respiratory Emergencies and Management)
9. Epiglottitis (page 1244; Respiratory Emergencies and Management)
10. Chest compressions (page 1243; Respiratory Emergencies and Management)

11. status asthmaticus (page 1244; Respiratory Emergencies and Management)
12. nasopharyngeal airway (page 1249; Respiratory Emergencies and Management)
13. Hemophilia (page 1255; Circulation Emergencies and Management)
14. Appendicitis (page 1257; Gastrointestinal Emergencies and Management)
15. Drowning (page 1261; Drowning Emergencies and Management)
16. blunt trauma (page 1264; Pediatric Trauma Emergencies and Management)
17. infection (page 1266; Pediatric Trauma Emergencies and Management)
18. Neglect (page 1270; Child Abuse and Neglect)

Crossword Puzzle

Critical Thinking

Short Answer

1. **T**–Tone

   I–Interactiveness

   C–Consolability

   L–Look or gaze

   S–Speech or cry (page 1228; Patient Assessment)

2. **Abnormal airway noise:** Grunting or wheezing

   Accessory muscle use: Contractions of the muscles above the clavicles (supraclavicular)

   Retractions: Drawing in of the muscles between the ribs (intercostal retractions) or of the sternum (substernal retractions) during inspiration

   Head bobbing: The head lifts and tilts back during inspiration, then moves forward during expiration

   Nasal flaring: The nares (the external openings of the nose) widen; usually seen during inspiration

   Tachypnea: Increased respiratory rate

   Tripod position: In older children, this position will maximize the effectiveness of the airway (pages 1228–1229; Patient Assessment)

3. Significant MOI—same MOIs as adults with the addition of:

   • Any fall from a height equal to or greater than a pediatric patient's height, especially with a headfirst landing

   • Bicycle crash (when not wearing a helmet)

   A history compatible with a serious illness

   A physical abnormality noted during the primary assessment

   A potentially serious anatomic abnormality

   Significant pain

   Abnormal level of consciousness, altered mental status, or signs and/or symptoms of shock (page 1235; Patient Assessment)

4. **70 + (2 × child's age in years) = systolic blood pressure (page 1239; Patient Assessment)**

5. **Pulse:** Assess both the rate and quality of the pulse. A weak, "thready" pulse is a sign that there is a problem. The appropriate rate depends on the patient's age; generally, except in the case of a newborn, anything over 160 beats/min suggests shock.

   Skin signs: Assess the temperature and moisture of the hands and feet. How does this compare with the temperature of the skin on the trunk of the body? Is the skin dry and warm or cold and clammy?

   Capillary refill time: Squeeze a finger or toe for several seconds until the skin blanches and then release it. Does the fingertip return to its normal color within 2 seconds, or is it delayed?

   Color: Assess the patient's skin color. Is it pink, pale, ashen, or blue?

   Changes: Changes in pulse rate, color, skin signs, and capillary refill time are all important clues suggesting shock. (page 1254; Circulation Emergencies and Management)

Ambulance Calls

1. Young children typically experience febrile seizures when their temperature rises rapidly. As with any call, you should assess airway, breathing, and circulation of this 2-year-old patient. Ensure that his airway is patent; assist him with breathing using a bag-valve mask and airway adjunct, as necessary; apply high-flow oxygen; and remove excessive clothing. The child's level of consciousness should improve. If the child's level of consciousness doesn't improve or if the child experiences additional seizure activity, then this is a very serious sign that should be relayed to the receiving emergency department. (pages 1260–1261; Fever Emergencies and Management)

2. Immediately open and suction the airway. Assess breathing and apply high-flow oxygen via nonrebreathing mask or bag-valve mask. Assess the patient further en route during rapid transport. Obtain the history from the grandmother en route. Reassess the patient's airway and vital signs en route as well.

3. Allow the child to remain in the mother's arms to decrease her anxiety. Offer oxygen via a nonrebreathing mask with the mother holding it. If she will not tolerate the nonrebreathing mask, use blow-by oxygen with her mother holding it.

Allow the mother to ride in the patient compartment of the ambulance to comfort the child. Provide rapid transport in a position of comfort with as much oxygen as she will tolerate. Continually assess the patient for signs of altered mental status and decreasing tidal volume; be prepared to assist ventilations. Obtain further history en route.

4. This infant is deceased, possibly as a result of SIDS. After you have quickly assessed the infant and made this determination, you must communicate the condition of the baby to the mother and family. This may be difficult, and they will possibly request resuscitation attempts regardless of your findings. This becomes a judgment call, which can be clarified by utilizing online medical direction and/or standing orders. You should survey the scene and document any history of recent illness, congenital conditions, and so forth. Be supportive of family members and assist them as appropriate. Calls involving infants and children can be traumatic experiences for emergency medical providers as well. Request debriefing as necessary and follow local protocols. (pages 1271–1273; Sudden Infant Death Syndrome)

Skills

Skill Drills

Skill Drill 34-1: Positioning the Airway in a Pediatric Patient

1. Position the pediatric patient on a(n) **firm** surface.
2. Place a(n) **folded** towel about 1-inch (2.5-cm) thick under the **shoulders** and **back**.
3. **Stabilize** the forehead to limit **movement** and use the head tilt–chin lift maneuver to open the airway. (page 1231; Patient Assessment)

Skill Drill 34-2: Inserting an Oropharyngeal Airway in a Pediatric Patient

1. Determine the appropriately **sized** airway. Confirm the correct size **visually**, by placing it next to the pediatric patient's **face**.
2. Position the pediatric patient's **airway** with the appropriate method.
3. Open the mouth. Insert the airway until the **flange** rests against the **lips**. **Reassess** the airway. (page 1247; Respiratory Emergencies and Management)

Skill Drill 34-3: Inserting a Nasopharyngeal Airway in a Pediatric Patient

1. Determine the correct airway size by comparing its **diameter** to the opening of the **nostril** (nare). Place the airway next to the pediatric patient's **face** to confirm correct **length**. **Position** the airway.
2. **Lubricate** the airway. Insert the **tip** into the right naris with the bevel pointing toward the **septum**.
3. Carefully move the tip forward until the **flange** rests against the **outside** of the nostril. Reassess the **airway**. (page 1248; Respiratory Emergencies and Management)

Skill Drill 34-4: One-Person Bag-Valve-Mask Ventilation on a Pediatric Patient

1. Open the airway and insert the appropriate airway adjunct.
2. Hold the mask on the patient's face with a one-handed head tilt–chin lift technique (EC clamp method). Ensure a good mask–face seal while maintaining the airway.
3. Squeeze the bag using the correct ventilation rate of 1 breath every 3 to 5 seconds, or 12 to 20 breaths/min. Allow adequate time for exhalation.
4. Assess effectiveness of ventilation by watching bilateral rise and fall of the chest. (page 1252; Respiratory Emergencies and Management)

Skill Drill 34-6: Immobilizing a Patient in a Car Seat

1. **Stabilize** the head in a(n) **neutral** position.
2. Place a(n) **short backboard** or pediatric **immobilization device** between the patient and the surface he or she is resting on.
3. Slide the patient onto the **short backboard** or pediatric immobilization device.
4. Place a **towel** under the back, from the **shoulders** to the **hips**, to ensure **neutral** head position.
5. Secure the **torso** first; pad any **voids**.
6. Secure the head to the short backboard or pediatric **immobilization device**. (page 1265; Pediatric Trauma Emergencies and Management)

SPECIAL PATIENT POPULATIONS

Chapter 35: Geriatric Emergencies

General Knowledge

Matching

1. E (page 1287; Changes in the Cardiovascular System)
2. C (page 1290; Changes in the Nervous System)
3. G (page 1291; Changes in the Nervous System)
4. I (page 1291; Changes in the Nervous System)
5. J (page 1292; Changes in the Nervous System)
6. F (page 1286; Changes in the Respiratory System)
7. D (page 1296; Changes in the Musculoskeletal System)
8. H (page 1297; Toxicology)
9. A (page 1296; Changes in the Musculoskeletal System)
10. B (page 1288; Changes in the Cardiovascular System)

Multiple Choice

1. C (page 1285; Common Complaints and the Leading Causes of Death in Older People)
2. A (page 1283; Introduction)
3. D (page 1284; Generational Considerations)
4. C (page 1284; Generational Considerations)
5. A (page 1284; Communication and Older Adults)
6. C (page 1285; Common Complaints and the Leading Causes of Death in Older People)
7. D (page 1301; Special Considerations in Assessing a Geriatric Medical Patient)
8. C (page 1291; Changes in the Nervous System)
9. A (page 1302; Special Considerations in Assessing a Geriatric Medical Patient)
10. A (page 1303; Special Considerations in Assessing a Geriatric Medical Patient)
11. D (page 1303; Special Considerations in Assessing a Geriatric Medical Patient)
12. B (page 1303; Special Considerations in Assessing a Geriatric Medical Patient)
13. C (page 1306; Trauma and Geriatric Patients)
14. A (page 1299; The GEMS Diamond)
15. D (page 1286; Changes in the Respiratory System)
16. B (page 1286; Changes in the Respiratory System)
17. A (page 1286; Changes in the Respiratory System)
18. C (page 1287; Changes in the Cardiovascular System)
19. A (page 1288; Changes in the Cardiovascular System)
20. D (page 1286; Changes in the Respiratory System)
21. C (page 1292; Changes in the Nervous System)
22. B (page 1289; Changes in the Cardiovascular System)
23. D (page 1290; Changes in the Nervous System)
24. D (page 1290; Changes in the Nervous System)
25. A (page 1291; Changes in the Nervous System)
26. D (page 1291; Changes in the Nervous System)
27. B (page 1293; Changes in the Gastrointestinal System)
28. A (page 1293; Changes in the Gastrointestinal System)
29. C (page 1294; Changes in the Gastrointestinal System)
30. C (page 1295; Changes in the Renal System)
31. D (page 1295; Changes in the Endocrine System)
32. A (pages 1296–1297; Changes in the Musculoskeletal System)
33. C (page 1297; Changes in the Musculoskeletal System)
34. B (page 1298; Toxicology)
35. D (page 1298; Behavioral Emergencies)
36. C (page 1305; Trauma and Geriatric Patients)
37. B (page 1299; Behavioral Emergencies)
38. D (page 1305; Trauma and Geriatric Patients)
39. B (page 1313; Elder Abuse and Neglect)
40. D (page 1306; Trauma and Geriatric Patients)
41. C (page 1310; Response to Nursing and Skilled Care Facilities)
42. D (page 1310; Response to Nursing and Skilled Care Facilities)
43. D (page 1311; Dying Patients)
44. D (page 1314; Elder Abuse and Neglect)
45. B (page 1314; Elder Abuse and Neglect)

True/False

1. T (page 1283; Generational Considerations)
2. T (page 1284; Communication and Older Adults)
3. F (page 1285; Common Complaints and the Leading Causes of Death in Older People)

4. T (page 1287; Changes in the Cardiovascular System)

5. T (page 1302; Special Considerations in Assessing a Geriatric Medical Patient)

6. T (page 1303; Special Considerations in Assessing a Geriatric Medical Patient)

7. T (page 1299; The GEMS Diamond)

8. F (page 1286; Changes in the Respiratory System)

9. F (page 1287; Changes in the Cardiovascular System)

10. F (page 1288; Changes in the Cardiovascular System)

11. T (page 1289; Changes in the Cardiovascular System)

12. T (page 1290; Changes in the Nervous System)

13. T (page 1291; Changes in the Nervous System)

14. F (page 1292; Changes in the Nervous System)

15. T (page 1293; Changes in the Gastrointestinal System)

16. F (page 1294; Changes in the Gastrointestinal System)

17. T (page 1295; Changes in the Endocrine System)

18. T (page 1296; Changes in the Immune System)

19. F (page 1297; Toxicology)

20. T (page 1299; Behavioral Emergencies)

21. F (page 1305; Trauma and Geriatric Patients)

22. F (page 1306; Special Considerations in Assessing Geriatric Trauma Patients)

23. T (page 1308; Special Considerations in Assessing Geriatric Trauma Patients)

24. T (page 1306; Trauma and Geriatric Patients);

25. T (page 1311; Dying Patients)

Fill-in-the-Blank

1. name (page 1284; Communication and Older Adults)

2. osteoporosis (page 1285; Common Complaints and the Leading Causes of Death in Older People)

3. Oxygen (page 1304; Special Considerations in Assessing a Geriatric Medical Patient)

4. Pneumonia (page 1286; Changes in the Respiratory System)

5. mucus production (page 1286; Changes in the Respiratory System)

6. Arteriosclerosis (page 1287; Changes in the Cardiovascular System)

7. aneurysm (page 1287; Changes in the Cardiovascular System)

8. left-sided (page 1288; Changes in the Cardiovascular System)

9. Presbycusis (page 1291; Changes in the Nervous System)

10. touch, pain (page 1291; Changes in the Nervous System)

11. Diverticulosis (page 1293; Changes in the Gastrointestinal System)

12. Pressure ulcers (page 1297; Changes in the Musculoskeletal System)

13. head injuries (page 1290; Changes in the Nervous System)

14. Bystander information (page 1307; Special Considerations in Assessing Geriatric Trauma Patients)

15. airway obstruction (page 1302; Special Considerations in Assessing a Geriatric Medical Patient)

16. flaccid abdominal wall (page 1308; Special Considerations in Assessing Geriatric Trauma Patients)

17. kyphosis (page 1309; Special Considerations in Assessing Geriatric Trauma Patients)

18. pelvic (page 1306; Trauma and Geriatric Patients)

19. Nursing homes (page 1310; Response to Nursing and Skilled Care Facilities)

20. Advance directives (page 1311; Dying Patients)

Fill-in-the-Table (page 1314; Elder Abuse and Neglect)

Fill in the missing parts of the table.

Categories of Elder Abuse	
Physical	• **Assault** • **Neglect or abandonment** • **Dietary (malnutrition)** • **Poor maintenance of home** • **Poor personal hygiene** • **Sexual assault**
Psychological	• **Benign neglect** • **Verbal** • **Treating the person as an infant** • **Deprivation of sensory stimulation**
Financial	• **Theft of valuables** • **Embezzlement**

Crossword Puzzle

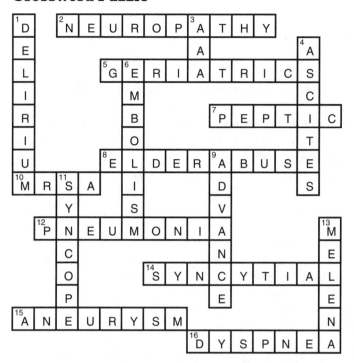

Critical Thinking

Short Answer

1. **1.** Hypertension
   2. Arthritis
   3. Heart disease
   4. Cancer
   5. Diabetes mellitus
   6. Asthma
   7. Chronic bronchitis or emphysema
   8. Stroke (page 1285; Common Complaints and the Leading Causes of Death in Older People)

2. **Motor nerves:** muscle weakness, cramps, spasms, loss of balance, and loss of coordination
   Sensory nerves: tingling, numbness, itching, and pain; burning, freezing, or extreme sensitivity to touch
   Autonomic nerves: affected involuntary functions that could include changes in blood pressure and heart rate, constipation, bladder and sexual dysfunction (page 1292; Changes in the Nervous System)

3. HHNS is a type 2 diabetic complication. It does not cause ketosis; instead, it leads to osmotic diuresis and a shift of fluid to the intravascular space that results in dehydration. HHNS does not present with Kussmaul respirations.

   DKA is a type 1 diabetic complication. It causes ketosis as a result of the hyperglycemia. The blood glucose is typically over 600 mg/dL in DKA, and patients tend to present with Kussmaul respirations. (page 1295; Changes in the Endocrine System)

4. Caregiver apathy about the patient's condition
   Overly defensive reaction by caregiver to your questions
   Caregiver does not allow patient to answer questions
   Repeated visits to the emergency department or clinic
   A history of being accident-prone
   Soft-tissue injuries
   Unbelievable, vague, or inconsistent explanations of injuries
   Psychosomatic complaints

Chronic pain without medical explanation

Self-destructive behavior

Eating and sleep disorders

Depression or lack of energy

A history of substance and/or sexual abuse (page 1313; Elder Abuse and Neglect)

5. **1.** Dysrhythmias and heart attack: The heart is beating too fast or too slowly, the cardiac output drops, and blood flow to the brain is interrupted. A heart attack can also cause syncope.

2. Vascular and volume changes: Medication interactions can cause venous pooling and vasodilation, the widening of a blood vessel that results in a drop in blood pressure and inadequate blood flow to the brain. Another cause of syncope can be a drop in blood volume because of hidden bleeding (such as an aneurysm).

3. Neurologic cause: Syncope can be a sign of transient ischemic attack or stroke. (page 1292; Changes in the Nervous System)

Ambulance Calls

1. This situation appears to be one of neglect and possible elder abuse. Perform a thorough assessment, especially if the patient is confused or is otherwise unable to express how or why she ended up on the floor. Ask for the patient's medical chart to obtain accurate information regarding her medical condition(s) and current medications. Immobilize her affected leg (and spine if needed) using the most comfortable methods possible. Geriatric patients need gentle care and many cannot tolerate conventional methods of splinting and immobilizing. Mechanisms of injury not viewed as significant in young, healthy patients can prove quite devastating or result in serious injury in older patients with frail skin and brittle bones.

2. Osteoporosis can be quite insidious in its onset. Individuals who were once relatively strong and healthy can suddenly find themselves with a fracture from something they may have done many times in the past. Postmenopausal, thin, Caucasian women are at higher risk of developing osteoporosis, and a spinal fracture in this scenario should be suspected. Perform an assessment to determine the presence of other injuries, provide full spinal immobilization, apply oxygen, and promptly transport this patient to the nearest appropriate facility. Always follow local protocols.

3. Hip fractures are a misnomer because true "hip fractures" are in fact fractures of the femur. You should determine if the mechanism of injury or suspicion exists for possible spinal fractures. Survey the scene to determine if there was a reason for the fall or if the break was spontaneous, giving the patient the impression of "tripping" on an object. If you believe that it was a spontaneous fracture, this patient suffers from extreme osteoporosis and likely sustained other fractures during the fall. If no spinal immobilization is deemed necessary, isolated hip fracture care requires an assessment of the patient's pulse, motor, and sensation of both lower extremities. You should also determine if the affected extremity is the same length or shorter than the uninjured side. It is also helpful to note if the leg is rotated inward, outward, or not at all. Immobilize the injured leg using blankets, pillows, and cravats or straps after placing the patient on a long backboard or scoop stretcher. After immobilization has occurred, reassess the pulse and motor and sensory functions of the injured extremity. Provide reassurance for the patient because many feel that hip fractures signal the loss of their independence. Always follow local protocols.

4. Patients with kyphosis are extremely uncomfortable when immobilized on long backboards. You should pad all voids using pillows, blankets, towels, or other appropriate forms of padding. Failure to adequately pad a patient's spine can result in increased pain and the inability of the patient to remain still. This can result in exacerbated injuries, as well as a very unhappy patient. Thoracic spine injuries and injuries to the ribs can make it difficult for patients to breathe without pain. Determine whether her shortness of breath is related to pain during inspiration and/or whether she has a history of respiratory disease, such as emphysema, chronic bronchitis, or asthma. Local weather conditions have likely contributed to her fall. Depending on the length of exposure to the elements, she could be suffering from hypothermia as well. Geriatric patients generally do not tolerate extremes in weather; avoiding extended periods of time in cold temperatures will minimize the likelihood for hypothermia.

Fill-in-the-Patient Care Report

EMS Patient Care Report (PCR)			
Date: Today's date	**Incident No.:** 011727	**Nature of Call:** Unknown medical emergency	**Location:** 222 Orchard Lane

Dispatched: 0843	**En Route:** 0843	**At Scene:** 0849	**Transport:** 0902	**At Hospital:** 0908	**In Service:** 0915

Patient Information	
Age: 78 years **Sex:** Male **Weight (in kg [lb]):** Unknown	**Allergies:** Aspirin **Medications:** Metoprolol, Lisinopril, Actos, metformin, Zocor, Celebrex, allopurinol, Lasix, K-dur, Plavix, and multivitamin **Past Medical History:** MI, CHF, hypertension, diabetes, arthritis, gout, high cholesterol **Chief Complaint:** Head pain

Vital Signs				
Time: 0853	**BP:** 110/68	**Pulse:** 86	**Respirations:** 20	**Spo$_2$:** 98%
Time: 0902	**BP:** 116/76	**Pulse:** 84	**Respirations:** 18	**Spo$_2$:** 100%

EMS Treatment (circle all that apply)				
Oxygen @ _15_ **L/min via (circle one):** NC (NRM) BVM	**Assisted Ventilation**	**Airway Adjunct**		**CPR**
Defibrillation	(**Bleeding Control**)	(**Bandaging**)	(**Splinting:** Full body/cervical immobilization)	**Other:**

Narrative

9-1-1 dispatch for 78-year-old man with an unknown medical problem. Local fire department was also dispatched for an assist per the dispatcher. Arrived on scene and was met by patient's wife at the front door who stated that patient was lying on the bathroom floor and she was unable to help him up. We were directed to the bathroom, where we found our patient lying supine on the floor in no obvious distress with a hematoma and laceration noted to his right forehead. Patient stated that he was on the toilet and must have fallen but cannot completely remember the incident. The patient denied any chest pain, dyspnea, N/V, dizziness, or sweating. The patient complained of "head pain," which he rated as a 4/10. The patient denied radiation of pain or neck pain. Cervical immobilization was manually maintained while immobilization supplies were gathered. The patient was fully immobilized onto a backboard to include cervical collar, longboard, and head immobilization device. Immobilization was assisted by fire personnel. Oxygen was applied at 15 L/min via nonrebreathing mask. Primary and secondary assessment performed, along with vital signs. The patient was secured to litter and taken to unit. Patient was transported to Mercy Hospital per his request. Reassessment of patient indicated his pain continued to be a 4/10. On arrival at facility, patient was stable. Care was transferred to ED staff. Verbal report was given to staff. Room 4. No further incidents. Unit cleaned and restocked. Crew went available and returned to station.**End of Report**

SPECIAL PATIENT POPULATIONS
Chapter 36: Patients With Special Challenges

General Knowledge

Matching

1. C (page 1330; Physical Disabilities)
2. H (page 1337; Patients With Medical Technology Assistance)
3. F (page 1324; Intellectual Disability)
4. J (page 1325; Intellectual Disability)
5. A (page 1337; Patients With Medical Technology Assistance)
6. D (page 1331; Bariatric Patients)
7. G (page 1327; Sensory Disabilities)
8. I (page 1337; Patients With Medical Technology Assistance)
9. B (page 1330; Physical Disabilities)
10. E (page 1333; Patients With Medical Technology Assistance)

Multiple Choice

1. C (page 1324; Intellectual Disability)
2. B (page 1324; Intellectual Disability)
3. D (page 1325; Intellectual Disability)
4. A (page 1325; Intellectual Disability)
5. A (page 1325; Intellectual Disability)
6. C (page 1326; Intellectual Disability)
7. D (page 1326; Sensory Disabilities)
8. B (page 1327; Sensory Disabilities)
9. D (page 1327; Sensory Disabilities)
10. A (page 1327; Sensory Disabilities)
11. A (page 1330; Physical Disabilities)
12. B (page 1330; Physical Disabilities)
13. C (page 1330; Physical Disabilities)
14. A (page 1331; Physical Disabilities)
15. B (page 1333; Patients With Medical Technology Assistance)
16. C (page 1334; Patients With Medical Technology Assistance)
17. D (page 1335; Patients With Medical Technology Assistance)
18. C (page 1335; Patients With Medical Technology Assistance)
19. B (page 1336; Patients With Medical Technology Assistance)
20. B (page 1337; Patients With Medical Technology Assistance)
21. A (page 1337; Patients With Medical Technology Assistance)
22. C (page 1338; Home Care)
23. D (page 1338; Hospice Care and Terminally Ill Patients)
24. A (page 1339; Poverty and Homelessness)
25. B (page 1332; Bariatric Patients)

True/False

1. T (page 1326; Intellectual Disability)
2. F (page 1327; Sensory Disabilities)
3. T (page 1331; Physical Disabilities)
4. F (page 1332; Bariatric Patients)
5. T (page 1333; Patients With Medical Technology Assistance)
6. T (page 1333; Patients With Medical Technology Assistance)
7. F (page 1333; Patients With Medical Technology Assistance)
8. T (page 1335; Patients With Medical Technology Assistance)
9. T (page 1336; Patients With Medical Technology Assistance)
10. T (page 1338; Patient Assessment Guidelines)

Fill-in-the-Blank

1. Autism (page 1324; Intellectual Disability)
2. shoulder (page 1327; Sensory Disabilities)

3. Hearing aids (page 1328; Sensory Disabilities)
4. sensorineural, conductive (page 1327; Sensory Disabilities)
5. Cerebral palsy (page 1330; Physical Disabilities)
6. vitamin B (folic acid) (pages 1330–1331; Physical Disabilities)
7. left ventricular assist device (page 1335; Patients With Medical Technology Assistance)
8. Shunts (page 1337; Patients With Medical Technology Assistance)
9. dehydration (page 1337; Patients With Medical Technology Assistance)
10. palliative care (page 1338; Hospice Care and Terminally Ill Patients)

Fill-in-the-Table (page 1333; Patients With Medical Technology Assistance)

Complete the missing information to the right of the mnemonic.

DOPE Mnemonic	
D	Displaced, dislodged, or damaged tube
O	Obstruction of the tube (secretions, blood, mucus, vomitus)
P	Pneumothorax, pulmonary problems
E	Equipment failure (kinked tubing, ventilator malfunction, empty oxygen supply)

Crossword Puzzle

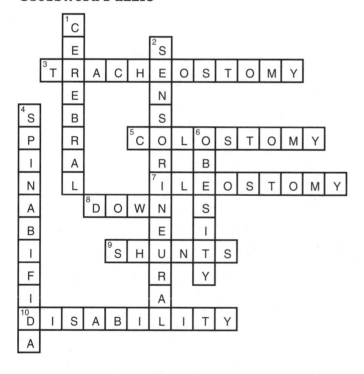

Critical Thinking

Short Answer

1. 1. Speak slowly and distinctly into a less-impaired ear, or position yourself on that side.
   2. Change speakers. Look for a team member with a low-pitched voice if you think pitch is the issue.
   3. Provide paper and a pencil so that you may write your questions and the patient may write responses.
   4. Only one person should ask interview questions to avoid confusing the patient.
   5. Try the "reverse stethoscope" technique: Put the earpieces of your stethoscope in the patient's ears and speak softly into the diaphragm of the stethoscope. (pages 1327–1328; Sensory Disabilities)

2. **1.** Make sure the hearing aid is turned on.

   2. Try a fresh battery, and check the tubing to make sure it is not twisted or bent. Ensure that the switch is set on M (microphone), not T (telephone).

   3. Try a spare cord for a conventional body type aid; the old one may be broken or shorted. Make sure the ear mold is not plugged with wax. (page 1328; Sensory Disabilities)

3. **1.** Behind-the-ear type

   2. Conventional body type

   3. In-the-canal and completely in-the-canal type

   4. In-the-ear type (page 1328; Sensory Disabilities)

4. **1.** Treat the patient with dignity and respect.

   2. Ask your patient how it is the best to move him or her before attempting to do so.

   3. Avoid trying to lift the patient by only one limb, which would risk injury to overtaxed joints.

   4. Coordinate and communicate all moves to all team members prior to starting to lift.

   5. If the move becomes uncontrolled at any point, stop, reposition, and resume.

   6. Look for pinch or pressure points from equipment because they could cause a deep venous thrombosis.

   7. Very large patients may have difficulty breathing if you lay the patient in a supine position.

   8. Many manufacturers make specialized equipment for morbidly obese patients, and some areas have specially equipped bariatric ambulances for such patients.

   9. Plan egress routes to accommodate large patients, equipment, and the lifting crew members.

  10. Notify the receiving facility early to allow special arrangements to be made prior to your arrival to accommodate the patient's needs. (page 1332; Bariatric Patients)

5. **1.** What type of heart disorder does the patient have?

   2. How long has this device been implanted?

   3. What is the patient's normal baseline rhythm and pulse rate?

   4. Is the patient's heart completely dependent on the pacemaker device?

   5. At what pulse rate will the defibrillator fire?

   6. How many times has the defibrillator shocked the patient? (page 1335; Patients With Medical Technology Assistance)

Ambulance Calls

1. An internal cardiac pacemaker is implanted under the patient's skin to regulate the pulse rate and rhythm. You should provide oxygen and airway management for this patient. Because the automated implanted cardioverter defibrillator is firing, it is likely that the patient has an underlying dysrhythmia. ALS should be contacted for a rendezvous. In addition, you should be prepared for this patient to go into cardiac arrest. Remember not to place AED pads directly over the implanted device. Transport immediately, maintain ABCs, and rendezvous with ALS.

2. Many patients with Down syndrome have epilepsy. Most of the seizures are tonic-clonic. Patient management is the same as with other patients with seizures. Because the patient has had two witnessed seizures, consider requesting ALS. It is likely the patient will seize again. In addition, use the parents and family as a resource for information; they are likely to be very familiar with the patient's medical history and complications. Maintain ABCs, apply oxygen, and assess for any potential injuries that may have occurred during the seizure. Be aware of the potential airway complications faced in patients with Down syndrome, such as a large tongue and smaller oral and nasal cavities.

Skills

Assessment Review

1. C (page 1324; Intellectual Disability)
2. D (page 1327; Sensory Disabilities)
3. D (page 1334; Patients With Medical Technology Assistance)
4. B (page 1337; Patients With Medical Technology Assistance)

EMS OPERATIONS
Chapter 37: Transport Operations

General Knowledge

Matching

1. D (page 1377; Air Medical Operations)
2. A (page 1353; Emergency Vehicle Design)
3. E (page 1372; Defensive Ambulance Driving Techniques)
4. G (page 1367; Phases of an Ambulance Call)
5. F (page 1352; Emergency Vehicle Design)
6. C (page 1367; Phases of an Ambulance Call)
7. B (page 1367; Phases of an Ambulance Call)

Multiple Choice

1. C (page 1352; Emergency Vehicle Design)
2. A (page 1352; Emergency Vehicle Design)
3. A (page 1353; Phases of an Ambulance Call)
4. B (page 1353; Emergency Vehicle Design)
5. C (page 1355; Phases of an Ambulance Call)
6. D (page 1355; Phases of an Ambulance Call)
7. A (page 1355; Phases of an Ambulance Call)
8. D (page 1361; Phases of an Ambulance Call)
9. B (page 1358; Phases of an Ambulance Call)
10. D (page 1359; Phases of an Ambulance Call)
11. A (page 1359; Phases of an Ambulance Call)
12. D (page 1361; Phases of an Ambulance Call)
13. D (page 1361; Phases of an Ambulance Call)
14. C (page 1363; Phases of an Ambulance Call)
15. C (page 1363; Phases of an Ambulance Call)
16. D (pages 1368–1369; Defensive Ambulance Driving Techniques)
17. B (page 1363; Phases of an Ambulance Call)
18. D (page 1370; Defensive Ambulance Driving Techniques)
19. B (page 1371; Defensive Ambulance Driving Techniques)
20. A (page 1375; Defensive Ambulance Driving Techniques)
21. C (page 1372; Defensive Ambulance Driving Techniques)
22. D (page 1374; Defensive Ambulance Driving Techniques)
23. D (page 1370; Defensive Ambulance Driving Techniques)
24. C (page 1375; Defensive Ambulance Driving Techniques)
25. C (page 1375; Defensive Ambulance Driving Techniques)
26. B (page 1375; Defensive Ambulance Driving Techniques)
27. D (pages 1363–1364; Phases of an Ambulance Call)
28. D (page 1366; Phases of an Ambulance Call)
29. C (page 1366; Phases of an Ambulance Call)
30. D (page 1370; Defensive Ambulance Driving Techniques)
31. D (page 1378; Air Medical Operations)

True/False

1. T (page 1354; Phases of an Ambulance Call)
2. F (page 1357; Phases of an Ambulance Call)
3. T (page 1376; Air Medical Operations)
4. F (page 1363; Phases of an Ambulance Call)
5. F (page 1375; Defensive Ambulance Driving Techniques)
6. T (page 1371; Defensive Ambulance Driving Techniques)
7. T (page 1379; Air Medical Operations)
8. F (page 1376; Air Medical Operations)
9. F (page 1378; Air Medical Operations)

Fill-in-the-Blank

1. jump kit (page 1359; Phases of an Ambulance Call)
2. Star of Life (page 1353; Emergency Vehicle Design)
3. hearse (page 1352; Emergency Vehicle Design)
4. First-responder vehicles (page 1352; Emergency Vehicle Design)
5. nine (page 1353; Phases of an Ambulance Call)

6. with due regard (page 1375; Defensive Ambulance Driving Techniques)

7. airway (page 1355; Phases of an Ambulance Call)

8. CPR board (page 1357; Phases of an Ambulance Call)

Labeling

1. Helicopter Hand Signals (page 1380; Air Medical Operations)

   A. Move right

   B. Move forward

   C. Move rearward

   D. Move upward

   E. Move downward

   F. Move left

Crossword Puzzle

Critical Thinking

Multiple Choice

1. A (page 1363; Phases of an Ambulance Call)
2. B (page 1363; Phases of an Ambulance Call)
3. D (page 1358; Phases of an Ambulance Call)
4. C (page 1365; Phases of an Ambulance Call)
5. A (page 1366; Phases of an Ambulance Call)

Short Answer

1. Type I: Conventional, truck cab-chassis with modular ambulance body that can be transferred to a newer chassis as needed

   Type II: Standard van, forward-control integral cab-body ambulance

   Type III: Specialty van cab with a modular ambulance body that is mounted on a cut-away van chassis (page 1353; Emergency Vehicle Design)

2. **1.** Preparation for the call
    2. Dispatch
    3. En route to scene
    4. Arrival at scene
    5. Transfer of patient to the ambulance
    6. En route to the receiving facility (transport)
    7. At the receiving facility (delivery)
    8. En route to station
    9. Postrun (page 1353; Phases of an Ambulance Call)

3. *Siren syndrome* is the term for the increase in anxiety of other drivers that commonly causes them to drive faster in the presence of sirens. (page 1372; Defensive Ambulance Driving Techniques)

4. **1.** To the best of your knowledge, the unit must be on a true emergency call.
    2. Both audible and visual warning devices must be used simultaneously.
    3. The unit must be operated with due regard for the safety of all others, both on and off the roadway. (page 1374; Defensive Ambulance Driving Techniques)

5. **1.** At the time of dispatch, select the shortest and least congested route to the scene.
    2. Avoid routes with heavy traffic congestion; know alternative routes to each hospital during rush hours.
    3. Avoid one-way streets. Do not go against the flow of traffic on a one-way street, unless absolutely necessary.
    4. Watch carefully for bystanders as you approach the scene.
    5. Once you arrive at the scene, park the ambulance in a safe place. If you park facing into traffic, turn off your headlights so that they do not blind oncoming drivers, unless they are needed to illuminate the scene. If the vehicle is blocking part of the road, keep your warning lights on to alert oncoming motorists; otherwise, turn them off.
    6. Drive within the speed limit while transporting patients, except in the rare extreme emergency.
    7. Go with the flow of the traffic.
    8. Always drive defensively.
    9. Always maintain a safe following distance. Use the "4-second rule."
    10. Try to maintain an open space or cushion in the lane next to you as an escape route in case the vehicle in front of you stops suddenly.
    11. Use your siren if you turn on the emergency lights, except when you are on a freeway.
    12. Always assume that other drivers will not hear the siren or see your emergency lights. (page 1370; Defensive Ambulance Driving Techniques)

6. A hard, level surface a minimum of 100 feet by 100 feet (30 m by 30 m).

    A clear site that is free of loose debris, electric or telephone poles and wires, or any other hazards that might interfere with the safe operation of the helicopter. (page 1378; Air Medical Operations)

Ambulance Calls

1. Fire departments have a distinct chain of command. You should obtain permission to place yourself en route to this medical emergency from your shift captain or appropriate fire officer. Just because a call is dispatched does not mean you should automatically place yourself en route to that location. The incident commander of the confirmed structure fire may need your immediate assistance on the scene. Because you do not know the nature of the medical emergency at this point, it would be prudent to place that decision in appropriate hands. Always follow local protocols and chain of command.

2. Ideally, you should be very familiar with your response area, and you should take time every shift to study local roads. This can be done individually or as a group shift activity. The larger your coverage area the more difficult it becomes to memorize addresses, especially if you are not native to the area. Regardless, you should be able to read maps quickly, and you should not rely on your memory to assist in locating a new address. To attempt to memorize all local streets is a good goal, but failing to consult with a map before leaving the station for reasons of pride is downright foolish. Ensure that each and every agency vehicle used in response to emergencies is equipped with local maps and other resources to ensure that you arrive promptly at emergency scenes. Utilize your local dispatch center for directions, if necessary.

3. Park your ambulance in a safe area and ensure your personal safety. Either you or your partner should handle traffic control until the police arrive. The person not handling traffic control should assess the patient. Provide patient care while ensuring personal safety and patient safety.

Fill-in-the-Patient Care Report

EMS Patient Care Report (PCR)			
Date: Today's date	**Incident No.:** 2011–8999	**Nature of Call:** MVC	**Location:** Hwy 12 and Nest Creek Rd.

Dispatched: 0512	**En Route:** 0513	**At Scene:** 0523	**Transport:** 0532	**At Hospital:** 0546	**In Service:** 0557

Patient Information	
Age: 41 years	**Allergies:** None
Sex: Female	**Medications:** Lisinopril
Weight (in kg [lb]): 90 kg (198 lb)	**Past Medical History:** TIA at age 36
	Chief Complaint: Facial pain following MVC

Vital Signs				
Time: 0532	**BP:** 142/100	**Pulse:** 100	**Respirations:** 16 Unlabored	**Spo$_2$:** 98%
Time: 0543	**BP:** 142/100	**Pulse:** 100	**Respirations:** 14 Unlabored	**Spo$_2$:** 98%

EMS Treatment
(circle all that apply)

Oxygen @ _15_ L/min via (circle one): NC (NRM) BVM	Assisted Ventilation	Airway Adjunct	CPR
Defibrillation / **Bleeding Control**	**Bandaging**	(Splinting)	**Other:**

Narrative

Dispatched on an emergency call to a motor vehicle collision on Hwy 12. Arrived on scene to find two vehicles involved and one injured driver (other driver denied any injury). Patient, 41-year-old woman with a swollen and bleeding nose, was contacted while still belted into the driver's seat of her damaged car. She was conscious and alert and followed directions appropriately. C-spine precautions were taken. The patient was properly secured to a long backboard, removed from the vehicle, and given high-concentration oxygen via nonrebreathing mask. Patient was loaded into the ambulance and was found to have no other obvious or stated injuries. Initial vital signs indicated elevated blood pressure, which the patient stated was normal; all other observations indicated that the patient was stable. While en route, I contacted the receiving facility to provide a report and completed a second set of vital signs to compare to the first and found no change other than a slightly lower respiratory rate. Transport was completed without incident. Once at the County Medical Center, the patient was transferred appropriately to the staff's care. I provided a full verbal report to the accepting nurse. Ambulance was then cleaned and restocked, and we returned to service without delay.**End of Report**

EMS OPERATIONS
Chapter 38: Vehicle Extrication and Special Rescue

General Knowledge

Matching

1. E (page 1390; Fundamentals of Extrication)
2. A (page 1396; Fundamentals of Extrication)
3. L (page 1391; Fundamentals of Extrication)
4. F (page 1390; Fundamentals of Extrication)
5. B (page 1399; Specialized Rescue Situations)
6. J (page 1402; Specialized Rescue Situations)
7. D (page 1396; Fundamentals of Extrication)
8. H (page 1400; Specialized Rescue Situations)
9. I (page 1399; Specialized Rescue Situations)
10. G (page 1403; Specialized Rescue Situations)
11. K (page 1403; Specialized Rescue Situations)
12. C (page 1394; Fundamentals of Extrication)

Multiple Choice

1. B (page 1389; Safety)
2. D (page 1391; Fundamentals of Extrication)
3. A (page 1392; Fundamentals of Extrication)
4. B (page 1390; Fundamentals of Extrication)
5. D (page 1392; Fundamentals of Extrication)
6. C (page 1393; Fundamentals of Extrication)
7. D (page 1394; Fundamentals of Extrication)
8. B (page 1390; Fundamentals of Extrication)
9. B (page 1394; Fundamentals of Extrication)
10. C (page 1395; Fundamentals of Extrication)
11. A (page 1395; Fundamentals of Extrication)
12. B (page 1396; Fundamentals of Extrication)
13. C (page 1399; Specialized Rescue Situations)
14. D (page 1401; Specialized Rescue Situations)
15. B (page 1402; Specialized Rescue Situations)

True/False

1. T (page 1403; Specialized Rescue Situations)
2. F (page 1400; Specialized Rescue Situations)
3. T (page 1400; Specialized Rescue Situations)
4. T (page 1398; Fundamentals of Extrication)
5. T (page 1399; Specialized Rescue Situations)
6. T (page 1391; Fundamentals of Extrication)
7. T (page 1398; Fundamentals of Extrication)
8. T (page 1397; Fundamentals of Extrication)
9. T (page 1393; Fundamentals of Extrication)
10. T (page 1394; Fundamentals of Extrication)
11. F (page 1398; Fundamentals of Extrication)
12. T (page 1396; Fundamentals of Extrication)
13. F (page 1396; Fundamentals of Extrication)
14. T (page 1395; Fundamentals of Extrication)
15. F (page 1394; Fundamentals of Extrication)
16. T (page 1390; Vehicle Safety Systems)
17. F (page 1391; Fundamentals of Extrication)

Fill-in-the-Blank

1. hazardous materials (page 1403; Specialized Rescue Situations)
2. rapid extrication (page 1395; Fundamentals of Extrication)
3. Entrapment (page 1390; Fundamentals of Extrication)
4. primary assessment (page 1397; Fundamentals of Extrication)
5. Size-up (page 1392; Fundamentals of Extrication)
6. hearing protection (page 1398; Fundamentals of Extrication)
7. EMS providers (page 1390; Fundamentals of Extrication)
8. firefighters (page 1390; Fundamentals of Extrication)
9. danger zone (page 1394; Fundamentals of Extrication)
10. battery (page 1394; Fundamentals of Extrication)

11. stabilized (page 1395; Fundamentals of Extrication)
12. protective gear (page 1389; Safety)
13. rescue team (page 1390; Fundamentals of Extrication)
14. Communication (page 1391; Fundamentals of Extrication)
15. leadership (page 1399; Specialized Rescue Situations)
16. fire-resistant blanket, backboard (page 1395; Fundamentals of Extrication)
17. specialized rescue (page 1399; Specialized Rescue Situations)
18. air transport (page 1400; Specialized Rescue Situations)
19. incident commander (page 1400; Specialized Rescue Situations)
20. Vibration (page 1401; Specialized Rescue Situations)
21. 4 feet (page 1401; Specialized Rescue Situations)
22. structure fire (page 1403; Specialized Rescue Situations)

Crossword Puzzle

```
¹A  C  C  E  S  ²S              ³S
              W        ⁴C        I
   ⁵S  I  T  U  A  T  I  O  N    M        ⁶E
              T        M        P         X
⁷H                     M        L         T
 A        ⁸D           A  ⁹G    E         R
 Z     ¹⁰S  C  B  A    N   R    A         I
 A        N           D   O    C         C
 R        G           E   U    C         A
 D     ¹¹S ¹²E  N  T  R  A  P  M  E  N  T
 O        I   R           S         I
 U        Z   Z           S         O
¹³S  A  F  E  Z  O  N  E              N
       U      N
¹⁴C  O  M  P  L  E  X  A  C  C  E  S  S
```

Critical Thinking

Short Answer

1. **EMS personnel:** Responsible for assessing and providing immediate medical care, performing triage and assigning priority to patients, packaging the patient, providing additional assessment and care as needed once the patient has been removed, and providing transport to the emergency department.

   Firefighters: Responsible for extinguishing any fire, preventing additional ignition, ensuring that the scene is safe, and washing down spilled fuel.

   Law enforcement: Responsible for traffic control and direction, maintaining order at the scene, investigating the crash or crime scene, and establishing and maintaining a perimeter so that bystanders are kept at a safe distance and out of the way of rescuers.

   Rescue team: Responsible for properly securing and stabilizing the vehicle, providing safe entrance and access to patients, safely extricating any patients, ensuring that patients are properly protected during extrication or other rescue activities, and providing adequate room so that patients can be removed properly. (page 1390; Fundamentals of Extrication)

2. **1.** Is the patient in a vehicle or in some other structure?

  2. Is the vehicle or structure severely damaged?

  3. What hazards exist that pose risk to the patient and rescuers?

  4. In what position is the vehicle? On what type of surface? Is the vehicle stable or is it likely to roll over? (page 1395; Fundamentals of Extrication)

3. **1.** Provide manual stabilization to protect the cervical spine, as needed.

  2. Open the airway.

  3. Provide high-flow oxygen.

  4. Assist or provide for adequate ventilation.

  5. Control any significant external bleeding.

  6. Treat all critical injuries. (page 1397; Fundamentals of Extrication)

4. **1.** Preparation

  2. En route to the scene

  3. Arrival and scene size-up

  4. Hazard control

  5. Support operations

  6. Gaining access

  7. Emergency care

  8. Removal of the patient

  9. Transfer of the patient

  10. Termination (page 1391; Fundamentals of Extrication)

5. **F**—Failure to understand the environment or underestimating it

  A—Additional medical problems not considered

  I—Inadequate rescue skills

  L—Lack of teamwork or experience

  U—Underestimating the logistics of the incident

  R—Rescue versus recovery mode not considered

  E—Equipment not mastered (page 1403; Specialized Rescue Situations)

Ambulance Calls

1. Unless there is an immediate threat of fire, explosion, or other danger, once entrance and access to the patient have been provided and the scene is safe, you should perform a primary assessment and provide care before further extrication begins. She is obviously alert and her airway is open. The first concern is to address the arterial bleeding, which is best managed with a tourniquet in this situation. You should direct your partner to take cervical spine control, and you should attempt to calm the patient and assess her mental status as you control the bleeding. Explain to her what you are doing and offer encouragement. Provide oxygen as needed and look for other life threats. Once these have been addressed, the extrication can continue and you should participate in the preparation for patient removal.

2. Entering the water could be a death sentence for you both. If you have a cell phone and/or department radio with you, your best course of action would be to inform incoming units of the boy's location and situation. It would be advisable to direct some responding units downstream so that if the boy should lose his grasp on the log, other responders will be available to retrieve him. If your department has areas that contain the possibility of swift water rescue (even if only seasonal), training should be conducted and appropriate helmets, throw bags, and life jackets should be made available for safe response. You must assess the scene before trying to effect immediate rescue operations. Many responders have been killed by "jumping into" all types of rescues without performing a scene size-up or using the proper gear. Don't become a victim. Doing so will only make you part of the problem.

3. Try to learn as much about the chemical as possible by having the dispatcher contact CHEMTREC or another agency to find out about possible effects to the patient. Prepare necessary equipment to manage the airway and ventilation. Be prepared to do CPR, if necessary. Have all equipment within reach. Once the patient is brought to you, rapidly begin to manage the ABCs and prepare for rapid transport.

Chapter 39: Incident Management

General Knowledge

Matching

1. H (page 1430; Recognizing a Hazardous Material)
2. N (page 1438; Recognizing a Hazardous Material)
3. B (page 1437; Recognizing a Hazardous Material)
4. J (page 1412; Incident Command System)
5. E (page 1438; Recognizing a Hazardous Material)
6. O (page 1415; Incident Command System)
7. L (page 1425; Disaster Management)
8. I (page 1437; Recognizing a Hazardous Material)
9. A (page 1429; Recognizing a Hazardous Material)
10. G (page 1430; Recognizing a Hazardous Material)
11. C (page 1420; Triage)
12. F (page 1428; Recognizing a Hazardous Material)
13. D (page 1420; Triage)
14. M (page 1412; Incident Command System)
15. K (page 1438; Recognizing a Hazardous Material)

Multiple Choice

1. B (page 1411; National Incident Management System)
2. D (page 1411; National Incident Management System)
3. A (page 1412; Incident Command System)
4. D (page 1414; Incident Command System)
5. A (page 1414; Incident Command System)
6. C (page 1416; EMS Response Within the Incident Command System)
7. B (page 1416; EMS Response Within the Incident Command System)
8. C (page 1417; EMS Response Within the Incident Command System)
9. D (page 1418; The Medical Branch of Incident Command)
10. B (page 1418; The Medical Branch of Incident Command)
11. B (page 1418; The Medical Branch of Incident Command)
12. A (page 1411; Introduction)
13. B (page 1421; Triage)
14. C (page 1421; Triage)
15. B (page 1421; Triage)
16. D (page 1421; Triage)
17. A (page 1422; Triage)
18. C (page 1414; Incident Command System)
19. A (page 1423; Triage)
20. C (page 1422; Triage)
21. A (page 1424; Triage)
22. C (page 1422; Triage)
23. B (page 1427; Recognizing a Hazardous Material)
24. D (page 1428; Recognizing a Hazardous Material)
25. C (page 1429; Recognizing a Hazardous Material)
26. C (page 1430; Recognizing a Hazardous Material)
27. B (page 1431; Recognizing a Hazardous Material)
28. A (page 1433; Recognizing a Hazardous Material)
29. D (page 1437; Recognizing a Hazardous Material)
30. B (page 1439; Recognizing a Hazardous Material)

True/False

1. T (page 1411; Introduction)
2. T (page 1411; Introduction)
3. F (page 1412; Incident Command System)
4. F (page 1416; EMS Response Within the Incident Command System)
5. T (page 1418; The Medical Branch of Incident Command)

6. F (page 1418; The Medical Branch of the Incident Command)

7. T (page 1419; The Medical Branch of Incident Command)

8. T (page 1422; Triage)

9. F (page 1423; Triage)

10. F (page 1426; Recognizing a Hazardous Material)

11. T (page 1427; Recognizing a Hazardous Material)

12. T (page 1429; Recognizing a Hazardous Material)

13. F (page 1430; Recognizing a Hazardous Material)

14. T (page 1436; Recognizing a Hazardous Material)

15. F (page 1441; Recognizing a Hazardous Material)

Fill-in-the-Blank

1. flexibility, standardization (page 1411; National Incident Management System)

2. span of control (page 1412; Incident Command System)

3. single (page 1413; Incident Command System)

4. planning (page 1414; Incident Command System)

5. Preparedness (page 1415; EMS Response Within the Incident Command System)

6. triage supervisor (page 1418; The Medical Branch of Incident Command)

7. Treatment supervisors (page 1418; The Medical Branch of Incident Command)

8. number, category (page 1421; Triage)

9. location, building (page 1427; Recognizing a Hazardous Material)

10. bulk, nonbulk (page 1428; Recognizing a Hazardous Material)

11. Storage bags (page 1429; Recognizing a Hazardous Material)

12. Control zones (page 1437; Recognizing a Hazardous Material)

13. warm zone (page 1438; Recognizing a Hazardous Material)

14. decontamination (page 1438; Recognizing a Hazardous Material)

15. intermodal tank (page 1429; Recognizing a Hazardous Material)

Fill-in-the-Table (page 1421; Triage)

Triage Priorities	
Triage Category	**Typical Injuries**
Red tag: first priority (immediate) Patients who need immediate care and transport Treat these patients first and transport as soon as possible	• **Airway and breathing compromise** • **Uncontrolled or severe bleeding** • **Severe medical problems** • **Signs of shock (hypoperfusion)** • **Severe burns** • **Open chest or abdominal injuries**
Yellow tag: second priority (delayed) Patients whose treatment and transport can be temporarily delayed	• **Burns without airway compromise** • **Major or multiple bone or joint injuries** • **Back injuries with or without spinal cord damage**
Green tag: third priority, minimal (walking wounded) Patients who require minimal or no treatment and whose transport can be delayed until last	• **Minor fractures** • **Minor soft-tissue injuries**
Black tag: fourth priority (expectant) Patients who are already dead or have little chance for survival; treat salvageable patients before treating these patients	• **Obvious death** • **Obviously nonsurvivable injury, such as major open brain trauma** • **Respiratory arrest (if limited resources)** • **Cardiac arrest**

Crossword Puzzle

```
1D I S A S 2T E R      3N I 4M S
        R              S
      5J O I N T      6L  D
  7P    A            8I C S
   I    G            A      9A
10M O 11R G U E    12W  I      C
    E        A    13S A F E T Y
    S        R    O        I
14D E C O N T A M I N A T I O N
    U        Z            N
    E    15S E C O N 16D A R Y
        N        R
17C O L D Z O N E    U
              18M C I
      19C A R B O Y S
```

Critical Thinking

Short Answer

1. Command and management

   Preparedness

   Resource management

   Communications and information management

   Supporting technologies

   Ongoing management and maintenance (pages 1411–1412; National Incident Management System)

2. 1. Check-in at the incident

   2. Initial incident briefing

   3. Incident record keeping

   4. Accountability

   5. Incident demobilization (page 1415; Incident Command System)

3. The total number of patients

   The number of patients in each of the triage categories

   Recommendations for extrication and movement of patients to the treatment area

   Resources needed to complete triage and begin movement of patients (page 1421; Triage)

4. An understanding of what hazardous substances are and the risks associated with them

   An understanding of the potential outcomes of an incident

   The ability to recognize the presence of hazardous substances

   The ability to identify the hazardous substances, if possible

   An understanding of the role of the first responder awareness individual in the emergency response plan

   The ability to determine the need for additional resources and to notify the communication center (page 1426; Introduction to Hazardous Materials)

5. The name of the chemical, including any synonyms for it

Physical and chemical characteristics of the material

Physical hazards of the material

Health hazards of the material

Signs and symptoms of exposure

Routes of entry

Permissible exposure limits

Response-party contact

Precautions for safe handling (including hygiene practices, protective measures, and procedures for cleaning up spills or leaks)

Applicable control measures, including personal protective equipment

Emergency and first-aid procedures

Appropriate waste disposal (page 1433; Recognizing a Hazardous Material)

Ambulance Calls

1. The 4-year-old should be triaged as first priority (red). The 27-year-old should be triaged as third priority (green). The 42-year-old should be triaged as fourth priority (black). (page 1422; Triage)

2. It is fortunate that this is occurring on shift change because members from two shifts are available to respond to this mass-casualty incident. Because this is a remote area, which implies extended response times, you should use this time to gather information from the crop-duster pilot/responsible parties regarding the substance and to notify all local hospitals. Area HazMat team members should be requested, and once the chemicals have been identified, appropriate first aid and other instructions should be relayed to the affected patients on-scene through the dispatch center. Law enforcement should be requested to cordon off the area to prevent more individuals, such as coworkers and family members, from entering the contaminated area. Consult HazMat team members and/or CHEMTREC for appropriate information, including medical treatment, PPE, and minimum distances that are required to avoid exposure to the identified substance. Do not enter the area unless you have been trained and have the proper equipment to do so.

3. The good news is that you are uphill from the possible hazardous materials. You should be uphill and upwind from contaminated areas (especially when dealing with an unidentified substance). Each chemical reacts differently to outside air, temperature, and other ambient conditions. You should immediately instruct all civilians along the road to move out of the immediate area and/or instruct them to wait in a specific location if you feel that they have already been contaminated by the substance. Do not allow the driver to contaminate the passersby. Immediately notify law enforcement, as well as the local HazMat team. Attempt to gain information regarding the shipment, keeping a safe distance (using binoculars, PA system to relay instructions, etc). Look for placards or other markings, and use the *Emergency Response Guidebook* in an attempt to ascertain what the truck is carrying. Prevent exposure to yourself and your crew and the members of the public. Always follow local protocols.

Skills

Assessment Review

1. C (page 1422; Triage)

2. B (page 1422; Triage)

3. A (page 1422; Triage)

4. B (page 1422; Triage)

Chapter 40: Terrorism Response and Disaster Management

General Knowledge

Matching

1. L (page 1457; Chemical Agents)
2. O (page 1457; Chemical Agents)
3. E (page 1463; Biologic Agents)
4. N (page 1458; Chemical Agents)
5. J (page 1467; Biologic Agents)
6. K (page 1466; Biologic Agents)
7. B (page 1457; Chemical Agents)
8. F (page 1462; Chemical Agents)
9. D (page 1457; Chemical Agents)
10. M (page 1467; Biologic Agents)
11. C (page 1463; Biologic Agents)
12. I (page 1468; Biologic Agents)
13. H (page 1463; Biologic Agents)
14. A (page 1471; Radiologic/Nuclear Devices)
15. G (page 1463; Biologic Agents)

Multiple Choice

1. D (page 1452; What Is Terrorism?)
2. A (page 1452; What Is Terrorism?)
3. B (page 1453; Weapons of Mass Destruction)
4. B (page 1453; Weapons of Mass Destruction)
5. A (pages 1454–1455; EMT Response to Terrorism)
6. A (page 1456; EMT Response to Terrorism)
7. B (page 1457; Chemical Agents)
8. C (page 1457; Chemical Agents)
9. A (page 1458; Chemical Agents)
10. A (page 1460; Chemical Agents)
11. A (page 1461; Chemical Agents)
12. B (page 1460; Chemical Agents)
13. A (page 1462; Chemical Agents)
14. B (page 1463; Biologic Agents)
15. D (page 1465; Biologic Agents)
16. D (page 1466; Biologic Agents)
17. C (page 1467; Biologic Agents)
18. A (page 1467; Biologic Agents)
19. A (page 1468; Biologic Agents)
20. B (page 1470; Biologic Agents)
21. B (page 1471; Radiologic/Nuclear Devices)
22. D (page 1473; Radiologic/Nuclear Devices)
23. B (page 1474; Incendiary and Explosive Devices)

True/False

1. F (page 1451; What Is Terrorism?)
2. T (page 1453; Weapons of Mass Destruction)
3. F (page 1454; EMT Response to Terrorism)
4. T (page 1454; EMT Response to Terrorism)
5. T (page 1455; EMT Response to Terrorism)
6. F (page 1456; EMT Response to Terrorism)
7. F (page 1457; Chemical Agents)
8. F (page 1457; Chemical Agents)
9. T (page 1458; Chemical Agents)
10. F (page 1459; Chemical Agents)
11. F (page 1461; Chemical Agents)
12. T (page 1459; Chemical Agents)
13. T (page 1463; Chemical Agents)
14. F (page 1464; Biologic Agents)
15. F (page 1465; Biologic Agents)
16. T (page 1466; Biologic Agents)
17. T (page 1467; Biologic Agents)
18. F (page 1468; Biologic Agents)
19. F (page 1469; Biologic Agents)
20. F (pages 1470–1471; Biologic Agents)
21. T (page 1472; Radiologic/Nuclear Devices)
22. T (page 1473; Radiologic/Nuclear Devices)
23. T (page 1474; Incendiary and Explosive Devices)

Fill-in-the Blank

1. domestic terrorism (page 1451; What Is Terrorism?)
2. weapon of mass destruction/casualty (page 1453; Weapons of Mass Destruction)
3. State-sponsored terrorism (page 1454; Weapons of Mass Destruction)
4. secondary infection (page 1458; Chemical Agents)
5. Cross-contamination (page 1455; EMT Response to Terrorism)
6. Route of exposure (page 1457; Chemical Agents)
7. contact hazard (page 1457; Chemical Agents)
8. Nerve agents (page 1459; Chemical Agents)
9. Off-gassing (page 1459; Chemical Agents)
10. Dissemination (page 1463; Biologic Agents)
11. Virus (page 1463; Biologic Agents)
12. viral hemorrhagic fevers (page 1465; Biologic Agents)
13. Anthrax (page 1466; Biologic Agents)
14. lymph nodes (page 1467; Biologic Agents)
15. botulinum (page 1467; Biologic Agents)
16. Points of distribution (page 1470; Biologic Agents)
17. radiologic dispersal device (page 1472; Radiologic/Nuclear Devices)
18. secondary blast injury (page 1474; Incendiary and Explosive Devices)

Crossword Puzzle

Critical Thinking

Short Answer

1. 1. What are your initial actions?
   2. Whom should you notify, and what should you tell them?
   3. What type of additional resources might you require?
   4. How should you proceed to address the needs of the victims?
   5. How do you ensure your own and your partner's safety, as well as the safety of the victims?
   6. What is the clinical presentation of a victim exposed to a WMD?
   7. How are WMD patients to be assessed and treated?
   8. How do you avoid becoming contaminated or cross-contaminated with a WMD agent? (page 1451; Introduction)

2. 1. Vesicants (blister agents)
   2. Respiratory agents (choking agents)
   3. Nerve agents
   4. Metabolic agents (cyanides) (page 1453; Weapons of Mass Destruction)

3. 1. Type of location
   2. Type of call
   3. Number of patients
   4. Victims' statements
   5. Pre-incident indicators (page 1454; EMT Response to Terrorism)

4. 1. Skin irritation, burning, and reddening
   2. Immediate intense skin pain
   3. Formation of large blisters
   4. Gray discoloration of skin
   5. Swollen and closed or irritated eyes
   6. Permanent eye injury
   7. If vapors inhaled:
      a. Hoarseness and stridor
      b. Severe cough
      c. Hemoptysis
      d. Severe dyspnea (page 1457; Chemical Agents)

5. 1. Shortness of breath
   2. Chest tightness
   3. Hoarseness and stridor due to upper airway constriction
   4. Gasping and coughing (page 1458; Chemical Agents)

6. 1. Salivation, sweating
   2. Lacrimation
   3. Urination
   4. Defecation, drooling, diarrhea
   5. Gastric upset and cramps
   6. Emesis
   7. Muscle twitching, miosis (page 1460; Chemical Agents)

7. 1. Shortness of breath and gasping respirations
   2. Tachypnea
   3. Flushed skin
   4. Tachycardia
   5. Altered mental status
   6. Seizures

7. Coma

8. Apnea

9. Cardiac arrest (page 1462; Chemical Agents)

8. 1. Fever

2. Chills

3. Headache

4. Muscle aches

5. Nausea

6. Vomiting

7. Diarrhea

8. Severe abdominal cramping

9. Dehydration

10. Gastrointestinal bleeding

11. Necrosis of liver, spleen, kidneys, and gastrointestinal tract (page 1469; Biologic Agents)

9. 1. Hospitals

2. Colleges and universities

3. Chemical and industrial sites (page 1472; Radiologic/Nuclear Devices)

10. 1. Time

2. Distance

3. Shielding (page 1473; Radiologic/Nuclear Devices)

Ambulance Calls

1. There is no confirmation regarding the nature of the explosion. It could have been caused by a number of hazards, but precautions should be taken any time there is the chance for a terrorist attack. No one should rush into the scene because terrorists have been known to deliberately target first responders by placing secondary explosive devices. Request all available resources, including local, state, and federal specialized HazMat and law enforcement agencies, to assist in this call. Notify all local and regional hospitals of the situation; assess the scene from a distance. Establish command and designate a staging area for incoming units. Enter the scene only when it has been determined to be safe. Regularly scheduled mock drills to include expected agencies to respond in this type of situation can greatly improve communications and the overall effectiveness and efficiency of response.

2. The presence of numerous people with the same signs and symptoms, who were in the same location at the same time, should immediately send up red flags. These patients were exposed to contaminated food, air, or water in which they ingested some sort of toxin. Ingestion of ricin can produce these signs and symptoms within 4 to 8 hours after exposure. It can be difficult to initially determine what substances caused these signs and symptoms, but through careful history taking and investigation of the patients' commonalities, the exposure can be found. Unfortunately, there is no vaccination or other specific treatment available for exposure to ricin. Only supportive measures for airway, breathing, and circulation can be applied.

3. Cyanide is colorless and has an odor similar to bitter almonds. It interferes with the body's ability to utilize oxygen and can result in headache, shortness of breath, tachypnea, altered levels of consciousness, apnea, seizures, and even death. Antidotes can be given but are rarely carried on ambulances. Patients' clothing must be removed to avoid exposure to the cyanide because it is released as a gas from the clothing fibers. For most patients, simply removing them from the source of cyanide and providing supportive therapy for their ABCs will be all that is needed. However, those with significant exposure may require aggressive airway intervention.

Skills

Assessment Review

1. C (pages 1464–1465; Biologic Agents)

2. B (page 1468; Biologic Agents)

3. D (page 1467; Biologic Agents)

4. A (page 1466; Biologic Agents)

THE TEAM APPROACH TO HEALTH CARE

Chapter 41: A Team Approach to Health Care

General Knowledge

Matching

1. H (page 1491; Dependent, Independent, and Interdependent Groups)
2. F (page 1497; Assisting With ALS Skills)
3. K (page 1496; Assisting With ALS Skills)
4. G (page 1500; Assisting With ALS Skills)
5. B (page 1500; Assisting With ALS Skills)
6. A (page 1491; Dependent, Independent, and Interdependent Groups)
7. I (page 1496; Assisting With ALS Skills)
8. M (page 1500; Assisting With ALS Skills)
9. D (page 1502; Assisting With ALS Skills)
10. C (page 1493; Effective Team Performance)
11. E (page 1493; Effective Team Performance)
12. N (page 1499; Assisting With ALS Skills)
13. O (page 1490; Types of Teams)
14. J (page 1495; Assisting With ALS Skills)
15. L (page 1491; Groups Versus Teams)

Multiple Choice

1. B (page 1491; Groups Versus Teams)
2. C (page 1493; Effective Team Performance)
3. C (page 1497; Assisting With ALS Skills)
4. B (page 1497; Assisting With ALS Skills)
5. D (page 1496; Assisting With ALS Skills)
6. B (page 1500; Assisting With ALS Skills)
7. A (page 1497; Assisting With ALS Skills)
8. A (page 1491; Groups Versus Teams)
9. B (page 1497; Assisting With ALS Skills)
10. A (page 1497; Assisting With ALS Skills)
11. C (page 1501; Assisting With ALS Skills)
12. D (page 1504; Troubleshooting Team Conflicts)
13. C (page 1489; An Era of Team Health Care)
14. C (page 1489; An Era of Team Health Care)
15. D (pages 1491–1492; Effective Team Performance)
16. D (page 1492; Effective Team Performance)
17. B (page 1501; Assisting With ALS Skills)
18. D (page 1495; BLS and ALS Providers Working Together)
19. B (page 1500; Assisting With ALS Skills)
20. D (page 1501; Assisting With ALS Skills)
21. D (page 1497; Assisting With ALS Skills)
22. C (page 1491; Dependent, Independent, and Interdependent Groups)
23. D (page 1494; Transfer of Patient Care)
24. B (page 1493; Effective Team Performance)
25. A (page 1500; Assisting With ALS Skills)
26. D (page 1499; Assisting With ALS Skills)
27. B (page 1497; Assisting With ALS Skills)
28. A (page 1497; Assisting With ALS Skills)
29. D (page 1495; Assisting With ALS Skills)
30. C (page 1490; Types of Teams)

True/False

1. T (page 1498; Assisting With ALS Skills)
2. F (page 1490; Types of Teams)
3. F (page 1490; Types of Teams)
4. T (page 1496; Assisting With ALS Skills)
5. T (page 1492; Effective Team Performance)
6. T (page 1495; BLS and ALS Providers Working Together)
7. F (page 1504; Troubleshooting Team Conflicts)
8. F (page 1499; Assisting With ALS Skills)
9. F (page 1500; Assisting With ALS Skills)
10. F (page 1501; Assisting With ALS Skills)
11. T (page 1500; Assisting With ALS Skills)
12. F (page 1500; Assisting With ALS Skills)
13. T (page 1495; BLS and ALS Providers Working Together)
14. T (page 1495; BLS and ALS Providers Working Together)
15. F (page 1496; Assisting With ALS Skills)

Fill-in-the-Blank

1. group (page 1490; Groups Versus Teams)
2. train, work (page 1490; Types of Teams)
3. sniffing position (page 1497; Assisting With ALS Skills)
4. gastric distention (page 1497; Assisting With ALS Skills)
5. Crew resource management (page 1493; Effective Team Performance)
6. Direct laryngoscopy (page 1496; Assisting With ALS Skills)
7. interdependent group (page 1491; Dependent, Independent, and Interdependent Groups)
8. Apneic oxygenation (page 1496; Assisting With ALS Skills)
9. team leader (page 1493; Effective Team Performance)
10. Community paramedicine (page 1489; An Era of Team Health Care)
11. Saline locks (page 1502; Assisting With ALS Skills)
12. Vascular access (page 1500; Assisting With ALS Skills)
13. Macrodrip sets (page 1500; Assisting With ALS Skills)
14. unstable (page 1499; Assisting With ALS Skills)
15. Endotracheal intubation (page 1495; Assisting With ALS Skills)

Crossword Puzzle

Critical Thinking

Short Answer

1. 1. Absence of an end-tidal CO_2 level.
   2. Decreasing SpO_2 level.
   3. Increasing resistance when ventilating.
   4. Other physical signs of poor ventilation and perfusion.
   5. Improper positioning or dislodgement of the ET tube. (page 1500; Assisting With ALS Skills)

2. 1. The patient comes first.

    2. Do not engage.

    3. Keep your cool.

    4. Separate the person from the issue.

    5. Choose your battles. (page 1504; Troubleshooting Team Conflicts)

3. **B**—Perform *BVM* preoxygenation.

    E—*Evaluate* for airway difficulties.

    M—*Manipulate* the patient.

    A—*Attempt* first-pass intubation.

    GI—Use a supra*Glottic* or *Immediate* airway if unable to intubate.

    C—*Confirm* successful intubation/*Correct* any issues. (page 1497; Assisting With ALS Skills)

4. Observe the access site for swelling, bleeding, discoloration, or leaking. Also, observe the IV tubing to see if it is improperly blocked, clamped, kinked, or if the bag of IV solution is empty. (pages 1502–1503; Assisting With ALS Skills)

5. 1. A common goal

    2. An image of themselves as "a group"

    3. A sense of continuity of the group

    4. A set of shared values

    5. Different roles within the group (page 1491; Groups Versus Teams)

Ambulance Calls

1. Do not be afraid to inform the paramedic that the leads have not been appropriately attached. You can save valuable time by simply relaying what you have seen. Sometimes EMTs can feel intimidated by the presence of paramedics and become afraid to speak out when they see something that doesn't appear right. Do not underestimate your ability to help because sometimes you may notice things that the paramedic does not. Everyone has the same goal of patient care and it is pertinent to point out those things that may interfere with this goal.

2. If successful intubation has occurred, you will hear equal, bilateral breath sounds and no sounds over the epigastrium. This endotracheal tube should be removed, and the patient should be ventilated with high-flow oxygen via bag-valve mask and the placement of an oral airway. Secondary placement devices should be utilized when assessing placement of the ET tube. Direct visualization of the ET tube passing through the cords along with the use of colorimetric devices and/or end-tidal carbon dioxide detectors can ensure that successful placement has been accomplished. If endotracheal intubation is not possible, consider the use of supraglottic airways such as the i-gel airway device, King LT airway, or laryngeal mask airway. Always follow local protocols.

3. You should immediately slow the IV to a TKO rate, raise the patient's head, and apply high-flow oxygen (or increase the current L/min). You may also consider the use of CPAP if the patient is alert enough to follow orders. Notify the receiving facility of the error. Healthy adults can handle the sudden influx of intravenous fluids without detrimental effects, but individuals who have diseased or otherwise weakened hearts, lungs, or kidneys do not possess the ability to cope with the fluid overload. To avoid this occurrence, check and double-check the drip chamber/flow rate to prevent accidental fluid boluses. Continuously monitor the patient.

Notes

Notes

Notes

Notes